Praise for the *Handbook of Human Performance Technology, Third Edition*

"This third edition of the seminal *Handbook* weaves in two decades of applied HPT experience to provide even more relevant guidelines to today's performance improvement practitioners as they continue the important work of leveraging an organization's most precious capital—its people—toward verifiable, measurable, and valuable outcomes."

—Clare Marsch, senior principal, global learning consulting, Convergys Learning Solutions

"The *Handbook of Human Performance Technology* is a valued resource for professionals who lead learning and performance improvement efforts in organizations. In this edition, top thinkers in our field take on the tough issues, summarize current thinking, and offer valuable new insights."

—Catherine M. Sleezer, CPT, Ph.D., professor, human resource/adult education, Oklahoma State University

"This *Handbook* not only bridges the gap between European and American performance improvement strategies, it also includes key multicultural approaches for change agents that focus on business results."

—Steven J. Kelly, CPT, managing partner, KNO Worldwide

"Taking the helm with the third edition, James Pershing ensures that the *Handbook of Human Performance Technology* retains its leading role in the field. Two aspects particularly resonate: a new classification of interventions at the worker and team levels and workplace and organizational levels, and a superb section on measurement and assessment, which concisely applies a variety of research and evaluation techniques specifically for use in our field."

—Saul Carliner, assistant professor, graduate program in educational technology, Concordia University, Montreal, Canada

"The *Handbook*'s clear and supportive structure and the high scientific and/or practical expertise of its authors makes this excellent documentation of HPT's mission, values, processes, and tools very beneficial and credible for both managers and HPT practitioners in work or social settings as well as academic readers with interest in state-of-the-art HPT related knowledge and experience."

—Verena Dziobaka-Spitzhorn, house of training/
head of learning and communication, METRO Cash &
Carry International GmbH, Germany

"The *Handbook* reflects the vast and diverse experience of the very best thinking and applications of HPT in the world today. It is an invaluable and comprehensive reference for anyone interested in improving human performance in the workplace."

—Christine Marsh, CPT, principal, Prime Objectives,
United Kingdom

"As the knowledge revolution takes hold, victory will go to the smartest organizations and societies. This must-have reference handbook provides consultants and business leaders with visual models, practices, and case histories to achieve measurable improvements in human performance and business results."

—Geoffrey A. Amyot, CPT, CEO, Achievement
Awards Group, South Africa

Handbook of Human Performance Technology

Third Edition

Principles, Practices, and Potential

James A. Pershing

Editor

Foreword by Harold D. Stolovitch and Erica J. Keeps

Pfeiffer

A Wiley Imprint

www.pfeiffer.com

Cataloging-in-Publication Data on file with the Library of Congress.

Acquiring Editor: Matthew Davis
Director of Development: Kathleen Dolan Davies
Production Editor: Nina Kreiden and Liah Rose
Editor: David Horne

Manufacturing Supervisor: Becky Carreño
Editorial Assistant: Leota Higgins
Illustrations: Interactive Composition Corporation

Printed in the United States of America
Printing   10   9   8   7   6   5   4   3   2   1

To Patricia Lorena, James Frederick, and Dara Lynn

CONTENTS

FOREWORD TO
THE THIRD EDITION

Human performance technology (HPT) is a professional field of study and application, the main purpose of which is to engineer systems that allow people and organizations to perform in ways that they and all stakeholders value. HPT is a derivative field that for over a half of a century has evolved from a number of disciplines, such as psychology, communications, neuroscience, management science, information science, economics, ergonomics, and measurement and evaluation. It is also the progeny of a number of applied fields, such as instructional technology, human resource development, organizational development, and industrial engineering.

Eclectic as this all sounds, HPT has grown to become a distinct specialty with its own international, national, and local professional societies as well as numerous publications, university programs, and certification structures that lend it credence. It has emerged as a domain of practice that is increasingly relevant, if not essential, for today's organizational success. The term *human performance technology* sounds somewhat dry and mechanistic. Hence, *human performance improvement* (HPI) has begun to appear in professional publications as a more acceptable euphemism. We view HPT as the rigorous means for achieving valued performance, that is, what we as performance-improvement specialists do, and HPI as the end result, that is, what we accomplish. Regardless of the terminology, HPT-HPI has come to represent a unique area of study, research, and professional practice, one that is worthy of recognition in the world of work and, more recently, in nonwork and social settings.

THE *HANDBOOK OF HUMAN PERFORMANCE TECHNOLOGY:*
A FOUNDATION DOCUMENT

Such an energetic field must, at points in its development, stop for a moment to consolidate its thinking, values, position, mission, direction, and practices and make a statement about what it is and why anyone should care. This statement serves three purposes: (1) to help its diverse scholars and practitioners disengage themselves from their daily, disparate, and pressing activities and reflect on who they really are as a family; (2) to inform the outside world of what the field is all about and why its existence is so excitingly important; and (3) to guide those entering the field and those responsible for informing new members on what and where to focus.

The statement HPT has made is this *Handbook of Human Performance Technology.* In 1988, the then National Society for Performance and Instruction (NSPI), now the International Society for Performance Improvement (ISPI), realized that while it was preaching HPT vigorously and vociferously, the message was not coming through very clearly. A stronger affirmation had to be made. A source document was necessary to inform the world of what HPT was all about. The result was the launching of a publication initiative. We were selected to be the parents of this publication, and our job was to give birth to a powerful HPT manifesto.

Here was our mission as it appeared in 1992 in the preface to the first edition of the handbook:

> What has been needed as a solid cornerstone for the field . . . is a major publication that clearly articulates, to the world and to HPT professionals, that we have arrived. That is the purpose of the *Handbook of Human Performance Technology:* to announce the existence of an emerging, highly relevant field, and to express what this field is about, where it comes from, what it does, and how its principles and practices can very significantly benefit organizations that seek outstanding results [Stolovitch and Keeps, 1992, p. xx].

Little did we realize what an undertaking this was to be, involving almost three years of intense work. Also, little did we anticipate its impact. Not only were the handbook's sales outstanding, it soon became the major textbook for university programs that were adding ever-increasing numbers of professionals to the field. The first edition also generated widespread, international enthusiasm for HPT. This resulted in a second edition, this time with a global thrust. What came out of this two-and-a-half-year effort was a markedly increased worldwide profile for HPT and many new adherents to the field from a host of nations.

However, as optimistic as we were about the staying power of the handbook, we certainly could not have predicted an entirely new, amazingly updated third edition some fourteen years after the first one. We view the contents of this outstanding, highly evolved volume with awe and admiration for what Professor Pershing and his authors have accomplished and strong emotion at seeing how far the field has evolved in so short a time.

HPT: HOW FAR WE HAVE COME

Speaking about our advances as a professional group, it is tremendously impressive to note the indicators of our dramatic growth. Witness the numerous books, chapters, periodicals, and articles dealing with HPT themes. Since 1992, publications have multiplied tenfold. The number of university programs and courses focused on human performance at work has burgeoned, and not only in the United States and Canada where the movement began, but also in Europe, the Middle East, Africa, South America, Australia, New Zealand, and throughout the world where there are people searching for ways to achieve organizational results valued by all. As an example, over the past year, we ourselves received requests for HPT guidance, suggested readings, and learning opportunities from countries including China, Mongolia, Uzbekistan, Malaysia, Singapore, Bangladesh, Romania, South Africa, Colombia, Israel, and Niger. In this listing, we do not even name the Western European countries, as they have now become normal fare, something we would not have said even ten years ago.

Along with the impact on publications and programs are the noticeable changes to professional societies and organizations that once were centered exclusively on training. The American Society for Training and Development, now ASTD, and VNU, publishers of *Training,* have begun to include the term *performance* in their taglines, including those for their various certificate programs. Recently a new magazine, *Workforce Performance Solutions,* sprang into existence, an offshoot of the *Chief Learning Officer* magazine. Also, let us not forget the emergence of the HPT certification program from the flagship organization for HPT, ISPI. The ISPI Certified Performance Technologist (CPT) program now has produced over one thousand CPTs worldwide. In contributing to growing the field, ISPI has also designed and developed a comprehensive set of professional development institutes for individuals and organizations interested in integrating HPT. Several large companies and organizations now have performance-improvement units. Prominent among these is the United States Navy Human Performance Center.

THE RELEVANCE OF HPT

While HPT has dramatically evolved since the first edition of the handbook, it is not one of those flash-in-the-pan fads that explodes on the organizational scene with blinding *éclat,* only to dissolve into forgotten history like a celebrity diet. Here is why HPT has stood and will continue to stand the test of time.

• *A concern with bottom-line results and return-on-investment (ROI) issues.* Yes, HPT possesses strong processes. Nevertheless, its central focus, as one of HPT's major founders, Thomas F. Gilbert, often stated, is *valued accomplishment,* meaning verifiable results that far exceed their costs. The ferociously competitive global marketplace drives organizations. In a world of limited resources, for-profit, nonprofit, and social welfare organizations all find themselves competing for these as well as scarce funds. Anything that can deliver high ROI and positive cost-benefit ratios as well as demonstrate impact supported by data immediately draws attention. This is HPT's *raison d'être.* HPT is bottom line and measurement conscious, imbuing it with ongoing relevance.

• *The high stakes of high investment.* As technology and communications innovations generally cause major changes to organizations, virtually any significant initiative demands the investment of large sums to ensure successful adoption. A new way of tracking customer buying behaviors can quickly mount into the millions of whatever currency one is using. Will the employees adapt well to it? Will the full potential of its promise be realized? These are the concerns of the enterprise. These are also the key issues with which HPT professionals deal.

• *The increased emphasis on measurement: Six Sigma and its relatives.* Long before Six Sigma, reengineering, and even total quality management appeared on the scene, there was HPT using a language very similar to all of these movements. HPT has always emphasized systemic analysis, systematic processes, holistic intervention design, and measurement. From time to time, individual practitioners may have been swayed by enthusiasms and fads, but not so for the field itself. HPT is about demonstrated hardcore results. If HPT could have a motto, it might very well be, "let data talk." Its caution would be, "beware enthusiasms!"

• *Systems thinking.* HPT is an applied offspring of general systems theory. Unlike science, which focuses on ever more minute phenomena viewed through the lens of a microscope, HPT employs a macroscope (de Rosnay, 1975) to examine all of the relevant elements that interact to affect the activities and outcomes of a system. Human performance is, as Gilbert (1996) suggested, valued accomplishment derived from costly behavior. To achieve valued accomplishment means analyzing all of the costly behavior elements and designing an integrated set of interventions that most efficiently generates desired and measured results. In our complex current and most likely future world, HPT possesses the appropriate viewpoint, processes, and validated tools to achieve constantly accelerating organizational goals.

• *Changes to departmental titles.* In the same way that *personnel* morphed into *human resources* and *accounting* into *finance, training* is in a period of transition to a new and more strategic state. The first transformational baby steps have been to *learning, learning services,* or *learning and development.* The bolder organizations have changed to *workforce development, workplace learning and performance, learning and performance support,* and even *performance enhancement.* What is in a name? Opinions abound. Nevertheless, changes in labels when accompanied by modifications and additions in activities, services, and deliverables certainly alter expectations and outcomes. The newer departmental or service titles appear to match more closely the needs of organizations. As such these augur well for evolved, more strategic, systemic roles than tactical training ever provided.

• *The interrelationship of HPT with human resource development (HRD), organizational effectiveness (OE), and organizational development (OD).* What we have asserted to date about HPT is in many ways true of other related fields. Gilley, Maycunich, and Quatro (2002) forcefully pointed out that the role of HRD professionals has been mainly a transactional one just as in the case of training. They encourage greater focus on becoming more transformational and performance focused. As they assert, "the challenges facing organizations require HRD professionals to adopt a role that improves firm performance, enhances competitive readiness, and drives renewal capacity and capability" (p. 25).

From the field of OE, we witness a growing emphasis on helping the organization fulfill its mission through a blend of sound management, strong governance, and a persistent redirection to achieving results. The concerns of OE sound markedly familiar to HPT professionals.

What is true for HRD and OE can also be repeated for OD. While OD generally operates at macro levels of organizations, its mission is that of increasing organizational effectiveness and health through planned interventions in the organization's processes or operations. OD may not adopt the engineering style of HPT; it is more characterized by its emphasis on communication and facilitation. However, its purpose, as with HPT, is to deliver valued organizational results, largely through people. This is not a far cry from HPT's concern with improving human performance.

These convergences, although seemingly threatening to the exclusivity of HPT's terrain, in fact only enhance its relevance. All desire valued performance. Each has its approach. HPT's is that of *engineer.* In this respect, it is well positioned for creating solid business cases for its activities and presenting data-based evidence of desirable outcomes. Increasingly, organizational decision makers demand this.

THE EMERGENCE OF HUMAN CAPITAL

Perhaps we should speak more of human capital's reemergence. Theodore Schultz, in 1979, and Gary Becker, in 1992, both won Nobel prizes in economics for their work in human capital. There was a brief period of excitement for this then-new concept in the early 1980s that quickly faded. However, in the last seven or eight years, the human capital theme has once again emerged as a serious and strategic business issue. A number of authors such as Davenport (1999), Edvinsson and Malone (1997), Fitz-enz (2000), Kravetz (2004), Pfeffer (1998), and Stewart (1997) have fanned the flames of human capital accounting and potential and have demonstrated the high returns to be derived from human capital management. By human capital, we mean the sum total of all knowledge, experience, and performance capability an organization possesses that can be applied to create wealth. The key words are *performance capability.* This is HPT's purview, and in this respect, the HPT professional, as portrayed throughout the chapters of this handbook, is above all a leverager of human capital. In fact, one might sum up the essential elements of this third edition of the *Handbook of Human Performance Technology* in the following ways:

- *The key mission of HPT:* the leveraging of human capital in the most efficient manner to achieve targeted, valued results.
- *The key process of HPT:* the engineering of valued and effective individual and organizational performance based on systemic, systematic, and scientific principles and demonstrated through credible measures.
- *The key roles of the HPT professional:* analyst, consultant, designer, evaluator, facilitator, project manager, management mentor, and, as required, organizational therapist.
- *The key contexts of HPT application:* the workplace or work setting. However, increasingly, HPT is being applied in social settings, for example, reproductive health in developing nations, community substance abuse programs, public education, and improved quality of life for the chronically ill and aged.

AND SO THIS THIRD EDITION OF THE *HANDBOOK OF HUMAN PERFORMANCE TECHNOLOGY . . .*

As you enter the pages of this remarkably impressive volume, you will be struck with how firmly the handbook still remains a foundation document. Now that it is in its third iteration, it has also assumed two new and extremely important roles: that of chronicler of HPT's progress as an evolving field and that of credible witness to HPT's ongoing relevance to organizations, workers at every level and of all stripes, and society at large. As was meant to be, it fulfills the role of authoritative guide and standard bearer for HPT's mission, processes, values, and practices.

Having twice stood in the shoes of editor James Pershing, we can appreciate the many months of tireless effort that he, the editors, and all of the contributors have invested to bring forth this important milestone that is the new handbook. It marks a significant moment in the history of HPT. It also represents a challenge for even greater HPT achievements in the years ahead.

February 2006   Harold D. Stolovitch
                                                        Erica J. Keeps
                                                  Los Angeles, California

References

Davenport, T. B. (1999). *Human capital: What it is and why people invest in it.* San Francisco: Jossey-Bass.

de Rosnay, J. (1975). *Le macroscope, vers une vision globale.* Paris: Le Seuil.

Edvinsson, L., and Malone, M. S. (1997). *Intellectual capital: Realizing your company's true value by finding its hidden brainpower.* New York: HarperCollins.

Fitz-enz, J. (2000). *The ROI of human capital: Measuring the economic value of employee performance.* New York: American Management Association.

Gilbert, T. F. (1996). *Human competence: Engineering worthy performance.* Washington, DC: International Society for Performance Improvement.

Gilley, J. W., Maycunich, A., and Quatro, S. A. (2002). Comparing the roles responsibilities, and activities of transactional and transformational HRD professionals. *Performance Improvement Quarterly, 15*(4), 23–44.

Kravetz, D. J. (2004). *Measuring human capital: Converting workplace behavior into dollars.* Mesa, AZ: Kravetz Associates.

Pfeffer, J. (1998). *The human equation: Building profits by putting people first.* Boston: Harvard Business School Press.

Stewart, T. A. (1997). *Intellectual capital: The new wealth of nations.* New York: Doubleday/Currency.

Stolovitch, H. D., and Keeps, E. J. (Eds.). (1992). *Handbook of human performance technology: A comprehensive guide for analyzing and solving performance problems in organization.* San Francisco: Jossey-Bass.

PREFACE

It is true; the one constant we can count on in this modern world is change. Since 1992, when Harold D. Stolovitch and Erica J. Keeps so ably coedited the first edition of the *Handbook of Human Performance Technology*, the world in which we live and work has undergone significant transformation. Several of these changes and their impact were captured in Stolovitch and Keeps's second edition of the handbook, published in 1999. However, when one compares and contrasts the first two editions of the handbook, one will note that there are constants in the forms of truisms and principles in the field of human performance technology (HPT) that transcend time. Our goal in producing this third edition of the handbook, some six-plus years after the second edition, was twofold: to capture the truisms and principles of HPT and to address what we judge to be some important transformations.

We purposefully established seven objectives to achieve these two purposes. In 2004 we worked with trusted formal and informal leaders in HPT, seeking their advice and counsel in setting the direction and content for the handbook. At HPT conferences and meetings we spoke in person with a number of individuals we judged to be established leaders in HPT. We sought their input and asked them to suggest others to contact. This led to our contacting a total of fifty individuals from whom we received valued advice in person, by e-mail, or over the telephone. Their input helped us to develop further objectives as well as to identify authors and to select members for the handbook editorial advisory board.

Given the interlude between the first two editions of the handbook and this third edition, the second objective was to have all new chapters. This objective has been met with fifty-five new information-rich chapters for this third edition.

A third objective was to have well-recognized leaders and subject-matter experts in HPT author at least one-half of the chapters. The reason for this objective was to give the handbook credibility and marketability. As a leading contributor to the field of HPT, the handbook must contain the ideas and views of our thought-and-practice leaders. Each of you may count differently; however, in our judgment, thirty of the fifty-five chapters have one or more authors that meet this criterion. The remaining chapter authors are emerging leaders in HPT or thought-and-practice leaders from fields closely aligned with HPT.

As a fourth objective, we sought diversity among the chapter authors, in terms of (1) demographics such as gender, years of experience in HPT, and nationality; (2) position, including academics, consultants, practicing professionals in business and the public sectors, and expertise representing a broad range of HPT interventions; and (3) what some affectionately dub old, new, and no guards in terms of perceived roles in the field of HPT and our flagship organization, the International Society for Performance Improvement. These judgments too will be in the eyes of the beholder. In our judgment we achieved our diversity objective.

Objective five had to do with a personal bias of mine, which stems from my years of experience in academia. I believe that knowledge is best advanced when it combines theory and practice and when we recognize that worthwhile ideas and views evolve from the in-depth study of and appreciation for the work of those who preceded us as well as from our contemporaries. In short, there are no giant leaps in knowledge development or practice in disciplines and fields of study associated with the social sciences. There are incremental steps, often forward, but sometimes backward, that come from synthesizing, integrating, and trying out the ideas or practices of others in different settings or ways. To this end, we were insistent that all chapter authors overtly acknowledge the impact of others on their work by citing and referencing the pertinent research, theoretical, and professional practice literature generously and accurately.

Our sixth objective also reflects a professional bias I have about the field of HPT. It is generally recognized that many of the principles and practices of HPT evolved from the field of instructional technology (IT). Over time, many performance technologists have expanded both the principles and practices of HPT, embracing ideas and views from a number of other academic and professional practice fields. However, the pervasiveness of education and training in HPT is substantial in my judgment. This dominance of IT in HPT exists in part for two important reasons. First, many practicing performance technologists and students of HPT have as their primary professional homes institutionalized programs that have education or training as a first line of business. There are not large numbers of organizations or academic programs with HPT as the single or even dominant focus. Second, education and training, especially when broadly viewed, are more often than not a part of the intervention set that performance technologists often settle upon to address performance issues. This is particularly true when one looks at primary or first-level interventions versus secondary or second-level interventions. Even if training is not a primary intervention, it often comes into play as other interventions are implemented. For example, retooling may be a logical choice to solve quality problems with a manufacturing process. However, the personnel responsible for implementing and using the new tooling may need formal or informal training or job aids to be effective. Whether this pervasiveness of education and training in HPT is real or perceived, I believe that it has existed for too long and has in part retarded the development and use of non-education interventions. Perhaps this is epitomized best by the number of HPT models and publications about HPT practice, including the first two editions of this handbook, that categorize or classify interventions as being of an instructional versus noninstructional nature. For this third edition of the handbook, we have chosen to address this issue by having parts of the book dealing with interventions designated as "Interventions at the Worker and Work Team Levels" and "Interventions at the Workplace and Organizational Levels." Four of the sixteen chapters in these two parts deal with some aspect of education and training. The others deal with a wide array of other interventions.

Finally, we had as our seventh objective the development of a brand new part for the handbook. For the first time, the handbook addresses issues related to a core practice of HPT, the gathering and analysis of data, and its transformation to information for use by performance technologists and their clients. We have a number of chapters devoted to performance measurement and assessment. We hope this added dimension is valued by our readers and contributes to improving the practice of HPT.

INTENDED AUDIENCES

As with the first two editions of the handbook, we believe that this third edition will appeal to a broad array of readers and users. We anticipate that human performance technology practitioners will use the handbook as their primary reference tool. We also believe that students and faculty in academic programs and those in professional development programs will use it as a textbook.

We anticipate that the ways we have treated and presented interventions will have greater appeal to a number of individuals and groups that are interested in performance improvement but come from disciplines and fields other than education and training. We are also hopeful that managers and executives in corporations, government, the military, and public agencies and organizations find that many parts of the handbook resonate with their goals to improve individual and organizational improvement.

Finally, we are confident that the well-established community of HPT practitioners, regardless of their experience and expertise, will find many chapters that challenge their thinking and rekindle their enthusiasm for our field of HPT. There is evidence that in the past the handbook has significantly reinforced the vitality and devotion that practicing HPT professionals have for our field, and we hope that this third edition continues to achieve this lofty goal.

OVERVIEW OF THE CONTENTS

Although all of the chapters are new, parts of this third edition of the handbook resemble the first two editions. Other parts are quite different. As before, we have leading HPT thinkers and doers sharing with the readers their experiences and views. We also have some authors who are familiar with HPT but are not mainstream performance technologists. They share with us a variety of perspectives about performance improvement that come from other fields and disciplines that are concerned with quality and effective performance in organizations.

The book itself is divided into seven parts. Some readers will read the book from beginning to end, obtaining a complete and comprehensive view of HPT. Others will be more interested in specific parts that align with their interests and practices. Still others will pick and choose among chapters in different parts of the book, being motivated by particular topics, authors they admire or want to learn from, and so on. The handbook will accommodate all of these approaches.

Part One, "Foundations of Human Performance Technology," has information about the practice of HPT as well as its more esoteric or academic attributes. The first three chapters paint a clear picture of what HPT is all about. The middle chapters deal with foundational ideas that support and justify practice. The last chapter is a comprehensive overview of the origins and history of the field that will provide readers with a sense of why and how HPT has evolved.

Part Two, "The Performance Technology Process," covers the main elements of HPT practice. It begins with explanations about strategic alignment, moves on to analysis, design, and change, and ends with evaluation. The symbiotic relationships of analysis and evaluation are made clear, and the importance of evaluation and accountability are evident given the two information-rich chapters that address evaluation issues.

Part Three, "Interventions at the Worker and Work Team Levels," is one of two parts that address HPT and related interventions. In Part Three, we have the first four chapters addressing the importance and criticality of instructional interventions. We have five more chapters that address critical interventions in the areas of mentoring, motivation, behavior in organizations, group performance, and performance support systems. These interventions exemplify problems and quality-improvement initiatives that focus on workers and work teams.

Part Four, "Interventions at the Workplace and Organizational Levels," is the companion part to Part Three. In Part Four, the focus moves to the workplace and organization. We have chapters that address established as well as new and emerging disciplines and fields of practice that complement and enhance the effectiveness of HPT. They include organizational development, learning organizations, knowledge management, communities of practice, workplace design, Six Sigma, and lean manufacturing. The authors strive to explain in detail these associated practices and show their relationships and value in partnering with HPT.

Part Five, "Performance Measurement and Assessment," presents information-packed chapters on collecting and analyzing data, a core process in HPT. The first chapter addresses issues related to quantitative and qualitative methods, showing the value of each. The next four chapters provide the readers with guidance on the mainstay means for collecting HPT data: questionnaires, interviewing, observing, and content analyses. The next chapter is a comprehensive overview of quantitative data analyses. Part Five wraps up with a treatise on the importance of evidence-based practice in HPT.

Part Six, "Performance Technology in Action," has much "how to" information. Several of the chapter authors make up a who's who of HPT. They share their wisdom and insight on a variety of practices, including transforming from learning to a performance function, partnering with management, project management, leadership in HPT, and consulting. There are two chapters that deal differently with the same topic, ethics. Given the state of affairs in our world today concerning corporate and government waste and malfeasance, these chapters seem most pertinent to HPT practice. Part Six ends with a chapter that provides an insider's view of HPT in practice. It is a military application and shows the power and value of HPT in a large organizational setting that deals with matters of life and death.

Part Seven, "Looking Forward in Human Performance Technology," presents a set of thought-provoking chapters. The authors challenge conventional thinking about HPT and help us to look forward, trying to envision the ways HPT may change and adapt to the future. We are provided with alternative ways to both think about and do HPT. Collectively, the authors present cutting-edge ideas and challenges that we must face as we move forward in developing our field of HPT, helping it to meet tomorrow's needs.

Given the expanding role of HPT in helping individuals, groups, and organizations meet the performance challenges of an ever-changing world, we have strived to reflect the stabilizing attributes of HPT as well as its potential transformations. Our new team of editors brings to you, our readers, fresh viewpoints that we hope advance the field and at the same time reflect its long-established strengths and foundations.

February 2006

James A. Pershing
Bloomington, Indiana

ACKNOWLEDGMENTS

Editing the handbook was a team effort. The core team members are the chapter authors who chose to expend the effort and the time to share with us in writing their knowledge and expertise about the field of human performance technology (HPT). Writing well is a laborious task, and this talented group of individuals has provided us with thought-provoking as well as valuable "how to" information that will advance the field of HPT. Their involvement, which often required substantive reorganization and rewriting of their chapters in response to reviewer comments and editorial suggestions, was central in helping to produce an integrated volume. I offer to the chapter authors my sincere appreciation and hope that the final product meets their expectations.

I also want to thank the seven part editors: Monique Mueller, Jim Hill, Karen L. Medsker, Mark J. Lauer, Jana L. Pershing, Debra Haney, and Darlene M. Van Tiem. This group of distinguished scholars and practicing professionals also constitute the handbook editorial advisory board. All of these individuals provided valued input in identifying and selecting authors, editing the content of chapters, and encouraging and challenging chapter authors to produce their best work. They also provided me with encouragement when I needed it and were very receptive to working with tight timelines and unexpected snafus. My appreciation goes to all seven editorial board members for their dedication and professionalism. I learned a lot from them.

I want to thank the International Society for Performance Improvement (ISPI) for its sponsorship and support in producing this volume. A special thanks goes to ISPI's elected leaders, who supported the production of this third volume, represented by ISPI presidents Guy W. Wallace (2003–2004), Donald T. Tosti (2004–2005), and Sivasailam Thiagarajan (2005–2006). Also a special thanks goes to ISPI staff, represented by April Davis, senior director and head of the book-publishing program, and Richard D. Battaglia, executive director. These ISPI elected members and staff provided valued resources and logistical support. Most of all, they granted the editorial board and me complete autonomy as we organized and produced the handbook to the best of our abilities.

Great appreciation goes to my wife, Patricia L. Pershing, and my Indiana University graduate assistant Alena R. Treat. Together, these two talented and patient individuals helped me to coordinate and set up systems to deal with the logistical aspects of this project. They also provided careful and thoughtful editing of the entire handbook manuscript. They made it feasible for me to invest the necessary time and effort to complete the project. Also, I want to recognize the material and moral support provided to me by my colleagues, graduate students, and the administration of my academic home, the Department of Instructional Systems Technology, School of Education, Indiana University.

My thanks to the very competent and professional staff at Pfeiffer: David B. Horne, the copy editor, for his careful and thoughtful editing of the handbook manuscript; Nina Kreiden, who managed the production of the handbook; Leota Higgins, senior editorial assistant; Matthew C. Davis, senior acquisitions editor; and Kathleen Dolan Davies, director of development. Their guidance, support, and advice at every step of the production process was valued and appreciated. They are very knowledgeable in their craft and insistent that quality be front and foremost in developing valued publications.

Producing a handbook of this magnitude is a major undertaking in time and effort. Frankly speaking, it is tedious and difficult work. My burdens were significantly lessened because of the input and support I received from the coeditors of the first two editions of the handbook, Harold D. Stolovitch and Erica J. Keeps. As I began working on this third edition, they graciously shared with me their working notes and production process templates as well as numerous insights as to what to expect and how to keep the process moving forward. Throughout the process they were available for consultation and moral support. The capstone of their support was their agreeing to write the foreword to this third edition. Harold and Erica, thank you very much.

J.P.

THE EDITOR AND
EDITORIAL ADVISORY BOARD

THE EDITOR

James A. Pershing
Professor
Department of Instructional Systems Technology
Indiana University
Bloomington, Indiana

EDITORIAL ADVISORY BOARD

Part One:
Foundations of Human Performance Technology

Monique Mueller
Chief Executive Officer
La Volta Consulting
Zurich, Switzerland, and Sitges, Spain

Part Two:
The Performance Technology Process

Jim Hill
Chief Executive Officer
Proofpoint Systems
Los Altos, California

FOREWORD TO
THE FIRST EDITION

In Memoriam
Thomas F. Gilbert
1927–1995

I offer my foreword in the hope that it can help readers focus the lenses they use to look at the *Handbook of Human Performance Technology,* which promises to offer a technology—a science, really—of human performance. At least I have had a lot of time to look at this subject in many different ways.

It has been almost thirty years now since I advertised my first workshop in "performance technology." At that time, I thought I had developed a sort of scientific way to improve human performance in the workplace. And what did I think I meant by that? A philosophy professor who is a friend of mine warned me, "You have a lot of jargon and excitement—but is it really a science, or just an urge?"

"Well, I can get results in the workplace," I huffed.

"Can you ever!" he said. "You get enough people to share your excitement, and they will improve something!"

He did not know how good a point he had made. Since then, I have discovered that job performance and job management are still so primitive that almost anyone can go into the workplace and find ways to improve performance, to a noticeable extent. An urge and some common sense will do quite well as a start. And why should the "modern" workplace not be primitive? It has been around only a hundred years or so. At Ford Motors, they are still using Henry Ford's original metal-stamping machines on the assembly lines, and there were no training development departments when I was born.

According to my dictionary, a *technology* is a system that applies the best techniques and sciences to a subject matter. Theoretically, we could have a technology of just about anything—a "cosmohirsutology," for example: how the heavens determine hair growth. Or perhaps we would prefer "hirsutocosmology": the way hair growth affects the movements of the stars. No bandwagons of this nature have come along recently, simply because they do not offer much opportunity to make a difference.

Does Human Performance Technology (HPT) pose a greater opportunity? Some economists claim that the best we can do is improve human productivity by no more than 4 or 5 percent, so why waste our precious days with Human Performance Technology? But economists look at large variables that few of us have any control over, like the weather, the aging of capital plants, government regulations, and foreign competition. A technology of human performance, however, focuses on those doing and managing the jobs, and here we find much greater potential for improving performance—the PIP, or the ratio of exemplary performance to the average. I have often discussed this elsewhere, but the rule-of-thumb PIP in the workplace runs about double: the top clerks perform 50 to 75 percent better than the average, and the spread in performance grows as jobs become more complicated. The top performers can usually be emulated because they typically do things more logically and systematically than others. That is why I call them *exemplary performers*—we can make examples of them. Obviously, then, there is a great opportunity to make huge differences in human performance, and not just the 10 or 20 percent improvement that almost any enthusiastic person walking in from outside might bring.

The opportunity is there, but it cannot be seized by our just saying that we have a technology. We must really have one and practice it systematically. If we can all agree that science is at the base of a technology, what are the characteristics of science, and does our effort here share them? I will use the characteristics of science to help polish the lenses through which you will be viewing this book.

SCIENCE HAS A CLEAR SUBJECT MATTER

Every science must be clear about its subject matter, and the science of human performance has not always been. From the start, there was an easy assumption that the focal part of our subject is human behavior, and this has caused a lot of confusion.

A subject matter has two parts: a focus (the philosophers call this the *dependent variable*) and the controls (they call these the *independent variables*). A little thought must lead us to abandon human behavior as our focal, dependent variable, since we have no interest in changing human behavior for its own sake alone. In fact, the more we think about it, the more we see that our focus is on human accomplishment, the valuable output of behavior, and that behavior itself is our independent variable. This may be very obvious when we talk about it, but it is not so obvious when we set out to practice our technology. I believe that the most difficult thing we as performance technologists have to do—or have our clients do—is focus on *accomplishments* rather than on human *behavior*.

Get a group of managers or HRD specialists together and ask them to identify the accomplishments expected in some rather simple jobs. You will find that this is not an easy task. Even bus drivers are often expected to move their buses quickly from one point to another (behavior), rather than deposit customers on time at their destinations (accomplishment). Cities that measure the *behavior* of their bus drivers tend to have too many customers complaining that buses did not stop for them. The following memory aid is about the most useful device I have found to help us distinguish accomplishment from behavior:

> *Behavior, you take with you;*
> *accomplishments, you leave behind.*

SCIENCE SIMPLIFIES

In getting us to focus clearly on improving human accomplishments, the contributors to this book are also making an effort to contribute to Human Performance Technology. The old philosophers of science insisted that scientific contributions be evaluated using a three-edged ruler: *parsimony, elegance,* and *utility.*

Parsimony, simply put, means *stinginess.* A good scientific concept should be relieved of any unnecessary baggage. It should never use three ideas to explain something if one idea will do as well. *Elegance* means that the pieces and parts of a scientific theory fit together coherently and that the science is not a messy jumble of eclectic ideas. *Utility* simply refers to the scientific contribution's usefulness—if not in the marketplace today, then at least in the development of the science.

If we look at the early development of Newtonian physics, we see how closely it adhered to these characteristics. The same is true of Skinner's rules of reinforcement: they explain the development of behavior patterns with great parsimony, elegance, and utility.

SCIENCE IS GROUNDED IN MEASUREMENT

Acceptable evidence about performance must rely on measurement. If science does nothing else, it measures, and we must become very good at measuring human performance. As a general rule, our clients in the workplace are not good at it, and here is where we can be of especially great help. We can have our greatest effects on human performance just by measuring performance correctly and making the information available.

There are three kinds of measurement, and we need them all. *Direct measures* are measures of quality, quantity, and costs (QQC). Quality measures concern such things as accuracy, class (quality beyond mere accuracy), and novelty. Quantity measures concern rate (speed of productivity), volume (where time is not critical), and timeliness. Cost measures concern labor costs, management time, and material costs. *Comparative measures,* once we know the critical QQC dimensions, can enlighten us by showing variance on performance. True exemplary performers can begin to suggest the PIP to us—roughly, the ratio of exemplary to average performance. Where exemplary performers are not available to give us estimates of the PIP, we must use our heads and our experience and begin to estimate what is possible. *Economic measures* are also necessary; direct and comparative measures of performance are not enough. We need to translate these measures into dollar values, or stakes. What is at stake for us in improving human performance? Performance engineers should acquire basic financial skills to become adequate at estimating financial worth. For example, they should know what a load factor is. (This is the number by which we multiply a person's wage in order to obtain a rough estimate of what it costs an organization to employ the person. If a maintenance specialist in a power company earns $15 an hour, for example, it actually costs the company about three times that hourly amount to employ him—in insurance, benefits, work space, utilities, supervision, training, and so on.)

One device that performance technologists should not use in measuring performance is the instrument called the *performance appraisal.* Look closely at one, and you will see that it is largely concerned with people's estimates of such vague behavioral traits as initiative, creativity, and attitude. Even if we could estimate those traits reliably, they would be poor correlatives of actual job performance. It is much easier to measure job performance directly than it is to rate such presumed correlatives.

SCIENCE IS CAREFUL OF ITS LANGUAGE

Physicists are careful when they use words like *velocity* and *speed,* because those words mean something slightly different. In the Human Performance Technology business, we need to be careful about some of our basic terms, and we can do this without creating jargon. For example, I use the term *exemplary performer*, since *top* or *peak performers* may have come to be known as such for reasons other than their performance. (Perhaps they buttered up the boss, cheated, worked eighty hours a day, or possessed some sort of genius, but we need not try to make examples of them.) To take another example, I use the word *accomplishment* because it connotes value. (*Outputs* can be malodorous and *results* disastrous.) It would be nice if we could settle on some basic terminology that really says what we want it to say.

ENGINEERING SCIENCE FOCUSES ON ITS
MOST PROMISING INDEPENDENT VARIABLES

How many kinds of things could influence our achieving exemplary standards of performance? The literature is full of suggestions, from leadership to motivation, from management sensitivity to self-esteem. I have concluded that if we make people's pay contingent on their performance, tell them clearly what we expect of them and whether they have delivered it, and give them excellent instruction when they need it, then they will mostly rise to exemplary levels of performance, no matter what else we do. If we get the three I's right—information, incentives, and instructional design—we will have done 95 percent of the job.

I am proud to have written the foreword to the *Handbook of Human Performance Technology*. As you read the book, I hope you will stay alert to how well these characteristics of a science have been considered.

Hampton, New Jersey   Thomas F. Gilbert
January 1992

FOREWORD TO
THE SECOND EDITION

"Good grief!" you might exclaim as you note the number of pages in this volume. True, there are a lot of pages, but then there is an incredible amount of worthy information at your fingertips. Fortunately, you don't have to read all the pages at once—or ever.

Were you to read this entire volume at a single sitting (prudence forbid!), it might be easy to feel overwhelmed by the sheer magnitude of the information, assertions, techniques, and procedures described herein. It would be easy to be awed by the seemingly boundless domain under discussion. And, although such an impression might have merit, it would be improper to conclude that learning one's way to the level of a competent practitioner in the performance craft would represent an insurmountable task. After all, just as it can easily be verified that the world of music is huge, one need learn only a minuscule fraction of what is knowable to become a very competent musician. And, though the domain of medical knowledge is beyond the ability of any single person to master, many practitioners provide useful services to their clients. Similarly, that there is much one *could* know about Human Performance Technology (HPT) should not deter one from an effort to become worthy in the field.

One also need not conclude that a lifetime of academic preparation is required to acquire the necessary skills. Many of the useful contributors to the field developed their expertise from the experience and coaching they received from mentors more professionally senior to themselves.

Thus it would be a mistake to conclude that formal training is the only door through which to enter the exciting and personally rewarding field of HPT, or even that the HPT classroom is where one will surely observe state-of-the-art HPT practices being modeled. Unfortunately, although there are now many graduate programs teaching aspects of HPT in our universities, few of their faculty members appear as yet to be applying much if any of that technology to their own instruction. It is as if they were still operating on the belief that telling is the same as teaching, as your own academic experience may confirm. Even so, there are many competent HPT practitioners who ply their profession from inside the walls of academe, and from whom you could learn a great deal.

WHAT IS HPT?

That is the question this volume will attempt to answer. In the chapters that follow, you will read about the nature of HPT, about the breadth of human performance problems being addressed, about the techniques and procedures used to solve these problems, about some of the research from which these techniques and procedures have been derived, and about some of the results achieved. This content will provide you with a solid foundation on which to build your own expertise in the field of human performance. (Note: though this volume is called a handbook, it isn't intended to serve as a how-to-do-it manual; it is left largely for you to decide which components and techniques will be applicable to your own world.)

Because this volume does not tell a story that must be read from beginning to end, you should feel comfortable reading the chapters in any order you find interesting. To provide a framework, however, a few words about the purpose and scope of the field may be helpful.

The term *HPT* refers to a powerful collection of techniques, procedures, and approaches intended to solve problems involving human performance. What kinds of problems? All kinds of problems, in all kinds of locations, for all kinds of people. Here is just a short sampling of the types of events that might trigger application of one or more HPT interventions, much as a leaky faucet or a decision to build a new house might trigger the need for a master plumber.

"These students have a bad attitude toward school."

"Production is down in the shipping department."

"These managers aren't motivated."

"My team doesn't believe that they've been empowered."

"It's taking too long to get these people up to speed."

"We're having way too many accidents."

"These people aren't taking charge of their own health and safety."

"Our Little League coach is a bully."

"My dog piddles on the carpet."

Each of these statements describes a symptom of a problem in need of attention, and each could benefit from the magic touch of HPT. That touch might involve any number of interventions (remedies), some involving instruction, and many not. But, regardless of the solutions applied, all are intended to improve the lives of their targets. There seems to be no limit to the types of human performance problems that can be profitably addressed, or the types of human situations that can be improved.

IT WASN'T ALWAYS THUS

It wasn't always thus. In earlier days, for example, every problem (or nonproblem) was treated with a single pill—instruction. Wrong attitude? Not motivated? Not authorized to do what they already know how to do? Not to worry; instruction will solve all. Instruction was seen as the remedy for almost every problem of human performance. The mantra seemed to be "If it moves, instruct it—and hang the cost, or the time required." This was hardly surprising, since there were as yet no techniques to facilitate systematic analysis for divining the cause(s) of a problem, nor was there an array of remedies (other than instruction) with which those problems might be solved.

The analysis issue became critical for me while working out of Paris during the 1960s. Though our company intended to solve performance problems mainly through development of programmed instruction solutions, it became clear that those who alleged to have "training problems" seldom presented problems that could be solved through instruction. In more than 80 percent of these client contacts, the appropriate remedy was something other than instruction. It was this reality that forced me to begin development of a performance analysis procedure that would quickly sort through the symptoms, identify the underlying problems, and point to relevant solutions.

Two years later, while I was managing a behavioral research laboratory for a large corporation, the same reality presented itself. My research program was designed to discover how close we could come to instantaneous development of instruction. The focus, in other words, was on severely shortening development time rather than on having an impact on delivery time. But it wasn't easy to complete the experiments. No sooner would we begin a speed run intended to quickly extract relevant information from a subject matter specialist (in a closed environment especially designed for the purpose) than we would discover that we were again faced with a problem that could (and should) be solved without instruction. Again and again we were asked to solve problems allegedly requiring instruction for their solutions, and again and again we discovered that something else would work better—and faster. This exasperation intensified the development not only of a performance analysis procedure but of nontraining solutions as well.

Other common practices of the day underline how far we have progressed in just three short decades. For example, until recently there was little or no concern with assessment of the results or outcomes of the treatments (interventions, solutions, remedies) being applied. Practitioners seemed far more concerned with the processes they were promoting than with their effects on the lives of their clients and their organizations. Evaluation tools were hardly thought to be needed when it was common knowledge that if students performed poorly or not at all, it was *their* fault—not the fault of the interventionists (for example, instructors), or of the materials, or of the procedures. Whatever the source of a failure, the finger was pointed squarely at the performers—it was always the student who got the grade. And what a diabolical grading system it was. Evaluation, such as it was, consisted of a comparison of the performance of one student (usually measured by a multiple-choice test) with that of another, rather than with an objective standard. (In the industrial arena, evaluation consisted mainly in end-of-course distribution of a "happiness sheet" intended to sample the warmth of the glow left behind by the instructors.) Thus it was that faulty measuring instruments were mated with faulty evaluation practices. The mantra "70 percent is passing" permeated the entirety of our educational system as though this magical number had been handed down from the gods themselves. Thus the conspiracy required that no matter how well students performed, at least some of them would be required to consider themselves inferior.

Instructors were often "selected" through a primitive incantation such as "You've been doing such a great job in your present assignment that now you are an instructor." And presto! With that incantation, a good artist or cabinet-maker or medical technician or salesperson was instantly transformed into an untrained, inexperienced instructor. University professors were similarly selected. Those with rich or promising publication track records and a willingness to work tirelessly on committees were judged qualified to teach—and ripe for promotion. It didn't matter much whether the teaching led to learning; after all, the Holy Grail of academe was the pursuit of publication, seldom the pursuit of academic excellence. And besides, if students didn't learn, it was their own fault. These outdated and mostly ineffective practices still exist, of course, but because of professionals such as those contributing to this volume, these practices are no longer the only option, nor are they in vogue.

BRIGHT WITH PROMISE

Currently available interventions present a much wider array of possibilities, from problem analysis to the selection, creation, and application of effective remedies. And the effectiveness of correct application of the technology is truly wondrous to behold. For example, not only can learning be guaranteed to take place and production problems to be solved, but health can be improved, self-efficacy can be made to soar, lifelong phobias can permanently be cured in less than half a day, public school students can be helped to grow two full grade levels in but a few weeks, and failure-oriented lives can firmly be put onto a path toward success. These are outcomes well worth the effort and, needless to say, they provide a great source of satisfaction to those who produce them.

Not only do currently available interventions present far more available solutions than the solution of instruction, but these interventions are also available from a broadening array of sources (which is especially gratifying when you know that instruction is often contraindicated as the primary intervention for improving performance). Human performance can be improved through proper design of buildings as well as of workstations; through improvement of mental and physical health; through redesign of tools and controls; through restructuring of the physical work environment as well as through redesign of the missions, policies, and structure of the organization; and through proper design and implementation of performance aids and incentive and feedback systems, to mention only some interventions. Today, when we think of performance improvement specialists, we no longer think only of instructors but also of health professionals, human factors engineers, tool and job aid designers, and architects. All these and more can have a profound effect on the successful performance of the wide array of clients with whom one might work (for example, students, workers, managers, marriage partners, parishioners, and so forth).

Interestingly, successful application of HPT often causes difficulties for HPT practitioners when their solutions prove too powerful (read: work "too well") for the establishment or client to tolerate—when, for example, those commissioning a project aimed at improving their instructional program discover that the best solution would be to abandon existing instruction in its entirety, or when it is discovered that unacceptable worker performance is caused not by deficiencies in the workers themselves but instead by the incompetence of their managers or by obstacles imposed by organizational policies and practices (for example, "Sorry, I'm not authorized to solve your problem"). And, all too often, the very livelihood of large numbers of people—in and out of government—depends on problems *not* being solved (for example, the drug "problem").

SCIENCE-BASED

That performance technology works as well as it does is no surprise, nor is it accidental. Just as medical practice is based on medical science, HPT prides itself on being science-based, on the derivation of its basic methodology from the best available research. Though there is no shortage of pseudoscience masquerading as sound practice, or of fads notable more for the dazzle of their processes and trappings than for the results they achieve, the field of HPT is moving rapidly toward the acceptance of science as the primary guide for the creation and perfection of its techniques. Research from the field of neuroscience, for example, not only has verified that the brain is not like a computer (when was the last time you deliberately moved information from one side of your brain to the other?) but also has provided us with a growing knowledge base from which to devise even more effective ways to accomplish our mission. It is this reliance on science as one of the arbiters of our success or failure that will expand the integrity of HPT as well as the power of its techniques.

But HPT is about a great deal more than just the prudent application of scientific research to the design of HPT interventions, for what good is the science-based design of an intervention if it is brutishly applied? What good is the application of a science-based procedure if the effectiveness of the treatment is impeded by unnecessary obstacles, or if the objects of the treatments are insulted, humiliated, or robbed of their self-esteem? What good is the application of a well-researched procedure if its best effect is too small to be easily noticeable? And how much should we value science-based practices applied more for evil than for good?

As you proceed through these pages, and then through your quest to become an exemplary HPT practitioner, it might be well to remember that accomplishment of your mission begins and ends with a concern for those human beings who will be the objects of your attention—with those who are the intended targets of your interventions. It begins with a deep respect for the lives and the agendas of those people, and with a profound concern that you not only do no harm but also do not impose (inflict?) yourself and your interventions on their lives when doing nothing would work just as well.

Nonetheless, keeping one's eye firmly on the ball is essential if we are to be perceived as effective and caring professionals. This is a mission that requires a focus on the well-being, existing abilities, and agendas of those with whom we interact rather than on the satisfaction of an urge to brandish the latest technique or hardware iteration as a glittering sword with which to skewer the objects of our attention. Among other things, this means attention to the wants and needs of clients—to the "business case" underlying our activities, to the refinement of our ability to interact tactfully, to the strengthening of our ability to function with discretion, and especially to our habit of acting reliably.

Those striving to become competent practitioners of the performance craft would do well, therefore, to remember that most of those who lose their jobs do so not because of an inability to perform their jobs but because of an absence of those critical social skills that lead to their performing reliably, politely, tactfully, discreetly, and responsibly. Those who lack these skill sets will always lose out against those who possess them.

THERE'S STILL WORK TO BE DONE

As you study the material contained herein, you might begin to think that the technology is now mature, that everything has been invented, that all the techniques have been honed to perfection, and that they have been applied to all applicable areas where they might conceivably improve performance. Nothing could be further from the truth. HPT is an evolving technology, and there's still much to learn, especially about how to disseminate the fruits of the technology to those who might benefit. For example, we have yet to make much of a dent in the bureaucracy that passes the laws and makes the rules. We have yet to attract the attention of those who create the rules that make it "illegal" to teach efficiently in our schools (for example, "70 percent is passing"), who pass the laws that require us to revere process over results, and who make the rules that confine the measurement of competence to the straitjacket of the multiple-choice test. We have yet to attract the attention of those institutions that package their wisdom into time-based chunks called "credit hours" and that have yet to require anything much in the way of instructional literacy on the part of the faculty members they employ. And we have yet to make a significant impact on those government agencies whose primary criterion for certification (and recertification) of competence in critical skills consists mainly of assessing the knowledge that may be necessary for supporting desired performances (rather than the performances themselves) and of counting the number of hours the student posteriors have been glued to classroom chairs.

It is clear that opportunities stretch as far as the eye can see, and not only for development of "new and improved" components of the technology itself. Opportunities exist for the improvement of the environments where people work and the places where they live. Opportunities exist for improvement in the performance of large systems as well as for improvement in the health, well-being, and performance of a single individual, a marriage, a family, or the family dog. And if you can but contribute to the elimination of a single obstacle to effective performance, you will have made a significant contribution to the betterment of the lives you touch. Happily, the contents of this volume will help you to do exactly that.

THE REWARD IS WORTH THE EFFORT

HPT provides a set of powerful tools with which we can and do perform humane acts of value for individuals and organizations alike. As long as we remember that these tools are intended to serve as means rather than as ends in themselves—as long as we remember to measure our success by the results we achieve rather than by the glitter of our processes—we will continue to grow in value to our mission, and HPT will justifiably be perceived as an enterprise worthy of acclaim. This volume will introduce you to the practitioners and the practices through which that accomplishment can indeed be achieved.

Carefree, Arizona   Robert F. Mager
January 1999

FOUNDATIONS OF HUMAN PERFORMANCE TECHNOLOGY

MONIQUE MUELLER

Nearly fifty years of research and practice with human performance technology (HPT) have led to a vast body of literature: theoretical concepts and models, case studies, and lessons learned from application. As HPT evolves, and a healthy debate on what it really entails continues, we have one certainty, that the field is alive and well.

Through experience and through the solid work of scholars and professional practitioners, HTP now is firmly grounded in a set of fundamental principles and a code of ethics.

The purpose of the chapters in Part One is to introduce these fundamentals. They are meant to orient the reader with an overview of what HPT is about, its practical application, the basic concepts and models, and the history and evolution of the field.

The first chapter, by James Pershing, provides a definition of the field and a process model. It explains in unambiguous terms what HPT is today. As with any serious professional field, future research and insights may make some knowledge obsolete and confirm other knowledge. For today, this is what we know and agree upon.

The next three chapters are devoted to the application of HPT. First, Roger Addison and Carol Haig take you on a journey through the key elements of a full performance process, with its pitfalls and how to avoid them, including guidelines and tools. This is followed by a chapter by Kenneth Silber and

Lynn Kearny, which ties HPT firmly into the world of business. Understanding the language of business is an essential prerequisite for successful performance improvement. This language is financial, the data mostly numeric, and the valued results economic. The chapter shows you how to learn your client's language and how to find, analyze, and use financial data for your HPT project. Chapter Four, by William Daniels and Timm Esque, is concerned with the essential concept of feedback. No other word in our field has been used and abused to such an extent. The authors build solidly on tried-and-true experience in the field, develop a detailed case study of a working feedback system in a large high-tech company, and share their insights on how to implement feedback for results.

Two subsequent chapters delve deeply into theory. First you will find a detailed analysis by Dale Brethower of the concept of systems thinking. *Be systemic* is one of the fundamental principles of HPT. Accordingly, systemic issues appear in most publications within HPT and within many other disciplines. This has created confusion about the definition of systems, sometimes for lack of a definition, often for excess of conflicting definitions. This chapter explains the meaning and value of being systemic. To illustrate and clarify the concept it tells you stories from various sources: fiction, a case study from a large company, and examples from the author's experience.

Chapter Six presents Roger Kaufman's model of HPT, which is probably the most inclusive. The author's quest is to provide meaningful results consistent with the fundamental principles of HPT. His view of meaningful results aims at looking for all elements involved: the world, society, companies, and individuals. Any change intervention should lead to a better future for all. At the very least, companies should try to do no harm to their environments. Kaufman puts the threshold high and expects you to be concerned as much with ethics as with the bottom line.

The final chapter, by Camille Ferond, takes a general look at both history and the future of humankind's struggle to improve its well-being, its knowledge, and its organizations. Within the field of HPT it summarizes the work of the main thinkers and explains how all of them build on prior knowledge to expand or invent new HPT models and tools.

Part One of this HPT handbook is designed to be an introduction to the key concepts of human performance technology. Readers who are new to the field or have little experience will become familiar with the essential ideas of HPT. Also, experienced professionals will find new and exciting views that put a different focus on HPT's crucial questions. Part One sets the stage for the remaining parts of the book, in which methodology, methods, and tools will be presented in detail and within different contexts of thought and application.

Our field is evolving and attracting interest from a large variety of sources. HPT can help to improve performance in all sectors of society, be they business, public, or nonprofit. Within the past decade the field has become more international. HPT will benefit vastly from research and practice from all over the globe. Thus far, the experience with HPT in a variety of countries is encouraging; we can therefore assume that HPT is effective independent of culture. Or, the other way round, that those cultural issues can properly be addressed within the HPT framework.

CHAPTER ONE

Human Performance
Technology Fundamentals

James A. Pershing

Ideas and conceptualizations of human performance technology (HPT) have
evolved over time. What we know about HPT today is timebound. It builds
upon the work of a number of academic and professional practitioners begun
in the United States in the 1950s and 1960s. Randell K. Day, in the book
*Performance Improvement Pathfinders: Models for Organizational Learning
Systems,* edited by Peter J. Dean and David E. Ripley (1997), presents the case
that the field of HPT evolved from the ideas of B. F. Skinner and his collaborators. "Many performance improvement pioneers got their start by attempting to
improve training and were heavily influenced by Skinner" (Day, 1997, p. 22).
Skinner was trying to explain how people operate in their environments. He
formulated the idea that people "learn to manipulate and control their environment by their responses to it" (Day, 1997, p. 23).

Susan Markle, an early collaborator with Skinner, worked on the development of teaching machines and accompanying instructional materials. These
activities and much experimentation by Markle and others on designing instructional materials led to the design and development of *programmed instruction*
(Day, 1997).

Early in the heyday of programmed instruction, Thomas Gilbert and Joe
Harless experienced instances in which well-designed instruction was failing to
have an impact on individual and organizational performance. Both Gilbert and
Harless came to recognize that training is but one factor that affects human performance. They questioned at the outset of design and development whether

training was the appropriate intervention to improve individual and organizational performance. These ideas are well articulated in Harless's 1970 book *An Ounce of Analysis (Is Worth a Pound of Objectives)* and Gilbert's 1978 book *Human Competence: Engineering Worthy Performance.* During the past fifty years, a plethora of individuals has influenced the growth and direction of HPT. Studying the ideas of these individuals and their evolving thinking is to see history in action (Argyris, 1970; Brethower and Smalley 1998; Coscarelli, 1988; Geis, 1986; Harless, 1970, 1988; Kaufman, 2000; Langdon, 1999, 2000; Mager and Pipe, 1984; Molenda, Pershing, and Reigeluth, 1996; Robinson and Robinson, 1989; Romiszowski, 1981; Rosenberg, 1996; Rossett, 1987, 1999; Rothwell, 1996; Rummler and Brache, 1995; Stolovitch and Keeps, 1992, 1999; Wile, 1996; Zemke and Kramlinger, 1982).

A DEFINITION OF HUMAN PERFORMANCE TECHNOLOGY

Defining a field is risky business. There are at least two hazards. The first has to do with time. Any definition is today's definition and may not fit as a definition for tomorrow. Second, many people are very familiar with the illustrious history and foundations of HPT. They will not agree with all of the elements or their emphases in any one definition. These points are exemplified in looking at a sample of definitions for HPT that have been offered over the past four decades (see Table 1.1). Cognizant of these risks, I offer the definition that I have developed and use with my clients and students:

> Human performance technology is the study and ethical practice of improving productivity in organizations by designing and developing effective interventions that are results-oriented, comprehensive, and systemic.

ELEMENTS OF THE DEFINITION

Following is a discussion of each of the key terms used in this definition of HPT. Understanding the meaning of each in the context of the overall definition is important.

Study

The use of the term *study* means that human performance technologists carefully examine and analyze questions that arise in understanding and applying their knowledge and skills. These questions involve both *how* to do HPT and *what* to do in given situations. This requires an understanding of the theoretical, empirical, and research foundations of the field.

Table 1.1. Sample of Definitions of Human Performance Technology from the Past Thirty Years.

Author(s)	Definition	Key Terms
Gilbert (1978, p. 18)	Human competence is a function of worthy performance (W), which is a function of the ratio of valuable accomplishments (A) to costly behavior (B).	• Accomplishment • Behavior • Competence
Ainsworth (1979, p. 5)	A cornerstone of performance technology is outcome signification—discovering valid, useful performance objectives and stating them in terms that are easily understood.	• Objective • Outcome signification
Stolovitch (1982, p. 16)	A field of endeavor that seeks to bring about changes to a system in such a way that the system is improved in terms of the achievements it values.	• Achievements • Change • System
Harless (In Geis, 1986, p. 1)	Human performance technology is the process of selection, analysis design, development, implementation, and evaluation of programs to most cost-effectively influence human behavior and accomplishment.	• Accomplishment • Behavior • Cost effective • Process
NSPI, via Coscarelli (1988, p. 8)	A set of methods and processes for solving problems—or realizing opportunities—related to the performance of people. It may be applied to individuals, small groups or large organizations.	• Processes • Realizing opportunities • Solving problems
Langdon (1991, p. 2)	Systematic application of identifying that a need exists to establish, maintain, extinguish, or improve performance in an individual or organization; defining the need; identifying, implementing, and networking appropriate interventions; and validating that the results are true improvements.	• Establish • Extinguish • Improve • Maintain • Systematic

(Continued)

Table 1.1. Sample of Definitions of Human Performance Technology from the Past Thirty Years. (*Continued*)

Author(s)	Definition	Key Terms
Stolovitch and Keeps (1992, p. 4; 1999, p. 5)	The application of what is known about human and organizational behavior to enhance accomplishments, economically and effectively, in ways that are valued within the work setting. Thus HPT is a field of endeavor that seeks to bring about changes to a system, in such a way that the system is improved in terms of the achievement it values.	• Accomplishments • Change to a system • Human and organizational behavior
Rothwell (1996, p. 29)	Human Performance Enhancement (HPE) is the field focused on systematically and holistically improving present and future work results achieved by people in organizational settings.	• Holistically • Present and future work • Systematically
O'Driscoll (1999, p. 97)	Systems thinking applied to human resource activities. (1) Systemic, (2) systematic, (3) grounded in scientifically derived theories and the best empirical evidence available, (4) open to all means, methods, and media, and (5) focused on achievement that human performers and the system value.	• Achievement • Derived theories • Grounded in science • Systems thinking • System value
Van Tiem, Moseley, and Dessinger (2004, p. 2)	The systematic process of linking business goals and strategies with the workforce responsible for achieving goals. Moreover, performance technology practitioners study and design processes that bring about increased performance in the workplace using a common methodology to understand, inspire, and improve. And finally, performance technology systematically analyzes performance problems and their underlying causes and describes exemplary performance.	• Achieving goals • Analyzes • Common methodology • Design processes • Study • Success indicators • Systematic process

(Continued)

Table 1.1. (*Continued*)

Author(s)	Definition	Key Terms
ISPI (2005b)	A systematic approach to improving productivity and competence, uses a set of methods and procedures—and a strategy for solving problems—for realizing opportunities related to the performance of people. More specific, it is a process of selection, analysis, design, development, implementation, and evaluation of programs to most cost-effectively influence human behavior and accomplishment. It is a systematic combination of three fundamental processes: performance analysis, cause analysis, and intervention selection, and can be applied to individuals, small groups, and large organizations	• Accomplishment • Competence • Cost effective • Process • Realizing opportunities • Solving problems • Systematic

A key to understanding the importance of the term *study* in HPT is the idea of disciplined and systematic inquiry. This involves asking questions and seeking answers about human performance in orderly and prescribed ways that follow organized sets of principles. It includes both quantitative and qualitative approaches to research as well as philosophical analyses, historical investigations, theorizing and theory building, model development, and evaluation.

From the beginning, systematic inquiry, including research and evaluation, has been the genesis for new ideas in HPT. Early on, the dominant paradigm for inquiry was studies that focused on *proving* that specific interventions were effective ways to improve individual and organizational performance. Today, the performance technology researcher and evaluator have added other paradigms or ways of looking at and approaching research and evaluation. These include understanding the complex world of people's experiences from their points of view as they function in natural or authentic settings (Mertens, 2005). Popular labels associated with these two paradigms are *quantitative* and *qualitative* research. In contemporary practice many HPT researchers and evaluators combine or blend these paradigms.

The importance of the term *study* in the definition is threefold. First, study is critical to understanding and improving the practice of HPT. Second, study is important to the selection, design, development, and testing of human performance interventions. Finally, it is important to avoid the trap of believing that we already know all that needs to be known about how and what to do in HPT. The continued growth of HPT is dependent upon performance technologists who think about the field, practice it, and do not become complacent by believing that the philosophy of HPT is set in stone, that its history has been written, its theories and models are beyond reproach, and how we ask and answer research and evaluation questions are one dimensional and tied to one research paradigm. *Study* we do, and *study* we must.

Ethical Practice

HPT has a long history of ethical standards and ethical practice (Dean, 1993; Watkins, Leigh, and Kaufman, 2000; Westgaard, 1988). The certified performance technologist (CPT) credential of the International Society for Performance Improvement (ISPI) emphasizes recent guidelines for ethical standards and ethical practice.

The CPT code of ethics includes (1) the principle of adding value for clients, their customers, and the global environment; (2) promoting and using validated performance technology strategies and standards that align with an existing body of theory, research, and practice knowledge; (3) working collaboratively with clients and being a trustworthy strategic partner; (4) continually improving one's proficiency in the field of HPT; (5) practicing integrity by being honest and truthful in representations to clients, colleagues, and others; and (6) maintaining client confidentiality and avoiding conflicts of interest (International Society for Performance Improvement, Certified Performance Technologist, 2002).

In this time of corporate scandal and international strife, there are increasing concerns about ethical issues in HPT. Nonethical behavior is detrimental to individuals, groups, organizations, the profession, and society. It undermines the work and good intentions of all who practice in the field. Key elements in ethical behavior are to *do no harm* to your clients, their customers, and the profession and to keep in the forefront serving the *good* of society.

Improving Productivity

To *improve* is to make better and involves enhancing quality and value. Productivity has both quality and quantity dimensions. It is the maximum value that an organization that delivers a particular product or service creates at a given cost using the best available management techniques, skills, technologies, and required inputs. "In a nutshell, productivity reflects results as a function of effort. In a classical sense, productivity is defined as a ratio such that the output of an effort under investigation is divided by the inputs . . . required to produce the output" (Brinkerhoff and Dressler, 1990, p. 16).

Productivity can be simply depicted as the relationships between inputs, processes, outputs, and feedback. "Inputs are the resources consumed in producing the goods and services of an organization" (Brinkerhoff and Dressler, 1990, p. 72), while outputs are simply the goods and services an organization produces. Processes are mechanisms organizations employ to convert inputs to outputs. Feedback is the means organizations use to calibrate the inputs, processes, and outputs. There are essentially three ways to increase productivity. An organization can hold inputs constant and increase outputs. Second, outputs can be held constant and inputs can be decreased. And finally, inputs can be decreased while outputs are increased. These combinations are achieved by modifying or changing inputs and processes.

Organizations

Organizations are enterprises that are dynamic, political, economic, and social systems with multiple goals. They are invented by, made up of, and serve the needs of people. People come together and create an organizational culture consisting of principles, ideas, and pronouncements that define an organization. They also create a structure that defines the roles, relationships, tasks, and duties of individuals and groups. Finally, organizations operate in a larger environment that requires the development of direct and indirect relationships with other organizations, including suppliers, distributors, stockholders, and others. Organizations are purposeful and serve the needs of their members and a public that values and consumes the organization's products and services.

Historically, HPT has had as its major focus individuals, including workers and managers. Over the years, several human performance technologists and management gurus have modified or changed this single focus on individual workers. Ideas from two pioneers exemplify this shift in thinking. Thomas Gilbert, in referencing organizational systems, observed that if you "put good people in a bad system, the system will dominate" (quoted in Dean, 1997, p. 63). W. Edwards Deming, a founder of total quality management (TQM), emphasized that workers are not the source of problems in organizations. Managers and those that lead organizations have the control and power to change and improve the structure of organizations, and problems rest with them, not the powerless worker (Petty, 1991).

So nobody works alone. People work in organizations and regularly interact with other individuals. Individuals belong to units or work groups and receive and give information, meet, and problem solve as part of and in the context of a group which is part of an organization (Hanson and Lubin, 1995). In short, people's needs are organizational needs and organizational needs are people's needs. The two are inextricably entwined.

Designing and Developing

Designing involves the preparation of a detailed plan for performance-improvement interventions. It includes completing a performance analysis, specifying objectives, identifying characteristics of the affected population, grouping and sequencing objectives, specifying characteristics of the interventions, and executing an evaluation process. Designers orchestrate and logically sequence a series of activities that solves problems and improves performance.

Production involves translating design specifications into actual interventions and strategies for implementing them. Performance design is often confused with performance development. The major difference is that design indicates what the performance should look like, whereas development indicates how to make it that way (Reigeluth, 1983).

Effective

Effective performance improvement produces desired results. It is achievement of purpose; doing the right thing and doing it right. Doing the right thing means that performance is aligned with the mission, goals, and purposes of the organization. This *strategic alignment* means that there is a direct and traceable relationship between a performance-improvement initiative and a declared goal of the organization.

Doing things right is subsumed with doing the right thing. It means achieving desired results with a minimum of inputs. So there is a hierarchy for effective and efficient behavior. Effective behavior is efficient, but efficient behavior may not be effective.

For example, a city builds a traffic bridge over a small river. The bridge is built to state and federal load and safety standards for minimal costs: it is built efficiently. However, a traffic bridge may not be the best solution to a strategic goal of the city: the movement of people. Mass transit may be a better solution. Or moving people across the river may become less important if zoning laws that restrict commercial and home building on the floodplain on the far side of the river are enacted and enforced. If the bridge is the best solution but building it takes decades versus months and nearly bankrupts the city with cost overruns delaying its use, it is not effective. Effectiveness is being correct and in so doing, doing things correctly.

Interventions

An intervention is a course of action taken to improve performance. It is planned and purposeful, and requires organizations and the people in them to behave differently. Interventions have to be proactively planned for and managed, and people must adapt to them. Interventions are designed and developed to respond to specific needs, which are gaps between where an organization is and where it seeks to be in the future.

Results-Oriented

An enduring and distinguishing principle of HPT is focusing first and focusing last on *results*. Results must be tangible and measurable, due to a performance improvement initiative, and must positively affect an organization. They must create value for the organization, its members, and its customers. In short, they must have a positive impact.

There are many types of results. Some focus on an organization's bottom line. Examples include increased production, reduced scrap, reduced backlog work, and reduced costs. Time savings also have an impact on the bottom line of an organization. The focus also can be on workers and work teams. Examples include reduction in accidents, increases in worker health and safety, improvements in morale and motivation, increases in knowledge and skills, and reductions in grievances and personnel turnover. Or the focus can be market-oriented, such as increased market share, maintaining and increasing satisfied customers and repeat business, long-term growth, and expanding partnerships. Finally, organizations can focus externally and serve and give back to the community by being good corporate citizens and avoiding externalities such as air and water pollution, worker exploitation, and wasting of natural resources.

All results must be legal, ethical, and morally defensible. Most important, they must be aligned with one or more of the values, missions, goals, and objectives of the organization.

Comprehensive and Systemic

To be effective, performance-improvement interventions must solve the whole problem; that is, be comprehensive. The interventions must also be integrated into the organization, which is being systemic (Irlbeck, 2002). In deriving a solution set and as the whole picture is uncovered as we seek to maximize effectiveness, there are inevitable trade-offs when only partial performance issues are identifiable or partial solutions are feasible.

All organizations are complex systems of multiple and mutually interacting components. These interrelated parts connect with one another to carry out the purposes of the organization. The parts of an organization are unified as a whole by complex sets of rules, principles, ideas, and methods that govern the interactions and behavior of the parts. There are also boundaries for organizations that separate them from other organizations.

Systemic interventions address organizational needs as a whole, especially with regard to an organization's vital processes and functions. Systemic problem solving looks beyond linear cause and effect by taking the perspective that a given cause and its effect cannot be separated or isolated from their context. It is a matter of holism versus reductionism (Douglas and Wykowski, 1999; Hallbom and Hallbom, 2005).

In explaining the idea of systemic thinking and problem solving, I find a useful analogy in the old game of "pick-up sticks." For those unfamiliar with this game, it often uses painted wood sticks that are about eight inches in length and look like oversized toothpicks. Twenty-five or so sticks come in a bundle, often stored in a tube. A player grasps the bundle of sticks and drops them on a table in a pile. The object of the game is to pick up as many sticks as possible, one at a time, without disturbing the rest of the pile.

Imagine each stick as a part or element of an organization. When dropped, the pile of entwined sticks represents the organization as a whole. Some of the sticks may not touch or they may only touch in simplistic and easy-to-manage ways. Other sticks will be piled in a complex web, and if disturbed or changed, they will move or disturb other sticks. In other words, there are *ripple effects* of moving or changing any one part of the organization, with some parts being more affected or sensitive to change than others. Moreover, as the pile of sticks is disturbed as a player touches and manipulates a given stick or part, the pile as a whole changes its form. Although not a perfect analogy, the game of "pick-up sticks" does illustrate the need for performance-improvement initiatives to be comprehensive and systemic.

PERFORMANCE-IMPROVEMENT MODEL

As with definition building, model building in HPT is risky. I often get the questions, Why are there so many HPT models? and Why has the field not settled on one model? In my judgment, the answer is threefold. First, if one looks back over time, as the field has matured and the ways organizations operate and are managed have changed, academics and practitioners have adapted their views and practices. The models they use reflect these changes. Second, organizations have different needs, vary in their orientations to HPT, and have HPT personnel from varying backgrounds. Because of this, performance technologists customize an HPT model that reflects their views and ways of doing performance improvement. Third, there is the view that some academics and independent consultants build models for self-promotion and as a marketing device.

The model I have built and use is a process model. It builds on the work of others, consists of a set of components that I find essential in doing HPT, and fits with my definition and view of the field. Use it as is, adapt it, or reject all or parts of it. Do not accept or use it without study. The graphic depiction is displayed in Figure 1.1.

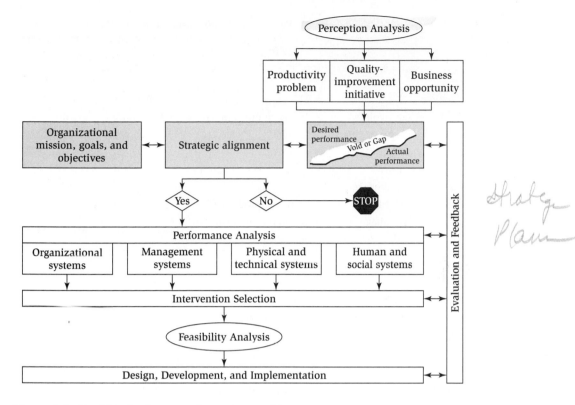

Figure 1.1. Pershing Performance Improvement Process.

Getting Started

As displayed in Figure 1.1, the *performance-improvement process* has a beginning. I find that individuals or a group in an organization move forward with one of three types of perceptions. They believe there are performance problems, they believe there is a challenge for quality improvement, or they believe that new or emerging business opportunities have arisen (see Table 1.2). Furthermore, they sense that there is a void or gap between where the organization is and where it ought to be. The void or gap is often perceived as the difference between present or actual performance and desired future performance.

Perception Analysis

Needs for performance improvements are identified on a daily basis in organizations. Given this frequent activity, how is a performance analyst to know which needs are important and deserve attention?

Different performance-improvement needs will have different perceived levels of importance within an organization. This leaves the question, Who has the

Table 1.2. Sample Performance-Improvement Initiatives.

Performance Problem	Quality Improvement Initiative or Challenge	Business Opportunity
• Backlogs	• Decrease inputs	• Acquire new business
• Customer complaints	• Increase outputs	• Acquire competitor
• Delivery delays	• Increase return on investment	• Enter new geographic market
• Employee absenteeism		
• Employee turnover	• Improve organizational climate	• Expand customer base
• Equipment downtime		• Expand product line
• Quality-control failure	• Improve processes	• Merge businesses
• Waste and breakage	• Reduce unit costs	
• Worker health and safety	• Speed up delivery	

correct perspective? For the performance analyst the key to this dilemma is found in the process of *perception analysis.*

The power of individual and group perceptions is well established in the literature on performance analysis, needs assessment, and organizational change (Hall and Hord, 1978; Eggen and Kauchak, 1997; Tafoya, 1983). If you are familiar with the idea that someone's perception is his or her reality, then you are familiar with the most basic reason for carrying out a perception analysis as part of the performance-improvement process. Individuals and groups within an organization may have widely varying understandings of the same situation, event, process, or need.

Perceived needs reside in the values, beliefs, opinions, and judgments people have about their work and the culture of their organization. Often they evolve from people's reactions to events or situations. In a way, they are like the vital signs of an organization as viewed by the very people who make up the organization. Such information helps gauge individual and group perceptions and possible ambivalence toward, support for, or resistance to an identified need and potential interventions. Perception analysis uses three guiding questions to reveal three important aspects of the need: who, how, and why?

The Who Question. The who question identifies which individuals and groups are involved in the performance-improvement initiative. At a minimum, a perception analysis discerns the sponsors, champions, and stakeholders.

Sponsors are people and groups with influence and power. They control the purse strings and have the authority to devote resources to a performance-improvement initiative. Their belief in and their willingness to support an initiative are vital to success. Champions are individuals or groups that lead the effort to improve performance. They are personally invested in the process and believe in its importance and potential. Stakeholders are individuals and groups either directly or indirectly affected by the performance-improvement initiative. They will include employees, owners, stockholders, customers, suppliers, and others. They have significant interest in the actions and effectiveness of the organization. Performance-improvement initiatives must have a strong sponsor and champion. These may be the same person or group. Stakeholder support is helpful. More critical, however, is to make sure that key stakeholders are not hostile toward an initiative or overtly intent on undermining the efforts.

The How Question. Perception analysis considers the origin of the need because the very nature of people's perceptions of a problem, quality-improvement initiative, or business opportunity is rooted in the originator's perceptions. This gets at the issue of ownership. If the performance analyst identifies a need or opportunity, it is considered proactive. This type of purposeful action by the analyst will need to be sold to affected individuals and groups so that they take ownership. If the initiative is perceived to be owned only by the analyst, it will falter or fail.

Reactive situations occur when individuals or groups identify a need or opportunity and seek assistance from performance-improvement specialists. The initiators have ownership. Challenges for the performance analyst come into play when the need or opportunity is misdiagnosed by the owners and the interventions are predetermined and do not meet the need. In such instances, the analyst must sell the rigor of the performance-analysis process.

The Why Question. The final perception-analysis question is Why is the perceived performance-improvement initiative important? This is essentially a matter of impact: impact upon individuals, groups, the organization as a whole, other organizations, and society. It is best answered in terms of the next component in the model, strategic alignment.

Strategic Alignment with Organizational Mission, Goals, and Objectives

A way to judge the importance of a perceived need is to ascertain its relationship to meeting the missions, goals, and objectives of the organization. This is *strategic alignment.* The essence of strategic alignment is looking for agreement between perceived needs and the goals and tactical behavior of an organization. Strategic alignment is a *state of affairs,* not an outcome. The assumption is that alignment leads to increased organizational effectiveness and performance-improvement initiatives that contribute to rather than conflict with strategic alignment. The performance-improvement analyst must ask, If this need is met, will this fit or conflict with the organization's missions and goals in the following ways?

- *Values:* Do the perceived need and potential interventions fit with the set of preferences and judgments concerning what individuals and groups in the organization deem as good or bad and desirable or undesirable?

- *Norms:* Will the proposed interventions support formal and informal guidelines for acceptable and unacceptable behavior standards that facilitate interactions between individuals and groups in the organization?

- *Culture:* Is there congruency with the prevailing values, beliefs, and expectations within the organization, including the ways the organization is managed, what is expected of its members, and goal attainment?

- *Structure:* Is there a rational cascade of goals, key processes, teams, and individuals so that outputs contribute directly to goal attainment and reward systems?

- *Performance:* Will the interventions help individuals and groups engage in goal-directed, results-oriented behavior?

- *Environment:* Are there external factors or demands from the environment that conflict with the proposed interventions? [Adapted from Semler, 1997]

Questions of strategic alignment are the most important in the performance-improvement process. Too often, nonaligned performance-improvement initiatives are undertaken, resulting in suboptimal behavior. Organizations are often caught up in expending resources and time in solving problems or seizing opportunities with little or no payback or contribution to organizational goals. Sometimes the outcomes have negative consequences and make things worse by addressing performance in a way that directly conflicts with organizational goals. If a performance-improvement initiative is not strategically aligned and causes suboptimal behavior by individuals or groups, as the model depicts, stop and move on to another project.

Performance Analysis

Performance analysis focuses on factors that drive individual, group, and organizational performance. The factors may be causes of problems, road maps to improve quality, or ways to exploit opportunities. They are the why questions, and the answers can be classified and analyzed in several ways.

In terms of classification, there are a number of popular HPT models that depict performance elements and suggest that analyzing performance gaps is often complicated and multifaceted (Gilbert, 1978; Langdon, 1999, 2000; Mager and Pipe, 1984; Molenda, Pershing, and Reigeluth, 1996; Robinson and Robinson, 1989; Van Tiem, Moseley, and Dessinger, 2004; Wile, 1996). The taxonomy of performance elements or classification scheme depicted in the performance-improvement-process model (Figure 1.1) synthesizes elements from models of five distinguished names in the HPT field: Harless (1970, 1988, 1997), Gilbert, (1978), Rossett (1999), Spitzer (1992), and Wile (1996). It also builds upon the work of Gilmore and Pershing (2001). The four elements are organizational systems, management systems, physical and technical systems, and human and social systems.

Organizational Systems. At the core of any organization is its economic status for present and future conditions, including financial stability and readiness for change. Its structure is important, including lines of communication, lines of command, span of control, and divisions of labor. Both formal and informal lines of communication are significant, as are relationships between management, employees, suppliers, customers, the community, and government. How people access information, methods of operation, and executive decision making are part of the organizational system (Gilley and Coffern, 1994). The goal in analyzing an organizational system is to look for ways to improve organizational viability and effectiveness.

Management Systems. At the heart of every organization are people who manage others. They provide guidance and direction to employees and serve as the interface with the organization's executives. The functions of managers are to delegate, develop personnel, conduct performance appraisals, and establish priorities. Managers need to have good listening skills, provide constructive feedback, and have productive relationships with the employees they manage. In short, they must be skilled at the art of managing and be supported at the organizational level as they do so (Gilley, Eggland, and Gilley, 2002). The goal in analyzing the management system is to improve management practices and techniques.

Physical and Technical Systems. Organizations of every type have facilities, equipment, and tools that surround its members. These need to be up to date and appropriate for the tasks that are performed. Facilities need to be of adequate size, properly lighted, well heated or cooled and ventilated, noise inhibitive, and so on. Equipment and tools need to be available, ergonomically sound, and safe. Facilities, equipment, and tools need to be well maintained (Rothwell, 1996).

All organizations have technical processes that combine and integrate people, machines, materials, and methods to produce a product or service (Mears, 1995).

These work activities consist of sets of interrelated tasks that produce results. The ideal is to minimize the variation in these technical processes. Information and engineered systems are often combined with various job aids and performance support tools that reduce system complexities and enhance the mental and physical capabilities of individuals and teams. Well-designed technical systems minimize worker fatigue and monotony, enhance safety, minimize physical distractions, and maximize the quality and quantity of outputs (Pipe, 1986). Productive organizations invest in the necessary facilities, equipment, tools, and technical processes to be effective.

Human and Social Systems. People in effective organizations are competent. They have the required skills, knowledge, aptitudes, and attitudes or beliefs to perform effectively whether individually or in groups. They know how to solve problems and work in teams. The organization has formal and informal on-the-job education and training systems in place to maintain and enhance the competencies of its members. These education and training systems have clear linkages with workplace applications.

Effective organizations also have effective systems for recruiting, hiring, orienting, advancing, and redeploying competent people. Often there are structured coaching and mentoring systems in place. There are also support systems in place to help workers be safe and healthy, and for emotional support. According to Gilley and Boughton (1996), a healthy work environment includes freedom from fear, positive interactions with others, personal involvement, trust, honesty, and self-esteem.

Effective organizations also have reward systems and incentives that support individual and team performance. Rules and regulations for worker compliance with policies, procedures, and work rules are clear and fairly administered.

Finally, there are systems in place that enhance collaboration and group dynamics. Examples include team and group work between management and labor, day and night shifts, home and field offices, technicians and engineers, and departments. In effective organizations, race, ethnicity, and gender are celebrated, and diversity adds to productivity (Hanson and Lubin, 1995). Productive organizations invest in their people and treat them well.

Order of the Four Elements. The order of the elements in the model, from left to right, has meaning. When carrying out a performance analysis, experience has taught me to look at all four elements but to look first at the organizational system, second at the management system, third at physical and technical systems, and finally at human and social systems. Over time, I have also learned that the order, again from left to right, has meaning in terms of level of difficulty in problem identification and problem solving. These experiences parallel what David Wile (1996) reported in presenting his classification scheme of seven elements: organization systems, incentives, cognitive support, tools, physical environment, skills and knowledge, and inherent ability.

How Is It Done? Performance analysis is a form of action research. Research involves "a problem to be investigated, a process of inquiry, and explanations that enable individuals to understand the nature of the problem. Research can also incorporate actions that attempt to resolve the problem being investigated" (Stringer, 1996, p. 5). In paraphrasing Denzin and Lincoln (1994), Stringer explains action research as follows:

> Its purpose is to assist people in extending their understanding of their situation and thus resolve problems that confront them. Put another way . . . action research provides a model for enacting local, action-oriented approaches to inquiry, applying small-scale theorizing to specific problems in specific situations [p. 9].

According to Stringer, this approach to research may be used to enhance work practices by reviewing goals and procedures, evaluating their effectiveness, and planning activities and strategies. It can help to "resolve specific problems and crises by defining the problem, exploring its context, analyzing its component parts, and developing strategies for its resolution" (1996, p. 13). Is this not the essence of the performance-analysis process?

For each of the four performance-analysis elements in the performance-improvement process model (Figure 1.1), the analyst will pose questions, collect data, analyze the data, and determine a response. These action research activities are akin to pieces in a complex puzzle (see Figure 1.2).

Intervention Selection

Once the performance gap and its underlying causes, means, or opportunities are identified, interventions can be selected. Performance problems, quality-improvement initiatives, and business opportunities are usually multidimensional, and more than one intervention is needed. Performance can be improved even more and maintained for a longer period of time when interventions across the performance-improvement technology spectrum are coordinated (Rosenberg, 1996).

According to well-established intervention design and selection principles, there are many different interventions to improve performance (Burke, 1982; Coleman, 1992; Deterline and Rosenberg, 1992; Holton, 1999; Langdon, Whiteside, and McKenna, 1999). Various authors have developed comprehensive classification and categorical schemes for major performance-improvement interventions. For a comprehensive understanding of several options, I recommend the *Intervention Resource Guide: 50 Performance Improvement Tools* (Langdon, Whiteside, and McKenna, 1999).

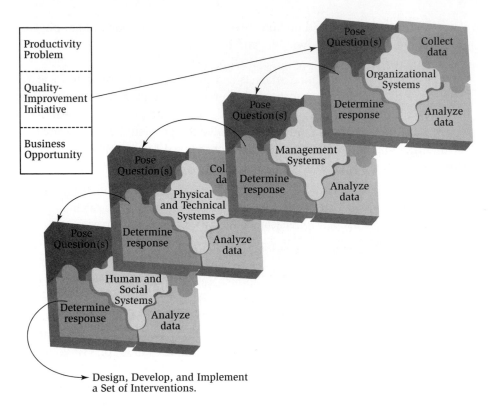

Figure 1.2. Analyzing Performance-Improvement Initiatives.

As early as 1970, Argyris developed three basic requirements for effective intervention selection: valid and useful information, free choice, and internal commitment. By valid and useful information, Argyris meant "that which describes the factors plus their interrelationship that create the problem for the client system" (Argyris, 1970, p. 17). By free choice he meant "the locus of decision making [is] in the client system" (p. 19) and the client is provided alternatives for action. No particular or specified action is automatic, preordained, or imposed. By internal commitment, Argyris (1970) meant that the client owns the choices made and feels responsible for implementing them.

Without careful planning, intervention selection can lead to disaster. To increase success, Spitzer (1992) suggests eleven principles that will enhance the successful selection of interventions. They can be summarized as follows. Choose interventions that

1. Are based upon a comprehensive understanding of the situation

2. Are carefully targeted

3. Are sponsor-based and supported

4. Employ a team approach

5. Are cost sensitive

6. Align directly with organizational priorities

7. Are well investigated and weighed against options

8. Are powerful

9. Are sustainable

10. Take implementation into consideration

11. Take an iterative approach to design, development, and implementation

Feasibility Analysis

This component of the model relates to identifying and assessing the probable or likely success of solution strategies or interventions. For most performance-improvement initiatives there is more than one intervention making an intervention set. The feasibility of each intervention as well as the bundle or set as a whole has to be analyzed (Stufflebeam, McCormick, Brinkerhoff, and Nelson, 1985; Harrison, 1994; Mitchell, 1998). These feasibility factors can be classified as practical, political, and cultural (Kirkey and Benjamin, 2005).

Practical factors include administrative capacity, costs, workplace readiness, available technology, and timing. Political factors include perceived benefits, leadership, stakeholder readiness, and organizational power structures. Cultural factors include employer and employee development, organizational culture, and readiness for change.

Some intervention sets or bundles of interventions will require articulation and coordination. For complex feasibility analyses, a decision matrix may be helpful. Table 1.3 displays a sample feasibility decision matrix.

Design, Development, and Implementation

Any performance-improvement initiative that is worth carrying through should produce results that convert a given performance from what it is into what it should be. The initiative will pass through three stages: design, development, and implementation. The design stage involves proposing objectives as well as means and strategies for achieving the objectives. The means include identifying content and substance, and delineating outcomes. Strategies include proposing cost-effective activities and actions to achieve the objectives. All of this leads to a design plan. The development stage involves the actual production of the interventions, including a project-management plan. The interventions and the accompanying administrative support system must be validated through pre- and pilot testing. The implementation stage involves the application of the tested interventions on a large scale. Each of these stages needs its own evaluation, approval, and feedback provisions (adapted from Romiszowski, 1981).

Table 1.3. Sample Feasibility Decision Matrix.

Consideration (estimated or projected)	Risk (R)*	Risk Weight (W)** (1 to 10)	Risk Index (I)
1. Projected return on investment (ROI): cost-effectiveness	Low = 1 Moderate = 2 High = 3	Low = 1 Moderate = 5 High = 10	$I = R \times W$
2. Strength of support	Low = 1 Moderate = 2 High = 3	Low = 1 Moderate = 3 High = 5	$I = R \times W$
3. Organizational change impact	Low = 1 Moderate = 2 High = 3	Low = 1 Moderate = 5 High = 10	$I = R \times W$
4. Barriers to implementation	Low = 1 Moderate = 2 High = 3	Low = 1 Moderate = 3 High = 5	$I = R \times W$
5. Number of interventions in intervention bundle	Low = 1 Moderate = 2 High = 3	Low = 1 Moderate = 5 High = 10	$I = R \times W$
6. Available resources (financial and human)	Low = 1 Moderate = 2 High = 3	Low = 1 Moderate = 3 High = 5	$I = R \times W$
7. Dependence on time, or urgency	Low = 1 Moderate = 2 High = 3	Low = 1 Moderate = 5 High = 10	$I = R \times W$
8. Number of sites or functions affected	Low = 1 Moderate = 2 High = 3	Low = 1 Moderate = 5 High = 10	$I = R \times W$
9. Number of people and groups affected	Low = 1 Moderate = 2 High = 3	Low = 1 Moderate = 5 High = 10	$I = R \times W$
10. Other _____	Low = 1 Moderate = 2 High = 3	Low = 1 Moderate = 3 High = 5	$I = R \times W$
Totals			

*Risk category descriptors can be modified. Numerical values assigned to the descriptors vary from low to high depending on the consideration; that is, whether it is more or less desirable.

**Weight assignments are made in consultation with clients and affected parties.

In most cases, the performance technologist orchestrates and manages this process. Cross-functional and interdisciplinary teams are brought together that have expertise in the various interventions. Within the team, or as separate members, there must be personnel with change-management expertise. Performance-improvement initiatives by their very nature lead to purposeful change involving the beliefs, attitudes, values, and structures of organizations. Such change will be adopted and become institutionalized only if it is planned and managed.

Evaluation and Feedback

Evaluation is the means to ascertain the worth or value of a performance-improvement initiative. It can be used to improve a performance-improvement process or to decide to discontinue the effort. It is also useful in judging the relative worth of performance-improvement alternatives. Two types of evaluation are *formative* and *summative*. Formative evaluation is used to make improvements as a performance-improvement initiative is being designed and developed. Summative evaluation is used to judge the worth or merits of a completed and fully implemented performance-improvement initiative.

There are five ways in which evaluation can be used in HPT:

1. As a means of *feedback.* As performance-improvement initiatives are being designed, developed, and implemented, one can measure progress against stated objectives, analyze what is working well and what is not working as expected, and identify potential barriers to implementation. If information products, training materials, job aids, or new tools and equipment are involved in the initiative, their usability can be assessed.

2. As a means of *control.* During development and implementation of initiatives and after they are completed, questions can be asked and answered concerning the value of the program to the organization as well as alignment issues. Measures of worth can be compared to measures of cost.

3. As a means of *power.* Evaluation data can be very powerful. These data are sometimes used politically in organizations. Given this reality, the HPT specialist must be certain that evaluation data are based upon sound evidence and are presented fairly and ethically.

4. As an *intervention.* The very act of evaluation affects the performance-improvement initiatives being evaluated. As evaluation questions are formulated, instruments for collecting data are designed and tested, and those that will be involved in the evaluation are identified, people begin to behave differently as they react to and prepare for the evaluation process. These reactions can

be positive and enhance the initiative, or they can be skeptical and lead to resistance to the initiative.

5. As a means of *research.* This is the most important and often the most overlooked role that evaluation can play in the HPT process. As performance-improvement initiatives are evaluated, data can be collected and analyzed in ways to add knowledge to HPT principles and practices and provide knowledge that can be generalized to future efforts. Evaluations can be designed to provide reliable and valid data to ascertain what worked, when, and how it worked. This information, when shared with the field, will advance practice.

IS THERE MAGIC IN HUMAN PERFORMANCE TECHNOLOGY?

There is no magic in HPT. There are no easy-to-use cookbooks or templates for doing HPT. To be an effective human performance technologist takes hard work and dedication to its study and practice. Each organization and its performance-improvement challenges are unique and require individualized study and attention. The clever title *Figuring Things Out,* a 1982 book by Ron Zemke and Thomas Kramlinger, best captures the job of the performance technologist. Zemke and Kramlinger explain that figuring things out is process oriented, and that there are political, strategic, tactical, and technical considerations that need to be taken into account as problems are matched with techniques. They explain in great detail research techniques and procedures including "time studies, task listings, S-R tables, behavioral frequency counts, behavioral algorithms, focus group discussions, one-on-one interviews, consensus groups, the critical incident technique, fault tree analysis, and much more" (pp. vi–x). Since 1982, other performance technologists and quality-improvement specialists have added to this tool list with data-gathering and analysis techniques such as mapping and indirect estimations, content or document analysis, the community forum, the nominal group technique, focus groups, DACUM, Delphi technique, concept mapping, cross-impact analysis, future wheels, fishbone diagramming, affinity diagramming, cause-and-consequence analysis, fault tree analysis, Pareto diagram, force-field analysis, control charting, deployment charting, benchmarking, and so on (Gilley, Eggland, and Gilley, 2002; Ishikawa, 1987; Juran, 1988; Langdon, 2000; Mears, 1995; Rothwell, 1996; Witkin and Altschuld, 1995).

At the core of HPT is formalized speculation: hypotheses or statements of conjecture about the relationships among variables are stated and tested.

Sometimes the variables can be quantified, and sometimes they are qualitative or contextual. In either case, data describing the variables and their relationships with other variables can be collected. These data can be transformed by analysis to information that can be used in decision making by performance-improvement technologists and clients. This is the essence of a basic action research routine:

- Look

    Gather relevant information: gather data

    Build a picture: describe and define the situation

- Think

    Explore and analyze: What is happening here? Speculate or hypothesize

    Interpret and explain: How and why are things as they are? Theorize

- Act or intervene

    Plan and report

    Implement

    Evaluate [Stringer, 1996, p. 16]

The behavior and actions of successful performance-improvement specialists may at times seem magical. In my judgment, if you scratch below the surface, you will find four success criteria. First, the HPT specialist recognizes that performance improvement is not something we do to or for organizations and their members; rather it is something we do with them. We are collaborators. "In the collaborative style, decisions regarding actions to take and implementation plans are all shared responsibilities" (Robinson and Robinson, 1995, p. 20). Second, HPT requires a team effort. The performance-improvement specialist is like an orchestra leader, coordinating and integrating the efforts of team members and clients that have cross-functional and interdisciplinary responsibilities and expertise. The third factor has to do with appreciation for and tolerance of iteration. As depicted in the performance-improvement-process model (Figure 1.1), evaluation and feedback connect the major elements of the model in a nonlinear or repetitive way. At any given time in the process, one may have taken five steps forward and have to go back two or three steps to collect and analyze new data and to change or modify responses to those data. Fourth, and related to the iteration requirement, is to avoid letting solutions or interventions prematurely drive the process. This is a particular problem when the client and project team members have expertise in or an affinity for specific interventions.

CONCLUSIONS

An immediate appeal of human performance technology is that all organizations are human performance systems. Organizations can be viewed as operational, process, technical, or financial systems, but they are still founded by and for people. HPT is symbiotic in that it views organizations and their members as one. Its foci, or units for analyses, are individuals or workers, units or teams, departments or divisions, branches or subsidiaries, and the community or society. It is a process that begins and ends with results and the ultimate goal of creating value for an organization, its members, and the society it serves. HPT has been applied in all sizes and types of organizations, including private businesses, government, social service and nonprofit organizations, educational institutions, and the military. The field of HPT has evolved over a period of fifty years, and as a whole the field itself is not a passing fad.

Is HPT a cure all or end all for all organizational challenges or problems? The answer is no. It is not an effective approach for organizations to use when they are involved in goal-free or goal-conflicted activities. If results are a nonissue, HPT will not help in planning or decision-making activities. It is often ineffective when predetermined or suboptimal interventions drive the process. Finally, the HPT process is data-driven. If clients are skeptical about data gathering and analysis or only accept data as valid if the data support their preconceived views of problems or improvement initiatives, then the HPT process will falter.

How does HPT distinguish itself from other fields and disciplines involved in improving organizations? (1) Largely, HPT is evaluation- and change-driven. At each stage of the performance-improvement process, activities and outputs are evaluated and focus on the ultimate target of organizational results. Solving problems, improving organizations, and actualizing opportunities by their very nature mean change. In HPT, before, during, and after the performance-improvement process, change is managed. (2) The characteristics of HPT are dynamic and ever-changing. It is not identified with one person or one institution. (3) When practiced properly, HPT is nonideological in two important ways. First, it draws upon a variety of research and evaluation methodologies, letting the questions posed drive the methods employed. Second, there is no intervention bias. The selection, design, development, and implementation of interventions are driven by organizational needs and capabilities. (4) Finally, as a field of practice, HPT is eclectic. It selects what is best from a number of fields of study in terms of theories, models, and practices including, but not limited to, applied math and statistics, communications and cybernetics, economics, folklore, general systems theory, human capital theory, human resource development and management, instructional systems design and technology, management science, political science, psychology, quantitative and qualitative research and evaluation methods, sociology, systems design, the engineering disciplines, and more.

There are concerns and challenges facing the field of HPT. In my judgment, prominent among them are three. The first concern has to do with one of the strengths of HPT. Being an eclectic field has a downside. Drawing upon the principles and theories of numerous academic disciplines and other fields contributes to a lack of clarity for HPT. Scholars and practitioners alike have had difficulty in clearly articulating and agreeing upon foundational issues: "It is now time to bring clarity to definitions for the field" (Irlbeck, 2002, p. 87). Second, HPT has been and continues to be a largely North American and European enterprise. Strides are being made in South America and the Asian Pacific Rim. With economies expanding all over the world and more international trade agreements materializing on a regular basis, HPT needs to increase its influence and impact globally. The third concern has to do with a new type of partnering for the field of HPT. There are other established and emerging disciplines and fields of study that have organized bodies of knowledge and practice that address issues of performance by individuals and organizations. Examples of established disciplines are organizational development, human resource development, health and safety, total quality management, instructional technology, and reengineering and restructuring. Examples of newer and emerging disciplines are appreciative inquiry, communities of practice, informatics, knowledge management, lean manufacturing, learning organizations, rapid development and reflection, Six Sigma, and sociotechnical systems. By partnering with individuals and other organizations that represent many of these areas, there are some potentially positive outcomes. Several of these areas are experiencing what training personnel experienced years ago as HPT evolved. They find that their field or interest area is solution-driven, and this does not always fully address performance-improvement needs. They too are looking for more comprehensive solutions and may be attracted to HPT. At the same time, all of these areas have perspectives, tools, insights, and sometimes established credibility with organizations that HPT professionals need to learn about and utilize. In short, experts from these areas often make natural team members or partners for performance-improvement initiatives, and if treated respectfully they will become enthusiastic partners. The International Society for Performance Improvement, the flagship organization for HPT professionals, is addressing this issue by forming professional communities within its ranks to broaden its membership base and to help its current members learn about and network with these companion disciplines and fields of study (Svenson, 2005).

In closing, this is an exciting time for the field of human performance technology. More and more evidence is being compiled through action research and the presentations of case studies that show the significant impact HPT can have on adding and creating value for all types of organizations and the people they serve. This evidence is exemplified in the *Got Results* presentations and publications of ISPI that "demonstrate how practitioners can and do use meaningful measures of performance outcomes to evaluate and make decisions about performance interventions and ongoing performance systems" (International Society for Performance Improvement, 2005a). Both ISPI and ASTD have published books of authentic case studies in performance improvement and closely aligned areas (Deterline and Rosenberg, 1992; Esque and Patterson, 1998; Hodges, 1999; Phillips, 2000; Rothwell and Dubois, 1998). Articles, monographs, and books abound that will help you explore and learn about this exciting and dynamic field. For starters, begin with the publications of ISPI: *Performance Improvement, Performance Improvement Quarterly,* and *PerformanceXpress.* The remaining sections and chapters of this handbook will also help you to gain greater insight into the field of human performance technology. In looking to the future, I find a statement by Joe Harless (1997, pp. iv–v) insightful: "[I]f today we are concerned primarily with improvement of human performance at work, can concern with human performance in *all parts of lives* be next?"

References

Ainsworth, D. (1979). Performance technology: A view from the fo'c'sle. *NSPI Journal, 18*(4), 3–7.

Argyris, C. (1970). *Intervention theory and method: A behavioral science view.* Reading, MA: Addison-Wesley.

Brethower, D., and Smalley, K. (1998). *Performance-based instruction: Linking training to business results.* San Francisco: Jossey-Bass/Pfeiffer.

Brinkerhoff, R. O., and Dressler, D. E. (1990). *Productivity measurement: A guide for managers and evaluators.* Thousand Oaks, CA: Sage.

Burke, W. W. (1982). *Organization development: Principles and practices.* Boston: Little, Brown.

Coleman, M. E. (1992). Developing skills and enhancing professional competence. In H. D. Stolovitch and E. J. Keeps (Eds.), *Handbook of human performance technology: A comprehensive guide for analyzing and solving performance problems in organizations* (pp. 634–648). San Francisco: Jossey-Bass.

Coscarelli, B. (1988). Performance improvement quarterly and human performance technology. *Performance Improvement Quarterly, 1*(1), 2–5.

Day, R. K. (1997). B. F. Skinner, Ph.D., and Susan M. Markle, Ph.D., the beginnings. In P. J. Dean and D. E. Ripley (Eds.), *Performance improvement pathfinders: Models for organizational learning systems* (pp. 22–44). Washington, DC: The International Society for Performance Improvement.

Dean, P. (1993). A selected review of the underpinnings of ethics for human performance technology professionals—Part one: Key ethical theories and research. *Performance Improvement Quarterly, 6*(4), 6–32.

Dean, P. J. (1997). Thomas F. Gilbert, Ph.D.: Engineering performance improvement with or without training. In P. J. Dean and D. E. Ripley (Eds.), *Performance improvement pathfinders: Models for organizational learning systems* (pp. 45–64). Washington, DC: The International Society for Performance Improvement.

Dean, P. J., and Ripley, D. E. (Eds.). (1997). *Performance improvement pathfinders: Models for organizational learning systems.* Washington, DC: The International Society for Performance Improvement.

Denzin, N. K., and Lincoln, Y. S. (Eds.). (1994). *Handbook of qualitative research.* Thousands Oaks, CA: Sage.

Deterline, W. A., and Rosenberg, M. J. (1992). *Workplace productivity: Performance technology success stories.* Washington, DC: National Society for Performance Improvement.

Douglas, N., and Wykowski, T. (1999). *Beyond reductionism: Gateways for learning and change.* Boca Raton, FL: St. Lucie.

Eggen, P., and Kauchak, D. (1997). *Educational psychology: Windows on classrooms* (3rd ed.). Upper Saddle River, NJ: Prentice-Hall.

Esque, T. J., and Patterson, P. A. (Eds.). (1998). *Getting results: Case studies in performance improvement.* Amherst, MA: HRD Press.

Geis, G. L. (1986). Human performance technology: An overview. In M. E. Smith (Ed.), *Introduction to performance technology* (Vol. 2). Washington, DC: National Society for Performance and Instruction.

Gilbert, T. F. (1978). *Human competence: Engineering worthy performance.* New York: McGraw-Hill.

Gilley, J. W., and Boughton, N. W. (1996). *Stop managing, start coaching: How performance coaching can enhance commitment and improve productivity.* New York: McGraw-Hill.

Gilley, J. W., and Coffern, A. J. (1994). *Internal consulting for HRD professionals: Tools, techniques, and strategies for improving organizational performance.* Burr Ridge, IL: Irwin.

Gilley, J. W., Eggland, S. A., and Gilley, A. M. (2002). *Principles of human resource development* (2nd Ed.). Cambridge, MA: Perseus.

Gilmore, E. R., and Pershing, J. A. (2001, April). *Don't miss! Identify all causes of that performance gap: A review of literature supporting a refinement of Wile's HPT model.* Paper presented at the annual meeting of the International Society for Performance Improvement, San Francisco.

Hall, G. E., and Hord, S. M. (1978). *Change in schools: Facilitating the process.* Albany, NY: State University of New York Press.

Hallbom, T., and Hallbom, K. J. (2005). *The systemic nature of the mind and body and how it relates to health.* Retrieved May 26, 2005, from www.nlpca.com/articles/article2.htm.

Hanson, P. G., and Lubin, B. (1995). *Answers to questions most frequently asked about organization development.* Thousand Oaks, CA: Sage.

Harless, J. H. (1970). *An ounce of analysis (is worth a pound of objectives)*. Newnan, GA: Harless Performance Guild.

Harless, J. H. (1988). *Accomplishment-based curriculum development*. Newnan, GA: Harless Performance Guild.

Harless, J. H. (1997). Foreword. In P. J. Dean and D. E. Ripley (Eds.), *Performance improvement pathfinders: Models for organizational learning systems* (pp. iii–v). Washington, DC: International Society for Performance Improvement.

Harrison, M. I. (1994). *Diagnosing organizations: Methods, models, and processes* (2nd ed.). Thousand Oaks, CA: Sage.

Hodges, T. K. (Ed.). (1999). *Measuring learning and performance*. Washington, DC: American Society for Training and Development.

Holton, E. F. (1999). An integrated model of performance domains: Bounding the theory and practice. *Performance Improvement Quarterly, 12*(3), 95–118.

International Society for Performance Improvement. (2005a). *Got results*. Resources and services. Retrieved June 8, 2005, from www.ispi.org.

International Society for Performance Improvement. (2005b). *What is HPT?* Retrieved June 10, 2005, from www.ispi.org.

International Society for Performance Improvement, Certified Performance Technologist. (2002). *Standards of performance technology and code of ethics*. Retrieved May 19, 2005, from www.certifiedpt.org/index.cfm?section=standards.

Irlbeck, S. A. (2002). Human performance technology: An examination of definitions through dependent and independent variables. *Performance Improvement Quarterly, 15*(2), 84–95.

Ishikawa, K. (1987). *Guide to quality control*. White Plains, NY: Kraus International.

Juran, J. M. (Ed.). (1988). *Quality control handbook* (4th ed.). New York: McGraw-Hill.

Kaufman, R. (2000). *Mega planning*. Thousand Oaks, CA: Sage.

Kirkey, D., and Benjamin, C. M. (2005, April). *Feasibility analysis: An instruction implementation reality check*. Paper presented at the annual meeting of the International Society for Performance Improvement, Vancouver, BC.

Langdon, D. (1991). Performance technology in three paradigms. *Performance and Instruction Journal, 30*(7), 1–7.

Langdon, D. (1999). The language of work. In H. D. Stolovitch and E. J. Keeps (Eds.), *Handbook of human performance technology: Improving individual and organizational performance worldwide* (2nd ed.) (pp. 260–280). San Francisco: Jossey-Bass/Pfeiffer.

Langdon, D. (2000). *Aligning performance: Improving people, systems, and organizations*. San Francisco: Jossey-Bass/Pfeiffer.

Langdon, D. G., Whiteside, K. S., and McKenna, M. M. (1999) *Intervention resource guide: 50 performance improvement tools*. San Francisco: Jossey-Bass/Pfeiffer.

Mager, R. F., and Pipe, P. (1984). *Analyzing performance problems: Or you really oughta wanna* (2nd ed.). Belmont, CA: Lake Publishing.

Mears, P. (1995). *Quality improvement tools and techniques*. New York: McGraw-Hill.

Mertens, D. M. (2005). *Research and evaluation in education and psychology: Integrating diversity with quantitative, qualitative, and mixed methods* (2nd ed.). Thousand Oaks, CA: Sage.

Mitchell, G. (1998). *The trainer's handbook: The AMA guide to effective training,* (3rd ed.). New York: American Management Association.

Molenda, M., Pershing, J. A., and Reigeluth, C. M. (1996). Designing instructional systems. In R. L. Craig (Ed.), *The ASTD training and development handbook: A guide to human resource development* (4th ed.) (pp. 266–293). New York: McGraw-Hill.

O'Driscoll, T. (1999). *Achieving desired business performance: A framework for developing human performance technology in organizations.* Washington, DC: International Society for Performance Improvement.

Petty, P. (Executive Producer). (1991). *The Deming of America.* One-hour video. Funded by Arthur Andersen and Company. Produced by Petty Consulting Productions.

Phillips, J. J. (Ed.). (2000). *Performance analysis and consulting.* Washington, DC: American Society for Training and Development.

Pipe, P. (1986). Ergonomics and performance aids. In *Introduction to performance technology.* Washington, DC: International Society for Performance Improvement.

Reigeluth, C. M. (1983). Instructional design: What is it and why is it? In C. M. Reigeluth (Ed.), *Instructional-design theories and models: An overview of their current status* (pp. 3–36). Hillsdale, NJ: Lawrence Erlbaum Associates.

Robinson, D. G., and Robinson, J. C. (1989). *Training for impact: How to link training to business needs and measure the results.* San Francisco: Jossey-Bass.

Robinson, D. G., and Robinson, J. C. (1995). *Performance consulting: Moving beyond training.* San Francisco: Berrett-Koehler.

Romiszowski, A. J. (1981). *Designing instructional systems: Decision making in course planning and curriculum design.* London: Kogan Page.

Rosenberg, M. J. (1996). Human performance technology. In R. L. Craig (Ed.), *The ASTD training and development handbook: A guide to human resource development* (4th ed.) (pp. 370–393). New York: McGraw-Hill.

Rossett, A. (1987). *Training needs assessment.* Englewood Cliffs, NJ: Educational Technology Publications.

Rossett, A. (1999). Analysis for human performance technology. In H. D. Stolovitch and E. J. Keeps (Eds.), *Handbook of human performance technology* (2nd ed.) (pp. 139–162). San Francisco: Jossey-Bass/Pfeiffer.

Rothwell, W. J. (1996). *Beyond training and development: State-of-the-art strategies for enhancing human performance.* New York: American Management Association.

Rothwell, W. J., and Dubois, D. D. (Eds.). (1998). *Improving performance in organizations.* Washington, DC: American Society for Training and Development.

Rummler, G. A., and Brache, A. B. (1995). *Improving performance: How to manage the white space on the organization chart* (2nd ed.). San Francisco: Jossey-Bass.

Semler, S. W. (1997). Systematic agreement: A theory of organizational alignment. *Human Resource Development Quarterly, 8*(1), 23–40.

Spitzer, D. R. (1992). The design and development of effective interventions. In H. D. Stolovitch and E. J. Keeps (Eds.), *Handbook of human performance technology: A comprehensive guide for analyzing and solving performance problems in organizations* (pp. 114–129). San Francisco: Jossey-Bass.

Stolovitch, H. (1982). Performance technology: An introduction. *Performance and Instruction, 21*(3), 16–19.

Stolovitch, H., and Keeps, E. (1992). What is performance technology? In H. D. Stolovitch and E. J. Keeps (Eds.), *Handbook of Human Performance Technology: A comprehensive guide for analyzing and solving performance problems in organizations.* San Francisco: Jossey-Bass.

Stolovitch, H., and Keeps, E. (1999). What is performance technology? In H. D. Stolovitch and E. J. Keeps (Eds.), *Handbook of Human Performance Technology: Improving individual and organizational performance worldwide* (2nd ed.). San Francisco: Jossey-Bass/Pfeiffer.

Stringer, E. T. (1996). *Action research: A handbook for practitioners.* Thousand Oaks, CA: Sage.

Stufflebeam, D. L., McCormick, C. H., Brinkerhoff, R. O., and Nelson, C. O. (1985). *Conducting educational needs assessments.* Boston: Kluwer Nijhoff.

Svenson, R. (2005). Human performance technology: Professional communities. *Performance Improvement, 44*(1), 6–8.

Tafoya, W. L. (1983). Needs assessment: Key to organizational change. *Journal of Police Science Administration, 11*(3), 303–310.

Van Tiem, D. M., Moseley, J. L., and Dessinger, J. C. (2004). *Fundamentals of performance technology.* Washington, DC: International Society for Performance Improvement.

Watkins, R., Leigh, D., and Kaufman, R. (2000). A scientific dialogue: A performance accomplishment code of professional conduct. *Performance Improvement, 38*(4), 17–22.

Westgaard, O. (1988). *A credo for performance technologists.* Western Springs, IL: International Board of Standards for Training, Performance and Instruction.

Wile, D. (1996). Why doers do. *Performance and Instruction, 35*(1), 30–35.

Witkin, B. R., and Altschuld, J. W. (1995). *Planning and conducting needs assessments: A practical guide.* Thousand Oaks, CA: Sage.

Zemke, R., and Kramlinger, T. (1982). *Figuring things out: A trainer's guide to needs and task analysis.* Reading, MA: Addison-Wesley.

CHAPTER TWO

The Performance Architect's Essential Guide to the Performance Technology Landscape

Roger M. Addison, Carol Haig

Some years ago, a company had a team of high-performing data-entry clerks that was known for consistently rapid production with very low error rates. These were skilled, dependable employees who had worked together for some time. When their company moved to a new and much larger building, the clerks were delighted with their workspace. They loved their spacious office, large wrap-around windows, and restful views of lush lawns and shady trees.

When they moved, they brought along all their existing office furniture, state-of-the-art computers, and other equipment. They settled into their wonderful new space and continued with their work. After a week or two, their manager reviewed the production reports and was surprised to see that the team's error rates had noticeably increased. He searched in vain for an obvious reason and could only conclude that the move had somehow disrupted the clerks' usual accuracy.

When this alarming trend continued through several reporting cycles, the manager decided the best course of action would be to retrain this group of skilled high performers because they obviously had forgotten how to do their jobs. So all the data-entry clerks were retrained. And, as you may have guessed, their substandard performance continued, with subsequent reports showing no reduction in error rates.

In desperation, the manager asked the Performance Consulting department for help, and a consultant paid him a visit. After the manager brought her up to date on events, the consultant asked to see all the reports from after the move and several sets from before to compare the clerks' performance.

After reviewing the reports, the consultant shared her findings with the manager. In the reports generated since the move to the new building she noticed a definite pattern of increased errors in the late afternoons. The manager could not immediately provide an explanation for this, so the consultant asked if she could spend a few days on the floor to observe the clerks and learn more about their jobs.

When her observations were complete, the consultant met with the manager to again share her findings. Those large, bright windows really let in lots of light. In the late afternoons, as the sun began to set, it created glare on the clerks' computer screens. Even though they knew their software well, it was easy to make mistakes and not see them; hence, the increased error rates.

The manager was somewhat embarrassed to have missed this obvious reason for poor performance, but the consultant helped him see the value of another pair of eyes when trying to diagnose a problem from inside the situation. She pointed out the power of observation in analyzing performance problems and confided that she never fully believed anything her clients told her until she went to see for herself. The manager forgave himself his oversight and was pleased to discover that window coverings were a relatively quick and inexpensive solution to a critical performance obstacle.

INTRODUCTION

In this chapter we welcome you to the territory of the seasoned performance-improvement professional. Join us as we journey across the region to explore the features of the "Performance Technology Landscape." In preparation for our travels, we will provide a packing list of helpful tools for the trip. We have selected them based on their usefulness to us in our combined sixty years of performance-improvement practice, coupled with the valuable work of such notables as Dale Brethower, Judith Hale, Paul Harmon, Lloyd Homme, Tom Gilbert, Robert Mager, Margo Murray, Geary Rummler, Harold Stolovitch, Don Tosti, and others. These practitioners are among those responsible for building the foundation of human performance technology (HPT); they have contributed to the principles of performance technology through their work and documented it in publications.

So get out your backpack and your walking shoes as we begin to chart our course and study the map of the Performance Technology Landscape.

THE PERFORMANCE TECHNOLOGY LANDSCAPE

Experienced travelers prepare carefully for a new journey by collecting maps and resource materials to plan their trip. Our map for this tour is the Performance Technology Landscape (Figure 2.1). It provides a framework

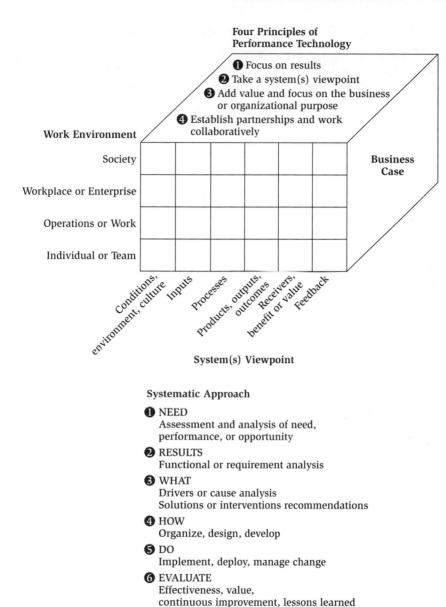

Figure 2.1. Performance Technology Landscape.

Source: Addison, 2004, p. 15.

for the work of HPT, an integrated-systems approach to performance improvement. Our resource materials include two key concepts that will prepare us for discoveries along the way: performance and human performance technology.

What Is Performance?

While many of us might think of performance as simply an activity on the Performance Technology Landscape, seasoned performance-improvement professionals add a critical component: a result. So performance equals activity plus result, as in reading a map, *activity*, and using it to find your destination, *result*. We further stipulate that the result must be of *value*. For example, reaching your destination enables a wedding to take place in which you are the groom. The value is in the importance of the wedding to all involved stakeholders: bride, groom, families, guests, and others.

In 2003 the International Society for Performance Improvement (ISPI) convened a Presidential Initiative Task Force to address critical issues in HPT. One of this group's many achievements was the further refinement of the definition of performance to include "those valued results produced by people working within a system" (International Society for Performance Improvement, 2004, p. 9).

What Is Performance Technology?

We define a technology as a set of empirical and scientific principles and their application. Performance technology (PT) is the technology that comprises all of the variables that affect human performance. We use PT in the workplace to identify the factors that enable workers to perform their jobs and to produce the desired results. Performance technology provides tools and processes to identify opportunities for improved performance, valued solutions, and return on investment, as well as the building blocks to construct new performance environments and systems. The HPT task force also suggested the following definition (International Society for Performance Improvement, 2004, p. 4) for HPT:

1. Focuses on valuable, measured results

2. Considers the larger system context of people's performance

3. Provides measurement tools that can be used repeatedly and will consistently show the same outcome

4. Describes programs and solutions clearly enough to be duplicated by others

Mapping the Performance-Improvement Journey

The Performance Technology Landscape is a topographical map for performance technologists, providing a multidimensional representation of the routes we can travel in pursuit of improved human performance and increased value to the client organization. A closer look at the Performance Technology Landscape calls out four noted landmarks to guide us on our journey: Principles of Performance Technology, Work Environment, System(s) Viewpoint, and Systematic Approach.

Principles of Performance Technology. Performance improvement professionals adhere to these principles in our work. We

- Focus on results, using our knowledge of the business we are supporting to link performance-improvement initiatives to business needs and goals and add value for the stakeholders
- Take a systems viewpoint that encourages consideration of all aspects of the organization's total performance system
- Add value to the organization or business by producing results that make a difference
- Establish partnerships with clients and other performance-improvement professionals to share skills, knowledge, creativity, and successes

By thinking systemically, we are able to identify and work with all the linkages in organizations as we strive to improve performance.

Work Environment. In organizations work is performed at three, and sometimes four, levels:

- Individual or teams: the worker level
- Operations: the work level
- Organization: the entire enterprise
- Society: the communities served, the world

We ensure that we correctly identify the level affected by the performance issue or opportunity so that our investigations are complete and our recommendations have a high probability of success.

Many organizations today acknowledge society as a fourth level in which they, as good corporate citizens, can make valuable contributions to the environment, the economy, and the communities they serve. This service may involve encouraging employees to contribute their efforts to local charities, such as the Volunteer Day program or the 78 Community Involvement Teams at Levi Strauss worldwide (Levi Strauss & Co., 2005). Another example is through active support of humanitarian issues, as with Hewlett Packard's Design-for-Environment program (HP Invent, n.d.) that provides environmentally sustainable products through recycling services, or the Siemens Arts Program (Siemens, 2005) that supports and advances local arts and culture in company locations around the world.

Performance-improvement professionals also work at the societal level, using HPT tools and techniques to address broad areas of need in the developing world (Haig and Addison, 2002).

Whenever possible, performance-improvement practitioners expand their work to the next highest organizational level to increase the impact of improved performance and add value for the organization. Many practitioners are accustomed to working with individuals or teams to improve performance. However, organizations realize broader, longer-lasting gains in performance improvement when changes are made in processes or across the enterprise, because these levels directly affect the customer.

System(s) Viewpoint. One way that we in HPT differentiate ourselves from other disciplines is with our systems viewpoint. HPT professionals consider that every organization is, by definition, a system, and that all components of that system are related. Therefore, when performance improvement is needed in one component we consider all of them in our investigation. This is often referred to as thinking systemically. Remember, we make the greatest impact on performance when we address the whole system.

As the Systems Model illustrates (see Figure 2.2) performance begins with inputs into a system, which are processed until the results reach the receiver; hence performance occurs from left to right. Performance-improvement specialists, however, work from right to left, beginning by clearly identifying the desired results of an initiative and then working backward through the model to inputs.

By thinking systemically we are able to view the enterprise as a complete system comprising the following components (adapted with permission from International Society for Performance Improvement, 2004):

Receivers: The system stakeholders who receive or are directly affected by the result.

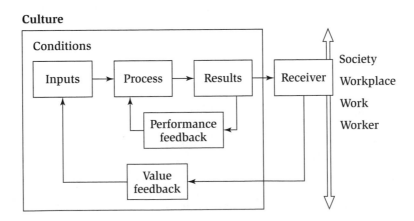

Figure 2.2. Systems Model.

Results: The accomplishment, or that which is produced or created by a process, including products and services.

Process: The sequence of actions in the value chain that produces the desired results.

The organizational or workplace level focuses on those processes concerned with the governance of the organization.

The operational or work level includes all the processes in the value chain as well as those that maintain them. The variables here take into account the specific activities and tasks and their sequence and flow. At this level we often look for broken connections and misalignments such as bottlenecks and disconnects.

The performer or worker level is focused on the actions of the individual. It therefore seems best to put the performer in the Process box in Figure 2.2. The variables to be considered are those internal to the performer that are relevant to the execution of the task. These include

- Skill or knowledge
- Motivation
- Other variables such as confidence, preferences, and practices

It may be useful to think of two types of processes. Some, such as sales or service, touch the customer. Others, such as employee payroll or recruitment, enable the organization to function. Ultimately, organizations require both types of processes to be effective.

Inputs: What initiates or directs an action or process, including customer requests, stakeholder demands, information, the strategic plan, tools and equipment, work schedules, assignments, and support.

Conditions: The surroundings or environment within which performance occurs, such as economic and market trends; industry norms; and the physical, business, and social environments.

Performance feedback: Information about the quantity or quality of outputs that is fed back to a performer, operational unit, or organization from within the system, and that can be used to make adjustments that will improve the results.

Value feedback: The same type of information as provided by performance feedback, but originating from outside the system. Sources may include end users, stockholders, the surrounding community, the media, and so forth.

Remember that performance feedback comes from within the system and value feedback from outside. A colleague explains the difference this way: when the chef tastes the soup, that is performance feedback; when the customer tastes the soup, that is value feedback (personal communication, Lynn Kearny, April 21, 2004).

Systems thinking is scalable and can be applied at any of the three organizational levels: worker, work, or workplace.

Systematic Approach. Performance-improvement professionals use a systematic approach to organize projects. They follow sequential steps and create a replicable process to identify needs and recommend solutions. The steps include

- *Need:* identify and review the problem or opportunity with the client
- *Results:* assess current performance against expected results and identify requirements for success
- *What:* identify sources of current performance and recommend solutions
- *How:* design and develop selected solution
- *Do:* implement approved solutions and put change-management processes in place
- *Evaluate:* monitor performance against the expected results defined initially

Finally, performance-improvement specialists take care to nurture and enhance the business partnerships they have established with their clients.

WHAT IS PERFORMANCE ARCHITECTURE?

It seems that a large organization had a sizable population of operations managers in desperate need of training. While they were mostly experienced employees, their work performance was deteriorating. They were consistently working extended hours, they were challenged to find the time to train new hires, and quite a few were on stress-related leaves of absence.

In response to the situation, a senior manager requested extensive additional training. Fortunately, the performance consultants assigned to the project had considerable performance technology experience. They were able to gather pertinent data, make observations, and diagnose critical alignment and priority issues that were having a negative impact on the operations managers' effectiveness.

The performance consultants found that the priorities of senior management were not consistent, and the operations managers receiving their directives were understandably confused about how to focus their work. With many staff vacancies to fill, and no efficient tools for teaching rudimentary tasks, many operations managers were simply doing low-level work themselves because it was faster than taking the time to teach a new employee.

Finally, many customer-service and problem-resolution tasks formerly handled by the operations managers had been moved into processing centers. A number of the operations managers had found it more expedient, and better for their customers, to continue to handle these issues personally rather than trust them to the processing centers, where response time was slow and accuracy not dependable.

With these and additional findings, the performance consultants were able to show that the operations managers had the skills and knowledge to do their jobs, thus ruling out training as a viable solution. They then recommended a cascading suite of solutions that included aligned priorities from senior management, delegation tools for the operations managers, and service-level agreements with the processing centers. The solutions were packaged into an offsite meeting exclusively for operations managers that showcased their concerns and gave them a prominent voice in the organization.

In addition to the improved performance of the operations managers, an unprecedented reorganization in the processing centers, and a significant shuffling of roles and responsibilities among senior management, results showed a decrease in the number of operations managers on leave and a considerable increase in customer satisfaction. Let us take a look behind the scenes and examine the tools that the performance consultants used.

Performance Systems

The performance-improvement professionals used performance-architecture tools to repair an existing performance system. They used two of our favorites, the Performance Map and the Iceberg Model, which we will introduce as we explore performance systems in more depth.

Let us begin with the notion of human performance as being those valued results produced by people working within a system. Many performance-improvement professionals have their roots in training. They have broadened their approach from delivering training to improving performance systems. Performance system design is not solution-driven and gives the practitioner the space to engage all relevant aspects of the total performance system in the development of the solution.

We frequently find ourselves in the business of repairing existing performance systems, as did the performance consultants in the operations managers' case. In some situations we may construct new performance systems. According to Tosti (2004), this is very much a back-to-the-future situation. He observes that the earliest practitioners of HPT were focused on building rather than repairing as a way to create new performance-improvement alternatives. As our discipline evolved, we became more concerned with identifying performance problems and fixing them, and moved away from inventing new performance systems. We would like to see among our HPT colleagues once again an increased emphasis on the building of performance systems.

Once, a team of performance-improvement specialists was asked to support a job redesign project. The position, "Manager of the Service Department," was renamed "Customer Service Manager," and refocused from a repair operation to emphasize the selling of customer services. This meant added management responsibilities for the incumbents, new customer service skills and knowledge for them to acquire, and a progressive shift in what had been a very traditional repair shop role. Wisely, the executive responsible for the job change initiative realized that the revamped position required a new performance system to support those in the job and enable them to be successful, and he asked the performance-improvement team to design it. One of the tools they used was the Performance Map.

Performance Map

Whether to solve a problem or to respond to an opportunity, the Performance Map's simple grid format is a useful tool for diagnosing performance-related issues (Figure 2.3). It is easy to explain to managers, who often pick up a pen and actively engage with the map.

The four key quadrants are

- *Structure:* the foundation of the organization
- *Motivation:* the emotions, desires, and psychological needs that incite action
- *Environment:* the external and internal conditions that affect the growth and development of the organization
- *Learning:* the increase of employee proficiency in a given area

The north-south axis looks at employee competence on a scale of 0 (low) to 10 (high). The east-west axis addresses the employee's confidence in her or his ability to do the job, also on a scale of 0 (low) to 10 (high).

As an example, when you and a manager have identified specific employees who have performance issues, you would follow these specific steps:

- Help the manager determine the identified employees' job competence by asking a question such as, What skills do employees need to complete the job? Ask the manager to rate the identified employees from 0 (no skills or knowledge) to 10 (highly skilled and knowledgeable).
- Next, ascertain the employees' level of confidence by probing for examples of accomplishments, behavior, attitudes, commitment, and contributions. You might say, "Tell me about the general attitude of employees toward this job." Again, ask the manager to rate the performers. Zero means your client has no confidence in the performers and 10, that he or she has total confidence in the performers. You may also want to ask the performers these same questions. In our experience we often get conflicting responses. This is a signal to you to clearly specify the gap between manager and performer.

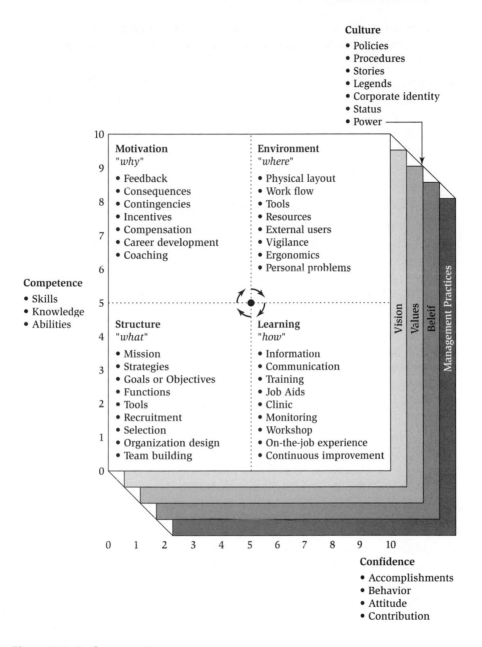

Figure 2.3. Performance Map.

Source: Addison and Johnson, 1997, p. 4.

- Mark the levels for both competence and confidence on the grid and draw the appropriate horizontal and vertical lines to connect the two variables.

- With such information, you can identify the quadrant in which the two variables intersect. This will help you to diagnose the most common areas of organizational problems or opportunities and prescribe a series of effective solutions. For example, if you identify a structural deficiency, possible solutions might include revisiting the mission statement or developing goals and objectives for the individual or group. Other quadrants will suggest other solutions.

- Regardless of which quadrant houses the issue, you need to consider the other three as you work toward a solution. Remember that you are operating in a performance system, and actions taken in one area will have an impact on the others. This is especially important if you have identified the Learning quadrant as the source of the performance issue. If a manager has a confident employee, a high performer who has the necessary skills and knowledge, you would want to engineer the environment for success so that the employee will continue to perform at a high level.

- Finally, consider the organization's culture as you identify solutions, to ensure that your prescription will do the job without unwanted side effects. Few elements of organizational life are as pervasive as culture; ignore this powerful force at your peril. We know from experience that performance-improvement recommendations and implementation plans must be culture-compatible, or they will be destroyed. When strategy meets culture, culture always wins.

Tip of the Iceberg

The Performance Map guides us to the probable source of our performance issue. Our second tool enables us to explore further and integrate performance-improvement solutions with all related components of the organization's performance system. The iceberg is a metaphor for much that can go wrong when we start with an assumed solution, at the tip, and create an organizational disaster because we neglect to consider all the layers of the iceberg below the surface (Figure 2.4).

Organizational Level. The Iceberg Model encourages us to start our work at the base organizational level with a cultural audit, so that we get to know the operational norms (Carleton and Lineberry, 2004). With this perspective we can more effectively analyze, diagnose, and prescribe performance-improvement solutions that will address the identified concerns and mesh with the organization's

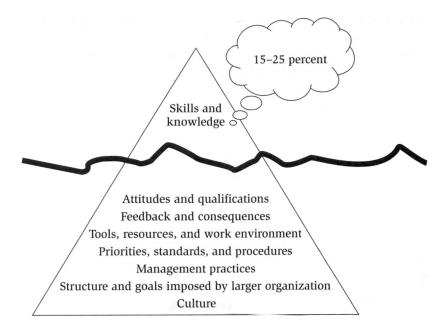

Figure 2.4. The Iceberg Model.

Source: Adapted from Harmon, 1984.

business practices. Understanding the environment avoids costly and time-consuming errors. The cultural audit is also a valuable precursor to using the Performance Map.

Structures and Goals. Moving up the model, we gather information about structures and goals—the organizational chart, for example—and such foundational elements as mission, vision, and values.

Management Practices. Next, we explore typical management practices. These are related to the culture, of course, and they tell us about the organization's customs and best practices. This helps us understand what is valued in management's performance and will inform how we interact with our client and present our findings.

Priorities, Standards, and Procedures. At this point, we narrow our focus to the work level as we look at priorities, standards, and procedures. Here we are interested in work processes, and the connections among work groups as tasks are performed.

Tools, Resources, and Work Environment. To be successful, workers require tools and resources. In addition, the work environment must support the processes to be completed. We want to learn about these elements to ensure that employees have what they need to do their jobs effectively.

Feedback and Consequences. Of course, workers need to know how they are doing, so we look next at the systems in place for feedback and consequences. Without these, employees are deprived of critical information about the quality and quantity of their work, and their motivation to perform is undermined.

Attitudes and Qualifications. We explore the attitudes and qualifications the organization looks for to select employees. Are these in alignment with all the other aspects represented in the Iceberg Model? If not, identifying the disconnects will yield valuable clues to the sources of issues and their possible resolution.

Skills and Knowledge. And so we reach skills and knowledge at the tip of the iceberg, the place where many clients begin their request for help from performance-improvement specialists. Learning and skill building live here and are vital solutions for situations in which employees do not know how to perform. Organizations should provide activities in this sector to orient new hires and introduce new products and services, systems, equipment, or other innovations. For all other circumstances, as the Iceberg Model has shown, the performance issue is at another level and the solution will be found nearby.

Other Models and Tools

There are many models and tools available to performance-improvement practitioners; we offer these as samples from among those we have found useful over the years. These models and tools are not meant to be all-inclusive. They allow us one view of organizations. However, no matter how appropriate the tools are for the task, they are useless to us and to our clients without the all-important link to the organization's business.

Evaluation

As performance-improvement professionals, we position our work in the context of critical business goals, requirements, or initiatives, and clearly tie what we do to one or all of these.

Identify the Business Requirements. We begin by learning from the client what critical business, process, or individual issues are of concern and how improved performance can affect what the client identifies as most important. This is what the client values, and to call out these elements at the beginning of an engagement is a hallmark of success in performance improvement. Another colleague begins every project by identifying the related business requirements and posting them at his desk as a reminder throughout the engagement (personal communication, Miki Lane, April 18, 2004).

Evaluation Planning. With the business need clearly identified, we move ahead with the performance-improvement project and plan what and when we will evaluate. This advance planning is key to successful evaluation. Legions of practitioners wait until implementation to go hunting for baseline information to compare with results. Then they attempt to evaluate those results only to discover the near impossibility of doing so at the end of the project.

The best time to plan how you will evaluate a solution is when you and your client agree on it. Performance-improvement specialists design evaluation to

- Show that the solution closes the identified performance gap
- Ensure that the solution relates to the business requirements
- Ensure that the solution has value and meaning for all groups that have a stake in the performance issue
- Compare results with the baseline information collected at project inception

Formative Evaluation. Successful performance-improvement initiatives usually include formative evaluation in the project plan. Because this type of evaluation occurs at each project milestone, wise performance consultants can take immediate corrective action, a practice that keeps everyone on track.

Summative Evaluation. This is the evaluation that determines whether or not a solution will be implemented, revised, or discontinued. It is usually conducted at the conclusion of the pilot or after a limited implementation.

Return on Investment (ROI). Finally, we want to provide our clients with meaningful measures, from their own data, to show that the investment the organization made to improve performance has paid off. Rummler (2004) suggests that if we accurately identify the critical business issue at the organizational level, the critical process issue at the work or process level, and the critical job issue at the worker or individual level, we will have the necessary metrics to measure success.

THE SAVVY PERFORMANCE-IMPROVEMENT PROFESSIONAL'S GUIDE TO SUCCESSFUL PERFORMANCE (TECHNOLOGY): A DECEPTIVELY SIMPLE LIST

One universally enjoyable travel activity is shopping for treasures to bring back home for family and friends, or to keep and use for one's own. The Performance Technology Landscape offers a variety of terrains with much to see and do. While you were busy absorbing new ideas and concepts we were quietly collecting a few valuable mementos we think all seasoned performance-improvement professionals should have.

In particular, we searched out the factors that, in our experience, will increase your chances of a successful implementation. Keep in mind that implementation is the hill upon which so many worthy solutions have met their untimely end.

Here is what we added to our travel bag (Addison and Lloyd, 1999):

- *Mission and vision:* What is the organization's purpose? Its goals? How does your performance-improvement project support and further the enterprise's reason for existence? Be sure these vital structures are in place before you begin your work and that you and your client can clearly tie them to your project.

- *Cultural audit:* As we have discussed, culture is a powerful driver in every organization. The performance-improvement professional assesses the internal climate at the project's inception to ensure that everything from daily project management to reports and recommendations are compatible with the environment.

- *Implementation team:* Choose your team members with care and ensure that you have several with a strong record of successful implementations. You can build the best performance-improvement solution in the world, and it will fail if your team lacks the necessary navigational skills.

- *Plans and contingencies:* Be prepared for anything! Take the time to envision everything that could possibly happen during your project and plan your responses. Then, should the unexpected occur, you will have many good ideas to draw from in response as well as the confidence to invent something on the spot if necessary.

- *Communication:* Do not keep your project a secret. The most successful performance-improvement endeavors are marked by consistent, clear communications to all stakeholders. Plan who should be informed, at what project milestones, and what communication vehicle you will use. And it is never too early to market a new endeavor.

- *Education:* Show your client, your subject-matter experts, your team members, and your performance-improvement colleagues how you are running your project. There is no magic, and all can benefit from learning how it is done.

- *Monitoring mechanisms:* Set up two way feedback and communication conduits so stakeholders can let you know what is working and what should be fixed. Then respond promptly to maintain the project's credibility and momentum.

- *Lessons learned:* A mistake is a powerful learning tool. While no one likes to make errors, leveraging learning from them is invaluable. Capture the project goofs and repair them. Then store that information in a useful format for the future.

- *Rewards and fun:* There are many small successes in a well-run project, and they should be acknowledged and celebrated. Find ways to recognize both individual team members and the whole group for their contributions. And do laugh and enjoy your work.

HEADING HOME

All journeys must come to an end, and we are pleased to have been your guides as you took in the features of the Performance Technology Landscape. It is time for you to think about what you saw in your travels and how you plan to put your new tools and models to good use as you work to improve performance. Perhaps a bit of prompting from us will help you organize your impressions to take home.

Landscape Model

Initially, we used the Performance Technology Landscape to orient ourselves to the world of performance improvement, gaining a better understanding of performance, performance technology, and critical supporting landmarks. We identified the four levels of organizations where we work and the value that performance-improvement professionals can add when we raise our efforts to the next-highest organizational level.

Systems Model

Because systems thinking is scalable and can be applied at any organizational level, we can expand or compress performance-improvement initiatives to meet business requirements. We explored the systematic approach to show the ways in which we, in performance improvement, distinguish ourselves from colleagues in related disciplines. And we saw that we always begin with the end in mind. That is, we identify the results to be achieved and work backward to inputs.

Performance Architecture

As we learned about performance systems, we moved from a training perspective to a performance-system perspective, bringing to light another way in which performance-improvement professionals differ from other practitioners.

We also discovered that although current practice appears to focus on repairing existing performance systems, we have a history of building them so that they can be put to valuable use for our clients today.

Performance Map and the Tip of the Iceberg

Next, we discovered the versatile Performance Map, a tool that provides a quick diagnosis and has special appeal for managers who find it easy to use. The organizational dimensions, particularly culture, are important to factor into any performance analysis.

The Iceberg Model illustrates, once again, that we think differently. By starting at the bottom with the culture factor, and working our way up to the tip of the iceberg, we can gain a very accurate understanding of an organization's performance system, and identify the critical linkages necessary to improve performance.

Feedback and Evaluation

Performance-improvement professionals tie their work to the organization's requirements and plan a series of evaluations at critical project milestones. We compile formative feedback to evaluate our progress during the project's life cycle and solicit summative feedback to determine the "go–no go" decision. By planning and conducting evaluations throughout the project, we are able to use the client's metrics to compile the ROI data that they expect to receive from us.

The List

Finally, of course, you have our recommended list of factors that guide you through a successful implementation of your project.

Travelers' Advisory

The savvy traveler distills the learnings from every journey and employs them to make the next trip smoother and more enjoyable. Following are our critical learnings from our many years of helping organizations improve performance. We share them as our final travel treasure for you:

- Keep up to date in your profession
- Surround yourself with smart people
- Cultivate a large and varied professional network

- Participate in a professional association
- Never hire anyone you would not like to have lunch with

We have enjoyed your company on this introductory trip and hope to see you again somewhere on the Performance Technology Landscape.

References

Addison, R. M. (2004). Performance architecture: A performance improvement model. *Performance Improvement, 43*(6), 14–16.

Addison, R. M., and Johnson, M. (1997). The building blocks of performance. *Business Executive, 11*(68), 3–5.

Addison, R. M., and Lloyd, C. R. (1999). Implementation: The glue of organizational change. *Performance Improvement, 38*(6), 8–11.

Carleton, J. R., and Lineberry, C. S. (2004). *Achieving post-merger success: A stakeholder's guide to cultural due diligence, assessment, and integration.* San Francisco: Jossey-Bass/Pfeiffer.

Haig, C., and Addison, R. M. (2002, October). Trendspotters: Snapshots from the field featuring Edgar Necochea and Rick Sullivan. *PerformanceXpress*. Retrieved January 25, 2006 from http://www.performancexpress.org/0210/.

Harmon, P. (1984). A hierarchy of performance variables. *Performance and Instruction, 23*(10), 27–28.

HP Invent (n.d.). *Design for environment.* Retrieved April 30, 2005, from www.hp.com/hpinfo/globalcitizenship/environment/productdesign/design.html.

International Society for Performance Improvement. (2004, March). *ISPI Presidential Initiative Task Force Final Report.* Silver Spring, MD: Author.

Levi Strauss and Co. (2005). *Social responsibility/Our commitment.* Retrieved April 30, 2005, from www.levistrauss.com/responsibility.

Rummler, G. A. (2004). *Serious performance consulting: According to Rummler.* Silver Spring, MD: International Society for Performance Improvement.

Siemens. (2005). *Corporate citizenship.* Retrieved April 30, 2005, from www.siemens.com/index.jsp?sdc.

Tosti, D. T. (2004). *Build or repair, or why I hate cause analysis (sometimes).* Working Paper. San Rafael, CA: Tosti and Associates.

Additional Resources

Addison, R. M., and Haig, C. (1999). Performance technology in action. In H. D. Stolovitch and E. J. Keeps (Eds.), *The handbook of human performance technology: Improving individual and organizational performance worldwide* (2nd ed.) (pp. 298–320). San Francisco: Jossey-Bass/Pfeiffer.

Addison, R. M., and Wittkuhn, K. D. (2001). HPT: The culture factor. *Performance Improvement, 40*(3), 14–19.

Conner, D. R. (1994). *Managing at the speed of change: How resilient managers succeed and prosper where others fail.* New York: Villard.

Gilbert, T. F. (1996). *Human competence: Engineering worthy performance* (ISPI tribute edition). Washington, DC, and Amherst, MA: ISPI and HRD Press.

Hale, J. (1998). *The performance consultant's fieldbook: Tools and techniques for improving organizations and people.* San Francisco: Jossey-Bass/Pfeiffer.

Harmon, P. (2002). *Business process change.* San Francisco: Morgan Kaufman.

Kaplan, R. S., and Norton, D. P. (2004). *Strategy maps.* Cambridge, MA: Harvard Business School.

Kotter, J. P. (1992). *Corporate culture and performance.* New York City: Free Press.

Rummler, G. A., and Brache, A. P. (1995). *Improving performance: How to manage the white space on the organization chart* (2nd ed.). San Francisco: Jossey-Bass.

Senge, P. M., Kleiner, A., Roberts, C., Ross, R., and Smith, B. (1994). *The fifth discipline fieldbook: Strategies and tools for building a learning organization.* New York: Doubleday.

Stolovitch, H. D., and Keeps, E. J. (2004). *Training ain't performance.* Washington, DC: American Society for Training and Development.

Trompenaars, F., and Turner, H. (1997). *Riding the waves of culture: Understanding cultural diversity in business.* Yarmouth, ME: Brealey.

Van Tiem, D., Moseley, J. L., and Dessinger, J. C. (2001). *Performance improvement interventions: Enhancing people, processes, and organizations through performance technology.* Silver Spring, MD: International Society for Performance Improvement.

Wittkuhn, K. D. (2004). Models, systemic thinking, and unpredictability in consulting. *Performance Improvement, 43*(6), 17–19.

Zemke, R., and Kramlinger, T. (1982). *Figuring things out: A trainer's guide to needs and task analysis.* Reading, MA: Addison-Wesley.

CHAPTER THREE

Business Perspectives for Performance Technologists

Kenneth H. Silber, Lynn Kearny

S ince the 1970s, many human performance technology (HPT) authors have been suggesting two ideas: (1) that a key component of success in HPT practice is the ability to consult well with clients, and (2) that a key component of consulting with HPT clients is to understand their business and their language (Bratton, 1995; Liang and Schwen, 1997; Deden-Parker, 1981; Deden-Parker, Bratton, and Silber, 1980; Hartt and Rossett, 2000; Hedberg, 1980; International Board of Standards for Training Performance and Instruction, 1999; International Society for Performance Improvement, 2002; Katz, 1978; Price, 1978; Silber, 1975, 1978a, 1978b, 1980a, 1980b, 1982a, 1982b, 1998, 2001; Silber and Bratton, 1984; Silber and Kearny, 2000, 2003; Summers, Lohr, and O'Neil, 2002).

These authors suggest that understanding a business includes understanding the industry in which the business operates, the strategic goals of the whole organization, the financial picture of the organization, and so on.

Yet in workshops and courses we have conducted over the past five years involving approximately five hundred HPT practitioners, we have found that fewer than 10 percent can answer very basic business questions about the organizations they work in or work with as consultants (Silber, 2001; Silber and Kearny, 2000, 2003). Among those basic questions is, Where can one find documentation about the organization, including documentation that is public and is required by the government? Other questions have to do with the strategic issues facing the organization, and how the HPT practitioners contribute to the organization's bottom line, or even what the bottom line is and how it is calculated.

Yet these HPT practitioners come to workshops to learn how to get clients to understand what we do. They seem to be missing the basic point: it does not add value, a key HPT component, for us to create extra work for the client in trying to understand what we are all about; instead it does add value for us to understand the client's business and language and present ourselves and our ideas in light of that understanding.

WHY UNDERSTANDING THE BUSINESS IS IMPORTANT

When we talk about *business* in this chapter, we are using an extremely inclusive notion of what a business is. It certainly includes the corporate sector, which is the normal concept we think of when we mention the word *business*. But a business is really any organization that offers a product or service to customers; that receives income directly or indirectly for products and services; that has expenses it must meet in order to create the products and services; that strives for its income to at least meet its expenses; and that has a strategy, processes, and people to make all this happen. Therefore business also includes nonprofit organizations, educational systems or institutions, financial institutions, hospitals, social service agencies, and so on.

When HPT practitioners present ideas and recommendations to clients, the clients must balance those ideas with many others they face in doing business. Clients must consider how other members of management will react to the ideas, how those ideas fit into the strategic direction of the organization, what resources the ideas will require, and what changes in the organization will be necessary to implement the ideas. They must think of all the elements of the organization that will be affected. The conversations clients have about these issues, both with themselves and with others, are carried out using business concepts and business language.

If HPT practitioners cannot understand these business concepts and the business language their clients use, how can they understand their client's most pressing problems? And if HPT practitioners make recommendations that do not take into account all the business issues the client faces, why should the client trust the recommendations?

The clients that we HPT practitioners deal with expect us to make recommendations that address their key goals and objectives, in language that they understand. They expect us to recommend actions that will not shipwreck other key business initiatives in their areas of responsibility, and they expect us to find out about these issues and take them into consideration. They expect us to be able to state both the cost and the payoff of a proposal we are making in business terms so they can evaluate it and make an informed decision so they can defend their action if challenged.

HOW HPT PRACTITIONERS CAN IMPROVE THEIR BUSINESS UNDERSTANDING

This chapter offers HPT practitioners a set of business ideas and vocabulary so we can talk with our clients in terms that they understand about the things that they care about. It provides us with tools for understanding the problems our clients are struggling with from their own perspective. It can help us build credibility and at the same time identify the business issues that are driving our clients' decisions. It will help us discover what metrics our clients are using to measure success, so we can make better decisions about what projects to tackle and so that we know how to ask for the data that we need. It will also alert us to the other parts of the business that our clients must take into consideration, and give us some idea of how changes we propose in one area might affect initiatives in another area.

Fortunately, we do not need to have an M.B.A. degree or an education in marketing or accounting to do all of this. With a good mind and a useful model, we can get enough of a high-level view of the organization to ask intelligent questions and figure out where to get the answers we need. Every organization has people who do have the background in finance, marketing, operations, information technology, and so on. Following the International Society for Performance Improvement (ISPI) standard on collaboration, we can partner with our clients to obtain greater detail where needed.

THE BUSINESS LOGICS MODEL

This chapter will explain the Business Logics Model, a high-level structure for assembling an overview of an organization. It will also give us a menu of metrics that organizations use to measure how they are doing in the different sides of the enterprise.

The Business Logics Model provides a systematic method for HPT practitioners to understand an organization. HPT practitioners can also use the model as the basis for building a scorecard with the current-state numbers filled in (Kaplan and Norton, 1996).

This model is *not* any of the following, though it has been misconstrued to be some of them: an HPT model; an organization problem-diagnosis model; an alignment model; or an HPT intervention guide.

The Business Logics Model is specifically designed *only* to help HPT practitioners understand the organizations they are working with. The model can be extended into serving as the basis for a current-state scorecard based on the metrics involved in the model. Of course, prudent HPT practitioners can use the information gathered in the Business Logics Model as a basis for many different types of HPT analysis, design, intervention selection, evaluation, and so on.

The Business Logics Model draws on many respected sources in the general business literature. The idea of business logic was adapted from Karl Albrecht's *The Northbound Train* (Albrecht, 1994). Albrecht pointed out, in his chapter on business logic and strategy, that each business has logic, or a set of ideas and assumptions, behind its approach to things. This logic may or may not be explicit, but it must be understood for the business to prosper. His idea of four basic kinds of business logic has since been extensively modified, including Michael Porter's writings on competitive strategy (Porter, 1998), Kaplan and Norton's *The Balanced Scorecard* (Kaplan and Norton, 1996), and many others.

Drawing on these sources, the authors of this chapter themselves developed and expanded the model and all the elements, graphics, and tools in it, incorporating both our own ideas and the recommendations of clients and colleagues in the field. We have tried out earlier versions successfully both with clients and with attendees at ISPI conference sessions and workshops.

Uses of the Business Logics Model

Most of us have been advised, upon deciding to go out as independent consultants, that before we called on a prospective client we should go to the local business library and do our homework on the client's business. Those of us who are internal consultants are exhorted to understand the business we are in. We can use the Business Logics Model to frame and organize this homework assignment. This research does not have to be done all at once: we can rough it out initially and fill in details over a period of time. Once we have most of the information filled in, we have done our homework. The model can be used to accomplish two things: understand a client organization and begin developing a scorecard for the organization.

To Understand a Client Organization. We can obtain a good overview of any organization by using the Business Logics Model and worksheets in this chapter to gather and organize high-level information about what that organization is trying to do and also what context it is trying to operate in. In so doing, we will use the logic and the language of the business rather than our own HPT models and jargon. This high-level view will simply help us describe all of the elements of the organization in business terms. We may find we have a better overview than do many of the functional managers within the organization, who tend to know a lot about their own areas of responsibility, but little about the organization as a whole. But remember, it is a descriptive tool, not a diagnostic tool. HPT is systems-based, and this model helps us to see and to understand the organization as a whole system.

To Develop a Scorecard for the Organization: Current and Desired. The metrics at the end of each "business logic" section provide a menu of possible measures. By partnering with our client and other experts in the organization, we can identify which of these measures are used by the organization to track its performance and which are targeted by the current year's goals. We use this information to construct a scorecard of key metrics, not unlike Kaplan and Norton's "balanced scorecard" (1996). For metrics that are targeted in the organization's goals, there will be both "should" numbers, the goals, and current numbers. How the organization is doing "today" is being tracked and stored somewhere in the organization.

We can think of this scorecard as a gap analysis. We want to find opportunities to do projects that will move closer to the goal numbers that are crucial to the organization. This is key to our client's survival, and should be a priority for us.

Overview of the Model

The Business Logics Model looks at business as something that can be viewed from different logical perspectives. Each logic focuses on a different aspect of the organization. As Figure 3.1 shows, the model describes the seven logics of an organization.

1. *External logic:* Opportunities and threats the organization faces, due to external forces in its own industry and general trends in the world around it

2. *Economic logic:* How the organization makes a profit and achieves growth

3. *Strategy logic:* The purpose of the organization, the direction it is moving in and its plans for getting there, and the organization's culture

4. *Customer logic:* How the organization attracts and retains customers

5. *Product logic:* How the organization's products and services appeal to customers, and how the organization differentiates itself from other, similar organizations

6. *Process logic:* How the organization creates, produces, and delivers its products and services

7. *Internal logic:* The organization's infrastructure; that is, how it organizes itself to accomplish its work

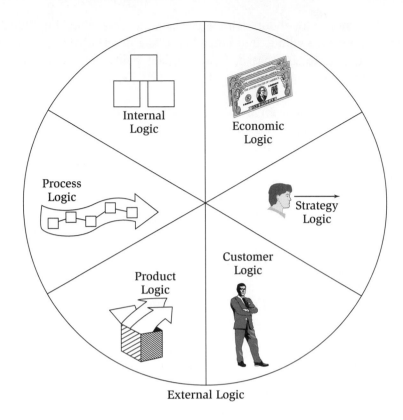

Figure 3.1. Business Logics Model.

As described previously, the Business Logics Model can also be represented as a version of the "balanced scorecard" (Kaplan and Norton, 1996). Figure 3.2 shows a matrix version of the model for identifying measures, targets, short-falls, and results for each of the "logic areas."

Gathering Data for the Various Logics and Metrics

A busy senior executive will expect us to have learned as much as possible about his or her organization before we show up for an initial meeting. We will gather more information as we start working with the organization—more than is practical to gain in a single interview. Here are some ways to obtain the information that are part of the model.

Documents. There are many published sources we can use to learn about a business before we ever talk to the client. Most organizations large enough to afford our services are required to publish information about themselves every

Logic	Measures	Target	Current	Gap	Performance Problems	Interventions	Measured Results
External							
Economic							
Strategy							
Customer							
Product							
Process							
Internal							

Figure 3.2. Business Logics Matrix.

year: to inform investors, governmental agencies who fund or oversee them, and other stakeholders. Possible resources include

- *Annual reports:* A high-level report of the organization's financial health, the annual report is increasingly used as a communication tool to reach many stakeholders.

- *10-K and Form 990 reports:* More-detailed reports published yearly by all publicly traded companies (10-K) and not-for-profit organizations (990), these list all the financial details, details about problems such as lawsuits, information about key patents and technologies, much of the business plan, names and contact information for officers, information about products and services, and more.

- *Hoovers:* This is a popular by-subscription investor publication that profiles all publicly traded companies. It gives several thumbnail analyses of each company with financial information; history; a brief thumbnail critique of management, strategy, and operations; and comparisons with the company's three top competitors. It is quick, pithy, and fun to read.

- *Libraries:* The main library in any city will have at least one business librarian and one research librarian. They are very helpful about identifying resources and showing how to use them.

- *The Web:* Visiting an organization's Website reveals what the organization wants investors, customers, and prospective employees to believe about them. A Website will communicate the image the organization is trying to project, and if it is well organized it will provide useful information about the organization's products and services.

People. An HPT practitioner can use internal experts and external networks, such as professional societies (for example, ISPI), business schools, the Chamber of Commerce, sports clubs, and local service organizations to make informal contacts for obtaining information about an organization. Once inside and working on a project, one can use interviews, focus groups, observation, and other information-gathering techniques in the HPT toolkit. For more details on these, see the section in this book on data-gathering techniques.

- *Managers:* Managers are a good source of information about the areas they are responsible for. However, unless the managers are highly placed or particularly alert and well tuned into the organization, we will find many of them narrowly focused on their own specialties.

- *Internal experts:* Specialists in various logics of the model are invaluable resources. Ask accountants or finance people to interpret the financial information for you, instead of spending hours puzzling over numbers.

- *Clients:* We may have knowledgeable clients in the same or a similar organization who can give us valuable insights, or at least useful contacts. Do not hesitate to ask.

Customers. External customers are the best source for information about how the organization's customer and product logic are actually playing out.

THE MODEL, LOGIC BY LOGIC

This section of the chapter will walk you through each logic of the model; remember that our goal is to understand the organization and not to prematurely jump to conclusions about gaps or causes of problems. For each of the logics, there will be a brief introductory paragraph and a reference to a figure that contains all the detailed information about the logic: the elements that make it up, definitions of the elements, examples of the elements, and, finally, measures that an organization can use to measure that logic.

The measures section of each figure can appear to be overwhelming if read as an algorithm; that is, that one must use *all* the measures mentioned. That is *not* the intent. The lists presented are a *menu* of possible measures an organization could use to determine the success of the organization in that logic. Our job is *not* to collect data for all the measures. However, the authors cannot predict in advance which will be the right measures for a specific organization. Therefore, the task of the model user is to find out from the client which measures the organization actually uses and cares about, then identify the metrics that are readily available. Some measures that the organization cares about may have one metric, some may have two or more metrics, and some might have no metrics at all. The final task is to secure the actual numbers for each metric.

External Logic

This view of the organization, "external logic," refers to the factors external to the organization that exert a large and important force on the organization. These are factors that the organization cannot control, though it may, in collaboration with others, influence them. They are factors, however, that the organization must understand well, since they have an impact on all the logics internal to the organization. There are two groups of factors: general societal trends and industry trends.

General Societal Trends. Trends that affect all aspects of society, as well as all industries in the society, are the general societal trends. The general societal trends include economic factors such as a recession; demographic factors such as people living longer; political and legal factors such as military actions;

TREND	EXPLANATION	EXAMPLES
Economic	What changes in the economy are affecting the business?	Inflation or recession (globally, not just in the United States), tax rates, interest rates, GDP
Demographic	What are changes in the population makeup?	Increased percentage of older people, migration of people from one country or region to another
Political and legal	What legislation, regulation, legal precedents, or political changes have occurred?	Admission of Eastern European countries to the European Union; laws related to pollution
Technological	What developments have occurred in science and technology?	Genetics, biotech, chemistry, physics, new materials (microfiber)
Sociocultural	What are changes in people's cultures, beliefs, desires, or actions?	Terrorism, increased global opportunities for women, AIDS/HIV

Figure 3.3. External Logic, General Societal Trends.

technological factors such as bioengineering; and sociocultural factors such as political shifts at local, state, and national levels. These trends are explained, with examples, in Figure 3.3.

Industry Trends. Trends that affect an industry as a whole, rather than just one company in it, are industry trends. Industry trends include the threat of new entrants (for example, is a another Google possible?); supplier bargaining power (for example, Microsoft controls prices for Windows); buyer bargaining power (for example, Wal-Mart controls the prices it pays); threat of substitutes (for example, Linux software replaces Windows); intensity of rivalry (for example, Sun versus Microsoft); and industry growth (for example, the airline industry versus the oil industry). These trends are explained, with examples, in Figure 3.4.

Key Opportunities and Threats. Just having these lists of trends is not enough. They must be summarized and translated into what they mean for the organization. The goal is to develop a list of the three to five major opportunities and threats presented to the organization by all these trends.

TREND	EXPLANATION	EXAMPLES
New entrants	How easy is it for new competitors to enter the industry (or to change the industry to enter it)?	The gasoline industry has low threat; the computer industry has high threat; the telephone industry had low threat (landlines), but cell phones made the threat high.
Supplier bargaining power	Are key suppliers few (and therefore have high bargaining power over supply and price) or many?	Oil suppliers have high bargaining power; pharmaceutical companies have high power until a patent runs out, then low power.
Buyer bargaining power	Are there many equal buyers, each with equal or low power, or few major buyers, with high power?	Wal-Mart and McDonald's have high buyer bargaining power.
Threat of substitutes	How likely is it the industry will be completely obsolete due to a new product that does the same thing and more?	Telephone and computer industries have high threat; for now, auto and oil industries have low threat.
Intensity of rivalry	How fiercely do firms in this industry compete?	Competition among software companies is high; competition among oil companies is low.
Industry growth	How rapidly is the industry growing (or shrinking)?	Biotech was expected to have rapid growth (so far has not); geriatric products have rapid growth.

Figure 3.4. External Logic, Industry Trends.

Opportunities are ways the organization can benefit from the trends. For example, the food industry saw the opportunity provided by the U.S. low-carb diet craze to introduce whole new lines of food products in grocery stores and restaurants, all at premium prices.

Threats, on the other hand, are ways the organization can be hurt by the trends. For example, a threat in the retail business is that Wal-Mart and Target will drive out of business not only small businesses but also large companies in certain product lines. Toys "R" Us, for example, did not see this threat, and recently was forced to go out of the toy business.

At this point we will have completed a good general external scan. Now we can shift our focus to an internal scan. This means identifying an organization's economic, strategy, customer, product, process, and internal logics. Because serious businesses start with finances, we too should start there.

Economic Logic

This view of the organization, "economic logic," focuses on how the organization gets profit and spends money. The factors in economic logic include cost structure (for example, the ratio of fixed to variable costs and direct-to-indirect costs); financial focus (for example, is the organization more concerned with cost of sales or general administrative costs, and how does it look at where its profit comes from?); and financial metrics (for example, does it measure return on assets or sales?).

Without understanding the factors in this logic, we will be unable to talk to senior executives in a meaningful way about how our proposed HPT interventions will affect the bottom line of the organization. For more information on understanding economic logic, we refer the reader to Stack (1994). These factors are explained, with examples, in Figure 3.5.

Strategy Logic

This view of the organization, "strategy logic," refers to how the organization views itself, its purpose, its direction, its unique skills, its growth, and how well all of these factors are aligned. It also includes how strategy is measured. This logic is akin to what business people call strategic planning or business alignment. The purpose of the model here is to highlight the key factors that an organization usually considers in its strategy, and to clarify what those factors are for the business in question.

Because managers and consultants can spend months debating the differences among certain strategy-related terms, we have grouped related ones together to avoid the debate and provided simple, but usable, definitions for each. These factors are explained, with examples, in Figure 3.6.

Customer Logic

How an organization finds and keeps customers is its "customer logic." It asks, Who are the organization's customers and how does the organization relate to them? This logic addresses questions about the organization's market strategy (for example, market segmentation and target market); its relationship-with-customers strategy (for example, encouraging a life-long customer); and metrics (for example, the percentage of new versus returning customers, or desired versus actual). These factors are explained, with examples, in Figure 3.7.

Cost structure	**Ask: Which is more of an issue for you, fixed or variable costs?** **What are the key ones you focus on? What are you doing to manage these costs?**	
	OPTIONS	**EXAMPLES**
	FIXED = Costs that are always incurred regardless of what the business is doing	Facilities, equipment, permanent staff
	VARIABLE = Costs that change with the volume of business that is available	Short-term rentals, raw materials, merchandise, temporary staff
	Organizations that have high fixed costs with relatively lower variable costs	Airlines, hospitals, refineries
	Organizations that have high variable costs, with relatively lower fixed costs	Retail stores, general contractors, small consulting firms
	Turbulence (rapid change) in the environment increases an organization's risk. Many businesses try to reduce risk by switching fixed costs to variable costs.	Downsizing, outsourcing, subcontracting, leasing

Figure 3.5. Economic Logic.

Financial focus	Ask: Which is more of a cost issue for you: COGS or SG&A—or is it both?	
	DEFINITION	**EXAMPLES**
	Cost of goods sold: The direct amount it costs to make and bring to market a product or service: • Research and development costs • Production costs • Distribution costs • Sales and marketing costs • Customer service costs	Companies concerned with process and supply-chain redesign for optimal efficiency and lowest cost, such as McDonald's and Wal-Mart
	Salaries, general, and administration: The costs a company has that are not directly related to one product but are costs of running the business as a whole; for example, • Information technology • Management • Human resources and training • Employee benefits • Facilities	Companies concerned with reducing fixed costs in administrative areas through outsourcing and downsizing, which is just about everyone

Figure 3.5. (*Continued*)

	Ask: How does the company analyze where its profits come from?	
Profit source	**OPTIONS**	**EXAMPLES**
	Profit margins by product sector—which product in its inventory (for example, desktop computers versus "extras") produces the greatest profits	Apparel (Gap) Electronics (Circuit City, Dell)
	Profit margin by customer type—new versus return	Retail (Circuit City, Nordstrom)
	Profit margin by market channel type—urban store versus suburban store versus the Internet; large store versus smaller store	Pharmacy chain (Walgreen, Target)
	Profit margin by geographical region	Retail (McDonald's)

	Ask: What are the key metrics your organization looks at to determine how well its customer logic is working?	
The financial picture: measures	1. Profit (overall; by market segment; by customer; by product type)	
	2. Costs (per unit; versus competitors)	
	3. Cash flow (length of "cash-to-cash" cycle)	
	4. Reinvestment (percentage; where)	
	5. Return on investment (benefits versus costs)	
	6. Return on capital employed (revenue to organization asset [employees, and so on])	
	7. Earnings per share/price to earnings ratio	
	8. Profitability:	
	• Return on investment (return on assets, return on sales, and return on equity)	• Operating margin • Gross margin • Net margin
	9. Solvency:	
	• Current ratio	• Total debt versus total assets • Debt-to-equity ratio • Efficiency • Asset turnover (receivables turn, payables turn, and inventory turn) • Collection period

Figure 3.5. (*Continued*)

	CHARACTERISTICS	EXAMPLES
Mission and vision	**Ask: Why does this company exist?** A mission is a statement of the specific purpose of the organization. A vision is a more affective, future-oriented statement of what the organization means. Missions and visions provide specific direction to the organization and people in it: • Mission statements should be specific and clear about the organization's industry, products and services, and customers—and even measurable. • Vision statements should express big, bold goals for the future—and talk about the affective side of the business.	**Mission** "**ComputerGeeks.com** is a leading direct-to-consumer e-Commerce site specializing in providing computer-related excess inventory, manufacturer-closeouts, high-demand and unusual computer components, and peripherals at highly discounted prices to tech-savvy, 'Geeky' consumers." **Vision** "**ComputerGeeks.com** is committed to offering tremendous savings on computer products and hosting a Website providing value-added content. Our aim is to amuse, inform, and entertain you—while providing amazing values—and to push the envelope of interactive Web functionality and secure on-line shopping ease."
Objectives and initiatives/tactics	**Ask: How do we get from here to there?** Objectives are specific, measurable, year-to-year goals that are steps in reaching the mission and vision. Initiatives or tactics (sometimes mislabeled "strategies") are the specific actions the organization is going to take to reach the objectives, and therefore the mission and vision. Objectives and initiatives should • Be specific and measurable • Be attainable and implementable • Be consistent from year to year (unless other elements of total strategy change) • Provide "line of sight" at all levels of the organization.	

Figure 3.6. Strategy Logic.

Culture	**Ask: What does the organization stand for both internally and externally?**
	CHARACTERISTICS **EXAMPLES**
	The study of "corporate culture" can include many things, depending upon whom you read. Most explanations include three key elements that can be our focus:
	Companies known (for better or worse) for their unique cultures include
	• *Values*—what the organization believes in, in terms of how it treats investors, employees, and customers and how it conducts business with other companies.
	• Enron • Microsoft • Wal-Mart • Google • Sony • Gap • Disney
	• *Beliefs or stories*—how an organization "sees" itself, in terms of the beliefs it has about role and destiny in the marketplace and the stories it tells about how it got started, what success is, the good it does, and what employees should do.
	• *Behaviors rewarded*—how an organization operationalizes the culture by rewarding behavior consistent with the culture and punishing behavior not consistent.
Core competencies	**Ask: What are we uniquely good at?**
	DEFINITION **EXAMPLES**
	Core competencies are those organizational skills and knowledge without which the organization could not exist, that the organization does better than anyone else, and that make the organization unique.
	Nike = marketing and R&D McDonald's = supply chain and marketing Amazon = tracking customer preferences and adjusting recommendations
	They are frequently not the obvious things the company is known for.

Figure 3.6. (*Continued*)

Growth strategy	**Ask: How are you growing the company?**	
	OPTIONS	**EXAMPLES**
	Acquisitions: Buying other businesses:	
	• To increase market share by buying a competitor	• Big banks (Wells Fargo)
	• To acquire expertise, distribution channels, and other resources	• Automotive (credit and insurance) (Ford)
		• Software developers (Microsoft and AOL)
	Internal growth: Adding "growth rings" to the business:	• Pharmaceuticals (Merck)
	• Grow by building facilities, hiring people to expand capacity	• Retail stores (Wal-Mart)
	• Acquire needed resources and expertise by developing them in-house or hiring to expand capabilities	• Manufacturing (Intel)
	Alliances: Expanding business by joint ventures and strategic alliances to reduce risk	• High tech (Apple partners)
		• Transportation (airlines, hotels, and car rentals)
		• Banks (Wells Fargo)
		• Grocery stores (Safeway)
		• Convenience retailers (Amoco)
		• Fast food (McDonald's)

Figure 3.6. (*Continued*).

Pricing strategy	**Ask: How are you pricing your product or service? What end of the market are you targeting? Why?** **OPTIONS** / **EXAMPLES** Top of the market: Charging the highest prices and competing on prestige, uniqueness, and perceived quality - Luxury cars (Lexus) - Designer clothing (Armani) - Exclusive privilege (first-class air travel) Mid-range: Minimize focus on price by staying in the middle of the pack - Internet service providers (AOL, AT&T Worldnet) - Most airlines (United) Low end of the market: Competing to be the low-cost provider - Superstores (Wal-Mart) - Commuter airlines (Southwest Air)
Alignment	**Ask: Are all the elements of strategy logic in alignment with one another and with other logics?** A simple notion, made complex recently, alignment asks, Are all the elements consistent with one another? and Is it clear how each element is derived from the preceding elements and guides the following ones? If the mission or vision is to be the low-cost leader, then are the prices the lowest, are the processes designed to minimize COG and SGA, are the stores located in the correct areas? If the vision is to push the envelope of interactive Web functionality, does the organization have the core competencies, culture, financial metrics, processes, and technology to do so?
Measures	**Ask: How do we measure how well strategy logic has been developed?** - Identified (yes, sort of, no) - Stated or documented - Clearly understood by all - Specific - Measurable - Consistent with other elements of strategy logic and with external and economic logics - Supported by the organization - Agreed to by people in the organization

Figure 3.6. (*Continued*)

Market strategy

Ask: How are you segmenting the market? (when relevant)

OPTIONS	EXAMPLES
Segment:	
Demographic groups	People fourteen to twenty-two years old (Old Navy Stores)
Psychographic groups	Upwardly mobile suburbanites (Pottery Barn)
How customers buy	Bulk purchasers (U.S. Steel)
How products are used	Commercial air transport (Boeing)

Ask: Which segment(s) are you going after? Why?

OPTIONS	EXAMPLES
Target:	
High-net-worth individuals because the product or service is costly to provide	Spas and luxury resorts (La Costa)
Teenage girls with disposable income	TV programming (Dawson's Creek)

Figure 3.7. Customer Logic.

Relationship versus transaction strategy	**Ask: Are you focusing on building a high volume of transactions, or more on developing long-term relationships with customers? Why?**
	OPTIONS **EXAMPLES**
	• High transaction volume • Fast food; superstores (McDonald's; Toys "R" Us)
	• Relationship: Frequent, ongoing contact • HMOs, health clubs, banks (Gold's Gym, Safeway, Chase)
	• Relationship: Infrequent, sole source • Capital equipment vendors, dentists, attorneys (Applied Materials)
Measures	**Ask: What are the key metrics your organization looks at to determine how well its customer logic is working?**
	• Size of market segment (*absolute, growth*)
	• Share of market (*absolute, growth, overall, in niche*)
	• New customers (*number, percentage, overall, in niche*)
	• Current customer renewal (*number, percentage*)
	• Complaints (*number, percentage, decrease, versus competition*)
	• Net profit per customer (*cost of sale versus profit from sale*)
	• Value (*perceived benefits versus cost*)

Figure 3.7. (*Continued*).

Product Logic

The way an organization develops and positions its products and itself to customers is its "product logic." It asks what kinds of products the organization develops, what makes them unique, and how customers see them as an organization. This logic addresses questions about product strategy (for example, making and selling niche products versus wide product ranges); differentiation (for example, is the product unique because of quality, novelty, timeliness, or low price?); company image (for example, building the "shopping experience" into stores); and metrics (for example, the number of defects, the first to market by so many days, and so on). These factors are explained, with examples, in Figure 3.8.

Process Logic

The economic, strategy, customer, and product logics that we have discussed are logics that our clients are used to understanding and working with, while they are logics that we, as HPT practitioners, are not used to working with. The situation is reversed for the last two logics, because it is in the areas of "process" and "internal logic" that HPT practitioners do most of their work.

Process logic refers to how the work in an organization gets done. It answers the question, How does the organization go about creating and providing the product or service? It describes the various processes in the organization, including research and development, production, supply chain and logistics, and postsale processes as well as metrics by which these processes can be measured. These factors are explained, with examples, in Figure 3.9.

Internal Logic

The second logic HPT Practitioners are used to working with is "internal logic," or the organization's infrastructure and support function. It includes the organization's internal structure, information systems, and learning and innovation. This logic represents the author's reframing of the traditional human resources role to focus on organizational learning and on managing the organization's investment in human capital. These factors are explained, with examples, in Figure 3.10.

WORKSHEETS AND HOW TO USE THE MODEL

A human performance technology handbook chapter on this topic would be incomplete without job aids and worksheets we can use to complete a "business logic" model for any organization. The worksheets in this section are intended to be used at a very high level, to obtain a quick, at-a-glance overview of an organization from a CEO's or general manager's point of view.

Product strategy	**Ask: How are you satisfying customer needs?**
	OPTIONS
	Niche focus: Narrowly focused product or service that people buy under specific circumstances
	Wide product range: A range of products or services that let you do more business with the same customers by meeting a variety of needs
	EXAMPLES
	Catering (Lawler Catering)
	Wetsuits (BodyGlove)
	Tropical vacations (Club Med)
	Investors reports (Hoovers.com)
	.com catalogues (Amazon.com)
	Department stores (Macy's)
	Software (Microsoft)
	General contractors (Ecker Enterprises)
Differentiation	**Ask: What is it about your product that makes it distinctive or unique? What are you doing to differentiate it?**
	EXAMPLES
	• Delivery service—know exactly where your shipment is at any time (Federal Express)
	• Personal computer—innovative product styling (Apple Computers)
	• Personal productivity software—most widely distributed, hence "readable" by more people (Microsoft)
Company image	**Ask: What is the image your company projects in order to appeal to customers? What is the company's reputation with its customers?**
	OPTIONS
	"The experience economy"
	Building customer loyalty through identity
	EXAMPLES
	Viacom (the experience of being in a movie)
	Nordstroms (the ultimate customer service experience)
	Southwest Airlines (the "be casual, be yourself" experience)

Figure 3.8. Product Logic.

Measures

Ask: What are the key metrics your organization looks at to determine how well its product logic is working?

1. Product or service:
   - Functionality (*number; novelty; time*)
   - Quality (*returns [number; percentage]; defects [number; percentage]*)
   - Price (*versus cost, competition, expectation*)
   - Timeliness (*versus purchase time, competition*)
   - Safety (*number of accidents*)
   - Volume (*production versus orders*)
   - Novelty (*absolute [number; percentage]; versus competition [number; percentage]*)
   - Differentiation (*which of above differentiate your product from competitors?*)

2. Company image:
   - Knowledgeable (*questions answered [number; percentage]*)
   - Innovative (*sales, service, finance [number; novelty]*)
   - Confident (*attitude conveyed*)
   - "Store environment" (*pleasant or unpleasant*)
   - Proactive (*number of questions asked, number of solutions generated; number of problems avoided*)
   - Helpful (*number of problems solved; number of problems welcomed*)

   - Speedy service (*cycle time; time out of service*)
   - Quality service (*number of revisions; number of callbacks*)

3. Relationship between company and customer:
   - Convenient (*steps involved [number, complexity, hassle]*)
   - Responsive (*problems solved [number; complexity; time]*)
   - Welcome given (*customer feelings [number; percentage; degree]*)
   - Thanks given (*percentage; timeliness*)
   - Guarantee (*amount; ease*)
   - After-sale service (*number of questions answered; loaners*)
   - Availability (*percentage of time available when needed*)
   - Team rapport (*number of arguments; problem-solving speed*)
   - Contracting (*number of steps, hassles, arguments*)
   - Drive out costs (*number of innovative ideas presented*)

Figure 3.8. (*Continued*)

	Ask: How do you provide new products and services?	
Research and development process (product development)	**OPTIONS**	**EXAMPLES**
	Develop new ones based on market research	A single lightweight device that will provide phone, Internet, and paging services (Cisco Systems)
	Invent new ones by pushing technology to new levels	The copper chip (IBM)
	Find existing or emerging ones and adapt them to your own strengths	The Macintosh graphical user interface adapted as Windows (Microsoft)
	Enhance your existing products or services by adding or extending features	Software (all known software companies)
Production, logistics processes, or both	Ask: What happens inside the organization to turn sales and raw materials into products and services delivered to the customer? What are the five to seven biggest cross-organizational flows of events, and what groups participate in the process?	
	Possibilities (Hammer and Champy, 1993)	**What department or groups are involved?**
	Product development (concept to prototype)	Engineering only? Or also marketing, manufacturing, customer service, training, finance, customers, and even suppliers?
	Sales (prospect to order)	Sales only? Or also finance, engineering, manufacturing, and customer service?
	Manufacturing (parts to product)	Manufacturing only? Or also engineering, sales, customer service, training, suppliers, and even customers?
	Order fulfillment (order to payment)	Shipping and accounts receivable only? Or also suppliers, finance, sales, manufacturing, engineering, customer service, and customers?

Figure 3.9. Process Logic.

Post-sale processes	Ask: Does your company provide post-sale support to customers? In what ways? (customer satisfaction, technical support, repair, updates, and returns)	
	POSSIBILITIES	**EXAMPLES**
	Minimal and reluctant	Many high-tech organizations, especially for Internet sales (let's not mention them)
	Passive reactive: complaint handling	Customer service and repair provided at customer's request (most automobile manufacturers)
	Active reactive: complaint transformation	Move heaven and earth to satisfy the customer (Nordstrom)
	Proactive: seek customers out and ask what could be better	Conduct regular focus groups of customers to solicit new product or service ideas and improvements (sporting goods manufacturers, such as for skis, mountain bikes, motocross, and so on)

Figure 3.9. (Continued)

Measures

Ask: What are the key metrics your organization looks at to determine how well its process logic is working?

1. R&D processes
   - Products created *(radically new, next generation, or enhancements: number of each; percentage of each; versus plan; versus competition)*
   - Cycle time *(absolute; versus last product, versus competition; versus customer requirements, time from initiation to payback)*
   - Process time *(absolute; versus last product, versus competition; versus customer requirements)*
   - Value-added activities *(percentage)*
   - Rework or waste *(unusable ideas [number; percentage])*
   - Coordination *(unproducoeable ideas [number; percentage])*
   - Innovative processes used *(percentage rapid prototyping, and so on)*
   - Cost *(absolute; versus last product, versus competition; versus customer requirements)*

2. Production or logistics processes
   - Quality *(variance [amount; percentage]; defects [number; percentage]; rework [number; percentage; time]; unusable products [number; percentage])*
   - Cycle time *(absolute; versus last product, versus competition; versus customer requirements)*
   - Process time *(absolute; versus last product, versus competition; versus customer requirements)*
   - Value-added activities *(percentage)*

   - Coordination *(order/supply/production/delivery match [number; percentage; timeliness; accuracy]; yield [percentage]; inventory [percentage time + or −])*
   - Innovative processes used *(percentage of rapid prototyping, and so on)*
   - Cost *(absolute; versus last product, versus competition; versus customer requirements)*
   - Supplier and interim customer satisfaction

3. Post-sale processes (repair or update and return)
   - Returns *(variance [amount; percentage]; defects [number; percentage]; untimely [number; percentage; time]; wrong order [number; percentage])*
   - Repairs/updates (amount needed [number; percentage]; done to customer satisfaction first time [number; percentage]; process cycle time)
   - Value-added activities *(percentage)*
   - Coordination *(order/supply/production/delivery match [number; percentage; timeliness; accuracy])*
   - Innovative processes used *(percentage of rapid prototyping, and so on)*
   - Cost *(absolute; versus last product, versus competition; versus customer requirements)*

4. Miscellaneous
   - Effectiveness and efficiency
   - Sustainability
   - Consumption of resources

Figure 3.9. *(Continued)*

Internal structure	**Ask: What does your organization chart look like? Why is it structured this way?**
	POSSIBILITIES **EXAMPLES**
	Profit centers — Self-contained profit and loss divisions
	Functional divisions — Marketing, R&D, manufacturing, human resources, and so on
	Geographic divisions* — Northeast region, Midwest, and so on
	Product divisions* — Adhesives, protective coatings, and so on
	*May also be self-contained profit and loss centers
Information systems	**Ask: What are five to seven key decisions most people in your organization have to make every day? How do they get the information they need to make those decisions?**
	POSSIBILITIES **EXAMPLES**
	People at every level get timely information in a form that helps them make their decisions. — Open data structures such as data warehouses and data marts are available throughout the organization, and people know how to use them. Data capture is efficiently designed and managed.
	Information exists and is accessible to decision makers, but is not useful. This is because it is out of date, incomplete, inaccurate, or not organized in a useful form for decision making. — Data capture is poorly organized or poorly managed. People charged with formatting the information are not accountable to end users. There is little or no feedback between those who structure data capture, those who input data, and the users.
	Information is centrally controlled. Decision makers often must act without access to information that exists within the organization's information system. — A central legacy system keeps information in functional stovepipes. Functional divisions and hierarchical authority levels constrain access.
	Information is squirreled away in independent systems throughout the organization. Decision makers either decide without information or must duplicate data collection and analysis activities performed by other groups. — Each part of the organization has computers and computer systems that were purchased and programmed independently. No one knows what anyone else has, and systems do not interface with each other. Some of the systems are technically incompatible. Duplication and holes abound.

Figure 3.10. Internal Logic.

Learning and innovation	**Ask: How does the organization acquire skills and knowledge?**	
	POSSIBILITIES	**EXAMPLES**
	Acquire capital:	
	Buy	Recruit for new skills
	Lease	Hire temps and contractors
	Develop	Train or educate the existing workforce
	Ask: How do you manage your investment in human capital?	
	Build value:	
	Job design	Decision making, control over success factors
	Infrastructure	Work environment, equipment, information, and safety
	Recruitment and retention	Planning, replacement strategies, career paths
	Continuous learning	Knowledge management (effective information system), double loop learning (constantly examining mistakes to learn and improve versus fix blame)
	Ask: How is your human capital acquisition and investment aligned with your core competencies?	

Figure 3.10. (*Continued*).

Measures

Ask: What are the key metrics your organization looks at to determine how well its Internal Logic is working?

1. Organization structure
   - Alignment with other logics (*percentage*)
   - Reward or recognition (*percentage, meaningful, satisfaction*)
   - Adequate information (*percentage, timeliness, usefulness, satisfaction*)
   - Safety (*accidents [number, cost, lost time]*)

2. Information systems

   A. Knowledge management
   - Knowledge strategy (*developed?, consistent with other logics?, satisfaction*)
   - Knowledge availability (*to who needs it [percentage, number], when needed [process time, cycle time]*)
   - Knowledge usability (*relevance [percentage, amount], accuracy [percentage, amount]*)
   - Knowledge effectiveness (*business problems solved [number, percentage], more accurate decisions made [number, percentage], more timely decisions made (cycle or process time reduction, on-time decisions made [number, percentage]*)

   B. System Performance
   - Quality (*variance [amount, percentage], defects [number, percentage], rework [number, percentage, time], unusable products [number, percentage]*)
   - Cycle time (*absolute, versus last product, versus competition, versus customer requirements*)
   - Process time (*absolute, versus last product, versus competition, versus customer requirements*)
   - Value-added activities (*percentage*)
   - Coordination (*business process match [number, percentage, timeliness, accuracy]*)
   - Innovative processes used (*percentage of rapid prototyping, and so on*)
   - Cost (*absolute, versus last system, versus competition, versus customer requirements*)
   - Supplier or interim customer satisfaction

Figure 3.10. (*Continued*)

Measures

3. Learning and innovation
   A. Job design
      - Involvement in decision making (*percentage, satisfaction*)
      - Reward or recognition (*percentage, meaningful, satisfaction*)
      - Adequate information (*percentage, timeliness, usefulness, satisfaction*)
      - Safety (*accidents [number, cost, lost time]*)
   B. Infrastructure
      - Adequate work environment (*match job design, match human needs, satisfaction*)
      - Adequate tools and equipment (*percentage, timeliness, usefulness, satisfaction*)
      - Safety (*equipment used [number, percentage], accidents or sick-time [number, cost, lost time]*)
   C. Recruitment and retention
      - Strategy (*buy, lease, develop, churn*)
      - Alignment with other logics (*percentage*)
      - Satisfaction (*management, employees*)
      - Have employees need (*percentage, quantity, quality*)
      - Acquisition, replacement, and redeployment
      - Efficiency (*cost per employee*)
      - Timeliness (*cycle time to fill, percentage filled by date needed*)
      - Accuracy (*length of stay of employee*)
      - Satisfaction (*manager with employee, manager with work, employee with work, employee with company, employee with manager*)

Figure 3.10. (*Continued*)

Measures
(*Continued*)

D. Career development
  - Career paths (*number, meaningful, satisfaction*)
  - Career planning (*frequency, follow-through, satisfaction*)
  - Competencies for job (*identified, meaningful, aligned, learning opportunities, satisfaction*)
  - Evaluation processes (*identified, followed, aligned, meaningful, satisfaction, growth focused*)
  - Learning (*identified, followed, provided, aligned, meaningful, satisfaction, growth focused*)

E. Continuous learning
  - Errors repeated (*number, percentage, time, cost, rework*)
  - Correction of errors (*time, cost, rework*)
  - Problems avoided (*number, cycle time*)
  - New processes created (*number, cycle time, accuracy*)

4. Miscellaneous
  - Effectiveness
  - Sustainability
  - Cost
  - Consumption of resources
  - Capability and capacity to dedicate resources over time
  - Support of major goals and harmony or integration with other initiatives
  - Diversity
  - Health and safety

Figure 3.10. (*Continued*)

They are designed to capture the information you gain about each of the logics. There are three worksheets: the "External Logic Worksheet," the "Business Logic Worksheet," and the "Measures Worksheet." They are displayed in Figures 3.11, 3.12, and 3.13, respectively.

The reader will note that there is room for only a few key words about each logic. This is to encourage high-level thinking and to ensure that we do not sink into details before we have the big picture. This is what we would use to do our homework, whether internal or external, before going to see a new client.

We would then check this analysis of the model's logics with our client to determine whether we had a valid understanding of the business, and, if not, get the client's inputs and perspectives right at the beginning of the project.

Once we have the worksheets filled out and validated, we can ask ourselves the questions at the bottom of each worksheet: what are the key opportunities and threats, what is the relationship among them, and how does the organization measure each?

Once we are involved in a project, we would construct a more detailed electronic version of these worksheets, in which we could keep adding information about the larger organization as the project progressed. As one colleague, an experienced business consultant, said, "My clients are always throwing this kind of information at me. The model gives me a framework for organizing it." It will help keep the big picture in view.

SUMMARY AND CONCLUSION

The completed Business Logics Model gives us a *business-eye view* of the organization. Once we have filled in the blanks we will know enough about a business to make intelligent observations and useful suggestions without getting ourselves labeled as one of those "time-wasting staff people." The best way to get people to understand and respect our expertise is to understand and respect theirs first. We will have the credibility that comes with knowing the score and being able to talk about it.

Having an understanding of the business's logic also puts us in a good position to be a valuable consultant for clients. With a good, complete, and accurate model of what the business is trying to do and how it is going about it, we are now in a better position using the clients' logic and their language to begin to make them aware of how the interactions of problems and initiatives across logics work. Furthermore, we are in a position to suggest ways of partnering with them to address the organization's performance problems.

Finally, and perhaps most important, we understand the metrics the organization uses to judge its success, we will be able to identify the gaps in those metrics, and we will be able to relate HPT interventions to closing those gaps.

Do an environmental scan for the business you are targeting: ☐ **Industry** ☐ **General Trends**

THE INDUSTRY	KEY THREATS	GENERAL TRENDS
Threat of new entrants?		Economic
Bargaining power of suppliers?		Demographic?
Bargaining power of buyers?	KEY OPPORTUNITIES	Political or Legal?
Threat of substitutes?		Technological?
The intensity of the rivalry?	Is the industry growing or shrinking? How fast?	Sociocultural?

- Considering your answers, what appear to be key threats and opportunities for this business?
- How can you test your assessment of the threats and opportunities?

Figure 3.11. External Logic Worksheet.

Assess and fill in the logic the business appears to be using.

ECONOMIC LOGIC	STRATEGY LOGIC	CUSTOMER LOGIC	PRODUCT LOGIC	PROCESS LOGIC	INTERNAL LOGIC

- Do the logics in the six columns support each other or are they contradictory?
- If they are contradictory, does this have some bearing on the problem you were asked to solve?
- How can you test your assessment that these are the business logic(s) the company is using?
- Now review the logic in the light of your environmental scan. Do the six logics seem to be consistent with external realities?

Figure 3.12. Business Logic Worksheet.

LOGIC	MEASURES	TARGET	CURRENT	GAP	PERFORMANCE PROBLEMS	INTERVENTIONS	MEASURED RESULTS
External							
Economic							
Strategy							
Customer							
Product							
Process							
Internal							

- For which logics does your business have measures? Circle them in the first column.
- What specific measures does it use for each logic? If you do not know, use the options at the end of each logic and ask. Write them in the second column.
- What is the target for each measure? Write it in the third column.
- What is the current number for each measure? Write it in the fourth column.
- What is the gap between target and current number for each measure? Write it in the fifth column.
- What are the measures with the greatest and most critical gaps? Note these in the sixth column.
- What interventions can be used to narrow the gaps? Note these in the seventh column.
- What results can be used to monitor success? Write these in last column.

Figure 3.13. Measures Worksheet.

Then we will truly be able to meet the ISPI standards for performance technologists of producing results and adding value by demonstrating how our HPT intervention closed the gap in key organization metrics.

References

Albrecht, K. (1994). *The northbound train.* New York: AMACOM.

Bratton, B. (1995). Professional competencies and certification in the instructional technology field. In G. J. Anglin (Ed.), *Instructional technology: Past, present, and future* (2nd ed.). Englewood, CO: Libraries Unlimited.

Deden-Parker, A. (1981). Instructional technology skills sought by industry. *Performance and Instruction, 20*(1), 14–15.

Deden-Parker, A., Bratton, B., and Silber, K. H. (1980, April). *Consulting skills for instructional developers.* Workshop conducted at the meeting of the Association for Educational Communications and Technology, Denver, Colorado.

Hammer, M., and Champy, J. (1993). *Reengineering the Corporation: A manifesto for business revolution.* New York: HarperCollins.

Hartt, D. C., and Rossett, A. (2000). When instructional design students consult with the real world. *Performance Improvement, 39*(7), 36–43.

Hedberg, J. (1980). Client relationships in instructional design. *Programmed Learning and Educational Technology, 17*(2), 102–110.

International Board of Standards for Training Performance and Instruction. (1999). *1998 instructional design competencies.* Retrieved December 1, 2004, from www.ibstpi.org.

International Society for Performance Improvement. (2002). *Standards for the certified performance technologist.* Retrieved December 1, 2004, from www.ispi.org.

Kaplan, R., and Norton D. (1996). *The balanced scorecard.* Cambridge, MA: Harvard Business School Press.

Katz, S. (1978). The politics of instructional technology. *NSPI Journal, 17*(7), 28–31.

Liang, C., and Schwen, T. (1997). Critical reflections on instructional design in the corporate world. *Performance Improvement, 36*(8), 18–19.

Porter, M. (1998). *Competitive strategy: Techniques for analyzing industries and competitors.* New York: Free Press.

Price, R. D. (1978, April). *Preparing instructional developers for the initial client conference.* Paper presented at the meeting of the Association for Educational Communications and Technology, Kansas City, Missouri.

Silber, K. H. (1975, April). *People skills involved in instructional development.* Paper presented at the meeting of the Association for Educational Communications and Technology, Dallas, Texas.

Silber, K. H. (1978a). Problems and needed directions in the profession of educational technology. *Educational Communications and Technology Journal, 26*(2), 174–185.

Silber, K. H. (1978b, April). *Training instructional developers for the 80s.* Paper presented at the meeting of the Association for Educational Communications and Technology, Kansas City, Missouri.

Silber, K. H. (1980a). The need for the study of approaches to training instructional developers. *Journal of Instructional Development, 4*(1), 2–3.

Silber, K. H. (1980b, April). *The need for the study of approaches to training instructional developers.* Paper presented at the American Educational Research Association National Conference, Boston.

Silber, K. H. (1982a). An analysis of university training programs for instructional developers. *Journal of Instructional Development, 6*(1), 15–27.

Silber, K. H. (1982b, April). *Training performance technologists/instructional developers: An analysis of university training programs.* Paper presented at the meeting of the National Society for Performance and Improvement, San Diego.

Silber, K. H. (1998). *Selecting performance improvement interventions that work to improve the organization's key metrics.* Chicago: Silber Performance Consulting.

Silber, K. H. (2001). *Seeing organizations through business glasses.* Workshop conducted at the meeting of the International Society for Performance Improvement. San Francisco.

Silber, K. H., and Bratton, B. (1984, April). *Interpersonal consulting skills.* Workshop conducted at the meeting of the National Society for Performance and Improvement, Atlanta.

Silber, K. H., and Kearny, L. (2000, April). *Seeing organizations through business glasses.* Workshop conducted at the meeting of the International Society for Performance Improvement, Cincinnati.

Silber, K. H., and Kearny, L. (2003, April). *Seeing organizations through business glasses.* Workshop conducted at the meeting of the International Society for Performance Improvement, Boston.

Stack, J. (1994). *The great game of business.* New York: Currency-Doubleday.

Summers, L., Lohr, L., and O'Neil, C. (2002). Building instructional design credibility through communication competency. *TechTrends, 46*(1), 26–32.

CHAPTER FOUR

Performance Improvement

Enabling Commitment to Changing Performance Requirements

William R. Daniels, Timm J. Esque

To improve human performance, it is important to respect a performer's ability and a necessity to choose individual performance requirements in the context of many competing choices. This is especially true for organizations with multiple layers of management hierarchy. For organizations to sustain excellent performance over time, individual performance requirements must be changeable while remaining realistic and aligned with the organization's purpose.

In this chapter we use the systems approach to simplify understanding the performer's many competing performance requirements. We give special attention to the interaction of two social systems that provide most of a performer's performance requirements: informal role sets and formal hierarchy. We illustrate, with a case, how especially effective organizations assist their performers in dealing with their many competing requirements to achieve rapid and long-lasting performance improvement. We conclude with some rules of thumb that make human performance technology (HPT) interventions more likely to empower organizations for performance improvement. As process consultants, HPT practitioners can help organizations create regular, frequent opportunities for performers to align their interdependent performance requirements and renew commitments to each other.

THE PRIMACY OF PERFORMANCE REQUIREMENTS

A system is a concept, a mental construct for understanding how things operate. When we view something as a system we look for the following generic components: "inputs, a processing system, processing system feedback, outputs, a receiving system, and receiving system feedback" (Brethower, 1982, p. 355). According to the systems perspective, every system controls itself by evaluating its outputs against the receiving-system requirements and making adjustments to its inputs and processing system. As it does so, we say the system is performing. We are particularly interested in *human* performance systems.

Applying the systems approach to human performance improvement helps us identify the key elements that must be considered. Juran and Gryna (1988) predicted a few key conditions that will lead to excellent, self-controlled human performance. The performers must

1. Know the performance requirements, the outputs desired by the receiving system

2. Know whether they are meeting those requirements, through feedback

3. Have the means and authority to change individual performance, inputs, and process in the event the requirements are not being met

The power of these conditions for causing performance improvement was demonstrated by Feeney's work with Emery Air Freight (Hall, 1972; Kopelman, 1982). The Emery Air Freight case therefore provides a good illustration of taking the systems approach to improving human performance.

In the late 1960s, due to concern over the productivity of its package-delivery function, Emery Air Freight, with input from the University of Michigan Bureau of Industrial Relations, set up self-control systems for performers who processed packages for shipping. The receiving-system requirements were discussed with small groups of performers, who were asked to state what they thought was a fair day's work in terms of what constituted effective use of containers.

Each performer was given a self-monitoring tally sheet and asked to make a tic mark on the sheet immediately after filling a container. The sheet divided up the day into hourly periods, so that by looking at the sheet and a clock, performers could tell if they were on track to meet the daily goal. Supervisors were instructed to check in with each performer at least twice a week, look at the performer's chart, and provide positive reinforcement every time they noticed a performer on track to meet the expectation.

In 70 percent of the offices, the average container use rose from 45 percent to 95 percent by the end of the first day. By applying these practices to three areas of performance, Emery Air Freight documented savings of more than $3 million in three years (Hamner, 1974; Daniels, 1995).

It is evident that each performer had always had the means and authority to meet these requirements. The cause for the change was in the shared commitment to clear performance requirements, established by using standards seen by the performers as reasonable to begin with, plus each performer's constant attention to performance feedback against those requirements. The authors have replicated this intervention many times with clients and achieved similar success (Daniels and Mathers, 1997; Esque and McCausland, 1997: Esque, 2001).

Other methods for implementing the same basic principles have been less successful. Based on these results, it should be noted that the key predictor of success is the performer's commitment to the output requirements. It should also be recognized that there are significant complications in securing this commitment, especially when the performance requirements are frequently changing.

ROLE SETS: STABILIZER OF HUMAN PERFORMANCE AND RESISTER OF PERFORMANCE CHANGE

Let us take the systems approach a few steps further. To alter a system's performance, all you have to do is change the requirements by which that system controls itself. For instance, to change the performance outputs of a heating system, you change the settings on the thermostat. Improving a human performance system (HPS) is not so easy. The difference is that an HPS decides whether or not to commit to the change in the requirements. If the heating system had this ability, it might say, "I do not like that thermostat setting, and if you do not stop playing around with it I am going to shut down and let you freeze." Most people would show little tolerance for such a mechanical heating system. But everyone has to find a way to deal with this autonomy as an inherent feature of a HPS.

HPT practitioners are not, by any means, alone in recognizing human autonomy as a stumbling block when trying to improve performance. Every parent wrestles with this issue as his or her infant attempts to escape dependency, fearfully botches up the experiments with independence, and finally settles down into a predictable and socially functional pattern of interdependence called adulthood. In addition, and based upon artifacts of human existence that span across time, it is evident that people often have found the autonomy of their adult neighbors to be a problem. Anything in the environment that is so powerful and unpredictable is also, to some extent, an intolerable problem. The positive side of recognizing these realities is that our species is thriving, so far, in spite of the problem. The species has already evolved reliable ways of getting people to stabilize their own behavior.

One of the most useful models of how people get each other to stabilize their own behavior is called role-set theory (Merton, 1957; Katz and Kahn, 1978). Role sets are very simple social systems that can be observed, in simplicity, among children at play or in primitive societies. Though they may be one of the most ancient of our social structures, role sets are still at work beneath the radar of organizations' formal systems of role definition.

The role-set model begins by picking an individual in the organization and asking the question, Why is that person acting that way? The answer, arrived at after many years of working with the model, goes as follows: every person's behavior expresses the choices being made to satisfy the requirements of the immediate role set.

For each individual, called *focal person,* there are three to eight people called *role senders,* who perceive themselves as having strong dependencies upon the performance of that individual. For these reasons, role senders pay attention to the focal person and attempt to influence the frequency with which their needs are satisfied (see Figure 4.1).

The relationship between the focal person and each role sender can be understood as a micro HPS. The role sender provides the receiving-system requirements and feedback. The focal person provides the resources, processing system, and outputs.

Role senders are not always clear about what they want from the focal person. Some of the needs are quite personal, perhaps embarrassing, and often unconscious. Furthermore, role senders' needs can suddenly change. In many cases the focal person is invited to engage in a guessing game about what the role senders want. Role senders will inform the focal person of wrong guesses

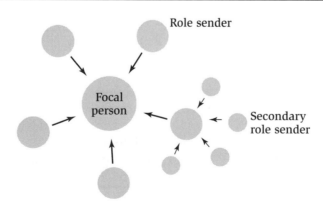

Figure 4.1. A Role Set.

by sending subtle and often ambiguous messages of disappointment or mild threats of punishment if another more accurate guess is not made soon. In these cases nonverbal messages are predominant: facial expressions, long silences, physical contact, or withdrawal. Actual punishments are often dealt in the forms of ridicule, criticism, withholding of favors and cooperation, gossip that assaults the focal person's reputation, and social exclusion. More positively, role senders may initiate small talk, engage in flattery, or perform favors to get the focal person's attention and keep the guessing game going. Occasionally a role sender actually talks to the focal person about these needs, but often these acts of communication are confrontational expressions of major disappointment. In most cases, a role sender gives the focal person a choice: "Give me what I want or I will do what I can to annoy and hurt you." If the focal person responds by attempting to satisfy these needs, a micro-HPS begins to function.

Collectively, all of a focal person's role senders are called the *role set*. The role set is therefore a complex HPS composed of the microsystems that operate between the focal person and each role sender. The only thing this set of role senders has in common is its focal person. Unfortunately for the focal person, the role senders rarely act as a group with a common set of requirements. Typically, the role senders do not even know each other. They certainly do not think together about what they want from the focal person. Nor do these role senders attempt to align expectations, or fit them to the limited resources at the disposal of the focal person.

The focal person is surrounded by this small group of people who pay attention and send frequent messages that register more or less consciously as punishment. The expectations are ambiguous, conflicting, and often unrealistic in terms of the focal person's time, energy, and talents. To diminish the punishment, the focal person experiments and discovers the behaviors that at least partially and temporarily satisfy one role sender at a time. However, when any one member of the role set tries to dominate the focal person's attention, other members intensify their threats and punishments until the focal person turns to take care of them. The focal person keeps turning from one member of the role set to another, depending on which one's message is most threatening. Eventually, the focal person learns to anticipate when and how to turn, and the behavior takes on a fairly predictable pattern.

Over time the role set members come to accept this pattern of behavior as the best they can get. They hone the efficiency with which they influence the focal person to an even more subtle set of signals. At this point, the focal person is in self-control and has complete responsibility for the pattern of behavior. Anyone or anything that tries to change the focal person's role reactivates the resisting forces of the whole role set. People learn that change equates to more pain; so they say "No thank you" when those outside their role sets offer suggestions for improvement.

Focusing only on one role set misses the truly extraordinary power of this social structure. All the role senders for a focal person are also focal persons in their own role sets. The role senders are trying to satisfy their role sets; and those similarly ambiguous, conflicting, and unrealistic requirements are the source of the role senders' demands on a focal person. The role senders take from the focal person what they can get to satisfy their own role sets. The focal person is at the center of many concentric rings of role sets. Suddenly we see an immense web of role sets binding every individual in a somewhat predictable and serviceable pattern of behavior. This is how individuals are knit into the social fabric of families, bands, tribes, organizations, city-states, nations, and cultures.

ALIGNING REQUIREMENTS ACROSS FORMAL AND ROLE-SET STRUCTURES

Taking this network of role sets into consideration provides new insight into why organizations have trouble in both establishing and aligning performance requirements, and in changing those requirements to improve performance. It shows what causes the difference between a formal job description and what any individual actually does after a few days on the job; role sets redefine jobs. It is now easy to see why it does not work when a boss tries to change a subordinate with training that occurs apart from the role set. The subordinate simply returns to the role set's relentless punishment for doing things differently. When the subordinate fails to improve after receiving a bad evaluation and being put on a program of corrective action, the role set escalates its counterthreats and puts the focal person in a world of pain. When the boss fires the subordinate, it is just the *coup de grâce*; the role set terminates the focal person first. Then, amazingly, the role set greets the new hire, and begins teaching that person the same role for which the predecessor was fired.

These are all illustrations of how the performance requirements of role sets and the formal organization's requirements usually compete with each other. This is an issue both for getting the organization aligned to one set of requirements and for getting it to adapt to changing requirements over time. As illustrated in Figure 4.2, the role set's structure is like a heavy, messy web that drapes itself all over the individuals inhabiting the nice, clean, logically arranged boxes of the organization chart. Touch any box, and the whole web vibrates with alarm; to move any box you have to drag the whole, heavy web. The web's messiness makes it very difficult to identify and change its performance requirements. The role set's subtle, very personal negative feedback keeps performers frozen in the current patterns of behavior. The organization constantly resists change, including all performance improvement.

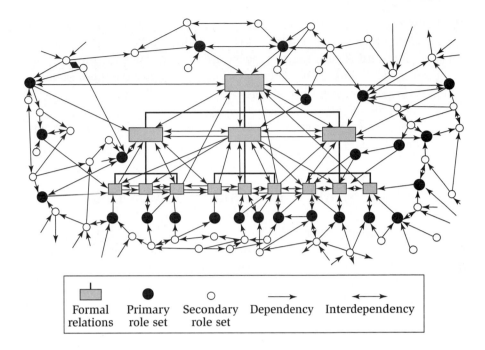

Figure 4.2. Formal Structure Draped by Primary and Secondary Role-Set Relationships.

On the positive side, role sets function like the organization's immune system, rejecting all new behaviors that might distract the organization from doing what it has always done to survive. Without a large part of the organization holding its performance steady, it is unlikely that the organization will be able to afford the risks of change and growth.

The objective for the formal organization is not to fight with the role-set structure but to find a way to align the role-set requirements with those that support the organization's purpose and its ongoing need to change performance requirements. To the extent that role-set requirements align with the formal organization's requirements, the organization will adapt to those changed requirements very reliably (Daniels, 1995). When the organization has processes of goal setting, budgeting, and work review that regularly encourage this alignment of both formal and role-set requirements, the organization has extraordinary adaptability and growth potential.

For insight into the nature of these alignment processes, we have found very helpful the guidelines articulated by Likert (1961, 1967) and his colleagues at the University of Michigan's Institute for Social Research. Likert noticed that only a few organizations could sustain a 20 percent compounded annual growth rate for three or more consecutive years while maintaining a personnel turnover rate that was lower than their industry average. Likert described, in behavioral detail, the management practices that supported the organizations that could meet this standard. These same practices are among those identified in more recent research (Collins, 2001). The authors of this chapter see these same practices as uniquely suited for bringing role-set and formal organizational performance requirements into alignment.

The authors will illustrate the alignment practices by sharing a description of a successful organization recently observed in India.

CASE STUDY: A SOFTWARE PROGRAM TEAM

The organization being described in this section is a program team within a software center in India. The center produces software for product groups within its European high-tech company, and also for external customers. This software center's revenue has grown at rates of more than 50 percent for the past four years and expects to continue growing at this rate for at least three more years. Its employee turnover rate is very low. The workforce is growing by 30 to 40 percent each year, and the organization is assimilating these new employees while continuing to improve the quality of its outputs and global reputation.

The authors will look at the three levels of one of the software center's six program teams. As shown in Figure 4.3, the program team is divided into eight project teams that manage the actual day-to-day performance of the 120 software engineers (SEs). All of the projects under the leadership of the manager of the

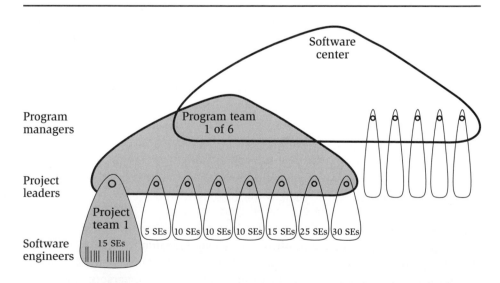

Figure 4.3. Software Center as Linked Teams.

program team are related to each other in that they produce software that controls components in consumer-imaging products. The program team currently serves six different customers. For each project, the program team defines the customer's project requirements, creates the project plan, acquires and allocates the necessary resources, and manages the project's progress to completion.

The purpose of this description is to show how this program team keeps its role set and formal performance requirements aligned. The description will start at the base with its SEs; that is, the individual engineers who write the software products.

The Monthly All Hands Program Meeting

At the beginning of each month, a meeting known as the All Hands Program Meeting is held. All of the 120 SEs working on the program team's eight projects come together in a large room. Also present are the program manager; all the project managers; the managers of support services such as human resources, quality, and finance; suppliers external to the program team; members of the marketing and sales groups; and sometimes external customer representatives. The membership of these meetings is intended to include all the contributors and stakeholders for the program's projects. Representatives of any skill, resource, or authority that can affect the program during the next month are personally present in the meeting. For many of the SEs and managers, there is a high probability that their entire role set, and many of their role senders' role sets, will be in the room. It is a unique opportunity to expose all these requirements and cause role senders to bring them into alignment with the organization's formal requirements.

The long-range plans for each project are displayed as milestones on separated rows of one large master chart. The first twelve columns of the chart in Figure 4.4 represent the weeks of the current quarter. The squares on the chart represent three to five key milestones identified for each month of each project. These milestones are represented by small, movable bits of paper placed on the appropriate project row and week. Their horizontal order represents the sequence in which the milestones will occur, and some of the slips are marked with red stickers to indicate their presence in the project's critical path. Future quarters are represented only as single columns with one or two macro milestones for each project row. The determination of milestones for this master chart will be described later as a function of the program team.

The program manager opens the meeting with a brief review of this master chart. The focus is then turned to the status of the projects as of the day of the meeting. Highlights are recognized and briefly celebrated.

In the next step the project teams consider the issues for the coming month in relation to the planning they are about to begin. Next, the project teams

	Jan				Feb				Mar						
	W1	W2	W3	W4	W1	W2	W3	W4	W1	W2	W3	W4	Q2	Q3	Q4
P1	☐			☐	☐	☐			☐						
P2		☐		☐			☐								
P3	☐			☐	☐	☐		☐							
P4			☐	☐	☐		☐						☐	☐	☐
P5			☐		☐	☐			☐				☐	☐	☐
P6		☐					☐						☐	☐	☐
P7		☐		☐	☐	☐	☐						☐	☐	
P8	☐	☐			☐	☐		☐	☐	☐					

W = week   Q = quarter   P = project

Figure 4.4. Master Chart of Project Milestones.

	Week 1					Week 2					Week 3					Week 4				
	M	T	W	Th	F	M	T	W	Th	F	M	T	W	Th	F	M	T	W	Th	F
MS			☐													☐				
SE1																				
SE2																				
SE3																				
SE4																				
SE5																				
SE6																				
SE7																				
SE8																				
SE9																				

MS = milestones   SE = software engineer

Figure 4.5. Project Chart of Weekly Deliverables.

separate into their respective groups. Each project team stands before a new, nearly blank chart representing the days of the next four weeks of its project work. As shown by the squares on the chart in Figure 4.5, the milestones that appeared on the project team's row of the master chart now reappear as the top line of these project charts. Each SE on the project team is assigned to one of the rows for the project chart.

For the next hour, the SEs in each project team will work together to detail the key weekly outputs that they will deliver to achieve their project's monthly milestones. As the SEs do this, they work the *Three Ds: deliverables, dependencies,* and *done.* The SEs make sure that all the necessary deliverables are accounted for, describing each one in writing on a small, sticky slip of paper. Then they attach the slips of paper to the correct SE's row, arranged in the proper sequence. The SEs responsible for the deliverables identify the dependencies, suppliers, and customers for each of their deliverables and define with their customers the requirements that will be used to determine that the deliverables are completed. When these discussions have been completed, each small slip of paper on the chart describes a deliverable, its producer, and its customer, and represents a personal commitment made between two or more SEs (Esque, 1999).

Thousands of decisions are made and confirmed to ensure that the month's milestones constitute reasonable expectations. The managers of the project teams are available to help resolve disagreements or capture issues that need higher-level, cross-team resolution. Whenever possible, the necessary higher-level managers meet with the SEs immediately to resolve these issues. More than a hundred people are engaged in these conversations simultaneously, and the room rumbles with the chatter. At the end of this hour almost all foreseeable issues for the next month have been resolved. Those that remain for further consideration are immediately assigned to task forces. The members of these task forces and all the project managers remain in the room to accomplish their tasks. Everyone else returns to their workstations, leaving their teams' monthly charts hanging on the wall as a record of their plans.

The task forces resolve their assigned issues. Then they rearrange the deliverables on the monthly charts as is necessary to reflect the resolutions. Immediately after these task force meetings, the project managers post the new monthly chart in their team's weekly meeting place.

Soon after the All Hands Program Meeting, the SEs break down the first week's deliverables into daily *micro-deliverables.* They expect to produce at least one specific micro-deliverable every two hours. They will have a simple daily to-do list of these three or four micro-deliverables, posted next to their computers, and mark them off as they are done. Each individual contributor's suppliers, customers, and project manager refer to these to-do lists to stay informed about each other's performance and adjust their own as necessary. To facilitate these interactions, interdependent performers are colocated whenever possible, often within the same cubicles, and the project managers are always located within view of the SEs.

There is urgency about getting that day's deliverables done. When a serious obstruction appears, it is quickly recognized and brought to the attention of those who are able to take corrective action. First, everyone in the immediate network of dependencies is alerted. The SEs make a large range of adjustments to their own performance and coordinate the adjustments with their colleagues. If the SEs are not able to resolve the problems among themselves, they call on their project manager, who, if necessary, will take the issue up to the program manager. Every effort is made to make the adjustments that will allow everyone to meet the day's expected deliverables. The intention is to remain on plan at the end of each day.

The Weekly Project Team Meetings

Toward the end of each week, the SEs in the project team meet with their project manager for about fifteen minutes. The meeting is held with everyone standing near the wall on which their four-week project chart is hanging. As the meeting begins, the SEs remove the slips representing the deliverables that their customers have agreed are done. If any intended deliverables remain not done, the manager leads a brief discussion with the group to solve the problem or problems. This is done by using extended work hours for the performer, making task force assignments, or delegating issues upward through the project leader to the program team's weekly work review. Whenever possible, a course of action is determined that will accomplish the task to be done before the next week begins.

Next the team turns its attention to the next week's planned deliverables. Things discovered or remembered during the current week that require adjusting the plan are discussed and approved by the group, and new slips of paper are added to the appropriate SEs' rows. Finally, the project manager sums up the group's performance status as it will be reported upward to the program team. For instance, the summary may simply state that the group has done thirty of its thirty-two weekly deliverables and has plans for catching up the remaining two.

The SEs return to their workstations and begin work on the next week's deliverables, including the adjustments agreed to in the meeting. The first few minutes are spent planning the next week as a new set of daily to-do lists. These are posted and then the work on each listed task begins. Each week passes as the one described above.

Because the SEs are never asked to make commitments beyond the next four weeks, and are offered the opportunity to reexamine these commitments on a weekly basis, the project charts and to-do lists take on a quality of stark realism and are quite reliable as feedback about the whole team's performance. All team members have reason to believe that if they stay on track with their daily to-do lists, the weekly and monthly milestones will be reached. *Shared confidence in the realism of the project's plan is essential to maintaining mutual trust and keeping honest communication flowing between SEs and between SEs and their managers* (Esque, 1999).

Thus far the description of this program team has focused on behavior at the level of its SEs and how they commit to output requirements, monitor themselves with feedback, and take corrective action when necessary. But it is important to notice that these human performance systems, though self-managed, are not operating in isolation. The work environment is permeated by planned, interpersonal interaction. There are many forums in which a large part of each SE's role set is likely to be present. The forums are explicitly focused on personal intentions and commitments. All team members are given frequent opportunities to work at removing ambiguity, conflict, and overload from their own role set requirements and to get the role senders lined up in support of each other's commitments to the organization's plans (Kahn, 1980). This is the key to the organization's ability to use the role sets' power to support its growth and change.

The Weekly Program Team Meeting

This description has already progressed from that of several SEs performing their key tasks to the integration of their outputs at the group level under a project manager. Now let us give attention to this same integration of role set and formal performance requirements for the project managers in the program team.

The members of this particular program team are the project managers and the managers of facilities maintenance, quality, marketing, finance, and human resources. It is a group of thirteen members and is led by the program manager. When a new member joins the program management team, the program manager will have made certain that the individual knows the purpose of the meeting: to make decisions about how to allocate resources for the accomplishment of the program's performance objectives and priorities. This purpose is usually explained in the hiring or promotion process, and reviewed again in a one-on-one discussion specifically focused on the requirements for performance in the program management team's meetings. These requirements are also summarized in a brief document called "Ground Rules for Management Team Meetings." The ground rules are briefly reviewed again with the whole team, as part of the welcoming ceremony the first time the new member attends a program management team meeting.

It is made clear that the new member will make the program team's objectives the highest priority of his or her management role. That is, the first priority of all the team members is to accomplish *all the program outputs,* not just the project or service outputs they individually manage on behalf of the program team.

As a corollary to this rule about accountability for all program outputs, each member is expected to participate on the assumption of shared ownership of all the program's resources. All members are responsible for knowing what is being done with these resources on all the projects. Managers are expected to request and offer resources, as necessary, to ensure that all the projects are accomplished with maximum efficiency.

The exercise of this authority and accountability is accomplished by participating in the program team's weekly work reviews. The primary purpose of these meetings is to decisively resolve the issues that are brought forward when it is discovered that milestones will not be accomplished with the current allocation of the team's resources. These issues are presented with a recommendation by the leaders of the troubled projects. The group resolves the issue using consultative decision making. The program leader is the decider. The members of the program team discuss the recommendation in order to ensure that the leader's decision will take into consideration all the probable consequences and possible solutions. The intent is to make every decision the best one possible in the context of the objectives and priorities of the program as a whole.

The procedure by which the program team accepts new projects is a further illustration of how the group exercises its shared authority and accountability. The entire program team works together in a special meeting to examine the customer specifications for potential new projects and assesses the program team's ability to provide the necessary resources. When the project is accepted, it is added to the program team's statement of performance objectives, which is, in fact, a list of the projects, their delivery dates, and their priority relative to all the other projects. Next, the members of the program team create the new project's plan by adding a row to the master chart and identifying the project's quarterly and monthly milestones. Finally, the program team selects the project's leader and the start-up team of SEs. These decisions are displayed at the next monthly All Hands Program Meeting, when the new project team will begin planning its first month of deliverables (Daniels and Mathers, 1997).

Again, notice how this program team's ground rules, its team approach to setting the requirements for each project and for the program as a whole, and its work-review process keep all the managers informed about each other's commitments and keep the requirements in front of the team for frequent reconsideration. These weekly program team meetings and the monthly All Hands Program Meeting effectively keep the manager's role set and formal performance expectations aligned. The same processes are being used by all the other program teams throughout the software center. The authors believe these processes for aligning the performance requirements account for the software center's unusual ability to manage its wide variety of projects, its diverse workforce, its demands for increased efficiency and quality, and rapid growth in volume of work and personnel.

GUIDELINES FOR HPT PRACTITIONERS

The authors have used the systems approach to understand how human performance is stabilized around a set of requirements coming from two major sources, the performers' role set and the formal organization's goals and objectives. Some practices have been described by which an organization sustaining continuous improvement and rapid growth makes it possible for performers to bring all these competing requirements into frequent reconsideration and alignment. The authors would like to conclude with a few suggestions about what HPT practitioners can use as guidelines when helping organizations adopt such practices.

Help the Client Focus on Its Process for Setting and Realigning Performance Requirements

Approach the task of organizational improvement as process consultants. No matter what symptoms concern the client, pay early attention to the *process* by which performance requirements are being set and aligned. Do not assume that the current processes are achieving this obvious responsibility; most are not. The client tends to assume that the requirements have already been made clear, and asks the HPT practitioner to "fix" the subordinate performers. This request for service should be seen as an invitation to be an ally with the client in competing for the subordinates' attention. To do so will escalate the intensity of the competition within all the performers' role sets and will probably only cause greater stress for the performers as they continue to choose their current pattern of behavior.

Instead, help the leader of the organization create the processes that permit all the other role senders to participate in setting the formal performance requirements. Give these other role senders a chance to articulate their needs, get their needs aligned with each other, and get the needs to fit the resources accessible to the performers. This is critical because the needs of all the role senders, including the leader, are being defined by their own role sets. It is this peculiar complexity of human performance systems that dictates our top few recommendations for HPT practitioners.

Get into the Real Meetings and Deal with the Real Issues

Get the focus of the intervention on the organization's current goal-setting and work-review systems. These current systems are the dysfunctional core of most organizational problems. First, these systems must be identified and exposed. The performers in these systems, managers and individual contributors, must acknowledge how their current interactions in fact lead to conflicting performance requirements and cause predictably unsatisfactory performances. Then the performers can reevaluate those requirements and change their commitments.

Notice that both *goal-setting* and *work-review* processes are necessary. The typical alignment intervention focuses only on goal setting, usually beginning with an annual executive strategic planning retreat followed by a cascade of goal-alignment sessions with each team of subordinate managers. This process almost always produces a wish list, more or less beautifully bound, and set on the reference shelf in each manager's office. Ninety day-to-day struggles later, it has little relevance to the systems that guide the organization's human performance. It is important to expose not only the requirements, but also the performance feedback elements of the current systems. Once exposed, the performers almost always find that the formal requirements and feedback systems are disconnected.

We find that it is better to approach the organization's performance requirements by focusing on its actual feedback systems. Rather than looking at the special meetings devoted to planning, look at the more frequent and regular meetings in which work review is, or should be, occurring. The most frequently held meetings, for instance the weekly staff meeting, are usually the ones that most fully expose the organization's dysfunctional performance feedback systems.

A good way to expose these systems for reconsideration is to get permission from the meeting leader to take over one of its sessions. Start the meeting by asking the members to work alone to write a brief description of their most pressing, *real* issue. Define an issue as something the member does not know how to resolve without additional allocation of resources. Ask the members to continue preparing for the meeting by drafting a recommendation about what resources are needed to resolve their issues and where those resources might come from. Finally, ask the members to write what outcomes they are trying to achieve by resolving these issues. When the members present these statements to each other, it raises all the right questions:

- What are we *really* trying to do?
- How important are these outputs to the meeting leader and the other members of this group?
- What is obstructing the delivery of the outputs?
- What can the group do about it?

While these are the right questions, the group, working alone, is usually less able to take corrective action than is desirable. The leader's and members' role sets are not readily available for participation. This leads to our next guideline.

Work with at Least Three Levels of the Hierarchy at Once

A three-level management meeting is the best opportunity to bring the role set and formal performance requirements into reconsideration and alignment. Get at least all the first-line managers, all the middle managers they report to, and the department head who leads the team of middle managers in a large room together. Start with all of the teams of first-line managers and their leaders sitting together. Ask everyone to work alone to prepare their issues, recommendations, and objectives as described above. Then ask the middle managers to lead a meeting with their first-line managers, using consultative decision making, to resolve as many of the team's issues as possible. All these meetings should happen simultaneously in the same room. Let the department head informally walk around to audit these meetings.

Next, bring the issues these lower-level teams cannot resolve up to the department head's meeting with the middle managers. Let the first-line managers observe, sitting behind their respective middle managers. Keep the focus on getting the issues resolved, the objectives clarified, and the resources properly allocated according to the department's priorities.

Then have the lower-level teams meet again to deal with implementing the resolution of issues passed down from the department head's meeting. Go through at least two of these rounds of passing the issues up and down. Just before each round of meetings, take a few minutes to offer advice about the procedures the teams need to use for preparation, decision making, and recording of the meeting's resolutions. Provide meeting process checklists with which the groups can evaluate their own procedures and conduct process-review discussions. In these ways, the clients learn and determine the department's preferred management practices while on the job, doing their managerial work. It is a form of *action learning.* Learning and implementation of the management practices is simultaneous.

It is very useful to follow up these management meetings with a set of lower-level meetings. This time, bring in all the individual contributors, first-line managers, and the middle manager to whom they report for about two hours. Share with them the objectives, priorities, and resolutions reached in the management meetings. Then ask the first-line managers to lead a meeting with their direct reports to plan their next four weeks of deliverables. All of these meetings should happen simultaneously in the same room. Use charting wherever it seems appropriate. Again, use at least one round of escalation and pass down so that individual contributors can see how they are linked into the management structure.

The point is to always examine and alter the process by which the organization sets its performance requirements. Learn the new processes while using and testing them. Get everyone in the room to watch and listen to each other, so that all the role senders have a chance to realign their expectations of each other. To make a lasting impact, these meeting practices must be implemented on an ongoing basis. The smaller meetings can be held weekly and the larger, three-level meetings once a month. Help your clients see these three-level meetings as a better way of doing the ongoing business of their organization.

CONCLUSION

Improving human performance systems is largely about changing the performance requirements and keeping them realistic for commitment. Because of the nature of role sets, this cannot be accomplished by addressing the performance of individuals or small groups in isolation. It also cannot be addressed by simply imposing new performance requirements on the organization's members, down through the formal organizational hierarchy. Instead, it requires regular, frequent opportunities for performers to align their interdependent performance requirements and renew commitments to each other. A key role for the HPT practitioner is to help organizations transform their regular meetings to accomplish this.

References

Brethower, D. M. (1982). The total performance system. In R. O'Brien, A. Dickenson, and M. P. Rosow (Eds.), *Industrial behavior modification* (pp. 350–369). New York: Pergamon Press.

Collins, J. (2001). *Good to great: Why some companies make the leap . . . and others don't*. New York: HarperCollins.

Daniels, W. R. (1995). *Breakthrough performance: Managing for speed and flexibility.* Mill Valley, CA: ACT Publishing.

Daniels, W. R., and Mathers, J. G. (1997). *Change-able organization: Key management practices for speed and flexibility.* Mill Valley, CA: ACT Publishing.

Esque, T. J. (1999). *No surprises project management: A proven early warning system for staying on track.* Mill Valley, CA: ACT Publishing.

Esque, T. J. (2001). *Making an impact: Building a top-performing organization from the bottom up.* Atlanta: CEP Press.

Esque, T. J., and McCausland, J. (1997). Taking ownership for transfer: A management development case study. *Performance Improvement Quarterly, 10*(2), 116–133.

Hall, E. (1972). *Business, behaviorism and the bottom line* [Motion Picture], The B. F. Skinner Film Series. Carlsbad, CA: CRM Productions.

Hamner, W. C. (1974). At Emery Air Freight: Positive reinforcement boosts performance. In H. L. Tosi and W. C. Hamner (Eds.), *Organizational behavior and management: A contingency approach* (pp. 113–122). Chicago: St. Clair Press.

Juran, J. M., and Gryna, F. M. (Eds.). (1988). *Juran's quality control handbook* (4th ed.). New York: McGraw-Hill.

Kahn, R. L. (1980). Conflict, ambiguity, and overload: Three elements in job stress. In D. Katz, R. L. Kahn, and J. S. Adams (Eds.), *The study of organizations.* San Francisco: Jossey Bass.

Katz, D., and Kahn, R. L. (1978). *The social psychology of organizations* (2nd ed.). New York: John Wiley and Sons.

Kopelman, R. E. (1982). Improving productivity through objective feedback: A review of the evidence. *National Productivity Review, 2*(1), 43–55.

Likert, R. (1961). *New patterns of management.* New York: McGraw-Hill.

Likert, R. (1967). *The human organization: Its management and value.* New York: McGraw Hill.

Merton, R. K. (1957). *Social theory and social structure.* Glencoe, Ill.: Free Press.

CHAPTER FIVE

Systemic Issues

Dale M. Brethower

This chapter supports a thesis: systemic issues are important, fundamental, and defining for the effective practice of human performance technology (HPT).

Here are two examples of systemic issues:

Example 1: My reading clinic colleagues and I taught a child to read. We were good reading teachers but not good human performance technologists at that moment. Our mistake was in thinking that a little girl's performance in school would be improved by teaching her to read. Good assumption, right? Wrong! She was not given the opportunity to read in school. Her very caring teacher knew she could not read and could not believe that she could have learned to read so quickly. She did not ask the child to read, believing that it would subject the child to further humiliation. Should we blame a teacher for preventing a child from being humiliated?

Example 2: Doug Meade successfully taught repair technicians how to make repairs. He was a good trainer but not a good human performance technologist at that moment: he had analyzed the skills necessary to make repairs, developed a course in which technicians learned the content, told supervisors what was in the course, and invited them to send people to the course. His mistake was in thinking that having the skills would improve performance on the job. It did not and for good reason: few of the people sent to the course ever performed the repairs they learned to make. The supervisors might have believed that having more skills was a good thing. Perhaps they wanted to develop their people. Should we blame supervisors for developing their people?

111

Nothing was wrong, per se, with the teacher's thinking or the supervisors' thinking. What was wrong was that neither Doug nor I were using human performance technology competently. We overlooked an important fact: *Performance occurs in a systemic context that supports performance, or not, and defines the meaning and value of performance.* If I scream "Fire!" it means one thing in a crowded theater and another thing if I am commanding a mock military battle. Context determines meaning and value.

Doug and I thought we understood the systemic context. Children must read to be successful in school, right? Repair technicians must have the knowledge and skill necessary to make common repairs, right? Fixing the knowledge and skill deficit will lead to improved performance, right? Wrong! We did not investigate systemic issues. Will they have the opportunity to perform? "Yes," we thought. "No" was the answer. What would also have to be changed to support the performance or make it valuable? We did not ask.

I made inquiries about other situations and learned systemic information about schools in Michigan. For example, schools lose special education funding if a special education student is successful enough to be placed in a regular classroom. Doug discovered an array of systemic issues related to work assignments: supervisors being evaluated on whether they support development of their people, compensation issues and safety issues that are relevant, and a whole lot more.

RELEVANCE OF SYSTEMIC ISSUES TO HPT CERTIFICATION STANDARDS

The importance of systemic issues has long been recognized, considered, talked about, and, too often, ignored by opinion leaders in our field. But now concern for systemic issues is written into the HPT Certification Standards. Systemic issues are a defining standard for our profession.

Here are the standards, as downloaded from the International Society for Performance Technology (2004). Emphasis is added to highlight four defining principles of HPT.

The ten standards are based on ISPI's four principles, following a systematic process, and agreeing to a code of ethics. They are summarized as follows:

1. *Focus on results* and help clients focus on results.
2. *Look at situations systemically,* taking into consideration the larger context, including competing pressures, resource constraints, and anticipated change.
3. *Add value* in how you do the work and through the work itself.
4. *Utilize partnerships or collaborate* with clients and other experts as required.

5. Be systematic in all aspects of the process, including the assessment of the need or opportunity.

6. Be systematic in all aspects of the process, including the analysis of the work and workplace to identify the cause or factors that limit performance.

7. Be systematic in all aspects of the process, including the design of the solution or specification of the requirements of the solution.

8. Be systematic in all aspects of the process, including the development of all or some of the solution and its elements.

9. Be systematic in all aspects of the process, including the implementation of the solution.

10. Be systematic in all aspects of the process, including the evaluation of the process and the results.

The first four standards capture ISPI's four principles: focus on results, work systemically, add value, and collaborate with others. They describe the essence of our work in HPT. The four standards, considered together, recognize that it is possible to do a performance-improvement project that is considered a success in one area of an organization even though it makes performance worse in another area or makes performance worse for the total organization. That is not what human performance technologists should be doing. The four principles must work together; it is necessary to meet all four to ensure that meeting any one of them is possible or worth the effort.

We in ISPI are proud of the remaining six standards because they were invented by and for our colleagues, but they have been invented elsewhere as well. Standards 5 through 10 are generic problem-solving standards written in language that connects them to our world. Together, these six "being systematic" standards, when combined with the first four standards, mean working within and addressing the systemic context of organizations, not simply working in a lockstep or systematic fashion.

Allow me to repeat, for emphasis, and then explain further: *if any one of the first four standards is not met, one is not doing human performance technology.*

1. Our first standard is to focus on results. Other professional standards often focus on means, such as using standard accounting procedures. The focus on results is an uncommon standard for professions, but an essential one for HPT.

2. The second standard requires attention to systemic issues. Much more will be said about it in what follows, as systemic issues are the focus of this chapter.

3. The third standard emphasizes adding value. Adding value requires focusing on a result that is worth more than it costs to attain. The standard is very basic and very powerful, but it is easier to provide lip service to it than to meet it.

4. The fourth standard specifies collaboration with clients and other experts. The standard is a necessary companion to a systemic approach. HPT is not something we do *to* clients but something we do *with* clients.

A systemic approach cannot be carried out within the confines of one narrowly defined organizational specialty or academic discipline. It cannot be carried out by one person or one champion or one small segment of an organization. Collaboration is necessary.

Here is an image to capture the meaning of the collaboration standard. Imagine the client for your project not as one person or executive, even a CEO or COO, or one division, but as a steering committee that represents the organization as a whole, including marketing, production and delivery, finance, human resources, and other key functions. The steering committee would have members that represent the formal and informal power structures and organizational structures.

It would be nice to have a powerful steering committee backing your every project, but it does not happen that way. It is not practical to put together a high-powered steering committee for every project. Now alter the image of client-as-powerful-steering-committee to make it more realistic.

Imagine that you create a de facto steering committee by interacting with the people who would be appropriate for a steering committee. Just ask for and listen to their views and integrate the views into the project work. For example, in my performance-improvement work within a university, improving the performance of a graduate program, I did not have an open invitation to drop into the president's office, the Vice-President for Research's office, the Graduate College Dean's office, the Arts and Sciences College Dean's office, the Psychology Department Chair's office, and the offices of the chairs of three or four relevant curriculum committees and three or four relevant budget committees whenever I wanted. Nor was I naive enough to ask the president to appoint a representative steering committee to support my efforts. No one gets the enthusiastic support of everyone at the top, not even the people at the top.

Acting as if the steering committee were real is more important than having the committee. Knowing who the key players are, one can work systemically by occasional interviews or chats, reading things the committee members write, listening to and checking out rumors, and making intelligent guesses. It is possible to be influenced by them simply by actively listening to them. It was easy for me, for example, to know what the president wanted. He was working to develop and communicate a strategic plan. Similarly, each of the other players was busy doing an important job that included formulating an agenda and pushing it. Listening works.

My point here is simple: one cannot work systemically by staying inside one's organizational box. Getting out of one's box is a choice, even though making the choice can bring internal political sniping and other nastiness down upon you and does not, by itself, ensure that you get value-adding results.

The next section shows an orderly way to work systemically to implement the first four HPT standards. It begins with a fictional story and moves on to a careful look at systemic issues within the framework of an actual organization as a system. The two stories are offered to illustrate the meaning and fundamental importance of systemic issues.

ORGANIZATIONS ARE SYSTEMS

Humans throughout the ages have communicated important concepts through stories. Two stories illustrate the concept of system, providing a context to articulate important systemic issues and to identify tactics that work, and those that do not work, in dealing with systemic issues.

Organizations as Systems in the Fictional World

In the Mesh is the title of a story and a fact of life that is emphasized in author John-Paul Sartre's existential philosophy. Sartre's 1954 story, or scenario, as he called it, begins by showing scenes of fighting, a revolution in progress. Jean Aguerra, a hated dictator, and his troops are outnumbered and surrounded. He orders a ceasefire and surrenders. He is escorted to a tribunal, then a firing squad. As the firing squad prepares to execute him, Aguerra smiles, fleetingly, sadly. *In the Mesh* is about the events that brought about the dictator's execution and his smile.

Flash back to another scene, about five years before. Jean Aguerra is in the scene, this time as the leader of the *revolutionaries.* He and his fellow revolutionaries burst in upon a dictator. They take him into custody, to a tribunal, and to a firing squad. Five years previous, Aguerra was the leader of the revolutionaries overthrowing a hated dictator. Now, five years later, he is executed as a hated dictator.

The scenario is set. How did the idealistic revolutionary of five years ago become transformed into a hated dictator? As the scenario unfolds we learn that Aguerra was not corrupted by personal power and greed as the revolutionaries believed. Aguerra was caught in a systemic mesh of realities, the realities one encounters in trying to implement ideals.

The plan: Nationalize the oil fields and turn over the profits to the people.

The reality: Who would develop the oil fields, pump the oil, pipe it to the sea, and transport it to market? Who would buy the oil and at what price? What would happen if other oil producers in other nations reduced their prices? Or pumped more oil?

The revolutionaries knew how to destroy. They could shout and shoot. But they did not know how to run an oil industry. Even had they known, they did not have the capital, the cash, and the connections. The oil industry operates in a value chain, in a mesh of connections. It operates within an infrastructure that the revolutionaries did not know existed. Aguerra found out about the infrastructure quickly. The former owners of the nationalized industry explained the situation. They could leave the country to Aguerra and his revolutionaries or they could stay and run the oil fields, under contracts that resulted in some, but not all, of the profits flowing to the people.

Perhaps Aguerra could train and develop his constituents to take over more and more responsibility for running the oil fields. But it would take time. Aguerra's revolutionary friends were not happy nor patient when their dreams of immediate oil profits were not realized.

There were, to Aguerra's dismay, similar problems with land reform. The people knew how to grow things and could do so in little plots of land, but could they work together to maintain the irrigation systems and the machinery and the markets? Or would there be disputes over who was to get which piece of land, who could travel across another person's land, who used the most water, who got what machinery? How could such disputes be resolved? The new landowners had guns and the will and skill to use them, but could Aguerra and the revolutionary council allow civil strife? Should they allow the carnage to ignite and spread, or should they send in the central police to throw shooters-of-neighbors in jail: and then what? Establish a judicial system, respected and known to be fair, and do it within a few weeks?

You can see the problems; there are systemic issues involved. One does not move swiftly and easily from governance by an oppressive dictator to a smoothly running government and economy. Just as it is easier to kill a goose than to raise a child, it is easier to overthrow a government than it is to govern. Aguerra discovered that a government operates in the mesh of many realities, the realities of people's hopes and dreams, the realities of an economic infrastructure, and the realities of an infrastructure for governance. That is true whether we are talking about one company or one country.

The former revolutionary found himself in the mesh of systemic realities. He ran out of political capital before he could wriggle out of the mesh enough to create the country he dreamed of. Why the smile as he was executed? Perhaps it symbolized understanding, knowing that the executioners would be caught in the mesh and follow him in his role as the star at an execution.

The lack of effective infrastructure and the competing interests that grew within the country had generated other systemic issues that Aguerra had to deal with or die. He could not do the job without the cooperation of others internally and without satisfying external interests. He could not succeed by using power; he lost it even as he tried to exercise it. He was functioning within a mesh of systemic issues. The systemic issues were captured in fiction, significant and interesting because the art mimics systemic reality.

Organizations as Systems in the Real World

This is the story of General Motors (GM) from 1918 to 1964 and its subsequent decline. The GM story is important to HPT for two fundamental reasons:

1. GM served as the laboratory for development of management consulting and organizational theory. GM built vehicles; observers such as Peter Drucker (Drucker, 1946) built organizational theory.

2. The GM story provides a case study that showcases systemic issues: key systemic features were put in place one by one, then removed.

The early history of General Motors is the history of a failed dream, the dream of a man named William C. Durant, who wanted to create a company that could build a car. He pulled together a number of companies that had a car to build, such as Buick and Chevrolet, and companies such as Hyatt Roller Bearings, Remy Electric, and ACDelco that built parts that went into cars like Oldsmobile, Cadillac, or Pontiac. Durant, good at making deals, created General Motors. Durant, not good at managing, twice ran GM nearly into bankruptcy before losing control of the company.

Durant lost control because General Motors was caught in a mesh of systemic issues.

Internal Systemic Issues. Three major internal issues faced General Motors:

1. The companies that Durant had acquired were headed by executives strong enough to build a company and strong-willed enough to want to continue doing things the way that had produced the successes.

2. The companies were part of GM on paper, but there was no internal infrastructure to support working together.

3. The companies within General Motors had a history of competing with one another and very little incentive for cooperating.

External Systemic Issues. Four major external issues faced General Motors:

1. There was no clear direction for how the company was to compete in the marketplace.

2. The cars from one GM division were competing with cars from another division as well as with cars manufactured by competitors.

3. GM was nearly bankrupt and had lost the confidence of investors who supplied capital and banks who supplied operating funds.

4. GM was facing a post–World War I economic slump; car sales were low all around the country.

General Motors brought in a new leader, Pierre duPont. The financial community knew duPont and trusted him. They would listen to plans for financial restructuring rather than just shut GM down and cut their losses. The leadership change was necessary to stay in business, but it did not solve the systemic problems: internal chaos and external economic downturn.

Enter Alfred P. Sloan, Jr., who had headed Hyatt Roller Bearing and then a collection of GM companies called United Motors. He had ideas about how General Motors might become a functioning organization (Sloan, 1963). Sloan, working with others, did several important things. Each has a complex story, but the critical business issue driving each was simple: GM had to adapt or die.

The Bonus Plan. Part of adapting was to give the executives an incentive for working together within GM instead of pulling out. Walter Chrysler and others had already left and formed competing companies. The bonus plan was carefully structured. If GM did well financially, there would be a substantial amount of money available for bonuses. If GM did not do well, there would be little or no money for bonuses. Each executive was paid a bonus according to the profitability of his division. An executive who maximized his division at the expense of others would get a larger share of a smaller amount. If GM did well and the division did poorly, the executive would get a small share of a larger amount. The plan was set up to ensure that each executive had a financial stake in how well GM did as a whole and in how well the division performed. In addition, the bonus was typically paid in GM stock rather than cash, another incentive for the executive to work to increase the value of GM stock. The bonus plan was an effective motivational device but it was not the solution; it could work if and only if a number of other things were done to fix GM so that it worked as a company.

The Organizational Structure. A major item was to introduce an actual organizational structure that ensured form would support function.

Sloan knew that any organizational plan would be met with great resistance, since GM executives had been competitors all their lives, and each would be looking to seize an advantage. Consequently, he articulated two principles, criteria that any structure must meet and, if met, would be acceptable to the executives. The principles were

1. Complete operating autonomy of the divisions
2. Central coordination of certain essential resources

The division executives liked the first principle. Pierre duPont, accustomed to centralization, and the Finance Committee, which believed in controlling the purse strings, liked the second principle. Both principles are essential. Together they achieve a systemic balance between centralization and decentralization.

When the organizational structure was drawn up it depicted each of the former companies as a division of GM. They were the core of GM and were shown as the largest and central part of the organization chart. Above the divisions was an operations committee that reported to the president. The operations committee's job was to help the divisions operate, not dictate to them. The division heads would have it no other way.

On one side of the organization chart were financial services, including the General Motors Acceptance Corporation, to make sure that people could get help financing their new car purchases. That looked good to the operating divisions. On the other side of the organization chart were several advisory groups. The advisory groups could advise the divisions. *That is all they could do.* The advisory group on engineering could not order the engineers to do anything. They held seminars to keep the engineers informed as to the latest in engineering and as to what was going on in other divisions. Attendance at the seminars was voluntary and the costs were charged back to the divisions. The advisory groups had to perform well to survive.

The organizational structure ensured a decentralized operation of GM. The divisional executives could run their divisions, benefiting from advice and financial services and within the constraints of the money available. The scheme provided freedom within a structure and the information necessary for making intelligent operating decisions.

The core of GM was making cars. The advisory groups and financial services were about making that possible. *Managing money well and managing knowledge well were and are essential for successful operation and innovation.* The operating divisions could, working together, get much better information about financial matters than each could have working separately. The organization structure was put in place to ensure that GM as a whole could be mightier than the sum of its parts. It ensured that it *could* but there was more to be done to ensure that it *would*.

How could the divisions be sure that each was being treated fairly in financial resource allocations? How could each divisional executive know that he was being treated fairly in bonus decisions? How could everyone know that each division was doing better as part of GM than it could independently? There were serious questions that required serious and credible answers. A system for measuring divisional performance and the performance of GM as a whole was required. GM needed a scorecard.

Keeping Score. Enter Judson Brown with a tool he brought with him from the duPont company: the duPont Return on Investment (ROI) formula. The tool supported reasonably precise calculations about how each division was doing as a commercial enterprise. But it took the support of the company president, Pierre duPont, the chair of the Executive Committee, Alfred Sloan, the chair of the Finance Committee, and a lot of work, to get the formula used. There were several legacy accounting systems in use and different ways of collecting numbers. Brown's task of getting credible numbers to plug into the ROI formula was an arduous one, but he succeeded.

GM now had a bonus plan to encourage cooperation and discourage subsystem maximizing, an organizational structure to get the parts working as a whole, and a yardstick for measuring financial performance. Missing was a strategic marketing plan to ensure that GM could succeed in the marketplace, earning the revenue to keep the whole thing going.

The Theory of the Business and Marketing Plan. Sloan called the marketing plan a theory of the business because it dealt with how one does business with respect to the two key elements of a marketplace: (1) customers and (2) competitors. The plan was simple, though it took time and deliberation to develop and even more time and deliberation to implement.

The plan: look at the buying power and wants of potential customers. Divide the market, arbitrarily, into bands from the lowest-priced cars to the highest-priced cars and make sure that GM had a car in each band. Ford, with its basic black, simple, and inexpensive cars, dominated the low end, so price the lowest-priced GM car just above them. Compete with Ford not on price but by appealing to customers to step up to a Chevrolet, with a slightly higher price and many more features. The overall GM plan was as follows:

- Put only one GM car in every price range to avoid competing with other GM cars
- Challenge competitors below the range with features
- Challenge competitors above the range with price

GM now had a response to the major systemic challenges. As Sloan put it, GM had the three requisites for success:

1. A theory of the business, the marketing plan
2. An organizational structure, including balancing centralization and decentralization to support the business

3. A yardstick, the duPont Return on Investment formula, to measure success

The theory of the business aligned GM's products with the marketplace. The organizational structure aligned GM's operation with its products and the marketplace. The advisory structure supported continuing innovation in the marketplace and continuous improvement of operations to keep the alignment. The yardstick enabled everyone to keep score regarding the financial health of the organization.

Unlike Jean Aguerra, who failed to establish the three requisites for success, Alfred P. Sloan, Jr., was kept on. He was a leader at GM from the crisis years just before and after 1920, through the Great Depression of the 1930s, and through the crisis of World War II. He served as president for several years, establishing the technical and informational infrastructure that supported informed and intelligent decision making by managers. He then served as chairman of the board, where he supported the operational leaders and stood in the way of efforts to make management decisions on the basis of favoritism or self-promotion. He relied on the yardstick, applying it to promoting executives based on yardstick performance, not on whether they exuded the charisma of leadership and not dependent upon their ability to get Sloan to like them.

From the post–World War I crisis years until Sloan retired in the early 1960s, GM rose from near bankruptcy and trailing Ford for market share to a position of dominance. General Motors had a 65 percent market share and a new strategic challenge, that is, avoiding being broken apart by running afoul of anti-trust laws.

The post-Sloan GM story is one in which key systemic features of GM were gradually dismantled. We have, from the position of hindsight, a remarkable opportunity to observe the reversal of fortunes as the systemic features were tampered with in the late 1960s and beyond. Success and the systemic features went together, supporting but not proving the notion that managing the systemic features caused the success.

The Dismantling and Decline. General Motors declined in market share and revenue as the marketing plan was undercut, the bonus plan undercut, the organizational structure compromised, and the yardstick ignored. The marketing plan was ignored by default as GM companies started competing directly with other GM companies. Chevrolet and Pontiac, the poorer cousins on the price and prestige ladder, each led the charge by attempting to transfer brand loyalty from GM loyalty to Chevrolet or Pontiac loyalty (Wright, 1979). Both divisions did so by building a wider range of cars so that Chevrolet and Pontiac competed head on with one another and also with Oldsmobile and Buick.

The bonus plan was undercut by the paying out of huge sums to executives when GM as a whole was not making much money, an activity that had the side effect of strengthening the anger of employees and their loyalty to the United Auto Workers. Without the bonuses, they opined, the cuts in employee wages could have been smaller and would have been more palatable. The organizational structure was compromised as people at headquarters stopped being advisers and started attempting to be controllers, by beginning to micromanage the job of the persons reporting to them. Many GM executives stopped being externally focused and became focused on internal politics.

Part of GM's decline had to do with increases in international competition. But part of the success of the international competition, in turn, had to do with GM alienating GM dealers across the land. Sloan had seen the dealers as an essential component of the marketing strategy and a source of intelligence about what was happening in the marketplace. He established policies to ensure that dealers were supported. He spent vacations in dealerships selling cars and keeping in touch with the marketplace and issues facing the dealerships. As GM policies changed from *support* the dealers to "squeeze the dealers," the alienated dealers became a great resource in the distribution of Toyotas, Nissans, BMWs, Volkswagens, and so on. The competitors did not have to build a distribution network, they only had to accept the one GM handed them by heavy-handed treatment of dealers. By the mid-1980s GM no longer had the market share to be concerned with anti-trust laws. They were now downsizing and worrying about economic survival.

No one thing produced GM's increasing success from 1920 through the 1960s. In my view, the success required attention to systemic issues. No one thing produced the decline. The decline of GM occurred, however, as systemic issues were ignored.

My points here are that, whatever else was going on,

1. Key systemic issues were not effectively addressed at GM around 1920 and GM was near bankruptcy: the baseline period.

2. When the systemic issues were addressed, GM prospered for more than forty years: the intervention period.

3. As the same systemic matters were ignored or addressed much differently, GM's fortunes declined: the reversal period.

In the Mesh and the GM story highlight systemic issues that I believe are vital for the successful, value-adding application of HPT. They are issues that anyone who attempts to practice HPT competently will experience sooner or later, usually sooner. In the next section I will enumerate some of the systemic issues and show specific connections between HPT concepts and systemic issues. As I do that, I will show some of the ways that systemic issues can be dealt with constructively.

POINTS OF THEORY AND SYSTEM PRINCIPLES IN THE STORIES

A major theme in each of the earlier stories is that we operate in a mesh of systemic variables. Jean Aguerra did not know how to deal with systemic issues and paid the price of ignorance. Neither the fictional Jean Aguerra nor the real Alfred P. Sloan, Jr., could escape that mesh. The mesh is there whether we know it or not.

The stories illustrate interconnectedness. In a system, everything is connected to everything else. Many things are necessary but none, by itself, is sufficient to ensure that the system works.

- Managing internal operations is necessary but not sufficient.
- Managing external relationships is necessary but not sufficient.
- Providing value to customers and other stakeholders, including employees and suppliers, is necessary but not sufficient.
- Managing money effectively is necessary but not sufficient.

Many things are necessary; no one thing is sufficient. Viewing organizations systemically requires looking at the interconnections among variables.

Points of Theory: The System

Consider this definition: *A system is a whole, its elements, and the interrelationships among the elements, between each element and the whole, and between the whole system and other systems with which it interacts.* That definition, and each of the others similar to it, is not a bad definition, just too densely packed to be very meaningful. Allow me to unpack it a bit.

Consider an airplane as a system. It is a whole. You can see it in a hangar, on a runway, or in the air. The elements are a million or so parts, clustered into subsystems for power, guidance, and the like. To understand the parts, we must understand the interrelationships among them, the interrelationships that make the airplane into a whole thing that flies. But if we want to understand the airplane-as-system, we must understand what makes the thing fly and a whole array of other things that determine how the airplane relates to its environment. The airplane, as system, is not just the complicated and expensive device. *A system is not only the elements, it is also the relationships.*

The essence of an airplane-as-system includes how well it flies and lands and carries cargo and how easy it is to repair and how it is perceived by the public and how many people buy tickets to fly on it. Thinking about the airplane-as-system we must consider the value of the airplane to an airline, the company that built it, the passengers, the crew, the ground crew, the gate crew, the competition, the local economy, and the company balance sheet.

Attempting to consider all the elements and relationships in a typical company could lead to a severe case of analysis paralysis and incapacitate the performance system analyst. What can we do instead? Only a few things:

1. Collaborate with others to ensure that important information is available.

2. Coordinate the work, by ourselves and others, through theory and knowledge of basic concepts and principles of systems.

3. Coordinate the work, by ourselves and others, through selective information about the system being considered.

4. Attempt to ignore systemic issues until the ignorance causes serious problems.

5. Attempt to know all about it.

While the last two techniques are common, so too is failure. A combination of the first three is more likely to be successful. To describe how to do them I must articulate six key points of theory, then three principles that help focus on the right selective information about the system.

Six Key Points of Theory

Six key points of theory describe and define the type of system that HPT deals with most, the adaptive system. An adaptive system is one that can *adapt* to changing circumstances in order to fulfill its purpose and one that can change its purpose to *adapt* to a changing world.

Theory Point 1: Definition. A system is a collection of elements and relationships, held together by a purpose in common.

- An airplane is a collection of elements and relationships constructed to achieve a small number of specific purposes. The relationships with external elements are part of the system; relationships with pilots who might fly it, mechanics who might maintain it, and customers who might benefit from services that can be provided by using it are all parts of the system. The external relationships are part of the system in the sense that they define the value and purpose.

- I am a collection of elements, body parts and skills, mostly, and relationships with family, friends, enemies, and employers that function to achieve a small number of specific purposes such as health and happiness. Who I am is defined in significant ways by the relationships with people external to me. I would not be who I am without the relationships with family, friends, colleagues, former students, and business contacts.

- General Motors is a collection of operating and support divisions plus many internal and external relationships, held together by a small number of specific purposes such as making cars and making money. The external relationships are captured, roughly, by business concepts such as brand image and market share.

Theory Point 2: Value Added. External relationships define the value added by the system.

- An airplane adds value only if it reliably and safely carries people and property to specific destinations.
- No matter how many good products GM builds, it adds no value if no one values the products.
- All the parts of an airplane have to work and have to be supported by many people to keep the machine operating reliably and safely.

Theory Point 3: Adding Value. Internal relationships are essential in providing the value to be added.

- Neither cars nor airplanes can be produced unless the parts of the manufacturing plant work together effectively.
- The parts of a manufacturing plan will not work together effectively without an appropriate internal infrastructure, including a management system and an appropriate pay system.
- The staff of a manufacturing plant or a human service agency will not work together effectively without an infrastructure, including a specific culture, that supports cooperation.

Theory Point 4: Alignment. Maintaining two interconnected sets of relationships, internal relationships and external relationships, is necessary for survival.

- If my heart and liver and stomach, and so on, do not work together, I am unhealthy or dead; if I do not maintain good external relationships, I will not survive very long.
- If the staff members of a human service agency do not work well together, the quality or efficiency of service will suffer.
- If each division of General Motors does not maintain good relationships with its customers and community and with other divisions of General Motors, the quality or efficiency of work will suffer.

Theory Point 5: Interconnectedness. Systemic variables are interconnected; systemic performance is multiply caused; there is no such thing as an independent variable in a living system. If the parts are *not* connected, they are not parts of the system.

- Interconnectedness was illustrated in the opening stories about learners: they had knowledge but lacked opportunity to perform. Instructional variables were connected to workplace variables only after we began working systemically.

- Interconnectedness was also illustrated in the *In the Mesh* and General Motors stories.

Theory Point 6: Adapting Through Feedback. The actions required to maintain each set of relationships cannot be predicted in advance, but must be guided by feedback.

- A consequence of *not* adapting through feedback was illustrated in *In the Mesh.*

- Adapting through feedback was illustrated in the General Motors story.

Adapting through feedback is something we experience every day of our lives. We live in a complex, changing, and only partly predictable world. Following a prescriptive plan when new information is available would be dangerously foolish. But it is possible to plan and anticipate and make contingency plans and alter them when new information is available. We manage effectively or at least muddle through reasonably well only by responding to and adapting through feedback.

Three principles can help us perform the inordinately complex task of managing all the variables necessary to improve or maintain the performance of a complex system. The first principle is obvious from Point 6.

Three System Principles

System Principle 1: Feedback. Feedback is information about performance that is used to guide performance.

Guide it to where? We hope toward worthy goals, but the principle operates even while guiding a system toward destruction. Furthermore, information about performance will guide performance only if it gets to the right person, at the right time, in the right form, and only if it is related to one or more specific goals. Data dumps are not feedback; neither are offering advice, criticism, or suggestions that are ignored. Attempting to punish or reward someone might be feedback if it guides performance, but it is not feedback if it does not guide performance.

Intelligent value-adding performance is possible only with adequate feedback; defective feedback yields defective performance, always.

System Principle 2: Value Set. There is a small set of interconnected variables that must remain within a narrow range of values if a living system is to survive or remain healthy.

The value set principle is exemplified in the health checks that occur each time a patient enters an emergency room or appears for treatment. Temperature, heart rate, blood pressure, and blood sugar levels must all be maintained within narrow ranges. There are a huge number of variables that affect value set variables, but if the value set variables are in range we can check out the linked variables in a more leisurely fashion.

The value set principle is also exemplified in the checking of financial statements that potential lenders and shareholders do before putting money into a company. Business managers and executives also monitor cash flow, profit margin, return on equity, and the like. Experts disagree on which variables constitute the best value set variables to monitor but agree that monitoring a few key variables is the way to go.

Value set variables must be maintained even as we adapt; if they are not, we die.

System Principle 3: Subsystem Maximization. It is impossible to maximize the functioning of a subsystem and the total system at the same time.

This principle is so vexing that it took me years to believe it, even though I knew that there are mathematical proofs of the principle. It took a long time and many examples to convince me that the principle works in the real world. The subsystem maximization principle is a root cause of all those so-called personality clashes that commonly occur between leaders or between departments, such as marketing and production, production and human resources, or accounting and everybody else. It is also a root cause of problems of governance and society that result from ideological and partisan efforts, but that is another story that is beyond the scope of this chapter. It might be that personalities are clashing, but the subsystem maximization principle suggests a fundamental reason why they clash: if each player is doing his or her best to do the job, there will be many clashes. Marketing has a different job than production, and neither, by itself, can add value to the total organization. There must be a product to market. Even if there is a product, if it is not purchased it adds no value to the producer or to a customer.

The subsystem maximization principle is one of the major, perhaps *the* major, sources of conflict in organizations. We each experience it on a daily basis in our own lives: we have several things that we simply must do; if we do any one of them as best we can, one or more or all of the others will not get done as well. When a child is ill, parenting maximizes for a time and interferes with performance at work or in maintaining other relationships. When there is a crisis at work, work demands maximize and interfere with all else that we should do. Much of the resistance we encounter when doing a change project is a manifestation of the subsystem maximization principle. We encounter resistance whenever what we do threatens a subsystem, that is, requires a change in routine operation.

For example, advertising a new product threatens the sales of existing products; however, if the new product is not advertised, sales projections will not be met, and, perhaps, the loan for new product development will be lost. Similarly, selling the product that generates the best commission for the salesperson will sometimes, if not always, interfere with selling the product that generates more revenue or a better profit margin for the organization or the product that establishes the organization's leadership in the marketplace.

The subsystem maximization principle means that doing the best work possible from the perspective of one part of an organization will make the organization as a whole do worse, guaranteed. Additional examples can be found every day by watching, reading, and listening to the daily news. It takes only a little practice to identify them and notice the enormous impact on our lives of well-intentioned attempts at maximization around one issue or one value.

LINKING THEORY, PRINCIPLE, AND PRACTICE

The six points of theory and the three system principles are not the only ones there are. I selected these nine because, taken together, they are comprehensive enough to be quite powerful. I also selected them because each principle and most or all of the points of theory connect to experiences each of us has every day; with practice, they can become intuitive.

Looking back, it is clear that these six points of theory and three principles were operating in every performance-improvement project I have been involved in during the past forty-plus years. In addition, the six points of theory and the three principles of systems seem to have been operating in nearly every one of the performance-improvement projects I have read about during that same forty years. At the beginning of the projects feedback has been defective, many people involved did not know the value set variables, the variables they knew about and tracked were not closely linked to value set variables, and they did not take into account the implications of the subsystem maximization principle. It was more common for people to attribute the effects of the subsystem maximization principle to personality conflicts or unspecified communications problems.

I do not see any way to collaborate effectively, consistently, and successfully with others in an organization without either an incredible amount of luck or without taking into account the six points of theory and the three systemic principles.

Dealing with Systemic Issues: Fundamental Questions

Acting as if we are attempting to achieve a result is an approach to selling as well as an approach to improving performance. Perhaps we should model by asking intelligent and systemic questions and allowing the intelligence, knowledge, and expertise of the client to persuade the client that systemic variables are worth attending to.

How to Take Systemic Issues into Account. I have included fundamental systemic questions in this section, in their generic form. They should not be used in that form. They can easily be modified to fit specific situations with a little practice (See Rummler, 2004, for examples). Tailoring the questions to the client language, beliefs, practices, and so on is quite important, so I will begin by showing the thinking behind the questions.

Regarding Theory Point 1, Definition, in any analysis, I want to know the purpose-in-common that holds the system together. If there is a mission statement or vision statement, I want to see it and find out if they are widely ignored words on paper or living documents. I want to know if the mission and vision are connected to value set measures, and if everyone is clear about the connections. I almost always find disconnects.

Regarding Theory Points 2, Value Added, and 3, Adding Value, I want to know who the customers and investors and suppliers are and how the organization adds value to them. I want to know if the people in the organization, suppliers of knowledge and the behavior that yields results, know how their performance adds value and to whom. I want to know if there are people who are unaware of how they add value and whether people generally believe that others in the organization really care about adding value.

Regarding Theory Point 4, Alignment, I want to know the plans and practices that are in place to know the status of, and improve, external relationships. I want to know the plans and practices that are in place and to know the status of internal relationships, such as the relationships between production or service delivery and support functions, or the relationships between leadership and management and between any person I meet and everyone else. I can find out a lot about all of this by asking a few questions and observing carefully on a tour of the organization.

Regarding Theory Point 5, Interconnectedness, I want to know the interconnections. How do people attempt to manage the interconnected value set variables? Do they see them as a set or do they pursue them as separated goals, perhaps assigned to different leaders or parts of the organization? An especially important set of connections is the set that relates specifically to Theory Point 2, Value Added. For example, if a company makes plastic penguins for amusement parks, the connections to the suppliers of plastic and suppliers of penguin molds and their designs are very important, as are the connections to plastic penguin distributors and to amusement parks and ultimately to the people who visit amusement parks. It is very important to understand the interconnections among the parts of the value chain that ensure that it is possible to make plastic penguins and supply them to the marketplace.

Regarding Theory Point 6, Adapting Through Feedback, I want to know how the executives know whether the organization is prospering, stagnating, or faltering. What value set numbers do they have and look at? I want to know how each person I encounter can tell whether or not they are doing a good job and whether or not they can tell if anyone cares about that.

It is clear how System Principle 1, Feedback, ties in: I go in guessing that many people get too little feedback, get the wrong feedback, or get the feedback at the wrong times. It is clear how System Principle 2, Value Set, ties in: I go in guessing that the feedback executives and everyone else gets is not well connected to value set variables. I know that is my bias going in so I look very diligently and explicitly for disconfirming evidence; I am very happy whenever I find it.

It might not be obvious how System Principle 3, Subsystem Maximization, fits in. Allow me to attempt to make it clear. I am always looking for conflict in the organization. First, I look for conflict between goals. In what ways do the goals conflict and how are the conflicts balanced? Goals conflict whenever those seeking to achieve them strive mightily for only one of the goals or supporting subgoals.

Second, I look for conflict between parts of the organization. In what ways do people believe they are misunderstood by almost everyone else in the organization or that others are just out for themselves?

Third, I look for conflict and cooperation between individuals. Who seems to get in their way when they try to do a good job? Who do they go to when they want to be sure something gets done? Do they understand that the variables required for success are interconnected, not manageable independently?

The six points of theory and the three system principles guide my observations and informal conversations. They guide what I talk about, ask about, and look for in an organization. They orient me as I learn about the people and the organization. They help in making the case for doing an analysis. They help in describing the tools I use in doing the analysis. I use specific tools for the analysis, then discuss the results, guiding conversations by the points of theory and system principles.

That said, here are some of the systemic questions I ask in doing an analysis. I ask the questions in casual conversations, and I ask them using specific HPT tools. I am very likely to use one or more of five tools, my Total Performance System Diagram (Brethower and Smalley, 1998; Brethower and Wittkopp, 1987; Lafleur and Brethower, 1998), Rummler's Supersystem Diagram (Rummler, 2004), Kaufman's Organization Elements Model (Kaufman, Oakley-Browne, Watkins, and Leigh, 2003), Gilbert's Performance Engineering Matrix (Gilbert, 1978), and Carleton and Lineberry's analyses of cultural issues (Carleton and Lineberry, 2004). I am also likely to use some form of cross-functional process maps (Rummler and Brache, 1995). I merely list the questions here with very little elaboration; explicating each would make this chapter far too long. However, the chapter in this book by Geary Rummler shows a practical and proven way to get them answered.

The Systemic Questions. This section discusses five systemic questions. Together, answers to the questions will help you to flesh out the most important attributes of a system. You will understand this list of questions and the importance of answering them more thoroughly after reading Rummler's chapter or Rummler (2004).

Systemic Question 1: What is the system performance?

System performance always involves use of scarce resources to generate products or services that, we hope, add value. Referring to the resources as "inputs" and the products or services as "outputs," we can ask about system performance as follows:

What are key inputs? The key inputs will be orders for goods or services, materials or supplies required to fulfill them, the money budgeted for the purpose, and the people assigned to the work.

What are the key outputs and how does each add value? The key outputs will be the goods or services provided to clients or customers.

Systemic Question 2: How does the system fit into the environment?

The inputs and outputs connect to the external environment. That is why they are so important, why we must know a lot about them if we are to understand the system and figure out how to improve its performance. The following set of questions helps us do that.

1. How does the system relate to closely linked systems?
2. How does the system add value to stakeholders?
3. How does the system relate to competitors?
4. How does the system relate to regulators?
5. What variables or indicators show how well the system is functioning to add net value?

Systemic Question 3: What are the parts of the system?

Systems have far too many parts to look at them one at a time. When I seek advice regarding an illness or about how to support health, I do not want the adviser to examine each cell in my body to determine if it is healthy, sick, well-nourished, or starving. I want advice organized around the major subsystems that compose my body and the value set variables connected to them. How is the cardiovascular subsystem working, and what should be done to make it work better? How about digestion and breathing and temperature regulation?

How do the primary processes function? A simple, useful, and reasonably accurate way to think of primary processes is that they are the processes that produce the goods and services offered for sale.

- How are inputs acquired and at what costs?
- How are outputs monitored?
- How are the processes monitored?

How do the support processes function? Support processes are those that support the primary processes. Human resources, quality assurance, accounting, maintenance, purchasing, data processing, and marketing are examples.

- How are inputs acquired and at what costs?
- How are outputs monitored?
- How are the support processes monitored?

Systemic Question 4: How are value set variables maintained?

This is a very important question but one that is often not asked and often not part of the formal analysis. I want to know the answer, always, so I talk with people about it. For example, I might ask questions about how good relations are with key suppliers of financial resources and about relationships with key customers. If the company has an investor relations department or a customer relations department, it might be worth asking how they maintain those relations. But where I get most of the information about value set variables is in asking the question, How do you know how well things are going?

Systemic Question 5: How do the governance processes function?

Governance processes are the policies and procedures and rules for governing what people do in an organization. Hiring, promotion, compensation, and budgeting are part of the governance infrastructure. They are a special category of support processes and are an extremely important aspect of governance in management. So a key question is, How do the management processes function?

Management processes are about establishing strategies and goals, allocating resources, providing feedback, providing tools and materials, and taking supporting and corrective action to support performance. Management processes are also about ensuring that primary processes achieve operational and strategic goals and that support processes support primary processes, and result only in constraints that are necessary to implement policies.

- *How are planning and resource allocation managed?* Once strategic and operational goals are in place at the organizational level, how do they cascade downward in the organization? How does information flow upward to show that goals are cascading downward or to show that changes in organizational goals are necessary, based on the constraints within which each part of the organization operates? How are money and people allocated to support goal attainment in each part of the organization? What are the data that are necessary to make the business case that resources should be allocated in specific ways?

- *How are corrective actions managed?* This is an extremely important area. Are corrective actions coercive or collaborative? What are the code words, such as does being "accountable" mean that you will lose your job if you do not make your numbers? Is it dangerous for a manager to identify problems and ask for help? Is it the manager's job to hold people accountable or to ensure that people have what they require in order to perform well?

- *How are sustaining actions managed?* This question is about success criteria and rewards, recognition, promotion, and the items that go into keeping up the good work for each part of the organization, each manager, and each worker.

THE HPT CERTIFICATION STANDARDS

Understanding systemic issues is essential before we recommend any course of action. Failure to do so is a failure to apply HPT as it is defined through the certification standards.

How Working Systemically Generates Documentation for the Standards

Suppose that we ask ourselves questions about the organization as a whole, about each part of the organization, about each initiative, and about each program. If we do that tenaciously, we will be off to a very good start in working systemically. By tenaciously, I mean asking questions such as, What are our goals? How do we add value and for whom? Who do we do harm to or who do we compete with? Where are we going if we do nothing? What must we stop doing if we are to meet future challenges? What must we do that we are not doing? How can we tell if we are getting better? How can we tell if we are doing worse? Additionally, we need follow up questions such as, Who agrees? Who disagrees? What evidence do we have? What evidence must we have to ensure that we know how things are going?

Obviously, if we ask questions tenaciously we will get answers and have a sense of how much we can trust the answers. But there is more to do to work systemically. We must model collaboration and systemic thinking and focusing on results and on adding value. How do we model systemic thinking? We do it by how we frame the questions and how we frame the answers.

Framing the Questions. We ask the questions in the client's language and about systemic issues. What are the company's outputs? How do the outputs add value and to whom? What are the closely linked systems such as the suppliers, the customers, the investors, the company's friends and enemies in the industry, the company's competitors, the people who refer clients, and so on?

We are asking the right questions if we are asking about matters that clarify for us the six points of theory, as they apply to the organization, and the three system principles.

We are asking the right questions if we are asking about inputs, outputs, feedback, primary processes, support processes, governance, and management practices. We know we are asking the right questions if we are asking about planning, resource allocation, corrective action, and sustaining excellent performance through feedback; incentives; and development of people, processes, and organizational support structures.

Framing the questions helps ensure that we get data relevant to systemic issues. But how can we be sure that we and our clients can cope with all that data to make informed decisions? We do it through two-way communications, active and reflective listening, appreciative inquiry, and every other way we know how based on what we know about human learning and about instructional design. And one thing we know about learning complex material is that we must find ways to make the apparently complex and disconnected appear straightforward and connected. We must construct pictures that convey at least a thousand words, and we must help people throughout the organization develop the same frame of reference so they can communicate efficiently and effectively. How do we do that? By the way we frame the answers.

Framing the Answers. Instructional designers have discovered time and again that a good graphic helps people understand complex concepts. We include two-by-two tables, Venn Diagrams, labeled circles, labeled boxes, and so on liberally in our instructional materials. We have developed the notion of reusable instructional objects to help us do so more efficiently.

The tools and templates that many of us use in doing analyses of systems are, in effect, reusable instructional objects. They are reusable templates for capturing reality. Our problem, in HPT, is not a lack of models or templates; it is having too many and having a tendency to develop more all the time.

The tools were invented, in the heat of the moment, in real projects to capture something that was systemically important so that clients would understand. I got better at doing so after explicit instruction from Rodger Stotz (personal communication, n.d.). Rodger said to me once at an ISPI conference, "Dale, here is how to do it. I collect the information from people, then organize it on the template. The first time they see the template, it contains their information. We talk about the insights they get from having their information there in an organized way. We talk about their issues." As soon as Rodger told me that, it was clear. When the information is introduced that way, the clients do not merely see the features of the template; they experience the benefits of using it!

A system, by definition, is the elements and relationships among them. Using the right template captures some of the elements and some of the key relationships and captures them in a way that enables people to discuss them intelligently. For example, one of the major reasons for inventing the total performance system diagram was to call attention to the fact that a specific company or work unit exists in a specific context. The diagram captures some of the context and raises the questions, What feedback do you get that tells you how satisfied your customers are? What feedback do you get that tells you how well you are meeting your production or service goals?

The answers are framed to link to results, systemic issues, and added value. The answers are developed collaboratively with the client. The documentation of that work provides documentation that is useful in keeping track of progress and in demonstrating that the HPT and certified performance technologist standards are being used in the project.

How Working Systemically Is Fundamental to HPT

Let me call your attention again to the wording of HPT standard number 3: Add value in how you do the work and through the work itself.

Adding value in how you do the work is modeling. Modeling is arguably the most powerful instructional technique in the HPT instructional toolkit. If we model systemic thinking, collaboration, focusing on results, or adding value, we are instructing. Think of it this way: every HPT project we do is an ongoing lesson in system thinking. Or, it is not.

How Failure to Work Systemically Produces Suboptimal Results

Sartre's fictional account, *In the Mesh,* showed clearly how failure to work systemically produces suboptimal results; in that example, not only for Jean Aguerra but also for the revolutionaries whose dreams were not fulfilled and for the nation. The story about teaching the girl to read without making sure she would have an opportunity to read, and about teaching people how to make repairs without ensuring that the people trained would be people who could use the skills, illustrate suboptimal results through failure to work systemically. The long rise and the slow decline in the fortunes of General Motors illustrate the difference between working systemically and not working systemically. Every failure of instructional impact illustrates how failure to work systemically produces suboptimal results. The management books about successes now that turn into failures later illustrate how failure to work systemically produces suboptimal results.

We discover additional examples of the effects of failure to work systemically almost every time we do a system analysis, an analysis to find the causes of and cures for performance problems *in that system.* If we find a knowledge deficit and correct it, we have done one part of our job. We must also help ensure that the other necessary performance supports are in place. If we find a defective process and correct it we have done one part of our job.

We must find the causes of that defective process; was it always defective? If not, what change in the organization, what deficiency in management, what other events brought about the defective process? How can we make sure that the new process has the management and budgetary support to continue to be effective?

How does failure to work systemically lead to suboptimal results? The answer is simple: it makes it very likely that we will miss one or more of the many interconnected variables that are necessary to support optimal results.

CONCLUSION

In each situation I have been in during my entire professional career, the choice has always been between working incompetently and working systemically.

I have, reluctantly, come to believe we have to make that choice in HPT. Working systemically gets us out of our box and rocks the boat; not working systemically keeps us locked in our box, helping to sink the boat or at least allow it to drift or take on water.

References

Brethower, D. M., and Smalley, K. (1998). *Performance-based instruction: Linking training to business results* (Chap. 9). San Francisco: Jossey-Bass.

Brethower, D. M., and Wittkopp, C. J. (1987). Performance engineering: SPC and the total performance system. *Journal of Organizational Behavior Management, 9*(1), 83–103.

Carleton, J. R., and Lineberry, C. S. (2004). *Achieving post-merger success: A stakeholder's guide to cultural due diligence, assessment, and integration.* San Francisco: Jossey-Bass/Pfeiffer.

Drucker, P. (1946). *The concept of the corporation.* New York: New American Library.

Gilbert, T. F. (1978). Human competence: Engineering worthy performance. New York: McGraw-Hill.

International Society for Performance Improvement. (2004). *Performance improvement standards.* Retrieved from www.certifiedpt.org/index.cfm?section = standards.

Kaufman, R., Oakley-Browne, H., Watkins, R., and Leigh, D. (2003). *Strategic planning for success: Aligning people, performance, and payoffs* (Chap. 4). San Francisco: Jossey-Bass/Pfeiffer.

LaFleur, D., and Brethower, D. (1998). *The transformation: Business strategies for the 21st century.* Grand Rapids, MI: Impact Groupworks.

Rummler, G. A. (2004). *Serious performance consulting: According to Rummler* (Chap. 2). Silver Spring, MD: International Society for Performance Improvement.

Rummler, G. A., and Brache, A. P. (1995). *Improving performance: How to manage the white space on the organization chart* (2nd ed.). San Francisco: Jossey-Bass.

Sartre, J. P. (1954). *In the mesh.* London, U.K.: Andrew Dakers.

Sloan, A. P., Jr. (1963). *My years with General Motors.* New York: Macfadden-Bartell.

Wright, J. P. (1979). *On a clear day you can see general motors.* Grosse Pointe, MI: Wright Enterprises.

CHAPTER SIX

Mega Planning and Thinking

Defining and Achieving Measurable Success

Roger Kaufman

Defining and then achieving sustained organizational success is possible. Doing so simply extends many of the concepts and tools that are applicable to human performance improvement. Defining and achieving organizational success by aligning what every organization uses, does, produces, and delivers with external value added is rational, practical, and vital. Doing so relies on three basic essentials, some of which are not yet in the conventional wisdom or conventional practice of human performance technology (HPT). But they should be and will be. These three essentials are

1. *A societal value-added frame of mind:* All people and all organizations are means to societal ends, and this approach to defining sustained success formalizes this commitment.

2. *A shared determination and agreement on where to head and why:* All people who can and might be affected by performance objectives must agree on purposes and the results criteria.

3. *Use and consistent application of pragmatic and basic tools:* Tools that are applicable to carrying out essentials 1 and 2 should be utilized.

WHAT IS THE SOCIETAL VALUE-ADDED PERSPECTIVE AND FRAME OF MIND?

The required frame of mind for defining and delivering success, the basic guiding paradigm for organizations, is simple, straightforward, and sensible. It involves seeing one's organization as the vehicle for adding measurable value for external clients and society. Within this shared societal value-added frame, everything one uses, does, produces, and delivers is linked to achieve shared and agreed upon positive societal results.[1] I call this societal frame of reference the "Mega" level of planning. Why is this vital? If you are not adding value to our shared society, what assurance do you have that you are not subtracting value? Beginning the planning process with Mega-level planning, in which the primary client and beneficiary of everything that is used, done, produced, and delivered by an organization is societal value, is the central focus in "strategic thinking." A central question that each and every organization should ask and answer is, *If your organization is the solution, what is the societal problem that you are addressing?*

This fundamental proposition is central to strategic thinking and planning, that is, Mega planning. It represents a shift from the usual focus only on one's self, individual performance improvement, or one's organization, to making certain that one also adds value to external clients and society. This basic question, directly or indirectly, should reappear throughout your thinking and work, for it keeps ends and means in perspective. Mega planning better ensures that you will be successful by making a useful contribution outside of the organization where you and your clients live and work.

It is this shared definition and commitment to where the organization should head, why it should go there, and how to tell when it is successful that is essential to this approach. Agreement on purpose is vital, and was identified as essential to successful organizational behavior by Peter Drucker (1993).

AN OVERVIEW OF THE BASIC CONCEPTS AND TOOLS FOR MEGA PLANNING

There are three basic tools, guides, or templates that will be helpful as you define and seek to achieve organizational success. Each is described in much greater detail in several books or articles I have authored or coauthored, several of which are listed in a special section at the end of this chapter. For our entry into Mega planning and strategic thinking, short descriptions of these three guides follow.

Guide One: Defining and Aligning Everything an Organization Uses, Does, Produces, and Delivers, and the Resulting Measurable Value Added

The Organizational Elements Model (OEM) defines, links, and aligns what any organization uses, does, produces, and delivers with external client and societal value added, that is, the Mega level. For each organizational element, there is an associated level of planning. Given that each and every organization has external clients to whom it must add measurable value, successful planning links, aligns, and relates all of the organizational elements.

Table 6.1 names and explains the organizational elements and the level of planning to which each element relates. It also provides examples for each. These elements are also useful for defining the basic questions every organization must ask and answer, as provided in Figure 6.1.

Table 6.1. The Five Levels of Results and Levels of Planning.

Name of the Organizational Element	Name of the Level of Planning and Focus	Brief Description	Example
Outcomes	Mega	Results and their consequences for external clients and society (shared vision)	Zero losses of life or permanent disabilities
Outputs	Macro	The results an organization can or does deliver outside of itself	Market share increased to at least 33 percent
Products	Micro	The building-block results that are produced within the organization	Each associate having and using the competencies required to meet performance requirements
Processes	Process	The ways, means, activities, procedures, and methods used internally	Training, applying Six Sigma
Inputs	Input	The human, physical, and financial resources an organization has available or uses	Budget, buildings, equipment, staff

QUESTIONS	Self-Assessment		Organizational Partners	
	NO	YES	NO	YES
1. Do you commit to deliver organizational results that add value to all external clients and society? (Mega/Outcomes)				
2. Do you commit to deliver organizational results that have the measurable quality and acceptance required by your external clients? (Macro/Outputs)				
3. Do you commit to produce internal results that have the measurable quality required by your internal partners? (Micro/Products)				
4. Do you commit to having efficient internal processes?				
5. Do you commit to acquire quality human capital, information capital, and physical resources? (inputs)				
6. Do you commit to evaluate and determine the following: A. How well you deliver products, activities, methods, and procedures that have positive value and worth? (process performance) B. Whether the results defined by your objectives in measurable terms are achieved? (evaluation and continuous improvement)				

Figure 6.1. Basic Questions Every Organization Must Ask and Answer.

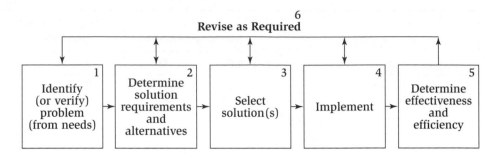

Figure 6.2. The Six-Step Problem-Solving Process.

Guide Two: Defining, Justifying, and Resolving Problems

Figure 6.2 depicts a six-step problem-solving model that includes step 1, identifying problems based on needs; step 2, determining detailed solution requirements and identifying, but not yet selecting, solution alternatives; step 3, selecting solutions from among alternatives; step 4, implementation; step 5, evaluation; and step 6, continuous improvement that involves revisions as required at each of the prior five steps. This is a process for identifying and resolving problems as well as identifying and actualizing opportunities.

Each time you want to identify problems and opportunities and systematically get from current to desired results and consequences, follow the six-step process. This process shows the functions, or building-block steps, and the order in which they are usually carried out. Following the process will get you from identified needs to ascertaining requirements for closing the gaps in results and will help you to identify possible ways and means to close the gaps.

Guide Three: Six Critical Success Factors
of Strategic Thinking and Planning

Displayed in Figure 6.3 is an essential framework for this approach and for Mega planning and thinking regardless of the type of organization.[2] Unlike conventional "critical success factors," these are factors critical to successful planning and that go beyond those things an organization must get done to meet its mission.

These six critical success factors (CSFs) for Mega planning are not targeted for any one organizational business but only for the planning process and concerns as detailed in Figure 6.3. The six CSFs provide ongoing guidance for anything you and your organization decide to use, do, produce, and deliver in order to ensure the provision of external value added. You use the CSFs to make sure that you are maintaining integrity of both *Mega* planning and *Mega* thinking.

To be successful, that is, to do and to apply Mega planning, you have to realize that yesterday's methods and results often are not appropriate for tomorrow.

CRITICAL SUCCESS FACTOR 1

Move out of your comfort zone and today's paradigms, and use new and wider boundaries for thinking, planning, doing, evaluating, and continuous improvement.

CRITICAL SUCCESS FACTOR 2

Differentiate between ends (what) and means (how).

CRITICAL SUCCESS FACTOR 3

Use, link, and align all three levels of planning and results:
- Mega/Outcomes
- Macro/Outputs
- Micro/Products

CRITICAL SUCCESS FACTOR 4

Prepare all objectives, including the ideal vision and mission, to contain precise indicators of both where you are headed and the criteria for measuring when you have arrived.

CRITICAL SUCCESS FACTOR 5

Define "need" as a gap between current and desired results, not as insufficient levels of resources, means, or methods.

CRITICAL SUCCESS FACTOR 6

Use an ideal vision as the underlying basis for all planning and continuous improvement, stating what kind of world, in measurable performance terms, you want for tomorrow's children.

Figure 6.3. The Six Critical Success Factors for Mega-Level Strategic Planning and Strategic Thinking.

Most planning experts agree that the past is only a prologue to today and tomorrow, and tomorrow must be crafted through new patterns of perspectives, tools, and results.[3] The tools and concepts for meeting the new realities of society, organizations, and people are linked to each of the six CSFs.

Additional details and the "how-tos" for each of the three guides are provided in the referenced sources at the end of the chapter. The three basic guides or templates should be considered as forming an integrated set of tools, much like a piece of fabric, rather than each guideline being used on its own. Each resource is valuable in obtaining and understanding the critical success factors. Together the resources paint a full picture.

Mega Planning: Getting Agreement

When doing Mega planning, you and your associates will ask and answer the questions shown in Figure 6.1. Interestingly, commitments to the questions in Figure 6.1 are important but not always automatic. Formalizing an agreement clears the strategic planning and thinking "air" and ensures agreement on direction. If there is nonagreement, which is sometimes the case, this requires that the differences must first be resolved. Then conversations about the costs of delivering on the answers to all of the questions compared with the costs of not delivering on all of them must be moved to resolution.

An answer of "yes" to all of the questions will lead you toward Mega planning and allow you to prove that you have added value, a proof that is becoming increasingly required for both public- and private-sector organizations. These questions relate to Guide One. They define each organizational element in terms of its label and the question each addresses.

Mega Planning Is Proactive

Many approaches to organizational improvement involve waiting for problems to happen and then scrambling to respond. Of course, like true love, the course of organizational success hardly ever runs smoothly. But there is a temptation to react to problems and to never take the time to plan so that surprises are fewer and successes are defined and systematically achieved before problems spring up. Figure 6.4 provides a job aid to consider any time you begin organizational planning.

THE SIX CRITICAL SUCCESS FACTORS IN BRIEF

As indicated earlier, Guide Three entails six critical success factors for strategic thinking and planning.

CSF 1: Use New and Wider Boundaries for Thinking, Planning, Doing, Evaluating, and Continuous Improvement

Move out of today's comfort zones. Look around our world. There is evidence just about everywhere we look that tomorrow is not a linear projection or straight-line function of yesterday and today. Thinking otherwise is what led, in part, some U.S. car manufacturers to squander their dominant client base by shoving unacceptable vehicles into the marketplace and some U.S. airlines to focus on shareholder value and ignore customer value. An increasing number of credible authors have told us and continue to tell us that the past is a

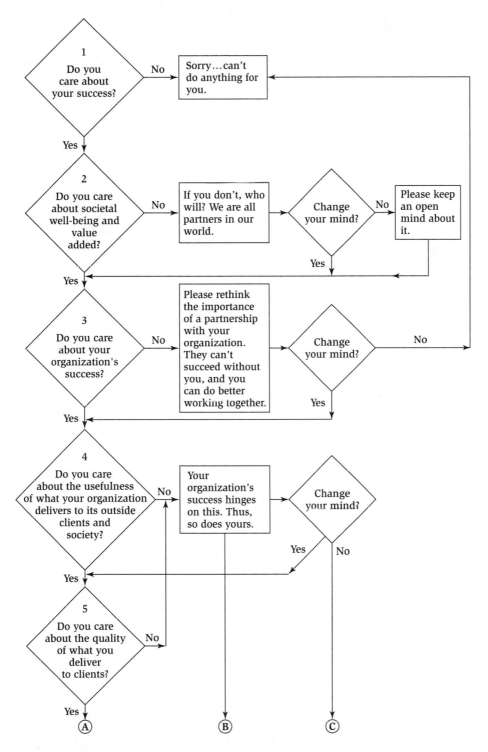

Figure 6.4. A Job Aid for Choosing What to Accomplish Before Attempting to Make Things Better.

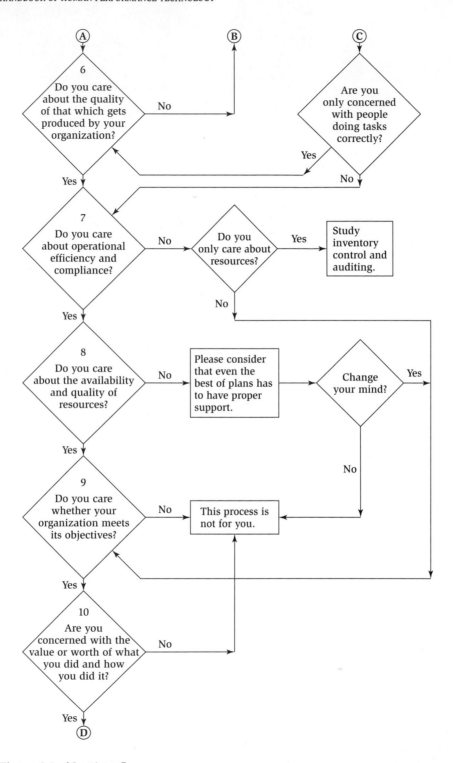

Figure 6.4. (*Continued*)

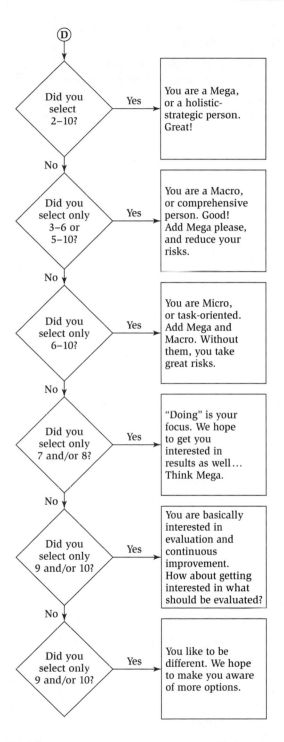

Figure 6.4. (*Continued*)

prologue and not a predictor of what the future will be like. In fact, old paradigms can be so deceptive that Tom Peters (1987) suggests that "organizational forgetting" must become conventional culture.

Times have changed, and anyone who does not also change is risking failure. It is vital to use new and wider boundaries for thinking, planning, doing, and delivering. Doing so will require getting out of current comfort zones. Not doing so will likely deliver failure.[4]

CSF 2: Differentiate Between Ends and Means by Focusing on "What" Before "How"

People tend to be action-oriented. We want to get going. In this dash to doing, we often jump right into *solutions* or *means* before we know the *results* or *ends* we must deliver. The importance of writing and using measurable performance objectives is something upon which most performance-improvement specialists agree. Objectives correctly focus on ends and not methods, means, or resources.[5] Ends, or the "what," sensibly should be identified and defined before we select the "how" of getting from where we are to our destination. If we do not base our solutions, methods, resources, and interventions on the basis of the results we are to achieve, what do we have in mind when we make the selections of means, resources, or activities?

Focusing on means, processes, and activities is usually more comfortable as a starting place for conventional performance-improvement initiatives. Doing so, though, can be seductive and dangerous. For example, imagine that you are in an unknown area and then are provided with a new automobile, keys in the ignition and fully fueled . . . but there are no maps for navigation and no guides for your journey as you start out. Similar is the situation if, for a performance-improvement initiative, you are provided process tools and techniques without a clear map that includes a definite identified destination along with a statement of why you want to get to the destination in the first place. Also, a risk for starting a performance-improvement journey with means and processes alone is the idea that there is no way of knowing whether your trip is taking you toward a useful destination. Furthermore, there are no criteria for telling you if you are making progress.[6]

It is vital that successful planning focuses first on results; that is, useful performance in measurable terms. By establishing purposes, measuring progress, and providing for continuous improvement toward the important results, the performance technologist can determine what to keep, what to fix, and what to abandon.

It is vital to focus on useful ends before deciding "how" to get things done. It also sets the stage for CSF 3, "use, link, and align all three levels of results" through application of the Organizational Elements Model (OEM) and for CSF 4, "prepare objectives to include indicators of how you will know when you have arrived." The OEM relies on a results focus because it defines what every

Table 6.2. The Levels of Planning and Results That Should Be Targeted and Linked.

Primary Client and Beneficiary	Name for the Level of Planning	Name for the Level of Result	Type of Planning
Society and external clients	Mega	Outcomes	Strategic
The organization itself	Macro	Outputs	Tactical
Individuals and small groups	Micro	Products	Operational

organization uses, does, produces, and delivers, and the consequences of those activities for external clients and society.

CSF 3: Use, Link, and Align All Three Levels of Planning and Results

As was noted in CSF 2, it is vital to prepare objectives that focus only on ends . . . never just on means or resources. There are three levels of results shown in Table 6.2 that are important to target and link.

There are three levels of planning and results, based on who is to be the primary client and beneficiary of what gets planned, designed, and delivered. For each level of planning there are three associated levels of results: Outcomes, Outputs, and Products.[7]

Using the three levels of planning, Mega, Macro, and Micro, and the three levels of results, Outcomes, Outputs, and Products, ensures that there is strategic, tactical, and operational alignment among what you and your organization use, do, produce, and deliver, and the value added for external clients. Strategic planning and thinking starts at the Mega level, tactical planning starts at the Macro level, and operational planning is at the Micro level.

CSF 4: Prepare Objectives, Including Those for the Ideal Vision and Mission, to Contain Precise Indicators of Where You Are Headed and How You Will Know When You Have Arrived

It is vital to state the *mission statement* plus *success criteria* precisely and rigorously, so that they clearly state where you are headed and tell how to know when you have arrived.[8] Statements of objectives must be in performance terms, so that one can plan how best to get there and how to measure progress toward the end.

Objectives, at all levels of planning, activity, and results, are absolutely vital. Everything is measurable, so do not kid yourself into thinking you can dismiss important results as being "intangible" or "nonmeasurable." It is only sensible and rational to make a commitment to measurable purposes and destinations. Increasingly, organizations throughout the world are focusing on Mega-level results.[9]

CSF 5: Define "Need" as a Gap Between Current and Desired Results and Not as Insufficient Levels of Resources, Means, or Methods

Conventional English language usage would have us employ the common word *need* as a verb or in a verb sense . . . to identify means, methods, activities, actions, and resources we desire or intend to use (Kaufman, Watkins, Triner, and Stith, 1998). Terms such as *need to, need for, needing,* and *needed* are common, conventional, and destructive to useful planning. Is this semantic quibbling? The answer is, absolutely not.

As difficult as it is to change our own behavior, and most of us who want others to change seem to resist change ourselves, it is central to useful planning to distinguish between "ends" and "means." We have already noted this in CSF 2. To do reasonable and justifiable planning we have to first focus on ends and not means, and second, use the term *need"* as a noun. *Need* as used in conjunction with useful and successful planning is only used as a noun that describes a gap between current and desired results.

If we use *need* as a noun, not only will we be able to justify useful objectives, but we will also be able to justify what we do and deliver on the basis of costs and consequences analysis. We will be able to justify everything we use, do, produce, and deliver. By using need as a gap in results we get a triple bonus:

1. The "what should be" criteria become the objectives to be obtained.
2. Evaluation criteria are thus "built in" because one only has to track the progress made from "what is" to "what should be."
3. By using this approach, one may price both the cost to meet the need (that is, to close the gaps in results) and also the cost to ignore the need. Doing this shifts responsibility for nonfunding to the person denying the funding.

This is the only sensible way we can demonstrate value added.

CSF 6: Use an Ideal Vision as the Underlying Basis for All Planning and Continuous Improvement

This is another area that requires some change from the conventional ways of doing planning. Again, we have to resist conventional wisdom.

An "ideal vision" is never prepared for an organization, but rather identifies the kind of world we want to help create for tomorrow's children. From this societal-linked ideal vision, each organization can identify what part or parts of the vision it commits to deliver and move ever closer toward achieving. If we base all planning and doing on an ideal vision of the type of society we want for future generations, we can achieve "strategic alignment" for what we use, do, produce, and deliver, as well as the external payoffs for our Outputs.

To do this we have to change some paradigms, change some old habits, and forget how things used to be done. We must abandon our current comfort zones.

CONCLUSION

To sum up, *Mega* thinking and planning is about defining a shared success, achieving it, and being able to prove it. It is not a focus on one's organization alone, but a focus on society now and in the future. It is about adding value to all stakeholders. It is responsible, responsive, and ethical to add value for all.

Notes

1. Many planning experts now agree with this perspective. I first proposed using a societal frame of reference as the primary focus for individuals and organizations in 1968 and 1969. This brought alarm and suspicion on the part of many "old paradigm thinkers." Some people are still concerned (Schneider, 2003; Winiecki, 2004). Such concerns seem not to be easily supported, as brilliantly pointed out by Brethower (2005). Thus, I have recently been joined in this call for such new paradigms by many future-oriented thinkers, including, but not limited to, those cited in the chapter and included in the references. These shifts in thinking to new paradigms or frames of reference that are radically different from the conventional wisdom are sprouting, as Joel Barker (2001) suggested they would when seen by the "paradigm pioneers" of our world.

2. Please realize that unlike many other presentations of critical success factors, these relate to and can be generalized to any organization, public or private. Most "critical success factors" discussed in the management literature refer to organization-specific factors related to a unique business. In contrast, these apply to any organization and are "above" any organization-specific factors.

3. Please note the differences between Mega results—actual societal value added— and Macro results, client satisfaction and payoffs for the organization such as market share or quarterly profits.

4. Interestingly, Peters (1987) states that it is easier to kill an organization than it is to change it.

5. Robert Mager (1997) set the original standard for measurable objectives. Later, Tom Gilbert (1978) made the important distinction between behavior and performance, that is, between actions and consequences. Recently, some "constructivists" have had objections to writing and using objectives because they claim

that objectives can cut down on creativity and impose the planner's values on the clients. This view, I believe, is not useful. For a detailed discussion on the topic of constructivism, please see the analysis by philosophy professor David Gruender (1996).

6. Jan Kaufman, my partner, provided this insight.

7. It is interesting and curious that in the popular literature, *all* results tend to be called "outcomes." This failure to distinguish among three levels of results blurs the importance of identifying and linking all three levels in planning, doing, and evaluating as well as in continuous improvement.

8. An important contribution of strategic planning at the Mega level is that objectives can be linked to justifiable purpose. Not only should one have objectives that state "where you are headed and how you will know when you have arrived," the objectives should also be justified on the basis of "why you want to get to where you are headed." While it is true that objectives only deal with measurable destinations, useful strategic planning adds the reasons why objectives should be attained.

9. For a more extensive explanation of these phenomena, see Kaufman, Watkins, Triner, and Stith (1998).

References

Barker, J. A. (2001). *The new business of paradigms* [Videocassette]. (Classic Ed.). St. Paul, MN: Star Thrower Distribution.

Brethower, D. M. (2005, February). Yes we can: A rejoinder to Don Winiecki's rejoinder about saving the world with HPT. *Performance Improvement, 44*(2), 19–24.

Drucker, P. F. (1993). *Management: Tasks, responsibilities, practices.* New York: Harper & Row.

Gilbert, T. F. (1978). *Human competence: Engineering worthy performance.* New York: McGraw-Hill.

Gruender, C. D. (1996, May–June). Constructivism and learning: A philosophical appraisal. *Educational Technology, 36*(3), 21–29.

Kaufman, R., Watkins, R., Triner, D., and Stith, M. (1998). The changing corporate mind: Organizations, visions, mission, purposes, and indicators on the move toward societal payoffs. *Performance Improvement Quarterly, 11*(3), 32–44.

Mager, R. F. (1997). *Preparing instructional objectives: A critical tool in the development of effective instruction* (3rd ed.). Atlanta: Center for Effective Performance. (First edition published 1969 as *Preparing Objectives for Programmed Instruction.*)

Peters, T. (1987). *Thriving on chaos: Handbook for a management revolution.* New York: Alfred A. Knopf.

Schneider, E. W. (2003, April). Applying human performance technology while staying out of trouble. *Performance Improvement, 42*(4), 16–22.

Winiecki, D. J. (2004, September). Rejoinder to "saving the world with HPT":
A critical, scientific and consultative reflection. *Performance Improvement, 43*(8),
30–34.

Additional Resources

Following are a number of references authored by Roger Kaufman or written by him with colleagues that provide details and in-depth rationale for mega planning and mega thinking.

Andrews, J., Farrington, J., Packer, T., and Kaufman, R. (2004, February). Saving the
world with HPT: Expanding beyond the workplace and beyond the business case.
Performance Improvement, 43(2), 44–47.

Kaufman, R. (1998). *Strategic thinking: A guide to identifying and solving
problems* (Rev. ed.). Arlington, VA, and Washington, DC: American Society for
Training and Development and the International Society for Performance Improvement. (Also published in Spanish: *El pensamiento estrategico: Una guia para
identificar y resolver los problemas.* Madrid: Editorial Centros de Estudios Ramon
Areces.)

Kaufman, R. (2000). *Mega planning: Practical tools for organizational success.*
Thousand Oaks, CA: Sage.

Kaufman, R. (2002, May–June). What trainers and performance improvement
specialists can learn from tragedy: Lessons from September 11, 2001. *Educational
Technology, 42*(3), 63.

Kaufman, R. (2003, February). Value, value, where is the value? *Performance
Improvement, 43*(2), 36–38.

Kaufman, R. (2004). Creating your own future: You are only thirty seconds away. In
A. Shostak (Ed.), *America moving ahead* (Vol. 2). Tackling tomorrow today series.
Langhorne, PA: Chelsea House Publishers.

Kaufman, R. (2004, October). Mega as the basis for useful planning and thinking.
Performance Improvement, 43(9), 35–39.

Kaufman, R. (2004, January). *Performance improvement: On vital signs and active
ingredients.* Retrieved October 4, 2005, from the American Society for Training and
Development's ASTD Links Website: http://www.astd.org/astd/Publications/
ASTD_Links/January2004/InPractice-HPI-Kaufman.htm.

Kaufman, R. (2004). War, peace, and connecting the dots: Observations about wars,
missed opportunities, and what we can do about it matters. In A. Shostak (Ed.),
*Making war/making peace: defeating terrorism/developing dreams: Beyond 9/11 and
the Iraq war* (Vol. 3). Langhorne, PA: Chelsea House Publishers.

Kaufman, R. (2005). *Seven deadly sins of strategic planning: How to get it right.*
Retrieved October 4, 2005, from http://www.ispigoldcoast.org/Seven%20Deadly%
20Sins%20of%20Strategic%20Planning-Ft%20%20Lauderdale%202005.pdf.

Kaufman, R., and Forbes, R. (2002). Does your organization contribute to society? In M. Silberman (Ed.), *The team and organization development sourcebook* (pp. 213–224). New York: McGraw-Hill.

Kaufman, R., Oakley-Browne, H., Watkins, R., and Leigh, D. (2003). *Practical strategic planning: Aligning people, performance, and payoffs.* San Francisco: Jossey-Bass/Pfeiffer.

Kaufman, R., Thiagarajan, S., and MacGillis, P. (Eds.). (1997). *The guidebook for performance improvement.* San Francisco: Jossey-Bass/Pfeiffer.

Kaufman, R., and Unger, Z. (2003, August). Evaluation plus: Beyond conventional evaluation. *Performance Improvement, 42*(7), 5–8.

Kaufman, R., Watkins, R., and Leigh, D. (2001). *Useful educational results: Defining, prioritizing, accomplishing.* Lancaster, PA: Proactive Press.

CHAPTER SEVEN

The Origins and Evolution of Human Performance Technology

Camille Ferond

The quest to achieve organizational success goes back to the beginning of civilization. Throughout history, leaders have had to adapt their attempts to safeguard organizational survival to the socioeconomic and political forces of their time (Dean, 1997b). The natural process by which organizations die often threatens the well-being and livelihoods of employees and at times of entire geographical areas, the local economies of which have come to depend on an organization. Early responses to such evolutionary processes have ranged from intuitive reactions to immediate circumstances, to the pursuit of numerous economic and psychological theories of human behavior (Gould, 1983). These efforts stimulated important insights into human nature and organizations, though they often lacked scientific support and were difficult to implement, leading to two successive paradigm shifts[1] in the field (Hayes, 2001; Frederiksen, 1982b; Mawhinney, 1992; O'Brien and Dickinson, 1982; Warren, 1982).

Furthermore, while change is a constant, the general agreement is that growth of technology and globalization have increased their rate, bringing about a new level of complexity to contend with. Today, engendering purposeful organizational change that is both timely and valuable to its stakeholders is an exceptionally difficult challenge. Also, many organizations seem to lie at opposite poles on a continuum between inertia that is a sure threat to survival and unsuccessful organization redesign initiatives that only result in, as Tosti (2004) calls them, a "temporary disruption of the system" (p. 5) (Carleton

155

and Lineberry, 2004; Dean, 1997b; Kaufman, Oakley-Browne, Watkins, and Leigh, 2003; Tosti, 2004).

A glance at the historical evolution of organizations illustrates the danger of inertia, such as the rise and fall of the United States steel industry and the ongoing struggle with the price of steel. Similarly, the number of United States automotive companies, which fell from thirty-three in the first decade of the twentieth century to three at present, dropped in part because of the ongoing challenges they faced from foreign competition. Ethical scandals at Enron, Global Crossing, Adelphia, HIH, ImClone, WorldCom, Tyco International, Parmalat, and Andersen, and even allegations about wrongdoing in the United Nation's Oil-for-Food program, illustrate the widespread and disastrous legacy stakeholders now have to bear (Hatcher, 2000; 2003a; 2003b; Kaufman, Oakley-Browne, Watkins, and Leigh, 2003; Lee, 2003; Mawhinney, 1992, 2001; Sidman, 1989). Also, the growing number of mergers and acquisitions, in spite of their high failure rate, shows that it takes more than large investments in resources and technology or inspirational leaders and theories to generate a culture that is apt to survive in today's environment (Carleton and Lineberry, 2004; Dean, 1997b; Frederiksen, 1982b; O'Brien and Dickinson, 1982; Tosti, 2004).

Human performance technology (HPT) challenges traditional inspirational theories and the subsequent mechanistic emphasis on causality with its linear structure (Hayes, 2001) with a robust scientific logic underpinning a conceptual foundation that offers scalable and prescriptive techniques rather than generic best practices (Tosti, 2004). Moreover, its procedures generate measurable performance-improvement interventions and maximize their effectiveness by aligning them with the dynamics of the human performance system. In this way, HPT gives leaders a clear competitive advantage by providing them with the means to make informed strategic decisions about what constitutes valuable change in any area of organizational functioning and for a broad set of stakeholders. Thanks to its consolidated multidisciplinary theoretical foundation and track record of successful applications on a growing scale, HPT is in a position to address performance management complexity (Kaufman, Oakley-Browne, Watkins, and Leigh, 2003; Rummler, 2004; Tosti, 2004).

The *organizational ecology* vantage point of this chapter borrows from theories of biology, cultural anthropology, and behavior analysis and will show that the field of HPT draws its strengths from the way it has evolved into a multidisciplinary field (Mawhinney, 1992, 2001). Moreover, thanks to its systemic vantage point, HPT is particularly suited to address the metacontingencies or "the relation between cultural practices and outcomes of those practices" (Glenn, 1991; p. 62 in Mawhinney, 1992) that affect the survival of organizations, which, in turn, allows the field to operate as a learning organization would (Dean, 1997b). Together, these features predispose HPT to address its own ongoing evolution and adaptation to changing times as a scientific field (Dean, 1997b). In fact, HPT cannot claim any single individual as its "parent," but is the fruit of the systematic and independent efforts of many pioneers who have developed and continue to develop techniques, assessment tools, and models of human performance across different disciplines. The pioneers of HPT, or rather the *pathfinders,* as others have called them, have been academicians, practitioners, or both who have used readily observable performance or behavior and accomplishments as their research and development base (Dean, 1997b). While pathfinders were guided by a unified behavioral theory and a shared view, data have been the driving force behind the conceptual foundation of the field (Dean, 1997b; Frederiksen, 1982b; O'Brien and Dickinson, 1982). In this way, HPT has been grounded in reality, which, in turn, has worked to shape further refinements of the technology throughout its evolution, using a rigorous underlying science. Throughout, ongoing interactions across disciplines have served as the human performance technologists' best defense against forming a small, self-referential group, enabling ongoing cross-fertilization and integration.

As a result, it is not surprising that after forty-three years of successive iterations of the scientific process, HPT made the paradigm shift to system theory and naturally evolved into a completely new multidisciplinary approach that is optimally adapted to addressing current organizational issues (Hayes, 2001). That is, an approach that goes beyond *best solutions* by putting in the service of organizations expertise capable of specifying the underlying performance logic for HPT interventions in specialization areas. Moreover, HPT's self-correcting features are more likely to guarantee the ongoing adaptations of the field to novel conditions, as learning systems are built to do (Frederiksen, 1982b; Tosti in Addison, 2003).

HISTORICAL ORIGINS AND EVOLUTION OF HPT

HPT is an outgrowth of the pragmatic philosophy that took hold in the 1950s. Nonetheless, earlier events that shaped the evolution of performance management are traced here to provide a perspective on the context in which past efforts occurred; their flaws; their significant contributions to successive thinking; and, where appropriate, how the HPT logic distinguishes itself from commonsense approaches. The next section will then take stock of where the field is by reviewing a variety of models of HPT. Finally, the review of HPT models will then serve as a springboard for a discussion of the future directions the field may take (Frederiksen, 1982b; O'Brien and Dickinson, 1982).

Changing Views of Performance Management from Antiquity to the 1950s' Intuitive Culture-Based Management

Some of the earliest historical records suggest that from the time of the Babylonians through the Middle Ages, work was taught by means of individual apprenticeships, after which it was controlled by simple forms of management by incentives. However, the industrial revolution exacerbated the shortcomings of spontaneous incentive schemes that tended to be based on local cultural practices rather than on performance per se. Also, more reliable approaches to managing the supply chain became necessary to make the transition from agriculture to more complex commerce and manufacturing organizations. The debate that ensued over how best to develop and deploy workers made its contribution to performance management by spurring the development of a number of economic theories.

Economic Theories. Unlike earlier periods, philosophical rationales abounded between the seventeenth and eighteenth centuries. They ranged from the *subsistence theory,* which held that hungry workers would be the most productive, to the *theory of the economic man,* which, following the lead of Adam Smith, held that productivity would increase if workers were paid based upon their performance. When Schoenhof (1892) reported evidence that higher wages indeed raised productivity while reducing cost, the stage was set to experiment with increasingly sophisticated profit-sharing schemes. For example, the *equilibrium theory* advocated a market approach to wage setting. However, the long-standing practice of cutting rates when workers improved their performance, preoccupation with job security, and peer pressure to restrict productivity undermined the success of incentive approaches.

Scientific Management. By the close of the nineteenth century, Frederick Taylor (1885, 1903, 1911) sought to address the flaws inherent in subjective performance standards by combining economic theories with time-and-motion studies. In fact, Taylor's provision of "a rationally defensible standard for establishing the rate with the amount of rewards clearly linked to levels of performance" (Peach and Wren, 1992, p. 17) is thought to be his most fundamental contribution to the field of human performance.

In this context, workers were expected to operate as mere extensions of machines and to optimize productivity and efficiency by submitting to the machine's purpose rather than the other way around. The resulting impersonal work environment provided fertile ground for later humanistic approaches and can be used as a backdrop against which to compare and contrast them (Frederiksen, 1982b; O'Brien and Dickinson, 1982).

Social Science Motivation Theories. The human relations approach to management has its roots in the 1920s and 1930s, when early performance theorists began to question the value of financial incentives. New studies focusing on the worker rather than on productivity began to emerge, such as the Hawthorne studies at Western Electric (Parsons, 1992). The resulting *social man* view suggested that other motivators could impinge on workers' productivity. People were no longer viewed as interchangeable machine parts, and management was thought to have to shift its concern from productivity alone to facilitating collaboration toward the achievement of a goal. People development became a focus of concern for the first time. Also, the *economic man* versus *social man* paradox, which would later be recaptured by McGregor's Theory X and Theory Y (1960), broadened the outlook on needs and stimulated the work of behavioral scientists (Frederiksen, 1982b; O'Brien and Dickinson, 1982).

In 1943, Abraham Maslow proposed his *psychological theory of needs,* which would have a great influence on the field of performance management. Maslow's ideas continued to be popularized by McGregor (1960) and Herzberg (1966). Maslow thought of needs as internal forces that produce internal tensions when activated. These tensions work to motivate the worker to act in such a way as to *satisfy* the need, thereby reducing the tension. Moreover, needs progress is a hierarchy and can only be satisfied in succession, ranging from basic needs to self-actualization (Frederiksen, 1982b; O'Brien and Dickinson, 1982).

While Maslow's hierarchy of needs seemed to provide a commonsense explanation of behavior, it enjoys little empirical support. Moreover, the applicability of the theory in work settings remains problematic, since it is impossible to directly observe, assess, predict, and therefore impinge upon need states. However, it is important to understand the legacy of Maslow's hierarchy of needs because it focused the attention of a generation of academicians and organizational practitioners on needs so much as to misguide them to thinking of *needs* as the cause of behavior rather than as a convenient hypothetical explanation (Frederiksen, 1982b; O'Brien and Dickinson, 1982).

O'Brien and Dickinson (1982) warned that need satisfaction neither causes nor explains behavior. In fact, even though Herzberg's (1966) adaptation of Maslow's hierarchy of needs to work settings identified useful contextual factors that can influence behavior, such as recognition, policies, and structures, these factors still failed to adequately address individual differences or to articulate how contextual variables have to be manipulated in order to maximize their effectiveness. Likewise, followers of Vroom's (1964) *expectancy theory* argue that a worker's behavior is mediated by an internal process of perceiving the probability that an event will occur. Yet it would be simpler and more objective to assess the role of specific learning histories and readily observable environmental variables on the worker's behavior in order to change the contingencies controlling them to promote performance if needed (Frederiksen, 1982b; O'Brien and Dickinson, 1982).

Thus, from an HPT standpoint, the reliance of motivational theories on internal states, needs, expectancies, and so on (Vroom, 1964) to explain behavior in some cognitive universe is cumbersome at best. Moreover, critics of such mentalistic approaches caution that attempts to modify attitudes, perceptions, and personalities have obscured the fact that changing attitudes is only a means to changing performance, not an end in itself. Finally, internal perceptions are beyond the reach of managers, yet engineering the probability of occurrences of targeted performances by manipulating their consequences is relatively straightforward. Hence, while humanistic theorists were instrumental in recasting workers as human beings rather than as disposable machine parts, the next section will show how behavioral psychologists did much more to fulfill the humanistic mission (MacCorquodale, 1974) while at the same time promoting productivity by outlining the behavioral principles necessary to directly change behavior (Frederiksen, 1982b; O'Brien and Dickinson, 1982).

HPT as an Outgrowth of the Pragmatic Philosophy

Behavioral psychology's departure from mentalistic theories that attempt to explain such mental constructs as thoughts, personality, attitudes, perception, needs, and motives, and its focus instead on observable behavior and its environmental control, mark the first paradigm shift in our field. That is, humbled by the inaccessibility of mental constructs to direct observation and hence scientific scrutiny, behavioral psychologists have adopted an engineering approach that is based on the precise description of observed behavioral relations within the context in which they occur (Frederiksen, 1982b; O'Brien and Dickinson, 1982).

Early Laboratory Experimentations. One of the earliest contributions to behavioral theory came from the Russian physiologist Ivan Pavlov (1849–1936). His classical conditioning experiment demonstrated that environmental stimuli could *elicit* involuntary responses, or reflexes, thanks to their biological relevance to our organism, just as a puff of air elicits eye blinking. Moreover, the association of two stimuli in respondent conditioning could account for conditioned social behavior without needing to appeal to internal motives and desires (Frederiksen, 1982b; O'Brien and Dickinson, 1982).

Edward Thorndike (1898), however, studied learning by manipulating the association between a stimulus and a response. He is credited for stipulating three *primary laws*. The first primary law essentially states that neural paths are established through practice, thus producing learning. The second primary law states that the more one practices a response, the greater the likelihood it will be maintained over time. Third, behaviors can be weakened or strengthened depending on whether they are repeatedly followed by either positive or aversive consequences. In other words, behavior is controlled by its consequences. Thorndike's primary laws would later become recognized as the foundation of programmed instruction (Day, 1997; Frederiksen, 1982b; O'Brien and Dickinson, 1982).

The American psychologist John Watson (1926) built on the work of Pavlov and Thorndike and advanced the field by advocating the assumptions and methods of behavior theory. Though Watson became widely recognized as the father of behaviorism, B. F. Skinner's contributions had the greatest influence on the development of HPT (Frederiksen, 1982b; O'Brien and Dickinson, 1982).

Since then, HPT has come to represent the convergence of a number of disciplines: behavior theory, systems analysis, communication, educational psychology, human resource development, psychology, instructional systems design and technology, management theory, and organizational design and development, to name a few. While describing the specific contribution of each discipline is beyond the scope of this chapter, the next section briefly outlines some of the models that have stood the test of time over the past four decades.[2]

Behavior Analysis. Skinner (1938, 1953, 1957) embraced Thorndike's *law of effect* and proceeded to conduct a large number of controlled laboratory experiments that served as the basis of *behavior analysis.* His experimental analyses highlighted the difference between Pavlov's *elicited* involuntary responses and the *operant behaviors* organisms emit in an effort to control their environment. Skinner showed that some events are instrumental in shaping operant behavior. For example, we will work for the opportunity to engage in favorite activities, setting the occasion for some operant behaviors rather than others. Likewise, rain is a *setting operation* for reaching out for one's umbrella when leaving the house (Day, 1997; Frederiksen, 1982b; O'Brien and Dickinson, 1982; Mawhinney and Mawhinney, 1982).

Skinner also demonstrated that events occurring both before a behavior, which he called "antecedents," and after, which he called "consequences," when combined are called "behavioral contingencies" and can be manipulated to influence the probability of occurrence of a behavior. Thus, Skinner described his basic unit of analysis as the three-term contingency of stimulus-response-consequence, whereby previous associations between antecedents and consequences set the occasion for specific responses. Such *functional analysis of behavior* allows the experimenter or change agent to determine not only which behavior is occurring but also what conditions maintain it, and to change it by changing its contingencies (Day, 1997; Frederiksen, 1982b; O'Brien and Dickinson, 1982; Mawhinney and Mawhinney, 1982).

Furthermore, building on the law of effect, Skinner demonstrated that positive and negative reinforcers—that is, pleasurable events or events occurring immediately after the behavior, allowing the organism to avoid or escape from aversive ones—work to increase the probability of occurrence of a behavior. Conversely, punishment following a behavior, either through removing a pleasant event or stimulus or from inflicting an aversive stimulus, reduces the probability of occurrence of that behavior. Also, the behavioral model defines consequences as reinforcing or punishing empirically (rather than a priori), on the basis of whether they had the effect of increasing or reducing the occurrence of a target response. In this way, the behavioral model accounts for individual differences and performance change within the same individual over time as a function of experience or learning history (Day, 1997; Frederiksen, 1982b; O'Brien and Dickinson, 1982; Mawhinney and Mawhinney, 1982).

Response classes are behaviors that are functionally related through their impact on the environment. For example, day-dreaming and doodling may be part of a "Let's relax or avoid this boring task" response class, while turning the doorknob or kicking the door both function to open doors. Analyzing response classes can generate a number of controlling variables. Moreover, it is important to track each response class because they may or may not vary together, and it is often useful to pinpoint which of the responses in a class are desired or not (Day, 1997; Frederiksen, 1982b; O'Brien and Dickinson, 1982; Mawhinney and Mawhinney, 1982).

Stimulus discrimination is evident when one response class that occurs in the presence of one set of stimuli does not occur in the presence of a different set of stimuli, such as daydreaming in a waiting room but not in a classroom. Conversely, *stimulus generalization* is evident when a response class occurs in the presence of novel stimuli that had not been reinforced before. The extent to which the organism is able to appropriately generalize or discriminate how to behave in certain situations depends on the similarity of the situation to others previously reinforced or punished (Day, 1997; Frederiksen, 1982b; O'Brien and Dickinson, 1982; Mawhinney and Mawhinney, 1982).

In addition, Skinner's studies on the effect of schedules of reinforcement on behavior demonstrated that the frequency and timing with which one delivers consequences are important. They yield systematic differences not only in the probability of occurrence of behaviors but also in the rate of acquisition of new repertoires and the maintenance of established ones. For example, it is important to provide lots of reinforcements in the acquisition stage because of the effort costs involved in doing something new. Also, the more one reinforces acquisition, the quicker the learning curve. Hence, it is important to structure the environment in such a way that it is very reinforcing in the early stages of learning. Intermittent schedules of reinforcement play an important role in maintaining and establishing permanence of newly acquired responses (Day, 1997; Frederiksen, 1982b; O'Brien and Dickinson, 1982; Mawhinney and Mawhinney, 1982; Sulzer-Azaroff and Mayer, 1991).

Skinner noted that traditional educational practices failed to leverage the law of effect by delaying feedback and reinforcement at times for as much as a week. For example, mathematical operations would provide hundreds of opportunities for natural reinforcement if feedback was provided at every step of the operation rather than just at the end. This observation alone revolutionized how instructional materials would be written (Day, 1997; Frederiksen, 1982b; O'Brien and Dickinson, 1982; Sulzer-Azaroff and Mayer, 1991).

Programmed Instruction. The Skinner Box, which Skinner used to study operant behavior under different schedules of reinforcement, allowed for direct ongoing observation and recording of *free operant* responses. His methodology earned him the credit for marking the onset of a truly scientific practice of psychology, thanks to the reliable and direct observational and measurement methods he provided (Day, 1997; Frederiksen, 1982b; O'Brien and Dickinson, 1982; Sulzer-Azaroff and Mayer, 1991).

Skinner made a major contribution to the technology of teaching when he extrapolated the principles behind the cumulative recording methodology to academic instruction by means of the *teaching machine*. The methodology was perfectly suited to record students' ongoing performance as they actively responded to programmed instructional material at their own pace. Moreover, cumulative recording provided the kind of ongoing immediate feedback instructors needed to make timely data-based curriculum decisions. For the first time instructors were able to respond to learners' needs immediately and to tailor instruction to individual needs in a classroom setting, thus increasing the quality and rate of learning in an unprecedented way (Day, 1997; Frederiksen, 1982b; O'Brien and Dickinson, 1982; Sulzer-Azaroff and Mayer, 1991).

Naturally, the quality of instruction depended on the quality of the instructional material, and programmed instruction became an area of research in its own right, starting with the work of one of Skinner's students, Susan Markel. Markel showed that students could learn in an error-free way by providing them with the opportunity to interact with the material in small, sequential, and easy steps or frames and to receive immediate feedback. This errorless learning method not only speeds learning but also reduces the amount of practice learners need and the number of errors that reemerge later. Moreover, not only is programmed instruction an effective way to teach simple discrimination and generalization, it is also instrumental in building response chains and complex responses (Day, 1997; Frederiksen, 1982b; O'Brien and Dickinson, 1982; Sulzer-Azaroff and Mayer, 1991).

In addition, Markel (1964), in her book *Good Frames and Bad: A Grammar of Frame Writing*, guided programmed instruction designers by outlining the skills, knowledge, and abilities along with procedural rules they need to follow. One of the critical differences between traditional material and programmed instruction is that the effectiveness of the latter is learner verified (Day, 1997). That is, the validation of the material is based on how students perform as a function of interacting with the instructional program (Markel, 1967).

Integrating Cognitive Psychology and Information Technology

Markel noted later that integrating the cognitive psychology concept of learning as information gathering leverages instructional effectiveness. In addition, the work of Gagné on *over learning* provided independent data corroborating findings reported in generative methods of instruction, such as fluency training, and precision teaching methods that were borne out of programmed instruction (Brethower, 2005). For example, Carl Binder (1978), another student of Skinner's, identified four conditions that could place a ceiling on fluency: (1) the type of measurement procedure used, (2) the type of testing procedures used, (3) preexisting deficits in tool skills, and (4) subcomponents of one's repertoire. Removing these artificial ceilings on performance reveals the true nature of learners' performance deficits or fluency level, thus guiding curriculum decision more objectively. Carl Binder's application of Skinner's free-operant methodology in precision training in areas such as product knowledge is an excellent example of current adaptations of programmed instruction.

Today the cost of producing and delivering programmed instruction is greatly reduced, thanks to technological advances including computer-assisted instruction (CAI), object-based authoring systems, computer-based training (CBT), CD-ROMs, and just-in-time on-line delivery. While the acceptance level of these technologies in the classroom has been disappointing, there are a growing number of technological innovations used for adults, such as on-line education programs and blended learning (Day, 1997).

Objectives and Learner-Centered Instruction. While behavior theory focused on response, Robert Mager's book *Preparing Instructional Objectives* (1975), helped to set behavior in proper perspective. His model ensures that behavior functionally relates to the circumstances in which it has to occur by defining objectives that describe the performance standard of specific behavior in terms of the context as well as its rate, topography, and criteria. For example, salespersons need to be able not only to describe products but also to do so accurately, succinctly, and clearly enough that customers can understand them. Moreover, Mager's learner-centered focus helped to build even more adaptive programs that could follow learners' progress starting at any point in a program and then guide the learner to address his or her specific knowledge gaps (West, 1997b).

Mager's model was instrumental in shifting the traditional focus from what instructors should do to what learners' desired performance repertoire should become in order to ensure that they meet the necessary performance standards of application. Thus, Mager is credited with having revolutionized training by demonstrating that developing measurable objectives based on desired performance standards could guide performance improvement (West, 1997b).

Accomplishments and Worthy Performance. With the emphasis on the bottom line, organizations cannot afford to track behavior alone lest their employees risk falling into what is known as the *activity trap*. The activity trap is evident when lots of people are very busy doing lots of things and checking them off on their "to do lists," independent of whether they are instrumental in meeting organizational goals. One way to avoid the activity trap is to keep track of the accomplishments that result from one's behavior. Daniels (1989) said that behavior is what you can see a person doing while a result is what they leave behind. Also, in his book *Human Competence: Engineering Worthy Performance,* Gilbert (1978) said that change agents have to understand the distinction between behavior and accomplishments because performance is the transaction between the two and could not be changed unless one knows which behavior leads to which result. Conversely, it is important to understand which work-related behaviors fail to contribute value to the accomplishment, so that they can be eliminated from the job routine. To find out if an accomplishment is valuable, one has to ask whether it fulfills the job, tasks, or function's purpose (Dean, 1997c; Gilbert, 1982).

Gilbert (1978) lists three criteria accomplishments have to meet. They must be (1) measurable, (2) observable, and (3) reliably verified. Also, accomplishments can be measured in terms of their quality, which in turn can be assessed in terms of accuracy, class, and novelty; their quantity in terms of rate, time, and volume; and their cost in terms of labor, material, and management. Thus, pinpointing behaviors and accomplishments helps to set expectations and provides constructive feedback as well as to make sure that the behaviors workers engage in are instrumental to the organizational mission (Dean, 1997c; Gilbert, 1982).

FIRST VISIBLE SIGNS OF HPT AND ITS SCALABILITY

Though most of the early applications of behavior analysis were in the areas of education and mental health, educators and mental health practitioners who encountered difficulties in implementing programs with students and clients resorted to the same principles to secure their full participation and to manage their performance (Frederiksen, 1982b; Mawhinney and Mawhinney, 1982). Also, in 1962, eager to apply laboratory findings to the field, a number of behavioral scientists and their students founded the National Society for Programmed Instruction (NSPI) for the purpose of establishing a forum to discuss and promote the evolution of human performance technologies. Today the association is known as the International Society for Performance Improvement (ISPI) and is supported by a number of other professional organizations such as the American Society for Training and Development, the International Federation of Training and Development Organizational Development (Rosenberg, Coscarelli, and Smith Hutchison, 1992), and the Organizational Behavior Management Network, a special interest group of the Association for Applied Behavior Analysis. In addition, a number of professional journals focus on HPT, including *Training, The Performance Improvement Quarterly, Performance Improvement, Performance Express, The Journal of Organizational Behavior Management* and the *OBM Network News.*

Researchers and practitioners who contribute to this body of knowledge by using behavioral principles to solve organizational problems through training and organizational change have been instrumental in establishing a track record for HPT. From a historical perspective, with few exceptions, HPT interventions of the 1970s tended to be small scale or short term and integrated behavior theory with system theory. This coupling worked to advance the field of HPT another step toward addressing large-scale, organizationwide issues in a systemic way (Brethower, 1982; Frederiksen, 1982a; Tosti, 2004; Zemke and Gunkler, 1982). Thus, Skinner is credited with providing the scientific rationale for studying behavior as well as with suggesting and inspiring many applications of behavior analysis and their theoretical ramifications (Frederiksen, 1982b).

Brethower's Five Performance Principles

Brethower's five performance principles (1982) expand on the basic behavior principles described in the behavior analysis section. As such, they are particularly useful, as they further illustrate how to make an intervention work at both the individual and group levels.

The first principle states that "[b]ehavior is a function of what a person brings to an experience and what the environment provides" (Brethower, 1997, p. 68). The second principle emphasizes the importance of establishing *stimulus control* to make sure that learning and performance are situated in a functional context. The third principle states that *discriminative control* is established by exposing the learner or the performer to multiple examples and counterexamples of which behavior can or cannot be generalized across situations. The fourth principle maintains that performance is controlled by its consequences. Thus, motivation is often a matter of managing consequences more effectively. The fifth principle addresses what Brethower calls *information control*. This principle suggests that performance is optimized when it benefits from good *intelligence gathering*. Thus performance feedback, its timing, its accuracy, and its frequency are important variables to consider when thinking about optimizing performance.

In fact, Brethower recalls that "individual performance and organizational performance, including workgroup performance, are inextricably interconnected so that constructive attention to one requires attention to both" (Brethower, 1997, p. 73). Thus, he states that the performance system accurately characterizes the nature of the interdependence between individual and organizational performance (Brethower, 1997; Mawhinney, 2001).

Behavior Systems Analysis as the Total Performance System

The integration of behavior systems analysis underlies the scalability of HPT, allowing for the analysis of performance in complex social systems made up of many individuals whose actions have an impact on the well-being of the organization (Austin, 2000; Rummler, 2004; Tosti, 2004). That is, it is indeed possible to move from one level of analysis to the next to address issues that impinge on the goal of the organization. Thus, behavioral systems analysis focuses "on the analysis of how the behavior of individuals combines to form a social organization" (Frederiksen, 1982b, p. 33). It addresses organizational issues in terms of the interdependency of subsections of the *system,* or *subsystems,* such as departments and how they function together toward the achievement of an organizational goal (Frederiksen, 1982b).

Kaufman, Oakley-Browne, Watkins, and Leigh (2003) draw attention to the distinction between a *system approach* and a *systems approach* as follows.

> *System Approach.* Begins with the sum total of parts working independently and together to achieve a useful set of results at the societal level—that adds value for all internal and external partners. We best think of it as the larger whole. . . .
>   *Systems Approach.* Begins with the parts of a system—subsystems—that make up the "system" [p. 341].

Also, Kaufman and others depict each approach as one half of a yin and yang diagram, with the system approach's external client and society focus complementing the systems approach's internal client and organizational focus. They go on to explain the implications of one approach versus another, stating that

> It should be noted here that the "system" is made up of small elements or subsystems, shown as "bubbles" embedded in the larger system. If we start at this smaller level, we will start with a part not a whole. So when someone says he or she is using a "systems approach" that person is really focusing on one or more subsystems and is unfortunately focusing on the part and not the whole. When planning and doing at this level, one can only assume that the payoffs and consequences will add up to something useful to society and external clients, and this is usually a very big assumption [pp. 341–342].

Hence, according to the system perspective, it is necessary to determine whether change at the behavioral level will be supported in the larger social system at the organizational level. For example, it would be futile to address tardiness if management failed to address the negative consequences of coming to work on time and to deliver consequences for tardiness.

Also, the extent to which a system is *permeable* depends on how open or closed it is to input from other systems or subsystems. For example, an organization is

more or less permeable to the external influence of the economy and sociopolitical events. Similarly, an organization that is part of a conglomerate is subject to
the influences of the conglomerate's policy requirements. Internal influences that
can permeate various levels of the organization include organizational influences,
personnel influences, and work factors. Likewise, performance factors including
working conditions, processes, outcomes, and their measures may also influence
and permeate various components of the organizational system. Thus, integrating
the empiricism of behavior theory with a system view serves to leverage the feedback process within the system model. Such a behavior systems analysis provides
more complete information about the status of the system than it would by relying either on a behavior theory or a system theory view alone. Also, the more complete the feedback, the more self-correcting and adaptive the organization will be
(Frederiksen, 1982a).

As a result, truly dynamic systems function in such a way that they can be
self-correcting. Subsystems provide feedback on the workings of the system,
informing it on eventual inefficiencies. That input can in turn be used to adjust
the workings of the system and to maximize efficiency. For example, it is possible to know how cost-effective a process is and how efficient the inputs and the
outputs are. Negative feedback can suggest opportunities to improve the system
by introducing the changes necessary to produce the required outputs. Even feedback systems can be identified as sources of malfunction, and feedback can be
improved in terms of its timing, quality, quantity, and type as well as whether it
should be delivered individually or in group, verbally or in writing (Frederiksen,
1982a; O'Brien, Dickinson, and Rosow, 1982). Hence, isolating deficiencies in
any of the system's components is instrumental in pinpointing performance gaps
and prescribing potential solutions at the system level (Brethower, 1982, 1997;
Frederiksen, 1982a).

However, Tosti (2000) suggests that a dynamic system "reject[s] any change
that is not linked to other key components of the system," whereby "the system
returns to steady state following a temporary disruption" as would failing to
take into account the effect of a change intervention on one component on the
other components of the system. Hence, it is important to assess an organization's *change potential* or agility (p. 56). Lasting change is best obtained by
designing the system so that ongoing changes in input, such as business drivers and feedback that monitors change as well as how change is being supported internally by employees, permeate the system, allowing it to effectively
adapt to changing demands on the organization (Malott, 1999; Warren, 1982;
Zemke and Gunkler, 1982; Tosti, 2000).

The contribution of behavior systems analysis is that it provides systematic feedback information in a way that enables HPT practitioners to align and join the personal stakes of individual members of the organization in order to fulfill
organizational missions. When natural reinforcers are lacking, such a sophisticated

feedback system can prescribe; other reinforcers, such as opportunities to engage in preferred or novel activities, bonuses, profit sharing, and so on, can be put in place to align individual performance toward a common goal. In this way, the behavior systems analysis contributes to HPT's ability to address complex human interactions (Warren, 1982; Zemke and Gunkler, 1982; Tosti, 2000).

Rationale for the Paradigm Shift from Mechanical Determinism to System Theory

The integration of behavior theory and system theory has worked to leverage the analytical power of both fields, yielding *behavioral* system analysis. While behavior theory and system theory share a bias for functional analyses, their differences from a philosophical point of view are noteworthy (Brethower, 1982; Frederiksen, 1982b).

Mechanical Determinism. As mentioned earlier, owing to its mechanistic emphasis, behavior theory offers scientific rigor by bringing the observable behavior of individuals into proper focus rather than dissipating performance interventions that focus on a search for internal mind states. However, Hayes (2001) contends that while mechanistic determinism is a relevant foundation for any branch of science and is instrumental at the investigative level, once taken out of the well-controlled laboratory setting it can paradoxically "keep unwitting company" (p. 359) with earlier mentalistic or dualistic conceptualizations of the mind. In fact, as shown earlier, while the mechanistic approach might effectively yield episodic changes in such stable environments, they would come short of engendering long-lasting changes in today's business environment.

That is, the need to conceptualize causality in terms of the beginning and ending of an event imposed by a linear structure is cumbersome in the context of an interrelated and perhaps cyclical whole. For example, a mechanistic approach cannot adequately describe the nonlinear impact of changes in the interrelation of metacontingencies such as economic, political, and natural resources on the well-being of an organization, culture, society, and the life cycle. It would either reduce the relation of one element to the other, or relegate one as the effect of the other, obliterating its independent status. Thus, natural resources might be reduced to the status of an economic resource on grounds that natural resources are a type of trade currency, economics is about trade, and so on. Also, the moment when the influence of one element on the other begins and ends is not subject to observation. Furthermore, with regard to life as an event, there is the appeal of being able to observe the events beyond one's own life experience. Requiring some sort of a continuation beyond the end of one's own experience is not amenable to direct observation. Thus, Hayes feels that an alternative interpretation of time is necessary to establish the philosophical grounds on which to describe performance in nondualistic terms.

Hayes (2001) suggests that addressing organizational issues requires a paradigm shift from the superfluous mechanistic invocation of causality and its implication of purpose to a system approach. She notes that mechanistic linear temporal relations whereby cause and effect occur in irreversible succession are ill-suited to address "the simultaneous concurrence of factors, promoting an understanding of events primarily in terms of spatial arrangements" that is relevant to organizational settings (p. 357). In addition, she suggests that the mechanistic attempt to isolate as few factors as possible to establish their status as independent causal or dependent effect variables is incompatible with the need to make sense "of the multi-factorial, ever expanding, fields of simultaneous interactions, which have become our new subject matter . . ." (p. 369) or of *performance logic,* as Rummler calls it (Rummler and Brache, 1995; Rummler, 2001, 2004).

System Theory. Carleton has written various articles about systems for ISPI. He states that

> A system is best characterized as a set of two or three elements that satisfies the following three conditions:
>
> 1. The behavior of each element has an effect on the behavior of the whole.
> 2. The behavior of the elements and their effects on the whole are interdependent.
> 3. However subgroups of the elements are formed, each has an effect on the behavior of the whole and none has an independent effect on it.
>
> A system therefore is a whole that cannot be divided into interdependent parts. Every part of a system has properties that it loses when separated from the system. Every system has some properties, its essential ones, that none of its parts do. Therefore, when a system is taken apart it loses its essential properties.
>
> To make an impact upon a system requires a systemic approach to deal effectively with all relevant parts of the system in concert. In effect, a solution is not one you "interject" into the system. Rather, it is one that is "aligned" to the overall system within which it has to exist. This applies to all things in the organization, from things as specific as reducing costs to things as complex as altering the culture or improving the leadership. Elements in a system must be dealt with systematically and in a systemic manner [2005, p. 2].

Thus, taking the system apart to maximize the efficiency of its elements separately from one another in a mechanistic way is unlikely to optimize the system. Alternatively, troubleshooting individual performance within the larger system allows HPT professionals to change the larger context so that it may better support and maintain changes within its subsystems. Tosti (2004) states that "[t]he approach accommodates the need to address complex problems/ solutions where problems at various levels are magnifying the consequences of problems at another level" (p. 8). The next sections will review models that adhere to this new paradigm (Brethower, 2001; Gilbert, 1982).

Behavior Engineering and PROBE Models

In keeping with the system approach, Gilbert's *Human Competence: Engineering Worthy Performance* (1978) model takes a bird's-eye view of the organization as a whole by looking at it from different vantage points. Also, the model speaks to Geary Rummler's comment, which Gilbert has captured into a principle: "Put a good performer in a bad system, and the system will win every time" (Gilbert, 1978; Rummler 2004, p. xiii).

Accordingly, Gilbert's model provides a means of conducting a functional analysis of what is going on in the organization in a way that reveals which stimuli, responses, and consequences account for the current performance of the organization. By the same token, it is diagnostic as far as the contingencies that sustain suboptimal performance. Thus, Gilbert's model reveals gaps in current and desired performance with the purpose of fixing environmental contingencies to promote excellence. Furthermore, he asserts that performance can only be maximized if the analysis and corresponding intervention transcend traditional hierarchy levels.

In fact, Gilbert's analysis starts by addressing contingencies at the organizational level and then proceeds to consider them at the individual level. At the organizational level, the behavior-engineering model raises questions in the stimulus category regarding whether the work environment provides the necessary information as input on how to perform a job. In the response category, the model inquires about the adequacy of the resources, such as tools, material, time, and so on. Finally, in the consequence category, the model seeks answers to questions about the types of incentives provided in the work environment, including money and nonmonetary performance-based incentives. At the individual level, questions about stimulus, response, and consequence could provide answers as to why people *don't know* (knowledge); *can't do* (capacity); and *won't do* (motivation) in performing their work appropriately, or why they cannot excel in it.

Thus, the analysis enables the objective assessment of performance blockers at both the organizational and the individual levels. Also, it is a means of defining the problem in terms of performance gaps or improvement opportunities. Finally, it is prescriptive in that it suggests which solution is most appropriate given the nature of the problem by clarifying whether a problem is best resolved by managing resources and contingencies or whether training is necessary to enhance employees' knowledge, skills, and attitudes.

Front-End Analysis

Joe Harless, a student of Gilbert, is credited with redirecting the training design process thanks to his emphasis on front-end analysis. His 1970 book *An Ounce of Analysis (Is Worth a Pound of Objectives)* built on previous work in the field and addressed transfer of training in a way that was unprecedented. The unique features of the Performance Improvement Process (PIP), outlined in the book, not only transformed trainers into true performance specialists who involved employees as change agents throughout the entire process but also included organizational alignment and a systematic analysis of performance gaps with the end in mind (Ripley, 1997).

The role of the performance specialists in preparing the PIP program is to provide up-front training for employees taking on an internal consulting role. Also, they guide them in the implementation of a number of supporting job aids, the creation of an audit trail of documentation worksheets describing the work and decisions taken throughout a process, and facilitation of the organizational alignment process (Ripley, 1997).

Change agents then organize the PIP by using that information to align organizational events with strategic and business goals. At this point in the PIP one can identify gaps in current performance as well as in performances that would be needed given new organizational goals. In this way, analysts are able to prioritize interventions on the basis of which shortfalls seem to yield the greatest return (Ripley, 1997).

The project alignment phase derives directly from the prescription of the preceding organization phase. It consists of laying out the preliminary plans for the target project without specifying any particular solution. The solution is derived by means of the front-end analysis, which consists of, as Harless would say, "all the smart things a manager, trainer, or consultant does *before* addressing a solution to a human performance problem" (in Ripley, 1997, p. 97).

Once gaps are clearly defined in terms of performance opportunities, the intervention phase ensues. At this point, the change agent's task is to choose the appropriate intervention, be it in the area of personnel selection, skills, and knowledge; environmental change; processes policies, procedures, or management practices; or motivation and incentives. In this way, Harless's model extends Gilbert's earlier behavior-engineering model by including the personnel selection category to better address the kinds of sudden changes in job requirements that are common in redesign and reengineering efforts (Ripley, 1997).

Implementation, per se, does not ensue, however, until the interventions are tested and revised. According to the results of the testing, change agents then engage in developing, validating, and pilot testing the tailored performance indicators. At the same time, a separate evaluation project addresses the process itself by focusing on whether change agents followed the systematic PIP process and whether it worked or needs to be better adapted to the specific context. Throughout, Harless's performance-engineering approach means that ongoing measurement monitors whether interventions produce the desired effect on performance. By the same token, it signals when changes call for a new cycle of front-end analyses, intervention, and evaluation to enable desired performance outcomes (Ripley, 1997).

Managing the White Space and Serious Performance Consulting

As in Gilbert's and Harless's models, Rummler and Brache's model, as described in their book *Improving Performance: How to Manage the White Space on the Organization Chart* (1995), as well as in the case studies illustrated in Rummler's *Serious Performance Consulting* (2004), attempts to grasp and diagnose the overall organizational context by means of the solution-neutral approach they call the "anatomy of performance" (AOP). This approach clarifies the organization's direction and then looks for misalignments and barriers in cross-functional processes to reveal how these may be driving suboptimal organizational performance. Thus, Rummler's holistic approach to organizations extends his colleagues' models because he not only addresses performance at the organizational and the personal levels but also captures the adaptive nature of organizations at the processes level as a diagnostic source for performance-improvement initiatives (West, 1997a).

Rummler and Brache's (1995) analysis further breaks down these three performance levels into three performance needs: goals, designs, and management. Rummler subsequently added *evaluation* as a fourth performance (2004), arguing that optimizing performance in any one of these components and subcomponents alone risks leaving it in a suboptimal context and weakens the system as a whole. Also, his performance-improvement process integrates interventions across all functions, independent of organizational hierarchy, by addressing the following issues across levels: the specification of the problem, improvement opportunities, actions that will be taken, and parts of the system that will be affected by the change. Following the process sequentially helps to produce tools and job aids that facilitate the diagnosis of performance gaps that transcend hierarchical silos (West, 1997a).

Rummler's performance logic links the result chain to critical business issues that take the supra-system into account. Such a transparent multilayer diagnostic approach is especially suited to address the complexity of today's global organizations and has the added advantage of preventing change agents from prematurely jumping to conclusions about solutions that may offer no more than mere symptomatic relief (Rummler and Brache, 1995; Rummler 2001; Rummler, 2004; West, 1997a).

The Organizational Scan, Performance Levers, and Alignment

Like Rummler, Tosti and Jackson's *organizational scan model* (1996) is concerned with how change in one component of the system affects the equilibrium of the rest of the system. Considering that an organizational system is permeable to both internal and external influences, Tosti and Jackson's organizational scan model aims to detect those factors or performance levers that mediate organizational performance and may be responsible for specific deficits. Moreover, the model takes the diagnostic process a step further by explicitly addressing receiving systems' needs and *values,* thus broadening its ecobehavioral vantage point. These additional features of the model enhance change agents' ability to plan interventions with a long-term view (Kolvitz, 1997).

More specifically, while Tosti and Jackson (1996) start at the organization level, they proceed to the work at the people level and probe into the input, conditions, processes, and outcomes across each level, much as their colleagues have. However, the organizational scan probes further into the receiving system components, including such factors as strategy, culture, and objectives. It also articulates the mediating role of *culture* on the quality and quantity of work produced. To this end, the model raises questions that enable change agents to evaluate whether their intervention is aligned with the current organizational realities. Thus, while the scan can reveal misalignments, it also supports change agents to make sure their interventions will become culturally embedded in the organization so that they may have a lasting effect.

In this way, the organizational alignment model not only articulates what needs to be done in the organization in order to fulfill its mission but also shows how the vision is to be accomplished. Tosti and Jackson suggest that results will be more or less easy to achieve as a function of alignment and provide a number of useful guidelines that will facilitate culture change while managing a cultural balance that will nurture the long-term impact of interventions (Kolvitz, 1997).

Strategic Planning for Success

Kaufman, Oakley-Browne, Watkins, and Leigh's *Strategic Planning for Success: Aligning People, Performance and Payoffs* (2003) is a strategic needs assessment model so comprehensive that it embraces both a front-end analysis approach and the organizational alignment model. As a front-end analysis, it is particularly significant in that it shifts the traditional paradigm by strengthening the link between ethical values and concerns at the societal level and related useful and justifiable organizational missions. Also, it takes into account how the goals and needs that derive from that link can be reconciled so that organizational strategies, goals, and activities may be aligned to yield results that will be worthy for both the organization and society. Kaufman and others define SMARTER goals as Specific, Measurable, Audacious, Results-focused, Time-bound, Encompassing, and Reviewed frequently. Thus, what distinguishes the model from others is that it addresses needs, or the *gap between current and desired or required results* at the Mega level as SMARTER high-payoff goals, in addition to the more traditional Macro- and Micro-level needs and suggests ways to reconcile the objectives at each level. Building on Peter Drucker's observation, Kaufman and others suggest that their model is not only concerned with doing things right but also with doing "the right thing" (p. 81).

The focus at the Micro level is on individual or small-group results such as task accomplishment. At the Macro level, the focus turns to organizational outputs such as finished products and services. Kaufman advocates shifting the focus to the Mega level, or societal payoffs and consequences that impinge on our quality of life, well-being, and survival. For example, Kaufman and others (2003) advocate focusing on socioeconomic self-sufficiency and ecological products. Moreover, they suggest that aligning Macro- and Micro-level results to Mega-level results will provide more justifiable rationales for organizational tactics, goals, and strategies and the methods we select to get intended results (Dean and Ripley, 1997c).

The Performance Learning-Satisfaction (PLS) Evaluation System

Swanson's *performance learning-satisfaction evaluation system* (PLS) (1996) addresses the fundamental flaws inherent in conducting interventions in the absence of a preestablished evaluation plan by connecting performance goals set at the beginning of an intervention to intervention outcome at the evaluation phase. He proposes that evaluation be conducted in any independent domain, including learning, performance, and satisfaction (Dean and Ripley, 1997b).

The performance domain can be evaluated in terms of whether it yields *business*, that is, productivity measures such as sales, number of widgets, and so on, or *financial* results, that is, subtracting the cost of performance from the value it generates. Objectives attained in the learning domain can be evaluated as having yielded either *mastery* of knowledge content, such as criterion scores on a multiple-choice test, or workplace-implementation *expertise*, such as behavior-based observations of what the performer can do. The satisfaction domain assesses the satisfaction of either *participants* in or *sponsors* of the intervention, such as standardized program evaluations completed using a Likert scale at the end of the program for participants and sponsors, respectively.

Furthermore, Swanson states that evaluation data can be collected before, during, and after the intervention. When within-group comparisons are not appropriate, data can be compared against performance standards or against preestablished norms. Thus, Swanson provides practitioners and researchers with a simple, valid, and adaptable evaluation method for any PIP (Dean and Ripley, 1997b).

Language for Work That Works

Danny Langdon's model (1995) is founded on the premise of language as unifying cultural medium and uses it as a vehicle to affect organizational culture.

He likens the language of work models metaphorically to elements of language including words, syntax, message, and medium. Accordingly, his model focuses on the six key words that best describe work within the performance paradigm: (1) inputs, (2) conditions, (3) processes, (4) outputs, (5) consequences, and (6) feedback. Describing the cycle of the performance paradigm provides the syntax, which explains how behavior evolves at every level of an organization and hence explains how to improve performance. Sharing the same language across the organizational hierarchy then aligns management and workers, enabling organizationwide performance improvement. In fact, the language of work serves to operationalize work applications throughout the organizational strata (Dean and Ripley, 1997a).

The Metamodel of Performance Improvement

With his *metamodel of performance improvement,* Dean (1997a) recalls that the list of state-of-the-art models does not stop here. While the metamodel of performance improvement encompasses models for framing, assessing, and analyzing performance like the ones described above, it also features a number of intervention models, including training, workplace performance technologies, systems and process redesign, and organizational culture. Likewise, articulation and experimentation continue with measures of testing, evaluating, and managing performance-improvement systems, models, and approaches to reconceptualize, apply, and install performance-improvement models, methods, and measures.

Currently, the field continues to use model building as a means of adapting HPT to the changing nature of organizations and their context (Chevalier, 2003; Wilmoth, Prigmore and Bray, 2002). Furthermore, Kaufman's work suggests that the field may now also be shaped by broader societal needs. Hence, the following sections will take a look at how the field may evolve over the next ten years as it gains acceptance in organizations around the world which are, in turn, shaped by the larger context of world events (Hatcher, 2000, 2003a, 2003b; Watkins, Leigh, and Kaufman, 2000).

TWENTY-FIRST-CENTURY HPT

Looking at the forces that have shaped and reshaped the nature of work is another way of looking at the conditions in which HPT has evolved and continues to develop (Skinner, 1986). These have included the shift from farmwork, well over one hundred years ago, to the factory, with today's farmworkers making up the minority of workers in the industrialized world. Automation and the consequent decline in the labor force created another shift, which today is also seeing an increase in the tertialization of the workforce in Western countries.

At the same time, emerging economies, including those of India and China as well as Eastern Europe and some North African countries, are attracting the relocalization of production. On the local scale, the new market environment applies pressure in areas depleted by the exportation of production to reinvent their economies. Likewise, the resulting growth, accelerated productivity, and excessive consumption are exerting unprecedented pressure on the environment both in terms of natural resource depletion and pollution. On a global scale, it is disturbing both the economic and ecologic equilibrium as we have known it.

Industrialized countries continue to struggle with economic recovery since the 2001 lows. The struggle has been finding expression in a rash of mergers, acquisitions, and takeovers as well as antiglobalization protests, strikes, and debates over which currencies should be adjusted, and whether to address the slower-than-projected rate of job creation by reducing the work week. The fact remains that widespread downsizing and outsourcing efforts have left both local governments and employers with a difficult legacy. Difficulties inherent in enforcing the thirty-five-hour work week and freezing pay in some European countries, while remaining competitive and developing the necessary infrastructure to attract businesses at the same time, are yet to find a solution. Also, issues such as job creation beyond low-paying temporary jobs and whether legislation alone will indeed spur entrepreneurship are generating bitter debate. For those individuals who are working full-time, issues such as work-life balance, job stress as they attempt to cover for others dismissed by downsizing, the absence of adequate time and training, and ever-increasing health care costs are current concerns. The cultures of some United States organizations now have an uncanny resemblance to the long-hour cultures that have been common in many Asian, United Kingdom, Spanish, and Italian organizations for decades. Talk of temporary work and overtime seem to have replaced talk of flex time. In addition, the problem of retention, given the increasingly high level of educated employees who require a certain type of challenge to preserve their level of interest, remains paradoxical (Thurkow, 2005).

Demographic issues include the growing number of women who continue to enter the workplace and the lag behind their male counterparts in pay, credit for the enterprises they create, and access to leadership roles even in spite of equal or superior educational levels (Amodio, 2005; European Professional Women's Network, 2005; Ministère de la parité et de l'égalité professionnelle, 2005). Also, women in some parts of the world still don't have equal access to the education necessary for comparable employment (Corporate Women Directors International, 2005).[3] In addition, handling the aging Baby Boomer population is translating into social security uncertainties and even into raising the retirement age in Europe. This is generating bitterness on the part of workers in a number of industrialized countries. At the same time, the post–Baby Boom gap threatens a talent-and-leadership shortage if it is not managed carefully

(Andrasik and McNamara, 1982). Finally, uncontrolled population growth and its associated disparity of wealth, chronic poverty, and hunger remain throbbing threats to economic and political stability (Bailey, 2000).

In fact, our world is becoming an increasingly dangerous place in which to live, with epidemic threats not only rising from the overcrowding in some urban areas but also due to increasingly resistant virus strains and deadly sexually transmitted diseases. In addition, the proliferation of weapons of mass destruction, terrorism, the threat from hazardous waste, and manmade earth warming and its associated natural disasters are issues national leaders strive to resolve at great cost and sometimes outright unsuccessfully (Bailey, 2000; Hayes, 2001).

While the Industrial Revolution marked a profound paradigm shift, and the shift from introspection to behaviorism which in turn shifted to system theory were others, society has gone through a number of cultural paradigm shifts including civil rights, the feminist movement, government breakdowns, the Asian stock market crash, state-sanctioned terrorism, safe sex, the personal computer, the Internet, national health crises, biotechnology, the European Union, climate changes, the terrorist attacks on September 11, 2001, and so on (Bailey, 2000; Kaufman, Oakley-Browne, Watkins, and Leigh, 2003). However, in 2001, Hayes cautioned that we should heed futurists' claim that we are in the midst of a paradigm shift of monumental proportions that is likely to be dramatic, with massive transitions in material condition, values, and social relations. Moreover, each has "enormous implications for the future of society" (Hayes, 2001, p. 369) that are magnified by the fact the rate of change is faster than ever and that it is now global. Therefore, the future development of HPT can be conceived of, against this background, in terms of how the field manages its current strengths, weaknesses, threats, and opportunities to address these metacontingencies in such a way as to safeguard its own adaptation and survival while adding value to humanity (Skinner, 1986).

Strengths

Though ISPI is currently engaged in a societywide open discussion aimed at clarifying HPT's value proposition, as described in the February 2003 issues of its journal *Performance Improvement* (International Society for Performance Improvement, 2003), the consensus is that the strength of HPT is its value proposition, no matter how members define it. In addition, HPT offers a perspective on how to address organizational change nonlinearly through its ability to handle ever-increasing complexity and to adapt to changing realities.

Understanding the commonalities across different realities gives HPT a relative head start on the learning curve, whereby the *what* to do may already be fairly well outlined in many areas. HPT professionals' abilities to adapt to the *hows* of implementation and to validate their contextualization could go a long way in stretching HPT beyond its American origins. Also, successful HPT implementations in multinational companies have already helped to establish the transferability of the technology across cultures and borders (Tosti, 1999a).

Weaknesses

Somewhat paradoxically, expectations that HPT would naturally expand with other successful management practices abroad through multinationals has met with a certain hostility to anything associated with *American management.* The extent to which such a stigma can be attached to HPT will constitute a cultural barrier to its progress abroad. To prevent this, change agents will have to make a special effort to develop and involve local professionals in the workplace and in academia. The true test that the profession is indeed both global and local lies in its ability to involve local professionals in guiding its contextualization to local laws and culture and in integrating their contributions into the core science of HPT (Andrasik and McNamara, 1982).

HPT is rarely presented in contrast with other change theories. Hence, there is a need to produce controlled experiments demonstrating HPT's potential to increase organizational agility (Tosti, 1999b)—that is, to produce lasting change and to make quick transitions to new states when needed. Yet organizational settings are rarely conducive to such experimentations. Also, empirically demonstrating the link between HPT's ethical and professional standards and sustainability faces the same problem and requires the kind of long-term intervention few organizations are inclined to pursue right now. As a result, it will take time until the data of enough independent replications can be corroborated to help decision makers appreciate the differential costs, benefits, and overall utility of HPT against other approaches.

Also, though HPT language is much less threatening than the language of behavior theory, most of the literature is in English, and few foreign applications have been published, creating a language and context barrier for non-English speakers (Kreitner, 1982). Even though more and more managers are becoming acquainted with HPT principles, standards, models, methods, and techniques, the widespread understanding and application of HPT is still lagging because it is vulnerable to language barriers and resistance to change (Berthold, 1982). In fact, Bailey cites examples of decision makers who had made important budget decisions while oblivious to what HPT has to offer. He suggested that if HPT remained unknown, it is perhaps due to our failure to tailor our message and present our products to their intended audiences, including the general public, decision makers at all levels of government, insurance companies, financial brokers, business and consulting firms, and the media. This long-standing *best kept secret* status has now extended over forty years, suggesting we seriously consider leveraging the know-how of experts in marketing and advertising to help us overcome this important shortcoming (Bailey, 2000).

Threats

While diversity is an important asset to HPT, our inability to reconcile diversity with regard to ethical values may threaten the accountability and acceptability of HPT (Andrasik and McNamara, 1982; Ferond and Stevens, 2005; Kaufman, Oakley-Browne, Watkins, and Leigh, 2003; Lee, 2003; Roehl, Murphy, and Burns, 2000; Sidman, 1989; Stewart, 2003; Watkins, Leigh, and Kaufman, 2000). While this is obviously relevant with regard to transnational security issues, which are mobilizing new institutional forms that require unprecedented levels of coordination in diverse environments, it is also relevant to business and non-profit organizations. Ongoing dialogue is necessary within our professional communities as to what it means to get on board with the principles articulated by organizations such as the International Society for Performance Improvement across cultural settings. Failing to establish mechanisms to safeguard the sustainability of local efforts to promote HPT would certainly halt the expansion of HPT internationally. It would also amount to a lost opportunity to enrich HPT as a science and technology, as the input of international professionals working in a broad variety of contexts is essential to the transfer of the technology into local realities, an important source of versatility for the field (Andrasik and McNamara, 1982).

Opportunities

The current business environment is so complex and challenging and the interconnections between business and society are so close, that nothing short of a scientific and multidisciplinary approach that encompasses a systemic view with a *Mega* outlook will suffice. Thus, HPT professionals have an opportunity to support leaders in implementing tailor-made solutions based on systematic and systemic needs analyses. As shown in the application section, the range of HPT interventions is only limited to the range of human activities. Thus, where we continue to be challenged with such issues as displaced workers, vocational training, stress management, retention, succession, sexism in the workplace, innovation, and entrepreneurship, HPT has a role to play in removing barriers to progress.

Likewise, while economic and technological development can no longer be seen as panaceas to social ills, HPT has an opportunity to help create a *sustainable society* by engendering the transformation of cultural practices that are threatening the ecosystem on which the future of society depends. To this end, HPT change agents might begin to address significant transitions in the near future, from exhaustible fossil fuel to renewable energy sources, maximal exploitation to maximal contribution, expansion to conservation, competition to cooperation, quantity to quality, and domination to partnership (Hayes, 2001; Stewart, 2003).

Instant access to information and increasingly sophisticated electronic performance support systems, afforded to HPT scholars and practitioners thanks to the information revolution, allow them to tap into highly specialized sources of knowledge, enabling both depth and breadth of knowledge to inform communication, problem solving, and decision making, in multidisciplinary functions and ongoing scholarship in the service of the end user (Andrasik and McNamara, 1982; Bailey, 2000; Hayes, 2001). Moreover, armed with their long-standing data-based approaches and the ability to show return on investment for many kinds of stakeholders, HPT professionals have an exceptional opportunity to meet organizational and societal demands and to raise levels of concern by making themselves heard in unequivocal terms. In this way, it would seem that HPT professionals have the means to influence important decision makers in both the public and the private sectors. To succeed in this endeavor, however, HPT needs to pursue an intensive policy of information management, development, dissemination, internationalization, and succession planning for the next generation.

Notes

1. See Kaufman, Oakley-Browne, Watkins, and Leigh (2003) for a discussion of paradigms.
2. The reader is encouraged to turn to the following for more detailed accounts: Dean (1997b); Mawhinney (1999); Dickinson and Mawhinney (2000); Dickinson (2000), and the original authors of the models, as well as Dale Brethower's (2005) *A History of HPT as a Chronology of Publication* at www.seekvaluedadded.net/chronohistory.doc.
3. See Jarema, Snycerski, Bagge, Austin, and Poling (1999) for an account of the participation of women in our field.

References

Addison, R. M. (2003). Performance technology landscape. *Performance Improvement, 42*(2), 13–14.

Amodio, A. (2005). Donne al timone delle aziende. *Il Sole-24 ore* (11), p. 10.

Andrasik, F., and McNamara, R. J. (1982). Future directions for industrial behavior modification. In R. M. O'Brien, A. M. Dickinson, and M. P. Rosow (Eds.), *Industrial behavior modification: A management handbook* (pp. 428–440). New York: Pergamon Press.

Austin, J. (2000). Performance analysis and performance diagnostics. In J. Austin and J. Carr (Eds.), *Handbook of applied behavior analysis* (pp. 321–350). Reno, NV: Context Press.

Bailey, J. S. (2000). A futurist perspective for applied behavior analysis. In J. Austin and J. Carr (Eds.), *Handbook of applied behavior analysis* (pp. 473–488). Reno, NV: Context Press.

Berthold, H. C. Jr. (1982). Behavior modification in industrial/organizational environment: Assumptions and ethics. In R. M. O'Brien, A. M. Dickinson, and M. P. Rosow (Eds.), *Industrial behavior modification: A management handbook* (pp. 405–427). New York: Pergamon Press.

Binder, C. (1978, September). Four kinds of ceilings. *Data-sharing newsletter.* Waltham, MA: Behavior Prosthesis Laboratory, 15, 1–2.

Brethower, D. M. (1982). The total performance system. In R. M. O'Brien, A. M. Dickinson, and M. P. Rosow (Eds.), *Industrial behavior modification: A management handbook* (pp. 350–369). New York: Pergamon Press.

Brethower, D. (1997). The knowledge base of human performance technology. In P. J. Dean and D. E. Ripley (Eds.), *Performance improvement pathfinders: Models for organizational learning* (pp. 65–83). Silver Spring, MD: The International Society for Performance Improvement.

Brethower, D. M. (2001). Managing a person as a system. In L. J. Hayes, J. Austin, R. Houmanfar, and M. C. Clayton (Eds.), *Organizational change* (pp. 89–105). Reno, NV: Context Press.

Brethower, D. M. (2005). *A history of HPT as a chronology of publications.* Retrieved June 12, 2005, from www.seekvalueadded.net/chronohistory.doc.

Carleton, J. (2005). System theory. In *Vector: Systemic solutions to business issues.* Retrieved June 12, 2005, from www.vectoreurope.co.uk/documents/2/BI_A4_Systemic_Solutions_to_Business_Issues_V1_4.pdf.

Carleton, J. R., and Lineberry, C. (2004). *Achieving post-merger success: A stakeholder's guide to cultural due diligence, assessment, and integration.* San Francisco: Jossey-Bass/Pfeiffer.

Chevalier, R. (2003). Updating the behavior engineering model. *Performance Improvement, 42*(5) 8–14.

Corporate Women Directors International. (2005). *Global 200: Key findings.* Retrieved June 12, 2005, from http://globewomen.com/cwdi/Global200_KeyFindings.htm.

Daniels, A. (1989). *Performance management: Improving quality and productivity through positive reinforcement.* Tucker, GA: Performance Management Publications.

Day, R. K., (1997). B. F. Skinner & Susan Markel: The beginnings. In P. J. Dean and D. E. Ripley (Eds.), *Performance improvement pathfinders: Models for organizational learning* (pp. 22–44). Silver Spring, MD: The International Society for Performance Improvement.

Dean, P. J. (1997a). A metamodel for performance improvement. In P. J. Dean and D. E. Ripley (Eds.), *Performance improvement pathfinders: Models for organizational learning* (pp.197–205). Silver Spring, MD: The International Society for Performance Improvement.

Dean, P. J. (1997b). The importance of performance improvement models in organizational learning systems. In P. J. Dean and D. E. Ripley (Eds.), *Performance improvement pathfinders: Models for organizational learning* (pp. 2–19). Silver Spring, MD: The International Society for Performance Improvement.

Dean, P. J. (1997c). Tom Gilbert: Engineering performance with or without training. In P. J. Dean and D. E. Ripley (Eds.), *Performance improvement pathfinders: Models for organizational learning* (pp. 45–64). Silver Spring, MD: The International Society for Performance Improvement.

Dean, P. J., and Ripley, D. E. (1997a). Danny Langdon: A language of work that works. In P. J. Dean and D. E. Ripley (Eds.), *Performance improvement pathfinders: Models for organizational learning* (pp. 172–196). Silver Spring, MD: The International Society for Performance Improvement.

Dean, P. J., and Ripley, D. E. (1997b). Richard Swanson: The PLS evaluation system. In P. J. Dean and D. E. Ripley (Eds.), *Performance improvement pathfinders: Models for organizational learning* (pp. 152–171). Silver Spring, MD: The International Society for Performance Improvement.

Dean, P. J., and Ripley, D. E. (1997c). Roger Kaufman: The needs assessment audit. In P. J. Dean and D. E. Ripley (Eds.), *Performance improvement pathfinders: Models for organizational learning* (pp. 142–151). Silver Spring, MD: The International Society for Performance Improvement.

Dickinson, A. M. (2000). The historical roots of organizational behavior management in the private sector: The 1950s–1980s. *Journal of Organizational Behavior Management, 20*(3/4), 9–58.

Dickinson, A. M., and Mawhinney, T. C. (Eds.). (2000). Organizational behavior management in the year 2000 [Special issue]. *Journal of Organizational Behavior Management, 20*(3/4).

European Professional Women's Network. (2005). Home page. Retrieved June 12, 2005, from www.europeanpwn.net.

Ferond, C. A., and Stevens, A. (2005, April). *Productive, profitable and sustainable, socially responsible development: Value-based 360° assessments lead the way!* Paper presented at the annual conference of the International Society for Performance Improvement, Vancouver, Canada.

Frederiksen, L. W. (1982a). *Handbook of organizational behavior management.* New York: Wiley.

Frederiksen, L. W. (1982b). Organizational behavior management: An overview. In L. W. Frederiksen (Ed.), *Handbook of organizational behavior management* (pp. 3–29). New York: Wiley.

Gilbert, T. (1978). *Human competence: Engineering worthy performance.* New York: McGraw-Hill.

Gilbert, T. (1982). Analyzing productive performance. In L. W. Frederiksen (Ed.), *Handbook of organizational behavior management* (pp.117–144). New York: Wiley.

Glenn, S. S. (1991). Contingencies and metacontingencies: Relations among behavioral, cultural, and biological evolution. In P. A. Lamal (Ed.), *Behavior analysis of societies and cultural practices* (pp. 39–73). Washington, DC: Hemisphere.

Gould, S. J. (1983). *Hen's teeth and horses' toes: Further reflections in natural history.* New York: W. W. Norton and Company.

Harless, J. H. (1970). *An ounce of analysis (is worth a pound of objectives).* Newnan, GA: Harless Performance Guild.

Hatcher, T. (2000). The social responsibility performance outcomes model: Building socially responsible companies through performance improvement outcomes. *Performance Improvement, 39(7) 18–22.*

Hatcher, T. (2003a). Introduction to PIQ's special ethics section. *Performance Improvement Quarterly, 16(2) 70–71.*

Hatcher, T. (2003b). Social responsibility as an ethical imperative in performance improvement. *Performance Improvement Quarterly, 16(2) 105–121.*

Hayes, L. J. (2001). Finding our place in a constructed future. In L. J. Hayes, J. Austin, R. Houmanfar, and M. C. Clayton (Eds.), *Organizational change* (pp. 349–371). Reno, NV: Context Press.

Herzberg, F. (1966). *Work and the nature of man.* Cleveland, OH: World Publishing Company.

International Society for Performance Improvement. (2003). Special issue: Clarifying HPT. *Performance Improvement, 42(2).*

Jarema, K., Snycerski, S., Bagge, S., Austin, J., and Poling, A. (1999). Participation of women as authors and participants in articles published in the Journal of Organizational Behavior Management. *Journal of Organizational Behavior Management, 19(1),* 85–94.

Kaufman, R., Oakley-Browne, H., Watkins, R., and Leigh, D. (2003). *Strategic planning for success: Aligning people, performance, and payoffs.* San Francisco: Jossey-Bass/Pfeiffer.

Kolvitz, M. (1997). Donald Tosti and Stephanie Jackson: The organizational scan, performance levers and alignment. In P. J. Dean and D. E. Ripley (Eds.), *Performance improvement pathfinders: Models for organizational learning* (pp.124–141). Silver Spring, MD: The International Society for Performance Improvement.

Kreitner, R. (1982). Controversy in OBM: History, misconceptions, and ethics. In L. W. Frederiksen (Ed.), *Handbook of organizational behavior management* (pp. 71–94). New York: Wiley.

Langdon, D. G. (1995). *The new language of work.* Amherst, MA: Human Resource Development Press.

Lee, M. (2003). On codes of ethics, the individual and performance. *Performance Improvement Quarterly, 16(2),* 72–83.

MacCorquodale, K. (1974). Behaviorism is a humanism. In F. W. Matson (Ed.), *Without/within: Behaviorism and humanism.* Monterey, CA: Brooks/Cole.

Mager, R. F. (1975). *Preparing instructional objectives* (2nd ed.). Belmont, CA: Pitman Learning.

Malott, M. E. (1999). Creating lasting organizational changes. *Performance Improvement, 32*(2), 33–36.

Markel, S. M. (1964). *Good frames and bad: A grammar of frame writing.* New York: Wiley.

Markel, S. M. (1967) Empirical testing of programs. In P. C. Lange (Ed.), *Programmed instruction: Sixty-sixth yearbook of the national society for the study of education: 2* (pp. 104–108.) Chicago: University of Chicago Press.

Maslow, A. H. (1943). A theory of motivation. *Psychological Review, 50,* 370–376.

Mawhinney, T. C. (1992). Evolution of organizational cultures as selection by consequences: The Gaia Hypothesis, metacontingencies, and organizational ecology. In T. C. Mawhinney (Ed.), *Organizational cultures, rule-governed behavior and organizational behavior management: Theoretical foundations and implications for research and practice* (pp. 1–26). New York: Haworth Press.

Mawhinney, T. C. (1999). An abbreviated history of OBM in ABA. *Journal of Organizational Behavior Management, 19*(1), 7–12.

Mawhinney, T. C. (2001). Organization-environment systems as OBM intervention context: Minding your metacontingencies. In L. J. Hayes, J. Austin, R. Houmanfar, and M. C. Clayton (Eds.), *Organizational change* (pp. 137–167). Reno, NV: Context Press.

Mawhinney, T. C., and Mawhinney, R. R. (1982). Operant terms and concepts applied to industry. In R. M. O'Brien, A. M. Dickinson, and M. P. Rosow (Eds.), *Industrial behavior modification: A management handbook* (pp. 115–136). New York: Pergamon Press.

McGregor, D. (1960). *The human side of enterprise.* New York: McGraw-Hill.

Ministère de la parité et de l'égalité professionnelle. (2005). Home page. Retrieved June 12, 2005, from www.femmes-egalite.gouv.fr.

O'Brien, R. M., and Dickinson, A. M. (1982). Introduction to industrial behavior modification. In R. M. O'Brien, A. M. Dickinson, and M. P. Rosow (Eds.), *Industrial behavior modification: A management handbook* (pp. 7–34). New York: Pergamon Press.

O'Brien, R. M., Dickenson, A. M., and Rosow, M. P. (Eds.). (1982). *Industrial behavior modification: A management handbook.* New York: Pergamon Press.

Parsons, H. M. (1992). Hawthorne: An early OBM experiment. *Journal of Organizational Behavior Management, 12*(1), 27–43.

Peach, E. B. and Wren, D. (1992). Pay for performance from antiquity to the 1950s. *Journal of Organizational Behavior Management, 12*(2), 5–26.

Ripley, D. E. (1997). Joe Harless, Ed.D. An ounce of analysis. In P. J. Dean and D. E. Ripley (Eds.), *Performance improvement pathfinders: Models for organizational learning* (pp. 92–107). Silver Spring, MD: The International Society for Performance Improvement.

Roehl, J., Murphy, S., and Burns, S. (2000). Developing a model for ethical dialogue and decision making. *Performance Improvement, 39*(5), 13–17.

Rosenberg, M. J., Coscarelli, W. C., and Smith Hutchinson, C. (1992). The origins and evolution of the field. In H. D. Stolovitch and E. J. Keeps (Eds.), *Handbook of human performance technology: A comprehensive guide for analyzing and solving performance problems in organizations* (pp. 14–31). San Francisco: Jossey-Bass.

Rummler, G. A. (2001). Performance logic: The organization performance Rosetta Stone. In L. J. Hayes, J. Austin, R. Houmanfar, and M. C. Clayton (Eds.), *Organizational change* (pp. 111–133). Reno, NV: Context Press.

Rummler, G. A. (2004). *Serious performance consulting according to Rummler.* Silver Spring, MD: The International Society for Performance Improvement and the American Society for Training and Development.

Rummler, G. A., and Brache, A. P. (1995). *Improving performance: How to manage the white space on the organization chart* (2nd Ed.) San Francisco: Jossey-Bass.

Schoenhof, J. (1892). *The economy of high wages.* New York: G. P. Putman & Sons.

Sidman, M. (1989). *Coercion and its fallouts.* Boston: Authors Cooperative.

Skinner, B. F. (1938). *Behavior of organisms.* New York: Appleton-Century.

Skinner, B. F. (1953). *Science and human behavior.* New York: Appleton-Century-Crofts.

Skinner, B. F. (1957). *Verbal behavior.* New York: Appleton-Century-Crofts.

Skinner, B. F. (1986). What is wrong with daily life in the western world? *American psychologist, 41*(5), 568–574.

Stewart, J. (2003). Ethics of PI: A polemical overview. *Performance Improvement Quarterly, 16*(2), 90–104.

Sulzer-Azaroff, B., and Mayer, G. R. (1991). *Behavior analysis for lasting change.* Chicago: Holt, Rinehart and Winston.

Swanson, R. A. (1996). *Performance-learning-satisfaction evaluation: An application of the three-domain evaluation model to performance improvement, human resource development, organization development and training and development.* Saint Paul, MN: Human Resource Development Research Center.

Taylor, F. W. (1885). A piece-rate system, being a step towards partial solution of the labor problem. *Transactions, A.S.M.E., 16*, 856–883.

Taylor, F. W. (1903). *Shop management.* New York: Harper & Row.

Taylor, F. W. (1911). *The principle of scientific management.* New York: Harper & Row.

Thorndike, E. L. (1898). Animal intelligence: An experimental study of the associative processes in animals. *Psychological Review* (Monograph Supplement No. 8). New York: Macmillan.

Thurkow, T. (2005). Doing more with less. *OBM Network News, 19*(1), 3–5.

Tosti, D. T. (1999a). Global fluency. *Performance Improvement, 38*(2), 49–54.

Tosti, D. T. (1999b). *Organizational agility.* Retrieved October 12, 2005, from Persona Global Website at http://www.personaglobal.com/progover_OA.asp.

Tosti, D. T. (2000). Systemic change. *Performance Improvement, 39*(3), 53–59.

Tosti, D. T. (2004, August). The power and glory of human performance technology. *OBM Network News, 18*(2), 5–8.

Tosti, D. T., and Jackson, S. (1996). *Organizational scan: A performance analysis model.* Unpublished manuscript, Vanguard Consulting, San Rafael, CA.

Vroom, V. H. (1964). *Works and motivation.* New York: Wiley.

Warren, M. W. (1982). Performance management and management performance. In L. W. Frederiksen (Ed.), *Handbook of organizational behavior management* (pp. 539–564). New York: Wiley.

Watkins, R., Leigh, D., and Kaufman, R. (2000). A scientific dialogue: A performance accomplishment code of professional conduct. *Performance Improvement, 38*(4), 17–22.

Watson, J. B. (1926). *Behaviorism.* New York: Norton.

West, J. (1997a). Geary Rummler: Managing performance in the white spaces. In P. J. Dean and D. E. Ripley (Eds.), *Performance improvement pathfinders: Models for organizational learning* (pp. 108–123). Silver Spring, MD: The International Society for Performance Improvement.

West, J. (1997b). Robert Mager: Learner-centered instruction. In P. J. Dean and D. E. Ripley (Eds.), *Performance improvement pathfinders: Models for organizational learning* (pp. 84–91). Silver Spring, MD: The International Society for Performance Improvement.

Wilmoth, F. S., Prigmore, C., and Bray, M. (2002, September). HPT models: An overview of the major models in the field. *Performance Improvement, 42*(8), 14–22.

Zemke, R. E., and Gunkler, J. W. (1982). Organization-wide intervention. In R. M. O'Brien, A. M. Dickinson, and M. P. Rosow (Eds.), *Industrial behavior modification: A management handbook* (pp. 565–584). New York: Pergamon Press.

PART TWO

THE PERFORMANCE TECHNOLOGY PROCESS

JIM HILL

The authors represented in this part of the handbook have come together to paint a broad picture of the performance technology process, which is, at its core, a means of adding order to systems. Throughout this book you are presented with a wide range of methods and techniques for successfully employing human performance technology (HPT). This section provides some structure regarding the flow and timing of the process and a depiction of the desired results in each major process phase.

In any endeavor, it is unlikely that order can be elegantly achieved with haphazard probes and their resulting interventions. So the HPT process has evolved over time to incorporate lessons from both general systems theory and systems analysis. Borrowing from the *Cambridge Dictionary of Philosophy* (1992), the seven chapters that make up this section of the handbook provide some introductory answers for two broad questions:

- How do we optimize and control a system while facing limited resource availability and balancing multiple objectives?

- What is the optimal arrangement of the parts of a system and how do they relate to each other?

Since the publication of Gilbert's 1978 seminal work, *Human Competence: Engineering Worthy Performance,* performance technologists have viewed their roles from an engineering perspective. Over the past forty-three years, they have created a results-oriented amalgam from a wide range of scientific fields to address increasingly complex performance issues at the job, process, and organizational levels.

That amalgam is best applied via an ordered approach, often referred to as ADDIE (analysis, design, development, implementation, evaluation). In the following text, you will find descriptions of the chapters that describe the milestones of our tour of the HPT process.

Ryan Watkins explores the alignment of performance improvement with the strategic direction of an organization. As an ancient proverb reminds us, "if we don't know where we're going, any road will get us there." In addition to worthy goals, clear strategy helps us determine what value we seek, so we know not only whether we are focused on the right things, but that those things are worth our attention.

Allison Rossett leads us on a journey through performance analysis. While you will sense a heavy bent toward evaluation through this part of the handbook, Rossett argues that it is well entwined with analysis. It is a logical perspective, but often forgotten in practice.

Ray Svenson takes over from Allison and helps us link analysis to the design of performance solutions. By staying focused on the critical performance issue and keeping the end in mind, the design of successful solutions can be made easier and more effective.

Guy Wallace gives us a detailed means of determining how best practices or mastery performance can be captured, documented, structured, and used to create solutions that minimize the time to expertise. In a time when the definitive word often comes from managers or outdated training materials, the use of top performers as *the* critical data source bears heavy consideration. There is a tremendous amount of research indicating that this approach leads to extraordinary performance results and the rapid development of legitimate experts.

Larissa Malopinsky and Gihan Osman provide yet another reality check with their focus on organizational change. The most well-intended solutions often go down in a blaze of ridicule, disdain, and apathy for want of a little stakeholder buy-in. These authors' commonsense approach helps performance technologists maximize their potential for success.

In the final two chapters, Robert Brinkerhoff and Joan Dessinger and James Moseley give us practical approaches to evaluate the success of our interventions and, more, the resulting success of our *post-change* organizations.

So, even in the layout of this part of the handbook, you will sense an attempt to provide a process for learning more about the HPT process. Engaging and practical, the presented authors do us and our organizational clients a great service by helping us add discipline and order to our performance-improvement initiatives.

References

Audi, R. (Ed.). (1992). The Cambridge dictionary of philosophy. Cambridge, UK: Cambridge University Press.

Gilbert, T. F. (1978). *Human competence: Engineering worthy performance.* New York: McGraw-Hill.

CHAPTER EIGHT

Aligning Human Performance Technology Decisions with an Organization's Strategic Direction

Ryan Watkins

Predictably, the specific roles and related tasks of performance technologists vary from organization to organization. In general, however, the function of the performance technologist is to provide leadership in the development and implementation of interventions that lead to and support the achievement of useful results for individuals and organizations alike. This organizational role can include everything from designing classroom training and evaluating performance reward systems to developing strategic plans and establishing mentoring programs. As a result of these diverse roles and responsibilities, performance technologists are continually being challenged to interpret the strategic goals and objectives of their organization as guides toward their own success and the success of their projects. From decisions regarding which products to recommend to potential clients to questions regarding the most effective delivery tools for training, all decisions in an organization should be aligned, either formally or informally, with the organization's strategic direction.

Organizations, however, are not always clear in their strategic direction. Torraco and Swanson (1995) suggest that "[b]usiness objectives themselves are almost as diverse in nature as the wide range of organizations that articulate them. Business objectives can span long- and short-term time frames, and can focus on broad business issues (for example, diversification in the defense industry in the post–Cold War era) or more specific issues (for example, reduction of employee turnover in company field offices)" (p. 11). While most organizations invest significant amounts of time and money in the development of strategic plans that outline their ambitions, more often than not these documents are left on bookshelves to gather dust rather than being used by employees as guides for daily decision making.

Consequently, strategic plans typically fail organizations in both their capacity to guide decisions and their accessibility to many employees (Mintzberg, 1994). This situation regularly leaves managers, supervisors, performance technologists, and others in the organization with few tools for defining what results are necessary for success: the accomplishment of results that are aligned with the strategic direction of the organization and its clients. Yet strategic direction remains an essential ingredient in decision making at all levels of an organization. Watkins, Triner, and Kaufman (1996) suggest that strategic plans frequently fail to guide decision making by focusing on processes instead of results. When strategic plans focus on processes, describing what employees should do rather than what results should be accomplished, they lose their ability to guide decisions by disempowering employees. As a result, it is important to determine the capacity of strategic direction to guide decision making in an organization.

While analysis is a frequent starting place of many human performance technology models (for example, Van Tiem, Moseley, and Conway, 2004), in the past little attention has been paid to the analysis of how the decisions that are made throughout a performance technology project can be aligned with the strategic direction of the organization and its clients. For performance technologists, the alignment of their decisions with the strategic direction of the organization should therefore begin with an analysis of the current goals and objectives of the organization, its partners, its clients, and the community it serves.

STRATEGIC DIRECTION

Strategic plans can and should provide practical guides for decision making at all levels of any organization. Nonetheless, most of us have copies of ineffective plans that are now destined to sit on our bookshelves for years to come. This is, unfortunately, far from the most effective way to provide guidance for decision making.

> To transform your organization into the one you envision takes more than great strategy and implementation; you also need to make the strategy an integral part of the very fiber of your organization. When we speak of this idea, we usually use the phrase "strategic alignment." Aligning everyone in your organization with your strategy is one of the most important things you can do beyond formulating and implementing great strategies [Bradford, 2002, p. 1].

With most organizations no longer relying on a large number of "middle managers" to provide direction and guidance for decision making, many employees are increasingly being expected to make critical decisions without clear guidance based on the strategic direction of the organization and its clients. The development of effective strategic alignment therefore begins with useful strategic planning. Strategic plans that provide a clear picture of the useful results to be achieved throughout the organization, without micromanaging decision making, are effective tools for aligning the performance of people with results that add value (Watkins, Triner, and Kaufman, 1996; Kaufman, Oakley-Brown, Watkins, and Leigh, 2003). In turn, strategic plans are most useful when they provide essential guidance for decision making, thereby aligning the actions of the employees with the goals of organizational leaders. As organizations continue to rely on the decision making of employees at all levels, it is becoming increasingly important for all employees to use the strategic direction of the organization to guide their daily decisions.

Unconventional Wisdom

Transforming organizational planning from a process that results in dusty binders on a shelf to one that generates useful guides for daily decision making can be challenging. Regularly, there are competing demands for limited resources, organizational politics, contending interests, institutional cultures, opposing ideas of what clients want, contrasting input from outside clients and suppliers, as well as other obstacles that all chip away at the potential contributions of a planning effort. In the end, through compromise and concession, strategic documents can end up offering little guidance for aligning decisions with the organization's strategic direction.

These obstacles, and others, can derail well-intended planning efforts unless one begins with strategic objectives that have broad appeal across many stakeholder groups. Instead of starting a planning initiative by discussing the tools, techniques, processes, suppliers, and other details of "how" the results of the organization can be accomplished, effective planning begins with the recognition of shared goals and objectives (Kaufman, Oakley-Browne, Watkins, and Leigh, 2003). The shared goals and objectives cannot, however, be limited to those of the organization; after all, organizations do not succeed without the support of their partners and the ability to make valuable contributions to their clients and their clients' clients.

As a consequence, effective strategic plans begin with some unconventional wisdom that starts outside of the organization (Kaufman, Stith, Triner, and Watkins, 1998; Kaufman, Oakley-Brown, Watkins, and Leigh, 2003). By defining the common goals and objectives both within the organization and among the stakeholders outside of the organization, strategic planning initiatives can begin to define the results that all agree must be achieved.

A Model for Effective Direction Setting

Among his reflections on healthy interpersonal relationships, the social philosopher and business leader Charles Handy (1999) adds, "It seems to be the same with organizations. The healthiest are those which exist for others, not for themselves" (p. 48). For organizations, this pragmatic perspective is applied through strategic planning initiatives that begin with the shared goals of the organization, its clients, the clients' clients, and the community they serve. By starting here, instead of in the details of daily operations, each of the partners can clearly view the common results they can accomplish together.

Kaufman, Stith, Triner, and Watkins (1998) and Kaufman, Oakley-Brown, Watkins, and Leigh (2003) recommend that organizations use an "ideal vision" as a sensible starting place for establishing effective strategic direction. An ideal vision is a tool for defining in measurable terms for the outcomes, or "Mega-level" results, that both internal and external partners can agree upon. Unlike vague vision statements, this vision focuses on the societal contributions that the organizations, together or separately, can make to clients, clients' clients, and others. By specifying only the results that are to be accomplished, the ideal vision can guide the strategic planning process away from the obstacles of preferred tools, techniques, suppliers, or other elements that focus on "how" the results will be achieved.

In place of the debatable preferences for how results will be achieved, the ideal vision clearly defines which results have to be accomplished and how they will be measured. Hence, discussions related to the process elements of the plan, the "how to," are then reserved for a time after the results to be accomplished, the "what," are defined in measurable terms. For sample ideal visions, see Kaufman and Watkins (1999), Kaufman, Stith, Triner, and Watkins (1998), and Kaufman, Oakley-Browne, Watkins, and Leigh (2003).

After coming to an agreement with stakeholders on the shared definition of what results, or "Outcomes," should be accomplished, organizations can then define the results, or "Outputs," they will achieve and how they will contribute to the common objectives previously defined in the Mega-level ideal vision. At this stage in the planning process, organizations define the measurable results they will contribute to their clients, creating a clear strategic alignment of the results they accomplish with the shared goals of the organization and its partners.

Still focusing entirely on the results the organization will accomplish, Kaufman, Stith, Triner, and Watkins (1998) and Kaufman, Oakley-Brown, Watkins, and Leigh (2003) refer to this as Macro-level planning, and the process typically results in a mission statement. By defining measurable results that are to be accomplished by the organization, such as discharging healthy patients or delivering safe and reliable automobiles, the Macro-level planning documents provide unambiguous objectives by which all decisions within the organization can be aligned. In other words, if an option does not measurably move the organization closer to the accomplishment of the results defined in the mission and vision, then other alternatives should be examined. Performance technologists and others in the organization can then initially look to the mission for clear guidance when making challenging decisions, knowing that it is strategically aligned with the shared goals and objectives defined at the Mega-level.

While an exclusive focus is maintained on the results to be accomplished, the next step in setting effective strategic direction is to align the results to be achieved by individuals, groups, teams, divisions, and projects with those identified at the Mega and Macro levels. Referred to as "Micro-level" planning by Kaufman, Stith, Triner, and Watkins (1998) and Kaufman, Oakley-Brown, Watkins, and Leigh (2003), the objectives defined in this stage of planning provide clear and measurable achievements that all employees can use in guiding their decision making. At this level of planning, organizational leaders should work with employees, clients, suppliers, and other stakeholders to determine what "chain of results" must be accomplished to achieve the results defined in the mission and vision, as shown in Figure 8.1.

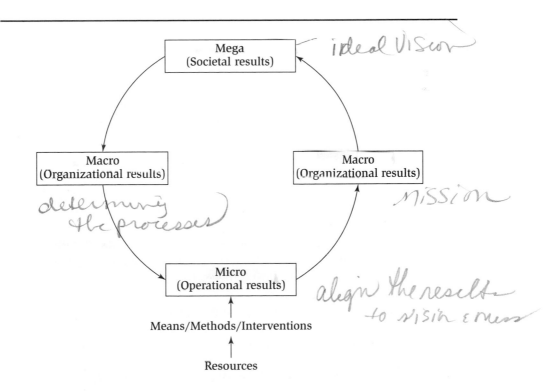

Figure 8.1. Chain of Results.

Source: Based on Kaufman, Oakley-Browne, Watkins, and Leigh, 2003.

First, the results to be achieved must be defined at the Mega level with partners internal and external to the organization; then results must also be defined at the Macro level, for the organization as a whole, and the Micro level, for the individuals and groups within the organization. Only then does effective strategic planning move to determining the "Processes," how these results will be accomplished, and "Inputs," what resources are necessary for implementing the processes. The complete framework can then be used by decision makers to ensure that the choices they make are adequately aligned with the strategic direction of the organization and its partners. After all, decision makers at all levels of an organization should be able to use the strategic direction established by the organizational leaders as guides in making daily choices. This is not to say, however, that strategic plans should make the decisions.

Strategic plans that do not provide clear and specific directions for making the decisions can frustrate employees. Yet effective strategic plans do not dictate how jobs are to be done, nor should they. Effective plans avoid describing the desired number of training hours employees will receive on new software systems, the skill requirements of newly hired workers, or the processes for creating a meaningful mentoring system. Instead, they provide clear statements about what results are expected, how success in accomplishing those results will be measured, and how the results are aligned with the organizational objectives as well as the goals of partners, clients, and clients' clients. By offering this guidance, without dictating processes or micromanaging, strategic plans can provide a guiding perspective for performance technologists and all employees in helping to define the results that are essential for success.

Consequently, aligning the strategic direction of the organization and its partners with the results to be contributed through effective performance technology interventions is essential. After all, if the processes a performance technologist implements, such as a training curriculum or rewards system, are not adequately contributing to the Micro-level results they are to achieve in order to support the organization in achieving its Macro- and Mega-level objectives, then the success of the project is in jeopardy.

Fortunately, the strategic direction established by the organization can provide indispensable input for the design of almost any performance technology. Moving forward with performance-improvement processes, such as performance analysis; cause analysis; intervention selection, design, and development; intervention implementation and change; and evaluation, can be risky without a clear analysis of how the performance intervention is linked and aligned with the strategic objectives of the organization.

Analysis of Strategic Direction

Too often strategic plans offer only vague, confusing, or contradictory guides to planning and decision making. Some plans are hidden between the revenues and expenditures pages of the annual report, while others seem to put forward only "pie in the sky" slogans or axioms that have little direct impact on the decisions employees have to make each day. As a result, a systematic analysis of the plans to ascertain the strategic directions they embody is essential.

Even with the best-written strategic plans it is often necessary to sift through the strategic plan's goals, objectives, and ambitions to determine which elements will have the most impact on the success of current and future performance initiatives. It is necessary to look beyond vague statements of triumph such as "number one in our market" or "first in quality" to identify the actual objectives that will define success. Since many strategic plans are not written as guides for employee decision making but are designed as marketing materials or quickly assembled platitudes to include in the annual report, asking the right questions requires thoughtful consideration.

When reviewing organizational plans, questions that are often useful include

- Are the strategic objectives of the organization that include Macro-level results aligned with clients and clients' clients' Mega-level results?

- Which organizational initiatives will have priority in the next five to ten years? How can performance technology support these initiatives?

- Which strategic objectives will performance technology initiatives contribute to the most?

- Can a direct or indirect relationship be demonstrated from the impact of performance technology initiatives that yield Micro-level results to the strategic objectives of the organization that yield Macro-level results?

- In light of the strategic objectives, how will the performance technology's impact on on-the-job performance be evaluated?

- In light of the strategic objectives, how will the performance technology's impact on organizational performance be evaluated?

- In light of the strategic objectives, how will the performance technology's impact on clients and clients' clients be evaluated (see Watkins, Leigh, Foshay, and Kaufman, 1998)?

Typically, the answers to each of the questions are not found in any single strategic planning document. Most performance technologists will have to survey a variety of organizational documents with information about visions, missions, annual progress, strategic plans, and so on, and possibly interview organizational leaders in order to find answers to these important questions. Meeting with clients, suppliers, and other partners that are not within the organization can also be valuable in seeking answers to these questions. Additionally, Robinson and Robinson (1996) recommend the following steps in developing a well-informed analysis of an organization's strategic direction:

- Read the annual report of the organization and work to understand it.

- Discuss with managers and others the ratios used to measure the operational health of the organization in order to compare current performance of the organization against goals.

- Identify the primary forces outside the control of the organization that will challenge the organization's ability to meet its business goals.

- Discuss the strategies and actions being taken by competitors and the implications of those actions for the organization.

- Skillfully use the business terminology of the organization [pp. 12–13].

Even when the appropriate resources for answering questions are identified, it typically pays to read "between the lines." Since many of the planning documents for an organization are public, and often available to both shareholders and other partners, the true objectives of the organization may be somewhat obscured in vague goal statements or concealed in what is not said. For example, while annual reports are often among the most valuable documents for answering questions about an organization's strategic direction, they are also often written in a manner that paints only a positive picture for shareholders. As a result, close scrutiny of financial investments, asset liquidations, or other changes in the organization often can reveal objectives that may not be written in the text of an annual report. Such scrutiny is important in helping the performance technologist find links from the strategic direction of the organization to the performance technology project.

When possible, it is most beneficial to establish a direct relationship between the results of a project and the strategic objectives of the organization and its clients; for example, project X brought about change Y. However, performance technologies are often more subtle in their contributions, and indirect relationships must be identified and demonstrated. Consequently, it is important to recognize that most performance technology projects cannot take credit for all of the success an organization has in achieving its objectives, nor can they take all the blame when performance discrepancies continue. Identifying the often unique definitions of *success* for each project is therefore an essential task for the performance technologist.

DEFINING SUCCESS

The *success* of any performance technology is ultimately defined by its ability to accomplish useful results for individuals and organizations alike. Sounds straightforward, does it not? Yet defining the *success* of performance technologies quickly becomes convoluted and challenging as we begin to analyze the criteria for *success* brought to the project by the multiple partners, sponsors, and clients that are necessarily drawn into any and all performance-improvement projects. For example, in a performance technology project there will likely be multiple players involved in the design, development, implementation, and evaluation of the technology, as well as the workers, supervisors, clients, clients' clients, and other stakeholders evaluating the results long after the project has concluded. Individuals and teams in each of these groups will have different perspectives on the success of the project.

Success is therefore difficult to define and accomplish; consequently, performance interventions that are not adequately aligned with the strategic directions valued by key partners stand little chance of being considered *successful* from these multiple perspectives. Generally, partners and stakeholders in projects will have both unique and shared criteria in defining *success*. As a result, for the performance technologist, recognizing and attending to the multiple strategic goals and objectives of the partners and stakeholders in the project are critical, and since it is unlikely that any performance interventions will completely meet the demands of each of these perspectives, prioritizing these various criteria for *success* is important.

For example, if after an analysis a performance consultant concludes that an instructional intervention is a necessary part of a performance technology solution, then there will be competing perspectives on the success of the project, including the following:

- *Learners:* For the performance technologist to be successful from the perspective of the learners, content such as lectures, activities, assignments, exams, and so on should have an engaging graphical interface, be easily navigated, facilitate interactions, and provide the necessary experiences for the required certification, as well as offer skills that can be used on the job the next day.

- *Client organization:* For the performance technologist to be successful from the perspective of the client organization, the time spent by employees in training must result in the transfer of knowledge and skills to on-the-job performance that adds value and improves the ability of the organization to serve its clients.

- *Clients' clients:* For the performance technologist to be successful from the perspective of the clients' clients, training must lead to more efficient and effective processes that reduce costs and lead to higher-quality products from the client organization.

- *Training facilitators:* For the performance technologist to be successful from the perspective of the training facilitator, the instructor-guide directions must be clear, a range of customizable features to meet the instructor's teaching preferences should be included, and course materials should include assessments for measuring learner performance.

- *Manager of performance technology projects:* For the performance technologist to be successful from the perspective of his or her manager, he or she must provide services to a growing number of clients, maintain professional skills through training and workshops, produce products that can be accepted by clients ahead of deadlines, and reduce costs where possible to increase profitability.

- *Organizational leaders:* For the performance technologist to be successful from the perspective of the organization's leaders, the technology process must be cost effective, ensure that services can be offered to a substantial market, provide services to a growing number of clients, and illustrate the latest uses of technological innovations.

With increased pressure to shorten turnaround times, to use quick-design models, and to develop rapid prototypes, addressing the various criteria for *success* from each of these perspectives has become increasingly challenging for performance technologists. Many approaches to performance improvement fail to include the valuable input from diverse external stakeholder groups in the initial design decisions and front-end analysis, and as a result performance interventions are typically developed to meet the criteria for success defined by a very limited number of project partners.

For instance, if in the previous example the consultant had focused only on the criteria for success defined by the client organization, then project decisions would have been at risk of failing other important partners in the project, including learners, the supervisors of learners, and the leadership of the technologist's own organization. Consequently, including multiple perspectives of *success* in the planning of any project is vital. To do this, technologists should (1) identify the essential partners and stakeholders in the project who will have a perspective on its *success,* (2) determine the criteria they will use to measure the *success* of the project, and (3) prioritize those criteria based on the cost of meeting the criteria versus the cost of not meeting their criteria. Table 8.1 recommends a useful format for identifying and prioritizing the criteria of *success* from multiple perspectives.

It is not expected, however, that any performance technology can meet the criteria of *success* applied by all stakeholders. After all, most projects have numerous partners and stakeholders that have their own priorities, making it next to impossible to define a single set of measures that will be the standards for *success.* For the performance technologist, this complexity offers the opportunity to both help the partners determine shared objectives and assist in the prioritizing of criteria that will be used to measure *success* as a project progresses. As a result, it is good practice for the technologist to work with partners and stakeholders from the onset of a project in determining what criteria for defining *success* are appropriate and measurable.

Table 8.1. Format for Assessing Multiple Perspectives on Success.

Stakeholder	Criteria of Success	Priority	Achieved (yes or no)
For example, supervisors of training participants	Worker will operate equipment using the latest safety measures	High	Yes
	Worker will demonstrate new safety measures to other workers	Low	No
	Worker will alert management to emerging safety hazards	High	Yes

Adding measurability to criteria, such as a reduced process time of three minutes or increased warehouse capacity of 45 percent, is another important task for most performance technologists. Without clear and specific guidelines as to how results will be measured, making decisions based on strategic objectives is difficult at best. In addition, having agreed upon measures for *success* defined at the beginning of any project can pay high dividends when it comes time to evaluate *success*. Last, with measurable criteria for *success* in hand, performance technologists can then work with partners and stakeholders to negotiate the strategic alignment among the groups and prioritize the results to be achieved.

How Is Your Success Defined?

Following are some essential questions you should ask at the beginning of any performance technology project. The answers to each question will help shape the strategic direction of the project and guide decision making by defining the multiple perspectives of *success*.

- Which partners and stakeholders will be in a position to make a judgment on the *success* of the project?

- Which partners and stakeholders are within the organization and which are external to the organization?

- How will you prioritize the differing perspectives among the partners and stakeholders?

- Are the criteria used by the partners and stakeholders conflicting?

- Can the objectives for the performance technology be prioritized and agreed upon by the partners and stakeholders?

- What informal criteria will you use to assess the *success* of the performance technology, such as team building, office morale, or promotions?

Making Decisions

As it is in many professions, decision making is at the foundation of nearly all human performance technology processes, from front-end analysis to summative evaluation (Chermack, 2003). As a result, most performance technology models include the use of performance data to support many of the decisions that have to be made during their application. For example, Van Tiem, Moseley, and Conway (2004) include the analysis of work, worker, work environment, and organizational environment as data are collected to support decisions related to "need or opportunity." Likewise, many performance technology projects rely on data collected through (1) interviews with groups including direct recipients, supervisors, managers, clients, and the clients' clients, (2) performance data regarding current and desired results at all levels of evaluation, and (3) estimates of return on investment of alternative interventions to support their decision making.

Furthermore, deriving the goals and objectives that drive the perceptions of a successful project also commonly requires the review and analysis of the strategic plans of the partner organizations and other stakeholders. In these documents, the performance technologist should identify long-term strategic objectives that can guide his or her decisions throughout the project. For example, if an organization's client is planning to grow international markets by developing new manufacturing facilities in Asia, then the performance technologist should survey the capacity of potential interventions to meet these requirements. Efforts to select one or more appropriate interventions could then include one or more of the following: cultural impact of proposed solutions, translation of training materials, and differing return-on-investment projections based on the costs of performance solutions in Asian markets. All of these would be useful considerations for performance initiatives if they are evaluated from a variety of perspectives on *success*.

HPT IMPLICATIONS

Like few other processes in an organization, performance technology projects regularly have the unique opportunity to align individual performance and decision making with the strategic objectives of an organization and its clients. Robinson and Robinson (1996) affirm that "someone in the role of performance consultant thinks in terms of what people must do if business goals are to be achieved" (p. 10). Yet sometimes the alignment of decisions with the goals of the organization is assumed, and other times performance is "suboptimized" when decisions are aligned only with personal or project goals instead of broader organizational objectives. Unfortunately, each of these paths increases the odds that the performance technology will not contribute the required results and that the project will not be perceived as a success from one or more perspectives. To neutralize these obstacles to success, our decisions at each phase of a performance technology project should be based on an analysis of the strategic objectives of the organization and its partners.

Table 8.2 illustrates a variety of questions that a performance technologist will typically ask at some point during the development and implementation of a performance intervention. Using the four major phases of the human performance technology model presented by Van Tiem and others (2004), the table offers

Table 8.2. HPT Considerations for Strategic Alignment.

Sample Decisions in Leading an HPT Project	*Suggested Steps for Strategic Alignment*
Phase One: Performance Analysis	
Which of the organization's strategic objectives are not being accomplished?	Review the strategic plan of the organization to verify the objectives. If objectives are not clear, work with the organization to develop an effective strategic direction.
How are the organization's strategic objectives measured?	Identify criteria currently being used to measure the achievement of strategic objectives. If measurable criteria are not associated with objectives, then work with the organization representatives to define the results they want to accomplish.
How are the organization's strategic objectives aligned with those of clients and clients' clients?	Review the strategic plans of clients and clients' clients.

(Continued)

Table 8.2. HPT Considerations for Strategic Alignment. (*Continued*)

Sample Decisions in Leading an HPT Project	*Suggested Steps for Strategic Alignment*
How are the organization's strategic objectives aligned with other internal departments or projects?	Determine the strategic objectives of internal departments and projects.
What are the gaps in individual or group performance?	Use the strategic objectives to establish the desired performance as a benchmark for evaluating current performance.
How should individual or group performance be measured?	Select measurement criteria for individual or group performance that are aligned with the objectives of the organization and its partners
What results are required of the project for the organization to be successful in accomplishing its objectives?	Use the strategic objectives of the organization and its partners to define the results to be accomplished by the performance technology project.

Phase Two: Cause Analysis

What current programs or projects are associated with the performance gap?	Expand your view of organizational structure and initiatives with a review of the current programs and projects associated with the performance.
Which future initiatives may be associated with the performance gap?	From the strategic plan, identify future initiatives that may have influence on the performance gap or that may be affected by the performance gap.
Are causes of the performance gap also associated with the accomplishment of other strategic objectives of the organization?	Review the organization's strategic objectives to determine other objectives associated with the causes of the performance gap.
How are the organization's suppliers (that is, partners), associated with the causes of the performance gap?	Review the strategic objectives of the partner organizations in relation to the performance gap.
Are the performance objectives at the individual or group level associated with the performance gap?	Analyze the performance objectives at the individual or group level to determine if misalignment is a cause of the performance gap.

Table 8.2. (*Continued*)

Sample Decisions in Leading an HPT Project	*Suggested Steps for Strategic Alignment*

Phase Three: Intervention Selection, Design, and Development

Which performance technology interventions can accomplish the required results?	Use the strategic objectives of the organization and its partners to define the results that must be accomplished by eligible performance technology interventions.
What criteria related to the required results will be used to evaluate alternative performance technology interventions?	Align the measurable criteria for evaluating alternative interventions with the measurement criteria used to assess the accomplishment of strategic objectives.
How does the selected intervention influence the accomplishment of the organization's strategic objectives in other departments or units?	Verify that the selected intervention will assist in the achievement of the organization's strategic objectives in other departments or units.
Are the specific decisions associated with the design of the intervention going to accomplish the necessary results?	Use the measurable criteria for measuring both project objectives and the organization's strategic objectives to determine if specific design decisions are going to achieve necessary results.
Are development plans consistent with the organization's strategic objectives?	Review the strategic plan of the organization to ensure that development plans are aligned with current and future initiatives.
How much time and how many resources should be devoted to this project?	Review the prioritized strategic objectives of the department and organization to determine the relative priority of the project in relation to other projects.

Phase Three: Intervention Implementation and Change

Are implementation strategies consistent with the organization's strategic objectives?	Review the strategic plan of the organization to ensure that implementation strategies are aligned with current and future initiatives.
What revisions to the original design of the intervention are necessary?	Determine if revisions will better support the achievement of the project's objectives and the accomplishment of the organization's strategic objectives.

(Continued)

Table 8.2. HPT Considerations for Strategic Alignment. (*Continued*)

Sample Decisions in Leading an HPT Project	*Suggested Steps for Strategic Alignment*
Can the organization's strategic objectives be used to promote the value of the changes brought with the performance technology intervention?	Coordinate the alignment of the selected intervention with the strategic objectives of the organization, its clients, and clients' clients.

Phase Four: Evaluation

Is the performance technology project successful from the perspective of the organization?	Determine the impact (that is, the measurable results of the project on the achievement of the organization's strategic objectives).
Is the performance technology project successful from the perspective of the organization's clients and the clients' clients?	Determine the impact (that is, the measurable results of the project on the achievement of the clients as well as the clients' clients' strategic objectives).
Is the performance technology project successful from the perspective of your partners in the design, development, and implementation of the project?	Determine the impact (that is, the measurable results of the project on the achievement of the strategic objectives of others associated with the project).
When and how should the performance technology intervention be revised?	Review any changes to the strategic objectives of the organizations, its clients, and the clients' clients, and continue to measure the impact of the intervention.
Are there unanticipated strategic benefits from the project?	Review the strategic objectives of the department and organization for new opportunities to accomplish useful results.

examples of how performance technologists can use the strategic directions of organizations and their partners to guide the decisions in each of these phases.

SUMMARY

The success of performance technologies is regularly assessed by their ability to achieve measurable results that are aligned with the strategic direction of the organization and its partners. As a result, the daily decisions made by performance technologists and others should be based, at least in part, on an understanding both of the strategic objectives set by the organization, its clients, and the clients' clients and of the criteria each partner will use to define *success*. Through effective planning at the Mega, Macro, and Micro levels (Kaufman, Stith, Triner, and Watkins, 1998; Kaufman, Oakley-Brown, Watkins, and Leigh, 2003), performance technologists can support this type of pragmatic decision making by guiding the development of strategic plans that offer clear and measurable descriptions of what results are to be accomplished and how those results are aligned with the objectives of the organization's partners. In addition, through the analysis of criteria used by each of the multiple partners to define *success*, performance technologists can better prioritize and use strategic objectives when making decisions. Together, these processes can support performance technologists in aligning their daily decision making with the strategic directions of the organization and its partners.

References

Bradford, R. (2002). Aligning employees with strategy. *Inc.Com.* Retrieved October 15, 2004, from www.inc.com/articles/2002/04/24063.html

Chermack, T. (2003). Decision-making expertise at the core of human resource. *Development Advances in Developing Human Resources, 5*, 365–377.

Handy, C. (1999). *Waiting for the mountain to move: Reflections on work and life.* San Francisco: Jossey-Bass.

Kaufman, R., and Watkins, R. (1999). An ideal vision to guide Florida's revision of the state comprehensive plan. In L. DeHaven-Smith (Ed.), *Charting Florida's future.* Tallahassee, FL: The Florida Institute of Government.

Kaufman, R., Oakley-Brown, H., Watkins, R., and Leigh, D. (2003). Strategic planning for success: Aligning people, performance, and payoffs. San Francisco: Jossey-Bass.

Kaufman, R., Stith, M., Triner, D., and Watkins, R. (1998). The changing corporate mind: Organizations, vision, mission, purposes, and indicators on the move toward societal payoffs. *Performance Improvement Quarterly, 11*(3), 32–34.

Mintzberg, R. (1994). *The rise and fall of strategic planning.* New York: Free Press.

Robinson, D. G., and Robinson, J. (1996). *Performance consulting: Moving beyond training.* San Francisco: Barrett-Koehler.

Torraco, R. J., and Swanson, R. A. (1995). The strategic roles of human resource development. *Human Resource Planning, 18*(4), 10–21.

Van Tiem, D., Moseley, J., and Conway, J. (2004). *Fundamentals of performance technology: A guide to improving people, process, and performance.* Washington, DC: International Society for Performance Improvement.

Watkins, R., Triner, D., and Kaufman, R. (1996). The death and resurrection of strategic planning: A review of Mintzberg's *The rise and fall of strategic planning. International Journal of Educational Reform, 5*(3), 390–393.

Watkins, R., Leigh, D., Foshay, R., and Kaufman, R. (1998). Kirkpatrick plus: Evaluation and continuous improvement with a community focus. *Educational Technology Research and Development, 46*(4), 90–96.

CHAPTER NINE

Analysis and More

Allison Rossett

Since the turn of the century, we have been confronted with new words and new expectations: *human capital, skill gap, war for talent, talent management, intellectual assets, competency management,* and *strategic impact,* among others. Whether you work in a school, a government agency, or a global pharmaceutical company, human capital management and people development are on your plate.

It is United States law, in fact. The United States Homeland Security Act of 2002, PL 107-296, mandated the establishment of a chief human capital officer in major government agencies. According to Friehl (2003), President Bush appointed Ronald James as the nation's first human capital officer for the Department of Homeland Security, the first government leader tasked with strategic responsibilities regarding talent, competence, and results. What will these new officers do? They will set workforce development strategy, assess worker needs, identify best practices, measure effectiveness, and develop a culture of continuous learning.

In the Center for Effective Performance May 2005 corporate newsletter, *Performance Edge,* Ann Parkman was quoted as follows:

> Accountability is a matter of growing importance in our industry. Training departments are being held accountable for the performance of employees and the resulting financial impact on the organization. It's up to the training director to be able to prove the ROI of training so that executives support future programs and can understand the value of training in business terms.

To develop a meaningful return on investment (ROI) for a program, Parkman stated that you must first have done the appropriate data collection on baseline performance measures. As she said in the February 2005 on-line newsletter, "This entails first conducting an analysis to determine the true measurable outcomes the program or course is intended to provide. The results of the analysis are then used to determine the ROI—or measurable business impact—of the effort."

That brings us to analysis. Analysis, in a nutshell, is the process used to figure out what to do. Chief human capital officers rely on it, as does each and every performance professional. It is how we look to many sources to establish direction for our efforts.

AN EXPANDING VIEW OF ANALYSIS: ANALYSIS AND EVALUATION

Here is one prevalent, current view of analysis, from a study conducted by Berk (2004, p. 36):

> Organizations provide the results of their learning analytics for many reasons. The most popular reason is to showcase the training's value to the organization. Another common reason is to indicate the quality of the training services provided. Additional reasons are because stakeholders request it or to justify large expenditures.

While we would never want to turn our backs on gathering data to make a case for delivering results, that is certainly not the only or even the best reason to perform analysis. The need reflected by respondents in the Berk study is omphaloskeptic. That is about our survival. It is driven by fear, not hope or strategy.

Opportunities for performance improvement abound. An Accenture (2003) study asked two hundred executives from companies in the United States, Europe, and Australia about their companies' top strategic priorities. The executives chose workforce-related priorities as four of the top five: these were "attracting and retaining skilled staff," "changing organizational culture and employee attitudes," "changing leadership and management behaviors," and "improving workforce performance." All of these priorities were chosen by more respondents than "industry consolidation," "cost reduction," and "competitive pressures." Three-quarters of responding executives reported that their companies had increased or maintained their human resource (HR) and training and development budgets over the past year. Of most concern, only 17 percent of the executives reported that they were very satisfied with the progress made on their training programs, and only one in four said they believed that most employees have the skills to execute their jobs at industry-leading levels.

What is to be done? For starters, it is critical to get a handle on what is needed, what is happening, what is not, and why. When more than half of the Accenture respondents say their companies never or rarely measure their training investments against employee retention, and slightly more than one-third said their companies never or rarely measure investments in human resources or training against customer satisfaction, there is much work to be done.

Parkman (Center for Effective Performance, 2005) urges data collection on baseline performance measures. This entails first conducting an analysis to determine the measurable outcomes the program or course is intended to provide. The results of the analysis are then used to determine the ROI, or measurable business impact, of the effort. Retention and customer satisfaction are likely to be high priorities.

We can and must do better. This can be achieved by using analysis to define and document meaning and need, to craft solutions systems, to intrigue people across the organization, and then to provide the basis for lean evaluation efforts and continuous improvement.

Table 9.1 compares analysis and evaluation. The contention here is that they are more similar than different. Sources, techniques, and approaches are the same, with the emphasis in analysis on what *ought* to be happening in means and ends and with more emphasis during evaluation on what has *already transpired*. Table 9.2 illustrates these ideas for an example of helping convenience store salespeople, after complaints and sales dips, to do a better job at customer service. For the front and rear end, the data gathering and gathered look much the same. What differs is the tilt and uses of the questions. The analyst will use the process to create the program. The evaluator will use it to make judgments and continuously improve the existing effort. In both cases, the professional uses data to enlighten the sponsor and enhance decisions. The most effective organizations will continuously ask and answer questions, gathering data and using those data to define possibilities and improve efforts. It is not so much a matter of first and last or front and rear; it's much more about being pervasive, applied, and transparent.

ANALYSIS GOALS AND REQUESTS

The overarching goal of analysis is to ascertain the attributes of excellent performance. Often the analyst must be both creative and persistent with clients in obtaining the necessary access and internal support to carry out a thorough analysis.

Table 9.1. Analysis and Evaluation: Close Kin.

	Analysis ← → Evaluation	
Purpose	*Planning* approaches	*Judging* approaches
Key questions	What *should* we do?	How *well* did we do it?
Why bother?	To get the right program in place for this organization at this time	To judge *existing* efforts, to determine what *has happened,* to continuously improve
From whom? From what?	Multiple sources, such as sponsors, best practices, customers, supervisors, experts, work product, results, and so on	Multiple sources, such as sponsors, best practices, customers, supervisors, experts, work products, results, and so on
How?	Review work products and the literature, conduct interviews or surveys, test, observe, conduct focus groups, and so on	Review work products and the literature, conduct interviews or surveys, test, observe, conduct focus groups, and so on
When?	Looking *forward*	Looking *backward* in order to go forward
Kinfolk	Defines and articulates promises about how things will change, get better	Determines if promises have been fulfilled and identifies opportunities to look once again, through analysis

Goals

1. Finding out the current status of performance from many sources, including sponsor, opinion leaders, published literature, job incumbents, content experts, supervisors, work products, records, and customers

2. Finding out what excellence looks like from these very same sources

3. Finding out why that performance is as it is, with an eye toward the individual and organizational factors that drive or impede performance

4. Tailoring approaches to the kind of request or requirement in the organization

Table 9.2. Analysis and Evaluation: Customer Service in Convenience Stores.

	Analysis ← →	*Evaluation*
Purpose	I've been asked to figure out how we should boost customer service in the stores across North America.	They asked me to look at the effectiveness of the current program, to judge where it is working and where not.
Key questions	Why tackle this now? What would it look like if we did this wonderfully well? What is our customer service message? Where are the opportunities to exercise great customer service? Where do we go wrong now? When it's great, why? When it isn't, why not?	How well did we execute the program, given the goals and objectives derived from the analysis? What are the reps' opinions about the customer service program? Are reps doing what is expected of them? What are the supervisors' opinions? What do they do? What do they fail to do? How does it affect our numbers? How does it affect customer satisfaction and purchases?
Why bother?	Yes, why? Where are we meeting goals? Where are we failing? Why? How can this program further strategic goals for the stores, such as an increase in purchases per visit?	How do we improve the program; boost service to customers; increase customer satisfaction, size of purchases, and repeat visits; provide data to direct improvement of the effort?
From whom?	Multiple sources, such as sponsors, best practices, customers, supervisors, published literature, and experts.	Multiple sources, such as sponsors, best practices, customers, supervisors, and experts.
How?	Review work products and the literature; conduct interviews, surveys, and focus groups; use secret shoppers.	Review work products and the literature; conduct interviews, surveys, and focus groups; use secret shoppers.
When?	Seven weeks before the program is launched, the analysis commenced.	As elements of the program are in place, data are gathered. A pilot is done in New England in six stores and customer satisfaction, supervisory checklists, sales, and secret shopper results are compared to matched stores in nonpilot regions.

5. Using what you find out in items 1 through 4 to plan solution systems and win organizational support

6. Using what you find out in items 1 through 4 to plan strategies to measure progress, judge worth, and continuously improve the effort.

Requests

Work does not always present itself as we might hope. The "ask" is often murky, vast, or trivial, and misconceived. That truth, however, does not give us permission to sniff or whiff at the opportunity. The sponsor has said, "We want a three-day class" or "Can you take this information-assurance course and put it on the Web?" or "I was thinking you could do something to increase ethics in our organization, maybe a half-day event to really rivet their attention." While every one of those "asks" begs for analysis and might even raise an eyebrow or two, they share a key attribute. They open the door. Each one enables professionals to look closer and determine sweet spots for performance improvement through analysis and evaluation. They also create an opportunity for customer education. Maybe the "ask" will be better next time, if the chief operating officer or vice president of sales have revelatory experiences.

Effective analysis and consultation depend on the questions we ask of sources (Block, 2000; Rossett, 1999). Sample sources are suggested in Table 9.2, for the customer service example. Questions, of course, are then linked to purposes: (1) defining that optimal or ideal state, (2) defining the actual or current state, (3) defining the drivers of performance or the barriers to that performance, and (4) then using what you have learned to conceive a solution system potent for individuals and the organization. More information about sources, questions, and stages is presented in Rossett (1999) and Rossett and Sheldon (2001), and about work with roots in Dewey (1933), Mager (1970), Tyler (1949), Harless (1970), Gilbert (1978), Kaufman and English (1979), Zemke and Kramlinger (1982), and Rossett (1987).

Figure 9.1 is a screen capture from a free Web tool (www.jbp.com/ rossett.html) that presents a sample analytical approach for the roll-out of a new automated ordering system. Note the stages, sources, and questions. When grappling with a roll-out, the introduction of some new idea or thing, the thrust of the effort is to figure out what "it" is, how the new system works, how it achieves critical goals, and how it meets the needs of people at work. Alternatively, Table 9.2 presented sources and approaches for a problem with customer service, when a professional looked to sponsor opinion, data on customer complaints, published literature, observations, and so on to figure out how to improve customer service in the convenience stores. Obviously, the place to start there was in defining the nature of the service problems and why they were happening. Solutions flow from there.

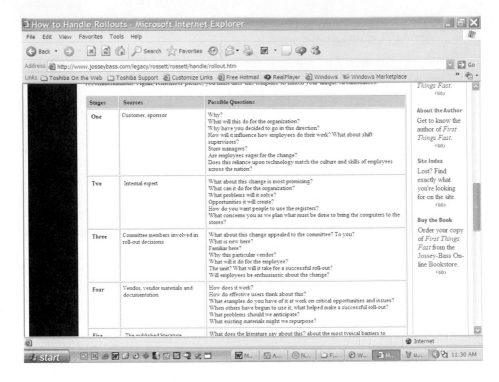

Figure 9.1. Analysis for a Roll-Out.

Let us look at yet another kind of requirement. Imagine that you are a new executive with responsibility for workforce development for a large, global petrochemical company. Nearly 1100 people worldwide sport titles that suggest they have substantial responsibility for learning and development. When you got the job, the chief operating officer said, "I want you to elevate the performance of our training people, or whatever you all are calling them this year. They have so many opportunities for offering great training now, what with technologies and all. Also, if someone in Asia Pacific does a great program, wouldn't it make sense to make that program widely available? Jobs are changing. We need best-in-breed practices here. What can we do to move that dispersed and diverse group forward?"

This is different from a request to bring a new system into play or to fix customer service problems. Here the focus is on a cohort of people and how to develop them in positive, nonspecific ways. Purposes are in play, as you can see in Table 9.3, based also on www.jbp.com/rossett.html but adapted to this broad tasking. Only the first stage of the analysis effort is shown here in Table 9.3. Subsequent stages of analysis would take this

Table 9.3. Analysis Questions for the Sponsor and the Chief Operating Officer.

Purposes	Source: Chief Operating Officer for a Petrochemical Company
Optimals	What do you envision these people will do over the next two, three, and four years? How is it different from what they do now?
Optimals	How do your expectations vary by geography?
Actuals	As you look at what your workforce learning professionals have been doing over the past year, what strikes you as positive, effective, and contributing to strategy? What concerns you? What demands improvement?
Optimals	Consider comparative global organizations. What are they doing in the arena? What kinds of programs catch your eye?
	I understand that you haven't looked at what is happening. Let me come back to you in a week with some descriptions and you can provide some reactions and guidance.
Drivers and causes	Why do you think that our people are not putting such programs in place? Do you think they know what to do? Do you think they know how to do it? Do we have the necessary technological infrastructure? Have we invested in their continuous development? Have we exposed them to best practices? Have we exposed them to clear expectations?
Drivers and causes	As we talk about shifting more to technology-based learning, I cannot help wondering how your professionals respond. Do you have any sense of that? Have any expressed eagerness to move in these directions?

professional to the literature, professional associations, and workforce learning professionals across the organization, to individuals identified as particularly effective, and to line-organization clients. Note that answers to the questions posed in Table 9.3 should eventually convert into measures for the executive and the learning organization, illustrating the neat link between analysis and evaluation.

OBSTACLES TO ANALYSIS

Blame It on the Organization

Most people work in organizations that take imperfect advantage of analyses and evaluations—organizations too often described as lacking in alignment. Symptoms of this problem are an array of initiatives issued by fiat and delivered by the training organization, with few discernible links to careers, competencies, conversations, appraisals, and, most important of all, results. Rossett and Czech (1996) found performance professionals disappointed in their organization's alignment and consistency. A few years later, Rossett and Tobias (1999, p. 37) found that 60 percent of professionals described their situations as "people across the organization come together to plan a solution system," with only 42 percent reporting that others in the organizations are comfortable when they bring people from different units together to plan solutions. Only 18 percent described their organizations as boundaryless. The study put an exclamation point on problems in the organization as performance professionals rely on analysis to play more strategic roles.

Blame It on the Executives

Saba CEO Bobby Yazdani (2004) put it like this in an article in *Chief Learning Officer* magazine:

> Change is continuous and rapid. Globalization and hyper-competition are having a profound impact on the ability of organizations to set and achieve long-term objectives on a sustainable basis. Due to these realities, management is challenged by limitations on the potential productivity of people, skills that are rapidly becoming obsolete and ongoing demographic changes in the workforce. Subsequently, executives have a renewed focus on the productivity and success of their employees.

That is the challenge and the opportunity. Executives are critical players. Alas, many fail workforce learning professionals, first through the initiating "ask," and then by not following up and aligning the effort. The Rossett and Tobias (1999, p. 36) study found that only 39 percent of responding professionals reported that "encouraging cross-functional solution systems" was typical of executives. And there is even more to ask of executives, from communicating clarity about expectations to establishing appraisal systems that link to strategy and learning to articulating a defined role for managers and supervisors.

Blame It on the First-Line Supervisors

Every effective analysis and evaluation should involve supervisors and managers in the mix. Why? They enjoy both proximity to the action and influence. Their view, words, and engagement are at the heart of transfer of training. In a comprehensive review of transfer into the workplace, Stolovitch (1997) emphasized the role of the supervisors. Do they second the message? Do they follow up with worked examples? Do they remind the employee why it matters? Do they help the employee anticipate where it is going to be difficult and suggest ways to work around the problems? When efforts result in little, often it is the first-line managers who failed to move outcomes forward. That is why it is important during analysis to determine their readiness, eagerness, and ability to be active in the effort.

Blame It on Ourselves

Analysis and evaluation occur, and their influence is less than desirable. When was the last time you were asked to do a substantive study before rolling out a program? When were you last asked to gather data to determine whether or how to tweak or applaud or terminate a program? Clearly, you cannot wait to be asked.

Rossett and Tobias (1999), in a survey of professionals attending International Society for Performance Improvement (ISPI) and American Society for Training and Development (ASTD) events, found that 62 percent used analysis to figure out what to do. While that is a substantial number, it is less impressive when viewed in light of the respondents. These are not random trainers; they are individuals attending professional conferences devoted to these concepts. Sugrue and Kim (2004) revealed a similar problem in ASTD's *The 2004 State of the Industry Report.* While 74 percent of respondents reported that they gather data on satisfaction, the numbers plummet for measurement of impact and results. Why?

Were analyses too lengthy or too perfunctory? Were results predictable? Were they vivid and substantiated? Were the solutions executable?

How about evaluations? Did a steady stream of data help managers and executives see into the organization and its performance? Were results actionable? Were they linked to what matters to managers and leaders, to outcomes, sales, errors, and customers? Do those to whom you are reporting perceive value, discuss it, and then elect to act on it?

Too often, the answers to these questions do not reflect well on us. What causes our failures? When we are successful, what has driven the good news? Table 9.4 reviews potential causes and uses our own technology to consider halting progress on analysis and evaluation. The causes and drivers listed in Table 9.4 would be relevant for thinking about customer service, leadership development, time management, software installation, or any problem or opportunity we might confront.

Each cause has solutions tailored to it. Table 9.5 makes the case, once again applied to our own performance, but with implications for every topic on earth.

Table 9.4. Performance Causes and Drivers.

Four Kinds of Causes and Drivers	Questions
Lack of skill, knowledge, or information	Do professionals know how to do analysis? Evaluation? Do they know where to seek information, how to gather it, and what to do with it, once it is in hand? Do they know how to adapt to changing circumstances? Are there examples to look at? Templates on which to rely?
Lack of motivation	Do professionals value analysis? Do they know why it is important to push back? Do they value evaluation and see good reasons for the effort? Do they feel confident that they know what to do and that doing it adds to professional prestige and influence?
Flawed incentives	What happens if professionals move in these directions? What happens if they do not? Are analysis and evaluation expected? Honored? Is this work included in appraisals? In career paths?
Flawed environment	Can professionals turn to examples, templates, job aids, and performance support tools to encourage their work in analysis and evaluation? Do supervisors and their efforts remind professionals that these activities are at the heart of professional practice? Do they themselves use these approaches?

TRENDS IN ANALYSIS

Data Hounds for Analysis and Evaluation

Perhaps the most telling trend is the one that rivets attention to data for analysis and evaluation. No doubt I am not the first who has noticed that front and rear activities grow ever more identified, as they should, and that data gathered in either cause is relevant for the other.

Some years back I visited a telecommunications company for curriculum specialists on analysis. After several days on that topic, conversation naturally moved to evaluation. "Didn't the evaluation data, in fact, provide grist for analysis too?" A manager walked me down the hall to a room chock full of gray cabinets. What do you think was in the cabinets? There were evaluations, tens of thousands of evaluations. While the organization just about always did evaluations that queried student satisfaction, the data being gathered meant just about nothing to the organization or its instructors.

Table 9.5. Causes and Solutions.

Causes	Interventions
Lack of skill, knowledge, or information	Education and training, in class and on-line
	Clarity about expectations
	Coaching, e-coaching, and mentoring
	Documentation, job aids, knowledge bases
	Communities of practice
	Performance support tools
	Captology
Lack of motivation	Education and training, in class and on-line
	Coaching, e-coaching, and mentoring
	Documentation, job aids, knowledge bases
	Communities of practice
	Performance support tools
	Captology
	Use of role models
	Early successes to instill confidence
	Participatory goal selection
Flawed incentives	Targeted policies
	Linked performance appraisals
	Development for managers and supervisors, and a defined role to play
	Incentives, recognition, and bonus plan
Flawed environment	Targeted hardware, software, tools
	Documentation, job aids, knowledge bases
	Communities of practice
	Performance support tools and captology
	Selection and job-person match
	Work and process redesign

A few years later, it was deja vu all over again when I visited a large government agency. There were lots of data, but no discernible impact.

Today, patience is wearing thin. Executives want to know what is happening and why. They seek targeted solutions resulting in tangible strategic benefits. They cannot have any of that without a steady stream of data from key sources.

Performance Consulting

Performance consulting and performance technology are not new to the profession. They have become the essence of the profession. Many forces have nudged performance forward and front and center, including a more robust ISPI, sturdy expansion for *Performance Express* (www.performancexpress.org), *Performance Improvement, HRD Quarterly,* and quickening interest in the Certification in Performance Technology (www.certifiedpt.org). When ASTD joined ISPI in offering that certificate, the trend become a force.

Ten years ago, performance technology was a good idea. Now it is a career path recognized, even expected, by the U.S. Coast Guard, the U.S. Navy, and IBM.

Converging Learning, Performance, and Work

- Does it make sense to send employees to a class to learn about their employee benefits, the features in a software package, or how to get around Bangalore?

- Should we rely on employee memory when critical, complex, or dangerous actions are involved in a lab, on an airplane, or in a nuclear plant?

- Should the organization invest in what it takes for employees to learn material by heart, especially when there is much to learn, the content changes often, a mistake is dangerous, and employees could and will take their expertise with them if they leave the organization?

- How often have you offered a course, on-line or in rooms, and then worried whether it would make any difference at all?

Surely these questions resonate. They are leading the profession to revisit old friends, documentation and job aids, and to consider new pals, performance support, workflow learning (www.internettime.com/workflow/intro_wfl.htm), and captology. (See edweb.sdsu.edu/people/ARossett/pie/index.htm for definitions.)

A customer service representative could not serve customers without a targeted Website. A real estate salesperson could not qualify customers without access to mobile data, materials, and rationale, all provided on his personal digital assistant. First-line supervisors schedule and improve their performance reviews by turning to their on-line tools. Uncle Harry tries to stop smoking again with support from QuitNet.com. What the employee or citizen needs in order to do the job is not necessarily in her or his brain. It is in the environment as a checklist, an on-line help system, a reminder, a database, an example, or even the supportive words of an on-line adviser or community. Support, learning, and work occur simultaneously and seamlessly. There's no need to worry about transfer; resources are within the context of work.

CONCLUSION

Technology, outcomes, competencies, results, accountability, systems, and *speed.* Today these are the words that buffet professionals in learning and performance improvement. Expectations are high, grow higher, and link us not just to learning but to what really matters—graduation rates, sales, safety, retention, and service. Meeting such expectations is the pivotal role we sought when we dubbed ourselves performance technologists, not trainers. The only way to play on that team, in that league, is with insights provided by analysis and evaluation.

References

Accenture. (2003, March). *The Accenture high-performance workforce study 2002/2003.* Retrieved January 9, 2005, from http://whitepapers.zdnet.co.uk/0,39025945, 60086430p-39000682q,00.htm.

Berk, J. (2004, June). The state of learning analytics. *Training and Development, 58*(6), 34–39.

Block, P. (2000). *Flawless consulting fieldbook.* San Francisco: Jossey-Bass/Pfeiffer.

The Center for Effective Performance. (2005, May). Return on investment (ROI), three words that strike fear in trainers: They don't have to if you have the right skills. *Performance Edge.* Retrieved February 12, 2005, from www.imakenews.com/ cepworldwide/e_article000281911.cfm?x=b11,0,w.

Dewey, J. (1933). *How we think.* Lexington, MA: Heath.

Friehl, B. (2003, May 13). Bush appoints his first human capital officer. *GovExec.com.* Retrieved March 11, 2005, from www.govexec.com/dailyfed/0503/051303b1.htm.

Gilbert, T. (1978). *Human competence: Engineering worthy performance.* New York: McGraw-Hill.

Harless, J. H. (1970). *An ounce of analysis (is worth a pound of objectives).* Newnan, GA: Harless Performance Guild.

Homeland Security Act of 2002. Pub. L. No. 107–296. Retrieved May 11, 2005, from www.access.gpo.gov/nara/publaw/107publ.html.

Kaufman, R., and English, F. W. (1979). *Needs assessment.* Englewood Cliffs, NJ: Educational Technology Publications.

Mager, R. M. (1970). *Goal analysis.* Belmont, CA: Pitman Learning.

Rossett, A. (1987). *Training needs assessment.* Englewood Cliffs, NJ: Educational Technology Publications.

Rossett, A. (1999). *First things fast: A handbook for performance analysis.* San Francisco: Jossey Bass/Pfeiffer.

Rossett, A., and Czech, C. (1996). They really wanna but . . . The aftermath of professional preparation in performance technology. *Performance Improvement Quarterly, 8*(4), 114–132.

Rossett, A., and Sheldon, K. (2001). *Beyond the podium: Delivering training and performance to a digital world.* San Francisco: Jossey Bass/Pfeiffer.

Rossett, A., and Tobias, C. (1999). An empirical study of the journey from training to performance. *Performance Improvement Quarterly, 12*(3), 31–43.

Stolovitch, H. D. (Ed.). (1997). Special issue on transfer of training-transfer of learning. *Performance Improvement Quarterly, 10*(2).

Sugrue, B., and Kim, K. (2004). *The 2004 ASTD state of the industry report.* Alexandria, VA: American Society of Training and Development.

Tyler, R. L. (1949). *Basic principles of curriculum and instruction.* Chicago: University of Chicago Press.

Yazdani, B. (2004, December). Managing people through learning. *Chief Learning Officer.* Retrieved February 12, 2005, from www.clomedia.com/content/templates/clo_feature.asp?articleid=739&zoneid=34.

Zemke, R. E., and Kramlinger, T. (1982). *Figuring things out: A trainer's guide to needs and task analysis.* Reading, MA: Addison-Wesley.

CHAPTER TEN

Requirements

The Bridge Between Analysis and Design

Ray Svenson

Our performance-improvement methodology requires that we conduct a performance analysis before we recommend and design a solution. This is true whether we are designing a simple learning module or a complex solution involving multiple components, such as training, feedback, consequences, processes, structure, staffing strategy, and so on.

Given this approach, how do we move from analysis to design and know that our design is appropriate, effective, and efficient? The best way to do this is to pause after the analysis and develop a set of requirements that the design must meet, get stakeholder acceptance of the requirements, and then evaluate and test the design alternatives against the requirements.

This is a best practice that is followed by architects and engineers for all kinds of systems, including buildings, computers, airplanes, refineries, and virtually any other product or system.

WHAT IS A REQUIREMENT?

A requirement is a technical statement about some attribute of the solution that can be validated and tested during design, development, and implementation. Requirements are derived from analysis data such as

- Performance-improvement opportunities or performance expectations for a new system

- Solution elements needed to achieve the performance-improvement opportunities or expectations
- Interfaces in the larger system to which the solution must be retrofitted
- Needs and wants of the stakeholders
- Geography: local, regional, national, and global
- Best practices for the class of indicated solutions
- Cost constraints and cost-effectiveness trade-offs

THE PERFORMANCE SYSTEMS ENGINEERING APPROACH USING REQUIREMENTS

The International Society for Performance Improvement Presidential Task Force report *Clarifying Human Performance Technology* (2004) produced the Performance Systems Engineering Approach (Figure 10.1).

If the solution is a simple one including only one element such as a training module, a job aid, or a feedback system, the process might look like Figure 10.2. Requirements play a role in each of the following steps:

- *Conduct analysis:* The analysis must be conducted in a way that elicits the data needed to formulate all of the requirements. More on this later.

- *Develop requirements:* In this step, the requirements are derived from the analysis data that was documented and reviewed with clients or stakeholders. More on this later.

- *Design the solution:* Here, one or more designs are created that satisfy the requirements, and one is chosen. More on this later.

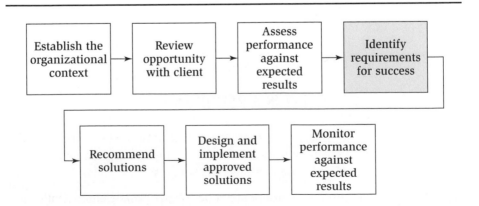

Figure 10.1. Performance Systems Engineering Approach.

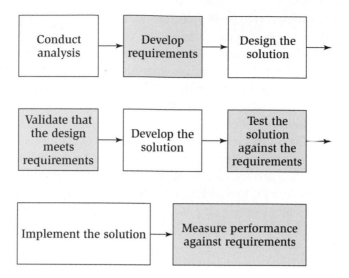

Figure 10.2. Simple Solution Example.

- *Validate that the design meets requirements:* Since we only have the design and have not yet developed the solution, it cannot be tested. Validation usually involves analyzing the design to make sure it meets requirements.

- *Develop the solution:* Develop the solution to fulfill the design with an eye always on the requirements.

- *Test the solution against the requirements:* With the solution in hand, it may be possible to test the solution against some of the requirements.

- *Implement the solution:* Pay special attention to the requirements when implementing the solution. The implementation monitoring system can be explicitly oriented to the requirements.

- *Measure performance against requirements:* The performance of the implemented solution should be measured against the requirements.

Naturally, there are feedback loops throughout this process. When it becomes apparent that the design, the developed solution, or the implemented solution do not satisfy the requirements, something must change. If the solution cannot be found that meets all requirements, then one set of requirements may need to be traded for the others. You can see that the requirements are the means of judging the design and carry all the way through to the final performance measurement. If the solution is a complex one with multiple elements, the requirements must cascade down to the elements.

Figure 10.3 shows a two-level solution. Many real solutions have three or more levels. The process for multilevel solutions is essentially the same as the simple, one-level solution in Figure 10.2. However, once we have an overall solution design, we must develop requirements for the solution elements and go through the same validation and testing with each element. Another difference in multilevel solutions is that the integrated design must be validated and tested against the requirements.

Requirements are even more important in multilevel solutions than they are in simple solutions. They are the major means of ensuring that when all the parts are put together, the interfaces will work and the overall solution will do the job.

In a multilevel solution in which different individuals or teams may be working on separate elements, there should be a system designer or system engineer

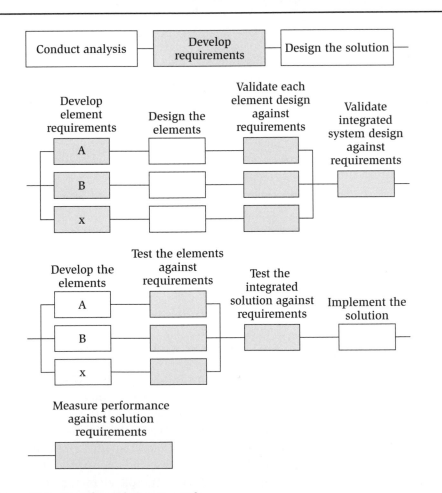

Figure 10.3. Complex Solution Example.

who owns the overall design and the cascade of requirements. The designers or developers of the elements work with the system designer to make trade-offs among the requirements where necessary and possible.

In a multilevel solution there should be top-down and bottom-up traceability of requirements. That is, the system designer should be able to look down from the top and see how the overall requirements will be met by the requirements at each level going down. The designer or developer at the lowest level should be able to look up the requirements cascade and see how meeting requirements at the bottom contributes to meeting requirements all the way up. Table 10.1 provides an example of a multilevel solution.

In this example, the highest level of requirements will be requirements for the entire sales training system. An example of a requirement at this level might be as follows: "The sales training system must enable new sales recruits to function independently as sales representatives within six months of being hired."

A related requirement at the next level for "curriculum" might be as follows: "The sales curriculum must contain the necessary learning experiences and certification tests to ensure that a new hire who meets the selection criteria specified in the performance model can satisfy the performance criteria, spelled out in the performance model, for independent performance as a sales representative."

Table 10.1. Multilevel Solution Example.

Level 1	Sales Training System			
Level 2	Performance Models	Curriculum	Training Organization	Support System
Levels 3, 4, 5 . . .	• Sales representative • Sales manager • Sales technical support	• Learning paths • Courses Modules Lessons	• Structure Instructional designer Instructor Media specialist Training manager • Processes Analysis Design and development	• Training center • E-learning system • Materials production

At the third level, a related requirement for the sales representative performance model might be as follows: "The sales representative performance model must spell out minimum selection criteria and minimum criteria for a sales representative to function independently." These requirements are in both vertical and horizontal alignment.

Categories of Requirements

Requirements come in many different categories. Following is a list of typical requirements categories.

- Functional or performance requirements
- Interface requirements
- Administrative requirements
- Best practices
- Geographical requirements
- Laws, regulations, policies, and standards
- Financial or resource requirements
- Aesthetic and cultural norms
- The "ilities"

The following paragraphs give a few examples of requirements in each category.

Functional or performance requirements are what the solution must accomplish. This is perhaps the most important category. Some examples of performance requirements include

- Reduce order-entry process or cycle time by at least 30 percent, from 1.5 hours to 1 hour.
- Reduce assembly errors for the motherboard assembly to less than one per thousand assemblies.
- Enable a learner to do x to y standard given z.
- Grow sales by at least 15 percent per year for the next three years.
- Recruit, select, and deploy enough qualified employees to meet the company's growth goals, including turnover replacements; quantitative requirements per population segment.

Interface requirements apply at the common boundaries with other systems with which the solution must interact; for example,

- The learning module must interface with
    Other modules in x curriculum
    The Learning Management System and Learning Content Management System

- The staffing process must interface with the training process, the performance-management process, the compensation process, and the career-and-succession-management process, and must use a job performance model and selection criteria shared with these other processes.

Administrative requirements derive from administrative policies, other rule sets, or administrative practices and preferences of the organization; for example,

- The solution must include automated daily, weekly, monthly, and yearly reports that provide

    Predictive performance measures

    Performance results for response time, unit cost, scrap, customer satisfaction, and production volume

    Workforce certification rates

    Workforce productivity

    System downtime and recovery times

- The solution must include self-managed work teams with a supervisory span of control to include at least three teams.
- The solution must conform to the existing union contract.

Best practices are proven design approaches or rules; for example,

- The solution must conform to validated best practices in instructional design.
- The solution must conform to accepted best practices in leadership development.

Geographical requirements derive from the geographical distribution of the organization's operations, customers, and employees; for example,

- The solution must be implementable globally.
- The curriculum must be translated into four principal languages and adapted to local practices in twenty-four countries.

Laws, regulations, policies, and standards are bodies of requirements that apply to the solution; for example,

- Equal Employment Opportunity (EEO) law and internal diversity policy
- Federal Aviation Administration (FAA) pilot certification requirements
- Internal instructional design standards

- Professional society standards
- Documentation standards

Financial or resource requirements provide financial and other resource constraints that must be met by the solution; for example,

- The cost to design, develop, and implement the solution must not exceed $5 million over the next three years.
- The benefit-cost ratio over three years must exceed 30:1.
- The solution must be implementable without adding staff.

Esthetic and cultural norms reflect practices and behavior constraints that fit "how we do things here." Examples of this category would include

- Trainees may not be off the job for training for more than two days at a time or more than six days in a calendar year.
- The solution must align with our policy of decentralized, operational decision making.
- The solution must be globally implementable in our four major business languages.

For the "ilities," some examples are

- *Operability:* the solution must be operable with our current talent mix.
- *Maintainability:* the system solution must be maintainable at less than 10 percent of initial cost per year.
- *Scalability:* the solution must be scalable to a business fifty times our current size.
- *Reusability:* the curriculum and courseware must be constructed of small, reusable modules or learning objects.

Deriving Requirements from Analysis Data

There are four parts to deriving requirements from analysis data.

1. Using requirements categories to shape the data collection and analysis
2. Deriving the requirements from the analysis
3. Reviewing all of the requirements for compatibility and making necessary trade-offs
4. Reviewing the requirements with stakeholders and clients for acceptance

Using Requirements Categories to Shape the Data Collection and Analysis. If you do not have the data, it is difficult or impossible to set good requirements. The best way to make sure you get the necessary data is to

- Review the list of requirements categories and decide which ones apply. Some of the requirements categories will almost always apply. For example,

  Functional or performance

  Interfaces

  Financial or resources

- Develop analysis questions and methods that will elicit the data you will need to formulate the requirements for each category.

Deriving Requirements from the Analysis. If you have used the requirements categories during analysis and paid attention to likely requirements while collecting and analyzing the data, the requirements writing step can be fairly easy. Following are some examples.

Example 1: Functional or performance. The analysis of an order-fulfillment process reveals opportunities that will make substantial performance improvement by redesigning the process. These include the potential to

- Shorten cycle time from five days to one day
- Cut errors from one per ten orders to one per one hundred orders
- Cut processing cost from $4.00 per order to $1.00 per order

The functional solution requirements practically jump out of this analysis.

Example 2: Interfaces. An analysis of a training and development system is conducted during the strategic redesign of the human resource development system. To meet the business goals of the company, it is revealed that training needs to have critical interfaces with the following other systems:

- Staffing
- Performance management
- Career and succession management
- Compensation and rewards
- The human resources information system
- The operational system in the workplace

The analysis further reveals critical attributes and opportunities at each of these interfaces that must be addressed to meet the needs of the business. Requirements are then written around the critical interface attributes and opportunities for each of these training system interfaces.

Reviewing All of the Requirements for Compatibility and Making Necessary Trade-offs. The initial requirements should be treated as a wish list. Often it is not feasible to simultaneously satisfy all of the requirements. For example, the functional process-improvement requirements suggest major improvements in cycle time, error rates, and cost per unit. However, achieving these new requirements may involve investing in technology that exceeds available resources. In this case, it is necessary to develop a set of performance requirements that can be achieved within the cost constraints or to offer multiple alternatives to the clients.

An important consideration here is to keep in mind that the compatibility of all of the requirements will be in question well into design and development and even implementation. Requirements must be reviewed for necessary trade-offs at all stages of the project, and clients must be kept informed of and approve the trade-offs. The final set of requirements after implementation may look substantially different from the initial requirements you derive from the analysis.

Reviewing the Requirements with Stakeholders and Clients for Acceptance. After the requirements are written, it is a good idea to review them and the analysis that produced them with clients and stakeholders. Based on this review, it may be necessary to adjust some of the requirements or add some new ones. This is an important validity-and-acceptability check. Similarly, as requirements are adjusted during design, development, and implementation, it is important to review the changes and their rationale with stakeholders and clients wherever possible.

THE VALUE OF EXPLICIT REQUIREMENTS

There are a number of ways that explicit requirements add value. Those associated with the processes of stakeholder approval, intervention design and development, and interventions are briefly discussed.

Stakeholder Approval

Analysts and designers often leave most requirements implicit. The more completely you can make them explicit and get stakeholder agreement before designing, the less rework or outright failure you will experience.

Get agreement from key stakeholders that the requirements are appropriate to the analysis findings and conclusions. Then, when your solution meets the requirements as you proceed through design, development, and implementation, everyone's needs should be satisfied unless the analysis was faulty. Explicit requirements help manage stakeholder expectations.

Design

Design could involve editing existing designs, combining existing design elements in new ways, or creating a major new design concept. In any case, there is never only one design that will meet the requirements. If you create a number of alternative designs, you can evaluate them against the requirements for best fit. This is usually an iterative process.

Development

The more measurable or testable your requirements, the easier it is to validate the solution for conformance and the less the risk of failure during implementation.

Implementation

The complete set of requirements gives you a way to measure implementation effectiveness, troubleshoot problems, and report payback for the solution.

EXAMPLES OF REQUIREMENTS FOR DIFFERENT KINDS OF PERFORMANCE SOLUTIONS

The examples provided in this section are incomplete by necessity. They are offered to demonstrate that the requirements approach works when designing and implementing any performance-affecting solution.

Instructional System Example

This example is an instructional system to train newly hired geologists and geophysicists for the exploration department of a major oil company. The entry trainees have master's degrees in geology or geophysics.

Level 1: The Exploration Training System

Functional: The trainees must be able to function independently within two years of employment following the standard exploration process and appropriately use all of the available best practices tools.

Interface: The training system must use the corporation's standard learning management systems and learning content management system.

Administrative: Trainees must not be away from their jobs for training for more than two weeks the first year and one week the second year; the remainder of the training must be on the job and related to real work assignments.

Best practices: The curriculum and training modules must be designed using the corporation's performance-based design and development processes.

Policies and standards: The standard exploration process, standard geologist and geophysicist responsibilities, and standard exploration tools must be incorporated.

Resource requirements: The training system may not add more than five additional employees.

Esthetics: The training system must be compatible with the independent learning style of geologists and geophysicists.

Maintainability: The training system must be easily updated to accommodate new practices, tools, and technology.

Level 2: The Exploration Curriculum

Functional: The learning paths through the modules must be flexible so that trainees can learn what they need to perform on their actual jobs at the time they need it.

Interface: The trainees and their on-the-job coaches must be able to use the learning management system to configure individual learning plans and track learning progress using the standard modules in the curriculum.

Level 3: Upside-Down Map-Reading Module

Functional: The trainee must be able to correctly read and interpret subterranean maps upside-down on a table while presenting results to a manager or project leader.

Interface: The module must be compatible with the learning content management system.

Organization Redesign Example

This example depicts the redesign of a product-development organization that is developing consumer electronics products.

Level 1: The Product-Development Organization

Functional: The organization must be capable of putting new products into commercial manufacture within twelve months of product conceptualization and approval to commence development.

Interface: Product conceptualization must be integrated between the product-development organization and the marketing organization with regard to product features, functionality, and cost.

Administrative: Product-development progress must be visible to management in marketing, sales, manufacturing, the supply chain, finance, and general management.

Best practices: Concurrent engineering practices must be incorporated.

Level 2: Product-Development Process

Functional: The process must be capable of meeting the twelve-month-cycle-time requirement.

Interfaces: The process must have approved interfaces with processes in marketing, manufacturing, materials, finance, and quality assurance.

Level 3: The Project Manager Job

Functional: The project manager must have control over the development resources assigned to the development team.

Interfaces: The project manager must have identified organizational interfaces within marketing, manufacturing, materials, finance, and quality assurance.

Qualification System Design Example

This example deals with the design of a new qualification system for operators and technicians on a major oil pipeline.

Level 1: The Qualification System

Functional: The qualification system must be able to qualify operators and technicians by testing actual or simulated performance on all critical tasks included in their specific job responsibilities against criteria established by acknowledged experts and agreed to by the company.

Interface: The qualification system must integrate with the operator or technician multilevel pay system; that is, technician pay grades must be linked to their level of qualification.

Administrative: The qualification system must be designed to be administered by the operator and technician community.

Best practices: The qualification system must be based on a detailed task analysis of each operator and technician role in each of the locations they serve.

Cost and resources: The development and implementation cost may not exceed $750,000, and the system may not add more than two employees to ongoing operations.

Level 2: The Testing System

Functional: All tests must be performance tests on critical tasks established through job analysis.

Interface: All tests must interface with the administrative system.

Administrative: Tests must be administered by a qualified evaluator.

Standards: All tests must conform to a standard test format.

Level 3: The Individual Test

Functional: The individual test must qualify the candidate by testing actual or simulated performance on one critical task, and satisfy established criteria for technical correctness, workmanship, and safety.

Administrative: The completed test must be signed and dated by the candidate and the evaluator and permanently filed in the administrative system.

Maintainability: Each test must be easily maintained for changes in technical content and performance criteria.

Usability: Each test must be easy to understand and use by the candidate and the evaluators.

Feedback System Example

This example is a feedback system for an assembly process in an electronics assembly plant.

Level 1: The Feedback System

Functional: The feedback system must provide real-time and trend-performance data on speed, quality, scrap, and downtime for the entire process and for each assembly step to management and to all personnel assigned on the assembly process.

Interface: The feedback system must interface with the plant information system.

Standards: The feedback system must be based on established process performance standards for the entire process and each assembly step.

Usability: The feedback data must be understandable and usable by management and by each person assigned to the process for analyzing and correcting performance problems.

Maintainability: The feedback system must be easily maintainable for changes in process performance standards, in the process and the product.

SUMMARY

Requirements are a valuable bridge between analysis and design. They are useful all the way through the design, development, and implementation processes to validate, test, and measure the efficiency of the solution to resolve the performance issues it was designed to address. Requirements are also a valuable asset for establishing client expectations and communicating with clients throughout the process. In addition, requirements are useful ingredients for bid specifications if all or parts of the solution design or development are to be contracted to third parties.

Reference

International Society for Performance Improvement. (2004). Presidential Task Force Report. *Clarifying Human Performance Technology.* The Report to the ISPI Board, March 31, 2004. Silver Spring, MD: International Society for Performance Improvement.

Additional Resource

An in-depth treatment of requirements for complex systems may be found in

CMMI Product Team. (2001). Capability maturity model integration for systems engineering/software engineering/integrated product and process development/ supplier sourcing, version 1.1. Pittsburgh, PA: Software Engineering Institute, Carnegie Mellon University. Retrieved May 11, 2005, from ftp://ftp.sei.cmu.edu/ pub/documents/misc/cmmi-beta/QA3-SE-SW-IPPD-Staged.pdf.

CHAPTER ELEVEN

Modeling Mastery Performance and Systematically Deriving the Enablers for Performance Improvement

Guy W. Wallace

The purpose of this chapter is to share an approach to developing quickly a consensus model of mastery performance and then systematically deriving the human and environmental enablers required to support that mastery performance. The model will also help in further assessing the importance and adequacy of the enablers for the current state, the future state, or both. The data allow one to determine which of the enabler gaps warrant closing based on the performance-improvement initiatives' projected return on investment (ROI).

This analysis approach is best used when some of the performers are already demonstrating high performance and others are not. Since 1982, I have used this evolving approach in over two hundred projects with Fortune 500 clients for instructional and noninstructional initiatives. I have trained and coached over 250 practitioners in the use of the application. Together, we have well over a thousand applications and a thousand stories to tell. In the course of such stories, one would discern much variation among these many practitioners in the exactness of the approaches used in both "modeling mastery performance" and "systematically deriving the enablers."

Modeling mastery performance is a robust approach; it is more about the data sets generated and less about the exactness of the process or method. I will cover the accelerated and other approaches to modeling mastery performance, and then will show how to systematically derive the enablers.

The chapter's content will start with an overview of the two major data sets of our focus, the "performance model" and the "enabler matrices," followed by an overview of the targeted usages of each in improving performance. Having completed the advanced organizer, the chapter then will move to the specific tools, techniques, and steps for generating the performance model and the enabler matrices data sets. Next, the two key teams needed to carry out performance modeling and enabler analysis efforts are explained, as are participant selection criteria and overviews of key roles in the analysis process. Finally, the chapter covers the potential impacts of the performance model and the enabler matrices data sets to the improvement requirements of an enterprise's targeted business processes as well as its processes for human-asset management and environmental-asset management.

Modeling mastery performance and systematically deriving the enablers generates data for use in downstream improvement efforts, including additional analyses, design, and development efforts.

INTRODUCTION TO THE KEY DATA SETS

The two key data sets are "performance models" and "enabler matrices." Respectively, they capture the model of mastery performance and the enablers of that mastery.

The performance model and the enabler matrices are two linked sets of data that are produced from the current-state view of master performers who have proven that high performance levels are attainable. The performance model and the enabler matrices can also be produced for a future-state view.

Performance Models

The performance-modeling process documents the requirements of the performers within the scope of the intended project and creates performance models. A performance model is the device used to capture ideal performance requirements. It is also used to document identified gaps from that ideal performance and their probable causes.

The performance model has two components: (1) areas of performance (AoPs), which are the segments of overall performance; and (2) enabler charts that capture the data details for each AoP segment (see Figure 11.1). Performance models may be developed for an organization, a function, a job, a task, or a process.

The information in a performance model includes a segmentation of overall performance into AoP segments, plus details regarding the expectations for outputs, their measures and standards, the tasks per output, and the roles and responsibilities per task for all involved performers. The ideal mastery performance is documented on the left side of the performance model chart. This information is then used to facilitate a structured and systematic gap analysis on the right side (see Figure 11.2).

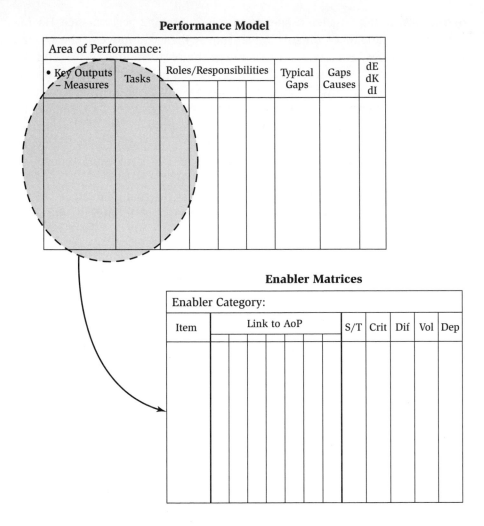

Figure 11.1. Deriving Performance Enablers.

The entire performance model data set, including the gap analysis data, is then used in analyzing and specifying both the human enablers and the environmental enablers that are necessary to achieve mastery performance.

Enabler Matrices

The enabler matrices document the human and environmental asset enablers required for mastery performance. "Human asset requirements enabler analysis" occurs when the requirements for the human assets are ascertained via a systematic review of the documented mastery performance outputs and tasks.

**The Most Convenient Stores
Store Management
Performance Model**

Area of Performance: A. Staff Recruiting, Selection, and Training

Key Outputs – Measures	Key Tasks	Roles/Responsibilities				Typical Performance Gaps	Probable Gap Cause(s)	dE dK dI
		1	2	3	4			
New staff hired - Timely - Qualified	Identify need for additional staff and complete internal paper work		✓	✓		Too few candidates	Poor recruiting Local economy Neglect to check references	dK dE dI
	Create and place local ads		✓				References do not provide key information	dE
	Select candidates for interviewing		✓			Poor choice		
	Interview and select candidates for offer		✓					
	Make hiring offer(s)		✓					
	Complete paperwork to fill the position		✓					

Role: 1 = District Manager
2 = Store Manager
3 = Assistant Manager
4 = Clerk

dE = deficiency – Environment
dK = deficiency – Knowledge or skill
dI = deficiency – Individual attribute or value

Key Outputs and Metrics or Measures: Describes what is produced from doing the job tasks and identifies key performance measures of each output

Key Tasks: Describes the key activities needed to produce the outputs

Deficiency:
dE = Environment
dK = Knowledge or skill
dI = Individual attribute or value

Probable Gap Cause(s): Identifies most likely causes for each typical performance issue or deficiency

Typical Performance Gaps: Identifies any typical ways the output or task does not meet performance standards

Roles and Responsibilities: Clarifies who is typically responsible for performing the tasks

Figure 11.2. The Performance Model Data Sets.

Human assets categories are

- Awareness, knowledge, skill
- Physical attributes
- Intellectual attributes
- Psychological attributes
- Personal values

"Environmental asset requirements enabler analysis" occurs when the requirements for all nonhuman assets are ascertained, again via a systematic review of the documented mastery performance. Environmental assets categories are

- Data and information
- Materials and supplies
- Tools and equipment
- Facilities and grounds
- Headcount and budget
- Culture and consequences

The systematic review of the data in the performance model charts facilitates the generation of the various enablers by enabler categories and their subcategories. For example, there are seventeen subcategories for the analysis of the "awareness, knowledge, and skill" category. These are displayed in Figure 11.3.

Later these captured data facilitate additional analyses. Examples include the validation of any complex interpersonal behaviors and root-cause identification for complex problem solving. These data can also be useful in assessing further the adequacy of enterprise support entities in the overall value chain in ensuring that the right human and environmental asset systems are available at the right place and at the right times to achieve and sustain peak performance.

Other Analyses Potentially Required

While it is my claim that the two sets of data in the performance models and enabler matrices are at the heart of analysis for any improvement effort, there are other analyses, such as financial, competitive, marketplace, strengths or weaknesses, opportunities or threats, legal, ethical, benchmarking, process mapping, activity-based costing, and so on, that may also be necessary at times.

1. Company Policies/Procedures/Practices/Guidelines
2. Laws, Regulations, Codes, Agreements, and Contracts
3. Industry Standards
4. Internal Organizations and Resources
5. External Organizations and Resources
6. Marketplace Knowledge
7. Product/Service Knowledge
8. Process Knowledge
9. Records, Reports, Documents, and Forms
10. Materials and Supplies
11. Tools/Equipment/Machinery
12. Computer Systems/Software/Hardware
13. Personal/Interpersonal
14. Management/Supervisory
15. Business Knowledge and Skills
16. Professional/Technical
17. Functional Specific

Figure 11.3. Enabler Analysis Categories for Awareness, Knowledge, and Skills.

INTRODUCTION TO THE DATA SET USAGES

The purpose of the analysis efforts of performance modeling and enabler analysis is to generate data and insights regarding performance-improvement potential and to assist in identifying the probable improvement levers. Performance-improvement initiatives can then be better planned, costs estimated, and the return on investment more accurately estimated before large investments in time and money are made.

Three Performance Variables That May Need Changing

With this approach, performance-improvement efforts take into account the following three major components of performance to leverage improvement:

- The process itself
- The enabling human assets
- The enabling environmental assets

The understanding of the ideal and actual for these three components is crucial, as any two or all three may be in need of improvement to leverage overall performance. These improvement levers are determined after the analysis has been completed and the ROI has been estimated for various improvement scenarios.

It may be that the process and human assets are fine, but if three-fourths of the performers lack one of the proper environmental assets, productivity will suffer. Imagine three-fourths of a company's loggers with dull saw blades due to budget constraints.

Process Design and Redesign

Process design and redesign are targeted at improving error reduction, cycle time reduction, and cost reduction. In other words, the goal is to be better, faster, and cheaper. Tools and techniques used in process design and redesign include process mapping, value stream mapping, statistical process control, process simplification, process automation, activity-based costing, and so on. Not all of the enterprise's systems or processes have to always be in tight statistical process control to produce the required outputs and deliverables necessary to achieve peak performance, but some do. Control will not make up for a bad business plan or reconcile with other conflicting goals within the enterprise. But it is still a critical component for actualizing the business plan. The stakes are high for high-impact processes, and the failure of a core business process is usually not a viable option, for it can result in the overall decline or death of the enterprise.

The performance model provides an illustration of both ideal process performance and actual process performance via its gap analysis, and can provide the basis for the targeting of improvement resources for various interventions, including design and redesign of the process itself. Either the process is designed to meet its current or future metrics, reflecting the balanced requirements of its many stakeholders, or it needs to be redesigned to do so. This is always the starting point: the process itself.

Human Asset Management Systems Changes

The human asset management systems (HAMS) provide the right human assets to the right processes at the right time and in the right quantity to enable the enterprise to operate at peak performance, as demonstrated by the master performers. Those HAMS are typically owned or shared with the human resources function and include

- Jobs and organization design systems
- Staffing and succession planning systems
- Recruiting and selection systems
- Training and development systems
- Appraisal and performance management systems

- Compensation and benefit systems
- Rewards and recognition systems

These human asset management systems must be aligned or realigned with the requirements of the enterprise processes and produce worthy outputs, as judged as appropriate inputs by the downstream customer and other process stakeholders. The HAMS are in place within the enterprise to ensure that human assets are in place with the following

- Awareness, knowledge, and skill
- Physical attributes
- Intellectual attributes
- Psychological attributes
- Personal values

Not all of the HAMS's processes have to always be in tight statistical process control to produce the required outputs and deliverables necessary to achieve peak performance, but some do. It is always situational.

Environmental Asset Management Systems Changes

The environmental asset management systems (EAMS) should provide the right nonhuman environmental assets to the right processes at the right time and in the right quantity to enable the enterprise process to operate at peak performance. If they do not, they will need to be improved to ensure that their own processes have the right human assets performing at peak levels and that they have the right environmental assets. The EAMS include

- Data and information systems
- Material and supply systems
- Tools and equipment systems
- Facilities and ground systems
- Headcount and budget systems
- Culture and consequence systems

Ownership of the EAMS varies to a much greater extent than for the HAMS. The ownership for the various types of data outputs, tangible and intangible, that become inputs further downstream is voluminous and is therefore difficult to ascertain quickly with 100 percent certainty. And not all of the EAMS's processes have to always be in tight statistical process control to produce the required outputs and deliverables necessary to achieve peak performance. The situation will again dictate what is necessary.

Next, we'll cover the process steps for producing our two data sets, the performance models and the enabler matrices.

THE PROCESS OF MODELING MASTERY PERFORMANCE

The process of modeling mastery performance involves first creating a segmentation of the overall performance and second, gathering and documenting details about each segment of performance.

In my experience, I have found it beneficial to model mastery performance in a group process in which eight to twelve master performers are brought together to generate a consensus model of mastery. It is best when the group is handpicked politically. This will be discussed in more detail later.

Establishing Areas of Performance

The first step of performance modeling is to establish the areas of performance (AoPs). AoPs can be one or both of the following: (1) "chunks" of the job, (2) "chunks" of the multiple enterprise processes within which most performers must perform. AoPs segment a job, process, or both for in-depth scrutiny. AoPs create a *systems* framework and frames of reference for all other data to be gathered and analyzed. Two examples follow; the first is an example of AoPs for a store manager at a convenience store (see Figure 11.4), and the second example is for an account representative (see Figure 11.5).

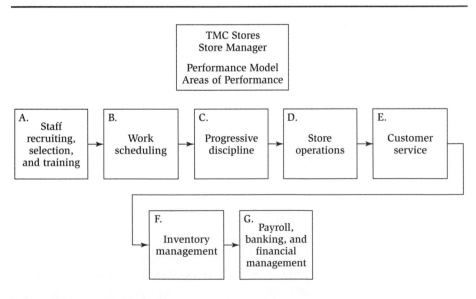

Figure 11.4. Areas of Performance for a Store Manager.

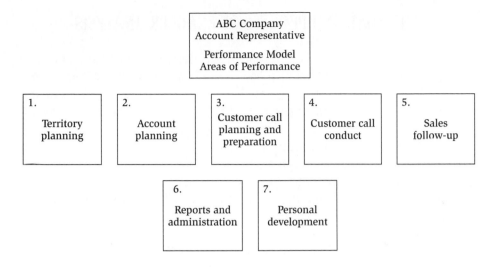

Figure 11.5. Areas of Performance for an Account Representative.

Creating Performance Model Charts

The performance model is created by obtaining the information described in the following lists and then documenting the answers on the performance model (see Figure 11.2).

The left half of a performance model chart describes *ideal* performance. This information includes

- The area of performance (AoP)
- Outputs produced and their measures, per AoP
- Tasks performed, per output
- Roles and responsibilities, per task

The information in the right half of a performance model chart captures and articulates *actual* performance via a gap analysis, and includes

- Typical performance gaps in which standards for measures at any level are *typically* not being met by job incumbents
- Probable causes of those typical performance gaps
- Differentiation of those probable causes into one or more of three categories of deficiency:

    dE: deficiency of environmental support

    dK: deficiency of knowledge and skills

    dI: deficiency of individual attributes and values

THE GOAL AND PROCESS OF ENABLER ANALYSIS

The goal of enabler analysis is to systematically derive the enablers of mastery performance and then document them on the enabler matrices. The enabler items captured are those that the analysis team of master performers and subject-matter experts (SMEs) believes lead to and enable mastery performance. These are enabler items that are not just *thought* to be needed but are *known* to be needed, by a consensus of master performers.

The enabler matrices link each enabler item back to the AoP or to the AoP output it enables as documented in the performance model. Thus, the performance model helps to ensure that the discrete enablers in the various enabler matrices are truly performance relevant.

Establishing Enabler Categories

The major categories for enablers are listed and defined in this section. Note that not all categories may be appropriate for your analysis effort, depending on the charter of your assignment and the intent of your project. It is better to adapt rather than adopt this listing for your situation. It is also good to gather only what you know you will definitely need downstream. Otherwise, you will be caught up in analysis paralysis; an attempt akin to boiling the ocean for a cup of tea.

Human Assets Categories. Awareness, knowledge, and skills come in many types and varieties. Further complicating the situation, one performer might need to be aware only of what other performers need to know, while another group of performers may need to obtain an actual skill level.

Physical attributes include factors such as the five senses: sight, hearing, touch, taste, and smell, as well as height, weight, strength, endurance, and so on. Psychological attributes include factors such as positive attitude, aggressiveness, risk taking, cautiousness, detail orientation, big-picture orientation, and so on. Intellectual attributes can include factors such as conceptual thinking, concrete thinking, strategic thinking, process thinking, and so on. Values can include customer satisfaction orientation, teamwork, diversity, fairness, honesty, work ethic, family, and so on.

Environmental Assets Categories. In performing their duties, job holders consume and use numerous information resources and tangible assets. These resources and assets are organized and disseminated through managed structures that have rules and regulations that govern their use.

- *Data and information:* include all of the work orders and instructions, the policies or procedures, and all data or information needed to enable job holders to perform

- *Materials and supplies:* provide all of the materials and supplies needed to enable job performance
- *Tools and equipment:* provide the tools, equipment, machinery, and vehicles needed to enable performers to perform at a level of mastery
- *Facilities and grounds:* provide the buildings, grounds, and facilities such as utilities for communications, power, water, and so on, needed to enable performance
- *Financial systems:* provide the capital and expense budgets and the headcount budgets to management, all of which are needed to enable and support job holders in performing
- *Culture and consequences:* provide and reinforce the enterprise cultural norms or goals, and all of the management reinforcements and extinguishments needed to encourage or discourage performance

Creating Enabler Matrices Charts

The process of systematically deriving the enablers uses a subset or adaptation of the list of predefined enabler categories and subcategories. Additional data points are gathered for each enabler item on the matrices (see Figure 11.6).

The data in the columns of the knowledge or skill matrix are best captured live by the facilitator, ideally during the same three-to-five-day meeting in which the performance model is built and with the same analysis team members. To develop enabler matrices, enabler items are identified via a review of each page of the performance model and then listed on the enabler matrices chart. Each enabler is linked back to each of the AoPs or outputs that it enables.

The *select and train* column on the human asset enabler matrices, for the awareness, knowledge, and skill category, which varies slightly from the other human- and environmental-asset enabler matrices, differentiates those items that are always attended to by the selection processes and not by the training processes. The analyst marks training items with a T and selection items with an S. The *criticality* column gives an assessment of the importance of the enabler item in terms of enabling mastery performance. The analyst marks each item as high (H), medium (M), or low (L) criticality as the analysis team consensus dictates. The *difficulty* column indicates how hard the analysis team assesses it will be for the typical targeted performer to grasp the awareness, knowledge, or skill related to this enabler item, or to otherwise acquire the attribute. The analyst marks each item H, M, or L. The *volatility* column is an assessment of the future amount of maintenance required by the enabler item. Volatility affects packaging, deployment, or distribution strategies for addressing the enabler gaps. The analyst marks this column H, M, or L.

The Most Convenient Stores
Store Manager
Knowledge/Skills Matrix

Knowledge/Skill Category: 1. Company Policies/Procedures

K/S Item:	Link to Area of Performance							Select and Train (S/T)	Criticality (H/M/L)	Difficulty (H/M/L)	Volatility (H/M/L)	Depth (A/K/S)
	A	B	C	D	E	F	G					
EEO	✗							T	H	M	L	K
Alternative action	✗							T	H	M	L	K
Vacation and day off policy	✗	✗	✗	✗				T	H	M	L	K
Discipline policy	✗		✗					T	H	H	L	K
Suspension procedure			✗	✗				T	H	L	L	K
Store hours policy	✗	✗		✗	✗	✗		T	H	L	L	K
Credit card sales procedure				✗		✗		T	H	L	L	K
New hire orientation procedure	✗	✗						T	L	L	L	K

Codes: Link to Area of Performance
A = Staff Recruiting, Selection, and Training
B = Work Scheduling
C = Progressive Discipline
D = Store Operations
E = Customer Service
F = Inventory Management
G = Payroll, Banking, and Financial Management

Depth of Coverage
A = Awareness
K = Knowledge
S = Skill

Criticality/Difficulty/Volatility
H = High
M = Medium
L = Low

AoP Link: Identifies the segment of the job or function where the knowledge or skill enables performance

K/S Item: Identifies the discrete knowledge or skill item

Depth: The level to which any training and development needs to go

Volatility: Ranks how often and significantly the knowledge or skill will change

Difficulty: Ranks how difficult the item is to learn

Criticality: Ranks the relationship between having the knowledge or skill and performance mastery

Select and Train: Denotes whether the item is a selection criterion or condition or whether it needs to be covered in training and development

Figure 11.6. Enabler Matrices Data Sets.

The final column on the human-asset enabler matrices, for the awareness, knowledge, and skill matrices, varies from the remaining human-asset matrices. Those for all of the environmental-asset enabler matrices indicate the depth needed by the HAMS within their systems or processes to ensure that the enabler item is sufficiently addressed. The analyst and team may decide that the appropriate depth is at the awareness level (A), the knowledge level (K), or the skill level (S) for the awareness or knowledge or skill category and H, M, or L for the other human-asset categories of physical attributes, intellectual attributes, psychological attributes, and personal values; and the same applies for all of the environmental asset categories. The data are then documented as appropriate for their downstream use.

THE PARTICIPANTS OR TEAMS AND THEIR ROLES

Rather than individual interviews or observations, a team approach to conducting the analysis efforts of modeling mastery performance and systematically deriving the enablers not only saves time but also creates ownership of the results by the participants. However, some situations do not lend themselves to assembling a group of master performers and others for a three-to-five-day meeting. The nonteam approach is discussed at the end of this section. In thinking about the nonteam approach, imagine the analyst doing all of the work of the analysis team alone as described later on. Furthermore, think about the analyst then having to sell the draft analysis outputs and conclusions to management and other key stakeholders, one person at a time. And then, imagine iterating through that process several times in an attempt to reconcile to everyone's satisfaction the specific words used. In short, it is best to choose the team approach when feasible.

The Team Rationale and Approach

The personal witness of most observers concerning what happens in the real world is quite often neither accurate nor deep enough. Many peers and clients have found that too often too partial a view is produced, informed more by the observer's ignorance than knowledge of the total performance context, the players, the rules, and the decision-making rubrics. This is especially a concern in complex situations.

The observation and documentation of the steps in the conducting of a credit card transaction by a cashier, for example, are not very complicated. However, much more complex are observing and documenting the activities of a product team leader who is facilitating a diverse team that is producing a business case and new product-development plan for eventual investment of $3 billion in a new automotive truck platform, then managing this team as well as additional teams through the implementation of the plan. Observing the latter example is very impractical if not almost impossible. And in reality, no one individual has all the information and insight for such complex cases. Furthermore, individual perceptions will differ depending on the knowledge and experience of the observer. If a mix of participants is involved in the analysis processes, group synergies will evolve, resulting in much greater detail and more accuracy than is feasible with a single observer.

If the participants are all credible and recognized as master performers, and they are selected based on their demonstrated abilities in meeting the appropriate business metrics for their roles, the resulting analysis data sets that are produced by their team will be credible. Who else would possibly know what complex mastery performance is, other than those who do it and demonstrate their mastery consistently? Also, who could credibly challenge one master performer's view other than another master performer?

However, it must be acknowledged that complex interpersonal behaviors may require additional validation for some downstream improvement efforts such as in training and development. It is true that individual master performers are often at a loss in explaining what they do. They tend to perpetuate myths garnered from their community of performers or from their own personal reflections on their performance. However, when they are put into a group process with their peers, with the direction of a good facilitator who knows how to both control and use those big egos in the room, a very rich, organized, and detailed picture of performance emerges. Furthermore, the creators of the picture increase their level of buy-in and ownership at each step of its development.

Any additional analyses, observations, and validations necessary can happen in the follow-up projects to design and develop the various interventions specified in the solution set. Significant improvements rarely involve one-dimensional solutions.

In creating the teams, it is important to ensure a diverse team of participants at two levels. A project steering team (PST), named appropriately to its task, should be formed to address the improvement effort from the business perspective, representing the enterprise's key management and stakeholders. An analysis team should be formed, handpicked by the PST, to include both master performers and SMEs.

Master performers are experienced in the very process context, rules, tasks, and knowledge of other players involved in the enterprise processes being targeted for improvement. SMEs are those who are knowledgeable in the theory of the process and tasks or some relevant enabler for it, but do not *do it* in their current job assignment.

Additionally, your team might benefit from involving supervisors, managers, and perhaps novice performers. While master performers are important because they have years of experience and understand the intricacies of performing the tasks on a daily basis, novice performers might be important to the team precisely because the tasks were recently new to them. Their perspective will often differ from older and wiser master performers as to what is needed and when.

Project Steering Team

Arguably the most important of the two teams is the project steering team (PST). It is composed of customers and other key stakeholders. The keys are recruiting, organizing, and communicating with the PST leader and its members. The successful selection and formation of the PST ensures better communication with the members both individually and collectively regarding project activities and results. PST members are charged with carefully considering the requirements of the project and then selecting members for the analysis team, assuming they don't kill the improvement initiative. After all, it is still a business decision to pursue improvement. Also, the project steering team is typically responsible for

- "Owning" the project
- Reviewing the project plan and directing the project
- Reviewing and providing feedback for all project documents and outputs
- Approving or redirecting the implementation plan
- Selecting all participants for subsequent or downstream phases of the performance-improvement project

The project manager uses the PST to test ideas and obtain sanctioning for all project activities. The members of the PST meet on a planned basis to review, debate, challenge, and modify the project plan. Ideally, the PST is composed of members who have a significant stake in the outcomes or processes for conducting the improvement project. Often, the most important role on the PST is that of chairperson.

The PST chairperson often becomes the owner of the project, the person with ultimate responsibility and accountability for making improvement happen. The project steering team chairperson is the key customer and interface with stakeholders. Early in the project, the chairperson provides key input for the development of the project plan and helps to identify other individuals who should be engaged up front in the conduct of the project.

In selecting candidates for the project steering team, a general rule is to identify individuals who might come forward at some later stage of the project and question or take exception to what is occurring. It is better to have sought their participation on day one of the project than to have these individuals raising questions or being nonsupportive at later stages of the project. Having them join the project after it is under way is less than ideal.

How many members should be on the PST? Generally, with fewer members, things move faster. However, with more members, there is less likelihood that any one individual could negatively influence the project, and a greater shared understanding can be achieved among diverse stakeholders regarding facts, opinions, biases, and so on. The number is a balancing act. Too few can be problematic, as can too many.

Establishing a formal PST ensures that key stakeholders "buy in" to the project plan politically, that it makes business sense, and that the outputs and planned tasks will be supported during and after the project. Having the PST members handpick all other team members goes a long way toward ensuring that the outputs produced by the various teams have credibility and political acceptability. That is extremely important because the data to be produced are voluminous, and the PST will be probably not be able to do a thorough review. They will need to rely on the inputs of others, the handpicked master performers. For them to choose people they have confidence in is akin to the idea that it is better to build in quality early than to attempt to inspect it in later. The PST is empowering that analysis team.

Analysis Team

The analysis team is used to define performance requirements and the enablers. The key responsibilities of the analysis team are to

- Provide input in analysis meetings regarding the missions, key outputs and metrics, tasks, and roles and responsibilities of ideal performance
- Provide input in the analysis meetings regarding the typical gaps in performance, such as outputs not meeting targeted metrics, as well as probable causes of the gaps and an assessment of the root causes
- Provide input in the analysis meetings regarding all human and nonhuman enablers required for mastery performance

The analysis team typically has between six and twelve members. Eight seems to be the best number. Fewer than six sometimes negates the team approach, and more than twelve becomes unwieldy in group forums. Ideally, the PST handpicks members of the analysis team, seeking

- Mastery of performance
- Credibility with the project steering team
- Credibility with the target audience they represent

The analysis team should be composed of members who can articulate and come to a consensus regarding the performance requirements of the job, task, or process. Collectively, team members will know the key enabling factors that affect their and others' performance. Individual members will themselves be master performers or subject-matter experts.

Individual master performers are known for their current expertise in today's performance situation, not the knowledge they had three years ago before they took a headquarters staff job. They have good reputations and are credible with their management and peers. They are often called on to help others who are in trouble in the organization. They are often peer coaches for the organizations' novices. They usually have strong egos and strong personalities, and facilitating them can often be a challenge for the meeting facilitator. These challenges need to be met, because the master performers' participation and input are critical to the success of the analysis effort.

Subject-matter experts are people who know a great deal about some aspect of the job or are knowledgeable about relevant issues, procedures, policies, tools, or problems. SMEs most often are knowledgeable about some aspect of performance, but not all of it. Typically they are not master performers unless they just recently have been performing the targeted performance to a level of mastery as recognized by the organization and their peers. SMEs often do *not* really know how to get the job done when faced with today's real-world barriers and issues, when to do a workaround, or when and how to plow right through barriers.

Downstream Teams for Performance-Improvement Design and Development

There are other teams that may be involved downstream of the up-front analysis effort. Often they include

- Design teams
- Development teams
- Pilot test teams
- Roll-out teams

The Nonteam Approach

As the goal is to capture consensus data, a nonteam approach involves interviews, observations, and then documentation of findings in a first draft report. Then a redo loop of reviews with the sources begins. This process is repeated until you achieve a consensus or run out of time and resources. It is much faster and easier, and perhaps even less expensive, to bring all the right people together in a team approach to create and approve the data sets.

THE IMPACT OF THE DATA ON THE ENTERPRISE PROCESSES

The impact on the enterprise processes from the data sets generated can be very specifically targeted. Again, there are three areas to consider for improvement:

- The process itself
- The enabling human-assets systems
- The enabling environmental-assets systems

Process Design and Redesign

Process design and redesign are targeted at improving one or more of the following: error reduction or elimination, cycle time reduction, and cost reduction. Tools and techniques used in process design and redesign include process mapping, value stream mapping, statistical process control, process simplification, process automation, activity-based costing, and so on. The goal is to simplify without increasing short-term or long-term negatives in either costs or cycle times.

This is done for the targeted process or processes deemed needful of improvement, *and* for those upstream value stream processes that also need to change and improve for the benefit of the downstream, targeted process. Those upstream value stream processes can and do include the HAMS and the EAMS.

The Impact of the Data on the Human-Asset Management Systems

The lack of any of the following enablers in the enterprise processes will typically be due to a failure of the human-asset management system:

- Awareness, knowledge, skills
- Physical attributes
- Psychological attributes
- Intellectual attributes
- Values

These human factors and enablers need to be present to some degree to meet the specific process needs. Meeting these needs helps manipulate the environmental factors and enablers, which in turn help to produce the desired outputs. These outputs are inputs to some downstream processes, including the process being targeted for improvement efforts. A potential "root cause" when any single HAMS process is deficient is that its own processes, that is, its HAMS and EAMS processes, or a combination of these, are themselves deficient. Again, the HAMS are

- Organization- and job-design systems
- Staffing and succession systems

- Recruiting and selection systems
- Training and development systems
- Performance appraisal and management systems
- Compensation and benefits systems
- Rewards and recognition systems

The human-asset management system places humans into processes in concert with the process needs. The performance model will be our first clue that improvement may be needed in the HAMS.

Organization- and Job-Design Systems Changes. The organization and job-design and redesign systems provide a set of job designs and organizational systems that are conducive to the needs of the process in its current and future volume. They are configured for the abilities and capabilities of the human performers who will be selected into those jobs, given the enabling environmental support available in the locations where the performers will perform. Data from the performance model that would suggest that there might be a need for a follow-up improvement effort include environmental deficiencies (dEs) on the performance model suggesting task overlap or gaps with other jobs, teams, and so on; lack of role clarity; or lack of clear expectations. The system would use the performance model and its data structure to document the process outputs for job, team, department, and function definitions and designs.

Staffing and Succession Systems Changes. Staffing and succession systems provide the strategies, plans, and mechanisms for staffing-plan development and succession strategies, plans, and mechanisms necessary to populate the organization's jobs with people in an efficient manner, providing career and growth opportunities where feasible. Data from the performance model that suggest that there might be a need for a follow-up improvement effort include dEs on the performance model suggesting lack of time whose root cause may be the lack of people, staff, and resources, or knowledge, and skill deficiencies (dKs) on the performance model in combination with dEs suggesting that the learning curve is steep for new performers.

Recruiting and Selection Systems Changes. The recruiting and selection systems provide the strategies, plans, and mechanisms for first recruiting and then selecting the best candidates in the right quantities, consistent with the staffing and succession plans, and populating the organization's jobs. Data from the performance model that would suggest that there might be a need for a follow-up improvement effort include dKs on the performance model suggesting that performers in the job are not competent in specific aspects of the job due to current knowledge or skill competence. New-to-the-job staff members, including those from external sources and from internal promotions and other internal personnel movements, either come up to speed in a reasonable time, or they do not. It might be the people selected for the job who do not have the capacity to acquire and use the new skills or perform using the correct interpersonal behaviors in complex situations.

Training and Development Systems Changes. The training and development systems provide the strategies, plans, and mechanisms to train and develop the new hires and incumbents consistent with performance requirements in the organization's jobs, as they have been designed. Data from the performance model that would suggest that there might be a need for a follow-up improvement effort include dKs on the performance model suggesting lack of knowledge and skill.

Performance Appraisal and Management Systems Changes. The performance appraisal and management systems provide the strategies, plans, and mechanisms for appraising the job task performance and managing of problems and opportunities, as appropriate and consistent with laws, regulations, codes, and enterprise policies or procedures. Data from the performance model that would suggest that there might be a need for a follow-up improvement effort include dEs on the performance model suggesting lack of timely feedback.

Compensation and Benefits Systems Changes. The compensation and benefits systems provide the strategies, plans, and mechanisms to ensure that the total pay and benefits attract and retain competent staff appropriate to the various labor markets for the various locations of enterprise operations, and are consistent with laws, regulations, codes, and labor contracts as well as enterprise policies or procedures. Data from the performance model that would suggest that there might be a need for a follow-up improvement effort include dEs on the performance model suggesting turnover whose root cause may be the lack of timely feedback or unfair evaluations or rewarding of others.

Rewards and Recognition Systems Changes. The rewards and recognition systems provide the strategies, plans, and mechanisms for providing nonmonetary and small monetary rewards and recognition to appeal to the ego needs of staff that are consistent with laws, regulations, codes, and labor contracts as well as enterprise policies or procedures. Data from the performance model, enabler matrices, or both that would suggest that there might be a need for a follow-up improvement effort include dEs on the performance model suggesting lack of rewards and positive consequences for performance to standards, or individual attribute and value deficiencies (dIs) on the performance model suggesting that the individuals are not motivated enough by the available reward system.

The Impact of the Data on the Environmental-Asset Management Systems

Processes must have a balance between human assets and environmental assets. These two complementary sets of assets need to be in place to ensure value-adding processes. Human assets work with or manipulate the environmental assets in order to *process* an output. One cannot effectively improve human assets without an understanding of the environmental factors in which humans perform. The lack of any of the following enablers in the enterprise processes will typically be due to a failure of the environmental-asset management system (EAMS):

- Data and information systems
- Materials and supplies systems
- Tools and equipment systems
- Facilities and grounds systems
- Financial systems
- Culture and consequences systems

Data and Information Systems Changes. The data and information systems provide all of the work orders and instructions, the policies and procedures, and all of the data or information needed to enable job holders to perform at a level of mastery. Data from the performance model that would suggest that there might be a need for a follow-up improvement effort include dEs on the performance model suggesting lack of information or data, poor timeliness of the data, or erroneous data.

Material and Supplies Systems Changes. The materials and supplies systems provide all of the materials and supplies needed to enable jobholders to perform at a level of mastery. Data from the performance model and enabler matrices that would suggest that there might be a need for follow-up improvement efforts include dEs on the performance model suggesting lack of adequate or correct types of materials or supplies.

Tools and Equipment Systems Changes. The tools and equipment systems provide the tools, equipment, machinery, and vehicles needed to enable jobholders to perform at a level of mastery. Data from the performance model and enabler matrices that would suggest that there might be a need for a follow-up improvement effort include dEs on the performance model suggesting lack of adequate quantities or quality of tools, equipment, machinery, vehicles, and so on.

Facilities and Grounds Systems Changes. The facilities and grounds systems provide the buildings, grounds, and facilities or utilities for communications, power, water, and so on needed to enable jobholders to perform at a level of mastery. Data from the performance model and enabler matrices that would suggest that there might be a need for a follow-up improvement effort include dEs on the performance model suggesting lack of or inadequate performance setting and environment such as proper lighting, temperature, air quality, storage, and so on.

Financial Systems Changes. The financial systems provide the capital and expense budgets as well as the headcount budgets to management that are needed to enable and support jobholders in performing at a level of mastery. Data from the performance model and enabler matrices that would suggest that there might be a need for a follow-up improvement effort include dEs on the performance model suggesting lack of staff or budget, or dKs on the performance model whose root cause would be lack of budget resources or time for training.

Culture and Consequences Systems Changes. The culture and consequences systems communicate and reinforce enterprise cultural norms and ensure that all of the management reinforcements and extinguishments needed are in place to encourage or discourage jobholders and enable them to perform at a level of mastery. Data from the performance model and enabler matrices that would suggest that there might be a need for a follow-up improvement effort include dEs on the performance model suggesting lack of any or enough rewards or positive consequences for performance to standard as well as real or imagined punishment for doing the work to standard. Other problems would be tolerance by management and peers for inappropriate or poor performance.

SUMMARY

The intent of this chapter is to share a proven approach for quickly developing a consensus model of mastery performance and then systematically deriving the human and environmental enablers required to support that mastery performance, the end purpose being the development of the performance model to assess the adequacy of an organization's current state, future state, or both. The process involves two key data sets: performance models and enabler matrices. Respectively, they capture the model of mastery performance and the enablers of that mastery.

The performance model and the enabler matrices are two linked sets of data that are produced for the current-state view by current master performers who have proven that high performance levels are attainable. Three performance variables are affected:

- The process itself
- The enabling human assets
- The enabling environmental assets

Key players and teams that are essential to the process are the project steering team, which is formed to address this improvement effort from the business perspective, and an analysis team that includes both master performers and subject matter experts. The players in these teams, with the models and data that they produce, can undertake performance-improvement initiatives that are cost effective and will yield a return on investment. This will help organizations to be competitive in today's global economy.

Resources

Rummler, G. A., and Brache A. (1995). *Improving performance: How to manage the white space on the organization chart.* San Francisco: Jossey-Bass.

Smith, K. R. (2001, Summer). On watch from the bridge. *Pursuing Performance, 4*(2), 4–5. Retrieved October 17, 2005, from www.eppic.biz/resources/res_newsletters.htm.

Smith, K. R. (2002, Spring). Laying the foundation for great human asset management systems (HAMS). *Pursuing Performance, 5*(1), 41–43. Retrieved October 17, 2005, from www.eppic.biz/resources/res_newsletters.htm.

Svenson, R. A., Kennedy, K. M., and Wallace, G. W. (1994). *The quality roadmap.* New York: Amacom.

Wallace, G. W. (2000). *Lean-ISD.* Naperville, IL: CADDI Press.

Wallace, G. W. (1999–2000, Winter). The AoP framework for management. *Lean-ISD, 3*(1), 1, 7–9. Retrieved October 17, 2005, from www.eppic.biz/resources/res_newsletters.htm.

Wallace, G. W. (2000, Fall). T&D systems view: 10 and 11 o'clock. *Lean-ISD, 3*(4), 19–22. Retrieved October 17, 2005, from www.eppic.biz/resources/res_newsletters.htm.

Wallace, G. W. (2000, Fall). Human asset management planning and management. *Lean-ISD, 3*(4), 27–28. Retrieved October 17, 2005, from www.eppic.biz/resources/res_newsletters.htm.

Wallace, G. W. (2000, Winter). Environmental asset planning and management. *Lean-ISD, 3*(5), 41–43. Retrieved October 17, 2005, from www.eppic.biz/resources/res_newsletters.htm.

CHAPTER TWELVE

Dimensions of Organizational Change

Larissa V. Malopinsky, Gihan Osman

The ability to change and innovate becomes an organization's competitive advantage in today's business world. Today, thinking strategically and developing capabilities for managing change within the specific organizational context are considered critical competencies both for middle and senior-level management and for human performance technology (HPT) professionals. Organizational change can happen at different levels and can take various forms. Organizations may initiate massive redesign of organizational structures and processes, or take incremental, evolutionary steps in attempts to find new directions and opportunities. Change can be strategically planned, or it can come as a reaction to unexpected external factors. Regardless of the form and cause of change, it is a complex, multidimensional process that requires collaborative efforts of executives, management, and human performance consultants who accept the challenging role of change agents in order to lead their organization through the pitfalls of the change process.

HPT professionals are actively involved in all stages of planning and implementing change initiatives, through conducting organizational analyses and identifying performance gaps, designing and managing change process, evaluating organizational performance during change implementation, communicating change-related strategic decisions to various organizational levels, and supporting individual members of an organization in challenges of change adoption. Therefore, it is critical that human performance technologists understand all aspects of the change process and develop strategies, methodologies, competencies, and skills necessary for becoming effective change leaders. The major domains of change agent expertise include

- Understanding the nature of change and its potential impact on organizations and their members
- Performing organizational diagnosis and making conclusions about compatibility of the proposed change with a company's culture, strategic goals, available resources, and business context
- Assessing organizational readiness to change and making strategic decisions regarding the scope and timelines of planned change projects
- Developing change-implementation plans and evaluation methods for assessing organizational performance during a change process
- Understanding the nature of resistance to change and individual change-adoption rates in order to develop support structures that would address informational, educational, and performance needs of all those affected by the change process

This chapter discusses these domains in some detail, emphasizing their relevance and specific application in organizational contexts, and offers strategic advice to those leading organizational change efforts.

UNDERSTANDING ORGANIZATIONAL CHANGE

Defining Organizational Change

The concept of organizational change assumes a fundamental organizationwide transformation that an organization undergoes in response to a changing environment, as opposed to minor organizational adjustments such as adding new personnel, modifying a specific program, or introducing a new technical procedure. Organizational change typically has an impact on organizational mission and vision, and involves restructuring of main operations, mergers and acquisitions, implementation of new technologies that affect all organizational levels, and new programs and tools such as total quality management or Six Sigma (Johansson, McHugh, Pendlebury, and Wheeler, 1994; Schermerhorn, Hunt, and Osborn, 2003).

Organizational change is usually caused by some major environmental factors or internal driving forces, such as changing markets, globalization, transition to a different product line, or a new organizational leadership. Today's organizations require employees to demonstrate ability to learn in a complex and dynamic working environment, and achieve success while experiencing stress and uncertainty accompanying continuous change (Pettigrew, Woodman, and Cameron, 2001; Schermerhorn, Hunt, and Osborn, 2003). Organizational performance specialists view change as an opportunity for learning and sharing new concepts and organizational practices.

Why Do Organizations Change?

Today's organizations are experiencing massive pressure to achieve performance and constantly innovate in highly unstable economic, political, and social environments. Rapid technological developments, increasing cost of natural resources, emergence of new international economic spheres, and an aging population are some of the factors that determine process innovation and change in organizations (Doppler and Lauterburg, 2001). While rapidly changing environments present new business opportunities for organizations, they also bring high risks. To survive and stay competitive, organizations and their members must react quickly to new environmental trends and be able to adapt to changing conditions quickly.

Forms of Organizational Change

Organizational change can be characterized from the following perspectives: (1) level of change: transformational versus incremental, (2) mode of change: proactive versus reactive, and (3) control of change: planned versus unplanned.

Level of Change: Transformational and Incremental. Some of the organizational change movements can be described as transformational or systemic change, resulting in a radical shift in organizational strategy including mission and vision, underlying values and beliefs, and transformation of organizational structure and its major components. Transformational change is often initiated by a critical event in the life of an organization, such as leadership change brought about by merger or acquisition or a failure in operating results. Since transformational change hits key functions in an organization, it requires the consultancy of change agents who can objectively assess how the proposed changes affect different levels and components of the organization. Change agents also provide plans for addressing the implications of those changes to help organizations avoid major setbacks and transform challenges into opportunities.

Another form of organizational change, incremental, is a form of organizational evolution, and it brings introduction of new technologies, new products, and new processes. Incremental change strategically explores new directions without fundamental shifts in organizational structure and culture (Nadler and Nadler, 1998). Continuous process improvement through incremental change is a critical capability of today's competitive business environments (Schermerhorn, Hunt, and Osborn, 2003). The role of the agent in incremental change might vary from recognizing opportunities for organizational development to designing plans to integrate the change through the provision of necessary information and training, and using influential members of the social network to mitigate resistance.

Some authors discuss transformational and incremental change as revolutionary versus evolutionary forms of organizational change, emphasizing the difference between major strategic shifts and step-by-step piecemeal approaches to improving organizational effectiveness (Field and House, 1995).

Mode of Change: Proactive and Reactive. Organizations more commonly engage in reactive change, responding to new strategic initiatives by competing firms, reacting to changing customer needs, or addressing internal needs for transformation caused by some type of crisis (Nadler and Nadler, 1998). However, some organizations initiate proactive change without obvious and immediate threats from external and internal environments. Proactive change is a characteristic of process and product innovations. Change agents search for opportunities to improve organizational performance and create needs among organizational members by pointing out the existence of desirable new ideas, then proceed to strategically select and resource some options in order to explore and ultimately implement them in a systematic way (Hellström, 2004; Rogers, 2003).

Control of Change: Planned and Unplanned. A proactive approach to changing organizational processes manifests itself in the form of planned change. Planned change is the result of focused efforts of change agents, people who lead and support change processes. It is conceived from the analysis of performance gaps, discrepancies between the actual and desired organizational processes, and behaviors of organizational members. The analysis of performance gaps reveals either problems that require immediate resolution or opportunities to be explored. Performance technology specialists are concerned with planned change processes for the purpose of systematically improving organizational effectiveness and performance of organizational members (Stolovitch and Keeps, 1999).

Process and product innovations are examples of planned change in organizations. Process innovations result in introduction and integration of new work methods and operations, while product innovations bring new or improved products and services. Both forms of innovation start with generating new ideas and experimenting with them in order to establish potential value and application. Once the value and the context of use are determined, organizations identify anticipated costs and benefits associated with the idea implementation and finally produce and market new products and services or implement new processes and methods (Rogers, 2003; Schermerhorn, Hunt, and Osborn, 2003).

Change does not always come as a systematic, planned action. Unplanned changes occur spontaneously and can be both positive and negative. A problematic documentation exchange between two functional areas in the company may prompt the organization to develop a new effective information-exchange strategy, while a dramatic rise in oil prices might cause bankruptcy and closure of a small transportation firm. When an organization experiences unplanned change, it is essential to act quickly and put every effort into minimizing negative consequences while maximizing any potential benefits, thus transforming unplanned change into an opportunity (Schermerhorn, Hunt, and Osborn, 2003). Although unplanned change is not initiated by change agents, it is essential that they take an active position in managing critical organizational situations by consulting executives on potential strategic solutions. They also conduct analyses of the impact of the problem on various organizational levels—business, legal, financial, cultural, and social—while assisting organizational members in their individual adaptation to change through a variety of adaptation strategies. Such adaptation strategies might include (1) visualizing potential successful outcomes of the change efforts, (2) creating power networks and peer influence groups, (3) providing those affected by change with comprehensive and up-to-date information about change, (4) providing just-in-time technical support, and (5) supplying training required by the changing organizational context (Dormant, 1997).

Organizational Forces and Targets for Change

The forces driving change in organizations can be found in the context of the relationships between an organization and its environment: changing competitors and markets, acquisition threats, and globalization. These are all examples of the forces that make an organization redefine its position in a dynamic external environment. The driving forces can also be focused on organizational life cycles with changes in organizational design, structure, tasks, or cultural values and beliefs in response to organizational evolution, increased workforce diversity, or process control and communication dysfunctions (Schermerhorn, Hunt, and Osborn, 2003). Organizations maintain their state of equilibrium by balancing driving and constraining forces that initiate or resist change, respectively (Lewin, 1958). When the driving forces are increased and a gap in organizational performance is identified, organizational leadership initiates the change through an unfreezing stage in order to close this gap between current and potential performance and achieve the state of equilibrium again (King and Anderson, 1995; Lewin, 1958).

The forces driving change can be directed toward various organizational components, including mission and vision, organizational strategy, technology, structure, people, and culture. However, when contemplating change in one organizational component, those who lead the change initiative must recognize that all these components are highly interrelated in the workplace, and, therefore, a change in one component will almost inevitably cause changes in others. Thus a technological change requires new skills, knowledge, and behaviors from organizational members in order for them to complete the new sets of tasks. Changes in tasks, in turn, will likely necessitate some modifications in organizational structure and ways in which the organizational members communicate with each other. It becomes critically important for organizational performance specialists to conduct a thorough analysis of the potential impact, both positive and negative, that the proposed change makes on different organizational components. This analysis must be completed before a change project begins, so organizations can plan for and address arising issues in a systematic way and avoid "quick fixes" and crisis-management situations (Nadler, 1987; Schermerhorn, Hunt, and Osborn, 2003).

Organizational Change Stages

According to Lewin (1952, 1958), an American social scientist who had a profound impact on the development of the theory and practice of organizational psychology, a planned change process has three distinct phases: unfreezing, changing, and refreezing. Lewin emphasizes the importance of the unfreezing and refreezing stages, and cautions against neglecting them in favor of the change stage.

Unfreezing. The "unfreezing" stage is concerned with recognizing conditions for change, and preparation of the organization for change. This stage is facilitated by various environmental influences, such as increased industry requirements to improve process and produce quality, or changing markets, and recognition of internal organizational problems and decline in performance. If managers fail to monitor their environments and recognize the important trends and situations that require change efforts, their organizations may experience failures and consequently lose their competitive edge. Organizations always benefit from the change agents who understand the importance of "unfreezing" in the change process and recognize early signals that change may be needed (Schermerhorn, Hunt, and Osborn, 2003).

Changing. The "changing" stage involves actions focused on modifying organizational elements, such as technology, structure, tasks, and culture. The success of this stage largely depends on how an organization was "unfreezing" while preparing for change. There are multiple factors that may affect this stage of the change process by facilitating or inhibiting change outcomes: feasibility of change agenda, degree of group and individual change required, leadership commitment, level of expectations about change outcomes shared by organizational members, and system readiness—availability of sufficient infrastructure, technology, and resources to support and sustain change (Malopinsky, 2004).

Refreezing. "Refreezing," the final stage in the change process cycle, focuses on sustaining the change outcomes and on their reinforcement and institutionalization. During this phase, organizations evaluate the costs and benefits associated with change program implementation and plan the next steps to increase change success over time. Neglecting the refreezing stage can lead to change not fully being implemented and failure in sustainability of organizational transformation efforts.

The concept of "unfreezing-changing-refreezing" is critical for successful management of organizational change. A change agent needs to find ways to increase the driving forces and reduce resistance in the unfreezing stage by diffusing information supportive of change through the social network, consulting top executives and management, and designing necessary implementation plans. During the changing stage, the change agent needs to provide support to the groups and individuals undergoing change within the organization, and make necessary adaptations to the change process. Evaluating and monitoring how the change process has been fulfilling the organizational goal and mission usually helps in reaching a point of new equilibrium between driving forces and resisting forces.

WHY MANAGE CHANGE?

Change is a lengthy, expensive, and complex process. This is especially true for large-scale organizational changes. The probability of a change initiative succeeding will increase with the application of change-management principles, strategies, and tactics. Examples of these would be assessing the readiness for change; determining key framing factors that might affect change implementation and its outcomes; aligning change projects with organizational systems, business goals, technologies, and culture; and assisting organizational members in the change-adoption process (Dormant, 1986, 1997). For an overview of the change-management process, see Figure 12.1.

PLANNING CHANGE

Though an opportunity for growth and development, change is often regarded as a complex and risk-laden endeavor that raises the level of uncertainty and might induce high levels of resistance. To ensure successful change implementation, organizational analysis followed by careful planning has to take place. The change agent's role at this point is helping management to develop comprehensive plans to address the needs of different groups and components involved in the change within the organization. The advice offered by a human

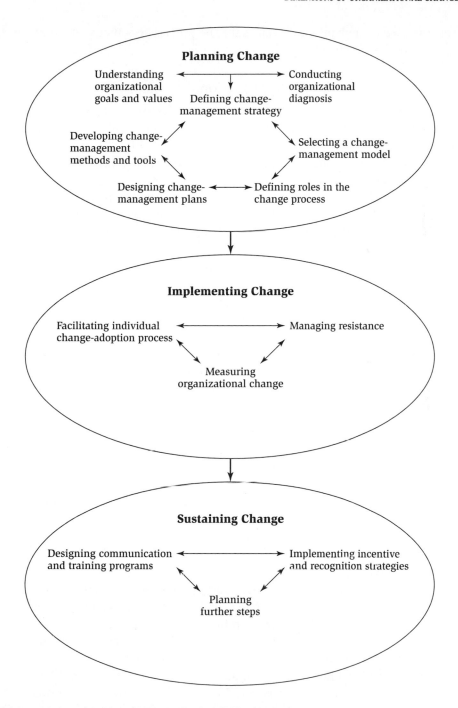

Figure 12.1. Managing the Organizational Change Process.

performance consultant may often make the process less time-consuming and more resource effective.

Understanding Organizational Goals and Values

The value system, or culture, of an organization determines how readily it will adopt change (Dormant, 1986). For example, some organizational cultures promote competitiveness while others encourage teamwork. The value system of an organization is not always explicitly advocated or consciously acknowledged by its members (Morgan, 1998). This does not, however, undermine its capacity to act as a powerful and often invisible force that can facilitate or hinder change. Organizational leadership and change agents should always consider organizational history and the values evolved and shared over time as well as information and work distribution flows. In hierarchical organizations that value compliance with authority, change decisions are usually made at the executive level and communicated in a traditional top-down approach. Independent work practices and democratic leadership values promoted in flat organizations make change by command less likely (Hiatt and Creasey, 2003; Schein, 1996). Such contrasting organizational value systems would require from change agents the development of different change-management strategies and tactics that would minimize resistance to change and ensure more successful change implementation (Hiatt and Creasey, 2003).

Conducting Organizational Diagnosis

Change should never be initiated without a comprehensive organizational diagnosis as a basis for decision making in a planned change process (Doppler and Lauterburg, 2001). Harvey and Brown (1996) define organization diagnosis as "a rigorous analysis of data on the structure, administration, interaction, procedures, interfaces, and other essential elements of the client system" (p. 123). The goal of an organizational diagnosis is to form a clear picture of the internal and external conditions of the organization based on data collected in a scientific, systematic way.

During the diagnosis period, it is important to examine whether the organization really needs the proposed change and to assess organizational readiness for change. Many organizations introduce changes they do not really need, while other organizations that would really benefit from a change initiative are more reticent to consider it (Doppler and Lauterburg, 2001). It is the role of the change agent to conduct a thorough analysis of organizational problems and needs, assess driving and restraining forces that may affect the process of change and its outcomes, evaluate readiness of all organizational components, and propose the course of action based on real, rather than contrived, assessment of organizational problems and needs.

Once an organizational diagnosis is performed, change agents engage in daily management activities using specific models and tools for facilitating change process and supporting organizational members during the transition period.

Defining Change-Management Strategy

Selection of the specific change-management approach is based on the comprehensive diagnosis of the organization's internal and external conditions, analysis of organizational culture and value systems, and the factors that may support or restrain change initiatives. Organizations may use different strategies for exerting influence over organization members in order to support the change process. These strategies use various bases of social power and evoke different behaviors of change agents resulting in different outcomes for the planned change process.

Force-Coercion. A force-coercion approach in managing organizational change uses legitimacy, rewards, or punishments as primary drivers in the change process. This approach is based on the assumption that organization members are generally motivated by self-interest, expressed in terms of potential personal gains and losses (Schermerhorn, Hunt, and Osborn, 2003). Change agents build supporting alliances with organizational leadership or use the formal authority of their position in an organization to induce change via an offer of special rewards, such as promotion or financial benefits, or via demonstration of negative consequences or threats of punishment. This strategy is used primarily in the traditional hierarchical organizations, in which strategic decisions are communicated downward to employees from the top management level. We argue that the benefits of this approach are limited to only the relatively quick solutions of minor organizational problems, since it does not allow organizational members to voice their expectations about change and develop shared understanding and agreement in regard to the outcomes that an organizational change agenda brings to their workplace.

Rational Persuasion. Change in organizations can also be introduced through the use of a rational persuasion strategy that is built on the assumption that if people are presented with rational argumentation and specific information and facts, they can be convinced that the change is beneficial for them (Schermerhorn, Hunt, and Osborn, 2003). When using the rational persuasion strategy, expert power and knowledge are mobilized by change agents to support specific actions and decision making in the organization experiencing change. The tactics used by change agents to influence the process of adoption of organizational change and ensure long-lasting support by all organizational members include (1) the use of successful change-implementation examples and best practices from other organizations, (2) analyses of the internal data clearly demonstrating the problems,

(3) the sharing of lessons learned from change projects implemented in the organization in the past, and (4) new strategic propositions supported by research findings (Malopinsky, 2004).

Shared Power. A shared-power approach to managing change assumes active involvement of people affected by a change in strategic planning and making decisions related to the change process (Garud and Van de Ven, 2002). Those change agents who use a shared-power approach in managing change recognize that organizational members act in accordance with the certain sociocultural norms and values accepted in their organization and that change not only brings new information and practices but requires people to review their norms, values, attitudes, and relationships in order to be active participants in the change process. This strategy is built on the principles of empowerment of those involved in the change process and is concerned with developing essential foundations such as shared goals and values and group norms to ensure sustainability and internalization of change efforts (Schermerhorn, Hunt, and Osborn, 2003).

Selecting a Change-Management Model

A variety of models can guide change agents in managing the process of organizational transformation. Some of them, such as the Performance Improvement Model (Rosenberg, 1990; Rummler and Brache, 1990), the Business Process Reengineering Model (Davenport, 1993), or the Total Quality Management Process Change Model (Drucker, 1991; Deming, 1986; Ishikawa, 1986), illustrate change as a cycle of iterative stages that change agents need to consider when helping organizations to change their strategies and practices. The McKinsey 7-S Framework explains change as a complex interaction between organizational components that must be given attention to ensure an effective change-management process and successful implementation of change projects (Kalman, 2001). Other models include the Burke-Litwin model (Burke, 1994), the Tichy Strategic Alignment Process Model (Tichy and Devanna, 1986), and the Weisbord Six-Box Model (Weisbord, 1976). It is critical that a change agent choose the appropriate model to use during a change project, based on careful analysis of organizational systems and assessment of organizational culture and values.

Developing Change-Management Methods and Tools

Selecting appropriate methods and tools for facilitating change activities is another essential task for a change agent. It is important to understand how these tools support an overall organizational business-improvement strategy in order to avoid superficial activities that do not bring expected results (Hiatt and Creasey, 2003; Malopinsky, 2004). The selection of methods and tools should be determined by the following critical aspects of a change-management process: (1) problem or opportunity identification, (2) organizational assessment, (3) project planning, (4) sponsor preparation, (5) communication and training, (6) implementation and measurement, and (7) resistance management (adapted from Hiatt and Creasey, 2003). These methods and tools need to target various participants of the change process: individuals, groups, whole organizations or their large components, and an organization's relevant environments (Doppler and Lauterburg, 2001). Here are just a few examples from a change agent's toolbox:

- Assessment of strengths, weaknesses, opportunities, and threats (SWOT) related to the proposed changes in organization (Houben, Lenie, and Vanhoof, 1999)

- Force-field analysis of driving and restricting forces that have an impact on change implementation (Lewin, 1951)

- S.C.O.R.E. (Symptoms-Causes-Output-Resources-Effects) model for analyzing a present and a future state of organization that helps to identify current problems, resources for addressing them, desired outcomes, and long-term impact of these outcomes on a changing organization (Dilts, 1996)

Organizational-development literature provides a wide variety of methods, tools, and procedures that can be adopted by change agents for the specific context of their organization and used for driving forward an organization's transformation and supporting individuals in their change efforts (Doppler and Lauterburg, 2001; Dormant, 1999; Rogers, 2003).

Defining Roles in the Change Process

Once the specific strategy for managing a change process is defined and justified, a change-management team is formed. It may include the sponsors of the change project, who provide leadership and allocate funding and resources for the change project; opinion leaders providing an expert assessment of the impact of change on the organization and communicating their concerns to various management levels in the organization; mid-level managers and nonmanagerial employees facilitating specific change-project activities; and HPT professionals as change agents who orchestrate change-project activities, facilitate communication among the members of a change-management team, and propose strategic directions and advice based on continuous assessment of the change-project progress and the rate of adoption of specific decisions by organizational members (Dormant, 1999; Rogers, 2003).

Executive Sponsorship. Sponsorship is vital for the success of a change-management initiative. The importance of defining change sponsors occupying high positions on the executive ladder and securing their commitment cannot be overestimated, as the change-management team would find it challenging to plan and implement change without the overt authorization of the organization's executive sponsors (Hiatt and Creasy, 2003; Dormant, 1999). The role of executive sponsors goes beyond initiating change; their support legitimizes the change process and gives authority to those in charge of implementing the change process, such as opinion leaders and change agents (Dormant, 1999). Organizational literature also suggests that the level of resistance to change within organizations is inversely proportional to the level of support of executive sponsorship (Schermerhorn, Hunt, and Osborn, 2003; Rogers, 2003).

Opinion Leadership. Unlike executive sponsorship, opinion leadership does not necessarily require a formal leadership position in the organizational system. Opinion leaders are members of the organization who exert influence on other organizational members by providing strategic advice to organizational leadership, sharing their professional expertise and experience, and advocating organizational culture and values (Dormant, 1999; Rogers, 2003). In addition to providing information, giving advice, and projecting judgments regarding the proposed innovation, opinion leaders adopt change early, thus serving as models to others. The success of change implementation in the whole organization is very often determined by the level of readiness to adopt change and the attitude to the specific change activities exhibited by opinion leaders.

Although opinion leaders play a critical role in organizational change, Rogers (2003) warns against overusing them; when associated too frequently with change, opinion leaders can be perceived by peer employees as professional change agents and therefore no longer a part of the organization. It is also important to consider working with different opinion leaders when planning and implementing different change initiatives: Dormant (1999) suggests that the person who might be an appropriate opinion leader for one intervention might not be for another.

The Change Agent. The change agent's role is central in the process of organizational transformation. The change agent may be a member of the organizational community or an external consultant specializing in organizational development and change management. HPT professionals are very often called on for this role, which encompasses a variety of activities, including initiating change as a result of a needs analysis, orchestrating planning, implementation, and management of the change initiative, or performing evaluation of the change impact on organizational processes and external environment. In some cases, the change agent is asked to investigate whether change is necessary or to evaluate the potential impact of specific change implementations.

Change agents work with organizational members at different levels of the organization, and they are expected to know how to use the social network of the organization to facilitate the change process. They work with executive sponsors to provide comprehensive organizational analyses, allowing sponsors to make concrete strategic decisions and define directions for change activities. They use opinion leaders as mediators for communicating critical information and minimizing resistance. In addition, the change agent might help in the formation of teams supervising the planning and implementation of change, and help the teams fulfill their roles through training and strategic guidance at various different phases of the change process (Dormant, 1999).

To be successful in their challenging role, change agents need to adopt some important strategies. First of all, they need to be able to assess organizational need and capability for change and consider potential drivers and barriers for change in order to suggest a feasible change process, a timeline, and resources. Negotiating, effective communication, and group management are other critical attributes of change agents' roles, as change agents rarely work in isolation and their success always depends on how well they can communicate important strategic decisions and lead change-management teams.

Designing Change-Management Plans

A number of change-management and implementation plans need to be developed before actual implementation takes place. Hiatt and Creasy (2003) suggest focusing on the following organizational domains when planning change implementation:

- *Communication:* Communication plans targeting different organizational groups are designed to ensure that potential adopters get the information that addresses their needs, and that they understand those messages in the way those messages were intended to be delivered.

- *Leadership support:* Creating sponsorship road maps will help executive sponsors remain active throughout the change-management process. The team in charge of change, especially change agents, needs to support sponsors if their fulfillments of leadership roles through specific planned activities are to be met.

- *Resistance management:* Resistance is a natural by-product of change; however, that does not imply that resistance should be left to take its own course. Change agents, in collaboration with organizational leadership, need to make some predictions about the level of resistance and identify potential resistance groups in order to plan activities that would minimize negative attitudes toward change.

- *Coaching:* Training supervisors to drive change is part of building change-management leadership. Supervisors are believed to have a great influence on their direct subordinates when it comes to minimizing the resistance regarding the personal impact of change.

- *Training:* Planning educational and training programs is needed to provide organizational members with the knowledge and skills necessary to implement change. The content and scope of training programs may vary widely across different units and levels in the organization.

IMPLEMENTING CHANGE

Change is highly complex; it is rarely unidimensional or unidirectional and can come from inside the organization as a result of an internally identified need or can be imposed on the organization as a result of external changes. Change can happen at different levels, varying from change on the level of the organization on one end of the continuum to that of the individual on the other end. Implementation in such a complex environment can be successful only if change agents carefully assess organizational context and plan all pivotal aspects of a change agenda. Table 12.1 presents organizational and individual aspects of a change-management program that need to be addressed before and during implementation of a change program.

Facilitating the Individual Change-Adoption Process

People affected by change have their specific roles and goals in the change process. They focus primarily on the implications that a change initiative makes on their position in the organization and their individual performance, and they tend to interpret information they receive in the light of their own beliefs, needs, and concerns (Rogers, 2003). Therefore, it is important for those in charge of

Table 12.1. Organizational and Individual Aspects of a Change-Management Program.

Organizational Aspects	Individual Aspects
• Analyzing organizational structures and processes	• Defining roles for organizational members in the change management process
• Defining change management strategies and methodologies	• Developing models for individual change management
• Creating change management plans	• Selecting methods and tools for helping organizational members participate in the change process
• Designing communication and training programs	• Designing incentive and recognition programs
• Evaluating the impact of a change program on organizational performance	

change to remember that any change initiative generally involves people, and the role of change agents is to ensure that the needs, concerns, and fears of organizational members are addressed and that all people are working toward the same goals and cooperating with each other to achieve desired results (Doppler and Lauterburg, 2001; Hiatt and Creasey, 2003).

Dormant (1999) suggests a number of factors that individuals or groups involved in organizational transformation of any kind consider in their assessment of change: (1) the advantages and disadvantages of the proposed change compared to previous or other change initiatives, (2) compatibility of the suggested change with current and past practices, (3) how comprehensible the suggested change is, (4) how adaptable the change is to the specifics of organizational context, and (5) the impact of the proposed change on the social networks within the organization. These perceptions are important because they influence the extent to which organizational units or individual members of organizations embrace or resist change.

The change agent can help the different units and members within the organization perceive the change initiative more clearly and precisely by providing accurate and abundant information. Potential adopters often have questions at this stage that a change agent can address more fully. It is thus important that the change agents be accessible to adopters to provide answers and give support when needed. Disseminating success stories of change implementation within the organization is also vital in shaping potential adopters' perceptions. Being aware of the idiosyncratic needs of individuals and groups within the organization is vital to providing effective help at this stage (Hiatt and Creasy, 2003; Rogers, 2003).

Adoption Stages

Members in organizations experiencing change are involved in intensive decision-making processes and communication of innovative ideas among different parts of the organizational system. Because change always creates a sense of uncertainty (Rogers, 2003), information exchange becomes critical, as it is supposed to help potential adopters become certain that the suggested innovation is advantageous for them and that they are capable of implementing it. However, this is a lengthy and gradual process, which Rogers describes as "diffusion," when ideas infiltrate the social system and subsequently result in the acceptance of change or the rejection of it.

Rogers (2003) suggests that the diffusion process consists of five different stages: (1) knowledge, (2) persuasion, (3) decision, (4) implementation, and (5) confirmation. The decision process does not always flow in a linear fashion. For example, in organizations that are highly autocratic in culture, adopters might start at the implementation stage and then move to other stages or skip certain stages altogether.

Knowledge. At this stage potential adopters receive information about the planned change. The information provided is generally limited to the existence of the change and its nature (Rogers, 2003). It is important for the change agent to understand that just becoming aware of a planned change initiative does not necessarily mean the potential adopters are ready to join it. This is especially true of more complex change projects that involve substantial uncertainty. The role of the change agent at this stage is to provide sufficient knowledge about the innovation or change initiative and to create a need for the change if none already exists.

Persuasion. The persuasion stage is characterized by affective reactions to the cognitive knowledge received previously; the potential adopters need to see the change as relatively risk free, compatible to their goals and values, and relevant to the context of their work. At this stage no decision is formed. The product of this phase is an inclination toward embracing or not embracing the change.

Rogers (2003) emphasizes the importance of social networks at this stage in change. Forming a positive or negative attitude about the change initiative is reinforced by examples of success or failure provided by influential elements with the organization. Another source of evidence is the opinions of peers. In the absence of evidence, the stage of inconclusive uncertainty tends to persist, and change is less likely to happen. The role of the change agent is to facilitate the diffusion of such evidence through the organization's social networks.

Decision. The decision to adopt or reject a suggested change is the next step in the process of making a decision about a change. This decision is formed as a result of activities in which individuals actively participate in a change project or passively observe it. According to Rogers (2003), individuals often seek to partially try out the change. If that trial is successful, the decisions for adoption tend to be positive and the actual adoption process is facilitated. If a trial is not feasible, individuals tend to look at examples of successful implementation of the suggested change by peers. The role of opinion leaders is vital at this stage.

Implementation. It is not until the implementation stage that change is really put into action. At the implementation stage, organizational members actively seek to answer many questions about how to realize some decisions and overcome some of the problems that might arise during the change-implementation process. This becomes even more of a problem if the change is organizational. The role of the change agent here is to act as a supporter and problem solver. The implementation stage concludes with what Rogers (2003) refers to as "institutionalization" or "routinization" of changed strategies and practices.

Confirmation. At the confirmation stage adopters reevaluate their decisions regarding the implementation of change. They collect more information to either support their adoption or challenge their previous decision. When negative information that challenges the implementation of changes becomes too substantial to ignore, discontinuance of the implementation often results. Discontinuance may happen in the form of replacement of one solution by another that adopters believe is more effective, or may result in disenchantment resulting from the lack of compatibility between the change and the organizational environment, or from the adopters' failure to use the change effectively (Rogers, 2003).

Adopter Categories

Individuals vary in their readiness to adopt change. The organizational literature suggests several categories of change-adoption levels: from innovators who adopt change early to laggards who are the last to accept change (Rogers, 2003; Dormant, 1999).

Innovators. Innovators are open to change, are comfortable with ambiguity, and are ready to take risks. According to Rogers (2003), innovators are inquisitive and actively seek information about suggested innovations. They develop elaborate social circles or networks that help in active information gathering and the sharing process. It is critical that innovators have sufficient credibility within their organization, so they can lead others through demonstrating interventions and serving as models (Dormant, 1999).

Early Adopters. Early adopters are regarded as among the most influential contributors to the adoption of innovation. They are often opinion leaders. Unlike the innovators, early adopters are more widely respected and accepted in their social system. This could partially be due to their careful approach to change. According to Havelock (cited in Dormant, 1986), early adopters often observe the adoption of change by innovators to assess potential success and pay attention to the objections and reservations of those who oppose change in order to evaluate potential failure risks. Such observations, followed by a trial period, lead them to form change-adoption judgments.

Early Majority. The early majority adopters, according to Rogers (2003), form one third of potential adopters and are thus said to adopt ideas before the average person in the social system. They do not lead the process but often watch the success of the trial implementation by innovators and early adopters. They provide the link between these two groups and those who are late in adopting the innovation.

Late Majority. The late majority, which also constitute one third of change adopters, follow the average person in the system in the adoption of change. Being skeptical of the change, they are often very hesitant to accept the proposed organizational changes. To be convinced of change benefits, they need to experience peer pressure to change and know that organizational leadership and the whole system surrounding them definitely favor the proposed change (Rogers, 2003).

Laggards. Last to adopt change are the laggards. These are the ones who resist change and voice their concerns regarding the change initiative (Dormant, 1986). Rogers (2003) suggests that laggards are often the isolated elements in the system and thus do not have access to the information resources provided by members of the organizational network. Moreover, they measure everything against the past and make decisions in terms of what has been done previously. Dormant (1986) suggests that change agents can help this traditional category of adopters embrace the change by listening to and addressing their concerns and by taking a careful, step-by-step approach to introducing advantages of the proposed change.

Managing Resistance

Any change initiative can meet some resistance from some organizational members who have various reasons to be reluctant to join change efforts. It becomes critically important for change agents to understand the causes of resistance and to assist organizational leadership in developing strategies for its successful management. Resistance management is especially critical in entrepreneurial, flat organizations where autonomy is often encouraged and obedience is no longer rewarded (Hiatt and Creasy, 2003).

According to Kotter and Schlesinger (1979), there are several reasons that might lead organizational members to resist change:

- Parochial self-interest, when people are concerned with potential negative implications of change for their interests and position within the organization and make every attempt to protect their status quo
- Misunderstanding or misinterpretation of goals and expected outcomes of the change initiative due to communication problems and limited availability of information related to change projects
- Low tolerance to change simply because certain people are very keen on stability and the security of their work and feel very uncomfortable with the uncertainty that change brings to their working environments
- Different perspectives on the reasons for change and positive and negative implications of the change process expressed by various employee groups and individuals.

HPT professionals and other organizational change agents can employ different approaches to minimize resistance to change and support employees during the difficult transition time: (1) development of educational and communication programs focused on various aspects of change, allowing employees to see the rationale behind the change efforts, (2) early and active involvement of employees in the change process, and (3) ongoing managerial support and incentives for contributions to change projects (Malopinsky, 2004; Schermerhorn, Hunt, and Osborn, 2003; Kotter and Schlesinger, 1979).

It is important to recognize that employees may exhibit resistance to the change itself, the specific change strategy, or the change agent (Schermerhorn, Hunt, and Osborn, 2003). Change agents must be prepared to address resistance at these levels by using different approaches. To minimize resistance to the change itself, change agents must ensure that the new process or strategy is not proposed for the sake of change but brings certain benefits to the organization and individuals working there. Change steps should be as simple as possible and compatible with the existing values and experience of organizational members.

The negative attitude to change can be caused by resistance to the specific approach used to implement the change: if a rational persuasion strategy is employed, change agents and organizational leadership need to ensure that the data used to support certain propositions are correct and complete and that the strategic argument is compelling; when using a shared-power approach, people leading the change should be aware of the possibility of being perceived as insincere and manipulative.

Resistance to the change agent might come from differences in education, age, position within the organization, and other factors (Schermerhorn, Hunt, and Osborn, 2003). Change agents should know about these potential causes of resistance and constantly monitor the feedback on change from all levels of the organization to be able to react quickly and propose solutions that minimize negative reactions. Certainly, careful up-front analysis of organizational values, traditions, culture, business agendas, and personal goals of those involved in change is beneficial for addressing the resistance issues as the change project progresses.

Measuring Organizational Change

Measuring progress and the status of change implementation is critical, as it allows organizations to objectively assess whether the change actually takes place. We cannot improve what we cannot measure. Continuous assessment of change-project status provides information about the present status of the organization, trends in organizational performance over time, and feedback on the measurement methods themselves that suggests which aspects of the change process need to be assessed differently.

When implementing change, organizations should develop metrics aligned with the key organizational goals and design the processes that allow for collecting and analyzing information about the change-implementation status. The change agent's role in this process is facilitating the design and implementation of a change measurement system, examining the outcomes of various measured processes and strategies, and communicating the results to organizational decision makers.

The measures or indicators for change progress should be selected to best represent the factors that lead to improved performance at various levels of an organization, including business processes, financial performance, organizational learning, and customer satisfaction. However, assessing "change in progress" can be a challenging task because not all aspects of the change can be measured quantitatively through financial and productivity indicators (Greenan and Mairesse, 2001). In addition to quantitative organizational effectiveness measures, such as Six Sigma (Pande, Neuman, and Cavanagh, 2001; Breyfogle, 2003), change agents need to look for measurement tools such as the Balanced Scorecard (Kaplan and Norton, 1996), the Half-Life method by Schneiderman (2004), or the Organizational Culture Inventory (OCI) model (Cooke and Szumal, 1993) that allow them to assess the "soft" aspects of change, for example, organizational culture and organizational learning.

DEVELOPING STRATEGIES FOR SUSTAINING CHANGE EFFORTS

To ensure commitment to change from various organizational units and individuals, change leaders need to demonstrate a positive impact of the change on the whole organization as well as on the working environment of individual members of the organization. Sustainability of the achieved results is the major concern of every change agent. It is not enough just to convince people to follow the change; efforts should be made to provide continuous support to the organization and its employees in the form of effective communication and training programs that target the complex change issues. It is also critical to recognize the successful change-implementation efforts through various reward programs in order to support employees' motivation and demonstrate the value of specific solutions for the organization.

Designing Communication and Training Programs

Communication of information lies at the core of any change process. Without the diffusion of information that tears down uncertainty and fear of the unknown novelty, change will not take root in the organization. It is important for the change agent to identify informational and educational needs of the different groups involved in the change process and to propose special communication and training initiatives that address those needs.

Harvey and Brown (1996) point out the importance of sending clear, adequate messages to the right people at the right time. Few people can deal with ambiguity, and in the absence of information, rumors rise to satisfy the need for information. Change agents need to consider every communication channel available, including informal social networks, for providing access to information about change at all organizational levels. Availability of complete, accurate, and up-to-date information might support potential adopters in embracing the change and help them to become active participants in the change-diffusion process.

It also becomes imperative to identify the gaps in skills and knowledge prerequisites to successful change implementation within the organization. The change agents need to ensure that all those involved in organizational change, and especially change-management leaders, receive adequate training to be able to participate in the change process and successfully manage it.

Implementing Incentive and Recognition Strategies

Employees find embracing change difficult despite adequate information, motivating opinion leaders, supportive executives, and available training. There is ample proof in the organizational literature that appropriate reward and recognition programs may facilitate better performance and increased individual commitment to change (Harvey and Brown, 1996). "Profit-sharing, bonuses, skill- and knowledge-based pay, gain sharing, and stock ownership" (Harvey and Brown, 1996, p. 165) are some of the motivating change-adoption strategies that change agents may offer for consideration to organizational change leaders.

PLANNING FURTHER STEPS

Change is an ongoing process, and once some decisions are made and some change propositions are realized and institutionalized, change agents engage in the evaluation of implementation experience and reflect on lessons learned with the purpose of planning further steps and continuous improvement. Change agents may encourage representatives of different stakeholder groups to evaluate the change experience in a systematic and objective way. The outcomes of this experience are the development of a shared understanding of the barriers and the enablers to change implementation and suggestions for future change efforts.

References

Breyfogle, F. W. (2003). *Implementing Six Sigma: Smarter solutions using statistical methods.* New York: Wiley.

Burke, W. W. (1994). *Organizational development: A process of learning and changing.* Reading, MA: Addison-Wesley.

Cooke, R. A., and Szumal, J. L. (1993). Measuring normative beliefs and shared behavioral expectations in organizations: The reliability and validity of the organizational culture inventory. *Psychological Reports, 72,* 1299–1330.

Davenport, T. H. (1993). *Process innovation: Reengineering work through information technology.* Boston, MA: Harvard Business School Press.

Deming, W. E. (1986). *Out of the crisis.* Cambridge, MA: MIT Center for Advanced Engineering Study.

Dilts, R. B. (1996). *Visionary leadership skills: Creating a world to which people want to belong.* Capitola, CA: Meta Publications.

Doppler, K., and Lauterburg, C. (2001). *Managing corporate change.* Berlin: Springer.

Dormant, D. (1986). The ABC's of managing change. In M. Smith (Ed.), *Introduction to performance technology* (pp. 238–256). Washington, DC: International Society for Performance Improvement.

Dormant, D. (1997). Planning change: Past, present, future. In R. Kaufman, S. Thiagarajan, and P. MacGillis (Eds.), *The guidebook for performance improvement.* San Francisco: Jossey-Bass.

Dormant, D. (1999). Implementing human performance technology in organizations. In H. D. Stolovitch and E. J. Keeps (Eds.), *The handbook of human performance technology: Improving individual and organizational performance worldwide* (2nd ed., pp. 237–259). San Francisco: Jossey-Bass/Pfeiffer.

Drucker, P. (1991). The new productivity challenge. *Harvard Business Review, 69,* 69–77.

Field, R. H., and House, R. J. (1995). *Human behavior in organizations: A Canadian perspective.* Scarborough, Ontario: Prentice-Hall.

Garud, R., and Van de Ven, A. H. (2002). Strategic change processes. In A. Pettigrew, H. Thomas, and R. Whittington (Eds.), *Strategy and management* (pp. 206–231). London: Sage.

Greenan, N., and Mairesse, J. (2001, June). Trying to measure organizational change: A first look at a matched employer-employee survey for French manufacturing. Paper presented at the Nelson and Winter Conference, Aalborg, Denmark.

Harvey, D., and Brown, D. R. (1996). *An experiential approach to organization development.* Upper Saddle River, NJ: Prentice-Hall.

Hellström, T. (2004). Innovation as social action. *Organization, 11*(5), 631–649.

Hiatt, J. M., and Creasey, T. J. (2003). *Change management: The people side of change.* Loveland, CO: Prosci Learning Center Publications.

Houben, G., Lenie, K., and Vanhoof, K. (1999). A knowledge-based SWOT-analysis system as an instrument for strategic planning in small and medium sized enterprises. *Decision Support Systems, 26*(2), 125–135.

Ishikawa, K. (1986). *Guide to quality control.* Portland, OR: Productivity Press.

Johansson, H. J., McHugh, P., Pendlebury, A. J., and Wheeler, W. A. (1994). *Business process reengineering: Breakpoint strategies for market dominance.* New York: Wiley.

Kalman, H. K. (2001). *Use of strategic planning process to reinvent corporate training: A case study in developing governance and organizational influence.* Unpublished doctoral dissertation, Indiana University.

Kaplan, R. S., and Norton, D. P. (1996). *The balanced scorecard: Translating strategy into action.* Boston: Harvard Business School Press.

King, N., and Anderson, N. (1995). *Innovation and change in organizations.* New York: Routledge.

Kotter, J. P., and Schlesinger, L. A. (1979). Choosing strategies for change. *Harvard Business Review, 57*(2), 106–114.

Lewin, K. (1951). *Field theory in social science.* New York: Harper & Row.

Lewin, K. (1952). Group decision and social change. In G. E. Swanson, T. M. Newcomb, and E. L. Hartley (Eds.), *Readings in social psychology* (pp. 459–473). New York: Holt, Rinehart & Winston.

Lewin, K. (1958). Group decision and social change. In E. E. Maccoby, T. M. Newcomb, and E. L. Hartley (Eds.), *Readings in social psychology* (pp. 197–211). New York: Henry Holt and Company.

Malopinsky, L. V. (2004). *Analysis of strategic change in manufacturing science & technology organization.* Technical Report. Indianapolis: Eli Lilly and Company.

Morgan, G. (1998). *Images of organization: Executive edition.* Thousand Oaks, CA: Sage.

Nadler, A. (1987). The effective management of organizational change. In J. W. Lorsch (Ed.), *Handbook of organizational behavior* (pp. 358–369). Englewood Cliffs, NJ: Prentice-Hall.

Nadler, D. A., and Nadler, M. B. (1998). *Champions of change: How CEOs and their companies are mastering the skills of radical change.* San Francisco: Jossey-Bass.

Pande, P. S. Neuman, R. P., and Cavanagh, R. R. (2001). *The Six Sigma way team fieldbook: An implementation guide for process improvement teams.* New York: McGraw-Hill.

Pettigrew, A. M., Woodman, R. W., and Cameron, K. S. (2001). Studying organizational change and development: challenges for future research. *Academy of Management Journal, 44*(4), 697–713.

Rogers, E. M. (2003). *Diffusion of innovations* (5th ed.). New York: Free Press.

Rosenberg, M. J. (1990). Performance technology: Working the system. *Training, 27*(2), 43–48.

Rummler, G. A., and Brache, A. P. (1990). *Improving performance: How to manage the white space on the organization chart.* San Francisco: Jossey-Bass.

Schein, E. H. (1996). *Organizational culture and leadership.* San Francisco: Jossey-Bass.

Schermerhorn, J. R., Hunt, J. G., and Osborn, R. N. (2003). *Organizational behavior.* Hoboken, NJ: Wiley.

Schneiderman, A. M. (2004). Half-life method. In K. Kempf-Leonard (Ed.), *Encyclopedia of social measurement*. Dallas: Academic Press.

Stolovitch, H. D., and Keeps, E. J. (1999). What is human performance technology? In H. D. Stolovitch and E. J. Keeps (Eds.), *The handbook of human performance technology: Improving individual and organizational performance worldwide* (2nd ed., pp. 3–23). San Francisco: Jossey-Bass.

Tichy, N. M., and Devanna, M. A. (1986). *The transformational leader.* New York: Wiley.

Weisbord, M. R. (1976). Organizational diagnosis: Six places to look with or without a theory. *Group and Organizational Studies, 1,* 430–447.

CHAPTER THIRTEEN

Using Evaluation to Measure and Improve the Effectiveness of Human Performance Technology Initiatives

Robert O. Brinkerhoff

This chapter presents practical guidance to help performance consultants and other professionals understand the role of evaluation in human performance technology (HPT) initiatives and use evaluation as a strategic tool for leveraging continuously improved value from HPT project efforts. The first section of the chapter reviews the function of evaluation in HPT, discusses some fundamental evaluation concepts, and suggests a strategic framework within which evaluation is viewed as an integral part of HPT practice. The second section describes five critical failure modes for HPT initiatives, explaining how each failure mode represents a typical and fundamental error that HPT practitioners can make and which, if not avoided, will undermine and thwart the value of the performance-improvement initiative. The third section presents a systemic framework, keyed to the failure modes, for designing and using evaluation to improve HPT project results and demonstrate their organizational impact. The chapter closes with a list of references and additional resources that readers can use to obtain more information about evaluation procedures and tools.

THE WHAT AND WHY OF EVALUATION

Evaluation is a normal and necessary component of everyday life. You cannot cross the street or operate an automobile without engaging in continuous evaluation, formulating expectations such as, "I need a clear and danger-free path to my destination." This involves collecting information about current states and conditions, such as, "Is there a car coming and is the truck ahead moving too slowly?" A driver processes and values the information to make a decision, such as, "Should I wait or should I slow down?" Similarly, informal evaluation is a normal and integral part of any organized activity, including an HPT effort. That is, clients and other people involved in the HPT initiative will be making continuous evaluative judgments and acting on them, perhaps deciding that your work is going well or deciding that it is flawed, making decisions to act on advice, regarding or ignoring information, and intervening and taking action as they choose.

The question is not whether your HPT efforts will be fraught with evaluation, but whether the evaluation information that people will use and act on is either flawed or worthy. You cannot avoid evaluation; you can only take steps to see that it is carried out more formally than haphazardly, and more or less well with more or less validity and fairness. If evaluation is done haphazardly, unfairly, and ineffectively, then the likelihood that the HPT initiative will fail is great, since decisions will be made based on erroneous and misleading information. If evaluation is done well—systematically, fairly, sensitively, and accurately—then the HPT initiative is virtually failsafe; it can only make a positive contribution.

Purposes for Evaluation

Above all, evaluation is for learning. Evaluation helps all stakeholders learn how, when, and why HPT works. It can help HPT consultants become more proficient and effective. It can help managers and other HPT clients learn to become more savvy consumers of HPT products and services and even to become better performance managers themselves. It can help organizations build capability in becoming more proficient in improving and leveraging performance into lasting and valuable outcomes. Beyond learning, there are two key additional purposes for evaluation.

Evaluation also serves accountability needs and interests, helping everyone involved in performance focus on what matters and steer their efforts toward valuable results. HPT efforts involve a considerable investment of time and fiscal resources. Evaluation helps assure clients and their constituents that their investors understand the potential benefit from investments in HPT efforts, not only increasing investors' commitment and buy-in, but helping investors to make wise decisions about where and how to spend their time and money. As HPT solutions are implemented and concluded, HPT leaders can provide progress reports that assure all involved that good progress is being made and that worthwhile results are being achieved, or not, as the case may be.

Finally, evaluation addresses quality improvement and assurance purposes. Systematic evaluation of plans and progress can get feedback to the right people at the right time to help them make decisions that increase the probability that

HPT efforts will yield durable and positive results. In the fast-paced work common in many organizations, it is increasingly likely that principles of good stewardship and thoughtful practice might be neglected in the hustle and bustle. A commitment to evaluation as part and parcel of the HPT process ensures that principles of good practice will be most thoughtfully applied.

Evaluation as Systematic Reflection

Evaluation is best defined as formalized and systematic reflection. Reflection is looking back; taking a pause in the action to ask how things are going. Are we headed in the right direction? Are things working the way we need them to? Reflection guides us to notice what is working, to take steps to keep it working, and to notice what is not working and take steps to change it. Evaluation is systematic in that we plan for it and commit resources to it. It is formal in that it is guided by rules of good scientific inquiry, done in the open and available to scrutiny. We plan for the "pauses" in action, and systematically reflect by formally assessing conditions and outcomes, nurturing what is working and changing what is not.

The function of evaluation in HPT initiatives is to make current and future HPT efforts more effective in improving individual and organizational performance. Evaluation can improve the effectiveness of current initiatives by collecting critical information about the nature and soundness of HPT activities, verifying assumptions and causal analyses, and helping stakeholders make decisions to steer the HPT initiative to the most successful possible conclusion. This sort of evaluation that helps steer initiatives to successful effect is often called "formative evaluation." Evaluation improves future HPT efforts by helping stakeholders investigate past efforts and decide what has worked and what has not, guiding them to allocate resources and organizational energy to subsequent efforts that have the greatest promise for paying off. Evaluation that helps stakeholders judge the worthiness of past efforts is referred to as "summative evaluation."

The Process of Evaluation

Evaluation entails asking questions, then collecting data to help answer these questions. We might ask, for example, whether a job aid we have designed for use by bank tellers is pitched at the right level and whether it can be readily understood by the typical teller. The data we collect to answer this question would be reactions of tellers toward drafts of the job aid, or opinions of expert job aid designers, or perhaps managers' opinions of tellers.

Some of the questions that evaluation asks are about concerns internal to the HPT process, such as whether an analysis of needs has uncovered adequate and accurate data on which to base a solution or whether a team of workers can make effective use of a computer-based help function. The questions asked vary from phase to phase in an HPT initiative, and might include the following:

- How important is the business need that the HPT effort is designed to address?

- What gains in performance are needed to justify the expense of an improvement effort?

- Which of several alternative HPT approaches is best?

- How well is the solution working so far? Is it on track?

- What changes should be made to keep the HPT effort on track and to make it more effective?

- How much good has the initiative done?

- What do clients think of the work and results that have been achieved?

- What lessons have been learned from this current work that should guide future practice?

Timely and accurate data collected in response to these and other questions will help all parties involved in the HPT process do their best work and get the best results. Alternatively, inaccurate data will get invalid answers to these questions and throw the HPT effort off track. Or time and money spent pursuing wrong or misguided questions will deflect inquiry from more important matters, frustrating HPT clients and practitioners and crippling their efforts. Thus, HPT practitioners need a sound and solid evaluation framework that helps them ask the right questions, and they need practical and valid evaluation methods that get timely, accurate, and complete data on which they can base solid answers to the evaluation questions they raise.

EVALUATION AS PART OF AN ITERATIVE HPT STRATEGY

HPT efforts, like many other consultative efforts and initiatives such as training, individual and group counseling, project management, and so on that are aimed at improving what people and organizations do, are imperfect sciences. Individual and organizational behaviors are driven by a complex nexus of factors: values, goals, interests, psychological motives, conscious and unconscious desires, fear, quests for achievement and status, greed, desire for fame and recognition, incentives, learned abilities and innate competencies, and so on. We have a good deal of knowledge about some of these factors and how they interact. Often we have some control over them. For other factors we have little knowledge and little control. There is more yet about the causes and influences of things that we have no knowledge about, though new information and theories emerge almost daily.

Evaluation is the handmaiden of good HPT practice. Since we know that we are always basing our plans on less-than-perfect knowledge, but that action to try something different is almost always necessary, a process of iterative cycles of trial, assessment, and learning-from-progress is the most practical and worthy path forward. This may strike some HPT purists as somewhat heretical, as it is a standing principle of HPT practice to base HPT interventions on a thoughtful and complete analysis of root causes of performance problems. It is not wise, of course, to move too quickly to implement a solution if one is not certain as to the causes of a problem in the first place. But the challenge relates to the meaning of the word *certain*. When it comes to understanding human behavior, certainty is a matter of degree, not an absolute. HPT practitioners may be more or less certain, but must accept the fact that there will always be some degree of uncertainty in any analysis of causes of performance problems. Thus, the decision of when to move from analysis to taking action must consider probabilities, not certainties. We will take action when we think we know enough, not when we know it all, as knowing it all is an unreachable goal. So then the question is, How much certainty is enough certainty?

Unfortunately for those who look for assurance, the answer to this relative question introduces yet another issue of relativity. The more important and pressing the performance problem and the higher the stakes involved in solving it, the greater the need for action. And as the need for action looms more important, then the pressure grows to move ahead to a solution, despite a lack of certainty as to exactly what is most sure to work. Imagine, for example, a company that sells high-technology products in a tightly competitive market. Imagine further that this company has invested in a new product on which it has "bet the business," and that the product has been launched as early as possible in an attempt to trump competitors. Now imagine that the sales force is not being successful in selling this new product. Every day of poor sales adds fuel to the fires of risk for larger failure, as competitors' products gain an increasingly greater foothold and the slope up to the new product's success becomes steeper. In this example, the need to act sooner rather than later is great, and the stakes are high: survival of the company. An HPT practitioner can ill afford to move slowly or hesitate in the face of uncertainty and must try something quickly.

Evaluation is the method we can use to answer the "when is enough, enough?" question; evaluation can help with this scenario by enabling a strategy of successive approximation, or what engineers might call "rapid prototyping." According to this strategy, when the need for action is great, the HPT practitioner does a hasty and admittedly less-than-complete analysis of needs, and moves very quickly to implement a solution. Because the solution is quickly put together and is not certain to work, the HPT leader may decide to limit risk and try out the solution on a small scale with just a minor portion of the salesforce. The HPT leader will then quickly and carefully assess the success of the hastily tried solution, gauging what parts of it work and what parts of it do not work. The learning from this first trial enables the HPT practitioner to quickly craft a second-generation solution that, while still put together in a rush and less than perfect, will at least be more effective than the first try. Again, the HPT practitioner will follow the second trial with evaluation and move through successive iterations of a solution until the problem performance is sufficiently improved.

Note that this rapid-prototyping process does not abandon the principle of basing performance problem solutions on a thorough analysis of needs. There is still a lot of analysis; it is just not all done before the creation and implementation of a solution design. Instead, evaluation is used to spread the analysis phase out and across several successive iterations of trial solutions. This not only enables quick responses but provides a more thorough and effective solution, because the HPT intervention is based on real, context-specific experience and learning.

An iterative development process is not just a response to pressure for quick action. It is a thoughtful policy based on the reality that a "perfect" solution is always out of reach. Even given vast amounts of time for an up-front analysis, the solution would *still and inevitably* be less than perfect because of two unavoidable facts of HPT life:

1. Some portion of the causes of human performance problems will always be a mystery, and thus all HPT solutions will address some of the causal factors but miss others.

2. The organizational context that introduces causes for performance problems is constantly changing, so that what is right in this moment may be wrong in the next moment.

THE FIVE FATAL HPT ERRORS

HPT efforts are no different than any other human endeavor: they can work well, or they can fail miserably. While some of the causes of failure may be in the hands of the gods, such as a cataclysmic disruption in the work of the organization or a drastic illness or accident suffered by the HPT team, most of the factors that make for success or failure are in the hands of the HPT practitioner and the HPT team. While there is a host of such potential causes and factors that can drive failure, it is useful to put these many causes into categories, for these categories provide a foundation from which to build a practical and easily understood evaluation framework.

Errors of Direction

This type of error consists of aiming the HPT effort at the wrong goals in the first place, such as trying to improve performance that would not add sufficient value to the organization even if it were improved, or making a mistake about the presumed business value of an apparent business goal or need. At any given time any organization has hundreds if not thousands of performance deficits, people not doing the right thing, or people performing at substandard levels. Some factory workers, for example, may be taking too long for lunch breaks, or a roofing contractor may make mistakes in putting together a cost proposal, or a sales person may fail to call on certain accounts. Of all of these many performance deficits, however, only a few may be worth correcting or improving, since only a few may make the greatest difference to the overall goal achievement of the organization. Given that HPT energy, attention, and resources are such that only a very few performance issues can be addressed, which among these is the most important and amenable to a solution? It is possible to improve performance in all sorts of ways, but only a very few of these are likely to truly pay off. The challenge for the HPT practitioner is to avoid the error of misdirection and invest HPT resources in the performance issue that is most likely to be solved in a way that will yield the greatest benefit to the organization. This challenge is further exacerbated by the fact that some performance issues might be very important to address but for certain reasons (for example, lack of political support, low likelihood for success, and so on) should not be the target for HPT attention.

Errors of Analysis

This type of error creeps in after the HPT practitioner has decided on a goal to address but for one reason or another fails to accurately identify the root causes of the performance issue. The focus, for example, may be on a branch travel office that is in the bottom 20 percent of effectiveness on a measure that tracks the conversion of visitors to a closed sale. The most profitable offices convert one out of eight visitors to a sale; this location has a conversion ratio of one sale per twenty visitors, putting it on a collision course with being closed down. The performance issue is important and needs to be addressed, and let us also assume for purposes of the example that there is the political support and other good will necessary to enlist support for tackling the problem. Now, the HPT practitioner must figure out what is causing the low conversion ratio. It could be a sales staff issue, a problem with management of the sales staff, a problem in the culture or design of the organization, a problem with marketing that is failing to bring in the right types of customers, a problem in store location, and so on, or some combination of any or all of these factors, or none of them. The HPT analysis challenge, of course, is to identify the right performance obstacles and issues, a challenge with room aplenty for error. Identification of the wrong causes will send the solution design off in the wrong direction.

Errors of Design

Assuming a valid performance issue and the correct analysis of causes, the next opportunity for error is with the design of a performance-improvement solution.

Here the HPT practitioner faces a complex challenge. The solution must be technically correct, in that it must be capable of resolving the performance issue. Perhaps, for example, the sales performance problem is due to a simple lack of skill on the part of the sales staff; assume, for instance, that they do not know how to do a good job of establishing rapport with potential customers and thus cannot understand their needs or objections. A training intervention might be technically capable of providing them with the skills. However, the designed solution must also be practical and compatible with the audience needs and interests; it must be capably "sold" to management so that their support will be provided, it must incorporate the right balance of practice and feedback, and so on. The HPT practitioner not only must be right in the selection and design of a solution but also must enlist the correct support and buy-in, forge the right alliances with key constituents, and so on. All of these complex factors are a part of the design for solving the performance issue. If any part of the design is flawed, the effectiveness of the HPT intervention is clearly at risk.

Errors of Implementation

Assuming all is correct in goals, analysis, and designs, the success of the HPT venture now relies on thoughtful and responsive implementation. The old adage of the best-laid plans of mice and men applies; there can be many a slip twixt plan and action. The more complex the HPT effort, the more likely it is that something will go wrong during implementation. At this point in our five-part framework, success bears heavily on project management—making the HPT project work. It will not matter how elegant and right the goals, analysis, and design are if the carefully laid plans never get implemented correctly or are let go through neglect or misguided management.

Errors of Sustained Impact

This type of error emerges at the point that all preceding work appears to have been done well. That is, the goal was correct, the analysis valid, the design workable, and the implementation faithful, but for some reason, performance just does not get adequately improved. Theoretically, this could not be logically possible if all previous errors had been completely avoided; had the HPT practitioner completed all the previous goal setting, analysis, design, and implementation with perfect accuracy and validity, then performance would have to improve to a worthwhile extent. If it did not, then either (1) something was really done wrong in goal-setting analysis or design or implementation, but it was mistakenly assessed to be right; or (2) something changed.

Either explanation is, of course, probable and likely. Most likely, both a previous error was made and also something changed. Organizational contexts are in continuous flux, so that what was an important goal last month may not be so important this month due to a change in the external competitive environment. Or new technology was introduced, or personnel changed, or factors influencing people changed, such as new opportunities or changes in family and career interests and needs. To avoid errors of this fifth type, HPT practitioners must continuously revisit earlier decisions and assumptions, changing plans and direction as needed, and flexing implementation according to shifting plans, capabilities, probabilities for support, shifting political dynamics, and so forth. The author still recalls vividly, for example, a project in which a series of job aids was being introduced to improve performance among call center staff in a sales and service operation. All was going well, and early implementation reports indicated good improvements in operator performance—fewer errors, reduced cycle time, increased sales, and so forth. A senior executive decision was made, however, to shift the business strategy toward a customer service and retention emphasis versus a sales revenue focus, and most of the job aids were no longer relevant, nor did improved sales results matter to the business leaders. As it turned out, there was not time to redirect performance, and the new company failed in the marketplace. The HPT initiative was, in the end, a failed effort, as it never really helped the business perform, though it did improve performance quite remarkably. However, had there been closer communication among ourselves, our HPT client, and the senior leadership of the company, we never would have gotten as far down this particular HPT road as we did, and we might have been able to shift performance direction soon enough to enable the business to succeed.

A FIVE-PHASE FRAMEWORK FOR EVALUATION OF HPT

The five-phase framework in Figure 13.1 is based on the five critical errors discussed in the previous section and is intended to guide evaluation thinking and practice for HPT practitioners. This framework can be used to monitor the

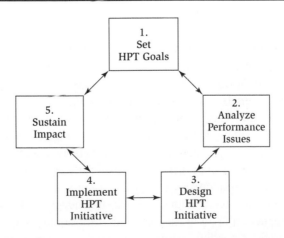

Figure 13.1. A Five-Phase Framework for Evaluation of HPT Initiatives.

evolution of an HPT initiative and to gather data that will help HPT practitioners keep their efforts on track to the most successful outcome. Each phase of
the framework suggests different evaluation questions and concerns, and each
phase likewise would entail different evaluation methods and types of data. But
together, the five phases provide a comprehensive and practical model for HPT
practitioners.

Note that the framework elements in Figure 13.1 are arrayed in a circular format. This emphasizes the fact that the process of implementing HPT evaluation
initiatives is an iterative process that cycles and recycles. Note also that the
arrows connecting the several phases are double-ended. This denotes the fact
that the phases themselves are interactive, and that HPT practitioners would
cycle back and forth between phases, not necessarily moving through the
process in a strictly stepwise fashion. A design for an HPT intervention, for
example, is of course based on the analysis of causes for the performance issue
that has been presented. During the design phase, particularly as stakeholders
react to suggestions for a plan to resolve the performance issue, it is very likely
that their consideration of plans for intervening will introduce new analytic
information. When a manager reviews a suggestion for a job aid intended to
support some aspect of performance, for instance, it may occur to that manager
that incentives for the particular performance are lacking, thus introducing new
consideration of causal analysis.

The remainder of this section describes each phase in more detail, providing
suggested evaluation questions that further define the inquiry to be pursued in
that phase, and also some suggestions for data-collection methods especially
useful in that phase.

Phase 1: Set HPT Goals

HPT always aims beyond just improving performance. Performance itself is neither good nor bad; it is a means to an end. Thus, the value of improving some
aspect of human performance can only be determined by looking at the consequences of the performance. Making more widgets per hour, for example, has the
consequence of greater widget production. It also has the consequence, perhaps,
of a more fatigued performer; making more widgets in an hour also results in a
reduction in raw materials available for making widgets, or some other product;
it also results in an increased supply of widgets which would have subsequent
consequences for the supply in the market and for storage of increased inventory;
likewise, making more widgets per hour means that labor is less available for some
other task, even though it makes more widgets for potential sale. The value of
these and all other consequences of the performance are always relative to the
goals and context of the organization in which the widget-making process resides.
Are more widgets needed? Could they be sold without reducing price and profit?
Is some other product needed more? Could labor be expended in some other

venture more profitably? The HPT practitioner can assess the worth of an HPT initiative only by asking and addressing these questions.

HPT practitioners will encounter many requests and opportunities for improving performance, only some of which are the most valuable and most worthy of further pursuit. Thus, evaluation at this stage is vital to be sure that the goals expressed or implied in the performance-improvement opportunity are truly worthwhile. Note that goals of performance-improvement projects are not always explicit. A performance-improvement process usually begins with a plea for help, or the surfacing of some performance problem. It is always possible to improve performance, but it may not always be worthwhile to do so. Thus, an HPT practitioner's first response to a plea for assistance should not be to ask How? or When? but Why? What argument is there that improving performance in the way suggested or requested would be a worthwhile effort? This may require considerable digging and intensive dialogue with a range of stakeholders. It will also require some persistent thinking from the HPT practitioner, as rarely will the client have thought through all of the potential consequences of improving performance. The true goals of an HPT effort are not just the goals expressed and hoped for by the client; the true goals are the sum of all the consequences that would ensue if the performance opportunity were to be pursued.

It should also be noted that, while this is always the first step in thinking through a performance-improvement initiative, assessment and confirmation of the goals should not be done just once at the beginning of the project. Rather, the goals, implicit and expressed, should be revisited throughout the HPT planning and implementation process, as organizational contexts change: key people who support the HPT effort may change jobs; marketplace dynamics may change; organization roles, goals, and structure may change; and so forth, any one of which could imply a new direction for the HPT initiative.

One of the first vital steps in phase 1 inquiry is clarifying and documenting the intended outcomes and purposes of the proposed HPT initiative so that the goals can be evaluated. The HPT practitioner will find that an especially useful tool for this step is something called an "impact map" (Brinkerhoff and Apking, 2001), which is a particular variant of the more general format known to evaluators as logic models (see, for example, Schmitz and Parsons, 1999).

Table 13.1 shows an impact map for a sample performance-improvement initiative in a hotel that had introduced a new system for customizing guest-room amenities according to special requests of guests. In this system, guests when checking in would be able to complete a brief form specifying any special requests for additional amenities such as spray starch for ironing clothes, nonfat milk for morning coffee, and so on. These data were entered into an intranet database by front-desk staff. Housekeeping staff were provided with training and a job aid that would enable them to access these request forms and take subsequent action to stock the guest room according to guest specifications.

Table 13.1. Impact Map for a Hotel Housekeeper.

Key Capabilities	Critical Actions	Key Results	Guest Services Business Unit Goals	Hotel Company Goals
Able to use new job aid to	Access guest request forms on intranet for assigned rooms and ensure complete understanding of guest requests	All guest rooms fully stocked with requested amenities	Complete guest satisfaction	A fully satisfying guest experience for each hotel guest
• Access intranet and retrieve all pertinent amenity request forms	Alert front-desk staff to any noncertified amenity requests	Guest requests for additional service fulfilled completely, accurately, and on time	All rooms ready for occupancy with no discrepancies	Increase return business rate an average of 20 percent across all guest categories
• Interpret and understand amenity requests	Check request forms daily for changes	Complete satisfaction of guest requests		Increase employee satisfaction
• Place amenities in proper room locations	Stock each guest room with requested amenities			
• Understand and apply all hotel standards for safe and fully equipped guest areas	Check guest rooms daily during cleaning and replenish amenities as needed			

This performance-improvement initiative was part of a larger guest-services initiative intended to contribute to greater guest satisfaction, which was in turn intended to promote repeat business, a key driver of hotel profitability.

Notice that the impact map in Table 13.1 shows the "logic" of the performance-improvement initiative. It explicates how a new capability, enabled by the job aid, is meant to be used in job performance (that is, critical actions), which is then intended to contribute to certain job results that are in turn intended to contribute to the achievement of business unit and overall organization goals. Because the impact map clearly articulates the logic, this logic itself, the intent and goals of the HPT initiative, can then be evaluated, the purpose of phase 1 inquiry. Because it enables clarification and assessment of the HPT goals, HPT practitioners are urged to always prepare an impact map for each of their initiatives. Once the map has been prepared, then there are a number of questions that can be asked about the validity and integrity of the logic.

Key Phase 1 Evaluation Questions

- What is the value of the organizational goals to which the HPT initiative is intended to contribute? Are they valid and worthy of pursuit?
- How does the value of the goal compare to the likely cost of improving performance?
- To what extent is the performance aligned with the values and culture of the organization?
- To what extent is there reason to believe that the performance targeted is likely to make a worthwhile contribution to the business goal?
- How reasonable is it to expect that the current role incumbents have the capability of improving their performance to the extent needed for success?
- To what extent is there political will and support necessary to sustain the performance-improvement initiative?
- To what extent are the performance and business goals supported by existing data?
- To what extent are the performance and business goals likely to be supported by senior managers and other key stakeholders?
- Is the performance targeted for improvement reasonable and likely to be accomplished?
- To what extent is the business goal aligned with organizational strategy, purposes, and values?
- To what extent are performance and business goals ethical and socially responsible?

Some Phase 1 Evaluation Methods

- Seek the opinions, as in a survey, for example, of key leaders and other stakeholders.

- Have a panel of experts and key stakeholders discuss and review the goals and performance-improvement targets.

- Interview the intended performers and their managers and discuss the goals and targets with them.

- Review existing performance data that support the goals.

- Have external experts review the goals and seek their opinions and perspectives.

Phase 2: Analyze Performance Issues

Analysis of performance issues and root causes is, of course, at the heart of HPT and is usually one of the core capabilities in which HPT practitioners have received extensive training and education. Despite the fact that most HPT practitioners are highly skilled in analysis, this phase begs for careful and thoughtful evaluation, since this analysis forms the foundation on which all of the HPT methods and tools needed will be built; if the analysis is flawed, the initiative has little to no chance for success.

The human performance environment is very complex, and, as we noted earlier, has many unknown as well as known elements (Rummler and Brache, 1995; Gilbert, 1996). More than likely, also, particular performers, such as the hotel housekeepers in our example, are not going to be able to improve their performance all on their own. Rather, they will need support, both from other people and from the system in which they work. If the housekeepers' supervisors, for example, do not understand the new guest-services initiative and how it works, they are more likely to subvert its purposes than to help accomplish them. Likewise, if the systems support staff in charge of the hotel's computer systems cannot help solve access and application problems, then there are likely to be performance problems. Other performance-environment elements would have to be effective, such as incentives for the housekeeper's and other staff to make the new process work, measurement and feedback to let them know how things are going, and so forth.

It is useful to think about the analysis phase, and thus evaluation of analysis, as focusing on three related but different levels of performance:

- *Primary performance needs:* these are needs to improve the specific behaviors and results of the performers themselves. For example, to "increase room readiness by 15 percent" is a primary performance need. Primary improvement needs must be clear, must be relevant to the goals to be achieved, and must be within the legitimate reach and control of performers.

- *Secondary performance-improvement needs:* these are the needs for changes that will enhance the capability of the immediate performers—in our example, the housekeepers. They may need a job aid, for example, or better feedback data, or a new skill. A secondary need is for some tool or personal attribute that directly increases the capability of the performers who are responsible for producing the performance represented by the primary performance need.

- *Tertiary performance-improvement needs:* these are needs to make changes in the people or systems that provide support to the direct performers. Very often, direct performers cannot change their behavior by themselves, but require external support. If, for example, the supervisors of the housekeepers were not very good at providing feedback, they may need training in feedback methods and skills in order to make the new guest-services system work. Or imagine that front-desk staff consistently made errors in inputting guest requests, thus meaning that housekeeping staff were not meeting guest needs because they were provided erroneous guest amenity requests. Imagine further that they made these errors because the amenity-inputting software was difficult to use or had inherent flaws. In this case, there would be a need, a tertiary-level need, to make changes in the software or to better train the front-desk staff.

As these few examples make clear, analysis of performance problems and needs is extremely complex, and performance-improvement efforts thus require many layers and levels of intervention. Almost never does a performance problem require just one simple fix, and there are many interconnected needs for change across several layers and levels in the organization. Furthermore, because of the interconnectedness of performance-system factors, a change in one element spreads like ripples across a pond, requiring changes in other elements, and so on. A worthy analysis must identify and make sense of the many factors and keep track of how they interrelate and interact.

Key Phase 2 Evaluation Questions

- Is the primary performance issue or need clearly defined and logically related to important goals?

- Have the correct causes of the primary performance issue or need been accurately identified?

- Have sufficient and logical secondary and tertiary performance needs been identified?

- Is the performance analysis sufficiently broad and comprehensive so that important factors are unlikely to have been overlooked?

- Is there good reason to believe that the causal factors, if they were addressed, would improve performance sufficiently to achieve goals?
- How valid and reliable are data sources used in the analysis?
- To what extent are data sources and factors free from bias and other sources of error?
- Did the analysis employ a valid and comprehensive analysis framework?

Some Phase 2 Evaluation Methods

- Present the analysis to some key stakeholders and ask them to review and critique it.
- Access research studies on similar performance and behavior issues and compare their causal factors to those you have identified.
- Make a performance-analysis checklist and have your analysis reviewed by peers and colleagues.
- Provide your analysis summary to one or more HPT experts and ask for their opinions and feedback.
- Validate your analysis by analyzing the performance of exemplary performers and confirm that the factors you identified are operative and important.

Phase 3: Design HPT Initiative

Once analysis is complete enough to move forward, the HPT practitioner begins to design an intervention, that is, the blend of performance-support procedures, methods, and tools that will best address the performance issues. HPT designs may be relatively simple or highly complex, though almost all will have multiple elements. Even our simple example of the hotel housekeeper could have several moving parts, for instance:

- A paper-based job aid (a checklist, for example) for use by housekeepers
- An on-line performance-support tool for front-desk staff to help them input guest preferences
- Training for housekeepers
- Training for front-desk staff
- Software for systems support staff to use
- Training for housekeeping and front-desk supervisors
- An incentive system to recognize and reward exemplary performance
- An orientation document or presentation for senior hotel management to solicit their support and buy-in

- A measurement process and associated feedback system to track progress and keep performers and other stakeholders informed

Behind each of these elements is an array of associated design steps and tasks. The checklist job aid for housekeepers, for example, would require validation to be sure it completely lists and describes proper locations for each amenity; the checklist would need to be shared with supervisors to gain their feedback and ideas for revision; the checklist format and language would need to be validated; a field test would be used to be sure it was user friendly and could be accurately interpreted and applied; a training session focusing on its use would need to be planned and scheduled; materials and exercises would need to be designed. In sum, an HPT design has a lot of interrelated parts and is likely to be more rather than less complex. It must be technically sound and carefully integrated.

In addition to having technical adequacy, that is, the right elements that are capable of improving performance, the design has to be practical and feasible. This will vary according to the organization. What would work in one organization may not work in another, since all organizations differ in their political nature, culture, work environment, sophistication, and so on. The HPT design a practitioner plans must be integrated with and suitable for use by the people for whom it is intended and aligned with their needs, interests, capabilities, values, and preferences. If it is in any way alien to these sorts of social contextual factors, it is likely to fail despite its level of technical elegance.

Key Phase 3 Evaluation Questions
- Is the design complete? Has it accounted for and addressed all important primary, secondary, and tertiary needs?
- How likely is it that the organization will be capable of making the design work? Is it compatible with existing procedures, tools, and systems?
- Are the technical resources (for example, computer, telephone, and information) available to make the design work?
- Is there likely to be sufficient managerial support for the HPT design?
- Is the HPT design cost-effective and efficient?
- Is there a reasonable and logical theoretical foundation for the design? Is it supported by HPT theory, research, and best practices?
- Is the design compatible with performers' capability levels, experience, culture, and other interests and needs?
- Is the proposed design the most cost-effective solution available?
- Is the design fully ethical and fair, and does it comply with all legal and human rights codes and guidelines?

Some Phase 3 Evaluation Methods

- Conduct a field test of the design with a small group of performers or in a single business unit.
- Make a checklist of all of the factors listed earlier that bear on design adequacy and effectiveness, and have key stakeholders review and critique the design.
- Conduct presentations and "hearings" on your design and solicit feedback and advice
- Have the design reviewed by some HPT experts.
- Have the design reviewed by senior managers.
- Compare the design to solutions tried by others and reported in research and practice publications.
- Present the design at a professional association meeting and solicit feedback.

Phase 4: Implement HPT Initiative

Evaluation of implementation is very much like good project management, and has two principal purposes:

1. *Steering:* to track implementation, assess progress, and provide feedback to HPT leaders so they can make ongoing revisions to ensure success
2. *Accountability:* to inform HPT leaders and stakeholders and assure them that the HPT resources are being used appropriately and that the initiative is being faithfully and professionally implemented

The steering purpose of evaluation at this phase is accomplished by careful monitoring of the HPT initiative, paying special attention to whether critical actions are being carried out and whether interim objectives and milestones are being met. The general process for implementation evaluation follows a discrepancy analysis model. That is, the design calls for certain actions, events, and milestones; the design prescribes what is supposed to be happening. Housekeepers, to return to the hotel example, should be referring to the checklist and placing the correct kind and amount of amenities in guests' rooms. The evaluation should check to see whether actual housekeeper performance matches this expectation. If there are discrepancies between intent and actual actions and results, then the HPT leaders should take action to reduce or eliminate the discrepancy.

An HPT practitioner can manage discrepancies elimination in two ways. One way to get rid of a discrepancy is to better control actual performance so that it comes closer to the expectations set forth in the design. Housekeepers, for example, might be further trained, or provided more assistance from supervisors to help them better meet expectations. Exercising greater control over performance is the most common way that discrepancies are resolved. But sometimes a discrepancy points out a flaw or oversight in the design. The expectation set forth in the design may prove to be not appropriate or otherwise misguided. If it appears that the intent itself was unrealistic, or if conditions have changed so that the original intent is no longer correct, then the performance expectations can be adjusted to better match what experience is teaching.

In an evaluation of a call center performance-improvement project, the HPT designers had called for a thirty-second reduction in call duration; this objective, it was felt, would allow for more calls to be completed in an hour but still meet customer information needs. As it turned out, the best that call center operators could achieve was a twenty-second duration reduction, on average. Calls cut short of this mark tended to impair customer service and increased the stress levels on operators to unreasonable levels. The call center managers, taking this emerging performance information into account, adjusted customer fee schedules so that fewer calls per hour would not undermine profits, and the project went forward with a new standard. As it turned out, the twenty-second reduction seemed optimum; customer service improved, profits improved, and staff satisfaction as indicated by absenteeism also improved.

It is also important during evaluation of implementation to monitor support and contextual variables to assess the extent to which key players in the HPT process are fulfilling their responsibilities. If, for example, desk staff are not faithfully inputting guest requests, then amenity stocking behavior will not meet guest expectations. Or, for another example, if managers are not providing employee time to have meetings to discuss progress, this could likewise undermine staff performance. Providing feedback to these several key players is a vital role for evaluation. It enables HPT leaders to use feedback to shape the behavior of these parties, recognize them for their contributions, and gently persuade them to live up to their promises.

Accountability is also served by evaluation of implementation. In this case, resource consumption is tracked and performance data recorded so that key stakeholders can be informed of progress and results. This helps demonstrate responsibility and accountability, and provides a way to keep all parties to the HPT effort focused on results and outcomes.

Key Phase 4 Evaluation Questions

- To what extent are interim milestones and objectives being achieved, on time and with sufficient quality?
- To what extent is the HPT effort operating on schedule and within budget?

- How completely and effectively are key stakeholders and others providing the resources and other support needed to enable success?

- To what extent are HPT tools and methods (for example, job aids) being deployed and used as they were planned? What needs for revisions are emerging?

- What revision needs are emerging to keep the HPT effort headed for success?

- What changes are occurring in the context of the HPT initiative that have implications for revision or redirection?

- To what extent is performance improving as HPT tools and methods are used?

- To what extent is the HPT effort meeting the needs, interests, and expectations of key stakeholders?

Some Phase 4 Evaluation Methods

- Use observations, interviews, and questionnaires to gather and review opinion and operating (that is, behavioral) data from users of HPT tools and methods.

- Monitor resource expenditure and compare it to schedules and achievement of interim objectives.

- Survey or otherwise seek the opinions of key stakeholders to gauge their satisfaction with progress to date and identify their concerns.

- Interview or otherwise seek opinions from customers (for example, managers of performers) to gauge their satisfaction and emerging concerns.

- Conduct regular project-review meetings to identify and resolve emerging HPT staff issues.

Phase 5: Sustaining Impact and Worthy Performance

This fifth and final phase of the HPT evaluation cycle focuses on the performance results and goals of the intervention. It asks, in essence, (1) what results the HPT initiative has achieved or contributed to, (2) whether these results and other emerging conditions indicate lasting outcomes of value, and (3) what if anything should be done to make this current or future HPT effort more effective. To some extent, this phase focuses on the outcomes produced and the extent to which client needs and interests have been positively addressed. This phase may also focus on the concerns and questions of the HPT practitioners themselves, asking what worked, what did not work, and what should be done in the future to get better results. Phase 5, like all other phases of the evaluation cycle, is aimed at learning. But in this case, the focus for inquiry is the results of the HPT effort and the conditions that helped or impeded the achievement of positive results, the most powerful and lasting lessons of the entire effort.

Phase 5 evaluation brings the evaluation cycle back to its beginning. At phase 1, the central question was, To what extent are the projected goals worthy of effort and likely to be positively affected? At phase 5, the focus is again on goals, but retrospectively. Now we ask whether the goals actually achieved are worthwhile and whether they are likely to be and are worth being sustained.

Phase 5 evaluation also confronts more directly the issue of causation. Causation was implicit at the early phases, especially in phase 1, goals; phase 2, analysis; and phase 3, design. All of these phases rest on the assumption that actions taken to improve performance will indeed be efficacious; that the HPT analysis and design are likely to lead to an impact on goals. At phase 5, causation is more explicitly examined, for at phase 5 we ask, What results did our efforts help achieve, and are they worthwhile? What worked to help achieve these goals? What did not? The client has always paid a price for the HPT effort, in time, money, and displaced resources. Both the client and the HPT practitioner must find out what these resources have bought, and decide finally whether the "purchase" was worth the expenditure.

There can be no final and indisputable proof, however, and the evaluation should not be held to this standard of proof. No amount of inquiry into human, social, and organizational behavior can ever account for the action of unknown factors and quantities. The criterion is for reasonable evidence that the HPT effort either helped or did not help to improve performance. Evidence for causation is more likely to be firm at the level of immediate performance outcomes than it is at the level of ultimate business results. We'll return briefly to our earlier example of a hotel seeking ultimately to improve repeat business. Part of the analysis in this example led to a conclusion that guest satisfaction was a primary determinant of whether a guest would decide to make a return visit to a hotel. This analysis can be quite definitively established through research and practice, and of course was the basis for making a decision to affect satisfaction in the first place. The next level of analysis determined that provision of amenities would help drive guest satisfaction. This in turn led to an assumption that meeting "customized" amenity requests as fulfilled by housekeepers would be helpful in driving satisfaction. Further analysis determined that housekeeper performance in stocking rooms to expectations could be facilitated by a combination of training for housekeepers, a job aid, a system for recording guest requests and summarizing them for housekeepers, training for front-desk staff in soliciting and inputting guest requirements, a measurement-and-feedback process, and so on.

Impact on the business goal of repeat business was, of course, the reason for all of this effort in the first place, and phase 5 evaluation should seek information about this impact. But we must also recognize that a number of prior performance objectives, a sort of "causal chain" of outcomes, would have to be achieved in order to make the intended contribution to the business goal. Thus, the evaluation has to carefully define the causal linkage and monitor the achievement of the interim and enabling outcomes, such as the extent to which front-desk staff gathered and recorded accurate guest-request information, or the extent to which housekeepers correctly interpreted guest requirements and placed the amenities in the guest rooms. If there is a break in this causal chain, then the achievement of the business goal is at risk, and steps should be taken by the HPT practitioner to resolve the breakdown. Imagine, for example, that evaluation showed that front-desk staff were correctly recording guest requests but also revealed that some guests were not getting their requested amenities. Imagine further that evaluation of housekeeper performance showed that they interpreted the requests correctly but that there was sometimes an insufficient supply of amenities available to place in rooms. Armed with these data, the HPT practitioner could investigate the breakdown in the supply process, and might discover that the hotel's purchasing staff was not kept adequately apprised of amenity demands and thus was not ordering sufficient quantities to consistently fill guest requests. In this instance, the "fix" would be obvious: implement a better process for communicating front-desk request information to the purchasing staff.

This example makes clear the fact that, while phase 5 evaluation is conceptually retrospective—that is, it looks back at performance through assessment of achievement of results—its evaluation activity does not wait chronologically until the end of the entire HPT effort. Instead, phase 5 inquiry overlaps and interacts with phase 4, and begins as soon as the HPT implementation has stabilized and interim results and outcomes are being achieved. In this manner, phase 5 aims to improve the achievement of HPT outcomes at the same time as it assesses the causal contribution to the achievement of business goals. Imagine, for example, that assessment of repeat business showed poor results; the hotel had not increased its percentage of repeat business except to a small degree. Yet, further imagine that all aspects of the HPT intervention, the amenity request and stocking procedure, had worked exactly as planned. In this case, it would appear that the operation, the amenity process, was a success, but that the patient, repeat business, died. This could, of course, be possible if some external force had overwhelmed the performance-improvement effort and affected repeat business. A nationwide catastrophe or economic slowdown, for example, could easily have a strong and negative impact on repeat business through drastic reduction of discretionary business travel. Does this mean that the guest-services initiative was a failure and should be discontinued? Not necessarily. Phase 5 evaluations, by looking at both the achievement of interim HPT outcomes and the eventual achievement of business goals can help stakeholders understand the initiative more completely, gaining critical knowledge about what worked and what did not. It is possible, for example, that the effect of the HPT effort on improving guest satisfaction would still be deemed a worthwhile investment on the part of the hotel despite the temporary economic scenario that was suppressing repeat business, since the increase in guest satisfaction might consolidate the hotel's competitive stature and position it for an increase in business and profits when the economy allowed a return to more discretionary business travel.

In sum, the charge for phase 5 evaluation is to measure and assess the achievement of outcomes, both good and bad, both intended and not, and to track achievement of outcomes from the most immediate, early objectives to the eventual impact on the broader business goals that were the reason for the HPT initiative in the first place. This will help stakeholders judge the worth of the HPT effort, make decisions to continue or improve or abort the effort, and also use the learning from this evaluative inquiry to build capability for more effective and successful HPT efforts in the future.

Key Phase 5 Evaluation Questions

- To what extent has performance in key roles and processes improved or not?
- What additional, unplanned-for outcomes have occurred that are a likely result of the HPT initiative?
- To what extent has performance on business goals and metrics that were the reason for the HPT effort improved?
- What parts of the HPT initiative worked, and what did not?
- What factors supported the success of the initiative and what factors impeded its success?
- What evidence is there that the HPT initiative elements contributed to or were the "causes" of improvements in performance?
- What should future HPT initiatives do differently?

Some Phase 5 Evaluation Methods

- Analyze performance records and work samples, if appropriate, and compare changes in them to data about when, where, and to what extent HPT interventions were used and applied.
- Survey performers and ask them what worked and what did not.
- Survey the bosses and customers of performers and ask them about results, changes, improvements, and shortfalls.
- Track and analyze business metrics to assess changes and improvements.
- Conduct "post mortem" reviews and discussions with HPT staff, performers, and other stakeholders.

- Conduct pre-post analyses and comparisons on key performance factors and metrics from before the HPT intervention occurred to conditions and metrics after it was used.

- Conduct comparative analyses of the performance of individuals and groups who made the most use of HPT tools and methods to those who made the least use of them; determine whether differences in performance varied as a function of amount and quality of HPT tool and method usage.

- Conduct pilot comparison group studies. Try the HPT interventions out on one group and withhold them from another group, and compare their performance before and after the HPT intervention.

- Conduct "success case" studies (Brinkerhoff, 2003) in which you find those who were most, and least, successful in improving performance. Then assess the value of the HPT effort when it works best, and determine how much more value could be achieved if more people were as successful as the most successful people. Identify the factors that seem to determine the difference between the most and least successful groups, and decide if they can be more effectively managed to get more success.

SUMMARY

Evaluation should pervade all the steps and phases of an HPT effort, with the purpose of both improving the effectiveness of the initiative and assessing and accounting for its impact. Evaluation is especially useful in HPT because it enables a "rapid prototyping" approach that allows HPT practitioners to quickly plan and implement HPT solutions even though the analysis of causes and influencing factors may be incomplete. Through progressive cycles of analyzing, trying solutions, and checking on how well they work, important and pressing client performance issues and problems can be quickly addressed at the same time that the HPT practitioner is learning how to make them even more effective and productive.

A useful framework for HPT evaluation is to apply a five-phase model. In phase 1, the goal of the HPT effort is evaluated to be sure that it is reasonable, worthwhile, important, and likely to be successfully affected by the planned HPT initiative. At phase 2, evaluation is applied to the analysis of performance issues and opportunities to be sure that accurate performance factors and causes are identified and that the analytic foundation for the HPT effort is sufficiently valid to enable a solution that is likely to work. At phase 3, evaluation is applied to the design for the HPT intervention, assessing its technical adequacy and the degree to which key support factors have been solidified—managerial buy-in, for example. Evaluation at this phase helps the HPT practitioners assure themselves and their clients that the design is practical, technically sound, and cost-effective. A phase 4 evaluation is used to monitor implementation of the HPT effort and help steer it to increasingly greater success. Phase 5 evaluations complete the HPT cycle, assessing the impact of the HPT initiative and determining what worked and what did not.

References

Brinkerhoff, R. O. (2003). *Success case method.* San Francisco: Berrett-Koehler.

Brinkerhoff, R. O., and Apking, A. M. (2001). *High-impact learning.* Cambridge, MA: Perseus.

Gilbert, T. F. (1996). *Human competence: Engineering worthy performance* (ISPI tribute edition). Washington, DC, and Amherst, MA: International Society for Performance Improvement and HRD Press.

Rummler, G., and Brache, A. (1995). *Improving performance: How to manage the white space in the organization chart* (2nd ed.). San Francisco: Jossey-Bass.

Schmitz, C., and Parsons, B. (1999). *Everything you wanted to know about logic models but were afraid to ask.* Battle Creek, MI: W. K. Kellogg Foundation.

Additional Resources

Phillips, J. J. (2003). *Return on investment in performance improvement programs* (2nd ed.). Woburn, MA: Butterworth-Heineman.

A very practical, though somewhat formulaic, practitioner's guide to conducting evaluations that result in quantitative estimates of financial values and benefits as compared to the costs of training and HPT initiatives.

Russ-Eft, D., and Preskill, H. (2001). *Evaluation in organizations: A systematic approach to enhancing learning, performance, and change.* Cambridge, MA: Perseus.

Provides a more thorough and scholarly, though also practical, coverage of several constructions, theories and approaches to evaluation.

Swanson, R. A., and Holwood, E. F. (1999). *Results: How to assess performance, learning, and perceptions in organizations.* San Francisco: Berrett-Koehler.

This is a solid and well-conceived approach to evaluation that many practitioners will find useful; many examples and tools are provided.

CHAPTER FOURTEEN

The Full Scoop on
Full-Scope Evaluation

Joan C. Dessinger, James L. Moseley

What is this thing called full-scope evaluation? What makes it different from just plain evaluation? Why is there a chapter devoted to full-scope evaluation in this handbook on human performance technology (HPT)? Is it something you ought to do?

The authors of this chapter believe that evaluation is more than a separate process box at the end of the HPT model; that is why we added relationship arrows when we expanded the model for *Fundamentals of Performance Technology* in 2000 and revised the arrows in the 2004 second edition (Figure 14.1). The arrows indicate that evaluation is, or should be, an integral and integrated part of the performance-improvement process; it should take place during all HPT processes: performance and cause analyses, intervention selection and design, and implementation and change.

This chapter will give you the full scoop on full-scope evaluation and will describe how you can integrate full-scope evaluation into the HPT process. So read on, and then make up your own mind whether you want to "do" full-scope evaluation.

WHAT EVALUATION IS; WHAT IT IS NOT

Evaluation wears many faces. It is integral to every aspect of life. Consider these examples: I visit my local grocery store to purchase Bing cherries. I take handfuls of cherries, but prior to placing them in a sack, I separate them. I look for

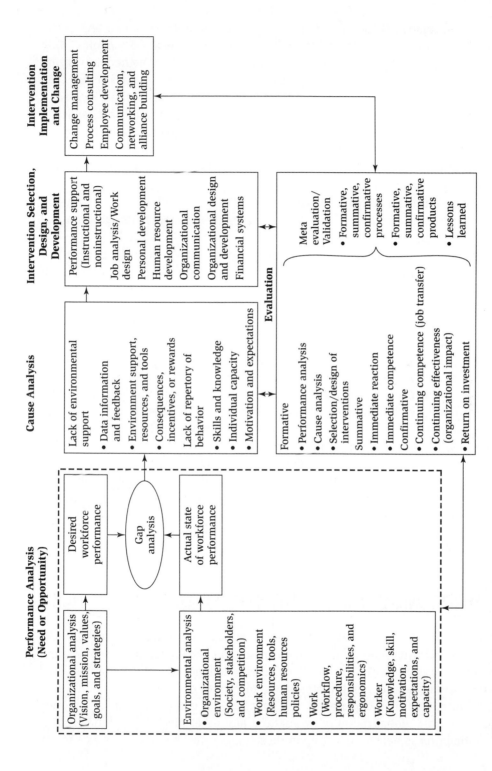

Figure 14.1. ISPI Human Performance Technology Model.

Source: Van Tiem, Moseley, and Dessinger, 2004, p. 3. Used with permission.

firmness, remove those that are blemished, and may even taste a few in the process. I then move to the meat counter to purchase steaks. My choices may include select choice or prime-grade quality, wet or dry-aged method, or varying amounts of marbling, and, if I really know my steaks, I may also consider the feed type, since corn creates buttery fattiness whereas grass yields a leaner steak.

I then go home and, while grilling my steak and eating a few cherries, I watch the Olympic Games. I form my judgment about a particular athlete's success. Then professional judges render their scores based on technical accuracy and aesthetics. The higher the score, the more likely the athlete will secure a place in the limelight.

In these three examples I have unconsciously and subjectively evaluated cherries, steaks, and an athlete. I have even made my judgments against a real set of criteria.

Evaluation in professional settings is similar to the evaluation choices we make on a daily basis. The evaluator renders a judgment of value or worth against a set of specific criteria. The evaluation is subjective; however, it is made more solid because we add measurement. For example, we may say that 93 percent of the participants agree that instructional objective number four gives them a good review of the history of evaluation or that thirty-six of the fifty participants feel confident that given a performance-support tool they could transfer a procedure to their job. Similarly, we need to evaluate individual performance, competence, organizational impact, and so forth in the business world not only by describing situations but also by comparing variables, predicting relationships, and showing significance, using evaluation that is peppered with robust measurement.

When we think about evaluation we often reflect upon accountability issues, all levels and kinds of objectives, budgeting priorities and constraints, pre- and post-performance and other testing, and the like. There is the tendency to equate these elements with evaluation. Beware! In themselves, they are not evaluation; however, all evaluation has elements of objectives, testing, budgeting, and accountability.

MILESTONES IN THE EVOLUTION OF EVALUATION PRACTICE

There are many milestones in the history of evaluation that reflect the social trends of the time: testing movement in schools, heavy reliance on measurement, experts relying on social science methodologies, creation of professional associations, development of standards and codes of conduct, competition in the United States precipitated by the space race accomplishments of the then Soviet Union, globalization of evaluation, and other pivotal benchmarks. It is not the purpose here to reflect upon these milestones; however, it is safe to say these activities influenced current evaluation theory and sound practice (Fitzpatrick, Sanders, and Worthen, 2004).

A seminal work in program evaluation is *Standards for Evaluations of Educational Programs, Projects, and Materials* by the Joint Committee on Standards for Educational Evaluation (1981). The standards focused on K–12 schools, and in 1994 they were expanded to include other settings as well. "The Joint Committee *Standards* is a set of thirty standards, each with an overview that provides definitions and a rationale for the standard, a list of guidelines, common errors, illustrative cases describing evaluation practices that could have been guided by that particular standard, and an analysis of each case" (Fitzpatrick, Sanders, and Worthen, 2004, p. 444). The quality of an evaluation study is judged by utility, feasibility, propriety, and accuracy.

Another pivotal benchmark that has influenced professional evaluation is the set of principles developed by the American Evaluation Association (AEA). The AEA guiding principles promote systematic inquiry about all aspects of evaluation, competence of evaluators, honesty and integrity of the evaluation process, respect for all stakeholders, and societal concerns focusing on diverse interests and values. HPT organizations have stepped up to the plate with their guiding principles, standards, and codes of conduct for all HPT processes, including evaluation; for example, the International Society for Performance Improvement (ISPI) and the American Society for Training and Development (ASTD) both have certification programs for performance technologists that include standards and codes of ethics (Van Tiem, Moseley, and Dessinger, 2004; American Society for Training and Development, 2005).

The individual who has contributed most to past and present evaluation thought and practice is Michael Scriven. Scriven coined the terms *formative evaluation* and *summative evaluation.* He provided several product-evaluation checklists that have shaped the consumer-oriented evaluation approaches over the years. Scriven also challenged our perspective with goal-free evaluation (Scriven, 1967). His current efforts in evaluation continue to guide and focus evaluation theory and practice.

Two individuals who are influencing the current practice of evaluation in the training and development and human performance technology fields are Jack Phillips and Carl Binder. Phillips extends the Kirkpatrick levels discussed later in this chapter by adding a fifth level called "return on investment" (ROI). This level takes a hard look at the monetary value of the results and costs for a program (Phillips, 1991). Binder, a frequent contributor to the ISPI publications *Performance Improvement* and *PerformanceXpress,* encourages human performance practitioners to employ sound evaluation practice and robust measurement. He sounds the alarm and cautions us that the survival of HPT means we need to plan for effective measurement because that is what drives business results (Binder, 2002).

There are a variety of pivotal monograph resources on formative and summative evaluation. However, there is only one resource on confirmative evaluation that addresses continuing efficiency, effectiveness, sustainability, value, and alignment: *Confirmative Evaluation: Practical Strategies for Valuing Continuous Improvement* (Dessinger and Moseley, 2003). Evaluators need to seamlessly add confirmative evaluation to their repertoire of knowledge and skills. Dessinger and Moseley's book is an on-the-job guide for planning and conducting confirmative evaluation to evaluate performance-improvement interventions three to twelve months after implementation.

EVALUATION MODELS

Evaluation models are blueprints for guiding and making evaluation decisions. Many of the models that are often applied within the HPT framework actually come from the Educational Technology (ET) or Instructional Systems Development (ISD) arenas and may be adapted to both training and nontraining interventions by creative HPT practitioners. The HPT practitioner benefits from a general understanding of the various models reported here along with an eclectic approach to their use and value.

Curriculum Evaluation Models

The literature reports a variety of curriculum evaluation models. Tyler, Provus, Hammond, Papham, Taba, Bloom, and others have followed the "straightforward procedure of letting the achievement of objectives determine success or failure and justify improvements, maintenance, or termination of program activities" (Fitzpatrick, Sanders, and Worthen, 2004, p. 80). Scriven and Komoski support a consumer-oriented approach using varieties of criterion checklists and product testing to address the consumer information needs of audiences, sponsors, clients, and stakeholders (Fitzpatrick, Sanders, and Worthen, 2004, pp. 100–111). Eisner suggests expertise evaluation where professional judgments of quality are required. Individuals such as Stake, Patton, Guba, Lincoln, and so on are participant-oriented, use a pluralistic approach, and are concerned with description, judgment, and context (Fitzpatrick, Sanders, and Worthen, 2004, pp. 129–151).

Training Evaluation Models

The literature also reports a variety of training evaluation models. The grand-daddy of all is the Kirkpatrick Model. Kirkpatrick focuses on four levels of evaluation: level 1, participant reaction; level 2, participant learning; level 3, on-the-job change in behavior; and level 4, final results of the training

(Kirkpatrick, 1994). Kirkpatrick is referenced by Hale (2004) and other HPT practitioners in terms of evaluating both training and nontraining performance-improvement interventions.

Other models, such as the CIRO Model, Hierarchy Model, Bell System Model, Contingency Model, Behavioral Science Model, Xerox Model, IBM Evaluation Model, and Saratoga Institute Model, are rooted in Kirkpatrick's four levels. For more information on these models, see Moseley and Dessinger (1998, pp. 233–260).

Eclectic Models

There are models that are more eclectic and flexible in their approach to evaluation. They can be used both in training evaluation and in human performance technology evaluation. The Kaufman, Keller, Watkins Model suggests a five-level approach to interventions: level 1, inputs such as human, physical, and financial resources and reactions such as perceived acceptability and efficiency of methods, means, and processes; level 2, acquisition, mastery, and competence; level 3, application or utilization within the organization; level 4, organizational results; and level 5, societal outcomes focusing on client responsiveness, contributions, and payoffs (Van Tiem, Moseley, and Dessinger, 2004).

Brinkerhoff's Six-Stage Model evaluates needs and goals that trigger an intervention; the design that addresses responsiveness to needs and goals; operation or the installation and implementation of an intervention in relation to the needs and design; the learning that takes place when interventions are first used; the endurance and sustainability of the intervention over time; and the payoff or the return on investment from the successfully implemented interventions (Van Tiem, Moseley, and Dessinger, 2004).

Stufflebeam's CIPP Model delineates context or planning, input or structuring, process or implementing, and product or recycling. CIPP is a comprehensive approach to evaluating at all stages of program development (Fitzpatrick, Sanders, and Worthen, 2004).

Full-Scope Evaluation: A Timely New Model

Unlike the models discussed previously, the Dessinger-Moseley Full-Scope Evaluation Model illustrates the benefits of integrating two processes, performance improvement and evaluation, in one iterative flow. The model blends formative, summative, confirmative, and meta evaluation into a seamless, iterative flow for making judgments about the continuing merit and worth of any performance-improvement intervention. Then the HPT practitioner skillfully diverts the flow into the mainstream HPT process, where it becomes part of, rather than a branch off of, the HPT process flow. The real scoop is that full-scope evaluation can be as deep and as wide as you and your stakeholders agree that it needs to be.

FULL-SCOPE EVALUATION: AN OVERVIEW

One way to gain perspective on full-scope evaluation is to zoom out to view full-scope evaluation in its entirety, and then zoom in on each of the four components and their foci. Zooming out gives us a holistic view or the full scoop; zooming in reveals the details.

Zooming Out: Definition, Purpose, and a Model

Since we first began to talk and write about full-scope evaluation, we have tried to develop a model that graphically reveals its iterative nature (Moseley and Dessinger, 1998) and establishes the purpose of full-scope evaluation through the use of foci: what each type of evaluation focuses on throughout its life cycle. The latest model (Figure 14.2) uses concentric circles and the concept of "foci" to illustrate how full-scope evaluation may be integrated into the HPT process. If it were feasible to do so on paper, we would set each circle spinning to intensify

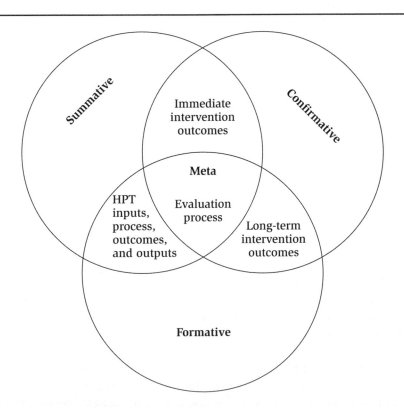

Figure 14.2. The Dessinger-Moseley Full-Scope Evaluation Model.

the concept of evaluation as spiraling concentric circles of activities that are always pulling in and sending out new information.

The Dessinger-Moseley Full-Scope Evaluation Model provides a holistic view of full-scope evaluation as it applies to the HPT process. The concentric circles illustrate the iterative relationship among the four types of evaluation, and the overlaps suggest that integrating evaluation throughout the HPT process makes it possible to focus on the full range of performance improvement: inputs, processes, outputs, and outcomes.

Within the overlaps are the foci of each type of evaluation. Beginning with the overlap between formative and summative evaluation, the model identifies the following foci:

- Formative evaluation focuses on the HPT processes of performance, gap, and cause analysis; intervention selection, design, development, and implementation and change; and the process outputs and outcomes.

- Summative evaluation focuses on immediate intervention outcomes, such as reaction, accomplishment, and immediate impact.

- Confirmative evaluation focuses on the long-term intervention outcomes of efficiency, effectiveness, impact, and value.

- Meta evaluation focuses on attributes of the evaluation process itself, such as validity, reliability, and accountability.

Zooming In: The Components of Full-Scope Evaluation

The four types of evaluation that make up full-scope evaluation are delineated by their purpose and timing. Table 14.1 illustrates the differences among the four types.

Formative Evaluation. Formative evaluation keeps us honest to ourselves and to the process right from the start. It judges the merit and worth of the processes we use to analyze, select, design, develop, and implement performance interventions, and the products or outcomes that result from the processes. For example, we formatively evaluate the design and development of a training program when we ask subject-matter experts to review the training materials for content completeness and accuracy or we pilot the training program with a sample audience to determine whether there are ambiguities in the content or presentation.

Summative Evaluation. Summative evaluation is the most familiar and most used type of evaluation. Using summative evaluation, we can judge how the participants and customers of the performance-improvement intervention felt about the intervention and the degree to which what we said would happen is

Table 14.1. Zooming In on the Components of Full-Scope Evaluation.

Type	Focus or Purpose	Timing
Formative	Improve performance intervention process and outputs	During analysis, selection, design, and development
Summative	Determine immediate user competency and immediate intervention effectiveness	During implementation and change
Confirmative	Determine continuing user competency and intervention effectiveness, efficiency, impact, and value	Three to twelve months after implementation of long-term intervention; that is, one year or more
Meta	Evaluate evaluation process and outputs	After confirmative evaluation is completed

Source: Adapted from Van Tiem, Moseley, and Dessinger, *Fundamentals of Performance Technology* (2004), p. 157. Used with permission.

really happening right now. Participant reaction surveys and knowledge or performance pre-post tests are examples of common summative evaluation tools.

Confirmative Evaluation. Confirmative evaluation is not just an "extension of summative evaluation" (see Table 14.1). Confirmative evaluation helps us go a step further and verify that what we said would happen has continued to happen after the intervention has been implemented for a year or more. The tools for gathering confirmative evaluation data include review of existing documentation such as formative and summative evaluation data, organizational impact data, and so forth; surveys; individual or group interviews; and observation. They also include more sophisticated techniques and tools such as ROI analysis.

Meta Evaluation. Meta evaluation also helps to keep us honest. We use it to evaluate how well we have been and are evaluating by judging the merit and worth of all our evaluation processes and products. Type 1 meta evaluation is concurrent, evaluate-as-you-go evaluation of the evaluation, and type 2 meta evaluation evaluates the evaluation after it is completed and focuses on whether the results are reliable and valid.

Zooming In: Full-Scope Evaluation Activities

There are seven major activities that contribute to any successful evaluation, including full-scope evaluation:

1. Plan the evaluation
2. Design and develop the materials
3. Collect the data
4. Analyze the data
5. Interpret the findings
6. Communicate the status of the evaluation activities and the findings, with recommendations for action
7. Document and archive information on the evaluation process and results

The activities that are most crucial to the success of full-scope evaluation are planning, communicating, documenting, and archiving the evaluation process and results.

Develop a Plan. Planning for full-scope evaluation is either proactive or reactive. Proactive planning takes place up front during the planning phase for the intervention. Reactive planning is the result of a trigger event that occurs during or after the intervention is implemented. Suddenly a stakeholder needs to measure the outcomes or prove the value of the intervention. In either case, planning should address and resolve the following issues:

- Who are the stakeholders for the evaluation? Who needs to know whether the intervention is successful?
- Why do the stakeholders need to know? To plan? Prove? Improve? Make decisions?
- What information do the stakeholders need to know to meet their needs?
- What evaluation objectives do we need to accomplish to meet stakeholder needs?
- What evaluation questions do we need to answer to meet stakeholder needs?
- What evaluation data do we need to collect to accomplish the evaluation objectives or answer the evaluation questions?
- What sources are required and available to provide the data we need?
- What resources such as people, technology, time, or money, are required and available to collect and analyze the data, and interpret and communicate the results?
- What data-collection techniques are most useful, given the evaluation objectives and the current context such as organizational culture, climate, and resources? Survey or questionnaire? Group or individual interview? Observation? Review of existing documents? Other . . . ?

- What analysis techniques are most useful, given the evaluation objectives or questions and the current context, such as organizational culture, climate, and resources? Informal analysis techniques may include focus groups, Delphi technique, Q Sort, and other qualitative techniques; formal analysis techniques may include frequency distributions, mean-mode-median, analysis of variance (ANOVA), multiple regression analysis, and other quantitative techniques.

- How and to whom should we communicate the results?

- How should we document and archive the evaluation processes and results so that they are useful for auditing this evaluation and guiding future evaluation efforts?

Planning is the most crucial activity for a successful full-scope evaluation because it establishes a strong foundation for why and how the evaluation will be conducted. Once the plan is in place, it is just a matter of using the plan as a road map for the remaining evaluation activities: collection, analysis, interpretation, communication, and documentation.

Communicate: Let Them Know You Are Still Around. Communicating the findings at each stage of full-scope evaluation is also crucial. Full-scope evaluation stays around longer than "regular" evaluation and requires long-term support from the organization and all the stakeholders. Provide information on the findings with recommendations for action so the stakeholders can use the information to make decisions related to performance improvement. If you are beginning to implement the next step in the evaluation plan, let everyone know when and why so they can arrange their schedules if necessary and begin to "think evaluation" again. There may be a gap of several weeks or even months between evaluations, and the stakeholders need to remain aware that evaluation is still an important part of the intervention process.

Document and Archive. Keeping accurate records and documenting what you are doing as well as what you have discovered throughout the evaluation is critical. Lessons learned may save time and money the next time around, may help to develop expertise in a novice HPT practitioner, and may even help you develop a business case for your next full-scope evaluation effort. The need for documenting and archiving both the evaluation process and the evaluation results is not as obvious as it sounds. Unless the organization has a good knowledge-management structure and practice in place or is affected by certification or regulatory standards, many stakeholders fail to see the usefulness of documenting and archiving information, and many practitioners skip this step.

THINKING INSIDE THE BOX

What makes full-scope evaluation work is that it is both iterative and integrated; the flow between types of evaluation is seamless, and, in most cases, it is better not to be "outside of the process box." Tables 14.2, 14.3, and 14.4 provide suggestions for how to integrate full-scope evaluation into the HPT process. Table 14.2 suggests ways to integrate formative, summative, and confirmative evaluation into the analysis stage of the HPT process; Table 14.3 presents similar suggestions for the intervention selection, design, and development stage, and Table 14.4 describes what to do during intervention implementation and change. When evaluation is integrated into the HPT process, the evaluation stage is no longer a separate entity, so it is not represented in this table.

IMPLEMENTING FULL-SCOPE EVALUATION
IN THE REAL WORLD

Car companies do it, chemical companies do it, companies dedicated to Six Sigma and other formal quality-improvement processes do it, and do it well. But, like Willy Loman, the protagonist in *Death of a Salesman,* those who do it feel they do not need to talk about it. Over the past six years we have asked close to 250 full-scope evaluation workshop participants the following question: Do you, your clients, or your organization do full-scope evaluation: formative, summative, confirmative, and meta? We have kept a tally of the replies, and Figure 14.3 shows how the replies spread over a continuum from Yes to Not Sure.

When pressed, even those who admit to "doing" full-scope evaluation do not like to provide specific case studies or discuss findings, or even share strategies. It is easier to document innovative formative or summative evaluation practices or Kirkpatrick's Levels 1 through 4, which certainly contain elements of full-scope evaluation, or even ROI studies. Part of this reticence on the part of practitioners may stem from the sensitive nature of the data collected during a full-scope evaluation. It can definitely bare the

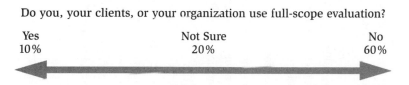

Figure 14.3. Continuum of Responses to the Full-Scope Evaluation Question.

Table 14.2. Integrating Full-Scope Evaluation into the Analysis Phase of the HPT Process.

Formative Evaluation	Summative Evaluation	Confirmative Evaluation	Meta Evaluation
Decide whether to conduct a formative evaluation:	Review the analysis outputs and outcomes to decide whether to conduct a summative evaluation:	Review analysis outputs and outcomes to decide whether to conduct confirmative evaluation:	Review analysis outputs and outcomes to decide whether to conduct meta evaluation:
• Do the organization and stakeholders need information on the value of the HPT process?	• Do the organization and stakeholders need information on immediate outputs and outcomes?	• Is it a long-term intervention?	• Are there certification, standards, licensing, or other external or internal accountability factors that require meta evaluation?
• If yes, for what purpose?	• If yes, for what purpose?	• Do the organization or stakeholders need to confirm long-term results?	• Does the organization have the resources for and desire to support meta evaluation?
• Does the organization have the resources for and desire to support formative evaluation?	• Does the organization have the resources for and desire to support summative evaluation?	• If yes, for what purpose?	If yes, plan the meta evaluation and select an internal or external evaluator
If yes, review the analysis inputs, process, outputs, and outcomes of the Analysis Phase to judge reliability, validity, and alignment with organization and stakeholder needs	If yes, gather information to align summative evaluation with organization and stakeholder needs	• Does the organization have the resources for and desire to support confirmative evaluation?	*Type One*: monitor and evaluate the evaluation processes, outputs, and outcomes of this HPT phase
		If yes, gather information to align confirmative evaluation with organization and stakeholder needs	*Type Two*: monitor (collect, review, archive) the evaluation data from this phase for future evaluation

Source: Joan Conway Dessinger, The Lake Group. Used with permission.

Table 14.3. Integrating Full-Scope Evaluation into the Intervention and Design Phase of the HPT Process.

Formative Evaluation	Summative Evaluation	Confirmative Evaluation	Meta Evaluation
Establish and monitor criteria for selecting and designing interventions	Design a summative evaluation plan for the intervention based on the analysis phase outputs and outcomes	Design a confirmative evaluation plan for the intervention	*Type One:* monitor and evaluate the evaluation processes, outputs, and outcomes for this HPT phase
Monitor and evaluate the selection, design, and development process	Develop the summative evaluation materials	Develop the first draft of the confirmative evaluation materials	*Type Two:* monitor, that is, collect, review, and archive the evaluation data from this phase
Monitor the alignment between analysis outputs, needs, objectives, and so on, and intervention selection, design, and development outputs	Design, develop, implement, and evaluate a pilot of the intervention	Monitor and collect the formative, summative, and meta evaluation data	
Plan and implement a stakeholder review, revise, and approve cycle for all the outputs of this phase			

Source: Joan Conway Dessinger, The Lake Group. Used with permission.

Table 14.4. Integrating Full-Scope Evaluation into the Implementation and Change Phase of the HPT Process.

Formative Evaluation	Summative Evaluation	Confirmative Evaluation	Meta Evaluation
If this phase involves redesign of the intervention, repeat the formative evaluation activities from the HPT select, design, and develop phase to evaluate the redesign process and outputs	Implement summative evaluation and review the summative evaluation outputs and outcomes Report the results to the stakeholders with recommendations	If this is a long-term intervention: • Implement confirmative evaluation three months to one year after implementation begins • Monitor, that is, collect, review, and archive, the evaluation data from this phase • Analyze results • Report findings to stakeholders, with recommendations • Revise confirmative evaluation materials if needed	*Type One Evaluation:* monitor and evaluate the evaluation processes and outputs for this HPT phase and report findings to the stakeholders *Type Two Evaluation:* • Monitor, that is, collect, review, and archive the evaluation data from this phase • When the intervention ends, evaluate all the formative, summative, and confirmative evaluation processes and outputs and report findings to the stakeholders

Source: Joan Conway Dessinger, The Lake Group. Used with permission.

soul of an organization, or at least of its performance-improvement activities. Getting approval from a large organization to release information on what could be considered part of the organization's strategic plan is often difficult and time consuming; that may also play a factor in the difficulty we have encountered over the years as we try to discover "real world cases" to include in presentations, articles, and books. Meanwhile, for those of you who want to "do" full-scope evaluation in your organizations, or at least add it to your repertoire of knowledge and skills, here are some tools for getting started.

Full-Scope Evaluation Toolkit for the HPT Practitioner

There are a number of books that will help HPT practitioners who need to add full-scope evaluation to their repertoire of knowledge and skills. Each of the resources blends theory with practical suggestions and performance-support tools for implementing evaluation. These books are listed after the reference list at the end of this chapter.

Another source of information is this handbook. Other chapters will provide information on and examples of how to use interviews, surveys, observation, data analysis, and other tools of the evaluation trade. Elsewhere in this book, our colleagues introduce the concept of appreciative inquiry. As appreciative inquiry becomes a useful and viable HPT intervention, you may decide to add it to your evaluation toolbox, along with participatory, stakeholder, and learning-oriented approaches to evaluation that all share similar assumptions, purposes, and methods (Coghlan, Preskill, and Catsambas, 2003).

Can You Get There from Here? The Future of Full-Scope Evaluation

Full-scope evaluation helps HPT practitioners conduct a major reality check on three important performance-improvement success factors: keeping the performance-improvement intervention aligned with organizational needs, adapting to change, and accomplishing the intended performance-improvement goals and objectives. Formative evaluation helps us focus on alignment and the intricacies of change management; summative and confirmative evaluation help us focus on accomplishments. Meta evaluation makes it possible for us to be accountable for the outputs and outcomes of our evaluation efforts.

Call to Action

Full-scope evaluation is not for the faint-hearted, but it is for HPT practitioners and clients who strongly believe in continuous improvement and accountability. So here is what HPT practitioners need to think, say, and do to make full-scope evaluation happen in the real world.

Make the Decision to Do Full-Scope Evaluation Based on Sound Analysis.
Remember, every intervention is different, and the scope may be more or less
"full," depending on the decision you make in the analysis phase (Table 14.2).
For example, if on the one hand the intervention is a one-time-only event, you
may want to do a partial full-scope evaluation with formative and summative
components only. On the other hand, the one-time event may be very costly or
have long-term outcomes that require confirmative evaluation in the future
and may even need a meta evaluation to justify regulatory or certification
requirements.

Exceptions to the Rule. Most full-scope evaluations are conducted for long-term
interventions and are not used for one-time events. However, there are exceptions to the rule. As an example, an international pharmaceutical company, or
Company Y, planned to close Plant X in the Deep South. To keep the plant going
until the paperwork could catch up with the closure, the company sent manufacturing work orders to plant X that its other plants were too busy to fill. Lo and
behold, Plant X did such an efficient and effective job manufacturing the product that Company Y decided not to close it down. Meanwhile, Company Y had
implemented a team culture at all levels, and Plant X had not been part of the
massive intervention implementation and change effort. So a decision was made
to move the company's annual meeting from New York City to Plant X's small
town and hire an outside training company to implement the team culture for
Plant X at the same time as the annual company meeting. The costs were
extremely high. They even involved remodeling the local motel. The company
asked for a full-scope evaluation plan to justify their investment in this one-time
event.

Accentuate the Positive. There are at least four benefits that HPT practitioners need to recognize, internalize, and disseminate to all stakeholders before
they can make a business case for implementing full-scope evaluation. The benefits are that full-scope evaluation

- Establishes and verifies the continuing merit and worth of a perfor-
  mance intervention
- Provides a foundation for long-term planning, proving, improving, and
  making decisions
- Supports the need for accountability for performance improvement
- Models and supports continuous improvement

Eliminate the Negative. In addition to proving the case for full-scope evaluation, HPT practitioners need to eliminate the barriers to implementation. In the
end, it is all about resources: time, money, and talent. If HPT practitioners

possess the knowledge, skills, and talent to plan full-scope evaluation activities that are both effective and efficient, save time and money, and produce recognized value-added results for the organization and the stakeholders, they can turn full-scope evaluation into a real-world part of HPT practice.

References

American Society for Training and Development (ASTD). (2005). *Standards and ethics*. Retrieved May 13, 2005, from www.astd.org/astd/Education/code_of_ ethics.htm.

Binder, C. (2002). Commentary: An open letter to my colleagues—how're we doing? *Performance Improvement, 40*(5), 6–9.

Coghlan, A. T., Preskill, H., and Catsambas, T. T. (2003, Winter). An overview of appreciative inquiry in evaluation. In H. Preskill and A. T. Coghlan (Eds.), *Using appreciative inquiry in evaluation* (New Directions for Evaluation, No. 100). San Francisco: Jossey-Bass.

Dessinger, J. C., and Moseley, J. L. (2003). *Confirmative evaluation: Practical strategies for valuing continuous improvement*. San Francisco: Jossey-Bass/Pfeiffer.

Fitzpatrick, J. L., Sanders, J. R., and Worthen, B. R. (2004). Program evaluation: Alternative approaches and practical guidelines (3rd ed.). Boston: Allyn & Bacon.

Hale, J. (2004, September). *Meaningful metrics*. Presentation at the International Society for Performance Improvement Performance-Based ISD Conference, Chicago.

Joint Committee on Standards for Educational Evaluation. (1981). *Standards for Evaluations of Educational Programs, Projects, and Materials*. New York: McGraw-Hill.

Kirkpatrick, D. (1994). *Evaluating training programs: The four levels*. San Francisco: Berrett-Koehler.

Moseley, J. L., and Dessinger, J. C. (1998). The Dessinger-Moseley evaluation model: A comprehensive approach to training evaluation. In P. J. Dean and D. E. Ripley (Eds.), *Performance improvement interventions: Methods for organizational learning*. Washington, DC: International Society for Performance Improvement.

Phillips, J. J. (1991). *Handbook of training evaluation and measurement methods* (3rd ed.). Houston: Gulf Publishing Company.

Scriven, M. (1967). The methodology of evaluation. In R. Tyler, R. Gagne, and M. Scriven (Eds.), *AERA monograph series on curriculum and evaluation: Perspectives of curriculum evaluation*. Chicago: Rand-McNally.

Van Tiem, D. M., Moseley, J. L., and Dessinger, J. C. (2004). *Fundamentals of performance technology: A guide to improving people, process, and performance* (2nd ed.). Silver Spring, MD: International Society for Performance Improvement.

Additional Resources

There are a number of additional resources not cited in this chapter that will help HPT practitioners who need to add full-scope evaluation to their repertoire of knowledge and skills. Here are our recommendations.

Combs, W. L., and Falletta, S. V. (2000). *The targeted evaluation process: A consultant's guide to asking the right questions and getting the results you trust.* Alexandria, VA: American Society for Training and Development.

Dessinger, J. C., and Moseley, J. L. (2004). *Confirmative evaluation: Practical strategies for verifying continuous improvement.* San Francisco: Jossey-Bass/Pfeiffer.

Geis, G. L., and Smith, M. E. (1992). The function of evaluation. In H. D. Stolovitch and E. J. Keeps (Eds.), *Handbook of human performance technology: A comprehensive guide for analyzing and solving performance problems in organizations* (pp. 130–166). San Francisco: Jossey-Bass.

Hale, J. (2002). Performance-based evaluation: Tools and techniques to measure the impact of training. San Francisco: Jossey-Bass/Pfeiffer.

Mark, M. M., and Pines, E. (1995). Implications of continuous quality improvement for program evaluation and evaluators. *Evaluation Practice, 16*(2), 131–139.

PART THREE

INTERVENTIONS AT THE WORKER AND WORK TEAM LEVELS

KAREN L. MEDSKER

M any HPT interventions intended to improve individual and group or team performance include instruction. This is true for at least four reasons: (1) many HPT practitioners are or were specialists in learning and teaching, including instructional design, training, and education; they are experts in designing, developing, implementing, and evaluating instruction; (2) a large body of research informs instructional practice; we know how to make learning happen; (3) managers and other HPT clients often prefer instruction as a method for improving performance; it is familiar and comfortable; and (4) instruction is truly needed in many situations; changing business needs, new knowledge, new technologies, and worker mobility create constant requirements for people to learn. In addition, other interventions often have an instructional component.

Consequently, the first four chapters of Part Three are about instruction. Michael Molenda and James Russell define instruction, distinguish it from information giving and cognitive support, and identify it as one important intervention within the broad array of performance-improvement interventions, such as job design, tools, incentives, and job aids. They point out that instruction should be used to bridge skill and knowledge gaps, and describe how instruction often can be used along with other interventions to meet performance challenges. The chapter describes procedural instructional design and development models, which typically advocate a systems approach to planning instruction, and specific lesson-design frameworks from a variety of theoretical perspectives. The authors also discuss method and media selection, current use of various instructional delivery systems, and evaluation of learning and impact resulting from instruction.

Next, Kenneth Silber and Wellesley Foshay explain how to design instructional strategies, using a cognitive psychology perspective. They begin by describing how learning occurs, based on information-processing theory. Then they describe different types of knowledge. A key principle is that different types of learning should be taught differently. Their cognitive instructional design model shows how different strategies can be used to help learners acquire facts, concepts, principles, mental models, and procedures, and solve well- and ill-structured problems. The authors include tables that illustrate their design principles with examples of declarative and procedural lessons.

Robert Appelman and John Wilson, in Chapter Seventeen, explain the power and roles of games and simulations. They provide details about the outcomes, aspects, and characteristics of games and simulations. They also discuss evaluation criteria for games and simulations.

In Chapter Eighteen, Jose Manuel Ochoa-Alcántar, Christy Borders, and Barbara Bichelmeyer take a look at the past, present, and future of distance education. They present a forthright discussion about the pros and cons of distance training, including information about planning and administering distance training programs.

In Chapter Nineteen, another type of education experience is presented. According to Margo Murray, mentoring is the deliberate pairing of two people with different skills and experiences, with the purpose of transferring those skills and experiences from one person to the other. The mentor's tasks are many and may include coaching. Today, different structures or formats are used in mentoring programs. For example, the mentor is not always older or more senior than the protégé; peer mentoring and reverse mentoring are two variations. This chapter describes several contemporary formats and provides specific examples. It also discusses success factors, pitfalls and ways to avoid them, and benefits of mentoring for the mentor, the protégé, and the organization.

Sometimes people fail to perform as desired, not because they do not know how, but because they do not want to. Richard Clark explores the issues of work motivation, which he demonstrates is a major problem in today's organizations. After defining motivation, Clark lists and describes the major motivation killers found frequently in organizations, following with universal principles of motivation, with research support for each. Another section of the chapter discusses financial incentives and their effect on performance. Finally, he offers advice on how to motivate teams.

Another intervention aimed at improving the performance of individuals and teams is to shift from a traditional, top-down, overt management approach to an unobtrusive approach that seeks to develop a shared set of values, norms, and beliefs. Anthony Marker's chapter points to alignment, or congruence between organizational goals and performer behavior, as a critical factor in organizational success. But how is alignment to be maintained, either in a growing organization or in a lean organization using self-managed teams? Marker shows how the unobtrusive model is more effective. He suggests guidelines for the HPT practitioner in getting manager buy-in, and steps for making the shift.

Because much of the work in today's organizations is being done by groups or teams, improving group performance is essential. Michael Cassidy and Megan Cassidy, in Chapter Twenty-Two, focus on the critical conditions for work-group productivity, such as who should be included, the roles and responsibilities within the group, and attention to technical and social dimensions of the group's work. The authors discuss operational, tactical, and strategic levels of group functioning. They also explain the benefits of modeling the problem or decision, lay out steps for guiding a group through a problem-solving or decision-making process, and describe common problems in work groups and ways to overcome them.

The final chapter in Part Three describes the latest thinking and practice related to performance support systems, or PSS. Authors Steven Villachica, Deborah Stone, and John Endicott define PSS broadly to include learning, guidance and tracking, task-structuring support, knowledge management, communities of practice, tools, and even motivational components: an integrated set of on-line and off-line methods and resources that support performance. As the authors point out, a large-scale performance support sytem could include most or all of the interventions described in this handbook. The chapter sets forth conditions for choosing PSS, variations on and other names for PSS, examples, benefits, and project-development considerations.

Part Three of the handbook includes a wealth of guidance for HPT practitioners for improving the performance of individuals and teams, backed by extensive research and the chapter authors' many decades of observations and experiences.

CHAPTER FIFTEEN

Instruction as an Intervention

Michael Molenda, James D. Russell

Although instruction is only one of many possible performance interventions, it is one of the most valuable, flexible, and frequently used. This chapter begins by placing instruction into the larger context of performance improvement. Next, it provides guides to planning instruction, with emphasis on selecting an appropriate lesson framework and then selecting appropriate methods and media within that framework. It also provides data on how different forms of instruction are being implemented currently in the workplace. It concludes with an overview of assessing learner outcomes and evaluating the impact of instruction.

INSTRUCTION AIMS AT IMPROVING CAPABILITIES

Instruction is a generic term referring to any effort to stimulate learning by the deliberate arrangement of conditions and experiences. Instruction is often viewed as covering a spectrum of efforts, ranging from very narrow in scope to very broad in scope and with purposes ranging from immediate application in the workplace to general personal development. Some advocate labeling the ends of the spectrum as "training" and "education." Stolovitch and Keeps (2002) refer to the aim of *training* as equipping learners to "consistently reproduce without variation" (p. 10). Figure skating, keyboarding, assembling a rifle, and remembering the multiplication tables are the sorts of repetitious, even mechanical, abilities that they would consider the subjects of training. They define *educa-tion,* on the other end of the spectrum, as efforts to achieve the broader goal of developing generalized abilities with underlying mental models and value systems. Leading project teams, responding flexibly to customer needs, and devising strategic plans are the sorts of complex abilities that could be viewed as goals of education. However, such distinctions are somewhat arbitrary, and both training and education can take place either in the workplace or in formal education institutions. The more generic term, *instruction,* encompasses the whole range of types, and so it is used here as a common denominator that can be used in different sectors to refer to the whole range of learning interventions.

The critical attribute of instruction is that it is directed at facilitating *learning.* Learning is defined as a persisting or quasi-permanent change in capability resulting from the learner's experience and interaction with the world (Driscoll, 2000). Instruction, therefore, has as its goal a lasting change in capability. This is a crucial point in distinguishing instruction from merely providing information.

Instruction can be defined as the arrangement of purposive and controlled events that lead to the achievement of some learning goal. The learning goal can range from recalling information to comprehending and applying principles to attaining mastery of physical skills to new attitudes, or many other types of outcomes, as is discussed later.

Instruction Is One of Many Performance Interventions

Training does not take place in a vacuum, but some training professionals behave as though it does. The corporate training literature tends to place learning, instead of performance, at the center of the universe, ignoring the impact of the many environmental factors surrounding performance in the workplace. Some involved in business consulting began to see the larger picture more clearly in the 1970s as they saw instruction-only solutions fail to have lasting effects on persistent business problems. The view began to emerge that instruction alone seldom was sufficient to enable people to become effective achievers, in society or in the workplace. Over time, a new perspective emerged that the goal should be the improvement of human performance, which could best be accomplished by combining instructional interventions with noninstructional interventions, such as enhanced incentives, better tools, job aids, more supportive organizational structures, and so on.

This handbook is based on this newer view, the human performance technology perspective. One way of depicting this approach is through a visual model developed by Molenda and Pershing (2004), shown in Figure 15.1.

The major theme of the Strategic Impact Model is that instruction alone seldom solves performance problems. Almost all performance problems are rooted in more than one cause, and although training or education may be part of the solution, other interventions, such as job redesign, incentive adjustments, job

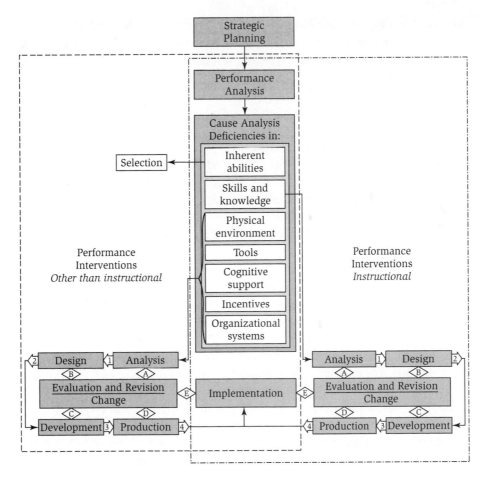

Figure 15.1. The Strategic Impact Model.

aids, better tools, or the like, are invariably required in order to make the instruction pay off. Instruction comes into play when people's performance is inhibited by the lack of needed knowledge or skills.

The model shows explicitly how instructional interventions and other sorts of performance interventions relate to each other, springing from a common performance analysis and converging in a common implementation phase. The model specifies an array of performance interventions, of which instruction is one. It incorporates the typology developed by Wile (1996) specifying seven sources of performance shortfalls: (1) inherent abilities, (2) skills and knowledge, (3) physical environment, (4) tools, (5) cognitive support, (6) incentives, and (7) organizational systems. This typology proposes that people fail to perform adequately in the workplace when they (1) lack the basic qualifications, such as intelligence, strength, or speed, to do the job; (2) lack the specific knowledge, skills, or attitudes; (3) are given surroundings that are detrimental to good work: hot, noisy, crowded, unsafe, having poor ergonomics, and so on; (4) don't have proper tools to do the job: obsolete machines, clumsy computer systems with faulty software, and so on; (5) lack job aids or electronic help systems that can provide information as needed; (6) have insufficient incentives: money, benefits, recognition, advancement opportunities, and so on; (7) struggle in an organizational structure with poor communication, weak leadership, oppressive supervision, and the like; or (8) some combination of two or more deficiencies.

The point is to keep constantly in mind that instruction is the solution to only one type of problem, the problem of lack of the sorts of knowledge and skills that can be learned. In many cases, people know how to do something but do not have the incentive to do it. Or they have the knowledge and incentive but do not have the tools to do the job well. Training will not give them the motivation or the tools.

Although instruction is just one tool among many in the performance-improvement toolbox, it is an extremely vital one. When addressing business problems or opportunities, the capabilities of the workforce are often the most important component, so training or education are frequently the keystones of the change process. Even when other interventions are at the center of a change, there is almost always some need for training or education to support those other interventions. For example, if the wordprocessing system is upgraded, implementing a tool intervention, the users will need some orientation to and practice on the new hardware or software, which would be an instruction-type intervention. Or in a shift from individual to team-based operation, which would be an organizational system intervention, supervisors will need extensive reorientation of their skills and values, which would be an education-type intervention.

Distinguishing Information Giving from Instruction

Information consists of facts, news, comments, and similar representations of knowledge. Receivers are not responsible for measurable, specific actions or performance as a result of being presented with information. Often the presentation, which may be live, printed, or on the Internet, is general in content, and its purpose is to give an overview of ideas or subject matter: to generate interest, to provide background information, or to give procedural details. Information can be presented in a memo, in the classroom, in the textbook, or on the Web.

Giving information, the presentation of content, is much different from and less than instruction, the arrangement of information and events to facilitate learning. In other words, "telling ain't training" (Stolovitch and Keeps, 2002). Trainees should not be expected to be responsible for the retention or use of information they have only seen or heard. Meaningful understanding, retention, and use require instructional activities, including practice with feedback. Active engagement with the material by questioning it, discussing it, or applying it to practice problems is the critical component of instruction. And, of course, there should be assessment to determine whether the trainees have mastered the objectives.

Distinguishing Cognitive Support from Instruction

It is easy to lose sight of the differences between two related interventions, cognitive support and instruction. Both deal with mental operations, and both may entail some presentation of information. In some cases, cognitive support can substitute for and complement instruction, but they are not equivalent.

An example can be found in the digital work environment, where people are near computer screens as they work. The computer system makes it possible to give them electronic help systems to provide advice as needed. The most common example is the help button built into most wordprocessing programs. If you don't know how to change the margins on a page you can click on the help button, type in some key words, and receive specific advice on how to do it.

Besides computer help systems, cognitive support is provided by other sorts of job aids, which can take many forms (Rossett and Gautier-Downes, 1991). A telephone directory saves you from having to memorize every phone number you might ever need. Tables in the back of statistics textbooks provide sequences of random numbers and charts to determine levels of significance. Nearly every appliance comes with a booklet of operating procedures; the power lawnmower has the most critical operation rules inscribed on the handle. Decision-tree charts can quickly help decide if an applicant qualifies for disability payments under Social Security.

There is a real distinction between mere cognitive support and instruction. The information provided by the job aid is not meant to be memorized. It is assumed that the user will look up the information on the rare occasions that it is needed. Alternatively, instruction is meant to lead to learning, a quasi-permanent change in capability. However, with computers, it has become possible to give ever more rapid and detailed advice in specific problem situations, to the point that the computer could be said to be coaching the user. This can lead into a grey area between telling and training. That is, with consistent use, the user could gradually internalize the advice of the help system, remembering more and more of the information provided. At this point the help system may be contributing to learning, although its aim is only to provide just-in-time assistance.

In the future, the line between cognitive support and instruction will be further blurred by the trend toward work-embedded training, instruction that occurs at the worksite. Employers are increasingly reluctant to take workers off the job for training, especially since there is a lot of evidence that the training that transfers to the job is the training that most closely resembles working conditions. Transfer of training increases as the practice is more realistic. So cognitive support may take on more and more of the traits of training, what some refer to as just-in-time training, and training may incorporate more and more cognitive supports, especially in the form of electronic performance-support systems, such as help systems.

PLANNING INSTRUCTION

There are two broad types of guides to the preparation of effective, appealing instruction. First, there are instructional design and development models, procedural guides that focus on the steps to be followed by the planners as they proceed from conceptualizing the problem to evaluating the success of the intervention. Such models attempt to specify what decisions need to be made and in what order. Models that follow the systems approach generally recommend the sequence of analyze, design, develop, implement, and evaluate. Based on this sequence, the acronym ADDIE is often used to refer to this family of models.

Second, there are lesson frameworks or templates for the structure of instructional units, which might be referred to as a lesson, unit, module, program, or other term. These frameworks specify the nature and sequence of learning activities that should be incorporated into any effective lesson. A familiar example is the Events of Instruction framework (Gagne and Medsker, 1996). Such lesson frameworks are vitally useful during the design stage, when planners are deciding how to structure the lesson or series of lessons. Particular lesson frameworks are better suited to particular sorts of objectives, so the team's choice may be guided by the types of outcomes that are being pursued.

Instructional Design and Development Models

In the world of formal education, teachers usually plan their own lessons, select or develop the instructional materials, conduct the classroom activities, assign and grade practice exercises, and develop and administer the tests. Their planning processes tend to be informal and pragmatic.

Alternatively, in business, military, and other large organizations, instructional processes are often allotted to different specialists: managers and supervisors decide on training needs, analysts conduct surveys and observations, designers create lesson blueprints and tests, production specialists create materials, trainers conduct the lessons, and evaluators measure the results. Coordinating the whole process may be a small team headed by an instructional design-development specialist.

Furthermore, organizations other than formal education institutions tend to place a higher value on efficiency and efficacy. Instruction must accomplish its goals for the organization to survive. To do this, instructional planning procedures must be efficient, and their results must be demonstrable. In complex organizations with many units and even multiple sites there must be a standardized process for carrying out instructional planning, to avoid expensive waste and duplication of effort. Thus, in organizational settings managers and training specialists prefer instructional design and development processes that follow a systems approach.

Systems Approach Models. The essence of the systems approach is to break the instructional planning process into small steps, to arrange the steps in logical order, then to use the output of each step as the input of the next. At the most general level, most planners agree that the major stages are analysis, design, development, implementation, and evaluation. Therefore, the outputs of the analysis stage—a description of the learners, the tasks to be learned, and a listing of the instructional objectives to be met—serve as input to the design stage, in which those descriptions and objectives are transformed into specifications or a blueprint for the lesson. Next, the design specifications serve as inputs to the development stage, where they are used to construct the materials and activities of the lesson. In the implementation stage the instructors, materials, activities, and learners come together to use the products of the development stage. Finally, those instructional activities are evaluated to determine whether the original objectives have been met and whether further instruction is necessary.

Another key attribute of the systems approach is a commitment to conducting evaluation and revision at each step of the design and development process. At each major decision point there is an opportunity to gather data to test that decision and other prior decisions to verify that the project is moving ahead toward a solution of the originally defined problem. If the results of a step are not satisfactory—for example, if trainees in a sample group are confused by the directions in the prototype of a new simulation exercise—then the design step must be repeated to find ways to clarify the directions. Of course, sometimes it happens that further analysis leads developers to shift the target objectives and continue in a different line. This process of repeating steps until satisfactory results are achieved is referred to as an *iterative* approach. Because of this commitment to evaluation at each phase of the process, the ADDIE label is a bit of a misnomer. Evaluation is not just conducted at the conclusion of training, but at the conclusion of each phase of development.

Numerous systems-approach models have been proposed. They differ in terms of the number of steps, the names of the steps, and the recommended sequence of functions. Gustafson and Branch's *Survey of Instructional Development Models* (1997) includes eighteen models. Their list is not intended to be exhaustive, but to be illustrative of the various ways of implementing a systems approach. Most organizations use their own home-grown model, often adapting or combining other models to guide their design and development activities.

The major steps of the systems approach are shown in Figure 15.2.

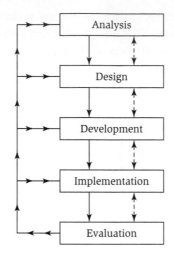

Figure 15.2. The Major Steps of the Systems Approach, Also Known as the "ADDIE Model."

Gagne, Wager, Golas, and Keller (2005) provide an expansion of these basic steps into a more detailed procedural guide:

I. Analysis
   a. First determine the needs for which instruction is the solution.
   b. Conduct an instructional analysis to determine the target cognitive, affective, and motor skill goals for the course.
   c. Determine what skills the entering learners are expected to have, and which will impact learning in the course.
   d. Analyze the time available and how much might be accomplished in that period of time. Some authors also recommend an analysis of the context and the resources available.

II. Design
   a. Translate course goals into overall performance outcomes and major objectives for each unit of the course.
   b. Determine the instructional topics or units to be covered and how much time will be spent on each.
   c. Sequence the units with regard to the course objectives.
   d. Flesh out the units of instruction, identifying the major objectives to be achieved during each unit.
   e. Define lessons and learning activities for each unit.
   f. Develop specifications for assessment of what students have learned.

III. Development
   a. Make decisions regarding the types of learning activities and materials.
   b. Prepare draft materials and/or activities.
   c. Try out materials and activities with target audience members.
   d. Revise, refine, and produce materials and activities.
   e. Produce instructor training or adjunct materials.

IV. Implement
   a. Market materials for adoption by instructors and potential learners.
   b. Provide help or support as needed.

V. Evaluate
   a. Implement plans for learner assessment.
   b. Implement plans for program evaluation.
   c. Implement plans for course maintenance and revision [p. 22].

The Dick and Carey Model. The most widely known and used ADDIE-type model is the one developed by Dick, Carey, and Carey (2005), shown in Figure 15.3. It is taught in most introductory courses at colleges and universities, it has been widely adopted, and it serves as the basis for other models. The model is typical of the overall planning process for instructional interventions in business, industry, government, and military training.

The Dick and Carey model begins with needs assessment to determine whether there is an ignorance problem. It then recommends analyzing the instructional content, the learners, the instructional context, and the context in which the skills will be applied. The initial analysis leads to the specification of objectives. A unique aspect of the Dick and Carey model is that it then recommends specifying the assessment instruments and methods aligned with those objectives, prior to designing the instruction. Their concept is that if the developers can be clear enough about what and how they will be testing, they will have a much better idea of what instructional strategies to select in the next step. After developing the instructional materials and procedures to implement the strategy, the model wraps up with evaluation and revision. It recommends first a formative evaluation of the instruction, small-scale testing of the early drafts of the lesson elements, followed by revision. Then a summative evaluation is conducted at the end of the actual lesson to determine whether the lesson achieved the expected learning results.

In the Dick and Carey model and other similar models the central focus is on the design phase, creating or selecting the methods and materials that will constitute the learner's experience. The steps of specifying objectives, selecting methods and media, and deciding on a lesson framework deserve special attention.

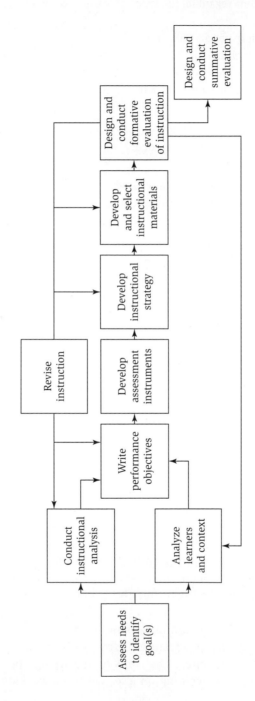

Figure 15.3. The Dick and Carey Model.

Specifying Goals and Objectives

Goals for instruction are typically classified under three broad headings according to the type of learning being pursued: cognitive, affective, and psychomotor. This classification system was proposed in Bloom (1956) and has continued to be the most popular taxonomy. Cognitive refers to intellectual skills, from simple knowledge of facts through complex problem solving. Affective refers to attitudinal and emotional changes, from the formation of preferences to complex value systems. Psychomotor refers to physical skills, including manual dexterity, athletic skills, and the like; the stem *psycho-* is included in this term to remind us that many physical skills also entail mental activity. Romiszowski (1981) proposes a fourth category, interpersonal, to cover objectives related to human relations, such as those involved in teamwork, sales, coaching, and supervision.

Sometimes it is difficult to classify a learning goal or objective into just one category because most real-world instructional objectives have cognitive, affective, interpersonal, and psychomotor aspects. It is difficult to conceive of any instructional objective that doesn't have some mental component, emotional overtone, or observable physical activity. For example, if the goal is to have the learner write a memo in proper format, this does entail the physical act of writing or keyboarding. Nevertheless, the focus is on the mental skill of remembering and applying the proper format, so this would be classified as a cognitive, not psychomotor, objective. Thus instructional objectives are classified according to which category of skill is being emphasized at any given time. Advocates of a systematic approach place great importance on clear specification of objectives at an early stage in the planning process, as the selection of instructional methods is to a great extent dependent on exactly what learning objective is being pursued.

Instructional Methods and Media

During the design phase, planners have to decide what methods to employ and what media channels to use to carry out the instruction. The term *method* simply means a way of doing something. An *instructional* method is a way of instructing or a way of involving learners in a particular sort of teaching-learning activity. Instructional methods are defined here as teaching-learning activities distinguished by the pattern of communication among teacher, learner, and different types of materials. For example, a presentation is a one-way information exposition by a teacher, or software substituting for a teacher, to a number of learners. A discussion entails free exchange of information among a group of learners. Instructional methods can be classified into about ten broad families: presentation, demonstration, tutorial, reading, reflection, discussion, expression, construction, drill and practice, and discovery-inquiry; these are shown visually in Figure 15.4.

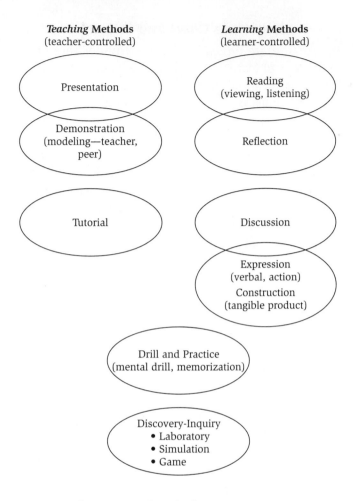

Figure 15.4. Typology of Instructional Methods.

Some of these methods are centered on activities controlled by the teacher or instructional system, such as presentations and demonstrations; others are more learner controlled, such as reading, reflection, and discussion; yet others can share or alternate control between teacher and learner, such as drill and practice and discovery-inquiry.

Table 15.1 gives a verbal definition of each category and shows typical formats in which these methods are embodied.

Media can be distinguished from methods. A medium is a channel that carries information between a source and a receiver (Smaldino and Russell, 2005). Today's electronic media are often made up of multiple sets of channels constituting the delivery systems through which messages are sent. Radio programs are broadcast through the air, then picked up by radios from which the program

Table 15.1. Methods, Their Definitions, and Their Typical Formats.

Methods	Definitions	Typical Formats
Presentation	One-way information flow from source (Teacher) to many receivers (Learners) • Typically verbal • May have visual supplement	Lecture, oral presentation • With display: whiteboard, overhead transparencies, handouts, PowerPoint slides Film showing Radio program Television program Video clip Statement made via audio or video conference
Demonstration	One-way information flow, featuring realistic "showing" rather than "telling" • May be human or device, Teacher or Learner • May be planned behavior modeling • May be unconscious modeling	Showing "how to do it" (live, recorded) • Teacher demo in music, dance master class • Video: sports skills Teacher as role model Peers as role models
Tutorial	Two-way interchange between Teacher and Learner • Learner exerts some control • Teacher must be able to respond flexibly	Apprenticeship Athletics: coaching Music: master class Mentoring Socratic dialogue Structured tutoring Branching programmed instruction Adaptive computer-assisted instruction Teacher-student exchange in Web chat Teacher-student exchange via e-mail
Reading	Learner engages with text or visual material • Material instructionally encoded • Learner controls pace	Reading textbooks, modules, handouts Reading Web pages, "tutorials" Linear programmed instruction or computer-assisted instruction Watching video, listening to audio Video-streaming on the Web

(Continued)

Table 15.1. Methods, Their Definitions, and Their Typical Formats. (*Continued*)

Methods	Definitions	Typical Formats
Reflection	Learner examines own performance and thoughts • Analyzes and may report	Coach-student dialogue Medical, psych: case conference Written • Short paper • E-mail to teacher • Post-class recap (+, −, ?) Evaluative checklist Debriefing: post-simulation or game, or field work "Think-aloud" protocol Small-group process analysis
Expression	Learner creates a verbal product or physical performance • Meant to express thought, feeling	Answers to study or quiz questions Essay, poem E-mail messages • Chat, bulletin board comments Performance: dance, speech Musical performance or composition
Construction	Learner creates a tangible product • Not a verbal message • Meant to express thought, feeling	Multimedia presentation Art: painting, sculpture Design: drafting, interior decor, lighting, landscape, architecture
Discussion	Two-way interchange among Learners • Teacher may initiate, monitor, not control	Seminar T-group Buzz group Debate (for participants) Panel discussion Reacting to someone's posting in a discussion forum Participating in a Web chat Participating actively in an audio or video conference
Drill and Practice	Learner practices skill repeatedly • May be internal memorization • Usually self-paced	Memorization drill Language lab Athletic practice, drama rehearsal End-of-chapter exercises Recitation Instructional game • Math, reading, spelling drills

Table 15.1. (*Continued*)

Methods	Definitions	Typical Formats
Discovery-Inquiry: Laboratory	Learner acts on real environment, raw materials • Usually self-paced exploration	Science experiment Studio art, drama Clinic (diagnosis, problem solving) Field work • Archeology, anthropology • Student teaching Case study (real instances) Project
Discovery-Inquiry: Simulation Game	Learner acts on *artificial* environment, materials, characters • May be group-based • Games include artificial rules, a goal, and competition	Physical simulator Decision-making simulation (policy) Social simulation • Role play, one-to-one • Group interaction (sociodrama) Business scenario (simulated case) Business game (competitive)

signals are conveyed through a speaker into the air to the listener's ear. Videotapes pass through playback devices, which send the recorded signals through wires to a TV set or monitor, generating images on a screen, which are scanned by the viewer's eye. These common electronic delivery systems illustrate the sometimes complex chain of senders, receivers, and channels comprising a given medium. Some media are much simpler, such as the human voice traveling through the air to the listener's ear. Whether simple or complex, the media themselves are merely channels through which almost any sorts of messages can be transmitted. They can be used effectively or ineffectively for instruction.

Sometimes people confuse media with methods. For example, the terms *e-learning* or *video-based instruction* might be used purportedly to describe what instructional methods are being used. However, although these terms tell you something about what communication channels or media are being used, they tell you very little about what teaching-learning activities or methods are being used.

E-learning simply refers to the use of words, images, and sounds that are filtered through some computer system and displayed on a viewing screen. Learners might interact with the display by clicking or scrolling with a mouse, touching a touch-sensitive screen, or typing on a keyboard. In the most prevalent type of e-learning, the learner simply reads verbal information on a screen, with the interaction limited to clicking on links or possibly on multiple-choice items, leading to more pages of text. In this case, the teaching-learning activity or *method* is simply reading, one of the most commonly used methods.

The Relationships among Methods, Media, and Learning. Although the issue is still debated in instructional technology circles, there is compelling evidence, both from research and from logic, that methods influence learning far more than media do. Clark (2001) convincingly argues this point, pointing to hundreds of media comparison studies and the meta-analyses of those studies. In research studies in which two different media are used to teach the same content, it usually turns out that the winning treatment is the one that uses more effective instructional methods. Even more certainly, when the studies are tightly controlled so that both media treatments use the same instructional methods, then a finding of no significant difference is inevitable.

The choice of medium does make a difference, of course. Different media can have definite cost and time advantages. If you want a thousand sales representatives scattered over eighty-five cities to participate in an interactive simulation exercise, it will probably be faster and cheaper to distribute the simulation on the Web than to arrange for live, face-to-face meetings, assuming the reps have access to Internet-accessible computers at work or home. The medium accounts for the savings in time and cost; the instructional method, simulation, accounts for the learning effect.

Certainly, some delivery systems are better suited to incorporate certain methods. A demonstration is easier to communicate by television than by radio. A book is better for reading than a computer monitor. Face-to-face interaction is better for discussion than a telephone. But these built-in disadvantages can be overcome with the investment of enough time, money, and ingenuity. A highly detailed verbal description, with sound effects, can approximate a visual demonstration. Given attention to font size and background color, printed material can be read from a TV screen. High-quality multiparty discussions can be done by telephone if planned well. With ingenuity, the normal bounds of a medium can be stretched to accommodate methods that are not really well-matched with that medium. To do this, though, requires additional effort, creativity, and cost.

Alternatively, the built-in advantages of a medium can be ignored by designers. Consider the use of television to show talking heads or shots of written material; these are not the most powerful instructional methods that television is capable of carrying. Again, media can be used well or poorly; they can incorporate effective or ineffective methods. The secret of *effective* instruction is the selection of methods suited to the particular content and objectives. The secret of *efficient* instruction is the selection of media that can carry the required methods to the largest number of learners at the lowest cost.

Models Versus Lesson Frameworks. There are, of course, other ways of viewing the design of instruction besides the systems approach. Dozens of alternative approaches are described in *Instructional Development Paradigms* (Dills and Romiszowski, 1997). However, most of these approaches actually are closer to lesson frameworks, as described in the following section, than to road maps for the entire instructional planning process. Approaches that attempt to portray the whole process tend to resemble the systems models, although using synonyms for the elements of the process.

Even within the systems-approach community, though, some practitioners and researchers feel that many instructional design and development models do not provide sufficiently specific directions on how to actually carry out each step, especially the crucial step of design—deciding how to construct the lesson (McCombs, 1986; Gordon and Zemke, 2000). Although such steps may not be specified within instructional design or development models, there is a related body of knowledge that does provide such guidance. There are a number of well-known, tested frameworks around which designers can flesh out the plan for the individual units or lessons.

LESSON FRAMEWORKS

A major decision at the design stage is to select an overall framework for the lesson or other instructional unit. Many different frameworks have been proposed, usually inspired by a particular theory of learning. Theories of learning attempt to describe what is going on as people learn. Deeper understanding of the learning process can suggest ways to shape instruction to fit more naturally with that process, giving rise to new instructional theories and new frameworks for structuring lessons. Four lesson frameworks that are well known and widely applied are explored here in some depth: behaviorist, cognitive, constructivist, and eclectic. Many other frameworks are explained fully in Reigeluth (1983, 1999), Davis and Davis (1998), and Medsker and Holdsworth (2001).

Behaviorist Framework

The first major post–World War II influence on thinking about lesson design was B. F. Skinner's innovation, programmed instruction, which he created to embody the principles of learning that he and others had discovered in the operant conditioning laboratory (Skinner, 1954).

Theory Base. Operant conditioning focuses on the observable behavior of the learner and the events that follow the behavior. The theory holds that any behavior that is followed by reinforcing events is more likely to be learned and exhibited in the future. Complex performances can be broken into smaller components and each component can be built up by practice followed by reinforcement.

Application of the Theory. To apply this theory to cognitive abilities, Skinner proposed using a framework called "programmed instruction." The programmed-instruction framework specified five major elements, according to Schramm (1962): "an ordered sequence of stimulus items; to each of which a student responds in some specified way, his responses being reinforced by immediate knowledge of results, so that he moves by small steps, therefore making few errors and practicing mostly correct responses, from what he knows, by a process of successively closer approximations, toward what he is supposed to learn from the program" (p. 2).

As research and practical experience accumulated, exemplified by Lumsdaine and Glaser (1960) and Glaser (1965), the robustness of many of these specifications came into question. That is, the sequence of experiences, the nature of the response, the timing of feedback, and the size of steps all appeared to be contingent on various learner characteristics and learning conditions. Since the specific formulaic elements of programmed instruction didn't seem to account for its success, developers began to see that the benefit was in the underlying principles. Programmed instruction's specifications were then broadened and simplified by Popham (1971) to four principles: "1. Provide relevant practice for the learner. 2. Provide knowledge of results. 3. Avoid the inclusion of irrelevancies. 4. Make the material interesting" (p. 171).

Instructional Pattern. The behaviorist approach today is characterized by precisely phrased performance objectives and breakdown of the learning task into small steps, each of which can be practiced and corrected until mastery is attained. This pattern can take the form of a self-study module in printed or computer-based form or a face-to-face session conducted by a coach or mentor with an individual learner or small group.

Methods. This approach favors methods that allow learners to progress at their own pace while getting feedback:

- *Reading,* including use of programmed texts, programmed audiovisual modules, and linear computer-assisted instruction (CAI)
- *Tutorial,* including on-the-job apprenticeship, structured tutoring, and adaptive CAI
- *Drill and practice,* including language labs, practice exercises embedded in Web lessons, and instructional games
- *Demonstration,* displaying the desired behavior to be learned, most likely in the form of behavior modeling (Bandura, 1969)
- *Discovery-inquiry,* including social simulations, role-play exercises, and computer-based scenarios.

Uses. The behaviorist approach is well-suited to skill development of the sort that Stolovitch and Keeps (2002) would place into the domain of training, routine tasks— simple or complex—that must be completed repeatedly with accuracy and efficiency. Intellectual skills of the lower levels, such as discrimination, concept learning, association, and chaining, which is automatically performing a multistep procedure, have been taught successfully with the behaviorist approach (Ertmer and Newby, 1993, p. 56). Such intellectual tasks are often embedded in a larger procedural skill lesson.

Cognitive Framework

In the decades since the 1960s, instruction has been informed increasingly by principles drawn from other sources, especially cognitive psychology. The cognitive approach emphasizes the importance of the learners' mental and emotional processes during the course of instruction. From this perspective, learners use their memory and thought processes to generate strategies as well as store and manipulate mental representations and ideas.

Theory Base. One branch of cognitive theory, information-processing theory, conceives the human learner as a processor of information, similar to a computer. In this view, represented by the work of Atkinson and Schiffrin (1968), sensory inputs are selected, encoded, and stored in short-term and possibly long-term memory. Later, well-stored information may be retrieved and used.

Another branch, assimilation theory, focuses on the human learner's cognitive structure and the processes whereby new information is integrated into the overall structure. Ausubel's schema theory (1980) views schemata as providing mental scaffolding, containing slots that can be filled in with particular cases. These schemata allow learners to organize information into meaningful units. This theory implies that the learner's cognitive structure at the time of learning is the most important factor in determining the likelihood of successful learning.

All branches of cognitive theory emphasize that the new knowledge must be meaningful to the learner if it is to be retained and used in the future. Another major cognitive theorist, Jerome Bruner (1966) promoted the value of learning by inquiry or discovery, discussed further on.

Application of the Theory. One cognitive approach, the expository strategy, involves instructional activities that present information to the learner or allow learners to read or view material and think about it, after which they practice applying it in some realistic form. The concerns revolve around attending to relevant messages, interpreting the new material, relating it to existing mental structures, and remembering it so that it can be retrieved later when needed. Designers must devise ways to gain the learner's attention, in competition with the many distracting stimuli in the environment. Then they want to present the new information in ways that will encourage melding it into the learner's existing mental structures or schemata. One instructional technique derived from schema theory is the advance organizer—a brief preview based on the learner's existing knowledge, which serves as a framework for new learning. Analogies, examples, outlines, and mnemonic devices also make new information easier to remember. To improve retention and use of combinations of knowledge and skills, it is helpful to embed practice in a realistic setting.

Another cognitive approach, the inquiry strategy, turns the expository strategy upside down. It begins by immersing learners in real-world problems, leads the learners to make hypotheses about these problems, and guides them to discover an answer. This approach is commonly found in management training; for example, in desert-survival simulations.

A rather complete and thorough set of cognitive prescriptions is offered by Foshay, Silber, and Stelnicki (2003) as "a cognitive training model" (p. 23). They offer seventeen specific tactics organized around the strategic phases of gaining attention, linking to prior knowledge, structuring the content, presenting the new knowledge, and strengthening the new knowledge through practice and feedback.

Instructional Pattern. Training and education based on the cognitive framework are likely to take the form of lectures or recorded presentations illustrated with audiovisual supplements. In many cases it is more efficient to package cognitive instruction for self-study in the form of textbooks, manuals, or Web documents. In any case, the pattern is likely to consist of a carefully constructed arrangement of information designed to attract and hold attention, to meld the new knowledge with the learner's previous knowledge, and to suggest ways of applying this new knowledge to practical use. The presentation will likely include opportunities to practice in the form of embedded quizzes, provocative questions, or other types of exercises.

Methods. The cognitive approach is likely to incorporate methods focusing on the presentation of information and learner interactions with the material and each other:

- *Presentation,* including illustrated lectures, videos, and PowerPoint shows
- *Reading,* including textbooks, training manuals, and Web so-called tutorials, which usually are not truly tutorial, in the sense of a rich two-way exchange
- *Demonstration,* including how-to-do-it demonstrations, video demonstrations, and peers or instructors serving as role models
- *Drill and practice,* including end-of-chapter exercises, recitation, and memorization drills such as spelling bees or other game-type activities
- *Discussion,* including debates, seminars, and buzz groups.

Uses. The cognitive approach is well suited to helping learners recall new information, comprehend how things work, and remember and use new procedures (Davis and Davis, 1998). It applies generally to objectives in the cognitive domain, particularly to tasks at the lower and middle levels of complexity.

A Constructivist Framework

A more recent educational theory, constructivism, revolves around the notion that "knowledge is constructed by the learners as they attempt to make sense of their experiences" (Driscoll, 2000, p. 376). Constructivism can be viewed as a philosophy, an epistemology, or an instructional orientation. The label has been used by theoreticians working in different realms. Even within education there is no comprehensive set of beliefs that is embraced by all constructivists. Beyond a certain set of core beliefs, constructivists diverge into several subgroups, some of which hold positions that are contradictory to others. This discussion focuses on the core beliefs that are most widely accepted.

Theory Base. A core philosophical belief is that while there is a real world out there, there is no meaning inherent in it; meaning is constructed by people and cultures. In terms of epistemology, then, knowledge is constructed from and shaped by experience, and understanding of the world is socially negotiated. The name, constructivism, is a reminder that whatever is done *to* the learner in the name of instruction, ultimately nothing happens until the learner takes those inputs and *constructs* some meaning from them. Hence, giving learners ownership of the knowledge is crucial. Furthermore, that knowledge is useful only to the extent that it is embedded in a real-world context. Generalizations stripped of their context are of little practical use (Duffy and Jonassen, 1992).

Application of the Theory. Prescriptive principles derived from constructivism include "1. Embed learning in complex, realistic, and relevant environments. 2. Provide for social negotiation as an integral part of learning. 3. Support multiple perspectives and the use of multiple modes of representation. 4. Encourage ownership in learning. 5. Nurture self-awareness of the knowledge construction process" (Driscoll, 2000, pp. 382–383).

Although Merrill rejects the constructivist label for his work, he proposes a set of instructional principles, which he calls "first principles of instruction" (2002a, p. 43), that are problem-centered, progressively more realistic, and focused on knowledge construction by the learner, as shown in Figure 15.5. These ideas are clearly aligned with the constructivist view. So until another representation of the constructivist perspective comes along that is at least equally coherent, Merrill's framework can represent this perspective.

Merrill's theory proposes four phases in the instructional process: (1) *activation* of prior experience, (2) *demonstration* of skills, (3) *application* of skills, and

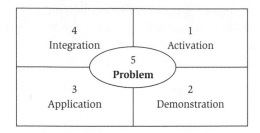

Figure 15.5. Visual Model of the Major Elements of Merrill's "First Principles."

---

(4) *integration* of these skills into real-world activities, with all four phases revolving around (5) a *problem*. Each of these five elements has supporting generalizations or principles, which provide the prescriptions for effective instruction. The broadest generalizations about each step of the instructional sequence are

1. *Activation:* Learning is facilitated when the learner is directed to recall, relate, describe, or apply knowledge from relevant past experience that can be used as a foundation for the new knowledge.

2. *Demonstration:* Learning is facilitated when the learner is shown rather than told.

3. *Application:* Learning is facilitated when the learner is required to use his or her new knowledge to solve problems.

4. *Integration:* Learning is facilitated when the learner can demonstrate his or her new knowledge or skill.

5. *Problem:* Learning is facilitated when the learner is engaged in solving a real-world problem [Merrill, 2002a, pp. 45–50].

Instructional Pattern. Merrill also proposes a simple framework for applying his first principles to training situations, called the "Pebble-in-the-Pond" model (Merrill, 2002b). The essence of his framework is to begin by imagining the simplest whole version of the task that the learner must be able to perform, the first ripple of the pebble dropped into the pond, then to identify the expanding ripples: "a progression of such problems of increasing difficulty or complexity such that if learners are able to do all of the whole tasks thus identified, they would have mastered the knowledge and skill to be taught" (p. 41). The focus on actual on-the-job problems makes this approach highly suited to immediate application on the job, one of the keys to retention and transfer of training. Merrill reports documented success in terms of better and faster learning.

Methods. Merrill's approach and other constructivist approaches tend to prefer methods that immerse learners in problematic situations:

- *Discovery/Inquiry*

  Includes laboratory-type activities, such as science experiments, field work, internships, and apprenticeships.

  Includes simulation and game-type activities, such as business games, social simulations, simulations of work situations, videogames, and other sorts of immersive environments, including virtual reality.

- *Tutorial*

  Includes face-to-face apprenticeship and mentoring; action-learning programs that emphasize action, reflection, and mentoring are a good example.

- *Reading*

  Includes particularly Web text with links connecting related ideas, known as hypertext, possibly incorporating sounds and motion images, known as hypermedia.

- *Expression*

  Includes multimedia productions, hypertext document construction, and other projects, especially those that are developed collaboratively.

- *Reflection*

  More than any other instructional approach, constructivism emphasizes the importance of learners' thinking back on their experiences, typically in the form of a game debriefing, dialog with a coach, keeping a journal, or the like.

Uses. The constructivist approach is well-suited to learning advanced skills high in cognitive complexity, particularly in domains that are not well structured, in which there may be many correct solutions to a problem, such as in management. Action-learning programs in executive education embody the constructivist approach by combining short, formal training sessions with longer periods of on-the-job work under the guidance of a mentor.

An Eclectic Framework

Lesson frameworks are seldom derived purely from one theory base. Although many frameworks reflect multiple influences, including Merrill's, Gagne's Events of Instruction framework is quite self-consciously eclectic, explicitly drawing on different theories.

Theory Base. Gagne, a leading translator of learning theory into instructional theory, proposed in early editions of his influential book *The Conditions of Learning* (Gagne, 1965, 1977) that the information-processing view and the assimilation view of learning could be combined with behaviorist concepts to provide a more complete approach to teaching different learning tasks.

Application of the Theory. Gagne's Events of Instruction framework suggests that certain mental operations must be carried out for successful learning, and it works best to do them in a certain order, at least when following an expository strategy. When following an inquiry strategy the middle steps may be done in reverse order. The best-known version of his framework has been a robust and influential outline for lesson design:

1. Gaining attention
2. Informing learners of the objective
3. Stimulating recall of prior learning
4. Presenting the content
5. Providing "learning guidance"
6. Eliciting performance
7. Providing feedback
8. Assessing performance
9. Enhancing retention and transfer [Gagne and Medsker, 1996, p. 140]

Instructional Pattern. Offered by Gagne as a general guide, this framework can be used to construct a lesson having a specific sequence: (1) gain the learners' attention by telling them or dramatizing the reason for mastering this skill; (2) tell them clearly what they are expected to be able to do after the learning session; (3) remind them of what they already know and how today's lesson adds to that; (4) demonstrate the new skill or present the new knowledge; (5) suggest mnemonic devices, ask probing questions, or give prompts that guide the learners in mastering the content; (6) make sure that the learners have a chance to practice the new knowledge or skill; (7) during the practice, confirm correct responses or desired performance and help them overcome mistakes; (8) test the learners' mastery by having them use the new knowledge, skills, and attitudes in realistic or simulated problem situations; and (9) help the learners connect their new skills with the job by giving them on-the-job practice or simulated practice involving varied problems.

Presenting instruction in this sequence exemplifies an expository or deductive approach: telling the learners "The Point"—the concept, rule, or procedure you want them to master—and then letting them apply The Point in some practice setting. Sometimes a discovery or inductive approach may be more effective, putting practice and feedback, steps 6 and 7, before steps 2, 3, 4, and 5. This way the learners discover The Point for themselves.

Adaptation: The "Universal Model" of Stolovitch and Keeps. The Events of Instruction template has been adapted and simplified by many authors. For example, Stolovitch and Keeps (2002) offer a "universal model for structuring any learning session" (p. 68), consisting of five major steps: (1) tell the learners the rationale for the lesson, (2) tell them the objectives of the lesson, (3) create learning activities that lead to attaining the objectives, (4) evaluate learner performance, and (5) provide feedback on how well they mastered the objectives. They reduce the nine steps to five, but keep the essence of Gagne's framework.

Adaptation: Russell's Objectives Alignment Framework. A further simplification, the Objectives Alignment Framework, developed by Russell, is shown in Figure 15.6. The salient elements of a learning session could be boiled down to three: objectives, activities, and assessments. *Objectives* describe what you want the learners to be able to do *after* instruction. *Activities* are what the learners do *during* instruction to help them learn the content, attitudes, or skills being taught; this usually entails practice with feedback. *Assessments* are how instructors determine if learners have mastered the content, attitudes, and skills being taught. As shown in Figure 15.6, all three components of the lesson structure are interrelated. Any one of the components can be used to begin constructing the lesson, and each of the three components is equally important. Some start with the objectives, then select or design the activities, and finally develop the assessment items. If the objectives are clearly stated, it will be fairly easy to develop both of the other components.

Others prefer to start with the activities. They select the readings, class discussions, small-group projects, games and simulations, and other learning activities. They can then develop objectives by answering the question, What will the

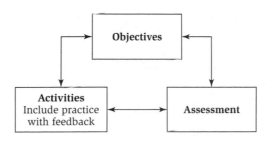

Figure 15.6. Visual Model of James D. Russell's Objectives Alignment Framework.

students be able to do after they complete these activities? Then they develop assessment methods that measure successful completion of the activities.

Finally, there are occasions when planners might start with the assessments. Perhaps the assessment will be some sort of company certification exam or an external government exam. The design and development team then selects activities that will enable the students to be successful on the exam. Using the completion of an exam as a method of assessment, they interpret the knowledge and skills required by the test as the lesson objectives.

In short, any one of the three components, if developed well, should lead to the other two. Regardless of where planning starts, all three components should be developed and all three must be aligned with each other; each component must fit with and support the other two. No matter how clear and ingenious the instructional activities are, they will not be the right activities if they do not give the learners practice in the skills on which they will be assessed. Similarly, if the test is not aligned with the objectives, managers will not be able to be sure that the learners have mastered the essential skills.

This Objectives Alignment Framework is probably the simplest and most robust expression of the framework first proposed by Gagne. It has the virtues of being well-tested in practice and easy to communicate to new instructors or designers.

Methods. The eclectic approach may be implemented through a combination of methods associated with the behaviorist, cognitive, and constructivist approaches.

Uses. The eclectic approach is well-suited to training goals that combine routine tasks and skills at the intermediate level; they are likely to include cognitive, affective, and psychomotor skills together.

DELIVERY ENVIRONMENTS FOR INSTRUCTION

Instruction can take place in many different environments, from a formal classroom to the actual workplace, and in many places in between or in combination. These delivery environments can be placed into three major categories: face-to-face classroom, which might be augmented by audiovisual media; distance learning that is telecommunications-based or computer-based; and independent self-study.

Face-to-Face Classroom Instruction

Potential Uses. The advantages of face-to-face instruction are obvious because the classroom has been and continues to be the most popular venue for instruction. The presence of an instructor and fellow learners gives a social dimension that is difficult to replace. Both the instructor and fellow learners can serve as behavior models and sources of inspiration. The ability to adapt spontaneously and flexibly to the group's needs, the ability to share stories, the opportunity to network, and simply having an appointment to learn give the classroom environment numerous advantages. It is especially appropriate for pursuing interpersonal skills, seeing demonstrations of skills, and practicing those skills with immediate feedback and corrective guidance.

Trends in Use. Despite many earlier predictions to the contrary, face-to-face classroom instruction is still the most universally applied format in the corporate realm, being used "always" or "often" at 91 percent of companies (Galvin, 2003, p. 31) with no significant downward trend over the preceding several years. The traditional audiovisual media used in face-to-face instruction show a pattern of slow decline, although video materials continue to be very widely used. Videorecordings are used always or often at 52 percent of responding organizations, according to Galvin (2003, p. 30). The traditional analog media are being replaced gradually by digital formats, including projection of Web pages and presentation software such as PowerPoint.

In terms of the percentage of *time spent in training,* instructor-led face-to-face classroom instruction occupied 69 percent of all training time in 2003, a decline of five percent from the previous year. Another ten percent of time was spent in classrooms with remote instructors, an increase of three percent since the previous year. Participation in computer-based learning occupied 16 percent of time, an increase of four percent over the previous year (Galvin, 2003, p. 22). So most organizations still use face-to-face classroom instruction, but trainees are spending a larger proportion of their training time in distance or computer-based learning, and the computer-based learning is increasingly delivered through the Internet or private intranets.

Distance Learning via Synchronous Telecommunications Media

Potential Uses. When it is impractical or expensive to bring learners together in one geographical location, but the attributes of face-to-face instruction are still needed, organizations turn to synchronous distance learning, typically through teleconferences transmitted over broadcast, satellite, or computer networks or through a cable television network that is owned or leased by the organization. This ensures that everyone gets the same message at the same time and allows real-time two-way exchange.

It is possible to arrange multipoint audio conferences via the Web; these can be combined with electronic whiteboards to allow collaborative learning at a fraction of the expense of other telecommunications options.

Trends in Use. A small proportion of organizations, 12 percent in 2003, used broadcast or satellite television to disseminate training programs to multiple sites (Galvin, 2003, p. 30). Two-way videoconferences distributed over satellite, cable, or the Web are used always or often for training at 22 percent of all organizations (Galvin, 2003, p. 30). They tend to be used as supplements to other forms of training or for special purposes, such as the introduction of new products or the roll-out of new tools at organizations with widely scattered locations.

Distance Learning via Asynchronous Computer-Based Media

Potential Uses. Asynchronous (not at the same time) delivery is suited to pre-recorded programs that need to be accessible all the time to many people for independent study. Typically, computer-based lessons have been transmitted over local area networks (LAN) or, more recently, through CD-ROMs or DVDs. Transmission via the Web is becoming increasingly popular. This form of distribution enables anytime, anywhere access. Some degree of interaction or even collaboration among learners is possible through discussion boards, chat rooms, instant messaging, or shared work spaces. The advantage of asynchronous group interaction is that participants have the time to think about questions or problems and can take time to formulate a response. Less assertive participants often find they have a better chance to get a word in edgewise in discussions that are asynchronous.

Trends in Use. Computer-based delivery systems have played a gradually expanding role in training over the past decade. In the early 1990s, this meant modules distributed via floppy disk or LAN. Since then distribution has migrated toward CD-ROM or DVD formats or, more recently, to the Internet or an organizational intranet. According to the 2003 *Training* survey, 45 percent of companies distributed instruction in digital storage media format. However, 63 percent used Internet or intranet delivery (Galvin, 2003, p. 30).

Games and Simulations

Potential Uses. Games and simulations are often seen as ideal pedagogical methods for learning to make decisions about complex business problems, for practice under realistic conditions, or for repetitive drills on facts or concepts to be memorized. They may be used in face-to-face classroom contexts or in immersive computer environments, so-called "micro worlds."

Trends in Use. About a quarter of all organizations use classroom-based games and simulations regularly. However, by using the computer to present the problems and select appropriate responses, more sophisticated programs can be run faster and less expensively than in face-to-face settings. Considering these potential advantages, it is perhaps surprising to see that computer-based games and simulations are used regularly within only about ten percent of organizations (Galvin, 2003, p. 31).

Independent Self-Study

Potential Uses. Programmed instruction, developed in the 1960s, dramatically demonstrated the possibility of packaging a wide range of subjects into modules for self-paced independent study. The requirement of continuously interacting with the material and getting feedback about progress at each step accounted partly for the success of this approach. More recently, independent study has been converted to delivery through interactive CD-ROMs or so-called Web tutorials, which typically are not truly tutorial but do present the content in a step-by-step form. This can be an attractive option because it allows learners to start and stop the program at any time and progress at their individual pace.

However, experience has shown that learners in the workplace tend to lose interest and drop out of such programs. There appear to be at least two factors at work. First, text-based materials can be repetitive and boring, with only superficial levels of interactivity. Second, self-study does not fit the way many adults prefer to learn. Adults tend to seek social learning settings; they want to hear stories about others' experiences, what works and what doesn't work.

When self-study is the most practical approach due to time and cost constraints, the loss of the human dimension can be overcome to some extent by employing video episodes in the program. The moving image is certainly preferable when teaching interpersonal skills or complex physical tasks or conveying messages from specific sources, such as a credible expert. Even for verbal material, a human with facial expressions and body language can hold interest far longer than can straight text.

Trends in Use. Since 2002, the *Training* survey has included self-study as a separate instructional context. Since then self-study based on print and audiovisual modules has been declining, while the use of Web-based self-study grew from 36 to 44 percent of organizations using it always or often, making it one of the most widely used instructional delivery environments (Galvin, 2003).

Blended Learning

In everyday parlance, trainers have tended to classify learning events into discrete categories: face-to-face classroom instruction, on-line learning, independent study, action learning, and so on. In fact, though, corporate training and education programs increasingly consist of hybrids; for example, face-to-face classroom meetings interspersed with Web-based team projects; satellite videoconferences followed by small-group discussions at remote sites; on-the-job action learning plus mentoring via e-mail. Combining conventional and on-line delivery has come to be recognized as a third alternative, referred to as blended learning. The advantages of combining formats are obvious. On-line activities offer self-pacing, standardization of information dissemination, and rapid deployment of new material, while face-to-face learning allows live human interaction, practice with feedback, team building, networking, and the other functions that are tied to people's emotional responses. There is a growing consensus that the future belongs to blended approaches.

Selecting Delivery Systems

In the instructional technology literature there is a long tradition of creating schemata for matching delivery systems with different learning objectives. A highly regarded guide from the audiovisual era is by Reiser and Gagne (1983). More recently, a group of training specialists and consultants (Pallesen, Haley, Jones, Moore, Widlake, and Medsker, 1999) have developed a delivery system selection model that attempts to take into account economic factors as well as the capabilities of each of the various categories of delivery systems and environments, including desktop multimedia, satellite, audiovisual media, teleconferencing, Internet or intranet, electronic performance support systems, and electronically enhanced live classrooms. They then assess the suitability of each for a range of different learning objectives. The result is a model that would be suitable for selecting appropriate delivery systems and environments for blended learning, helping to decide which elements of a lesson or course could be delivered electronically and which would work better in a face-to-face classroom environment.

EVALUATING INSTRUCTION AND ASSESSING LEARNER OUTCOMES

Evaluation and assessment may be aimed at two basic targets: the instruction itself and the learners. For each target, three phases of evaluation may be used: formative, summative, and confirmative. Consequently, there are six different categories of evaluation and assessment (Hellebrandt and Russell, 1993).

Formative Evaluation of Instruction

Formative evaluation of instruction is done during the development of the materials in order to improve them. Often this type of evaluation is called "learner tryout and revision." This type of evaluation is done while the materials are still in draft form.

Summative Evaluation of Instruction

Summative evaluation of instruction is designed to determine the ultimate effectiveness of the materials. Often this process is called "validation" or "verification." It is conducted after the materials have been developed and have been used by the trainees. A major issue is what should be measured to determine success. A widely accepted framework is Kirkpatrick's four levels model (1998), which proposes that one could evaluate program success by any of four criteria: (1) the reaction or satisfaction of learners, (2) the attainment of learning objectives, (3) the on-the-job behavior changes that follow instruction, or (4) organizational results, the overall impact of the instructional program on the organization's goals or the so-called bottom line. Managers would be most interested in the fourth level of evaluation, the return on investment. The selection of any of these targets could be justified, but the choice is often made out of convenience rather than out of careful consideration of the demands of the situation. There is widespread agreement that the first level, learner reaction, is the one most often tapped, simply because it is the easiest sort of information to gather and it satisfies the trainer's immediate concern: is my audience happy?

Confirmative Evaluation of Instruction

Confirmative evaluation of instruction is conducted some time after initial implementation of the instruction, perhaps months or years later. The purpose is to determine whether that lesson or program is still enabling trainees to meet the original objectives. The evaluation process may determine that the content has changed since the original development of the material or that the characteristics of the target audience have changed. In either case, the materials would need to be revised.

Formative Assessment of Learners

Formative assessment of learners is conducted to diagnose learning problems and may result in prescribing some sort of enrichment or remediation. It occurs during instruction and uses self-check, progress tests, nongraded quizzes, or instructor observation.

Summative Assessment of Learners

This form of assessment is conducted at the end of instruction to give a certification of competency. It can be viewed as a sort of final exam administered to measure trainee achievement. These assessments can be paper-and-pencil or performance-based, and they can be norm-referenced, learners compared to each other, or criterion-referenced, with learners compared to an objective standard of competence. Outside of formal education settings, criterion-referenced tests are usually the more appropriate choice. Shrock and Coscarelli (2000) argue forcefully that because test scores can affect people's careers and life paths, it is imperative to follow systematic procedures in developing and administering tests, so that tests can withstand legal challenge. They provide a fourteen-step process for criterion-referenced test development, a process that yields valid and reliable measures of people's mastery of specific competencies. Another comprehensive guide to preparing effective tests, administering tests, analyzing the results, and reporting and using test results is provided by Westgaard (1999).

Confirmative Assessment of Learners

Sometime after completion of instruction, usually months or years later, learners may be retested to confirm whether they have maintained their competence demonstrated during summative assessment immediately after the instruction.

CONCLUSION

In the past, instruction was probably overused as a panacea for virtually any and all problems of human performance in the workplace. Now it is seen as one intervention among an array of performance interventions, to be used when there is a clear indication of an ignorance problem.

Another common misconception is that instruction is somehow improved when it is conveyed through a newer media-delivery system. Computer-based delivery systems can distribute lessons faster and possibly more inexpensively, but they lead to better learning only if they employ better instructional methods.

In the corporate realm, a standardized approach to developing instruction is often beneficial, streamlining the planning process and ensuring some consistency across different times and locations. Adopting or adapting a particular instructional design and development model is a common means of improving instructional planning, and a systems approach model is most often chosen. A weak link in the use of such models is the design stage. It is a complex task to select and apply powerful instructional methods and strategies to widely varying objectives, diverse learners, and different working situations, with different delivery systems available.

Designers do not have to start from scratch. They can borrow frameworks, such as the behaviorist, cognitive, constructivist, or eclectic frameworks, to help organize a lesson or module. These are robust generic frameworks that have been proven in practice. At the very least, they can turn to a simple template such as Russell's Objectives Alignment Framework to make sure that at least there is alignment among the lesson's goals, its activities, and its test; this alone makes a huge difference in the effectiveness of a lesson.

Learners can participate in instruction in a variety of delivery environments, from face-to-face classrooms to on-line tutorials to on-the-job, work-embedded training. There is a trend to move training as close as possible to the work situation, both to save time off the job and to increase the likelihood that the worker will actually use the new knowledge and skills. Distance learning and self-study formats can be vehicles for moving instruction closer to just-in-time. This can be effective as long as everyone remembers that telling isn't teaching, and that the mere transmission of information to the worker is not equivalent to providing instruction. Neither face-to-face classroom instruction nor distance learning is effective unless learners are actively engaged with the material and have opportunities to practice with feedback.

In the end, it is impossible to determine if the design decisions were the right ones without valid evaluation. Formative evaluation of instruction and assessment of learners allow early detection of flaws before final development and implementation. Summative measures allow managers to determine whether the training hit the mark in terms of benefits over costs. This is how instruction can prove its value.

References

Atkinson, R. C., and Shiffrin, R. M. (1968). Human memory. A proposed system and its control processes. In K. Spence and J. Spence (Eds.), *The psychology of learning and motivation* (Vol. 2). New York: Academic Press.

Ausubel, D. P. (1980). Schemata, cognitive structure, and advance organizers: A reply to Anderson, Spiro, and Anderson. *American Educational Research Journal, 17,* 400–404.

Bandura, A. (1969). *Principles of behavior modification.* New York: Holt, Rinehart and Winston.

Bloom, B. S. (Ed.). (1956). The taxonomy of educational objectives, the classification of educational goals, handbook I: Cognitive domain. New York: David McKay.

Bruner, J. S. (1966) *Toward a theory of instruction.* Cambridge, MA: Belknap.

Clark, R. D. (2001). *Learning from media: Arguments, analysis, and evidence.* Greenwich, CT: Information Age.

Davis, J. R., and Davis, A. B. (1998). *Effective training strategies.* San Francisco: Berrett-Koehler.

Dick, W., Carey, L., and Carey, J. O. (2005). *The systematic design of instruction* (6th ed.). Boston: Allyn & Bacon.

Dills, C. R., and Romiszowski, A. J. (Eds.). (1997). *Instructional development paradigms.* Englewood Cliffs, NJ: Educational Technology Publications.

Driscoll, M. P. (2000). *Psychology of learning for instruction* (2nd ed.). Boston: Allyn & Bacon.

Duffy, T. M., and Jonassen, D. H. (Eds.). (1992). *Constructivism and the technology of instruction: A conversation.* Hillsdale, NJ: Lawrence Erlbaum Associates.

Ertmer, P. A., and Newby, T. J. (1993). Behaviorism, cognitivism, constructivism: Comparing critical features from an instructional design perspective. *Performance Improvement Quarterly, 6*(4), 50–70.

Foshay, W. R., Silber, K. H., and Stelnicki, M. B. (2003). *Writing training materials that work.* San Francisco: Jossey-Bass/Pfeiffer.

Gagne, R. M. (1965). *The conditions of learning.* New York: Holt, Rinehart and Winston.

Gagne, R. M. (1977). *The conditions of learning* (3rd ed.). New York: Holt, Rinehart and Winston.

Gagne, R. M., and Medsker, K. L. (1996). *The conditions of learning: Training applications.* Fort Worth, TX: Harcourt Brace College.

Gagne, R. M., Wager, W. W., Golas, K. C., and Keller, J. M. (2005). *Principles of instructional design* (5th ed.). Belmont, CA: Thomson/Wadsworth.

Galvin, T. (2003, October). 2003 industry report. *Training*, 21–45.

Glaser, R. (Ed.) (1965). *Teaching machines and programmed learning, II: Data and directions.* Washington, DC: Department of Audio-Visual Instruction, National Education Association.

Gordon, J., and Zemke, R. (2000, April). The attack on ISD. *Training, 37,* 43–53.

Gustafson, K. L., and Branch, R. M. (1997). *Survey of instructional development models* (3rd ed.). Syracuse, NY: ERIC Clearinghouse on Information and Technology.

Hellebrandt, J., and Russell, J. D. (1993, July). Confirmative evaluation of instructional materials and learners. *Performance & Instruction, 32*(6), 22–27.

Kirkpatrick, D. L. (1998). *Evaluating training programs: The four levels* (2nd ed.). San Francisco: Berrett-Koehler.

Lumsdaine, A. A., and Glaser, R. (Eds.). (1960). *Teaching machines and programmed learning: A source book.* Washington DC: Department of Audio-Visual Instruction, National Education Association.

McCombs, B. L. (1986). The instructional systems development (ISD) model: A review of those factors critical to its successful implementation. *Educational Communication and Technology Journal, 34*(2), 67–81.

Medsker, K. L., and Holdsworth, K. M. (Eds.). (2001). *Models and strategies for training design.* Washington, DC: International Society for Performance Improvement.

Merrill, M. D. (2002a). First principles of instruction. *Educational Technology Research and Development, 50*(3), 43–59.

Merrill, M. D. (2002b). A pebble-in-the-pond model for instructional design. *Performance Improvement, 41*(7), 39–44.

Molenda, M., and Pershing, J. A. (2004). The strategic impact model: An integrative approach to performance improvement and instructional systems design. *TechTrends, 48*(2), 26–32.

Pallesen, P. J., Haley, P., Jones, E. S., Moore, B., Widlake, D. E., and Medsker, K. L. (1999). Electronic delivery systems: A selection model. *Performance Improvement Quarterly, 12*(4), 7–32.

Popham, W. J. (1971). Preparing instructional products: Four developmental principles. In R. L. Baker and R. E. Schutz (Eds.), *Instructional product development* (pp. 169–207). New York: Van Nostrand Reinhold Company.

Reigeluth, C. M. (Ed.). (1983). *Instructional-design theories and models.* Mahwah, NJ: Lawrence Erlbaum Associates.

Reigeluth, C. M. (Ed.). (1999). *Instructional-design theories and models: A new paradigm of instructional theory, Volume II.* Mahwah, NJ: Lawrence Erlbaum Associates.

Reiser, R. A., and Gagne, R. M. (1983). *Selecting media for instruction.* Englewood Cliffs, NJ: Educational Technology Publications.

Romiszowski, A. J. (1981). *Designing instructional systems: Decision making in course planning and curriculum design.* London: Kogan Page; New York: Nichols (1984).

Rossett, A., and Gautier-Downes, J. (1991). *A handbook of job aids.* San Diego: Pfeiffer.

Schramm, W. (1962). *Programmed instruction: Today and tomorrow.* New York: The Fund for the Advancement of Education.

Shrock, S., and Coscarelli, W. (2000). *Criterion-referenced test development* (2nd ed.). Washington DC: International Society for Performance Improvement.

Skinner, B. F. (1954). The science of learning and the art of teaching. *Harvard Educational Review, 24*(1), 86–97.

Smaldino, S. E., and Russell, J. D. (2005). *Instructional technology and media for learning.* Upper Saddle River, NJ: Pearson Education.

Stolovitch, H. D., and Keeps, E. J. (2002). *Telling ain't training.* Alexandria, VA: American Society for Training and Development.

Westgaard, O. (1999). *Tests that work: Designing and delivering fair and practical measurement tools in the workplace.* San Francisco: Jossey-Bass/Pfeiffer.

Wile, D. (1996). Why doers do. *Performance & Instruction, 35*(2), 30–35.

CHAPTER SIXTEEN

Designing Instructional Strategies

A Cognitive Perspective

Kenneth H. Silber, Wellesley R. Foshay

A comprehensive treatment of the cognitive approach to instructional design would go well beyond the scope of a single chapter, of course. This chapter will focus on one of the most critical parts of the design process, the definition of instructional strategies. We apply current cognitive-based research on teaching and learning to formulate instructional strategies for the different knowledge types one typically addresses in training.

THE COGNITIVE APPROACH TO DESIGNING INSTRUCTIONAL STRATEGIES

How Learning Occurs from a Cognitive Point of View

There are many theoretical models in cognitive psychology about how learning occurs (Anderson, 1995a, 1995b; Ausubel, 1968; Best, 1989; Hannafin and Hooper, 1993; Klatzky, 1980; Zechmeister and Nyberg, 1982). Though there are differences among them, they generally agree on how learning occurs. According to these models, there are several components of the mind, and each is involved in the learning process in certain ways. The components are perception and sensory stores, short-term memory, and long-term memory.

Perception and Sensory Stores

Perception is selective. There is more stimulation in the environment than we are capable of attending to and of encoding or internally translating for storage in memory. Therefore, we only attend to certain things because they are either (1) related to what we already know, or (2) so novel they force us to attend to them.

Limits of the sensory stores. Our sensory stores are capable of storing almost complete records of what we attend to, but they hold those records *very briefly.* During that very brief time before the record decays, we do one of two things: (1) we note the relationships among the elements in the record and encode them into more permanent memory, or (2) we lose the record forever.

Short-Term or Working Memory

Rehearsal. When information is passed from the sensory stores to memory, we mentally rehearse it. Examples include repeating phone numbers several times, or creating associations to names, such as Ted with the red hair, to help memorize them when you first hear them at a party. The former, simply repeating the information over and over, is called *passive rehearsal.* It does not seem to improve memory as well as rehearsing the information in a *deep and meaningful* way, like the latter way of creating associations.

Limited capacity. There seems to be a limit on the amount of information we can rehearse at one time. The classic Miller Principle (1956) shows . . . that we can remember seven plus or minus two bits of information at most, and that to remember more we have to "chunk" or group information in manageable sizes. The findings of this study still seem to apply, with some modifications of how you define a "bit," element, or a "chunk" (Sweller, 1999).

Format. At this point, the information is not yet organized and encoded, but there is some evidence that there are separate spaces for storing and rehearsing verbal information and visual and spatial information.

Long-Term Memory

In general, theorists believe that long-term memory is organized based on context and experience. That means we encode, store, and retrieve information in the way we have used knowledge in the past and expect to use it again in the future. There are several phenomena psychologists agree on about what strengthens the memory process.

Memory strength. Information in memory has a characteristic called *strength,* which increases with practice. There is a *power law of learning* that governs the relationship between the amount of practice and response time or error rates. The formula is *Strength = Practice to Power x.*

Elaboration. Elaboration means adding information to the information we are trying to learn. It involves tying the new information to existing information, or creating a new knowledge structure that combines the old and new information.

Chunking. Memories are stored not as individual bits or as long strings of information, but in "chunks." Chunking divides large amounts of information into logical groups of about three to seven items. The more complex the information, the smaller the chunks should be.

Verbal and visual information. It seems we encode verbal and visual information differently in memory. We use a linear code for verbal information and a spatial code for visual information. We remember visual information very well, especially if we can place a meaningful interpretation on the visuals.

Associations and hierarchy. Information is organized in memory, grouped in a set of relationships or structures, for example, hierarchically. Using such a structure makes it easier for us to remember, because there are more related pieces of information activated when we search for information.

By comparison with computers, humans can remember far fewer separate pieces of data, but are much better equipped for pattern recognition skills such as analogical reasoning, inference, and comprehension of visual and verbal languages.

Types of Knowledge

When they discuss learning, cognitive psychologists often draw distinctions between different categories of knowledge. The biggest distinction is between *declarative* knowledge and *procedural* knowledge: declarative knowledge is knowing *that,* and procedural knowledge is knowing *how.* The basic difference between the two types of knowledge is that declarative knowledge tells you *how the world* is, while procedural knowledge tells you *how to do things in the world.*

There are different types of declarative and procedural knowledge. Declarative knowledge includes facts such as names, concepts such as groups or categories, and principles and mental models, or how the world works. Procedural knowledge varies by *degree of structure,* on a continuum from well-structured, such as algorithmic knowledge with fully defined inputs, processes, and outputs, to ill-structured, such as design knowledge with undefined inputs, processes, and outputs.

THE COGNITIVE INSTRUCTIONAL DESIGN MODEL

The model for the cognitive approach to instructional design (Foshay, Silber, and Stelnicki, 2003) describes the five learning tasks learners have, according to cognitive psychologists. For each learning task, it describes the two to five lesson elements trainers must put in their lessons to help learners accomplish the learning task. They provide the blueprint for the lesson structure modeled here. The instructional strategies recommended here are based in mainstream cognitive psychology (Anderson, 1995a), sometimes called the cognitive information processing view of learning. While the research on which the model is based is sound regardless of one's philosophical approach, this model is *not* based in the cognitive inquiry or problem-based learning approaches (Medsker and Holdsworth, 2001). More complete descriptions are available in Foshay, Silber, and Stelnicki, 2003. See also Foshay, 1986 and 1991; Foshay and Gibbons, 2001; and Foshay and Kirkley, 1998. Portions of the model are based on Dick and Carey, 2001; Bonner, 1988; DiVesta and Rieber, 1987; Gagne, 1985; Gagne, Briggs, and Wager, 1992; Merrill, 1983; Reigeluth, 1999; and Reigeluth and Stein, 1983.

The model is a way to

- Synthesize and summarize the components of a well-designed lesson
- Relate what learners have to do to learn, to what you as a designer have to do to help them to learn
- Present a general framework for instructional design up front, with the notion that each subsequent component will teach how to apply this framework to teaching a certain type of knowledge
- Provide a job aid that you can use as you design training

The Cognitive Instructional Design (ID) Model, shown in Table 16.1, has two columns and five rows. The left-hand column lists the five tasks learners have to do in learning, one in each row:

1. Select the information to attend to
2. Link the new information with existing knowledge
3. Organize the information
4. Assimilate the new knowledge into the existing knowledge
5. Strengthen the new knowledge in memory

The right-hand column lists the seventeen elements of a training lesson that you design to help learners accomplish the five learning tasks. In each row, the table lists and describes briefly the lesson elements that relate to each of the five learning tasks. Eight of the seventeen elements are the same for all categories of knowledge and appear in boldface roman in the table. The other nine elements vary by type of knowledge and appear in boldface italic in the table.

The elements on the right side of the model are purposely *not numbered*. The reason for this is that within any row, you can manipulate the sequence of the elements the situation calls for. To accomplish the learning task, it is crucial that all elements listed in any row be included. However, within a given

Table 16.1. The Cognitive Instructional Design Model.

What Learners Must Do to Learn	*Elements Trainers Must Use to Help Learners Learn*
1. Select the information to attend to Learners must heighten their attention and focus it on the new knowledge being taught because that new knowledge is seen as important and capable of being learned.	**Attention.** Gain and focus learners' attention on the new knowledge. **WIIFM.** Tell learners "What's in It for Me" in the new knowledge. **YCDI.** Tell the learners "You Can Do It" in learning the new knowledge.
2. Link the new information with existing knowledge Learners should put the new knowledge in an existing framework by recalling existing or old knowledge related to the new knowledge, and linking the new knowledge to the old.	*Recall.* Bring to the forefront the prerequisite existing (old) knowledge that forms the base on which the new knowledge is built. *Relate.* Show similarities or differences between the new knowledge and old knowledge, so that the new knowledge is tied to the old.
3. Organize the information Learners must organize new knowledge in a way that matches the organization already in mind for related existing knowledge to • Make it easier to learn • Cut mental processing • Minimize confusion • Stress only relevant information.	**Structure of content.** Present the boundaries and structure of the new knowledge, in a format that best represents the way the new knowledge itself is structured. *Objectives.* Specify both the desired behavior and the knowledge to be learned. **Chunking.** Organize and limit the amount of new knowledge presented to match human information-processing capacity. **Text layout.** Organize text presentation to help learners organize new knowledge. **Illustrations.** Use well-designed illustrations to assist learners' organization and assimilation of new knowledge.
4. Assimilate the new knowledge into the existing knowledge Learners must integrate the new knowledge into the old knowledge so that these combine to produce a new, unified, expanded, and reorganized set of knowledge.	*Present new knowledge.* Using a different approach for each type of knowledge, present the new knowledge in a way that makes it easiest to understand. *Present examples.* Demonstrate real-life examples of how the new knowledge works when it is applied.

Table 16.1. The Cognitive Instructional Design Model. (*Continued*)

What Learners Must Do to Learn	*Elements Trainers Must Use to Help Learners Learn*
5. Strengthen the new knowledge in memory Learners should strengthen the new knowledge so that it will be remembered and can be brought to bear in future job and learning situations.	*Practice.* Involve learners by having them do something with the new knowledge. *Feedback.* Let learners know how well they've done in using the new knowledge, what problems they're having, and why. **Summary.** Present the structure of content again, including the entire structure of knowledge. *Test.* Have learners use the new knowledge again, this time to prove to themselves, you, and their employer that they have met the objectives of the training. *On-the-job application.* Have learners use new knowledge in a structured way on the job to ensure they "use it, not lose it."

row, it is not crucial that they be done in a particular order. For example, you could begin a lesson with any of these sequences:

- Attention → WIIFM → YCDI
- Attention → YCDI → WIIFM
- YCDI → WIIFM → Attention
- YCDI → Attention → WIIFM
- WIIFM → Attention → YCDI
- WIIFM → YCDI → Attention

USING THE MODEL TO BEGIN ANY LESSON

For any category of declarative or procedural knowledge lessons, learners must select the information to attend to (Keller, 1987; Keller and Burkman, 1993; Wlodkowski, 1985). The first three lesson elements help them do this. These elements are familiar to most, so a brief summary is provided here:

- *Attention.* Provide appropriate cues and signals to learners to help them focus and retain the stimuli related to the relevant new knowledge.
- *What's in it for me (WIIFM).* Show learners how the learning is important to them personally, jobwise, or to their careers.

- *You can do it (YCDI)*. Instill a sense of confidence in learners that they can learn the lesson content and use it on the job.

USING THE MODEL TO TEACH FACTS

Issues

Facts do not exist in isolation. They are stored in long-term memory in networks that are based on those relationships, and retrieved through those networks. The networks in which these facts are stored are created, and related to one another, based on the context in which the facts are learned and used. Facts are best retrieved in the same context in which they are learned. We learn facts by building onto existing networks of facts.

General Strategies for Teaching Facts

Context. Present both the learners' existing knowledge structure and the new facts, and show how the facts and knowledge structure relate in the context of a meaningful use of the facts. Give learners a hint about which existing networks to recall and add onto. Teach and practice facts in a context, preferably the context in which you expect them to be used; in the case of training, this is usually the job setting and tasks.

Objectives. When writing objectives for fact-level teaching, use verbs such as *state, define, recite,* or *list*.

Job aids. Depending on how the facts are used, consider giving learners a job aid so that they can look up facts as needed, rather than requiring them to memorize large amounts of information.

Embedding. If the number of facts to be taught at once is limited to a very few, perhaps just one or two chunks, consider embedding fact teaching within the teaching of other kinds of learning.

Teaching Facts Using the Lesson Elements

Recall. Stimulate recall by the learner of all those appropriate knowledge structures that will include the facts to be learned. One function of Ausubel's "advance organizer" (Ausubel, 1968) is to recall previously learned knowledge on which the new knowledge is based.

Relate. Relate the new facts to the knowledge structures you just got the learner to recall. To increase likelihood of recall, use a context that is similar to the one the learner will be in when the facts will be used. Again, a portion of the "advance organizer" emphasizes bridging or linking the new knowledge to the old by emphasizing the similarities and differences between them. Use verbal statements, images, tables, and so on to point out the relationships you want the learner to form. What is important is that the relations be meaningful to the learner within the structure of the task.

Structure of content. State how you have structured the facts for easy learning. This helps the learner get prepared to receive the new facts and relate them to appropriate existing networks of facts in memory. This is the place in the lesson at which you present the structure of the facts to the learner. Remember that it is best if the structure is directly related to how the facts will be used. An iconic rather than verbal representation works best.

Objectives. State both the desired content and behavior.

Assimilate

Present new knowledge. Present facts within structures. First, provide cues that signal the structure. These cues need to be distinctive, meaningful, and related to the learner's existing networks of facts. Where appropriate, use visual images of the facts, maps, diagrams, colors, tables, typography, and even sounds to provide additional cues to the learner about the structure of the facts. Follow these guidelines for what cues to include and the sequence in which to include them:

- *Step 1.* Show the facts.

    Use the structure you presented above.

    Establish links to what the learners already know.

    Reinforce the way the structure will be used.

- *Step 2.* Explain the structure.

    Include an explanation of the structure you presented.

    If possible, retain the display of the facts during the explanation, to help support encoding and storage, or memorization.

Strengthen

Practice. In fact learning more than most types of content, practice is crucial. It is crucial to aid the learner both in building the new fact network and in retrieving it at the appropriate time. Follow these guidelines for building in practice:

- Use only questions that present the cues the learner will use "on the job."

- For wrong-answer feedback, restate the structure rule the learner violated, if possible, as well as the factual association.

- Practice first within the structure you presented, even if it is only a list, and then intermix items from different parts of the structure. At the beginning, keep the total number of facts being practiced at one time to one structure or list of seven or fewer facts, then broaden out until the entire structure of facts is being practiced.

Feedback. Let learners know how well they have done in using the new knowledge, what problems they are having, and why.

Summary. Present the structure of content again, including the entire structure of facts. But you do not need to list each individual fact.

Test. Have learners use the new knowledge again, this time to prove to themselves, you, and their managers that they have met the training objectives.

On-the-job application. Have the learners use new knowledge in a structured way on the job to ensure they "use it, not lose it."

USING THE MODEL TO TEACH CONCEPTS

Issues

A concept is a group of things such as objects, events, or abstract ideas that have some features in common. The features a thing *must* have to be part of the concept are named *critical features* or *critical attributes*. Other features may be present, although their form can vary among members of the group. These are called *variable features* or *variable attributes*. A third type of feature that may be present is irrelevant to whether things are in the group or not, so they are called *irrelevant features* or *irrelevant attributes* (Fleming and Bednar, 1993; Tiemann and Markle, 1983).

Learners store in memory an idealized *prototypical example.* However, learners usually need additional examples to understand a concept.

A change in one or more critical attributes in a concept creates a different but related concept. These are called *coordinate* concepts. In addition, most concepts are part of or *subordinate* to other concepts, and have concepts that are part of or *superordinate* to them. These relationships create knowledge structures.

General Strategies for Teaching Concepts

Teach individual concepts and their knowledge structures, to help the learner create a correct knowledge structure that allows for the correct application of the prototypical example or critical and variable attributes to easily categorize new examples. Teach, relate, and differentiate several related new concepts at the same time, rather than teaching one concept at a time. Discuss a prototypical example of each concept, its critical and variable attributes, and its relationships to other concepts in the knowledge structure. Then give additional examples and nonexamples as needed, including analogies (Stepich and Newby, 1988). Do *not* present a narrative definition, but instead give a bulleted list of attributes of a single concept or an attribute matrix for all the related concepts.

Teaching Concepts Using the Lesson Elements

Link

Recall. Recall existing concept structures that the learner needs in order to understand the new concept knowledge you are teaching.

Relate. Relate the concepts you are teaching to their place in concept structures the learner already knows.

Organize

Structure of content. The structure of content should show the relationship between five to nine new concepts. If the concept structure is larger than that, show those that are at the high level. Wherever possible, the structure should be iconic rather than semantic.

Objectives. The objectives should describe both the behaviors to be learned and the knowledge to be understood.

Assimilate

Present examples and present new knowledge. Follow these guidelines:

- *Step 1.* Show the concepts, using a sequence that includes prototype examples, followed as needed by definitions and contrasts, and additional examples. Focus on presenting the prototype example. Use abstract diagrams or definitions when needed to highlight key attributes. Otherwise, use realistic video, photos, or illustrations.

- *Step 2.* If learners need more help in understanding the concepts, then you need extensive presentation and practice on the parts of the definition:

    Compare and contrast to show the logical relationships between the concepts.

    Use a hierarchy or a contrast table to make the comparisons visible and easy to see.

- *Step 3.* Present as many additional examples as needed to assure appropriate generalization, while avoiding errors of misconception, overgeneralization, and under-generalization. Use these principles to select and construct the examples:

    Include initial practice by having learners label and classify the examples.

    Contrast examples of one concept with those of others you are teaching, or those that the learner already knows.

    Keep all examples in view, if possible, or present them in close succession.

Sequencing

- Start with *close in* examples that are similar to the prototype example, then include more *far out* ones.

- After presenting some positive examples, mix positive and negative examples.

Range

- Use a range of examples that emphasize the variability of positive examples.
- Remember that in a coordinate concept set, any positive example of one concept is a negative example of all the others.
- Be sure to use examples across the whole concept structure at once, not just isolated concepts.

Strengthen

Practice and feedback. Practice with additional examples. Use these principles to build the practice (Tosti, 1990):

- Begin by having the learner classify or construct additional examples. Use the same practice formats as earlier.
- Examples used in practice must be new to the learner and not used previously.
- Use realistic contexts, preferably including simulations or scenario-based exercises.
- Include context and irrelevant information, so the learner is required to select only the relevant information.
- Include prompts and cues not found in the real world only when essential, or for wrong-answer feedback.
- Let the learners know how well they have done in using the new concept knowledge, what problems they are having, and why.
- In wrong-answer feedback, include an explanation of the attribute missed.

Summary. Present the structure of content, showing the critical and variable attributes or the prototypical example.

Test. Have learners use the new knowledge again to prove to themselves and upper management that they can perform the training objective.

On-the-job application. Have learners use the new knowledge in a structured way on the job to ensure they "use it, not lose it."

USING THE MODEL TO TEACH PRINCIPLES AND MENTAL MODELS

Learners construct mental models by synthesizing their knowledge of facts, concept, and principles into a model, often hierarchical, with causal relationships. Mental models are constructed for a particular purpose, and are very context bound. For example, mental models of trees and how they function will differ if you create them based on being a forester, an ecologist, a tree surgeon, or a tree worshipper. Solving problems involves constructing, modifying, or otherwise manipulating a mental model of the problem.

General Strategies for Teaching Principles and Mental Models

Relate principles to one another and to existing knowledge in mental models. Help learners learn or create mental models that are related to the context in which they will be using the knowledge, and synthesize their declarative knowledge well enough to use it as the basis for problem solving.

How to Teach Principles and Mental Models Using the Lesson Elements

Link

Recall. Recall existing declarative knowledge structures such as facts, concepts, principles, and mental models that the learner needs to understand the new principles and mental model knowledge you are teaching.

Relate. Relate the principles and mental model you are teaching to existing knowledge structures such as facts, concepts, principles, and mental models the learner already has and the context in which the new mental model will be used.

Organize

Structure of content. The structure of content should show the complete new mental model, including context, principles, and structure, and should incorporate existing mental models, concept structures, and facts.

Objectives. The objectives should require the learner to use the principles in some way. Most common is to have the learner *predict* what will happen next when observing or manipulating an object or scenario, or explain why something happened or why a particular decision is, or is not, justified. In response to a Why? question, the correct answer is often close to a statement of the relevant principle. Note that the event being observed or manipulated can be real or in a game or simulation, and it can be a normal or abnormal function.

Assimilate

Present examples and new knowledge. Follow these guidelines:

- *Step 1.* Show the principles in action, using prototypical examples in the form of stories both about how the principle works when it works and how it works when it does not work. People usually remember the prototype, idealized or first example, not the principle or mental model in verbal form. Make stories credible, vivid, and straightforward enough to highlight key principles. Tell the stories verbally with testimonials, or with realistic video, photos, or illustrations.

- *Step 2.* State the principles involved in the mental model and the mental model itself:

    Present the context for the principles and the mental model.

    Present the principles as "if . . . then . . ." statements or "because . . ." reasons.

    Display all principles in the mental model simultaneously to facilitate comparison and contrast, or to show how the principles fit together in the mental model.

    Show how the principles integrate with existing mental models, concept structures, and fact structures to create the new mental model.

    Show what the mental model looks like, with some kind of diagram.

    Be sure you are representing the system at the level of detail on which the learner will be operating. For example, do not show a full schematic diagram if a block diagram of the system shows what the learner will be manipulating. You should have determined the correct level of detail in your task or content analysis.

- *Step 3.* Present as many additional examples as needed to ensure that all applications of the mental principles and mental model in the desired context are exemplified.

Strengthen

Practice. Ask questions that require application of the principles to new situations. For example, you can ask the learner to

- Predict how the system will respond to something the learner does or observes.
- Explain by stating the reason why the system behaved as it did.
- Generate or select another example of the system's behavior.

Feedback. Let the learners know how well they have done in using the new knowledge, what problems they are having, and why.

Summary. Present the structure of content, showing the complete new mental model, including context, principles, and structure and incorporating existing mental models, concept structures, and facts.

Test. Have the learners use the new knowledge again to prove to themselves, the trainer, and the employer that they can perform the training objective.

On-the-job application. Have the learners use new knowledge in a structured way on the job to ensure they "use it, not lose it."

USING THE MODEL TO TEACH PROCEDURES OR WELL-STRUCTURED PROBLEM SOLVING

Only use this instructional strategy if the well-structured problem solving you are teaching is not likely to go out of date, is not like many other procedures you are teaching, and must be recalled from memory because it is too time critical, complex, or critical to be simply looked up.

General Strategies for Teaching Procedures and Well-Structured Problem Solving

Be sure to identify both the declarative and procedural knowledge components of skills. Give each appropriate instructional emphasis and make the relationships clear. When you teach the well-structured procedural components, first introduce the real problem-solving context for the procedure, then either alternate between teaching declarative and procedural knowledge, or integrate the two. Use direct or deductive teaching strategies for declarative knowledge and well-structured problem solving. When teaching well-structured problem solving, allow learners to retrieve the procedure if appropriate, for example, from a reference card. If the procedure is frequently used, encourage memorization of the procedure and practice until it is automatic. Within a problem exercise, help the learners understand or define the goal, then help them to break it down into intermediate goals. Use the errors learners make in problem solving as evidence of misconceptions, not just carelessness or random guessing, and, if possible, determine the probable misconception and provide feedback to correct it. If transfer is a goal, use multiple contexts for each procedure, and ask questions that encourage the learner to grasp the generalizable part of the skill across many similar problems in different contexts. Plan a series of lessons that grow in sophistication from novice-level to expert-level understanding of the knowledge structures used. If speed of performance or cognitive load is an issue due to problem complexity, stress, fatigue, and so on, add extensive practice to build automaticity, or automatic performance. Always include practice situations that allow the learner to choose the procedure from among other alternatives or to recognize that it is needed. The requirement for contextualized learning means that procedures always require a simulation or some kind of on-the-job-training or apprenticeship. As with any kind of learning, the amount of practice depends entirely on the criterion. Additional issues are discussed in Jonassen (1997, 2000), Mayer (1993), and Newell and Simon (1972).

The sequence of instruction described here is not the only one that has been shown to be effective. For example, backward chaining works. Discovery-based or inductive strategies also may be acceptable if certain conditions are met.

Teaching Procedures or Well-Structured Problem Solving Using the Lesson Elements

Link

Recall. Recall concepts, principles, and mental models needed to represent the procedure.

Relate. Relate the concepts, principles, or mental models to the purpose of the procedure.

Organize

Structure of content. Name and number the steps in the procedure and highlight any branches.

Objectives. Objectives should describe both the behaviors to be performed and knowledge to be learned. Inform trainees of the objective at an appropriate time during the presentation.

Assimilate

Present new knowledge and examples. Follow these guidelines:

- Show a worked-out example that is a prototype example as an application of the procedure.

- Include an explanation of each step in the procedure at the level of detail appropriate to what the learner already knows.

- Introduce, then show, the individual steps, each with its own explanation.

- Point out the cue that signals the beginning of the step, the action, and the feedback that shows the step has been correctly completed.

- Relate the steps to facts and concepts as the steps use them. Teach the concepts and facts as they occur if the learner does not know them.

Strengthen

Practice. Practice using additional examples. Present a new problem scenario and ask the learner to select or recall the procedure from among alternatives. Broaden the practice to include content and irrelevant information so the learner is required to select only the relevant information.

Feedback. Let the learners know how well they have done in using the new knowledge, what problems they are having, and why.

Summary. Restate the structure of content, such as the entire procedure.

Test. Have the learners use the new knowledge again, this time to prove to themselves, the trainer, and the employer that they have met the performance objectives of the training.

On-the job application. Have learners use new knowledge in a structured way on the job to ensure they "use it, not lose it."

USING THE MODEL TO TEACH ILL-STRUCTURED PROBLEM SOLVING

Issues

The following issues are key in teaching problem solving (Clark, 1998).

Problem space definition. When learners are presented with a problem, the first thing they must do is represent it in their minds. They must create a mental representation of the initial state, goal state, constraints, and so on of the problem. After recognizing there is a problem in the first place, learners now try to figure out what kind of problem this is. What they create is called a *problem space.*

The most difficult part of the task of ill-structured problem solving, and one that contrasts greatly with well-structured problem solving, is this defining of the problem space. Unlike with well-structured problem solving, the learner cannot just try to match the new problem with problems encountered in the past and use that match to define the problem space. The problem, by definition, is difficult, if not impossible, to classify. It is defined by the context or situation that presents it, and not by a specific set of declarative and procedural knowledge that one has learned. Therefore the problem space must contain information about many possible initial states, goal states, operations, and constraints of the problem. It also must contain a great deal of declarative and procedural knowledge that might be related to the problem.

Check the results—reflect. In ill-structured problem-solving, since the solution is almost always one of many possible solutions, it is important for the learners to be able to justify why they came to the solution they did. This involves both checking the results of implementing the solution, to see if it solved the problem, and, more important, reflecting on the process of getting to the solution.

This reflection activity is uniquely important to ill-structured problem solving. Reflection on the process becomes part of the mental model that is stored along with the problem and its solution. And it is the reflection on the process that aids both in more effective problem solving the next time and in generalization of the process to new and related problems.

Errors in learning ill-structured problem solving. The problems people have in learning to do problem solving include

- Defining the problem space too narrowly, or incorrectly.
- Assuming the problem is like another they have already solved when it is not.

- Not seeing that a problem is in fact like one they have already solved.

- Defining the problem in terms of the solution.

- Searching for an algorithm that will provide a simple solution to the problem when only heuristics will work.

General Strategies for Teaching Ill-Structured Problem Solving

Emphasize ill-structured problem solving when delayed transfer is a goal of instruction. For ill-structured problem solving, the main training tasks are (1) problem-space definition, (2) generating the heuristics to solve the problem, and (3) reflection over the problem-solving process (Silber and Stelnicki, 1993). Most of the strategies for well-structured problem solving apply, with the exceptions and additions listed here.

Use inductive teaching strategies to encourage synthesis of mental models for ill-structured problem solving. Within a problem exercise, help the learners understand or define the goal, then help them to break it down into intermediate goals. Plan a series of lessons that grow in sophistication from novice-level to expert-level understanding of the knowledge structures used. Encourage the learners to use their declarative—that is, context—knowledge to define the goal or properties of an acceptable solution and then invent a solution. Allow many right strategies and solutions, and compare them for efficiency and effectiveness. Ask questions and make suggestions about strategy to encourage learners to reflect on the problem-solving strategies they use. Do this either before or after the learner takes action. This is sometimes called cognitive coaching. Note that *minimalist* or discovery-based strategies may be acceptable under some circumstances.

In designing simulations, games, and exploratory environments, begin by modeling the process of building a strategy, using the cognitive coaching techniques previously discussed, then change the problem and let the learner invent a strategy. Then change the whole problem space and let the learner invent a similar strategy.

Teaching Ill-Structured Problem Solving Using the Lesson Elements

Link

Recall. Recall related declarative knowledge that is part of the mental model and procedures that are analogous to the one you are teaching in whole or in part.

Relate. Relate the current procedure to what the learner already knows about the mental model and the analogical procedures.

Organize

Structure of content. Show the mental model for a heuristic or a class of abstract problems. Develop an abstract diagram or other representation of how the components in the problem space interact. Present *worked examples* of typical problems, and then articulate the strategy steps used to solve the problems. Worked examples can take many forms, including "think-alouds" and step-by-step solutions. Note features of the problem that are unique to that problem, as opposed to those that are typical of a class of problems. Not all of the typical features or exceptions need be covered in these initial worked examples as long as they are covered elsewhere in the activity. Be sure that the cognitive processes such as cues and decisions are made clear in the example as well as in the performance.

Objectives. Tell the learner that the purpose of the lesson is to understand a particular general procedure for solving a particular broad class of problems that you name.

Assimilate

Present new knowledge and examples. Follow these steps:

- *Step 1.* State the class of problems to which the heuristic applies.
- *Step 2.* Show the heuristics.
- *Step 3.* Show the steps or general approach of each heuristic.
- *Step 4.* Explain that the heuristic is a guide the learner can use to generate a specific solution or procedures for a problem.
- *Step 5.* Teach the underlying principles, or stimulate recall on them.
- *Step 6.* Since problem representation is a major part of problem solving, the heuristic may have two major subparts, or two heuristics: one for representing the problem and one for solving the equation. Both heuristics need to be taught and practiced.
- *Step 7.* Show a specific example of application of the problem, such as a worked example, emphasizing the key decisions and information used in the step-by-step application of the procedure.

Strengthen

Practice. Practice using a range of similar problems. Use scenario-based simulations and games, on-the-job mentoring, or on-the-job training. Use these principles:

- If necessary, provide part-task practice of relevant algorithmic methods, such as facts, concepts, principles, and rote procedures. Part-task practice can be wrapped into the scaffolding of the whole skill practice described in the next step.
- Provide scaffolded practice. Scaffolded problems can take several different forms. One way is to ask the learner to provide part of a

solution and ask the learner to do the rest, such as by interrupting a think-aloud or completion problem, in which we present a partial worked solution and ask the learners to complete it. Also possible are interactions in which the sensitivity of feedback triggers is modulated, so that in early problems, feedback would be available at every step, and in later problems feedback would only be available for the final output.

- Provide significant support to the learner on initial problems, slowly withdrawing that support until the learner is doing the whole task independently.

- As you scaffold, do *not* distort the basic logical structure of the strategy. Each practice should be a complete beginning-to-end use of the strategy. Make the problem easier by providing direction, eliminating irrelevant detail, avoiding branches for special cases or extra steps, and avoiding or clarifying points of confusion.

- Provide a range of problems, including prototypical problems, problems that require unusual uses of the heuristic, and problems in which the heuristic is an inappropriate choice, or nonexamples.

- Provide a range of contexts.

- Do not increase problem difficulty while decreasing support. Modulate both difficulty and support, but only one at a time.

- Be sure to include features that expose anticipated learner misconceptions.

Feedback. As you engage in dialogue with the learner about how he or she has defined each of the basic problem characteristics, ask the learner to explain why he or she made the decision, and what knowledge he or she used to make the decision.

- Listen to the explanations for errors that reveal flaws, such as gaps or misconceptions in the learner's mental model of the problem space. When you find one, point it out to the learner.

- Look at the sequence of steps the learner is going through, and check it against the heuristics identified in the cognitive task analysis. When the learner skips a step, does a step out of order, or does a wrong or unnecessary step, first ask the learner to reflect on the strategy in use, that is, "Are you sure you want to do that now?" If that does not cause the learner to correct the error, state the missing heuristic to the learner, that is, "You do not have enough information to do that yet. Remember that < heuristic >." If that does not work, then model the solution and include a "think-aloud" explanation of why the solution is as it is, that is, "Here is how I think about problems like this. . . ."

Summary. The structure of content is the fully generated heuristic for problem solution. If possible, the learner should generate it.

Test. Problem solving has to be tested with a performance-based strategy: the only way to find out if a learner can solve problems is to have the learner solve problems of realistic complexity and in realistic contexts, without extra scaffolding. You can do this with well-designed simulations, hands-on exercises, role plays, and projects. Consequently, paper-and-pencil testing formats usually favor open-ended—that is, divergent or essay—questions that are scenario-based. In many content areas, however, paper-and-pencil formats are too limited to capture the context and complexity of the desired performance. In these cases, on-line simulations and various kinds of live group exercises, role plays, and projects are needed depending on the content area.

On-the-job application. In the first few weeks following training, make sure the learner encounters a wide range of tasks that are of typical difficulty and that are representative of the objective. It is helpful to have the learner do some tasks and review, critique, and troubleshoot similar tasks done by others.

TEACHING LESSONS COMBINING DIFFERENT TYPES OF LEARNING

It is rare for instructional designers to actually design and create separate lessons for each type of knowledge; this approach is too fragmented and takes too much lesson time. It is also rare for them to combine the lessons for all given types of knowledge into one lesson; this approach creates context, but moving back and forth among the different elements within the lesson becomes confusing to the learner.

The approach the authors recommend is to combine individual lessons into two lessons: one combining all the relevant declarative knowledge and a second combining the procedural knowledge. This approach provides context without overloading the learner.

A sample set of lessons that show how the events are combined when lessons contain multiple types of learning is shown in Table 16.2, for declarative knowledge, and Table 16.3, for procedural knowledge.

Table 16.2. Combined Declarative Knowledge Lesson.

Declarative Knowledge Lesson Elements	Sample Lesson Element Description

Lesson Overview and Mental Model Presentation

1. Select

Attention. The attention component should explain that you are teaching concepts and principles that you need to solve the problem just presented in the scenario.

Attention. After the title screen, begin the lesson with a video clip of people in a confusing store meeting; then show them emerging from the meeting and complaining about it. Ask, "Has this ever happened to you?"
- If yes, go on.
- If no, state "You've been lucky so far. It will."
- Continue: "Good meetings begin with a plan. That's what we'll concentrate on in this lesson."

WIIFM. Establish the context in which the problem is solved. This should be the framework for all explanations, examples, and practice throughout the lesson.

WIIFM. "Actually, < characters in meeting video > don't have to suffer through meetings like this. By understanding the elements of good meetings, you'll be able to ensure that this bad experience doesn't happen to your groups. Your store meetings can be a valuable way to make things work better, and to beat the competition."

YCDI. Build the learners' confidence that this is a skill they can learn by showing them how they have already done similar things.

YCDI. "Planning meetings well isn't much harder than planning them badly, it's just a matter of knowing what to do. It's a skill any successful professional develops, and you can, too."

2. Link

Recall. Recall related declarative knowledge that is part of the mental model, and concepts that the learner already knows and that are analogous to the one you are teaching, in whole or in part.

Recall. "You probably already know many of the concepts involved in planning from other contexts:

   < Show visual [hierarchy or actual graphic] which is first approximation of the structure of content. Have learner click on each element for a label. >

- Agenda
- Decision making
- Record keeping
- < And other components the learners already know >."

Relate. Relate the mental model to what the learner already knows, often by use of an analogy.

Relate. "Planning a meeting is like planning a party, a card game, or a home-improvement project.

Table 16.2. (*Continued*)

Declarative Knowledge Lesson Elements	Sample Lesson Element Description
	Click on the drawings below < of planning a party, and so on > to see what they have in common. In each of these examples, you see that planning involves • Why you're doing it • What you'd like the goal to be • Who's going to be involved • The time, place, and expense • The steps to follow from beginning to end."
3. Organize	
Structure of Content. This should show the mental model, including concepts, principles, and skills.	*Structure of Content.* < Show complete visual diagram of the parts of a successful meeting, with arrows that show how they interact. Pop on each meeting plan part and arrow as you name it, until the whole model is built. >
Develop an abstract diagram or other representation of how the components in the problem space interact, present *examples* of typical concepts and principles, or both.	*Alternative Using Example* • "Here's an example of a plan for a successful meeting. Roll your cursor over each part, and you'll see that part's name. Roll your cursor over the arrows, and you'll see what to call the ways the parts interact." • < Show example store meeting plan parts with arrows that show how they interact. When the learner rolls the mouse pointer over each part or arrow, its name pops up. > • "When all names have been displayed, activate the 'go on' icon."

Principle Lesson 1

1. Select	
Attention. Transition to first principle (*WIIFM* and *YCDI* are redundant and are omitted).	*Attention.* "Take a look at the first arrow in the diagram. It stands for the first rule for successful meetings < the rule of meeting purpose > . Click on it to see how it works."

(*Continued*)

Table 16.2. Combined Declarative Knowledge Lesson. (*Continued*)

Declarative Knowledge Lesson Elements	Sample Lesson Element Description
2. Link	
Recall and *relate*. This is a great time for an analogy—transition to first principle (*WIIFM* and *YCDI* are redundant and are omitted).	*Recall* and *Relate.* < Show video of basketball team in huddle. > "When you're playing basketball, the first thing you have to know is how points are awarded. Having a clear meeting purpose is like knowing how you'll score points."
3. Organize	
Structure of Content. Show how the principle fits in the mental model.	*Structure of Content* < Show mental model, with first arrow (purpose) highlighted, and pop on the plan parts it connects to. > "When you have a clear purpose, it's possible to develop all these parts of the plan: agenda, participants, logistics. . . ."

Concept Lesson 1

1. Select	
Attention. Transition to first concept structure (*WIIFM* and *YCDI* are redundant).	*Attention.* "Let's see what the different purposes of meetings are and what they mean."
2. Link	
Recall and *relate*. Another great place for an analogy.	*Recall* and *relate.* < Show posterized still photo of basketball video. > "Meetings are like discussions you have with your teammates in a basketball game. Sometimes you're just talking about how the game is going. Sometimes you need to decide what play to use . . . and so on. Just as different conversations have different purposes, so do meetings."
3. Organize	
Structure of Content. Show the concept structure.	*Structure of Content* < Bring up diagram next to basketball photo. > Diagram of meeting purposes should include these components, indicating the arrangement from simple to complex, and with information flow coming in, going around within, and coming out of each.

Table 16.2. (*Continued*)

Declarative Knowledge Lesson Elements	Sample Lesson Element Description
	< Pop on components individually: >
	• Information sharing
	• Discussion
	• Project review
	• Operations review
	• Decision making
	• Problem solving
Objective	*Objective.* "At the end of this lesson, you'll know the differences between meetings with these six different purposes—you'll be able to define them and pick out examples of each."

Fact and Concept Lesson 1

(Remember that only "Present Definitions" is needed when teaching facts. Examples are needed for teaching concepts.)

4. Assimilate

Present Explanations (for facts).

Step 1. Show the facts. Use the structure you presented earlier.

Step 2. Explain the structure. Include an explanation of the structure you presented.

Present Definitions: Learner Chooses Sequence.

< Delete basketball visual. Add one meeting icon for each meeting purpose. > "Click on each meeting purpose icon to see its definition."

Information sharing. Objective or content is to disperse news, intelligence, policy, and so on, to appropriate participants.

Discussion. Objective is to share various points of view about an issue.

Project review. Objective is to examine or reexamine proposed current projects as to soundness, management, progress, and success.

Operations review. Objective is to systematically examine the soundness, management, progress, and success of business procedures and processes.

Decision making. Objective is to choose among several options to proceed with an action.

Problem solving. Objective is to consider a question or statement or situation proposed for solution and achieve a resolution to it.

(*Continued*)

Table 16.2. Combined Declarative Knowledge Lesson. (*Continued*)

Declarative Knowledge Lesson Elements	Sample Lesson Element Description
5. Strengthen	
Practice. For fact, learners define. For concept, they select or classify.	*Practice (facts).* First, define each of these meeting types: • Information sharing • Discussion • Project review • Operations review • Decision making • Problem solving *Practice (concepts).* "Here are some more meetings. See if you can correctly identify the purpose of each one." < Show eight video clips of meetings, each followed by the question, "What meeting purpose did the example show?" >
Feedback. For each incorrect answer, provide an explanation that corrects the probable misconception that caused the learner to select that choice. For each correct choice, tell the learner the choice is correct. Then move on to the next example and question.	*Feedback.* < Give an example of incorrect answer feedback. > "This is not an example of decision-making, because the participants are sharing information, but they are not trying to reach consensus."
Summary. Place the concept structure back into the mental model.	*Summary.* < Show the full mental model, with the concepts just taught highlighted. > "So now you can see all the types of meeting purposes and how they relate to the rest of the meeting plan."
Test. This is a great time for progressively more far-out positive examples and close-in negatives.	*Test* **< Fact test >** "Define the six types of meetings." **< Concept test >** "Here are some more meetings. See if you can correctly identify the purpose of each one." < Show video clips of meetings, followed by question asking "What meeting purpose did the example show?" >

Table 16.2. (*Continued*)

Declarative Knowledge Lesson Elements	Sample Lesson Element Description
	< **Score test** >
Transition. Back to the principle	*Transition.* "Now let's see how the meeting purposes drive the rest of the parts of the meeting plan."

Principle Lesson 1

4. Assimilate	< Continue with full mental model graphic, but change highlighting to include principle arrow. >
Present Principle. Using the concepts just taught, *present +/− examples* of operation.	*Principle.* "If a clear-cut meeting purpose is specified, then you can clearly specify the meeting plan's participants, logistics, and agenda."
	Example. "Here's Ginny." < Show video still. > "Let's see how she decides on the participants, logistics, and agenda for her meeting."
	< In audio, play narrative in which Ginny introduces herself and explains her meeting's need, how she decided on a purpose, and how she used the purpose to decide on the participants, logistics, and agenda. Pop on handwritten notes listing participants and agenda items as she talks. >
5. Strengthen	
Practice. Predict or explain; this is a great time for simulation.	*Practice.* "Here's George planning another meeting in the same company." < Show example. > < Ask these questions > : • How do you think he decided on his agenda, logistics, and participants? • Did he do it right? • If not, why not? • How do you think the meeting will go?
Feedback. Give diagnostic feedback as in concept lessons.	*Feedback.* Be sure the system provides diagnostic feedback for wrong answers! < Repeat with as many examples as the learner needs to correctly explain and predict. >
Summary. Place principle and related concepts back into the mental model.	*Summary.* < Show the mental model diagram, with concepts and related principle highlighted. > "So now you can see how a clear meeting purpose really drives the rest of the meeting plan."

(Continued)

Table 16.2. Combined Declarative Knowledge Lesson. (*Continued*)

Declarative Knowledge Lesson Elements	Sample Lesson Element Description
Test. Same as "Practice."	*Test.* Provide scenario-based examples for which the learner needs to correctly explain and judge the purpose (in the agenda) and predict the outcome.
Transition. To the second principle.	*Transition.* "Now let's take a look at the second principle of meeting planning: ensuring that you have the right participants."

Principle Lesson 2

1. Select

Attention. Make the transition to first principle (*WIIFM* and *YCDI* are redundant).	*Attention.* "Take a look at the second arrow in the diagram. It stands for the second rule for successful meetings < the rule of correct attendees > . Click on it to see how it works."

2. Link

Recall and *Relate.* This is a great time for an analogy.	*Recall* and *Relate.* < Show video of football team in huddle. >
	"When you are playing football, the second thing you have to know is what types of players you need to put on the field at any given time. Knowing which participants need to be at a meeting to accomplish a purpose is like having a clear idea of the football team composition."

3. Organize

Structure of Content. Show how the principle fits in the mental model.	*Structure of Content.* < Show the mental model, with the second arrow (purpose) highlighted, and pop on the plan parts it connects to. >
	"When you have the right participants, it is possible to accomplish the purpose of the meeting."

Concept Lesson 2

1. Select

Attention. Make the transition to the first concept structure (*WIIFM* and *YCDI* are redundant).	*Attention.* "Let's see what the different types of meeting participants are and what they can do."

2. Link

Recall and Relate. This is another great place for an analogy.	*Recall* and *Relate.* < Show posterized still photo of football team on field. >

Table 16.2. (*Continued*)

Declarative Knowledge Lesson Elements	Sample Lesson Element Description
	"Participants are just like players at different positions in a football game. Some play offense, some defense, one is the main play caller, some perform special functions. Just as teams have different types of players, so do meetings."

3. Organize

Structure of Content. Show the concept structure.	*Structure of Content* < Bring up diagram next to football photo. > < The diagram of meeting participants should include these participants, indicating the arrangement from least to most influential, and with information flow coming in, going around within, and coming out of each. > < Pop on participants individually: > <ul><li>Subject-matter experts</li><li>Stakeholders</li><li>Decision makers</li><li>Decision influencers</li><li>Appropriate participants</li><li>Facilitator</li><li>Chairperson</li></ul>
Objective	*Objective.* "At the end of this lesson, you'll know the differences between these types of meeting participants. You will be able to define them and pick out examples of each."

Fact Lesson 2

(Only "Present Definitions" is needed)

4. Assimilate

Present Definitions.	*Present Definitions: Learner chooses sequence.*
Step 1. Show the facts. Use the structure you presented earlier.	< Delete football visual. Add one participant icon for each meeting participant. > "Click on each meeting participant icon to see its definition."
Step 2. Explain the structure. Include an explanation of the structure you presented.	*Subject-matter experts.* Individuals with highly specialized skills or knowledge in specific fields or subjects.

(*Continued*)

Table 16.2. Combined Declarative Knowledge Lesson. (*Continued*)

Declarative Knowledge Lesson Elements	Sample Lesson Element Description
	Stakeholders. Individuals who have a vested interest in meeting decisions, outcomes, or actions.
	Decision makers. Those empowered with making judgments, reaching conclusions, and having the institutional authority to make decisions that stand as final.
	Decision influencers. Those who directly or indirectly may shape decisions by reason of their expertise, vested interest, or other factors.
	Appropriate participants. Subject-matter experts, stakeholders, decision makers, and influencers; that is, all those needed to achieve a meeting's objective(s).
	Facilitator. Individual who specializes in running groups gathered for specific purposes. In most cases this individual participates only indirectly in a meeting's business by moving things along.
	Chairperson. Individual who runs the meeting and participates in discussion and decisions.
4. Assimilate *Present Definitions.* *Present Examples.* Note that in this medium, sequence of definitions (fact lesson above) and examples (concept lesson here) can be learner controlled unless you deem a particular sequence to be critical to understanding.	*Present Examples: Learner chooses sequence.* < Meeting participant icons are still on screen. > "Click on each meeting participant icon to see an example of that person in a meeting." < Each example is a video clip. > • Subject-matter experts • Stakeholders • Decision makers • Decision influencers • Appropriate participants • Facilitator • Chairperson

Table 16.2. (*Continued*)

Declarative Knowledge Lesson Elements	*Sample Lesson Element Description*
5. Strengthen	
Practice. For fact, learners define. For concept, they select or classify.	*Practice (facts).* First, define each of these meeting types: • Subject-matter experts • Stakeholders • Decision makers • Decision influencers • Appropriate participants • Facilitator • Chairperson *Practice (concepts).* "Here are some more participants in the meeting. See if you can correctly identify who each one is." < Show eight video clips of a meeting, each followed by the question, "What type of participant is (participant name)?" >
Feedback. For each incorrect answer, provide an explanation that corrects the probable misconception that caused the learner to select that choice. For each correct choice, tell the learner the choice is correct. Then move on to the next example and question.	*Feedback.* < Example of incorrect answer feedback > "Perhaps you thought Joe is the chairperson because he spoke the most. But a chairperson doesn't necessarily have the most to say; it's *what* the chairperson says that defines this role. Try again."
Summary. Place the concept structure back into the mental model.	*Summary.* < Show the full mental model, with the concepts just taught highlighted. > "So now you can see all the types of meeting participants and how they relate to the rest of the meeting plan."
Test. This is a great time for progressively more far-out positive examples and close-in negatives.	*Test.* "Define the seven types of participants." (**Fact test**) "Here are some more meetings. See if you can correctly identify the roles of the people in the meeting." (**Concept test**) < Show video clips of meetings, followed by the question, "What type of meeting participant did the example show?"

(Continued)

Table 16.2. Combined Declarative Knowledge Lesson. (*Continued*)

Declarative Knowledge Lesson Elements	*Sample Lesson Element Description*
Transition. Back to the principle.	**< Score test >** *Transition.* "Now let's see how the meeting participants influence the rest of the parts of the meeting plan."

Principle Lesson 2

4. Assimilate	< Continue with the full mental model, but change highlighting to include the principle arrow. >
Present Principle. Using the concepts just taught, *present +/− examples* of operation.	*Principle.* "You must have meeting participants from all categories in a meeting for it to be successful; if any are missing, the meeting is likely to fail." *Example.* "Here's Ginny." < Show video still. > "Let's see how she decides on the participants to invite to her meeting." < In audio, play narrative in which Ginny introduces herself and explains her meeting's purpose and how she decided on which participants in the organization to invite and why. Pop on handwritten notes listing participants as she talks. >
5. Strengthen	
Practice. Predict or explain; this is a great time for simulation.	*Practice.* "Here's George planning another meeting in the same store." < Show example. > < Ask these questions > : • How do you think he decided on his participants? • Did he do it right? • If not, why not? • How do you think the meeting will go?
Feedback. Provide diagnostic feedback as in concept lessons.	*Feedback.* Be sure the system provides diagnostic feedback for wrong answers! Sample feedback message: "George only invited four people to his meeting, so you may think that he couldn't possibly have people in each role. But remember that one person can fill more than one role. Try again." < Repeat with as many examples as the learner needs to correctly explain and predict. >

Table 16.2. (*Continued*)

Declarative Knowledge Lesson Elements	Sample Lesson Element Description
Summary. Place the principle and related concepts back into the mental model.	*Summary.* < Show the mental model diagram, with concepts and related principle highlighted. > "So now you can see how having the right meeting participants is necessary for a meeting's success."
Test. Same as practice.	*Test: Practice.* "Here's George planning next month's meeting for his store." < Show example. > < Ask these questions > : • How do you think he decided on his participants? • Did he do it right? • If not, why not? • How do you think the meeting will go?
Transition. To the second principle.	*Transition.* "Now let's take a look at the third principle of meeting planning, ensuring that you have the agenda items." (Note: This and the rest of the principle lessons, and their subordinate concept and fact lessons, will *not* be illustrated here since the pattern repeats.)

Mental Model Testing and Lesson Summary

5. Strengthen

Practice and *Test.* Practice the concepts and principles taught so far and provide feedback. Activities should include classification or generation of examples, and prediction and explanation of system behavior (a good way is to ask questions such as, "Why do you have to do this?" or "What would you have to do if . . . ?").

Practice. "Here's Dani planning another meeting for her store." < Show example of Dani planning a meeting employing all the principles and concepts (purpose, participants, agenda, and so on). >

< Ask these questions > :

- How do you think she decided all the meeting elements?
- Did she do each element right?
- Did the whole set of elements fit together correctly?
- If not, why not?
- How do you think the meeting will go? Why?

Summary. Refer back to the mental model.

Summary. < Show complete visual diagram of the parts of a successful meeting, with arrows that indicate how they interact. Pop on each meeting plan part and arrow as you name it, until the whole model is built. >

Table 16.3. Combined Procedural Knowledge Lesson.

Ill-Structured and Well-Structured Problem-Solving Lesson Elements	Sample Lesson Element Description
1. Select	< Well-structured procedure for planning a routine meeting. >
Attention. The attention component should explain that you are teaching a specific procedure for solving a type of problem, even if some of the problems are new.	*Attention.* "Now let's put it all together, and start planning some meetings! There are lots of variations, but here's a simple way you can use to plan a meeting."
WIIFM. Review the context in which the problem is solved.	*WIIFM.* "There's a temptation to 'pooh-pooh' this procedure or to shortcut some of the steps. Even the pro's follow this procedure; as you will learn, it ensures meeting success!"
YCDI. Build their confidence.	*YCDI.* "It's a simple procedure—a lot like the ones you probably use already for planning other kinds of events, from group outings and carpools to vacations to household projects."
2. Link	
Recall and *Relate.* Recall related declarative knowledge that is part of the mental model used in the procedure and the analogous procedure(s).	*Recall and Relate.* "Planning a meeting is just like the way you would plan a dinner party." < Show stills of steps of planning a party. > "First you have to decide why you want to have it, then you decide whom to invite, then you decide when to have it, then what food to serve, and so on. In planning a meeting you have to do essentially the same steps."
	< Party steps dissolve to meeting steps automatically or as mouse goes over steps. >
	"You have already learned what to call these steps and the principles involved in doing them."
	< Show the mental model of meeting elements from the "Declarative Knowledge" lesson. >
3. Organize	
Structure of Content. Show the structure of the procedure.	*Structure of Content.* "Now let's see how you do the steps, in order to figure out how to plan your meeting."
	< Show procedure diagram > :
	1. Clarify the meeting's purpose(s).
	2. Choose appropriate participants.
	3. Establish the date, time, and length of meeting.
	4. Arrange for room set up and equipment.

Table 16.3. (*Continued*)

Ill-Structured and Well-Structured Problem-Solving Lesson Elements	Sample Lesson Element Description
	5. Create the agenda. It must include all the information from steps 1 through 4 and any additional meeting activities. 6. Send the agenda to all concerned. 7. Appoint the person responsible for taking minutes and the person responsible for providing a permanent official record of the meeting.
State the Objective.	*Objective.* "You'll be able to plan meetings just like Ginny does."

4. Assimilate

- Present examples and knowledge.
- Show a worked-out example. Include an explanation of each step. Introduce and then show the individual steps, each with its own explanation. Point out the cue that signals the beginning of the step, the action, and the feedback that shows the step has been correctly completed.
- Relate the steps to facts and concepts as the steps use them.

Model It. "Let's rejoin Ginny as she plans her meeting, and we'll see how she uses these seven steps to plan her meeting. Click on each step to see what she does."

< Clicking on each of the steps plays a video clip with Ginny explaining her thought process as she performs the step. Handwritten notes appear that show the output of each step. >

"Now let's look at each step in detail. Click on each step to learn how to do it."

< Show each step. Explain how to do it, and show another positive example. >

< Each of the steps is accompanied by a second positive example that shows how Ginny applies the technique of that step to plan her meeting. Begin this sequence by introducing Ginny's scenario: > "Now let's look at another example of how people use this strategy to plan their meeting. Ginny needs to decide how to plan a meeting for < describe scenario >."

1. *Clarify the meeting's purpose(s).*

   Recall the types of meeting purposes and the principle of aligning everything with purpose.

   < Show video clip of Dani doing the first step of the procedure and verbalizing aloud the purpose of her meeting. >

(*Continued*)

Table 16.3. Combined Procedural Knowledge Lesson. (*Continued*)

Ill-Structured and Well-Structured Problem-Solving Lesson Elements	*Sample Lesson Element Description*
	< Show the list of substeps for doing this step as she verbalizes them: >
	• Think about the need that prompted the meeting.
	• Match the need with the six meeting purposes using a job aid.
	• Decide which purpose will match the need best.
	• Select the purpose.
	2. Choose appropriate participants.
	Recall the types of meeting purposes and the principle of aligning everything with purpose.
	< Show video clip of Dani doing the second step of the strategy and verbalizing aloud why she's doing it that way as well as what she's doing. >
	< Show the list of substeps Dani is using for doing this step as she verbalizes her thought process: >
	• Think about the purpose of the meeting.
	• Match the need with the seven meeting participants using a job aid.
	• Decide who in the organization fulfills each of the meeting participant categories for this meeting purpose.
	• Decide who in the organization could be a back-up for each participant category in case the primary person is not available.
	• If there is no person to fill the category, go to the project leader to have an additional person added to the project.
	3–7. < Repeat for all strategy steps. >
	8. Appoint the person responsible for taking minutes.

Table 16.3. (*Continued*)

Ill-Structured and Well-Structured Problem-Solving Lesson Elements	Sample Lesson Element Description

5. Strengthen

Practice and *Test*. Practice the procedure steps taught so far and provide feedback.

Summary. Refer back to the mental model.

Practice and *Test*. "Now you try it. Here's the setup:"

< Show scenario. It opens with the following narrative over the visual of a small group of people discussing hiring matters. >

"You are part of a human resource team at Knox Company. The team has decided to do some work process redesign and has asked you to set up the work process redesign team and the first meeting. Decide what you should do first as leader of the team. Type in your answer after the question and click on 'What's the answer.'"

"What steps do you think would be best for planning this meeting?"

< Answer: A list of steps that is like the standard procedure. >

"What should you do for the first step?"

< This format continues until all the steps of the procedure for planning a meeting are covered. >

Transition. To the ill-structured problem-solving lesson.

Transition.

"Now that you've practiced planning a meeting in a simple situation, let's see what happens when you have to plan a meeting in a situation that is not so cut-and-dried—one in which you have to do things on the fly and create your own procedure."

< Here the lesson generalizes to an ill-structured procedure for planning nonroutine meetings. >

1. Select

Attention. The attention component should explain that you are teaching a general strategy for solving a class of problems, even if some of them are new.

Attention.

< Show video clip: Joe home in bed asleep; phone rings in middle of night; governments in three of the fifteen countries in which his company has global offices have found a serious defect in one of the company's products and are

(Continued)

Table 16.3. Combined Procedural Knowledge Lesson. (*Continued*)

Ill-Structured and Well-Structured Problem-Solving Lesson Elements	*Sample Lesson Element Description*
	going to shut them down; it's only a matter of time till the other twelve countries do the same. Joe and Joyce call an emergency meeting at 8 A.M. Eastern time of all the people needed to fix this and come up with a plan by noon to address the crisis. >
WIIFM. Establish the context in which the problem is solved. This should be the framework for all explanations, examples, and practice throughout the lesson.	*WIIFM.* "This could be you facing this new kind of problem. What would you do in this kind of situation?"
YCDI. Build confidence.	*YCDI.* "You can solve this problem because you already have the skills to figure what elements need to be brought together and how to bring them together. You need to develop your own procedure for planning this unusual meeting, by applying the principles of meeting planning that you already know."
2. Link	
Recall. Recall related declarative knowledge that is part of the mental model, and procedures that are analogous to the one you are teaching, in whole or in part.	*Recall.* "You already know the strategy for planning a meeting and the related principles and concepts."
	< Show the mental model of meeting elements from the "Declarative Knowledge" and "Procedure" lessons. >
	"But this situation is different. There isn't time to use the routine process for planning this meeting, and you have to act before you know all the details. The problem you are facing is one of a class of problems you will face throughout your career—one where it's easy to solve if you have the time and resources, but in reality you do not have all the elements you need to solve the problem and you have to create a way to solve it while you are missing some of the key elements.
Relate. Relate the current procedure to what the learner already knows about analogous procedures.	*Relate.* "This is like cooking when the main ingredients did not arrive, the store is closed, the refrigerator power is off, and the gas stove is 'on the fritz.' It's like playing football when five

Table 16.3. (*Continued*)

Ill-Structured and Well-Structured Problem-Solving Lesson Elements	*Sample Lesson Element Description*
	of your top players are injured, the weather is abysmal, none of your plays is working against the opposition, and you are forced to play one man short in a 'must-win' game. "Conventional recipes and plays will not work."

3. Organize

Structure of Content. This should show the mental model for a heuristic for a class of abstract problems. Develop an abstract diagram or other representation of how the components in the problem space interact.	*Structure of Content.* "In an emergency business situation, you have to juggle these elements that are crucial to resolving the crisis."

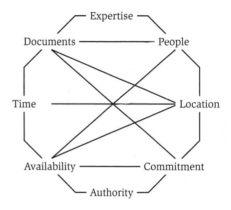

"There are five guidelines for manipulating these elements:

1. Most crucial
2. Sequence
3. Difficulty
4. Cost
5. Expertise"

Objective. State the ill-structured objective.	*Objective.* "The purpose of this lesson is to understand a general procedure for creating a meeting for a particular type of problem—getting people together to solve an emergency."

(*Continued*)

Table 16.3. Combined Procedural Knowledge Lesson. (*Continued*)

Ill-Structured and Well-Structured Problem-Solving Lesson Elements	*Sample Lesson Element Description*
4. Assimilate • State the class of problems to which the heuristic applies. • Show the heuristics. • Show the steps or general approach of each heuristic for representing, then solving the problem. • Explain that the heuristic is a guide. • Recall the underlying principles. • Show a specific example of application of the problem.	*Present Knowledge and Example.* "You already know from prior lessons that you need these elements to make good business decisions, and where each of these elements can reside in an organization." < Show example and definition and where they reside by moving the mouse over them. > 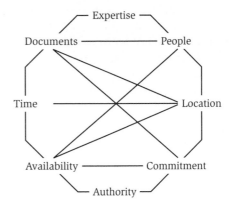 "So what do you do in a crisis when you cannot have all of them?" "Some guidelines are as follows: • Based on the type of crisis, decide which are most important; for example in this crisis, authority to make decisions, and expertise about what to do are the most important elements. • Based on the type of crisis, decide if you can access the elements in sequence instead of simultaneously; for example, in this crisis, you need expertise and documents first, and might need authority after some recommendations have been developed." "Watch Joe and Joyce as they think through how to resolve this crisis and plan a series of meetings."

Table 16.3. (*Continued*)

Ill-Structured and Well-Structured Problem-Solving Lesson Elements	Sample Lesson Element Description
	< Show video of Joe and Joyce brainstorming; show "think-aloud" balloons of the principles as the video shows each; show both negative uses of heuristics, with Joe and Joyce correcting themselves and explaining why to each other, and positive examples. >
	< Show final plan on screen with mental model. >
	< Play audio of Joe and Joyce presenting this plan to the CEO, including their reasoning. >
5. Strengthen	
Practice and *Test*. Provide scaffolded practice, supporting the learner on initial problems, slowly withdrawing that support; provide a range of problems, including prototypical problems, and a range of contexts; modulate both difficulty and support, but only one at a time.	*Practice* and *Test*. "Using what you know about meeting plans and your experience in planning routine meetings, how should you go about planning this emergency meeting? Click on the planning steps you need to take, and place them in order. If you need to skip a step, drag it to the trash can."
	< Learner selects planning steps and places them in order. For each step that is dropped in the trash can, ask, "Why do you think you should not do that step this time?" >
	< For each step that is dragged into the plan, ask, "Why do you think you should take the time to do that step?" >
	< If the plan will generate all the components of the mental model, then show the following scenario: >
	"It's 8 A.M., and the meeting participants assemble. They're looking harried, and no one has slept well. The boss looks at the learner and says, 'OK, looks like a good plan for this meeting—let's go!'"
	< If the strategy will not lead to a sound meeting plan, then run the following scenario: >
	"It's 8 A.M., and the meeting participants assemble. They're looking harried, and no one has slept well. The boss looks at the learner

(*Continued*)

Table 16.3. Combined Procedural Knowledge Lesson. (*Continued*)

Ill-Structured and Well-Structured Problem-Solving Lesson Elements	Sample Lesson Element Description
	and says, 'We've got an emergency here, and your plan will just waste our time. I'll take over from here.'"
Summary. Repeat the mental model.	*Summary.* < Repeat the mental model diagram. >
	"You can see that no matter how flexible you need to be to accommodate the situation, any planning strategy that gets you all the components of a good meeting plan will work. Now you're ready to try it on your job."
On-the-Job Application. In the first few weeks following training, make sure the learner encounters a wide range of tasks that are of typical difficulty and are representative of the objective.	*On-the-Job Application.* < Give the learner a checklist (rubric) recording the next meeting she or he plans, and rating how well the meeting went. The next week, bring the learners back together to recount their meeting planning processes and why they did it that way, and to judge the effectiveness of the meetings that resulted. Discuss how to do it differently next time. >

SUMMARY AND CONCLUSION

A basic principle of instructional design is that different types of knowledge are taught best with different types of instruction: there is no one best way to teach everything. This chapter showed how a basic lesson structure can be adapted to teaching three types of declarative knowledge and the range of procedural knowledge structure. Typically, training needs to include both procedural and declarative knowledge, and it is common for the full need to include all of the types of knowledge discussed here. It is also common, therefore, for a given instructional solution to teach the knowledge types in combination. We have explained and given examples of how this can be done while maximizing efficiency and minimizing redundancy. Taken together, we believe the strategies described here will result in maximally effective instruction that is also optimally efficient to design, develop, and use.

Successful use of the strategies in this chapter depends on a careful prior analysis of the knowledge types and structures to be learned, often called a *cognitive task analysis,* as well as a careful analysis of the learner's prior knowledge, frame of reference, motivation, and confidence. These strategies are generalizable across media: with suitable adaptation, they work in platform training or in a variety of on-line approaches from instructor-led distance education to tutorial computer-based training and simulation. They also carry substantial implications for assessment, which are beyond the scope of this chapter. A fully competent instructional designer will need to develop skills in all of these areas to effectively apply the strategies presented here.

Of course, a chapter such as this can provide only a summary. To encourage you to learn more about these strategies, we have included in our references section a number of current resources to add to your bookshelf, and to your knowledge structure.

References

Anderson, J. (1995a). *Cognitive psychology and its implications* (5th ed.). New York: W. H. Freeman.

Anderson, J. (1995b). *Learning and memory.* New York: Wiley.

Ausubel, D. (1968). *Educational psychology: A cognitive view.* New York: Holt, Rinehart & Winston.

Best, J. (1989). *Cognitive psychology* (2nd ed.). St. Paul, MN: West Publishing Company.

Bonner, J. (1988). Implications of cognitive theory for instructional design: Revisited. *Educational Communications & Technology Journal, 36*(1), 3–14.

Clark, R. (1998). *Building expertise.* Washington, DC: International Society of Performance Improvement.

Dick, W., and Carey, L. (2001). *The systematic design of instruction* (5th ed.). New York: HarperCollins.

DiVesta, F., and Rieber, L. (1987). Characteristics of cognitive engineering: The next generation of instructional systems. *Educational Communications & Technology Journal, 35*(4), 213–230.

Fleming, M., and Bednar, A. (1993). Concept-learning principles. In M. Fleming and H. Levie (Eds.), *Instructional message design* (2nd ed.). Englewood Cliffs, NJ: Educational Technology Publications.

Foshay, W. (1986). *ASI instructional design standards.* Arlington Heights, IL: Advanced Systems Inc.

Foshay, W. (1991, May). Sharpen up your schemata. *Data Training,* pp. 18–25.

Foshay, W., and Gibbons, A. (2001). *Teaching and designing problem solving: An assessment.* Bloomington, MN: PLATO Learning.

Foshay, W., and Kirkley, J. (1998). *Principles for teaching problem solving.* Bloomington, MN: PLATO Learning.

Foshay, W., Silber, K., and Stelnicki, M. (2003). *Writing training materials that work.* San Francisco: Jossey-Bass.

Gagne, R. (1985). *Conditions of learning* (4th ed.). New York: Holt, Rinehart & Winston.

Gagne, R., Briggs, L., and Wager W. (1992). *Principles of instructional design* (4th ed.). New York: Holt, Rinehart & Winston.

Hannafin, M., and Hooper, S. (1993). Learning principles. In M. Fleming and H. Levie (Eds.), *Instructional message design* (2nd ed.). Englewood Cliffs, NJ: Educational Technology Publications.

Jonassen, D. (1997). Instructional design models for well-structured and ill-structured problem-solving learning outcomes. *Educational Technology Research and Development, 45*(1), 65–94.

Jonassen, D. (2000). Toward a design theory of problem-solving. *Educational Technology Research and Development, 48*(4), 63–85.

Keller, J. (1987). The systematic process of motivational design. *Performance & Instruction, 26*(8), 1–7.

Keller, J., and Burkman, E. (1993). Motivation principles. In M. Fleming and H. Levie (Eds.), *Instructional message design* (2nd ed.). Englewood Cliffs, NJ: Educational Technology Publications.

Klatzky, R. (1980). *Human memory: Structure and processes* (2nd ed.). San Francisco: Freeman.

Mayer, R. (1993). Problem-solving principles. In M. Fleming and H. Levie (Eds.), *Instructional message design* (2nd ed.). Englewood Cliffs, NJ: Educational Technology Publications.

Medsker, K., and Holdsworth, K. (2001). *Models and strategies for training design.* Washington, DC: International Society for Performance Improvement.

Merrill, M. (1983). Component display theory. In C. Reigeluth (Ed.), *Instructional-design theories and models.* Hillsdale, NJ: Lawrence Erlbaum Associates.

Miller, G. A. (1956, March). The magical number seven, plus or minus two: Some limits on our capacity for processing information. *The Psychological Review, 63*(2), 81–97.

Newell, A., and Simon, S. (1972). *Human problem solving.* Englewood Cliffs, NJ: Prentice-Hall.

Reigeluth, C. M. (1999). *Instructional-design theories and models, a new paradigm of instructional theory: Vol. 2.* Mahwah, NJ: Lawrence Erlbaum Associates.

Reigeluth, C. M., and Stein, F. (1983). The elaboration theory of instruction. In C. Reigeluth (Ed.) *Instructional-design theories and models.* Hillsdale, NJ: Lawrence Erlbaum Associates.

Silber, K., and Stelnicki, M. (1993). Deep in the head of experts: What's there and how to get it out. *NSPI Bulletin.* Montreal: National Society for Performance and Instruction.

Stepich, D., and Newby, T. (1988). Analogizing as an instructional strategy. *Performance & Instruction, 29*(9), 21–23.

Sweller, J. (1999). Instructional design in technical areas. *Australian Education Review,* No. 43. Victoria, Australia.

Tiemann, P., and Markle, S. (1983). *Analyzing instructional content: A guide to instruction and evaluation.* Champaign, IL: Stipes.

Tosti, D. (1990, April). Feedback revisited. Session presented at the 1990 National Conference of the National Society for Performance and Instruction, Toronto, Ontario, Canada.

Wlodkowski, R. (1985). *Enhancing adult motivation to learn.* San Francisco: Jossey-Bass.

Zechmeister, E., and Nyberg, S. (1982). *Human memory: An introduction to research and theory.* Monterey, CA: Brooks/Cole.

CHAPTER SEVENTEEN

Games and Simulations for Training

From Group Activities to Virtual Reality

Robert L. Appelman, John H. Wilson

There have always been controversy, confusion, excitement, and passionately held opinions about the topic of games and simulations. Many people view games as being devoid of content and structured only for entertainment, while, for example, flight simulators are viewed as essential training tools for airline pilots. Some people say that videogame simulations are useless, nonconstructive forms of entertainment, and that games especially are detrimental to youths and a complete waste of time for an adult population (Bandura, Ross, and Ross, 1961; Barmazel, 1993; Griffiths, 1999; Herz, 1997). Yet others claim that only through games and simulations will we ever be able to reach the engagement, learning, and performance levels educators and trainers have been seeking for centuries, thus targeting games and simulations as the latest panacea for instruction and performance interventions (Crawford, 1984; Gee, 2003; Gibbons, Fairweather, Anderson, and Merrill, 1998; Rollings and Ernest, 2000; Thiagarajan, 1994).

For there to be such widespread opinions, there must also be some element of truth feeding each point of view, and this makes it particularly difficult for human performance technologists to decide if and when to use a simulation or game, and to determine which of the many modes of delivery would be appropriate to meet their training goals in specific contexts. The purpose of this chapter is to assist in the selection process. We plan to do this by first addressing the definitions of games and simulations, then introducing selected case studies of implementation, followed by a focus on strategies for development. By laying out these options, development variables, and examples of successful use, we aim to help you be able to determine the potential of games and simulations for meeting your performance-intervention needs and determine if the return on the development and implementation investment will balance out to the positive side of the equation.

CLASSIC PERCEPTIONS OF GAMES

The first thing that usually pops into someone's mind when the word *game* is mentioned is some activity that is strictly nonwork-related, is done by choice, is "fun and entertaining," and will not require any recall of the game play for future nongame use. A trainer implementing a game as an intervention must immediately confront these perceptions by addressing the facts that a game is being used for something work-related, that there is no choice but to play, and that there is an expectation to remember and reflect upon the game play. The aspects of the game being fun and entertaining may still be the case, but determining just what "fun" is and what "entertaining" is usually requires some deeper analysis and redefining on the part of both the trainer and trainee. Both fun and entertainment are primary motivators that the trainer may use to increase the engagement and focus on the topic at hand.

OUTCOMES, ASPECTS, AND CHARACTERISTICS OF GAMES

To sort out just what a game is requires delineating the difference between what happens during an activity or game and what outcomes result from the experience with that game. For instance, fun, entertainment, learning, and improved competency are all *outcomes* of a game. Game elements such as the specific tasks, consequences, and available interactions are *aspects* of a game. There are specific combinations of these aspects that are targeted at certain outcomes, and these become *characteristics* that define games from other forms of solutions. Six characteristic are present in all games:

1. *Challenges:* goals and tasks
2. *Rules:* instructions that govern how the game works
3. *Interaction:* the user's relation with aspects of the game
4. *Contrivance:* modification of realism to benefit game play
5. *Obstacles:* elements of the game encountered
6. *Closure:* an end to the game

Outcomes

Discussions surrounding needs within an organization, performance problems, lack of information, or even too much information will begin to frame desired *outcomes* that the selected intervention is to generate. Establishing an outcome first is pivotal because it will be the yardstick for success of any decisions made in selection and implementation of the intervention, be it a game, simulation, or direct instruction. Games may achieve many desired *outcomes,* such as

- Increased skill
- Understanding the implementation of a process
- Deeper understanding of relationships and concepts
- Awareness of cross-training needs

Aspects and Characteristics

The elements of the game, from the arrangement of people in a group to game-board arrangement to virtual rooms and avatars that are placed in virtual space, are all *aspects* of a game. The *aspects* are what a player interacts with to achieve the optional or required tasks that a player may perform while engaged in gameplay. These *aspects* are the variables of the game designer, who manipulates them to achieve the desired *outcomes*. All games will have aspects with some degree of challenges, rules, interaction, contrivance, obstacles, and closure.

Challenges. If there is no *challenge* to a player, then boredom ensues and little benefit is reaped from the experience. Presenting tasks in which players must compete with each other or work together to overcome obstacles in their path may present engaging *challenges.* Drawing upon previous knowledge and skills, the ability to seek and find new information or solutions, or forming new relationships and strategies to solve problems may all be *challenges* that make a game engaging.

Rules. The *rules* of the game also create a *challenge* in a game. In a role-play game, a rule may be "You may not speak until you hear a direct question," or, on a board game, "You may only move the number of spaces shown on the dice," or, in a virtual game, "You may only get into a room after you have completed a specific task." The *rules* of a game work in harmony with the tasks to achieve specific *outcomes*. In a team-based game a facilitator may state rules at the beginning of an activity, but depending on how the game is progressing, the facilitator may also change or add rules. When facilitators are absent, then the rules must be more rigid and embedded in the *instructions* that accompany a game, or within the artificial intelligence (AI) of a virtual game.

Interaction. If players do not *interact* with a game, then they are not playing, they are passive observers. This does not mean that passive observation cannot be part of what a player is asked to do during gameplay, but if there is no *interaction* through dialogue and decision making, then there is no gameplay. What makes a game engaging is the interaction with the *aspects* of the game.

Often it is the need for more and more interactive aspects of a game that causes game designers and implementers to stretch their resources and skills. As with challenges in a game, if the interactivity for a player is too low, then boredom ensues.

Contrivance. If you could really fail, offend someone, lose your job, or even get physically hurt, then the game would not be fun, nor would it be a constructive activity. In a game there is a suspension of significant negative consequences to gameplay such that new doorways may be opened for people to explore. To this extent any game has a certain amount of *contrivance* to allow the players freedom to try things that they may not do otherwise, or to just have fun interacting with critical elements. However, for any game to be an effective intervention there needs to be some correspondence, however fleeting, to the player's real day-to-day existence.

Obstacles. For there to be challenges, there need to be obstacles along the gameplay path. These obstacles may be anything or anyone that must be dealt with in order to proceed through the game. They could be psychological in nature, as when a person must overcome a self-efficacy issue relating to communication with authority figures, or they might involve learning the operation of a piece of equipment, or, in a virtual military training scenario, to decide if a game character encountered must be terminated somehow. In training scenarios, each obstacle represents a decision point for the player on how to proceed to the end goal. Strategic placement of obstacles along a gameplay path is a key design decision of the game designer.

Closure. There is always a temporal aspect to a game that places boundaries around the beginning and ending of a game. If the endtime is reached prior to the player completing all the objectives, or if someone "wins" before the end of the game, then the gameplay is over. Being within these boundaries is the aspect of *in-game* play. *Outside-game* activities focus on what occurs before or after in-game play. Closure may come to the in-game play, but outside-game activities must still progress to resolution and understanding of what happened during gameplay. The degree of contrivance of the game must then be extrapolated to the real day-to-day existence of each player. The meaning of why the activity was carried out must then be discussed, so that the desired outcomes and a true sense of closure and understanding can be achieved.

WHAT ARE SIMULATIONS (SIMS)?

Simulations began when people started to role play events that occur in real life. Whenever one proceeds into an activity that somehow mirrors a process, place, or event, a simulation strategy is being used to some extent. The modality of a *sim* may extend from arrangements of people to a sophisticated game like virtual spaces, and may even use both modalities in a blended learning context called "mixed reality."

Simulations are receiving special attention because of the computer capabilities to create realistic models of people, places, and things. This makes it possible to use simulation strategies in a virtual mode to mirror more situations than could have been possible prior to this capability, and even to consider using virtual space to mirror interpersonal interactions and decision making. Like games, all cases of sims will be directed toward particular outcomes and will have certain aspects that are unique to a specific context. All will have varying degrees of the common characteristics, and players will engage in interactions and activities similar to games. However, there are subtle yet significant differences found in the targeted outcomes and structural characteristics of a simulation, compared to those of a game.

Outcomes

Outcomes are one of the primary discriminators between games and sims. Fun and entertainment may be important outcomes of a game, but they are not primary outcomes of a simulation. How a person "plays" a sim is more important than where he or she ends up, since completion or winning is not one of the characteristics. Thus the ability of the player to make critical judgments and decisions during sim-play and reflect on each of them is one of the primary outcomes. Just as with games that are being used for training purposes, the scaffolding around a simulation of outside-sim activities is just as, if not more, important than the inside-sim activities.

For example, during a role-playing simulation, real emotions may surface and decisions made may cause equally strong reactions from the players. Reflection after the simulation is critical to bring out these interactions to the level of understanding desired for the targeted outcomes. Likewise, in a flight simulator the actions of the sim pilot that result in a crash may seem devastating enough to the one who caused it, but unpacking the sequence of decisions made and pointing out the good and bad ones is where the learning occurs.

Aspects: Why Not Characteristics?

Simulations are made of elements that have more relationship to real-world attributes than is necessary in games. The degree of correspondence of any attribute of an element within a simulation to its counterpart in the real world is called "level of fidelity." Attributes may have exact physical character-istics, matching specific people in actual places—for example, the person in a sim actually looks like the manager "George Smith," which is high fidelity—or attributes may have only metaphoric characteristics that match—for example, the person only looks slightly humanoid, with a label of "manager," which is low fidelity. In a team-based activity, another person would only try to emulate the interpersonal communication appropriate to the manager, which is medium fidelity.

For outcomes that require high correspondence between the actions during sim-play and the actions during actual performance, the level of fidelity of crit-ical aspects must be high, such as with flight simulators. Conversely, when reflection of sim play during outside-sim activities is more critical, then the level of fidelity could be lower, such as with customer sales training, in which the strategic choices of the player within generic contexts are the focus.

Often, various aspects of the sim have increased levels of fidelity due to the concern for maintaining user engagement and motivation. Even though this increase may not directly affect an outcome, it may increase elements of fun and entertainment necessary to keep the user on task. However, such decisions by the designer to inflate the fidelity come at a price, since every step in fidelity will most likely multiply the development cost. An iterative rapid prototyping development process will assist in determining the appropriate final fidelity level of the simulation.

Characteristics

All simulations will have different weights of the following six common char-acteristics, depending on the desired outcomes.

Challenges. Challenges in a sim may be game-like in nature, but the focus on how one deals with each challenge will reflect more on "success" than on get-ting to the end of a game. Real life presents many challenges, and reconfigur-ing these same challenges in a simulated context can engage learners in producing innovative outcomes, thus developing new strategies and tactics for application outside of the simulation.

Models. Simulations are based on models of reality, and these models act like rules in a game. For instance, "laws of physics" dictate that an object will fall at 9.8 meters per second, and if while training in a virtual environment pre-dicting when an object hits the ground is critical, then the physics model that controls the path of the object must have a high level of fidelity. If when an object hits the ground is not a critical factor, but only just that it drops, then the physics model can have lower fidelity. Similarly, if a team activity is being used to simulate the cooperation necessary between departments in a specific company, then the management model of that company must be used. If the goal is to examine alternatives to cooperation strategies, then more general models may be used or even manipulated during the sim play.

Control. In education we speak of learner-centered instruction and learner control. In both games and simulations there are player characters (PC), the people playing, and nonplayer characters (NPC), who are either following a script or are programmed by the AI of the game or sim. PCs of the sim must feel they have control of variables within the given model, or else they feel more like an NPC just acting out a script. Without control there are no decisions to make, so each element the PC controls is a critical design decision. The control may be to create or select a response to another person, to actuate a piece of equipment, or simply to move forward with a decision to engage.

Manipulation. *Manipulation* is more than control, it is how and to what degree you control. There are many variable aspects within a simulation, and the player's choice of which ones and how they are manipulated is a critical focus of a sim. One variable in a sim may be to negotiate with people. If an outcome of the sim is to create a support base for your plan of action, then you may choose to seek and find every possible person within the boundaries and negotiate their support. Other players may select specific people to negotiate with and not contact others, thus manipulating the variable by degree of use.

In the simulation "Zoo Tycoon," animal habitats are created by the PC that may have adequate food, shelter, and desired space to satisfy a specific animal. Manipulation of these variables is extensive, such that the PC may reduce food, space, and even shelter to find at what point the animal dies. This is important knowledge that may only be found in a simulation in which the underlying model allows authentic consequences from such manipulations.

Authenticity. Just as we spoke of individual elements having levels of fidelity, the setting, actions, and relationships of these elements may be described as having levels of authenticity. Simulations must have authentic variables, actions, and consequences for sim-play, but the levels of authenticity in all areas may vary. For instance, if a desired outcome is to appreciate the variety of skills that each team member has, each team member could take on the role of a different zoo aquarium fish or crustacean, thus needing to learn about the others' capabilities and characteristics. In this case the contextual authenticity may be low, but the variable of variety of skills, combined with the player actions of selection, could match real strategies and tactics that engage the desired learning from the resulting consequences. Toward the other end of the scale, such as with flight simulators, not only must the physics models and the visual and auditory input be authentic, but also the kinesthetic input of gravity and momentum variations must be of very high fidelity, thus placing this within a high level of authenticity.

Consequences. Consequences are the result of the control and manipulation in a simulation by the PC within the operational limitations of the existing model. They also are the result of outside-sim activities allowing reflection and learning. Consequences for high-risk topics such as military training and medical contexts may be immediate and could bring an end to the simulation, for example, if someone dies in the sim. In other cases, the consequences may not be as apparent until debriefing after sim-play, when the results of the player decisions are posted and the composite of all player actions results in a major consequence. The feedback to the player during a sim is a design variable that can greatly affect the degree of learning from a sim. The designer may provide help, coaching, warnings, and so on as the simulation proceeds, but the goal in a sim is not to avoid failure but to understand decisions and resulting consequences. Thus, iterative simulation modules often use reflection periods in conjunction with complex scenarios and tasks.

CASE STUDIES

Following are brief examples of interventions using a variety of games and simulations. We will begin using the term *mode* when distinguishing between the form of delivery of these interventions. Face-to-face, team-based, computer-driven virtual, or a combination of actual face-to-face mixed with computerized information in a mixed-reality delivery are all different modes. Our intent is that the following case studies will provide some concrete examples of how specific outcomes have been met using these modes of interventions.

Training on Insurance Benefits for Helpline Trainees

The Need. A large midwestern insurance company that receives hundreds of phone inquiries daily for clarifications and handling of claims and claim information identified a training need to improve the content knowledge about the benefits offered and also to provide clear, accurate information to policyholders. Because of the relatively boring content, the need for understanding at a significant depth, and the desire to increase team effectiveness, a group game activity was selected as the intervention mode to use on a cohort of new trainees.

Face-to-Face Team-Based Game Activities. Part of any group dynamic is major hurdles to overcome, such as any group member's fear of failing in front of peers and supervisors. This has the effect of limiting innovation and creative logical reasoning, and in general allowing only "safe" answers to surface. Fear of saying something stupid has the effect of squelching team interaction and sharing, because even if one person does know an answer to something, he or she may not get a chance to share it if no one else feels confident enough to ask. Efficiency of group management and finding ways to cover massive amounts of content, such as that in a complete listing of insurance benefits, was a major concern with this intervention strategy. In this case there was a requirement to bring the trainees to a significant depth of understanding of benefits, to train them to find information quickly and respond clearly to inquiries, and to help them achieve an accuracy level similar to an expert response.

Prior to the activities, everyone was asked to read the primary information source on the benefits and become as familiar as possible with the contents. This brought the entry level of everyone at least up to the "familiarity with content" level. You will note that the emphasis of these activities and "games" is to keep the learner active at all times with some level of cognitive processing through the introduction of frequent small challenges. That is why there are many short tasks and team interactions that keep things constantly moving. Following are three activities out of six that followed each other in rapid succession.

Activity: Open Book. To provide an orientation focus, each participant was asked to review the benefits for five minutes, then write ten questions on separate index cards for ten minutes. The group then separated into teams and each set of questions was collected from one team and given to another. During the next ten minutes the team selected the five best questions and discarded poorly worded ones or anything redundant or unclear. During the next ten minutes questions prepared earlier were read, and team members gained points for their team if they responded correctly. The highest-scoring team won and gained applause from the rest of the group. Note: this activity in no way requires that anyone ask a stupid question or even fail, but instead deep analysis and evaluation of the questions allow for confirmation that in fact someone in each group could generate good questions. To reinforce teamwork, a team wins, but not any individual.

Activity: Q & A. Next the focus was on mastery of the content by asking questions again, but specifically those that were confusing or hard to understand. The participants were asked to write two questions that related to the confusing topic and then exchange them with other participants, who then did the same. Participants read the questions they held at the end of the exchanges, thus concealing the identity of the original question writers. During the next twenty minutes the group received accurate answers in response to the questions. The last few minutes were devoted to writing individual reflections on the most important personal learning the exercise fostered. The reflection comments were mixed up and a few of them read. Note: there was no consequence for asking "stupid questions," and no individual was singled out, yet the most difficult portions of the content were analyzed by the entire group and personal reflection was shared.

Activity: Best Answers. Next the focus was on application and evaluation of the knowledge acquired so far. Participants had five minutes to respond individually to an open-ended question about benefits. They formed groups, and then the answers from one group were given to another group for analysis. Before the answers were collected, though, each participant put a code number on his or her response. The group then discussed the answers given to their group and selected the best response. The "best answers" were read and discussed, and the code number was shared so that the person who wrote it received applause. This was repeated for another open-ended question. Then the teams wrote their own open-ended questions, and participants from other teams responded with answers. Note: a simple individual code protects all participants from exposure to failure and from the fear of providing "stupid" questions or responses. The teams work together on problem solving, and the activity ends with team-to-team competition with very authentic challenges.

This mode of game and simulation depends heavily on a facilitator's skill to keep things moving, to foster a collaborative exchange among groups, and to capitalize on the game-like exercises to reduce stress and anxiety with the difficult content. This mode also allows for the most variation and accommodation to individual responses of the participants during the game experience in comparison to any other mode, and when individual responses must be judged for innovation and also accuracy, the facilitator has the opportunity to do so. Training facilitators and preparing detailed scripts are necessary if this mode is to be disseminated across large numbers of employees being trained (Thiagarajan, 1994, 2004).

Pre- and Post-Test Simulations for Pharmaceutical Sales

The Need. The sales department in a pharmaceutical company was developing a new sales methodology that it was going to unveil to its salesforce during the annual sales conference. This new methodology was drastically different from the current sales model, and the company wanted to gain an understanding of how well the salesforce could perform using this new model before it was finalized and fully implemented. The salesforce was widely distributed over a large area, and there was no time to conduct the preliminary assessment during the sales conference.

The solution was to incorporate the mode of an on-line sales simulation in which each salesperson could engage using his or her personal computer. The first simulation that the salesforce completed was a few weeks before the sales conference.

Pre- and Post-Test Sims. In the pretest simulation, each salesperson interacted with a receptionist, nurse, and doctor at the doctor's office. The goal was to build good sales relationships with each of these individuals and to investigate the environment of the office to help build these relationships. Each salesperson completed the simulation by making decisions that reflected his or her usual method of working with individuals in the doctor's office. Data on their performance were collected through an on-line learning management system.

The salesforce attended the conference and learned about the new selling methodology. They were then instructed to complete a second simulation, or post-test, in which they made a second virtual visit to the doctor's office to build relationships with the receptionist, nurse, and doctor. The pre- and post-test simulations were identical in their objectives, but the content differed between them.

Results. The company management was able to see how the salesforce performed using the new methodology they had been taught at the conference. The scoring showed that the salesforce significantly improved in their performance from the pretest to the post-test by applying the new methodology. In areas where the salesforce did not perform well, remediation was given to help improve performance and reinforce the newly learned methodology.

Algorithmic Strategy Simulation for Resource Management

The Need. A company that wanted to train its management on effective resource allocation had several field staff and customers to which it could apply time, training, materials, incentives, and other resources. The company used a model that reflected optimal resource management as the basis for the simulation. Strategy simulations that use algorithms to simulate real-world processes have been used for years in the business community to better understand problems and to train managers to perform well, so the mode of a computer-driven simulation was selected for this intervention.

A Simulation Blended with E-Learning. Because several hundred calculations were required for each action in the simulation, the company decided to develop a computer-based strategy simulation that could effectively process the data. Instead of being a distributed on-line simulation, this simulation was built to be used in conjunction with an instructor-led course on resource management. At the beginning of the course, the participants were asked to use the simulation and allocate resources to staff and customers for four simulated financial quarters. The effects of their resource management appeared in the form of product market share in the simulation. After completing the first four financial quarters, most of the participants saw a decrease in their product's market share. The instructors next taught the participants the principles of effective resource management, and then had the participants use the simulation again for another four quarters.

Results. Most of the participants saw a dramatic increase in their market share after applying the principle taught in the course. One group, however, did not. Upon investigation, the instructors learned that this group had cultural conflicts with the way that resources were allocated to field staff in the simulation. The fact that the simulation reflected the effects of this conflict helped the instructors to further teach this group about appropriate resource management and to develop a solution to their cultural conflict with the company's methodology. Accurately simulating the resource management methodology better prepared each participant to put these principles in place in the field, saving the company time and resources.

Porting Real Data into Virtual Space for Automobile Design and Manufacturing

The Needs. The specific outcomes of interventions are common to most manufacturing companies, such as shortening the development period, optimizing the "fit" of different components that integrate into one unit, providing the most productive feedback to the designers on the results of design decisions, arriving at the most efficient process of fabrication, and testing the results of these decisions through formative evaluation. BMW has initiated efforts to integrate virtual reality (VR) tools and strategies at appropriate points along their process and integrate them among traditional tried-and-true methodologies. This *mixed-reality*-mode strategy has allowed many of their goals to be realized (BMW Group, 2004).

Virtual Reality Sims. The VR mode is created for designers first through the use of 3D computer-assisted-design (CAD) software programs that allow them to make design decisions through a graphic interface on a computer screen. These decisions are coupled to reality by making this virtual environment mimic actual dimensions of the real world such that when a line is drawn on the screen it is measured to whatever level of scale necessary. This allows the designer to create any object at any size and then "size" it to fit a preexisting form by simply scaling it to a desired size. The exact dimensions of the final object are then measured for manufacturing purposes.

This process may be considered a simulation, since all characteristics of a sim are present. The challenge is to create an object that follows the functional and formal requirements to be integrated into the gestalt of the finished automobile, and the model is the program that controls what you may do in this virtual environment. The designer has control of what is attempted and the level of manipulation of the critical variables is high. The level of authenticity is high because measurements in the VR space must match the final measurements of the real object, and the results of the designers' decisions have significant consequences as other designers around the world attempt to integrate the object into their own process.

Results. Standardization of tools, data file formats, and telecommunication protocols have allowed BMW to create a design database available to any of its design centers around the world. This amalgamation of data is analogous to a virtual manufacturing center and has contributed to reducing the development period of a new model from six years in the past to just 2.5 years today (BMW Group, 2003).

DESIGN AND DEVELOPMENT

In the broadest sense, the human performance technology (HPT) process of analysis, design, implementation, and evaluation has direct application to what we will condense here to the analysis, design, and development of any form of game or simulation intervention. Yet, as George Geis pointed out in 1986, this process is highly iterative and rarely follows a linear path, but rather describes looping recycling patterns that continually feed new information into the design process at each stage.

While in the process of designing a game, the formative feedback from upper management could indicate a mismatch between the value of the need for this intervention and the investment allocated to complete it. Such information would affect the scope of each phase of the process and require rethinking each strategic decision. As development complexity increases, the need to extend patterns of iterative communication in an ever-increasing spiral, from the development team, through the organization, and out to the target population, becomes more critical (Spence, 2002; Toth, 1997). There is also the need to visit each center of focus of the analysis, design, and development process, to flow from mega strategic decision making through the macro tactical planning, and to implement through the micro operational tasks within each focus center. It is this outward expansion that must coexist with the inward decision making from mega to micro that creates the often difficult tension associated with analysis, design, and development.

Analysis Focus

An *analysis focus* centers on defining the workplace context and comparing this to ideal conditions through needs, task, and gap analysis. Such a focus might reveal several factors that are contributing to a performance problem, such as a lack of communication along organizational lines or a lack of respect or morale among employee groups, fostering the need for attitude changes among individuals or groups. It could identify different groups who need training or access to specific resources. This analysis focus should also identify the propensity for the use of innovative modes of game and simulation interventions at all levels of the organization. Not only must the development team be enthusiastic, but the spiral out through the upper management and target population must at least demonstrate acceptance of their use. The extent of the gap found between the actual and desired performance, coupled with the level of acceptance to use these modes of intervention, will correlate with the scope of the interventions prescribed during a *design focus*. There are certain specific factors that need to be quantified in this analysis focus. They are highlighted in the following sections.

Your Trainees. The number and distribution of participants can have great influence on what modality is chosen for delivery. If the group is small, less than a few hundred participants, then the developer might consider more face-to-face interactions, if that modality fits the need of the simulation or game. Although face-to-face delivery often has recurring resource needs such as the cost of facilitators and space for training, the small size of the group makes this modality ideal. For large group sizes, several hundred to thousands or tens of thousands, standalone and computer-based modalities such as 2D and 3D simulations and games can be a better choice. While computer-based games and simulations can have higher up-front costs than face-to-face games and simulations, these costs are spread across a larger group of participants and so can be less expensive than face-to-face training when the group size reaches the thousands.

The distribution of the participants is another important factor. If the group is located in a central area, where travel costs are not high, then face-to-face modalities can make a lot of sense. However, if the group is highly distributed, 2D and 3D computer games and simulations can be very effective for delivery, since they can be sent electronically to the participant's location via the Internet or other types of electronic delivery, decreasing travel costs.

Motivation, Knowledge, and Entry Level. Often overlooked in many training interventions, the motivation level of the participants is critical in making design and development decisions for games and simulations. Often games are used because of low motivation levels on the part of the participants, as described earlier in the chapter. The lower the motivation for a given topic, the more important the group engagement in the game or sim will be. Motivation can also help in making decisions about fidelity, particularly in simulations. Higher visual fidelity can be more engaging to the participants and can draw them into the experience. Alternatively, highly motivated participants may need less fidelity, because they are motivated to "make the jump" between more symbolic representations and reality.

Another important consideration with motivation is whether the simulation or game is a mandated experience or not. If it is mandated, then participation is more readily assured, but if it is not mandated, then the designer should include more motivational elements in the game or sim to encourage participation. Also, mandated games and simulations can often be designed to be more challenging, since the participants will need to "stick with it" in order to the complete the experience. Non-mandated games and simulations often need to have frequent rewards for the participants to keep them engaged in the experience so that they do not leave.

Game design and simulation design are highly affected by the knowledge and skill levels of the participants as they pertain to the topic covered in the game or sim. Is the topic new for the average participant, or does it build on existing knowledge and skills? How comfortable are the participants with the topic? Answering these questions often can help a designer decide whether face-to-face modalities or human-facilitated electronic delivery might be more effective, or if standalone modalities might be better. Obviously, good human facilitators can respond to participant concerns much more effectively than can a programmed computer or other technology, but good facilitators can be expensive and difficult to find in large numbers. 2D and 3D computer games and simulations, however, can be programmed with expert responses and are easily reproduced.

Design Focus

A *design focus* is a plan to address any needs or gaps found while one is in an analysis focus. Gaps in employee attitude might suggest the need for consensus building, culture development, skill training, or team building, while organizational analysis might reveal the need for change management, group reorganization, process improvement, or intracommunication modifications. All of these specific outcomes become the driving force throughout the entire HPT process. The design focus must specify these outcomes in a clear and specific manner, such that they can be called in for comparison against any major strategic, tactical, or operational decision that will guide the design and development of the game or simulation intervention. In this model of design and development, the evaluation component of the HPT process is embedded in every center of focus specifically to test conformance with the prescribed *outcomes*.

In a design focus the strategic question becomes, What type of experience should we place our participants in that would allow for appropriate challenges with issues, interactions with critical variables that result in meaningful consequences relative to this outcome? At a more micro tactical level is the question about further defining the experience as a game or simulation. This tactical question evaluates the importance of game characteristics such as competition-like challenges, with content that is possibly more contrived and fun, versus simulation characteristics that are more authentic, with a greater focus on decision making during play. Questions about the participants' need to interact through more rule-based game-like actions or through simulated variables to achieve the desired consequences must also be addressed in a design focus. At the most micro operational level are those decisions that tie together specific aspects of the experience, such as sequence of events, encounters with specific obstacles or people, and descriptions of the play-by-play details within the game or simulation experience.

Outcomes Targeting Training or Evaluation

A critical strategic design decision in the development of a game or simulation is deciding where outcomes lie on a training-and-evaluation continuum from low to high (see Table 17.1). This low-to-high continuum represents how much the designer wants a given outcome to be taught to the participants and to what extent the participants should be evaluated on a given outcome.

This has important tactical considerations, particularly in simulations. Simulations that are designed to teach more than to evaluate will have more frequent debriefing and feedback on performance throughout the experience. Conversely, simulations that are primarily meant to assess the performance of the participants on a given set of objectives will have less debriefing and feedback on performance and likely not until the end of the experience. This training-and-evaluation continuum is important for a designer to consider, given the dichotomy between training and evaluation when it comes to debriefing and

Table 17.1. Training-and-Evaluation Continuum.

Aspect	Training	Evaluation
Participant content familiarity	Low	High
Level of detail	Low	High
Level of fidelity	Low	High
Level of authenticity	Low	High
Frequency of debriefing	High	Low
Degree of feedback	High	Low
Complexity of experience	Low	High
Degree of problem solving	Low	High
Degree of experimentation	High	Low
Consequences of failure	Low	High

feedback. If the designer provides a deep level of debriefing and feedback, while useful for training purposes, this feedback may actually help to improve performance by providing hints, strategies, and tactics. This level of feedback is not typically desired in evaluative simulations, in which the participants should not be assisted so that performance can be more accurately measured.

When considering participant actions, the different purposes of training and evaluation affect the demand for fidelity in the simulation. As mentioned earlier, the level of fidelity of critical aspects of the game or sim may vary depending on the degree to which they must have detail that reflects real-world imagery. Toward the training end of the continuum, less fidelity is needed based on participant actions, since debriefing and feedback can be used to get the participant back on the right track. But toward the evaluation end of the spectrum, more fidelity is required, since the participant should witness the outcome of his or her actions, which requires more paths through the experience and the development of more content. Since debriefing and feedback are less frequent, the experience must simulate reality at a higher level of fidelity. When imagery is not important, such as when simulating a phone call between two individuals, then less fidelity is needed. However, when imagery is critical to the core objectives of the game or simulation, such as accurately identifying an enemy vehicle, then the level of fidelity is important. With computer-based games and simulations, more visual fidelity typically means more time and costs for development, but this is not always the case if the designer can target the key content aspects for which level of fidelity needs to be high.

Game and Simulation Rules and Models

The importance of understanding what is to be modeled in the game or simulation cannot be underestimated. In a game, the rules are the driving factor for scaffolding, and in a simulation the model determines what can or cannot be done. Because many games and simulations need very detailed designs in order to achieve a high level of authenticity, a thorough understanding of the concepts for the rules or model is critical. For example, if a designer wanted to model the throwing of a ball in a virtual environment, an exact understanding of physical and gravitational forces would be necessary for the simulation to work authentically. However, rarely have rules been clearly stated, nor are models as straightforward as the scientific principles of gravity and physics. In the beginning the designer often will not know the intricacies of what is to be simulated. For example, if a designer wanted to simulate a discussion between a salesperson and a client, and wanted the client to respond to the salesperson in an authentic manner, he or she would need an understanding of common client reactions to sales tactics. This type of knowledge is nebulous and is often spread across the collective understanding of the sales staff rather than gathered in a single location. Harder still is designing simulations or games that are based on complex models, such as the effects of resource allocation on the market share of a given product. These models can be even harder to define because of the multitude of variables that affect the final outcome. For this purpose, the designer must know where and to whom he or she can turn for information that can help to build an accurate model with a high level of authenticity. Sometimes this exists already, such as in the ball-and-gravity example, but oftentimes the designer will need to seek it out in the form of subject-matter experts. The designer needs to make an honest assessment of how much is known about the model to be used and what resources are needed to get the model to a state where it can be used for a game or simulation.

Determining the rule set or model to be used can also have influence on the modality of the game or simulation. If the designer encounters a set of do's and don'ts, then a game intervention might work best; however, if a set of if-then decisions is encountered, a simulation might meet the outcomes better. Models that involve interpersonal communication and emotional engagement may be more suited for face-to-face simulations or games in which reading facial expression and voice tone are more easily accomplished, while complex models that rely on thousands of calculations to predict the outcome of participant actions often need to be delivered via computer technologies.

Play Time, Apperception of Content, and Complexity

Games and simulations can take as little as a few minutes and as long as weeks or months to complete. The participant may be exposed to only a small fraction of the content, or may progress through the majority of it, depending on the way the game or sim is designed. A key concept here is the difference between the perception of the game from the designer's point of view and the view of the participant. To the designer the game or sim will have multiple paths a participant can take, and all these paths must be developed, even though any given participant might not experience all paths. A participant can only traverse a game or sim along a linear path, even though they might back up to a decision node and progress in a different direction. The branching remains the same, but the time of play increases. Attempting to anticipate what a participant will do within a game or sim is the difficult part of design in these modes. A designer should consider how long, on average, it should take participants to complete the game or simulation. Often, the longer the experience, the more time and resources that are required to build it.

Debriefing and Feedback Complexity

Appropriate and timely feedback to players is a primary advantage of face-to-face modalities. The amount and type of debriefing and feedback provided in a virtual mode will determine the mode's complexity as well as the time and resources needed to develop it. The more frequent debriefing and feedback or correlation to the participant's actions, the more content that must be written for the feedback. For example, if the participant can make four different choices, there may need to be four different types of feedback based on the choice that was made. In addition, while immediate feedback likely will deal only with a few variables, summative feedback may potentially deal with the combination of several variables over time, making the debriefing and feedback more complex.

Development Focus

Within the *development focus* are three basic phases of planning, creation, and implementation. Although these phases do have a strong linear coupling, an iterative development model flows through them a number of times, generating ever-increasing degrees of functionality and fidelity. This is also referred to as a rapid prototyping model that allows for natural milestone events in which formative evaluation may occur, allowing other members of the organization to have input. Although the general path through the development focus is the same for all modes, each mode of delivery is unique enough to warrant individual descriptions of the development focus (Appelman, 2000; Bethke, 2003; Toth, 1997; Tripp and Bichelmeyer, 1990).

Time and Resources

After the participants, purpose, and model of a simulation and game have been determined, the designer must also consider the time and resources available for development. Games and simulation can be very inexpensive to create or extremely expensive, and the designer should have an understanding of which mode is being dealt with. In an emergent form of a spiraling development model, it is easy to spiral out of control if there is no overall plan or experience in developing whatever mode is being targeted. A spiral model requires a team of experts, in subject matter, in instructional design, in mode design, and project managers, all of whom are willing to keep coming together to evaluate and redirect the development toward the desired outcome. Conferences, Web resources, and publications are increasingly available for detailed exploration into this complex development process (ACM SIGGRAPH, 2005; Bethke, 2003; DIGRA, 2005; IGDA, 2005; IMRC, 2005: ISAGA, 2005; NASAGA, 2005; Rollings and Ernest, 2000; Zimmerman and Salen, 2004).

Performance Tracking and Scoring

As with other types of training and evaluation, designers should consider how participant performance will be tracked and scored. This can be as simple as facilitator observation or self-reporting, or as complex as reporting performance scores to an on-line learning management system for analysis and reporting. Performance tracking and scoring are determined largely by the modality of the game or simulation delivery, but their importance cannot be understated. Tracking participant performance not only helps deliver accurate feedback during the simulation or game, but also helps to have more effective debriefing sessions after the simulation or game is completed. The good news is that in a virtual world, everything is data and very easy to capture and report. The question will be what to report in light of the desired outcomes, and who to report it to. The more accurate, timely, and pertinent the performance data the more likely that effective feedback and instruction can be provided to improve performance.

ROI AND SUMMARY

Throughout this chapter we have attempted to identify variables that illuminate the similarities and differences between games and simulations, as well as to provide discussion that would engage you in the decision-making process, matching your training needs with these modes of interventions. As you approach your own needs, we suggest you fully understand the opening definitions and then move to the "training-and-evaluation continuum" matrix, where you can begin matching your context needs with cells in the matrix. As the description of your particular solution takes shape, the case studies and specific discussion areas will be good question-generating exercises that will require you to ask critical questions of your mode and participant experiences to produce the desired training outcomes.

A key decision of whether to use a game or sim is the "cost of failure"; stated simply, the cost of failure is the "cost" that an organization or individual would pay if an individual or group of individuals fails at a given task in the real world. This cost might be missing a sales quota or not accurately assembling a piece of machinery. It can be as benign as not answering phone calls in time or as serious as a pilot losing his life in a plane crash. The high cost of failure in terms of human life and equipment is the reason why military forces around the world have some of the most sophisticated simulations and games known to man.

The final recommendation is to avoid selecting a game or simulation because it just seems like a neat thing to do, or because your employees would like to have "fun" learning (Appelman and Goldsworthy, 1999; Crawford, 1984; Thiagarajan, 1994). Instead, determine where both your organization and participants are with respect to role playing, using technology solutions in training, and even familiarity with playing videogames. Experimenting with these different experiential modes would provide you with some evaluative information that could point to a development starting point (Herz, 1997; Summers, 2004). Perhaps it would be best to develop first some face-to-face group activities, then move to some off-the-shelf training modules. If you have a population that is amenable to high-tech solutions, then you could consider creating some simple low-fidelity branching PowerPoint games to become familiar with the development decisions discussed here. Once you feel you have reached a critical confidence level of support from your organization and employees, that would be a good time to look for game and simulation development companies that could work with you to determine the best level of fidelity and authenticity for your context.

While many are touting the value and potential for learning of games and simulations (Amory, Naicker, Vincent, and Adams, 1998; Crawford, 1984; Filho, Hirata, and Yano, 2004; Gee, 2003; Gibbons, Fairweather, Anderson, and Merrill, 1998; Jones, 2003; Klabbers, 2003; Kommers, Rödel, Luursema, Geelkerken, and Kunst, 2003; Rollings and Ernest, 2000), the main goal is for you and your design team to experience these rich learning environments yourselves. You need to examine the characteristics of content density, what is challenging, the experience of low-consequence failure, and how rewarding it can be to achieve a goal in a game, or to reflect on the consequences of your experience in a simulation. Even if you decide it is not for your organization at this time, you will be making that decision from experience, and you will know when the time is right for these immersive learning environments.

References

ACM SIGGRAPH. (2005). Retrieved May 20, 2005, from the SIGGRAPH 2005 home Website: www.siggraph.org.

Amory, A., Naicker, K., Vincent, J., and Adams, C. (1998). *Computer games as a learning resource.* Retrieved July 11, 2002, from www.und.ac.za/und/biology/staff/amory/edmedia98.html.

Appelman, R. (2000). An iterative development model: A genesis from pedagogical needs. *International Journal of Continuing Engineering Education and Life-long Learning, 10*(1, 2, 3, 4), 136–141.

Appelman, R., and Goldsworthy, R. (1999, February). *The juncture of game and instructional design: Can fun be learning?* Paper presented at the Association for Educational Communications and Technology annual conference, Houston, Texas.

Bandura, A., Ross, D., and Ross, S. (1961). Transmission of aggression through imitation of aggressive models. *Journal of Abnormal and Social Psychology, 63,* 575–582.

Barmazel, S. (1993, Sept. 3). Video games: Asians in Canada say they promote hatred. *Far Eastern Economic Review,* 37.

Bethke, E. (2003). *Game development & production.* Plano, TX: Wordware.

BMW Group. (2003). *Virtual reality in car production.* Retrieved March 18, 2005, from www.bmwgroup.com/e/nav/?/e/0_0_www_bmwgroup_com/homepage/0_home.shtml.

BMW Group. (2004). Retrieved March 18, 2005, from the *BMW Group Research and Innovation Network* Website: www.bmwgroup.com.

Crawford, C. (1984). *The art of computer game design.* Emeryville, CA: Osborne/ McGraw-Hill.

DIGRA. (2005). Retrieved May 20, 2005, from the Digital Games Research Association Website: www.digra.org.

Filho, W. A., Hirata, C. M., and Yano, E. T. (2004). GroupSim: A collaborative environment for discrete event simulation software development for the World Wide Web. *Simulation, 80*(6), 257–272.

Gee, J. P. (2003). *What video games teach us about learning and literacy.* New York: Paulgrave Macmillan.

Geis, G. L. (1986). Human performance technology: An overview. *Introduction to performance technology.* Washington, DC: National Society for Performance and Instruction.

Gibbons, A., Fairweather, P., Anderson, T., and Merrill, D. (1998). Simulation and computer-based instruction: A future view. In C. R. Dills and A. J. Romiszowski (Eds.), *Instructional development paradigms* (pp. 1–63). Englewood Cliffs, NJ: Instructional Technology Publications.

Griffiths, M. (1999). Violent video games and aggression: A review of the literature. *Aggression and Violent Behavior, 4*(0), 203–212.

Herz, J. C. (1997). *Joystick nation: How videogames ate our quarters, won our hearts, and rewired our minds.* Toronto: Little, Brown.

IGDA. (2005). Retrieved May 20, 2005, from the International Game Developers Association Website: www.igda.org.

IMRC. (2005). Retrieved May 20, 2005, from the Indiana Mixed Reality Consortium Website: www.imixedreality.org.

ISAGA. (2005). Retrieved May 20, 2005, from the International Simulation and Gaming Association Website: www.isaga.com.

Jones, S. (2003). *Let the games began: Gaming technology and entertainment among college students.* Unpublished manuscript, Pew Internet and American Life Project, Washington, DC.

Klabbers, J.H.G. (2003). Simulation and gaming: Introduction to the art and science of design. *Simulation and Gaming, 34*(4), 488–494.

Kommers, P., Rödel, S., Luursema, J., Geelkerken, B., and Kunst, E. (2003). *Competency-based learning surgical interventions by navigating in virtual reality case spaces.* Retrieved October 1, 2004, from users.edte.utwente.nl/kommers/ DiMEpage/VR1.htm.

NASAGA. (2005). Retrieved May 20, 2005, from the North American Simulation and Gaming Association Website: www.nasaga.org.

Rollings, A., and Ernest, A. (2000). *Andrew Rollings and Ernest Adams on game design.* Boston: New Riders.

Spence, L. (2002). *Software engineering.* Retrieved December 15, 2004, from osiris.sunderland.ac.uk/rif/linda_spence/HTML/contents.html.

Summers, G. J. (2004). Today's business simulation industry. *Simulation and Gaming, 35*(2), 208–241.

Thiagarajan, S. (1994). How I designed a game and discovered the meaning of life. *Simulation and Gaming, Silver Anniversary Issue* (Part 2), 529–537.

Thiagarajan, S. (2004). *Introduction to U.S. benefits: Facilitators guide* (Version 1). Bloomington, IN: The Thiagi Group.

Toth, K. (1997). *Software engineering best practices.* Unpublished manuscript presentation, Intellitech Consulting Inc. and Simon Fraser University, Vancouver, Canada.

Tripp, S., and Bichelmeyer, B. (1990). Rapid prototyping: An alternative instructional design strategy. *Educational Technology Research and Development, 38*(1), 31–44.

Zimmerman, E., and Salen, K. (2004). *Rules of play: Game design fundamentals.* Harvard, MA: MIT Press.

CHAPTER EIGHTEEN

Distance Training

José Manuel Ochoa-Alcántar, Christy M. Borders,
Barbara A. Bichelmeyer

Thirteen years ago, a chapter titled "Distance Education Systems" in the first edition of the *Handbook of Human Performance Technology* defined distance education as encompassing "the transmission of educational, instructional, or training programming to two or more people at two or more locations separated by space or in time" (Wagner, 1992, p. 513). While we may argue today that distance training can be transmitted to even a single person and a single location, the 1992 definition continues to have merit and is generally very similar to our understandings and discussions of what distance training is today. In this chapter, we use the terms *distance education* and *distance training* interchangeably, preferring the term *distance training* for human performance technology contexts. Though the 1992 definition provides a basic explanation of distance education, we currently have a broader conceptual vision due to advancements in access to Internet technology and the many options that are now used for the distribution of distance training that were not previously available.

In the conclusion of that chapter, the author stated rather prophetically that "distance education is a technology application that eventually may provide HP technologists with novel ways of solving instructional and training problems, specifically those associated with resource need and access speed" (Wagner, 1992, p. 525).

Wagner (1999) also wrote a chapter for the second edition of the *Handbook of Human Performance Technology*, in which distance learning and distance education were discussed as alternatives to traditional, face-to-face training. In that chapter, Wagner also described "distributed learning" as the convergence of "audio, video, and data-transmission media into a single integrated digital 'pipeline'"(p. 630).

The second edition also included a chapter titled "Emerging Trends in Instructional Interventions," which focused on the concept of a virtual class (Winer, Rushby, and Vázquez-Abad, 1999). The authors described the virtual classroom as an entity that would provide "a technology-mediated environment where people can meet, talk, access, work with a wide range of resources, and learn. In doing so, it starts to move us away from the shackles of learning in a fixed place at a prescribed time" (p. 875). Amusing in retrospect, these authors stated that "the virtual class sounds like something from a work of science fiction" (p. 875), a view that provides context for just how much progress has been made in the area of distance education during the past six years.

One topic not addressed in that edition that is currently an emerging field is "blended learning," a rapidly evolving approach to education that blends the best features of face-to-face learning environments with the best of distance learning experiences. The purpose of this chapter is to create a bridge between the past and the future by exploring the reasons behind the burgeoning growth of distance education, documenting the current status of distance learning systems in corporate environments, identifying the issues that affect the use of distance learning systems in corporations, and providing an introduction to blended learning.

DISTANCE TRAINING: A NOVELTY OR A REAL SOLUTION?

The use of information technology has caused a revolution in education. Whether it is just one course or an entire academic program, learning opportunities that were not previously available to students locally are now offered via the World Wide Web. This revolution has given rise to difficult questions about the value of distance training as compared with face-to-face or residential training in terms of effectiveness, efficiency, humanness, and access, to mention a few concerns.

Whatever answers to these difficult questions ultimately emerge, current proponents of distance training see it as an important avenue to provide "more than just an opportunity to unite students from different locations in a common educational goal. It serves as a bridge from the often theoretical basis of academic studies to the real-world practices necessary for success outside university walls" (Gibbons and Brenowitz, 2002, p. 355).

Is the Excitement about Distance Training Justified?

Just because new technologies, especially the World Wide Web, are popular does not mean that they are the solution for everything, nor does the popularity of distance training mean that it is better than traditional face-to-face training. The traditional classroom and the on-line classroom both have their benefits and disadvantages. However, the novelty and popularity of electronic media may lead people to assume that distance training is the long-expected solution to all problems faced in education. Hill, Wiley, Nelson, and Han (2004) note that "few technologies have had such a global impact; further, few technologies have impacted such a wide range of sectors in our society across and within various socioeconomic groups. This is particularly true for the World Wide Web (Web). Business to education, youth to elders, world powers to third world countries—all have felt the impact of the Web" (p. 433).

The excitement about Web-based distance training might be justified in part because the field is so new, but there is no conclusive evidence that on-line instruction is the same, better, or worse than teaching face-to-face. On one hand, advocates of the newer technologies offer many promises (DeCorte, Verschaffel, and Lowyck, 1994). On the other hand, it is still too early to judge new technologies as failing because they are still in development. Applying new technologies in education and corporate settings is in the early stages and it continues to grow. We are still unsure as to whether distance training will be a decent alternative to traditional education or a real revolution in education.

How Is the Distance Training Format Different from Traditional Instruction?

Hill, Wiley, Nelson, and Han (2004) note that "While [distance training] efforts hold much promise for the future of technology, particularly for learning, some researchers contend that the majority of the educational uses of these tools simply replicate classroom practice" (p. 453). Though some may argue that distance instruction is no different than traditional instruction, Romiszowski and Mason (2004) have identified several practices that differentiate distance instruction from traditional instruction and that, perhaps, only Web-based distance instruction can offer: (1) it allows instructors to teach from anywhere; (2) it allows for the possibility of increased enrollment in education or training activities without a need for more physical infrastructure; (3) it provides for asynchronous activities that allow flexible time management; (4) it allows students to learn from anywhere; (5) it allows for flexible scheduling; (6) it offers the possibility for learners to analyze their own interactions through the use of text threads; and (7) it offers the possibility for learners to see a display of their group dynamics.

The list provided by Romiszowski and Mason includes features that are related to administration and economy of the system, as well as to teaching and learning activities. We will discuss these features related to teaching and learning before proceeding to the administration of distance programs.

Teach from Anywhere. By definition, distance training means that the instructor does not need to be physically present to teach a particular class, and the rest of the world does not need to be physically present to take advantage of the instructor's particular and valuable knowledge. The instructor can teach from wherever he or she is to students wherever they are, and the teaching and learning interactions are not limited to a single classroom.

Asynchronous Activities and Learn from Anywhere. Distance training allows students to access courses, materials, information, and classmates anywhere and anytime. While face-to-face training requires people to be in a specific place and time, participating in synchronous activities, Web-based instruction allows the students to communicate and collaborate at different times when it is convenient for them. This convenience makes learning accessible to individuals who may not have been exposed previously to the instruction, such as full-time workers and those separated by geography. The asynchronous feature of Web-based distance instruction is the key feature that distinguishes this new generation of distance technology from previous generations of video-based distance courses.

The Possibility for Learners to Analyze Their Own Interactions. An on-line class allows people the opportunity to participate at their own pace, without pressures such as time limits or speaking in front of a group, and gives each student an equal standing in the class. When students analyze their interactions, such as those recorded through threaded discussions, this opportunity opens a window for reflection about their own processes of learning. They can see what they have been doing and how they have done it. They can see their interactions, their participations, and their postings, all of which allow students to see their growth from the beginning to the end of the course. Having their interactions in a written format allows students to articulate, concentrate, and reflect deliberately.

The Possibility for Learners to See a Display of Their Group Dynamics. Group dynamics play a key role in problem-based, learner-centered, and constructivist educational experiences, and Web-based training allows students and instructors to see their interactions and reflect on them. This makes the process accountable and digestible.

Why Are These Features Valuable?

The value of the features explained in the preceding section is to make training more convenient in regard to time and place. No barriers of geographical separations interfere with people getting an education; people from anywhere are able to receive education of almost any kind. Rigid scheduling is not convenient to busy individuals who desire training but cannot move to another location to participate in a residential program because of their occupations. Second, making training a more reflective process allows people to be aware of what they are doing, enabling them to be more active rather than passive in their own learning process. Being more active equals being more involved, and who does not want to have more involved students? Business and industry today require workers who are able to take initiative and to think critically, and distance training fosters these capabilities.

How Much Evidence Is There to Support Claims of the Distance Advocates?

A comprehensive summary of research on the topic of computer-mediated communication in on-line learning environments can be found in Romiszowski and Mason's 2004 chapter titled "Computer-Mediated Communication" in the second edition of the *Handbook of Research for Educational Communications and Technology.*

Given that Web-based training technologies are still very new, it should not be surprising to find that research in this area is currently lacking in both quantity and quality. More research is needed that identifies the effects of distance technologies and environments on learning, and a more coherent framework is needed in order to allow the results from these studies to be used for appropriate comparisons (Berge and Mrozowski, 2001; Gall and Hannafin, 1994).

There is still much to learn about distance training: "The use of the tool, as well as the research practices surrounding it, [is] in need of expansion if it is to reach its potential as a platform for educational innovation" (Hill, Wiley, Nelson, and Han, 2004, p. 453).

Hill, Wiley, Nelson, and Han (2004) point out that there is no one best way, but rather many appropriate ways to improve practices in education and training. They believe that the question related to distance training that we should be asking now is, "What are the best ways to teach students within specific contexts and under certain conditions?" (p. 453). The current issue for which we need to develop our understanding has to do with when the use of Web-based instruction becomes more beneficial for the student, as opposed to when traditional face-to-face instruction is of most benefit to students. Similarly, we need to know which practices are most suitable for different types of instructors and students, and how we can best use this information to improve teaching and learning.

The World Wide Web is still new, particularly in its use as a format for education. Students, instructors, and researchers all have much to learn about this educational environment and the technologies that support it. It is too early yet to make judgments about the worth of this developing process: we need to continue researching and learning from direct exploration. We will likely be both surprised and disappointed with the eventual findings of research, but in either case, we need time to see what research will reveal.

THE STATUS OF DISTANCE TRAINING

Distance training is no longer exclusively used by colleges and universities. Its influence has expanded to all levels and types of education and to all aspects of our daily lives. Families, K–12 education, and corporations are now engaged in Web-based distance training. Oblinger and Rush (2003) have estimated that "corporate America's adoption of e-learning has come at a much more rapid pace than in higher education" (p. 593). What might be the reasons behind the widespread and rapid adoption of distance training technologies? We could cite many, but the most important might be the simple fact identified by Ruttenbur, Spickler, and Lurie (2000) that the workforce must be rapidly updated, and distance training technologies provide an effective, efficient, and economical means to address this need.

Oblinger and Rush estimated in 2003 that the 2004 worldwide corporate e-learning market would exceed $23 billion. This would represent an annual growth rate of 68.8 percent from 1999 through 2004, with North America being accountable for two-thirds of this growth. "In a time of shrinking budgets, distance learning programs are reporting 41 percent average annual enrollment growth. Thirty percent of the programs are being developed to meet the needs of professional continuing education for adults" (Gunawardena and McIsaac, 2004, p. 355). Dolezalek (2004, October) calculated that the total training budget spent in the United States in 2004 was $51.4 billion (see Figure 18.1).

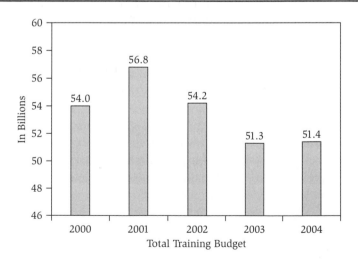

Figure 18.1. Total Training Budget Spent in the United States in 2004.
Source: Adapted from Dolezalek, October 2004.

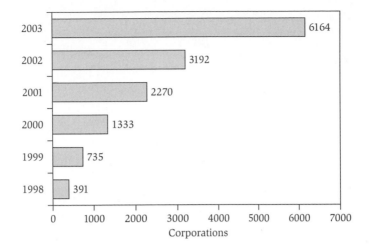

Figure 18.2. Number of Corporations Offering Distributed Learning Courses.

Source: Adapted from Moe, 2002.

The number of corporations offering distributed learning courses to employees has been growing rapidly (Moe, 2002), with a total of 6,164 companies in 2003, almost two times the number that offered in the previous year (see Figure 18.2). The e-learning market is in its early stages and not old enough to be considered well established. Results from a survey designed to depict the state of e-learning provide evidence that this market is growing rapidly (see Figure 18.3). Nearly 80 percent of survey respondents reported that they have adopted e-learning within the past four years (Hequet, 2003).

Hequet also reports that e-learning is offered to the majority of employees in 56 percent of the organizations that responded to the survey, while 45 percent of those organizations offer e-learning to select employees, and 26 percent of the organizations offer e-learning to customers, resellers, partners, and suppliers. E-training is not, however, the panacea for every training need. It does have limitations, among them, to mention a few, up-front investment required of an e-learning solution is larger due to development costs; technology issues that play a factor include whether the existing technology infrastructure can accomplish the training goals and whether additional tech expenditures can be justified; cultural acceptance is an issue in organizations in which people may be predisposed against the use of computers at all; reduced social and cultural interactions among people; suppression of communication mechanisms; and elimination of peer-to-peer learning. It appears, from the same survey conducted by Hequet (2003) about e-learning (see Figure 18.4), that the principal limitations on e-learning are cost and learner motivation.

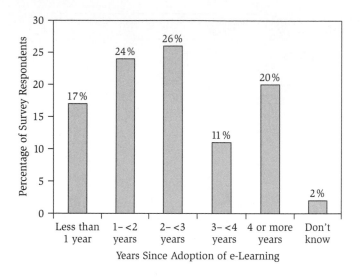

Figure 18.3. Rate of e-Learning Adoption by Corporations.

Source: Adapted from Hequet, 2003.

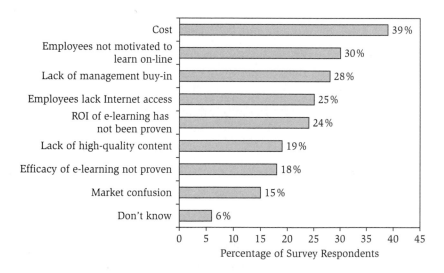

Figure 18.4. Limiting Factors on Use of e-Learning in Corporations.

Source: Adapted from Hequet, 2003.

Dolezalek (2004, October) conducted a survey of corporate training organizations to determine the comparative usage of e-learning courses and traditional face-to-face training. She found that 31 percent of technology-based training programs were delivered by outside contractors and 69 percent by inside staff, while

Table 18.1. Frequency of Use of Instructional Methods for Corporate Training.

Methods	Never Used	Seldom Used	Often Used	Always Used
Most Used				
Classroom with instructor, traditional	3%	13%	67%	18%
Public seminars	8%	40%	48%	4%
Self-study, Web-based	16%	42%	37%	6%
Least Used				
Classroom with instructor, virtual	40%	41%	17%	2%
Computer-based games	50%	41%	9%	1%
Virtual reality programs	81%	16%	2%	0%

Source: Adapted from Dolezalek, October 2004.

26 percent of the traditional training programs were delivered by outside contractors and 74 percent by inside staff. With regard to the development of technology-based training programs, 41 percent were developed by outside contractors and 59 percent by inside staff. Thirty-five percent of the traditional training programs were developed by outside contractors and 65 percent by inside staff.

Regarding the amount of interaction in training courses, Dolezalek (2004, October) found that 29 percent of trainees interacted with a human instructor while the rest (71 percent) interacted only with a computer. The most frequently used instructional formats for corporate training were (1) the traditional classroom with instructor, (2) public seminars, and (3) Web-based self-study courses. The least-used format for corporate training was the virtual classroom in which students were engaged in virtual reality programs (see Table 18.1).

WHY CORPORATIONS ARE ADOPTING DISTANCE LEARNING

Traditionally, educational institutions and corporate training have had clear and distinct boundaries, but in the recent past, educational institutions have been reaching out to adult learners as never before in order to increase revenues by meeting the needs of lifelong learners. Green (2000) reports that most current distance students are adult professionals who are looking for additional training. According to a 1999 survey by the National Center for Education Statistics, just over 50 percent of adults ages forty-five to fifty-four, 37 percent of adults ages fifty-five to sixty-five, and 20 percent of adults aged sixty-five or over are taking distance classes (U.S. Department of Education, 2002; Waits and Lewis, 2003; Wirt, Choy, Rooney, Provasnik, Sen, and Tobin, 2004). Continuing education is the fastest growth area within the educational marketplace.

Human resources and training departments in corporations of all sizes have come to the same realization as educational institutions: (1) the need for learning does not stop after an employee becomes comfortable in a new position; and (2) rapid advances in technology and the exponential growth of information require constant and continuous development for employees. To address this situation, companies are looking for ways to offer the ongoing training that employees request and require. Continuing education and training serve as means to personal advancement for employees, as well as means to keep or increase competitive advantage for the company. Berge (2003) posits that lifelong learning is now the standard for everyone: "Our global society is moving into the Knowledge Age, where technology dictates that we will live, work, and learn differently than we did in the Industrial Age. The new age demands more skills, knowledge, learning, and re-learning" (p. 601). The recognition that companies need to become learning organizations stems in part from employers' growing awareness that employees cannot come to a job today knowing all that is needed to be successful, and that school does not prepare individuals for all the needs that will emerge in the workplace. A workforce that has employees with the ability to learn on their own and be responsible for that learning is now needed, and distance training is a viable strategy for developing a learning organization.

Berge (2003) has also identified a number of other reasons that are driving companies to use distance training. Most practically, the need to train hundreds or thousands of employees who are located in different geographical areas with the same content at the same time is a better fit for distance training than for face-to-face instruction. Second, traditional face-to-face methods of training and education incur higher costs in terms of housing and transportation, while the lower cost of distance training is attractive to employers. Third, face-to-face training requires employees to be available for a set period of time on particular days, which may interfere with the completion of regular and normal work tasks and activities. The lack of time during work hours is a great deterrent for traditional training, but the asynchronous nature of distance training may help to overcome this obstacle by allowing training to occur when it is convenient for each employee. Finally, distance training is offered in a modular format so that training can occur "just-in-time," making it highly relevant to employees and supporting the learning that is critical to the success of the organization.

PLANNING AND ADMINISTRATION OF DISTANCE TRAINING

For the reasons stated earlier, we conclude that the distance training provided by an organization may be an essential element in improving the performance of employees. To remain competitive, organizations are placing more emphasis on distance training. The success of distance training initiatives is contingent on the planning and management that support these efforts. In this section, a brief description of the administrative team responsible for distance training is provided, and the functions of the team as well as the possible obstacles it might face along the way are delineated.

Functions of the Distance Training Administrative Team

In addition to the obvious need for expertise in maintaining the technology that makes distance instruction possible, the distance training initiative requires expertise in technology-based instructional strategies such as the facilitation of on-line discussion, collaboration, and learner engagement. Also, because the trainees who take distance learning courses have widely varying technology skills, it can be expected that trainees will need assistance at some point in navigating their way through the landscape of the distance training experience.

The administrative team generally consists of individuals who have expertise to support the hardware and software used for the distance training environment, who have expertise in the design and delivery of technology-based training, and who are able to provide learner support for all aspects of the distance training experience. The team is responsible for building the bridge from the traditional face-to-face training experience to the newer technology-based distance training experience, so that learners become comfortable in this new environment. Some of the key functions that the administrative team must take on in addressing this responsibility include to

- Conduct needs analysis for distance training
- Evaluate strategies and technologies for the delivery of distance training
- Determine needs for equipment, facilities, policies, and cultural change
- Research to discover successful models used elsewhere
- Determine incentives for designers, instructors, and developers and students
- Estimate costs of distance training and compare with traditional training
- Identify barriers for implementation and address these barriers
- Assess results of distance training initiatives
- Report findings and propose recommendations to improve distance training

According to Dolezalek (2004, April), the distance training implementation team can expect to spend a significant portion of its time on integration issues, making sure that the course content integrates with the technology-based learning management system and other systems within the company, such as the human resource information system, compliance recording systems, and e-mail systems.

Potential Issues and Obstacles to Be Addressed by the Administrative Team

The administrative team should expect to face obstacles as it works to integrate the distance training initiative into the organization's existing structures. Some of the typical obstacles to successful integration of distance training that may need to be addressed by the administrative team include buy-in, access, support services, legal issues, and evaluation of distance training initiatives.

The administrative team, because it allocates the funds that make the distance training initiative possible, should ensure that the organization's leaders believe in these initiatives. Similarly, employees are generally resistant to organizational change if there is not clear communication about the change and opportunity for employees to be involved with the change. The administrative team should therefore work to engage employees in the initiative to bring distance training into the organization.

The administrative team needs to ensure that all learners have the technology that will be needed to access courses, and that all instructors and trainees have the technical expertise to appropriately use the distance training technologies. It is important to minimize as much as possible any intimidation or fear on the part of employees regarding the initiative.

The administrative team is generally responsible for determining what support services will be needed for learners and how those services will be made available. Support services might include the availability of resource repositories, and systems for registration, payment, and advising related to training activities.

The administrative team will also need to consider and develop policies regarding legal issues such as copyright and intellectual property as they relate to distance training materials. The administrative team should work toward agreements for how legal issues related to distance training will be addressed within the organization.

Most important, the administrative team will need to determine how to evaluate the effectiveness of distance training. There is currently no consensus in the academic literature about how best to evaluate distance learning in terms of process or outcomes. Measures and indicators for success of the distance training initiative will need to be identified.

Stages of Organizational Capability for Distance Training

Solid program planning and program management will be the keys to program effectiveness and efficiency. In Figure 18.5, Schreiber (1998) describes four stages of organizational capability.

If an organization is in the early stages of transition or is experimenting with distance training options, Johnson (2004) provides recommendations for the types of content that are most suitable for making the transition from face-to-face to

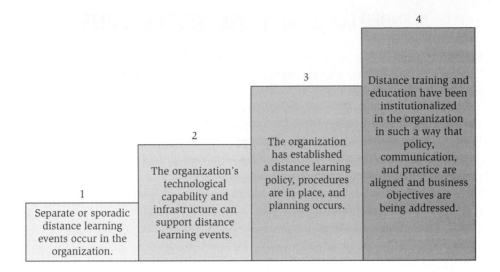

Figure 18.5. Stages of Organizational Capability.

Source: Adapted from Schreiber, 1998.

distance learning formats during the early stages of a distance training initiative: the administrative team should consider migrating from face-to-face to distance training for content that

- Reaches the greatest number of employees
- Is covered infrequently at very remote locations
- Is considered prework to other training activities
- Changes so frequently that it is difficult to keep the employees up to date
- Puts the learners in harm's way
- Requires expensive equipment or is difficult to set up the training
- Requires significant drill and practice to achieve mastery
- Is linked to regulatory compliance or certification
- Requires consistent delivery

The preceding information has been provided to support the many organizations that are just beginning to venture into the use of distance learning as a means to support employee performance. Though distance training is still a relatively new activity for many organizations, the next "new thing" is on the horizon, and so the final section of this chapter will introduce the phenomenon of blended learning and discuss its potential for corporate training.

BLENDED LEARNING: A LOOK INTO THE FUTURE

In an article by Stephanie Sparrow in the magazine $T+D$ (2004), it was reported that according to a transatlantic survey of 150 U.S. and 118 British learning professionals by Balance Learning Ltd., a global provider of comprehensive blended learning solutions, blended learning is the delivery method of choice. According to the survey, blended learning is viewed as the most effective and efficient form of training in the United States. The results show that 77 percent of the U.S. organizations currently use blended learning, and that it accounts for 16.1 percent of all training in the United States.

Blended learning has been compared metaphorically to brewing coffee. Johnson (2003) states that finding the appropriate components of blended learning is likened to "brewing the right mix," which refers to choosing the most suitable elements to ensure a successful training situation that can include multiple delivery methods, such as instructor-led training, e-learning courses, and printed and electronic media, among others.

Blended learning can be defined as a mixed model of learning in which all available technologies, from traditional printed materials through electronic documents, both on-site and in distance lectures, are used to deliver learning and to create educational experiences that are successful and that try to accommodate the best qualities of every environment and medium with the resources that the organization and the learner have at their disposition, creating a balanced combination of learning environments.

Adult learners have unique characteristics that set them apart: Learning environments that combine Internet learning with the face-to-face experiences sought by many adult learners have advantages over pure traditional classrooms and totally on-line situations. Blended learning has been recognized as an effective alternative that can combine the best features of each model, helping to foster rapport among participants and decrease "psychological" distances and isolation (Ausburn, 2004).

IBM (IBM Learning Solutions, 2004), a global services organization, recently implemented an internal blended learning training module for its employees. Based on the belief that people learn in different ways, IBM's methodology uses four distinct educational approaches. Each approach works with the other approaches to enable employees to be more productive and to help create value for the organization. IBM's blended learning system combines Web-based, interactive, collaborative, and face-to-face learning. This blended learning structure coordinates movement from one learning experience to the next so that each learning experience emphasizes and builds on the last. The four learning approaches are

1. *Learning from Information.* Performance support and reference materials are frequently used as a starting point. They tend to be Web-based

and take advantage of on-line information transfer. This allows an employee to access only the materials that are relevant to his or her job function. Allowing the learner to move at his or her own pace maximizes interest and motivation and empowers the user to learn the material quickly and comprehensively.

2. *Learning from Interaction, Simulation, or Games.* This type of learning enables an employee to focus on practicing with real-life scenarios, and is typically conducted on-line. Using a "learning from information" approach, it is self-directed and involves specific modules, interactive games, coaching, and layered simulations. These practice cases provide a multitude of possible choices that help employees master specific competencies at their own pace.

3. *Collaborative Learning.* This approach allows employees to work with their peers in virtual classrooms, e-labs, and collaborative sessions to build awareness through live, on-line conferences and teaming. This learning approach is typically threaded, meaning there is an expert who posts the scenarios and continually focuses the discussions.

4. *Classroom-Based Learning.* Face-to-face discussions regarding information gained through the other learning approaches help the employees understand important lessons learned. This approach includes classroom sessions, mentoring, role-playing, and coaching.

According to IBM reports, the introduction of a blended learning approach has saved the organization $24 million annually in deployment costs of IBM's new-manager training program, Basic Blue. IBM also reports that five times as much content was delivered through the blended learning approach as was delivered by the previous new-manager program (IBM Learning Solutions, 2004).

SUMMARY

The use of information communications technology is becoming widespread in corporations today. Worldwide, companies are committing themselves to maximizing the potential of the new technologies, to enhancing their training needs and programs, and to best reaching different, diverse, and geographically separated populations. The commitment to distance training requires both an enabling policy framework and an understanding of the way it can be integrated into the training process. E-learning, on-line learning, and blended learning have surpassed their status of "newness" to establish one more option to answer a need for information, formation, and personal growth.

We have seen that the unique features of Web-based technologies that allow for asynchronous communication between individuals who are widely dispersed across various geographical locations has led to the widespread and rapid adoption of distance education. It has been noted throughout this chapter as well that corporations are following the lead of educational institutions in adopting the use of these distance technologies for the training and education of large numbers of employees. Additionally, we introduced a new phenomenon, known as blended learning, which seeks to integrate the best features of face-to-face and distance training environments, and reported on a model for blended learning from IBM, a multinational corporation. If IBM's success with blended learning is replicated by other corporations, we can be assured that blended learning will experience the widespread and rapid adoption that we are currently seeing with distance training technologies.

References

Ausburn, L. (2004). Course design elements most valued by adult learners in blended online education environments: An American perspective. *Educational Media International, 41*(4), 327–337.

Berge, Z. L. (2003). Planning and managing distance training and education in the corporate sector. In M. G. Moore and W. G. Anderson (Eds.), *Handbook of distance education.* Mahwah, NJ: Lawrence Erlbaum Associates.

Berge, Z. L., and Mrozowski, S. (2001). Review of research in distance education, 1990 to 1999. *The American Journal of Distance Education, 15*(3), 5–19.

DeCorte, E., Verschaffel, L., and Lowyck, J. (1994). Computers and learning. In T. Husen and T. N. Postlethwaite (Eds.), *The international encyclopedia of education* (2nd ed.). Oxford: Elsevier Science.

Dolezalek, H. (2004, April). Dose of reality. *Training, 41(4),* 28–34.

Dolezalek, H. (2004, October). The 23rd annual industry report. *Training, 41*(10), 20–36.

Gall, J., and Hannafin, M. (1994). A framework for the study of hypertext. *Instructional Science, 22*(3), 207–232.

Gibbons, T. C., and Brenowitz, R. S. (2002). Designing and using a course in organization design to facilitate corporate learning in the online environment. In K. E. Rudestam and J. Schoenholtz-Read (Eds.), *Handbook of online learning.* Thousand Oaks, CA: Sage.

Green, J. (2000). The online education bubble. *American Prospect, 11*(22), 32–35.

Gunawardena, C. N., and McIsaac, M. S. (2004). Distance education. In D. H. Jonassen (Ed.), *Handbook of research for educational communications and technology* (2nd ed.). Mahwah, NJ: Lawrence Erlbaum Associates.

Hequet, M. (2003, September). The state of e-learning market. *Training, 40*(8), 24–28.

Hill, J. R., Wiley, D., Nelson, L. M., and Han, S. (2004). Exploring research on Internet-based learning: From infrastructure to interactions. In D. H. Jonassen (Ed.), *Handbook of research for educational communications and technology* (2nd ed.). Mahwah, NJ: Lawrence Erlbaum Associates.

IBM Learning Solutions. (2004). *IBM's learning transformation history.* Retrieved March 14, 2005, from www.306.ibm.com/services/learning/solutions/pdfs/learning_transformation.pdf.

Johnson, G. (2003, December). Brewing the perfect blend. *Training, 40*(11), 30–34.

Johnson, G. (2004, February). Conversion anxiety. *Training, 41*(2), 34–40.

Moe, M. T. (2002, December). *Emerging trends in postsecondary education—The view to 2012.* Presented at the Driving Post-Secondary Education Conference, Washington, DC.

Oblinger, D. G., and Rush, S. C. (2003). The involvement of corporations in distance education. In M. G. Moore and W. G. Anderson (Eds.), *Handbook of distance education.* Mahwah, NJ: Lawrence Erlbaum Associates.

Romiszowski, A., and Mason, R. (2004). Computer-mediated communication. In D. H. Jonassen (Ed.), *Handbook of research for educational communications and technology* (2nd ed.). Mahwah, NJ: Lawrence Erlbaum Associates.

Ruttenbur, B. W., Spickler, G. C., and Lurie, S. (2000). *E-learning: The engine of the knowledge economy.* Memphis, TN: Morgan Keegan.

Schreiber, D. A. (1998). Organizational technology and its impact on distance training. In D. A. Schreiber and Z. L. Berge (Eds.), *Distance training: How innovative organizations are using technology to maximize learning and meet business objectives* (pp. 3–18). San Francisco: Jossey-Bass.

Sparrow, S. (2004, November). Blended is better. *T + D, 58*(11), 52–55.

U.S. Department of Education. (2002). *The condition of education 2002* (NCES 2002-025). Washington, DC: U.S. Department of Education, National Center for Education Statistics, U.S. Government Printing Office.

Wagner, E. (1992). Distance education systems. In H. D. Stolovitch and E. J. Keeps (Eds.), *Handbook of human performance technology: A comprehensive guide for analyzing and solving performance problems in organizations.* San Francisco: Jossey-Bass.

Wagner, E. (1999). Beyond distance education: Distributed learning systems. In H. D. Stolovitch and E. J. Keeps (Eds.), *Handbook of human performance technology: Improving individual and organizational performance worldwide* (2nd ed.). San Francisco: Jossey-Bass/Pfeiffer.

Waits, T., and Lewis, L. (2003). Distance education at degree-granting postsecondary institutions: 2000–2001 (NCES 2003–017). Washington, DC: U.S. Department of Education, National Center for Education Statistics, U.S. Government Printing Office.

Winer, L., Rushby, N., and Vázquez-Abad, J. (1999). Emerging trends in instructional interventions. In H. D. Stolovitch and E. J. Keeps (Eds.). *Handbook of human performance technology: Improving individual and organizational performance worldwide* (2nd ed.). San Francisco: Jossey-Bass/Pfeiffer.

Wirt, J., Choy, S., Rooney, P., Provasnik, S., Sen, A., and Tobin, R. (2004). *The condition of education 2004* (NCES 2004–077). Washington, DC: U.S. Department of Education, National Center for Education Statistics, U.S. Government Printing Office.

CHAPTER NINETEEN

Innovations in Performance Improvement with Mentoring

Margo Murray

The use of mentoring relationships as a strategy for performance improvement has been proven to work in all types of organizations. Since 1970, some researchers and practitioners have tracked results to demonstrate the added value of greater competence, stronger confidence, and loyalty of participants involved in mentoring processes. In updating this chapter of the handbook, I will include the key success factors for effective mentoring processes. In addition, I will describe some contemporary formats of people interactions that are being called mentoring.

Myths still abound when people describe mentoring processes. There are so many different structures and activities being called "mentoring" that it must be time to clarify what is mentoring and what is not mentoring. Let us start with definitions. When I began design of the first facilitated mentoring processes, in the late 1960s, the popular dictionaries showed *mentor* only as a noun.

Men·tor *n* [Greek] 1. A friend to whom Odysseus, when setting out for Troy, entrusted his house and the education of Telemachus. 2. [F] Hence, a faithful counselor [*Webster's New Collegiate Dictionary,* 1958, 2nd ed.].

Going to the latest on-line dictionaries we find a general definition, without as much as a nod to the Greeks or the French:

men·tor *n* somebody, usually older and more experienced, who provides advice and support to, and watches over and fosters the progress of, a younger, less experienced person [*Encarta World English Dictionary,* 1999].

A second definition acknowledges contemporary usage with a transitive verb definition:

> men·tor *vt*: to act as a mentor to somebody, especially a junior colleague
> [*Encarta World English Dictionary*, 1999].

These definitions are already outdated in current mentoring practices, in which the mentor is not always older, a senior, and the protégé is not always younger, a junior. Some of the most effective mentoring results are gained in pairs who are peers with different skill sets. Other examples are seen in which the mentor is newer to the organization, younger, and is bringing state-of-the-art skills needed in the organization.

In an attempt to bring some clarity to the foundation for discussion and examples used in this chapter, I will start with basic concepts and definitions of the terms. When I am relating an example from an organization's mentoring process, I will employ terms used by participants in that organization. When striving for clarity and common understanding, I will use the terms that most clearly distinguish the roles and functions. The popular and frequently used terms are not always the grammatically correct ones.

Our working definition of mentoring is, "a deliberate pairing of a more skilled or experienced person with a lesser skilled or experienced one, with the agreed-upon goal of having the lesser skilled person grow and develop specific competencies" (Murray, 1991, p. xiv). Often there is a lot of formality and bureaucracy applied to human resources and personnel programs. To avoid this with the mentoring processes, I chose the term *facilitated,* and defined it as "a structure and series of processes designed to create effective mentoring relationships, guide the desired behavior change of those involved, and evaluate the results for the protégés, the mentors, and the organization" (Murray, 1991, p. 5).

Training magazine reported that 77 percent of the "Top 100" companies have formal mentoring programs (Barbian, 2002). The article cited many different formats and designs of the rated companies' mentoring processes. Some were targeted to specific groups and some were open to all employees. When I tried to get data on results, I found that many of those companies had conducted a pilot program for a few pairs and had only anecdotal data on the results.

Most of the published accounts of mentoring experiences are described in positive terms by both protégés and mentors. Occasionally, we do hear and read about some experiences that were unpleasant or destructive for the protégés and some that were less than rewarding for the mentors. Those negative experiences are most often reported from mentoring relationships that were informal, usually happenstance, and with no specific discussion or mutual agreement about the expectations of either partner. A Catalyst organization survey reported that only 23 percent of women and 17 percent of men are satisfied with the number of mentors in the workplace who provide them with career advice (Witt, 2004).

Table 19.1. **Key Success Factors for Informal Versus Facilitated Mentoring.**

Key Success Factors	Informal Mentoring	Facilitated Mentoring
Business goals	Mentoring is not tied to goals; relationships are not tracked.	Mentoring is linked to existing business initiatives; results are measured.
Internal ownership of program	Ownership is unclear; there is little support or coordination.	Ownership is by project coordinator(s) who are skilled in communication, negotiation, mediation, and evaluation.
Development of protégé's skills and behaviors	Mentoring is often a more generalized relationship, with less-specific focus.	Mentoring is focused on skill development and transfer of experience; also is linked to individual development plan.
Comprehensive orientation of protégés and mentors	There is no orientation; generic training is not linked to the specific needs of the pairs.	There is comprehensive orientation to focus on roles, key success factors, the mentoring process, and goals.
Ongoing support for mentoring pairs	There is no structured support.	FMP coordinators facilitate, mediate, and provide resources as needed.
Measured results	There is little or no follow-up, with mostly anecdotal data.	Baselines are established during needs assessment; periodic evaluations measure results; results are linked to business goals.

When there is ongoing concern for return on investments of all types, a systematic approach to any performance intervention is necessary. It cannot be left to a lucky accident to develop employees to full performance potential. The information presented in Table 19.1 illustrates the comparative key success factors of informal and facilitated mentoring (Murray, 2001b).

More and more managers and leaders are turning to mentoring as a strategy for improving human performance in leaner, flatter organizations. An exceptionally competent workforce is seen as the most promising competitive advantage when technology has leveled the playing field for many businesses. Wide ranges of entering levels of knowledge and skills of workers make classroom instruction both ineffective and inefficient. Limited time for the myriad tasks in every worker's job makes it essential for each learning experience to be focused on specific individual needs and skill gaps. Supervisors do not support "fluff training." Some organizations are now describing themselves as "learning organizations" with the same fervor that many expressed when describing themselves as a "total quality organization." The criteria for attaining the stature of learning organization are even fuzzier than for total quality. With many products and services there is a quality measure that can be communicated to performer, vendor, or customer with sufficient clarity to make it feasible to achieve. I have yet to hear any proponent of the learning organization goal articulate performance indicators in a way that observers would agree was an accurate description. A facilitated mentoring process, integrated into the culture of the organization and aligned with other human performance improvement processes, can create a continuous learning climate and earn the description of "learning organization."

The impact of a mentoring process can be measured by tracking trends in the goals, needs, and opportunities of the organization. For example, an organization has a goal of increased profits through sales. A mentoring process is implemented to shorten the cycle time for salespeople to meet sales goals. The salespeople being coached by a mentor increase their sales significantly over other salespeople who do not have mentors. Our clients cite other positive measures such as increased retention of the right people who feel valued because of having a mentor. Another client measured reduced costs of on-the-job accidents when automotive service technician mentors wore their protective gear more consistently.

Individual learning and skill development can be measured with specific performance and development objectives, both before and after the mentoring experience. Kevin Wilde, vice president and chief learning officer for General Mills, relates the importance of individual development plans: "Part of the value proposition here is great development" (Ellis, 2004, p. 22).

MENTORING: THE PROCESS, ROLES, AND TASKS

In current excellent practices with facilitated mentoring, the term *mentoring* describes the *process* that deliberately pairs two people with different skills and experiences with the objective of transferring those skills and experiences from the one who has them to the one who needs them.

Mentor is the *role* taken on by someone who is willing to help someone else learn and grow by agreeing to interact with this person to transfer experiences and skills. Mentors may perform several tasks in the process of their interactions with protégés.

These role *tasks* include but are not limited to tutoring, coaching, listening, counseling, teaching, modeling, giving feedback, demonstrating, giving information, facilitating desired performance, and guiding. To clarify what mentors may do in carrying out their agreed roles with their protégés, following are several examples of actual pairs in which the mentor is performing one or more of these tasks.

Tutoring: A graduate new hire engineer in petroleum exploration brings state-of-the-art technical knowledge in petrochemical engineering, particularly using computer modeling. She is paired with a mentor who is a highly skilled, experienced engineer who tutors her in how to communicate and negotiate effectively with contract designers of equipment. The role of mentor could shift at any given moment, for example, when the new hire passes on current technical applications.

Coaching: A sales representative in a sports apparel distribution firm has set an objective to strengthen her sales skills in order to improve sales results in her territory. Her mentor agrees to accompany her on sales calls to observe and coach her while interacting with a customer. Coaching is done just before the task is to be performed and by subtle and timely interventions during the sales call.

Listening: A personnel relations manager feels drained by the constant bombardment of complaints about company policy and procedures. He wants the mentor, who may be a peer or a colleague in another department, to just listen to his venting of his own frustration with policies that he must interpret, but that he sees no way to change at this time. He wants the mentor to keep these gripes in confidence.

Counseling: A recent college graduate is hired into a small public accounting firm. This "junior" is immediately assigned to a series of short-term auditing, tax-planning, and consulting engagements with clients, each led by a different engagement manager. Her "senior" mentor, having experience in all functions, fills the gap in counseling on career options in the firm by assisting her in exploring all the options and selecting an area of specialty before being promoted to senior.

Teaching: An electrical design engineer in an aerospace company sets a long-term career goal to become a general manager. His mentor, the controller, agrees to teach him how to develop financial analyses and business proposals.

Modeling: A commodity manager has an objective of gaining exposure to and awareness of upper-management activities. She asks her more experienced mentor to allow her to observe her mentor's modeling of appropriate behavior with higher-level executives at business social events.

Giving feedback: A territory representative knows every feature and benefit of the product being sold. His goal is to further develop skills in handling customer visits effectively. The action plan agreed to with the mentor includes having the mentor observe several customer visits and give feedback on the quality of the interaction with the customer.

Demonstrating: A copy center manager has a long-term career goal of working in public relations, which will require good presentation skills. Her mentor invites her to a professional society meeting to watch him demonstrate how to make an effective presentation. Following the event they discuss the strengths and areas for improvement for the mentor.

Guiding: A technical services center representative has a development objective of learning how to prioritize career goals, and articulate and quantify mini steps to achieve the long-term goals. The mentor takes on the role and task of guiding the protégé in the process of determining the investment the protégé is willing to make in his own career development.

Giving information: A warehouse supervisor aspires to be the manager in her building. Her mentor provides information on company policies and procedures that managers must follow and interpret to their subordinates.

Facilitating desired performance: An experienced project coordinator recognizes that he turns some people off with his abrupt way of demanding progress reports. His mentor agrees to facilitate the development of project-management skills, and to focus on the project coordinator's style of communication and interaction with members of the project teams.

Feedback and coaching: A combination of these two tasks is often applied by the perceptive mentor. A petite, Asian information technology specialist is frustrated during a meeting when her inputs are seen as sabotage by the project team. Her mentor coaches her to seat herself in the line of sight of the meeting leader to more easily gain recognition. She is also coached to make her recommendations early in the discussion before the other team members are committed to a potentially less effective strategy or solution.

One additional point may help to distinguish mentoring from on-the-job training. The immediate supervisor of the function or group conducts most on-the-job training. It is sometimes delegated to a team leader or the lead performer, and the objective is to produce or refine skills needed for performance on the current job.

EVOLUTION OF THE MENTORING CONCEPT

The principles and practices of modeling and mentoring have been key elements in the continuity of art, craft, and commerce from ancient times. In arts and crafts guilds a young person was apprenticed to a master who was considered to be excellent in the trade or profession (Murray, 1991, 2001a). The master taught, coached, and guided the development of skills in the trade or art. To become a master, the apprentice's skills were judged from a work sample, such as a painting, or even a horseshoe. The word *masterpiece* originated from this sample of skillful work.

The traditional picture of a mentor was of an older, long-service person who selected his own protégés and took these lucky individuals firmly under one wing to guide their life-time career development. This picture has finally faded. Occasionally there may even be a dark side to mentoring relationships. I have heard about mentors who use the protégé for work projects, take credit for the work, sometimes abuse the relationship and the mentoring partner, and refuse to let go when the protégé has outgrown the relationship. Mentors often complain that the *neophytes* attached themselves to their coattails and expected to be carried along to success with little personal effort. That describes what we would define as a *role model* or *sponsor* (Murray, 2001a).

The skills required of the new masters are as different from those of the apprentices of yore as the high-tech clean room is from the blacksmith shop. Yet the process by which the skills are learned, one to one, is very much the same. Certainly mastering an art, craft, or profession increases one's marketability in diverse workplaces. Flexibility is essential when workplaces include people from dozens of different cultures. Enabling the transfer of the requisite skills and experiences in a facilitated mentoring process can strengthen this flexibility.

Different Structures Called Mentoring

Many different formats and structures are called "mentoring." I will briefly describe a few of the more popular ones and mention some of the pluses and questionable aspects of each.

Facilitated One-to-One Pairings. This format has proven to be a cost-effective strategy for transferring skills and experiences. Ideally the match is based on assessed and perceived skill deficiencies or lack of experience of the protégé. The mentor selected for the match is one with mastery level in the needed skills and the desired experience.

Pluses
- Coaching is targeted to specific skills and competencies.
- The protégé's privacy is protected.
- Both achieve maximum efficiency of time.
- Coaching sessions are easily scheduled.
- Results are measured.

Questionable Aspects
- The mentor may have limited time for one partner.
- There is deep investment in an individual employee.

Reverse Mentoring. *Reverse mentoring* is a term used by some corporations and agencies to describe a process of pairing a lower-level, sometimes newer person with a higher-level executive or administrator. The purpose is usually to provide an opportunity for the senior person to get direct input from the "shop floor."

Pluses

- People may learn about the organization's direction.
- The mentor's ego is stroked.
- The protégé feels valued.

Questionable Aspects

- Lower-level people will not "rat on" their bosses.
- Both parties are accused of favoritism.
- Expectations are often thwarted. The mentor is not at all likely to violate policies or bypass standard procedures for promotions or plum assignments.
- The protégé is the target of jealousy by peers.
- The protégé will not reveal areas of needed growth, and thus does not grow.
- There is no measurement of outcomes.

Group Mentoring. Organizations using what they call "group mentoring" are citing shortages of mentors as the reason to create groups. Protégés see this as an easy opportunity to network with their colleagues. They find safety and anonymity in the group, particularly if they are reluctant to voice dissatisfaction with policies or procedures to their bosses.

Pluses

- The mentor's time is spent with more people.
- It helps expand protégés' networks.

Questionable Aspects

- Employees are unlikely to express skill deficiencies in a group.
- Competitiveness is increased.
- There is no measurement of results.
- Time is wasted for some participants who already have the skills being discussed.

Circle Mentoring. Patterned after the quality circles, *circle mentoring* is another term used for group processes. Usually the participants are peers who are coming together periodically to exchange ideas and strategies. The Mentoring Company, the organization that developed and trademarked Mentoring Circles, uses storytelling in circles in which participants share with one another their successes and failures (Tahmincioglu, 2004). What one person has learned can be passed on to the others, thus saving trial-and-error learning for some. The downside is the same as for group processes.

Pluses

- Peers can network.
- Sharing lessons are learned.

Questionable Aspects

- Employees are unlikely to express skill deficiencies in a group.
- Feedback is not specific.
- Competitiveness is increased.
- There is no measurement of results.
- The return may not justify the time invested.

Whether the mentoring pairing is up, down, or sideways, the objective of skill and experience transfer remains the key. As cited in the listings of pluses and questionable aspects above, in some formats this transfer is unlikely to happen.

ECONOMIC IMPACT OF SKILLS LOSS

The lack of basic skills throughout much of the workforce, and the growing shortages of workers with specific skills that are increasingly needed, create a danger that the American economy will drift into what economists call a "low skills equilibrium." . . . [T]his can set in motion a cycle that will have destructive effects throughout our economy, and for a long time to come [Task Force on Workforce Development, 2004. p. 5].

Mentoring processes can be designed and implemented to support a wide range of business imperatives. Technical and professional skills transfers are prime examples. Susan Meisinger, president of the Society for Human Resource Management, cites this skills shortfall as a major reason for "offshoring" and alerts businesses that "A skilled workforce is vital for America's future economic health" (Meisinger, 2004, p. 12). With the imminent retirement of baby boomers in the United States and other countries, there will be a huge loss of investment in intellectual capital. This loss can be avoided by having retirees become mentors and passing on their skills and knowledge before departure.

Cultural Due Diligence

Global firms and organizations hiring employees with widely differing ages, education, cultural experiences, physical abilities, gender, and ethnic backgrounds are experiencing severe impact on results when the lack of awareness and sensitivity to these differences results in breakdowns in communication. Articles in recent professional journals have added religion and sexual preference to the lists of subjects for manager and supervisor training. Even unintentional offenses may result in loss of customers or legal actions. A very common problem is substandard performance due to misunderstanding of assignments when the language or communication style is different. For decades, organizations in the United States have tried mass approaches to these issues with mixed results. The popular social responsibility training of the 1960s, race relations seminars of the 1970s, T-groups of the 1980s, and diversity workshops of the 1990s have for the most part failed or fallen short of desired outcomes. The increasing diversity of the workforce (U.S. Department of Labor, 1999) will necessitate that people value the differences between themselves and others in the organization, and realize that strength comes from having multiple ways of solving problems and seizing opportunities. Preaching at groups of people that they really "oughta wanna" like people who are different from themselves has not worked. Informal mentoring relationships have actually exacerbated the problem, as many self-appointed mentors proceeded to clone themselves in their protégés. Deliberately pairing people who are different in education, age, culture, gender, or whatever has resulted in both partners coming to respect and value their differences. When working together one to one with an agreed goal, it is easier to see the strength that derives from diversity. Mentors who are matched with partners in different countries often comment on how the international experience is helping them communicate with all members of their work teams more effectively.

Professional or Technical Skills Transfer

Rapid changes in technology have leveled the playing field for many businesses. At the same time, those technological advances have made traditional training in group courses or classes less effective and certainly inefficient. When the extant knowledge and skills vary widely, group training that is aimed at the average learner probably hits the mark for only about 15 percent of the participants. The other 85 percent are forced to sit through "nice to know," or irrelevant, content. At the very least, some find the pace too fast, while others are bored with the slowness. Some find the learning process to be of an appropriate style and others are confused or annoyed by it. When training is focused on specific technical or professional skills deficiencies, the motivation to learn is much higher and the process more efficient.

Mentoring processes are often designed to match technicians or professionals who are peers in order to facilitate the transfer of skills two ways. This broader skills base makes each of the participants more flexible and more readily assignable to a different function in the organization. Obviously, this increases their value to the organization as well as their ability to sustain their motivation for peak performance.

KEY ELEMENTS TO MAKING MENTORING WORK

The keys to implementing and sustaining an effective mentoring process track with those of any successful performance-improvement process:

- Identification of need, goal, opportunity, and readiness
- Planning and design: alignment with other performance support and improvement strategies
- Communication to all stakeholders
- Agreements on criteria for matching mentors and mentees
- Orientations and training for participants
- Development plans, which are essential to healthy relationships
- Evaluation and continuous improvement

The types of organizations that have implemented facilitated mentoring processes run the gamut from those in the aerospace industry to universities. The added business value they seek varies just as widely. The following notable examples were selected from more than fifty organizations that I have studied, all of which have facilitated mentoring processes in place.

Banking: When a rapidly growing bank put an aggressive marketing strategy in place, it changed the core skill sets required of officers and managers. New managers with marketing and sales experience and skills were recruited from financial institutions such as brokerage firms, from sales jobs in real estate, and from management positions in retail merchandising. The gaps in their experience and skills were in the banking services and products (Wells Fargo Bank, 1998). A "map" of development was designed involving mentors, who coach on specific skills needed as well as help put into the context of retail banking the competencies already possessed by the new managers.

Community foundation: Even before the federal laws were passed to limit the time that welfare benefits would be provided to needy families, some community foundations saw a need to help people develop job seeking and keeping skills. In a midwestern city a community group obtained funding from the Kellogg Foundation to pilot test a mentoring process for women on welfare.

The targeted women were each matched with a successful—that is, employed—female mentor. Formal training sessions were scheduled for the mentors and mentees; their subjects ranged from home expense budgeting to how to resist an aggressive salesperson at the door. Mentees reported successes in obtaining jobs, going back to school, and ending abusive personal relationships.

Computer manufacture, sales, and service: A large computer manufacturing company's reengineering efforts created a strategy of customer solution selling, to improve results in this highly competitive industry. Previously, there were specialists with hardware, software, and customer services skills. The mentoring process matched these specialists across functions to enable them to transfer their special skills and experiences. The lead coordinator reported that on eleven essential job skills, protégés increased their measured skill levels by an average of 61 percent (Duncan, 1995). In addition, these participants demonstrated measured gains in nine of eleven career-effectiveness skills measured with a skills-assessment instrument.

Financial: The credit card division of a bank experienced unacceptably high turnover in the Customer Service Representative position. Quality and productivity results were also below standards. A comprehensive job and task analysis revealed that all new hires were scheduled for twenty days of training in a lock-step-format, trainer-led and -paced program. The target population analysis showed that many of the new hires had extensive customer service experience, some had strong computer skills, and a few had actual credit card product knowledge. The training format was revised to be learner-oriented, with a combination of trainer modeling, self-study with print materials and computer help screens, and coaching with a mentor. Areas for mentor coaching included defusing the anger of customers with questions about their bills, navigating through complicated computer screens of customer history, and job performance planning with supervisors. In less than six months the average training time dropped to fourteen days, retention of desired employees increased, and the quality of service improved.

Health care product distribution: In a health care product warehouse, a mentoring process was implemented to improve retention of warehouse workers and to improve communication across functions. Results were that 18 percent of the warehouse workers were promoted or made lateral moves into other functions in the company in the first year (Garcia, 1994).

Highway engineering: An aging workforce in manager and higher-level administrator ranks caused an engineering agency to examine why they were losing bright young engineers after four years on the job. The formal training ran about twenty-seven months, so these losses meant a high cost to the agency. Employees saw that older, longer-service people tended to identify and bring along people very much like themselves in terms of education, gender, and ethnicity. The message sent to those outside that group was that there would be no opportunity for them, so they left. The regional administrator made the decision to implement a mentoring process that would make these valuable developmental experiences equitably available to everyone in the organization.

Information systems: I was asked to train mentors for a supplier of large-scale information systems. The average sales cycle was nine months. Mentors were experienced salespeople, and it was thought that they would not be willing to coach new salespeople for fear of adding to the competition for their own jobs. The orientation workshops for these mentors communicated the benefits they would get from taking on this added role. One mentor joyfully related to other mentors that his partner, or protégé, closed her first big deal in just three weeks!

RETURN ON INVESTMENT: PERCEPTION AND REALITY

Since 1971, I have conducted workshops and collaborated with clients on implementation of mentoring processes in Argentina, Australia, Egypt, Ethiopia, Finland, India, Ireland, Korea, Pakistan, Philippines, Taiwan, Trinidad, The Netherlands, Sweden, the United States, and Venezuela. In the *readiness assessment* phase of this work, we ask clients to identify expected benefits to mentors, protégés, and the organization. At the beginning it is essential to dispel prevailing myths and clarify whether expectations can become reality. This process also enables us to capture baseline data for evaluation of the unique benefits of mentoring to an organization and the participants.

Unless a clear linkage can be made to organizational goals, needs, and opportunities, it is highly unlikely that a mentoring process will survive. Unique benefits to the supervisors or team leaders of both mentors and protégés are often overlooked.

In the following paragraphs are a few examples of the many benefits reported by mentoring participants in many countries in a wide range of organizations, such as manufacturers, oil refineries, municipal and superior courts, telecommunication, transportation, financial, and many others.

Benefits to protégés are the first to come to mind. These benefits are expressed in various ways in the organizations and cultures within which we work. The following results have been measured through analysis of development plans, checkpoint surveys, and self-report of participants. They are grouped into some specific categories, with verbatim comments noted.

Greater understanding of business objectives: Increased organization awareness and a clearer understanding of corporate culture and goals are often cited as gains by participants in mentoring processes. Exploring these phenomena revealed that mentors are much more likely to provide information on the mission, goals, and future direction of the organization than are line supervisors.

Some protégés also describe a deeper sense of accountability and feeling that their contributions matter.

Focused development: When learning activities are focused on specific diagnosed needs, skill development is far more effective and efficient. Learning from a mentor's experience avoids costly and demotivating trial and error. Mentors can put into context the importance of training, which fosters more rapid use of relevant skills. One protégé in a small engineering firm said, "In one hour of coaching with my mentor I solved some problems I had been struggling with for four months."

Learning in a nonthreatening environment and process: Fear is a fierce obstacle to learning. Few of us would tell our bosses about all of our weaknesses or lack of experience. Mentors provide safe environments to practice skills. "I found it was OK to be wrong, learn from my mistakes, and ask stupid questions. I could be real."

Productivity: Appraisal and evaluation ratings are higher. This may be partly attributable to the protégés' greater skills with planning, negotiation, and feedback when interacting with their supervisors. Another possible variable is the "Hawthorne effect," that any extra attention improves performance (Franke and Kaul, 1978).[1]

Possible advancement: Advancement is accelerated with guided career paths and without time-consuming, irrelevant assignments. With clarity of direction, people are more likely to develop skills for taking on greater responsibilities. Even when there are few promotional opportunities, greater competence, confidence, and visibility make people more competitive for every opportunity. The Tasmanian Department of Justice perceived that women were not competing successfully for management positions. Development plans included a combination of individual coaching with mentors and group training in areas of common needs. Evaluation after twelve months showed that three mentees, or protégés, had taken up extra tertiary studies; two had been transferred to more challenging positions; one was promoted to middle management; and one had been reclassified to a higher grade level.

Political savvy: Participants report they gain greater insight into the maze of politics in their organizations. This makes them feel more confident and powerful as the mentoring process accelerates their acceptance as an insider.

Career resiliency: "The smart and successful will be preparing for career resiliency" ("Margo Murray on Mentoring," 2002, p. 1). Directed learning activities shorten the cycle time in gaining experience to work effectively in different functions. When changes in markets, products, services, or the economy cause some functions, or entire jobs, to disappear, people with broader experience and multiple skills will land on their feet in a different function or a new organization.

Increased visibility: With the hectic pace of demanding jobs, line managers are, perhaps understandably, lax in giving each of their subordinates the visibility and exposure that may be beneficial. "In the mentoring process I feel noticed and visible; it has expanded my network base immensely."

Increased valuing of diversity: Exposure to different cultures broadens our understanding of the increased strength of varied approaches. A very weak organization is created when everyone is educated in the same schools, solves problems in the same way, and has the same narrow view of the world.

Team building: Learning to work closely with another person tends to make it easier to be a contributing member or a leader of a team. "I found that it strengthened my ability to work more effectively with my team."

Fuzzier benefits reported by protégé participants: "It was good to have a sounding board," "Gives me another avenue for information," new friendships, fun, "I feel that the organization cares about me," "I feel welcomed," increased loyalty, receipt of honest feedback, "My mentor had more confidence in me than I had in myself."

Benefits for the Mentor

One of the greatest challenges for a performance technologist in implementing and sustaining a mentoring process is the task of recruiting good mentors. In Finland and Canada, we found that shy people were reluctant to volunteer as mentors yet readily agreed when invited to participate. Even more of a challenge is how to reward mentors in appropriate ways to maintain their motivation to keep agreements with their partners. Some of the key personal and professional motivators a facilitated program can offer are the following.

Enhanced influence in the organization: Mentors are respected for the value they add in the development of future leaders of the organization. Mentors extend their influence on the mission and direction of the organization through their partners.

Developmental needs of the mentors are met: The mentor's skills in coaching, performance planning, and feedback are honed by working with protégés with varied skills and experiences. Protégés often teach their mentors new skills.

Professional assistance on work projects: The protégé may have a technical skill relevant to a project the mentor wants to have done. When a task can be taken as a learning experience by the protégé, additional work is accomplished for the mentor, although I caution that such tasks must be relevant to the development objectives of the protégé, not just working as an extra pair of hands for the mentor. As a mentor once said, "I am amazed at the creative and innovative input the protégé brought to this project."

Maintenance of motivation: "I was just burned out with more and more of the same old work," stated one mentor. "The fresh viewpoint of my partner sparked my enthusiasm and motivation."

New perspectives about the organization from the protégé's fresh point of view: Often managers and executives are shielded from problems at operating levels when there is fear among employees that the messenger will be shot.

Problems and issues are more openly discussed when there is a bond of trust with a mentor.

Having ideas challenged: Experienced and competent people may become complacent about decisions they make and strategies they use. It can be a career-limiting move for a subordinate to challenge a superior's decisions or actions. Working with a protégé who asks *why* something is done a particular way may cause the mentor to examine approaches used and find they are outdated and ineffective. Many mentors urge their partners to challenge their thinking, and apparently enjoy the intellectual exercise more than the passive "Yes, boss" often heard from their direct reports.

Organizational Benefits

In lean times, and when most organizations are trying to do more with less to stay competitive, no program will be supported unless it contributes to the overall desired results.

Our thirty-plus years of experience and current research reveal some significant and exciting outcomes of *facilitated* mentoring relationships. The impact on the work environments as a result of mentoring experiences is remarkable. When people are more competent, knowledgeable, and confident, they contribute more to the bottom-line results of the organization. In Finland a female lawyer new to the banking world was responsible for specific reform projects in the bank. A chief with extensive experience outside banking and now in bank management was matched as her mentor. They acknowledged the value of the experience: "We discussed many ideas at first felt to be too wild, then brought them into concrete forms." As a result of this collaboration, costly projects unsuitable to the banking environment were avoided (Petäjäniemi and Mansukoski, 1998).

Multiskilled, flexible people add greater value to downsized, leaner, and flatter organizations. They can move across functions and work with different technologies. Furthermore, they are more loyal to the organization, more likely to sustain their own motivation, and more likely to support necessary change.

Organizations are now implementing evaluation processes to measure the impact of the mentoring process on the organizations' results, as well as on the skills and experience levels of the protégés and the mentors. Following are some of the measured results attained in facilitated mentoring processes.

Increased productivity: Improved performance and productivity are reported by both mentors and protégés. Protégés' skills are strengthened, enabling them to work more effectively and efficiently. Developmental projects carried out by protégés often assist mentors with their work.

Cost-effective development of skills: Most mentors report that the coaching of protégés is done on their own time, at no out-of-pocket cost for the organization. When mentoring is used as an alternative training strategy, employees get to competency quicker at less cost than in classroom training formats. When training is individually based and self-paced, it is "just in time" training.

Cost avoidance: The Sacramento Superior and Municipal Courts reported savings of over $6,000 when a protégé working with a mentor to prepare for the job of electronic recording monitor discovered that she did not like or want the job (Capaul, 1996). Terminating the six-week training process after short meetings between the protégé and the mentor not only saved the courts potential training costs, it saved the self-esteem and job satisfaction of the protégé, who avoided a wrong career move.

Recruitment efforts: Prospective employees are attracted to a firm that offers facilitated growth and development. A recruiter told me he interviewed more than one hundred business school graduates for management trainee positions in a large paper pulp manufacturing business in Canada. He was surprised to hear two-thirds of them ask if the company had a mentoring process.

Increased retention: The best and brightest people stay with a company that cares about their development. A doctoral dissertation study of high-technology firms revealed it cost $577,000 to replace an entry-level engineer who left after one year (Melnarik, 1998). Although the high-tech job situation has changed drastically since that study, the cost of replacing contributing employees is still significant. Alternatively, with better career counseling, sometimes the people who are good losses leave sooner.

Enhanced image of the organization: Public recognition that the organization provides a caring, developmental environment, including a mentoring process, can enhance the corporate image. Most of the "Top 100 Companies" have mentoring processes in place (Barbian, 2002, p. 38).

Achieving strategic goals: In the performance-improvement projects we have carried out, the evaluations show that organization results are better when everyone knows the targets. Sharing mentors' experiences helps others avoid making the same mistakes. More competent and confident employees produce better results, creating a competitive edge. During a time of rapid change in one company a participant commented, "This process gave us an element of stability, and gave me an anchor, in a time of chaos."

Benefits to Supervisors

It often surprises coordinators to find that supervisors of protégés recognize that they can benefit directly by having their people work with a mentor. This is a sensitive area, and a potential pitfall, if not managed well. It is essential that all managers and supervisors of intended participants be briefed on what the mentoring process is and is not, and on the roles and responsibilities of all participants. Otherwise, it is easy for the supervisor to feel resentment and to feel threatened by having this third person involved with a subordinate.

Supervisors have reported these types of benefits: "It gave me another resource for supporting employee development." "I'm stretched pretty thin with day-to-day operations and have little time for people's career development; this helped." "I was promoted to this job on the basis of my technical expertise, and have had no training in career development stuff." "My employee got better with performance planning and communicating with me. That helped both of us." From one organization I received a copy of a message sent from the supervisor to the mentor expressing thanks for helping with a serious communication and motivation problem that the supervisor had not been able to handle.

PITFALLS AND PREVENTIVE ACTIONS

In workshops I facilitate at international conferences, I often ask the audience to play a game of "Ain't It Awful!" With any new idea or intervention, you can always count on someone to counter the proposal immediately with, "Yes, but it won't work here because. . . ." Brainstorming about "ain't it awful, that won't work here" surfaces potential pitfalls. Once these pitfalls are articulated, they can be tackled with one or more problem-solving strategies to determine how to prevent them from jeopardizing the potential success of the new program. Following are just a few of the potential pitfalls, and the strategies that may prevent them, gleaned from work done by many dedicated coordination team members in the MMHA Mentoring Coordinator Development Institute.

Pitfall: It has been tried before.

- Clarify exactly what the facilitated mentoring process is.
- Get people who are pro and con involved in development.
- Show that mentoring is what our competitors are doing.

Pitfall: There is a lack of adequate resources.

- Show proof that it reduces training costs.
- Relate benefits to organization goals and objectives.
- Present a success case: best practice, benchmarking.
- Show cost avoidance with better retention of staff.

Pitfall: Protégés are not willing to risk being open.

- Have the pair sign a confidentiality agreement.
- Establish level of disclosure on both sides.

Pitfall: Program is viewed as for certain people; it is exclusive.

- Clearly define the business case for the process.

- Establish clear, thorough communication as to what it is and what it is not.
- Align the mentoring process as one human resource strategy.
- Offer resources used in the process to others.

Pitfall: There is a lack of mentors.

- Provide a clear process for volunteering.
- Communicate the benefits for mentors.
- Protégés nominate several choices to be mentor.
- Tie performance as a mentor to the mentors' key results areas and reviews.

Pitfall: The ideal or only pairing is across a great geographical distance.

- Leverage technology: use e-mail, faxes, and telephones.
- Establish a budget for travel.
- Schedule coaching sessions during other meetings or vacations.

Pitfall: There is potential for the "tall poppy" or "heir apparent" syndrome.

- Use briefings to communicate goals and objectives.
- Design for open entry, open exit, and individual applications.
- Get all stakeholders involved in the process.

Pitfall: There is conflict between the mentor and the protégé's supervisor.

- Clearly define roles and responsibilities.
- Emphasize benefits to both.
- Communicate the rewards for the supervisor.

Pitfall: It is difficult to maintain mentor commitment.

- Review "1001 Ways to Reward and Recognize."
- Provide formal evaluation and credit.
- Reward with "face time" with executive who has status.
- Tie to team performance bonus.

Pitfall: It is seen as the "flavor of the month" or a "magic potion."

- Link to organization goals.
- Make it a consistent part of management responsibility.
- Be sure the process includes regular reviews, publicized successes.
- Get high-level support for three years minimum.
- Show how mentoring is aligned with other human performance technology strategies.
- Provide feedback on results, success stories.

One pitfall in any mentoring process, whether pairings are facilitated or informal, is that the mentor may take on an advocacy role for the protégé. Organization policies may restrict the extent of this advocacy. For example, in one federal agency, a board or panel of administrators decides all promotions. The mentoring process guidelines explicitly prohibit any mentor from participating on the promotion board when that mentor's protégé is a candidate for the promotion.

A more likely situation is that the protégé expects the mentor to take on the advocacy role. The role of the mentor is a critical subject in discussion of the agreement between the pair. When no policies constrain such advocacy, the mentor must describe exactly how support for the protégé may be demonstrated.

SYSTEMATIC DESIGN

Analysis: This phase of the "front end" work we have chosen to call a "readiness assessment." Some organizations want to have a mentoring process in place just to say they have one, whether or not it fills an assessed need. Performance technologists have learned, sometimes by bitter experience, that a client often wants something that is not necessarily needed. To avoid the obvious turn-off of a client, and the loss of business, calling the needs assessment a readiness assessment is often more acceptable. The purpose is still to determine the needs, goals, and opportunities the organization is facing when considering a facilitated mentoring process. This assessment includes scanning the work environment to identify commitment to and support for mentoring, as well as any indicators of resistance or objection to the proposed process. We strive to interview the top managers, administrators, decision makers, and opinion setters in one-to-one sessions. The objective is to get the widest range of opinions and expectations. In addition, we elicit data on goals, needs, and opportunities the organization is facing that may or may not be supported by a mentoring process.

Design and production: One of the critical success factors for mentoring is that the process be designed to fit the environment and culture of each unique organization and the identified target populations of participants. As with any performance-improvement intervention, it is essential to conduct a pilot test of the design and implementation processes to ensure they will achieve desired outcomes reliably. Good instructional design strategies are vital to selecting and producing the relevant and adequate resources needed by participants. For example, mentors matched with a protégé on the basis of the protégé's job-specific skill deficiency may lack the requisite skills in coaching and feedback, making it necessary to design skill practices to fill these gaps.

Data gathered in the readiness assessment phase enables us to design relevant briefings and orientations for the mentoring process participants.

Implementation: Any instructional or nontraining performance-improvement intervention must have an implementation plan. A critical success factor for a mentoring process is a communication plan, which ensures that everyone who needs to know something about the mentoring process gets that information on a timely basis. A well-designed mentoring process has a coordination team to administer it and ensure that it is sustained as a viable strategy for improving human performance and results.

Evaluation and continuous improvement: Evaluation of mentoring processes, and mentors, may take several forms. First, an evaluation process for the process itself must be planned at the beginning. Key baseline data must be captured before information about the proposed process begins to contaminate it (Murray, 1991, 2001a). The evaluation plan must be crafted to capture only data you intend to use. Begin by asking the question, What will we do with the data?

Examples of useful data include those needed to

- Report impact of the process on organization results
- Continuously improve the design of the process
- Determine that the mentoring pairs are meeting development objectives in the transfer of skills and experiences

In addition, mentors' effectiveness must be evaluated by the mentor and protégé jointly agreeing on progress in transferring skills, willingness to share information, and the degree to which agreements about time and focus are kept.

CHALLENGES OF SCALING UP

When a mentoring process pilot has resulted in benefit to the organization and the participants, most want to expand the process to include key groups of employees. Some believe it is only fair to open the process to all employees. This presents a challenge when the workforce numbers in the thousands. Some organizations have implemented software systems to allow participants to create their own matches on-line. The results are mixed. Protégés do have more control over whom they seek as a mentor. However, they may choose because they want a sponsor rather than on the basis of assessed skill deficiencies. Popular mentors are often overwhelmed with requests. Some who are not well-suited to the mentor role do volunteer. The initial match is only the first step in the process. If the participants are not prepared for a successful interaction—orientation and training—they will not have a good experience. "Training both mentors and mentorees for their roles in the mentoring process is vital to the success of the program . . ." (Drahosz, 2004, p. 101).

An on-line matching process was implemented by one of the U.S. military branches in 2000, and has continued to be available. We were told by the administrator that usage by participants is not tracked or evaluated.

When there is no monitoring and tracking of what is happening with the pair, many of the pitfalls described above are likely to occur. Worse yet, with no evaluation there is no evidence that the several-thousand-dollar investments had any meaningful return.

CONCLUSION

Probably the most beneficial application of a mentoring process in the near future will be selecting mentors to transfer tacit knowledge. Every organization has an enormous investment in the intellectual capital of its experienced employees. Knowledge management, including the systematic cost containment of intellectual capital, will be demanded of the executive team by astute corporate boards of directors.

Results of mentoring processes are not accidental; they do not happen by chance or magic. The key to ensuring desired results and continuity of the mentoring process is to use all the best practices of human performance technology in the needs assessment, planning, design, implementation, and evaluation stages. Mentoring must be closely linked to the mission, goals, and priority strategies of the organization. Standalone programs are extremely vulnerable to economic downturns, budget cuts, and changes of affection. Only integrated, facilitated processes linked to current and future mission and business imperatives can be expected to stand the buffeting of the winds of change. Rapidly changing environments demand multiskilled, flexible workers, and mastery levels of core competencies. A mentoring process facilitates the essential performance improvement.

Note

1. Individual behaviors may be altered because the performers know they are being studied. This phenomenon was demonstrated in a research project (1927–1932) at the Hawthorne Plant of the Western Electric Company in Cicero, Illinois. This result of this series of research studies, first led by Harvard Business School professor Elton Mayo, is commonly called the Hawthorne Effect.

References

Barbian, J. (2002, March). A little help from your friends. *Training, 39*(3), 38.

Capaul, J. (1996, Winter). *Mentoring applied: A successful self-implementation.* Retrieved October 28, 2005, from MMHA The Managers' Mentors Web site: http://www.mentors-mmha.com/newsletter2.html.

Drahosz, K. W. (2004). *The keys to mentoring success.* Washington, DC: The Training Connection.

Duncan, M. (1995, Fall). Mentoring applied. *Manager's Mentor,* pp. 1–3.

Ellis, K. (2004, December). Individual development plans: The building blocks of development. *Training, 41*(12), 20–25.

Franke, R. H., and Kaul, J. D. (1978). The Hawthorne experiments: First statistical interpretation. *American Sociological Review, 43,* 623–643.

Garcia, J. (1994, April). *The mentoring experience.* Rocklin, CA: Whitmire Distribution Corporation.

Margo Murray on mentoring. (2002, June). *Allstate Insurance Newsletter,* p. 1.

Meisinger, S. (2004, November). Shortage of skilled workers threatens economy. *HR Magazine, 49*(11), 12.

Melnarik, C. S. (1998). *Retaining high-tech professionals: Constructive and destructive responses to job dissatisfaction among electrical engineers and non-engineering professionals.* Unpublished Doctoral Dissertation, Walden University, Minneapolis.

Murray, M. (1991). *Beyond the myths and magic of mentoring: How to facilitate an effective mentoring program.* San Francisco: Jossey-Bass.

Murray, M. (2001a). *Beyond the myths and magic of mentoring: How to facilitate an effective mentoring process* (2nd ed.). San Francisco: Jossey-Bass.

Murray, M. (2001b, March). Energizing employees with mentoring: They keep staying, and staying, and staying. . . . *Performance Improvement, 40*(3), 34–38.

Petäjäniemi, T., and Mansukoski, S. (1998). *Mentorointi* (Author interview with program director). Finnish Institute of Public Management, Helsinki, Finland.

Tahmincioglu, E. (2004, November). Logging on to link mentors, proteges; Keyword: matchmaking. *Workforce Management Online.* Retrieved November 30, 2004, from www.workforce.com/section/11/feature/23/89/52/index.html.

Task Force on Workplace Development. (2004, April 20). *Learning partnerships: Strengthening American jobs in the global economy.* Washington, DC: The Albert Shanker Institute and The New Economy Information Service. Retrieved May 18, 2005, from www.ashankerinst.org/Downloads/TF%20Report%20Apr-2004.pdf.

U.S. Department of Labor. (1999). *The state of the American worker.* Annual Report, Fiscal Year 1999. Washington, DC: Government Printing Office.

Wells Fargo Bank. (1998, January). *Corporate officer development* (Performance improvement consulting project). Oakland, CA: MMHA The Managers' Mentors.

Witt, L. (2004, September 28). Answer central: Entrepreneurs can have mentors, too. *Fortune Small Business.* Retrieved May 16, 2005, from www.fortune.com/fortune/smallbusiness/answercentral/0,15704,702741,00.html.

CHAPTER TWENTY

Motivating Individuals, Teams, and Organizations

Richard E. Clark

*Motivation is [defined] in terms of selection
of pursuits from competing alternatives, intensity
of effort, and persistence of exertion.*
—Bandura, 1991, p. 158

Solid evidence supports both the need for and the benefits of motivational programs at work. For the past two decades the most comprehensive surveys of attitudes toward work demonstrate a disturbing but consistent lack of motivation among employees at all levels in all types of organizations. Approximately 50 percent of North American workers confess that they do only the minimum to avoid being fired, and about 80 percent admit that they could work "much harder" (Spitzer, 1995; Buckingham and Coffman, 1999). Popular wisdom would suggest that managers in top organizations are more motivated than line workers, but this seems not to be the case. In two recent combined surveys of eighty thousand managers in four hundred organizations, the Gallup Organization found that the motivation of managers is as low as that of the people they supervise (Buckingham and Coffman, 1999). Other studies have reported clear links between organizational change cycles and work motivation, suggesting that as the momentum and extent of organizational change increase over time, work motivation decreases (Storseth, 2002).

Another body of studies testing different motivational strategies, conducted in small and large organizations, supports the claim that a well-designed and

---

Some of the ideas presented in this article are taken from R. E. Clark and F. Estes, *Turning Research into Results: A Guide to Selecting the Right Performance Solutions,* Atlanta, CEP Press, 2002; from R. E. Clark, "Fostering the Work Motivation of Individuals and Teams," *Performance Improvement,* 2003a, *42*(3), pp. 21–29; and from other published and unpublished work by the author. Please address questions or comments to Richard Clark by e-mail at clark@usc.edu.

carefully implemented motivational program can have a very positive effect on performance. Condly, Clark, and Stolovitch (2003) reviewed all well-designed motivation studies conducted in business and government settings and reported that when employees were offered money for improving their performance, individual performance increased an average of 20 percent over the short term, about three months, and over 40 percent in longer-term programs, from six months to a year. Even more dramatic was their report that team performance increased over 40 percent, even in short-term programs. Similar reports of performance benefits from motivational programs have been described in book-length reviews by Bandura (1997), Buckingham and Coffman (1999), Clark and Estes (2002), and Pintrich and Schunk (2002).

Because nearly all performance-improvement efforts are currently focused on training, we should be asking about the relative increase in performance benefits we could expect from adding motivational-improvement programs to our organizational toolkits. A recent comprehensive review by Arthur, Bennett, Edens, and Bell (2003) of research on the impact of training on performance over the past forty years reported an average 19 percent performance gain overall. The percent gain was lower in studies that were more adequately designed. The authors pointed to evidence that the factor that seemed to prevent training from having a greater impact on performance was the motivation to transfer and use the skills that had been learned. The greatest benefit they reported was in the area of interpersonal skills training, which resulted in a 27 percent performance gain.

It appears that motivation programs are at least as effective as training in boosting performance by individuals and teams. While most large organizations have formal training units and make a considerable investment in training each year, motivation seems not to be on anyone's radar at the moment. Is motivation the vehicle that will take us to the next level in performance improvement? The purpose of this chapter is to provide a current overview of what we know about work motivation. After defining motivation and describing how to identify a motivation opportunity, the causes of and solutions to a number of common motivational issues will be discussed. An attempt will be made to distinguish between individual, team, and organizational motivation issues.

WHAT IS MOTIVATION?

All motivational performance analyses begin by examining progress on three goals: starting, persisting, and investing mental effort. Motivational performance gaps occur when performance goals are not achieved because of problems with one of the three motivational goals: (1) when we avoid starting or refuse to start something new, or something familiar that we have not done for some time, this is an active-choice failure; (2) when we stop or pause when working on something that is important and switch our attention to a different task, this is a persistence failure; and (3) when we refuse to work smart and invest mental effort to succeed at a novel challenge and instead use old and familiar but inadequate solutions to solve a new problem, this is a mental effort failure (Clark, 1999; Pintrich and Schunk, 2002). According to most of the top experts in motivation, one or more of these three conditions must exist for us to say we have encountered a motivation problem or opportunity. Motivation is the psychological and social process that starts and maintains goal-directed performance. It energizes our thinking, fuels our enthusiasm, and colors our positive and negative emotional reactions to our surroundings. Motivation helps us generate the mental effort that drives the application of our knowledge and skills to solve problems and seek opportunities. When we need to learn something new to achieve a goal, motivation provides the initiative and keeps us moving when we encounter difficulties. Without motivation, even the most capable expert will fail. Motivation nudges us to convert intention into action and start doing something new or to restart something we have stopped. It also controls our decision to persist at a specific work goal in the face of distractions and competing priorities. Finally, motivation leads us to invest more or less mental and physical effort to enhance both the quality and quantity of our work.

It is crucial to note that motivation does not directly influence work performance. Instead, motivation leads us to use our knowledge and skills and apply them effectively to work tasks. It is the force that initiates, starts, energizes, and continues the application of our experience and expertise. Successful performance always involves the cooperation of motivation and knowledge in supportive work environments. Without adequate knowledge, motivation alone does not increase useful performance. Thus, adequate motivation is necessary but not sufficient for effective performance.

What Causes Motivation?

After more than a century of research and argument, motivation researchers and practitioners now begin to agree that nearly everyone is willing to start, persist, and invest maximum effort in activities that they believe will make them more successful and effective. Whatever we think gives us more control is motivating, and, conversely, whatever takes away our control limits or destroys our motivation. We all value the goals, working conditions, and incentives that we believe will contribute to our success. We avoid situations that will prevent us from achieving our goals. For example, money is a nearly universal motivator because it can be exchanged for most, if not all, of the things most people define as "success." Whether we call motivational tools "reinforcement," "incentives," "drivers," "inducements," or some other quasi-technical name, they only motivate when they are perceived as giving us more control and making us more successful or effective. Conversely, we avoid conditions that we think will delay, inhibit, or prevent control or success.

What makes motivation a complex issue is that different individuals, groups, and cultures have very different beliefs about what exactly defines control, success, or effectiveness. People working in teams may define success differently than when they are working alone. The same person may be motivated very differently in different settings; for example, when he or she is with family as opposed to relaxing with friends, or working at his or her job as opposed to volunteering services in the community. Each of these settings might present a significantly different set of motivational expectations. While our multicultural workforce may add variety that further complicates motivational planning, even people who are members of the same family or culture express a dizzying variety of individual definitions of "success" and "beliefs" about the factors that enable and inhibit success.

One way to think about the many personality types described by the Myers Briggs Type Indicator, the "Big Five" (Digman, 1990), and many of the other working and thinking style measures available today is that they reflect our personal values. Some people value reflective, analytical, and organized approaches while others value impulsive, expressive, and intuitive strategies. Some people who are confronted with barriers decide to stand fast and overcome them, and others quickly decide to avoid and withdraw. Many people work for money and recognition, and others work for the sheer joy of doing something well or learning something new. Some of us are very effective at regulating our own motivation by ignoring demotivators and creating the conditions that lead to personal success. Nearly all of us depend on coaches and friends for occasional motivational support. Most of us work with different values and styles in different situations. How can we make sense of such breathtaking variety and turn it to our benefit as performance technologists?

In any given situation in which we want to increase work motivation, we must determine what will convince people to start doing something new or different, increase their persistence at an important task, and invest mental effort. They must believe that the motivator driving their enhanced performance will directly or indirectly contribute significantly to what they need to feel successful and effective. The motivator that works has to cost less than the value of the increased performance, and it must meet current ethical and legal requirements. While it might appear that motivators have to be tailored to the different "here and now" demands of individuals, in fact there are more or less universally effective motivators and demotivators. It appears that there are a finite number of powerful, cost-effective, ethical, and legal strategies for increasing work motivation for nearly everyone. The list begins with common organizational practices that have been found to destroy motivation for many people and ways to eliminate them.

1. Act in a way that is perceived as dishonest, hypocritical, or unfair.

2. Provide vague, impossible, and constantly changing performance goals.

3. Impose arbitrary and unnecessary rules, policies, and work processes.

4. Support constant competition among everyone in the organization.

5. Point out people's mistakes and criticize them for errors.

Figure 20.1. Five Motivation Killers.

What Kills Motivation in Organizations?

There are at least five elements of work environments that most researchers agree are the main destroyers of motivation (see Figure 20.1).

While a discussion of what kills motivation is a negative exercise, it is critical to emphasize that some very common and popular features of organizations hurt the work motivation of many people who work in them. Among the most common motivation killers are the following five practices:

1. Act in a Way That Is Perceived as Dishonest, Hypocritical, or Unfair. Organizations and individuals do not have to lie or cheat or be unfair; they only have to be perceived to be doing so to destroy motivation. Managers often feel that they must tell "innocent untruths," refuse to keep promises as work conditions change, and favor their friends or punish their enemies. Most of us do not believe that when we do these things we are perceived by many people to be "lying" or being "hypocritical" or "unfair." People at work are all adults, right? This is the way the world works, so get over it, right? Yet what we think about our own behavior is much less important than how our behavior is perceived by those around us. The real question is whether or not we want to act in a way that conforms to our beliefs about organizations and how they work or act in a way that is effective because it motivates people to perform better.

Private perceptions control personal motivation. When people perceive their treatment as unfair, dishonest, or hypocritical, the best we can hope for is that they will act maturely, ignore those conditions, and work hard despite it all. Yet even the most mature people are not going to work as hard when they experience dishonest and unfair behavior directed at them personally. Trust is difficult to gain and very easy to lose. Typically, organizational dishonesty and unfairness are viewed as an invitation to respond in the same manner (Bandura, 1997). Motivation is enhanced when everyone in an organization avoids even the appearance of unfairness, prejudice, dishonesty, or hypocrisy.

2. Provide Vague, Impossible, and Constantly Changing Performance Goals. Vagueness and inconsistency in a work environment lead most people to assume that anything goes. Impossible "stretch goals" also damage motivation (Locke and Latham, 2002). While experienced and mature people assume that the stretch goals are only urging them to work harder, impossible-to-achieve goals damage motivation for most. Goals must be challenging and difficult; easy goals are not motivating despite what some people believe. Work goals should not be described in a way that leads people to perceive them as impossible to achieve. Vague goals are as destructive as impossible goals. In the absence of a clear vision leading to well-defined business and performance goals, people substitute their own goals, and their goals may not support the organization. Without clear performance goals and feedback, people are not committed to work and are not inclined to give their best effort (Locke and Latham, 2002). Increased work motivation is supported by concrete and challenging work goals that are focused on the near term; that is, today, this week, or this month.

3. Impose Arbitrary and Unnecessary Rules, Policies, and Work Processes. Many studies point to the huge variety of arbitrary, disliked, and seemingly unnecessary rules and cumbersome policies as one of the major demotivators at work (for example, Spitzer, 1995). Why not ask people which work rules they dislike the most and, if changed, would motivate them to work harder and increase their commitment to their jobs and the organization? Check to see what evidence exists for the benefit of very unpopular rules and be clear about the trade-off between what might be lost if they were eliminated and what is gained if they are maintained. For example, what is gained from rules that prevent people from decorating their workspace in ways that suit them? Do we have solid evidence, beyond our preferences, that dress codes are necessary and that they add significant value to a business? How many of these rules stem from preferences or arbitrary decisions about taste that have no business value? How much of people's behavior must you control to achieve business goals? Even the most competent and personally motivated people tend to quit trying in the face of what they perceive to be arbitrary barriers. One way to motivate people and simplify organizational work processes is to eliminate all unnecessary and arbitrary rules, policies, and procedures.

4. Support Constant Competition among Everyone in the Organization. Focused competition with competing organizations is a very motivating experience for most people. Competition within an organization produces mixed results. While salespeople seem to thrive on it, there are many instances when internal competition between individuals and work teams has harmed organizations. Constant, intense rivalry within an organization is most often destructive because it focuses attention and energy away from business goals. For example, the U.S. National

Academy of Sciences surveyed all of the research on organizational team-building strategies (Druckman and Bjork, 1994). The performance-improvement methods they surveyed attempted to get members of work teams to bond, collaborate, and work efficiently toward common goals by competing with other teams. When the Academy released its findings, it was surprising to learn that many of the most popular team-building programs had succeeded in increasing collaboration and cooperation among team members, but the teams were competing in a nearly suicidal fashion with other teams in the same organization. This type of misdirected, competitive behavior at work happens in many contexts. Organizations should consider the possible unintended side effects of encouraging wide-scale internal competition. A more motivational approach to competition within an organization is to encourage people to compete with themselves by asking them to exceed their own personal best in critical areas of their job.

5. Point Out People's Mistakes and Criticize Them for Errors. Too many managers seem to believe that to "keep people on their toes" they have to watch carefully until someone makes a mistake and then jump on them. Or, to "keep people in line," remind them of their past mistakes whenever they are acting independently or seem overly satisfied with something they have done. Both of these strategies are motivation killers. When most people are faced with negative, critical feedback, they react with anger or feel depressed, and many simply stop trying. Negative emotion is not only a notorious motivation killer, it also leads to acts of revenge. Buckingham and Coffman (1999) reported that about 17 percent of the managers in their sample were so angry at the way they had been treated that that they were actively trying to hurt the organization.

Two comprehensive international reviews of performance feedback research studies found that negative feedback that focused on mistakes actually depressed performance (Kluger and DiNisi, 1998; Bandura and Locke, 2003). This happened in one-third of all feedback research studies conducted both in natural settings and in the laboratory. In another third of the studies, vague performance feedback had no impact. Feedback improved performance in only one-third of the studies. Effective performance feedback was focused on describing and closing the gap between goals and current performance. When feedback emphasizes negative qualities of the performer, performance deteriorates. The finding that poor feedback was obvious in two-thirds of all well-planned research studies suggests that it may even be more prevalent in practice, since researchers tend to select typical strategies to test in experiments. Motivate people by giving them feedback that begins with descriptions of what they have accomplished and the goal they were attempting to reach, and then discuss ways that the gap between the two can be closed.

> 1. Help people develop levels of self-confidence in their work skills.
>
> 2. Create a positive emotional environment at work.
>
> 3. Ask people to accept and value their own performance goals.

Figure 20.2. Motivators That Work for Everyone.

What Helps Motivation? Universal Motivators That Work for Everyone

Many of the strategies that contribute most to developing motivation are relatively easy to implement and cost very little (see Figure 20.2). The three motivational pressure points that work for everyone are realistic levels of self-confidence, positive emotional climates, and strong personal values for work tasks.

1. Help People Develop Appropriate Levels of Self-Confidence in Their Work Skills. A primary motivational goal is to support people in achieving a high level of personal confidence in their belief about their own ability to achieve performance goals in the work setting. People's belief about whether "I have the skills required to succeed at this task in this context" is perhaps the most important factor in their commitment to work tasks and the quality and quantity of mental effort they invest in their work. It is important to focus self-confidence on specific types of tasks. Good evidence suggests that general self-confidence is not as critical for work motivation as is task-specific confidence (Bandura, 1997).

When people lack confidence that they can succeed at a specific goal, they will not choose to tackle that goal. If they have started to work on the goal, they may find a way to convince themselves to switch to less vital tasks, invest very little mental effort, or argue about their assignment. If people are overconfident, they will not invest much mental effort in tasks and also not take responsibility when they fail or make mistakes. If people are good at something, they believe that mistakes or failures must have been caused by someone or something else. Everyone needs very high levels of confidence about their job skills. However, if overconfidence turns to arrogance, they can be tempted to ignore their mistakes and treat even very novel challenges as if they are routine and familiar.

To help people build self-confidence we must constantly check with them to learn their concerns. The real danger here is that we might believe that others are "like us" and so will respond positively to the confidence builders that we prefer. The best assumptions are that people are not like us, that other people are most likely to be motivated by very different values than our own, and that other people's values are not "wrong or stupid," only different. The most motivating attitude toward other people's values is understanding and respect. We do not have to agree with other people or share their values to respect their right to hold different beliefs and styles. Keep in mind that as confidence increases, commitment to performance goals also increases.

People who are overconfident, however, make mistakes and may not take responsibility for them. They misjudge the tasks they face as familiar and well within their skill level when in fact those tasks are novel challenges that require them to develop new strategies. Overconfidence can lead them to refuse to change their view when they are not successful at the tasks. Overconfident people tend to blame others, their equipment, and fate for the mistakes they make. They need to see that the strategies they are using are not working and that the tasks they face are novel and require new approaches (Clark and Estes, 2002).

2. Create a Positive Emotional Environment at Work. Emotions are usually ignored in discussions about motivation, but they are very important. Positive emotions such as happiness, humor, and joy support and enhance work commitment. Negative emotions such as anger, extreme frustration, and depression kill it. Yet it is not necessary for everyone to be happy in order to be committed. It is more important that people are not excessively unhappy, angry, or depressed about work issues. Anger and depression focus much of our attention on past negative events and not on future goals. The matter seems very straightforward. Organizations will benefit from helping people maintain the level of positive emotion that supports their maximum commitment.

Yet different people sometimes have very different ideas about what helps them have positive emotions or get rid of negative feelings. Even if people were more like each other, we cannot always do a great deal to modify extremely negative work emotions. Emotions are not always event-based. Because of biological reasons or early life experiences, some people simply react more quickly with strong anger or depression to routine events they perceive as negative than do others. The effort invested in creating a positive, enjoyable work climate can pay off in increased work commitment for many people, because the result is less negativity about work.

Gordon Bower (1995) has surveyed the research on the impact of a positive mood on performance. Bower emphasized asking people what would make their work environment more enjoyable. His research could be summarized as recommending the following ways to support positive emotions toward work for everyone:

- Engage people in decisions about the esthetic design of their shared workplace. Invest in a bright, lively, positive environmental design. Let people decorate their personal workspace and themselves if the decoration will not interfere with other people or violate important policy.

- Allow people to listen privately to music while they work if listening does not decrease work efficiency or interfere with the work of others.

- Eliminate rules and policies that reduce work enjoyment without providing a measured benefit that is greater than the loss of commitment they cause. Ask people what policies, if modified, would increase their enjoyment.

- Encourage everyone, including supervisors and managers, to be enthusiastic, positive, and supportive. Cynical, negative, pessimistic, and "sour grape" styles may be fashionable in some organizational cultures, but they do not encourage positive emotion or work commitment for anyone.

3. Ask People to Accept and Value Their Own Performance Goals. All of the advice on performance motivation up to this point can be viewed as ways to enhance people's beliefs that if they make a strong commitment to and persist at the achievement of their performance goals, they will become more effective. Locke and Latham (2002) have studied work goals for over a quarter century. Their evidence suggests that while people do not have to choose their own work goals in order to be motivated by them, a personal intention to succeed at assigned goals is very motivating. Commitment to goals is somewhat contingent on our confidence that we can achieve the goals we are assigned. Personal confidence and our job- and task-related emotions are intimately connected with goal commitment. Our confidence is a measure of our belief about how our own ability will combine with organizational processes to support, or prevent, our success and effectiveness. Some of our strongest job-related emotions are the product of our reasoning and experience about how effective or ineffective we have been and will continue to be in our work environment.

DIFFERENT TYPES OF VALUES FOR WORK GOALS

Values are one of the powerful ways people express their views about what they expect will make them effective or reduce their effectiveness. People value what they believe helps them, and they reject what they believe stands in their way. Values can be viewed as preferences that lead people to more quickly adopt a course of action and persist in the face of distractions.

Of course, different people have different values. Yet research on values and performance suggests that there may be ways to identify types of values and connect them to work goals. The goal here is to increase people's work commitment by suggesting connections between their own values and the benefit of achieving work goals. Eccles and Wigfield (1995) present evidence that most people use three different types of values.

Interest value: People will more easily and quickly choose to do what interests them the most. Many people are generally interested in mastering a new skill or adding to their expertise. This more "intrinsic" interest pattern often characterizes the most effective workers. Others are more interested in impressing managers with their capability. This more "performance"-oriented style can also be useful under some conditions. It is useful to suggest connections between performance goals and people's natural interests whenever possible. Suggest that their goals represent an "opportunity to do something that interests you," such as master a new area or get a manager's attention.

Skill value: Most people seem more willing to do those things that they believe challenge one of their special skills. So people who see themselves as more analytical like brain teasers and difficult analytical problems and tasks. People who see themselves as more artistic and style conscious like tasks that involve esthetic decisions and design challenges. To support skill value, suggest connections between performance goals and people's special abilities by suggesting that they are "good at this kind of task" and that it is an "opportunity to show your skills in this area."

Utility value: So much of what we do is chosen not because we love it or can excel at it but because we want the benefits that come when we finish and to avoid the negative consequences of avoiding or delaying. This is called "utility value," and it shifts a person's focus from means to ends. It asks people to focus on the benefits of finishing the task and not on their lack of interest or discomfort about the means to reach the end. It is one of the ways we justify enduring something we do not like to get something we do like or avoid something that would be worse. Utility value can be enhanced by describing the realistic benefits of completing a less desired task or goal and the risks of avoiding it. Do not inflate either the benefits or the risks.

FINANCIAL INCENTIVES THAT CREATE VALUE

Another highly effective way to increase motivation for work is to provide financial incentives for exceeding past performance. Some question whether offering people pay or gifts tied to exceptional performance actually motivates them beyond the type of strategies we have described already. The overall results of the large body of studies that are published in reputable journals suggest that cash and other tangible incentives can be very powerful and relatively inexpensive ways to increase the value people place on work goals (see Figure 20.3 and the study by Stolovitch, Clark, and Condly, 2002, including their references for other, similar studies).

To most researchers who study this question, the evidence is clear that financial or other tangible incentives, for example, vacations or luxury gifts, can

1. Quota plans give additional pay for exceeding a previous level.

2. Piece-rate plans pay for increasing quantities of work products.

3. Tournament plans pay winners in "same job" competitions.

4. Flat-rate plans are similar to salary.

Figure 20.3. Four Types of Incentive Programs.

significantly increase people's work performance by increasing their motivation. For the incentives to provide maximum benefit, the performance level must be very challenging and not routine or easy, but also not perceived as impossible. In much of the research, an impossible task is defined as one for which the probability of success is less than 15 percent.

Types of Financial Incentive Programs

There are a variety of types of financial incentive programs. Following are four prominent types.

Quota Plans. When organizations use a "quota plan," they appear to get the largest motivational benefit. Quotas offer additional bonus pay for work that exceeds a previous level achieved by the individual, team, or organization, or by another organization. Quota schemes seem to give incentives the highest impact on performance.

Piece-Rate Plans. The second most effective use of tangible incentives is in piece-rate plans, in which a set amount of output, for example, the manual assembly of one electronics board, is tied to a set rate of pay. Quota and piece-rate schemes are often combined to get the benefit of both approaches. In the combined schemes, people have an incentive to do more than simply exceed their past performance. The farther they go, the more they get.

Tournament Plans. The third-ranking incentive approach is "tournament plans," in which pay is linked to performance rankings based on competition between people doing the same job. This plan is often used to motivate sales staff. The factors that are thought to diminish the effects of tournament incentives are the fact that only capable people tend to "play." Those who feel they will not "win" tend to avoid this kind of scheme, so it may attract only top performers and overconfident people. Another problem here is that competition sometimes leads to attempts to sabotage the efforts of competitors, thus reducing the overall benefit to the organization. The lack of impact of tournament schemes may be one of the main reasons why competition is not often an effective motivator.

Flat-Rate Plans. "Flat rate" or "fixed pay" schemes are the least effective overall. "Work for a set salary" is the best example of a flat-rate incentive system. Here we pay people for full-time work, usually pegged at forty hours a week. Ironically, very few studies have found motivational advantages for the most common tangible incentive system used worldwide.

Disputes about Incentive Systems

Many of the disputes about pay incentives focus on evidence, drawn largely from studies with children in classrooms, that our personal interest in work tasks decreases when tangible incentives are used to reward work. The argument is that paying people to do what they would do anyway because they are interested in the job switches their motivation away from a fascination with the task to the pay they are promised for performance. In the future, the argument goes, people who are paid more for interesting work will work for extra pay and not because they are interested. The best advice is not to provide tangible incentives to people who are already achieving business goals without tangible rewards, unless there is an excellent financial reason to exceed business goals at the possible risk of future "interest" motivation. The best evidence is that giving cash or other tangible incentives to adults for increased work actually increases people's interest in their jobs (Stolovitch, Clark, and Condly, 2002) but may decrease the interest of younger children in study and schoolwork contexts (Pintrich and Schunk, 2002).

MOTIVATING TEAMS

Motivating a team is often more challenging than motivating a single individual. Individuals within teams operate with a different set of goals, values, beliefs, and expectations. Yet the variety of team member personalities can be a positive force if each performer contributes his or her unique capabilities when and where they are needed.

Teamwork potentially allows a number of individuals to achieve more when they collaborate than when they work separately. Conversely, team differences are destructive when, for example, prima donnas refuse to cooperate or members loaf because there are more people available to do the job, leaving them feeling less visible.

Most of the suggestions for motivating teams are exactly the same as those suggested for motivating individuals (see, for example, Clark, 2003b, 2004, and 2005; Clark and Estes, 2002). The next section describes five research-tested motivation strategies focused exclusively on the unique qualities of teams.

Why Is Team Motivation Different from Individual Motivation?

The first critical issue in team motivation is to be clear about the definition of "a team." Nearly everyone who studies teams emphasizes that it is unnecessary to use team-motivation strategies when teams are defined as any group of two or more people with similar skills who are simply working together to achieve a common goal (Bandura, 1997). For a team to exist, for motivational purposes, team members must play different roles or bring different skills to the table. Those different skills must be required to achieve team goals. So a team is an interdependent group of individuals, each possessing a different set of skills, but who collectively possess all of the skills required to achieve team goals.

For example, while each member of a sports team may have played all of the different positions on the team in the past, individuals specialize in the one or two positions where they excel. Since everyone cannot play every position during competition, they must depend on each other. This is true in most professions. Lawyers have experience in litigating and negotiating, but they tend to specialize in one or the other. Support teams built around litigating include, for example, specialists in jury selection, research on the legal issues involved in a dispute, background investigations, and courtroom strategies.

Many different types of teams are formed within and between organizations for various purposes. Some teams are project-based, chosen to respond quickly to rapidly changing conditions and to disband after a project is completed. Other teams are formed to take advantage of customer-related expertise in different organizations. Networked or virtual teams tend to serve over longer periods of time, depending on their success, and are assembled by brokers who serve as coordinators. Many varieties of these teams exist, three types of which have been named in this paragraph, and each of them presents unique motivational challenges and issues for members and managers. The subject of this section is motivational strategies that appear to work with all teams, regardless of their focus, makeup, or lifespan.

What Motivates Teams?

Teams, like individuals, are motivated by whatever they believe will help make them successful in achieving their most important goals. Yet teams must also share some collective beliefs if they are going to be successful. The role of team managers and leaders, or team members in leaderless teams, is to achieve the following five motivational goals, summarized in Figure 20.4.

1. Foster Mutual Respect among Teammates. Teams in which one or more members believe that they are working with people who lack adequate skills to achieve team goals have a major motivational problem. In some cases, this belief is simply incorrect. Highly competitive people sometimes distort the real situation and develop the self-protective view that one or more other people on their team are inadequate. Competitive spirit is good. Bolstering self-confidence

1. Foster mutual respect among teammates.

2. The team must believe weaker members are working hard to improve.

3. Require team members to collaborate with others.

4. Hold individual team members accountable.

5. Direct the team's competitive spirit outside the team and the organization.

Figure 20.4. Team Motivation Strategies.

at the expense of others is immature and destructive of team efforts. Bandura (1997) describes many studies in a variety of fields showing that "weak link" doubts about team member expertise have significantly reduced team effectiveness. Even though all team members vary in their expertise levels, when mutually supportive confidence is in place, less able team members tend to perform significantly better and work hard over time to increase their skills. Since individual team members tend to be self-focused and so think more about their own contributions and ability, team members need to be reminded about the skills of other members. One effective way to accomplish this task is to actively attribute successes to each team member's expertise and attribute missteps or mistakes to temporary lapses and external causes.

When it is obvious that someone cannot measure up and that no amount of "reframing" their mistakes will be accepted by the group, the person with inadequate skills must be transferred as soon as possible if team motivation and performance are suffering. It is most important that the confidence team members have in each other's expertise is the only factor that accounts for their success in high-pressure situations. Bandura, after a long review of the research on sports teams, concludes that "in pressure-packed overtime matches where contestants are evenly matched and a mistake brings sudden death defeat . . . perceived (group) efficacy emerges as the sole determinant of overtime performance" (1997, p. 383). He goes on to suggest that the same is true for all teams that are in competitive situations.

What happens when you can not replace a weak link?

2. The Team Must Believe Weaker Members Are Working Hard to Improve. Occasionally teams must accommodate members who are novices or for some reason are not able to do the best job for the team. When teams cannot replace weaker members with more skilled people, what works best to preserve team motivation? Jackson and LePine (2003) have studied this controversial question over many years. They have recent and solid evidence that when team members believe that their weakest member is merely inexperienced, or has faltered for some uncontrollable reason, for example, illness, accident, or a family crisis, and can improve, they will give support provided that the person is investing his or her best effort to improve.

The biggest motivational challenge on a team is faced by the weakest members. They must believe that what they contribute to the team is vital to the team's success and that the other members expect them to improve and succeed. Feedback to members who are working to improve must emphasize effort and not ability. When they make progress, it is best to attribute the progress to effort. When no progress is forthcoming, they need to be urged to "get busy," to "get serious and work harder." Avoid attributing success or failure to ability. Belief that performance is due to ability tends to discourage hard work. Why would anyone work harder if they believe they cannot do it because they lack the ability, or that their achievement is due to ability and not to effort? When weak links work hard and gain skills, they need to know that their team appreciates their effort and notices the result and its impact on the team's progress.

In many teams the motivational challenge is not a weak link but instead a lack of cooperation and collaboration.

3. Require Team Members to Collaborate with Others. Healthy teams are made up of team players who cooperate with each other. One uncooperative person can damage the motivation of even the most capable team. The obvious examples are the arrogant, self-focused prima donnas who invest most of their effort in making themselves look good with managers and clients, at the expense of the team. Less obvious, but equally destructive, are the outwardly supportive but silently devious "back stabbers," whose primary goal is to make their own work highly visible. Selecting people with a history of effective collaboration helps to avoid these problems. Yet very capable people are sometimes competitive and self-focused.

One of the biggest challenges facing team leaders and coaches is to promote a sense that despite differences, when the chips are down, the team will cooperate. Achieving this goal requires the development of a cooperative environment. Debriefing a team after either a success or a stumble should involve a description of the sequence of interactions among members that may have led to a positive or negative outcome. The more that members learn to see team results over time as due to interactions among them, and not exclusively to their own solitary contributions, the more they will focus on cooperation (Bandura, 1997; Druckman and Bjork, 1994).

Developing cooperative confidence also requires that coaches and team leaders learn to blunt the negative impact when members begin to complain that one of their team is consistently avoiding obvious opportunities to collaborate. Here also it is helpful to attribute successes to each team member's cooperation and attribute selfish missteps or mistakes to temporary lapses, such as a misperception of the situation, and to external causes. But when it is obvious that someone cannot measure up, and that no amount of "reframing" their mistakes will be accepted by the group, the uncooperative person must be transferred to an individual performance situation if team motivation and performance are suffering.

Is it possible to find out that someone is not measuring up if the team performance is evaluated without assessing the contributions of individual members?

4. Hold Individual Team Members Accountable. One of the first team-motivation studies (described in Williams, Karau, and Bourgeois, 1993), performed just after 1900, established the phenomenon that has been called "social loafing." When people pulled as hard as possible against a rope connected to a strain gauge, their best effort was recorded. When another person was added to the rope and two people pulled together, each person invested less effort in a collaborative effort than they did when he or she was alone. As more people were added to the rope, each person pulled less forcefully. When interviewed, most people seem unaware that they are not working as hard in a group situation as they did when alone.

In the past century, this phenomenon has been replicated and verified in an amazing range of research studies that represent a broad range of work and educational settings, populations, and tasks, including knowledge work (Williams, Karau, and Bourgeois, 1993). The overwhelming evidence for social loafing actually led to early suggestions that people work alone unless teamwork is essential. Recently, a research team found a relatively simple and powerful solution for this problem. For a discussion of the history and current studies, read Williams and others, 1993. When the individuals on a team believe that their individual contributions to the team are being accurately and fairly assessed, social loafing seems to completely disappear. Therefore, the advice to all organizations is to always evaluate the contributions of the individual members of a team and make certain that every team member is aware of the evaluation process and results.

The final team-motivation strategy is to encourage and focus their competitive spirit.

5. Direct the Team's Competitive Spirit Outside the Team and the Organization. Competition can be highly motivating for individuals or teams. Salespeople seem to thrive on it, and many people who are raised in Western cultural traditions seem to like a bit of it. One of the most common motivational team-building exercises favored by organizational consultants is a field experience in which teams compete with other teams in order to bond and build team spirit. These events are scheduled offsite and ideally are held in unfamiliar, often rural settings to eliminate familiar surroundings and therefore interrupt habitual patterns formed at work for relating to others. Teams are challenged to do something highly novel such as build structures or navigate difficult terrain to reach a target sooner or more effectively than other teams. Individuals are asked to notice how hard they are working, how much they are collaborating, and whether they have a real desire to win.

In general, team-building exercises have been found to be very effective, but they also have a potentially ugly, unintended side effect. Druckman and Bjork (1994) reviewed all studies of team building for the U.S. National Academy of Sciences. The variety of team-building methods they surveyed shared the common goal of attempting to get members of work teams to bond, collaborate, and work efficiently toward common goals by competing with other teams. They concluded that many different approaches worked, but they were surprised to find that after team-building exercises, a significant number of teams were competing in a nearly suicidal fashion with other teams in their own organization. Stories include misguided team members who were found to be modifying or deleting the electronic files, intentionally "misplacing" or rerouting team resources, and spreading negative rumors about members of other teams in their organizations. Apparently, fostering constant, intense rivalry can help when it is directed at the organization's competition, but it can also support a destructive level of internal competition and focus attention and energy away from organizational goals. The obvious motivational issue in this situation is to make certain that team-building exercises focus the team's competitive energy on competing organizations, not on other teams in the same organization.

CONCLUSION

We should no longer tolerate the fact that the culture and practices common in most organizations cause one out of every two employees to do only what they must to keep from being fired. While psychologists estimate that approximately one in twenty employees has serious emotional problems such as depression and substance abuse issues that limit their motivation despite our best efforts, most people are willing to increase their enthusiasm for work. The most conservative estimates, based on carefully conducted field studies, suggest that it is reasonable to expect a 20 percent increase by most employees in nearly all types of organizations. The size of the impact is almost identical to the measured average performance gain due to all of the training carried out in organizations (Clark, 2004). Team-based organizations can hope for even greater gains. The programs implemented to accomplish these gains actually grow in impact over time as they become rooted in the culture of an organization. They also appear to cost much less than the benefits realized from the performance gains that they produce, although more research is needed on the economics of motivational programs. One way to visualize the potential impact is to imagine the benefits for your organization if all of the employees choose to work one extra day a week.

Some of the most powerful motivational programs can be implemented on individual and team levels by line managers, provided that careful analysis precedes implementation and that results are monitored and measured. Many of the most powerful motivational strategies require changes primarily in the way that work goals are developed and communicated, the way that performance is rewarded, and the strategy that managers use to give feedback, show interest, and encourage people.

References

Arthur, W., Bennett, W., Edens, T. S., and Bell, S. T. (2003). Effectiveness of training in organizations: A meta-analysis of design and evaluation features. *Journal of Applied Psychology, 88*(2), 234–245.

Bandura, A. (1991). Human agency: The rhetoric and the reality. *American Psychologist, 46,* 157–162.

Bandura, A. (1997). Self-efficacy: The exercise of control. New York: W. H. Freeman.

Bandura, A., and Locke, E. A. (2003). Negative self-efficacy and goal effects revisited. *Journal of Applied Psychology, 88*(1), 87–99.

Bower, G. H. (1995). Emotion and social judgments. Monograph published by the Federation of Behavioral, Psychological and Cognitive Sciences as part of the Science and Public Policy Seminars, Washington, DC.

Buckingham, M., and Coffman, C. (1999). *First break all the rules: What the world's greatest managers do differently.* New York: Simon and Schuster.

Clark, R. E. (1999) The CANE model of motivation to learn and to work: A two-stage process of goal commitment and effort. In J. Lowyck (Ed.), *Trends in corporate training.* Leuven, Belgium: University of Leuven Press.

Clark, R. E. (2003a). Fostering the work motivation of individuals and teams. *Performance Improvement, 42*(3), 21–29.

Clark, R. E. (2003b, August). How effective is training? A new summary of the past 40 years of training field research and evaluation. *PerformanceXpress,* pp. 1–4. Retrieved from International Society for Performance Improvement Web site: www.ISPI.org.

Clark, R. E. (2004, March). The "ten most wanted" motivation killers. *PerformanceXpress,* pp. 1–3. Retrieved from International Society for Performance Improvement Web site: www.ISPI.org.

Clark, R. E. (2005). Five research-tested group motivation strategies. *Performance Improvement, 44*(1), 13–16.

Clark, R. E., and Estes, F. (2002). *Turning research into results: A guide to selecting the right performance solutions.* Atlanta: CEP Press.

Condly, S., Clark, R. E., and Stolovitch, H. S. (2003). The effects of incentives on workplace performance: A meta-analytic review of research studies. *Performance Improvement Quarterly, 16*(3), 46–63.

Digman J. M. (1990). Personality structure: Emergence of the five-factor model. *Annual Review of Psychology, 41,* 417–440.

Druckman, D., and Bjork, R. (Eds.). (1994). *Learning, remembering, and believing: Enhancing human performance.* Washington, DC: National Academy Press.

Eccles, J., and Wigfield, A. (1995). In the mind of the actor: The structure of adolescents' achievement task values and expectancy-related beliefs. *Personality and Social Psychology Bulletin, 21,* 215–225.

Jackson, C., and LePine, J. (2003). Peer responses to a team's weakest link: A test of LePine and VanDyne's model. *Journal of Applied Psychology, 88*(3), 459–475.

Kluger, A., and DiNisi, A. (1998). Feedback interventions: Toward the understanding of a double-edged sword. *Current Directions in Psychological Science, 7*(3), 67–72.

Locke, E. A., and Latham, G. P. (2002). Building a practically useful theory of goal setting and task motivation. *American Psychologist, 57*(9), 705–717.

Pintrich, P., and Schunk, D. (2002). *Motivation in education: Theory, research and applications* (2nd ed.). Englewood Cliffs, NJ: Merrill.

Spitzer, D. (1995). *SuperMotivation.* New York: AMACOM.

Stolovitch, H., Clark, R. E., and Condly, S. (2002). *Incentives, motivation and workplace performance: Research and best practices.* Silver Spring, MD: International Society for Performance Improvement.

Storseth, F. (2002). Maintaining work motivation during organizational change. *International Journal of Human Resources Development and Management, 4*(3), 267–287.

Williams, K., Karau, S., and Bourgeois, M. (1993). Working on collective tasks: Social loafing and social compensation. In M. A. Hogg and D. Abrams (Eds.), *Group motivation: Social psychological perspectives* (pp. 130–148). London, UK: Harvester Wheatsheaf.

CHAPTER TWENTY-ONE

Shifting Organizational Alignment from Behavior to Values

Anthony W. Marker

One of the greatest challenges for a modern organization is that of keeping all its members moving in the same direction and continuing to do their jobs in accordance with the organization's goals, missions, and values as the business grows. Yet as growth occurs, the hierarchical distance often increases between those setting the goals and those producing the bulk of the organization's products and services. The greater the distance between those two organizational functions, the greater the opportunity for communication to become garbled, distorted, or simply lost. Think of the childhood game "Telephone," in which a message is passed down a chain of people, and where the message starting out at one end of the chain may be very different from the message heard by the last person at the end of the chain. The same is true of organizations that have several layers of management separating strategic decision makers from those directly involved with producing goods and services. When this distortion or loss of communication exists in organizations, it is nearly always coupled with problems in maintaining alignment between the organization's culture, strategy, values, and behavior. The head of the organization can no longer reliably control the organization's hands and feet.

A result of this communication loss, particularly in recent years, has been a trend by choice or economic necessity toward flatter and leaner organizations. Organizations now actively work to eliminate extra layers of management. One major benefit of this trend is the shorter lines of internal communication that make it easier to keep an organization aligned. Improved communication can reduce costs and product cycle time. However, even with shorter communication lines, getting all of an organization's resources working toward a single goal can be both costly and time consuming.

The organizations of today strive to maintain ever-greater symmetry of alignment. No matter what the trend, human performance technology (HPT) professionals have many tools at their disposal to help organizations continue to maintain an alignment between management and workers: knowledge-management systems, human resource (HR) policies, documentation, and training being just a few of the possibilities. One valuable approach for gaining a greater degree of organizational alignment, described in detail in this chapter, is to pass control of daily operational decisions and behavior down the organizational hierarchy from senior managers to the work teams. This approach greatly enhances strategies such as flattening organizational structure by putting the decisions and control of behavior right where those decisions must be made. Miscommunication can be reduced and alignment can be promoted between management and work teams. It is a bit like the head, senior management, trusting the hands, the teams, to decide what to do mostly on their own.

However, simply passing control down to workers will likely *not* resolve the complex organizational alignment issues HPT professionals hope to resolve. Having passed that control down, how can the head feel certain that the hands will make decisions that match the head's values and goals? How can senior managers in an organization make sure that teams and individual workers will make choices about behaviors that are consistent with the organization's goals and values? To understand the answers to these questions, it is important to more clearly understand the nature of the alignment problem.

WHY ALIGNMENT MATTERS

For the past twenty or thirty years, organizations have been experiencing an increase in competition, as well as increasing customer and societal expectations. Organizations often feel competing pressures to remain flat and lean while at the same time growing the organization and its business.

Alignment in Lean Organizations

Streamlined, or flat, management structures are often inadequate to cope with the increasing demands and pressures of modern business. Organizations are continually forced to find ways to increase the efficiency of production, the quality of their products and services, and the speed at which they deliver them (Cummings and Molloy, 1977). This organizational challenge has become so ubiquitous and so accepted in the past few years that it has become almost trite to voice it; organizations, and the people in them, are asked to do more and more with the same or fewer resources. While the push for cost efficiency, quality, and speed may be a commonly recognized concern, its pervasiveness does not diminish the importance of the human performance interventions that organizations rely on to further their goals.

Along with an increasing pressure to perform well, the tasks involved in keeping an organization functioning have become increasingly dynamic, interdependent, and complex. Whereas flattening an organization by removing layers of management will certainly decrease the distance between management and workers, it does not address the increasingly complex and interwoven tasks caused by the recent speed and complexity of business. Simply flattening the organizational structure, without also aligning the culture, values, and norms of the organization, is unlikely to lead to the necessary increases in efficiency and effectiveness.

Alignment in Growing Organizations

Leaner, smarter, and more efficient organizations are becoming more common but eventually even these need to grow larger when they run up against their maximum output using current resources. As organizations grow, tasks tend to become differentiated and specialized. For instance, let us examine the example of a small, two-person seafood department that suddenly grows to five or six people. With an increased staff, instead of two people sharing all the tasks, certain members on the team are likely to be assigned to tasks requiring higher levels of skill, such as filleting fish. This specialization lets the department hire more-skilled workers for specialized tasks and less-skilled workers for simpler tasks. As tasks become more specialized, the workers performing those tasks understand each other's tasks less and less; keeping those people connected, aligned, and moving toward common goals and with shared values becomes more difficult and expensive. It is a classic circular problem. In order to survive, organizations must grow, which in turn leads to specialization and pressure to centralize control and to add layers of management. Specialization and layers of hierarchy, however, lead to misalignment, which then requires decentralization of control and flatter organizational structures.

How then do HPT professionals help organizations grow their business while maintaining their alignment? While there are no foolproof solutions, as a first step it is safe to say that performance interventions often need to help pass greater control over daily activities down to teams that are closer to where the real work actually takes place; teams need a greater degree of autonomy over their daily operational behavior. More than that, those teams need to be *empowered* in order to increase their task motivation. Kirkman and Rosen (1999) suggest that empowered teams are characterized as having "increased task motivation resulting from an individual's positive orientation toward his or her work role" (p. 58). Yet to pass control down to teams, the organization must first make sure its values, norms, and beliefs are aligned. Additionally, giving up power and control is something that many managers are hesitant to support, since they may feel that letting go of the reins will result in the organization running off course. While misalignment, in either lean or growing organizations, is a problem that can be corrected, the solutions demand that HPT professionals have a better grasp of how organizational alignment and control work.

Identifying Alignment-Intervention Warning Signs

Alignment gets all the organization's resources working in concert and moving in the same direction. It stands to reason that misalignment is a serious threat to an organization's ability to achieve its goals in environments where the pace and nature of business is fast, furious, and constantly changing. In one way or another, many of the organizational challenges that HPT professionals are asked to address lead back to the issue of organizational alignment; getting the organizational goals, behaviors, and values to match up. Some examples (adapted from Xavier, 2002) of warning signs that the goals, behaviors, and values might be misaligned include complaints from

- Managers who suggest that workers
    - Do not perform up to expectations
    - Have difficulty in delivering quality results
    - Do not have a clear idea of what tasks come next
    - Do not perform in accordance with the organization's stated values
- Workers who suggest that managers
    - Have not provided clear guidance about performance or behavior
    - Have not communicated exactly what is expected of them
    - Are holding teams accountable for outcomes over which the teams have little or no control

Teams: Defining Self-Management and Empowerment

As stated earlier, one means of flattening an organization's structure is by passing control from management down to work teams. The behaviors that managers tend to pass down are typically immediate behaviors, or what Parsons (1969) describes as operational-level behavior and decisions. This means that managers might allow the team to control aspects of its own work process, such as scheduling, work assignments, compensation, feedback, and, occasionally, how the work is accomplished. Ouchi (1977) suggests that in organizations with large hierarchies the greatest area of control loss, misalignment of values, and behavior in our terms is in the area of relatively routine activities such as getting workers to show up to work on time, observe dress codes, and provide for customer needs. It is over these functions that management often passes control to teams, which explains the descriptor *self-managing* that is applied to such teams. They have the power, or autonomy, to make certain types of decisions.

Are self-managed teams *any* teams that take control over these aspects of their work environments and tasks? Typically the answer is no. Self-managed teams tend to be teams that are assigned to complete a relatively whole task, or portion of a larger task. In addition, self-managed team members usually have the necessary mix of skills required to complete their tasks and contribute to the team's goals (Hackman, taken from Cummings, 1978). Further, Manz and Sims (1987) have suggested that "the use of self-managing groups involves a shift in focus from individual work methods of work performance to group methods" (p. 106).

Sharing Control in Order to Increase It

Why does shifting control over operational behaviors, that is, task autonomy, down to self-managing teams alleviate loss of control? A cohesive group, aligned with an organization's goals and working toward a single objective, can better allocate its resources to deal with changes in its work environments than can individuals who are assigned responsibility for a smaller, more isolated, portion of that environment or task (Susman, taken from Manz and Sims, 1987). In other words, the self-managed team can collectively see enough of the picture to keep the team members aligned with the organization's goals, more than can individuals working on smaller pieces of the task.

Traditional management structures tend to align employee behavior and outputs with the overall organizational goals from outside the work group. This form of management structure depends on controlling the team's alignment without directly participating in the team's tasks. When this type of structure is depicted on an organizational hierarchy chart, such managers may appear to be part of the team, but often, such team membership can be more in *name* than in *fact*. There can still be an "us versus them" perception of the relationship, particularly among team members. While such external top-down approaches to managing alignment used to be successful, current environmental pressures vastly reduce their effectiveness.

Once the team members themselves are given collective control over their operational-level behaviors, then the alignment of the team's values with the greater organizational goals is actually maintained from the *inside* rather than from the outside. Manz and Sims (1987) suggest that because alignment is being maintained from the inside of the work team instead of from the outside, self-managing teams are actually characterized by higher levels of control and alignment at the group level. Once control has been shared with the team, performance pressure is no longer being exerted from outside the team in a ratio of one controller to many team members. Several team members are generally exerting pressure on each other for performance, and the ratio changes to that of many controllers to many team members. One would expect, in such a situation, that the aggregate level of control in such a situation would increase; after all, now many team members are all serving as internal monitors of the team's behaviors.

Empowered Teams

Empowered teams further extend possibilities for adding organizational alignment. Kirkman and Rosen (1999) suggest that there is a difference between self-managing teams and empowered teams. While both self-managing and empowered teams share the dimension of task autonomy, that is, control over operational-level behaviors, empowered teams are further characterized by increased perceptions in three other dimensions: self-efficacy, added value, and impact. These latter three dimensions are somewhat parallel to the last three of four dimensions of motivation described in Keller's (1983) well-known ARCS model of relevance, confidence, and satisfaction. Transforming self-managing teams into empowered teams relies on successfully going beyond mere task control toward aligning the team's values, beliefs, and norms to those of the overall organization. As Dainty, Bryman, and Price (2002) put it, "Empowerment represents a shift towards a greater emphasis upon trust and commitment in the workplace" (p. 334).

THE NATURE OF CONTROL: GETTING BEYOND MERE AUTONOMY

When task autonomy is passed down to the team, how does the organization as a whole maintain alignment of that team's behavior with the organization's values? The answer is that management must shift its alignment efforts from the control of behaviors to the control of values, norms, and beliefs.

Alignment Approaches

There are two approaches to creating or maintaining an alignment of a team's behavior with the organization's values: (1) overt alignment, and (2) unobtrusive alignment.

Overt Alignment. The older and more traditional approach, overt alignment, relies on management's maintaining control over the operational-level behaviors. Overt alignment is directive in nature and results, at least theoretically, in a clean and unblemished line between the directions issued by a manager and the behavior of a worker. The manager directs that workers engage in, or avoid, specific behaviors, and the decisions about those behaviors rest with the manager.

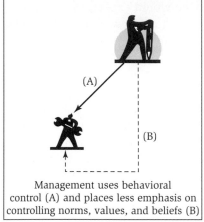

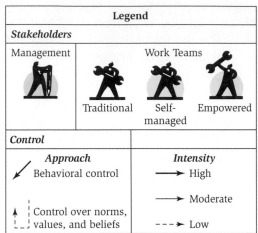

Figure 21.1. Traditional Team Control.

Source: Marker, 2001, p. 15.

Alignment of behaviors to values is maintained by management from outside the work team but at costs to efficiency and effectiveness. Unobtrusive alignment relies on shifting the emphasis of control from behaviors to the control of values.

An illustration of how the traditional approach to alignment is used to control a work team can be found in Figure 21.1. The heavy line (A) extending from management to the work team represents the overt alignment of a team, or rather the direct control over the team's behavior. The dotted line (B) that comes up from underneath the team is meant to represent unobtrusive alignment and the way in which the control of norms and values supports the team and provides a foundation for the team's decision making. The intensity of those lines illustrates the emphasis of each of those types of approaches to alignment in a given situation. In Figure 21.1, high emphasis is placed on the overt alignment of behavior and low emphasis is placed on the unobtrusive alignment of values; thus a traditional managerial structure is depicted.

An example of traditional management exerting overt alignment over a team can be illustrated using the case of the seafood department of a grocery store. One of the seafood manager's primary goals is to make sure that the department meets its sales goals. To achieve these goals, the manager will control operational-level behaviors such as

- Assigning employees to perform each of the various functions and tasks, including serving customers, cleaning, stocking shelves, or cutting and preparing fish

- Deciding when to order additional product so that a balance is maintained between keeping the displays full and keeping the products fresh
- Deciding shifts and hours for the team members
- Pricing fish appropriately so it sells
- Monitoring the quality of the fish and deciding when to discard old stock

The manager exerts direct control over the team members by making decisions and directly assigning tasks and behaviors. Such control often extends to when, where, and how the tasks will be performed. A single person, the manager, is typically in charge of making sure that behaviors are aligned with the organization's values.

Unobtrusive Alignment. Unobtrusive alignment, however, relies on the control of a team's norms, values, and beliefs. These values and norms serve to guide decision making and, *by extension,* behavior. Therefore, unobtrusive alignment relies on guiding the decisions teams make as opposed to directly controlling their behavior.

When we speak of unobtrusive alignment affecting norms, values, and beliefs, to what are we really referring? McGrath (1984) defines norms as "sets of expectations about what someone 'ought' to do under a given set of conditions. Violation is negatively sanctioned" (p. 200). Norms are rules or standards designed to guide member behavior (Bales, 1958; Feldman, 1984; Trevino and Victor, 1992). Feldman suggests that teams generally only enforce norms that are associated with something important to the group, such as those things that affect group survival, facilitate task accomplishment, contribute to group morale, or express the group's central values.

There is ample evidence to suggest that aligning a team's norms will be effective in aligning that team's behavior:

- Groups consider loyalty an important norm (Katz and Kahn, 1978).
- Groups prefer to handle the misconduct of team members themselves (Greenberger, Miccli, and Cohen, 1987).
- Members of self-managing teams tend to define their work roles in terms of their ability to contribute to the team's primary task rather than in relation to a specific job (Manz and Sims, 1987).

Instead of dictating a specific behavior, unobtrusive alignment strives to develop a set of shared norms and values to draw on to make decisions about how to act in a given set of circumstances. The end goal is to influence a team's behavior indirectly by influencing value systems the team uses to make choices and decisions instead of directly managing the behavior itself.

Let us return to our example of the seafood department and examine how it might work if the emphasis is shifted away from overt alignment and toward unobtrusive alignment. Instead of the seafood manager dictating specific behaviors, as before, the members of the seafood team would be given responsibility for meeting certain goals regarding how much profit they need to bring in given specific time, quality, and budget frameworks. The daily decisions about how to meet those goals would then fall to the team members; they would decide who worked on what shifts, who performed certain tasks, what products were sold and how they were displayed, and other operational behaviors. The types of norms and values might include

- Putting customer service first
- Selling only the freshest fish
- Obeying health and safety regulations
- Observing store guidelines about the storage and display of products
- Maintaining the highest standards of cleanliness

Unobtrusive alignment is directly linked to an organization's culture. In fact, Child (1984) referred to the control of norms and values as "cultural control." This type of organizational alignment from culture to values to behavior is necessary. He suggests, "When unpredictability, complexity, and information processing are very high, then decision-making may have to become diffused throughout the organization, formalization is more of a hindrance than a help, and management's best bet is probably to rely on cultural control" (p. 167). In other words, when organizations are experiencing a great deal of change and competition, it is even more important that organizations align their culture, strategies, values, and behaviors to deal with uncertainty.

By focusing on norms and values instead of behaviors, the management's emphasis shifts from defining specific behaviors to defining what *classes* of behavior to engage in or avoid. Unobtrusive control provides boundaries rather than shackles. The result is a team that is free to choose new and innovative strategies for dealing with its environment and tasks. This does not guarantee that such empowered teams will innovate, but it does free them to do so.

An examination of these types of approaches to alignment quickly reveals that they must simultaneously exist in greater or lesser proportions within all organizations. Pure forms of either overt or unobtrusive alignment are likely to be theoretical at best. However, we can see the distinction between organizations that rely on the more traditional overt alignment and those shifting to a more unobtrusive approach to alignment. Figure 21.2 illustrates that the way traditional management structures emphasize overt alignment differs from how organizations using self-managed teams tend to emphasize unobtrusive alignment.

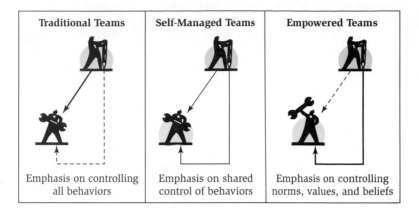

Traditional Teams	Self-Managed Teams	Empowered Teams
Emphasis on controlling all behaviors	Emphasis on shared control of behaviors	Emphasis on controlling norms, values, and beliefs

Figure 21.2. Management Approaches to Alignment.

Source: Marker, 2001, p. 18.

Alignment and Its Link to Power

If it is just a matter of shifting emphasis, why do so many organizations still place so much reliance on overt approaches to alignment? The reason is likely the tight link of control to power. Power is essentially the ability to obtain a desired output. If an organization is going to *empower* teams, then management is going to need to pass some of this power down to those teams. However, power redistribution is not without its problems. Russ Forrester (2000) put it this way:

> The most common mistake made by organizations looking to empower frontline employees is to take too lightly what they are asking the managers in the middle to do. Many top executives seem to believe that managers and supervisors who have been exercising the most power will, at the declaration of an empowerment program, readily pass that power on as easily as if they were asked to pass the muffins. That is a momentous misunderstanding [p. 70].

Perceptions of power loss by managers are important for implementation reasons. Getting a manager to give up certain amounts of control to a team is one thing, and might be accomplished based on a purely logical argument. However, convincing managers to give up *power* is "stunningly hard" (Forrester, 2000, p. 70). HPT professionals must keep in mind the continuing, and perhaps increasing, personal needs of these middle managers for control, achievement, recognition, and security.

Control and power are, in turn, linked to perceptions of authority and responsibility. Hind (1992), described the connection between the two this way:

> So why is there reluctance for managers to delegate responsibility? One of the key reasons is an inability to recognize the difference between responsibility and accountability. Responsibility has been described as the ability to respond.

Accountability can be described as being able to be held accountable in the long run. Responsibility requires a detailed understanding of narrow issues. Account-ability requires a less detailed view of much broader issues. The former is dynamic and easily measurable over short time periods; the latter is passive, less easy to measure, and not so easy to control. Delegation therefore, is the art of changing responsibilities into accountabilities—short-term responding into long-term accounting [p. 39].

The results of transferring one without transferring the other are reasonably clear. Granting an individual or group responsibility for the completion of a task, for instance, without also granting the authority necessary to complete that task is a sure recipe for disaster. Likewise, granting authority for an action with-out also making the bearer of that authority responsible for the outcome is asking for trouble. The result can be that management is reluctant to release authority, or control and power, in our parlance, while work teams given responsibility for fulfilling a task are sure to need that authority. How does one overcome these problems?

Power and the Horn of Plenty. One potential way to encourage managerial buy-in to an unobtrusive alignment approach lies in helping managers under-stand that power is not a finite resource. If it were, then managers might have legitimate personal and organizational concerns about giving up the behavioral control associated with an overt alignment approach. However, if you can pro-vide a convincing argument to management that transferring control to a team can actually increase management's control over the overall level of organiza-tional alignment, then you are much more likely to get their buy-in and willing participation for shifting from a behavior- to a values-based approach.

There is evidence going back to the late 1950s that suggests that participatory work designs, in other words, those designs in which teams control their own oper-ational behavior, actually result in a higher aggregate level of organizational control as compared with organizations using nonparticipatory work designs (March and Simon, 1958). Tannenbaum (1961) suggested a similar impact on organizational control. This idea of increasing organizational power through participatory man-agement, or self-management, is illustrated in Figure 21.3.

By passing the authority down to several team members who are internal to the work group, we are actually getting an increase in control over that team's behavior. Why then do we not see all organizations using participatory man-agement structures? Recent trends suggest that more organizations *are* shifting to participatory management models. However, the transfer of control required for unobtrusive approaches to alignment can prove difficult. That is where HPT professionals can provide assistance.

Managing Perceptions of Power Shifts. Delegating and transferring control is one thing, but getting management to give up something as dear and at the

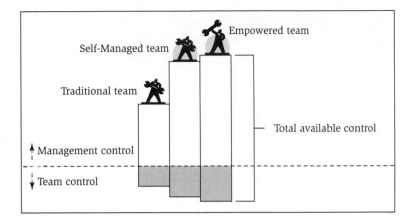

Figure 21.3. Perceived Control Levels.

Source: Marker, 2001, p. 19.

same time elusive as power is quite another. If HPT professionals can make a convincing case that giving up control may lead to managers realizing an increase in power and organizational alignment—and the resulting cost savings—they may be able to make significant progress in overcoming potential managerial resistance.

When control is delegated to teams, the obvious conclusion is that power has been passed downward as well. To a certain extent that is true. The question is, What kinds and amounts of power have been passed to the teams? The control over overt behaviors tends to be for relatively minor operational decisions and actions, though this need not always be the case. Decisions regarding shifts, task distribution, and such are comparatively minor when seen from an organizational perspective. Yet teams that are given control over these aspects of their work are likely to feel both more freedom and more power. If management then shifts its focus to unobtrusively shaping the team's norms and values to more closely align with those of the organization, then the corresponding increase in unobtrusive control may well result in an even higher aggregate level of power and control within the organization as a whole.

SHIFTING TO AN UNOBTRUSIVE APPROACH

HPT professionals are often the ones faced with making the theory of empowerment into a reality. You may be asked to provide training, create job aids, or perhaps help teams design policies and procedures for dealing with new processes. Unless you pay attention to the actual transfer and delegation of control between management and the team, you may well run into difficulties. The Tannenbaum and Schmidt Continuum of Leader Behavior (Tannenbaum and Schmidt, 1958) outlines seven levels of delegated control that a manager can transfer to a team. The manager

- Makes the decision and announces it
- Sells the decision
- Presents the ideas and invites questions
- Presents the tentative decision subject to change
- Presents the problem, gets suggestions, makes the decision
- Defines limits; asks the group to make the decision
- Permits subordinates to function within limits defined by the superior

These levels range from the lowest level of delegation, where the manager makes the decisions and simply announces them to the team, to the highest level of delegation, where the manager delegates to the team, within specific boundaries set by the manager, the authority to identify problems, develop possible options, and decide on a solution. However, it is not enough to know these levels of delegation. HPT professionals must ensure that the conditions required for a level of delegation to occur actually exist. Toward that end, let us look at a model that proposes some possible scenarios.

The model illustrated in Figure 21.4 suggests that there are three routes along the path to successfully shifting from an overt alignment approach to an unobtrusive alignment approach, and hence to the conditions necessary for healthy and well-functioning self-managed teams. Two of those routes result in a misalignment due to imbalances in autonomy. The top route results in too much control, or over-control, while the bottom route results in too little, or under-control. In both cases the results are conditions that are in a misalignment of an organization's values and behavior at the managerial and work-team levels. The central route, however, suggests that a careful shift from overt to unobtrusive alignment can result first in self-managing teams with behavioral task autonomy and then eventually in empowered teams with greater commitment. By helping organizations avoid the pitfalls of over-control and under-control, HPT professionals can help managers pass behavioral control down to teams and eventually move from self-managed teams to the greater paybacks promised by empowered teams.

Over-Control

The first route illustrates what is likely to happen if management gives the team responsibility for fulfilling their goals without giving them the autonomy or overt control over their behavior that is necessary to successfully attain those goals. If responsibility is delegated to the team, then management must shift its own control

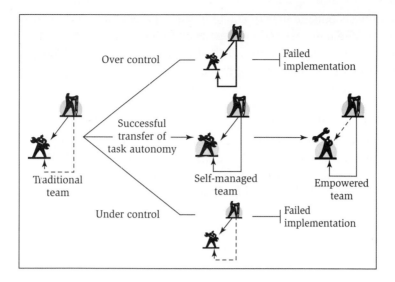

Figure 21.4. Impact of Alignment Approaches on Team Transition.

Source: Marker, 2001, p. 20.

away from behaviors and toward norms and values. Failure to make this shift will likely lead to a situation in which members of the team experience over-control. They are required to fulfill obligations and functions for which they have control over neither behaviors nor values. The result is likely to be a deadening effect and rising frustration in which team members go through the motions with no real buy-in to the process. Under these types of conditions, it is quite possible that team members will experience symptoms of work exhaustion, such as reduced job satisfaction, reduced self-esteem, reduced organizational commitment, increased turnover, and diminished personal accomplishment (Moore, 2000). Members of our seafood team, under such conditions, might well be aware of ways to increase productivity but feel no empowerment to make changes or even participate in a decision process leading to potentially profitable missed opportunities.

Under-Control

The second route to failure is brought about when management delegates responsibility down to a team *with* the requisite authority over their overt behavior but *without* establishing an unobtrusive approach to control and guide the team's decisions. The result may well be a team that feels empowered but also ill prepared to make the decisions needed to perform. Again, this can lead to frustration and a reduction in both performance and participation in the process. While injurious to the team, any decisions that cause the team to behave in ways outside the organization's acceptable limits are likely to be catastrophic to the manager and perhaps even to the organization as a whole. For example, in the instance of our seafood team, team members might decide to keep the fresh fish in stock longer than is allowed by company policy in an effort to stretch resources to meet profit margins.

Balancing the Transition to Autonomy

Establishing conditions for the successful shift from an overt approach to alignment to an unobtrusive approach requires a careful shift from control of behaviors to the control of norms and values. Even when this is accomplished, the team must consist of members who have enough skill, maturity, and experience to take on that control. The complexity inherent in such changes explains, at least in part, why shifts in control structures toward self-management are so often perceived as either only partially successful or in some cases outright failures. Therefore, the shift to an unobtrusive alignment approach is a process that is likely to take place over a span of time measured in years, rather than days, weeks, or even months. While skills and knowledge are part of an intervention of this type, HPT professionals will recognize that at the heart this is a systemic change implementation with significant affective components.

Moving on to Empowerment

Once the organization has successfully gotten past the significant hurdle of passing down autonomy, it is time to empower teams and unobtrusively align the organization according to shared norms, values, and beliefs. Russ Forrester (2000) suggests several steps that transfer power gradually and in a less threatening manner:

1. Grow team members' power first by knowledge, skills, and access to information.

2. Build team members' confidence by allowing them to practice in risk-free situations such as case studies, simulations, and supervised trials.

3. Avoid overwhelming the system by delegating power and autonomy from the top gradually down.

4. Limit risk to managers and team members alike by delegating low-risk projects and decisions first and then working up to higher-risk situations.

Finally, for these initiatives to work, HPT professionals must make sure that the overall organizational system supports the change rather than working against it. HR policies that reward the old behavior, managers who reverse decisions made by the teams, excessive work demands, and other systemic factors can all be fatal to organizational efforts to shift alignment to an unobtrusive approach.

CONCLUSION

The greatest challenge for HPT professionals, when faced with organization shifts in the alignment approach, is likely to be identifying the indicators early enough to take action. Once a problem has been correctly identified, then steps can be taken to design interventions that will manage the necessary shift and transfer of control from one set of stakeholders to another. The trap to be avoided, as in so many interventions, is one of misdiagnosis by either the HPT professional or a client. The pain of an organizational control issue can easily be mistaken for a policy or training issue if the root cause is not recognized. Therefore, HPT professionals need to pay particular attention to those situations in which frictions over responsibility, authority, goals, or empowerment rise to the surface and demand attention. When these issues arise, they are signs that some deeper and potentially systemic problem needs to be addressed and that band-aid-type fixes such as simple training or policy changes are less likely to have the long-term desired impact.

Summary of Main Points

Here is a brief summary for HPT professionals of some of the main takeaways from this chapter:

- The interconnections between alignment, control, power, authority, and responsibility all suggest that an overall systems approach is necessary when dealing with such complex problems; systemic change of this kind involving interventions that address organizational structure, training, supports, and policies may take months or years to fully implement.

- When evaluating a particular organizational problem, anticipate that the greater the distance between management and production, the greater the risk of communication distortion and the misalignment of cultures, values, and behaviors.

- Diagnose organizational structure issues early if possible to avoid addressing symptoms rather than causes.

- Help management to understand that shifting control of behaviors to work teams does not guarantee success.

- Aid management in paying attention to both overt alignment of behaviors and unobtrusive alignment of norms and values. Finding the right balance can be a challenge.

- Training is often an essential component in the transition to self-managed teams; team members need to be experienced, skillful, and mature to effectively take on many of the common functions of self-management.

- Anticipate resistance based on perceived loss of power and try to inform stakeholders about the possibilities for expanding power and alignment through sharing and delegation.

- Transfer task autonomy and power gradually.

- Make sure that the overall system is not working against the transition and that the change is aligned with the organization's culture and goals.

References

Bales, R. F. (1958). Task roles and social roles in problem solving groups. In E. E. Maccoby, T. M. Newcomb, and E. L. Hartley (Eds.), *Readings in social psychology.* New York: Holt, Rinehart, & Winston.

Child, J. (1984). *Organization* (2nd ed.). London, UK: Harper & Row.

Cummings, T. (1978). Self-regulating work groups: A socio-technical synthesis. *The Academy of Management Review, 3*(3), 625–634.

Cummings, T. G., and Molloy, E. S. (1977). *Improving productivity and the quality of work life* (Praeger Special Studies). Westport, CT: Greenwood.

Dainty, A. R., Bryman, A., and Price, A. D. (2002). Empowerment within the UK construction sector. *Leadership and Organization Development Journal, 23*(6), 333–342.

Feldman, D. (1984). The development and enforcement of group norms. *Academy of Management Review, 9*(1), 47–53.

Forrester, R. (2000). Empowerment: Rejuvenating a potent idea. *The Academy of Management Executive, 14*(3), 67–80.

Greenberger, D. B., Miceli, M. P., and Cohen, D. J. (1987). Oppositionists and group norms: The reciprocal influence of whistle-blowers and co-workers. *Journal of Business Ethics, 6*(7), 527–542.

Hind, M. (1992). The challenge of managing people. *Logistics Information Management, 5*(4), 38–41.

Katz, D., and Kahn, R. L. (1978). *The social psychology of organizations.* New York: Wiley.

Keller, J. M. (1983). Motivational design of instruction. In C. M. Reigeluth (Ed.), *Instructional theories and models: An overview of their current status* (pp. 383–434). Mahwah, NJ: Lawrence Erlbaum Associates.

Kirkman, B., and Rosen, R. (1999). Beyond self-management: Antecedents and consequences of team empowerment. *Academy of Management Journal, 42*(1), 58–74.

Manz, C., and Sims, H. (1987). Leading workers to lead themselves: The external leadership of self-managing teams. *Administrative Science Quarterly, 32*(1), 106–128.

March, J., and Simon, H. A. (1958). *Organizations.* New York: Wiley.

Marker, A. (2001). The roles and relationships of training, rewards and control in an organizational change: A human performance field study. *Dissertation Abstracts International, 62*(2), 669. (UMI No. 3005403.)

McGrath, J. E. (1984). *Groups: Interaction and performance.* Englewood Cliffs, NJ: Prentice-Hall.

Moore, J. E. (2000). Why is this happening? A causal attribution approach to work exhaustion consequences. *The Academy of Management Review, 25*(2), 335–349.

Ouchi, W. (1977). The relationship between organizational structure and organizational control. *Administrative Science Quarterly, 22*(1), 95–113.

Parsons, T. (1969). On the concept of political power in Bell. In D. Edwards and R. Wagner (Eds.), *Political power: A reader in theory and research.* New York: Free Press.

Tannenbaum, A. (1961). Control and effectiveness in a voluntary organization. *The American Journal of Sociology, 67*(1), 33–46.

Tannenbaum, R., and Schmidt W. H. (1958). How to choose a leadership pattern. *Harvard Business Review, 36*(2), 95–101.

Trevino, L. K., and Victor, B. (1992). Peer reporting of unethical behavior: A social context perspective. *Academy of Management Journal, 35*(1), 38–64.

Xavier, S. (2002). Clear communications and feedback can improve manager and employee effectiveness. *Employment Relations Today, 29*(2), 33–41.

CHAPTER TWENTY-TWO

Principles and Practices
of Work-Group Performance

Michael F. Cassidy, Megan M. Cassidy

The final draft of The International Society for Performance Improvement (ISPI) Presidential Initiative Task Force report (2003) defines human performance technology (HPT) as an integrated systems approach to improving performance. The varied implications of this definition are described in the report as well as other sources, including Stolovich and Keeps (1992). Human performance technology's domain unambiguously includes the goal of improving people's performance in organizational settings, as individual performers or actors, and acting in cohort with others to fulfill organizational obligations. The focus of this chapter is on the collaborative aspect of human performance.

One of the dominant and sustained organizational practices in the past decade has been the adoption of work teams to complete organizational objectives. The use of work groups is an inherent characteristic of process improvement, change management, reengineering, reinventing government, the learning organization, contemporary management and leadership theory, and so forth. Work groups have become part of the fabric of organizational life. It has been estimated, for example, that two-thirds of Fortune 500 companies use work groups in their organizations (Sivasubramaniam, Murry, Avolio, and Jung, 2002).

Workers are now often expected to function, formally or informally, in intact work groups or teams, and to demonstrate the often-cited research finding that groups have the potential of exceeding the individual contributions of their most knowledgeable and skilled members (Katzenbach and Smith, 1999;

Reagan-Cirincione, 1994). Yet, despite an empirically supported link between group performance and organizational performance, the expectation of improved group performance is often unfulfilled (Reagan-Cirincione, Schuman, Richardson, and Dorf, 1991). In turn, the promise of enhanced organizational performance is unfulfilled.

Meetings, the typical vehicle for intragroup communication and decision making, are fodder for the daily comics. Their inefficiencies are the subject of private hallway, lunch, phone, and e-mail conversations. The impact of poorly functioning work groups on organizations, however, can be substantial, resulting in interpersonal conflict and decreased productivity (Jehn, 1997). Yet the use of work groups persists, perhaps in part because when they *do* work their output reflects the creativity, richness, and commitment to action that is difficult to achieve when a single person dictates a solution or action plan to others. When work groups are properly designed and implemented, they benefit organizations by effectively meeting performance challenges in the workplace (Katzenbach and Smith, 1999).

Perhaps the most significant value of a group lies in the potential of its diversity: the leveraging of relevant differences in perspectives that individual group members bring to collaborative organizational tasks. While homogenous groups may initially be more efficient than heterogeneous groups, the advantage vanishes quickly (Watson, Kumar and Michaelsen, 1993). Maznevski's research (1994), for example, supports the notion that meetings attended by people in a variety of roles and status levels result in greater acceptance of input and advice and have a salutary impact on problem-solving strategies. Hambrick, Cho, and Chen (1996) identify a positive relationship between functional and educational heterogeneity in top management teams and the magnitude of the organizations' competitive actions. A study of Canadian banking branches (Ng and Tung, 1998) identified a higher level of organizational performance in racially mixed branches than in primarily Caucasian branches. We do not wish to oversimplify the issue of diversity and work-group performance. The literature is substantial and growing. The specific condition under which diversity of group membership positively affects group work is complex. The literature and our experience, however, suggest that diversity can contribute substantially to group and organizational performance when it is employed to challenge assumptions, question practices, and develop solutions not previously considered.

Work teams succeed when certain circumstances are present. However, when one or more of these conditions is not met, the team risks failure and frustration. This chapter is directed specifically at both team members and facilitators to help them determine which characteristics lead to effective team functioning. In particular, our aim is to provide insight into determining when it is appropriate to convene a group meeting, how to identify social and technical factors associated with group performance, and how to select approaches that will improve the likelihood of team success. We use the terms *group* and *team* interchangeably, but we limit consideration to *task groups:* groups whose basic reason for being is to complete a task in support of organizational goals, and whose work involves some level of interaction, primarily in a face-to-face setting. In addition, we exclude nominal groups, insofar as they are groups in name only: Delphi groups, because their process generally minimizes interaction among members; focus groups, due to their emphasis on gathering rather than acting on information; and groups whose primary purpose is social or therapeutic. Social groups, for example, be they formal, such as a fraternity, or informal, such as a group of persons who convene irregularly to share company, exist principally as vehicles for social networking. Therapeutic groups may be formed as part of a clinical treatment program. Groups that are formed primarily to do something in support of organizational goals, however, whether they are permanent and intact, or convened for a fixed period to complete a given assignment, are unique in a number of regards. We begin with a consideration of some fundamental issues associated with group performance, and next present a sequential, normative model for designing and implementing a task-group intervention. Our focus is predominantly on groups with an established purpose of problem solving or decision making. Nonetheless, this scope is broad, encompassing any circumstances in which a set of persons is involved in and actively engaged in acting upon data or applying judgment. Examples include planning groups, design teams, management teams, and so forth.

Before beginning, we offer a final clarification. The format of any handbook is such that only a cursory treatment of a given subject is feasible. The balance between scope and depth is a difficult one to realize. We attempt to be sufficiently broad to encompass the key dimensions of work-group performance, and to provide sufficient detail to be of practical use to the reader. The details, however, may not always be sufficient, and in such instances we recommend that readers turn to the many published sources available.

THE CONTEXT OF GROUP PERFORMANCE

When Is a Group Necessary?

There is no algorithm for answering the question, When is a work group necessary? The decision to employ a group is influenced as much by sensitivity to organizational norms as by the need to engage a range of expertise. For example, an organization in which members have expressed dissatisfaction with senior management, arguing that they have an insufficient role in key decisions, may benefit from the use of a representative team chartered to make recommendations. This approach may, from a strictly technical perspective, offer little additional benefit. Some heuristics do exist, however, that provide counsel on when to employ a group. Perhaps the most widely cited guidance on when to convene a group or when to make a decision autonomously comes from Vroom and his associates (Jago and Vroom, 1980). Their Contingency Model of Leadership Behavior suggests that multiple persons should be involved in the decision-making process if the decision relates to goals not universally accepted by organizational members, acceptance of the decision by organizational members is imperative for successful implementation, and there is no guarantee that the decision made by the leader will be accepted by the subordinates.

Gordon (1993) presents similar guidelines, adding that members' previous experiences working together and the availability of time are additional supporting factors in the team-based approach. We adopt a somewhat different perspective on the time-availability criterion. It is our experience that when an organization is in crisis and time to resolve the issues is short, convening a meeting of decision makers, stakeholders, experts, and other relevant parties may prove the best approach for a supported outcome that effectively addresses the issues. Reasons for this perspective are addressed throughout this chapter.

What Are the Requisite Conditions for a Successful Work Group?

How does one define success in terms of a work group? The issue is problematic. As argued by McCartt and Rohrbaugh (1995), groups in which members work harmoniously and efficiently sometimes produce bad decisions. By contrast, groups that are largely contentious and whose members engage in personal attacks on one another may ultimately have superlative outcomes. Simply, *good* groups can produce bad decisions just as *bad* groups may produce good decisions. Using the output of a group as the criterion of success is inherently tautological. How then might success be measured? In general, well-functioning groups, those in which emotional conflict is minimized and conflict related to the cognitive dimensions of the task is maximized and managed, have a higher likelihood of generating well-thought-out and supportable outcomes (Pelled, Eisenhardt, and Xin, 1999). Success, therefore, may best be assessed on the basis of *how* a group functions. Several conditions have been identified as necessary, albeit not sufficient, conditions for enhancing group processing. We describe these in the following paragraphs.

Groups should possess a clear charter. While this condition is seemingly obvious, a group is sometimes convened with an underlying ambiguity regarding the group's purpose or its level of authority. For example, it may be unclear whether the group has been convened to develop a high-level strategy or to create a detailed implementation plan. Making the charter of the group explicit has the associated benefit of signifying group efficacy to its members, and elevating confidence in success (Mohammed and Ringseis, 2001). Clearly establishing group goals, both proximal and distal, has also been linked to enhanced group performance (Weldon and Yun, 2000).

Second, groups should be issue or problem focused. Groups sometimes fall prey to the trap of not making the tacit explicit or accepting assumptions that may not be accurate. A potential consequence is the risk of developing detailed and time-consuming solutions to a misdiagnosed problem. For example, a manager becomes alarmed when she observes that sales have been steadily declining over several months. She convenes a group to fix the problem. At the first meeting, someone from the finance department proposes that the decline in sales began at approximately the same time that the advertising budget had been cut. The group readily agrees to this observation and its attention turns to solving the advertising problem. In reality, however, the root cause for the decline in sales actually encompasses several factors: poor cycle time, increased market competition, and poor customer support. The reasons for misdiagnosis are myriad. Sometimes, for example, they emerge from a sense of social pressure to conform, explicit or implicit censorship of ideas that diverge from the norm, or a shared illusion that the group is impervious to failure (Manz and Neck, 1997). This is not meant to suggest that a group may not be convened with the specific charter of diagnosis, but simply that when charged to address an issue, the group sometimes fails to address the problem adequately before advancing to the solution stage.

Finally, clearly defined roles and responsibilities are essential for a group to work effectively. Each team member should understand his or her specific role and the roles of all other members. Some members may be asked to participate because they have knowledge pertinent to the task not possessed by others. Others may be involved to represent the perspective of a particular organization unit. Clarifying *what* people are responsible for in group activities is just as important as clarifying *why* they are involved.

Salas, Bowers, and Edens (2001) investigated flight crew behaviors during flight mishaps and found that avoidable errors are sometimes the result of role ambiguity among lower-ranked officers, specifically as their role relates to the legitimacy of questioning a decision of a superior officer. For example, at Houston International Airport in 1996, a departing aircraft slid along the runway during takeoff. This near-fatal error was traced to a subordinate officer's decision not to question the senior officer's decision despite the junior officer's perception of a problem. The subordinate officer apparently believed it inappropriate to question the judgment of his superior. One way of avoiding potential problems associated with status differences within a group is to make explicit the role that each member is expected to play.

GROUP ROLES

Group Leader

A group leader is the person with primary responsibility for stewardship of the group as it executes its work. The group leader is often the most senior-ranking member in the group, but not necessarily. Nanus (1996) argues that the team leader is responsible for creating a goal for the group, gaining commitment from group members, and creating the necessary organizational or group changes to fulfill the goal. In this latter sense, the leader plays a key role in linking the work of the group to the larger organization and acting as a conduit for the bidirectional flow of information. As suggested by Likert (1967), the leader acts as a lynchpin for bridging organizationally disparate groups. Nutt (1976) describes the function as one of coalescing. McFadzean and O'Loughlin (2000) argue that the absence of a group leader leads to a decrease in performance and an increase of struggle for dominance among group members. When there are options regarding who will assume the role of leader, it may be useful to attempt to match the leader's style with the specific parameters of the group. Myrsiades (2000), for example, suggests that directive leadership is more compatible with large groups that thrive on structure and that lack topic knowledge, motivation, experience and time. Someone with a reserved style may be better suited to small and knowledgeable groups that are tolerant of uncertainty, experienced in intragroup interaction, motivated, and not under pressure to reach a decision quickly.

Subject-Matter Experts

Often groups need to include persons possessing expertise critical to the group's deliberations for some or all of their meetings. These carefully selected subject-matter experts function best within the group when they do not have genuine ownership in the group's decisions. For example, we recently facilitated a budget-setting activity involving several groups in an organization. Each team represented a specific technical function within the overall organization. While each group was able to argue the substantive impact of varying budget allocations on the technical work of its own functional unit, the overall success of the project required the involvement of financial personnel, organizationally distinct from the technical groups. In addition, the task required that management conduct a comprehensive review across functional units.

Facilitator

Schwarz (2002) suggests that one of a facilitator's primary responsibilities is to help the group increase the effectiveness of its interaction. An effective facilitator removes from the group the burden of managing the process, thereby permitting it to concentrate on the substance of the issues with which it is tasked. The positive impact of a facilitator on a group's performance has been widely documented (McFadzean and O'Loughlin, 2000; Phillips and Phillips, 1993; Anson, Bostrom, and Wynne, 1995; Wheeler and Valacich, 1996; Nelson and McFadzean, 1998). An effective group facilitator inevitably faces the difficulty of reconciling two potentially conflicting tasks: allowing the group to function efficiently and controlling, in reality or in perception, the group's activities. Facilitators operate in the three levels of group performance described later in this chapter: operational, tactical, and strategic. Facilitators are instrumental in designing and executing the meeting, developing a suitable model or structure for the group to approach its task, engaging participation of all group members regardless of status, and so forth (Frey, 1995; McFadzean and O'Loughlin, 2000).

We have been asked on several occasions to facilitate groups in which the members, the agenda, meeting length, and other important elements of the design had already been set. In virtually all instances, we declined the opportunity, and regretted afterward those rare instances in which we accepted. It is our experience that groups in general, especially those that are grappling with contentious issues, are best served when the design of the meeting emerges from the needs. Establishing a design and then involving a facilitator places the proverbial cart before the horse. A well-conceived design, however, is not infrequently discarded in response to the dynamics that emerge in the actual meeting. The lead author once facilitated a meeting of senior managers and the organization's board of directors. The group was convened with the primary purpose of selecting future organizational initiatives. In preparation, interviews were held with each attendee, including the board members. Several decisions recently made by the board had been met with strong resistance from senior managers. At a preparatory meeting with board members, the facilitator was informed that these decisions were irrevocable. The meeting was thus designed to take into account these immutable decisions. Within the first thirty minutes of the general meeting, however, when questioned about a specific decision, one of the board members remarked somewhat meekly, "Well, I guess *nothing* is set in granite." The other board members nodded in silent agreement. The event precipitated the need to revise radically the meeting design in real time.

One final guideline about facilitators is in order: do not facilitate any group in which you have, or may be perceived to have, a stake in the outcome. The central tenet in this guideline is that someone external to the organization is largely immune from accusations of partiality. In this regard, the colloquial definition of a consultant as someone who borrows your watch to tell you the time, and then keeps your watch, may be apt for some facilitators as well. An alternative to using external facilitators is to engage someone adequately prepared from another part of the organization, and to return the favor when needed.

Decision Makers and Stakeholders

As suggested earlier, it is essential that the person or persons with legitimate organizational authority for a decision be actively involved in the decision-making process. In addition, representatives of key stakeholding groups affected by the decision must be involved. If one or more key players refuse to participate, the most senior manager is advised to make explicit that those abstaining are relinquishing the opportunity to shape the decision and will have to live with the consequences. In one situation in which we participated, a particularly weak executive-level manager permitted two of four senior-level managers to abstain from a critical three-day strategic planning session involving approximately two dozen persons representing all functional units. In a management session scheduled after the large meeting with the purpose of developing a follow-up implementation plan, the two managers absent from the general sessions each stated that they could not support the plan. No justification was given. The executive manager, holding that unanimous support was essential, acquiesced, and the strategic plan was abandoned. Several months later, the executive manager was dismissed from his position.

Sensitivity to Social Dynamics

Task-group work has two broad dimensions: technical and social. The technical dimension comprises issues related to how a meeting is structured, the roles of participants, length, and so forth. The social dimension, in contrast, concerns the interaction of psychologically complex individuals with one another in a social forum, may involve their attempts at dominance or territoriality, may reflect their emotional attachment to specific solutions (Jehn, 1997), and so forth. Schein (1996) effectively argues that the stage for organizational failure is set when the dynamics of relationships among human beings are ignored or viewed as irrelevant.

In a group environment, the personal goals of individual members need to be balanced with the goals of the organization (Ariely and Levav, 2000). Individuals may, for example, identify themselves more closely as members of a particular functional or demographic group with goals that are ostensibly out of alignment with the goals of task groups of which the individuals are also members.[1] The technical dimension, if well managed, facilitates healthy cognitive conflict. Cognitive, or task-group, conflict arises when multiple persons view the same situation from different perspectives, even when their individual goals and values may be in harmony (Bose and Paradice, 1999). Effectively managed cognitive conflict positively affects group performance (Jehn, 1997).

McFadzean (2002) suggests that properly facilitated conflict also can reduce "group think,"[2] enhance inventiveness, and permit examination of the issues from a variety of perspectives. Napoleon Bonaparte is alleged to have remarked that those who failed to oppose him, who acquiesced to his views without question, were his worst enemies, yet within the social arena also lies the danger of conflict of an interpersonal nature. The objective of anyone designing or facilitating a task group, therefore, is to facilitate cognitive conflict and to manage social conflict.

LEVELS OF GROUP PLANNING

A potentially useful organizing scheme for teamwork is to distinguish between three levels of planning and execution, as depicted in Figure 22.1. The continuum shown at the top of the figure is grounded in Simon's work (1987).

As the complexity and uniqueness of a given task increases, so does the importance of addressing tactical and strategic issues. For example, a team that meets weekly obviously needs to consider operational issues, but if the meeting is largely to discuss emerging issues of importance to the group, tactical and strategic issues may be less critical. In other situations, however, all three levels may need to be addressed if the team is to complete its task successfully. A merger of two organizations, as an illustration, may prompt key individuals to meet and to develop a new strategic plan. While operational issues—such as ensuring that the meeting room is sufficiently large to accommodate all attendees—are important, they pale in relation to the more substantive issues of managing undefined status relationships among players. Proper management of these relationships facilitates group exploration of emerging opportunities, constraints, and so forth.

Planning Levels	Simple Routine → Complex Novel		
	Operational	**Tactical**	**Strategic**
Examples	Adequacy of physical environment	Effectiveness of facilitative strategies	Exploring the problem space: focusing on root causes versus symptoms
	Adequacy of media	Ensuring full participation of attendees	Exploring the solution space: considering all viable options
	Sufficient time to complete tasks	Managing status differences among participants	Selecting evaluation criteria
			Correctly modeling the decision

Figure 22.1. Levels of Planning for Effective Task Groups.

Operational

At the simplest, operational-level issues relate to the physical needs of the group. These include environmental factors such as the size of the room, availability of media, legibility of projected media, and so forth. While relatively straightforward, operational issues are not unimportant. Considerable attention has been given in the literature to factors such as the seating configuration, lighting, location onsite or offsite, and so forth (Myrsiades, 2000; Doyle and Straus, 1982). Myrsiades (2000) requested that respondents list circumstances that negatively affect a meeting and subsequently lead to ineffectiveness or inefficiency. The operational characteristics of the worst possible meeting conditions included continuous interruptions from outside parties, group members leaving and entering the room throughout the meeting, the meeting exceeding its predetermined ending time, poor ventilation, classroom style configuration, and so on.

Tactical

The tactical dimension largely involves the management of social and psychological dimensions of a meeting. Given that facilitation was discussed earlier in the chapter, we will focus primarily on tactical issues related to the status and participation of group members.

Status relates to the hierarchical positions people occupy in organizations, and the potential impact of those different levels on group functioning. The example cited previously concerning the flight crew's performance is an instance of the undesirable impact of status on team performance. Hollingshead (1996) suggests that those who may provide the most benefit to the group may be intimidated by higher-status members, and, as such, refrain from contributing despite the potentially significant impact of their contributions. Some have argued for homogeneity in level among group members as a response to the potentially negative impact of status (McFadzean, 1998; McFadzean, 2002; Pinsonneault and Kraemer, 1990; Belbin, 1981).

While we recognize that status differences present a very real problem, we believe the solution does not lie in pursuing homogeneity but rather in managing heterogeneity. Unequal status is but one potential threat to group performance. Participants, for example, may come from different sectors of the organization. Each sector may hold an unspoken but universally acknowledged place in the pecking order. What is the best way to address these issues? The answer, we believe, lies in the technical dimension of the group, specifically, the use of techniques that help to eliminate or mitigate these factors. For example, a simple solution to the status problem is to ask each participant to record his or her ideas on a sticky note and place it on the wall for review by the group, thereby eliminating initial association of the idea with its owner. In a less threatening environment, the use of an "oral round robin," in which each participant sequentially proposes an idea, may mitigate the adverse impact of status.

Another tactic for dealing with issues of status and participation is decomposition, which refers to the segmentation of an issue into smaller elements that then may be considered rationally. For example, one of the authors was asked to facilitate a session of approximately twenty persons representing varying hierarchical levels and sectors of the organization. The goal of the meeting was to choose between two existing technologies for a new service the organization was interested in developing. There were strident advocates of each technology in the meeting. Our approach was to identify the criteria against which the two potential solutions would be evaluated and then to rate each technology against each weighted criterion. This decompositional approach permitted the group to consider each technology's performance against each criterion. Differences in opinion became narrowly focused. If someone asserted, for example, that a specific service might be implemented more rapidly with one technology, the rationale for the assertion was solicited. Unbundling the issues helped the group to deal rationally rather than emotionally with them. Identifying the criteria, assigning weights to them to reflect differences in importance, and applying the criteria to evaluate each technology illustrate the use of structure. At the close of a very long day, the group unanimously agreed that one technology was superior to the other and should be adopted. One participant remarked that while it was not the decision he was hoping for, it was derived fairly, was auditable, and was one that he could defend to his management.

Structure is another potentially effective tactical approach to managing issues of status and participation in groups. An example of this, sometimes referred to as the *sucker effect,* occurs when perceived involvement and commitment from some group members may influence the satisfaction of other members. According to Maznevski (1994), for a group to be effective, each member must believe that every individual in the group is participating fully and enthusiastically. If group members perceive that there is a loafer within the group they will subsequently decrease their level of involvement and performance rather than carry that individual. The use of structure, however, may be effective in eliminating the issue by making explicit the actual contributions of group members. For example, recording the tasks each group member has agreed to do, and making this public, may pressure the social loafer to volunteer for his or her share of the work. If this does not occur, and there appears to be an unequal distribution of work among participants, the facilitator can legitimately note the perceived inequality and ask for clarification or explanation.

Strategic

The literature provides ample guidance on the operational and tactical levels of group planning and performance. The strategic level, however, is less well represented. It is, however, potentially the most critical, insofar as it concerns the fundamental intellectual framework within which groups approach tasks.

As Simon (1987) and others have proposed, decisions should emerge from an iterative process encompassing several interrelated steps. Intelligence, or gathering relevant data, is the point of departure. The second step entails exploring the problem area thoroughly and attempting to distinguish root causes from symptoms. Third, the criteria against which potential solutions will be evaluated need to be developed and defined for consistency in interpretation. A robust set of potentially viable solutions should be generated. These potentially viable solutions should be evaluated against the criteria, and, finally, the preferred solution should be examined to assess how robust it is under varying circumstances. This is known as sensitivity analysis. Building on this scheme, we present in the next section a model for executing these strategic functions. While admittedly iterative, the model is intended to be applied sequentially.

MODELING THE PROBLEM OR DECISION

We assume that all relevant data have been collected and reviewed prior to convening the group. Realistically, however, in *acting* upon the data collected, unanticipated questions sometimes arise, necessitating additional and unavailable data. It is also important to caution against giving water to someone drowning.

Decisions that involve a single, clearly defined criterion for which there are reliable and valid data do not require a group's judgment. If, for example, the only criterion at play in choosing to relocate to site A or site B is total annual operating cost, and site B is less costly than site A, the decision is simple. In reality, however, affairs are rarely so simple or simplistic.

Modeling is essentially structuring a problem or issue in a way that maximizes group performance in task completion. We advise considering how to model the task prior to convening the group. Not unlike the point made above that the need for additional data may emerge, sometimes, despite the best intentions and effort, the model initially chosen may need to be switched for another during the process.

Table 22.1 is a simple decision-making table for choosing between two alternative models. While we do not claim that these options are exhaustive, our experience is that they are appropriate for a majority of organizational issues.

Table 22.1. Matching Models and Circumstances.

Condition	Recommended Model
The choice is among a discrete set of options.	Multi-attribute
Options are not inherently discrete, but may be combined in different ways reflecting varying ways of allocating limited resources.	Cost/benefit or resource allocation

Some choices are inherently discrete, as presented in the earlier example regarding the selection of one of two vying technologies. When an organization has only one open position and two excellent candidates, the choice is clearly dichotomous. This is similar to the dilemmas we may face in choosing among several automobiles when we can only afford to purchase one, or grappling with the choice of two computers that use different and incompatible operating systems. When faced with such choices, a multi-attribute or criteria-modeling approach can be a very effective way of approaching the decision (Cook and Hammond, 1982). Bose and Paradice (1999) define a multi-attribute modeling approach as a technique wherein exact values of each decision maker in the group are clarified and compared. An example of a value tree, representing hierarchically nested attributes or criteria, is shown in Figure 22.2. The overall value of the options under consideration is assessed using each level in the model. This figure was generated by HiView, a groupware program designed for multi-criteria decision making at the London School of Economics.

By contrast, many decisions can be modeled effectively by examining various combinations of alternatives and associated resources required to pursue them. For example, budgeting across multiple units within an organization

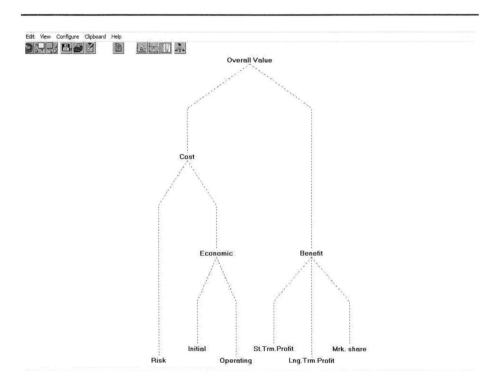

Figure 22.2. Example of a Value Tree.

File Edit View Configure Clipboard Analysis Help

	1	2	3	4	5	6	7
Plumbing	Porosity	Level 1					
Roof	Leave as is	Patch	Asphalt - new	Tin roof - new	Shake shingles	Italian Tile	
Kitchen	SQ	microwave	change floor	Sears Best!	Change cabinets	KRUPS etc	Gourmet
HVAC	SQ	Shared fan	Use fireplace	AC window units	Solar system	New HVAC	
Landscaping	SQ	Cut grass	Lawn service	Pond	Rose garden		
Flooring	SQ	Clean carpets	Pro. clng.	Carpet tiles	Pro. carpet		

Figure 22.3. Example Created in a Decision-Making Course.

when approached this way may facilitate team members considering increasing or decreasing allocation based on different benefits to the organization. In some instances, decisions that are not inherently discrete are conceptualized as if they were. To use a mundane example, a family decision for a vacation location may be unnecessarily cast as the beach or the mountains, when a compromise may be achievable which combines the options into a different package.

Figure 22.3 shows an example created in a decision-making course. In this scenario the students pooled their resources and purchased a house in need of much repair. The sewer pipe, for example, is leaking or evidencing porosity; the roof is leaking; the kitchen has not been remodeled since the early 1950s; and so forth. The underlying concept is that there are limited resources, and that the members of the group hold differing values regarding how to spend those limited resources. Each horizontal row in the model represents an investment area, and each cell within the area represents a different level of investment, bounded by the least and the most anyone in the group would consider acceptable.

The roof area, for example, ranges from ignoring the leak to installing an expensive tile roof. The table was made with another program developed through the London School of Economics, Equity. Both Equity and HiView were created to help groups model typical organizational decisions and facilitate decomposition, weighting, sensitivity analysis, and so forth.

Structuring encourages the group to consider investment levels potentially greater and less than what they may have initially entertained. In addition, each option is evaluated against cost and benefit criteria. The individual arguing for the Italian tile roof, for example, is compelled to make explicit why her desired option is more or less beneficial than other options in the row. The process encourages rational evaluation and discourages emotional conflict.

Defining Criteria

Choices, either individual or group, inherently involve the application of criteria to the available options. This seemingly straightforward task, however, is often complicated by failure to make the criteria explicit, failure to operationalize criteria, and failure to distinguish the relative importance of each criterion. A necessary but not sufficient condition for success is that all members of the team understand the measures they will be using to evaluate options.

If the criteria are not specified or not operationalized, there is a strong risk of disagreement arising from insufficient communication. For example, if a new strategic venture is being considered, and benefit to the firm is identified as the primary criterion, one member may interpret benefit as market share and another may interpret it as short-term profitability, while a third person may be defining it as long-term growth. A colleague of one of the authors relates an incident in which he was facilitating a group in a rural area of New York State regarding development of rural land. With frustrations rising among the two constituencies, one supporting development and the other opposing it, he asked each group to define *development* in operational terms. Perhaps not surprisingly, each group was using a different definition. Quickly, the group was able to reach a common acceptable definition and, by so doing, came to realize that they agreed with one another more than they disagreed.

There is a similar need for explicitness in identifying the relative importance of each criterion. For example, a university department team is charged with selecting a new faculty member to replace a retiree. The team identifies a list of several criteria, including a strong record of research, excellence in teaching, and success in grant proposal writing. Each criterion may have a different weight for each member of the selection team. Were they to discuss the relative importance of each criterion and apply them to the candidates, they might develop a structure similar to the one shown in Table 22.2. The values beneath

Table 22.2. Candidate-Evaluation Matrix.

	Candidates	
Criteria	A	B
Research Weight = 35	4 × 35 = 140	7 × 35 = 245
Teaching Weight = 45	6 × 45 = 270	4 × 45 = 180
Grants Weight = 20	2 × 20 = 40	7 × 20 = 140
Total = 100	Total = 450	Total = 565

each criterion represent the relative importance of the criterion agreed to by the group. Each of the two candidates is evaluated on a 1 to 7 scale, with higher numbers representing better performance against the criterion. In total, candidate B, with an overall score of 565, dominates candidate A.

Exploring the Problem Space

As described earlier, groups sometimes embark on the design of solutions without questioning whether they are tackling the root cause of the problem or merely the symptoms. A large body of literature is devoted to why this phenomenon occurs, and equally large amounts have been written on how to avoid the problem. Beach (1997) and others use the term *framing* to describe this phenomenon. Framing entails interpreting events based on previous experience, available data, the specific context, and often the role the person assumes in the situation. It is a way of dealing efficiently with limited information-processing capacity. Someone who is under suspicion for committing a crime, for example, may be perceived, incorrectly, to be guilty based on his or her fidgety behavior (Vrij, 2000). The classic film *Twelve Angry Men* depicts an excellent example of faulty framing; the plot centers on a dissenting juror in a murder trial who slowly manages to convince the other jurors that the case is not as clear as it seemed in court. As another illustration, Russo and Schoemaker (1989) describe a situation in which an organization's engineers investigated a problem and quickly concluded it to be of the same type as one they had recently encountered. The diagnosis was incorrect and the manager estimated a loss of $2.6 million resulting from fixing something that was not the real cause of the problem. While framing has its advantages in efficiency, it may lead to undesirable consequences.

Numerous well-documented techniques are helpful in challenging a group's frames and helping them think through an issue critically, including cognitive mapping, influence diagrams, Ishikawa diagrams (Ishikawa, 1982), value trees, and so forth. We briefly address one such technique, force-field analysis. As documented by Cummings and Worley (2001), force-field analysis stems from Lewin's change model (Lewin, 1952). Lewin postulated that organizations are subjected to two forces: one that is pushing for change and one that is pushing against change. A strength of the technique is that it helps make both forces explicit in regard to a particular organizational goal, as well as facilitating a structured discussion on what the organization might do to intensify positive forces and reduce the impact of, or eliminate, negative forces.

An organization has experienced a recent increase in employee turnover. In an effort to stem the loss of valuable employees and reduce the associated costs, a cross-functional group is formed to assess the situation and make recommendations. As a point of departure, the group examines the organization's attrition data for the past several years and compares its turnover rate with industry statistics. The data confirm that there has been a marked increase over

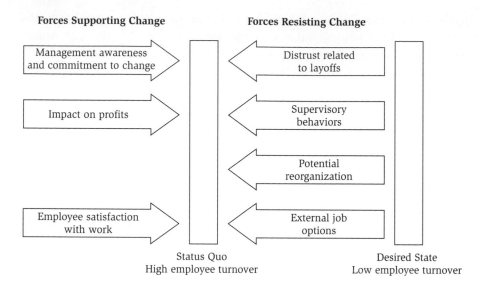

Figure 22.4. Force-Field Analysis Example.

time, and that the current rate compares very unfavorably with other companies in the industry. As a way of better understanding the reasons for employee turnover, the group uses a force-field analysis diagram, an example of which is shown in Figure 22.4.

The group begins by identifying some factors that it believes may facilitate the desired change of moving from the current state of unacceptably high turnover to the desired state of reduced turnover. In turn, it identifies forces working against change. What begins to emerge is a better understanding of what may be working for and against change, as well as questions about some of the assertions. For example, while there may be clear and persuasive evidence of management's commitment as well as an adverse impact on the organization's profitability, evidence of employees' satisfaction with their work may be anecdotal, requiring the review of extant data or the collection of new data. Over the course of several meetings, the group begins to develop a better sense of what is symptomatic and what is likely at the root of the issue. The benefits of this and related techniques include identification of potential forces, the impetus for targeted hypothesis testing, identification of relationships between opposing factors, identification of potential actions that might facilitate the desired change, and clarification and development of relevant metrics.

Exploring the Solution Space

As groups may fail to give sufficient attention to root causes, they also sometimes fail to search for potentially better solutions than the ones immediately at hand. Simon (1987) used the term *satisfying* to describe this phenomenon, identifying a course of action that is good enough. In large part, Simon argues that this behavior is less the result of laziness than a function of the inherently limited information-processing capabilities of humans. Our world, he suggests, is one bound by rationality (Simon, 1955).

The notion of decomposition, introduced earlier, is an inherent element of challenging assumptions regarding what should be included in the universe of potential solutions. To return to the house-improvement issue, in this example the facilitator challenges the group to expand its list of potential options as well as to define realistic anchors. In a budgeting exercise, for example, each department representative may enter the meeting using the current year's budget as the anchor. The facilitator presents challenges, such as the following: If your budget were cut by 50 percent, what would you not be able to accomplish? If your budget were increased by 10 percent, what would you be able to do that you cannot currently do? The process of diverging from the status quo encourages the group to identify new options and to consider both the costs and the relative benefits of each.

Conducting Sensitivity Analyses and Resolving Disagreements

Reason, consistently applied within a structured process involving decomposition, can be an extremely effective device for managing emotional discord. Humans, thankfully, are not clones of the quintessentially logical Mr. Spock of *Star Trek* fame. If a member's personal goals, for example, are at odds with the decision the group appears to be nearing, an oft-heard response is to suggest that the emerging outcome is the consequence of a specific parameter with which he or she disagrees. One particularly effective technique for addressing this issue is applying sensitivity analysis. In this context, this approach assesses how robust a choice is to changes in the relative importance of the criteria.

In Table 22.2 we presented the results of a faculty hiring team's evaluation of two candidates. Candidate B, with a total of 565 points, is clearly superior to candidate A given the criteria, their weights, and the ratings. Assume, however, that a member of the hiring team has a strong preference for candidate A and expresses to the others that there must be something wrong with the way things were done. He argues that the group was too harsh in evaluating candidate A's research record, and suggests raising the rating from a 4 to a 5. In this simplified example, the dissident faculty member would presumably see the consequence of this change, but in the complexity of more realistic situations, such modifications would not be quite so apparent. The group acquiesces and recalculates the total. Candidate A now has 485 points, and is still dominated by candidate B. Put more simply, the dominance of candidate B over A is insensitive to the change in the rating.

In an actual situation, an astute facilitator would probe to determine if one or more important criterion had been omitted, if the weights actually reflected the department and university's goals, and other relevant issues. It is important to stress that the structured process effectively diverted a potentially contentious confrontation by emphasizing rationality.

Communicating Results and Garnering Support

One of the primary advantages of teamwork is the involvement of multiple actors. Those involved in the decision-making process have likely achieved an understanding of compromises reached and the reasons for reaching them. Those outside the meeting have not so benefited. Therefore, unless the team comprises the entire organization, or the decisions made are of no consequence to others, it is essential to try to engage those not directly involved. The word *communication* is derived from the Latin *communicare,* to make common. The connotation is an active sharing between two or more persons. The behaviors of some, however, suggest an interpretation that condones an "I told them, therefore I communicated" perspective.

The taxonomy of the affective domain (Krathwohl, Bloom, and Masia, 1964) sheds an interesting perspective on the issues of communication and commitment. The domain comprises five hierarchically ordered levels: receiving, responding, valuing, organization, and characterization by a value or value complex. Our experience suggests that this framework may be useful in partially explaining why organizational changes often do not succeed as anticipated. A senior management team, for example, meets repeatedly in a face-to-face, structured meeting format similar to what we have been describing. Over the course of two full days the group's members are compelled to challenge their assumptions about causes, options, benefits, costs, criteria, and so forth. At the end of the meeting, the group reaches consensus about what and how changes should be made.

We speculate that the group has been engaged in affective learning. The truth, however, wrought by them in an intensive process, is now dictated to the organization as a whole. Not being afforded the same opportunity to internalize the need for change or the attractiveness of the solutions identified, organizational members resist. To be effective, organizational members need to learn in the same manner in which those in the meeting learned. Involving affected persons throughout the process is essential. What we have proposed in this chapter encompasses documenting not only the decisions themselves, but also the processes used in reaching the decisions. Both may be necessary if change is to be accepted with lessened resistance.

SUMMARY AND CONCLUSIONS

Were task groups not as prevalent as they are in organizations, Scott Adams, the creator of *Dilbert,* would have much less material with which to work. Groups have the potential of outperforming any individual, but to realize this promise, certain conditions need to be met. We have argued for explicitness in virtually all aspects of group design. These range from the reason the group is formed to the roles and responsibilities of its members. We presented a three-level structure for planning and implementing groups and have argued that as the complexity and impact of the decision increases, so also does the need to attend to less tangible and more strategic issues related to defining the root issues, defining potential solutions, and evaluating those solutions within an appropriate structure using clear and relevant criteria. Group performance can be exemplary, but both the technical and social dimensions within which people work collaboratively must be actively addressed.

Notes

1. It is beyond the scope of this chapter, but a growing body of literature emerging from social identity theory addresses this topic of conflicting goals (Brickson, 2000; Hogg and Terry, 2000).

2. Group think is the phenomenon wherein the need for group members to identify with a group dominates the approach to the group task. The group members ultimately develop a narrow perspective. Group think frequently results in a decrease in group performance (Mann and Putnam, 1990).

References

Anson, R., Bostrom, R., and Wynne, B. (1995). An experiment assessing group support systems and facilitator effects on meeting outcomes. *Management Science, 41,* 189–208.

Ariely, D., and Levav, J. (2000). Sequential choice in group settings: Taking the road less traveled and less enjoyed. *Journal of Consumer Research, 27,* 279–290.

Beach, L. R. (1997). *The psychology of decision-making: People in organizations.* Thousand Oaks, CA: Sage.

Belbin, R. M. (1981). *Management teams: Why they succeed or fail.* London, UK: Heinemann.

Bose, U., and Paradice, D. B. (1999). The effects of integration cognitive feedback and multi-attribute utility-based multicriteria decision-making methods in GDSS. *Group Decision and Negotiation, 8,* 157–182.

Brickson, S. (2000). The impact of identity orientation: Individual and organizational outcomes in demographically diverse settings. *Academy of Management Review, 25,* 147–149.

Cook, R. L., and Hammond, K. R. (1982). Interpersonal learning and interpersonal conflict reduction in decision-making groups. In R. A. Guzzo (Ed.), *Improving group decision making* (pp. 13–72). New York: Academic Press.

Cummings, T. G., and Worley, C. G. (2001). *Organization development and change* (7th ed.). Cincinnati: South-Western College Publishing.

Doyle, M., and Straus, D. (1982). *How to make meetings work: The new interaction method* (Jove edition). New York: Berkley Publishing Group.

Frey, L. R. (1995). *Innovations in group facilitation: Applications in natural settings.* Cresskill, NJ: Hampton Press.

Gordon, J. R. (1993). *A diagnostic approach to organizational behavior.* Boston, MA: Allyn & Bacon, pp. 348–356.

Hambrick, D. C., Cho, T. S., and Chen, M. (1996). The influence of top management team heterogeneity on firms' competitive moves. *Administrative Science Quarterly, 41,* 659–685.

Hogg, M. A., and Terry, D. J. (2000). Social identity and self-categorization processes in organizational context. *The Academy of Management Review, 25,* 121–141.

Hollingshead, A. B. (1996). Information suppression and status persistence in group decision making: The effects of communication media. *Human Communication Research, 23,* 193–220.

Ishikawa, K. (1982). *Guide to quality control.* Tokyo: Asian Productivity Organization.

ISPI Presidential Initiative Task Force. (2003, December). Final report. Silver Spring, MD: International Society for Performance Improvement.

Jago, A. G., and Vroom, V. H. (1980). An evaluation of two alternatives to the Vroom-Yetton normative model. *Academy of Management Journal, 23,* 347–355.

Jehn, K. A. (1997). A qualitative analysis of conflict types and dimensions in organizational groups. *Administrative Science Quarterly, 42,* 530–557.

Katzenbach, J. R., and Smith, D. K. (1999). *The wisdom of teams: Creating the high-performance organization.* New York: HarperBusiness.

Krathwohl, D. R., Bloom, B. S., and Masia, B. B. (1964). *Taxonomy of educational objectives: The classification of educational goals. Handbook II: Affective domain.* New York: David McKay.

Lewin, K. (1952). Group decision and social change. In E. Newcombe and R. Harley, R. (Eds.), *Readings in social psychology* (pp. 459–473). New York: Henry Holt.

Likert, R. (1967). *The human organization.* New York: McGraw-Hill.

Mann, G. J., and Putnam, K. B. (1990, December). Motivating and managing staff groups, practitioners forum. *Journal of Accountancy,* 108–110.

Manz, C. C., and Neck, C. P. (1997). Teamthink: Beyond the groupthink syndrome in self-managing work teams. *Team Performance Management, 3,* 18–40.

Maznevski, M. L. (1994). Understanding our differences: Performance in decision-making groups with diverse members. *Human Relations, 47,* 531–553.

McCartt, A. T., and Rorhbaugh, J. (1995). Managerial openness to change and the introduction of GDSS: Explaining initial failure and success in decision conferencing. *Organizational Science, 5,* 569–584.

McFadzean, E. S. (1998). *The attention wheel: How to manage creative teams working.* Paper No. 9823, Henley Management College, Henley-on-Thames.

McFadzean, E. (2002). Developing and supporting creative problem-solving teams: Part 1: A conceptual model. *Management Decision, 40,* 463–476.

McFadzean, E., and O'Loughlin, A. (2000). Five strategies for improving group effectiveness. *Strategic Change, 9,* 103–114.

Mohammed, S., and Ringseis, E. (2001). Cognitive diversity and consensus in group decision making: The role of inputs, processes, and outcomes. *Organizational Behavior and Human Decision Process, 85,* 310–355.

Myrsiades, L. (2000). Meeting sabotage: Met and conquered. *The Journal of Management Development, 19,* 870–885.

Nanus, B. (1996). Leading the vision team. *The Futurist, 30,* 20–23.

Nelson, T., and McFadzean, E. S. (1998). Facilitation problem-solving groups: Facilitator competencies. *Leadership and Organization Development Journal, 19,* 72–82.

Ng, E.S.W., and Tung, R. L. (1998). Ethno-cultural diversity and organizational effectiveness: A field study. *The International Journal of Human Resource Management, 9,* 980–995.

Nutt, P. C. (1976). Models for decision making in organization and some contextual variables which stipulate optimal use. *Academy of Management, 1,* 84–97.

Pelled, L. H., Eisenhardt, K. M., and Xin, K. R. (1999). Exploring the black box: An analysis of work group diversity, conflict, and performance. *Administrative Science Quarterly, 44,* 1–29.

Phillips, L. D., and Phillips, M. C. (1993). Facilitated work groups: Theory and practice. *Journal of the Operational Research Society, 44,* 533–549.

Pinsonneault, A., and Kraemer, K. L. (1990). The effects of electronic meetings on group processes and outcomes: An assessment of the empirical research. *European Journal of Operational Research, 46,* 143–161.

Reagan-Cirincione, P. S. (1994). Improving the accuracy of group judgment: A process intervention combining group facilitation, social judgment analysis, and information technology. *Organizational Behavior and Human Decision Process, 58,* 246–271.

Reagan-Cirincione, P., Schuman, S., Richardson, G. P., and Dorf, S. (1991). Decision modeling: Tools for strategic thinking. *Interfaces, 21,* 52–65.

Russo, J. E., and Schoemaker. P.J.H. (1989). *Decision traps: The ten barriers to brilliant decision-making and how to overcome them.* New York: Simon and Schuster.

Salas, E., Bowers, C. A., and Edens, E. (2001). *Improving teamwork in organizations: Applications of resource management training.* Mahwah, NJ: Lawrence Erlbaum Associates.

Schein, E. H. (1996). Culture: The missing concept in organization studies. *Administrative Science Quarterly, 41,* 229–240.

Schwarz, R. (2002). *The skilled facilitator.* San Francisco: Jossey-Bass.

Simon, H. A. (1955). A behavioral model of rational choice. *Quarterly Journal of Economics, 69,* 99–118.

Simon, H. A. (1987, February). Making management decisions: The role of intuition and emotion. *Academy of Management Executive,* pp. 57–64.

Sivasubramaniam, N., Murry, W. D., Avolio, B. J., and Jung, D. I. (2002). A longitudinal model of the effects of team leadership and group potency on group performance. *Group and Organization Management, 27,* 66–95.

Stolovitch, H. D., and Keeps, E. J. (1992). What is human performance technology? In H. D. Stolovitch and E. J. Keeps (Eds.), *Handbook of human performance technology: A comprehensive guide for analyzing and solving performance problems in organizations* (pp. 3–13). San Francisco: Jossey-Bass.

Vrij, A. (2000). *Detecting lies and deceit.* West Sussex, UK: John Wiley and Sons.

Watson, W. E., Kumar, K., and Michaelsen, L. K. (1993). Cultural diversity's impact on interaction process and performance, comparing homogeneous and diverse task groups. *Academy of Management Journal, 36,* 590–603.

Weldon, E., and Yun, S. (2000). The effects of proximal and distal goals on goal level, strategy development, and group performance. *The Journal of Applied Behavioral Science, 36,* 336–344.

Wheeler, B. C., and Valacich, J. S. (1996). Facilitation, GSS and training as a source of process restrictiveness and guidance for structured group decision making: An empirical assessment. *Information Systems Research, 7,* 429–450.

CHAPTER TWENTY-THREE

Performance Support
Systems

Steven W. Villachica, Deborah L. Stone,
John Endicott

Human performance technology (HPT) practitioners face increasing pressures to close ever-changing performance gaps, support a growing flood of new products and services, and keep workers productive, all within shrinking budgets and timelines. Performance support systems (PSS), also called electronic performance support systems (EPSS), offer a powerful means of meeting these pressures. Combining any and all conceivable interventions, PSS offer significant opportunities to improve measurably the performance of people and organizations.

INTRODUCTION

We begin this chapter by outlining our approach to investigating PSS. We then offer a detailed description of PSS concepts and terminology. Next, we address four ways that PSS can vary. We then provide examples of PSS, followed by a discussion of how PSS can benefit organizations. After discussing development considerations, we conclude with our insights regarding the future of PSS.

The authors thank Gloria Gery and Gary Dickelman for the generous contribution of their expertise during personal and phone interviews. We also would like to thank Kim Moore of Brandon-Hall.com for information she provided. Last, we would like to thank Sylvie Vanasse and IBM Australia for providing PSS examples used in this chapter.

Authors' Approach

As we noted in 1998, the "field of PSS is moving too fast for articles in the peer-reviewed professional literature to keep up . . ." (Villachica and Stone, 1998a, p. 443). This remains the case today, when there are even more articles, presentations, technical reports, opinion papers, and case studies. While the number of descriptions of PSS is increasing, the professional literature includes few peer-reviewed studies that investigate PSS in business and governmental settings or evaluate their return on investment (ROI). Accordingly, we have based this chapter on the following sources:

- Our own experience creating PSS
- Our colleagues' comments in telephone interviews
- An extensive search of on-line databases and the World Wide Web
- A review of related articles appearing in business trade publications and presentations made at professional conferences

Description of PSS

This section describes PSS by providing definitions, discussing how PSS fit with other performance interventions, and noting when PSS should be used. We have not changed our definition of PSS as an optimized body of integrated on-line and off-line methods and resources providing what performers need, when they need it, in the form they need it in, so that they can perform in ways that meet organizational objectives (Villachica and Stone, 1999). This definition is broader in scope than the computer-centric definitions that appear in the professional literature, as illustrated in Table 23.1.

The existence of numerous and different definitions for PSS and EPSS, used interchangeably in this chapter, reflects considerable confusion over concepts and terminology. Carliner (2002) notes that this situation arose from similar design strategies emerging from different disciplines, such as user-centered design and minimalism, which compete for the leading role in formulating future PSS conventions and practice. The idiosyncratic experiences of EPSS authors also contribute to this situation. However, while the details vary, these sources agree about the goal of PSS: expert-like performance from day 1 with little or no training. There is also agreement regarding the means for PSS to reach this goal: creating a zone in which performance can occur to standards that meet organizational objectives. Such a zone emerges with the intersection of representations appropriate to the task, appropriate to the person, and containing critical features of the real world, as depicted in Figure 23.1. There is also widespread agreement that maintaining performance within this zone requires users to be able to learn, use, and reference necessary information within a single context and without breaks in the natural flow of performing their jobs.

Table 23.1. Sources, Types, and Definitions of EPSS.

Source	Definition
Gery (1991)	EPSS provide whatever "is necessary to generate performance and learning at the moment of need . . . to make it universally and consistently available on demand any time, any place, and regardless of situation, without unnecessary intermediaries involved in the process. . . . [They] integrate information, tools, and methodology for the user" (p. 34).
McIntire (2002)	EPSS provide employees with tools and on-line support they need to get their jobs done without the involvement of another person. There is no distinction between the learning and application environments.
Carliner (2002)	EPSS are "part online help, part online tutorial, part database, part application program, and part expert system" (p. 400), all of which are integrated in the form of a system. EPSS can also help capture knowledge and best practices for dissemination across the entire organization.
Dickelman (2003)	Describes EPSS using the phrase "business performance through human performance." In this framework, EPSS mean the rapid construction, deployment, and maintenance or the right processes and content to enable the largest possible competitive advantage with the smallest possible expense. In his view, EPSS are about "getting the right process right—quickly and continuously" (Foreword).
Kaplan-Leiserson (n.d.)	The entry in ASTD's Learning Circuits glossary provides two different definitions of EPSS. The first is a computer application linked directly to another application to train or guide users as they complete tasks constituting the target application. The second definition is more general in nature, describing a computer or other device that gives workers information or resources to help them accomplish a task or achieve performance requirements.
Ruyle (2004)	EPSS are computer-based job aids that provide just-in-time, just-what-is-needed assistance to performers on the job. EPSS typically include one or more of the following features: <ul><li>Database of job-required information organized to optimize clarity and facilitate rapid access</li><li>Calculators and wizards that simplify and automate procedures that would otherwise be performed manually</li><li>Decision-support modules that help users solve problems</li><li>Embedded tutorials and simulations that provide instruction in work related concepts and procedures</li></ul>

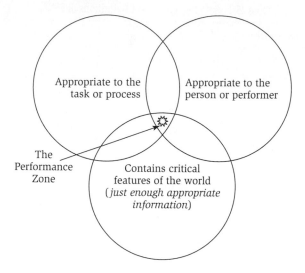

Figure 23.1. The Performance Zone.

Source: Dickelman, 1995, 1996.

Fit with Other Performance Interventions. As PSS still encompass one of the widest possible ranges of HPT, a large-scale application could use all or most of the methods and interventions appearing in the *Human Performance Technology Handbook.* While smaller PSS applications may reside entirely on computers, larger applications can consist of integrated, contextualized on-line and off-line components. Figure 23.2 depicts a partial listing of the potential components of a performance support system.

When Used and Not Used. Our experience suggests that HPT practitioners should consider using PSS when all of the following conditions are present.

- *Multiple performance gaps.* Performance gaps often appear in packs, and they typically interact with each other. For example, a lack of adequate feedback at the level of the worker often means a lack of streamlined processes at the level of the team and lost productivity to the organization. PSS can systemically address multiple gaps and the interacting relationships among them.

- *Multiple solutions.* Multiple gaps usually require multiple interventions to close them. A streamlined process also provides feedback to the individual worker. PSS can integrate these solutions, contextualize them so users understand what they are doing, and provide on-demand access to learning, information, and tools.

- *Project team alignment with business drivers and objectives.* Owing to their visibility within the organization and associated development

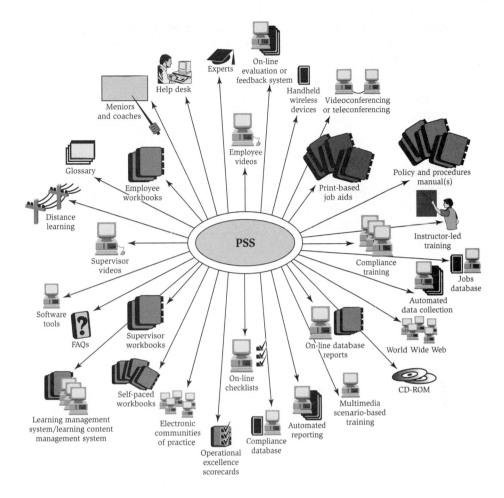

Figure 23.2. Partial Depiction of Potential PSS Components.

costs, practitioners must align their efforts to create PSS with strategic business objectives and key decision makers. Without this alignment, the PSS will go unimplemented or, at best, remain a toy solution to the problem they were designed to solve.

- *Sponsorship for crossing silos.* Aligning with the business and employing systemic and systematic approaches typically require PSS to cross between the silos that arbitrarily separate departments and the activities they perform. Without adequate sponsorship that can mandate change from the top down, a PSS development effort can stall when it encounters sufficient organizational inertia.

- *Acceptance of collaborative development approaches.* PSS implementation will stall without adequate bottom-up support from the user community. To facilitate change management while ensuring accurate performance requirements and appropriate designs for meeting them, the PSS development effort should employ collaborative, prototyping-based development approaches. Accordingly, the sponsor and the client organization must be willing and able to provide release time of key managers, supervisors, and job incumbents.

- *Willingness to employ formative evaluation.* By its very nature, collaboration can increase the scope of a PSS development effort. Client organizations and project teams should employ robust formative evaluation to shape project deliverables during the early phases of the effort, when changes are less expensive to make and more money is available in the budget. Collaborative activities such as prototyping and usability testing can also provide empirical data that can direct the revision process. The client organization and the project team must be amenable to making decisions based on their alignment with business objectives and collected data, rather than on personal preference and past practice.

BASIC CONCEPTS AND TERMINOLOGY

This section discusses basic concepts and terminology. Building from the work of Gery (2002), Rossett (2002), and Carliner (2002), we offer a big-tent, or hybrid, taxonomy of PSS components comprising a variety of integrated performance interventions, which is depicted in Table 23.2. Depending on the nature of the performance requirements, HPT practitioners can build PSS that employ learning; guidance and tracking; task-structuring support; knowledge management; and communities of practice, tools, and motivation. A discussion of each component follows.

Learning

Learning refers to changes in the declarative, strategic, and procedural knowledge that people store in long-term memory and demonstrate in performance (Jonassen, Beissner, and Yacci, 1993). In short, learning means the ability to

- Know or believe something new
- Recall previously forgotten knowledge
- Organize knowledge differently
- Perform tasks that were not possible before

Many workers' jobs are in a constant state of flux, as change itself increases at a steady rate. Continual learning is a fundamental job requirement. Employees are constantly encountering new situations, information, and technologies.

Table 23.2. Hybrid Taxonomy of PSS Components.

Carliner (2002)	Rossett (2002)	Gery (2002)	Hybrid
Skills and knowledge	Learning		Learning
Resources	Guidance and tracking		Guidance and tracking
	Information support and coaching	Task-structuring support	Task-structuring support
	Knowledge management	Knowledge	Knowledge management
		Data	• Knowledge • Data
	Interaction and collaboration	Communications and collaboration	Communities of practice
		Tools	Tools
Motivation			Motivation

As a result, they must upgrade their skills by practicing them and responding to feedback until they reach mastery and can transfer their new skills to the job. To meet this demand within a job context, big-tent PSS can include e-learning in its various forms as well as off-line learning, such as instructor-led courses, mentoring and coaching, and on-the-job training.

Guidance and Tracking

Formerly called *computer-managed instruction,* guidance and tracking components enable managers and users to monitor learning progress. Guidance and tracking systems enable end users, supervisors, and the larger organization to prescribe instruction, monitor the user's progress, and record certification data. Organizations can also employ these systems to identify the most frequently requested resources, which usually correspond to the most in-demand skills and knowledge. The data these systems collect can greatly facilitate both needs analysis and evaluation, including the calculation of ROI.

Task-Structuring Support

Task-structuring support spares end users from having to constantly ask, "What next?" Effective support aids both novice and expert, enabling them to perform their jobs with little or no training. For novices, this support acts like the temporary beams that support a building under construction, until human performance can stand on its own. Such support is, therefore, called *scaffolding* (Collins, Brown, and Holum, 1991). Effective PSS provide both strategic and tactical levels of scaffolding.

Strategic scaffolding helps novices solve problems they are facing for the first time. Such scaffolding can take the form of high-level task descriptions, goal statements, rules of thumb, process flow diagrams, or worked examples (Chandler and Sweller, 1991) that help users determine

- Why am I doing this?
- How do experts think about this?
- What decisions do I need to make?
- How do I monitor my progress to see if I am performing the task correctly?
- How do I know I have finished the task correctly?
- What should the end result look like?

Tactical scaffolding provides support for novice users who need help using the software itself and can include

- Descriptions of screens, windows, fields, and buttons constituting the software
- *Tool tips* that specify software components as users place a cursor over them
- Definitions of key terms
- Advisers who tell users what they can do or model the performances of experts
- Cue cards that provide step-by-step instructions while helping users make decisions
- Wizards that completely or partially automate the completion of a task, based on inputs that users provide

Novice and expert alike will benefit from two other forms of task support that affect the user interface of PSS, that is, the aspects of the software that users see and interact with to input data and control the operation of the software (InfoStreet, Inc., 1999). To minimize novice training and ensure experts' ease of use, the user interface of PSS should employ a flow that matches that of the job. The sequence of screens, displays, windows, fields, and buttons that appear in the software should match the natural workflow and logic of the job. To minimize the time otherwise spent looking for information, the PSS also should filter the information available to users. When such support is built into the system, users see only the images, text, features, and menu options that apply to the task at hand and their individual profiles. Users do not have to spend time finding what they need to perform their jobs. With both forms of task support, the computer has adapted to the needs of the user, rather than vice versa.

Knowledge Management

Knowledge management (KM) is about capturing and disseminating intellectual capital and expertise, especially in environments characterized by change or when key workers are leaving and taking vital knowledge with them. It is about making knowledge active (Gary Dickelman, personal communication, October 19, 2004). KM includes both data mining, that is, searching electronic databases, and the collection and dissemination of best practices. KM systems also make knowledge manifest in contextualized ways, so that users can actually employ it. To be useful, context-specific knowledge must be built into the systems, user interfaces, tools, and processes that make up users' jobs. Jonassen (2003) describes two such KM applications. The first consists of a diagnostic tool technicians can use to troubleshoot problems they are experiencing. The second consists of a case library technicians can use to input observed symptoms of a given problem and compare them to those in similar situations.

Communities of Practice

A community of practice (CoP) is a group created, usually on an informal basis, to capture and share expertise, methods, tools, and techniques in a specific area. Members use the CoP to develop their knowledge and address recurring problems they encounter in their field (Lave and Wenger, 1994). By including members of different but related disciplines, communities of practice encourage their members to view their work in novel ways. Members are generally self-selected and share an evolving culture, language, vocabulary, stories, and agreement on best practices. Kaplan (2002) cites the following benefits of communities of practice:

- They create an informal setting for learning. Because employees learn about 70 percent of job-required knowledge outside of formal training (Henschel, 2001), it is prudent to maximize opportunities for such learning.
- They are effective at capturing tacit knowledge that cannot be delivered in other ways. In other words, a CoP brings out how things really get done.
- In addition to capturing more tacit knowledge, a CoP can be a powerful tool for disseminating it to the community at large, increasing an organization's overall effectiveness.

PSS can support such communities of practice by providing chat rooms, contextualized archival materials, access to knowledge brokers, and support for coaching and mentoring.

Tools

Tools include applications designed to automate and otherwise support specific job functions. Their main purpose is to reduce or eliminate routine, time-consuming tasks, freeing up more time to solve problems and make decisions. Simple examples include notepads, calculators, spreadsheets, and templates. High-end examples include report-generating engines that pull together disparate information in a database the user has completed into a finished, formatted product. The highest-end tools can be indistinguishable from other types of components, such as task-structuring or knowledge-management systems. Well-designed tools can eliminate or reduce the need for training, resulting in faster time to proficiency. By providing a standard set of resources, they also minimize nonstandard performances and resulting rework.

Motivation

Motivation is a vital component of PSS. There is no substitute for a motivated, engaged team that *wants* to perform. Users must actively choose to perform their job tasks, persist until they are completed, and invest the appropriate level of mental effort to complete them to standard (Condly, Clark, and Stolovitch, 2003). Willingness and persistence are often influenced by the consequences users experience. Appropriate performances need to be reinforced in meaningful ways so they will continue to occur in the future. Inappropriate performances need to result in consequences that will make them less likely to occur. A user interface that follows the natural workflow of the job reinforces the use of the PSS, while one that does not follow the workflow can actually punish its users, who must adapt to the way the PSS require them to perform their job. PSS also can help users calibrate the level of necessary mental effort required to perform a task. For example, a performance support system helping users troubleshoot a problem with a broken assembly line could provide information describing the frequency, criticality, diagnostic difficulty, and repair difficulty associated with each option for repairing the line.

VARIATIONS

Given the number of potential components, PSS can be expected to vary widely. While the goal of PSS remains providing contextualized support at the moment of need, they vary across four different factors: the extent to which their components are integrated, the scale at which they support performance, whether they can be worn on the body, and the nomenclature by which they are described.

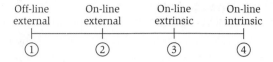

Figure 23.3. Continuum of Integration for Performance Support.

Source: Villachica and Stone, 1999.

Integration

The first factor is integration, the extent to which performance support is woven into the applications and the jobs users perform. In the previous edition of the *Human Performance Technology Handbook,* we described a continuum of integration of PSS components, as depicted in Figure 23.3. Although our experience leads us to believe that the right-hand side of the continuum produces the greatest performance gains and return on investment, our literature review yielded no studies comparing the overall efficacy of the two approaches.

Sponsorship and timing continue to affect the extent to which HPT practitioners can direct their efforts toward the right side of the integration continuum. With inadequate sponsorship for their efforts, HPT practitioners usually arrive on the scene after the application has been created. By then, the only possible performance support is a bolt-on system. With sponsorship for collaboration across the disciplines and stakeholders affected by the application, performance support can become part of the application itself, resulting in intrinsic PSS.

Scale or Level

The second factor is the scale of the PSS, or the level of performance they serve. Although this chapter on PSS resides within the part of the handbook that addresses the worker and the work team, PSS can be scaled to any level of performance, including larger organizations and entire enterprises. As enterprisewide software becomes more commonplace, so will the enterprisewide performance support that is built into these applications.

Wearability

The third factor along which PSS vary is the extent to which they can actually be worn by the user. With increased miniaturization and computing power, users can now access on-line PSS using a variety of delivery options, including desktop and laptop computers, personal digital assistants (PDAs), and wearable computing components. Stone and Villachica (2001) report a system that employed a variety of automated formatting engines to provide market results to institutional traders and their customers using their computers, fax machines, and PDAs. Likewise, anyone dealing with parcel delivery service sees carriers using PSS residing on PDAs to track package receipt and pickup, while customers can track their shipments and billing via desktop computers, laptops, PDAs, or Internet-equipped cell phones.

Wearable PSS and software applications typically consist of head-mounted displays, PDAs, and wireless connections to databases and back-end software. The Agricultural Technology Research Program of Georgia Tech's Research Institute has employed mobile computing technologies to develop better ways of providing real-time and immediate data storage and information access for mobile plant personnel. The resulting Factory Automation Support Technology uses speech recognition to record data in meat-processing plants (Gobert, 2002). Users include managers, supervisors, auditors, production personnel, and maintenance personnel who would otherwise need to use their hands to access such support as they manipulated product or machinery. Users can access the PSS anywhere in the plant as they perform their jobs. Other wearable applications include PSS for mechanics who maintain Honda and Cadillac vehicles (Adkins, 2003a; Barron, 1999), U.S. Army National Guard maintenance technicians who service tanks (Barron, 1999), and dermatologists who can collaborate remotely while accessing databases of medical records and laboratory results (Gobert, 2002).

Nomenclature

The last factor on which PSS vary is the rapidly expanding nomenclature they employ. In addition to the term *knowledge management,* PSS also appear under five other common aliases.

Business Process Integration Tools. As their name implies, business process integration (BPI) tools provide intelligent tools for designing business processes while connecting them to underlying applications. Most BPI products contain a software engine that works as a meta application that invokes and passes data among the enterprise's underlying applications, based on core and enabling processes (Gruden and Strannegard, 2003). Common reasons for using BPI include connectivity, process automation, and decision support.

One BPI package, ProCarta by ProCarta, Inc., sits on top of existing enterprise IT software to link existing knowledge assets to mission-critical business processes. Cited as the 2003 EPSScentral.net extraordinary PCD tool, ProCarta was described by Gloria Gery as "the most extraordinary software I have seen" (EPSScentral.net, 2004).

Enterprise Application Integration. With most organizations using a myriad of different, stovepiped systems from different vendors, enterprise application integration (EAI) attempts to integrate all of them so that they work together and exchange data, methods, objects, and processing power. EAI is a close relative of knowledge management; indeed, Adkins (2003b) predicts that EAI will soon absorb knowledge management, which will become one of many features of EAI products.

Composite Applications. Composite applications attempt to place existing data that are locked away in an organization's legacy systems on-line, so that they are available to the employees and customers who need them. For example, thanks to the advent of e-commerce, customers expect up-to-date information about pricing, availability, and order status. Meanwhile, employees need to update customer information in a legacy data store with a difficult-to-use interface. Composite applications make such data accessible, either by replacing the entire legacy systems or introducing new systems that replicate the legacy systems' logic. Regardless of the method chosen, a successful composite application will make data available to end users in the form in which they need it.

Portals. Gery defines a portal as "an integrated, single point of access to knowledge, data, tools, communications and task support" (2003b, p. 9). They can be built for an entire organization, a role such as sales representative, a function such as a learning center, a task such as purchasing a product, or to access and use data such as those in an inventory. Advantages include collection and aggregation of data, classification, improved representation, filtration, integration within a site, and integration among other portals.

In other words, a portal pulls together resources from a variety of systems, personalizes them, and makes them available, on demand, in the form that users need. Cheese and Ives (2002) predict that portals are the "desktops of the future" and submit that to be effective, they must enable employees to view the knowledge they need, use that knowledge to make decisions, and then act on those decisions through integrated applications.

Decision Support Systems. Decision support systems (DSS) help managers answer relevant questions (Power, 1997). At the enterprise level, DSS are linked to large data warehouses and designed with an intimate understanding of users' goals, priorities, and strategies. DSS have become widespread over the past ten to twenty years, producing variants such as business nervous systems that compile and digest input on what is happening within the organization, helping managers to identify areas that need attention, and business intelligence systems that provide coherent data on external, strategy-affecting events. The medical community uses DSS to help create exercise regimens for arthritis patients (Minor, Reid, Griffin, Pittman, Patrick, and Cutts, 1998) and to facilitate doctor-patient collaboration in treating pediatric asthma (Porter, 2001).

PSS EXAMPLES

To demonstrate PSS concepts and variability in action, we provide examples of on-line-external and on-line-intrinsic PSS.

On-Line External Example

Figure 23.4 and Table 23.3 depict an on-line-external performance support system developed by IBM for a major utility company in Australia that had successfully merged and consolidated three back-office systems. It provides context-sensitive on-line help for enterprise resource planning systems such as SAP and PeopleSoft. Linked to an extensive back-end database, the system user interface calls up and displays on-line help resources, including business process overviews, flow charts, and procedures. Its screen design provides cognitive support by providing visual cues such as graphics and colors for different types of information, while its menu bar provides quick access to document information such as page references and file names.

The system user interface is browser-based, and PeopleSoft users can quickly and easily access its step-by-step, task-specific instructions by one of the following options:

- Directly from the client's home page on the intranet site. This enables users to locate business process information and help without having to log on to PeopleSoft.

- By clicking the "Help" hyperlink in PeopleSoft or SAP. This method allows users to display context-sensitive on-line help for tasks related to the page they are viewing. Users also can resize the window or make it disappear and reappear.

On-Line-Intrinsic Example

Figure 23.5 and Table 23.4 depict an on-line-intrinsic, prototype performance support system developed by DLS Group, Inc. for the U.S. federal government. It provides a blueprint for delivering context-sensitive performance support for people who interpret satellite imagery. Designed to work as a user interface integrating data from different legacy systems, the system allows analysts to select an assignment, review the information associated with it, conduct ad hoc queries, analyze the data they have collected, and review or release the analyses for dissemination. The screen design provides a variety of forms of cognitive support for this problem-solving activity, including the use of different background colors that correspond to each phase of the analytical process and quick access to contextualized information, training, and on-line tools. The system works as the analysts' desktop application, eliminating the need to use multiple software systems to complete their analytical assignments.

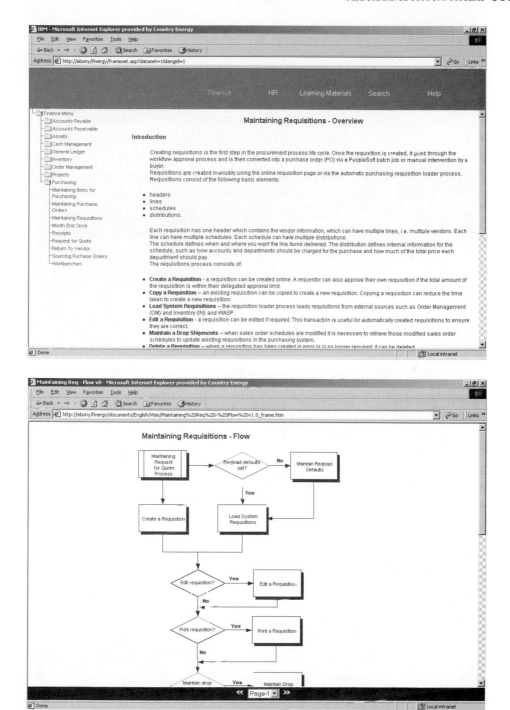

Figure 23.4. Screen Samples from IBM Performance Support System.

Table 23.3. IBM Performance Support System Description.

Performance Support System	Description
Project goal	Leverage the best-practice processes within the enterprise resource planning application and support end-to-end implementation of the software and its corresponding business processes
Target audience	Three thousand users who fill sixteen different roles related to finance, human resources, and payroll
Components	Web-based learning and context-sensitive on-line help for fourteen PeopleSoft modules, plus the development and delivery of a train-the-trainer program and related documentation
Development effort	Three months

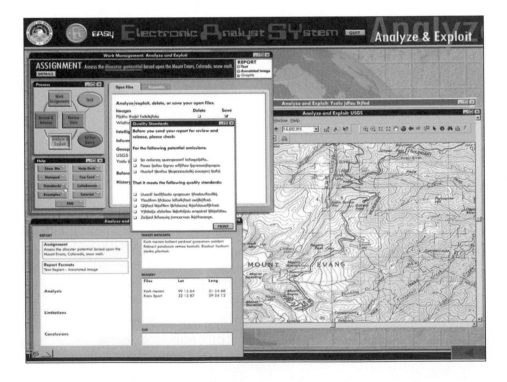

Figure 23.5. Screen Sample from EASY.

Table 23.4. EASY Performance Support System Description.

Performance Support System	Description
Project goal	Support the performance of people who interpret satellite imagery for the federal government of the United States by
	• Replacing stovepiped software systems with a seamless, common look and feel
	• Providing end-to-end support for job processes that parallel workflow
	• Providing both strategic (problem-solving) and tactical (software use) levels of on-line support
	• Filtering and preloading the information users need for ready access.
Target audience	The number of users who gather, analyze, and disseminate imagery for assorted agencies is classified.
Components	Workflow-based user interface with context-specific access to training, information, advice, and tools. On-line training consists of short, Web-based tanning modules. Information components include worked examples, knowledge nuggets, glossaries, demonstrations, cue cards, standards, and access to human knowledge brokers. Tools include a powerful search engine and automated report assembly tools.
Development effort	One and a half months.

BENEFITS OF PSS

Why the interest in the various forms of PSS? Simply stated, the benefits of PSS improve the performance of people and organizations. The benefits of PSS arise from supporting performance at the time of need. Altalib (2002) reports a variety of benefits from PSS that HPT practitioners can measure, including

- Increased productivity arising from just-in-time support, such as reduction in time required to perform a task or increase in units produced or items processed
- Reduced costs rising from decreased or eliminated training
- Improved worker autonomy that reduces the burden on support teams
- Improved quality arising from standard work practices, including reduced numbers of errors and waste

- Improved knowledge capitalization, including the capturing and leveraging of skills, knowledge, and best practices
- Decreased system maintenance costs
- Improved morale, including reduced absenteeism

Other benefits can include increased revenue, decreased novice ramp-up time to competent job performance, decreased or eliminated costs associated with informal mentoring, when users get help by asking the person next to them, and improved internal and external customer satisfaction. Additional information describing the beneficial impact of PSS appears on the Website describing performance-centered design winners (http:www.epsscentral.com/news/pcdawards) and in Table 23.5.

PROJECT-DEVELOPMENT CONSIDERATIONS

Although the potential benefits of PSS are great, creating the system that realizes them requires HPT practitioners to be aware of several development considerations, including collaboration, design, implementation, and evaluation.

Collaboration

The first consideration is collaboration. The creation and successful implementation of PSS requires successful collaboration within the core development team and with the end user population. Owing to the increased scope of PSS efforts, a larger cast of characters must be responsible for building them. Describing a team developing on-line, intrinsic PSS development, Huber, Lippincott, McMahon, and Witt (1999) suggest a group comprising a project manager, a system integrator and architect, object-oriented designers, software developers, software engineers, and knowledge engineers. Gary Dickelman (personal communication, October 19, 2004) suggests that teams creating on-line extrinsic or intrinsic performance support systems must minimally possess expertise in three core areas: business-process analysis and improvement, such as reengineering; human-factors engineering or usability science; and the architecture and management of hypertext, information, and knowledge.

Describing rapid application development (RAD) strategies, Martin (1991) suggests project managers employ small teams comprising specialists with advanced tools, that is, SWAT teams. Using this approach, a SWAT team for a particular PSS effort would consist of two to four people, including a project manager, a PSS architect, designers, and developers. Additional expertise, such as that of software architects, software developers, and graphic artists, rotates in and out of the team as needed (Villachica and Stone, 1998b). This team should have previous success working together; good collaboration skills; and tools composed of proven

Table 23.5. Impact Data Reported for PCD Winners.

Year	Description	Reported Impact
1997	TREE, a performance support system that helps teachers plan, organize, and manage their work. Using TREE, teachers can group students in meaningful ways and develop lesson plans with common objectives.	• Ease, efficiency, and accuracy of the instructional tasks that grouped students performed • Dramatic reduction in teacher training time
1998	The GoldWing 1500 Electrical Troubleshooting performance support system assists Honda service technicians in servicing and troubleshooting the electrical system of GoldWing 1500 motorcycles. It consists of three major sections: • Troubleshooting and diagnostic procedures • Repair and replacement procedures • Interactive schematics	• Reduced service costs • Improved technician productivity • Improved consistency of task performance • Decreased call volume for technical support • Improved efficiency and efficacy of technician troubleshooting • Decreased training time and costs with corresponding increase in training efficacy • Improved access to timely information about changes in products and processes • Preserved and disseminated technician expertise • Improved customer satisfaction
2000	The Eventful performance-centered event management application helps users to manage the administration and operations of an event-based sales business. This software allows users to manage suppliers and inventories, manage customer relationships, manage press relationships, conduct sales events, and process sales statements and accounts.	• Improved productivity

(Continued)

Table 23.5. Impact Data Reported for PCD Winners. (*Continued*)

Year	Description	Reported Impact
2001	Step 7 Lite helps automation specialists engineer and program solutions to automation problems arising in the manufacturing industry.	• High user satisfaction rising from usability testing • Improved design efficiency
2002	The Integrated Sensor Radio Frequency Identification System alerts transportation logistics workers to in-storage and in-transit exceeded limits for conditions such as temperature, pressure, and humidity that can be corrected to prevent damage to high-value assets.	• Reduced inventory of lost engines • Reduced instances of stored ready-for-issue and non-ready-for-issue assets reaching "beyond economic repair" status or complete loss due to corrosion • Decreased costs to refurbish containers • Decreased loss rates for engine containers because of tracking, inventorying, and full or empty status errors
2003	The e-Learning Development Resource Center provides the training community of the U.S. Internal Revenue Service with enterprisewide, single-point access to a wide variety of e-learning information, tools, templates, guides, and other resources. To this end, it provides task support, content knowledge, data, tools, collaboration, and integration capabilities.	• Improved access to a community of practice • Increased levels of course consistency and compliance • Leveraged expertise regarding courseware design, streamlined development processes, and the production of better courseware
2004	Business Plan Developer assists interns creating business plans for the National Park Service. Specifically, it helps users get started, collect and analyze information, and generate appropriate reports.	• Reduced training time from five days to one • Improved efficiency of data collection • Improved ease, consistency, and quality of business plans • Substantial cost savings

Source: http:www.epsscentral.com/news/pcdawards.

processes, templates, code, content libraries, and applets such as macros or engines that automate the completion of various tasks. Smaller PSS efforts require the work of a single SWAT team. Larger efforts require the coordinated work of multiple SWAT teams working on different PSS components.

Design

The second PSS consideration is design. Owing to the abstract nature of the integrated components constituting a performance support system, collaborative prototyping-based design approaches are a must. Using RAD, the PSS project team can collaborate with end users to create and review iterative prototypes depicting the system. In addition to allowing the changes to the design before they become too expensive to make, prototyping also helps ensure adequate representation of the breadth and depth of the final system prior to the development effort. Subsequent usability testing ensures that the system design the project team created will be acceptable to other end users. Brown (2002) suggests that usability testing also helps identify and correct usability issues early, ensure repeated visits to the Website or system application, and provide formative evaluation data. By conducting a post-mortem workshop addressing the final prototype arising from the usability test, the PSS team can baseline project roles and accountabilities, development processes, and metrics prior to the development effort. During the development phase, the team can then concentrate on increasing its efficiency rather than coping with increasing costs of changing the performance support system as it moves into pilot testing, implementation, or maintenance.

Guiding these efforts are two core design strategies: performance-centered design (PCD) and minimalism. First articulated by Gery (1995) and subsequently modified by Marion (2002), PCD seeks to create PSS and other software that demonstrate specific attributes that improve their ease of use and organizational impact. These attributes appear in Figure 23.6. Using PCD, designers embed knowledge into the interface that users would otherwise need to access externally. Furthermore, they structure that knowledge to mirror the thought processes, interactions, and decisions involved in the task the tool is supposed to support. In essence, the tool *becomes* the task (Dickover, 2002).

Supplementing PCD is minimalism, a design strategy based on the contention that users will begin interacting with a new or unfamiliar application immediately, rather than waiting until they have received formal training (Carroll, 1990). Because of this natural predisposition to act before understanding, the minimalist approach suggests users will obtain greater benefit from targeted yet limited assistance, rather than from all-encompassing on-line support. Under the minimalist approach, it is critical that designers possess a complete and thorough understanding of what users need to accomplish a job. Through the use of RAD strategies such as collaborative analysis and design, prototyping, usability

Clarifying the Work Context

1. Establish and maintain a work context
2. Aid goal establishment
3. Structure work process and progression through tasks and logic
4. Institutionalize business strategy and best approach

Optimizing the User Interface

5. Contain embedded knowledge in the interface, support resources, and system logic
6. Use metaphors, language, and direct manipulation of variables to capitalize on prior learning and physical reality
7. Reflect natural work situations
8. Use appropriate vehicles to convey information
9. Provide information visualizations where helpful
10. Provide alternative views of the application interface and resources

Optimizing Interactivity

11. Observe and advise
12. Show evidence of work progression
13. Provide contextual feedback
14. Provide support resources without breaking the task context

Optimizing Automation

15. Accommodate performer diversity by layering or individualizing information
16. Provide access to underlying logic
17. Automate tasks
18. Allow customization
19. Provide obvious options, next steps, and resources

Optimizing Knowledge Access and Use

20. Provide an appropriate search function
21. Provide sufficient maps of and paths to information
22. Ensure quick and easy navigation
23. Facilitate communication through appropriate tools
24. When possible, capture and reuse knowledge

Being Consistent

25. Employ consistent use of visual conventions, language, visual positioning, and other system behavior

Figure 23.6. Attributes of PCD.

Source: Gery, 1995, and Marion, 2002.

testing, and similar field research techniques, designers can identify the minimal, essential tasks that users need to accomplish right away.

Implementation

The third PSS consideration is implementation. The changes to job roles and activities arising from PSS mean that their implementation cannot be approached as an afterthought. It takes time to ensure that the organization is ready to adopt the PSS, educate users about what PSS are, communicate what they will do, brand the PSS, market them, and strategize flawless logistics that make their implementation transparent. For these reasons, the implementation effort for PSS must begin on day 1 of the project, if not before (Stone and Villachica, 2003).

Evaluation

The last PSS consideration is evaluation. Given their large scale and intensive use of technology, PSS tend to involve development costs well beyond those of traditional documentation and training. For this reason, documenting ROI is critical in making a case for PSS. Practitioners should be able to demonstrate that the new system meets the performance needs of workers in ways that postively affect the organization's financial performance. Practitioners should be able to show that the impact of the benefits a performance support system generates is greater than the cost of creating it. In spite of our views on the importance of ROI, our review of the literature yielded few discussions of such results. Only Endicott, Villachica, and Stone (1998) and Villachica and Stone (1998a) provide published ROI data associated with implemented PSS. Neither of these book chapters was a formal evaluation study appearing in the peer-reviewed professional literature.

Given the risks associated with PSS development, evaluation should be an ongoing activity that begins on day 1 of the project. Hale (2004) describes a three-point model that lends itself to performance support system evaluation at the worker, work, and workplace levels. The first point occurs when HPT practitioners measure need during or before the analysis phase. Outputs at this point include either a rationale for action or a business case that calls for action, sets the baseline, defines goals and gains, identifies success measures, and confirms the feasibility of the effort. The second point occurs during the creation and implementation, when practitioners measure their in-process efforts to recommend corrective actions based on formative evaluation data or predictive indicators. The third point occurs after implementation, when practitioners report results, including impact and ROI data.

Elements of RAD support all three points in Hale's model. During an initial alignment workshop that precedes the analysis phase, project teams establish critical success factors that are aligned with business objectives, as well as their corresponding measures. During design and development efforts, the project team collects baseline metrics associated with the measures, establishing a baseline. Data collected during collaborative analysis and design workshops, prototyping, and usability tests provide information for formative evaluation. After implementation, summative evaluation collects subsequent data to compare against the baseline. Depending on the needs of project decision makers, this summative evaluation could collect data describing the impact of the performance support system on the organization, the return on the organization's investment, or the overall quality of the system, such as what worked well, what could be improved, potential breaks in the chain that links the system and its components to job performance, and organizational results.

ANOTHER LOOK TOWARD THE FUTURE

This chapter on PSS is the second that has appeared in the *Handbook of Human Performance Technology.* In the previous edition, we noted that predicting what would happen in the future is a risky venture (Villachica and Stone, 1999). We asked whether PSS represented a fad or a real contribution to the field. We said they were real and here to stay. We also stated that we believed that PSS would "move out of their current niche status to grow in importance for HPT practitioners. Given the increasing appearance of PSS on the job, HPT practitioners may well conclude that their primary role, rather than to create isolated performance interventions, is to create systems that support workplace and organizational performance" (p. 460).

With hindsight, we realize our predictions have had a mixed record. PSS are not only here to stay; in some ways they have matured and come of age. Writing of PSS, Gery (2003a) noted that "Improved design of software *for use* or work performance is occurring. We are finally seeing some software that is truly performance centered. We are achieving both performance and learning in the same context" (p. 1). She contends that such improvement occurs owing to

- Business strategies dependent on customers' willingness and ability to use PSS

- Inability to assume that training would be required, let alone completed

- Large-scale use of customer Websites, leading to questions and problems requiring help desk staffing requirements that could overwhelm an organization

Likewise, Dickelman (2002) also maintains that PSS have matured, noting the extension of performance support principles to new user populations and applications. He also notes that disciplines outside the mainstream of performance support have become aware of its tenets and begun applying them to their own domain. However, progress on some fronts has not extended to others. Our prediction concerning PSS becoming central to HPT practitioners now seems naively optimistic.

In spite of the progress of PSS and performance-centered design appearing in a variety of new places, practitioners and client populations remain confused about PSS. Dickelman notes (personal communication, October 19, 2004) that many still think of PSS as things or technology, rather than as an advocacy or point of view that serves to integrate the many disciplines that support performance: "It is about the organizational mapping of business processes, human factors, and hypertext. It is about cross-discipline cooperation. We have the technology. It is getting all that stuff in the same place at the same time to support performance." In other words, our focus as HPT practitioners should not necessarily be on PSS or EPSS. Our focus should be on using systemic and systematic approaches to create multiple, integrated interventions that support and improve performance in meaningful ways. When appropriate, performance support will follow.

References

Adkins, S. (2003a). Radical learning technology happening now. *Training and Development, 57*(11), 65–72.

Adkins, S. (2003b, December 23). Top ten trends for 2004: It is all about productivity now. Dramatic productivity gains from new technology dominate the landscape. *Workflow Institute Newsletter.*

Altalib, H. (2002). ROI calculations for electronic performance support systems. *Performance Improvement, 41*(10), 12–22.

Barron, T. (1999). The future of maintenance training. *Technical Training, 52*(11), 12–17.

Brown, C. (2002). Usability testing in Internet time. *Performance Improvement, 41*(10), 40–46.

Carliner, S. (2002) Read me first: An introduction to this special issue. *Technical Communication, 49*(4), 399–404.

Carroll, J. M. (1990). *The Nurnberg funnel: Designing minimalist instruction for practical computer skill.* Cambridge, MA: MIT Press.

Chandler, P., and Sweller, J. (1991). Cognitive load theory and the format of instruction. *Cognition and Instruction, 8*(4), 293–332.

Cheese, P., and Ives, S. W. (2002). Desktops of the future. *Outlook 2002, 2,* 73–75.

Collins, A., Brown, J. S., and Holum, A. (1991). Cognitive apprenticeship: Making thinking visible. *American Educator: The Professional Journal of the American Federation of Teachers, 15*(3), 6–11, 38–46.

Condly, S. J., Clark, R. E., and Stolovitch, H. D. (2003). The effects of incentives on workplace performance: A meta-analytical view of research studies. *Performance Improvement Quarterly, 16*(3), 46–63.

Dickelman, G. J. (1995). Things that help us perform: Commentary on ideas from Donald A. Norman. *Performance Improvement Quarterly, 8*(1), 23–30.

Dickelman, G. J. (1996, September–October). Gershom's law. *CBT Solutions Magazine.* Retrieved from www.pcd-innovations.com/law/.

Dickelman, G. J. (2002). Performance support matures. *Performance Improvement, 41*(10), 5–6.

Dickelman, G. J. (2003). *EPSS revisited: A lifecycle for developing performance-centered systems.* Silver Spring, MD. International Society for Performance Support.

Dickover, N. (2002). The job is the learning environment: Performance-centered learning to support knowledge worker performance. *Journal of Interactive Instruction Development, 14*(3), 3–14.

Endicott, J. E., Villachica, S. W., and Stone, D. L. (1998). KICS: Best practices caught in the web. In T. Esque and C. Binder (Eds.), *Case studies in performance improvement.* Washington, DC: International Society for Performance Improvement.

EPSScentral.net. (2004, August 17). *EPSScentral Announces Winners of 2004 PCD Awards.* Retrieved December 6, 2004, from http://epsscentral.com/2004PCDAwardsPress.

Gery, G. (1991). *Electronic performance support systems: How and why to remake the workplace through the strategic application of technology.* Tolland, MA: Gery Performance Press.

Gery, G. (1995). Attributes and behaviors of performance-centered systems. *Performance Improvement Quarterly, 8*(1), 47–93.

Gery, G. (2002). Performance support—Driving change. In A. Rossett (Ed.), *The ASTD e-learning handbook: Best practices, strategies, and case studies for an emerging field* (pp. 24–37). New York: McGraw-Hill.

Gery, G. (2003a). Ten years later: A new introduction to attributes and behaviors and the state of performance-centered systems. In G. J. Dickelman (Ed.), *EPSS revisited: A lifecycle for developing performance-centered systems* (pp. 1–3). Silver Spring, MD: International Society for Performance Improvement.

Gery, G. (2003b, July). *Supporting the development and use of eLearning: Designing and building portals.* Paper presented at the University of Wisconsin Distance Learning Conference, Madison.

Gobert, D. (2002). Designing wearable performance support: Insights from the early literature. *Technical Communication, 49*(4), 444–448.

Gruden, A., and Strannegard, P. (2003, January). Business process integration: The next wave. *eAI Journal,* pp. 8–12.

Hale, J. (2004, October). *Evaluating performance improvement solutions.* Paper presented at the Training Fall Conference & Expo incorporating Online Learning, San Francisco. Available at www.trainingfall.com/handouts/handout_182280.doc.

Henschel, P. (2001, Fall). Understanding and winning the never-ending search for talent: The manager's core work in the new economy. *LineZINE.* Retrieved from http://www.linezine.com/7.2/articles/phuwnes.htm.

Huber, B., Lippincott, J., McMahon, C. L., and Witt, C. (1999). Teaming up for performance support: A model of roles, skills, and competencies. *Performance Improvement, 38*(7), 10–14.

InfoStreet, Inc. (1999). *InstantWeb Online Computing Dictionary.* Retrieved December 13, 2004, from www.instantweb.com/foldoc/foldoc.cgi?query = user + interface.

Jonassen, D. H. (2003). Instructional design for learning to troubleshoot. *Performance Improvement, 42*(4), 34–38.

Jonassen, D. H., Beissner, K., and Yacci, M. (1993). *Structural knowledge: Techniques for representing, conveying, and acquiring structural knowledge.* Hillsdale, NJ: Erlbaum.

Kaplan, S. (2002, August). Building communities: Strategies for collaborative learning. *Learning Circuits.* Retrieved December 13, 2004, from www.learningcircuits.org/ 2002/aug2002/kaplan.html.

Kaplan-Leiserson, E. (Compiler). (n.d.). Glossary. *Learning Circuits.* Retrieved December 13, 2004, from http://www.learningcircuits.org/ASTD/Templates/LC/ LC_ OneBox.aspx?NRMODE = Published&NRORIGINALURL = %2fglossary& NRNODEGUID = %7bA1A2C751-7E81-4620-A0A3-52F3A90148EB%7d& NRCACHEHINT = NoModifyGuest#E.

Lave, J., and Wenger, E. (1994) *Situated learning: Legitimate peripheral participation.* Cambridge, UK: Cambridge University Press.

Marion, C. (2002). Attributes of performance-centered systems: What can we learn from five years of EPSS/PCD competition award winners? *Technical Communication, 49*(4), 428–443.

Martin, J. (1991). *Rapid application development.* New York: Macmillan Publishing Company.

McIntire, D. (2002). Question: Can you explain the differences between e-learning, EPSS, and online help? *Learning Circuits.* Retrieved from http://www. learningcircuits.org/2000/nov2000/geek1.htm.

Minor, M. A., Reid, J. C., Griffin, J. Z., Pittman, C. B., Patrick, T. B., and Cutts, J. H. (1998). Development and validation of an exercise performance support system for people with lower extremity impairment. *Arthritis Care and Research: The Official Journal of the Arthritis Health Association, 11*(1), 3–8.

Porter, S. C. (2001). Patients as experts: A collaborative performance support system. *Proceedings of the AMIA Annual Symposium,* 548–552.

Power, D. J. (1997). What is a decision support system? *DSstar, The On-Line Executive Journal for Data-Intensive Decision Support, 1*(3). Retrieved October 20, 2004, from http://dssresources.com/papers/whatisadss/index.html.

Rossett, A. (2002). Waking in the night and thinking about e-learning. In A. Rossett (Ed.), *The ASTD e-learning handbook: Best practices, strategies, and case studies for an emerging field* (pp. 3–18). New York: McGraw-Hill.

Ruyle, K. E. (2004, October). EPSS: A 20-year retrospective. *Performance Xpress.* Retrieved October 25, 2005, from http://www.performancexpress.org/.

Stone, D. L., and Villachica, S. W. (2001, September). *Beyond toy web sites: PSS design strategies for integrating a marketing presence, on-line services, e-learning, and operational support.* Paper presented at the Silicon Valley Chapter of the International Society for Performance Improvement, Mountain View, California.

Stone, D. L., and Villachica, S. W. (2003). And then a miracle occurs! Ensuring the successful implementation of enterprise-wide EPSS and e-learning from day one. *Performance Improvement, 42*(3), 42–51.

Villachica, S. W., and Stone, D. L. (1998a). CornerStone: A case study of a large-scale performance support system. In P. J. Dean and D. E. Ripley (Eds.), *Performance improvement interventions: Performance technologies in the workplace* (pp. 437–460). Washington, DC: International Society for Performance Improvement.

Villachica, S. W., and Stone, D. L. (1998b). Rapid application development for performance technology: Five strategies to deliver better interventions in less time. In P. J. Dean and D. E. Ripley (Eds.), *Performance improvement interventions: Performance technologies in the workplace* (pp. 343–399). Washington, DC: International Society for Performance Improvement.

Villachica, S. W., and Stone, D. L. (1999). Performance support systems. In H. D. Stolovitch and E. J. Keeps (Eds.), *Handbook of human performance technology: Improving individual and organizational performance worldwide* (2nd ed.) (pp. 442–463). San Francisco: Jossey-Bass/Pfeiffer.

PART FOUR

INTERVENTIONS AT THE WORKPLACE AND ORGANIZATIONAL LEVELS

MARK J. LAUER

Human performance technology (HPT) has a long history of addressing performance problems and opportunities in groups. With many of its roots in fields devoted to how humans interact and work together, it is no surprise that this fourth part of the handbook looks at interventions at the workplace and organizational level. The chapters in this section provide the reader with an assortment of interventions from a variety of HPT perspectives. In this diversity, we can clearly see the *big tent* nature of HPT.

In Chapter Twenty-Four, Brian Desautels explores how organizations need to identify, analyze, and eliminate obstacles that have a negative effect on the achievement of their business deliverables. With HPT having roots in organizational development (OD), many elements in this chapter will be familiar to practitioners. However, the particular business perspective that is presented will make a valuable contribution to all readers' knowledge base.

In Chapter Twenty-Five there is a detailed explanation of Senge's five disciplines that are essential for the creation of a learning organization. Authors M. Jeanne Girard, Joseph Lapides, and Charles Roe link the five disciplines to HPT and introduce the systems learning model (SLM). First developed at the Department of Engineering Professional Development at the University of Michigan-Dearborn, the SLM demonstrates how systemic thought and collective learning have a positive impact on organizational performance.

Moving on from the discussion of learning organizations, Chapter Twenty-Six examines knowledge management (KM) and the role performance technologists can play in its operation. Debra Haney demonstrates that HPT practitioners are well-suited to play an important role in KM in their organizations. Specifically, most KM systems mirror both project-management actions and the steps found in the ADDIE model. These are both familiar activities for performance technologists.

Chapter Twenty-Seven complements Chapter Twenty-Six by looking at the crucial role a community of practice (CoP) can play in identifying and nurturing practices within an organization. Authors Sasha Barab, Scott Warren, Rodrigo del Valle, and Fang Fang explain how a CoP can support the efforts of a particular group or department to design and develop an organizational structure so as to facilitate the emergence of a community if one does not already exist.

In Chapter Twenty-Eight, Karen Medsker explores the need for HPT practitioners to understand how the physical environment can affect human performance in the workplace. With a special emphasis on ergonomics, she centers the discussion on the tools and setting factors found in the workplace environment.

The final chapters of this part of the handbook, Chapters Twenty-Nine and Thirty, examine two different philosophies that are shaping the emerging focus on quality factors in global business: Six Sigma and lean manufacturing. Chapter Twenty-Nine provides a comprehensive explanation of the philosophy, tools, and processes commonly involved in Six Sigma efforts. The article demonstrates that Six Sigma and HPT are complementary approaches to improving performance within the quality-improvement paradigm. As proof, authors Darlene Van Tiem, Joan Dessinger, and James Moseley cite eight specific concepts and practices a performance technologist can import from Six Sigma to enhance his or her performance-improvement work.

Chapter Thirty describes in detail the philosophy, processes, and tools commonly found in lean manufacturing. Joachim Knuf and Mark Lauer explain that in a lean system, performance excellence is viewed as the normal state, and problems and opportunities need to be recognized and addressed at the operational level. Therefore, in a lean system HPT practitioners need to have a special focus on providing the knowledge and tools to workers at the operational level so as to realize the goal of excellence as being the norm.

If there is a common theme that runs through all seven of these chapters, it is this: organizations today have to continually improve if they are to survive. Whether this principle is explicitly stated or quietly inferred, each chapter discusses actions that can be taken on an ongoing basis to improve organizational performance.

Continuous improvement is a standard part of the work of the HPT practitioner. We constantly evaluate our work and feed that information back into our interventions to improve them. While this section highlights the big tent nature of the field, it also illustrates one of its fundamental commonalities. This is but one reason HPT practitioners are particularly well-suited for the changing nature of business today.

CHAPTER TWENTY-FOUR

The Impact of Organizational Development

Brian Desautels

Organizational development (OD) applies human performance technology (HPT) methodologies to a whole system rather than just to components of the system. In this chapter, I will define OD and study a case in which the complexities of an issue cross the entire organization, including its culture, operation, and systems. I will examine how OD uses the same results-oriented approach that HPT uses to achieve a sustainable solution to the issue.

When an organization requests an OD intervention versus other interventions, usually the reason is the perceived scope of the issue, such as a companywide restructuring, or because of the complexity of the issue, such as its effect on multiple departments, multiple systems, or multiple geographies. Similarly, OD interventions often consist of multiple subinterventions, such as reengineering processes, plus job redesign plus training plus new reward mechanisms.

Nonetheless, we may find the OD practitioner using the HPT methodologies when performing his or her work. However, the OD practitioner will always approach the problem without any preferred solution in mind, such as training, but instead will seek to clearly understand the issue and its cause first, then customize a solution and an evaluation plan to ensure the likelihood of a successful solution.

CASE SCENARIO

X-Press is a large software developer of operating systems and applications, located in the United States. The company began as an aggressive entrepreneurial start-up populated by technical enthusiasts who were passionate about their industry. Their culture and work environment reflected that aggressiveness; employees were given large goals and were expected to deliver. Long hours were required to produce those deliverables, and people worked twelve, fourteen, sixteen hours a day, seven days a week, to make them happen.

The culture proclaimed that the company hired only the smartest people in the world. Training was not necessary, the organization said, because smart people could figure out what was needed. Training took time to locate, to attend, and to implement. Figuring out a better way was faster.

The company thrived; its products and reputation in the market were extremely positive. Employee attrition was very low, in comparison both with its industry and with other, nonsoftware industries. Employees found the environment more motivating than previous jobs for two reasons:

1. They believed that the work that they were doing was making the world a better place.

2. The stock options that they received when hired, and additional options they received every year, looked to make them wealthy beyond their expectations.

Today, X-Press has grown into a huge global organization with fifty-five thousand employees worldwide. However, attrition is rising to historic highs, about 8 percent annualized, and climbing. Competitors who are developing niche software applications have established office locations within the same geographic areas as X-Press and are aggressively recruiting X-Press employees. In addition, X-Press stock leveled off about five years ago. Employees who joined early and made millions have left. Subsequent employees, who expected to make millions and have not, hide their disappointment by working harder, hoping to bring back the glory days of a hot stock.

Last, the CEO is worried about X-Press becoming a large, cumbersome company unable to provide the rapid responsiveness to the market that allowed it to grab market share and excel as it did in the early days. To keep employees agile and focused, he has implemented a program that identifies and terminates the bottom 10 percent of the employees for performance each year. These bottom 10 percent are not counted in the attrition rate.

Managers across X-Press are rushing to the recruiting department inside the company's human resources department. The managers are complaining to the CEO that the recruiting people are not finding qualified candidates to fill the empty positions. Deadlines are being missed, and, for those still here, work hours are increasing to well beyond the already high levels. The recruiting people are upset as well, complaining that managers need to do something to slow the attrition rates. Additionally, the recruiting department is finding that the decline rate, when offers to candidates are given but declined, is also running at historic highs. Both the recruiting people and the managers are running to the compensation department asking for increases in the salary structures and increases in signing bonuses, which have not been used recently due to the soft economy over the previous few years. The compensation people reply that X-Press is already paying very aggressively compared with others in the labor market—more than 15 percent higher than the average rate paid.

Susan, the human resources director, walks down the hall to talk the situation over with the corporate manager of organizational development, Jason. Susan knows that this situation is not manifesting itself as a recruitment issue; nor should it be fixed by a compensation solution that has a short-term resolution but is likely to cause bigger problems eventually. The problem is that the organization is not designed for success any more. A new design is needed to be implemented quickly.

WHAT IS ORGANIZATIONAL DEVELOPMENT?

Organizational development is an overarching approach to identifying and removing obstacles in the environment that are having a negative impact on an organization's ability to reach its deliverables. OD uses a deliberate methodology for aligning the organization's performance components to enable the organization to achieve business deliverables. These components typically include processes, knowledge and skill and attribute requirements, resources, people practices or policies, and available consequences. This methodology analyzes the ideal state of the total environment that contributes to produce a deliverable to quality standards, and then compares the results of the analysis against the current environment. The resulting gap would be closed or compensated for through OD strategies. OD is similar to the approach used by HPT:

> OD is effort planned, organization-wide, and managed from the top to
> increase organization effectiveness and health through planned interventions in
> the organization's processes, using behavioral knowledge [Fitz-enz, 2002, p. 213].

Every OD project's focus, and every OD solution, is driven by its contribution to the deliverable. Said another way, the deliverable, once clearly defined with performance standards, dictates the required contribution from the performance components. Without a stated definition of the deliverable, the performance components are likely to be miscued.

OD must also endeavor to ensure that the system components complement one another, so that when effort is applied appropriately by the employee, for example, that effort will produce the expected business deliverable. This reality recognizes that when a faulty OD intervention leaves any performance component shy of its requirement, the result for the system is zero long-term value. When any component is unfulfilled, such as when attrition removes effort, the result is devastating. Similarly, solutions applied to the wrong component, such as giving cash rather than training to an employee lacking the required knowledge, are useless solutions.

OD considers the whole system when choosing an intervention. The OD perspective is concerned with improving the effectiveness of the whole system and, in turn, endeavors to improve the effectiveness of the whole organization. It uses a systematic methodology for increasing value by continuously improving efficiencies and deliverables. An organizational development approach should be used when

- Dynamic and agile responsiveness is required by the organization.
- The situation is occurring within a high-complexity environment.
- The organization is experiencing broad-scope situations requiring team collaboration.

In addition, the very nature of the culture itself may force a more effective organizational design. Situations within the culture that may drive an organizational redesign include

- No common direction exists or the strategy has been changed.
- No apparent decision-making criteria exist, resulting in decisions that are in conflict.
- No measurable success factors exist.
- Sharing information between team members is critical.

OD considers the impact of the culture on the system because

The fact is that the solution is often sub-optimized or lost because of failure to acknowledge the humanity involved. . . . OD is a planned intervention aimed at improving individual and organizational health and effectiveness [Fitz-enz, 2002, p. 214].

DEFINING THE IDEAL STATE

Organization development begins its involvement by conducting a work system analysis. As mentioned earlier, all OD interventions are targeted to ensure that the necessary contribution to the development of the deliverable occurs, either by removing obstacles or by providing interventions that compensate for a shortcoming. For this reason, all analyses are to be performed in correlation to the functionality and standards of the deliverable.

Defining Deliverables

The work system analysis begins by defining the deliverable in the ideal state, meaning as if all factors were contributing perfectly. This action is simpler in product industries, where one can hold the output in one's hand, versus in the knowledge industry, where the output may be ambiguous and difficult to define.

OD sees deliverables as falling within two buckets, each with its specific owner:

1. *External:* These are the deliverables that leave the organization for the marketplace. They can be a product, a press release, a fine, advice, or trash, for example. Most often these external customers define the deliverable in broad terms, with the organization providing its differentiating uniqueness. When OD is defining the work system for an external deliverable, marketing and engineering representatives may be invited to participate.

2. *Internal:* These are deliverables that leave one work system to become resources in another work system. Examples include component parts, reports, advice, policies, and programs. Most often, these internal customers define the deliverable in fairly narrow constraints, which are then customized in minor ways by the subordinate system. OD works with the superordinate system to define the deliverable and, concurrently, with the subordinate system to ensure that it can be built. Representatives from both systems may be invited to participate [Ulrich, 1997].

Defining Processes

Once the deliverable is defined, the process tasks and steps can be identified to ensure that the deliverable can be produced. OD will pull together a team to analyze and diagram the process, often using a whiteboard. During this exercise the team will identify the following:

- Process tasks and steps
- Owners of process tasks and steps
- Handoffs between process steps and between owners

The team will also build quality control considerations into the process to ensure that the process has been effectively implemented and sustained.

OD will also drill further into the process as designed on the whiteboard. It must be clear that the handoff between steps and between owners is recognized as the point at which one person's deliverable becomes another person's resource. Failure to fully articulate subordinate deliverables will result in incorrect action being performed by the subordinate system, which may yield an ineffective outcome for the organization.

Defining Knowledge, Skills, and Attributes

The articulation of the processes drives the alignment of the knowledge, skill, and attribute (KSA) requirements to organization deliverables. Because process steps are specific tasks to be performed, and because tasks require knowledge and skills plus other contributors to be performed effectively, OD can identify the specific KSAs required to produce the deliverables. OD looks for an articulation of specific requirements rather than broad statements such as a degree in this or a certification in that.

OD will look at the KSA requirements against the organizational criteria used for assessing *talent fit* to determine if an effective assessment device is being correctly and consistently applied.

Concurrent with the review of the talent assessment, OD will look at the criteria used for assessing *cultural fit* to determine if both the work style and uniqueness are appropriate and if the cultural assessment device is being correctly and consistently applied.

Defining Resources

Beyond the knowledge and skill requirements, OD will again review the process and deliverables to determine if the required resources, including equipment and materials, are available in the environment at the correct time and place. Like KSA requirements, the articulation of the process drives alignment of the resources with the organization deliverable. Required resources fall into two categories:

1. Resources that constitute the deliverable, as flour is to bread
2. Resources that contribute to the building of the deliverable, as an oven is to bread

OD will ensure that an identification and alignment of required resources has occurred. Generally, however, OD does not involve itself with the actual identification or acquisition of either category of resources. Nonetheless, OD becomes very concerned with the availability of these resources and whether the deliverable can be built from the resources, considerations that directly affect the performance of both the individual and the organization.

Defining Effort or Execution

OD must now determine whether the existing environment will encourage sustainable execution, through managed consequence, by the employee. OD must first ascertain if the environment provides continuous process and resource availability and improvement. In other words, if employees choose to execute their duties and responsibilities, is what is needed available? Or, by contrast, are the resources and processes so unavailable that a reasonable employee will choose to decline to perform the required duties? This OD action is different than defining what is required; it is now asking if these components are easily available at the moment of performance.

OD assesses the visibility and actuality of a performance-reward linkage. In other words, OD assesses whether the employee will feel rewarded for performing the requirement or punished in some way. Furthermore, OD would assess the presence of cultural support mechanisms, or a lack thereof, to identify what they are and the type of consequences they apply.

At this point, OD has defined the deliverable in clear, measurable standards. In turn, these clear deliverables have driven a clear articulation of process requirements, knowledge and skill requirements, and requirements for additional resources, and have scoped an environment that will encourage sustained employee contribution through the use of targeted consequences.

DEFINING THE CURRENT STATE

OD turns the analysis now to describe the current state of this work system. Generally, the same analysis questions are used when defining the current state as were used during the definition on the ideal state, only the focus is now on what the environment shows today. For example, OD previously asked, Ideally, what are the knowledge requirements for that deliverable? OD now asks, Currently, what knowledge and skills are available?

OD's assessment of the current state will collect information on the clarity of the deliverable; the actual process used today; the alignment of present knowledge, skills, and attributes; the availability of required resources; and the present reward incentives.

X-Press Current State: Deliverables

Deliverables are slipping due dates. A new version of X-Press's operating system, featuring a massive upgrading of its functional capabilities, has slipped significantly past its target ship date. X-Press responded to the missed ship date by lowering its sights on what new functionality will be available, losing some image in the market. Still, it is projected to miss the ship date by three years, giving competing makers of operating systems the opportunity to show the stability of their environments.

Individual employees watch as the required deliverables continue to grow on their plates. New deliverables are added but, because of the attrition problems, none are taken off. X-Press has not guided managers to plan realistically. Indeed, the missed ship date has increased sensitivity about missing ship dates for other products.

X-Press Current State: Processes

X-Press had rewarded employees in the past for making a deliverable happen, regardless of how it was made. The most effective process became the self-directed process workaround, which consisted of the employee hand-carrying his or her need straight to the department head and waiting for a response, regardless of whatever else was being worked on. The workaround became so prevalent that normal processes became useless.

X-Press Current State: KSAs

At X-Press, there is a joke about a manager of software developers demanding that all candidates have an undergraduate degree in computer science, thus eliminating Bill Gates, who does not have a college degree, from further consideration.

Specifically, the manager was in need of someone who could code in C++. As the manager was requiring the computer science degree, the recruiting department spent most of its time finding candidates with degrees, rather than focusing on candidates with C++ coding experience, regardless of degree.

X-Press Current State: Resources

Generally, the only resource that is unavailable to this system is additional headcount. All tools, materials, reports, hardware, or software are either available or will be purchased.

X-Press Current State: Effort or Execution

The environment had changed significantly over the years from highly motivating to demotivating. In its early days, two true perceptions were present:

1. Employees believed that the company was changing the world in a positive way.
2. The stock was rising in value in such an accelerated manner that employees were getting wealthy.

These two perceptions were so true and visible that X-Press's large amount of deliverables were attained because of employees' supercharged response to a supercharged environment. Please note that, even in a supercharged, highly motivating environment, this level of employee contribution was not sustainable. Employees contributed until their stocks vested and they were wealthy, about five years, and then they retired from X-Press.

During this discussion at X-Press, the OD specialist discovered that, even if employees worked a fourteen-hour day, they would hear negative comments about missing an important e-mail that may have been delivered after the fourteen-hour day. The result of this is not the gratification of contributing well beyond an eight-hour day, but rather punishment for having missed a late message.

Today at X-Press, both of the original situations are no longer true. Breakthrough software innovations have been replaced by annual updated versions of older applications, and employees no longer passionately feel that they are changing the world. The second situation, becoming wealthy and retiring in five years, is no longer possible. The highest stock prices were reached five years ago.

As a result of today's perceptions, the ability to create a supercharged and motivating environment is greatly diminished. In addition, the CEO's plan to reduce the number of nonproductive employees actually created nonproductive employees instead. Innovation became viewed as too risky by employees. This program was viewed and felt by them to be punishing. The effect was that employees who saw no reason to work as hard as the supercharged environment formerly required shut down on the job. They began to see employment opportunities at competing companies where the pay was the same and competitors were requiring only forty hours of work rather than the sixty hours required at X-Press.

ORGANIZATIONAL DEVELOPMENT AND CLOSING PERFORMANCE GAPS

The difference between the ideal state and the current state is the performance gap. While the performance gap defines a need that in turn explains why the deliverable is not met, OD must be aware that the deliverable may not be met due to a combination of shortcomings causing a number of gaps across the performance components.

At this point, OD first reviews the system to determine if there are any false indicators masking performance gaps. Sometimes, employees demonstrate Herculean effort to produce a deliverable despite a lack of resources or a broken process. Such a false indicator suggests that the system is effective when it really is not. In these cases, OD will usually note an overcontribution from the performance component: effort. All overcontributions should be considered unsustainable; simply put, even with a potential for extremely high rewards, overcontribution by an employee will only be sustained until the reward threshold is reached or the potential for high reward is removed. Over long periods of time there will also be issues of employee burnout.

Once it is determined that the deliverable is or is not achieved, OD continues to

- Assess the performance gap
- Determine positive and negative environmental influences
- Monitor the workplace to determine if production of the deliverable can be sustained

Each of these performance components, of course, has the potential to show performance gaps between the current and ideal state. With the performance gaps identified, OD begins to design interventions that either will compensate for the targeted piece missing from the performance component or will close the gap fully.

OD achieves this by creating the criteria for selecting the solution needed to close the gap. Criteria for selecting an effective solution design include that it be deliverable-oriented, process-oriented, or people-oriented. Furthermore, the solution must be feasible and cost effective: the price of the solution must be less than the cost of the gap.

DESIGNING ORGANIZATIONAL DEVELOPMENT SOLUTIONS

The work of designing a solution is driven by the system requirements of the deliverable in the ideal state. OD solutions respond to any change to the deliverable by building a correlated change to the processes; the resources; or the employee contribution, either in the knowledge and skills component or in the amount of effort required. Change requirements correlated to the employee contribution are usually managed from within people practices or human resource policies.

In some circumstances, changes to the design, functionality, or production of the deliverable require technological changes. In turn, these technological changes affect the whole system and are likely to require changes to other system components: new processes, new knowledge requirements, and different levels of employee effort.

To OD, all work is driven by the requirements of the deliverable but within the context of organizational culture and structural change. Changes in market direction or market position can affect systems such that their formerly effective deliverables are now no longer competitive in the market. In addition, organizational vision and principles, which help guide and develop an organization, may become hindrances blocking the organization from where it needs to be today. The evolution of both the culture and the organizational structure may be restricted while out-of-date visions and principles remain in place.

The new or reengineered process is considered effective within the whole system when the process works horizontally across the components of the required performance, such as from receiving dock to shipping dock, and vertically from individual deliverable to organization deliverable, such as from software tester to the software development department.

Horizontal fit requires that all performance components correlate to the deliverable. There is a single deliverable with articulated specifications, related knowledge and skill requirements, implemented process steps, identified required resources, and rewarded effort to execute toward the deliverable. Each system component interacts with the other system components; the relationship between these components must be balanced, with each component contributing as designed. If any component fails to be fully present, an overcontribution from another component may result. Overcontribution by any individual component is never desired because it places unsustainable stress on that component while producing false indications of success.

Vertical fit requires that deliverables correlate to the resource requirements of the higher-level, superordinate work system. Each subordinate work system is, in fact, a contributing derivation of the overarching organizational strategy and goal. However, it is through the effective interplay of subordinate systems that OD links individual and work-group contributions to the organization's strategies and goals.

Designing OD Solutions Aimed at Process Deficiencies

Generally, OD solutions aimed at process deficiencies fall into either of two strategies:

1. *Process design:* The whiteboard is wiped clean, and the process is designed as if it were the first day that the organization existed. A team of stakeholders is brought together and designs a process unconstrained by how the process has existed in the past. Every station along the process is questioned for its necessity and is eliminated or modified as appropriate. Designing the new process begins with clearly articulating the deliverable, then mapping out the process by which the deliverable will be built or completed. Once mapped, ownership stations and related points of handoffs can be identified.

2. *Process reengineering:* The flow of the existing process is laid out on the whiteboard, and all the locations where the bottlenecks are occurring are highlighted. These bottlenecks are then analyzed for a

determination of the causes of the bottleneck. The causes are then removed by reengineering the flow of the process, or compensated for with additional training or resources.

Designing OD Solutions Aimed at KSA Deficiencies

KSA deficiencies are solved in one of two ways:

1. *Eliminate the need for the knowledge:* If possible, a change to the system process or an addition of targeted resources can eliminate the need for a specific skill.

2. *Provide targeted training solutions:* Various training solutions, from developing the training inside the organization to buying the training externally, are available. Commonly used training designs include

   - Performance aids
   - Self-study programs
   - Classroom training
   - Mentoring
   - Distributed and distance learning

The OD specialist will call on the training specialist to identify need-to-know information, design program materials, design evaluation devices, and implement. Generally, OD performs organizational readiness studies to determine how the organization needs to be prepared to use the new knowledge and skills. The studies often consist of holding small-group meetings with members of the target population to gather data about how the new deliverable requirements are viewed, the likely effectiveness of the process, and any changes to the reward system and jobs.

Designing OD Solutions Aimed at Resource Deficiencies

Driven by the resource requirements identified during the design of the process, deficiencies are commonly solved through one of two paths:

1. *Internal:* The internal path commonly requires interaction between two system owners, such as the accounting department and IT. OD recognizes the interdependency of separate systems within an organization and further recognizes that the deliverables of one system may become the needed resource of another system. For example, the on-line accounting system requires the availability of the accounting software, an IT deliverable. OD may find that the cause of the unavailable resources may reside in another system and, to resolve it, involves the owner of the other system.

2. *External:* If the resource is unavailable inside the organization, two paths can be used for solving the deficiency: use internal resources to build the needed resource or buy it from the outside.

Designing OD Solutions Aimed at Effort Deficiencies

If we view employee effort as a contribution to the development of a deliverable, it becomes easier to see effort as something measurable. We can determine whether the employee contribution meets, exceeds, or falls short of using the remaining performance components together and whether the deliverable is produced to specification.

Contribution must be viewed as execution, the energy required to pull the other components into an action aimed at a given deliverable. Contribution is both an emulsifier pulling the other components into something new and a multiplier that changes the components into something that they were not before. An ax and a log do not result in a stack of firewood without a contribution of the energy needed to swing the ax.

When we view execution in terms of contribution, then measure the contribution received and contrast it with the contribution required, we can determine if any additional intervention is needed to compensate for any shortcoming. OD recognizes that the organization can encourage a required level of contribution, but it cannot force that contribution to happen. As effort is a contribution, the employee is encouraged through reward to a high level of sustained contribution and discouraged from executing short of that level through consequences applied by the organization.

As stated earlier, while the organization cannot force contribution, it can design the system so that the employee is encouraged, or motivated, to contribute to the deliverable to the extent required. In addition to the availability of organizational rewards or consequences, OD can assess the workplace to determine if there are cultural or social elements, operational procedures, or misperceptions that may be either encouraging or discouraging the desired level of employee contribution.

OD says that when the requirements of the deliverable change, the performance components contributing to the deliverable must change. Conversely, if the performance components change, the deliverable will change unless there is compensation for the shortcomings in those changed components.

IMPLEMENTING THE OD SOLUTION

At this point, the OD solution is managed as an internal change project. The project requires a team comprising the key project stakeholders within the organization. OD identifies the constituency team that necessitated the change and assigns ownership responsibilities.

Assigning Ownership of Deliverables

In general, someone with operational responsibilities owns the deliverable and the process. For the deliverables, however, the question of who owns the deliverables has as many considerations as input into its definition:

- Marketing, if the deliverable exports to the market
- Management in the superordinate organization, if the deliverable is a resource to another's deliverable
- Manager, who receives the deliverable
- Employee, who produces the deliverable

Human resources (HR) representatives are included on the team because, generally, they have responsibility for obtaining the necessary knowledge, skills, and attributes and for providing an environment that the employee finds motivating. HR's role is not only to help solve the problem but to ensure that the solution does not cause difficulties elsewhere in the organization (Ulrich, 1997).

The procurement department may have responsibility for ensuring that the needed resources are available. Procurement typically makes the following decisions regarding acquisition of the required resources:

- Make or buy the resource
- Ensure budget compliance
- Deliver the required functionality to ensure utilization

Finally, someone from senior management, which has a significant stake in the projected results, should be identified as an internal sponsor. Sponsor responsibilities typically include building organizational support and championing the cause at the highest levels within the organization.

Managing the Project

Project-management actions apply to the development and implementation of the OD intervention. The five key actions owned by the project manager, once the team is identified, are

1. *Planning:* The implementation of the OD intervention needs to be planned, specifically as to what needs to happen by whom, when, and in what sequence.

2. *Piloting:* This refers to first alpha testing the intervention in laboratory conditions, then beta testing with an audience reflective of the audience that will ultimately be affected by the solution. When the change to the organization includes changes to the processes, it may be

required that a simulated environment be created so that work flows can be tested without affecting daily operations. As an alternative, a segment of the work can be flagged to follow a new flow for testing purposes while all other work follows the usual flow so as not to disturb the organization too dramatically.

3. *Communicating:* Thought must be given to all support mechanisms required by the new work system. Changes to the deliverable must be communicated by the manager. For shortcomings in KSAs, training must be provided. For changes to the process, flow charts must be revised and training must be provided. For changes to resources, notification of their availability and training, if needed, on how to operate must be provided. To ensure a smooth acceptance of the changes to the system, communication will need to be provided in a scenario-based style to ensure that employees understand the inherent rewards that accompany these changes.

4. *Scheduling and roll-out:* As with any plan, the roll-out activities need to be sequenced for success. Scheduling must include the effective date of the implementation. Then scheduling back to the first day will ensure that the employees understand the changes under way and their role in receiving or supporting those changes.

5. *Developing measurement criteria:* What will tell you that the intervention was successful? While OD lists this as the last of the five implementation actions, success is usually identified during the opening conversation when the client is asked, What makes you think that you have a problem? OD will say that both the analysis and the evaluation pivot off the deliverable. Measurement then ultimately must evaluate if the deliverable has been met.

Overcoming Resistance

OD also looks at the environmental influences that may randomly or predictably have an impact on the effectiveness of the implementation. The work system was designed under laboratory conditions, perfect and protected. Eventually, the system was tested under a simulated circumstance, a little less perfect and a little less protected. Now, however, the intervention is being implemented organizationwide in an environment where change may be resisted.

OD approaches the organizationwide implementation with knowledge of the cultural attributes of the environment. Resistance is a random influence that can nonetheless be anticipated. Focus groups can be pulled together during the beta period to review the new work system, which allows OD an opportunity to identify areas of resistance.

OD uses the information surrounding resistance by ensuring that it is managed effectively toward full assimilation into the workplace. OD may need a management sponsor to perform the following supportive activities:

- Reinforce or amend its current cultural principles
- Make visible its commitment to the changes and explain the expected positive impact on the organization
- Provide visible supports for the changes, which may include flow charts and performance aids
- Commit, on a daily basis, to the system being supported as designed. Adherence may include positive rewards for performing to the new processes and negative feedback for failing to participate.

MEASUREMENT AND EVALUATION

OD places paramount consideration on the need to measure and evaluate the effectiveness of the new work system. Before implementing the intervention, OD will identify its leading and lagging indicators of effectiveness.

A leading indicator is measured nearly immediately, or within thirty days, after implementation of the intervention. These indicators are meant to show right away if any impact is being realized. Examples of leading indicators include post-tests, production rates, error rates, and complaint rates.

A lagging indicator focuses more on whether the desired deliverable and supporting performance are being sustained as designed. Lagging indicators tend to look at many of the same indicators but at sixty or ninety days. In addition, lagging indicators may also include audits of the intervention's impact on organization performance, profitability, quality, and so on.

Both leading and lagging indicators are used to measure effectiveness of the intervention within two organizational realms: business and culture. Again, the timing of an audit varies by the intervention and can occur immediately after implementation, at thirty to ninety days, or even one year later.

Examples of business indicators that could be audited are

- Increases in organizational complexity or bureaucracy
- Responsiveness
- Profitability
- Customer satisfaction

Examples of cultural indicators that could be audited are

- Collaboration
- Talent and other resources

- Leadership
- Employee participation
- Link between employee contribution and organizational objectives

Examples of operational indicators that could be audited are

- Productivity goals
- Integration of business functions or components
- Competitive advantage

Previously, the question of sustainability of the performance and deliverable was raised. Simply put, if the work produced a change that was not sustainable, OD failed in its task. Assessments of the sustained effectiveness of the intervention usually occur at ninety days and one year after the intervention.

Assessing sustainability is different in its focus than the evaluations that were performed postintervention with the leading and lagging indicators. At this point, sustainability is questioned in terms of its ability to hold up under the random and predictable influences that enter the work environment.

These influences, referred to as "emergent influences," are managed by monitoring the work environment for their existence and impact. Emergent influences can be predictable or random. Examples of predictable influences are new policies, new product lines, changes to legislation, and so on. "Predictable" means that the owner can see the change coming and that the change is likely to have an impact on the work system. Examples of random influences are storms that disrupt, resources in your system that are not delivered or software that crashes, the devaluing of employee stock options, and so on.

Monitoring the environment is the only way to detect these influences and their potential effect. Discovering a predictable influence allows the deliverable owner to respond to the influence and compensate for its impending impact. Compensating means either allowing the influence to be absorbed into the system freely or safeguarding the system from the influence. If the influence is allowed to affect the system, the OD specialist will recommend methods to compensate for the impact at the point of interaction with the performance component to ensure that the state of the system remains ideal.

Anticipating a random influence allows the owner to take preventive action. Preventive actions are a list of compensating factors that can be implemented if the influence occurs. Inventory compensates for disruptive storms, backup data files compensate for crashed software, stock grants may compensate for stock options, and so on.

The key point to sustainability assessments is that the assessment is an ongoing practice. Given that all work environments are dynamic, the possibility of emergent influences is a constant threat; therefore, the ability to respond quickly and effectively allows the production of the quality deliverable to be sustained.

CONCLUSION

I began this chapter by stating my view that OD and HPT share much common ground. When well applied, both OD and HPT use results-oriented approaches and both take a systems view of organizations. OD and HPT use the same or similar processes and problem-solving tools. The major distinction is that OD applies these principles and methodologies to a whole system, while HPT more often deals with components of the system. I introduced a case scenario to illustrate the attributes of OD. In conclusion, I return to the case of X-Press.

X-Press: Designed OD Solutions

The analysis conducted by the OD specialist revealed that the underlying cause of the attrition was that the enormous requirements of the employee deliverable required an amount of employee effort that was unsustainable; the specialist discovered little issue with the organizational processes; availability of resources; or the required knowledge, skills, and abilities. Simply put, the workplace was now a demotivating environment rather than a highly charged, motivating environment. Employees were less willing to work long hours for smaller rewards than the historic millions that had been made through stock options by their predecessors.

A number of compensating actions were possible. First, the historically high demands of the deliverables could have been reduced; because the rewards were less, the demands should have been reduced similarly. Second, some role adjustments could have been made that differentiated between basic duties and high-level requirements and provided promotional opportunities that would be viewed as a motivating environment.

The guidance that OD provides here is the assertion that compensating actions must be applied to the environment to ensure that

- The workplace is found motivating by the employee, to encourage contribution.
- The required level of contribution is examined to determine that the requirement is sustainable.
- The deliverable, system components, and required employee contribution are aligned and sustainable.

The starting point for building this whole system is articulating what the expectations are that the employee is being asked to deliver. Expectations are both the activities to be performed and the standard to be measured against. These expectations represent the metrics by which the employee will be measured and, implied within those metrics, the reward that will be delivered upon attainment.

Pressure will be applied by the employee to lower the metric while maintaining the level of reward. This pressure is inherent within the reality surrounding the question of what must be present in the environment so that an employee will find it motivating. Generally, factors that are seen as competitive in the labor market are seen as reasonable by the workforce, rewards congruent with historical practices within the organization are seen as reasonable, and the clarity with which the rewards are understood by the employees helps ensure its effectiveness.

Workplace consequences must be balanced relative to the deliverable to be effective. The OD specialist found that X-Press was giving small rewards for an extraordinary deliverable. In addition, some employees were receiving high rewards for work that had less impact than the work of others. The recommendation was to align rewards realistically to the work performed so that employees clearly understood those rewards.

Generally, positive and negative consequences, which are applied to the workplace to encourage employees to perform toward the defined levels and away from undesired performance, fall into two broad categories: compensation and noncash equivalents, and recognition. Compensation and other noncash equivalents include

- Base pay
- Bonuses
- Stock (grants or options)
- Time off

Examples of recognition are

- Publicly received awards
- Inclusion in a desired committee
- Dinner with the CEO

The final factor to consider when building an environment that encourages an employee to contribute is the impact of that consequence upon the sustained production of the deliverable. The OD specialist recommended the use of targeted bonuses, avenues for professional visibility such as presenting at conferences, and dinners with the CEO, all of which were to encourage employees to stay (Ulrich, 1997).

X-Press: Implementation Plan

Clearly, the OD solutions were targeted at reducing the attrition rate. From the beginning, throwing additional cash toward employees was determined to be contrary to the organization's market strategy, which was already paying above-market rates, and OD supported the observation that cash would not yield the level of sustainability X-Press desired.

First, OD recommended that existing processes be frozen without changes for one year, to determine whether they could work as designed. Concurrently, all process owners would instruct their teams that processes must be followed. The environment that created the self-directed workaround processes had also created a trading floor mentality in which whoever shouted the loudest got satisfied; chaos and slowness affected those who did not shout as loud, causing frustrations for employees who tried to follow written procedures. By freezing the processes and eliminating the workarounds, the OD specialist sought to encourage cooperation between employees and reduce frustrations.

Second, OD asked the training department to conduct a training needs analysis within specific groups to determine if the skills needed to support the processes were in place. While the initial workplace review suggested that the knowledge requirements were being met appropriately, confusing process workarounds may have given false indications of where the knowledge level was. The goal was that time wasted as the employee tried to figure out solutions to simple procedural problems could be recouped by providing the needed skills up front. Plus, employees attending common classes could then use common language and procedures to improve workload balance. Upon completion of the needs analysis, appropriate interventions would be designed, if needed.

Third, the CEO's "Bottom 10 Percent Performance Program" was shelved. The program had created a negative, punishing, and paranoid environment that caused employees to want to leave. The stock situation was not replaced, but a program aimed at setting realistic expectations for wealth was established. Most important, a "Top 25 Percent Performance Program" aimed at identifying priority projects for outstanding employees was created. The program's purpose was to recognize projects considered critical to overall goals, and that were in jeopardy of failing, which could be made successful by assigning the projects to the outstanding employees.

X-Press: Evaluation of Effectiveness

The key evaluation points were the effectiveness of the deliverable in terms of quality, quantity, timeliness, and cost. Because X-Press was a knowledge-based business, the problem of employees leaving became the primary focus of the targeted interventions; the impact on the operation caused by the disappearing knowledge was huge. The analysis showed that, because an overcontribution of effort was required from employees to reach the deliverables, these employees refused to sustain the effort and left. With the increasing attrition rate, effort became empty in certain systems, causing requests for even higher demands of contribution from the employees who stayed.

To achieve balance within the system, to reduce the demand for unsustainable overcontribution, interventions were implemented into correlated performance components: processes were reengineered, knowledge was added, and the work environment was modified to be more rewarding and less negative.

Impact of OD Solutions on Attrition

Within six months, the annualized attrition rate flattened. After another six months, the rate dropped to 4 percent (from 8 percent) annualized.

References

Fitz-enz, J., and Davison, B. (2002). *How to measure human resources management* (3rd ed.). New York: McGraw-Hill.

Ulrich, D. (1997). *Human resource champions.* Boston: Harvard Business School Press.

CHAPTER TWENTY-FIVE

The Fifth Discipline: A Systems Learning Model for Building High-Performing Learning Organizations

M. Jeanne Girard, Joseph Lapides, Charles M. Roe

*T*he *Fifth Discipline,* written by Peter Senge (1990), introduced organizations to the concepts and practices of organizational learning. According to Senge, learning organizations are

> organizations where people continually expand their capacity to create the results they truly desire, where new and expansive patterns of thinking are nurtured, where collective aspiration is set free, and where people are continually learning to see the whole together [Senge, 1990, p. 3].

Senge argues that only organizations that are flexible, accepting of change, and creative in adapting to it will succeed in the global economy. Accordingly, all organizations and businesses should be learning organizations. The questions for human performance technology (HPT) practitioners are when and how to use fifth discipline interventions. This chapter will respond to these basic questions.

Organizational learning embraces the concept of *connectivity* through the practice of five essential disciplines. It emphasizes that *change* is the only constant, and it uses the five disciplines to help people acquire some level of comfort in dealing effectively with change.

Senge identifies the five disciplines as

- *Systems thinking:* Viewing an organization structure or process from a holistic perspective

- *Personal mastery:* Maintaining both a personal vision and a clear picture of current reality

- *Mental models:* Making assumptions or generalizations that influence perceptions, understandings, and actions taken
- *Shared vision:* Rather than exhibiting compliance, creating and sharing a picture of the future that fosters genuine commitment
- *Team learning:* Aligning and developing team capacities to create the results desired by the team members

Practicing the five disciplines helps to create a learning culture that is characterized by its clear and consistent openness to new ideas and experiences, encouragement of responsible risk taking, and willingness to acknowledge failures and learn from them. The learning organization's structures, values, policies, practices, and systems support and accelerate learning for all employees. This often results in continuous improvements in products and services, the structure and function of individual jobs, teamwork, and management techniques. Besides positively contributing to an organization's financial bottom line, a learning culture often fosters increased feelings of trust, creativity, camaraderie, and teamwork within the organization.

To become a learning organization, institutions need to discover how to tap employee commitment and encourage continuous learning throughout the organization. Although everyone has the capacity to learn, the organizational structures in which employees have to function are not always conducive to the learning process. Work deadlines focus employee attention on daily tasks and often leave little time to reflect on operational challenges and on any effective strategies to deal with them. One possible plan of action to assist in creating a continuous learning culture is to begin with the discipline of *systems thinking.*

SYSTEMS THINKING: THE HEART OF THE LEARNING ORGANIZATION

One of the greatest accomplishments in Senge's work is his use of *systems theory.* Systems theory addresses the whole by examining the interrelationships between the parts. Systemic thinking is the conceptual cornerstone of *The Fifth Discipline.* When leaders are able to view their organizations from a holistic perspective, actions are usually more appropriate and effective. In most of our organizations "we learn best from our experience, but we never directly experience the consequences of many of our most important decisions" (Senge, 1990, p. 23). Leaders often tend to believe that cause and effect are linear and relatively close to one another. This belief causes them to look for actions that deal with challenges and correct them in a relatively short period of time. However, when viewed within the context of systems theory, short-term improvements often generate significant long-term costs. Senge concludes,

> The systems viewpoint is generally oriented toward the long-term view. That's why delays and feedback loops are so important. In the short term, you can often ignore them; they're inconsequential. They only come back to haunt you in the long term [Senge, 1990, p. 92].

The discipline of systems thinking is a direct link between *The Fifth Discipline* and human performance technology. Rosenberg (1999, p. 137) indicates that HPT is "an offspring of general systems theory applied to organizations." The systems approach advocated by HPT requires practitioners to adopt a total systems perspective in examining organizations by emphasizing the interconnections and interdependencies of the elements of the organization. In developing interventions to improve human performance, practitioners rely on general systems process models such as ADDIE: analyze, design, develop, implement, and evaluate (Rosenberg, 1999).

THE REMAINING CORE DISCIPLINES IN GREATER DEPTH

As stated previously, systems thinking and the four other learning disciplines constitute the core disciplines of organizational learning. A description of each of the remaining disciplines follows.

Personal Mastery

"Organizations learn only through individuals who learn. Individual learning does not guarantee organizational learning, but without it no organizational learning occurs" (Senge, 1990, p. 139). Personal mastery is the discipline of "continually clarifying and deepening our personal vision, of focusing our energies, of developing patience, and of seeing reality objectively" (Senge, 1990, p. 7).

> People with a high level of personal mastery live in a continual learning mode. They never "arrive." . . . But personal mastery is not something you possess. It is a process. It is a lifelong discipline. People with a high level of personal mastery are acutely aware of their ignorance, their incompetence, and their growth areas. And they are deeply self-confident. Paradoxical? Only for those who do not see the "journey is the reward" [Senge, 1990, p. 142].

Mental Models

Mental models are "deeply ingrained assumptions, generalizations, or even pictures and images that influence how we perceive and understand the world and how we take action" (Senge, 1990, p. 8). We are often unaware of the impact of such assumptions on our actions, and thus a fundamental objective is to develop the ability to both reflect *in* action and reflect *on* action.

> The discipline of mental models starts with turning the mirror inward; learning to unearth our internal pictures of the world, to bring them to the surface and hold them rigorously to scrutiny. It also includes the ability to carry on "learningful" conversations that balance inquiry and advocacy, where people expose their own thinking effectively and make that thinking open to the influence of others [Senge, 1990, p. 9].

Organizations developing the capacity to work with mental models must create and support opportunities for people to learn new skills and develop new orientations. "Learning to recognize the internal politics and game playing that dominate traditional organizations is essential to the success of organizational learning. In other words, it means fostering openness" (Senge, 1990, pp. 273–286).

Shared Vision

The capacity to create and share a picture of the future is one of the most powerful characteristics of effective and inspired leadership. Such shared visions have the power to be uplifting and to encourage experimentation and innovation.

> When there is a genuine vision (as opposed to the all-too-familiar "vision statement"), people excel and learn, not because they are told to, but because they want to. But many leaders have personal visions that never get translated into shared visions that galvanize an organization. . . . What has been lacking is a discipline for translating vision into shared vision—not a "cookbook" but a set of principles and guiding practices. . . . In mastering this discipline, leaders learn the counter-productiveness of trying to dictate a vision, no matter how heartfelt [Senge, 1990, p. 9].

Team Learning

Team learning is viewed as "the process of aligning and developing the capacities of a team to create the results its members truly desire" (Senge, 1990, p. 236). To build on the disciplines of personal mastery and shared vision, people need to learn to be able to act together. When teams learn together, Senge suggests, not only can there be good results for the organization, but members will grow more rapidly than might have occurred otherwise.

> The discipline of team learning starts with *dialogue*, the capacity of members of a team to suspend assumptions and enter into a genuine *thinking together*. To the Greeks *dia-logos* meant a free flowing of meaning through a group, allowing the group to discover insights not attainable individually. . . . [It] also involves learning how to recognize the patterns of interactions in teams that undermine learning. . . . Team learning is vital because the teams, not individuals, are the fundamental learning units in organizations. This is where the "rubber meets the road"; unless teams can learn, the organization cannot learn [Senge, 1990, p. 10].

LINKS TO HUMAN PERFORMANCE TECHNOLOGY

Human performance technology is a "systematic process of linking business goals and strategies with the workforce, and is responsible for achieving the goals" (Van Tiem, Moseley, and Dessinger, 2000, p. 2). HPT provides processes for linking people to their organizations in mutually beneficial ways. HPT is about supporting *learning, communications,* and *governance for performance support.* Organizational learning in general and the systems learning model (SLM) in particular attempt to accomplish similar aims. The primary activity of HPT practitioners is to determine the organization's needs through the analysis of organizational systems, process, and human performance systems. Following this analysis, HPT designs, develops, and implements the activities that will help to accomplish the desired objectives. Typical *learning interventions* designed by HPT practitioners could be in skill development, technology training, soft skills development, the use and practice of the tools of *The Fifth Discipline,* and so on.

HPT practitioners maintain and facilitate organizational *communications* by offering process consulting; facilitating dialogue sessions; developing team-learning activities; and enhancing the connections between people, management, workers, and the various departmental specialists who are working on product development or solving challenging problems.

Using *gap analysis,* HPT practitioners develop and advocate for instructional and noninstructional performance-support structures, human resource development, job analyses, and organizational design and development. HPT practitioners also ensure the implementation of their interventions, network, build alliances, provide employee assistance, and develop the organizational structures to sustain the changes. In short, HPT implements the SLM.

THE AUTHORS' EXPERIENCE
WITH ORGANIZATIONAL LEARNING

The authors' experience with organizational learning (OL) comes from their affiliation with the University of Michigan-Dearborn's College of Engineering and Computer Science (CECS). Through its Department of Engineering Professional Development (EPD), the college offers organizational learning courses, seminars, and workshops designed for engineering and technical employees. Various organizational learning offerings have been available at EPD since 1996. The organizational learning knowledge discussed here reflects the authors' experience in working with organizations that have applied OL techniques in the workplace.

The Basis of the Authors' Work

To begin to understand organizational learning, it is easiest to reflect on your own learning as individuals. Generally, learning takes place when the following things occur:

- You do something or have some experience.
- You reflect on the consequences of the action you took.
- You allow this reflection to influence your next actions.
- You reflect on the consequences of the actions you took based on your earlier reflection.
- You repeat the cycle, building expertise and experience into new learning.

We can use a similar cycle to describe organizational learning. When we collectively engage in this cycle with other people we can develop a cycle to create new knowledge and then transfer this new knowledge into swift meaningful action. The *systems learning model* illustrates how systemic thought and collective learning have a positive impact on the actions, leading to effective results. Created by EPD at the University of Michigan-Dearborn's CECS, the model is a natural consequence of the college's intrinsic belief in systems thinking and its experience in teaching organizational learning competencies to over one thousand learners (see Figure 25.1).

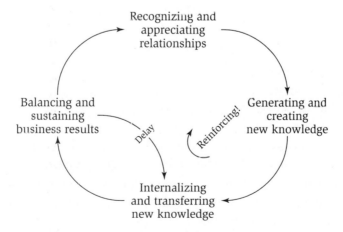

Figure 25.1. The Systems Learning Model.

Source: Waves of Change Partnership. Used with permission.

Table 25.1. Systems Learning Model Quadrants.

Quadrant	Step	Activity	Focus of Tools
Recognizing relationships	1	Focus with laser-like precision for maximum results to discover relationships	Interactions Interdependencies Interconnections
Generating new knowledge	2	Reduce delay by infusing new learning in mission-critical systems, not all of them	Mental models Diverse perspectives Learning styles
Transferring knowledge	3	Use swift, meaningful actions to inspire people, manage change, and infuse practical skills	Project management Scenario planning Systems thinking
Balancing and sustaining results	4	Recognize, review, and refocus efforts on the next set of mission-critical problems	Feedback reports Systems audits Operating models

Source: Waves of Change Partnership. Used with permission.

Using the SLM we create the ability to engage with others, to make links with the four quadrants, and to explore basic orientations and values and their linkages to organizational behaviors and beliefs. The quadrants, each quadrant's associated activities, and recommended tools for each quadrant are described in Table 25.1.

We know that people have mental maps that influence the various ways that they plan, implement, and review their actions. To fully appreciate the implications of this, we require a process model. This model involves three core elements:

- *Governing variables:* The factors that people are trying to keep within acceptable limits. A number of variables are likely to have an impact on such factors. Thus, any situation can trigger a trade-off among governing variables.

- *Action strategies:* The movements and plans used by people to keep their governing variables within the acceptable range.

- *Consequences:* The results of an action. Consequences can be both intended and unintended. In addition, they can affect the self or others [Anderson and Johnson, 1997].

These elements are illustrated in the single-loop learning graphic (see Figure 25.2).

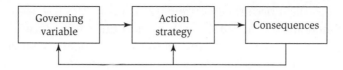

Figure 25.2. Single-Loop Learning Graphic.

When the consequences of the employed strategy match the person's intentions, then the *theory in use* is confirmed. This is due to the alignment between intention and outcome. However, there may also be a mismatch between intention and outcome. In other words, the consequences may produce unintended outcomes. This can misalign or work against the person's governing values. A commonly cited example is the *Challenger* space tragedy, in which engineers passed over a faulty "O ring" design, repeatedly intent on the goal of meeting space program deadlines. Argyris (1999) contends that such defensive routines are a product of the limited learning system that we create in our organizations based on single-loop learning. These variables lead to behaviors and actions that are primarily aimed at avoiding embarrassment or threats, such as the following:

- Advocating our views without encouraging inquiry; hence, remain in unilateral control and hopefully win

- Unilaterally saving face, our own and other people's; hence, minimize upsetting others or making them defensive

- Designing and managing situations unilaterally to maintain control

- Evaluating the thoughts and actions of others in ways that do not encourage testing the validity of the evaluation and our own thoughts and actions

- Attributing causes for whatever we are trying to understand without necessarily validating them

- Engaging in defensive actions such as blaming, stereotyping, and intellectualizing to suppress feelings

A paradox comes about because these kinds of variables reward limited learning and give rise to negative consequences, control games, and mixed messages. So, without intending to, we start to create environments that foster defensive routines, and as a consequence our work results are not what they could be. Why? Simply put, because we are disabling learning and foregoing knowledge that could be brought to bear on solving complex problems and making more robust decisions. Why do we all seem to act in accordance with these variables? First because they are based on variables that were instilled in us in childhood and reinforced through most of our early education and work experiences. This makes it very difficult to change because changing *requires that we explore strongly embedded values and assumptions within our own way of being.* Second, we have collectively constructed a system that is self-reinforcing, making it extremely difficult for us to change the system unless we fully understand and confront it.

We can only begin to break this cycle of defensive routines if we are able to engage a new set of governing variables and strategies that elicit behaviors which help create and support an entirely different and more open working environment. This set of variables and strategies would be things such as the following:

- Governing variables

    Providing valid information

    Encouraging free and informed choice

    Being internally committed to the choice and vigilant monitoring of the implementation of the choice in order to detect and correct error

- Resulting strategies

    Share power and cocreate situations

    Inquire such that we actively strive to test our theories publicly, making our inferences apparent; and we actively seek to reduce blindness about our own inconsistency and incongruity

    Do not save face or protect ourselves or others by withholding information

    Exhibit less defensiveness and instead act as facilitators, collaborators, and choice creators [Argyris, 1999]

Single- and Double-Loop Learning

When something goes wrong, many people look for another strategy that will address and work within the governing variables. In other words, given or chosen goals, values, plans, and rules are *operationalized* rather than questioned. This is *single-loop learning.* An alternative response is to question the governing variables themselves and to subject them to critical scrutiny. This is described as *double-loop learning.* Such learning may then lead to an alteration in the governing variables and thus a shift in the way in which strategies and consequences are framed. This is how Argyris and Schön (1978) describe the process in the context of organizational learning.

Single-loop learning is like a thermostat that learns when it is too hot or too cold and turns the heat on or off. The thermostat can perform this task

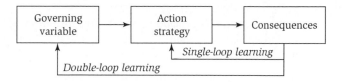

Figure 25.3. Double-Loop Learning Graphic.

because it can receive room temperature information and take corrective action. Double-loop learning occurs when errors are detected and corrected in ways that involve the modification of an organization's underlying norms, principles, policies, and objectives. This process can be represented quite easily by a simple amendment to the initial representation of theory in use by viewing the double-loop learning graphic (see Figure 25.3).

The focus of much of our work around the systems learning model has been on how organizations may increase their capacity for double-loop learning. We believe that double-loop learning is necessary if practitioners and organizations are to make informed decisions in the rapidly changing and often uncertain context of today's global economy. As Edmondson and Moingeon (1999, p. 160) state:

> The underlying theory, supported by years of empirical research, is that the reasoning processes employed by individuals in organizations inhibit the exchange of relevant information in ways that make double-loop learning difficult, and all but impossible, in situations in which much is at stake. This creates a dilemma, as these are the very organizational situations in which double-loop learning is most needed.

Exploration of the systems learning model helps to move people from a single-loop learning mentality to a double-loop learning orientation and practice. The significant advantages of double-loop learning include the ability to call upon good-quality data and to make inferences. It looks to include the views and experiences of participants rather than seeking to impose a view on the situation.

The focus of our systems learning model is the formulation and implementation of intervention strategies. This involves moving through six phases of work (see Figure 25.4).

By running through this sequence and attending to key criteria suggested by practicing double-loop learning, organizational development is possible. The process entails looking for the maximum participation of clients, minimizing the risks of candid participation, starting where people want to begin, and designing methods so that they value rationality and honesty.

Phase 1	*Map the problem as participants see it.* This includes the factors and relationships that define the problem, and the relationship with the organization's living systems.
Phase 2	*Have the participants internalize the map.* Through inquiry and active engagement with the participants, the facilitators, and coaches work to develop a true picture of the organization.
Phase 3	*Test the model.* This involves looking at what *predictions* can be derived from the model and reviewing organizational practice and history to see if the predictions can be verified.
Phase 4	*Create solutions to the problem and simulate them to explore their possible impact through the lens of the systems learning model.*
Phase 5	*Implement the solutions.*
Phase 6	*Evaluate the impact.* This allows for the correction of errors as well as generating knowledge for future designs.

Figure 25.4. Systems Learning Model Intervention Phases.

Source: Waves of Change Partnership. Used with permission.

THE TOOLS OF ORGANIZATIONAL LEARNING AND SYSTEMS LEARNING

Check-In, Check-Out

Check-in is a powerful conversational tool. It evolved from the practice of *dialogue* but has taken on a life of its own as an effective way to begin and conclude meetings. Although a simple process, it often deepens conversations, making them more powerful and meaningful. The check-in process requires that people sit in close proximity to one another, commonly with chairs set in a circle. People each then speak on any subject that they wish to share with the group, being uninterrupted until they have shared all of their thoughts. Commonly, people make comments about what happened to them just before the meeting, other issues that are of concern, or their feelings about the upcoming meeting. Since the main idea is that no opening subject is inappropriate, people have the freedom to speak about what they wish. When finished speaking, participants verbally signal the end of their comments by saying something such as "I am in" to the group, and by passing some object to the person next to them in the circle. The passed object serves as a visual reminder to other group members that the speaker has the floor and should not be interrupted.

The passed object can be any meaningful object or soft toy. One popular check-in object is a *koosh* ball. The central focus is that everyone participating in the process listens to the speaker without interrupting or making judgments about the speaker's comments. Participants also have the option of passing or not participating. The real leverage in this process resides in the aspect of *listening*. Check-out uses the same format as that of check-in. People signal that they are finished speaking by verbally signaling the end of their comments, "I am out," and by passing the conversational object along to the next person.

Dialogue: Raising the Level of Knowledge in a Team

As William Isaacs (1993, pp. 24–39) notes in *Taking Flight: Dialogue, Collective Thinking and Organizational Learning,* dialogue is a method of group conversation designed to increase inquiry into mental models and their underlying beliefs and assumptions. *Generative dialogue* utilizes no agendas or meeting minutes. *Strategic dialogue,* however, focuses on a specific question and can occur as follows: a group of invited participants sit in a circle, and after some initial introduction to the concept of dialogue they "check in." This process differs from the check-in process used for general meetings because participants focus their comments on a particular topic framed by the facilitator. Often, the comments are recorded on flip charts by designated, nonparticipating scribes. Following check-in, participants review the recorded comments during the check-in, continuing with facilitator guidance and the recording of participant comments. The group continues the dialogue process until it is no longer productive. During the dialogue, participants abide by the following rules:

- Begin with check-in.
- Speak to the center; do not address your comments to specific people.
- Listen.
- Postpone judgments.
- Suspend certainties.
- Inquire into assumptions.
- Listen to yourself, both speaking and thinking.
- Balance advocacy and inquiry. This means to go ahead and speak your mind, but keep an open mind and truly try to understand other positions.
- Conclude with check-out: this uses the same format as check-in, only with less emphasis on answering strategic questions.

Strategic dialogue is not about agreement or consensus. It is about listening for deeper understanding and insight. The goal is not to establish action plans, although they may be outgrowths of the process, but to acquire an understanding of and greater insight into the mental models of the participants and how they influence strategy. Commonly, the process requires about three days, with at least two of the days occurring consecutively.

Causal-Loop Diagrams

The causal loop has its roots in the discipline of systems thinking. A *causal-loop diagram* (CLD) is an illustration of the *cause-effect-cause* relationships between factors which over time generate the dynamic behavior of the system being considered. As such, a CLD depicts the arrangement of the important parts of a system's structure. A *causal link* within a CLD is marked with a single-head arrow, or *link,* denoting the direction of causality between causes and effects. To make same relationships explicit, some CLD diagrams will display an *s* at the arrowhead to indicate that the variables move in the *same* direction. A loop implies feedback, or circular causality. A sample CLD on collaboration is depicted in Figure 25.5.

Thinking with Hexagons

The basic *thinking-with-hexagons technique* is quite simple. At first, it seems similar to brainstorming. Someone assumes the role of facilitator to guide the process. Participants are invited, in turn, to share ideas that are relevant to a specific focus question. The thinking-with-hexagons technique is significantly better than typical brainstorming sessions because

- The purpose of the session is explicit, and the focus question is very clear and visible.

- Each participant is given a few moments of quiet time to record his or her answers to the focus question, thus empowering those who may have a more introverted nature.

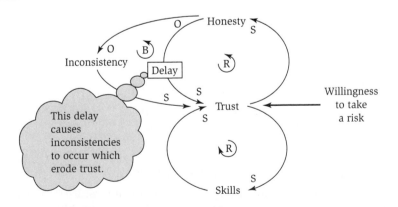

Figure 25.5. Collaboration Causal-Loop Diagram.

- The ideas are captured on small, hexagon-shaped sheets of notepaper similar to post-it notes. Using the hexagon-shaped paper provides opportunities to easily move the ideas around and link them to other ideas.

- Everyone has a chance to participate equally, and each person's ideas are given equal weight when offered to the group. Instead of stopping with the idea-generated lists, ideas are arranged into clusters that share a commonly related concept.

- Due to the graphic nature of the process, participants see the bigger picture.

- New ideas are created by forcing a *synthesis* idea from two or more other ideas.

- Participants are enabled to see the systems perspective by giving them the opportunity to discuss, and then explicitly describe, how the clusters are related to one another.

Advocacy and Inquiry

The term *advocacy* refers to making our thinking process visible and publicly testing our assumptions and conclusions (Senge, 1990; Senge, Kleiner, Roberts, Ross, and Smith, 1994) through the use of the following three techniques: (1) giving examples to illustrate thinking, (2) sharing the data or steps used to reach conclusions, and (3) thinking systemically so that the person providing the information recognizes that others may have a different view (Smith, 2001).

Inquiry involves asking others to make their thinking processes visible (Senge, 1990; Senge, Kleiner, Roberts, Ross, and Smith, 1994). It also involves three techniques: (1) encouraging challenges, (2) probing others' thinking, and (3) seeking others' views (Smith, 2001).

Ladder of Inference

Understanding the *ladder of inference* (Argyris, 1982; Argyris, Putnam, and McLain Smith, 1985) is crucial to increase organizational learning. It uses the tools of advocacy and inquiry. The ladder of inference can be seen as a continuum in which data, facts, and events are on one end, and action, theories, and synthesized concepts are on the other end. The ladder of inference is illustrated in Figure 25.6 (Senge, Kleiner, Roberts, Ross, and Smith, 1994).

Those readers familiar with *grounded theory methodologies* (Glaser and Strauss, 1967) may recognize the concept of how raw data are synthesized into theory. Most people communicate at the abstract or high end of the ladder of inference because they make statements that may mean something to some but may be interpreted differently by others. The ladder of inference can provide a focal point for understanding how learning can help or hinder organizations.

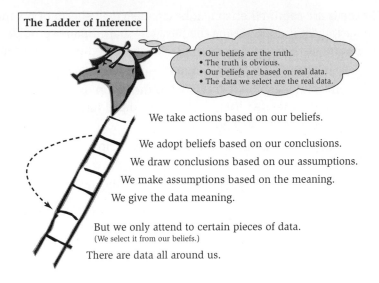

Figure 25.6. The Ladder of Inference.

When people speak too high on the ladder of inference, understanding is limited. Providing facts and raw data from the lower end of the ladder of inference helps clarify the speaker's thinking, thus giving the listener the opportunity to individually interpret the information.

Reflection

Communication and openness involve both self-reflection, which focuses on being honest with oneself about a situation, and participatory reflection, which means pushing the group to clarify and evaluate the assumptions underlying how work gets done within the organization. Taking the time for reflection is constructive. Reflection is central to the principle of adult learning. Reflection on our experiences allows us to formulate questions, acquire new perspectives, and expand our thinking. Introspection is the driving force behind organizational learning, organizational growth, and continuous improvement. We believe that effective learning is impossible without continuous reflection that is based on scientific inquiry. Scientific inquiry in our context consists of seven practical steps:

1. Record observations.
2. Compare observations and convert observations to measurements.
3. Introduce common reference.

4. Identify and separate variables.

5. Formulate a hypothesis.

6. Convert a hypothesis to a theory.

7. Elevate a theory to the status of law.

We believe that practical knowledge and research-based knowledge are interconnected and reciprocal. Our inquiry processes are based on the understanding that certain aspects of human experience cannot be understood through the simple collection of data. Rather, one must be inside the experience and in dialogue with those having the experience to properly explore, understand, and interpret the experience. We believe that research that values the voice of practitioners provides an important and unique perspective on organizational learning. Participatory action research done by practitioners develops "a higher degree of self-determination and self-development capability" (Elden and Chisholm, 1993, p. 125), or what Schön (1987) calls the "reflective practitioner."

Reflective practice requires particular characteristics. Dewey (1933) pointed out that good reflective practice is guided by wholeheartedness, directness, open mindedness, and responsibility. This means that reflective practitioners are enthusiastic about their subject matter, committed to learning, and open to new ways of seeing and understanding the world around them.

Operation Adventure

Operation Adventure is a program using graduated group and individual experiential challenges (Gibson, 1999). The program is administered and led by the staff of the Athletics and Recreation Department of the University of Michigan-Dearborn (UM-D). Operation Adventure, in conjunction with *The Fifth Discipline,* is a structured activity based on the principle of challenge by choice in experiential learning activities. The purpose of using Operation Adventure for organizational learning is to provide a laboratory for practicing the disciplines of personal mastery and team learning. It provides the learners with a structured, facilitated, and safe environment such as a "high ropes" course or a climbing wall to test their resolve and expand their capabilities in creating the results they truly seek (Senge, 1990). This is accomplished by conquering as many obstacles as the participants choose. For some learners, it may mean climbing up a ladder to a platform thirty-five feet off the ground, appropriately protected with harness and safety lines, standing there for a period of time, and returning by executing a "leap of faith," attached to a belay system, thus gently floating back to the ground. Each of the learners accomplishes the essence of personal mastery by attaining his or her goals, in the context of the reality of operation adventure.

The Beer Distribution Game

This is a game in which teams of participants manage each level of a distribution chain. There are four levels in the system: retailer, wholesaler, distributor, and factory. Each week, the players at each level receive shipments of beer from their suppliers, fill as many of their customers' orders as possible from their inventory, and place new orders for beer with their suppliers. The goal is to keep company costs as low as possible while meeting customer demands. The purpose of the game is to give participants insight into the behavior of a distribution system and to illustrate the difficulties of developing a robust strategy for managing even the simplest of systems. More fundamentally, the players systematically explore the consequences of various strategies and learn the dynamics of supply chains and the principles for effective management.

Clearness Committee

In *The Courage to Teach,* Parker Palmer (1998) describes how he adapted a Quaker structure that is called the "clearness committee" to help people resolve their dilemmas. The clearness committee is a process that invites people to help each other with personal problems or dilemmas while practicing inquiry, confidentiality, and the discipline of dialogue. The process is detailed as follows:

1. A learning circle is convened involving a maximum of ten participants. If the learning community is relatively new, the session will begin with a check-in. A volunteer is selected who will serve as the focus person.

2. The facilitator solicits agreement from the learning circle to honor confidentiality. Each member of the circle is required to respond affirmatively to this request.

3. The focus person presents a dilemma or a problem that requires attention.

4. Using *inquiry,* the learning circle inquires from a position of *total objectivity* and questions the focus person. The individual then responds by explaining or clarifying the dilemma or problem.

5. The circle is cautioned to avoid giving advice. They are reminded to ask questions from a position of total objectivity.

6. The clearness committee is adjourned after thirty to forty-five minutes or sooner.

7. The facilitator will invite the focus person to accept advice if any member of the group volunteers to provide it and the focus person agrees.

8. Debriefing the clearness committee usually focuses around the difficulty in asking objective questions and avoiding providing advice.

Organizational Engineering: I-OPT

Using information-processing methodologies, *organizational engineering* (OE) focuses on the understanding, measurement, prediction, and guidance of the behavior of groups. It does not contradict what is being done with psychological instruments, but rather extends it. The relationship between OE methods and psychological instruments is one of correlation. Because its focus is on how people make decisions, OE is less threatening than traditional psychological testing, and because its focus is on evolving group relationships, the effects of past baggage brought to the team by its members play a limited role.

The basic instrument of organizational engineering is the I-OPT survey. It is a survey and not a test. I-OPT is an acronym for *input-output processing template.* It suggests that the profile that is generated from an individual's survey responses is a strategy that the individual chooses to use to navigate life and work rather than a fixed aspect of the individual's personality. This is in contrast to the typical psychological orientation of *I am.* OE postulates that, just like individuals, groups must develop decision-making strategies to be effective. These strategies can be measured and influenced.

In the OE paradigm, people use different templates to filter the massive amount of information that might affect their decisions. The choice of the filter influences the nature and character of the input information and, as a result, the nature of the responses.

The other side of the information-processing paradigm is the output. The outcome of whatever processing a person does is described in OE by the concept of *mode.* Salton (1996) postulates that, at the extremes, individuals have the option of using two modes. The first is the *action* mode. In this mode a person's behavioral response is directed by addressing a particular issue using expedient strategies that *may* resolve the issue. In business, a person in an action mode might use a telephone and call a customer before deciding exactly what needs to be said to the customer.

Another available mode is *thought.* In this realm a person's response is an idea, plan, assessment, evaluation, or judgment. The response does not directly affect the issue but is rather a step along the way toward affecting it. The thought response is intended to give direction to subsequent action.

In today's information-based society, the ability to live on the output of the thought mode is even more available than in the past. Thought is as viable a survival strategy for individuals as is action. However, for society as a whole, action is more valuable than thought. It may be possible for a species to survive without much thought. It will not survive without action. OE theory points out that input and output can be linked without considering the exact methods and mechanisms people use. This is accomplished by using the concept of strategic posture, or *style.* In effect, the various methods and modes combine

Table 25.2. I-OPT Style Characteristics.

Reactive Stimulator (RS)	The pure RS is an action-oriented individual. RSs typically work with low detail, are tightly focused on near-term objectives, and seek tangible results. They operate in the action mode using unpatterned methods.
Logical Processor (LP)	The pure LP is methodical and action-oriented. Such individuals are naturally detail-oriented and work best when assignments are clear and precise with well-defined expectations. LPs operate in the action mode using structured methods.
Hypothetical Analyzer (HA)	The pure HA is a problem solver. HAs focus on problems and their solutions. Their primary concern is identifying the best way to address a situation, with a typical output being a plan, assessment, evaluation, or judgment. HAs operate in the thought mode using structured methods.
Relational Innovator (RI)	The pure RI is an idea generator. Relationships between divergent ideas are quickly identified. Seemingly disparate ideas, concepts, and innovation are quickly integrated into coherent theories and systems. The RI operates in a thought mode using unpatterned methods.

Source: Adapted from Salton (1996). Used with permission.

to create characteristic behavior patterns that are the result of the interactions between the dominant input templates and the dominant output form template. This is illustrated in Table 25.2.

Strategic Thinking

Strategic thinking is inherently different from ordinary thinking. Mintzberg (1994) says that strategic thinking is a particular *way* of thinking with specific and clearly discernible characteristics. It synthesizes intuition and creativity to produce "an integrated perspective of the enterprise" (Hamel and Prahalad, 1989, pp. 63–76). One can refer to strategic thinking as "crafting strategic architecture" (Public Service Commission of Canada, 2004). Strategic thinking involves thinking and acting within a certain set of assumptions and potential alternative actions as well as challenging those existing assumptions and alternative actions, potentially leading to new and more appropriate responses. This is illustrated in Figure 25.7.

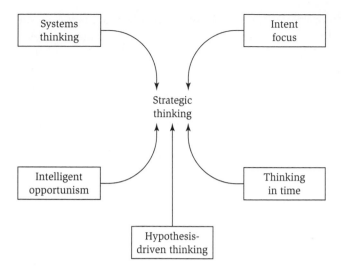

Figure 25.7. Strategic Thinking.

Source: Adapted from Liedtka, 1998. Used with permission.

Liedtka's model (1998) defines strategic thinking as a particular way of thinking with very specific and clearly identifiable characteristics. The model illustrates the five elements of strategic thinking: systems thinking, intent focus, intelligent opportunism, thinking in time, and hypothesis-driven thinking. Each of these will be discussed briefly in the following sections.

Systems Thinking. A strategic thinker has a mental model of the complete system of value creation from beginning to end and understands the interdependencies within the chain. Senge (1990) also stresses the significance of mental models in influencing our behavior. According to Senge, people fail to put new insights into practice because they conflict with deeply held internal images of how the world works, images that limit us to familiar ways of thinking and acting. That is why the discipline of managing mental models, surfacing, testing, and improving our internal pictures of how the world works can be a major breakthrough.

Intent Focus. Hamel and Prahalad (1989) note that *strategic intent* implies a particular point of view about the long-term market or competitive position that a firm hopes to build over the next ten-plus years. It implies a competitively unique point of view about the future. It offers employees the promise of exploring new competitive territory, and it states a goal that appeals to the emotions and that employees perceive as inherently worthwhile. Direction, discovery, and destiny are the attributes of strategic intent. Liedtka (1998) indicates that strategic intent creates the focus that allows individuals within an organization to collectively leverage their energy and to focus attention so they can resist routine distractions and provide focus for as long as it takes to achieve a goal.

Intelligent Opportunism. Intelligent opportunism involves the idea of openness to new experiences that allow organizations to take advantage of alternative strategies that may emerge as more relevant to a rapidly changing business environment. In practicing intelligent opportunism, organizations must consider the input from lower-level employees or more innovative employees. According to Hamel (1997),

> If you want to create a point of view about the future, if you want to create a meaningful strategy, you have to create in your company a hierarchy of imagination. And that means giving a disproportionate share of voice to the people who have until now been disenfranchised from the strategy-making process. It means giving a disproportionate share of voice to the young people . . . [and] . . . to the geographic periphery of your organization, because typically, the farther away people are from headquarters, the more creative they are: they don't have the dead hand of bureaucracy and orthodoxy on them. And it means giving a disproportionate share of voice to newcomers [Hamel, 1997, quoted in Lawrence, 1999].

Thinking in Time. Thinking-in-time strategy, according to Hamel and Prahalad (1994), is not solely driven by the future but by the gap between the current reality and the intent for the future. Strategic intent signifies a sizeable stretch for the organization, to the extent that current resources will not be enough, forcing the organization to be more inventive and to make better use of resources. By connecting the past with the present and linking this to the future, strategic thinking is always thinking in time. Neustadt and May (1986, p. 251) state that thinking in time has three components:

- Recognition that the future has no place to come from but the past; hence the past has predictive value.
- Recognition that what matters for the future in the present is departure from the past, including alterations, changes, and diversions from familiar flows.
- Continuous comparison, an almost constant oscillation from the present to the future to the past and back, heedful of prospective change, concerned to expedite, limit, guide, counter, or accept the change as comparisons to the past, present, and future suggest.

Hypothesis-Driven Thinking. The fifth element of strategic thinking recognizes the process as one that is *hypothesis-driven*. Like the scientific method, strategic thinking embraces hypothesis generation and testing as core activities. According to Liedtka (1998), this approach is somewhat foreign to most leaders. The scientific method accommodates both creative and analytical thinking by using iterative cycles of hypothesis generating and testing. Hypothesis generation poses the creative question, What if . . . ? Hypothesis testing follows up with the critical statement, If . . . then, and evaluates the data relevant to the analyses. This process allows the organization to pose a variety of hypotheses, without sacrificing the ability to explore novel ideas and approaches.

Scenario Planning

Scenario planning was developed and is used to assist companies in making expensive, long-term decisions in uncertain situations. A scenario is an account of a possible future. Scenario planning uses a set of contrasting scenarios to explore the uncertainty surrounding the future consequences of a set of decisions. Ideally, scenarios should be constructed by a diverse group of people for a specific purpose. Scenario planning is appropriate in systems when there is a lot of uncontrollable uncertainty.

Scenario planning is able to incorporate a variety of quantitative and qualitative information in the decision-making process. Considering this diverse information in a systemic way leads to better decisions. Furthermore, the participation of a diverse group of people in a systemic process of collecting, discussing, and analyzing scenarios builds shared understanding. The general steps to scenario planning are

1. Identify a diverse group of people to provide a variety of perspectives.
2. Conduct interviews or workshops with participants concerning what they see as significant shifts in the economy, technology, politics, or society.
3. Cluster these different views into common groups and look for patterns.
4. Generate a list of the best ideas from the patterns noticed in step 3.
5. Create stories or descriptive scenarios of what the future might hold based on the list of generated ideas.
6. Determine how each scenario will affect the organization based on the group's collective perspective.
7. Establish a set of warning signals that will provide an indication that a particular scenario is beginning to emerge.
8. Establish a process to monitor, evaluate, and review scenarios throughout the planning cycle.

EVALUATING THE SYSTEMS LEARNING MODEL

How are we to evaluate the systems learning model? First, we can say that there has been a growing research base concerning the model, including its facilitation and coaching strategy; however, the research is still limited. The process and the focus on *reflection in action* appear to bear fruit in terms of people's connections with the systems learning model and their readiness to explore personal and organizational questions.

Second, the approach assumes that "learning takes place in a climate of openness where political behavior is minimized" (Easterby-Smith and Araujo, 1999, p. 13). This is an assumption that can be questioned. It can be argued that organizations are inherently political, and that it is important to recognize this. Organizations can be seen as coalitions of various individuals and interest groups, where "organizational goals, structures and policies emerge from an ongoing process of bargaining and negotiation among major interest groups" (Bolman and Deal, 1997, p. 175). Perhaps we need to develop theory that looks to the political nature of structures, knowledge, and information.

Third, the facilitation and coaching strategy is staged. Why should things naturally operate in this order? We argue that, rather than operating in phases, interventions of this kind involve a number of elements or dimensions working at once.

THE UM-DEARBORN ORGANIZATIONAL LEARNING COURSE

UM-D's three-credit-hour organizational learning graduate course is titled "Building Highly Performing Learning Organizations." The purpose of the course is to introduce the learners to OL concepts.

The students are required to review and report on research related to organizational learning. They are also required to prepare a position paper that advocates the adoption of organizational learning practices in their respective workplaces. In addition, the students submit a final examination that requires their responses to the following four questions: (1) What did you learn in this course? (2) How do you know that you learned what you say you learned? (3) How do you show what you learned to others? and (4) What will you do with what you learned?

In some ways, the course is a traditional graduate course, but in many ways it is very different. In fact, one of the students suggested that this course should come with a warning: "It will change your life" (Lapides and Kachhal, 2000, p. 5).

One departure from traditional university instruction is that the learners sit in a circle on comfortable executive chairs in a room full of toys, pictures, and music. All sessions begin with a check-in, during which the learners typically are asked to enter the learning circle by sharing their thoughts coming into the class and their reflections about the previous session. The check-in practically and symbolically moves the learners from their daily routines to the learning tasks. At the end of the class session the learners participate in a check-out. During the check-out the learners share what worked for them in the session, or what did not, and what surprised them. They are also asked to provide a key learning highlight. The check-out is also a way to evaluate the learners' perception of the effectiveness of the session. Each session has a dialogue framing the discipline that is being introduced.

EVALUATING THE EFFICACY OF THE COURSE

To ascertain the efficacy of the course, a random sampling of final course examinations from 275 students who participated in the UM-D organizational learning graduate course between 1996 and 2001 was summarized. The examination required that students respond to what they learned in class and how they would use this new knowledge in the workplace. Follow-up telephone interviews with twenty-five members of the sample group were then conducted to determine what students did with what they learned and to what extent their efforts penetrated their organizations. The following questions were used to determine the efficacy of organizational learning with this population:

1. What is the impact of an introductory, albeit experiential, organizational learning course on learners and the organizations they represent?

2. To what extent are individuals who take this course able to sustain organizational learning in their organizations?

The course is designed to provide an experiential learning platform for the core competencies of organizational learning. With one voice all continue to practice the *core theory of success* (Kim, 1997), as illustrated in Figure 25.8.

Students related how OL concepts have benefited them in their work and personal lives. The impact on the organizations in which they work, however, appears minimal. Another result that emerged from this course is the practice of personal mastery in terms of commitments and successes in balancing work and home life while adhering to a personal vision.

If there is any axiom in this course, it is that *all changes begin with you.* The theme of the interviews supports this concept because the majority of the learners indicated that they took the initiative and started to *walk the talk* about organizational learning. The sad side of this exploration is that sustaining organizational learning in the environment of manufacturing and human services

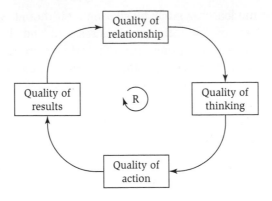

Figure 25.8. Core Theory of Success.

Source: Kim, 1997. Used with permission.

is still a dream. Sustaining organizational learning can occur only where upper-level management is completely invested in sustaining organizational learning. It is our opinion that to achieve the sustainability of organizational learning, organizations must have a critical mass of people who have learned the principles and practices. These people must work for an organization that values and supports them.[1]

Note

1. The research to examine the relationship between the learning organization concept and the financial performance of several firms was undertaken by Ellinger, Ellinger, Yang, and Howton (2002). To assess this association, the authors obtained managerial responses to the Watkins and Marsick Dimensions of the Learning Organization Questionnaire instrument along with both perceptual and objective measures of the firms' financial performance. Results suggest a positive association between the learning organization concept and the firms' financial performance. HPT practitioners may use the findings of this research to support the case for implementing organizational learning initiatives.

References

Anderson, V., and Johnson, L. (1997). *Systems thinking basics: From concepts to causal loops.* Waltham, MA: Pegasus Communications.

Argyris, C. (1982). *Reasoning, learning, and action: Individual and organizational.* San Francisco: Jossey-Bass.

Argyris, C. (1999). *On organizational learning* (2nd ed.). Malden, MA: Blackwell Business.

Argyris, C., and Schön, D. (1978). *Organizational learning: A theory of action perspective.* Reading, MA: Addison-Wesley.

Argyris, C., Putnam, R., and McLain Smith, D. (1985). *Action science: Concepts, methods, and skills for research and intervention.* San Francisco: Jossey-Bass.

Bolman, L. G., and Deal, T. E. (1997). *Reframing organizations: Artistry, choice and leadership.* San Francisco: Jossey-Bass.

Dewey, J. (1933). *How we think: A restatement of the relation of reflective thinking to the educative process* (Revised ed.). Boston: D. C. Heath.

Easterby-Smith, M., and Araujo, L. (1999). Current debates and opportunities. In M. Easterby-Smith, L. Araujo, and J. Burgoyne (Eds.), *Organizational learning and the learning organization.* London: Sage.

Edmondson, A., and Moingeon, B. (1999). Learning, trust and organizational change. In M. Easterby-Smith, L. Araujo, and J. Burgoyne, J. (Eds.), *Organizational learning and the learning organization.* London: Sage.

Elden, M., and Chisholm, R. F. (1993). Emerging varieties of action research: Introduction to the special issue. *Human Relations, 46*(2), 121–142.

Ellinger, A. D., Ellinger, A. E., Yang, B., and Howton, S. W. (2002). The relationship between the learning organization concepts and firms' financial performance: An empirical assessment. *Human Resource Development Quarterly, 13,* 5–21.

Gibson, M. (1999). *Operation Adventure.* Brochure. Retrieved October 30, 2005, from University of Michigan-Dearborn Web site: http://www.umd.umich.edu/athletics/Operationadventure/OA-basic%20brochure.pdf.

Glaser, B., and Strauss, A. (1967). *The discovery of grounded theory: Strategies of qualitative research.* London: Wiedenfeld & Nicholson.

Hamel, G. (1997). In R. Gibson, (Ed.), *Rethinking the future: Business, principles, competition, control, leadership, markets and the world.* London: Nicholas Brcaley.

Hamel, G., and Prahalad, C. K. (1989, May–June). Strategy intent. *Harvard Business Review,* 63–76.

Hamel, G., and Prahalad, C. K. (1994). *Competing for the future.* Boston: Harvard School Press.

Isaacs, W. (1993). Taking flight: Dialogue, collective thinking, and organizational learning. *Organizational Dynamics, 22*(2), 24–39.

Kim, D. (1997). What is your organization's core theory of success? *Systems Thinker, 8*(3), 1–2.

Lapides, J., and Kachhal, S. K. (2000, June). *Indicators for organizational learning sustainability.* Paper presented at Discovering Connections: A Renaissance Through Systems Learning Conference, Dearborn, Michigan.

Lawrence, E. (1999, April 27). *Strategic thinking: A discussion paper.* Retrieved January 15, 2005, from Public Service Commission of Canada Web site: www.psc-cfp.gc.ca/research/knowledge/strathink_e.htm.

Liedtka, J. (1998, October). Strategic thinking: Can it be taught? *Long Range Planning, 31*(1), 120–129.

Mintzberg, H. (1994). *The rise and fall of strategic planning.* New York: The Free Press.

Neustadt, R., and May, E. (1986). *Thinking in time: The uses of history for decision-makers.* New York: Free Press.

Palmer, P. J. (1998). *The courage to teach: Exploring the inner landscape of a teacher's life.* San Francisco: Jossey-Bass.

Public Service Commission of Canada. (2004). *Our areas of research, strategic thinking (2004).* Retrieved January 15, 2005, from www.psc-cfp.gc.ca/research/knowledge/strathink_e.htm.

Rosenberg. M., J. (1999) The general process of human performance technology. In H. D. Stolovitch and E. J. Keeps, E. J. (Eds.), *Handbook of human performance technology: Improving individual and organizational performance worldwide* (2nd ed.) (pp. 137–318). San Francisco: Jossey-Bass/Pfeiffer.

Salton, G. J. (1996). *Organizational engineering: A new method of creating high performance human structures.* Ann Arbor, MI: Professional Communications, Inc.

Schön, D. (1987) *Educating the reflective practitioner.* San Francisco: Jossey-Bass.

Senge, P. (1990) *The fifth discipline: The art and practice of the learning organization.* New York: Doubleday/Currency.

Senge, P., Kleiner, A., Roberts, C., Ross, R., and Smith, B. (1994). *The fifth discipline fieldbook: Strategies and tools for building a learning organization.* New York: Doubleday.

Smith, M. K. (2001). Chris Argyris: Theories of action, double-loop learning and organizational learning. *The encyclopedia of informal education.* Retrieved January 28, 2005, from www.infed.org/thinkers.argyris.htm.

Van Tiem, D., Moseley, J., and Dessinger, J., (2000). *Fundamentals of performance technology: A guide to improving people, process and performance.* Washington, DC: International Society for Performance Improvement.

CHAPTER TWENTY-SIX

Knowledge Management, Organizational Performance, and Human Performance Technology

Debra Haney

Τhe purpose of this chapter is to present to human performance technology (HPT) practitioners an intervention that can greatly benefit from their involvement: knowledge management. Knowledge management (KM) encompasses different aspects of an organization: people, culture, process, structure, leadership, technology, and measurement. This chapter provides an overview of KM, including its purpose, a brief history, current terms and concepts, and similar organizational initiatives that are connected to KM, such as organizational learning. It presents a framework for establishing a KM system in an organization, emphasizing the HPT skill set, and, finally, gives a list of resources for further information.

BASIC CONCEPTS AND TERMINOLOGY

In the early 1970s nobody was talking about knowledge management. In 2025 perhaps nobody will be talking about it, except for historians. However, the challenge in managing effective and purposeful communication of what individuals in organizations know will remain (Drucker, 1993). The actions involved in KM, even if they are termed *organizational development* actions or by the name of some other type of HPT intervention, will be an ongoing part of organizational success. HPT has a role in those actions, whatever they are called, and HPT professionals have a stake in that success.

Data, Information, and Knowledge

What is knowledge? Knowledge is composed of contextualized information, cognition, and skills. It is the ability to productively use information. Knowledge is what you know, and what you know how to do: your cognition and skills. This type of knowledge is stored in your head, and is often considered tacit because people cannot always articulate exactly what they know. Knowledge is also contextualized information that can be stored in databases and documents. It exists on both individual and collective levels. Those collective levels can be teams, departments, divisions, or the entire organization. Knowledge currently is believed to add more value to a company than land, labor, or capital, which are the traditional bases of wealth acquisition.

Knowledge is different from simple data and information because it is highly organized, meaningful to specific situations, and can be acted on easily. It is more useful than basic data or information because it is contextual (see Figure 26.1).

Trying to work smart is something each one of us does on the job already, both at an individual level, for ourselves, and at a higher organizational level, for our team, department, and company. KM is a more formalized and structured approach, with explicit strategic intent, than one person just informally knowing what needs to be shared, learned, or known. If employees just informally share what they know to the best of their ability, the very informality of the process means that it cannot be easily controlled by the organization. Knowledge management is the process of controlling or directing the creation, identification, organization, storage, dissemination, and maintenance of knowledge in order to support strategic goals. Those strategic goals can be for different organizational levels. Working smart is not a new idea. Sharing what one knows is

Least Useful ← → Most Useful		
Data	**Information**	**Knowledge**
Unorganized facts and figures that must be interpreted to be meaningful	Organized, meaningful facts	Contextualized information, productive skills, and cognition. Knowing how, what, why, and when to act
Example: The last quarter's production was ten thousand units.	Example: The last quarter's production of ten thousand units was down ten percent from the previous quarter.	Example: The last quarter's decreased production was not scheduled (and therefore management will take action)

Figure 26.1. The Data-Information-Knowledge Continuum.

not new either, and, unfortunately, hoarding what one knows for personal benefit is also not new. What is new is the term *knowledge management.*

Coordination and Communication

Coordinating the knowledge of individual employees with the goal of benefiting the organization has been and is still a perennial topic in business literature because it is difficult to do (Hayek, 1945). With the increasing role of information technology, the potential benefits of coordinating knowledge in an organization are seen as more attainable (Porter, 1990). Since the 1970s, researchers and practitioners in companies in Europe, Japan, and North America have taken the lead in developing KM systems and programs (Kobayashi, 1986; Stewart, 1997). The names of respected contributors make up an international KM who's who list: Alvesson, Sweden; Leonard-Barton, United Kingdom; Nonaka and Takeuchi, Japan; Nevis, DiBella, and Gould, United States; Sveiby, Sweden; and Wiig, United States. In addition to being a global topic, KM is also an interdisciplinary one. Organizational development, information technology, and HPT have all contributed to KM's development and use.

Currently, KM is used in one form or another in thousands of private corporations, public institutions, and government offices around the world (Alvesson, 2004; Andersen, 1996). The number and type of industries that use and benefit from KM is surprising: British Petroleum, Chrysler, Electricité de France, Harley-Davidson, IBM, Merck, Nissan, Royal Bank of Canada, Sears, the U.S. Army, and the U.S. Navy, to name a few. The range of organizations using KM gives an indication as to how adaptable it can be. This adaptability does not come cheaply, however.

Costs and Results

The costs for implementing and then maintaining a KM system are difficult to estimate. How do you decide how much of your company's new information technology system or personnel time is dedicated to just KM? On an individual company basis, the highest estimates of actual costs were 8 percent to 10 percent of revenues for consulting companies (Bair, Fenn, Hunter, and Bosik, 1997). Most of it seems to be spent on installing information technology. The results from an information technology approach to KM can benefit a company, but they do not always do so. Increasing profits, decreasing costs, or both, can indicate that the KM system is benefiting the organization.

KM has an impressive record of documented successes (Edvinsson and Malone, 1997; Stewart, 1997). *The Knowledge Management Practices Book* (Andersen, 1996) documents the KM actions and results of over one hundred organizations worldwide. The brief examples in Figure 26.2, taken from the *Knowledge Management Practices Book,* show the range of possibilities.

Some of these examples may not seem to be KM but rather other types of organizational actions, such as shared decision-making processes in Cin-Made, team

Knowledge-Management Action	Result
Cin-Made, manufacturers of cardboard and metal containers, adopted open-book management and involved workers in problem solving.	Productivity has more than doubled.
Mid-States Technical Staffing, an engineering company in Davenport, Iowa, decided to allow employees to share in budget decision making.	Company expenses were running 15 percent below their previous levels.
Chaparral Steel, the tenth largest U.S. steel producer, changed its pay structure to reward accumulation of skills as well as performance.	Chaparral has an absentee rate one-quarter of the industry average.
Hewlett-Packard brings new products to market quickly because of its ongoing, team-based innovation.	Sales have risen to $4 billion a year, and profits have grown by 30 percent.
BSG Alliance/IT spends 5 percent of its revenues on training its consultant employees, who, in turn, focus intensely on customers.	The company has doubled its revenues almost each year.

Figure 26.2. Examples of Knowledgement-Management Success.

innovation in Mid-States Technical Staffing and Hewlett Packard, compensation structure in Chaparral Steel, or training in BSG Alliance/IT. KM overlaps and is linked with other initiatives because it takes place in the context of an organization and shares the same organizational aspects or components: personnel, processes, structure, technology, and so on. In the Figure 26.2 examples, KM was accomplished partially through shared decision making, team innovation, compensation structure, and training. What these organizational actions are termed is not as important as the results. KM is based in the open communication of ideas, observations, and creativity. It supports new ways of doing business. It is adaptable to different types of organizations, with different goals and constraints. One style or approach to KM does not fit all organizations.

Symptoms of Problems

Knowledge management is an intervention that provides, in most cases, incremental improvement in organizational processes. Although all organizations potentially could benefit from it, in the reality of budget planning and resource allocations, not all organizations will choose to implement a KM system. Justifying the need for it to a company's executives requires evidence. Evidence of KM problems falls into three categories: hoarding knowledge, reinventing the wheel, and making poor or slow decisions. Here are some examples that I personally have witnessed.

- *Hoarding knowledge:* A senior claims processor retires, and then immediately starts working for the same company as a consultant because nobody knows how to do the job as well as he.

- *Reinventing the wheel:* Two training departments in the same company and in the same building, each supporting a different client group, independently design almost identical templates.

- *Making poor or slow decisions:* A business opportunity is lost to a competitor because the proposal writers could not find the documentation they needed even though it existed on a company database.

These three categories of problems—hoarding, reinventing, and poor decisions—exist in every organization. The issues are to what extent the problems exist and to what extent they have been institutionalized, either formally through procedures or informally through culture. Even after a KM system has been implemented, the problems will not necessarily go away. According to a survey by Wah (1999), in organizations that had implemented KM, the most important obstacles to effective KM were reported as measuring results, getting people to seek best practices, and getting people to share what they knew: better ways to do the job, the names of coworkers who knew those best practices, and what worked and did not work in previous projects. People, their motivations, decisions, and behavior, are key to knowledge management in both success and failure.

ORGANIZATIONAL LEARNING, COMMUNITIES OF PRACTICE, AND INTELLECTUAL CAPITAL

KM is linked to organizational learning, communities of practice, and intellectual capital. Although the terminology has changed over time, these terms refer to processes, relationships, and concepts that are basic to organizational life. Think of this scenario: an employee returns from a seminar and enthusiastically wants to share what he has learned with other in the department. At this point, what he has learned is individual knowledge. Then, if he shares what he has learned with others throughout the department, which is his community of practice, his individual knowledge becomes organizational knowledge at the department level.

A community of practice is a group with a single common interest, some shared understanding and assumptions, and collective knowledge of strategic importance to the members. Those members pool their knowledge and information; they learn from each other; and, together, they invent, discover, and learn more than they could individually. A community of practice often is the conduit between individual knowledge and organizational knowledge. A department of HPT practitioners is an example of a community of practice. An individual can belong to more than one community of practice at a time. Many performance technologists belong to the communities of instructional design, information technology, and organizational development. The boundaries of a community and questions of who belongs and who does not are debatable points (Brown and Duguid, 1998; Lave and Wenger, 1992). Some authors think that a community can only exist within a single employing company—Xerox, for example. Others think that a community can exist with members from different companies—the International Society for Performance Improvement (ISPI), for example. From a practical perspective, we individually should decide which communities we belong to and who our fellow members are. For example, I view myself as belonging to the ISPI community, among others. An inclusive perspective on membership is more useful than an exclusive perspective, because it allows us to be members of more communities in which we can contribute and learn.

If an employee learns something that can be communicated without great difficulty to coworkers, it is explicit knowledge. If, however, it is difficult to communicate, then the knowledge is tacit. If, later on, as a result of department members having learned the new technique, the department processes have changed, then organizational learning has occurred.

Organizational learning is a process of changing processes, routines, and procedures based on knowledge contributed by a member or community in order to improve them. This process is a prime contributor of explicit knowledge to organizational KM. Organizational knowledge is the sum of knowledge that is

- Owned by the organization, for example, a patented, explicitly documented process

- Rented by the organization from the individual who owns it, for example, a senior accountant's expertise

It resides in people, processes, structures, and communities as well as in patents, files, company records, and databases. In theory, all members of the organization have access to the organizational knowledge. In reality, all members do not have access. However, KM helps give more members greater access to organizational knowledge.

Another term for organizational knowledge is *intellectual capital* (Sveiby, 1997). Intellectual capital is the sum of an organization's intangible, nonphysical assets. These intangible assets are linked. According to Sveiby, human assets lead to structural assets internal to the company, which in turn can lead to intellectual property, which can lead to external structural assets. In other words, employees invent something that can be patented, marketed, and sold to clients (see Figure 26.3).

Type of asset	Human Assets →	Internal Structural Assets →	Intellectual Property →	External Structural Assets
Description	Employee knowledge, skills, and abilities	Standard operating procedures and processes	Patents and copyrights	Customer loyalty and joint venture partnerships
Example	Employees teaching each other better ways of working	Chaparral Steel's SOP for making a specialty steel	Eli Lilly's insulin patents	Saturn's loyal car owners and repeat buyers

Figure 26.3. Intellectual Capital Asset Types.

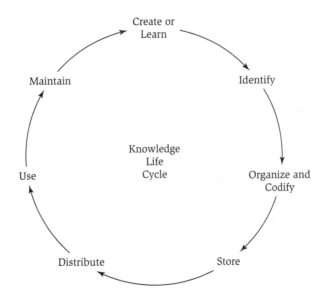

Figure 26.4. The Knowledge Life Cycle and Its Processes.

THE KNOWLEDGE LIFE CYCLE

It can be helpful to think of knowledge as something that grows, changes, and has different phases, from creation to obsolescence. Organizations exist in dynamic environments, change is constant, and what was useful to know last year may not be useful next year. Organizational knowledge must change to keep up. Knowledge management has different processes to support these different life cycle phases (see Figure 26.4).

Create or Learn, and Identify

The knowledge life cycle starts with acquiring knowledge. Acquisition can happen in different ways: through creating, learning, or purchasing. Identifying what is important and what can be useful to different parts of the company can happen before, during, and after acquisition. In terms of sharing knowledge located in one part of the company with other parts of the company, identifying that knowledge occurs after the initial acquisition.

Organize and Codify

Once the knowledge is acquired and identified, it must be organized in a way that is meaningful to the users. This frequently involves including an explanation of the context: giving the circumstances in which the knowledge was acquired as well as the circumstances in which it would be useful. This includes providing context and background, stating the main points and benefits, deleting extraneous material, translating the language or reducing the language-level difficulty, linking the knowledge to related items, and so on. Codification converts the contents into a format that can be stored, maintained, and accessed in organizational repositories—for example, changing contents stored on Macintosh software to PC software, or copying paper documents on American letter format sheets to European L4 format sheets so the contents can be placed in standard binders located in an office in Brussels.

Store

Storing knowledge usually, but not always, takes place by putting it on a server or in a database that can be accessed by the users. Storing the knowledge must be done in a manner that is safe from accidental deletion, sabotage, and espionage and that allows easy and rapid access by proper users. This involves cataloging decisions—how the knowledge and information will be organized—and repository decisions—where and in what form the contents will be stored. Repositories include people's minds, databases, and documents.

Distribute

Distribution or dissemination can occur in many ways; not all of them involve computer technology. The two categories of dissemination are active, known as *push technology,* and passive, known as *pull technology* (Stewart, 1997). Push technology sends the content to the recipient at the decision of the sender. Examples include mandatory scheduled training, an e-mail to a distribution list of recipients, or a companywide meeting called by the chief executive officer. Pull technology makes the content available to the recipient at the decision of that recipient, for example, through a topical database that the user accesses at his or her own volition, or by attending a brown bag luncheon for which attendance is invited but not required. Electronic performance support systems (EPSS) can be either active or passive, depending on how they are structured. For both push and pull technologies, providing easy, secure, and appropriate access to the knowledge is part of distribution.

Use

Knowledge is used by being applied to work activities that support or produce the organization's products and services.

Maintain

Because of the dynamic environments that organizations exist in, knowledge and its supporting processes cannot be static and unchanging. Both the content and the KM system need to be maintained. Knowledge will need to be updated, changed, added to, deleted, or replaced. The KM system requires maintenance; this includes not just the technology but all the other aspects involved, especially personnel, processes, and structures. Maintenance activities are monitoring, tracking, measuring, and evaluating contributions and usage. How often—a quantity measure—and how effectively—a quality measure—the content is used should be monitored. Maintenance includes the training, coaching, and support of the users of the system. The ongoing management of content, databases, and other KM systems is also a maintenance responsibility.

ORGANIZATIONAL CONTEXT

KM does not exist alone, unconnected to other organizational initiatives or daily organizational processes. It is a part of ordinary organizational life. To be as effective as possible, a KM system should be explicitly connected to other organizational programs and processes. HPT interventions are a natural fit for KM. As with any type of organizational system, a KM system should be closely aligned with the interests and needs of the stakeholders: management, information technology, human resources, and especially the end-user personnel.

CRITICAL SUCCESS FACTORS

KM depends on various organizational aspects or components (Davenport, De Long, and Beers, 1998). These aspects are the critical success factors (CSFs): people, culture, process, structure, leadership, technology, and measurement. Notice that these CSFs are the same ones found for other organizational initiatives, and are familiar to HPT practitioners. In a KM system, each CSF needs to be assessed in order to best plan for its part in the implementation and maintenance strategies. A KM project or initiative that does not take all seven CSFs into account will not be as successful as one that does. Taking into account is not the same as controlling all the CSFs; the degree of control will vary with the project and the organization. As with other HPT programs, actively networking and gathering support before the project starts will increase your success in a KM project.

- *People* refers to personnel and their skills, cognition, and productivity. People issues are those that concern the intrinsic and extrinsic motivations to learn, share, and use others' contributions; hoarding knowledge; and the belief that knowledge is power.
- *Culture* refers to the values, behaviors, and beliefs of an organization and its members. Some cultural issues that affect KM are the overall climate of trust in an organization and the degree to which making mistakes is acceptable. Many KM consultants have found that the most difficult factor to work with is usually organizational culture, because it is resistant to change (Bair, Fenn, Hunter, and Bosik, 1997; Ruggles, 1998).
- *Process* refers to both the preexisting work processes and the specific KM processes. Process issues deal with when, where, how, and why people share. Common examples of KM processes are including more documentation, sharing insights and discoveries, and conducting post-event analysis of what went wrong and what went right. An example of changing a work procedure is to include, at the end of a project, a write-up of what went well, what did not, and why. This write-up should be shared not only with all the members of the project team but with people who will have similar roles in future projects. An example of adding a separate procedure is to schedule regular, not necessarily long or frequent, meetings to share important items with the department or team. Most of us already have meetings to do this. The difference is in the strategic goal of the meeting. A meeting that supports KM has different topics of discussion than the usual department information meetings. The KM meeting topics are those that increase the skill set of the attendees, making them more productive.
- *Structure* refers to organizational alignment and designated resources, such as a half-time knowledge manager or steward for a department, as well as standard human resource structures such as recruitment, training, competency modeling, performance evaluation, and compensation, both for personnel with primary KM roles and for other employees who will have some KM responsibilities in addition to their regular roles. Figure 26.5 presents generic KM responsibilities for regular employees. The responsibilities increase in scope and difficulty as the personnel levels and competence increase. Notice how similar the language and progression of these are to items commonly used in both job descriptions and performance reviews. Figure 26.6 presents KM responsibilities specific to an employee with a primary KM role. The difference between KM

The *new Employee* will

- Identify his or her own knowledge needs and goals
- Recognize the appropriate resources and tools to use, depending on the type of information required
- Identify appropriate people who can answer questions

The *Experienced Employee* will

- Recognize knowledge gaps as an individual or as a project team member
- Access the appropriate resources and tools for continuous improvement
- Recognize the opportunity to gain information when it presents itself
- Recognize appropriate opportunities to share

The *Project Manager* will

- Close knowledge gaps as an individual or as a project team member
- Facilitate and reward knowledge sharing among team members
- Contribute consistently to the organization's knowledge sharing
- Build a network of contacts to access for various information needs

The *Department Manager* will

- Monitor to identify employees' knowledge needs
- Contribute observations, insights, and content to the organization's knowledge sharing from internal and external sources
- Facilitate knowledge sharing between teams and departments

Figure 26.5. Examples of KM Responsibilities for Regular Employees.

The *Knowledge Management Coordinator* will

- Collect, assess, and organize key methods, processes, marketing presentations, successful proposals, and so on
- Identify and post content from external sources, such as research groups and Internet Websites
- Develop and maintain employee yellow pages of expertise
- Promote and educate employees on knowledge-sharing resources, processes, and technology
- Work with experts within and outside of the organization to capture "best practices"
- Manage and monitor discussion databases
- Respond to information requests from employees

Figure 26.6. Examples of KM Responsibilities for KM-Specific Employees.

responsibilities for regular employees and KM employees is a difference of both degree and kind.

- *Leadership* involves both financial sponsorship and championship, including leading by example: walking the talk. Leaders should overtly participate in KM activities such as using content from a KM database or sending an e-mail containing the observations of what went well and what did not in a project.

- *Technology* refers to communication and information hardware and software: computers are obvious, but videoconferencing, telephones, and voicemail can also function as KM supports. An emphasis on technology is found in many KM implementation approaches. This is not because technology is the best way to approach KM implementation, but because technology is the easiest to base a strategy on. It is also much easier to sell to management, partly because it is the most politically neutral factor and approach. Paradoxically, it can be the most expensive KM factor to implement and then maintain, especially if the other factors, primarily people, culture, and processes, are not taken sufficiently into account. Technology by itself will never produce a successful KM system, because it is only a mechanism for storage and communication and does not address issues of who, when, where, how and why: the process issues.

- *Measurement* is concerned with deciding what needs to be measured, and on what level: individual, team, department, division, or organization, as well as with deciding on the appropriate metrics for doing so. In this discussion, measurement is not concerned with calculating market value of intellectual capital. It is only concerned with assessing the knowledge workers' and the knowledge-based organizations' expertise and productivity.

People, culture, and process factors are closely linked and are critically important to KM. An approach based primarily on these three soft-technology factors will help ensure success. Although all factors must be taken into account when implementing KM, some factors are more important than others. Which factors are more important than others depends on the unique characteristics and situation of the organization.

KNOWLEDGE MANAGEMENT AND HUMAN PERFORMANCE TECHNOLOGY

KM has been researched and written about from a variety of perspectives. Management, organizational development, information technology, and HPT each have claimed some aspects of KM as their own. From a practical viewpoint, all of these disciplines contribute to KM, and we can learn from them all. From the

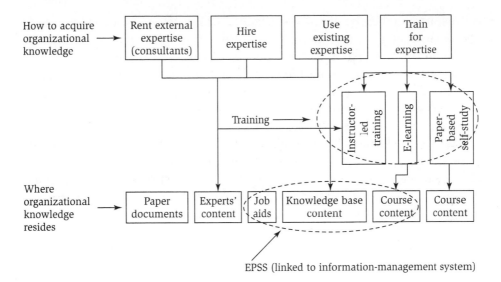

Figure 26.7. Knowledge Management, EPSS, and Training.

HPT perspective, KM is an HPT intervention. It is closely related to several mainstream HPT interventions: performance support, EPSS, training, and content management. HPT practitioners are well-positioned to contribute to KM in their organizations. The actions in implementing and maintaining a KM system will seem familiar to many of us because they are similar to both standard project-management actions and the ADDIE steps: analyze, design, develop, implement, and evaluate. Figure 26.7 shows the relationship between KM and several other HPT interventions. The same content or knowledge that is used in training is also available to the KM system and EPSS. Note that the genesis of knowledge is always in people, although it may reside in many different places and media.

Many of us act as change agents within our organizations and have ongoing roles in marketing and communication to stakeholders. In connection with this, HPT practitioners are experienced in partnering with members of other functional groups such as information technology (IT), human resources (HR), and department managers. All these skills are needed in a KM system.

ESTABLISHING A KNOWLEDGE-MANAGEMENT SYSTEM

A KM system needs to be first implemented and then maintained. Although this may seem obvious, many organizations make the mistake of focusing on the implementation, especially of the information technology component, and not allocating enough resources for maintenance. Both starting and continuing the system need to be planned. To be useful, a KM system must be tailored to fit the organization's needs and resources. No one-size-fits-all approach will be successful. A KM system can be designed to successfully support a team, a department, or larger organizational units. If the funding or executive support is not available to implement a system for the entire organization, think in terms of implementing a system for departments or teams.

For simplicity and ease of understanding, this chapter presents a KM project-design approach based in the implementation project steps, similar to ADDIE: assess, design, develop, prototype and pilot, implement, and, last, maintain. Change management, flexibility, and information gathering should be constants during all the steps. Another constant should be evaluation, so you can easily correct as you go. Note that the following is a starting point and is not inclusive of all aspects you should address in your organization. KM, like any other initiative or project, is specific to the organization. Tailor the following framework to fit your needs.

Assess

Establishing a KM system starts with assessing the organization's current state. The current state, with all its strengths, weaknesses, opportunities, and threats (SWOT), will always be the starting point. The organization can be assessed at the level of team, department, division, or entire company. While conducting the assessment, also look for opportunities to network and build support. The more you assess the actual current state in the beginning, the better your KM system design will be, because it will be based more in reality and less in wishful thinking.

What to Assess and Identify. The following are items that should be assessed and identified.

- KM project resources

    Skills, resources, and roles needed for implementation personnel. This will include personnel from HR, IT, sponsoring leadership, and representatives from the department or community in which the KM system will be implemented. If you do not know which department will be the location for the system, identify some likely candidates and identify representatives, from managers and employees you know are favorably disposed to KM, from those areas. KM project resources are listed first because you must manage yourselves first.

    Skills, resources, and roles needed for KM personnel in the maintenance phase.

- Goals and priorities of KM. Not everything is important enough to spend resources on, so think in terms of what is likely to be an easy success, or what will be a popular choice with sponsors, or what will best support strategic goals. Find out what employees want to know and learn. Be realistic.

- Liaise with HR to identify desired KM competencies and employees who possess them.
- All critical success factors. See the discussion further on.
- Current competencies, training, and gaps in employee skills.
- Benchmarks from external sources. This will also be a good source for ideas on what to focus on, how to implement, and how much time implementation will take.
- The level or levels of organization the KM system will support.
- Key stakeholders: sponsors, users, and opponents.
- Communities of practice.

  Their current process for creating and sharing

  The knowledge that is necessary for each community

  The community or group in which to pilot the KM system: low-hanging fruit

How to Assess. Assessing an organization's readiness for a formal KM system will be familiar to many HPT professionals because it is a type of front-end analysis. Assessment methods are interviews, review of existing documents, observations, and surveys or questionnaires. Figure 26.8 gives a few quick and easy assessment items that can be used in a survey, based on the seven CSFs most involved in KM. This table is a starting point; practitioners should change, add, or delete items from it to fit their situations. Any items that will be added should follow the same positive logic in sentence structure so that a single response structure can be used. For example, adding the item "People are afraid to speak their minds" would be confusing to the survey-taker because the logic is opposite the other items. Instead, use "People are confident in speaking their minds." Responses to the items can be structured as simple Yes or No, or as five-point Likert scale responses.

The simpler and the shorter the survey is, the better the response rate will be. A single baseline survey, containing the same items for all audiences, is recommended to establish clear patterns of opinions that different audiences may have. Subsequent surveys, with different items, can be tailored to different target audiences. The audiences of information technology staff and company executives, for example, can provide useful information on different topics.

Post-Assessment Decisions and CSFs. The most important decision that needs to be made after assessment is not how to implement, but whether to implement. If you find out that you do not have sufficient interest, sponsorship, funding, or other resources, then postpone continuing until these deficiencies

People
- People are eager to learn more in order to do their jobs better.
- People ask questions and challenge the standard operating procedure.
- People respond quickly to requests for help.
- People know what the core competencies of the organization are.

Culture
- Making mistakes is acceptable.
- People trust each other.
- People are comfortable in communicating work problems to their supervisors.
- The organization is flexible and receptive to new ideas.

Processes
- There are well-defined processes for storing and accessing knowledge.
- Attention and resources are given to finding out what people don't know.
- Training is based on employee competencies.
- Employees are evaluated on sharing their ideas and using others' ideas.

Structure
- The organization has a chief knowledge officer.
- The organization has formal knowledge management staff.
- There are regularly scheduled meetings to share knowledge in each department.
- Everyone has some knowledge-management responsibilities.

Leadership
- Leaders and managers openly promote knowledge sharing.
- Leaders demonstrate knowledge sharing in their actions.
- Learning and sharing support organizational competencies.
- Knowledge management is part of the organization's business strategy.

Technology
- Company databases, intranets, or both are used to store best practices.
- All employees have access to computers.
- The technology is "user-friendly."
- Technology supports virtual teams and collaboration.

Measurement
- Employees are evaluated on their contributions to what their colleagues know.
- The department has formal KM responsibilities for its members.
- The company commits resources to knowledge management.
- The company has linked knowledge management to the bottom line.

Figure 26.8. Sample Baseline Assessment Instrument Items.

have been corrected. The temptation may exist to go ahead anyway, without sufficiently addressing deficiencies or problems. If you give in to this temptation, you will be planning for failure, not success, and damaging your credibility in the organization. A common experience after assessment is that any preliminary plans for implementation will need to be changed.

In KM, the caveat to building on strengths is a reminder of the importance of people, culture, and process CSFs; these are the key to KM. If any of these act as a serious constraint, then building on the strength of another factor, or even a combination of factors, will not be effective. Knowledge activities, such as creating, learning, sharing, and making decisions about the usefulness of something, are uniquely human ones. Technology is often promoted as a KM system in itself. However, technology is only a means or mechanism for storage and communication. By itself, technology cannot be a KM system.

If people, culture, and process CSFs are strengths in an organization, then building on these while developing the other factors is one possible strategy. If they are constraints, then strong structures and technology will be unused or underused in KM. Building on them will not achieve success if barriers in personnel, culture, or processes prevent people from actively contributing to and benefiting from the KM system. Constraints based on people, culture, and process should be addressed before improving already strong structures or technology.

Design

After assessing, the KM implementation team needs to decide on which knowledge gaps to address first, and what kinds of knowledge would be most useful, easy to implement, and maintainable. Define a preliminary goal and then examine the overall pattern of constraints and supports. Conventional wisdom suggests building on strengths, while planning on strengthening weaknesses or working around constraints. I recommend that a small-scope pilot be designed first before rolling it out to other communities, departments, or the organization itself. Other decisions should be made in terms of all the CSFs and the time frame.

- Involve key stakeholders and end users in development.
- Design tactics incorporating all KM factors.
- Think in terms of change management and creating to build awareness, interest, and buy-in.
- Build on existing processes, structures, relationships, and so on. Design KM actions to be embedded in existing business processes. Identify existing technologies that can be used for knowledge sharing, for example, e-mail.
- Design new roles, responsibilities, networks, performance standards, and incentives. For example, include KM contributions in employee performance evaluation.

- Create processes for using and contributing to the organization's knowledge.
- Design meetings, both formal and informal, for knowledge sharing.
- Design training, job aids, and EPSS.
- Design corporate "yellow pages" that list personnel and their expertise.
- Design KM staff competencies.
- Assist in increasing the user-friendliness of computer technologies for repositories and communication.
- Design simple and easy-to-use measurement criteria for the KM system.
  Track recruitment and retention of valuable, highly skilled employees.
  Track both contributions to and usages of knowledge items.
  Track the number of employee certifications and college degrees.
  Design evaluation of training at Kirkpatrick's (1998) levels 2 and 3.
  Track both stories of failures and stories of success.
- Design workshops to inform and create buy-in.
- Design a prototype process of limited scope and high impact.

Develop

- Involve key stakeholders and end users in development.
- Develop multiple items for all CSFs for the prototype, especially culture, processes, and people, including roles and responsibilities, performance standards, and incentives.
- Develop workshops to inform and create buy-in.

Prototype and Pilot

- Involve key people and end users in all prototyping activities.
- Advertise: communicate the KM project.
- Take a leadership role: sponsoring, marketing, and leading by example.
- Present workshops to inform and create buy-in.
- Implement the small-scale KM pilot.
- Encourage sharing by public recognition.
- Document what went well and what did not go well at the time to maximize the accuracy of the observations.
- Evaluate the results, adjust and correct problems, and plan on a larger scale roll-out.
- Communicate the successes and continue to build awareness, interest, and buy-in.

Implement

- Involve key people and end users.
- Assign staffing for permanent KM roles.
- Implement all the CSF items.
- Advertise and communicate KM use internally and externally.
- Work with and support existing communities of practice through marketing and resource allocation.

Maintain

When implementation ends and maintenance begins is not clear-cut. That transition may occur at different times for different actions. At no time will maintenance be a static state without changes or adjustments. The organization and its knowledge needs will continue to change, and the KM system must evolve to keep pace. Creating, learning, and identifying knowledge are not actions that end in implementation. HPT skills and strengths will continue to be needed during maintenance due to the ongoing need for change management, flexibility, information gathering, and evaluation. A useful way to look at maintenance is as a time to continue to improve or expand the system.

THE FUTURE OF KNOWLEDGE MANAGEMENT

Knowledge management is maturing into a generally, but not universally, accepted organizational-improvement intervention. The future of KM will depend on its track record of success or failure. The term *knowledge management* may not even be in use twenty years from now, and other hot topics in management will have center stage. However, the challenge in increasing organizational effectiveness by managing what employees know and how they share it will continue. In the near future, as the limits of how technology can support KM are better known, attention will shift to people, process, and culture as the CSFs with the most leverage. Focusing on those CSFs, especially people, with their motivations, perceptions, fears, decisions, and actions, will require increasing HPT participation.

CONCLUSION

Successfully implementing and maintaining a KM system is based on

- Having a plan: assess, design, develop, prototype and pilot, implement, and maintain.

- Incorporating CSFs: people, culture, process, structure, leadership, technology, and measurement.

- Taking into account all knowledge processes: creating, learning, identifying, organizing, codifying, storing, distributing, maintaining, and using.

- Fulfilling important needs and expectations of the organization and employees.

- Tailoring solutions to the organization's situation, strategic goals, and resources.

- Commitment to ongoing change management, flexibility, information-gathering, and evaluation.

The growing body of literature about KM will support HPT practitioners in implementing systems, both large and small, in organizations. HPT practitioners are well-positioned to contribute to KM in their organizations because of their skill set and the linkage of KM to existing HPT interventions.

References

Alvesson, M. (2004). *Knowledge work and knowledge-intensive firms.* Oxford, UK: Oxford University Press.

Anderson, A. (1996). *The knowledge management practices book.* Chicago: Arthur Andersen and the American Productivity & Quality Center.

Bair, J., Fenn, J., Hunter, R., and Bosik, D. (1997). *Foundations for enterprise knowledge management* (Strategic Analysis Report R-400-105). Stamford, CT: Gartner Group.

Brown, J. S., and Duguid, P. (1998). Organizing knowledge. *California Management Review, 40*(3), 90–111.

Davenport, T. H., De Long, D. W., and Beers, M. C. (1998). Successful knowledge management projects. *Sloan Management Review, 39*(2), 43–57.

Drucker, P. F. (1993). *Post-capitalist society.* New York: HarperCollins.

Edvinsson, L., and Malone, M. (1997*). Intellectual capital: Realizing your company's true value by finding its hidden roots.* New York: HarperCollins.

Hayek, F. A. (1945). The use of knowledge in society. *American Economic Review, 35*(4), 519–530.

Kirkpatrick, D. L. (1998). *Evaluating training programs: The four levels* (2nd ed.). San Francisco: Berrett-Koehler.

Kobayashi, K. (1986). *Computers and communications: A vision of C&C.* Cambridge, MA: MIT Press.

Lave, J., and Wenger, E. (1992). *Situated learning: Legitimate peripheral participation.* New York: Cambridge University Press.

Porter, M. E. (1990). *The competitive advantage of nations.* New York: Free Press.

Ruggles, R. (1998). The state of the notion: Knowledge management in practice. *California Management Review, 40*(3), 80–89.

Stewart, T. (1997). *Intellectual capital: The new wealth of organizations.* New York: Doubleday/Currency.

Sveiby, K. E. (1997). *The new organizational wealth: Managing and measuring knowledge-based assets.* San Francisco: Berrett-Koehler.

Wah, L. (1999, April). Behind the buzz. *Management Review, 88*(4), 17–26.

Additional Resources

Websites

As of publication, these four Websites were active and well-established. However, given the ephemeral nature of the Web, these sites may not be available in the future. All the Websites contain links to other KM sites.

- www.kmresource.com

  The Knowledge Management Resource Center: a comprehensive collection of KM resources. Well-organized and well-described, so it is easy to find what you need.

- www.brint.com

  Brint offers general overviews on many different topics, and integrates knowledge management with business, technology, and HPT issues.

- www.cio.com/research/knowledge

  CIO is an on-line magazine for "information executives." Its knowledge-management section is well-organized, with content topically chunked for easy access.

- www.sveiby.com

  Sveiby Knowledge Associates is one of the first Websites devoted to KM. Karl Sveiby is one of the founders of current knowledge-management work and calculating values of intellectual capital. This site contains useful overview content as well as more specific, detailed KM and intellectual-capital content.

Printed Resources

Haney, D. S., Lauer, M., and Wells, C. (2001, April). HPT and HR roles in knowledge management. *Papers of the 39th ISPI International Conference,* San Francisco.

A short overview of the topic, useful for orienting others with no background in KM; gives KM tactics for HPT and HR roles; definitions of common terms.

Skyrme, D., and Amidon, D. M. (1997). *Creating the knowledge-based business.* London, UK: British Intelligence, LDT.

Practical and action-oriented. Gives numerous and detailed examples of KM programs from different industries.

Wiig, K. (1993). *Knowledge management foundations: Thinking about thinking and how people and organizations create, represent, and use knowledge.* Arlington, TX: SCHEMA Press.

One of the earliest, and best, books on the topic. The first of three books in the knowledge management series. Shows the connection between KM and other organizational developments.

CHAPTER TWENTY-SEVEN

Coming to Terms with Communities of Practice

A Definition and Operational Criteria

Sasha Barab, Scott J. Warren,
Rodrigo del Valle, Fang Fang

Over a decade ago, Jean Lave and Etienne Wenger (1991) published a highly influential book about communities of practice that has since spurred numerous efforts to harness the power of "community" to support learning. This has led to the development of many innovative learning environments that move beyond didactic pedagogical models in which there exists an all-knowing teacher-trainer, or instructional context, responsible for transmitting content to the isolated mind of some learner employee. From a practical standpoint, this movement is both valuable and consequential. However, from an intellectual standpoint and with the goal of advancing the science of what is known about supporting learning, there are few criteria for distinguishing between a *community* of learners and a *group* of individuals learning collaboratively.

Predicated on research in fields such as anthropology, education, and sociology, and on our own work as instructional designers, we adopt the definition of a community advanced by Barab, MaKinster, and Scheckler (2004): "A persistent, sustained social network of individuals who share and develop an overlapping knowledge base, set of beliefs, values, history and experiences focused on a common practice and/or mutual enterprise" (p. 55). Barab, Kling, and Gray (2004, p. 3) state in their introduction to an edited volume devoted to understanding communities in the service of learning that "[t]oo little of the education literature provides clear criteria for what does and does not constitute community; the term is too often employed as a slogan rather than as an analytical category." It is the intention of this chapter to advance clear criteria that others can use in evaluating to what extent and in what manner a particular context constitutes "community" or, to adopt the term advanced by Lave and Wenger (1991), a *community of practice* (CoP).

Central to the work of Lave and Wenger is the concept that learning stems from meaningful or legitimate participation by individual learners or employees as part of the community as a whole. Furthermore, there is a history of knowledge that is embraced and learned by new members through their *legitimate* participation in the completion of meaningful shared goals. For instance, in a business environment, a certified performance technologist (CPT) may be asked to determine if a community exists in a dysfunctional sales department. If a community exists, then older, established sales representatives and managers can be expected to have experiences and understandings that have evolved from one generation of salespeople to the next since the inception of the department. Sometimes the knowledge is reified as company documents that elucidate rules of behavior for interacting with clients and other professionals. In other instances, it comes in the form of nonreified, tacit knowledge that is learned by new employees in the form of verbal warnings, guidelines, or other communicated understandings and practices that allow new members of the salesforce to interact and participate in meaningful ways to complete sales tasks and goals.

Just what a community is and which characteristics of the community as well as of one's participation in a community are relevant to the learning process are unclear. Such clarity is exactly what is needed for those interested in designing or using something like community to support learning and to improve performance. In a human performance technology (HPT) setting, this may mean that the CPT must be able to identify the presence of an existing community through the incidence of particular criteria. If no community is detected in a particular group or department through observational techniques, interviews, or other research methods, such criteria should guide the CPT as he or she works to design structures to support the use, development, or emergence of a community. However, without guidelines for what communities of practice are and which characteristics of community contribute most to the organization's performance and learning, the CPT has no place from which to begin.

Clearly, *community* is a complex term and one that resists a single particular definition or meaning. In advancing this characterization and resultant criteria, we do not claim that it is possible to have some invariant structure that must be applied and is relevant to each actualization of community. There are likely groups that do not fit the earlier definition but are, upon direct observation, communities. Even with this appreciation, it is our belief that the concept of "community" can be useful for analytical work when studying corporate groups. Furthermore, to benefit the goal of scientific advancement, it is necessary that we as a field develop a shared appreciation and common meaning for terms that we are individually and collectively using to describe learning and practice environments. Without such a shared interpretation it becomes difficult to discuss meanings across projects or even to characterize the significance of a term within one's own project.

The intent of this chapter is to ground the concept of a community in the literature related to social-psychological constructs, how people learn, and performance improvement, while explaining why a community may be important in the context of performance improvement and assessment. Furthermore, we draw on the earlier definition to advance six criteria with respect to analyzing to what extent and in what manner a CoP is present: (1) a common practice and shared enterprise; (2) opportunities for interaction and participation; (3) mutual interdependence; (4) overlapping histories, practices, and understandings among members; (5) mechanisms for reproduction; and (6) respect for diverse perspectives and minority views. Finally, we provide practical information regarding the evolution of such communities and suggestions for anyone wishing to promote communities of practice.

WHY BOTHER WITH A CoP?

Stemming from the work of anthropologists, there is a long social-theoretical history of the concept of community that has informed the work of studying community development in sociology and education research. This history often focuses on village-scale communities in which kinship was a basic organizing element. However, more recent work has centered on the shared purpose and practices of professional work groups or organizations and does much to inform the study of community in business and human performance settings. The latter was the original focus of Lave and Wenger (1991), who coined the term *community of practice* as a means of communicating the importance of activity in binding individuals to communities and of communities to legitimizing individual practices.

It is this line of thinking that led to Lave and Wenger's (1991) discussion of *legitimate peripheral participation,* in which the primary motivation for learning involves participating in authentic activities and creating an identity that moves one toward becoming more centripetal to a CoP. In reflecting on their examination of four different communities, they stated

> [Community does not] imply necessarily co-presence, a well-defined identifiable group, or socially visible boundaries. It does imply participation in an activity system about which participants share understandings concerning what they are doing and what that means in their lives and for their communities [1991, p. 98].

While this work has proven useful, human performance designers and technologists interested in creating something like community to support learning are still in need of guideposts or criteria that they can use to help guide the community-related design processes.

Theoretical, Practical, and Psychological Underpinnings of Communities of Practice

Over the past two decades there has been a shift in the learning literature from a cognitive view of mind and learning that emphasizes individual thinkers and their isolated minds to a more *situated* perspective that acknowledges the role of the physical and social context in determining what is known, thus emphasizing the social nature of cognition and meaning (Brown, Collins, and Duguid, 1989; Greeno, 1998; Resnick, 1987). A core assumption underlying the situated perspective is an appreciation for the reciprocal character of the interaction in which identities, as well as cognition and meaning, are considered to be socially and culturally constructed (Barab and Duffy, 2000; Lave and Wenger, 1991). Lave (1993) advanced the belief that "developing an identity as a member of a community and becoming knowledgeably skillful are part of the same process, with the former motivating, shaping, and giving meaning to the latter, which it subsumes" (p. 65). As described by Wenger (1998), it is within the interaction that practice, meaning, identity, and community emerge and evolve, all of which interactively constitute context (see Figure 27.1). The focus in terms of learning is on facilitating engaged *participation,* not simply knowledge *acquisition.*

An important point about Wenger's conceptualization is that one could replace learning with the content of any other circle and the overall diagram would not lose its meaning. This social view of learning involves whole persons

Figure 27.1. Dialectical Relations Central to the Learning Process.

in social contexts, and is a process of constructing practice, meaning, and identity all in relation to a CoP (Barab and Duffy, 2000; Lave, 1993, 1997; Walkerdine, 1997; Wenger, 1998). Such a framework offers a radically different notion of the process of learning, one that we believe offers a powerful framework for the HPT community. Of crucial importance are the interrelations among community, practice, meaning, and identity; making learning and practice not just jobs but an integral part of who one is as a person.

Knowledge Conceptualization

Cook and Brown (1999) stated that there are four relevant forms of knowledge: explicit, tacit, individual, and group. Traditionally, an "epistemology of possession," the dominant paradigm in the organizational literature, tends to focus on individual explicit knowledge and treats it as something people *possess*. Although this epistemology can also include forms of tacit and group knowledge, these forms of knowledge are seen as second level. In the traditional paradigm, if there is such a thing as implicit or group knowledge, what matters is how we make it explicit so it can be "possessed" by the individual (Nonaka, 1994). When expanding our view of knowledge to include an "epistemology of practice" (Cook and Brown, 1999), along with adding "knowing," tacit and group knowledge become distinct and equally important forms of knowledge for the life of a community. There is a tacit knowledge that is part of the action and there is group knowledge that is part of the group practice and does not "belong" to any specific individual. Both are forms of group and tacit knowledge that cannot be possessed and transmitted in the traditional sense. It is participation within a CoP that eventually brings newcomers to those forms of knowing.

Knowledge and knowing depend on each other and are mutually enabling; according to Cook and Brown (1999, p. 381) "knowledge is a tool of knowing" that we use as we interact with the social and physical world. It is in the interaction of knowledge and knowing that groups can generate new knowledge and ways of knowing. This interaction is what Cook and Brown (1999, p. 383) have called "the generative dance between knowledge and knowing," a dance that can be a great source of organizational change and innovation, and for which a CoP can be a fruitful environment. At the same time, this process is essential to the life of a CoP, its definition and reproduction cycles are based on this generative dance, and newcomers become old-timers as they learn to participate in them (Barab and Duffy, 2000).

Benefits of a CoP

Communities of practice may exist all around us in a corporate setting, but what are the benefits of encouraging, supporting, or spurring their growth and development? How will a business, the members of an existing CoP, or individuals not currently part of a CoP increase their overall performance as a result of promoting these organizations?

Hubert Saint-Onge and Debra Wallace (2003, p. 4) identify three major strategic challenges that companies confront today: "(1) escaping the limits of performance to keep growing at an accelerated pace, (2) applying knowledge in different ways, in multiple places, across the organization to constantly innovate, and (3) building an environment where learning is the norm to acquire capabilities at a faster rate." Wenger, McDermott, and Snyder (2002, p. 14) note that communities of practice have a number of benefits for organizations, such as

- Connecting local experts and isolated professionals

- Diagnosing and addressing business problems that are organizationwide

- Analyzing knowledge-related sources of uneven performance across the organization to bring all units to the standard of the highest-performing unit by determining best practices

- Linking and coordinating previously disconnected activities that deal with comparable knowledge domains

In a business economy that values knowledge as the key to achieving success, these communities allow for improved access to and sharing of tacit knowledge as well as explicit knowledge that employees hold about best practices while adding short- and long-term tangible and intangible value to the whole organization. Short-term, tangible value includes improved, more rapid solutions to immediate problems, reduced development times, and increased innovation. Over the longer term, improved problem-solving skills; stronger trust relationships across the organization; and sense of ownership of product, practices, and community have tangible and intangible benefits that will improve the organization for the unforeseeable future.

The presence and encouragement of well-functioning communities of practice might hold a number of other advantages for any company, especially those organizations primarily reliant upon knowledge development, management, and sharing. Etienne Wenger and William Snyder (2000) state that communities of practice "can drive strategy, generate new lines of business, solve problems, promote the spread of best practices, develop people's professional skills, and help companies recruit and retain talent" (p. 140). The question remains: How can a CoP do this?

Driving Strategy and Spreading Best Practices. The structure of a CoP places the responsibility for developing new strategies for improving performance on the shoulders of those who are responsible for implementing innovative practices. By encouraging or implementing communication structures and technologies that allow for improved knowledge sharing among practitioners, teams, and departments, employees in the trenches share their daily concerns, problems, and solutions with one another, resulting in best practices being adopted. If the communication structures are implemented in such a way that management is also in the communication loop with practitioners, the best practices should also spread beyond the immediate community. This may occur through forums such as business roundtables, meetings with other corporate executives, or other managerial communities of practice and noncommunity-oriented groups (Saint-Onge and Wallace, 2003; Wenger and Snyder, 2000; Wenger, McDermott, and Snyder, 2002).

Developing Professional Skills, Recruiting, and Retaining Talent. Recognition of employees' "best practices" by management also allows for the support of employee learning, as those responsible for tailoring professional development programs select or develop learning experiences that support best practices while encouraging communication among practitioners that allows for peer support and further innovation. From a financial standpoint, much money is wasted on faddish, massive professional development programs that are based on what a manager or CPT perceives as what the employees need to be more effective. With the existence of a well-functioning, highly communicative CoP, employee practitioners identify and express what kinds of learning programs and initiatives would be of most benefit to their daily work. In addition, the existence of a CoP may also allow for the identification of employees with specialized knowledge and skills who should be singled out for leading and developing learning activities, encouraging the development of cohesive structures in fledgling communities, or communicating with senior management regarding the needs of practitioners.

Building Relationships and a Sense of Connection. The mentoring and peer support provided by a CoP as new and talented employees enter the company are expected to provide these new hires with a sense of belonging and identity that help combat possible feelings of isolation and lack of connection to the collected, tacit, and explicit knowledge held by veteran employees. In organizations without this sense of community, this sense of alienation often leads to the premature resignations of well-intentioned brilliant employees with innovative ideas who feel that they may be supported more effectively elsewhere. Whether recognition of individual achievement and innovation comes from management or peers, its effect can be substantial and powerful for employees, and a CoP is an excellent forum for both forms of recognition.

In addition to those advantages suggested by Wenger and Snyder (2000), Verna Allee (2000) notes a number of benefits, as presented in Figure 27.2. We see these benefits, in addition to those mentioned earlier, as highlighting the potential value of designing for a CoP.

For Business
- Helps drive strategy
- Supports faster problem solving both locally and across the corporation
- Aids in developing, recruiting, and retaining talent
- Builds core capabilities and knowledge competencies
- More rapidly diffuses practices for operational excellence
- Cross-fertilizes ideas and increases opportunities for innovation

For the Community
- Helps build common language, methods, and models around specific competencies
- Embeds knowledge and expertise in a larger population
- Aids in the retention of knowledge when employees leave the company
- Increases access to expertise across the company
- Provides a means to share power and influence with the formal parts of the organization

For the Individual
- Helps people do their jobs
- Provides a stable sense of community with other internal leagues and with the company
- Fosters a learning-focused sense of identity
- Helps develop individual skills and competencies
- Helps a knowledge worker stay current
- Provides challenges and opportunities to contribute

Figure 27.2. Benefits of Communities of Practice.

COMMUNITIES OF PRACTICE: SIX CHARACTERISTICS

Considering the potential benefits of communities of practice for the organization, it becomes relevant for any CoP-related intervention to be able to analyze
to what extent and in what manner a CoP is present in the organization before
and after the intervention. The following characteristics are based on an examination of the literature, emergent understandings from a number of community-
based research projects, and from our diverse set of experiences as participants
in corporate and educational communities both on-line and face-to-face.
Following each explanation of these six central aspects of CoP, we provide
three statements, that is, criteria, that operationally define each aspect. These
criteria can be used to better understand the extent to which a particular
context embodies one of the six characteristics of a CoP. Taken as a whole,

these six characteristics and eighteen criteria can be used to illuminate the extent to which a particular group has those aspects associated with a CoP. These criteria are by no means intended to guide a CoP design. As will be stressed in the next section of the chapter, as communities of practice emerge, we can support or encourage them, we can design "for" them, but we cannot design them.

A Common Practice and Shared Enterprise

Political sociologist Robert Bellah and his colleagues originally conceived of a community as "a group of people who are socially interdependent, who participate together in discussion and decision making, and who share certain practices that both define the community and are nurtured by it" (Bellah, Madson, Sullivan, Swidler, and Tipton, 1985, p. 333). This common practice or mutual enterprise is what binds the community as something larger than the individual. The extent to which someone is or is not a member is dependent on the person's overlap with this common core. Furthermore, such overlap legitimizes the practices of the larger community. Various practices are meaningful or legitimate to the extent that they are associated with and advance the core enterprise of the community.

For example, the sales department in a corporation mentioned earlier will have several practices or activities that most or all members of the team are engaged in, such as developing sales plans; communicating with clients; interacting with other members of the sales team; reading professional literature; participating in team and client meetings; interacting with members of the marketing, finance, contract, and engineering departments; and preparing periodic reports for management. Not all members may be required to participate in all of these practices or activities, but there will be common practices that overlap for members of the sales team, and identifying such overlaps will be an important task for the CPT when determining whether there is a CoP.

The presence of such overlapping practices and activities is a necessary but not sufficient condition for the presence of CoP. Lave and Wenger (1991) posit that learners participate as part of a community of practitioners in their movement from newcomers to full participation in that movement and not only in the overlapping practices that are unique to a CoP. Barab, Kling, and Gray (2004) broadly categorize practitioners as those with a common practice or mutual enterprise. Limiting participants in a CoP only to those that have a similar career or occupation would necessarily exclude a great number of potential communities of practice that may share a common enterprise, for example, contract negotiators, marketing team members, or special interest groups. We acknowledge both common practices and mutual enterprises as having the potential to unite a group, and view professional organizations, corporate teams, or groups with an overlapping cause as *possibly* constituting a community.

We have established three characteristics of a common practice or shared enterprise that can be used to assess the degree to which a community has an observable common practice or shared enterprise. The three guiding or evaluative criteria are

- The group exhibits observable activities and interactions that reflect common practices or mutual enterprises.

- Group members identify themselves as sharing common practices or mutual enterprises.

- The group has produced artifacts that detail common practices or mutual enterprises.

Opportunities for Interaction and Participation

Because activity and participation are at the core of the idea of a CoP (Barab and Duffy, 2000; Lave and Wenger, 1991), it seems evident that providing opportunities for interactivity, as in "acting" with others, and participation is essential to any CoP and environment designed to support a CoP in the service of learning. Unless there are tools and opportunities to share the mutually defined practices, beliefs, and understandings, that common pursuit of a shared enterprise is not possible. It is important to emphasize that the need for a CoP to provide opportunities for interaction and participation not only refers to the tools and channels that can support participation and interaction among them, but also, and first of all, refers to the real and meaningful social opportunities to interact and participate.

As designers and not simply anthropologists, we are interested in designed structures for supporting communities and at the same time acknowledging that communities are more than any set of technical structures. Kling (2000) introduced the term "socio-technical interaction networks (STIN)," which focuses on both the social and technical aspects and on how they interact. The STIN framework stresses that it is technology in use, and not just the tool, in the context of the social world that is important. Similarly, Barab, MaKinster, and Scheckler (2004) point out that in designing community it is the human-to-human interaction as mediated by computer interactions, and not human-to-computer interaction, that is a challenge in designing for communities. In this sense, when examining designed communities one should not overly focus on the most obvious pieces of the on-line or other tool-mediated aspects of the community such as Websites, lists, forums, meetings, bulletin boards, manuals, and so on, but on how those tools are providing support for real interaction and participation; on how they are actually being used and not just on the theoretical potential they have. This criterion goes beyond usability issues and focuses on sociability issues (Preece, 2000). This is not to say that usability is not relevant, but that it is only one aspect, and that it should be measured in the context of sociability and participation. The three guiding or evaluative criteria for opportunities for interaction and participation are

- The context provides meaningful opportunities for social, that is, human-to-human, interaction in which "newcomers" and "old-timers" are in fact engaged.

- The context provides opportunities for "newcomers" and "old-timers" to meaningfully participate.

- The interaction and participation opportunities are structured in a way that directly refers to the common practice of the group.

Mutual Interdependence

Communities are more than a collection of individuals; through interconnections between context, processes, or resources individuals can become a part of something larger, which helps provide a sense of shared purpose as well as an identity for the individual and the larger community (Barab and Duffy, 2000). Communities, whether face-to-face or on-line, are drawn together through the principles of "commonality" and "interdependence." Commonality involves a process of working together in common areas and interests and, in the process, forming a bond or identity with one another and with the group as a whole. Interdependence implies depending on one another for information, knowledge organization, or shared problem solving. A desirable feature of a CoP is that varying demands and expertise exist at different levels of competency where participants can scaffold one another through the sharing of information and abilities. It is mutual interdependence that defines community, not hierarchy.

It is not simply the community members who are a part of something larger. The community itself functions within a broader societal role that gives it, and the practices of the community members, meaning and purpose. If the community isolates itself from the societal systems of which it is a part, then both the individuals and the community become weaker. "This interdependent perspective prevents communities, from small families to nations, from becoming worlds unto themselves" (Shaffer and Anundsen, 1993, p. 12). This interdependent perspective also prevents individuals from becoming worlds unto themselves. With each newly appropriated practice, individuals become more central to and constitutive of the community and in a fundamental way develop a self that is partly constituted by their participation and membership in the CoP. The three guiding or evaluative criteria for mutual interdependence are

- The group includes members who have diverse expertise and knowledge.

- Members depend on one another for participation, shared problem solving, and completion of group tasks.

- The group functions within a broader societal role that gives it, and the practices of the group members, meaning and purpose.

Overlapping Histories, Practices, and Understandings among Members

Communities are more than the simple coming together of people for a particular moment in response to a specific need or for a class. Successful communities have an overlapping cultural and historical heritage that, in part, captures their socially negotiated meanings. This includes shared goals, understandings, and practices. These overlapping meanings, while being continually negotiated anew, are also inherited from previous community members' experiences in which they were hypothesized, tested, practiced, and socially agreed upon. "The negotiation of meaning is a productive process, but negotiating meaning is not constructing it from scratch. Meaning is not pre-existing, but neither is it simply made up. Negotiated meaning is at once historical and dynamic, contextual and unique" (Wenger, 1998, p. 54). The learner has access to and functions in the context of this history of previous negotiations as well as responsiveness from the current context on the functional value of a particular meaning.

One of the important benefits of functioning as part of a community is that through this heritage the practices and understandings are viewed as legitimate. When taught using a traditional instructional context, rules and behavior expectations can feel arbitrary, artificial, and even unnecessary. However, when one learns through participation in the community over time, these norms and understandings are a natural and legitimate part of one's participation. Through meaningful contributions to and valuing of the community histories, practices, and understandings, individuals become legitimate members of the community. In fact, being knowledgeable and skillful becomes intertwined with community membership and the development of one's self. Members develop this sense of self through engagement in the socially agreed upon discourse and practices of the community and in the context of the values of that community, as they become members of the community (Bereiter, 1994, 1997). Three guiding or evaluative criteria for assessing the presence of overlapping histories, practices, and understandings among members are

- There are mechanisms for the development of new, socially agreed upon goals, practices, and understandings.
- There is a core knowledge base that defines what practices and meanings are associated with the group.
- Members of the group know each other or about each other, and about those contributions that other members have made.

Mechanisms for Reproduction

A community is constantly reproducing itself so that new members contribute, support, and eventually lead the community into the future, but do so in the context of the existing agreed upon practices, goals, and understandings. In this manner, communities are continually replicating themselves with new members moving from peripheral participant to core member through a process of enculturation (Lave and Wenger, 1991). Reproducibility, in which newcomers are able to become central to and expand the community, is essential if the community is to have an overlapping cultural heritage. It is a process that is continually occurring in all communities of practice. Simply consider the experiences of most corporations: new hires apprentice with more seasoned employees, working closely at their elbows. Eventually, they begin to appropriate the company practices, and they move from the position of apprentice to more experienced employee, but they are still very much dependent on the codified knowledge of the company as displayed in books and manuals.

Over time, newcomers learn the more informal "stories" of the company and begin to develop their own experiences that give nuance to company policies and more formal processes. Eventually, they must fill the role of "old-timers," and they enter a new level of learning. They begin to expand the thinking of the community of which they are a part (Cook and Brown, 1999). They come to mentor junior hires in the ways of the company. They continue to learn this process and, perhaps more important, grow more confident in their contributions to the company and in their sense of self with respect to their jobs. During this process, they appropriate and contribute to the negotiation and reification of meanings. It is through this cycle that a CoP and the individuals that constitute the community reproduce and define themselves. It is also these reproduction cycles that define learning and participation as well as one's place in the company hierarchy. Any discussion of participation and learning within a CoP must consider the individual's position with respect to the corporate trajectory of the social and power structures of that community. Assumedly, and ignoring other sociopolitical obstacles, it is one's position in relation to the community trajectory from novice to expert that defines a particular member's ability with respect to community practices (Barab and Duffy, 2000). We have established three characteristics to help assess when a community has the mechanisms for reproduction typical of a CoP:

- The group contains both newcomers and more experienced experts.
- The group has a history that has continued beyond the completion of a particular problem or task.
- The group passes through multiple cycles, with newcomers becoming old-timers.

Respect for Diverse Perspectives and Minority Views

There is much evidence that has urged us to confront negative attitudes and adverse behaviors toward minorities by a dominant group in a community's practice. Bennett (1995) has suggested that "despite the fact that we live in a polycultural society, most of our schools remain monocultural" (p. 77).

Furthermore, he warned that the ignorance of cultural attributes runs the risk of misinterpreting "differences in modes of communication, participation, and world view," which are vital for academic and social success (p. 77). To build a healthy CoP, it is important that the design *for* the CoP reflect the rich cultural diversity of the community's population and increase an equal communication among members with various histories, interests, priorities, and concerns. Diversity creates opportunities for character development by teaching tolerance and respect for people and by encouraging concern for equity. A culturally diverse coalition that values and nurtures people from all backgrounds is worthy of active participation. Scholars and practitioners have demonstrated how culture and national values shape the construction of identity within the community, and have suggested setting up ethical standards for involvement of on-line discussion boards (Flicker, Haans, and Skinner, 2004), building on-line learning from an international perspective (McIsaac and Gunawardena, 1996), and incorporating mixed communication systems to increase the contact and understanding among different groups (Etzioni and Etzioni, 1999).

In our efforts to characterize communities of practice, an emphasis is placed on respect for diverse perspectives and minority views. Healthy community functioning should increase an awareness of the cultural diversity of the coalition in a community and thus create an environment that helps the members to understand all its dimensions and make a commitment to nurture cultural diversity. One can think about this characteristic in terms of respect, diversity, and acceptance of minority views. Respect could be demonstrated by the politeness a member shows when he or she challenges a perspective, or by the tolerance a member displays toward an opposite point of view, or by a member's readiness to accept an innovative viewpoint. Diversity is defined in terms of individual differences that play an important role in the culture and operation of organizations. The dimensions of diversity include age; educational background; ethnicity; race; social class; religion; and national, regional, or other geographic differences of origin. Minority views refer to the perspectives that are held by members whose cultures are underrepresented in the group, a challenge to a dominant perspective, or an innovative view that has not been normally accepted. The guiding or evaluative criteria for respect for diverse perspectives and minority views are

- The environment provides even and fair opportunities for members from different backgrounds to participate in and make contributions to the group practice.
- Members show politeness toward diverse and minority perspectives in the group.
- Members are satisfied that their individual perspectives have been fully understood and respected.

THE EMERGENCE OF A CoP

Throughout this chapter we have adopted a cautious vocabulary when referring to the ability to create a CoP. The essence of a CoP is that it emerges from among those who share a common practice. At the essence of a CoP, there are core characteristics that cannot be artifacts created by a design or intervention team. They are instead existing characteristics of human groups that may be expanded and supported in order to generate environments that are intended to foster learning in the context of communities of practice.

We cannot, using design techniques, create mutual interdependence, overlapping histories, or shared understandings. Much of the time, we will be in a situation in which we "design for" a CoP and do not "design" a CoP. Therefore, many of the essential characteristics of a CoP will be present, at least implicitly, in the human groups with which we work. In this context, any design and intervention effort becomes an attempt to stimulate the existence of essential CoP characteristics in an already existing group and expand them to promote learning and improved performance. Often, the goal will be to create the tools and foster the environments that promote the existence and preservation of an existing, perhaps incipient CoP. One cannot create a CoP unless there is an existing group of individuals who already share a practice. What matters is how that existing context can be used in the service of learning and performance improvement.

For Lave and Wenger (1991), participation in a CoP *is* learning, especially for newcomers, in the form of legitimate peripheral participation. The challenge then becomes to support the emergence or expansion of communities by developing the necessary scaffolds that will support members in participating in the movement along the communal trajectories. It is in this path that we can move from traditional practice fields to communities of practice (Barab and Duffy, 2000). In this sense, if the conditions are present, the CoP approach to learning could be used both as an effective intervention and as a more holistic organizational approach. It will depend on the context and the needs of the organization. As Schwen and Hara (2004, p. 164) have clearly stated, communities of practice are about "learning as a living experience of negotiating meaning—not about form. In this sense, they cannot be legislated into existence or defined by decree. They can be recognized, supported, encouraged, and nurtured, but they are not designable reified units."

Promoting a CoP

There are two general orientations to the development of a CoP, though from a theoretical standpoint, it has been argued that there is only one that allows for natural evolution of a real community. The first is a bottom-up approach in which the facilitator works to encourage the evolution and communicative strength of an *existing* fledgling CoP that is at a stage in which it may flourish, falter, or dissipate, depending on the depth of the need for a problem solution and the communication of the practitioners involved. This approach is by far the most common and is considered by many theorists and CPTs to be the only approach that allows for the development of a cohesive and beneficial community that allows for employee-participant ownership rather than management-mandated attendance (Saint-Onge and Wallace, 2003; Wenger, McDermott, and Snyder, 2002). Leadership in a bottom-up approach comes from the naturally emergent coordinators who are respected by the group, and innovation may come from any participant.

The second approach, from the top down, is initiated by and based on the *perceived needs* of practitioners, as elicited by needs analyses conducted by a CPT, or by the expressed wishes of management. It has been argued that this approach results in more difficulty in yielding a community because the levels of trust among participants may not evolve due to fear of reprisal by manager-initiators if concerns and ideas expressed are met with resistance (Barab, Kling, and Gray, 2004; Saint-Onge and Wallace, 2003; Wenger, 1998; Wenger, McDermott, and Snyder, 2002). This may stymie innovation and limit the possible benefits of any community. Furthermore, members of the group may never develop a sense of ownership, as they may view the group as being owned or driven by management, which will further limit the possible advantages expected from developing a CoP or CoP-like group (Schwen and Hara 2004).

Each approach is detailed further in the following sections. Regardless of the approach, the important point is that communities of practice are living entities and must be allowed to grow over time. While there have been a number of models that have been put forth to describe this growth trajectory, one of the most relevant for this community is that posed by Wenger, McDermott, and Snyder (2002) (see Table 27.1). In their model, a CoP passes through five stages: potential, coalescing, maturing, stewardship, and transformation. These stages begin with a group of common needs, identifying their overlap to a full-fledged community with most of the six characteristics described earlier.

Bottom-Up Development: Emergent and Designed. Wenger, McDermott, and Snyder (2002) use a gardening metaphor to illustrate that a CoP cannot be forced but can be cultivated like a garden. In this garden, the seeds are already planted in the form of shared individual needs and overlapping practice. The CPT's role is to provide the necessary support—in the garden, water, food, and sunlight. A CoP cannot be managed as project teams and other more traditional work units are managed because an overly strong hand can easily take the sense of ownership and cohesion away from the practitioners. This kind of development *encourages* the emergence of community due to a group's shared sense

Table 27.1. Five-Stage Developmental Model for Communities of Practice.

Stage	Description
Potential	Employees with similar problems and needs identify each other and contemplate the formation of a community for support.
Coalescing	The community begins to take shape through shared activities and practices intended to meet the needs of community members.
Maturing	Members plan directional strategy, set standards, and participate in joint activities. Members now value the community. The overall focus and role of the CoP solidifies.
Stewardship (formerly *Active*)	The community begins to plateau. The core membership (old-timers) begins to decline as legitimate peripheral participants move to more central roles. This may occur due to natural changes in focus and membership of the CoP or realignment of values.
Transformation (formerly *Dispersion*)	Members start to leave the community once its use or values no longer align with their own. New members join and the process either begins again or the community disperses.

Source: Adapted from Wenger, McDermott, and Snyder, 2002.

of need, rather than *forcing* individuals to associate due to management's perception that a need exists.

While there is no one way to develop a CoP, Wenger, McDermott, and Snyder (2002) suggest several design principles that should be kept in mind as one works to foster a nascent community.

1. Design for evolution.
2. Open a dialogue between inside and outside perspectives.
3. Invite different levels of participation.
4. Develop both public and private community spaces.
5. Focus on value.
6. Combine familiarity and excitement.
7. Create a rhythm for the community.

These principles each act as reminders that the facilitator has a number of different roles when working to promote a CoP. Possible roles include the following:

- *Mind reader:* You will be expected to anticipate the future needs of the community related to communication and reification of best practices as it grows.
- *Operator:* This role entails maintenance and improvement of the channels of communication among members as well as nonmembers.
- *Cheerleader:* The job here is to encourage and implement strategies and structures that allow for participation in community activities regardless of the centrality of membership of an individual.
- *Organizer:* Work with building managers for adequate space and time for community members to interact and communicate in a comfortable fashion.
- *Assessor:* Determine whether the community activities are yielding sufficient gains for the individuals, community, and company. If not, adjust your strategies and tactics to improve community results.
- *Magician:* Make the community members feel a sense of enjoyment about what they do without taking them too far out of their comfort zone. Make them aware when their group contribution makes a big difference.
- *Conductor:* Provide a sense of connection to a familiar pattern of interacting with one another that allows the community members to know what to expect in terms of their interactions with each other on a daily basis.

Top-Down Development: Created and Designed. If the impetus for creating and designing a CoP where one does not currently exist comes from management or a CPT, it requires a rapid relinquishing of power and ownership as the roles of leader and participant are transferred to group members. Again, the metaphor of the garden is appropriate; one should not force the group to work together too much early on, as this is likely to give them too much exposure to sunlight and might result in burnout. If the members are given too few chances to interact, the community will die off due to a lack of its key nutrient, interaction. The goal here is to facilitate and encourage communication that the individuals will likely make if given the opportunity. In addition, the same principles and roles discussed for the bottom-up approach should be used to encourage the formation of a CoP in the top-down approach.

Lingering Questions about Communities of Practice

For a CPT, there are a number of questions that crop up regarding communities of practice. How will you know when to facilitate a CoP? What types of problems, new business initiatives, or quality-improvement goals would tip us off to go with a CoP? What elements must be in place that will allow for the design of support mechanisms that will allow for the emergence of a CoP? How is it done in an organization and by whom? None of these questions has simple answers, but there are some guidelines that may provide direction.

What Does the Legitimate Peripheral Participation (LPP) Cycle Look Like in Practice? Let us consider the example of a newly hired contract negotiator at a medium-size large-truck transmission producer who we will call Susan. Susan enters a workplace in which there are already fledgling communities of practitioner—negotiators who have explicit knowledge and practices reified in manuals as well as strong stores of tacit knowledge and best practices that have been in place for some time. The manager, Peter, introduces Susan to Project Team 9, which consists of Mark, Therese, and their leader, Tom. Mark was hired about a month earlier, Therese has been in the company for about a year, and Tom has been a negotiator with the firm for nearly five years.

Tom informs Susan of a number of best practices that the team engages in that may be different from those of other groups. Over the course of the next few weeks, legitimate peripheral participants Susan and Mark encounter a number of situations that are unfamiliar and discuss strategies and solutions with core old-timers Therese and Tom, who convey a large amount of additional information about best practices and solutions. This allows for improvement of the team's performance in the next set of negotiations and causes a rethinking of the group's conception of best practices.

A few months later, Tom is given a promotion and moved to another division, Mark is made leader of another team, while Therese is made leader of Team 9. Two new hires, Jack and Martha, are brought on the team within a few weeks of one another. Jack and Martha become legitimate peripheral participants while Susan and Mark move toward being more core members and share their tacit knowledge of best practices with Jack and Martha as the need arises to solve problems. This is a limited, simple example of the cycle a CoP may go through, and most communities of practice are much larger than this example. However, it does paint the picture of the movement of members from LPP to core participants over time.

When Should I Facilitate a CoP? The answer to this question begins with an examination of the goals and needs of the organization. Does the organization have as its goals the increase of its knowledge-management and acquisition capabilities? Is the company working to overcome limitations in performance that prevent it from rapid growth and capitalization (Saint-Onge and Wallace, 2003)? Is innovation a key strategy used to advance the worth of its products, knowledge base, and everyday practices? Is learning new skills and information at the heart of the needs of the corporation? If the answer to any of these questions is affirmative, a CoP may be beneficial for meeting the organization's goals and needs.

Who Should Lead a CoP Initiative? Leadership may come from any level in the organization, whether it is the CPT attempting to improve performance at the behest of management, a manager perceiving a need for improved communication and cohesion among employees, or leaders of an existing and fledgling community. What determines this is who the community is willing or able to work with on a daily basis. In many instances, it is important that the leader not be someone whom community or group members find threatening, inflexible, or overly powerful, as they may be unwilling to participate due to feelings that their positions may be threatened if they speak up or suggest innovations.

Warnings and Cautions: What Experience Tells Us about Working with Communities of Practice

The fact that a CoP cannot be created, only "recognized, supported, encouraged, and nurtured" (Schwen and Hara, 2004, p. 164) makes it necessary to offer some cautions and warnings to be considered when working with or for a CoP. Drawing from their experiences and the literature, Schwen and Hara present specific cases of failed communities of practice, including a high-technology company, consulting firms, and legal firms. Schwen and Hara (2004) have pointed out five cautionary notes about working with a CoP. Although their effort refers especially to on-line communities and their support tools, their work is equally valid for other forms of community. We summarize their contributions and offer some realistic perspectives to remind the reader that working with a CoP is challenging, just as it is with any "living" entity.

Prescriptive Versus Descriptive. This common distinction in the instructional design literature is very valuable in this context. Lave and Wenger's (1991) original formulation about communities of practice was essentially descriptive, and therefore cannot be viewed as a prescription for the design of a CoP. To understand how a CoP works does not allow us to predict how a community will work if designed or facilitated to become a CoP. This does not mean that we cannot use this knowledge to guide our efforts to support, encourage, and nurture a CoP. In addition, we can use the principles and the characteristics presented in the previous section of this chapter to evaluate the effectiveness of existing CoP-related efforts.

Ready-Made Versus Communities-in-the-Making. CoP theory and situated cognition in general are most useful when working with an existing community. Experiences related to and the literature regarding the design of communities of practice from the ground up are limited. We hope this chapter to be our small contribution in this regard. In this sense, what is known about the more advanced development stages may not necessarily be useful for early stages of CoP development. Therefore, designers should use great caution and judgment when deciding to move forward with the design of a community.

Knowledge of Possession Versus Knowing in Practice. This theoretical distinction made earlier in this chapter is also to be taken as a cautionary note. Communities of practice are essentially centered on participation and knowledge-in-action or knowing rather than transmissible declarative knowledge. It should therefore be at the core of design efforts intended to support communities of practice.

Mid-Level Social Theory Versus Micro Learning Theory. Communities of practice as a situated cognition theory is at middle level as a social theory. It does not provide a specific pedagogy, and it is not a methodology to be followed. Additionally, combining a mid-level theory such as communities of practice with a specific micro learning theory, such as a specific educational method, may not produce the expected results. For example, emphasis on a detailed curriculum, extensive learning objectives, and knowledge objects may reveal a focus on a traditional method that is not necessarily supported in a CoP environment. It may at the same time show a focus on knowledge of possession.

Motivated Members Versus Unwilling Subjects. When working with a CoP, it is essential to focus on the authentic motivation of its members. They should not be viewed as the "subject" of an intervention. CoP members' intentions should always be considered as essential in any design effort. The work of the design team should not mean a loss of decision power for the participants. However, this is often not the case in CoP initiatives. Community members' intentions and needs are sometimes threatened or not considered, which subverts the social foundation of the CoP.

CONCLUSION

The CoP perspective suggests a reformulation of what it means to know and learn, from a dualist representational theory separating knowing from that which is known to one that pairs practice and meaning within context. This then suggests dialectic, as opposed to dualistic, relations among practice, meaning, context, and identity. The term *community of practice*, advanced by Lave and Wenger (1991), was introduced to capture the importance of activity in fusing individuals to communities and of communities in legitimizing individual practices. In their work, learning is conceived as a trajectory in which learners move from *legitimate peripheral participant* to *core participant* in the CoP. This work has garnered the interest of many human-performance and educational efforts. Nevertheless, all those interested in developing and examining a CoP, including on-line communities and especially instructional designers and human performance technologists interested in creating or using existing communities to support learning, need guideposts or criteria to guide their design and evaluation process.

We hope it has become evident throughout this chapter that the context in which the CoP grows is critical. Success depends less on any one technical structure and more on the potential for human-to-human interaction. In this sense, it will be the product, scaffold, or technology *in use,* not just the tool, that is critical to the potential success of a particular CoP. We have discussed some of the in-use characteristics that distinguish a community of learners and a group of individuals learning collaboratively. Even though having this set of guideposts or design criteria for a CoP is a step forward, from a performance-improvement perspective there is still the need to learn more about when it makes sense to design for a CoP. What are the problems, needs, goals, or opportunities that would call for an effort to develop or support a CoP? We hope that this discussion provides some useful responses to these questions and we look forward to learning about the efforts of others and how our experiences are useful to others.

Appendix: Guiding or Evaluative Criteria for Examining a Designed CoP

1. *A Common Practice and Shared Enterprise*
   - The group exhibits observable activities and interactions that reflect common practices or mutual enterprises.
   - Group members identify themselves as sharing common practices or mutual enterprises.
   - The group has produced artifacts that detail common practices or mutual enterprises.

2. *Opportunities for Interaction and Participation*
   - The context provides meaningful opportunities for social, that is, human-to-human, interaction in which newcomers and old-timers are in fact engaged.
   - The context provides opportunities for newcomers and old-timers to meaningfully participate.
   - The interaction and participation opportunities are structured in a way that directly refers to the common practice of the group.

3. *Mutual Interdependence*

- The group includes members who have diverse expertise and knowledge.

- Members depend on one another for participation, shared problem solving, and the completion of group tasks.

- The group functions within a broader societal role that gives it, and the practices of the group members, meaning and purpose.

4. *Overlapping Histories, Practices, and Understandings among Members*

- There are mechanisms for the development of new, socially agreed upon goals, practices, and understandings.

- There is a core knowledge base that defines what practices and meanings are associated with the group.

- Members of the group know each other or about each other, and about those contributions that other members have made.

5. *Mechanisms for Reproduction*

- The group contains both newcomers and more experienced experts.

- The group has a history that has continued beyond the completion of a particular problem or task.

- The group passes through multiple cycles, with newcomers becoming old-timers.

6. *Respect for Diverse Perspectives and Minority Views*

- The environment provides even and fair opportunities for members from different backgrounds to participate and to make contributions to the group practice.

- Members show politeness toward diverse and minority perspectives in the group.

- Members are satisfied that their individual perspectives have been fully understood and are respected.

References

Allee, V. (2000). Knowledge networks and communities of practice. *OD Practitioner: Journal of the Organizational Development Network, 32*(4). Retrieved October 28, 2005, from http://www.odnetwork.org/odponline/vol32n4/knowledgenets.html.

Barab, S. A., and Duffy, T. (2000). From practice fields to communities of practice. In D. Jonassen and A. M. Land (Eds.), *Theoretical foundations of learning environments* (pp. 25–56). Mahwah, NJ: Lawrence Erlbaum Associates.

Barab, S. A., Kling, R., and Gray, J. H. (2004). *Designing for virtual communities in the service of learning.* New York: Cambridge University Press.

Barab, S. A., MaKinster, J., and Scheckler, R. (2004). Designing system dualities: Characterizing a web-supported teacher professional development community. In S. A. Barab, R. R. Kling, and J. Gray, J. (Eds.), *Designing for virtual communities in the service of learning* (pp. 53–90). New York: Cambridge University Press.

Bellah, R. N., Madson, N., Sullivan, W. M., Swidler, A., and Tipton, S. M. (1985). *Habits of the heart: Individualism and commitment in American life.* Berkeley, CA: University of California Press.

Bennett, C. I. (1995). *Multicultural education: Theory and practice* (3rd ed.). Boston: Allyn & Bacon.

Bereiter, C. (1994). Implications of postmodernism for science, or, science as progressive discourse. *Educational Psychologist, 29,* 3–12.

Bereiter, C. (1997). Situated cognition and how to overcome it. In D. Kirshner and J. A. Whitson (Eds.), *Situated cognition: Social, semiotic, and psychological perspectives* (pp. 281–300). Mahwah, NJ: Lawrence Erlbaum Associates.

Brown, J. S., Collins, A., and Duguid, P. (1989, January–February). Situated cognition and the culture of learning. *Educational Researcher,* 32–42.

Cook, S., and Brown, J. S. (1999). Bridging epistemologies: The generative dance between organizational knowledge and organizational knowing. *Organizational Science, 10*(4), 381–400.

Etzioni, A., and Etzioni, O. (1999). Face-to-face and computer-mediated communities: A comparative analysis. *Information Society, 15*(4), 241–248.

Flicker, S., Haans, D., and Skinner, H. (2004). Ethical dilemmas in research on Internet communities. *Qualitative Health Research, 14*(1), 124–135.

Greeno, J. G. (1998). The situativity of knowing, learning, and research. *American Psychologist, 53,* 5–17.

Kling, R. (2000). Learning about information technologies and social change: The contribution of social informatics. *The Information Society, 16*(3), 217–232.

Lave, J. (1993). Situating learning in communities of practice. In L. B. Resnick, J. M. Levine, and S. D. Teasley (Eds.), *Perspectives on socially shared cognition* (pp. 17–36). Washington, DC: American Psychological Association.

Lave, J. (1997). The culture of acquisition and the practice of understanding. In D. Kirshner and J. A. Whitson (Eds.) *Situated cognition: Social, semiotic, and psychological perspectives* (pp. 63–82). Mahwah, NJ: Lawrence Erlbaum Associates.

Lave, J., and Wenger, E. (1991). *Situated learning: Legitimate peripheral participation.* New York: Cambridge University Press.

McIsaac, M., and Gunawardena, C. N. (1996). Distance education. In D. H. Jonassen (Ed.), *Handbook of research for educational communications and technology.* New York: Macmillan.

Nonaka, I. (1994). A dynamic theory of organizational knowledge creation. *Organization Science, 5*(1), 14–37.

Preece, J. (2000). *Online communities: Designing usability, supporting sociability.* Chichester, UK: John Wiley and Sons.

Resnick, L. B. (1987). Learning in school and out. *Educational Researcher, 16,* 13–20.

Saint-Onge, H., and Wallace, D. (2003). *Leveraging communities of practice for strategic advantage.* Boston: Butterworth-Heinemann.

Schwen, T. M., and Hara, N. (2004). Community of practice: A metaphor for online design? In S. A. Barab, R. R. Kling, and J. Gray, J. (Eds.), *Designing for virtual communities in the service of learning.* New York: Cambridge University Press.

Shaffer, C. R., and Anundsen, K. (1993). *Creating community anywhere: Finding support and connection in a fragmented world.* Los Angeles: Tarcher/Perigee.

Walkerdine, V. (1997). Redefining the subject in situated cognition theory. In D. Kirshner and Whitson, J. A. (Eds.), *Situated cognition: Social, semiotic, and psychological perspectives* (pp. 57–70). Mahwah, NJ: Lawrence Erlbaum Associates.

Wenger, E. (1998). *Communities of practice: Learning, meaning, and identity.* New York: Cambridge University Press.

Wenger, E., and Snyder, W. (2000). Communities of practice: The organizational frontier. *Harvard Business Review,* January–February, 139–145.

Wenger, E., McDermott, R. M., and Snyder, W. M. (2002). *Cultivating communities of practice: A guide to managing knowledge.* Boston: Harvard Business School.

CHAPTER TWENTY-EIGHT

Workplace Design

Karen L. Medsker

Human performance technologists use models such as Gilbert's Behavior Engineering Model (Gilbert, 1978, 1982) to diagnose causes of performance gaps and to identify categories of interventions that may improve performance. Gilbert identified factors associated with the performer—skills and knowledge, capacity, and motivation—and factors found in the environment—data or information, tools and setting, and incentives. This chapter discusses the *tools and setting* category of environmental factors, including physical and psychological elements that affect human performance in the workplace. Although the typical performance technologist is not usually an expert in furniture design, acoustics, or space planning, awareness of how the physical environment can affect performance and create potential ergonomic problems is essential. Just as we work with compensation specialists to design interventions in the incentive category, so also should we work with ergonomic experts and facilities managers to ensure effective physical working conditions for our clients. At a minimum, performance technologists can call attention to workplace design issues to raise awareness among employees and management.

Today's organizations cannot afford to ignore workplace design or to consider investment in the physical workplace only as a cost to be minimized. Because 75 to 85 percent of business expenditures are related to staffing, and only 5 to 10 percent are for property and operating costs, even small improvements in ergonomic enhancements for the physical workplace can easily and quickly offset investments in facilities by improving productivity (Oseland, 2001). When physical conditions in the workplace improve, and measures that are appropriate to the business and its objectives are used, productivity usually increases in areas such as processing time, rates of absenteeism or turnover, number of new customers, deadlines met, and customer satisfaction ratings. Workplace design can improve performance by as much as 15 percent (Kearny and Smith, 1999; Oseland, 2001). The economic benefits of these productivity increases typically offset the costs of workplace upgrades in less than two years. For example, Oseland (2001) describes a project considered by IBM to be a major success in workplace design. In 1999, part of the software company Tivoli Systems, which was acquired by IBM, was moved to a new workplace that was designed according to IBM's *e*-place standards. These standards focused on high-quality yet space-efficient, nonterritorial working environments. The productivity gains, measured in reduced downtime, offset the facilities investment in less than one year.

THE ERGONOMIC APPROACH TO WORKPLACE DESIGN

In part, workplace design is based on the science of ergonomics. According to Muchinsky (2000, p. 459), "ergonomics (or human factors psychology) is the study of the interface between individuals and their work environment. The environment may be a work tool or piece of equipment or the spatial surroundings in which work is conducted." The work environment includes many elements, such as location, equipment, furniture, storage, layout, light, sound, proximity, air quality, and decor. Since environmental elements are more malleable than people and are also less costly, it makes sense to adapt the work environment to the requirements of people and their job tasks. Such adaptation is known as the ergonomic approach to workplace design.

Because performance or productivity results from a complex set of factors, we must be careful when drawing conclusions about the causes of productivity gains. Did productivity improve as a direct result of the physical changes, or indirectly because the changes triggered a morale boost based on feelings that the company cares about its employees? Psychological factors such as motivation, employee expectations, preferences, and perceptions of reality play a significant role in work performance, productivity, and satisfaction. Nevertheless, many studies have shown that, directly or indirectly, workplace improvements have positive effects on performance and satisfaction. See, for example, the many success stories on the Steelcase, Heschong Mahone Group, and Humantech Websites listed in Figure 28.1.

You need not be an expert in workplace design to help yourself, your colleagues, and your clients achieve better designed work environments. As a performance technologist, you can identify situations in which the physical

Website	Description
www.sleepfoundation.org	The National Sleep Foundation focuses on all aspects of sleep research, the importance of sleep, and sleep problems and disorders. Their Website includes strategies for shift workers.
www.epa.gov/iaq/pubs/sbs.html	The U.S. Environmental Protection Agency's Website features information on sick building syndrome, as well as many links and resources related to indoor air quality.
www.ergonomics.ucla.edu	The Website for the Office of Environment, Health and Safety at the University of California, Los Angeles, includes sections on chairs, workstation setup, back safety, exercises, and office and laboratory ergonomics.
www.office-ergo.com	The Website for Ankrum Associates' Office of Ergonomics Training discusses back pain, eyestrain, and ergonomic products, and offers lists of links and periodicals. It also includes a good list of tips for making ergonomic change within an organization.
www.ergopen.com	The Website for ErgoPen, a Division of BIC, USA, describes the ergonomic pen and features cool pictures.
www.baddesigns.com	The Website of Michael J. Darnell's Bad Human Factors Design features a scrapbook with illustrated examples and presents an entertaining review of poorly designed tools and other everyday things.
http://ergo.human.cornell.edu	The site for Cornell University Ergonomics Web presents a collection of research reports, conference presentations, and ergonomic guidelines. It also includes research on an ergonomic mouse.
www.microsoft.com	Microsoft's Website offers articles and findings from surveys linking workspace design to productivity.

Figure 28.1. Selected Websites Related to Workplace Design.

www.chrisfoxinc.com	Chris Fox's Website presents a summary of research findings that connect the office environment to productivity.
www.steelcase.com	Steelcase is a major manufacturer of office furniture and components for workplace interiors. Steelcase's Website features a knowledge library containing workplace survey results, articles on workplace design, and case studies showing improved bottom-line measures.
cbe.berkeley.edu/resources	The Website for the Center for the Built Environment at the University of California, Berkeley, features research on indoor environmental quality, including topics such as speech privacy, human comfort model, ventilation and productivity, and team space and collaboration. The site includes many publications in PDF format.
www.h-m-g.com	The Heschong Mahone Group, energy consultants who do building science research, provide results of research on the connection between daylight and productivity on their Website.
iwsp.human.cornell.edu	The Website for the International Workplace Studies Program at Cornell University includes research on how innovative workplace strategies contribute to individual, team, and organizational effectiveness.
www.officeproductivity.co.uk	The Office Productivity Network, a consortium of leading UK businesses with government support, features best-practice buildings and productivity research on their Website.
www.humantech.com	Humantech, a consulting firm specializing in occupational ergonomics, offers ergonomics manuals, training programs, and analysis tools. The Humantech Website includes client success stories with quantified results.

Figure 28.1. Selected Websites Related to Workplace Design. (*Continued*)

www.ifma.org	This is the Website for the International Facilities Management Association, which certifies facility managers, conducts research, provides educational programs, recognizes facility management degree and certificate programs, and produces World Workplace, the largest facility-management-related conference and exposition.
www.ashrae.org	This is the Website for the American Society of Heating, Refrigerating, and Air-Conditioning Engineers, an international membership society whose mission is to advance the arts and sciences of heating, ventilation, air conditioning and refrigeration, and related human factors to serve the evolving needs of the public and ASHRAE members.
www.allaboutosha.com	All About OSHA's Website provides resources to help employers understand and comply with Occupational Safety and Health Administration (OSHA) regulations and implement safety training programs.

Figure 28.1. (*Continued*)

workplace interferes with job performance or improvements in workplace design that could enhance performance. You may even have opportunities to work with a team to plan a new space. Observations and interviews with performers often reveal simple but important ergonomic issues that require attention. Smith and Kearny (1994) present systematic procedures and job aids for working with people to improve their work environments. Although complex changes may require intervention by experts in ergonomics or facilities management, the performers themselves, with your systematic guidance, can often make simple but effective workplace improvements.

To organize the many topics related to workplace design, this chapter is divided into sections that address the following standard questions:

- *Who?* This section presents performer characteristics that are essential considerations in workplace design.
- *What?* This section discusses how task characteristics should influence workplace design.

- *Where?* Based on previous discussion of the performers and their tasks, this section describes principles of workplace design.
- *How?* How easily or well people perform depends partly upon the design of the tools and information available to them. This section shows that performers must also learn to work smarter, following best ergonomic practices.
- *When?* This section shows how work schedules present another set of physical and psychological issues that affect performance.
- *Why?* Benefits of sound workplace design, to employers and employees, are summarized in this section.

Figure 28.1 contains an annotated list of Websites relevant to workplace design.

WHO?: HUMAN REQUIREMENTS IN WORKSPACE DESIGN

Work environments have often been designed around the needs of machinery or equipment, particularly in manufacturing environments; office environments have often been designed for the convenience of managers who felt required to supervise closely the workers for whom they were responsible. Today we recognize the importance of designing workplaces to accommodate the needs of the people doing the work. As performance technologists, we should consider the physical needs of workers as we conduct performance analyses, assess causes of poor performance, and seek opportunities to realize higher performance goals.

Common Work Environment Needs

Most people have similar issues with their work environments. The following are the major common concerns (Smith and Kearny, 1994):

- Privacy and stimulation
- Interaction with others
- Physical comfort and safety
- Personalization
- Control or influence

Privacy and Stimulation. In today's information economy, most people perform knowledge work rather than physical labor. Knowledge work, and most physical work as well, requires people to think. Thinking demands the worker's attention, and attention is a limited commodity for the human mind. An indicator of this limit is the number of items a person can hold in mind at one time: seven, plus or minus two (Miller, 1956). Thus privacy, or protection from extraneous stimuli that distract the worker, is a common need.

DeMarco and Lister (1997) found that the performance of software developers correlated strongly with the relative quietness and privacy of the workspace, with freedom from unwanted telephone calls and other interruptions. The same research, and research conducted by IBM (Fox, 2004), found a correlation between the amount of office space per developer and developer productivity.

Alternatively, lack of stimulation can also interfere with work performance. Consider that extreme stimulus deprivation is a form of punishment and even torture. Stimulation may take many forms, including color, interior decoration, light, airflow, background noise, music, artwork, outdoor views, and proximity to other people. The right balance between privacy and stimulation should be matched to the worker and the task.

Interaction with Others. People at work need to interact with others to complete work tasks or to enjoy a social break from work tasks. Yet interaction with others can waste time and obstruct productivity. Workers need to be able to control when, where, and with whom they interact and to limit interaction as needed. When interaction is needed, a well-designed environment allows convenient access to the appropriate persons, a comfortable, well-appointed space for meeting, and sufficient privacy.

Physical Comfort and Safety. To work comfortably and safely, workers need the right space, surfaces, seating, equipment, tools, storage, and lighting. They also need clean air, ventilation, heating and cooling, protection from harmful or distracting sounds and smells, and workplaces free of harmful bacteria, dampness, mold, mildew, and so forth. In the United States, the federal government's Occupational Safety and Health Administration (OSHA) regulations protect workers from many workplace hazards. But workers and employers can go beyond basic health and safety requirements to create workplaces that facilitate maximum performance. By educating workers on safety issues and supporting their ability and freedom to design or tailor their own workspaces, employers also give more autonomy, which, in turn, increases job satisfaction.

Personalization. People are more comfortable and motivated at work when they are allowed or encouraged to personalize their workspaces (Smith and Kearny, 1994). The ability to rearrange furniture, raise or lower a work surface, select equipment, acquire ergonomic aids such as back supports and footrests, and obtain additional storage enables people to feel at home in their workspace. Freedom to hang family pictures or artwork, have plants, or display travel memorabilia also contributes to a sense of ownership and comfort in one's individual workspace. Less common is the freedom to paint the walls a color that enhances the mood of the individual. Some workplaces even allow employees to bring their pets to work. Customizations such as these may present prohibitive practical problems for facilities managers working within standardized environments; yet they may be possible in less formal settings.

Control or Influence. Underlying the previously mentioned needs is the need to have some control, or at least influence, over one's environment. If I cannot paint my cubicle, can I at least hang colorful posters? While I have no door to close, is there a conference room or library where I can work with concentration? If the cubicles are too small or too public to hold a small meeting, is the cafeteria open for private conversation with coffee? Having some choices gives individuals a feeling of autonomy instead of possibly feeling powerless or trapped. Hackman and Oldham's Job Characteristics Model (1976) identified five core dimensions that affect job performance and satisfaction: skill variety, task identity, task significance, feedback, and autonomy. While autonomy concerning job content and methods is central, control or influence over one's workspace can provide an additional component of autonomy.

Variable Work Environment Needs

While people at work have common needs, the ways these needs manifest themselves vary considerably among individuals. Variables that affect workspace design may be categorized as physical and cognitive.

Physical Variables. People vary in size, strength, and physical abilities. Those who purchase workplace furniture and equipment should not assume that one size fits all. Adjustable furniture can often adequately accommodate individual differences. For example, chairs with adjustable seat height and back position, desks with adjustable work surfaces, and computer monitors that change positions are readily available. In addition, low-cost or cost-free modifications are possible. For example, one six-foot-five-inch tall performance analyst invented a low-cost solution for his too-low work surface; he raised his desk by setting the legs on concrete blocks.

The U.S. government's Americans with Disabilities Act (ADA) requires that reasonable accommodations be made in the workplace for individuals with disabilities. Furniture and equipment to accommodate special needs are now readily available, as well as *assistive technologies* designed specifically for those with visual, hearing, or other impairments. All workers, including those with declared disabilities, should have the opportunity to ask for, and, if the request is reasonable, to acquire what they need to work effectively and comfortably.

Cognitive Variables. Building on the work of several psychologists (Mehrabian, 1976; Anderson, 1980; O'Donnell and Eggemeier, 1986), Smith and Kearny (1994) identified a continuum of *screening* behavior based on how well individuals control their attention to work tasks in the presence of distracting stimuli. *High screeners* ignore extraneous stimuli and focus on their tasks more easily, whereas *low screeners* have more difficulty ignoring extraneous stimuli and thus need more protection to focus on their work. According to Smith and Kearny, most people can identify where they fall on this continuum, and can accurately describe their privacy needs when working on various types of tasks. For example, office mate A, a high-screener, enjoys having the radio on while working and may be relatively unbothered by office mate B's phone conversations. Office mate B, a low-screener, has great difficulty working with the radio on and during office mate A's phone conversations. Sensitivity to these differences may lead to the switching of offices or behavior modification.

WHAT?: TASK REQUIREMENTS IN WORKSPACE DESIGN

As important as worker variables are, so are the variable requirements of specific tasks. An individual worker has different environmental requirements when performing different tasks. As performance technologists, we often conduct task analyses to determine how tasks should be done as a basis for process design, job design, job-aid design, and training design. Another factor to consider during task analysis is the physical environment required to perform the tasks well. Consider both mental and physical aspects of tasks to identify these environmental requirements.

Mental Aspects of Tasks

Mental aspects of work tasks may be placed on a continuum from routine to complex.

Routine Work. "Linear and straight-ahead, routine work uses prescribed repetitive procedures to reach a clear and well-defined goal" (Smith and Kearny, 1994, p. 14). Once the tasks are learned, routine work may also be described as automatic. Examples include packing boxes, making photocopies, simple data entry, washing dishes, and hand-rolling cigars. Since routine work makes few demands on the worker's attention, distracting stimuli may not degrade performance. Typically, routine tasks enable workers to recover quickly from interruptions. Performance on routine tasks may suffer because workers are bored and allow their minds to wander, or they become dissatisfied with such unengaging work. For high-screeners (and even for low-screeners), added sensory stimulation can help (Smith and Kearny, 1994). For example, listening to music may provide welcome stimulation for routine manufacturing tasks. The stuffing of information packets may be aided by conversations among the stuffers.

Complex and Creative Work. "Lateral and exploratory, complex mental work requires that new information be combined with existing information. The goals and procedures of complex work are often unclear" (Smith and Kearny, 1994, p. 15). Problem solving, designing, and decision making are in this category of work. Examples include designing a marketing campaign, writing a research report, planning a lesson, working with an employee to set career goals, and choosing the color scheme for a room. Creative work often involves both divergent and convergent thinking, each of which makes different demands on the performer (Kearny and Smith, 1999). Divergent thinking often requires a higher stimulus environment and interaction with others, whereas convergent thinking more often requires individual concentration in a quiet environment. In either case, complex and creative work requires higher levels of attention than does routine work. Distractions often degrade and delay performance, and workers find it difficult to recover from interruptions. For example, scientific and engineering thought is characterized by being in *flow*, which may take fifteen minutes or longer to regain following an interruption (Glen, 2003). Low-screeners, in particular, need sensory protection or privacy when they engage in complex or creative work, and even high-screeners may be helped by added protection.

Physical Aspects of Tasks

Whether tasks require heavy physical activity, such as construction work, or are primarily sedentary, such as office work, they all have a physical impact. To prevent or reduce potential physical harm, the work environment must be carefully designed in light of the task characteristics. Along with providing safety equipment and practices to help workers in high-risk situations avoid catastrophic injuries such as falls, electrocution, and chemical spills, injury prevention in lower-risk situations should also be a major concern. For example, cumulative trauma disorders, repetitive motion syndromes, and musculoskeletal injuries are common among people who sit at computer workstations for significant portions of their days (Ostrom, 1993). Correct body positioning, arrangement of equipment and furniture, task variation, and sufficient rest breaks are important in helping people avoid injuries.

Even in office environments, lifting and bending can cause injuries. One software engineer suffered long-term back injury when he lifted a book off the floor from a sitting position in his swivel office chair. Workers should lift limited weight loads and should be trained to observe correct lifting and bending postures. Since employee knowledge is so important in preventing injuries, enlightened employers schedule regular ergonomics training sessions.

Group and Team Tasks

While individual work spaces are critical, we must also consider the space needs of *groups* and *teams.* For our purposes, a *group* is a number of individuals who work together toward a common goal but whose performance is not interdependent. One example is a call center, in which all performers are doing similar tasks while working independently. In this case, we might plan the space so that the workers can see and communicate with each other. Individuals may have specialized or advanced knowledge into which others may tap. Socializing between calls may boost morale. Seeing and hearing others work may provide welcome stimulation and relieve boredom. Additional features might include notice boards and display screens that are visible from all of the individual workstations. At the same time, however, we would want to arrange the workstations and the acoustic features of the room such that noise from other calls does not interfere with people's work.

In a *team*, members are likely to perform different tasks, thus *interacting* to advance the team toward a common goal. Teams often need interactive work sessions and meetings. An example is a software design and development team. The team members may work together on an overall design, work separately on specific modules, then reconvene to review and integrate their work. Teams need spaces that are conducive to team interactions: comfortable conference furniture, whiteboards, walls for permanent display of work products, wireless LANs, and Internet connections.

WHERE?: WORKSPACE PLANNING

Workspace planning should be based on the needs of performers and the requirements of their tasks, as summarized in previous sections. Important design issues include the following:

- Noise reduction
- Heating, ventilation, and air conditioning (HVAC)
- Furniture
- Storage
- Lighting
- Color
- Music

Additional topics include spaces that facilitate collaboration, building location, indoor air pollution, and the design of home offices. While performance technologists usually do not have control over these factors, they may be part of a team to design or redesign workspaces, or they may consult with decision makers. For example, when performance technologists conduct performance analyses, they may recommend changes in the work environment, along with other recommendations involving feedback systems, training, and personnel selection.

Noise Reduction

Noise is unwanted sound. Exposure to loud noise, 95 to 110 decibels, the level of an average factory or a crying baby, causes blood vessels to constrict, heart rates to increase, and pupils to dilate. Continuous exposure to loud noise may cause high blood pressure, impair emotional well-being, and induce stress. Exposure to intense noise over time usually causes people to lose part of their hearing. In one study, textile mill employees experiencing high noise exposure had more disciplinary actions, accidents, absenteeism, and lower productivity and quality of work (Noweir, 1984). The U.S. government limits permissible sound levels for industrial workers: 90 decibels (db) for an eight-hour day; 100 db for a two-hour period, and 110 db for a thirty-minute period. Noise problems are most prominent in non-office environments such as factories, construction zones, power plants, and airports. In these environments, workers are protected from hearing loss by headphones or earplugs. Some employers even hire employees with partial or total hearing loss for jobs in noisy environments. In some cases, noisy equipment can be reengineered or placed in a segregated area away from people.

Noise is a major issue even in offices. Noise levels in open offices can cause measurable physiological signs of stress and reduce work motivation. Background noise can also impede communication, forcing workers to come closer to each other or yell. DeMarco and Lister (1997) concluded from their studies of over six hundred software developers from ninety-two companies that noise negatively affected productivity of these workers. In one study of seven office buildings, acoustics was the major source of dissatisfaction, with 72 percent of workers reporting that lack of speech privacy had a negative effect on their productivity (Center for the Built Environment, 2003).

While open or landscaped offices have become the norm, they create noisy workspaces. Ramon Venero (personal communication, December 15, 2004), facilities manager for the Society for Human Resource Management in Alexandria, Virginia, stated that higher workstation divider panels, while providing more visual privacy, do not work effectively to reduce noise. Solutions include sound-masking technology that introduces pink noise into the environment, and quiet areas where employees can retreat to perform tasks that require concentration. Employers of high-end knowledge workers are increasingly offering their workers multiple work settings, including both open and closed spaces and home-based work options, to allow workers to choose based on the task at hand and their individual work styles (Cantrell, 2001).

Heating, Ventilation, and Air Conditioning

Discomfort from heat is usually a combination of high temperature, high humidity, and low airflow. Air conditioning is the obvious and now almost universal solution for indoor workplaces, since it addresses temperature, humidity, and airflow. However, in many workplaces air conditioning temperatures are too low in the summer, thus forcing workers to wear sweaters or jackets indoors and to take outdoor breaks in order to warm up. Appropriate levels of air conditioning are needed to maximize physical comfort.

Heat stress is a problem for those who work outdoors in summer and for people who work around heat-producing equipment. Heat stress decreases performance not only on strenuous tasks but also on tasks requiring mental skills such as problem solving. Schultz and Schultz (2002) reported that temperatures at 90 degrees F interfere with perceptual motor tasks, strenuous motor tasks, and even sedentary mental tasks. The negative effects grow worse over time. Where air conditioning, ventilation, and dehumidification are not possible, workers should be given more breaks or be relieved by other workers.

Cold, including wind chill effects when activities are outdoors, also creates negative effects on comfort and performance. Performance on manual tasks decreases as fingers become numb. Discomfort resulting from cold reduces concentration on mental tasks and negatively affects performance. Outdoor tasks in cold conditions require special protective clothing and footwear, short exposures with frequent indoor breaks, and relief by other workers.

Low humidity causes people to feel cooler, so maintaining proper humidity in winter is necessary for indoor comfort. Forced air heat dries office air. Computers, printers, and fax machines increase heat and static electricity, which can dry out office air. Most office buildings do not have humidifiers, so installing them will help with the problem.

The primary complaint office workers have about their work environment is that it is too cold or too hot. Such complaints represent about 80 percent of all service requests to facilities departments (Ramon Venero, personal communication, December 15, 2004). Even mild discomfort can be distracting. Although most office workers perform in climate-controlled conditions, offices on the sunny side of the building can be too warm and offices on the shady side can be too cool. Up-to-date HVAC systems, where available, can mitigate these effects. Allowing employees in particularly cold areas to have space heaters is not recommended, since such equipment overloads electrical circuits and increases the risk of fire.

Furniture

Many of us have seen ergonomic drawings that show appropriate dimensions and alignment of a person sitting or standing at a computer workstation, yet many of us use workstations that fail to meet these specifications. The results of poor ergonomic workstation design or posture can be fatigue; pain in the wrists, back, neck, and shoulders; or even more permanent conditions such as carpal tunnel syndrome. Adjustability, a key feature of ergonomically-designed furniture, is needed for table height, screen height and viewing angle, keyboard height and angle, chair seat height, and chair back inclination. Adjustable furniture allows for differently sized users and allows users to change positions during long periods of work. Workers must be trained to use the full functionality of their ergonomic furniture, however. At least one chair comes with its own CD-ROM tutorial on using its capabilities.

Storage

An often overlooked ergonomic problem in the workplace is inadequate storage. People waste time and lose concentration while they are looking for a reference book, a tool, or a document. They also waste valuable work surfaces by using them for storage. For one manager, the office sofa, which was intended for meetings, housed piles of documents. To design adequate storage, keep the worker's tasks in mind. What inputs and tools are needed, where, and how often? Arrange materials in a way that is logical to the performer. Keep the work area decluttered by archiving or disposing of materials no longer needed. Consider individual style preferences: organized piles on shelves versus vertical or horizontal file cabinets.

Lighting

Two types of lighting should be considered in a workspace. First, ambient or general lighting should be sufficient for moving around safely and finding things in the space. General lighting should provide a pleasant atmosphere and should not cause headaches. Task lighting should provide sufficient illumination for the proper accomplishment of specific tasks. For example, reading, working at a computer, and connecting electrical wires may each require specific task-lighting features.

Light intensity or brightness should suit the task and the age of the worker. Generally, older workers need brighter light, and tasks requiring attention to small details require brighter light. Another important factor is the distribution of light. Illumination should be distributed over a work area, rather than concentrated over the specific task. A natural tendency is to look around, potentially causing eyestrain if the worker's eyes have to readjust frequently to different light levels. Indirect or reflected light provides illumination throughout a work area without the bright spots and glare that can result from direct lighting. Glare reduces visual efficiency, can obscure vision, and contributes to eyestrain. Shield people from extremely bright light sources and minimize glossy surfaces that reflect light.

Regardless of the adequacy of artificial light, people want natural light and to see outside. Satisfaction and performance may improve with access to windows or skylights. For example, the Australian National University's Human Resources Division (2003) recommends the use of windows and skylights in workplace design. Apparently, humans have a basic psychological need to know what is going on outside, and a little understood but pervasive biological need for natural light, which increases alertness. A research study by the Heschong Mahone Group demonstrated that test scores were 26 percent higher for college students studying in a building with windows compared with students studying in windowless spaces, and that sales were 40 percent higher in stores with skylights than in windowless stores (Libby, 2003). These results demonstrate what we know from our own experiences: people seek windows, natural light, and outside views.

Color

According to Shultz and Schultz (2002), no empirical evidence exists to support the claims that certain colors increase productivity, reduce accidents, or raise morale. However, color may be used successfully in the workplace to

- Act as a coding device; for example, red for danger
- Prevent eyestrain, due to reflective properties of different colors
- Give the impression of greater space and openness
- Influence perception of temperature; blue and green equal cool; yellow and red equal warm
- Give employees a morale boost through repainting a dingy area

Music

Many employees prefer to listen to music as they work and believe it makes them more productive. Schultz and Schultz (2002) say that research supports the idea that music in the workplace can effect a slight increase in productivity for jobs that are relatively simple and repetitive, but not for more complex types of work. These results seem logical when you consider that music can have either relaxing or arousing effects. When tasks are monotonous, psychological arousal is welcome; but for tasks that require steady concentration, either no music or music that relaxes may be helpful. To complicate the issue, people have a wide variety of musical tastes, and what one person finds relaxing may annoy another person. High-screeners may experience music differently than low-screeners. The Workplace Doctors (2004) summarize research showing mixed results: one study supports the positive effects of music for all types of work; others demonstrate positive effects only when the listener is able to choose the music.

Given the variety of worker preferences and task requirements, one practical suggestion is to allow employees to wear earphones and listen to music of their choice. If safety is a concern, or if job tasks require monitoring sounds in the environment such as ringing phones, then consider the use of single earphones.

Spaces That Facilitate Collaboration

Cantrell (2001) describes several concepts in space design currently in use by leading companies to encourage collaboration, creativity, and productivity:

- Open spaces that encourage informal and unplanned communication: lounges, outdoor patios and walking areas, wide stairwells and escalators, kitchens, and coffee bars.

- Spaces designed specifically to accommodate meetings of global teams, including state-of-the-art teleconferencing facilities.

- Activity-based work settings that provide choices: small private offices, group offices, brainstorming areas, presentation areas, and library areas to be used as needed.

- Walls, furniture, and equipment that can easily be moved and rearranged as needed for specific group or team activities and can be customized based on the type of work performed.

- Smaller, decentralized facilities that house between eight and thirty-five employees, with the goal of fostering entrepreneurial spirit and team identity.

- Dedicated team areas that permit personalization and storage of the team's working documents and artifacts, thus supporting team identity and morale.

- Seating arrangements placing people together according to personality rather than function to increase morale; or seating people from multiple functions together, such as engineering and marketing, to increase communication and reduce time to market.

Building Location

The workplace location can have major effects on job satisfaction and loyalty to the employer. These results, in turn, often affect attendance, turnover, commitment to work goals, and ultimately performance. For example, some employees prefer urban workplaces because they are close to restaurants, shops, public transportation, and cultural resources. For those who live in the city, commutes are minimized. Suburban dwellers often prefer a suburban work location, because it requires less commuting and can be more relaxed. If economically feasible, employers should consider the types of workers they want to attract and locate accordingly. If longer commutes are the rule, then employers can diminish dissatisfaction by subsidizing commuting costs and facilitating car and van pools. A worker who arrives at work already tired from a long commute is less likely to begin the day at peak performance.

Cantrell (2001) points out that some companies locate in certain cities, regions, or countries to increase the interaction of employees with people and ideas outside the walls of the organization. For example, high-technology firms gain cutting-edge sharpness by locating in Silicon Valley, and automakers identify trends by locating in New York and London.

Indoor Air Quality

The U.S. Environmental Protection Agency cautions that indoor air may carry many times more harmful pollutants than outdoor air. In a work environment, sources of pollutants include the following:

- Mold and mildew resulting from dampness
- Bacteria transmitted through air conditioning and ventilation ducts
- Chemicals from carpets, upholstery, and draperies
- Solvents, adhesives, paint, insulation, and other materials used during building construction and maintenance
- Cleaning products that people bring from home
- Emissions from trucks at loading docks
- Cigarette smoke from outdoor smoking areas
- Microwaves and other emissions from kitchen and office equipment
- Chemicals that people use to do their work, such as radiation for medical technicians, lead for painters, and arsenic for chemical plant workers

These and many other pollutants become more dangerous when buildings have insufficient supplies of outside air. Where energy-saving measures have made buildings tighter, these pollutants have more opportunity to build up and cause harm. Solutions include use of environmentally friendlier building and furnishing materials and cleaning supplies, as well as greater ventilation. U.S. government regulations require that all office buildings exchange 100 percent of interior air volume every ten hours. In addition, modern office environments have carbon dioxide sensors in the return air stream and adjust and increase fresh air intake as the day goes on (Ramon Venero, personal communication, December 15, 2004). Indoor air quality (IAQ) should therefore not be a problem if government regulations are followed and buildings are managed by competent facilities managers with expert HVAC contractors. Elsewhere, performance technologists may need to raise the issue of possible IAQ problems if people are complaining or getting sick.

The Home Office

According to a U.S. Bureau of Labor Statistics study (2002), about twenty million people in the United States worked at home at least one day per week in 2001. About half of these individuals were salaried workers who also had offices at work but who work, on average, seven hours per week at home due to the nature of their jobs or to catch up. About 17 percent are directed by their employers specifically to work at home, and 30 percent are self-employed. Recruiting and retention advantages, reduced absenteeism and turnover, reduced costs for office space, and increased worker productivity and satisfaction are all reasons why employers support working at home. Employees like working at home because it eliminates or reduces commuting time, cuts their costs associated with commuting, reduces air pollution, enables them to concentrate and be more productive, and allows them to enjoy increased personal and family time. Technology makes it all possible.

Employers and home-based workers do not always recognize that all of the requirements of ergonomic office space apply at home. One employee of a large multinational company was assigned to work at home full time after many years in the office. This individual set up his computer and other office equipment on a folding table without a keyboard tray and sat on a folding chair. His home office was in the basement, away from family distractions, but it lacked proper lighting. Weeks elapsed before the local telephone company finally installed properly his high-speed Internet service and an additional line for faxing. To avoid situations like this one, employers should provide guidance and support for setting up home-based offices. Some employers conduct yearly visits to ensure that supportive work environments exist in their employees' homes. Home-based workers should also be proactive in setting up ergonomically sound offices (Goldstein, 2004). Performance technologists could play a role in setting and enforcing standards, creating job aids, and educating employees who are assigned or allowed to work at home.

HOW?: WORKING SMARTER ERGONOMICALLY

How people work involves selecting the best tools, using them properly, and employing recommended ergonomic practices while performing tasks. Performance technologists can play a role in selecting tools that are worker friendly, devising solutions such as job aids and training when tools are not as user friendly as they should be, and educating workers about ergonomic practices such as posture and breaks.

Ergonomically Designed Tools

Tools vary greatly, from simple hand tools such as screwdrivers to heavy equipment such as bulldozers to electronic equipment such as control panels and laptop computers. In all cases, the human interface with the tool should be considered in its design and use. Industrial organizations and equipment manufacturers typically employ ergonomic experts to help design tools and equipment. In office environments, tools consist primarily of computer hardware and software.

Hand Tools and Machinery. Engineering psychologists have for many years considered the design of hand tools and machines to be an important part of workplace design. The user should be able to use the tool while maintaining a neutral wrist position, and without flexing or deviating the wrists. Ergonomically designed tools decrease the incidence of wrist injuries, reduce muscle fatigue, and lessen workers' feelings of discomfort (Ostrom, 1993).

Computer Hardware. A survey conducted by a market research company for Microsoft Hardware (2004) found that the U.S. workforce is spending more time using computers than ever. Nearly half of the respondents who use computers said they spend eight or more hours per day at the computer. Nine out of ten respondents said the design of their workstation directly affects their productivity. Earlier researchers found that individual performance is 25 percent higher when employees use ergonomically designed workstations (Pheasant, 1991).

People who spend much time in front of a computer screen often complain about eyestrain. Researchers believe that the following factors may affect eyestrain for computer users:

- Size of the screen
- Degree of flicker
- Rate at which characters are generated
- Illumination and glare in the workspace

Thus, bigger screens with higher-quality displays and proper illumination in the workspace are keys to effective workstations.

Computer Software. Software designed with usability in mind can greatly enhance productivity, reduce training costs and time when learning new software, and reduce untold frustration among computer users. Principles of people-friendly software design are the subject of ongoing research. Ben Shneiderman, a leading researcher in human-computer interaction, gives principles and practices for effective design of direct-manipulation systems such as spreadsheets, virtual environments, menus, forms, dialogue boxes, programming languages, natural-language computing, interaction devices such as keyboards and pointing devices, error messages, displays, on-line help, tutorials, multiple-window strategies, synchronous and asynchronous cooperative work systems, Website design, and many other features of human-computer interactive systems. Underlying design principles include his "Eight Golden Rules of Interface Design" (Shneiderman, 1998, pp. 74–75):

1. *Strive for consistency.* This principle applies to required action sequences, terminology, color, layout, capitalization, fonts, and so forth. Consistency minimizes user confusion.

2. *Enable frequent users to use shortcuts.* Special keys, abbreviations, and macros are common means to achieve shortcuts. Frequent users also like short response times and fast display rates.

3. *Offer informative feedback.* Users want the computer to acknowledge their input. The feedback should be minor for small, frequent actions and more substantial for major actions.

4. *Design dialogues to yield closure.* Feedback should inform users that they have completed a group of actions; this frees them to move on to the next group of actions.

5. *Offer error prevention and simple error handling.* The interface should make it easy for a user to submit error-free information—for example, a menu versus a fill-in. If the user makes a mistake, the system should offer simple, specific instructions for recovery.

6. *Permit easy reversal of actions.* Users are less anxious if they know their errors can be undone.

7. *Support internal locus of control.* Users, especially experienced ones, want to be in control of the system and have it respond to their actions; users primarily should initiate actions rather than respond to the system's actions.

8. *Reduce short-term memory load.* The magic number seven plus or minus two is the limited number of chunks of information a person can hold in working memory (Miller, 1956). Keep displays, codes, and sequences as simple as possible, with on-line access available to information that may be forgotten.

As human performance technologists, we can encourage the design or selection of software that, to the extent possible, meets the criteria for effective human interface design. Failing that, we can develop training or job aids to compensate for the less than perfectly designed software system.

Ergonomically Designed Information

Information used by the performer, including printed job aids, electronic help screens, instruction sheets, reference manuals, reports, forms, search findings, and even books, should be ergonomically designed, that is, designed for ease of use by the intended performer. Performance technologists frequently design such information.

Rossett and Gautier-Downes (1991) give excellent and detailed advice on the design of job aids. The type of job aid chosen, its structure, wording, illustrations, packaging, and placement are all critical to ensure that the job aid is effective and efficient.

Systems such as Information Mapping (Horn, with Nicol, Kleinman, and Grace, 1969) give helpful ways to analyze, organize, and present information in documents, both print and electronic. Use of special formatting, layout on the page, headings, illustrations, and marginal cues provide better reading comprehension, efficiency in learning, and faster retrieval of information from a document. Jonassen (1985) and Hartley (1985) present research-based principles for designing user-friendly text. For example, pages should end when thoughts end, rather than after a certain number of lines; ragged right margins provide easier comprehension than right-justified text. Tufte (2001) illustrates principles of information design, including the visual display of quantitative information for readability, comprehension, and the effective communication of ideas.

Educating Workers

Human performance technologists can contribute strongly to ergonomic practices in the workplace by helping workers change their own behavior. Job aids and training can help workers in the following areas:

- *Use their ergonomic furniture properly.* Adjustable furniture provides its intended benefits only when employees know how to use it. Workers should be able to adjust their furniture to achieve proper alignment.

- *Use proper body posture.* Back and wrist injuries can often be avoided through good working posture. People need to understand the reasons for recommended posture and the risks of poor posture. They may also need periodic reminders to establish good habits.

- *Use frequent breaks and stretches.* Computer users should look away from their screens every ten minutes, focusing their eyes on something farther away. They should get up and walk around every thirty minutes. Stretches, some of which can be done sitting at the workstation, can help alleviate back, neck, and shoulder strain. Other stretches require getting up but can be done in the cubicle or office. A wall chart of diagrams showing recommended stretches is a good reminder.

WHEN?: WORK SCHEDULES

Worker health, morale, and performance can be affected not only by where and how they work but also when. Performance technologists may consult on the establishment of work schedules or may recommend changes when performance analyses uncover possible ill effects of existing work schedules. Alternative work schedules, shift work, and twenty-four-hour operations are trends with potential performance benefits and pitfalls.

Alternative Work Schedules

Flexible working hours, often known as flextime, is a popular alternative work schedule now offered by most U.S. employers. Typically, employees must be present during specific core hours, such as 10:00 A.M. to 2:00 P.M., but they may, with supervisory approval, set their own starting and stopping times while still working the required number of hours per day. The research findings on flextime are generally positive, with no serious negative affects on satisfaction, productivity, absence, or turnover reported as yet (Muchinsky, 2000). The positive effects include easier travel and parking; less role conflict, especially for parents with children at home; and greater feelings of control in the workplace.

Another alternative work schedule is the compressed work week. Instead of working eight hours a day, five days a week, employees on a compressed schedule may work ten hours a day, four days a week. Coleman (1995) recommends avoiding the three-day weekend, opting instead for something like one day off, two days on, two days off, two days on each week. According to Coleman, this approach helps avoid burnout and actually improves performance and productivity of workers. A slightly less compressed version gives the employee a total of five days off during every two-week period. A more compressed schedule has employees, typically police officers and nurses, working twelve-hour shifts, typically midnight to noon or noon to midnight. Fatigue, with the potential for more errors and accidents and lower productivity, is a risk with compressed schedules. This risk must be balanced against the demands of the business and the potential positive effects on employee attitudes resulting from reduced commuting time and larger blocks of time off. Research results are mixed, and researchers caution that the success of compressed schedules depends upon the type of organization and the people in it (Muchinsky, 2000).

Shift Work

Shift work means working hours other than the standard 8:00 A.M. to 5:00 P.M. For example, swing shift, 4:00 P.M. to midnight, or night shift, 11:00 P.M. to 7:00 A.M. Shift work is necessary when an organization provides services or produces goods around the clock. Sometimes shift work requires a worker to rotate among more than one shift, such as two weeks on day shift, two weeks on swing shift, and two weeks on night shift. Theirry and Meijman (1994) found that shift work has several aversive affects on workers, and some shift-work patterns have more negative affects than others. Physical and psychological symptoms such as sleeping problems, digestive system disorders, fatigue, feelings of overload, and nervousness may result. In addition, workers have family and social problems because they are often unable to assume normal partner and parenting roles in the family or to participate in community and social activities as they would like. Because shift work can have such a major impact on workers' physical and mental health, morale, and productivity, psychologists conduct research to determine which individuals may tolerate shift work more readily (Muchinsky, 2000). For example, Akerstedt (1990) found that older workers and those with natural morning personalities have more difficulty than others adjusting to shift work.

The Demise of the Forty-Hour Week: The Rise of 24 × 7

Almost no one in the United States works what used to be the standard forty-hour work week: eight hours per day, five days per week (Bonné, 2004). The average U.S. worker puts in forty-six hours per week, according to a National Sleep Foundation study (2001), and 38 percent work more than fifty hours per week. Some of this work is done at home, on weekends, during travel, and even on vacation. Although survey findings vary, most studies agree that either U.S. workers are working longer hours, or they *perceive* that they are. Several factors have contributed to this phenomenon:

- Downsizing of organizations, with the result that each worker must do more

- Rise of productivity; the average worker actually does more

- Globalization of organizational responsibilities, with colleagues and clients spread across several time zones

- Growing expectations by customers that services will be available twenty-four hours per day, seven days per week

- Increasing use of technology, including Internet resources, e-mail, laptop computers, cell phones, and fax machines, making work available anytime, anywhere

- Greater acceptance of flextime, with workers setting their own hours and teleworking from home offices. Often there is no definite quitting time

- Increased number of in dual-career couples, with the resulting crunch at home with household chores and children. This situation leads to the *perception* of longer working hours

Potential effects include workaholism and burnout, neglect of family roles and responsibilities, health problems, and declines in productivity.

WHY?: POTENTIAL BENEFITS OF WORKPLACE DESIGN

As we have seen in previous sections, competent workplace design can benefit both workers and employers because ergonomic factors have an impact on morale, health, performance, and the bottom line. Human performance technologists can play a significant role by raising awareness, identifying workplace-related barriers to optimum performance, consulting with experts, and recommending practical solutions.

Benefits for Workers

Attention to workplace design, sometimes even with minor and inexpensive improvements in the work environment, can bring significant improvement in these important areas:

- Comfort
- Convenience
- Safety
- Health
- Productivity
- Job satisfaction
- Morale

If changes are made by management or consultants, workers feel that the organization cares about them. If workers themselves are involved in the analysis, design, and implementation of ergonomic features, they also gain a sense of empowerment. Working together on ergonomic planning projects may also increase team spirit, trust, communication, and loyalty in the organization. Physical improvements, when accompanied by psychological and social boost engendered by the initiatives, work together to heighten productivity and job satisfaction.

Benefits for Employers

The benefits experienced by their employees are, of course, benefits to employers as well. In addition, employers stand to benefit in a number of other ways. Whether as a direct result of the ergonomic changes or indirectly as morale and satisfaction increase, workplace design or improvements may benefit employers in the following ways:

- Improved quality of products and services
- Increased revenue
- Shortened cycle time
- Greater customer satisfaction
- Reduced health care costs
- Compliance with government regulations
- Fewer workers' compensation claims
- Reduced liability
- Reduced absenteeism and turnover
- Savings in recruitment and training costs

- Savings in direct labor costs
- Reduced waste and scrap
- Enhanced reputation as an employer

Everyone wins and no one loses when workplace design is taken seriously, approached systematically, and based on research-based principles of ergonomics.

SUCCESS STORIES

Humantech, Inc., the largest U.S. workplace ergonomics consulting firm, supplies many human performance ergonomics success stories that illustrate actual benefits to employers and employees. Visit their company Website to explore how ergonomic solutions brought about the following quantifiable, and usually quite dramatic, benefits to Humantech's client organizations (Humantech, 2004):

- Increased revenue; for example, Verizon
- Increased throughput or yield; for example, Lucent and TRW
- Shortened cycle time; for example, Textron and Honeywell
- Increased productivity; for example, Ligon Brothers
- Improved quality; for example, Corning
- Cost avoidance; for example, Corning
- Reduced injuries and accidents; for example, Corning and TRW
- Reduced absenteeism; for example, Verizon
- Savings in worker's compensation costs; for example, Verizon and Honeywell
- Lowered rates of musculoskeletal disorder; for example, Verizon and Textron
- Savings in direct labor costs; for example, Textron
- Reduced scrap; for example, Honeywell

References

Akerstedt, T. (1990). *Psychological and psychophysiological effects of shift work.* Retrieved June 1, 2005, from www.ncbi.nlm.nih.gov/entrez/query.fcgi?cmd – Retrieve&db = pubmed&dopt = Abstract&list_uids = 2189223&query_hl = 1.

Anderson, J. R. (1980). *Cognitive psychology and its implications.* San Francisco: Freeman.

Australian National University, Human Resources Division. (2003). *Natural lighting in the workplace.* Retrieved June 1, 2005, from http://info.anu.edu.au/hr/OHS/Hazard_Alerts/_Natural_Lighting_in_Workplace.asp.

Bonné, J. (2004). *Are we done with the 40-hour week?* Retrieved June 1, 2005, from www.msnbc.msn.com/id/3072426.

Cantrell, S. (2001). *Choices in workplace design for high-end knowledge work.* Retrieved June 1, 2005, from www.smarttech.com/facilitydesign/feature.asp.

Center for the Built Environment. (2003). *Speech privacy in offices.* Retrieved June 1, 2005, from www.cbe.berkeley.edu/research/acoustics.htm.

Coleman, R. M. (1995). *The 24 hour business: Maximizing productivity through round-the-clock operation.* New York: American Management Association.

DeMarco, T., and Lister, T. (1997). *Peopleware: Productive projects and teams.* New York: Dorset House.

Fox, C. (2004). *The impact of the office environment on productivity.* Retrieved June 1, 2005, from www.chrisfoxinc.com/OfficeEnvironmentAndProductivity.htm.

Gilbert, T. F. (1978). *Human competence: Engineering worthy performance.* New York: McGraw-Hill.

Gilbert, T. F. (1982). A question of performance. Part 1: The probe model. *Training and Development Journal, 36* (4), 21–29.

Glen, P. (2003). Leading geeks: How to manage and lead people who deliver technology. San Francisco: Jossey-Bass.

Goldstein, R. (2004). *Home office ergonomics.* Retrieved June 1, 2005, from www.allfreelancework.com/articleho3ergonomics.php.

Hackman, J. R., and Oldham, G. R. (1976). Motivation through the design of work: Test of a theory. *Organizational Behavior and Human Performance, 16,* 250–279.

Hartley, J. (1985). *Designing instructional text.* New York: Nichols.

Horn, R. E., with Nicol, E., Kleinman, J., and Grace, M. (1969). *Information mapping for learning and reference.* Cambridge: I.R.I. Horn, R.E. (A.F. Systems Command Report ESD-TR-69–296).

Humantech, Inc. (2004). *Client results and case studies.* Retrieved June 1, 2005, from www.humantech.com/Level2/publications_resourses/client_results.htm.

Jonassen, D. (Ed). (1985). *The technology of text: Principles for structuring, designing, and displaying text.* Englewood Cliffs, NJ: Educational Technology Publications.

Kearny, L., and Smith, P. (1999). Workplace design for creative thinking. In Stolovitch, H. D. and Keeps, E. J. (Eds.), *Handbook of human performance technology: Improving individual and organizational performance worldwide* (2nd ed.). San Francisco: Jossey-Bass/Pfeiffer.

Libby, B. (2003, June 17). Beyond the bulbs: In praise of natural light. *New York Times.* Retrieved October 31, 2005, from http://query.nytimes.com/gst/health/article-page.html?res = 9C06E3DF1238F934A25755C0A9659C8B63.

Mehrabian, A. (1976). *Public places and private spaces.* New York: Basic Books.

Microsoft Hardware. (2004). *Nine out of 10 employees link workspace design to their productivity.* Retrieved June 1, 2005, from www.dezignare.com/whatshot/2004june/28.ergonomics.html.

Miller, G. A. (1956). The magical number seven, plus or minus two: Some limits on our capacity for processing information. *Psychological Review, 63*(2), 81–89.

Muchinsky, P. M. (2000). *Psychology applied to work.* Belmont, CA: Wadsworth/Thomson Learning.

National Sleep Foundation. (2001). How long is the average work week in the U.S.? Retrieved June 1, 2005, from www.libraryspot.com/know/workweek.htm.

Noweir, M. H. (1984). Noise exposure as related to productivity, disciplinary actions, absenteeism, and accidents among textile workers. *Journal of Safety Research, 15,* 163–174.

O'Donnell, R. D., and Eggemeier, F. T. (1986). Workload assessment methodology. In K. R. Roff, I. Kaufman, and J. P. Thomas (Eds.), *Handbook of perception and human performance,* Vol. 2. New York: Wiley.

Oseland, N. (2001, October). To what extent does workplace design and management affect productivity? Presented at the 2001 British Institute of Facilities Management annual conference.

Ostrom, L. T. (1993). *Creating the ergonomically sound workplace.* San Francisco: Jossey-Bass.

Pheasant, S. (1991). *Ergonomics, work and health.* London, UK: Macmillan.

Rossett, A., and Gautier-Downes, J. (1991). *A handbook of job aids.* San Diego: Pfeiffer.

Schultz, D., and Schultz, S. E. (2002). *Psychology and work today.* Upper Saddle River, NJ: Prentice-Hall.

Shneiderman, B. (1998). *Designing the user interface: Strategies for effective human-computer interaction.* Reading, MA: Addison-Wesley.

Smith, P., and Kearny, L. (1994). *Creating workplaces where people can think.* San Francisco: Jossey-Bass.

Thierry, H., and Meijman, T. (1994). Time and behavior at work. In H. C. Triandis, M. D. Dunnette, and L. M. Hough (Eds.), *Handbook of industrial and organizational psychology,* Vol. 4 (2nd ed., pp. 341–413). Palo Alto, CA: Consulting Psychologists Press.

Tufte, E. R. (2001). *Visual display of quantitative information.* Cheshire, CT: Graphics Press.

U.S. Bureau of Labor Statistics. (2002). *Work at home in 2001.* Retrieved June 1, 2005, from www.bls.gov/news.release/homey.nr0.htm.

Workplace Doctors, The. (2004). *What type of music is best for the workplace?* Retrieved June 1, 2005, from www.west2k.com/wpdocs/q71.htm.

CHAPTER TWENTY-NINE

Six Sigma

Increasing Human Performance Technology Value and Results

Darlene M. Van Tiem, Joan C. Dessinger,
James L. Moseley

Envision Six Sigma as a single-lane brick road, with productivity and profitability as the final destination. In turn, picture human performance technology (HPT) as a multiple-lane thoroughfare with improved performance at the end of the journey. Now, shut your eyes tight, and voilà! Both roads blend into one yellow-brick superhighway. Got the picture? Good! Join us as we take a journey along these roads to illustrate how blending Six Sigma and HPT can help organizations improve their bottom line.

This chapter will travel the Six Sigma and HPT roads and focus on the applications of both Six Sigma and HPT. The chapter will suggest that blending Six Sigma and HPT can facilitate the ultimate goals of performance improvement, productivity, and profitability at the end of each destination or project. Along the way the similarities and differences between HPT and Six Sigma theory and practice will be visited. The journeys along the Six Sigma and HPT routes will be outlined to provide a view of how these roads sometimes flow well together and sometimes diverge and then converge again. For example:

- It is straight ahead for both roads when it comes to business-centric thinking, but the HPT lanes welcome hitchhikers, all levels of the workforce within the organization, while the Six Sigma lane starts and stops with senior management.

- HPT moves up the hill to view the forest, that is, takes a holistic approach to problem solving, while Six Sigma is likely to take side roads through the forest to analyze the trees.

- There are many forks on the yellow-brick highway during the portion of the journey that involves data-gathering or decision-making activities for Six Sigma and HPT.

- Six Sigma focuses on external customer service requirements, while HPT in its travel along varying lanes may address internal customers—that is, personnel within the organization—as well as external customers.

SIX SIGMA BACKGROUND

Motorola first developed the Six Sigma philosophy and practice in the early 1980s, when the company realized that products produced correctly the first time rarely failed in customer use. Motorola developed strategies and systems to virtually eliminate defects and trademarked Six Sigma. However, Motorola did not enforce the trademark, so Six Sigma is used today by many companies. As a result of Motorola's efforts, the company was among the first organizations to win the Malcolm Baldrige National Quality Award. The Baldrige Award is one of three coveted global-quality awards focused on U.S. manufacturing, service, and small business. The award is presented annually by the U.S. president to organizations that "enhance the competitiveness, quality, and productivity of U.S. organizations for the benefit of all residents" (National Institute of Standards and Technology, 2004).

In the mid-1980s, Asea Brown Boveri, Allied Signal, Kodak, IBM, and Texas Instruments founded the Six Sigma Institute, which extended the application and commercialization of Six Sigma. Jack Welsh, former CEO of General Electric, also publicized GE's accomplishments and advances using Six Sigma. For those unfamiliar with the technical meaning of the term Six Sigma, it is a *data-driven* methodology for eliminating defects that seeks to drive manufacturing and service efforts so that there are six standard deviations between the mean and the nearest specification limit in any process.

SIX SIGMA AS A PHILOSOPHY AND A PRACTICE

Six Sigma is both a philosophy and a practice. Six Sigma values the improvement of business and organizational processes and also provides "a methodology that an organization uses to ensure that it is improving its key processes" (Brassard, Finn, Ginn, and Ritter, 2002, p. 1).

Philosophy

As a philosophy, Six Sigma focuses on continuous quality improvement as viewed through the eyes of the customer. It provides a shared mental framework and common language for the workforce to achieve business excellence and high profitability (Jing and Li, 2004). "Creativity and individualism take a back seat to ensuring that each process step is in control and capable" (Elliott, 2003, p. 30). In other words, each process continuously provides outstanding outcomes and is capable of sustaining outstanding results.

Practice

As a practice, Six Sigma is a performance-improvement intervention that focuses on reducing the variation in product or service quality. The goal of Six Sigma is to produce product or service at a 99.999 percent perfection level (Van Tiem, Moseley, and Dessinger, 2001). Statistical measurement and analysis are at the core of Six Sigma, along with precise problem solving and decision making. "Less than four unsatisfactory customer experiences in one million opportunities" is the goal Six Sigma seeks (Eckes, 2003, p. 1). This rate is based on customer requirements or specifications, and sound measurement techniques (Van Tiem, Moseley, and Dessinger, 2001). As an improvement approach, Six Sigma is also a human performance technology intervention used as a solution to challenging quality-related problems.

BENEFITS OF SIX SIGMA

In a *Quality Digest* survey, a majority of the respondents who implemented Six Sigma equated the use of Six Sigma with "success" and felt that training was the key to successful Six Sigma implementation (Dusharme, 2003). Products and services provided by organizations using Six Sigma improve dramatically, resulting in less waste or scrap and rework, which in turn leads to lower costs. Products or services perform better and last longer. Customers are happier and more likely to remain loyal. Organizations gain measurable ways to track performance improvement and identify processes that are working well. Organizations using Six Sigma also focus on managing processes at all organizational levels, linking senior executives' priorities to operations and the front line in a team-based, collaborative approach. Improvement in customer relationships also results from actively addressing customer needs based on customer feedback concerning product or service defects and concerns. Six Sigma aligns efficiency and effectiveness with such customer needs, resulting in increased stockholder and customer satisfaction.

Six Sigma is popular precisely because it "delivers measurable, tangible economic benefits" (Brisgaard and Freisleben, 2004, p. 57). For example, Ford Motor Company initiated Six Sigma worldwide in early 2000, resulting in an impressive economic advantage of over $1 billion by 2004. Ford's first priority was to improve customer satisfaction, rather than cost cutting. In the first three years, Ford saved approximately $675 million globally, with half coming in 2002. By 2003, Ford had doubled the 2002 cost reduction by mid-year (over $300 million), primarily through improvements to business functions (Holtz and Campbell, 2004).

Six Sigma is becoming the de facto standard as a systematic practice to enforce process standardization and improve quality. "Increasing customer sophistication and the constant demand for improved product quality are changing the rules for sustaining and growing profitability for manufacturers. Global competition, fierce price wars, and eroding brand loyalty are exerting pressure on virtually every business function and process . . ." (Ramakumar and Cooper, 2004, p. 42).

BARRIERS TO IMPLEMENTING SIX SIGMA

Of course, there are barriers to using Six Sigma. Six Sigma can stretch an organization's three basic resources, time, money, and people, by increasing the cost to analyze, measure, and track product or service output and problem-solve further improvements. In addition, complete and total commitment from top management is essential to success because of the exacting nature of Six Sigma.

Small companies often perceive Six Sigma as a privilege affordable only to Fortune 500 + organizations. As *Quality Digest* reports, "it takes money [and] dedicated people-power" to implement Six Sigma (Dusharme, 2003, p. 30). This may be one of the reasons why there are rumors that Six Sigma is "on the wane" and why the Six Sigma hall of fame includes only large companies such as Dell, Dow, Ford, GE, Motorola, and W. R. Grace (Dusharme, 2003, p. 30). On the flip side, Pruitt, Van Tiem, and Doyle (2002) report that a small, 478-bed medical center in Kentucky saved over one million dollars when they implemented Six Sigma processes and tools.

SIX SIGMA TECHNIQUES

There are three basic techniques or methodologies that are used to implement the Six Sigma process. Each technique is an acronym for the steps that occur during its implementation, and each technique has a slightly different focus:

1. DMAIC is an acronym for Define, Measure, Analyze, Improve, and Control. DMAIC is the most common Six Sigma technique and is used to analyze and improve the quality of an *existing* program, process,

product, or service, such as manufacturing an automobile or repairing a computer.

2. DMADV stands for Define, Measure, Analyze, Design, and Validate. It is a variation of DMAIC that is used to create a *new* or completely *redesigned* program, process, product, or service based on customer requirements, such as an environmentally friendly refrigerator or a healthy hamburger. In DMADV, the improvement team defines the factors that the customer feels are critical to quality (CTQ) and then designs a program, process, product or service to satisfy the identified CTQs (Brassard, Finn, Ginn, and Ritter, 2002, p. 10).

3. DMEDI means Define, Measure, Explore, Develop, and Implement. DMEDI is a variation of DMADV that focuses on *exploring other options,* alternatives, risk factors, what-if scenarios, and so forth before development and implementation, such as creating a heat shield for outer space travel.

SIX SIGMA AND THE ISPI HPT MODEL

To understand how HPT practitioners can benefit from using the Six Sigma philosophy and techniques, a clear understanding of the International Society of Performance Improvement (ISPI) HPT Model is essential (Van Tiem, Moseley, and Dessinger, 2004) (see Figure 29.1). The model portrays HPT as a comprehensive, systematic, problem-solving approach to performance improvement that includes analysis, intervention selection and design, intervention implementation and change, and evaluation. The model also shows that HPT is systemic, analyzing the organization, environment, work, and worker to discover the root of a problem. HPT incorporates many disciplines and methodologies to deliver interventions such as communication, job design, coaching, compensation, culture, fiscal planning, balanced scorecards, and so on. The overall purpose is to move the organization in a positive way and resolve complex performance problems.

Table 29.1 indicates how the process steps within each of the three Six Sigma techniques parallel the four process steps of the ISPI HPT Model. Table 29.2 illustrates the similarities between DMAIC and the HPT process activities. DMAIC is used here because both DMAIC and HPT focus on improving an existing program, process, product, or service. The major difference is the emphasis of DMAIC on improving quality and the emphasis of HPT on improving human performance. Notice that there are elements in the DMAIC process that fit into more than one step of the HPT process.

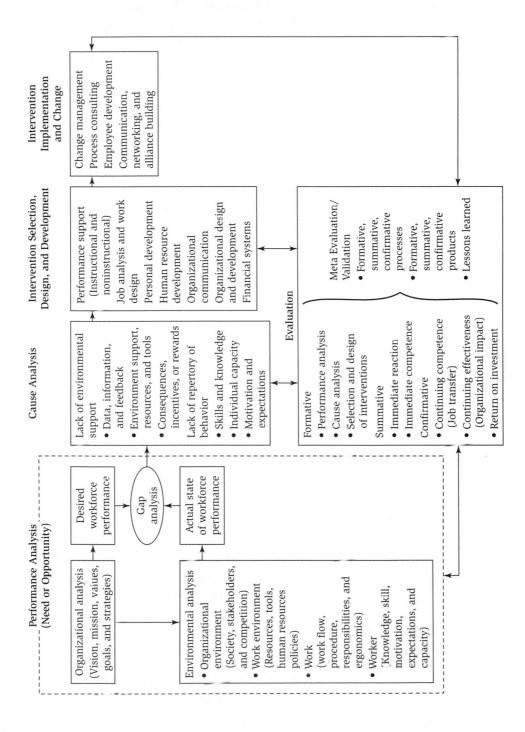

Figure 29.1. Human Performance Technology Model.

Table 29.1. Human Performance Technology and Six Sigma:
Parallel Constructions.

ISPI HPT Model	Six Sigma Process Steps
Analysis: Performance, gap, and cause	Analyze
	Define
	Measure
	Explore
Intervention selection, design, and development	Design
	Improve
	Explore
Intervention implementation and change	Implement
	Improve
Evaluation	Measure
	Control

Source: Joan Conway Dessinger, The Lake Group, 2004. Used with permission.

Table 29.2. Human Performance Technology and DMAIC Process Activities.

HPT	DMAIC
Analysis of Performance, Gap, and Cause • Analyze the organization's vision, mission, values, goals, strategies, and so on to determine the desired performance • Analyze the environment: the organizational environment, the work environment, the work, and the worker, and determine the actual performance • Conduct a gap analysis of desired versus actual performance • Conduct a cause analysis to determine the cause of the gap if one exists	Define • Define the purpose and scope of the program or product • Map and understand the process • Collect and understand customer needs and requirements Measure • Gather baseline data to provide a clear focus on the current situation • Determine the extent of the quality problem and the deviation from customer needs or requirements Analyze • Identify the cause of the quality defects • Confirm with data: cause and effect analysis

(Continued)

Table 29.2. (*Continued*)

HPT	DMAIC
Intervention Selection, Design, and Development • Select the most appropriate performance-improvement intervention(s) (performance support, work design, personal development, and so forth) • Design or develop the processes and materials required to implement the intervention	Improve • Create possible solutions for the root causes of the quality defect • Select the most appropriate solutions • Develop the processes or materials required to implement the solution
Intervention Implementation and Change • Use appropriate change-management techniques to implement intervention • Use process-consulting techniques • Focus on employee-development issues • Use communication, networking, and alliance building to support implementation efforts	Improve • Implement the solutions • Follow PDCA: Plan-Do-Check-Act Control • Maintain the solution: standardize and institutionalize • Collect and act on lessons learned • Plan for continuous improvement
Evaluation • Conduct formative evaluation of HPT analysis, and selection, design, and development processes • Conduct summative evaluation of the immediate performance-improvement outputs and outcomes • Conduct confirmative evaluation of long-term outputs and outcomes • Conduct meta evaluation to judge the "goodness" of the evaluation efforts • Communicate results and make recommendations for improvement	Improve • Pilot (PDCA) the solutions • Measure the results • Evaluate the benefits Control • Monitor performance • Create a process for updating procedures if necessary • Summarize and communicate lessons learned • Make recommendations for future quality-improvement efforts

Source: Joan Conway Dessinger, The Lake Group, 2004. Used with permission.

A SIX SIGMA TOOLBOX FOR THE HPT PRACTITIONER

Six Sigma is, in itself, a management tool that helps executives "set corporate objectives based on customer requirements and financial targets (Pruitt, Van Tiem, and Doyle, 2002). Six Sigma also relies on analysis, measurement, and other tools that are familiar to those involved in analysis, problem solving, performance improvement, or quality initiatives (Pande, Neuman, and Cavanagh, 2000).

The tools described in this section are similar to those in the Six Sigma toolbox provided to a DMAIC team by a major global manufacturer. The DMAIC team was charged with improving the quality of an existing product; however, the same tools would be useful for improving any program, process, or service. The toolbox in this chapter includes suggestions for when and how an HPT practitioner can use each Six Sigma tool to improve performance as well as quality.

These tools are used widely for Six Sigma and are not unique to any particular improvement situation. The toolbox is not exhaustive by any means; it simply reflects one large organization's approach to DMAIC. It allows the toolbox user to pick and choose from a variety of tools based on time, individual expertise, and the availability of the resources required to use the tools most effectively. For a more detailed description of Six Sigma tools, see Brassard, Finn, Ginn, and Ritter, 2002.

Tool: Benchmarking

Benchmarking is a continuous and systematic process for identifying, documenting, and evaluating best business, work, or industry practices before integrating them into an organization. Best practices are those methods, core competencies or strategic business capabilities, that help an organization to achieve superior performance and meet customer requirements. Benchmarking should include an action plan for integrating best practices.

HPT application: Use benchmarking when the purpose of the performance improvement intervention is to improve an organization's performance in the marketplace. Benchmarking helps you to get ideas from the experiences of other organizations.

Tool: Critical to Quality

Critical to Quality (CTQ) identifies the critical customer requirements (CCRs) for a program product, process, or service. CCRs may include cost, size, availability, and so forth, and should be quantifiable and measurable. If the program, process, product, or service meets or exceeds CCRs, it is perceived to be "quality."

HPT application: Use CTQ when customer satisfaction is an important component of the selection and design of a performance-improvement effort.

Tool: Design of Experiments

Design of Experiments (DOE) is a tool that facilitates selection of an experimental design to analyze multiple process variables and discover the one or more variables that affect quality and performance. For example, the variables that affect the success of a car dealership salesperson may include gender, experience, product knowledge, marketing and other organizational support, commission schedule, and so forth.

HPT application: Use DOE during cause analysis when you need to systematically or statistically determine which variables have an effect on performance.

Tool: Fault Tree Analysis

Fault Tree Analysis is a logical, structured, graphical tool that can help identify potential causes of system failure before the failure actually occurs. Fault trees are used for analyzing complex components and systems to determine potential errors in a design, predict reliability, assess effects and risks, and assess the probability of failure.

HPT application: Use Fault Tree Analysis during analysis and performance-intervention development to develop more reliable, maintainable programs, processes, products, or services and to determine the probability of design errors.

Tool: Failure Modes and Effects Analysis

Failure Modes and Effects Analysis (FMEA) is a systematic design or process-review technique that is used to find the weaknesses in designs *before* the design is created or implemented. The technique is an applied form of problem solving that focuses on how to anticipate and minimize the risk of failure.

HPT application: Use FMEA to create a new or redesign an existing process or product.

Tool: Multi-Generational (Product) Plan

The Multi-Generational (Product) Plan (MGP or MGPP) is a template that helps teams forecast up to three releases or generations of a product or service. MGP makes it possible to document and use current business competencies or lessons learned from one generation of a product or service to benefit the following generations.

HPT application: Use MGP or MGPP for defining and shaping a new program, process, product, or service concept that must survive through multiple generations.

Tool: Flowcharting

Flowcharting is used to graphically analyze, record, and communicate business process reengineering and total quality management (TQM) efforts. Flowcharting software provides the shapes, connectors, and so forth to develop professional flow charts. Micrografx Flowchart, also known as ABC Flowcharter, Flowcharter 7, and iGrafx Flowcharter 2000I, is Microsoft Office compatible and can import diagrams created in Microsoft's Visio. See also the following tool, Process Mapping.

HPT applications: Use Micrografx Flowchart or other flowcharting software to analyze and illustrate the flow of an existing process or plan the flow of a new process. It also allows users and stakeholders to become actively involved in design or redesign activities.

Tool: Process Mapping

Process Mapping uses flow charts, matrices, or a combination of graphics to identify and illustrate the main sequence of activities, discover and highlight bottlenecks and redundancies, eliminate unnecessary steps and nonvalue-added (NVA) activities, and clarify critical connections across individual operations and departments (Brue, 2002, pp. 115–116). Process Mapping helps designers and stakeholders to view the entire enterprise as a system of interrelated people, technology, and processes.

HPT applications: Use process mapping to identify and illustrate the flow of an existing process, redesign an existing process, or plan the flow of a new process. If carried out over an extended period of time, it helps to pinpoint areas for continuous improvement.

Tool: Modeling and Simulations

Modeling is used to set up and experiment with "what if . . ." scenarios in a risk-free environment before creating or changing an existing process or creating a new one. Arena and Aspen Custom Modeler are examples of process modeling and simulation software that help to evaluate a new or modified process, system, or operation.

SPAR is a software tool for performing reliability modeling. Reliability is the probability that a plant, system, process, or component will perform its intended function in a given environment for a defined period of time. Reliability modeling enables a decision maker to evaluate alternatives based on data rather than opinion. It also helps to establish measurements for the business case.

Simulations are interactive real-time or virtual computer-based reproductions of a process. Simulations conduct risk-free tests of a process design to determine flaws or optimum conditions early in the design process in order to pinpoint areas for improvement and test solutions over and over until they are right.

HPT applications: Use modeling or simulations when the performance-improvement intervention involves work or process design or redesign and the required time, expertise, and system resources are available. Modeling is useful when the performance-improvement initiative involves a complex system and reliability is a critical factor. Simulations are extremely useful when planning large-scale new processes; however, computer-based simulations take time and technical expertise to plan and execute. Plan to spend approximately 80 percent of the time finding and prioritizing the data and information, and 20 percent of the time building and executing the simulation and reporting the results.

Tool: Project Management

Project Management includes planning and maintenance activities. Project planning systematically determines what needs to be done, when it needs to be done, who should do it, and how it should be done. Project maintenance activities monitor and track the progress of the initial plan, troubleshoot and resolve problems, and ensure that deliverables are completed on time, within specifications, and within budget. There are a variety of tools available for project management, including project plan templates, GANTT charts, matrix diagrams, software such as Microsoft Project, and so forth (Martin and Tate, 1997).

HPT applications: Projects also drive HPT improvement efforts and use of project planning and maintenance tools are important for all performance-improvement efforts.

Tool: Quality Functional Deployment

Quality Functional Deployment (QFD) is a planning and decision-making tool that originated in Japan in 1972. The process is used to design, manufacture, and market products or services based on customer requirements. The basic design tool for QFD is the House of Quality, a graphical, conceptual map based on the needs of the customer. Four "rooms" record and show relationships among customer needs, product or service design requirements, targets and limits, and competition. There are software packages available for setting up the houses—for example, QFD Design and QFD Capture.

HPT applications: Use QFD support interventions that involve technology selection, process simplification, and risk assessment. QFD is useful when the team members prefer a hands-on graphical approach to intervention analysis, selection, and design.

Tool: Statistical Analysis

Statistical analysis methods are tests to identify and categorize variations, relate the variations to work environment, and determine whether the process or product can meet customer requirements. Some of the statistical methods and tests used for Six Sigma include classic statistical tests such as t-test, ANOVA (analysis of variance), correlation, and regression analysis. JMP and other computer software programs simplify the use of statistical methods. JMP links statistical methods with interactive graphics. Program features include basic descriptive statistics as well as customizable graphics and data and file management with links to Microsoft Excel, Microsoft Access, and Oracle.

HPT applications: Use statistical methods when quality, standardization, or certifications are important elements of performance improvement. The software can help you create, import, calculate, plot, manage, and analyze statistical data. Note: the available computer system must support the software, and the organization must be able to understand and benefit from detailed statistical analysis and reporting.

Tool: Structure-Tree Diagram

A Structure-Tree diagram is a graphical reproduction. The trunk of the tree represents a goal, process, problem, or category. The tree branches are used to illustrate increasing levels of details. Structure-Tree Diagrams are helpful during Quality Functional Deployment to verify customer information and identify the need for additional detail.

HPT applications: Use Structure-Tree Diagrams to verify that actions or elements link directly to the accomplishment of a goal or process or to trace and identify root causes of problems, create implementation plans, and identify effects.

Tool: TRIZ

TRIZ is an acronym for the Theory of Inventive Problem Solving. In its simplest form, TRIZ is a five-step problem-solving process that focuses on conflict and contradiction:

1. Transform the problem into a distinct system conflict model
2. Formulate a contradiction
3. Analyze the contradiction
4. Analyze available system resources
5. Define the ideal way to resolve the contradiction using available system resources

TRIZ is based on laws related to engineering system evolution and is often integrated with other Six Sigma problem-identification tools such as FMEA and QFD.

HPT applications: Use TRIZ in engineering or other systems-based environments where the team members find algorithms and hypotheses user friendly and helpful in solving problems. In the hands of an expert, TRIZ can accelerate program, process, product, or service design and development.

Tool: Voice of the Customer

Voice of the Customer (VOC) is a systematic method for identifying, understanding, and prioritizing customer expectations, wants, needs, requirements, and priorities. VOC is the first step in Quality Functional Deployment. VOC is also linked to other tools in this toolbox; for example, Structure-Tree Diagrams are useful for planning customer interviews and plotting customer responses to determine whether they are complete and contain sufficient detail.

HPT applications: Use VOC when customer input is vital to the success of the performance-improvement initiative. It also helps improve communication with customers and increase customer buy-in.

Tool: Verification-Validation Plan

Verification-Validation Plans are part of the Six Sigma action-planning process. They focus on how to collect and evaluate scientific and technical information to determine whether the action plan, when properly implemented, will effectively eliminate or control the identified causes of failure.

HPT applications: Use a Verification-Validation Plan when you need to prove that there is a direct impact on the bottom line. A detailed plan will speed up the collaboration process and supply the design team with metrics and feedback to measure the results.

A Final "Tool": General Guide to Selecting and Using Tools

Selecting the right tool for the right task is the key to successfully integrating Six Sigma tools into HPT practice. The matrix in Table 29.3 illustrates when the various tools in this specific toolbox were most frequently used during a typical DMAIC cycle, and when they could be used during the HPT cycle.

The literature on Six Sigma is a valuable source of more detailed information on how to use the various tools discussed in this section, especially the Six Sigma Memory Jogger (Brassard, Finn, Ginn, and Ritter, 2002). Just entering the name of a tool in an Internet search will also produce a plethora of information.

ROLES AND RESPONSIBILITIES

While tools are important to the successful practice of Six Sigma, people are its greatest resource. Six Sigma flourishes because there are definite roles and responsibilities throughout organizations. The roles described in Table 29.4 are consistent in all Six Sigma efforts and are key to Six Sigma success. Well-defined roles provide checks and balances, the appropriate expertise, and sufficient coaching and oversight to enforce and sustain the Six Sigma culture. In addition, organizations can learn from the experiences of other organizations to maximize benefit from effort. Roles are defined by organizational level, by appointment, and also by specific training. Although each level is essential, senior executive commitment and champions are the most significant factors for success of Six Sigma efforts.

Table 29.3. Using Six Sigma Tools for a DMAIC and an HPT Project.

Tools	DMAIC					HPT			
	Define	Measure	Analyze	Improve	Control	Analyze	Select, Design, Develop	Implement, Change	Evaluate
Benchmarking	✓	✓	✓	✓	✓	✓			
CTQ	✓	✓				✓			
DOE			✓	✓		✓		✓	✓
Fault Tree Analysis		✓	✓		✓	✓			✓
FMEA				✓	✓	✓		✓	✓
JMP		✓	✓	✓	✓	✓		✓	✓
MGP or MGPP	✓						✓		✓
Flowcharting		✓				✓	✓		
Modeling and Simulations		✓	✓	✓		✓	✓		
Process Mapping	✓	✓	✓	✓	✓	✓	✓		
Project Management	✓	✓	✓	✓	✓	✓	✓	✓	
QFD	✓	✓	✓	✓	✓	✓		✓	✓
SPAR	✓	✓	✓	✓	✓	✓			
Statistical Analysis	✓		✓		✓	✓			✓
Structure-Tree		✓				✓	✓		
TRIZ			✓	✓		✓		✓	
VOC	✓	✓				✓			✓
Verification-Validation				✓	✓	✓	✓	✓	✓

Table 29.4. Six Sigma Roles and Responsibilities.

Roles	Responsibilities
Senior Executives	• Create vision • Define strategic goals and measures • Establish business targets • Create positive environment and enforce accountability
Senior Deployment Champion	• Manages Six Sigma throughout organization • Designs Six Sigma infrastructure and support systems • Uses performance goals for business units • Reports progress and acts as liaison to senior executives • Establishes communication plan with deployment champions
Deployment Champions	• Responsible for deployment within division or business unit • Work with leaders to determine goals and objectives and ensure alignment • Identify opportunities that are aligned with business goals • Facilitate prioritization of projects • Establish and execute training plans • Develop unit or division communication plans • Report deployment status to senior deployment champion • Select project champions and remove barriers for teams
Project Champions	• Select and mentor black belts • Lead project identification, prioritization, and project scope • Remove black belt barriers and align resources • Work with deployment champions and process owners
Master Black Belt	• Expert on Six Sigma tools and concepts • Trains black belts and ensures proper application of methodology and tools • Coaches and mentors black belts and green belts • Maintains training material and updates as appropriate • Assists champions and process owners with project selection, project management, and Six Sigma administration
Black Belt	• Responsible for leading, executing, and completing projects • Teaches team members the Six Sigma methodology and tools

(*Continued*)

Table 29.4. Six Sigma Roles and Responsibilities. (*Continued*)

Roles	*Responsibilities*
	• Assists in identifying and refining project opportunities • Reports progress to project champions and process owners • Transfers lessons learned to other black belts and organization • Mentors green belts
Process Owner	• Is team member • Takes ownership when project is complete • Responsible for maintaining project goals • Removes barriers for black belts
Green Belt	• Trained in a subset of Six Sigma methodology and tools • Works small scope projects, typically in own work area • Effective member of black belt's team
Finance Champion	• Estimates and certifies project savings • Establishes clear criteria on hard and soft savings • Works with deployment champions to identify project opportunities • Assigns financial representative for each black belt team
Information Technology Champion	• Ensures computer and software adequacy • Works with black belt teams to access data from databases • Works with black belt teams to ensure electronic project tracking to collect, store, analyze, and report project data • Provides training on project tracking to black belt team • Develops reporting system to keep executives and champions informed about progress meeting goals and targets
Human Resources Champion	• Works with project champions to develop master black belt, black belt, and green belt selection process • Develops career path transition process for master black belts and black belts • Works with senior deployment champion and project champions to determine rewards, recognition, and performance appraisal for master black belts, black belts, green belts, and Six Sigma teams

Source: Adapted from Six Sigma Academy, 2002, pp. 7–10.

THE IMPACT OF CULTURE ON SIX SIGMA IMPLEMENTATION

Eckes (2001) identifies the three components of Six Sigma as strategic, tactical, and cultural. Organizational culture is one of, if not the biggest, challenges in a Six Sigma effort because Six Sigma requires discipline and continuous commitment from senior management to succeed. Normally, improvement initiatives work if a work group or department chooses to increase quality, responsiveness, or other factors.

Six Sigma is a proven management philosophy that must be accepted and sustained within the culture to be effective. Eckes' formula, $Q \times A = E$, suggests that the excellence (E) of Six Sigma results is equal to the quality (Q) of technical and strategic Six Sigma activities multiplied by cultural acceptance (A) (Eckes, 2001). In other words, culture has a profound effect and is a multiplier for predicting success.

Resistance to Six Sigma is normal and should be planned for. For example, systems and structures need to adapt to the Six Sigma mind-set. Rewards and recognition need to support Six Sigma results by creating consequences for shoddy output and positive compensation for quality. In a manufacturing setting, for example, the number of parts completed should not always be rewarded if the parts are not meeting specifications and could cause problems in use. Measurement of culture, that is the acceptance of Six Sigma, is as important as measurement of processes and defects. Six Sigma will fail if leadership support from senior executives through first line supervision is not strong and clear. In addition, bottom-line success comes from Six Sigma structure, black belts and green belts speaking the language of upper management (Brisgaard and Freisleben, 2004). (In Six Sigma nomenclature, "black belts" and "green belts" refer to individuals who have undergone specific training to assume leadership roles at varying levels in Six Sigma initiatives.) Like Six Sigma, consistent attention to culture enables successful organizations to realize the value of HPT improvement efforts as well.

"Blame the process, not the person" has become a quality mental mantra or mind-set. Six Sigma commits to improving the process, not blaming any particular employee. If processes are good, then employees are not likely to fail. However, employees are often steeped in traditional problem solving, which can lead to employees feeling overwhelmed by detail. This "high alert" problem focus can lead to emotional fallout due to intense questioning and improvement statements that can make the workers feel that they are major contributors to the problem, rather than the process being the problem (Balestracci, 2003).

Culture and the Pyramid of Quality

According to Grinnell's Pyramid of Quality, which was originally published as the Human System Optimization for Quality model, culture is the basis of quality

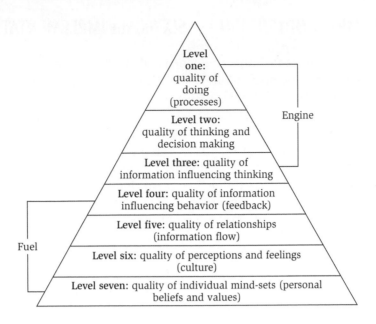

Figure 29.2. Pyramid of Quality.

efforts. Care needs to be taken to nurture all of the foundational and relationship levels to create and sustain a quality or Six Sigma culture (Grinnell, 1994).

Grinnell created the Pyramid of Quality (Figure 29.2) to understand the human aspects of quality; to illustrate that foundational or engine levels relate to minimizing resistance through awareness, knowledge, thinking, and behavior; and to show that information flows through relationships or fuel levels of quality.

According to Balestracci (2003), the engine or foundational levels are the bottlenecks or the factors that restrict improvement. Engine or foundational levels focus on doing or the processes that employees use to do their jobs and are directly related to organizational results, thinking and decision making that support doing, or the quality of information influencing doing. Fuel or relationship levels are related to (1) the value of using personal feedback to influence employee behavior; (2) the quality of relationships through which information flows; and (3) the quality of perceptions and feelings that influence employees' relationships with others, including coworkers, other departments, management, and organizational culture.

Culture-Oriented Six Sigma Application from the Health Care Field

The health care field has adopted culture-oriented continuous improvement as a way to promote fiscal responsibility and increase effectiveness. Health care organizations are beginning to embrace Six Sigma in order to improve clinical outcomes, reduce the costs of health care, improve patient satisfaction, and ensure nonexistent error rates. Dr. Martin D. Merry, physician, consultant, and learning facilitator on health care quality, medical staff leadership, and organizational transition describes current medical practice as using a craft model:

> That means we have this enormously complex system still largely formed on a pre-industrial revolution craft model: Train the craftsperson (physicians, nurses, and so on), license them, supply them with resources, then let them alone as they care for patients. This model—leaving much of the design of actual patient care up to the craftspeople—arguably worked, probably up until the mid-20th century [Merry, 2003, p. 32].

Following GE's Six Sigma success, GE Medical Systems took Six Sigma to their customers. One Six Sigma success is Commonwealth Health Corporation. Within three years of its Six Sigma implementation, Commonwealth Health Corporation, a 478-bed medical center in Kentucky, reinvigorated the culture. This new cultural approach resulted in an $800,000 reduction in costs, 20 percent improvement in employee satisfaction, and elimination of over 90 percent of order processing errors in a single division. The medical center then extended their Six Sigma efforts, resulting in improvements valued in excess of $1.5 million (Lucier and Seshadri, 2001, p. 45).

INTEGRATING SIX SIGMA AND HPT

Remember how the chapter started out by picturing Six Sigma blending in with HPT to form a yellow-brick highway leading toward improved performance, productivity, and profitability? Integrating Six Sigma and HPT strategies can make it possible for HPT practitioners and the organizations they work for and with to take business-centric journeys on the diverging and converging highway in the direction of improving the bottom line (Van Tiem, 2004).

Six Sigma

Six Sigma proponents seek to eliminate waste and improve performance in the workplace. It is a disciplined approach that "at its heart is a statistical method that involves drawing up an optimum specification for each of the processes within the organization, then using statistical analysis to reduce defects in the processes, products, and services to almost zero" (*Business: The Ultimate Resource*, 2002, p. 572). Since Six Sigma is based on statistical tools and techniques from quality management, it uses a more defined and precise decision-making process to improve productivity and increase profitability than do more general improvement initiatives, such as HPT, total quality management, or continuous improvement.

A hallmark of Six Sigma is its consistent terminology and roles. Six Sigma practitioners know the functions that individuals designated as green belts, black belts, master black belts, and so on play as change agents. Consistent terminology and roles provide a common language and mental models within an organization's culture. People similarly know their roles and responsibilities when Six Sigma teams spring into action, thereby providing common practice in the decision-making process.

Human Performance Technology

Human performance technology is a set of methods and procedures and a strategy for solving problems or realizing opportunities and challenges related to the performance of people. It is a systematic combination of four fundamental processes: (1) performance, gap, and cause analyses; (2) intervention selection, design, and development; (3) intervention implementation and change; and (4) evaluation. HPT applies to individuals, small groups, and large organizations. In 1992 the International Society for Performance Improvement published an ISPI HPT model designed by Deterline and Rosenberg to illustrate the HPT process. Van Tiem, Moseley, and Dessinger (2004) revised the ISPI HPT model to reflect current thinking and practice and to align it with the Performance Technology Standards and the Certified Performance Technologist credential.

The hallmark for HPT is its emphasis on analysis. A human performance technologist conducts a thorough performance analysis, which includes organizational and environmental analyses and leads to gap analysis. The practitioner then determines the reason for the gap by conducting a root cause analysis. The cause analysis is often rooted in both environmental factors and individual behavior. Once the performance analysis and the cause analysis are completed, the model guides the practitioner to intervention selection, design, development, implementation, and change. Intervention options, including Six Sigma, are extensive. Full-scope evaluation, which includes formative, summative, confirmative, and meta evaluation, is employed throughout the process for appropriate checks and balances.

The Case for Integration

Since HPT is comprehensive and combines interventions or solutions from many disciplines, an HPT practitioner can integrate Six Sigma, along with communications, strategic planning, performance management, balanced scorecards, and other approaches to effectively improve an organization's profitability and quality (Pruitt, Van Tiem, and Doyle, 2002; Minuth, 2003). Both Six Sigma and HPT, when presented in the context of a business problem, are appropriate foundations for problem solving. Six Sigma and HPT follow similar analysis to evaluation approaches. Six Sigma's tenets follow a disciplined five-phase approach known by the acronyms DMAIC, DMEDI, or DMEDV. HPT follows an enhanced ISPI HPT model that guides the process from beginning to end.

The languages of Six Sigma and HPT are languages of the customer or client. Both approaches help individuals and organizations reach their ultimate improvement goals, yet there are different techniques and roles along the way.

Six Sigma measures specific solutions while HPT looks at problem resolution more holistically. While Six Sigma focuses more on customer impact and having the customer define quality, HPT primarily relates to the individual, the organization, and society. Six Sigma requires active involvement of senior executives to champion the business efforts, whereas HPT seems more flexible and recommends high-level support. Six Sigma uses primarily quantitative data to support its efforts. HPT uses both qualitative and quantitative data, frequently with a greater emphasis on qualitative methodologies (Banchoff and Stebbins, 2004). To demonstrate organizational value, ". . . [Six] Sigma measures improvement by a shift in sigma value and cost savings, HPT can 'dollarize' improvement by ROI" (W. D. Pruitt, personal communication, September 19, 2004).

The authors acknowledge that Six Sigma is several steps ahead of HPT in terms of business focus. However, the most basic difference is that Six Sigma focuses on process while HPT focuses on outcomes. By focusing on outcomes and results, HPT is more flexible in considering options, including nontraditional or "out-of-the box" ideas. Creativity and innovation are expected, leading to many breakthrough solutions. While Six Sigma uses creativity and innovation, process analysis serves as the focal point, leading to more measured and incremental change.

CONCLUSION: HPT PLUS SIX SIGMA EQUALS SUPERHIGHWAY TO PERFORMANCE IMPROVEMENT

Six Sigma and HPT have much to offer organizations in their quest for improving and maintaining optimal performance. Since both are systematic and systemic processes affecting outcomes and results, they should be viewed as comprehensive and complementary approaches to accomplishing a job with efficiency and effectiveness within the fabric of a quality culture. With all its collective efforts on quality, performance, productivity, and competitive advantage, Six Sigma can improve the way our customers and HPT practitioners think about and manage business.

HPT practitioners can benefit from adopting concepts and practices from Six Sigma to conduct their own HPT practice of performance improvement. These specifics are worthy of consideration:

1. Six Sigma begins with the understanding that what is not measured is not known and, consequently, cannot be improved. HPT can benefit from Six Sigma by incorporating and implementing robust measurement within every step of the HPT process.

2. Six Sigma, with its commitment to customer quality, is already an established technique for doing business leading to operational excellence. HPT is relatively new, and the HPT mind-set could benefit from a business-centric approach to solving the problems, opportunities, and challenges of work, worker, and workplace accompanied by an organization culture that creates value.

3. There is a Six Sigma culture throughout organizations that embrace the philosophy. This disciplined philosophical thought process permeates every aspect of the organization culture. HPT could benefit from an organizationwide culture in which teamwork and added value are the norm rather than the exception.

4. There are defined roles assumed by Six Sigma participants, such as green belts, black belts, champions, process owners, and so forth, who become specialists due to rigorous training and practice. HPT practitioners could profit from more precise role definitions and common language accompanied by enhanced commitment to customers.

5. Six Sigma prides itself on costs saved, defects reduced, unwanted variation decreased, customer satisfaction, and loyalty improvements. HPT practitioners should ground themselves in the know-how of Six Sigma and add it to their repertoire of essential performance-improvement interventions whenever it is appropriate, timely, and cost-effective.

6. While evaluation is part of both processes, Six Sigma uses more quantitative data to drive evaluation decisions. HPT could profit by embracing more quantitative data-gathering approaches using statistical and analytical tools for accurate measurement.

7. Finally, Six Sigma practitioners emphasize analysis and finding root causes through a disciplined five-phase approach of defining, measuring, analyzing, improving, and controlling. HPT practitioners similarly are involved in performance analysis, cause analysis, and intervention selection and design. There is a growing tendency among novice HPT practitioners, however, to eliminate cause analysis because it takes too much time and is too demanding. Where would Six Sigma be today if it did not capture and complete root cause analysis?

In addition, we as HPT practitioners can and should champion the use of Six Sigma to widen the yellow-brick highways and byways that lead to the "Land of Performance Improvement." We can become so knowledgeable about Six Sigma that when the appropriate performance-improvement opportunity arises, we can plug in Six Sigma techniques. For example, Ford Motor Company and other Six Sigma companies promote HPT and learning by providing master black belt, black belt, or green belt training and certification opportunities for selected members of their Instructional Technology and Human Performance Technology Departments.

References

Balestracci, D. (2003, November). Handling the human side of change, *Quality Progress, 36*(11), 38–46.

Banchoff, E., and Stebbins, B. (2004, May and June). HPT and six sigma team up for improved customer satisfaction (two parts). *ASTD Links* (electronic newsletter). Retrieved October 29, 2005, from http://stebbins-consulting.com/hpt/hpt_6sigma/astdinks_article1.pdf. Alexandria, VA: ASTD.

Brassard, M., Finn, L., Ginn, D., and Ritter, D. (2002). *Six sigma memory jogger II: A pocket guide of tools for six sigma improvement teams.* Salem, NH: Goal/QPC.

Brisgaard, S., and Freisleben, J. (2004, September). Six sigma and the bottom line. *Quality Progress, 37*(9), 57–62).

Brue, G. (2002). *Six sigma for managers.* New York: McGraw-Hill.

Business: The ultimate resource. (2002). Cambridge, MA: Perseus.

Dusharme, D. (2003). Survey: Six sigma packs a punch. *Quality Digest, 23*(11), 24–30.

Eckes, G. (2001). *Making six sigma last: Managing the balance between cultural and technical change.* New York: Wiley.

Eckes, G. (2003, November–December). Making six sigma last (and work). *Ivey Business Journal Online* (University of Ontario). Retrieved October 29, 2005, from http://www.iveybusinessjournal.com/article.asp?intArticle_ID = 453.

Elliott, G. (2003, October). The race to six sigma. *Industrial Engineer, 35*(10), 30–36.

Grinnell, J. R. Jr. (1994, November). Optimize the human system. *Quality Progress, 27*(11), 63–68.

Holtz, R., and Campbell, P. (2004, March). Six sigma: Its implementation in Ford's facility management and maintenance functions. *Journal of Facilities Management, 2*(4), 320–330.

Jing, G. G., and Li, N. (2004, February). Claiming six sigma. *Industrial Engineer, 36*(2), 37–40.

Lucier, G. T., and Seshadri, S. (2001, May). GE takes six sigma beyond the bottom line. *Strategic Finance, 82*(11), 40–47.

Martin, P., and Tate, K. (1997). *Project management memory jogger: A pocket guide for project teams.* Salem, NH: Goal/QPC.

Merry, M. D. (2003, September). Healthcare's need for revolutionary change. *Quality Progress, 36*(9), 31–39.

Minuth, L. (2003, December). *Human technology and six sigma: Analyzing models for improvement.* Unpublished manuscript, University of Michigan-Dearborn.

National Institute of Standards and Technology. (2004). Baldrige National Quality Program. Retrieved December 23, 2004, from www.quality.nist.gov.

Pande, P. S., Neuman, R. P., and Cavanagh, R. R. (2000). *The six sigma way: How GE, Motorola, and other top companies are honing their performance.* New York: McGraw-Hill.

Pruitt, W. D., Van Tiem, D. M., and Doyle, T. R. (2002). *Six sigma: Product improvement and culture change at Auto Alliance.* World Congress paper #2002–01–0766. Allentown, PA: Society for Automotive Engineers.

Ramakumar, A., and Cooper, B. (2004, February). Process standardization proves profitable. *Quality, 43*(2), 42–46.

Six Sigma Academy. (2002). *Black belt memory jogger: A pocket guide for Six Sigma success.* Salem, NH: Goal/QPC.

Van Tiem, D. (2004, February and April). Six sigma and HPT: Mutual Benefits (two parts). *PerformanceXxpress* (electronic newsletter). Retrieved October 29, 2005, from http://www.performancexpress.org/0404/mainframe0404.html. Silver Spring, MD: International Society for Performance Improvement.

Van Tiem, D. M., Moseley, J. L., and Dessinger, J. C. (2001). *Performance improvement interventions: Enhancing people, processes, and organizations through performance technology.* Silver Spring, MD: International Society for Performance Improvement.

Van Tiem, D. M., Moseley, J. L., and Dessinger, J. C. (2004). *Fundamentals of performance technology: A guide to improving people, process, and organizations* (2nd ed.). Silver Spring, MD: International Society for Performance Improvement.

CHAPTER THIRTY

Normal Excellence

Lean Human Performance Technology and the Toyota Production System

Joachim Knuf, Mark Lauer

The field of human performance technology (HPT) is establishing itself rapidly at the intersection of a number of disciplines that are all invested in various ways in investigating and promulgating methodologies that make human effort in the workplace more effective. What distinguishes HPT from prior organizational practice, originally associated with the Taylorist "scientific management" practices of the Fordist or mass-manufacturing era (Taylor, 1911; Tsutsui, 1998), is not simply a reaffirmation of the essential unity of physical and intellectual effort that had been severed by the counterproductive segregation of work and its management, but a foundational commitment to an ethic of value that guides the design of work systems. The definition of such value is ultimately collaborative within the value chain and, in any case, permanently emerging as system dynamics change in response to physical, organizational, economic, social, and intellectual factors. It is not simply effectiveness that is sought by HP technologists, but the delivery of work that is relevant and meaningful to all its constituents. The central role of value in the lean work system ensures that HPT serves as an enabler of value generation benefiting society rather than as an instrument of raw performance extraction at the hands of the owners of the means of production. Ultimately, of course, only equitable systems are sustainable and likely to produce both a satisfactory return on capital *and* a high quality of life for those who work in and those who depend on them.

In this chapter, we focus on some HP technologies embedded in the Toyota Production System (TPS), which has given rise to a family of manufacturing or business systems that are generally described today as "lean." The quality of leanness, elusive in both concept and practice, is usually described negatively, as the absence of waste. However, we want to demonstrate its ultimate grounding in the ethic of value. For the purposes of this chapter a business system is considered lean if all of its constituents and relationships fully satisfy the value definition of its output by the recipient, expending the minimum of effort necessary while yielding an income sufficient to the long-term competitive viability of the system and respecting and empowering its people as well as protecting the environment. It is important to understand that leanness is not a teleological property of a system and thereby an absolute. There is no lean end-state. Instead, lean systems react to the pressures of their competitive markets by continuously developing new intellectual, organizational, behavioral, and physical resources that reduce required effort and maintain the integrity of both the system and its value proposition. The reduction and elimination of waste plays an obvious contributing role. Lean systems are therefore autopoietic; that is, they evolve in a process of self-determination that demands continuous reflection on all current activities, especially communication and learning exchanges, while closely monitoring the system environment. Self-determination is partly strategic and centralized, partly decentralized and local, consigning necessary decisions and resources to their appropriate place in the organization by continuously balancing the requirements of reactive speed and of strategic alignment, all with a view to value optimization.

The relativity of leanness to the requirement of a customer and to the principle of respect protects human performers and the environment against exploitative practices. Mature lean systems seek to achieve pace before speed, build to order rather than to capacity, restrict their output to actual consumption, are adaptive instead of rapacious, are flexible rather than dogmatic, seek simplicity, show minimal social and functional segmentation of processes, prefer horizontal to vertical organization, emphasize communication and transparency internally and externally, regard empowered people as their main asset, and execute their processes preferably in teams that produce both material and intellectual outcomes. Lean systems are epigenetic systems that evolve with sensitivity to previous states. Note that epigenesis is not a linear process in which new ideas accumulate over time, "but rather . . . a system of concepts and experiences recursively connected and in continual evolution" (Bertrando, 2000, p. 85). A signature practice of lean systems is continuous improvement, or *kaizen*, "the little engine that could."

The literature on TPS and lean systems, or in Europe, "lean production," has grown rapidly, especially after the establishment of Toyota's first wholly owned manufacturing plant in Georgetown, Kentucky, in the mid-1980s (Abo, 1994,

1998; Besser, 1996; Bremner and Dawson, 2003; Cooper, 1995; Cusumano, 1985; Imai, 1986; Kenney and Florida, 1993; Liker, 1997, 2004; Monden, 1993a, 1993b; Ohno, 1988a, 1988b; Schonberger, 1982, 1986; Schreffler, 1986; Shingo, 1988, 1989; Spear and Bowen, 1999; Taylor, 1990; Womack and Jones, 1996; Womack, Jones, and Roos, 1990; Yasuda, 1991). However, technological discussions dominate these publications, whereas human and system perspectives have not fared equally well (Besser, 1996; Knuf, 1995, 1996, 1998; Kochan, Lansbury, and MacDuffie, 1997; Parker, 2003; Springer, 1997, 1999; Wood, 1993). Moreover, not everything that has been written is enlightening, nor is it ultimately consistent. Studies purporting to represent the reality of lean work life have been conducted too often in environments that do not really deserve that name, even though some lean shop-floor tools may have been in use (Delbridge, 2000). Labor relations and human resource management topics have shown particular polarization (Babson, 1995; Fucini and Fucini, 1990; Green and Yanarella, 1996; Hampson, 1999; Harrison, 1994; MacDuffie, 1995; Moody, 1997; Rinehart, Huxley, and Robertson, 1997; Springer, 1999). In general, there is a distinctive lack of actual research on lean human performance. This is due in part to the small number of companies that have mature lean systems, in part to the reluctance of these companies to allow access to what they perceive to be the source of their competitive advantage, and in part to a general failure in the research and professional communities to understand the substantive distinctions between mass manufacturing and lean systems.

It seems appropriate to attempt to remedy this situation and unravel the lean system with a view to what it can teach us about human value generation or "worthy performance" (Gilbert, 1996). We will attempt to tie the features of this work system to themes of interest to students and practitioners of HPT. Along the way we hope to add to the more common focus on performance outcomes, in particular performance gaps, problems, and interventions (Carr, 1995; Dick and Wagner, 1995; Foshay and Moller, 1992; Harless, 1995; Rosenberg, 1990), a process dimension stressing the opportunities dormant in regular work-system design. Ultimately, of course, the technologies of human performance must be returned to the performers themselves so that they can create and then improve work systems in which behaviors always default to correct behaviors and where excellence is normal!

GENESIS AND EPIGENESIS OF THE LEAN SYSTEM

Originating in Japan at the end of World War II, the lean philosophy and the tools and practices derived from it were a direct response to the severe financial and material limitations under which Toyota and other Japanese auto manufacturers struggled (Fujimoto, 1999; Ohno, 1988a, 1988b; Reingold, 1999;

Toyoda, 1987). The system crystallized in an environment of social crisis, economic need, and material poverty, energized by an entrepreneurial mandate to match the highest existing production standards within a short period of time (Ohno, 1988a) and then fueled by the serendipitous surge of demand following the outbreak of the Korean War. At that time the avant-garde of Japanese industry had already experimented with Western management approaches for fifty years or so (Tsutsui, 1998) and was about to receive further assistance from U.S. quality gurus such as Deming and Juran (Aguayo, 1990; Deming, 1986; Gabor, 1990; Tsutsui, 1996). However, many of the solutions to the postwar economic challenges were homegrown or greatly reinterpreted and modified Western imports. To what extent characteristics of national culture played a role in all this remains a matter of opinion; the successful establishment of Toyota transplant organizations in many countries around the world would argue against a culture-determinist view (Besser, 1996; Knuf, 1995).

The Toyota Production System did not develop from a carefully designed master plan. It emerged a little at a time and then proceeded to evolve from the steady stream of ideas and experiments of the dedicated members of a company that was fighting for a way to survive (Yasuda, 1991). In this respect, nothing has changed at Toyota; *kaizen* continues the epigenesis of TPS today. In addition, TPS originated as a growing accumulation of more or less discrete elements and could not be considered an integrated system suffusing all aspects of business until about two decades from its inception. Today, while TPS is writing its own future, other companies are adding to the lean system, contributing the unique extensions required by its many derivative applications in industries characterized by products of high variety, of low volume, and with unique design and engineering requirements, as well as in those using not discrete but constantly flowing materials, such as chemical, pharmaceutical, or food processing. Furthermore, we observe highly interesting efforts to leverage lean systems into transactional environments, for example, accounting (Cunningham and Fiume, 2003; Maskell and Baggaley, 2003) or engineering and product development (Itazaki, 1999; Sobek, Liker, and Ward, 1998; Ward, Liker, Cristiano, and Sobek, 1995), as well as into service industries, health care (Panchak, 2003), government, and education.

Several attempts have been undertaken to unravel the building blocks of the lean system (Liker, 2004; Schonberger, 1982, 1986; Spear and Bowen, 1999). We advocate a different view, one that is serious about an assertion often heard but never fully explained. We will treat the lean system as a business *philosophy*. We propose that like all philosophies the lean philosophy is grounded in a plausible, parsimonious, discrete or independent, and consistent or noncontradictory set of foundational assumptions or axioms. These assumptions give rise to a small number of derivative principles, and these principles in turn guide the actions, behaviors, and practices that form the performance technology of the system. This whole lean philosophy attaches to a specific business model, which we will characterize first before discussing three foundational assumptions and four principles of the lean philosophy. Some of the important actual performance technologies are also described.

LEAN FOUNDATIONAL ASSUMPTIONS

The lean business model acknowledges the reality that, at least in industrialized societies, the days of unlimited demand for mass-produced goods are waning. Lean systems are conceived around the construct of a relational customer, not that of an anonymous commodity market that may or may not absorb product, with any absorption uncontrollable by the manufacturer, hence necessitating substantial, and expensive, inventories of finished goods to meet high absorption, respectively costly campaigns, and ultimately obsolescence of products under low absorption. Commodity markets do not allow a sufficiently targeted value definition, as customers and their demands are unknown. Conversely, customer anonymity makes it impossible for the manufacturer to compete on grounds other than price, whereas lean companies can tune combined product and service offerings to other, known, customer value propositions, for example, convenience, availability, after-sales services, life-cycle support, innovation, ecological concerns, esthetics, and so on. Many companies find that it is this very ability to offer additional services that enables them to retain and eventually grow their customer base. The relativity of all elements of the lean system to a specific customer value proposition is its central feature; in the terms of systems theory, value functions as the "strange attractor" that reveals the order ultimately inherent in a chaotic system (Gleick, 1987; Wheatley, 1999).

The lean system provides a unique business and work environment. It is built around a small number of fundamental assumptions or axioms that distinguish it from the Fordist world of mass manufacturing. Most important, lean systems are about *value generation and growth.* It is a satisfactory value definition that ultimately authorizes all production and support activities throughout the value chain, the partnership of suppliers, manufacturers, and distributors. Only superior value can ensure that customers return and provide future income opportunities to all the members of that value chain. Mass production economics looks upon the price of goods and services as the sum of material and production cost plus desired profit. The ability of a company to show a profit is hence a function of the price it can command for its product. Such thinking was reasonable at a time when market demand was unlimited, quality was driven by proprietary technologies or privileged knowledge, and producers had high control over consumer behavior. Cost control was primarily a tactical pursuit, that is, occasional and opportunistic. From the lean economic perspective the price of a product or service is assumed as already fixed by the market, where innovations typically manage to assert themselves only briefly against imitation products of comparable functionality and quality. Given a fixed price, profit is then a direct function of cost control. In other words, the lean enterprise identifies the production process as the major source of sustainable income, fortunately one that is under its exclusive control, aided by its partners in the value stream. Total value chains compete in the marketplace, not so much companies by themselves (Christopher, 1998).

The second foundational element of the lean system is its relational nature: *relationships* between the members of the organization itself, between different functions and departments, and externally among the various partners in the value chain. Lean organizational structures and processes of manufacturing, as well as support functions, rely fundamentally on strong relationships of individuals and groups, of business units, and partners. Evidence can be found in the basic team organization, which is characterized by the smooth and synergetic collaboration of a small number of operators in a well-defined work area, supported by a team leader who also spends a significant amount of time on the line. Similarly, larger units collaborate, such as functional domains in concurrent design and engineering. Continuous improvement of the production system is largely in the hands of *kaizen* teams and quality circles, whose membership is voluntary. The salaried staff typically rotates through different areas of responsibility on a scheduled basis, thereby supporting the lateral integration of all elements of the system. Furthermore, the assembly of products depends on the just-in-time delivery of parts and components manufactured by a closely integrated network of internal and external suppliers.

Given the importance of relationships, lean companies typically offer extensive training programs to enhance their members' knowledge and abilities in this area, among them courses in communication, listening, presentation skills, effective meetings, small-group interaction, and, of course, the basics of the lean system and behavior (Knuf, Haney, and Lauer, 2003; Knuf and Lauer, 2004). For the same reason, they send out people to visit partner plants and suppliers for internal or external benchmarking (Knuf, 2000). Finally, relationships work best if power is distributed and shared. Lean companies provide for the broad delegation of decision-making and problem-solving authority to the operational interface and encourage the involvement of team members in all work-management issues, building trust and commitment.

Both relationships and value are mediated by the final foundational element of the lean system, its *people*. Lean companies could not function without the constant attention of people at all levels of the organization to the system of work. In the lean system people are the ultimate source of authority. Operators are empowered to make important decisions about the work they do. They routinely stop production to address problems and quality issues the moment they are recognized. Moreover, they determine the rate of workplace and process improvements by contributing ideas that result in safer, more ergonomic, simpler, and less costly work. Last, but by no means least, only people are capable of learning, so the continuous evolution of the lean system depends on their efforts: teaching cascades through the organization and is strategically supported by strong communication pathways and the use of dialogue, narratives, and other means (Knuf, 1999).

LEAN PRINCIPLES

Given the value definition originating with a customer and the importance of relationships and ultimately of people in delivering value, we can now identify a small number of derivative principles that guide the daily activities of the lean system. Prominent among them is doing everything *just in time.* Value to the customer is maximized if production and associated transactional activities necessary to produce what the customer has ordered are arranged along a unidirectional timeline. This timeline is characterized by a regular and sustainable pace and minimal interruptions from internal sources, such as equipment breakdowns and mistakes, or external sources, such as shortages of materials supplied by a vendor. Production and transactional activities are typically tightly coupled (Glassman, 1973; Weick, 1976), migrating pertinent decisions as close as possible to the respective activity, thereby allowing maximum participation from local members of the organization under conditions of ideal visibility of the elements of the situation. All activities are triggered and then paced by a customer demand, not by a forecast. This creates a tight coupling that is attractive to any business, that of expenditures with revenue. In the lean world tight coupling applies to cash-to-cash cycles.

Lean systems continuously strive for stability. The principle of *stability* is balanced dynamically by *continuous learning and improvement,* or *kaizen.* In a lean environment, stability comes in many forms. Examples include the following:

- Sophisticated employee selection and assessment processes, followed by extensive and ongoing education and training (Knuf, Haney, and Lauer, 2003; Knuf and Lauer, 2004), comprehensive use of personal development plans, proactive evaluation methods, and organizational development efforts help standardize work behavior at all levels of the organization. Education broadens and deepens knowledge and understanding; training reduces the variability in human performance.

- Investments in people make sense, as long-term employment is protected to the greatest extent possible. Compensation systems that ensure high satisfaction with working conditions and careful work design maximize the sense of personal accomplishment from a job well done.

- Lean supply-chain management creates stability in the flow of purchased components. Negotiated long-term relationships with major and backup suppliers ensure that mutual investments in the production efforts among all members of the value chain pay off in reduced fluctuation and reliable availability while keeping inventories low.

- Production control tools clearly signal daily requirements to the workforce and update everyone about their performance against the plan. This provides full visibility of production obstacles and of any overtime that will be required to close the production gap.

- Maintenance personnel keep equipment in excellent working order and address any problems at the earliest point of manifestation. Plants are scheduled to run two shifts only, with overtime buffers between them, leaving several hours for overnight plant and equipment maintenance. Production workers participate in the maintenance effort by monitoring settings on tools and equipment and confirming the quality of the parts they are producing.

- An *andon,* or stop line, enables workers to signal any deficiency at the very moment it is discovered. An *andon* board alerts support staff to the area, and the deficiency is rectified with full participation of the workers. This particular lean tool is an important element in ensuring quality at the source, that is, within the manufacturing process itself, where the optimum configuration of materials, skills, and expertise as well as functional support is available to fix problems just in time.

A final principle underlying the lean system that we want to mention here is *respect for people.* The activities we are describing in this chapter clearly require considerable degrees of personal dedication, discipline, and physical-paired-with-intellectual effort. This effort can only be voluntary or discretionary, so it has to be elicited as a behavioral response to the culture and actions of the organization.

ELEMENTS OF LEAN HUMAN PERFORMANCE TECHNOLOGY

Next we describe some of the ways in which the lean work system is designed to maximize *normal* human performance. In this respect, what we propose here may differ in emphasis from the more typical assignments of human performance technologists. For their lean colleague, the goal is not so much to provide specific interventions, or an intervention capability within an existing organizational process, or to close gaps between given and optimal performance. Lean systems should produce very high levels of performance as a norm and preferably by default rather than choice. Only exceptions should need to be managed, steadily decreasing over time as systems mature. Lean systems and their subsystems should be designed to learn and self-correct where the minimum effort is required, that is, *at the level of their operations,* including, of course, those in the transactional realm. As a result, human performance technologies for performance assurance and continuous improvement must be provided to the workers in preference to external experts as the workforce matures. Gaps are addressed within this normal process immediately and locally as they emerge. Since HPT is rational and scientific, the lean system has to contribute broad capabilities, including data collection and the use of analytical tools to support this effort.

The following descriptions of lean human performance technologies reside at a general level. We seek to capture the essence of a number of central process features that have to be in place to call a work system or enterprise "lean." The grounding of the various technologies in the foundational assumptions and principles described previously will be apparent with a closer reading. It is this grounding in the lean philosophy, and then the everyday, living engagement of all members of the organization with that philosophy, that ultimately secures reliable responses at the behavioral level that are consistent and sustainable across the total process and allow the leveraging of intellectual resources to its continuous improvement. The overall integration of the technologies speaks to the strongly syntagmatic nature of the lean system: it excels at creating smooth interfaces in a highly complex horizontal process array concatenating many dissimilar elements, such as people, machines, materials, information, knowledge, functions, organizations, and capital.

Pull and Flow

As noted, all production commences in response to a specific customer order. The objective is to link all required activities effectively to flow the order toward the customer. This typically entails the close physical collocation of the different workstations through which the product will flow, often in dedicated work cells. In the ideal case, when an order arrives, the product is removed for shipment, not from a warehouse where it has been stored but directly from the final station in the production chain. At the same time, the previous station removes a product from upstream to work on. This process reaches back to the beginning of the production chain and initiates the pulling of materials and components from external vendors in successive moves all the way through the tiers of suppliers to the origins of the value chain. All such movements of product and associated services are synchronized by technical and logistic means in a minutely calibrated pace or *takt.*

With this just-in-time principle at work, the lean system is also known as a *pull system,* because it does not rely, as does the mass-manufacturing push system, on starting as much product as possible on the basis of a forecast and then running all workstations at maximum capacity to achieve high asset utilization and absorption rates. Only what has been sold to the customer will be produced. Pulling product on demand reduces cost and leads to the discovery of many kinds of waste, including expensive inventories of finished products that might go out of fashion or become obsolete. Where large batches of product built to inventory are defective, such masked defects will only become apparent when the first units from that batch are shipped and rejected by the customer. In-process corrective action becomes practically impossible.

More than customer value is realized in pull and flow systems. In a just-in-time environment, relationships are crucially important and define the ultimate productivity of the value chain. The best relationships are reciprocal, a form of dynamic stability we find in the lean world. No work process is more or less important than any other. Furthermore, this performance principle extends to the network of mutual customers and suppliers both inside and outside the organization.

Superior flow also leads to an increase in quality. This occurs in two basic ways. First, quality problems are discovered quickly because the parts flowing through the manufacturing process are not coming from built-up inventory. Instead they are pulled from the station immediately preceding it. If there is a quality problem, it is quickly detected. And this leads to the second benefit to quality. If there is good flow there is little need to build up inventory, which masks quality problems. Finally, flow leads to shorter delivery lead times. An organization with good flow delivers products on the customer's schedule more easily because there are reduced levels of work-in-progress and smaller batch sizes, often one single piece only.

Single-Piece Flow

By incorporating the principles of just-in-time production and stability, the technique of single-piece flow fulfills all three lean foundational assumptions. Single-piece flow is relational in that it links all operators, suppliers, and production steps and produces value by reducing inventory cost. As a technology, it reduces lot sizes to the essential minimum. Product is moved from station to station, determined in quantity and kind by customer demand with the needed materials flowing individually and evenly to those stations. This is advantageous because it allows the fastest turn-around of products in response to changing customer demands. Where customers require products in specific mixes, single-piece flow makes such production schedules possible. This is a complete reversal of mass-market, large-batch production thinking, where economies of scale are relied on to control cost and enhance competitiveness.

Still, some technological aspects of production are not as flexible as others. For example, in changing the dies in large presses, changeover times will have to be distributed across several production *takt*-time units, leading to the undesirable buildup of in-process inventory. These batches can be much smaller, however, as long as operators are skilled in adjusting the tooling quickly. Setup reduction is a continuous learning process that can yield astounding results. In the case of a thousand-ton press used by Toyota, setup times were reduced, step by step, from a high of four hours to three minutes (Suzaki, 1987); note that this learning process spread out over twenty-five years of sustained effort.

Setup Reduction or Quick Changeover

Performance technologies supporting quick changeovers and setups of equipment—for example, single-minute exchange of dies (Shingo, 1985)—support the ability of the lean system to react with minimal delays. Several forms of waste, such as excessive inventory and waiting, are eliminated in this process, and customer value increases proportionally.

Mastering quick changeover involves a number of connected elements. First, the process must be closely studied and documented; then, the workers responsible for changeovers must be carefully trained on the standard procedure to be used. This is supported by detailed and strongly visual standardized instructions. Finally, all necessary tools, attachments, and other needed equipment must be available. It is essential that any speed gain never come at the cost of safety.

The changeover process is unique for each piece of equipment. However, analyzing a changeover for redesign follows a general process. The first step in quick changeover is to *make a record* of exactly how a changeover is currently done. This requires operators and setup specialists to perform an actual changeover, which may be videotaped and observed in every detail. All steps performed in the changeover must be documented, and numbered in the correct sequence. Descriptions must be detailed, and the amount of time taken by each step must be recorded carefully. It is important that this record reflect the differences between internal components of the changeover (activities that can only take place when the machine is shut down, such as removing and replacing the die) and external components (things that can be prepared or done while the machine is still producing parts, such as preparing the necessary tools). Also noted are the problems that become apparent during the changeover, like excessive walking time, adjustments, availability of all tools and components, waiting, and other forms of waste. Downtime can be reduced by making many of the internal changeover process steps external, so they can be performed while the equipment is still producing parts. Some of the ways in which this can be done are to bring out equipment such as tools and dies early, locate all tools and materials that will be needed near the machine, and ensure that the people required for the changeover are available. Finally, many machines use bolts to secure changeable parts. In a lean system, this fastening method is often supplanted by simpler clamping devices.

Total Productive Maintenance

While on the topic of the role of equipment in the lean work system, we will explain another technology common in the lean environment, total productive maintenance (TPM). Traditionally, maintenance has been the responsibility of a specific group of employees. In the lean system, maintenance becomes the responsibility of all workers. This serves three basic purposes. First, it improves equipment reliability. If individual equipment reliability improves, then the entire production process becomes more reliable. Second, it helps maintain good flow. If the production process is reliable, *takt* time is more readily maintained and flow improves. And finally, TPM increases safety. If equipment is well maintained, the risk to employees who must work around it is reduced.

In most lean systems, TPM has five core elements, the first of which is *cleaning*. Operators clean their equipment, making it much easier to identify maintenance problems. This is coupled with *inspection*. Operators inspect their equipment on an ongoing basis. The earlier a problem is identified, the less likely flow will be degraded. Next, *check sheets* must be created. When cleaning and inspecting, workers keep track of the time it takes and the steps that need to be followed to properly clean and inspect the equipment. From this, a check sheet is created that is used as a historical record to understand and determine how much time it takes to clean and inspect each vital point of the equipment. As in all aspects of lean work, *skill development* is another important element. Team members increase their maintenance skill levels in order to be able to take on more complex maintenance procedures with their equipment. Finally, operators are given more *advanced maintenance training* that allows them to increase their ability to predict machine failures and take corrective action before the machine goes down.

TPM involves several other elements, of which we want to explain two. First, *single-point lessons* are training aids that show a particular maintenance point on a piece of equipment that needs to be cleaned and inspected. Second, *three-part tags* help communicate that there is a problem with a piece of equipment that cannot be fixed during the scheduled TPM period. The tagging process is straightforward: first, a worker places one tag on the equipment in the approximate location of the problem. This tag describes the problem the equipment is experiencing. Then, a second copy of the tag is given to the production schedulers. A third copy of the tag resides with the supervisor of that area. This tag is used for the planning of the repair. The benefit of using a three-part maintenance tag system is that it makes all associated maintenance activities concurrent. If TPM is done correctly, it will reduce unexpected downtime to negligible levels.

Kanban

As a product is pulled and flows step-by-step toward the customer, raw materials and components will be needed at workstations. For the close coordination of supplies to their points of use, a specific lean technology is available. The *kanban* technology was inspired by the experience of one of the founding figures of TPS, Taiichi Ohno, in visiting American supermarkets (Ohno, 1988a). He noticed that shelves were continuously restocked as product was removed. Much as customers leave behind money so the supermarket can order new product, shop floor operators who remove materials leave behind a *kanban,* or order card, which authorizes material handlers to restock the location. Similarly, *kanban* cards can enhance the flow of a product from station to station. The number of *kanban* cards is determined by the amount of material in the system, the speed of its consumption, lag factors deriving from the resupply turnaround time, and the various administrative processes to move cards and send out orders. Toyota is adopting e-kanbans to streamline the system. The use of *kanban* takes a lot of the guesswork out of production and also helps eliminate waste in the production process. Ultimately, *kanban* is a supply-chain communication tool; it controls inventory visually, makes scheduling easy, and supports the reduction of waste. This supply-chain technology also accomplishes prompt first-in-first-out stock rotation, which reduces spoilage cost.

Kanban cards contain information about the nature of the product, the place where it is used, and the location where it is kept. Some *kanbans* circulate between stations in a plant and are therefore referred to as "in-house" or "move" *kanbans.* Other *kanbans* connect the plant with a supplier's plant, to signal that more parts are needed. These *kanbans* are also called "interplant" or "replenishment" *kanbans.* There are five basic *kanban* signals.

- *Cards* can authorize employees to move or make an item. Here the *kanban* is a returnable order form. It comes attached to a container of materials and often is a neverending ticket that keeps circulating. As a worker begins to use material from the container, the card is sent back to the station that produced the parts, which authorizes that station to make the same quantity of the same parts. The system will not function if cards are not returned promptly or if they are mislaid or lost. Good discipline is essential to the success of card use as a *kanban.*

- *Containers* can authorize an employee to make an item. Sometimes a container is used without a special card attached to it. In this case, the container itself becomes the *kanban.* As a workstation consumes parts produced by another station, the empty container is sent back to that station. When it arrives, that station is now authorized to make just enough parts to fill the containers and then send them back to the station that needs them.

- *Flags* can signal the need to start making an item. Flags or similar signals mark the level at which parts inventory will have to be replenished so that the consuming workstation does not run out. They are found typically in lot production and not where there is a container for a container-replenishment system.
- *Squares* or other shapes can be considered reserved parking spaces for containers or carts with materials; as a location is vacated by the removal of materials in a workstation, the empty space signals the need to produce more parts to keep the space filled. No parts can be produced until space is available, thereby keeping inventory levels low.
- *Computer screens* can authorize production and can display production directions. In this case the consumption and replenishment of materials and parts is regulated electronically, usually by operators scanning bar codes as they consume materials.

Kanban is one of the performance technologies by which employees manage their own work. Shingo (1988) claims that managing this information flow eventually will allow producers to adopt a nonstock production system that will eliminate all waste from this aspect of manufacturing. *Kanban* regulates the exchange of products in the supply chain, underscoring the relational nature of the lean system.

Takt Time

Takt time, from the German *Takt,* or musical meter, has been referred to several times already. As a lean technology that steers the flow of product through the manufacturing process, it exemplifies the principles of just-in-time and stability and promotes value and relationships. The *takt,* or pace of production, is determined by the number of products that have been sold and need to be manufactured. *Takt* time therefore is a technology that allows the matching of production pace to the pace of customer sales. By taking the total available operating time, that is, regular overall work time minus breaks, maintenance, cleanup, and so on and dividing it by the daily total demand for product, a figure is derived that forms the basis of all steps to produce a component or product. The *takt* time prescribes the total sojourn of the product in any workstation. All workstations have to be synchronized through careful workload leveling. Use of the *takt* time technique sets demanding standards for production, and any deficiency in the process will surface promptly and lead to learning and improvement.

Following is an example. Assuming a standard eight-hour work shift, allowing thirty minutes for breaks and cleanup, with a required quantity of one thousand units per day, daily operating time is the following:

$$7.5 \text{ hrs } (8 \text{ hrs } - 30 \text{ minutes}) \times 60 \text{ (minutes)} \times 60 \text{ (seconds)} =$$
27,000 available seconds in a workday. The resulting takt time is
$$27,000 \div 1000 = 27 \text{ seconds.}$$

In its purest form, *takt* time is determined by the customer. If customer demand increases to two thousand units in a given shift, *takt* time drops to 13.5 seconds in the example above. Likewise, if customer demand drops, *takt* time increases. Incidentally, *takt* time can be difficult for workers to embrace initially; the technology goes against what most workers have had drilled into them since the day they stepped on the mass-manufacturing line: make it fast, and make as much as possible.

Takt times vary considerably by industry; whereas the automobile sector figures its *takt* in seconds, production progress on airplanes or ships may be measured in days or weeks. In any case, *takt* provides a numerical basis for procedural discipline and adherence to the system and is hence a driver for quality and productivity. Without a strong *takt* image, it is difficult to create a sense of timeliness and urgency in the production environment.

Leveled Production: *Heijunka*

Just-in-time production and adherence to *takt* time benefit if some leveling techniques, or *heijunka,* can be introduced to mediate between demand *peaks* and the work process. In the absence of such mediation, people, equipment, and material capacities would all have to equal the historically highest customer demand. This is obviously very expensive and hence wasteful.

Creating technologies for leveled production is a complex task that is influenced by market characteristics, the nature of the relationships with customers, the technological capabilities of the manufacturing system, the product mix and order cycle, and other factors. Accordingly, solutions differ. Toyota effectively uses a three-step order buffer to level its production both in terms of demand levels and sales proportions of its models (Toyota Motor Corporation, 1996; Toyota Motor Manufacturing, 1999). Their leveling effort relies on strong relationships in the value chain. First, Toyota dealers inform the company about their anticipated sales for the following month, providing an overall framework for resource planning at all points in the supply chain. Dealers base their figures on their own yearly and monthly experience, but they also add flexibility to the distribution network as a whole. They can affect production leveling by increasing sales through both internal and external promotions or decrease sales by not having enough cars in stock. Second, Toyota dealers transmit actual sales every ten days, and these figures provide the basis for detailed production plans in the plant itself and among all suppliers. Finally, some adjustments in specifications, such as vehicle color, can be made with as little as three days' lead time.

Other companies have developed production-leveling techniques suitable to their own environments. Among them we find the use of multiskilled workers who can be assigned to different product families as needed; modular production lines that can be set up quickly to satisfy temporary demands; variable *takt* times speeding or slowing production; a flexible, temporary workforce that can be added to the core workforce as needed; partnerships with other manufacturers to handle overflow at demand peaks; promotional packages or price adjustments to influence order volume directly; use of time not needed for production to hold continuous learning or improvement activities; and many others. Leveled production improves relationships among all people in the organization and of all partners in the supply chain, as cyclical stress buildup is avoided, and it creates value by averting the inefficiencies of inventory, equipment, and overtime or staffing demand peaks.

Andon

But what happens when, in this elegantly ordered flow of production steps, something goes wrong? The *andon* technology is part of a visual control system that empowers operators to stop production the moment a defect or other problem is detected. It is related to the error-preventing *pokayoke* technology described in the following section.

Team members are trained especially to use a defect-signaling system, the famous *andon* cord, or its equivalent, a stop button. This action summons immediate team leader support to a local problem situation and also notifies everybody in the work environment by the use of prominently displayed signal boards that communicate current production conditions publicly. If attempts at correction are ineffective within the time period the work piece spends in the affected area, production in the next segment of the process, and then successively wider adjacent areas, comes to a halt until a remedy is found. Applied conscientiously, this process avoids the production of defective parts or assemblies.

From the Fordist perspective of mass manufacturing, the *andon* technology gives rise to much concern. After all, it empowers team members to stop production, and that has the potential to make it impossible to predictably achieve business goals. Instead, it is much more common that team members need to be continuously encouraged to use the system, as they dislike disruption of their work. This disruption is essential to reaching the high-quality goals as well as effective cost control, as the cost of repairs increases dramatically as soon as a defect has escaped from its point of origin. *Andon* lines are typically connected to a computer, which takes note of the process that has occasioned their use. Data can then be aggregated at higher levels to initiate proactive reengineering efforts aimed at eradicating the root causes of recurring problems.

As a performance technology, *andon* demonstrates all four TPS principles. It is applied just in time and improves just-in-time product flow step-by-step; allows corrective intervention in machine-based processes, demonstrating the priority of operators over machines and thereby giving respect to people; and adds stability to the process by promoting continuous learning about sources of defects. The people axiom is hence strongly evident in *andon,* as is that of value. Relationships are validated by the focused collaboration of team members and team leaders on problems of common concern.

Pokayoke

To minimize the need for disruption, to reduce mistakes and errors and the resulting scrap and rework, the technology of *pokayoke* is designed to create a work environment that is replete with failsafe devices. The use of *pokayoke* creates stability in the production process, supports just-in-time product flow, and leads to continuous learning and improvement based on organizational routines and events (Knuf, 1996).

The failsafe devices of *pokayoke* ensure that operations are mistake proofed by the widest application of sensors, go or no-go fixtures, and other technical means. Product design supports these efforts by removing sources of error from the product. *Pokayoke* technologies help control waste by supporting quality at the source, and they bring to bear the intelligence and experience of empowered operators who notice and address abnormalities in the process. *Pokayoke* is similarly applicable in production support environments. Sales representatives can be given spreadsheets that require the collection of certain types of information from the customer and that will not allow data entry to progress until required fields have been filled.

According to Ohno (1988a), the technique of *pokayoke* derived directly from Toyota founder Sakichi Toyoda's auto-activated looms, which were designed to stop upon recognizing a break in a thread. Similarly in TPS, an infrared beam or a mechanical feeler might be employed to measure a critical dimension of a product, so that interruption of the beam by an odd-sized piece would alert an operator to this abnormal condition. Stopping production the moment a defect is detected has the added advantage of preserving the state of the production environment that has caused the defect, facilitating problem solving and learning. Incorporating error-detection capability into equipment also allows the use of human labor for value-adding work, not for watching machines cycle.

5S

Two related technologies address the overall preparation of the physical plant to accommodate lean work processes. The first one of these, 5S, has been described as the housekeeping component of TPS; the name derives from the original Japanese terms *seiri,* or sifting; *seiton,* or sorting; *seiso,* or sweeping; *seiketsu,* or spick and span; and *shitsuke,* or worksite discipline. By reducing a great deal of waste from the shop floor, this technology prepares the organizational environment for other aspects of the lean transformation. Fundamentally, however, 5S is much more than a housekeeping exercise. It is the source of much learning about the organization of work and hence a major resource for *kaizen.*

As noted, the first *S* denotes *sifting* and the second *S* denotes *sorting,* which may lead to the third *S, sweeping,* which is akin to scrapping. Everything on the shop floor and in the office is examined for its purpose, and unnecessary items are removed. Workers straighten the materials and tools that survive the initial sort. All items are stored in easily accessible locations, and these locations are clearly marked. For example, shadow boards that show their outline are set up to store tools. Any tool not in its place is in the hands of an operator. The fourth S is the actual cleaning operation. Work surfaces, floors, equipment, and everything else are scrubbed *spick and span.* This S is also a reminder to fix up the facility; paint floors, walls, and ceilings; and install good lighting. The final S involves workplace discipline, including standardization. Practices and rules for workplace maintenance are formulated for all areas of the plant and workers are trained to follow them, which is *systematization* (Knuf and Lauer, 2004), clearly a cultural element that requires constant vigilance.

Visual Management

Related to the technology of 5S is that of visual management. Visual tools and controls encode crucial information about production processes, outcomes, and work environments. They allow people to provide stability by making available information just in time when it is needed, enhance continuous learning and improvement, and thereby create value. Visual techniques support all others in TPS and contribute to the overall simplicity of operations (Greif, 1991; Hirano, 1995).

In TPS, a visual message is essentially public. It is not restricted to a group of individuals or specialists or to a particular level of hierarchy. Since visual messages can be observed by everyone working in a given area or passing through it, current operational conditions become evident and can be addressed or celebrated. It is desirable to keep manufacturing and office operations in a visual relationship. At the Mercedes-Benz plant in Vance, Alabama, the central office extends like a second floor island into production space. A band of interior windows provides an uninterrupted panorama of all shop-floor activities, and support staff can literally keep an eye on crucial production conditions from their desks.

Standardized Work

The technologies just described relate to aspects of the lean production system itself. Members of the organization certainly play a major role in their design, use, and continuous improvement. The preeminent performance technology undergirding the lean system, however, is standardized work. Standardized work applies the principles of just-in-time, respect for people, stability, and continuous learning. It strongly represents the influence of all three axioms. It is the most efficient way known to manufacture a product. Standardized work in lean production is established where the actual work is done, and it must be documented in detail.

Standardized work means that operators execute all steps of the process in the same manner, time after time in the prescribed sequence, with the prescribed tools and equipment, within the prescribed pace or *takt* time, and safely. Standardized work brings stability and thereby quality to the manufacturing process and, in turn, provides the basis of continuous learning and improvement.

The value of standardization in the lean work system is not necessarily obvious; indeed, this value can be overshadowed by the more visible practice of *kaizen*, the energetic pursuit of newness. But as Ohno (1988a) writes:

> We have eliminated waste by examining available resources, rearranging machines, improving machining processes, installing autonomous systems, improving tools, analyzing transportation methods, and optimizing the amount of materials at hand for machining. High production efficiency has also been maintained by preventing the recurrence of defective products, operational mistakes, and accidents, and by incorporating workers' ideas. All of this is possible because of the inconspicuous standard work sheet [p. 21].

TPS employs training and many visual-management tools to support standardized work. Textual instructions, schematics, and pictures demonstrate the proper work process. Simplicity translates into effectiveness.

If there is a pivotal technique in TPS, it is standardized work. All principles and axioms apply here. The relentless pursuit of perfection, driven through *kaizen* techniques, dissipates the effect of innovations if they are not supported by a stable base to which production can return if the trial-and-error process of learning has fallen short of its objective (Knuf, 1996).

Kaizen

The human performance technologies described so far create and guarantee the current capability of the lean work system. The future capability of that system is ensured by another technology, that of continuous improvement, or *kaizen*. *Kaizen* is without doubt the most popular and widely acclaimed technology in the TPS arsenal (Imai, 1986; Japan Human Relations Association, 1989, 1990; Suzaki, 1987). There are many companies that use *kaizen* as a standalone intervention and erroneously claim to have implemented lean manufacturing.

Grounded in all three axioms, *kaizen* combines and balances the principles of stability and of continuous learning. *Kaizen* uses multiple analytical and synthetic tools to advance to a higher level of effectiveness in the organizational process, which in turn defines the next work standard. Analytical tools include statistical control methods, flow charting, conventional measurements of time, effort and cost, problem-solving protocols like fishbone or Ishikawa diagrams and the routine of 5Y, or "five why?," the five-fold examination of causes. Synthetic tools include brainstorming, nominal groups, various forms of modeling, and the eventual hands-on reorganization of the manufacturing process itself.

Of considerable popularity at the time of writing is the so-called *"kaizen event"* or *"kaizen* blitz."* This is a program lasting several days, up to a week, during which operators and external experts and consultants take on a medium- to large-scale redesign of their work process. In general, *kaizen* events aim for a big breakthrough effect, and in this manner they differ from the gradual and incremental *kaizen* of the TPS. Womack and Jones (1996) refer to this form of activity as *kaikaku,* or "upheaval."

There are both advantages and disadvantages that attach to large-scale *kaizen* events. On the positive side, they allow the immediate harvest of many ripe opportunities. They also issue radical challenges to accepted operational wisdom and can hence push through conventional thinking with considerable force. On the negative side, they are more difficult to sustain as a learning and improvement mode since they consume considerable energies, and they can disrupt the alignment of dependent processes. It is our opinion that a policy of continuous smaller steps, supported by extensive conceptual and practical training, undertaken by team members themselves, is most often the preferable approach (Knuf, Haney, and Lauer, 2003). Indeed, small steps invariably also lead to major improvement opportunities, but in doing so they preserve a better sense of both ownership and strategic direction.

To sum up, *kaizen* is a team function. To reach new levels of performance, the joint commitment of team members is necessary and cannot be replaced by the intervention of external experts (Brooks, 1994). The team needs far-reaching authority in its approach to *kaizen* but also multifunctional support from the organization. The key to continuous *kaizen* successes lies in the improvements in the workplace itself: as they facilitate the daily work of people, the self-rewarding nature of this technique quickly becomes evident and sustains the practice.

CONCLUSION

At the beginning of a new millennium we are getting ready to leave behind a mode of industrial work dominated by mass markets and the easy availability of resources and energy. The new workforce has grown up in a period of affluence and security and demands a democratic workplace that provides meaningful work through empowerment, participation, and self-development. Work has to satisfy complex economic, social, and psychological needs. More and more, job security is sought not in large systems but in the qualifications individuals gain through continuous learning and improvement and through a demonstration of their own ability to perform.

The Toyota Production System and the various lean systems derived from it provide an important milestone in this development. Lean axioms reflect deep human needs, and they satisfy the demands of society for products of highest quality and value. We believe that the lean philosophy contains the seeds for a postindustrial model of work whose outlines we are just beginning to discern.

The new work will again be people work, much of it done in teams. Many teams will be self-organizing and multiskilled. By rotating leadership, they will seek out and complete tasks in appropriate social, organizational, informational, and material arrangements, matching their own complexity and performance ability to the requirements of the task. This will be enabled by high levels of task and process competence, and by innovative organizational support structures that facilitate access to knowledge resources; provide work environmental and reward flexibility; observe competence, learning needs, and fairness in fast-changing project assignments; and promote very high levels of trust. Teams will be not only self-directed, but eventually semi-autonomous, in that they may take over more and more business functions of the organization as well. The organization that leverages the collective potential of its employees to the highest degree will prevail in a fiercely competitive global market. And since the initial advantage of the team is its ability to turn around a task expediently, even small organizations will, over time, and in the absence of accidents, outperform larger and less capable ones in their own economic niche.

As a milestone, TPS is but one example of this new model of work. While we have much to learn from it, we have to add to it the experience of other organizations, other industries, and other workplaces. This is truly a millennial project. It demands our support but also our critical awareness as we move beyond clear transactional systems into organizational forms of notable fuzziness in which the relationships between people and organizations will become more and more ambiguous and potentially chaotic. Ownership of the means of production, intellectual assets, and complex value definitions in ever-changing markets will ultimately require a positioning of human performance technologies at all levels of the organization for the promise of normal excellence to be fulfilled.

References

Abo, T. (1994). *Hybrid factories: The Japanese production system in the United States.* New York: Oxford University Press.

Abo, T. (1998). Hybridization of the Japanese production system in North America, newly industrializing economies, South-East Asia, and Europe: Contrasted configurations. In R. Boyer, E. Charron, U. Jürgens, and S. Tolliday (Eds.), *Between imitation and innovation: The transfer and hybridization of productive models in the international automobile industry* (pp. 216–230). New York: Oxford University Press.

Aguayo, R. (1990). *Dr. Deming: The American who taught the Japanese about quality.* New York: Lyle Stuart.

Babson, S. (Ed.). (1995). *Lean work: Empowerment and exploitation in the global auto industry.* Detroit: Wayne State University Press.

Bertrando, P. (2000). Text and context: Narrative, postmodernism and cybernetics. *Journal of Family Therapy, 22,* 83–103.

Besser, T. L. (1996). *Team Toyota: Transplanting the Toyota culture to the Camry plant in Kentucky.* Albany, NY: State University of New York Press.

Bremner, B., and Dawson, C. (2003, November 17). Can anything stop Toyota? An inside look at how it's reinventing the auto industry. *Business Week,* pp. 114–122.

Brooks, A. K. (1994). Power and the production of knowledge: Collective team learning in work organizations. *Human Resource Development Quarterly, 5*(3), 213–235.

Carr, A. (1995). Performance technologist preparation: The role of leadership theory. *Performance Improvement Quarterly, 8*(4), 59–74.

Christopher, M. (1998). *Logistics and supply chain management: Strategies for reducing cost and improving service.* London, UK: Prentice-Hall.

Cooper, R. (1995). *When lean enterprises collide: Competing through confrontation.* Boston: Harvard Business School Press.

Cunningham, J. E., and Fiume, O. J. (2003). *Real numbers: Management accounting in a lean organization.* Durham, NC: Managing Times Press.

Cusumano, M. A. (1985). *The Japanese automobile industry.* Cambridge, MA: Harvard University, Council on East Asian Studies.

Delbridge, R. (2000). *Life on the line in contemporary manufacturing: The workplace experience of lean production and the "Japanese" model.* Oxford, UK: Oxford University Press.

Deming, W. E. (1986). *Out of the crisis.* Cambridge, MA: MIT Press.

Dick, W., and Wagner, W. (1995). Preparing performance technologists: The role of the university. *Performance Improvement Quarterly, 8*(4), 34–42.

Foshay, W. R., and Moller, L. (1992). Advancing the field through research. In H. D. Stolovitch and E. J. Keeps (Eds.), *Handbook of human performance technology: A comprehensive guide for analyzing and solving performance problems in organizations* (pp. 701–714). San Francisco: Jossey-Bass.

Fucini, J., and Fucini, S. (1990). *Working for the Japanese.* New York: Free Press.

Fujimoto, T. (1999). *The evolution of a manufacturing system at Toyota.* New York: Oxford University Press.

Gabor, A. (1990). *The man who discovered quality.* New York: Penguin.

Gilbert, T. F. (1996). *Human competence: Engineering worthy performance* (ISPI tribute edition). Washington, DC, and Amherst, MA: International Society for Performance Improvement and Human Resources Development Press.

Glassman, R. B. (1973). Persistence and loose coupling in living systems. *Behavioral Science, 18,* 83–98.

Gleick, J. (1987). *Chaos: Making a new science.* New York: Viking.

Green, W. C., and Yanarella, E. J. (1996). *North American auto unions in crisis: Lean production as contested terrain.* Albany, NY: State University of New York Press.

Greif, M. (1991). *The visual factory: Building participation through shared information.* Portland, OR: Productivity Press.

Hampson, I. (1999). Lean production and the Toyota Production System—Or, the case of the forgotten production concepts. *Economic and Industrial Democracy, 20,* 369–391.

Harless, J. (1995). Performance technology skills in business: Implications for preparation. *Performance Improvement Quarterly, 8*(4), 75–88.

Harrison, B. (1994). *Lean and mean: The changing landscape of corporate power in the age of flexibility.* New York: Basic Books.

Hirano, H. (1995). *Five pillars of the visual workplace.* Portland, OR: Productivity Press.

Imai, M. (1986). *Kaizen: The key to Japan's competitive success.* New York: McGraw-Hill.

Itazaki, H. (1999). *The Prius that shook the world: How Toyota developed the world's first mass-production hybrid vehicle.* Tokyo: The Kikkan Kogyo Shimbun, Ltd.

Japan Human Relations Association. (1989). *Kaizen Teian 1: Developing systems for continuous improvement through employee suggestions.* Portland, OR: Productivity Press.

Japan Human Relations Association. (1990). *Kaizen Teian 2: Guiding continuous improvement through employee suggestions.* Portland, OR: Productivity Press.

Kenney, M., and Florida, R. (1993). *Beyond mass production: The Japanese system and its transfer to the U.S.* Oxford, UK: Oxford University Press.

Knuf, J. (1995). Changing organizational cultures in the lean manufacturing environment. In K. Saito (Ed.), *Principles of continuous learning systems* (vol. 1, pp. 57–82). New York: McGraw-Hill.

Knuf, J. (1996). Transformational learning and change: From the practice of lean manufacturing to the culture of continuous improvement. In K. Saito (Ed.), *Principles of continuous learning systems* (vol. 2, pp. 55–88). New York: McGraw-Hill.

Knuf, J. (1998, January). *Rethinking competitive advantage: The strategic benefits of organizational learning and work-centered leadership.* 2nd International Conference on Corporate Reputation, Identity, and Competitiveness, January 16–17, 1998, Rotterdam School of Management, Erasmus University, The Netherlands.

Knuf, J. (1999, April). Rethinking corporate communication. In R. Varey (Ed.), *Excellence in communication management.* Proceedings of the 4th International Conference on Marketing and Corporate Communication, April 7–9, 1999. Salford, United Kingdom.

Knuf, J. (2000). Benchmarking the lean enterprise: Organizational learning at work. *Journal of Management in Engineering, 16*(4), 59–71.

Knuf, J., and Lauer, M. (2004). *The 5S system for workplace improvement.* Bloomington, IN: PKI.

Knuf, J., Haney, D., and Lauer, M. (2003). *Lean 101: Lean manufacturing foundations for work teams.* Bloomington, IN: PKI.

Kochan, T. A., Lansbury, R. D., and MacDuffie, J. P. (1997). Introduction. In T. A. Kochan, R. D. Lansbury, and J. P. MacDuffie (Eds.), *After lean production: Evolving employment practices in the world auto industry* (pp. 3–8). Ithaca, NY: ILR Press.

Liker, J. K. (Ed.). (1997). *Becoming lean: Inside stories of U.S. manufacturers.* Portland, OR: Productivity Press.

Liker, J. K. (2004). *The Toyota way: 14 management practices from the world's greatest manufacturer.* New York: McGraw-Hill.

MacDuffie, J. (1995). Human resource bundles and manufacturing performance: Organizational logic and flexible production systems in the world auto industry. *Industrial and Labor Relations Review, 48*(2), 197–221.

Maskell, B., and Baggaley, B. (2003). *Practical lean accounting: A proven system for measuring and managing the lean system.* New York: Productivity Press.

Monden, Y. (1993a). *Toyota management system: Linking the seven key functional areas.* Portland, OR: Productivity Press.

Monden, Y. (1993b). *Toyota production system: An integrated approach to just-in-time.* Norcross, GA: Industrial Engineering and Management Press.

Moody, K. (1997). *Workers in a lean world: Unions in the international economy.* London, UK: Verso.

Ohno, T. (1988a). *Toyota production system: Beyond large-scale production.* Cambridge, MA: Productivity Press.

Ohno, T. (1988b). *Workplace management.* Portland, OR: Productivity Press.

Panchak, P. (2003, November). Health care. *Industry Week, 252*(11), 35–40.

Parker, S. K. (2003). Longitudinal effects of lean production on employee outcomes and the mediating role of work characteristics. *Journal of Applied Psychology, 88*(4), 620–634.

Reingold, E. (1999). *Toyota: People, ideas, and the challenge of the new.* London, UK: Penguin Books.

Rinehart, J., Huxley, C., and Robertson, D. (1997). *Just another car factory? Lean production and its discontents.* Ithaca, NY, and London, UK: ILR Press.

Rosenberg, M. J. (1990). Performance technology: Working the system. *Training, 27*(2), 42–48.

Schonberger, R. (1982). *Japanese manufacturing techniques: Nine hidden lessons in simplicity.* New York: Free Press.

Schonberger, R. (1986). *World class manufacturing: The lessons of simplicity applied.* New York: Free Press.

Schreffler, R. (1986). Toyota's success: Inside Japan's industrial Godzilla. *Automotive Industries, 166,* 62–65.

Shingo, S. (1985). *A revolution in manufacturing: The SMED system.* Portland, OR: Productivity Press.

Shingo, S. (1988). *Non-stock production: The Shingo system for continuous improvement.* Portland, OR: Productivity Press.

Shingo, S. (1989). *A study of the Toyota Production System from an industrial engineering viewpoint.* Portland, OR: Productivity Press.

Sobek, D. K. II, Liker, J. K., and Ward, A. C. (1998). Another look at how Toyota integrates product development. *Harvard Business Review, 76*(4), 36–50.

Spear, S., and Bowen, H. K. (1999). Decoding the DNA of the Toyota production system. *Harvard Business Review, 77*(5), 96–106.

Springer, R. (1997). Rationalization also involves workers: Teamwork in the Mercedes-Benz lean concept. In K. Shimokawa, U. Jürgens, and F. Takahiro (Eds.), *Transforming automobile assembly: Experiences in automation and work organization* (pp. 274–288). Berlin and New York, NY: Springer Verlag.

Springer, R. (1999). The end of new production concepts? Rationalization and labour policy in the German auto industry. *Economic and Industrial Democracy, 20,* 117–145.

Suzaki, K. (1987). *The new manufacturing challenge: Techniques for continuous improvement.* New York: The Free Press.

Taylor, A. (1990). Why Toyota keeps getting better and better and better. *Fortune, 122*(13), 66–75.

Taylor, F. W. (1911). *The principles of scientific management.* New York: Harper.

Toyoda, E. (1987). *Toyota: Fifty years in motion.* Tokyo: Kodansha International.

Toyota Motor Corporation. (1996). *The Toyota production system.* Tokyo: Internal Public Affairs Division.

Toyota Motor Manufacturing. (1999). *1999 information kit.* Georgetown, KY: Toyota Motor Manufacturing, Kentucky, Inc.

Tsutsui, W. M. (1996). W. Edwards Deming and the origins of quality control in Japan. *Journal of Japanese Studies, 22,* 295–325.

Tsutsui, W. M. (1998). *Manufacturing ideology: Scientific management in twentieth-century Japan.* Princeton, NJ: Princeton University Press.

Ward, A. C., Liker, J. K., Cristiano, J. J., and Sobek, D. K. II. (1995). The second Toyota paradox: How delaying decisions can make better cars faster. *Sloan Management Review, 36*(3), 43–61.

Weick, K. E. (1976). Educational organizations as loosely coupled systems. *Administrative Science Quarterly, 21,* 1–16.

Wheatley, M. J. (1999). *Leadership and the new science: Discovering order in a chaotic world.* San Francisco: Berrett-Koehler.

Womack, J. P., and Jones, D. T. (1996). *Lean thinking. Banish waste and create wealth in your corporation.* New York: Simon and Schuster.

Womack, J. P., Jones, D. T., and Roos, D. (1990). *The machine that changed the world: The story of lean production.* New York: HarperCollins.

Wood, S. (1993). The Japanization of Fordism. *Economic and Industrial Democracy, 14,* 533–555.

Yasuda, Y. (1991). Forty years, twenty million ideas: The Toyota suggestion system. Cambridge, MA: Productivity Press.

PART FIVE

PERFORMANCE MEASUREMENT AND ASSESSMENT

JANA L. PERSHING

Central to the human performance technology (HPT) field is the ability to effectively measure and assess performance-improvement initiatives. Because HPT is based on a total-system perspective in examining organizations, it calls for a variety of ways to analyze and assess data before making recommendations and decisions aimed at improving results. This total systems process is commonly referred to as the ADDIE (analysis, design, development, implementation, and evaluation) process. Since the ADDIE process emphasizes testing ideas through empirical observation and measures, it relies on quantitative methods such as experiments and correlational studies. However, depending on the organizational problem at hand, qualitative data-collection techniques such as unstructured observation and unstructured interviews may be more appropriate for answering a specific research question.

Regardless of the type of methodology employed, the ADDIE process is an applied research technique applicable to solving organizational problems. For the ADDIE process to serve its purpose, all information-gathering tools should be considered before selecting an appropriate methodology. More important, appropriate standards of rigor should always be followed in an effort to produce information that is useful to the performance-improvement technologist.

The chapter authors in Part Five bring together a unique combination of scholarship, consulting, and applied experience in business and industry. Drawing from their expertise in measurement and assessment, their contributions to this handbook entail seven chapters that address various methods and analytical tools available to the performance specialist.

Part Five begins with a commentary on quantitative and qualitative methods, acknowledging that the HPT field relies heavily on quantitative data-collection techniques. In addition to addressing several misunderstandings about qualitative methods, Jana Pershing in Chapter Thirty-One discusses the benefits of mixing or blending methodologies. In Chapter Thirty-Two, Sung Heum Lee presents an overview of one of the most-often-used data collection methods in HPT, the written questionnaire. In addition to summarizing the types of questions and scales included in questionnaires, this chapter provides specific guidelines for constructing effective questionnaires that will yield useful and reliable information for the performance specialist. Jana Pershing deals with a commonly employed survey method, the interview, in Chapter Thirty-Three. In addition to describing the types of interviews that are useful to performance technologists, the chapter also explains the advantages and limitations of interviewing in person versus over the telephone.

In Chapter Thirty-Four, the method of observing is addressed in great detail by authors James Pershing, Scott Warren, and Daniel Rowe. Various types of observation are discussed, including their strengths and weaknesses. Chapter Thirty-Five describes an underused yet potentially powerful method for the performance analyst or evaluator, content analysis. In addition to explaining what it is, author Erika Gilmore includes several concrete examples of how to use content analysis in a variety of performance-improvement initiatives. Given the emphasis on quantitative methods in HPT, Chapter Thirty-Six provides an important overview of basic and advanced analysis techniques for examining, analyzing, and making decisions about quantitative data. Author Mary Norris Thomas also explains where data analysis fits into the larger research process. Finally, in Chapter Thirty-Seven, Ruth Colvin Clark addresses the challenges that HPT practitioners face in gaining professional status through evidence-based practice, including the process of accessing and evaluating evidence as well as influencing clients who also consider themselves experts in performance and learning.

The chapters in Part Five, taken together, provide the performance analyst or evaluator with a thorough overview of varied methodological approaches for solving organizational problems. In addition to describing cornerstones in the HPT field such as written questionnaires and interviewing, less commonly employed methods such as observing and content analysis are also addressed. Since the primary goal of the ADDIE process is to collect valid and reliable information, Part Five also illustrates the importance of selecting an information-gathering tool that is appropriate to answering a research or evaluation question.

CHAPTER THIRTY-ONE

A Commentary on Quantitative and Qualitative Methods

Myths and Realities

Jana L. Pershing

Central to the field of human performance technology (HPT) is the *a*nalysis, *d*esign, *d*evelopment, *i*mplementation, and *e*valuation (ADDIE) process, an applied and practical research technique applicable to solving organizational problems (Molenda, 2003).[1] The ADDIE process emphasizes testing ideas through empirical observation and measurement (Rosenberg, 1999). As such, it lends itself to scientific research based on deductive reasoning, relying heavily on quantitative data-collection techniques such as experiments, correlational studies, and surveys, including questionnaires.

Given this emphasis on quantitative methodology and data, several myths and misunderstandings about qualitative methods have arisen in the HPT field, culminating in the rejection by some of qualitative research as not *real science*. These myths include (1) the belief that the philosophical positions of quantitative and qualitative research are fundamentally incompatible; (2) the perception that quantitative research is more rigorous than qualitative research; (3) the oversimplification of qualitative research as all the same and the consequent failure to recognize the range and diversity of qualitative research methods; and (4) the assumption that quantitative methods yield quantitative data and, conversely, that qualitative methods yield qualitative data. In addition to describing the value of both quantitative and qualitative methods for analysis and evaluation in HPT, this chapter addresses the benefits of mixing or blending the methodologies.

MYTH 1: THE PHILOSOPHICAL POSITIONS
OF QUANTITATIVE AND QUALITATIVE RESEARCH
ARE INCOMPATIBLE

The HPT field and the ADDIE process are both rooted in behaviorism and cognitive psychology, which are post-positivist in their orientation to research. *Post-positivism* is a social science paradigm characterized by the idea that, through observation and measurement, objective reality can be understood.[2] Post-positivism lends a natural bias toward experimental designs and quantitative methods because they are deterministic and rely on establishing cause and effect. Quantitative research designs begin with identifying a problem to be investigated, outlining research objectives and questions, constructing hypotheses to be tested, and outlining assumptions and limitations. Quantitative methodologies use *deductive reasoning*, which involves the testing of hypotheses derived from theories and subsequent verification of those theories. Data analysis involves the testing of hypotheses by *induction*, that is, the use of statistical methods to form probabilistic generalizations.

In contrast, qualitative methodologies are based on *constructivism,* which posits that reality and meanings are socially constructed by humans as they interact with the world in which they live. As a consequence, the backgrounds and experiences of researchers themselves will influence how they interpret the environment that they study. Constructivism lends itself to qualitative methodologies, which tend to use inductive reasoning. *Inductive reasoning,* in turn, involves making observations, ascertaining patterns, identifying general principles, and generating theories. The process begins with identifying the general purpose of a study and then outlining a basic conceptual or theoretical framework. Details are not specified beforehand but are instead driven by data and research findings. Because qualitative research methods are concerned with context and natural settings, they have emergent research designs based on the data or phenomena under investigation.

A fundamental difference between inductive and deductive reasoning is that deduction moves from the general principles to specific conclusions, whereas induction goes from the specific observations to general conclusions. Deductive methods assume that conclusions or research findings must be true if all assumptions and premises are true. In the end, a problem is solved with known probability. In contrast, qualitative methods assume that conclusions are probably true, but not necessarily, even if all premises are true.

As a result of the different philosophical positions of the two approaches, the tone or discussion of findings from quantitative and qualitative studies will vary. Discussions of quantitative research findings tend to be unbiased, impartial, and express a scientific attitude with a writing style that is precise and clear. In

Table 31.1. Philosophical Positions of Quantitative, Qualitative, and Blended Research.

Quantitative	Blended	Qualitative
World is made up of observable and measurable facts	Things are a matter of degree	Reality is socially constructed and ever changing
Results are knowable within probability	Rejects idea of duality	Recognizes multiple realities
Uses advanced techniques	Neither paradigm is superior to the other	Interactive link exists between researcher and participants
Objectivity is central	Is pragmatic	
Is interventionist	• Is question-driven	Is naturalistic
Is decontextualized	• Best answers may require both approaches	Is contextual

contrast, qualitative research findings are intentionally unfiltered, clarify bias and subjectivity, and are designed to make readers reflect, mirror the ideas and expressions of subjects, and illustrate the complexity of ideas and issues at hand.

It should be noted that the emphasis on quantitative methodologies is not unique to the HPT field. In fact, quantitative research designs have been used from the beginning of social and human science research, whereas qualitative research has only emerged during the past thirty or forty years (Creswell, 2003). Upon initial observation, the philosophical positions of quantitative and qualitative research appear incompatible. However, in some instances, the best answer to an organizational question or problem may require both; that is, a *mixed* or *blended* research design. Although mixed methods are relatively new and developing (Creswell, 2003), the philosophical position of blended approaches is that neither quantitative research nor qualitative research is superior to the other. Instead, blended designs emphasize a pragmatic approach to research, assuming that the question should drive the method. Mixed approaches contain both quantitative and qualitative data-collection techniques. Table 31.1 summarizes the primary characteristics of quantitative, qualitative, and blended research designs.

MYTH 2: QUANTITATIVE RESEARCH IS MORE RIGOROUS THAN QUALITATIVE RESEARCH

Although the philosophical positions vary, this does not mean that quantitative research is better than qualitative research or, conversely, that qualitative research is better than quantitative research. All methodologies ultimately seek to explain *why*. The process by which this question is answered will, of course, vary depending on

Table 31.2. Study Focus of Quantitative and Qualitative Methods.

Quantitative	Qualitative
Identify testable and confirmable theory	Understand context of human behavior
Ground in theoretical assumptions	Discover meaning as portrayed and constructed by individuals
Focus on objectivity	
Use inductive reasoning	Recognize subjectivity and bias
• Derive hypotheses from theory	Use inductive reasoning
• Test hypotheses	• Make observations
• Assess, refine, and extend theory	• Ascertain patterns
Post-positivist Paradigm	• Identify general principles
	Interpretive or Constructivist Paradigm

whether quantitative or qualitative methodologies are used. Table 31.2 depicts the differences in the foci of quantitative and qualitative methodologies as well as general steps involved in both methodologies. Depending on the purpose of a study, both approaches may be extremely useful to the HPT researcher so long as all methods are employed rigorously.[3]

Populations and Samples

The misconception regarding the lack of rigor in qualitative research is, in part, related to differences in the sampling of populations. Quantitative research typically involves selecting a representative, *probability sample* of the population that one is interested in studying. Basic probability sampling simply refers to a process that ensures that each case in the population has an equal chance of being included in the sample. The advantage of random sampling is that research findings may be generalized to the entire population from which the sample was selected, which is why in part quantitative research is regarded as unbiased or objective.

In contrast, qualitative research typically involves selecting a nonprobability or *purposeful sample.* Expert judgments may be employed to select a sample that is considered representative or typical of the population or, conversely, may be selected because cases are viewed as outliers or atypical. In either case, the goal of purposeful sampling is to identify cases that best represent the phenomenon being studied. Although the findings derived from nonprobability samples may not be generalized to the population from which the sample is selected, they may be either more appropriate or practical depending on the purpose of the study.

Table 31.3. Population and Sampling Issues in Quantitative and Qualitative Research.

Quantitative	Qualitative
Define the population	Ascertain context
Use a probability sample	Use a nonprobability sample
Seek representation	Be purposeful
If using a convenience sample,	• Be representative
• Reverse the process	• Use a range of variation
• Project sample to population	Typical
• Ascertain population represented	Outliers
Generalize	Use cases that represent phenomenon being
Post-Positivist Paradigm	studied
	Interpretive or Constructivist Paradigm

It should also be noted that nonprobability samples are sometimes selected simply because the cases are conveniently available. *Convenience sampling* is considered quick, easy, and inexpensive and is typically used in the early stages of research when generalizability is not an issue. However, convenience sampling should be avoided in both quantitative and qualitative research if possible since it does not adhere to widely accepted guidelines regarding scientific rigor.

Regardless of how samples are selected, the quality of data obtained from both quantitative and qualitative studies is the central issue. Table 31.3 summarizes the primary differences between populations and samples in postpositivist and interpretive or constructivist approaches.

Standards of Rigor

The myth that quantitative methods are more rigorous is also related to the misconception that quantitative research produces valid and reliable information while qualitative research produces neither. However, the question is *not* whether quantitative research is more rigorous than qualitative research, but rather whether the standards of rigor for each research method are followed. Standards of rigor for quantitative research typically focus on the validity and reliability of data obtained. *Validity* refers to *goodness of fit*, or whether a study measures what one intends to measure. Methods of validity assessment include face validity, content validity, concurrent validity, and predictive validity. *Reliability* refers to stability and consistency, or whether similar results are obtained from repeated applications of an instrument—for example, a questionnaire. Valid measures are always reliable, but highly reliable measures are not necessarily valid.

Similar to the issue of validity are questions about the *credibility* and *transferability* of data obtained in qualitative studies. In other words, measuring what one intends to measure is also a central concern and may be assessed through processes such as triangulation of data or peer review (Eisner, 1998). Because repeated applications of research instruments are uncommon in qualitative studies, the standard of rigor for consistency focuses on the *dependability* of data rather than its reliability, that is, whether similar results are obtained through coding and recoding or by examining interobserver agreement.

When standards of rigor are not followed, or when research is conducted poorly, both quantitative and qualitative methods will yield information that does not measure what one intends and is therefore of little use. Conversely, when conducted rigorously, both methods will produce data that are useful to the performance-improvement technologist. In sum, both quantitative and qualitative methodologies have parallel or equivalent concerns, albeit different ways of addressing them given their different underlying philosophical approaches.

MYTH 3: QUANTITATIVE RESEARCH EMPLOYS A VARIETY OF METHODOLOGICAL APPROACHES, WHILE QUALITATIVE METHODS ARE ALL THE SAME

In the field of HPT, research practitioners and organizational members are familiar with the range and diversity of quantitative methods available for use. Rather than references to *quantitative research,* the approach is instead specified—for example, *experimental research* or *survey research.* Another consequence of over-relying on quantitative research is the oversimplification of qualitative methods. In other words, qualitative research is considered simple, as if it denotes a specific methodology, when in actuality qualitative methods are as varied as quantitative methods. Qualitative data-collection methods typically include interviewing, participant observation, nonparticipant observation, case studies, ethnographies, content analyses of archival data, and historical and narrative studies. Given the range and diversity of these methods, the issue is *what type* of qualitative method is employed rather than *whether* the method is qualitative.

Knowing the specific type of method, however, is not the same as knowing whether the method is qualitative or quantitative. In other words, the over-reliance on quantitative methods has also resulted in a polarization or false dichotomization of quantitative and qualitative methods and the corresponding implication that an approach must be of one kind or the other. Although some methods are strictly quantitative, such as experiments, others are exclusively qualitative, such as ethnographies. The most commonly employed approaches used in HPT can be either. Table 31.4 summarizes major research methods,

Table 31.4. Major Research Methods.

Quantitative	Both or Mixed	Qualitative
Experimental	Case study	Ethnographic
Quasi-experimental	Content (document) analysis	Grounded theory
Correlational	Observation	Naturalistic observation
Causal comparative or ex post facto	Clinical	Participatory
	Evaluation studies	Phenomenological
Single case or single subject	Survey (questionnaire)	Biographical
	Historical and narrative studies	
	Focused interview	
	• Individual	
	• Group	

including the most frequently used techniques for gathering information in HPT: written questionnaires, interviews, and observation (Rossett, 1999).[4]

- *Written questionnaires* are the most frequently used means of gathering data and, in some instances, the only method (Pershing, 2003). They are an effective survey research method for gathering information from a large number of people relatively quickly and inexpensively. Although questionnaire items are typically closed-ended, they may also include open-ended or semistructured items. This is explained more in a later section of this chapter titled "The Case of the Written Questionnaire."

- *Interviews* are a survey research method for collecting information from respondents through interactive, real-time communication on the telephone or in person. They are used as either a standalone procedure for producing information for subsequent analysis or in conjunction with other data-gathering methods. Like written questionnaires, interviews may be structured, semistructured, or unstructured. (Refer to Pershing, 2003, for more detail.)

- *Observation* is a research method for collecting information about people's behaviors and skills in the workplace or in other natural settings. Types of observation vary depending on the level of participation of the researcher, ranging from *nonparticipation,* such as watching a videotape, to *complete participation,* such as a teacher observing students live in a classroom. (See Mertens, 1998, for more detail.) Observing behaviors is typically a precursor to distributing written questionnaires or conducting interviews.

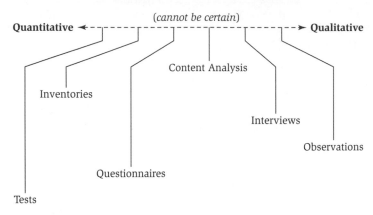

Figure 31.1. Methodological Continuum.

Without examining the data-collection process and instrument for a particular research study, it is inaccurate to assume that a research method is either qualitative or quantitative. Instead, it is more accurate to refer to a methodological continuum in categorizing the extent to which a specific approach is likely to be quantitative or qualitative or, perhaps, to possess characteristics of both in the case of mixed approaches (refer to Figure 31.1).[5] It should also be noted that the term *research method* encompasses the entire research process, beginning with the development of a research question and ending with the analysis and presentation of findings. *Data-collection methods* are an integral part of the overall research process, but this term refers specifically to the technique employed for obtaining information (Thomas, 2003).

Consider the case of the written questionnaire; is it quantitative, qualitative, or mixed? Not only are written questionnaires a popular and versatile data-gathering method in education and training (Clardy, 1997), they are the most frequently used means of collecting information and, in some instances, the only method (Swanson, 1983; Witkin and Altschuld, 1995). For example, as part of the implementation phase of the ADDIE process, questionnaires are used to gather information about preferred delivery options or possible barriers to the delivery of a performance-improvement intervention. Likewise, in carrying out evaluation studies, questionnaires are the preferred method for obtaining participants' reactions to training and performance-improvement programs (Lee and Pershing, 2002).

Although written questionnaires typically employ quantitative data-collection techniques, sometimes they possess characteristics of both. That is, questionnaire items fall into two broad categories: closed-ended and open-ended. *Closed-ended* items provide respondents with a fixed set of response alternatives.

Examples include yes or no, multiple choice, rankings, and items with word- or numeric-based rating scales (Babbie, 1990; Pershing and Pershing, 2001). *Open-ended* items require that the respondents answer using their own words. Examples include fill-in-the-blank items, short answers, and essay-type responses.

Closed-ended questionnaire items yield quantitative data because they are structured with response alternatives. Respondents choose one or more response categories designed to elicit information from memory. Such items are easy to complete and provide the same frame of reference for all respondents. They are also easy to code during data analysis, making the processing of responses straightforward.

While there are clearly advantages to closed-ended items, they also have some drawbacks. For example, response alternatives may not reflect respondents' actual attitudes about a topic, in which case the respondents may provide answers when they have no opinion or knowledge about the matter at hand. Another possibility is that respondents may not understand an item and therefore elect not to respond. Unless item response categories are carefully thought through, they may not cover the full range of possible responses.

In contrast, in responding to open-ended items, respondents answer using their own frames of reference and their own words. They are provided an opportunity to express their opinions and convey their judgments. For emotion-laden topics, respondents may use open-ended items to express personal feelings. As a consequence, analysts and evaluators are more apt to gain insight and understanding about respondent's opinions and attitudes. For consumers of the information provided, there is the benefit of hearing the opinions of respondents in their own words.

However, open-ended questionnaire items require more time on the part of respondents and researchers. Thoughtful responses take time and effort to write. Furthermore, respondents may not be capable or comfortable in writing narrative responses. Narrative responses also take time to read and content-analyze, since accuracy in coding and summarizing information can be a difficult and laborious process. *Content analysis* consists of several research techniques for systematically analyzing the content of written, spoken, graphical, and pictorial communications (see Babbie, 2004; Strauss, 1987). It provides a means to analyze and describe the narrative responses to open-ended items in questionnaires.

As an alternative, mixed questionnaires contain both closed-ended and open-ended questions. Moreover, *semistructured* items include questions that provide a fixed set of response choices in addition to one or more unrestricted response categories so that respondents may answer using their own words. Structured responses produce highly specific information, while unstructured comments allow for additional probing that tends to yield more in-depth information (Clardy, 1997). Refer to Figure 31.2 for an example of three alternative ways to structure a questionnaire item.

Open-Ended

In your judgment, what problems face purchasing departments in the next five years?

_____

_____

_____

Closed-Ended

Listed below are three problems some people believe purchasing departments will face in the next five years. In your judgment, how serious is each one?
(Circle your response)

(a) Hiring qualified workers	Very	Somewhat	Not at all
(b) Keeping up with technology	Very	Somewhat	Not at all
(c) Finding reliable suppliers	Very	Somewhat	Not at all

Semistructured

In your judgment, which one of the following problems facing purchasing departments in the next five years is the *MOST* serious?
(Circle the number for your response)

1. Hiring qualified workers

2. Keeping up with technology

3. Finding reliable suppliers

4. Other (please specify) _____

Figure 31.2. Alternatives for Structuring a Questionnaire Item.

MYTH 4: QUANTITATIVE METHODS YIELD QUANTITATIVE DATA, AND QUALITATIVE METHODS YIELD QUALITATIVE DATA

The assumption that quantitative methods yield quantitative data and, conversely, that qualitative methods yield qualitative data is rooted in a failure to distinguish between the terms *methods* and *data*. Broadly defined, a methodology refers to a scientific procedure through which data are obtained, whereas *data* refers to the information, measurements, or statistics obtained through

Table 31.5. Quantitative and Qualitative Date Analysis.

Quantitative (numbers)	Both or Mixed (numbers)	Qualitative (words and symbols)
Measures of relative position	Frequency counts	Coding (reducing and organizing)
Measures of association	Graphic presentations	Constant comparatives
Standard deviation	Percentages and proportions	Negative-case and discrepant-data analyses
Inferential statistics	Ranges	Synthesizing
Meta analyses	Means, medians, and modes	Identifying significant patterns
	Cross tabulations	Discovering what is important

those procedures. In other words, methods are the means through which data are collected and analyzed.

In addition to mixed methods, which are likely to produce both quantitative and qualitative data, quantitative methods will sometimes yield qualitative data. For example, as discussed in the previous section, written questionnaires may include open-ended survey questions, requesting narrative responses. Alternatively, qualitative methods may, on occasion, yield quantitative data. For example, participant observation could involve tallying the frequency of responses to open-ended questions or compiling information on the demographic characteristics of the group under observation—for example, calculating the proportion of men and women in the group. Table 31.5 summarizes data analysis techniques for quantitative, qualitative, and mixed research designs.

A Case Example: Content Analysis of Medical School Reaction Evaluations

The case example that follows describes a research project that evaluated fifty reactionnaire forms regularly administered by a prestigious medical school to ascertain if they were designed to yield useful information (see Pershing and Pershing, 2001). The term *reactionnaire* refers to an end-of-instruction evaluation form completed by learners. The research method involved three researchers performing content analyses on each reactionnaire form over a two-week period. Every form was systematically assessed for construction, content, and layout.

Three separate evaluation forms were used to perform the content analyses: criteria for reactionnaire development, dimensions of reactionnaire, and question construction. The first evaluation form was used to perform three tasks: (1) assess the general layout or appearance of each reactionnaire; (2) ascertain whether fundamental components were included on each reactionnaire, such as introductory and closing statements, directions for filling out specific sections of the reactionnaire, and a statement about anonymity or confidentiality; and (3) evaluate what types of questions and response formats were used, such as closed-ended versus open-ended questions.

As summarized in Table 31.6, the content analysis found no introductory statement on thirty-six (72 percent) of the forms. Six forms (12 percent) had fully developed statements that met some of the criteria for a good introductory statement, and only one of the six forms with a fully developed introductory statement adequately dealt with the issue of confidentiality. In addition to assessing fundamental elements of reactionnaire design, three other general areas of survey design and development were examined, including question dimensions, question construction, and question response formats. All analyses yielded similar results in terms of the number and corresponding percentage of forms that failed to adhere to widely accepted guidelines and rules that apply to questionnaire development and design. More important, the content analysis identified weaknesses so that appropriate revisions could be made for the benefit of evaluators, instructors, and learners.

Table 31.6. Case Example: Content Analysis of Medical School Reactionnaires.

Fundamental Elements of Reactionnaire Design	Number (N = 50)	Percentage
Introductory Statement		
None	36	72
Minimal	08	16
Full explanation	06	12
Closing Statement		
None	39	78
Yes	11	22
Directions		
None	15	30
Minimal	27	54
Fully developed statement	08	16
Anonymity or confidentiality logically dealt with		
No	46	92
Yes	04	08

Source: Pershing and Pershing, 2001.

In sum, *content analysis* of documents refers to the processes of locating and analyzing facts or trends in already existing documents (Witkin and Altschuld, 1995). Because of the plethora of existing work-related documents and artifacts within organizations, document analysis lends itself particularly well to the field of HPT. Not only is it a useful prelude to planning and carrying out the collection of new data using techniques such as interviews, questionnaires, and observations; it also allows performance analysts and evaluation professionals to ground their front-end analysis and evaluating criteria in performance and accomplishment. Last, although document analysis will often yield qualitative data, the aforementioned case example illustrates how a qualitative method like content analysis can sometimes produce quantitative data.

CONCLUSION

The over-reliance on quantitative methods in the field of HPT and widespread use of written questionnaires has resulted not only in misunderstandings about quantitative and qualitative methods but also potentially missed opportunities in conducting needs analysis research and evaluation studies. In other words, the primary goal of the ADDIE process is to collect valid and reliable information regardless of the type of methodology employed. Moreover, the method employed should be driven by the research questions rather than being selected because of preconceived notions about scientific rigor. Effective research designs take the following steps:

- Specify the research question.
- Select the most appropriate methodology for answering the research question; examples include written questionnaires, interviews, participant observations, and document analyses. *Remember the range and diversity of both quantitative and qualitative methods available for use.*
- Determine whether the methodology is quantitative, qualitative, or mixed in its orientation and research design. *Keep in mind that the philosophical positions of quantitative and qualitative research are not necessarily incompatible.*
- Decide on instrumentation as well as population and sampling issues based on the methodology selected. *Follow the appropriate standards of rigor regardless of whether the methodology is quantitative, qualitative, or mixed.*
- Select an appropriate data-analysis technique depending on the data collected rather than on the method employed. *In other words, remember that quantitative methods sometimes yield qualitative data, while qualitative methods sometimes yield quantitative data.*

Finally, although mixed or blended approaches are in their infancy relative to quantitative and qualitative research methods, they draw on the strengths of both, thereby minimizing the corresponding limitations of each (Johnson and Christensen, 2004).

Notes

1. For an in-depth explanation of the genesis and meaning of the term *ADDIE,* see Molenda, 2003.

2. Post-positivism is rooted in *positivism,* which is a paradigm characterized by the assumption that social behavior can be studied in the same way as phenomena in the natural world. For more detailed discussions of *post-positivism* and *constructivism,* see Mertens, 1998.

3. *Rigor* refers to following widely accepted standards and guidelines for conducting research, regardless of the type of methodology employed. See Babbie, 1990, and Singleton, Straits, Straits, and McAllister, 1988, for discussions regarding standards of scientific rigor for various methodological approaches.

4. See Mertens, 1998 for a comprehensive discussion of types of major research methods, including the methods listed in Table 31.4.

5. The term *methodological continuum* refers to the broad range of methods available for use in the HPT field, with controlled experiments on the quantitative end of the continuum and observation research on the qualitative end (Shrock and Geis, 1999).

References

Babbie, E. (1990). *Survey research methods.* Belmont, CA: Wadsworth.

Babbie, E. (2004). *The practice of social research.* Belmont, CA: Wadsworth.

Clardy, A. (1997). *Studying your workforce: Applied research methods and tools for the training and development practitioner.* Thousand Oaks, CA: Sage.

Creswell, J. W. (2003). *Research design: Qualitative, quantitative, and mixed methods approaches.* Thousand Oaks, CA: Sage.

Eisner, E. W. (1998). *The enlightened eye: Qualitative inquiry and the enhancement of educational practice.* Upper Saddle River, NJ: Prentice-Hall.

Johnson, B., and Christensen, L. (2004). *Educational research: Quantitative, qualitative, and mixed approaches* (2nd ed.). Boston: Allyn & Bacon.

Lee, S. H., and Pershing, J. A. (2002). Dimension and design criteria for developing training reaction evaluations. *Human Resource Development International, 5*(2), 175–197.

Mertens, D. M. (1998). *Research methods in education and psychology: Integrating diversity with quantitative and qualitative approaches.* Thousand Oaks, CA: Sage.

Molenda, M. (2003). In search of the elusive ADDIE model. *Performance Improvement, 42*(5), 34–36.

Pershing, J. L. (2003). Interviewing to analyze and assess performance improvement initiatives. *Performance Improvement, 42*(6), 30–36.

Pershing, J. A., and Pershing, J. L. (2001). Ineffective reaction evaluation. *Human Resource Development Quarterly, 12*(1), 73–90.

Rosenberg, M. (1999). The general process of human performance technology. In H. D. Stolovitch and E. J. Keeps (Eds.), *Handbook of human performance technology: Improving individual and organizational performance worldwide* (pp. 137–138). San Francisco: Jossey-Bass/Pfeiffer.

Rossett, A. (1999). Analysis for human performance technology. In H. D. Stolovitch and E. J. Keeps (Eds.), *Handbook of human performance technology: Improving individual and organizational performance worldwide* (pp. 139–162). San Francisco: Jossey-Bass/Pfeiffer.

Shrock, S. A., and Geis, G. L. (1999). Evaluation. In H. D. Stolovitch and E. J. Keeps (Eds.), *Handbook of human performance technology: Improving individual and organizational performance worldwide* (pp. 185–209). San Francisco: Jossey-Bass/Pfeiffer.

Singleton, R., Straits, B. C., Straits, M. M., and McAllister, R. J. (1988). *Approaches to social research.* New York: Oxford University Press.

Strauss, A. L. (1987). *Qualitative analysis for social scientists.* New York: Cambridge University Press.

Swanson, R. A. (1983). *Analysis for improving performance: Tools for diagnosing organizations and documenting workplace expertise.* San Francisco: Berrett-Koehler.

Thomas, R. M. (2003). *Blending qualitative and quantitative research methods in theses and dissertations.* Thousand Oaks, CA: Corwin Press.

Witkin, B. R., and Altschuld, J. W. (1995). *Planning and conducting needs assessments: A practical guide.* Thousand Oaks, CA: Sage.

CHAPTER THIRTY-TWO

Constructing Effective Questionnaires

Sung Heum Lee

Written questionnaires are popular and versatile in the analysis and evaluation of performance-improvement initiatives. They are instruments that present information to a respondent in writing or through the use of pictures, then require a written response such as a check, a circle, a word, a sentence, or several sentences.

Questionnaires can collect data by (1) asking people questions or (2) asking them to agree or disagree with statements representing different points of view (Babbie, 2001). As a diagnostic tool, questionnaires are used frequently for needs assessment, training-program evaluations, and many other purposes in HRD practice (Hayes, 1992; Maher and Kur, 1983; Witkin and Altschuld, 1995).

Questionnaires are an indirect method of collecting data; they are substitutes for face-to-face interaction with respondents. Questionnaires provide time for respondents to think about their answers and, if properly administered, can offer confidentiality or anonymity for the respondents. Questionnaires can be administered easily and inexpensively, and can return a wealth of information in a relatively short period of time (Babbie, 1990; Smith, 1990; Witkin and Altschuld, 1995). They are useful for estimating feelings, beliefs, and preferences about HRD programs as well as opinions about the application of knowledge, skills, and attitudes required in a job. Questionnaires can generate sound and systematic information about the reactions of participants to an HRD program as well as describe any changes the participants experienced in conjunction with the program.

It is important that questionnaires be designed properly to satisfy their intended purposes. To be used as an analysis and evaluation tool in measuring participants' attitude or feelings about performance improvement, questionnaire items have to meet a high degree of applicability, accountability, and technical quality (McBean and Al-Nassri, 1982). This means that the questions asked should be suited to the intended purposes of improving performance and should show high levels of statistical validity and reliability. This chapter covers developing and administrating questionnaires for analysis and evaluation in the field of human resource development (HRD). It focuses on the essential elements for designing a good questionnaire and administrative issues to improve the effectiveness of collecting information using questionnaires.

THE PROCESS OF QUESTIONNAIRE CONSTRUCTION

Questionnaire construction is one of the most delicate and critical research activities in the field of HRD. Asking the right questions, questions that provide valid and reliable information for making a decision, testing a theory, or investigating a topic, is probably as much of an art as any aspect of HRD research (Payne, 1951). A well-made questionnaire has several attributes. It is well-organized, the questions are clear, response options are well-drawn and exhaustive, and there is a natural order or flow to the questions that keeps the respondent moving toward completion of the questionnaire. These desirable attributes, though deceptively simple when they occur in a quality questionnaire, are the result of a great deal of painstaking development work. According to Peterson (2000), there are seven distinct tasks that are needed to achieve such a result. Each of these tasks requires a series of decisions and activities:

1. Review the information requirements necessitating a questionnaire.
2. Develop and prioritize a list of potential questions that will satisfy the information requirements.
3. Assess each potential question carefully.
4. Determine the types of questions to be asked.
5. Decide on the specific wording of each question to be asked.
6. Determine the structure of the questionnaire.
7. Evaluate the questionnaire.

As these tasks imply, an analyst or evaluator must be systematic when constructing a questionnaire. Each task of the process must be completed before subsequent ones are undertaken. The following sections focus on the first three tasks, which provide a foundation or context for constructing a questionnaire. Discussion of the remaining four tasks is integrated into later sections of the chapter.

Review the Information Requirements Necessitating a Questionnaire

The first step in constructing an effective questionnaire is to review and understand the information requirements of the problem, opportunities, or decisions that led to the need for a questionnaire. Such information identification will depend on the nature of the project goals as they pertain to human performance improvement and HRD. Theory and previous research will be major guides in this area, as will conversations with knowledgeable individuals. It is also at this initial stage that the population of interest that will be studied needs to be identified. In particular, the first thing to do when reviewing information requirements is to be sure that any unusual terms, constructs, and jargon have the same meaning to you as a performance technologist as they do to a project sponsor or client (Peterson, 2000). Unless you understand the information requirements—what information is needed and how that information will be used—no attempt should be made to construct a questionnaire; the results would be of little value.

Develop and Prioritize a List of Potential Questions That Will Satisfy the Information Requirements

Assuming that a decision has been made to use a questionnaire to gather information as a result of a conscious and deliberate process, it is then necessary to translate the information into questions that can elicit the desired information. These questions should be as specific as possible. The more specific the questions are, the easier their evaluation will be, and the easier it will be to translate the questions into a form that can be readily administered in a questionnaire. Each potential question should be screened with respect to (1) how the answers to it will be analyzed, (2) the anticipated information it will provide, and (3) how the ensuing information will be used. Part of the screening process consists of prioritizing the questions according to their information relevancy.

Assess Each Potential Question Carefully

Potential questions surviving the preliminary screening process should then be examined for their administrative viability or how participants might react to them. Each potential question should be evaluated by posing three sequential interrogatives: (1) Can participants understand the question?, (2) Can participants answer the question?, and (3) Will participants answer the question? For a question to be administratively viable, the answer to each interrogative must be "yes." When evaluating the administrative viability of a potential question, an analyst or evaluator should consider the mode of administration that will be used and the characteristics of the participants. Most potential questions are amenable to being self-administered or other-administered.

ESSENTIAL ELEMENTS IN CONSTRUCTING A GOOD QUESTIONNAIRE

According to Swisher (1980), the following criteria are important in constructing quality questionnaires: format and layout, question writing, question sequencing and organization, and a cover letter. Covert (1984) also suggests a checklist for developing questionnaires: title, introductory statement, directions, demographic section, writing items, and structure and format. Covert suggests that the most important part is the question items: the more clear and understandable the questions, the better the results.

Analysis and evaluation in HRD programs seek both quantitative and qualitative data that must be analyzed and interpreted for meaning. The type of data analysis necessary is usually decided on when an analysis or evaluation is planned (Phillips, 1997). There are three steps that must be carefully thought through at the beginning stages of questionnaire development: (1) the specification of the questions to be answered, (2) the operationalization of the specific concepts for data analysis, and (3) the selection of appropriate data-analysis methods. Variables must properly represent the concepts expressed in the questions, and statistical techniques must be appropriate for the variables and their measurement level (Weisberg, Krosnick, and Bowen, 1996). If these three steps are followed, it will facilitate appropriate analysis of the data.

Combining the advice of the aforementioned authors, one might conclude that at least five essential elements should be considered in designing and developing a good questionnaire for improving performance in HRD programs: (1) introduction, directions, and closing; (2) question construction; (3) question format and rating scale; (4) questionnaire layout or format; and (5) data analysis.

Introduction, Instructions, and Closing Statement

A questionnaire should contain introductory statements, clear instructions, and a closing statement as appropriate.

Introduction. An introductory statement may include information about the general purpose, a request for cooperation, and information about anonymity or confidentiality procedures. This information can be presented at the beginning of the questionnaire or in a cover letter. If a cover letter is used, a short introduction should also be printed on the questionnaire so that the questionnaire is self-sufficient (Plumb and Spyridakis, 1992).

"Anonymity" means that there is no feasible way to identify a respondent. In other words, the questionnaires are administered in such a way that the analyst or evaluator cannot identify a given questionnaire with a given respondent. It also means that there is no identifying information asked for and questions are structured in such a way that one could not match responses with a particular individual. These are difficult criteria to meet. When they are not feasible, one can offer the respondents confidentiality. This means that the analyst or evaluator will not report data or information that ties given individuals with their responses. If anonymity or confidentiality can be provided, the respondents need to know this up front. If not, they need to be told that the questionnaire is not anonymous or confidential.

The cover letter or introductory statement is the analysts' or evaluators' chance to ask for cooperation from participants. It should be clear and brief, given the goal of using as little of the respondents' time as necessary. If a questionnaire is arranged into content subsections, it is useful to introduce each section with a short statement concerning its content and purpose (Babbie, 1990).

An example of an introductory statement included on a questionnaire is shown in Figure 32.1. Additional information to consider for an introduction or a cover letter can include an appeal for cooperation, a few words to introduce the analysts' or evaluators' credibility, and information about deadlines. Expressed deadlines increase questionnaire response rates (Spitzer, 1979).

Instructions. Every self-administered questionnaire should begin with instructions on completing it. For closed-ended questions, including multiple choice, yes or no, and rating scales, respondents should be given instructions about answer formats, such as placing a check mark or an X in the box beside the appropriate answer or writing in their answers when called for. For open-ended questions such as fill-ins, short answers, and essays, respondents should be given some

---

As the one-week human resource development (HRD) program comes to a close, please share with us your frank reactions about this HRD program. Your input will help us to evaluate our efforts, and your comments and suggestions will help us to improve future programs. As director of the HRD Department, I appreciate your taking time to respond. This questionnaire will take about ten minutes to complete. I will read your answers carefully. All responses to the questionnaire will remain anonymous. If you want to obtain a summary of the results, please let us know and we will share them with you. Thank you for your cooperation!

Figure 32.1. Example of a Questionnaire Introductory Statement.

guidance as to whether brief or lengthy answers are expected. If a given question varies from the general instructions pertaining to the whole questionnaire, special instructions for that subsection will be required to facilitate a proper response (Babbie, 1990). Instructions should be complete, unambiguous, and concise.

Closing Statement. A questionnaire also needs a closing statement that thanks participants for completing the questions. A closing statement is also related in part to logistics. Questionnaires could include what to do with completed answers (Dixon, 1990). An example is, "When you have completed the questionnaire, please return it to the blue box located at the front exit of the room."

Question Construction

Writing questionnaire items is more an art than a science (Neuman, 1997; Payne, 1951; Sheatsley, 1983). It takes skill, practice, patience, and creativity. Neuman (1997) suggests two main principles for developing questions: "avoid confusion and keep the respondent's perspective in mind" (p. 233). There is a temptation to add superfluous words and items to a questionnaire, but developers are urged to resist the temptation.

Questionnaires should be short, containing only questions that yield answers that are actually going to be used in the analysis or evaluation. Avoid "interesting" and "nice to know" questions (Psacharopoulos, 1980). Also avoid including questions that appeared on prior or similar questionnaires, unless they pertain directly to the objectives of your study. Interesting, nice-to-know, and everyone-else-asks-them types of questions are the biggest culprits in questionnaires that the users judge to be long and laborious. The wording of questions is a critical factor in the respondent's interpretation of questions. Kent (1993, p. 78) provides three conditions to maximize the possibility of obtaining valid responses:

- Respondents must understand the questions and understand them in the same way as other respondents.
- Respondents must be able to provide the answers.
- Respondents must be willing to provide the information.

Analysts and evaluators of HRD programs want all respondents to read and understand in the same ways the same questions, but it is difficult for the question developer to make the questions equally clear, relevant, and meaningful to all respondents (Neuman, 1997). An extensive review of research on guidelines for questionnaire construction (Babbie, 1990, 2001; Biner, 1993; Brace, 2004; Dixon, 1990; Kent, 1993; Labaw, 1980; Lees-Haley, 1980; Maher and Kur, 1983; Moran, 1990; Neuman, 1997; Newby, 1992; Oppenheim, 1992; Pershing, 1996; Peterson, 2000; Rea and Parker, 1992; Richardson, 1994;

Sheatsley, 1983; Smith, 1990; Spitzer, 1979; Thomas, 2004; Weisberg, Krosnik, and Bowen, 1996), can be summarized by noting that there are a number of general principles of question writing that need to be used to avoid common errors in writing items for questionnaires. These principles will enable analysts and evaluators to design questionnaires that will yield better responses. Following is a selection of "do's," or appropriate use, and "do nots" that are sound guidelines for writing good question items for analysis and evaluation in HRD programs.

Write Simple, Clear, and Short Questions. Ambiguity, confusion, and vagueness bother most respondents (Neuman, 1997). To avoid these problems, questions for questionnaires should be simple, clear, and kept as short as possible. The longer the question, the more difficult is the task of answering. Fewer words are better than more, and shorter questions produce higher response rates (Pershing, 1996; Sheatsley, 1983). Although there is no magic number of words, Payne (1951), for one example, insists on using twenty-five or fewer words for a question.

Make Specific and Precise Questions. Specific questions are usually better than general questions because of their accuracy and similar interpretation by all respondents. Question items should be worded specifically with a particular audience in mind: the group you expect to answer the questions (Lees-Haley, 1980). The more general the question, the wider will be the range of interpretations (Converse and Presser, 1986). Questions with specific and concrete wording are more apt to communicate the same meaning to all respondents. Avoid words that may be interpreted differently by each respondent, such as "frequently," "most," "sometimes," or "regularly" (Dixon, 1990; Pershing, 1996).

Use Appropriate Language. Questions should be worded at the appropriate level for respondents. Professional jargon, slang, technical terms, and abbreviations can carry many different meanings to respondents who vary in life, work experiences, and education (Edwards, Thomas, Rosenfeld, and Booth-Kewley, 1997; Neuman, 1997). Avoid questions with such terms unless a specialized population is being used as respondents. If the questionnaire is designed for a specialized group, it is acceptable to use the jargon or technical terms of that group, provided all respondents are familiar with them.

Ensure Respondents' Ability to Answer. Respondents must be competent to answer questions. In making questions, we should continually ask ourselves whether the respondents are able to provide useful information (Babbie, 1990, 2001). Asking questions that few respondents can answer frustrates the respondents and results in poor-quality responses. Asking the respondents to recall past details, answer specific factual information, and make choices about something they know little or nothing about may result in an answer, but one that is meaningless (Neuman, 1997).

Include Only One Topic or Idea per Item. Each question should be related to only one topic or idea. Items that contain two separate ideas or try to combine two questions into one are called "double barreled" questions (Babbie, 1990, 2001; Neuman, 1997). The problem with double-barreled questions is that agreement or disagreement with the item implies agreement or disagreement with both parts of it. The best way of dealing with double-barreled questions is to break the item up and list each part as separate items, that is, one question per idea or topic. As a general rule, whenever the word *and* appears in a question or statement, question developers should check whether they are asking a double-barreled question.

Use Appropriate Emphasis for Key Words in the Question. The use of appropriate emphasis tools such as boldfaced, italicized, capitalized, or underlined words or phrases within the context of a question can serve as a constructive way to clarify potential confusion within the questionnaire (Rea and Parker, 1992). Appropriate emphasis for key words can add clarity to questions.

Take Care with Sensitive Questions. Asking sensitive questions on questionnaires has always been a difficult issue (Edwards, Thomas, Rosenfeld, and Booth-Kewley, 1997). People vary in the amount and type of information they are willing to disclose about their salary, race, ethnicity, and so on. In dealing with these kinds of sensitive questions, special care should be taken. It is also necessary to consider avoiding questions that use words or phrases of regional terminology or that reflect occupational or social class differences (Pershing, 1996).

Avoid Negative Questions or Double Negatives. The appearance of a negation, for example the word *not,* in a questionnaire item paves the way for easy misinterpretation. Double negatives in ordinary language are grammatically incorrect and confusing (Neuman, 1997). Questions with double negatives are also confusing and difficult to answer. A double negative question may ask respondents to disagree that something in a question statement is false or negative. This situation can result in "an awkward statement and a potential source of considerable error" (Sheatsley, 1983, p. 217).

Avoid Biased or Loaded Questions and Terms. The way in which questions are worded, or the inclusion of certain terms, may encourage some respondents more than others. Such questions are called "biased or loaded" and should be avoided in question development (Babbie, 1990, 2001; Neuman, 1997). Words have implicit connotative as well as explicit denotative meanings. Titles or positions in society can carry prestige or status, and can bias questions. There are many ways to bias a question, such as identification of a well-known person or agency and social desirability. Words with strong emotional connotations and stands on issues linked to people with high social status can color how respondents hear and answer questions (Neuman, 1997).

Avoid Questions with False Premises or Future Intentions. Respondents who disagree with the premises will be frustrated when attempting to answer a question. If it is necessary to include questions with a potentially false premise, the question should explicitly ask the respondents to assume the premise is true, then ask for a preference. Answers to a hypothetical circumstance or future intentions are not very reliable, but being explicit will reduce respondents' frustration (Kent, 1993; Neuman, 1997). In general, questions for analysis and evaluation should be specific and concrete, and should relate to the respondents' experiences.

Question Format and Rating Scales

Question Formats. Questionnaire item responses fall into two general categories: (1) closed-ended, or structured, fixed-response questions; and (2) open-ended, or unstructured, free-response questions. In closed-ended questions, including those with multiple choice, yes or no, and true or false answers, and questions with rating scales, respondents are asked to select their answer from a fixed set of response alternatives. Closed-ended questions are very common in questionnaires designed for analyses and evaluations because of a greater uniformity of responses and easy administration. Their main drawback can be in the structuring of responses (Babbie, 1990; Edwards, Thomas, Rosenfeld, and Booth-Kewley, 1997; Weisberg, Krosnick, and Bowen, 1996).

Open-ended questions, such as those requiring fill-ins, short answers, and essays, ask respondents to provide answers to questions using their own words. They provide respondents an opportunity to answer using their own frame of reference without undue influence from prefixed alternatives (Sheatsley, 1983; Weisberg, Krosnick, and Bowen, 1996). In answering and interpreting open-ended questions, there is the problem that some respondents will give answers that are irrelevant to the purposes of the analysis or evaluation.

Sometimes questionnaire developers combine closed-ended responses with an open category or option. Such questions are called "semistructured," and they are used when the questionnaire developer is concerned that the set of closed-ended options is not exhaustive.

Closed-ended questions take longer to develop, require a single specific answer or choice from several specified options, and take a shorter time to complete by the respondents. Open-ended questions provide in-depth responses and

Table 32.1. Characteristics of Closed-Ended and Open-Ended Questions.

Question Type	Advantages	Limitations
Closed-ended	Easier and quicker to answer More likely to get answers about sensitive topics Easier to code and statistically analyze Easier to compare different respondents' answers Easier to replicate	Frustration without desired answer Confusing if many response choices are offered Misinterpretation of a question without notice Simplistic responses to complex issues Blurred distinctions between respondents' answers
Open-ended	Opportunity for respondents to give their opinion Unanticipated findings to be discovered Adequate for complex issues Creativity, self-expression, and richness of detail are permitted Respondents' logic, thinking processes, and frames of reference are revealed	Different degrees of detail and irrelevance in answers Difficulty with response coding Difficulty with comparison and statistical analysis A greater amount of respondent time, thought, and effort is necessary Requires space for answers

unanticipated information, take longer to be completed by the respondents, and take longer to analyze. Each form of question has advantages and limitations (Babbie, 2001; Neuman, 1997; Sudman and Bradburn, 1982). Table 32.1 summarizes advantages and limitations of the two major types of question formats.

Rating Scales. A rating scale yields "a *single score* that indicates both the direction and intensity of a person's attitude" (Henerson, Morris, and Fitz-Gibbon, 1978, p. 84). Because the scoring method for most rating scales is based on the idea of measuring the intensity, hardness, or potency of a variable (Dwyer, 1993; Neuman, 1997), each item must differentiate those respondents with a favorable attitude from those with an unfavorable attitude. In addition, the question items must allow for expression of a broad range of feelings, from strongly favorable through neutral to strongly unfavorable.

According to Weisberg, Krosnick, and Bowen (1996), if a rating scale is to be used in a questionnaire, three decisions must be made. The first decision is how many points to include in the scale. It is usually a good idea to construct scales with fewer than seven points, because psychological research indicates that people have difficulty reliably making more than seven distinctions (Miller, 1956). The second decision is whether to provide a middle alternative in a scale. It is generally good to include a middle alternative because it represents the best description of some respondents' feelings. The third decision is how many points to assign to the labeled words. Verbal labels help to clarify the meanings of scale points for respondents. It is best not to mix labeling words with numbers.

There are several measurement techniques that have been used to assess beliefs, attitudes, and intentions (Fishbein and Ajzen, 1975). However, three major rating scales are commonly used in questionnaire development: (1) Thurstone, (2) Likert, and (3) the semantic differential.

Thurstone Scaling. Thurstone equal appearing interval scales, originally developed by Thurstone and Chave (1929), are based on the law of comparative judgment. Several steps are needed to arrive at a series of statements, each with its own weight or value. The Thurstone technique begins with a set of belief statements regarding a target subject. An analyst or evaluator can construct an attitude scale or select statements from a longer collection of attitude statements. Next, these statements are classified into one of eleven categories or dimensions from most favorable to neutral to least favorable through a judgment procedure of subject-matter experts (Miller, 1991). Third, the analyst or evaluator computes a mean or median rating and assigns the value to the statement. Statements are discarded if the assignment of the statement is variable across experts. The Thurstone scale is then developed by selecting statements with a scale value evenly spread from one extreme to the other, that is, 1 to 11 (Edwards and Kenney, 1946; Edwards, Thomas, Rosenfeld, and Booth-Kewley, 1997; Miller, 1991). An example of a Thurstone scale is shown in Figure 32.2. Although the weights or values in parentheses are not provided to respondents, they indicate the Thurstone values assigned to each question item.

Thurstone scaling approximates an interval level of measurement (Miller, 1991). Developing a true Thurstone scale is considerably more difficult than describing one (Nunnally, 1978). Nevertheless, economy and effectiveness of data reduction, if adequately developed and scored, are its strengths. The method is not often used by analysts and evaluators today because of the labor intensiveness of the dimension-construction process and the need for a large number of content experts to do the item rating and sorting (Babbie, 2001; Edwards, Thomas, Rosenfeld, and Booth-Kewley, 1997).

Likert Scale. Rensis Likert's scale (1932), called a summated rating or additive scale, is widely used and very common in questionnaires because of its easy construction, high reliability, and successful adaptation to measure many types of affective characteristics (Edwards and Kenney, 1946; Nunnally, 1978). On the Likert rating scale, a respondent indicates agreement or disagreement with a

---

Below are five statements about the training materials used in this human resource development program. Please indicate your feeling by circling either "A" or "D" for each statement. There are no right or wrong answers.

A = Agree, or agree more than disagree   D = Disagree, or disagree more than agree

Training Materials Used in This Human Resource Development Program

- Training materials are enjoyable. (5.5)   A   D
- Training materials are simple. (1.3)   A   D
- Training materials are traditional style. (2.8)   A   D
- Training materials are up-to-date. (10.7)   A   D
- Training materials are well organized. (7.3)   A   D

Figure 32.2. Example of Thurstone Scaling.

Below are five statements about the training materials used in this human resource development program. Please indicate your opinion by circling "SA," "A," "U," "D," or "SD." There are no right or wrong answers.

SA = Strongly agree   A = Agree   U = Undecided   D = Disagree
SD = Strongly disagree

Training Materials Used in This Human Resource Development Program

- Training materials are enjoyable.   SA   A   U   D   SD
- Training materials are simple.   SA   A   U   D   SD
- Training materials are traditional style. SA   A   U   D   SD
- Training materials are up-to-date.   SA   A   U   D   SD
- Training materials are well organized.   SA   A   U   D   SD

Figure 32.3. Example of Likert Scale.

---

variety of statements on an intensity scale. The five-point "strongly agree" to "strongly disagree" format is used. Responses are then summed across the items to generate a score on the affective instrument. An example of the Likert scale is presented in Figure 32.3.

The simplicity and ease of use of the Likert scale are its real strengths. The Likert scale can provide an ordinal-level measure of a person's attitude (Babbie,

2001; Miller, 1991). Gathering and processing the Likert responses are efficient. When several items are combined, more comprehensive multiple-indicator measurement is possible. The rating scales have the advantage of providing data that use values rather than merely categories (Edwards, Thomas, Rosenfeld, and Booth-Kewley, 1997). This feature can provide greater flexibility for data analysis.

The Likert scale has a limitation. Different combinations of several items may result in the same or similar overall score or result, and therefore the response set presents a potential danger (Neuman, 1997). To effectively combine items to enhance the measurement of a characteristic, items included in the same dimension should have a strong relationship to the characteristic they are supposed to measure, and the items should be logically related to each other.

Other modifications to anchor rating scales are possible: people might be asked whether they approve or disapprove, or whether they believe something is almost always true or not true. Table 32.2 gives additional sets of anchors that can be used with Likert-type questions for questionnaires (Bracken, 1996; Edwards, Thomas, Rosenfeld, and Booth-Kewley, 1997; Gable and Wolf, 1993).

Semantic Differential Scale. Charles Osgood's semantic differential scale (1952) provides an indirect measure of how a person feels about a concept, object, or other person. The scale measures subjective feelings about something by using a set of scales anchored at their extreme points by words of opposite meaning (Edwards, Thomas, Rosenfeld, and Booth-Kewley, 1997). To use the semantic differential, an analyst or evaluator presents target subjects with a list of paired opposite adjectives in a continuum of five to eleven points. Respondents mark the place on the scale continuum between the adjectives that best expresses their perceptions, attitudes, feelings, and so on. The results of semantic differential scales can be used to assess respondents' overall perceptions of various concepts or issues. Examples of semantic differential scales are presented in Figure 32.4.

Studies of a wide variety of adjectives in English found that they fall into three major classes of meaning: evaluation, or "good-bad"; potency, or "strong-weak"; and activity, or "active or passive" (Neuman, 1997). Of the three classes of meaning, evaluation is usually the most significant. Semantic differential scales yield interval data that are usable with virtually any statistical analysis. However, it is often difficult to give concise written directions for semantic differentials, especially to respondents unfamiliar with the rating scale.

Questionnaire Layout or Format

Questionnaire layout or format is just as important as the wording of questions (Babbie, 1990, 2001). The appearance and arrangement of the questionnaire should be clear, neat, and easy to follow. Often respondents seem to decide whether or not they will participate based on the appearance of the

Table 32.2. Various Likert-Type Response Formats.

Type of Scale	Points with a Scale Continuum				
	5	4	3	2	1
Agreement	Strongly agree	Agree	Neither agree nor disagree	Disagree	Strongly disagree
Frequency	Always	Often	About half the time	Seldom	Never
Importance	Very important	Important	Moderately important	Of little importance	Unimportant
Truth	True	Often true	True about half the time	Seldom true	False
Satisfaction	Very satisfied	Satisfied	Neither satisfied nor dissatisfied	Dissatisfied	Very dissatisfied
Effectiveness	Very effective	Effective	Neither effective nor ineffective	Ineffective	Very ineffective
Quality	Very good	Good	Average (Barely acceptable)	Poor	Very poor
Expectation	Much better than expected	Better than expected	As expected	Worse than expected	Much worse than expected
Extent (Likelihood)	To a very great extent	To a great extent	To a moderate extent	To a small extent	To no extent (Not at all)
Strength	To a very great strength	To a great strength	To a moderate strength	To a small strength	To no strength

questionnaire (Moran, 1990). A professional appearance with high-quality graphics, space between questions, and good layout improves accuracy and completeness, helps the questionnaire flow, and gets a higher response rate (Kent, 1993; Neuman, 1997; Spitzer, 1979; Swisher, 1980).

An efficiently constructed questionnaire will also facilitate the processing, tabulation, and analysis of the data (Harty, 1979). A questionnaire should be spread out and uncluttered, with a lot of "white space" to make it appear less formidable (Babbie, 1990, 2001; Moran, 1990; Weisberg, Krosnick, and Bowen,

Please read each pair of adjectives below that describes the training materials used in this human resource development program. Then place a mark in the box between them that comes closest to your first impression or feeling. There are no right or wrong answers.

How do you feel about the training materials used in this human resource development program?

Enjoyable	☐	☐	☐	☐	☐	Unenjoyable
Simple	☐	☐	☐	☐	☐	Complex
Traditional	☐	☐	☐	☐	☐	Modern
Out-of-date	☐	☐	☐	☐	☐	Up-to-date
Organized	☐	☐	☐	☐	☐	Unorganized

Figure 32.4. Examples of Semantic Differential Scales.

1996). Squeezing as many questions as possible onto a page makes the questionnaire shorter in pages, but the clutter may result in overlooked questions or in respondents deciding not to participate. This means it is important to leave enough room for answers to be written out.

It is also important that instructions be distinguishable from the questions themselves. A convention to follow is "use capitals underlined for instructions, capitals for the responses, and lower case for the questions themselves" (Kent, 1993, p. 83). Responses are usually listed one underneath the other, and the response categories are placed in columns.

Questionnaire layout is especially crucial for self-completed and mailed questionnaires because there is no person available to interact with the respondent. Instead, the questionnaire's appearance persuades the respondent to answer. Mailed questionnaires should include a polite and professional cover letter on letterhead stationery, identification of the analyst or evaluator, telephone or facsimile numbers for questions, and a statement of appreciation for participation (Neuman, 1997).

While the actual physical length of a questionnaire is important, the respondent's perception of its length is more important (Swisher, 1980). The developer should keep the questionnaire as short as possible without sacrificing the other criteria for format and layout. The format and layout must be physically and logically consistent. The length of a questionnaire should reflect the purposes of the analysis or evaluation.

Data Analysis

Data analysis of questionnaires involves coding questions and responses and deciding how to aggregate the data for use by the analyst or evaluator. Using simple frequency counts for closed-ended questions or using a categorization of the written answers to open-ended questions often suffice (Newby, 1992). Based upon Kent's suggestions for qualitative data reduction (1993, pp. 165–166), open-ended questions can be analyzed with the following activities:

- Paraphrasing and summarizing what respondents have answered
- Classifying responses into suitable categories
- Converting questionnaire data into quasi-quantitative data
- Undertaking content analysis

The response patterns for closed-ended questions can be presented in graphs or histograms. Items that use scales can be reduced to a mean response for purposes of comparison. Data for open-ended questions can be reported in the form of quoting extracts from the text, producing checklists or tables, or rearranging or reordering lists (Kent, 1993). It may be necessary in some cases to use more complex inferential statistical analyses of data from questionnaires if the respondents represent a sample and there is a need to generalize to the larger population.

USEFUL ADMINISTRATIVE GUIDELINES FOR USING A QUESTIONNAIRE

Self-completion questionnaires, whether paper-based or electronic, benefit from the absence of an interviewer from the process. This removes a major source of potential bias in the responses and makes it easier for a respondent to be honest about sensitive subjects. A questionnaire can either be delivered by e-mail or be accessed via a Web page. Each form of media provides its own opportunities in terms of questionnaire construction, but equally each has its own drawbacks (Brace, 2004; Fehily and Johns, 2004; Thomas, 2004).

In addition to the elements of a good questionnaire development, there are several helpful administrative guidelines to improve the effectiveness of using questionnaires to collect data in the analysis and evaluation of HRD programs (Newby, 1992; Phillips, 1997). Useful administrative guidelines for using questionnaires for improving HRD programs can be briefly summarized, based on the suggestions of Phillips (1997).

Explain the Purpose of a Questionnaire. Spell out for the respondents the questionnaire's use as part of an HRD analysis or evaluation project, including how the results will be put to use. This is not always understood by respondents, and it is useful to explain to them who will see the results and how the results will be used in the organization.

Have a Neutral Person or Third Party Administer the Questionnaire. In some cases, it is important and helpful to have a person other than the analyst or evaluator administer the questionnaire. A program coordinator or study sponsor instead of the analyst or evaluator can be used. This method increases the objectivity of the feedback on the HRD program and decreases the likelihood of the analyst or evaluator being perceived as reacting unfavorably to criticism expressed in feedback. This idea particularly extends to instructors in the administration of course evaluations at the end of a program.

Provide a Copy of the Questionnaire in Advance. For lengthy questionnaires covering HRD programs that span days or weeks, it is helpful to distribute the questionnaire early in the program so that participants can familiarize themselves with questions and statements. Respondents should be cautioned not to reach a final conclusion regarding their input until the end of the HRD program data-gathering activities.

Consider Quantifying Program Ratings for Comparisons. Analysts and evaluators often find it advantageous to attempt to solicit feedback from questionnaires in terms of numerical ratings. Although questionnaire data are still subjective, overall numerical ratings can be useful in monitoring performance and making comparisons with other, similar programs.

Provide Enough Time for Completing the Questionnaire. A "time crunch" can cause problems if participants are asked to complete a questionnaire in a rush at the end of an HRD program or data-gathering activity. To avoid this problem, analysts and evaluators should provide ample time to complete the questionnaire in a scheduled session as feasible. Pretesting the questionnaire will provide guidance as to how much time will be required. If the questionnaire is mailed, time information should be included as part of the introduction or instructions.

CONCLUSION

This chapter explores a range of design and administrative issues regarding the construction of questionnaires. Constructing effective questionnaires involves a concerted effort, a certain amount of time, and careful attention. When a questionnaire appears to be clear and logical to the respondents and those who will use the data that the questionnaire provides, this is invariably the result of a long and often complicated process of development and tryout. Well-designed questionnaires cannot be developed in a short time or at the last minute. A questionnaire is only as good as the questions it contains. When the design guidelines presented in this chapter are followed, the questionnaire becomes a powerful diagnostic and evaluation tool for the performance-improvement professional.

References

Babbie, E. R. (1990). *Survey research methods* (2nd ed.). Belmont, CA: Wadsworth.

Babbie, E. R. (2001). *The practice of social research* (9th ed.). Belmont, CA: Wadsworth.

Biner, P. M. (1993). The development of an instrument to measure student attitudes toward televised courses. *The American Journal of Distance Education, 7*(1), 62–73.

Brace, I. (2004). *Questionnaire design: How to plan, structure and write survey material for effective market research.* London, UK: Kogan Page.

Bracken, D. W. (1996). Multisource (360-degree) feedback: Surveys for individual and organizational development. In A. I. Kraut (Ed.), *Organizational surveys: Tools for assessment and change* (pp. 115–143). San Francisco: Jossey-Bass.

Converse, J. M., and Presser, S. (1986). *Survey questions: Handcrafting the standardized questionnaire.* Newbury Park, CA: Sage.

Covert, R. W. (1984). A checklist for developing questionnaires. *Evaluation News, 5*(3), 74–78.

Dixon, N. M. (1990). The relationship between trainee responses on participant reaction forms and posttest scores. *Human Resources Development Quarterly, 1*(2), 129–137.

Dwyer, E. E. (1993). *Attitude scale construction: A review of the literature.* Morristown, TN: Walters State Community College. (ERIC Document Reproduction Service No. ED 359 201.)

Edwards, A. L., and Kenney, K. C. (1946). A comparison of the Thurstone and Likert techniques of attitude scale construction. *Journal of Applied Psychology, 30,* 72–83.

Edwards, J. E., Thomas, M. D., Rosenfeld, P., and Booth-Kewley, S. (1997). *How to conduct organizational surveys: A step-by-step guide.* Thousand Oaks, CA: Sage.

Fehily, A. M., and Johns, A. P. (2004). Designing questionnaires for nutrition research. *British Nutrition Foundation Nutrition Bulletin, 29,* 50–56.

Fishbein, M., and Ajzen, I. (1975). *Belief, attitude, intention and behavior: An introduction to theory and research.* Reading, MA: Addison-Wesley.

Gable, R. K., and Wolf, M. B. (1993). *Instrument development in the affective domain: Measuring attitudes and values in corporate and school settings* (2nd ed.). Boston: Kluwer Academic.

Harty, H. (1979). Questionnaire design and administration. *New Directions for Institutional Advancement: Surveying Institutional Constituencies, 6,* 45–57.

Hayes, B. E. (1992). *Measuring customer satisfaction: Development and use of questionnaire.* Milwaukee, WI: ASQC Quality.

Henerson, M. E., Morris, L. L., and Fitz-Gibbon, C. T. (1978). How to measure attitudes. Beverly Hills, CA: Sage.

Kent, R. A. (1993). *Marketing research in action.* London, UK: Routledge.

Labaw, P. J. (1980). *Advanced questionnaire design.* Cambridge, MA: Art Books.

Lees-Haley, P. R. (1980). *The questionnaire design handbook.* Huntsville, AL: Lees-Haley Associates.

Likert, R. (1932). *A technique for the measurement of attitudes.* New York: Columbia University Press.

Maher, J. H., and Kur, C. E. (1983). Constructing good questionnaires. *Training and Development Journal, 37*(6), 100, 102–108, 110.

McBean, E. A., and Al-Nassri, S. (1982). Questionnaire design for student measurement of teaching effectiveness. *Higher Education, 11*(3), 273–288.

Miller, D. C. (1991). *Handbook for research design and social measurement* (5th ed.). Newbury Park, CA: Sage.

Miller, G. A. (1956). The magical number seven, plus or minus two. *Psychological Review, 63,* 81–97.

Moran, B. B. (1990). Construction of the questionnaire in survey research. In J. Robbins, H. Willett, M. J. Wiseman, and D. L. Zweizig (Eds.), *Evaluation strategies and techniques for public library children's service: A sourcebook* (pp. 155–158). Madison, WI: University of Wisconsin.

Neuman, W. L. (1997). *Social research methods: Qualitative and quantitative approaches* (3rd ed.). Boston: Allyn & Bacon.

Newby, A. C. (1992). *Training evaluation handbook.* San Diego: Pfeiffer.

Nunnally, J. C. (1978). *Psychometric theory.* New York: McGraw-Hill.

Oppenheim, A. N. (1992). *Questionnaire design, interviewing and attitude measurement* (New ed.). London: Pinter.

Osgood, C. E. (1952). The nature and measurement of meaning. *Psychological Bulletin, 49*(3), 197–237.

Payne, S. L. (1951). *The art of asking questions.* Princeton, NJ: Princeton University Press.

Pershing, J. A. (1996). *Critiquing a reactionnaire.* LG training workshop handout. Bloomington, IN: Indiana University.

Peterson, R. A. (2000). *Constructing effective questionnaires.* Thousand Oaks, CA: Sage.

Phillips, J. J. (1997). *Handbook of training evaluation and measurement methods: Proven models and methods for evaluating any HRD program* (3rd ed.). Houston: Gulf.

Plumb, C., and Spyridakis, J. H. (1992). Survey research in technical communication: Designing and administrating questionnaires. *Technical Communication, 39*(4), 625–638.

Psacharopoulos, G. (1980). Questionnaire surveys in educational planning. *Comparative Education, 16*(2), 159–169.

Rea, L. M., and Parker, R. A. (1992*). Designing and conducting survey research: A comprehensive guide.* San Francisco: Jossey-Bass.

Richardson, T. E. (1994). Using questionnaires to evaluate student learning: Some health warnings. In G. Gibbs (Ed.), *Improving student learning: Theory and practice* (pp. 499–524). Oxford, UK: The Oxford Centre for Staff Development.

Sheatsley, P. B. (1983). Questionnaire construction and item writing. In P. H. Rossi, J. D. Wright, and A. B. Anderson (Eds.), *Handbook of survey research* (pp. 195–230). San Diego: Academic.

Smith, M. J. (1990). *Program evaluation in the human service.* New York: Springer.

Spitzer, D. (1979). Remember these dos and don'ts of questionnaire design. *Training, 16*(5), 34–37.

Sudman, S., and Bradburn, N. M. (1982). *Asking questions: A practical guide to questionnaire design.* San Francisco: Jossey-Bass.

Swisher, R. (1980). Criteria for the design of mail questionnaire. *Journal of Education for Librarianship, 21*(2), 159–165.

Thomas, S. J. (2004). *Using web and paper questionnaires for data-based decision making: From design to interpretation of the results.* Thousand Oaks, CA: Corwin.

Thurstone, L. L., and Chave, E. J. (1929). *The measurement of attitude.* Chicago: University of Chicago Press.

Weisberg, H. F., Krosnick, J. A., and Bowen, B. D. (1996). *An introduction to survey research, polling, and data analysis.* Thousand Oaks, CA: Sage.

Witkin, B. R., and Altschuld, J. W. (1995). *Planning and conducting needs assessment: A practical guide.* Thousand Oaks, CA: Sage.

CHAPTER THIRTY-THREE

Interviewing to Analyze and Evaluate Human Performance Technology

Jana L. Pershing

In the field of human performance technology (HPT), the written questionnaire is the most frequently used means of gathering data and, in some instances, is the only method (Swanson, 1983; Witkin and Altschuld, 1995). Despite the centrality of questionnaires, relying exclusively on one method of data collection provides limited information about performance-improvement initiatives in organizations. Furthermore, because written questionnaires sometimes fail to obtain valid and reliable information, a variety of methodologies should be considered (Witkin and Altschuld, 1995). A less frequently used survey method that is a useful information-gathering tool, particularly in the preliminary stages of analyzing and assessing performance-improvement initiatives, is the *interview* (Swanson, 1983).[1]

In addition to providing information to develop items for written survey questionnaires, interviews may also be used as either a standalone procedure for producing information for subsequent analysis and evaluation studies or in conjunction with other data-gathering methods. Moreover, the personal contacts established during interviews allow for an open dialogue, thereby providing the performance analyst and evaluator the opportunity to acquire in-depth information not readily available through nonverbal survey research methods. This chapter begins with an overview of three types of interviews that are useful to performance technologists: structured, semistructured, and unstructured. It also explains how to conduct interviews and describes the advantages and limitations of interviewing in person, or face-to-face, versus on the telephone.

WHY CONDUCT INTERVIEWS?

The interview is a type of survey research method for collecting information from respondents through interactive real-time communication on the telephone or in person. Because personal contacts are established between the interviewer and respondents, interviews typically involve sharing ideas, engaging in dialogue, and problem solving (Kubr and Prokopenko, 1991). This can be particularly useful when information is overly detailed or technical. For the performance technologist, interviews are also typically used as a first step in collecting information for an improvement initiative (Swanson, 1983). Last, they may provide ways to obtain peripheral information that may be linked directly or indirectly to the causes and effects associated with a performance-improvement initiative (McClelland, 1995).

In contrast to written questionnaires, interviews may be conducted to collect in-depth narrative information by encouraging respondents to talk about their feelings, attitudes, and opinions concerning their jobs and the organization (Kubr and Prokopenko, 1991). They also provide a means for respondents to explore their own solutions to personal and organizational problems, which may be beneficial when addressing emotionally charged issues. In a systematic performance-improvement initiative, interviews are seldom used as the only method for gathering performance-improvement information (Swanson, 1983). Instead, they may be employed for the following reasons: (1) to provide information to develop questions for a written survey questionnaire, (2) as a stand-alone method for producing information for subsequent analysis and evaluation, or (3) in conjunction with other data-gathering methods to correlate and validate information obtained through multiple data-gathering methods.

Advantages

The interview has several general advantages for organizations seeking to collect data on performance-improvement initiatives. They include the following:

- Interviewers can seek clarification when respondents' answers are unexpected or ambiguous.
- Interviews serve as an effective rapport-building opportunity.
- Interviewing allows for a wider range of subjects, for example, unanticipated issues that may arise when following up on a response.

Disadvantages

As with any method of data collection, there are also disadvantages to interviewing. Specific drawbacks include the following:

- Interviewers may bias or lead respondents.
- An interviewer's note-taking can distract respondents.

- Interviews tend to be expensive and time-consuming.
- The results of analyzing interview data are often difficult to summarize, particularly if semistructured or unstructured questions are asked.

TYPES OF INTERVIEWS

As noted earlier, there are three types of interviews that are applicable for gathering performance-improvement information: structured, semistructured, and unstructured (Clardy, 1997). The depth and extent of information and feedback being sought for a particular performance-improvement initiative or evaluation study will determine which type to use (Zemke and Kramlinger, 1982). After the type of interview to conduct has been decided, questions can be designed to gather information about several job-related issues, including job activities, job problems, respondents' perceptions and feelings, and personal and background information (Rossett, 1987). It should also be noted that with the exception of responses to structured questions, data obtained from interviews is typically more qualitative than quantitative (Clardy, 1997). Table 33.1 summarizes the types of information commonly sought using interviews.

Table 33.1. Types of Information Sought Using Interviews.

Type	Examples
Job-specific information	Activities and events that take place on the job
	Job achievements
	Work results
Problems and issues	Problems on the job
	Ideas for performance improvement
	Causes and solutions for poor performance
Respondents' perceptions and feelings	The most- and least-liked parts of the job
	Information about people's experiences and behaviors
	Working relationships with coworkers, managers, and staff
	Work-related values, attitudes, opinions, and preferences
Personal information	Personal goals and interest in obtaining more knowledge and skills
	Work-related habits and practices
	Biographical and background information

Structured Interviews

Structured or standardized interviews are similar to written questionnaires in that they use a set of fixed questions with fixed-response categories covering a specific area or topic (Kubr and Prokopenko, 1991). They are effective when the goals of the performance-improvement initiative or evaluation study are clear. Questions can only be constructed after the performance technologist knows something about the performance problem or business opportunity. Structured-interview questions are concise and singularly address the issue at hand. Because some people are more visually oriented, it is sometimes recommended that response options be given in writing so that respondents can fully consider the range of answers. Depending on the desired depth and degree of information being sought, structured interviews normally last no longer than twenty minutes (McClelland, 1995).

Semistructured Interviews

Semistructured interviews include questions that provide a fixed set of response choices in addition to one or more unrestricted response categories so that the respondents may answer using their own words. Structured responses produce highly specific information, while unstructured comments allow for additional probing that tends to yield more in-depth information (Clardy, 1997). The primary advantage of semistructured interviews is that they provide response options that respondents may select expediently, while also acknowledging that sometimes a response may fall outside the fixed options. However, a drawback includes the possibility that respondents will simply choose from the fixed options even if a response does not exactly fit. Semi-structured interviews are similar to written survey questionnaires that employ both closed-ended and open-ended questions. They typically last thirty to sixty minutes.

Unstructured Interviews

Unstructured or conversational interviews are used when the depth of information being sought is broad and nonspecific (Kubr and Prokopenko, 1991). They are similar to the written survey questionnaire format of open-ended questions. They are also similar to questions asked in brainstorming sessions and are, there-fore, often used during the early stages of a needs assessment or evaluation study. Unstructured interviews are particularly valuable for investigating personal issues that are potentially emotional or sensitive (McClelland, 1995). A primary advantage includes allowing respondents to answer questions in their own words rather than with a predetermined set of response options. This type of interview also allows interviewers to seek clarification or more complete and detailed responses. However, coding and analyzing unstructured interview data can be challenging. Depending on the number of questions and the length of

Table 33.2. Examples of Question Types.

Types	Examples
Structured question	*Over the past three months, have you considered quitting your job?* _____ Yes _____ No _____ Not sure
Semistructured questions	*I am interested in the following background information:* *What is your position?* _____ Manager _____ Supervisor _____ Team Leader _____ Other—specify _____ *How many years have you been with the company?* _____ Specify number of years *Have you occupied the same position during this time?* _____ Yes _____ No *If no, how many positions have you held?* Explain_____
Unstructured questions	*What do you think are the reasons for decreased production rates over the past six months?* *What are the strengths of your salespeople?*

respondents' answers, they may last anywhere from twenty minutes to two hours.

Table 33.2 provides examples of structured, semi-structured, and unstructured questions.

METHODS OF INTERVIEWING

Depending on the type of questions asked, interviews may be conducted either on the telephone or face-to-face. Telephone interviews are more affordable but are also less personal, lending themselves to structured and semistructured questions (Lavrakas, 1998). In contrast, face-to-face interviews are more expensive but allow for in-depth discussions about a topic (Zemke and Kramlinger, 1982).

In-person interviews are conducive to open-ended questions or semistructured questions.

Telephone Interviews

Telephone interviews are particularly useful for seeking general information about a project or specific feedback on one or two straightforward issues. They may also be used to acquire an initial response or confirm the support of people already committed to a project. Because of savings in time and money, telephone interviews are especially beneficial when there is need to interview several people or for touching base with those who have little or no influence on the success of the outcomes of a project.[2] Advantages of conducting telephone interviews are numerous:

- Interviewers can clarify unclear or ambiguous questions for respondents.
- Respondents are more relaxed with an unfamiliar interviewer. In turn, more relaxed respondents are typically more truthful or forthcoming when responding to questions.
- Interviewers can use scripted questions and take notes without distracting respondents.
- Interviewing on the telephone expedites the collection of information and is less expensive than interviewing in person.

Despite their advantages, telephone interviews are not appropriate for all situations. Disadvantages include the following:

- Interviewers have few opportunities to place respondents at ease since small talk and informal conversations often do not work well over the telephone.
- Interviewers cannot assess respondents' reactions to questions by examining their body language. In other words, interviewers must rely exclusively on verbal responses rather than on nonverbal cues.
- The scope of questioning is limited since respondents tire quickly. In other words, interviewers have limited opportunities to probe for thoughtful, insightful, or in-depth responses.
- Respondents can be difficult to reach by telephone.
- Respondents may be reluctant to participate, especially when the interviewer is unknown or when there is no incentive.

Face-to-Face Interviews

In contrast to telephone interviews, face-to-face interviews are useful for seeking in-depth information about a project or for addressing difficult, complex, or controversial subject matter. Because in such interviews rapport is more easily established, they may also be used to enlist support from distressed respondents or to garner support from individuals who are critical to the success of the outcomes of a project. In some cases, such interviews are used when it is necessary to show respondents illustrated materials that are relevant to the interview. Because face-to-face interviews are more expensive to conduct, they are typically used to acquire information from only a few key individuals or when a problem being addressed is costly. Advantages of conducting interviews in person include the following:

- Interviewers can more easily clarify unclear or ambiguous questions for respondents.

- Interviewers can gain insights and ideas from respondents through spontaneous and unexpected responses.

- Interviewers can observe nonverbal cues such as body language to assess a respondent's reaction.

- Interviewers can adapt to the individual conversational styles of various respondents by changing the tone and style of the interview questions.

In contrast, face-to-face interviews have the following disadvantages or limitations:

- Respondents may be distracted by the interviewer's note-taking.

- In speaking to someone in person, respondents may question the confidentiality of the interview and, therefore, may not be as truthful or forthcoming in their answers.

- Face-to-face interviews are an expensive type of survey method given the extensive time involved in surveying several respondents.

- Respondents may be reluctant to agree to a face-to-face interview unless they have an incentive to participate.

THE PROCESS OF INTERVIEWING

As a precursor to conducting interviews, the analyst typically searches for information on the performance problem or business opportunity under consideration. Prior studies, books, journal articles, magazines, and literature reviews in the subject area are useful. Sometimes focus groups are conducted as a way to provide insights prior to developing questions, especially when issues are vague and undefined.[3]

Step 1. Determining the Objectives of the Interviews

Because of the time and expense involved in conducting interviews, the first step is to determine the information being sought. For example, performance technologists may be interested in asking questions about one or more of the following issues:

- Optimal performance
- Actual performance problems
- Feelings about performance
- Solutions to performance problems
- Business opportunities and barriers to implementing solutions

The analyst should use standard terms to draft the objectives, taking care to keep them clear, direct, and concise. Objectives should be shared with the champions of the performance-analysis initiative, and their comments should be incorporated before finalization.

Step 2. Preparing for the Interviews

After the analyst determines the primary objectives and whether interviews will be conducted face-to-face or by telephone, the second step involves preparing for the interviews. This includes six important procedures:

Procedure 1: Select Respondents. Decisions must be made concerning both the specific purposes of the interviews and the population or sample of respondents to be interviewed. A *population* refers to all people within a group, for example, all employees of a company, whereas a *sample* is a subset of a population. Interviewing respondents from a sample is done when limited resources or time make interviewing an entire population impractical, or, in some cases, when everyone in a population may not be available to be interviewed.[4]

Procedure 2: Develop Protocol. A protocol or script that aids in carrying out the interviews must be developed. Creating the protocol includes developing a cover sheet with space for pertinent information about each respondent, for example, name, role, address, and telephone number. Also included in the protocol is necessary logistical information, such as the time and place of the interview, directions, and contact person. An opening statement should be drafted that explains the purposes of the interview, clarifying the target group of the study and the uses to be made of the information collected. The statement should also indicate the estimated time for conducting the interview and provide an explanation concerning issues of confidentiality. Figure 33.1 presents an example of a telephone interview cover sheet including an introduction and call record.

The body of the script should also be prepared; at this point, the questions are developed. For specific examples of types of questions asked during interviews, see Table 33.3. It is important to script the interview questions to ensure continuity

---

TELEPHONE INTERVIEW COVER SHEET
With Introduction and Call Record

International Corporation, LTD
Training and Development Department
October 26, 2005

Name:_____

Phone#:_____ + _____ + _____

Street:_____

City:_____ State:_____

Zip:_____

Hello. Is this the (last name)_____ residence?

(If "NO": *The number I was calling is_____ ,*

and I am calling for (first and last name)_____.

IF WRONG NUMBER, TERMINATE WITH: *I am sorry to have bothered you.*

This is (interviewer's name) _____ *at the International Corporation, LTD in Great Place, Montana. We are doing a study on the need for* (topic) _____.

You were selected in a random sample of our product distributors.
(Go to next page.)

Call Record

Date	Time	Interviewer	Result	Code for Recalls

CODE FOR RESULT:
NA = no answer
VM = voice mail
PIC = partially completed
AM = answering machine
WR = will return (note when)
CP = cellular phone
DISC = disconnected
NH = not home
IC = interview completed
WN = wrong number
REF = refused (when, why, at what point)

CODE FOR RECALLS:
A = Respondent not selected
B = Respondent selected, not interviewed yet
C = Have talked to respondent (give any information helpful for recall interview)

Figure 33.1. Telephone Interview Cover Sheet.

Table 33.3. Types of Questions Asked in Effective Interviews.

Question Subjects	Examples
Optimal conditions	What do you believe ought to be going on?
	How do you think things should work in the organization?
	Given your personal experiences, what do you believe should be occurring?
Actual conditions	Can you provide an actual detailed example of how your fellow employees are performing? Or not performing?
	Explain how the organization is functioning.
	What problems can you identify? Or opportunities?
Feelings and beliefs	How do you feel about the work being done?
	Do you believe others feel the same way as you?
	Do you believe the problems being investigated need to be investigated?
Cause(s)	In your judgment, what are the causes of the problems you have identified?
Solution(s)	How would you suggest that the problems be solved?
	Do you have ideas for expanding the business opportunities for the organization?

Source: Adapted from Rossett, 1987.

in the process from one interview to the next. If the number of questions is few and they are not overly complex, it is best for the interviewer to memorize them. Otherwise, he or she should either write them down on interview forms, leaving room for note-taking, or use note cards, for example, one card per question. Another useful suggestion for questionnaire development includes combining closed-ended and open-ended questions to break up the monotony in the interviewing process. Questions should also be sequenced or ordered from general to specific and should be clustered topically. Also make certain that questions *do not* ask for information that is already known or readily accessible. Doing so will destroy the credibility of the interviewer. More important, avoid questions that intrude into the respondent's personal or professional affairs.

After questionnaire development, a script is prepared for concluding the interview that includes both wrap-up and thank-you statements. When appropriate, the analyst or interviewer should also offer to share information with the respondent when the study is completed.

Procedure 3: Prepare a Timetable. Prepare a timetable for conducting the interviews. In doing so, factor in the likelihood that additional interviews that occur later may build upon information from those preceding them, particularly with open-ended and semistructured interviews. At least forty-five minutes should be scheduled between interviews to review, record, and process notes. When face-to-face interviews are to be conducted, build in advance time to schedule rooms for carrying out the interview. In addition to providing privacy, rooms should be free of interruptions and situated near the activity being examined. Locations where the interviewer and respondent are on equal terms are preferable over private offices. Avoid scheduling interviews as part of a luncheon or dinner since snacking and eating tend to interfere.

Procedure 4: Conduct a Pilot Test. Review the interview design and plans with another, more experienced analyst or interviewer. This process may include testing the protocol on a neutral party and revising it based on the third-party feedback.

Procedure 5: Train Interviewers. After interviewers are selected, they must be trained.[5] Training includes learning the language of the people to be interviewed and practicing the delivery of questions in a conversational yet business-like tone. If during the questioning documents or records are going to be referenced, assemble copies for the interviewer to take to the interview.

Procedure 6: Schedule Interviews. It is important to schedule appointments that are convenient for the respondents. When scheduling, also inform them of the purpose of the interview. It is often useful to send a letter or memo to each respondent three or four days prior to the interview, stating the purpose of the interview and providing logistical information, including the date and time as well as location for face-to-face interviews. If deemed useful, have the letter written and signed by an authority figure, emphasizing the importance of the interview.

Step 3. Carrying Out Each Interview

Carrying out the interview involves not only conducting the interview but also opening and closing it. In the step 3 section, all procedural instructions are directed to the person carrying out the interview, whether the analyst or a separate associate.

Procedure 1: Open the Interview. Opening the interview is the first task in carrying out an interview, beginning with the interviewer introducing him- or herself to the respondent. For face-to-face interviews, begin the dialogue with a friendly smile and a few interesting or casual remarks to enhance communications toward forming a favorable relationship. The respondent should then be provided with a detailed explanation about the purposes and structure of the interview and should be assured about issues pertaining to confidentiality. It is important for the interviewer to arrive at least five to ten minutes before an interview is scheduled to begin. Also, the interviewer should become familiar with the dress code for the place of employment of the respondent, and dress accordingly.

Procedure 2: Conduct the Interview. Conducting the interview is the primary task involved in carrying out the interview. General guidelines that should be adhered to during the course of the interview include encouraging the respondent to talk as much as possible, avoiding interrupting, avoiding arguments or debates, avoiding the stating of one's own opinions, and not dominating the conversation. Interview questions should be directed toward obtaining pertinent information while also allowing the respondent's own line of thought to emerge. An interviewer should be honest about his or her competence in the subject matter at hand and should always demonstrate an appreciation for the points of view and perspectives of the respondent.

Since one of the primary purposes of interviewing is to supplement information already obtained, identify and investigate any inconsistencies, ask specific questions to allow for quantitative or closed-ended responses, and distinguish hard facts from personal opinions. When questions are answered vaguely, pursue them in a pleasant manner until they are fully clarified. Furthermore, when the respondent is too theoretical, conceptual, or uses jargon, seek clarification by asking for concrete examples and explanations.

Above all, remember that interviewers are prone to thinking faster than interviewees talk. Avoid interrupting and completing the sentences of the respondents and instead stay focused on their words in spite of how deliberately or slowly they may express their thoughts and ideas. In addition to paying close attention to the respondent's explanations, refrain from asking strong or direct questions too early in the interview. As an alternative, begin by building upon information already available or by using closed-ended questions that are not designed to provoke. Open-ended questions are more useful in the middle and end stages of the interviewing process after a rapport has been established. Some helpful hints for question-asking throughout the interview include giving the respondent time to think, respecting silence, and summarizing long responses. Conversely, the following should be avoided at all costs: sarcasm, correcting facts or data, and contradicting the respondent.

The process of *note-taking* deserves mention. Before beginning, ask the respondent about taking notes or using a recorder, and when tape-recording interviews, honor off-the-record requests. For complex questions and long responses, write down key ideas and information while remembering to accurately use the words of the respondent. At the end of the question, read your notes back to the respondent. For simple questions and short responses, jot down abbreviated notes quickly and write more extensive notes immediately following the interview.

Procedure 3: Close the Interview. Ease into closing the interview rather than abruptly ending it. After summarizing the main points of the interview, conclude with some positive comments and provide an overall evaluation of the results. In addition to thanking the respondent, ask whether there is anything else he or she would like to add by asking one more open-ended question. Examples of closing questions include the following:

- What has not been covered and should be?
- You seem to have a thorough understanding of _____. What else would you like to add?
- What are we overlooking in our performance analysis or evaluation?

If it is anticipated that the need may arise, ask the respondent's permission to follow up to confirm or clarify information provided during the interview or to gather further data.

Procedure 4: Record the Interview. The analyst or interviewer should record the interview notes immediately following the interview by finding a private place and taking the time to type up the respondent's answers. Keep in mind that reviewing notes and writing about interviews typically takes twice as long as conducting the interview (Mertens 1998; Swanson, 1983).

Step 4. Concluding the Interviewing Process

The overall interviewing process should be discontinued when the information gathered from several respondents becomes repetitive, particularly when open-ended interviews are being conducted (Babbie, 1990). In other words, when the responses of two or three interviews are similar and nothing new is being learned, it is time to bring closure to the interviewing process. As a guideline, redundant information will likely manifest itself after four to six interviews for a homogenous group of respondents. For heterogeneous groups, the number of interviews required before achieving redundancy may double or triple.

If necessary, follow up with respondents to obtain further clarification or needed data before ending the interview process. Also remember to respect the trust and confidence of the respondents. While organizing notes and data collected, conceal the identity of those interviewed, taking precautionary measures to remove information that would overtly identify a particular respondent.

Step 5. Compiling and Analyzing Results

Given the nature or quality of the information collected, select appropriate data-analysis procedures. For quantitative or closed-ended data, use descriptive statistics and graphically depict the numbers or percentages. For qualitative or open-ended data that need further judgments or comparisons by subject-matter experts, consider using affinity and fishbone diagrams. In contrast, conduct a content analysis to compare and contrast qualitative data.[6] Throughout the analysis stage, develop and report the following: numbers and percentages, consistent themes and ideas, and key differences and disagreements.

SUMMARY

Interviewing is less commonly used than written survey research methods in part because the method is time-consuming. Yet it serves as a useful information-gathering tool, particularly in the preliminary stages of analyzing and evaluating performance-improvement initiatives. In addition to providing information to develop questions for written survey questionnaires, interviews may also be used as a standalone procedure for producing information for subsequent analysis and evaluation studies. They may also be implemented in conjunction with other data-gathering methods to correlate and validate information obtained from multiple sources. The depth and extent of information being sought for a particular performance-improvement initiative will determine whether structured, semi-structured, or unstructured interviews should be conducted. In turn, the types of questions asked will determine whether interviews should be conducted on the telephone versus in person or face-to-face.

In closing, the primary purpose for conducting interviews is for the HPT analyst or evaluator to acquire in-depth information that is useful. In contrast to written questionnaires, the personal contacts established during interviews allow for an open dialogue in which respondents are encouraged to talk about their attitudes and opinions concerning their jobs and the organizations in which they work.

Notes

1. This chapter is an adapted version of an article published in *Performance Improvement* (Pershing, 2003).

2. Computer technology has advanced the way in which telephone survey research is conducted, including randomly generated dialing and automatic database storage of survey responses. For more information on computer-assisted telephone interviewing, see Babbie, 2001.

3. Focus groups, also commonly referred to as *group interviews,* involve a facilitator leading a discussion with ten to twelve participants who are knowledgeable about an organizational issue. For more information about using focus groups as a precursor to developing interview questions or conducting them for other research purposes, see Rossett, 1987, and Witkin and Altschuld, 1995.

4. See Babbie, 1990, for detail regarding sampling procedures and types of samples, for example, probability and snowball sampling.

5. For further information on training interviewers, including the issues of hiring and firing, see Babbie, 1990, and Bok van Kammen and Stouthamer-Loeber, 1998.

Regarding background characteristics of interviewers, such as gender, and the question of *who can interview whom?* see Mertens, 1998.

6. For information on compiling and analyzing interview data, refer to Mertens, 1998, and Zemke and Kramlinger, 1982. Also see Strauss, 1987, for more detailed discussions about analyzing open-ended interview data.

References

Babbie, E. (1990). *Survey research methods.* Belmont, CA: Wadsworth Publishing Company.

Babbie, E. (2001). *The practice of social research.* Belmont, CA: Wadsworth Publishing Company.

Bok van Kammen, W., and Stouthamer-Loeber, M. (1998). Practical aspects of interview data collection and data management. In L. Bickman and D. J. Rog (Eds.), *Handbook of applied social research methods* (pp. 375–397). Thousand Oaks, CA: Sage.

Clardy, A. (1997). *Studying your workforce: Applied research methods and tools for the training and development practitioner.* Thousand Oaks, CA: Sage.

Kubr, M. and Prokopenko, J. (1991). *Diagnosing management training and development needs: Concepts and techniques.* Geneva, Switzerland: International Labour Office.

Lavrakas, P. (1998). Methods for sampling and interviewing in telephone surveys. In L. Bickman and D. J. Rog (Eds.), *Handbook of applied social research methods* (pp. 429–472). Thousand Oaks, CA: Sage.

McClelland, S. B. (1995). *Organizational needs assessments: Design, facilitation, and analysis.* Westport, CT: Quorum.

Mertens, D. M. (1998). *Research methods in education and psychology: Integrating diversity with quantitative and qualitative approaches.* Thousand Oaks, CA: Sage.

Pershing, J. L. (2003). Interviewing to analyze and assess performance improvement initiatives. *Performance Improvement, 42*(6), 30–36.

Rossett, A. (1987). *Training needs assessment.* Englewood Cliffs, NJ: Educational Technology Publications.

Strauss, A. L. (1987). *Qualitative analysis for social scientists.* New York: Cambridge University Press.

Swanson, R. A. (1983). *Analysis for improving performance: Tools for diagnosing organizations and documenting workplace expertise.* San Francisco: Berrett-Koehler.

Witkin, B. R., and Altschuld, J. W. (1995). *Planning and conducting needs assessments: A practical guide.* Thousand Oaks, CA: Sage.

Zemke, R., and Kramlinger, T. (1982). *Figuring things out: A trainer's guide to needs and task analysis.* Reading, MA: Addison-Wesley.

CHAPTER THIRTY-FOUR

Observation Methods for Human Performance Technology

James A. Pershing, Scott J. Warren, Daniel T. Rowe

One of the more underused and undervalued methods for collecting data about human performance is observation. Observation methods have a number of purposes and advantages. Examples include (1) obtaining first-hand information about task performance in a work setting, (2) evaluating and assessing task, individual, and group processes, (3) identifying communication structures that degrade performance, (4) confirming quantitative performance findings, and (5) comparing predicted performance to actual performance. The data that result from using observation techniques include information about specific procedures and work processes that can be visually observed and noted when evaluating overall performance objectives, team interactions, and actual performance (Clardy, 1997; Phillips, 1991; Robson, 2002; Witkin and Altschuld, 1995). This information can be used to identify needs related to performance improvement, the analysis of managerial behavior, and the relationships between individuals and teams, as well as the interactions among units in an organization. Observation allows direct noting and recording of the difference between actual performance and expected performance on a single task or a series of tasks (Clardy, 1997; Phillips, 1991).

This chapter will provide a number of insights into the use of observation as an important method for collecting human performance technology (HPT) data. It provides an overview of the observation method, compares and contrasts commonly used observation techniques, details the different roles of the observer in using these techniques, discusses various types of instruments used in various observation processes, and suggests tips for completing successful observations. In addition, it will provide a rationale for and recommended methods of analysis to be used with collected data and discuss the inherent limitations of the method. Finally, as a means of overcoming possible problems, we examine alternatives to the most prevalent forms of observation and suggest future directions for the use of observation as a viable and important HPT datacollection method.

HISTORY OF THE METHOD

Simple, direct observation methods have been used to contrast expected outcomes of a task with actual outcomes throughout history. Observation is the fundamental basis of science and strives to describe *what is.* Collection of observational data must precede comparative and experimental methods before they can be applied in science (Clardy, 1997; Gall, Borg, and Gall, 1996; Robson, 2002; Witkin and Altschuld, 1995).

Observational methods have dominated the early periods of most scientific disciplines, including the physical and social sciences. Since the earliest research of Copernicus and Kepler in the fields of astronomy, geology, physics, and chemistry, as well as that of others in the discipline of biology, observation and comparison have always been central to or supportive of experimental methods.

Despite advances in quantitative methods used to produce objective measurements within established physical science disciplines, observation is still used to produce important knowledge. Given the centrality of observation within empiricist data-collection techniques in the natural sciences, the social sciences have followed suit (Hollis, 1994).[1] Empirical observation, which originated in anthropological and archeological studies, has been used for hundreds of years to describe differences and similarities between cultures in the field of social sciences (Bernstein, 1976; Brinkerhoff, 1987; Denzin and Lincoln, 2003; Hollis, 1994; Robson, 2002). These early studies were intended to provide objective accounts regarding the practices and behaviors of various social groups and relate them to the practices of the cultural group to which the observer belonged.

Since then and over the past two centuries, more formal and systematic structures for data collection and analysis have been implemented in order to improve the validity and reliability of data gathered by visual observation.[2] During the course of the last half century, validity improvement methods such as triangulation have rendered the resulting descriptive data much more useful than had previously been possible (Gall, Borg, and Gall, 1996). In addition, the use of multiple, trained observers to determine agreement has generated higher reliability of findings based on reported observer data (Carspecken, 1996; Clardy, 1997; Denzin and Lincoln, 2003; Phillips, 1991; Robson, 2002).

OBSERVATION IN HUMAN PERFORMANCE TECHNOLOGY

The observation method is flexible in that it can be applied to a variety of human performance technology situations including needs, task, and job analysis as well as formative, summative, confirmative, and usability evaluations. Its flexibility allows for the collection of both qualitative and quantitative information, depending on the circumstances and purposes of the observation. The use of observation as a primary method of data collection allows qualitative and quantitative HPT researchers and evaluators to gather data in order to make sense of a novel situation, to understand what happened in a system prior to an intervention, and to examine what happened since that intervention. In other circumstances, observations allow researchers to "gather details of optimal and actual performance and to infer the cause(s) of performance problems" (Rossett, 1987, p. 156). Further, observation may be useful in recording actual skill use when dealing with customer service training (Clardy, 1997; Phillips, 1991).

Robson (2002) notes three major uses of observation methods in the social sciences that are particularly applicable to HPT research. The first is for *unstructured exploration,* to identify possible issues that underlie a particular problem or dysfunctional situation prior to establishing hypotheses about solutions. Another use of observation is as a *supportive* or *supplementary* method for framing major issues identified using other collected data sets provided by interviews or questionnaires. Last, observation may be used as a *primary* means of data collection, especially in instances when the information to be identified is essentially descriptive, such as a case study in which other methods will supplement the observation. The observation method is especially useful as a supplementary or primary tool because it yields "a richness in perception and awareness often missing from surveys and interviews" (Clardy, 1997, p. 27). It is also important to note that observation measures alone are seldom recommended as the sole method of data-gathering in any research methodology (Clardy, 1997; Gall, Borg, and Gall, 1996; Witkin and Altschuld, 1995).

OBSERVATION TECHNIQUES

This section will provide an overview of the techniques and methods that are traditionally used in observational studies. Each of the methods and techniques reviewed can be implemented in an HPT setting to gather valid and reliable data given an appropriate context and purpose. The section begins with a comparison of unstructured and structured observational methods. Next, the discussion moves to an overview and comparison of direct- and indirect-analysis observation techniques. The section concludes with an introduction to unobtrusive observational measures.

Unstructured and Structured Observation Methods

The three major uses of the observation method, as identified by Robson (2002), parallel the specific observation techniques that have traditionally been used in HPT situations. The techniques of the observation method for application in HPT are often described and distinguished by the amount of structure the observer uses in carrying out an observation. For the purpose of unstructured exploration, as defined by Robson (2002), an HPT researcher would use an unstructured observation technique. In an *unstructured* observation, the observer purposefully conducts the observation without a specific checklist or guide directing what is to be observed. Conversely, during a *structured* observation the observer knows exactly the behaviors and performances to look for. Structured observations can be used in both the supplementary and primary roles that Robson defines. The amount of structure depends on the purposes and the goals of the study.

Unstructured Observations. Unstructured observations are characterized by a lack of predetermined tasks and activities on which to focus during the observation; the observer simply takes in as much as possible. The unstructured method is therefore most useful when the purpose of the observation is to gather exploratory data in novel situations and to observe newly occurring phenomena. Jorgensen (1989) writes, "[T]he basic goal of these largely unfocused initial observations is to become increasingly familiar with the insiders' world so as to refine and focus subsequent observation and data collection" (p. 82). Researchers find that the unstructured nature of this method makes it most useful during the initial stages of data collection.

In order to be most effective, the observer using this technique should enter the observation environment with few, if any, preconceived ideas regarding the phenomena or activities being observed. Some researchers recommend that the observer begin the observation with a blank sheet of paper and simply record his or her initial impressions and observations. The data gathered during unstructured observations often include information about the primary actors and their interactions, notes on the processes and protocols, descriptions of the work environment, and other initial impressions. Once the data from these observations have been compiled and carefully analyzed, they can serve as a foundation for strategically planning other data-gathering techniques, including structured observations.

Structured Observations. An observer using structured methods enters the observation environment with a specific plan for purposive, focused, and often systematic observations. There are a variety of structured-observation techniques that can be used to collect an array of data. These techniques include (1) frequency counts, (2) task listings, (3) time and motion, (4) stimulus-response tables,

Table 34.1. Observational Techniques.

Observation Method	Method Description	Appropriate Use Criteria
Frequency counts	Define the limits and bounds of the behavior being counted (What counts? What does not count?). Define the period of time of the observation. Record the specific behavior per standard time period.	Logic of task not evident (behaviors are those that are not likely to follow specific conditions).
Task listings	Record, in list or outline form, the duties of a specific job. Break the duties out into tasks, subtasks, and task elements.	Highly repetitive task and few choices to make. Speed is not important or is not under performer's control.
Time and motion	Similar to the task listing method. Record information about how long it takes to perform the tasks and subtasks of the behavior.	Highly repetitive task and few choices to make. Speed is important and is under the performer's control.
Stimulus response tables	Record observable behavior and determine the stimuli for each action. Separate and classify the stimulus items and the response items. Create a table diagramming the process.	Moderately repetitious task and moderate number of choices to make under specific conditions.
Algorithms	Record observable behavior (consider "think-aloud" in special instances). Ask questions to define the sequence. Define operations, procedures, decisions, and discriminations. Create an algorithmic flow chart.	Moderately repetitious task and high number of choices. Especially useful in describing and recording the necessary steps of a task.

(Continued)

Table 34.1. Observational Techniques. (*Continued*)

Observation Method	Method Description	Appropriate Use Criteria
Artifact analysis	Examine the artifact to understand its role in behavior performance. Most useful as supplement to other observation methods.	Visible artifacts involvement for tasks such as tools, products, and so on.

Source: Adapted from Zemke and Kramlinger, 1982.

(5) algorithms, and (6) artifact analysis. Table 34.1, adapted from the work of Zemke and Kramlinger (1982), includes a brief description of each technique as well as suggestions for proper application. The appropriate technique for any given situation is determined by the purpose of the study. The performance technologist should take care to select an observation technique that yields the type of data that will inform the overarching questions and purposes of the study. Rossett (1987) gives the following pragmatic advice to the observer: "Be clear about why you are going into the field. Select a way of observing which will provide valid results. Design an observation guide that gets you what you need" (p. 170).

Direct and Indirect Observations

The previous section discussed the level of structure needed for the varied purposes of observations. Another issue the performance technologist (PT) must consider is how to go about conducting the observation. Most observers use a direct-observation approach. As the name implies, the direct observation involves "placing oneself in a setting or situation to watch and record events as they occur" (Clardy, 1997, p. 27). In the case of direct observations, the researcher must determine the role the observer will play in the observation. Direct observation may not be possible, or even desirable, given the circumstances and context of the observation. In some cases, researchers choose an indirect observational technique in which the behaviors and performances are recorded on video- or audiotape and reviewed by observers at a later time. Both direct and indirect methods can be used to conduct either structured or unstructured observations. As stated previously, the decision to use a direct approach or an indirect approach is based on the circumstances and purposes of the observation. Each technique has strengths and weaknesses that should be considered during the planning stages of observational research.

Direct-Analysis Observations. The direct-analysis observation technique is the traditional and most widely applied method for conducting HPT observations. Direct observations allow the researcher to conduct the observation experience onsite and first hand. The direct-observation technique allows the observer to take in the whole of the observation while simultaneously focusing on important details. In addition, the observer can be flexible and adaptive to circumstances and unexpected situations that arise during the observation period. The onsite and first-hand nature of direct-observation techniques permits the performance technologist to form immediate impressions about the observation and to give immediate feedback when appropriate.

The role of the observer in conducting direct-analysis observational data collection can change depending on the observation model chosen and the purposes, goals, and circumstances of the observation. According to Gall, Borg, and Gall (1996) and Robson (2002), there are four possible roles that can be taken by an observer:

1. *Complete observer:* The performance technologist is expected to detach him or herself from the setting and participants to maintain an objective viewpoint.

2. *Complete participant:* In this instance, the performance technologist is either an authentic member of the group under observation or is converted to full membership during the course of the study. Practitioners of critical ethnographic methods often fall into this category (Carspecken, 1996).[3]

3. *Observer participant:* Comparable to the complete observer role, the performance technologist's only purpose is to collect data, and interactions are incidental and unrelated to the content of participant discussions.

4. *Participant observer or marginal participant:* This role is closer to the complete participant role, given that the observer develops an identity with the group and engages in some meaningful interactions but does not take part in those activities that are considered core to the group's identity and cohesion.

There are two important principles that the observer must consider when implementing direct-analysis observations. During these observations the performance technologist must be able to observe the performance while simultaneously recording data. This concern is especially true of the roles in which the observer also serves as a participant. A well-trained and experienced observer is able to take detailed notes without missing a moment of important action. In addition, the observer must be able to view the performance holistically while simultaneously focusing on subtle details. Some performance technologists refer to this skill as the ability to see the forest *and* the trees. In short, direct-analysis observations require a well trained and experienced observer to observe and record reliable data.

Indirect-Analysis Observations. A number of valuable tools are available for collecting data for indirect-analysis observations. These tools range from audio- and videotapes, computers, and other electronic hardware to more traditional paper-and-pencil tools such as behavior checklists, coding schemes, and observation guides (Clardy, 1997; Gall, Borg, and Gall, 1996; Phillips, 1991).

In carrying out observations, it may be impossible to train enough observers to capture all of the actions that happen concurrently throughout the workday (Gall, Borg, and Gall, 1996; Phillips, 1991). Furthermore, the observer may feel that it is important to have access to multiple viewings of important events for the purposes of sharing with other observers or the participants themselves. Audio- or videotaping may help to address such needs. If there are concerns about the reliability of coding, recording methods are an excellent means of allowing for repeated reviews of observations when training observers, conducting observer agreement checks, or even member checks in which the participants verify that they agree with the established codes or interpretations of recorded behaviors. Other computer tools exist, such as keystroke recorders and software that allow the observer to view what the participants are doing on their own computers. All of these tools are valuable, but there are ethical concerns with audio- and videotaping and in using these computer tools that need to be addressed.

There are limitations to these indirect observational techniques. Using video-cameras and audiorecorders tends to increase, and sometimes even double, the time and cost of the observation (Newby, 1992). In addition, audiorecorders and videocameras are limited in what they can record. It is hard for an observer viewing a videotape to observe anything other than what is displayed in the camera frame. Another concern addressed by Newby is that the presence of the video-camera and camera operator may be more intrusive to the work environment than an observer. Videorecording may be considered an invasion of privacy and can cause participants to react in unpredictable ways due to nervousness and concerns for privacy. While there are many times when such recordings might be beneficial, participant consent may be difficult to acquire. In addition, institutional review boards are wary of allowing concealed cameras unless there is an insurmountable need for such tactics. In spite of these negatives, the indirect method may be preferable when minute or subtle actions are being observed or in circumstances in which multiple observers are desired.

Unobtrusive Measures

In instances when there is a serious threat to reliability due to observer impact on participant behaviors, unobtrusive measures can be useful for overcoming this threat (Clardy, 1997; Phillips, 1991; Robson, 2002; Witkin and Altschuld, 1995). The term *unobtrusive measures* is often used interchangeably with the term "observation methods" or "nonreactive measures" in the observation methods literature (Brinkerhoff, 1987; Clardy, 1997; Denzin and Lincoln, 2003; Gall, Borg, and Gall, 1996; Robson, 2002; Witkin and Altschuld, 1995). However, what differentiates unobtrusive methods is that the data collection is conducted in a natural setting, and participants are not informed that they are being observed.

One way to implement unobtrusive measures is to train an observer who is unknown to the participants. The observer could sit in on formal meetings, informal meetings, or even lunch meetings held outside the office. The observer can then collect data without scrutiny from the participants. The participants would most likely act naturally because they are unaware that their actions are being formally observed and recorded. Additional examples of unobtrusive methods that may be appropriate include using programs that capture keystrokes on participant computers, observing patterns of employee cohesion into social groups, and counting the number of interactions between members of different divisions who are working together on a project and comparing those to interactions between other members of the same division.

A novel example of an unobtrusive observation measure concerned the intermittent use of library resources in a reading room. Nightly, a very light and undetectable harmless powder was placed on shelving to see which materials were accessed and used on a daily basis. Unobtrusive methods are many and varied and often are limited only by the imagination and creativity of the performance technologist.

As noted, in instances in which observer impact on participant behavior is considered a serious threat to reliability, unobtrusive methods can help if conducted effectively (Brinkerhoff, 1987; Witkin and Altschuld, 1995). Furthermore, other threats to reliability can be reduced. One example of a reduction of threat would be the problem of observer bias or omission due to either positive or negative past experiences with the participants. Such threats to reliability may be eliminated by limiting or eliminating personal interaction between the observers and the employees under observation.

Three limitations exist related to unobtrusive measures: (1) the validity of such measures is uncertain, (2) reliability is not easy to determine, and (3) there are thorny ethical issues surrounding the use of concealed methodologies (Brinkerhoff, 1987; Gall, Borg, and Gall, 1996; Robson, 2002; Witkin and Altschuld, 1995).

Many unobtrusive measure techniques lack consistency, making validity difficult to confirm. The establishment of validity with unobtrusive measures is often only established by comparing the *actual outcomes* of a project with those *previously predicted* by the unobtrusive measures.

Despite the fact that reliability can be computed for some unobtrusive measures, these computations are often of limited use to other researchers. This is typically the case because the results are sometimes overtly specific to the set of behaviors or attitudes under consideration and therefore do not generalize well to other populations or contexts (Robson, 2002; Witkin and Altschuld, 1995). However, over time, additional measures of reliability can be established that are relevant to the specific study. The more measures of reliability that are collected, the simpler it becomes to obtain estimates of reliability that generalize to different data sets collected in the future.

Finally, one of the more difficult issues related to unobtrusive measures is that of ethical considerations related to the consent of participants and privacy issues (Gall, Borg, and Gall, 1996; Robson, 2002; Witkin and Altschuld, 1995). If a participant is observed with unobtrusive measures, there can be no informed consent. The moment the participant is informed that he or she is being studied, the unobtrusive measures are no longer unobtrusive and advantages related to overcoming threats to reliability are lost. Related to questions of invasion of privacy, most research review committees will not view data collection conducted in public spaces such as open meetings, work areas, or restaurants as constituting an invasion of privacy. However, observing participants' home behaviors or private actions in nonbusiness settings such as locker rooms, or recording private phone calls may be considered a threat to privacy and may not be approved.

In order to gain approval for unobtrusive measures that have the propensity for violating privacy or informed consent policies, several conditions must be met: (1) participants will not be subject to risk, (2) anonymity of participants is upheld, (3) the study cannot be successfully conducted *with* informed consent, and (4) the benefits of the findings from the study will be significant (Robson, 2002; Witkin and Altschuld, 1995).

OBSERVATION INSTRUMENTS

Upon selection of appropriate observation methods and techniques, the performance technologist should begin to prepare the observation guides and other related instrumentation. As noted previously, unstructured observations do not require observation guides; a blank sheet of paper or blank notecards usually suffice. Semistructured and structured observations are enhanced by the development and use of a strategically created observation guide, used during observations to record and organize data. In addition, observation guides help the observer maintain focus on the predetermined objectives or schemes of the observation.

The key to creating and implementing a successful observation instrument is to align the items on the observation instrument with the overall research or evaluation objectives. Newby (1992) states that "[observers] need to design your behavior observation instrument to match your particular evaluation needs. [Observers] do this by basing the categories for observation on the objectives of the training activity" (p. 198). During the process of creating the observation instrument, the performance technologist should create an observation alignment matrix to ensure that the items in the observation instrument match the objectives for the study. Typically, in the left-most vertical column of the matrix, the performance technologist lists each of the research or evaluation objectives, including major questions. As headings for the remaining columns from left to right, the performance technologist lists the specific indicators to look for during observation that relate to each objective or question. This approach will help to ensure that the observation instrument is designed to note important observations as well as minimize gaps or holes in the data. An additional strategy for creating effective observation instruments is to base the elements noted in the observation guide on conclusions drawn from the analyses of data collected during unstructured observations or other methods. This approach grounds the instrument in the context and environment in which it will be used and links the guide to the unique behaviors or performances that have been deemed worthy of observation.

The precise scope of the observation directly affects the design of the observation instrument. Again, the scope of the observation should be aligned with the goals and purposes of the research or evaluation study. The observation guide should be limited in scope so as to allow the observer to be successful and efficient. After all, it is difficult, if not impossible, to take in all that is occurring in a worksite. At the same time, the scope must be sufficiently robust to gather data that will be useful to the purposes of the study.

Standard forms with established validity may exist that match the observer's research or evaluation goals (Gall, Borg, and Gall, 1996). Existing forms have the benefit of reducing preparation time for observations and allow for comparisons between past observations and the current study. The degree to which comparisons can be made depends on the performance technologist's judgment regarding the fit between the two situations. A problem with existing forms is that often several variables that are important to the current research question or evaluation are not adequately covered in the form. Modification of existing forms is acceptable, though it becomes more difficult to make comparisons between the current study and other studies that used the same form. Furthermore, revalidation and estimates of reliability should be conducted when existing forms are modified.

Self-created checklists and forms are the remaining possibility when seeking data through observation. Such measures are discussed in detail in the Reviewing Data section of this chapter.

In summary, there are a number of variables that must be considered when designing observation guides. These variables are weighted by the purpose of the observation, the observation techniques, and the types of data to be collected. Rossett (1987) records the major variables that must be accounted for when creating observation instruments: "[Guides should be] simple to understand and use, linked to the purposes of the observation, limited in scope, accommodating qualitative and quantitative aspects of the situation, allow for comments and impressions as well as miscellaneous data to be added, a blueprint for follow up needs" (p. 165).

As a final note, it is advisable to take time immediately after an observation period to look at your notes and guides. During this time, the observer should clarify any notes or markings as well as add commentary where needed. Some observation guides require the observer to make "final thought" comments on the guide immediately after the observation.

ESTABLISHING RELIABILITY

In many instances, there will be a number of work situations that need to be studied concurrently. A performance technologist cannot be in all places at once and must instead rely upon more than one trained observer (Carspecken, 1996; Clardy, 1997; Gall, Borg, and Gall, 1996; Phillips, 1991; Robson, 2002). Using a standard observation form, training multiple observers, and engaging observation team members in practice situations can address this obstacle.

However, how can one ensure that data collected by different people is reliable? Without establishing observer reliability, it is difficult to claim that the data reported are consistent and can be generalized to other comparable settings, contexts, or subjects. Three types of observer reliability are explained by Frick and Semmel (1978):

Criterion-related observer reliability: This is simply the degree to which the trainee observers' scores have agreement with the expert observer and creator of the validated observation instrument. Meeting this type of reliability standard provides the expectation that the trainees' and the experts' understanding of the relevant variables are the same. Such reliability is commonly established through the coding of the same taped segment by both the trainee and the expert followed by a comparison of the similarities and differences in the sets of codes.

Intra-observer reliability: This relates to the internal consistency of a rater-observer's coding. The method for establishing reliability in this instance is the same as that used in criterion-related observer reliability, except that the comparison is made between the observer's ratings during one time segment, a given day for example, compared with ratings on the same tape during another time segment, say a few days later.

Inter-observer reliability: In this instance, reliability is established *during* the course of actual data collection. If there are one hundred sets of observations to be conducted by ten observers, ten sets must be observed by all ten observers and their ratings are checked for levels of agreement among all observers.

PARTICIPANTS

There are a number of different models by which participants may be chosen for observation as part of a performance inquiry. However, there are a few guidelines related to the general characteristics one might expect from the participants and how a performance technologist should go about selecting participants for observation.

Characteristics of Participants

Participants may have a number of different characteristics due to the varying reasons for the observation. In some instances, participants may vary in their centrality to the specific issue or problem under consideration. Lave and Wenger (1991) discuss two types of participants: *legitimate peripheral participants* and *core participants,* or *"old-timers."* In any business or learning community, both kinds of participants are going to exist and are important for study using observational methods.

Legitimate peripheral participants are those that may not be central to the project or team under consideration, either due to inexperience or due to their being involved in nondirect or support roles (Lave and Wenger, 1991). The role of marginal peripheral participants in contributing to any dysfunction under study by a performance technologist may not immediately be recognized due to the tangential nature and complexity of their limited interactions with the core team in which the problem is evident. However, after observing the interactions between such participants and those considered core to the team, their role in either contributing to the problem or solving it may become more readily apparent. For example, during the observation of a sales team meeting, the interactions among sales team members may be significant. However, when input is requested from participants who are members of the contract team, the actions and behavior of the sales team members may suddenly shift. These contract team members, while not core members of the sales team being studied, may need to be included in the revised scope of the investigation. These seemingly tangential participants obviously could have an impact on both the problem and the behavior of the core participants, and studying them in conjunction with the sales team members may be beneficial to identifying problems and finding solutions.

Core participants are those who naturally fall within the scope of the study based on either the perceptions of the managers who called for the study or the perceptions of the performance technologist responsible for establishing the scope of the study. These participants have a direct impact on decision-making processes, interpersonal communications, and general work expected to be generated by the team in question (Clardy, 1997; Lave and Wenger, 1991;

Riel and Polin, 2004). Initially, core participants may be identified based on the substance of their contribution to the team. Core participants will often be those of most interest for individual observation of task completion or later for follow-up interviews.

Determining Which Participants Need to Be Involved

How do performance technologists determine which participants they should include in their observations? Commonly, a manager will identify a group or team for which a problem has arisen and capture the initial scope for the observation. However, an analysis should be conducted to identify key stakeholders as well as peripheral or support participants who may affect group processes (Clardy, 1997; Phillips, 1991) Usually during initial team or group observations, those participants most important for further study will surface. If not, other techniques such as interviews and document analysis will yield information that guides the performance technologist to core and peripheral members from which he or she may gain more relevant data during observations.

Concerns Regarding Participant Cooperation

Not all participants will consent to observation. Others may develop concerns regarding the observation during the course of the inquiry. In either instance this is a problem, especially if the subject is considered to be core to the dynamics of a team or unit under study. Sometimes, without the benefit of data collected by observing this particular subject, observations of other team members will be of less use due to lack of context for their interactions, utterances, and actions that involve the noncooperative subject.

Participants cannot be coerced into participation, and when any member says that they are uncomfortable continuing with their involvement in the observation, the observation should come to an end (Carspecken, 1996; Denzin and Lincoln, 2003; Gall, Borg, and Gall, 1996; Robson, 2002). If there is important and irrefutable evidence that the team member's cooperation is necessary to paint a complete picture of the situation, unobtrusive measures may be called for, contingent on approval by the institutional review board of the organization.

THREATS TO OBSERVER RELIABILTY

There are a number of possible threats to the reliability of data collected during observations. These threats can take the form of effects of the observer on the observed, observer personal bias, rating errors when using rating scales, observer contamination, observer omissions, observer drift, and reliability decay (Clardy, 1997; Gall, Borg, and Gall, 1996; Phillips, 1991; Robson, 2002). A description of each of these threats and their possible impacts on collected data follows.

Effects of the Observer on the Participants

Unless the observer is somehow hidden from participants, the observer is likely to have an impact on their behavior. Participants may act differently than they would ordinarily, exhibiting behaviors that they believe the observer expects. Unfortunately, this can result in unstable data because they do not represent normal behaviors of participants or normal interactions of the group. It is possible to mitigate these impacts by attending meetings prior to data collection so that group members have time to adjust to the observer's presence. Furthermore, not revealing details about the purpose of the observations to the participants may keep them from being inclined to adjust related behaviors.

Observer Personal Bias

Observer personal bias is a well-known concept and stems from individual observer prejudices related to the issues or participants under study. Having observers partake in reflective writing may help identify bias prior to actual observations and may reduce this tendency or at least allow the performance technologist to be aware that such bias may exist in reported data.

Rating Errors

Rating errors fall under three main categories. *Errors of leniency* are those in which the rater gives high ratings to most participants regardless of performance. *Errors of central tendency* are those in which observers rate all participants at the middle of the rubric's scale. The *halo effect* is one in which the observer forms initial impressions about an individual participant and applies these impressions to subsequent observation ratings.

Observer Contamination or Expectancy Effects

Reliability issues such as observer contamination or expectancy effects happen when the observer has prior knowledge of external data that influences observation, such as employee records, past performance reviews, or supervisor bias (Gall, Borg, and Gall, 1996; Phillips, 1991; Robson, 2002). This issue may be avoided by requiring supervisors and participants to refrain from providing data prior to observation. While a performance technologist must make recommendations based on all available data, the timing and sequencing of *when* the information is received can make a difference.

Observer Omission

Observer omission occurs when the observer fails to note a behavior due to one of any number of causes, such as personal bias, simple failure to notice an infrequent behavior, or more than one behavior occurring concurrently, preventing another behavior from being noted. Tendencies to such omissions may often be overcome through training and practice.

Observer Drift

As observer skills degrade over time, reliability also begins to fade. Periodic training and retraining can address this issue.

Reliability Decay

Data presented at the end of an observation period tend to be less reliable than data that are collected early. Persistent checks on observers and intermittent retraining can help overcome this problem.

ANALYZING OBSERVATION DATA

By the time the data-collection phase of an observation is completed, and depending on the observation instruments and specific measures used, a number of data sets will most likely have been collected (Gall, Borg, and Gall, 1996). To analyze these data, there are several different ways in which the raw information may be interpreted, patterned, and brought to bear on the research or evaluation questions.

Compiling Data

When compiling data, it is best to begin with *descriptive observations* of the setting, people, and events in order to frame the research (Robson, 2002). Table 34.2 demonstrates and defines the variety of foci appropriate for descriptive observations.

With descriptive data, the researcher's goal is to report in chronological order an account of the events observed. This information will provide an understanding of certain key and supporting events that occurred as well as events that preceded and followed them (Clardy, 1997). Once accounting has been documented, it is important to propose a theoretical framework and set of hypotheses that explain what happened and to help develop the story that evolved during the course of the observation. It is important that this framework be derived from the descriptive story rather than on nonscientific "hunches."

Furthermore, depending on the strength and number of key events or understandings that evolve from the observations, refinement of the initial research or evaluation questions and hypotheses may be warranted. Based on such changes, further *focused observations* may yield better data from stakeholders and participants who loom large in the descriptive story and have the most impact on the team or problem in question (Robson, 2002).

Table 34.2. Foci for Descriptive Observations.

Activities	Any activities taken part in by actors; can include group actions
Actions	Specific, individual actions performed by participants during the course of the observation that may be recognized as being separate from group activity
Actor goals	The explicit objectives given by participants related to their final target outcomes
Chronology	The order in which the observed activities and actions take place during the larger observation
Emotional expressions	Expressed utterances of emotion or feelings related to activities, actions, goals, events, other participants, and so on
Events	Specific meetings, planned interactions
Participants	Names, code names, or personal details observed that are important for identifying actors in the setting
Physical objects	Relevant objects in the room with which the actors may be expected to interact
Space	Physical setting in which the observation takes place (for example, a diagram of room layout)

Source: Adapted from Robson, 2002.

Reviewing Data

As discussed previously in the instrumentation section of this chapter, a number of choices exist for recording and reviewing data collected through observation. Each choice has its own strengths and limitations and depends on whether it makes sense to conduct *structural analysis, reflective analysis,* or *interpretational analysis* (Gall, Borg, and Gall, 1996; Robson, 2002).

Structural Analysis. Structural analysis focuses specifically on conversation segments or utterances to identify patterns inherent in collected data (Gall, Borg, and Gall, 1996). As with interpretive analysis, there are computer programs that identify repeated patterns in text and allow for organizing coded segments and utterances into distinct fields. Both computer-mediated discourse analysis and critical ethnographic methods incorporate structural analyses into their broader methods of analysis.

Reflective Analysis. Of the three kinds of observation analysis, *reflective analysis* is the most subjective. Such analysis involves the observer making personal judgments about the data in order to develop categories and descriptions. The use of this type of analysis comes from the hermeneutical research tradition, which involves the study of interpretive understanding or meaning from a certain standpoint or situation (Mertens, 1998). This approach engenders consideration of all data throughout the entire length of a set of observations. Unless the performance technologist takes part in longitudinal observations in an organizational environment as a participant or participant observer (Frick and Semmel, 1978), this may be the least useful of the three types of analysis due to the length of time it takes to collect and analyze data and its largely subjective nature.

Interpretational Analysis. Interpretational analysis is sometimes referred to as "phenomenological analysis." It is commonly used to discover underlying patterns, themes, and categories that are relevant to the phenomena or trends under study (Gall, Borg, and Gall, 1996). Such analysis will most commonly be conducted using computer databases that contain raw data collected during observations. Once the text has been entered into the database, segments, or meaningful units, should be developed. Segment length can range from phrases to several pages of text, and each observation involves very different breaks in meaning. From segmentation, analysis moves into the development of an appropriate coding scheme for the data. This series of specific, descriptive codes will eventually be placed within larger categories prior to allowing for the identification of emergent, larger themes that encompass both the codes and categories. The establishment of category and coding schemes follows.

Predetermined or Existing Coding Schemes. These schemes are often available off the shelf. They allow for ratings of participants that are framed by the original research or evaluation questions (Gall, Borg, and Gall, 1996; Robson, 2002). Such coding schemes may have diverse scope covering global or general ratings of participant behavior based on the context of the entire observation. Or they may be as small in scope as ratings of participants' speed at a miniscule task completion such as tightening a bolt in repeated succession. Many organizations have developed their own coding schemes and instruments that have well-established validity and reliability. A concern when using such schemes is interobserver or inter-rater reliability, because such constructs are often heavily reliant on the skills and knowledge of individual observers. Reaching high interobserver reliability may require lengthy training periods on each instrument or coding scheme. A further limitation is that it may be difficult to find a coding scheme that addresses a particular research or evaluation question. If the coding scheme and the question are incongruent, the two should not be used together.

Checklists and Category Systems. Category systems are distinguishable because they use a small number of items that are much more general than those used in checklists and they can be used to maintain a relatively continuous record (Clardy, 1997; Robson, 2002). An example of a category scheme may

Table 34.3. Sample Category Scheme and Observation Schedule.

Category Scheme for Sample Staff Meeting

Individual behaviors	These behaviors, carried out by an individual team member during the meeting, have no apparent bearing on the discussion or agenda points. This may include attending to other work, checking e-mail, or other off-task behaviors.
Group behaviors	Such behaviors as group discussion, debate, or departmental or subteam reports are those that affect the entire team, and while the action may only involve one member, the impact on the group is clear.
Decision-making behaviors	This category includes all behaviors undertaken either by individuals or by the group that have a decision-making component.
Social behaviors	Social behaviors include interactions among staff members that have no direct bearing on assigned tasks and are unrelated to work. These may include inquiries into family health, weekend, events, and so on.
Other behaviors	Any behaviors that do not fit categories one through four that seem to have bearing on the research question should be included here.

be found in Table 34.3. Checklists simply provide a large number of items that can be marked as either observed or not. Many available checklists and category systems include readymade coding schemes that are valid and reliable.

Independently Established Coding Schemes. If there are no coding schemes available that can be appropriately adopted or adapted to the specific needs of the project, creating one's own is another option (Robson, 2002). When establishing a coding scheme for use with observation data, it is important to begin with identification of behaviors that the researcher believes will lead to answers to the established research or evaluation questions. Table 34.4 lists a number of potential categories of behavior identification to facilitate matching data coding and observation objectives.

Coding sequences may center on *events, states, sequence intervals, time sampling,* or *concurrent events. Event coding* occurs whenever a predetermined event takes place in the raw data (Robson, 2002). For example, each time any employee in a staff meeting makes a negative statement regarding a proposal without providing an alternative, the behavior would be coded. *State coding* may be used when one wants to identify changes in the physical state of a

Table 34.4. Developing Codes and Coding Schemes.

Nonverbal behaviors	Characterized by physical movements and no language use
Spatial behaviors	Characterized by individuals moving toward or away form one another
Extralinguistic behaviors	Characterized by language use that is loud, interrupting, or spoken at a rapid rate
Linguistic behaviors	Characterized by content-specific speech including the use of specialized and technical languages

Source: Adapted from Smith, 1975, in Robson, 2002, p. 327.

team member, such as when the member changes from silent computer work to verbal phone conversations. Noting the length of time spent in each state may also be beneficial. *Sequence intervals* are predetermined periods by which all observations are divided. In some instances, it makes sense to use thirty-second intervals and use a code to describe, as accurately as possible, what happened during that set time interval. In other instances, especially when long periods occur between changes in topic or long silences between interactions are the norm, using longer time intervals would be appropriate, though time sampling may be a better coding scheme. *Time sampling* should not be used for showing sequences of events. It works better for recording representative samples of behaviors over short periods of time, followed by longer periods in which another coding scheme is used, or no coding is conducted. For example, five minutes of recording, fifteen minutes without recording. *Concurrent coding,* also known as *cross-classifying events* (Robson, 2002), is used to record not only an important event, such as an argument between two team members, but those behaviors that immediately precede and follow the event. Analysis of such codes may lead to better understanding of conflicts and decision-making procedures.

Drawing Conclusions

The reliability of the conclusions drawn from codes that are established for data analysis will depend heavily on interobserver agreement about the meanings and interpretation of the codes. Those codes that repeatedly occur throughout collected data and are observed by multiple observers at different times are the codes that will be the most reliable and valid. Such codes are expected to be specific, and smaller codes should be absorbed as repeated themes that occur throughout the series of observations (Carspecken, 1996; Denzin and Lincoln, 2003). For instance, if an observer notes that Manager A exhibits anger toward Employee B, these observations may fall into the larger theme of "Manager A's interaction difficulties." This is especially true if Manager A exhibits anger toward Employee C, apathy toward Employee D's ideas, and confusion regarding Employee F's suggestions. Finally, established themes should be categorized as they apply to the research or evaluation questions.

Once these themes have coalesced, conclusions regarding possible interventions, needs for further study, and other items may be made. However, further reliability and validity work must take place prior to presenting such conclusions.

Validity may be established using *triangulation,* a method of validating qualitative data or observations by using corroboration of multiple data-collection methods to help eliminate bias or reliance upon a single source of information for the drawing of conclusions (Frick and Semmel, 1978; Robson, 2002). For example, if qualitative observation methods are the primary means of collecting data, quantitative data collection using a survey, combined with follow-up interviews with participants to confirm themes and established codes, should follow. These follow-up interviews are commonly known as *member checks.* Another method involves having a more experienced performance technologist review the established themes and categories to see if they are in agreement or if they note persistent bias on the part of the observer. As an alternative, the more experienced performance technologist can develop his or her own codes and themes independently and then compare the levels of congruence between the patterns found in each set of analyses (Carspecken, 1996; Gall, Borg, and Gall, 1996; Robson, 2002).

TIPS FOR CONDUCTING SUCCESSFUL OBSERVATIONS

To this point, this chapter has included an overview of the observation method as an appropriate technique for gathering data in HPT settings. It has also provided an overview of methods and techniques available to performance technologists as observers. The major sections of the chapter have briefly discussed the keys to successful application of particular methods and techniques. The purpose of this concluding section is to offer a synthesis of the general suggestions for carrying out successful observations. Phillips (1991) posits that the observation method is sometimes misused and misapplied in evaluation situations and therefore abandoned. By following the tips and guidelines that follow, the observation method can be correctly applied in HPT settings.

The most frequent suggestions for proper use and implementation of the observation method are: (1) thoroughly train the observers, (2) plan observations systematically and strategically, (3) prepare and use a carefully designed observation instrument, and (4) use multiple observers when possible (Zemke and Kramlinger, 1982; Clardy, 1997; Phillips, 1991; Rossett, 1987).

The research methods literature on the observation method also features tips and suggestions for conducting effective observations. These include suggestions that are applicable at different stages of the observation process. The following list summarizes these additional suggestions:

- Take complete notes. Avoid censoring and judging (Clardy, 1997).
- Be attentive to misinformation and aware of reactivity (Clardy, 1997).
- Do not miss the ordinary by looking for the unusual (Clardy, 1997).
- Take measures to minimize the effect of the observer on the environment (Phillips, 1991).
- Be aware of preconceptions and how they could affect the observation (Rossett, 1987).

Another useful set of suggestions is a list of characteristics for a successful observer created by Rossett (1987), which provides a set of characteristics an observer can use as a self-assessment. These characteristics are

- *Curiosity:* The observer should attempt to begin each observation with an open mind and without bias.
- *Patience:* The observer should be willing to wait and silently watch as the observation takes its natural course. In addition, the observer must avoid coaching or interrupting the action unless it is part of his or her predetermined observer role.
- *Tact:* An experienced observer should be able to explain the purpose of the observation to those being observed in a way that reduces any anxiety of those being observed.
- *Ability to blend in:* The skilled observer should situate himself or herself in the observation environment so as to draw as little attention as possible.
- *Ability to multitask:* A successful observer should have the unique ability to record observational data without missing a moment of the action.
- *Ability to see the structure through the detail:* The observer should be able to make holistic observations of the action while simultaneously focusing on small details.

As a final note, remember that any structured observation method, while appropriate in many instances, should also be viewed in light of its inherent weaknesses. Fitzpatrick, Sanders, and Worthen (2003) list some of the drawbacks to the structured observation method. First, structured methods are most effective when carried out by trained and experienced observers. Most companies do not have a corps of qualified observers at their disposal to send into the field to collect data through observation. Second, when using multiple observers, it is difficult to ensure inter-rater reliability. Third, the logistics of site selection and access are difficult and time consuming. Fourth, it is extremely difficult to avoid reactivity, that is, changes in behavior by subjects in the presence of the observer during any type of observation.

CONCLUSION

Observation methods should be considered as a viable and reliable alternative for HPT contexts. Performance technologists should carefully consider the context and objectives of data-gathering initiatives as they decide specific methods to apply. This chapter is intended to serve as a reference that performance technologists can use to make decisions about the specific methods to use and how to effectively implement those methods. As the observation method is applied more frequently, researchers and performance specialists will be able to further adapt and perfect specific methods and techniques for appropriate application in HPT contexts.

Notes

1. The empiricist perspective relies heavily on experiment and observation-based research. It also refers to the belief that the experimental and observation approaches to research lead to the apprehension of true knowledge.

2. *Reliability* refers to the consistency with which a test or observation measures a certain attribute or behavior from one incident to the next. For example, repeated measures of a specific phenomenon should generate identical or similar results. *Validity* refers to the ability of a test or observation to measure what it is actually intended to measure.

3. *Ethnographic research* refers to direct-observation methods used for describing social and cultural phenomena. Ethnographic studies often involve the researcher becoming either a full or partial participant in the phenomenon being described.

References

Bernstein, R. J. (1976). *The restructuring of social and political theory* (6th paperback ed.). Philadelphia: University of Pennsylvania Press.

Brinkerhoff, R. O. (1987). *Achieving results from training.* San Francisco: Jossey-Bass.

Carspecken, P. F. (1996). *Critical ethnography in educational research.* New York: Routledge.

Clardy, A. (1997). *Studying your workforce: Applied research methods for the training and development practitioner.* Thousand Oaks, CA: Sage Publications.

Denzin, N., and Lincoln, Y. (Eds.). (2003). *The discipline and practice of qualitative research* (2nd ed.). Thousand Oaks, CA: Sage.

Fitzpatrick, J. L., Sanders, J. R., and Worthen, B. R. (2003). *Program evaluation: Alternative approaches and practical guidelines* (3rd ed.). Boston: Allyn & Bacon.

Frick, T., and Semmel, M. I. (1978). Observer agreement and reliabilities of classroom observational measures. *Review of Educational Research, 48,* 157–184.

Gall, M. D., Borg, W. R., and Gall, J. P. (1996). *Educational research: An introduction* (Vol. I., 6th ed.). White Plains, NY: Longman Publishers.

Hollis, M. (1994). *The philosophy of social science: An introduction.* Cambridge, UK: Cambridge University Press.

Jorgensen, D. L. (1989) *Participant observation: A methodology for human studies.* Newbury Park, CA: Sage.

Lave, J., and Wenger, E. (1991). *Situated learning: Legitimate peripheral participation.* Cambridge, UK: Cambridge University Press.

Mertens, D. M. (1998). *Research methods in education and psychology: Integrating diversity with quantitative and qualitative approaches.* Thousand Oaks, CA: Sage.

Newby, T. (1992). *Training evaluation handbook.* San Diego: Pfeiffer.

Phillips, J. J. (1991). *Handbook of training evaluation and measurement methods: Proven models and methods for evaluating any HRD program* (2nd ed.). Houston: Gulf.

Riel, M., and Polin, L. (2004). Online learning communities: Common ground and critical differences in designing technical environments. In S. A. Barab, R. Kling, and J. H. Gray (Eds.), *Designing for virtual communities in the service of learning* (pp. 16–50). Cambridge, UK: Cambridge University Press.

Robson, C. (2002). *Real world research: A resource for social scientists and practitioner-researchers* (2nd ed.). Malden, MA: Blackwell.

Rossett, A. (1987). *Training needs assessment.* Englewood Cliffs, NJ: Prentice-Hall.

Smith, H. W. (1975). *Strategies of social research: The methodological imagination.* London: Prentice-Hall.

Witkin, B. R., and Altschuld, J. W. (1995). *Planning and conducting needs assessments: A practical guide.* Thousand Oaks, CA: Sage.

Zemke, R., and Kramlinger, T. (1982). *Figuring things out: A trainer's guide to needs and task analysis.* Reading, MA, Addison-Wesley.

CHAPTER THIRTY-FIVE

Using Content Analysis in Human Performance Technology

Erika R. Gilmore

One of the most commonly used, if not overused, analogies in human performance technology (HPT) literature is that of describing various analysis and intervention methods as "tools in the toolbox" of the performance-improvement professional. However, at the risk of sounding clichéd, the analysis method explored in this chapter is just that, a quite critical tool in a toolbox teeming with a variety of other techniques and practices.

Content analysis can be used in nearly every performance-improvement initiative that we undertake in our profession, whether we are engaged in daily organizational performance-improvement activity or performing scholarly research in the field. In fact, most of us likely have performed some form of data examination similar to content analysis, even if we did not think of it as content analysis and even if we did not use a systematic or rigorous approach. To improve the significance and applicability of content-analysis activities upon which HPT professionals embark, this chapter will define content analysis, explore where it is typically situated in the HPT process, discuss how to conduct appropriate content analyses, and survey some examples of content-analysis work.

WHAT IS CONTENT ANALYSIS?

Content analysis has been defined in an assortment of ways by different authors in different fields. Given the array of available definitions, it is necessary to explicitly define content analysis for purposes of this chapter. While there are other characterizations of content analysis in the literature, the meaning offered here is appropriate because of its accuracy, relative generality, and ability to encompass most situations that a human performance technologist might encounter.

According to Thomas (2003), "The process of content analysis entails searching through one or more communications to answer questions that the investigator brings to the search" (p. 57). Key elements of this definition include the following ideas:

- *Process:* Effective content analysis involves multiple steps and requires a systematic approach; this is parallel with the overall HPT process.

- *Searching through communications:* Sometimes referred to as document analysis or extant data analysis (Pershing, 2002), content analysis can be performed using multiple forms of communication. This often occurs with textual documents, but visual and verbal communication may be studied as well. Regardless of the type of communication under investigation, detailed searching and examination of the information and messages within is the hallmark feature of content-analysis methodology.

- *To answer questions:* Content analysis does not occur randomly or without planning; the analyst must have a question or hypothesis in mind before beginning the investigation (Neuendorf, 2002). This characteristic of content analysis is consistent with the central HPT principle of grounding our analysis, intervention, and evaluation work with goals and performance objectives. Content analysis is no different; we must begin with a purpose in mind (Pershing, 2002).

It is important to note that some authors deliberately define content analysis as a quantitative research methodology (Neuendorf, 2002), while others refer to content analysis as a qualitative approach to data collection and analysis (Grandzol, Eckerson, and Grandzol, 2004). Authors in each camp have explicit reasons for embracing their definitions and overtly rejecting the opposite label. For example, the rich history of content analysis in media studies involving the numerical counting of occurrences of variables under study is pitted against some researchers' contention that studying and exposing emerging themes in communications is inherently qualitative.

Regardless of these arguments, such classification is largely insignificant for the purposes of this chapter and for content or document analysis in HPT. Of central importance is delineating the basic content-analysis process, while highlighting ways to maximize its usefulness in the field. Thus, this author purposefully chooses to avoid labeling content analysis as either a quantitative or qualitative research approach to avoid perpetuating the frequent misunderstanding and misapplication of these terms. For additional information on the distinction between qualitative and quantitative research and methodologies, refer to Chapter Thirty-One, "A Commentary on Quantitative and Qualitative Methods."

WHERE DOES CONTENT ANALYSIS FIT IN THE HPT PROCESS?

Content analysis is a versatile means of data collection and analysis that can be useful at multiple points during the HPT process. Using general analysis terms, Pershing (2002) advises that this technique is useful in "strategic alignment studies, context analysis, front-end and needs analysis, and performer or learner analysis" (p. 42).

Specifically looking at the International Society for Performance Improvement HPT model, as cited in Wilmoth, Prigmore, and Bray (2002), suggests that content analysis can be used effectively in at least four of the five key phases of that basic process model:

1. Performance analysis

2. Cause analysis

3. Intervention selection and design

4. Evaluation

Of all of the phases in the HPT process, content-analysis methods are employed most rarely during the intervention implementation and change phase; therefore, that phase will not be discussed in this chapter.

Using Content Analysis During Performance Analysis

Prevalent use of content analysis in the HPT process occurs during the performance analysis stage. This is often the starting point in a performance-improvement initiative. It includes analyzing factors in the performance environment and conducting a gap analysis between the actual and desired state of performance. This is when analysts "begin by learning the expectations and requirements of the organization" (Van Tiem, Moseley, and Dessinger, 2004, p. 6).

According to Pershing (2002), content analysis conducted at this early point in a performance-improvement venture involves review of "information to make inferences about past and current organizational and employee performance" (p. 36). This examination of existing documents, work records, or other artifacts is a useful precursor to later analysis efforts that may involve the creation of new data-collection instruments and the collection of new data (Pershing, 2002). In other words, initial content-analysis results can guide analysts in developing precise and meaningful interview, observation, or survey protocols later in the HPT process.

For example, an organization might initially request solving the problem of high worker's compensation claims. A natural starting point might be content-analyzing reports, accident claims, and other relevant artifacts to discover the nature and extent of the problem. The resulting information would then guide the next steps in the HPT process, learning why the problem exists and what might be done to improve it.

Another reason Pershing (2002) recommends content analysis during the early phase of performance analysis is that it "allows performance analysts and evaluation professionals to ground their front-end analysis and evaluation criteria in performance and accomplishment" (p. 36). This short statement presents a simple idea, but it bears notice because it reinforces the duty that HPT professionals have to anchor their work in performance data and concrete outcomes as opposed to mere speculation or ill-defined expectations. See Figure 35.1 for examples of organizational communications that could be examined during a content-analysis effort.

Using Content Analysis During Cause Analysis

While content or document analysis is more often employed during performance analysis, it can also be a part of cause analysis. During a typical performance-improvement initiative, the analyst will perform cause analysis concurrently with or immediately following the performance-analysis phase. Van Tiem, Moseley, and Dessinger (2004) explain that cause analysis searches for in-depth understanding of how organizational and individual performer attributes contribute to the defined performance gap. Content analysis is an effective way "to consider the information, data, and feedback" (p. 6) present in an organization, thus providing insight and definition into the causes of performance gaps. Clark and Estes (2002) support this view, explaining that "Adequate analysis of the reasons why goals are not being met (or identifying opportunities to increase performance) requires the review of many kinds of work records and other performance data" (p. 43).

For example, reviewing historical results of employee-attitude surveys administered in an organization may inform the cause analysis in a performance-improvement initiative. Logically, we know that without accurate determination of the causes of performance gaps, our chances of designing and implementing lasting improvements are poor at best, and nonexistent at worst. Thus, HPT practitioners must consider content analysis, in addition to techniques such as interviews and questionnaires, as they work to understand the causes behind the existence of performance gaps.

Accounting	
Audit reports	Payroll records
Purchasing records	Budgets
Balance sheets	
Customer Service	
Call records	E-mails
Letters	Comment cards
Organizational or Operations	
Memoranda	Procedures
Project time logs	Strategic plans
Productivity reports	Organizational charts
Human Resources	
Attendance reports	Turnover records
Exit interviews	Performance appraisals
Employee handbooks	Training records
Grievance records	Safety records
Legal	
Customer contracts	Security agreements
Employee contracts	Vendor agreements
Insurance policies	
Quality Assurance	
Scrap reports	Defect rates
Rework records	
Engineering	
Time studies	Design documents
Drawings or blueprints	Requests for quotes or proposals
Maintenance records	
Sales	
Sales projections	Marketing plans
Actual sales reports	Ad campaigns

Figure 35.1. Examples of Communications That Can Be Content-Analyzed in Organizations.

Source: Adapted from Pershing, 2002.

Using Content Analysis During Intervention Selection and Design

Another critical stage of the HPT process is that of intervention selection and design. This is the juncture at which solutions are chosen and constructed (Van Tiem, Moseley, and Dessinger, 2004). While the majority of intervention options will not rely on content analysis to take shape, content analysis can still be used effectively in this phase.

Consider a performance gap related to incorrect job changeovers in an organization. Performance analysis revealed the extent of the problem in measurable terms, and cause analysis revealed that changeover instructions are communicated in unstructured shift-to-shift "pass down" notes left from one supervisor to the next shift's supervisor. Content analysis would then be likely to reveal the unstructured nature of the notes. After the performance-and-cause analysis, a planned intervention is needed to create an easy-to-use but standardized pass-down form that will communicate both the necessary changeover instructions as well as the other informal nonchangeover-related information that supervisors need to share. A thorough content analysis of historical pass-down notes could be an effective technique for devising an improved format and subject-matter schema for communicating changeover instructions between shifts.

Using Content Analysis During Evaluation

Evaluation in HPT can benefit from content analysis nearly as frequently as does the performance-analysis phase. This primarily is due to the relationship between analysis and evaluation, in which objectives and criteria for success are established during the initial analysis phase and measured in the evaluation phase. It is common for the same data sources and variables to be reviewed during evaluation to gauge results; therefore, if content analysis was used early in the HPT process it may also be an appropriate technique to assess the impact of the interventions that have been put into place. Recall the workman's compensation example described earlier. During the evaluation stage of that particular performance-improvement initiative, the evaluator will probably content-analyze the same types of reports and accident claims after the solution implementation to see what trends emerge and if the performance gap has been lessened or eliminated.

PERFORMING CONTENT ANALYSIS

Regardless of when it is applied in the HPT process, conducting content analysis involves the same basic steps. There are also some noteworthy advantages and limitations of content analysis, as well as some key considerations that

HPT professionals should bear in mind as they plan and carry out content analyses.

Steps in the Content-Analysis Process

Pershing (2002) suggests the following sequence of actions. While they are presented as steps, it is useful to preface contemplation of them with Creswell's (1998) explanation of the analysis process as one that occurs "in analytic circles rather than using a fixed linear approach" (p. 142). This iterative context is important to remember and is executed more adeptly over time with practice and experience.

1. Articulate the purpose.
2. Decide on a specific type of analysis.
3. Prepare for the analysis.
4. Code documents.
5. Sort and sift.
6. Make discoveries.
7. Think about things.
8. Report findings.

Articulate the Purpose. Pershing and Lee (1999) emphasize that before starting content or document analysis the analyst must establish the rationale and goal for the analysis. Is this a performance problem or a quality-improvement initiative? What should the analysis achieve, and what will happen with the results of the analysis? In addition to answering these questions prior to beginning analysis, Pershing and Lee (1999) recommend that the champion or sponsor of the analysis be informed, supportive, and able to offer input.

Decide on a Specific Type of Analysis. Several types of content-analysis methods may be used depending on the analysis goals and available documents or artifacts (Pershing, 2002). Pershing, who uses the term *document analysis* as an umbrella term synonymous with the way *content analysis* has been used in this chapter, identifies three separate approaches: labeled tracking, content analysis, and case-study aggregation.

Labeled tracking requires "testing a formulated hypothesis by identifying tracks, that is, facts, found in documents or records" (Pershing, 2002, p. 38). The analyst's hypothesis will be either supported or rejected, depending on the tracks deemed present or absent during the analysis.

Content analysis as a specific type of document analysis is explained by Pershing (2002) as involving classification of information found in documents. Multiple analyses should be involved using the same methodical analysis process, which should be "systematic, generalizable, and quantifiable" (p. 39). The key feature is looking for information that can be classified into categories in a replicable manner; thus another term for this approach might be *content categorization.*

The third type of analysis Pershing (2002) describes, *case-study aggregation,* is a comparative approach. Different instances or cases are reviewed to compare and contrast information contained within them to learn how the similarities or differences relate to the purpose of the study.

Prepare for the Analysis. In addition to selecting a specific analysis method, the analyst must determine the source, type, location, and quantity of documents or artifacts to be studied (Pershing and Lee, 1999). While this may seem a simple step in the process, it is an important and sometimes intricate effort. Avoid delays, disruptions, and incomplete analysis by answering the following questions before you begin analysis (Pershing, 2002; Pershing and Lee, 1999):

- Who has access to the necessary documents or artifacts?
- Where will they be analyzed, and can they be moved?
- Do the documents contain sensitive or proprietary data?
- What confidentiality agreements are needed?
- Who should be consulted if additional documents or different types of documents are needed after analysis begins?
- Is training needed for analysts to examine the documents or artifacts?
- Is there built-in bias in the documents that might affect the data or coding scheme?

Code Documents. After establishing a purpose, deciding on an analysis method, and completing essential logistical preparations, the important work of coding may begin. Coding is the key means by which documents or artifacts are examined. Pertinent content within documents is identified and labeled during the coding process (Pershing, 2002). Pershing describes three common approaches to coding that enable analysts to draw out meaningful data from the content-analysis process: objective, heuristic, and in-between.

Objective coding occurs when words or elements in documents "can be counted, compared, and treated numerically" (p. 40). This is a very straightforward approach to coding in which "coded words represent facts and can be treated as surrogates for the text" (p. 40). This coding scheme is held constant and is more rigid than the next two coding approaches.

Heuristic coding relies on "flags or signposts" that highlight important elements of the documents or artifacts being analyzed. It is common for heuristic code-words to develop and change as the analysis progresses. This flexible yet still methodical technique enables thorough and far-reaching analysis of communications, with the full coding scheme emerging as the analysis is performed.

In-between coding is commonly used because an analyst's initial coding scheme may not be completely appropriate or of sufficient scope for the content encountered during the document analysis. This is acceptable, and it is natural to modify an objective coding scheme as new and important data or themes become evident in the communications under study.

No matter which coding approach is used, training people who will serve as coders is a critical element of the content-analysis process (Neuendorf, 2002). A codebook is the name of the tool frequently used in content analysis to document and define variables being assessed, and it is typically paired with a coding form. A coding form is the document upon which the data are recorded (Neuendorf, 2002). Refer to Figure 35.2 for an example of a coding form. Consistent coding has implications for reliability, which is discussed later in this chapter.

Sort and Sift. Once coding is complete, the iterative process of sorting and sifting begins. This allows the analyst to notice similarities and differences and bring order to the data collected (Pershing, 2002). Sorting and sifting happens just as its name implies; it "includes breaking the data down into discrete parts and grouping them according to the coding schemata" (p. 40). Do not be reluctant to recode some of the data consistent with the appropriate coding scheme, as it is natural to notice new ideas and experience evolving patterns of thinking during this process (Pershing and Lee, 1999).

Make Discoveries. Once the data have been ordered through sorting and sifting, the analyst must discover and chart patterns from the data. Such discoveries may take the form of describing data as processes, types, sequences, wholes, categories, or classes. As Pershing (2002) notes, "This process involves searching for both 'wholes' as well as 'holes' in the data" (p. 40).

Think about Things. The last step of the content-analysis process that happens before data are summarized and reported requires the analyst to "think about things." A deceptively simple-sounding step, this requires the analyst to make sense of what has been uncovered and organized. It is possible that in looking for patterns and making generalizations at this stage, the analyst may need to revisit the coding, sorting and sifting, and discovery steps until no new discoveries surface (Pershing, 2002). This is another iterative process that can be facilitated by considering additional factors beyond the mere presence and

Wile Model Coding Sheet

Case: _____
Date: _____
Coder: _____
Unit of Analysis: _____

Problem/Opportunity _____
Description: _____

Problem/Deficiency/Opportunity/Symptom/Cause

Description		Primary/ Secondary	Manifest/ Latent	Page Number
	1 Org Systems			
	2 Incentives			
	3 Cognitive Support			
	4 Tools			
	5 Physical Environment			
	6 Skills/ Knowledge			
	7 Inherent Ability			

Intervention/Planned Intervention

Description	Primary/ Secondary	Manifest/ Latent	Page Number

Figure 35.2. Example of a Coding Form Based on Wile's HPT Model.

Source: Adapted from Wile, 1996.

frequency of content and ideas. Analysts should think beyond the straightforward and reflect on the meaning of consistent or inconsistent patterns within and across the coded data (Pershing, 2002).

Report Findings. Concluding a content analysis requires documentation of results. Pershing (2002) recommends including the following elements in the report:

- State the original problem, question, or goal of the analysis.
- Describe the documents or artifacts studied, including number and type.
- Explain the coding process and categories defined.
- Describe the patterns that materialized from the analysis.
- Provide details of findings; this may include summaries of data that were counted, descriptive stories, or detailed pattern descriptions.
- Relate assertions and implications for the content analysis, and, as appropriate, the broader HPT initiative at hand.

Each of the eight process steps can be defined and conducted with painstaking detail, but HPT professionals must adjust and perform content analysis appropriately within the time and resource constraints of their environment and the project they have undertaken. This is consistent with the perpetual balance that practitioners must strike when carrying out systematic methods such as the HPT process.

The detailed systematic approach for content analysis documented here might seem at first glance too rigid and painstaking. However, it has been presented in more flexible and accommodating terms than other more explicitly scientific-method-based descriptions found in the literature (see, for example, Neuendorf, 2002). Furthermore, the content-analysis flow offered here provides the necessary framework to complete the task properly, particularly for novices. It is natural for the skilled practitioner to become more adept over time, improving efficiency and making the lines between the steps appear somewhat blurry to the untrained observer.

Combining Content Analysis with Other Methods of Data Collection and Analysis

In addition to content analysis, performance technologists have opportunities that call for the use of other data-collection techniques. During a single performance-improvement initiative, an analyst might use any combination of content analysis, interviews, focus groups, observation, and questionnaires. This is normal and usually desired. Depending on the problem or opportunity being analyzed, the objectives of the analysis, and the available resources, content analysis can be effectively combined with other data-collection and analysis methods in several ways.

Possible scenarios include using document analysis as

- A starting point for an improvement initiative, reviewing documents and records to gain insight into the situation at hand.

- A way to organize and interpret narrative data collected from open-ended questions on surveys or other assessment tools.

- An evaluative tool to compare pre- and postintervention states, focusing on possible measures such as reaction, learning, transfer or behavior change, or business impact (Pershing, 2002).

- A tool to triangulate data collected using other means (Neuendorf, 2002), to discern convergence or divergence with the results generated by the original data source(s).

Despite its illuminating and explanatory value, content analysis is rarely used as a standalone analysis technique for addressing performance-improvement problems or opportunities (Pershing and Lee, 1999). Consider and combine other factors and data sources to ensure the most accurate, comprehensive analysis or evaluation effort.

Within the context of considering possible methodological combinations, it is important to assess the advantages and disadvantages of each method. Carefully weighing the benefits and drawbacks in light of the specific performance-improvement initiative, setting, timeline, and resource situation will help determine whether content analysis is an appropriate method to employ.

Advantages

Human performance technologists continually encounter situations that require assessing performance in the past and present, and subsequently devising plans to improve the state of performance in the future. Content analysis is an excellent way to gather information about historical performance. The information gleaned is desirable because it directly reflects and explains work processes and products as they were originally documented using authentic organizational means, whether informal or formal. According to Pershing (2002), "Information gathered from documents is often more credible than information or data obtained via interviews, questionnaires, or observation, because the data are historical and often viewed as objective evidence" (p. 41).

Content analysis can also be a low-cost data-collection and analysis technique. Analysts can save both time and money in many cases because the information to be analyzed already exists, and sometimes the data may be sorted and analyzed with the help of computers. In some instances content analysis may be the only viable way to acquire the needed information. For example, it would not make sense to interview manufacturing operators to find out departmental productivity percentages for the previous year; document analysis of productivity data would be a more effective approach.

Fraenkel and Wallen (1996) highlight another very important benefit of content analysis, that it "is a method that permits researchers to study human behavior unobtrusively" (p. 11). Aside from time spent working with appropriate organizational personnel to obtain required documents or artifacts, performance-improvement professionals who are conducting content analysis need little assistance or interaction with people in the organization. The examination of documents often can be completed independently.

Limitations

When selecting content analysis, HPT professionals should be aware of several limitations. First, any research or analysis method that relies so heavily on human reporting and interpretation is subject to limitations. This does not render content analysis useless, but the nature of the human element must not be overlooked.

The integrity of data used for content analysis can be compromised in several ways, so analysts and evaluators must be aware of potential weak points if they choose this path (Pershing, 2002). For example, documents or other artifacts may be subject to alteration or editing. This could occur when someone wants to improve the appearance of individual or organizational performance, either during document composition or afterwards.

While the historical focus of documents used in content analysis is often an advantage, it makes content analysis an inappropriate choice for situations, however rare, in which historical data are inconsequential. At minimum, content analysis is insufficient by itself when the analysis or evaluation cannot be completed effectively with only historical information.

Simple logistics can also present pitfalls to content analysts, including physical accessibility problems, confidentiality issues, complex recordkeeping practices, incomplete document sets, and outdated documents (Pershing, 2002).

Successful performance of content analysis can be, as mentioned earlier in this chapter, more challenging than it might appear on the surface. Analysts need to work closely with document owners to gain a clear understanding of the terms and classifications of information contained in the archived communications they will analyze. This includes understanding definitions, formulas, and data sources, particularly in the context of the performance or evaluation issue under study. Without such understanding, a novice analyst may misread the information and jeopardize the value of the analysis. Likewise, Pershing (2002) notes that the analyst must have enough subject matter familiarity "to apply pertinent historical information to current problems" (p. 42).

The advantages of content analysis make it an ideal tool for an array of situations, but like any technique, limitations accompany the benefits. Performance-improvement professionals who select and carry out content-analysis methods will increase the meaning and success of their efforts if they keep limitations of the methodology in mind and adapt accordingly as needed.

Validity and Reliability of Content Analysis

Validity and reliability must be constant considerations during any data-collection and analysis process, and content analysis is no different. While analysis efforts will vary in terms of the standards required for validity and reliability, practitioners and scholars alike should take sufficient measures to maximize the validity and reliability of their content-analysis work within a given situation.

If our data collection and analysis are valid, it generally means that we have measured and analyzed what we have intended to measure. To enhance validity, analysts must take care in defining the variables they will study. Well-prepared codebooks and coding forms supported by good definitions of what coders should be looking for during analysis are necessary.

If our work is reliable, we should expect to obtain the equivalent results time and again if we conduct the analysis more than once. To check reliability, use multiple analysts or coders and then determine the degree to which their results agree (Fraenkel and Wallen, 1996). This is sometimes called inter-rater reliability or intercoder reliability (Neuendorf, 2002). A similar approach, though perhaps less practical in many HPT initiatives because it is more time-consuming, is using the same analyst to evaluate the data at two separate times (Fraenkel and Wallen, 1996).

Even during an abbreviated content-analysis study that might be considered preliminary to a larger HPT initiative, reliability is vital. Neuendorf (2002) stresses that "without the establishment of reliability, a measure cannot be considered valid" (p. 141). HPT professionals cannot avoid consideration of these two important characteristics of data collection and analysis, especially when performing content analysis.

EXAMPLES OF CONTENT-ANALYSIS WORK

Innumerable opportunities for content analysis exist within the realm of HPT, both in applied and research settings. The following case examples will offer more concrete guidance to HPT professionals as they look for ways to apply content-analysis methods for performance-improvement and advancement of the field.

Case 1: Improving Safety Performance

Situation. A large distribution organization noticed a sharp increase in the number of on-the-job injuries sustained by employees each month. The injury increase seemed isolated to one distribution center that had been known historically to have the best safety record in the entire organization, but the monthly trend had been increasing sharply for at least six months. The safety coordinator was asked to report to the local general manager and regional safety manager the specific causes of the injury-rate increase and proposed actions to reverse the trend.

Content-Analysis Approach. Working with the safety coordinator, the performance-improvement specialist assisting with the investigation planned a content-analysis approach to begin determining the causes of the injury rate increase. Documents selected for analysis included accident reports from the twenty-four-month period prior to the injury increase, as well as accident reports from the six-month period of degraded safety performance. Coding the reports involved documenting the type of injury, location of the injury on the body, date, shift, work area at which it occurred, and job task being performed when the injury occurred. Each of these variables was counted, categorized, and then further studied to uncover patterns in the circumstances surrounding the injuries. From that point, the investigators collected additional data to flesh out the probable causes and develop solutions that would set the distribution center back on the path of being best-in-company when it comes to safety performance.

Case 2: Improving Scheduling in Response to Attendance Fluctuations

Situation. A small manufacturing plant experienced unusually high rates of absenteeism, but a short-term solution to eliminate the absenteeism was not viable due to contractual obligations between the company and the labor union. Until the primary performance problem of high absenteeism could be addressed, management hoped to modify the plant production scheduling strategy to better fit the pattern of absenteeism that seemed to exist among employees. This short-term adjustment was desired to improve the efficiency of resource utilization and streamline the production process.

To better understand the perceived cycle of employee absenteeism and attendance, the plant manager requested concrete data that might enable schedulers to anticipate peak times of attendance and absenteeism and adjust production schedules accordingly. By adjusting production schedules the organization would realize many interim performance benefits until the root cause of high absenteeism could be addressed via the contractually negotiated attendance policy.

Content-Analysis Approach. Historical timecard and shift absentee records were used to track and chart attendance trends during the previous thirty-six months. Analysts noted that there were no appreciable changes in the number or identity of personnel during this time. Therefore a three-year span was selected to capture any potential attendance spikes that might be attributed to time of year. In addition to annual and monthly attendance figures, the analysts also analyzed the documents to pinpoint day of week, time of day, and shift trends that existed within the data set. The identified patterns of attendance and absence were summarized and reported to the plant manager and schedulers to enable them to better plan and meet production demands while maximizing the efficient use of labor and other supplies. Notice that this analysis scenario involved a preliminary or interim solution, but the data may also prove valuable when the real causes and elimination of the attendance gap are addressed during the future collective-bargaining process.

Case 3: Defining Performance Objectives for Employee Training

Situation. An organization that operated a network of telephone call centers just devised a new performance-improvement strategy that combines the successful completion of training and a formal qualification assessment before new employees are allowed to perform their call-answering jobs independently. Prior to this initiative, new employees only were required to complete formal training before assuming their full-time job responsibilities; there was no formal assessment of their knowledge or performance skills prior to placing them on the job. Given the existence of fairly robust training materials, the director of organizational learning and performance hired a performance-improvement consultant to devise formal qualification assessments that could be used in conjunction with the existing instructional program.

Content-Analysis Approach. The performance-improvement consultant worked with the client to determine that the instruments for assessment needed to combine knowledge tests and performance checklists. The skills and concepts included in the instruments needed to be derived from the objectives and material in the existing training packages; therefore, the consultant selected content analysis of those extant data sources as the first step in creating formal qualification assessments. In addition to coding the manifest documentation of learning objectives, the consultant looked for more latent content in the material to comprehensively identify the skills, facts, and conceptual themes on which the new employees should be formally assessed.

The consultant also requested access to company policies and standard operating procedures to analyze the performance requirements set forth in those documents and protocols. These data, when considered in tandem with the data from training packages, provided a sound foundation for the development of appropriate qualification instruments. Using content analysis in this situation enabled the organization to capitalize on several types of readily available information for the development of a new intervention to improve employee performance.

Case 4: Assessing the Efficacy of an HPT Model

Situation. A researcher in the field of HPT was intrigued by the fact that literature in the field is peppered with a multitude of models. This multiplicity can make it difficult for scholars and practitioners to know which models are best or most appropriate for use. While many of the models surveyed contained similar elements, the researcher believed some were different to the extent that they seemed to be notably more helpful or accurate than others. In a relatively young field like HPT, the researcher focused on the importance of identifying sound models as a foundation upon which to define and guide theory and practice. To identify such a model, she began a study of one prominent model to assess its efficacy as a central model in the field.

Content-Analysis Approach. HPT models are inherently general, designed to represent a process or framework of variables. The researcher chose a content-analysis technique to compare the generality of the model with the specificity of HPT in action as a means of judging value and applicability. The data set comprised published case studies explaining complete, nonfictional performance-improvement initiatives. The codebook was derived from components of the model the researcher was evaluating. Data collection required multiple coders to document the presence of model elements in the text of the cases. The coders completed initial coding of each case independently, and the individual results were subsequently analyzed together as a means of assessing reliability. Data analysis was completed for each case, and then a cross-case analysis was employed, thereby using content analysis to identify frequencies, patterns, and themes at more than one level. Composite results and conclusions concerning the model's efficacy yielded information that the researcher could draw upon to make recommendations for improving the model, thus increasing its value in the field.

SUMMARY

Practitioners and scholars interested in learning more about content analysis have many resources to which to refer, as the information presented in this chapter is a mere fraction of the available explanations and instructions for completing very simple to highly complex content analyses. Nonetheless, the power of content analysis in HPT is significant, and it may be underapplied in the field if it is not well-known or understood.

This chapter served a dual purpose, explaining what content analysis is within the context of HPT and offering guidance about how to conduct a useful content analysis in HPT. Professionals in the field, novice and experienced alike, can refer to this chapter to clarify their approach and direct their efforts. It should enable them to draw effectively upon the valuable data embedded in the many work samples, reports, and organizational communications that are readily available to support meaningful, attainable performance improvements in organizations now and in the future.

References

Clark, R. E., and Estes, F. (2002). *Turning research into results: A guide to selecting the right performance solutions.* Atlanta: CEP Press.

Creswell, J. W. (1998). *Qualitative inquiry and research design: Choosing among five traditions.* Thousand Oaks, CA: Sage.

Fraenkel, J. R., and Wallen, N. E. (1996). *How to design and evaluate research in education* (3rd ed.). New York: McGraw-Hill.

Grandzol, J. R., Eckerson, C. A., and Grandzol, C. J. (2004). Beyond no significant difference: Differentiating learning outcomes using multidimensional content analysis. *DEOSNEWS, 13*(8). Retrieved October 25, 2005, from http://www.ed.psu.edu/acsde/deos/deosnews/deosnews13_8.pdf.

Neuendorf, K. A. (2002). *The content analysis guidebook.* Thousand Oaks, CA: Sage.

Pershing, J. A., and Lee, S. H. (1999). Document analysis. In J. A. Pershing and S. H. Lee, *Analyzing needs for performance improvement: Processes and core competencies* (pp. 10-1 to 10-13). Bloomington, IN: EMRA.

Pershing, J. L. (2002). Using document analysis in analyzing and evaluating performance. *Performance Improvement, 41*(1), 36–42.

Thomas, R. M. (2003). *Blending qualitative and quantitative research methods in theses and dissertations.* Thousand Oaks, CA: Corwin Press.

Van Tiem, D. M., Moseley, J. L., and Dessinger, J. C. (2004). *Fundamentals of performance technology: A guide to improving people, process, and performance* (2nd ed.). Silver Spring, MD: International Society for Performance Improvement.

Wile, D. (1996). Why doers do. *Performance and Instruction, 35*(1), 30–35.

Wilmoth, F. S., Prigmore, C., and Bray, M. (2002). HPT models: An overview of the major models in the field. *Performance Improvement, 41*(8), 16–24.

CHAPTER THIRTY-SIX

Quantitative Data Analyses

Mary Norris Thomas

Data analysis is an aid to thought, not a substitute.
—Green and Hall, 1984, p. 52

D o you measure performance or consider performance measures taken by others? If yes, then you probably have engaged in quantitative data analysis. Performance technology is a measurement-oriented field of practice. We engage in measurement when we diagnose problems, when we perform assessments, when we track quality indicators, and of course when we conduct evaluations. We may wish to compare performance measures to standards or benchmarks, determine whether events are related, evaluate the effectiveness of programs, or predict outcomes.

We base decisions on many ways of knowing, such as experience, intuition, reasoning, and authority. Quantitative methods add empiricism to these ways of knowing. The results of quantitative data analysis help us to make decisions. Keep in mind, however, that the results of data analysis do not make the decisions. People use and interpret data to make decisions.

QUANTITATIVE DATA-ANALYSIS PROCESS

The quantitative data-analysis process begins with inspecting collected numerical data and ends with a decision. Data analysis is itself part of a larger research or evaluation process. Before collecting data, plan the measures you will take and from whom, the instruments you will use, the analyses you will perform, and your rules for making decisions about your data. Do this in an orderly and well-organized fashion so that another investigator could replicate your study. The plan may be in the form of a formal research proposal or part of a project proposal to a client accompanied by a timeline and budget. The basic steps of data analysis are

1. Inspect collected data.
2. Calculate appropriate statistics.
3. Make statistical decisions about the analyzed data.
4. Interpret the results.
5. Draw conclusions.

These analysis steps illustrate that the number-crunching part, step 2, is rather minor compared with the thought required before and after statistics are calculated. Germane to each step is to ask, What does this mean?

MULTIPLE MEANINGS OF STATISTICS

The term *statistics* is used in multiple ways. Statistics can refer to values of common usage, such as a baseball player's batting average, or to government statistics such as the consumer price index. In a broader sense, statistics refer to a mathematical discipline. In quantitative data analysis, statistics refer to techniques for summarizing, analyzing, interpreting, displaying, and calculating statements about data. In this way, we apply statistics as the "technology of the scientific method" (Daniel and Terrell, 1986, p. 2).

Statements about statistics are statements of probabilities. We apply probability theory deductively, going from a general theory to the specifics of an observation to estimate the odds of obtaining a particular result given certain conditions. Then we apply decision theory to create decision rules to make inferences and deduce decisions about this probability. We make decisions about what may be true under conditions of uncertainty, without having taken every measurement possible. For example, applying probability theory, we calculate the probability that a measured performance improvement occurred as a result of an intervention rather than just by chance. Using decision theory, we formulate probability-based decision rules. However, it is up to us to make the decision. Neither probability theory nor decision theory tells us how to decide (Hays, 1973). Only you can make the inductive leap from your specific observations to the general nature of the event.

Statistical Significance Versus Practical Significance

This brings us to the important distinction between statistical significance and practical significance. Perhaps you have encountered the phrase, "the results are statistically significant." Such statements of statistical significance are simply statements of probability. Practical significance, however, refers to the value or meaningfulness of the results.

It's Greek to Me

Do statistics look like Greek to you? If so, you are quite correct. Much of statistical notation uses Greek letters. Plus, comprehending the multitude of statistical terms may feel like learning a foreign language. And, yes, the equations may appear a bit scary. But mastering, or even just making friends with, statistics is not about the math. Hand-held calculators will do the math. Basic spreadsheet programs such as Microsoft Excel will do the math and draw the graphs. Statistical software packages such as SPSS will do the math, draw the graphs, and generate reams of outputs. However, only you can relate the statistical results to your problem and draw meaningful conclusions.

FUNDAMENTALS

Basic Terms and Notations

Statistical techniques broadly are divided into descriptive statistics and inferential statistics. Descriptive statistics refer to single values that describe a data set, such as the mean or average. Inferential statistics refer to test statistics that yield probabilities about the data, which help us to make inferences.

Usually we measure a sample, or a portion or subset, of a set of data rather than the entire set, which is known as the population. This brings us to yet two more uses of the word *statistic*. From the sample data, we calculate summary measures called statistics. A sample mean or average is a statistic; in this case it is a descriptive statistic. The term *test statistic* refers to inferential techniques for calculating the probability of obtaining a given descriptive sample statistic. Table 36.1 summarizes these basic terms.

If we measure all members of a population, then we have population values or parameters. When we have measured or observed every occurrence of an event, then we have measured the entire population. For example, if we wish to know the average age of all employees in Acme Brick Company, then we must collect data on all Acme Brick employees. But if there are 250,000 employees, then it is more efficient to randomly select a few birthdates and use sample measures to estimate the population values. Random selection or sampling is like drawing names from a hat, when each name has the same chance of being drawn.

Measurement and Meaningfulness

Measurement theory provides conventions (Townsend and Ashby, 1984; Siegel, 1956) that help us to preserve the integrity of our data. There are at least two

Table 36.1. Fundamental Terms.

Term	Definition
Descriptive statistics	Values that describe a data set
Inferential statistics	Test statistics that yield probabilities about a sample statistic and that help us make inferences about a population parameter
Sample	The portion or subset of a population that is measured
Population	The entire set of individuals, events, or items under consideration
Statistic	A summary value calculated from sample data used to estimate the population
Parameter	A summary value that describes or represents an entire population

procedural problems to avoid. First, if something meaningful is to emerge from data analysis, then something meaningful must be input (Stevens, 1972), or, to put it more crudely, garbage in, garbage out. There is a second undesirable procedure: meaningful data in, garbage out. This occurs when analyses are performed that just do not make sense. Statistical formulas are blind and will accept all numbers indiscriminately. At every step, you must invoke the test of meaningfulness.

Consider this classic example: the average American family has 2.47 children. What is wrong with this statement? This is an example of performing a mathematical operation, division, that is inappropriate for the scale of measurement. Sure, calculators will perform division, but calculators do not interpret the result. You must interpret the result. The operation of division in this example results in 2.47, a number that is meaningless because it is not possible to have forty-seven one-hundredths of a child; children only occur in whole numbers. Therefore, the average or mean is meaningless. In this case, the appropriate measure of central tendency is the mode, the most frequently occurring number, because its calculation does not involve division.

Measurement involves the assignment of numbers to objects or events according to rules or conventions (Stevens, 1972). This act of measurement results in a scale. There are at least four ways in which measurement scales can be constructed: as nominal scales, ordinal scales, interval scales, and ratio scales. Properties of each type of scale are summarized in Table 36.2.

Some consider subjective rating scales, such as the strongly agree, agree, disagree, and strongly disagree variety, to be somewhere between ordinal and interval scales of measurements. It is a matter of debate whether the intervals

Table 36.2. Scales of Measurement.

Scale	Permissible Operations	Definition	Example
	Nonparametric scales have no metrics or quantitative intervals between the categories or rankings.		
Nominal Naming, categorizing, or counting occurrences	= Equivalence or equal to	Nominal scales are naming scales and represent categories when there is no basis for ordering the categories. It is meaningless to add, subtract, multiply, divide, or even rank order categories. We can count the frequencies that each category occurred.	• Gender • Job classification • Eye color • Business industry type
Ordinal Rank order	= Equivalence or equal to > Greater than < Less than	Ordinal scales have categories that can be ordered, but the magnitude of the difference between categories is unknown. Here we only know whether two rankings are the same, greater than, or less than, one another. But we do not know how large or small the interval is between any of the rankings.	• Opinion (agree, don't care, disagree) • Class ranking (1st, 2nd, 3rd) • Preference (1st choice, 2nd choice, 3rd choice) • Grade (freshman, sophomore, junior, senior)
	Parametric Scales have metrics or quantitatively meaningful and equal intervals between numbers.		
Interval Quantitative intervals, but no zero point	= Equivalence or equal to > Greater than < Less than + Addition − Subtraction	Interval scales are numerical, the distance between successive numbers is equal, but there is no true zero because the starting point is arbitrary. Without a true zero point, we cannot say that there is none of the property being measured, nor can we compare proportions or ratios.	• Standardized test scores • Quality indices • Temperature

(Continued)

Table 36.2. Scales of Measurement (*Continued*).

Scale	Permissible Operations	Definition	Example
Ratio Has a true zero point	= Equivalence or equal to > Greater than < Less than + Addition (multiplication) − Subtraction (division) : Ratios and proportions	Ratio scales are the easiest to understand because they are numbers as we usually think of them. The distance between adjacent numbers is equal, and a score of zero means that there is none of whatever is being measured. We can add, subtract, multiply, and divide measures on a ratio scale.	• Money • Time • Height

between successive ratings are equal. For example, Likert or Likert-type response scales are ordinal because they solicit responses to words, and words are qualitative, not quantitative. Technically, the scale is ordinal, not interval, because there are no metrics or quantitative intervals between the words. However, research indicates that respondents tend to interpret these types of rating options as interval scaled (Lehmann, 1989). What does the scale of measurement have to do with statistical data analysis? Different statistics are appropriate for different scales of measurement.

Data Types

We distinguish between two types of data: categorical and numerical. When we collect categorical data, we may count the frequency of occurrence of qualities or categories. For example, managers are a category of employee, trucks are a category of vehicle, and strongly agree is a category of opinion.

Numerical data are quantities, such as salary, cycle time, or turnover rate. There are two types of numerical data, discrete and continuous. Data that are only whole numbers are discrete numbers. For example, the number of employees is a discrete number because people only come in whole numbers. In contrast, data that can take on any value between successive whole numbers are continuous. For example, depending on the instrument, we could measure height to any number of decimal places. Someone could be 64 inches in height if measured to the nearest inch, or 63.75 if measured to the nearest one hundredth of an inch. The association of data type to measurement scale is shown in Table 36.3.

Table 36.3. Data Types and Scales of Measurement.

Data Type	Measurement Scale	Example
Categorical	**Nonparametric**	
Discrete	Nominal	Political Party: ☐ Democrat ☐ Independent ☐ Republican
	Ordinal	Customer Satisfaction: ☐ Unsatisfied ☐ Neutral ☐ Very Satisfied
Numerical	**Parametric**	
Continuous	Interval	Score on Scholastic Aptitude Test (SAT): _____ Score
Discrete	Ratio	Complaints filed last month: _____ Number
Continuous		Last year's annual gross sales: $_____

DESCRIPTIVE TECHNIQUES

Descriptive techniques help us visualize and summarize data. Tables and graphs help us visualize differences among groups, associations among variables, or trends over time. Descriptive statistics, such as the mean, reduce data to a few numbers or descriptors. The key here is choosing descriptive techniques that best represent the data and therefore preserve the scale of measurement. For practical assistance using statistical and graphing functions in Microsoft Excel, see *Statistics for Managers Using Microsoft® Excel* by Levine, Stephan, Krehbiel, and Berenson (2005).

Tables and Graphs

Typically, tables contain quantities or numbers, whereas graphs illustrate relative differences among the quantities. Most spreadsheet applications have table and graphing functions. However, you must specify the type of table and graph to draw. Contingency tables, also called cross tabulation or cross tabs, are useful for organizing cross-classified data. Common types of graphs include frequency polygons, bar graphs, pie charts, line graphs, and scatter plots. Generally, bar graphs are preferred for discrete data, whereas line charts are recommended for continuous data (Ary, Jacobs, and Razavieh, 2002). Suggestions for when to use which type of graph are provided in Figure 36.1.

Tables and graphs not only help us to organize and visualize data, they also are efficient and effective ways to communicate data. The best graphs are those that have a clear purpose, accurately represent the data, and are self-explanatory (Levine, Stephan, Krehbiel, and Berenson, 2005; Tufte, 2002).

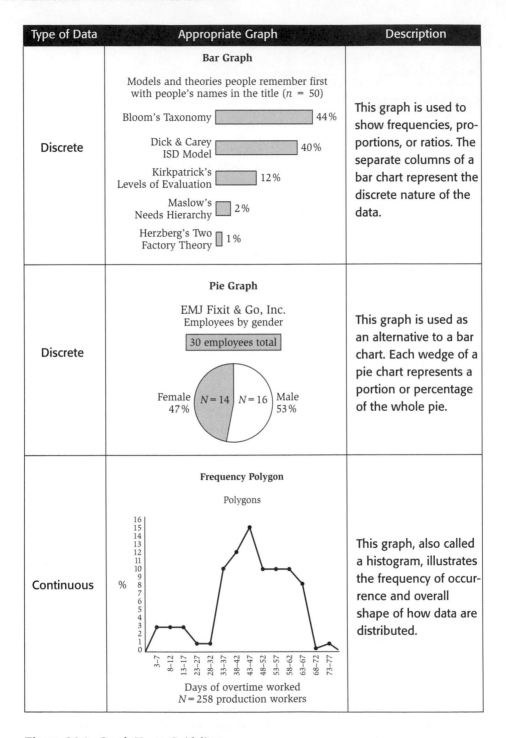

Type of Data	Appropriate Graph	Description
Discrete	**Bar Graph** Models and theories people remember first with people's names in the title ($n = 50$) Bloom's Taxonomy — 44% Dick & Carey ISD Model — 40% Kirkpatrick's Levels of Evaluation — 12% Maslow's Needs Hierarchy — 2% Herzberg's Two Factory Theory — 1%	This graph is used to show frequencies, proportions, or ratios. The separate columns of a bar chart represent the discrete nature of the data.
Discrete	**Pie Graph** EMJ Fixit & Go, Inc. Employees by gender 30 employees total Female $N = 14$ 47% / Male $N = 16$ 53%	This graph is used as an alternative to a bar chart. Each wedge of a pie chart represents a portion or percentage of the whole pie.
Continuous	**Frequency Polygon** Polygons % (16–0) 3–7, 8–12, 13–17, 23–27, 28–32, 33–37, 38–42, 43–47, 48–52, 53–57, 58–62, 63–67, 68–72, 73–77 Days of overtime worked $N = 258$ production workers	This graph, also called a histogram, illustrates the frequency of occurrence and overall shape of how data are distributed.

Figure 36.1. Graph Usage Guidelines.

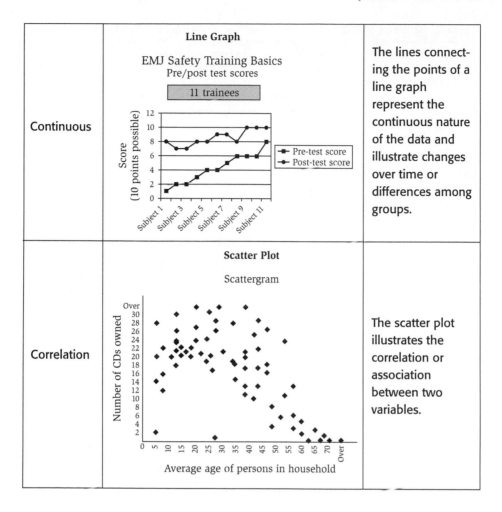

Figure 36.1. (*Continued*)

Descriptive Statistics Appropriate for Each Scale of Measurement

Measures of central tendency describe what most of the scores are like. Measures of dispersion represent variation or differences among observations. A third class of descriptors, correlation, represents the degree of relatedness among two groups of observations. Which descriptive statistics should you use? The best answer is the ones that best represent your data. Again, we invoke the primacy of measurement because it sets the bounds on preserving meaningfulness (Stevens, 1972). Table 36.4 summarizes some descriptive statistics appropriate for each scale of measurement (Siegel, 1956; Stevens, 1972; Siegel and Castellan, 1988).

Table 36.4. Descriptive Statistics Appropriate for Each Scale of Measurement.

Measurement Scale	Descriptive Statistic		
	Central Tendency	Dispersion	Relatedness
Nominal	Mode	Number of categories	Contingency coefficient C
Ordinal	Median	Percentile	Spearman's *rho*, Kendall's *tau*
Interval	Mean	Standard deviation	Pearson's *r*
Ratio	Mean	Standard deviation	Pearson's *r*

Measures of Central Tendency

Descriptors that represent most of the data are measures of central tendency. These measures identify the center or balance point of a distribution. Three ways to specify the center point include the mode, the median, and the mean.

Mode. The mode is the most frequently occurring score in a data set. In a bar graph, the bar with the highest frequency count is the mode. Properties of the mode include the following:

- It requires no calculations other than counting.
- It is not affected by extreme scores.
- It may not exist; for example, this data set, 85, 80, 75, 83, 87, is uniformly modal, because all scores occur with the same frequency.
- It may have more than one mode; for example, this data set, 4, 6, 9, 4, 7, 4, 5, 10, 9, 6, 9, is bimodal, because both 4 and 9 occur three times and are both modes.

Median. The median is the midpoint of a distribution, with half of the scores above and half the scores below. Properties of the median include the following:

- Each data set has only one median.
- It is not affected by extreme scores.
- It is more likely to vary from sample to sample, and therefore can be less reliable than the mean.

Mean. The mean is the average of all scores in a data set. Properties of the mean include the following:

- It is familiar to most people.
- Each data set has only one mean.

- It takes into account every score.

- It is fairly reliable; of the three measures of central tendency, the mean is least likely to vary from sample to sample.

- It is, however, greatly influenced by extreme scores.

Measures of Dispersion

While measures of central tendency tell us about similarity, measures of dispersion tell us about difference or variation. Common measures of dispersion include the range, the semi-interquartile range, and standard deviation.

Range. The range is the quickest but least informative measure of dispersion. The range is simply the difference between the largest and smallest values, and therefore takes only these two values into consideration. In this data set, 85, 82, 73, 61, 45, the values range from 85 to 45, or a forty-point range.

Semi-Interquartile Range. The semi-interquartile range specifies the range of the middle 50 percent of rank-ordered scores and is calculated as half of the difference between the seventy-fifth percentile, or Q3, and the twenty-fifth percentile, or Q1. The formula for the semi-interquartile range is $(Q3 - Q1)/2$. A set of scores with a wide semi-interquartile range has greater variability than a set of scores with a narrow semi-interquartile range. As previously mentioned, the median is the appropriate measure of central tendency for data sets with extreme scores. In such cases, the semi-interquartile range is the appropriate measure of dispersion because it is not as sensitive as the range to extreme values.

Standard Deviation. Although we have reduced the data to a single measure of central tendency, such as the mean, we still need to know how representative this number is. How well does it describe the data? We need to know how much each data point varies from the mean, called dispersion or deviation. The standard deviation uses all of the observations and is the average of how much each data point differs from the mean. The standard deviation is tedious to calculate by hand, but readily available using hand-held calculators or spreadsheet applications such as Excel.

Large standard deviations are associated with wide spreads, and small standard deviations are associated with narrow spreads. For example, if the standard deviations of the ages of people in two populations are fifteen years and two years, respectively, then we know that the first population has much greater age variability than the second population. But how do we interpret a single standard deviation? One way is to indicate the percentage of values that fall within a specified number of standard deviations from the mean. When the distribution is bell-shaped or normal, then

- 68 percent of all values will be within one standard deviation from the mean.

- 95 percent of all values will be within two standard deviations from the mean.

- 99.7 percent, or nearly all values, will be within three standard deviations from the mean. Perhaps you are familiar with the term *Six Sigma*. Sigma, or Σ, refers to standard deviation, and six refers to the spread of six standard deviations, three below the mean plus three above the mean.

Consider the following example. If the ages of a population are normally distributed with a mean of 30 and standard deviation of 10, then 68 percent of the population will be in the age range of 30 ± 10, or 20 years of age to 40 years of age; 95 percent will be in the age range of 30 ± 20, or 10 years of age to 50 years of age; and nearly all will be in the age range of 30 ± 30, or 0 years of age to 60 years of age.

In summary, dispersion is the degree of spread or variability within a set of scores. The range is useful, but it cannot stand alone as a measure of spread because it takes into account only two scores, the maximum and the minimum. The standard deviation is a commonly used measure of spread. It takes every score into account, is not misrepresented by extreme scores, and is used in many formulas in inferential statistics. But the standard deviation is not a good measure of spread in highly skewed distributions, when the distribution is not symmetrical and therefore not a normal distribution. In such cases, the standard deviation should be supplemented by the semi-interquartile range.

Normal Distributions

When we know both the mean and the standard deviation, we can describe the distribution of values within a data set, specify the relative positions of values within a data set, and compare values across different data sets. A commonly used distribution is a normal distribution. Normal distributions are bell-shaped and symmetrical, and the mean, median, and mode are identical. The shape of the bell may be pointy or rather flat depending on the deviation of scores from the distribution's mid point. Figure 36.2 illustrates these characteristics of normal distributions. Values close to the mean occur more frequently and form the hump of the bell, while values further from the mean occur less frequently and form the tails of the distribution.

Normal distributions play a key role in statistics as the basis, for example, for percentile rank and standard scores, as well as for probabilities associated with inferential statistics. Such information has practical application in distinguishing a reliable occurrence from a fluke occurrence, assessing differences among individuals or groups, or predicting how often an event may occur.

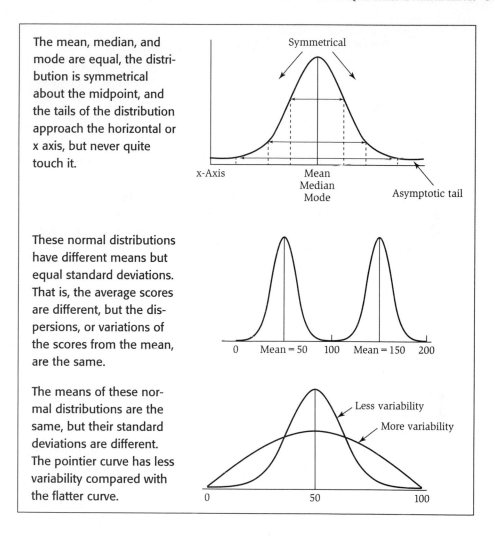

The mean, median, and mode are equal, the distribution is symmetrical about the midpoint, and the tails of the distribution approach the horizontal or x axis, but never quite touch it.

These normal distributions have different means but equal standard deviations. That is, the average scores are different, but the dispersions, or variations of the scores from the mean, are the same.

The means of these normal distributions are the same, but their standard deviations are different. The pointier curve has less variability compared with the flatter curve.

Figure 36.2. Characteristics of Normal Distributions.

Skewed Distributions

The term *normal,* as used in normal distribution, can be a bit misleading. In this context, *normal* refers to a theoretical or ideal state. A given data set may not conform to this ideal. Rather a given data set or even the entire population may have an asymmetrical or a skewed distribution. If the data bunch or skew off center, then the distribution is not symmetrical and one tail is longer than the other (see Figure 36.3). The distribution of math scores for physicists, for example, tends to be positively skewed or bunched toward the right tail because few people in the middle or low ranges tend to be physicists.

Positive skew	Negative skew
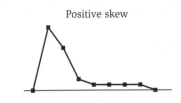	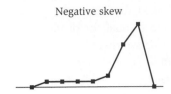
A positively skewed distribution has a long tail in the positive or right-hand direction. The mean is greater than the median, and therefore the median better represents central tendency than does the mean. For example, household income tends to be positively skewed, and this demographic is reported as median household income. Most households earn a modest income, but some earn quite a bit more, and a small number make many millions of dollars per year.	A negatively skewed distribution has a long tail in the negative or left-hand direction. The mean is less than the median. Imagine a distribution of final grades for a class in which most students received A's and only a very few did poorly. This distribution has a large negative skew.

Figure 36.3. Skewed Distributions.

Much of inferential statistics is based on the assumption that population values are normally distributed, even if the distribution is in fact skewed. To make inferences about such cases, we draw on the central limit theorem. In the long run, given sufficient samples, the means, not the individual data points, of repeated sample data sets would form a normal distribution. This theorem says nothing about the form of the population distribution, the sample data sets, or the individual data points, but simply that the sampling distribution of the means would be approximately normal (Hays, 1973).

Measures of Relatedness

Measures of relatedness, or correlation, represent the degree to which two variables are related, hence, co-relation. A good way to visualize a co-relationship is by creating a scatter plot. When two variables are perfectly linearly related, the points of a scatter plot fall on a straight line. In such cases, values of one variable can be perfectly calculated or predicted given values of the related variable. However, with behavioral data, there rarely is a perfect linear relationship between variables. Instead, the points tend to scatter, and the greater the scatter, the weaker the relatedness between the variables. Figure 36.4 illustrates two variables that have a strong positive relationship.

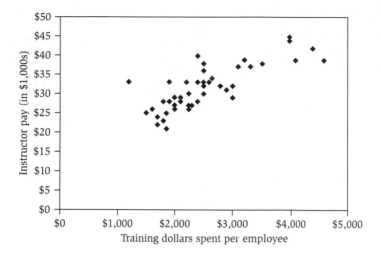

Figure 36.4. Sample Scatter Plot with Positive Correlation.

Table 36.5. Types of Co-Relationships.

If X	And Y	Then the Correlation Is	Example
Increases in value	Increases in value	Positive or direct	The taller one gets, X, the more one weighs, Y.
Decreases in value	Decreases in value	Positive or direct	The fewer car accidents one has, X, the lower one's insurance premium, Y.
Increases in value	Decreases in value	Negative or inverse	The brighter the light, X, the smaller one's eye pupil becomes, Y.
Decreases in value	Increases in value	Negative or inverse	The less sleep one gets, X, the more errors one makes, Y.

There are four ways that two variables, X and Y, can relate. Table 36.5 summarizes these four types of relationships. A correlation quantifies a linear relationship between variables, even if the true relationship is curvilinear. In fact, few relationships are simply linear. If we were to take sufficient measurements, we may find that what appeared to be a linear relationship is in fact curvilinear. We just happened to take measures on a linear stretch of the curve. Figure 36.5 shows examples of scatter plots of curvilinear relationships.

A correlation indicates that the variables share something in common. However, it is important to emphasize that correlation does not mean causation. For

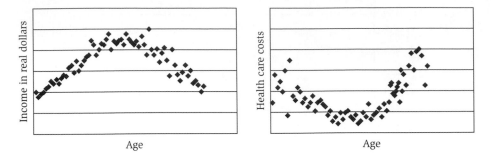

Figure 36.5. Sample Scatter Plots of Curvilinear Relationships.

example, there is a strong positive relationship between the number of fire-fighters sent to a fire and the amount of damage done. Does this mean that the firefighters cause the damage? Well, maybe. But it is more likely that the bigger the fire, the more fire damage and the bigger the fire, the more firefighters are sent. In this example, the variable "size of the fire" correlates with both the number of firefighters sent and the amount of damage done.

When variables to be correlated are parametric and measured on an interval or ratio scale, then the familiar Pearson's r product-moment correlation coefficient is appropriate. When measured in a population, the Pearson product-moment correlation is designated by the Greek letter *rho*, ρ. When computed in a sample, it is designated by r, hence, Pearson's r.

Pearson's r reflects the degree of linear relationship between two variables and ranges from $+1$ to -1. The strength of the relationship is indicated by the absolute value, ignoring whether the coefficient value is positive or negative, such that the larger the number, the stronger the relatedness. That is, as the absolute value of r approaches 1, the dots are more aligned in a straight line. Conversely, as the absolute value of r approaches 0, the dots are more scattered. The direction of the relationship is indicated by the sign, positive or negative, of the coefficient.

A correlation coefficient is packed full of information. We can tell the strength of the relationship and the direction of the relationship. We can also calculate the proportion of variance accounted for. The coefficient of determination is the proportion of variance in one variable accounted for by the variance in the other variable. The coefficient of determination is simply the squared value of the correlation coefficient, or r^2. For example, if the correlation coefficient, r_{xy}, is $+0.2$, then the coefficient of determination is 0.2^2 or 0.04, and we have accounted for 4 percent of the variance. The coefficient of alienation is the opposite of the coefficient of determination. The coefficient of alienation is the proportion of variance in one variable unaccounted for by variance in the other and is 1 minus the coefficient of determination. For example, if the coefficient of determination is 0.04, then the coefficient of alienation is $1 - 0.04$, or 0.96. This means that 96 percent of the variance is unaccounted for and that 96 percent of the variability between X and Y is not related.

INFERENTIAL TECHNIQUES

Descriptive statistics distill data sets to single numbers. Those numbers describe the data at hand. Inferential statistics help us to go beyond the data at hand to make inferences or generalizations about a broader state, say an entire industry, given that we only measured a few instances, say a sample of companies within that industry. The key word here is *inferential,* as in to draw a conclusion by reasoning from the evidence. That is, we infer something about an entire population based on evidence collected from a sample of that population. For example, from having observed only a sample, we may wish to answer questions such as these about an entire population:

- Does an observed event differ from an expected value, such as a standard or benchmark?
- Did an intervention improve performance and will it again in the future?
- Will a given assessment measure predict future performance?
- Is there a pattern of change over time?

When making almost any decision, there is risk. Tests of statistical significance simply yield risk estimates or probabilities of making an incorrect decision (Kirk, 1968, 1972). We use these probabilities to help make decisions. From these decisions, we make inferences about whether the observed values may be due to chance or random error, and whether those same values are likely to exist in the population from which the data were sampled. It is by this path that we judge whether the results are replicable or reliable as well as valid, generalizable, or representative of the population. Remember, however, that inferential statistics make neither the decisions nor the inferences. We make them.

Which Inferential Test to Use When

Two frequently asked questions are, Which statistics should I use? and What do the results mean? The answer to both questions is, it depends. First and foremost, consider the purpose of the investigation: What are you investigating? Who will use the data to make decisions about what? What are the implications of these decisions? What are the consequences of making an incorrect decision? The appropriate test statistic depends on the research question, the nature of the data, and the number and type of groups or variables.

Some commonly used inferential tests of statistical significance are listed in Table 36.6 (Graziano and Raulin, 2004; Lehmann, 1989; Siegel, 1956). To use

Table 36.6. Which Inferential Test to Use When.

Data Type and Scale	Differences			Relatedness
	One Group	Two Groups	Three or More Groups	
Nonparametric				
Nominal	Chi-Square Goodness of Fit Test	**Independent groups** Chi-Square Test for Independence **Dependent groups** McNemar Test for Changes	**Independent groups** Chi-Square Test for Independence **Dependent groups** Cochran Q Test	Contingency Coefficient C
Ordinal	Kolmogorov-Smirnov One-Sample Test One-Sample Runs Test	**Independent groups** Median Test Mann-Whitney U Test Kolmogorov-Smirnov Two-Sample Test **Dependent groups** Sign Test Wilcoxon Signed-Ranks Test	**Independent groups** Kruskal-Wallis ANOVA **Dependent groups** Friedman ANOVA	Spearman's *rho* Rank Correlation Coefficient Kendall's *tau* Rank Correlation Coefficient
Parametric				
Interval or Ratio	z-test t-test	**Independent groups** Independent groups t-test **Dependent groups** Dependent groups t-test	**Independent groups** Independent groups ANOVA **Dependent groups** Repeated measures ANOVA	Pearson's r Correlation Coefficient Regression

this table, identify whether you are examining differences or relatedness among variables, whether the data are nonparametric or parametric, the number of different measures being taken, the number of groups being compared, and whether the groups are independent or related.

There are conditions or assumptions related to choosing, calculating, and interpreting statistics. Assumptions generally relate to the scale of measurement, the number of observations or sample size, how the data are distributed, and the variation among groups (Hays, 1973). As with descriptive statistics, inferential test statistics broadly fall into one of two categories, nonparametric or parametric inferential tests of statistical significance.

Nonparametric tests require fewer assumptions compared with parametric tests. Nonparametric statistics yield exact probabilities, except when estimates are available for large sample sizes, regardless of the shape of the distribution (Siegel, 1956). Therefore, assumptions about the shape of the distribution or about equality of variance are not required. Furthermore, nonparametric tests accommodate small sample sizes.

Parametric tests require the most stringent assumptions and are the most powerful. Parametric tests estimate the probability of an observed value using the probabilities of a normal distribution as the point of reference. This is known as the assumption of normality. Generally, sample sizes of at least thirty are recommended for parametric tests. Violating these statistical assumptions may distort the resulting probabilities and therefore may affect a decision. Although slight deviations in meeting assumptions may not radically affect an outcome, the debate as to what constitutes a slight deviation (Siegel, 1956) appears ageless. For example, parametric tests generally accommodate sample sizes less than thirty, if the data are approximately normally distributed.

Common to both parametric and nonparametric tests are the assumptions that each member of the population has an equal and independent chance of being selected for the sample and that the measurements are independent. General characteristics of nonparametric and parametric inferential tests are summarized in Table 36.7 (Siegel, 1956).

Hypothesis Testing

A test of statistical significance, or hypothesis testing, is a rather regimented process of designating and applying decision rules to choose between two competing or mutually exclusive hypotheses. A hypothesis is an informed guess about the relationship among variables, such as, "I think turnover rate varies by industry." To test this speculation, it is translated into two competing statistical hypotheses, a null hypothesis, H_0, and an alternative hypothesis, H_1. The null hypothesis is the one that is tested and that the investigator does not believe to be true. The alternative hypothesis is the one that the investigator does believe to be true, and it is the only option that remains tenable if the null hypothesis is rejected.

In traditional hypothesis testing, we do not test the hypothesis that we believe to be true. Instead, we test the null hypothesis. When a statistically significant result is found, then the null hypothesis is rejected and the alternative

Table 36.7. Characteristics of Nonparametric and Parametric Inferential Tests.

Nonparametric Inferential Tests	Parametric Inferential Tests
There are fewer assumptions, compared with parametric techniques.	There are more assumptions, compared with nonparametric techniques.
There is no assumption of normality (shape of the distribution) or equality of variance.	Distribution must meet assumptions of normality and equality of variance.
Sampling is assumed to be random, with each member of the population having an equal and independent chance of being selected for the sample.	Sampling is assumed to be random, with each member of the population having an equal and independent chance of being selected for the sample.
Measurements are independent.	Measurements are independent.
They will accommodate small samples less than thirty.	Sample size recommended is at least thirty per group.
They accommodate nominal and ordinal data.	Data are interval or ratio.
They are generally easy to calculate.	Calculations can be complicated.

hypothesis is accepted by default. By this logic, rejection is a good thing. A finding of statistical significance indicates that the chances are small, say less than 5 percent, that the calculated test statistic occurred by random error or chance. Alternatively, if the differences are within chance limits, then we conclude that there is insufficient evidence to reject the null hypothesis.

Hypothesis Testing Steps. The basic steps for statistical hypothesis testing are the following:

1. State the statistical hypotheses, H_0 and H_1.
2. Identify the test statistic.
3. State the statistical decision rule.
4. Calculate the test statistic.
5. Make a statistical decision.
6. Interpret the results.

Begin by stating the statistical hypotheses. Next, identify the appropriate test statistic. The appropriate test statistic depends on the hypotheses, the nature of the data, and the number and type of groups or variables. This brings us to the third step. A statistical decision rule is a statement of your criteria for rejecting

Table 36.8. Hypothesis Decision Matrix.

Actual State of H_0	*Your Decision*	
	Accept H_0 *The process is safe.*	*Reject H_0* *The process is NOT safe.*
H_0 is true. There is really no difference. The process really is safe.	**Correct Decision** H_0 is accepted when there really is no difference. You decide correctly that the process is safe, and it is implemented.	**Incorrect Decision** H_0 is rejected when there really is no difference, a Type I error (α). You decide incorrectly that the process is unsafe, and it is not implemented.
H_0 is false. There really is a difference. The process really is not safe.	**Incorrect Decision** H_0 is accepted when there really is a difference, a Type II error (β). You decide incorrectly that the process is safe and you implement the unsafe process.	**Correct Decision** H_0 is rejected when there really is a difference. You decide correctly that the process is unsafe and not to implement it.

the null hypothesis, H_0, and accepting the alternative hypothesis, H_1. The statistical decision rule includes the level of significance α, or alpha level, and the criterion value of the test statistic. Begin by considering the consequences of the possible outcomes. There are two choices: reject the null hypothesis or do not reject the null hypothesis. As shown in Table 36.8, these two choices have four possible outcomes. There are two ways to make a correct decision plus two ways to make an incorrect decision.

The consequences of an incorrect decision must be evaluated. Consider the example in Table 36.8. You are testing a new process. The new process is more efficient, but it may be unsafe. You record accidents in two groups. Group A performs the new process and Group B performs the old process. The hypotheses are

- H_0: There is no difference in the frequency of accidents, A = B.
- H_1: Frequency of accidents is greater in Group A performing the new process compared with Group B performing the old process, A > B.

You would make a Type I error if you concluded that the new process does increase the frequency of accidents when in fact it is safe. This would not be a deadly conclusion because the new process would not be implemented. You would make a Type II error if you concluded that the new process is safe when in fact it increases accidents. Clearly, this is an outcome to avoid.

This brings us to the alpha level, α, or level of significance. When we compute an inferential test statistic, we determine the probability of obtaining a value this extreme or more extreme when the null hypothesis is true. If this probability is small, then we reject the null hypothesis, we accept the alternative hypothesis, and we say the test statistic is statistically significant. But what counts as small? You, the investigator, must set the criterion probability, which is the level of risk you are willing to take. This is referred to as the alpha level, or level of significance. We could set any value for alpha between zero and one, but the most common are

- $\alpha = 0.05$, a 5 percent chance of making an incorrect decision.
- $\alpha = 0.01$, a 1 percent chance of making an incorrect decision.
- $\alpha = 0.001$, a 0.1 percent chance of making an incorrect decision.

An example of the alpha level stated in a decision rule is, Reject H_0 if the calculated test statistic is equal to or greater than the criterion value of test statistic, given $\alpha = 0.05$. The statistical decision is whether or not to reject the H_0 based on the stated decision rule.

The last step, interpret results, is the most valuable one. Here the investigator translates the statistical decision into the real-world problem, thus making the transition from statistical significance to practical significance.

Although tests of statistical significance add another bit of information for decision making, both the process and the result of hypothesis testing have limitations. A statistically significant result says nothing about its magnitude or importance. Such information is provided by measures of effect size.

Effect Size. Tests of statistical significance simply estimate probabilities of making incorrect decisions. The level of significance tells us nothing about how different the two groups are. That is what measures of effect size quantify. Measures of effect size quantify the magnitudes of the differences among groups, such as the effect of an intervention or treatment or strengths of association or correlation among variables. In this way, effect sizes are important inputs to informed decisions regarding the practical significance of results.

Measures of effect size are available for a variety of inferential statistics, such as for tests of group means, for correlations, for homogeneity of variance, and for nonparametric statistics when data are nominal, ordinal, or skewed (Hays, 1963; Kirk, 1996; Rosenthal, 1994; Rosenthal and DiMatteo, 2001; Vaughan and Corballis, 1969; Winer, 1971; Wolf, 1986). Guidance on how to choose, calculate, and interpret measures of effect size is summarized in Wilkinson and American Psychological Association Task Force on Statistical Inference (1999).

Cohen (1988) provides the following guidelines for interpreting effect sizes: 0.20 is small, 0.50 is medium, and 0.80 is large. However, the context must be considered. For example, a correlation coefficient, which also serves as the effect size, of 0.75 is considered low for equivalent forms reliability of an achievement test (Ary, Jacobs, and Razavieh, 2002). However, a correlation of 0.75 would be considered quite high for the relationship between an aptitude measure such as the Scholastic Assessment Test (SAT) or American College Testing (ACT) and college grade point average (GPA). Correlations between SAT or ACT scores and GPA typically are about 0.40, and less than Cohen's guide for a large effect.

Chi-Square Tests

Chi-square, Greek letter chi or χ^2, is a nonparametric test for comparing differences among frequency counts of categorical variables. The scale of measurement is nominal, and the data are discrete, whole-number frequency counts. Because a chi-square test does not assume that the data are normally distributed, it is appropriate for skewed distributions and for sample sizes smaller than thirty. But chi-square should not be used when any expected frequency is less than one or when more than 20 percent of the expected frequencies are less than five. Important assumptions in using chi-square are that each observation must be independent of every other and each observation may be counted in only one category.

A chi-square tests whether a statistically significant difference exists between an observed number of objects or responses falling in each category and an expected number.

$$\chi^2 = \frac{\Sigma \ (\text{Observed Frequency} - \text{Expected Frequency})^2}{\text{Expected Frequency}}$$

The difference between observed and expected frequencies for each category is calculated. If the observed, O, and expected, E, frequencies are similar, then the difference, $O - E$, is small and the value of chi-square is small. If the difference between the observed frequency and the expected frequency is large, then the value of chi-square is large. Roughly speaking, the larger the value of chi-square, the more likely it is that the null hypothesis is false. See Figure 36.6 for an example.

t-Tests

A t-test is a parametric inferential test appropriate when the data are interval or ratio, the assumptions for parametric tests are met, a single variable is being measured, and a maximum of two groups are being compared. Although a sample size of at least thirty is recommended, t-tests accommodate smaller sample sizes, given that the data are approximately normally distributed. A t-test may be used to test statistical significance for means, proportions, variances, or correlations. An independent-groups t-test compares measures for two unrelated or independent groups, such as whether average customer wait times are statistically different for two different call centers. A dependent-groups t-test compares measures within a single group, such as whether the average customer wait time is statistically shorter following equipment upgrades compared with before equipment

Situation	Does the current year's distribution of employee performance ratings differ from last year's distribution of performance ratings? The number of employees who were rated last year was 600 and the number of employees rated in the current year is 650. The chi-square test for goodness of fit compares the frequency distributions of cases falling into categories or levels of a single classification variable collected from a single group to an expected distribution. In this example, the comparison variable, performance ratings, has three categories: exceeds, meets, and fails job requirements.
Frequency Distribution	Frequency distribution of performance ratings in each rating category for the current year's ratings, the observed frequencies, compared with the previous year's ratings, the expected frequencies.

	Exceeds Job Requirements	Meets Job Requirements	Fails Job Requirements	Total
Observed Frequency (from current year)	78 (12%)	546 (84%)	26 (4%)	650
Expected Frequency (from previous year)	48 (8%)	540 (90%)	12 (2%)	600
Total	126	1,086	38	1,250

1. State the statistical hypotheses.	H_0: $F_o = F_e$. The current year's distribution of employee performance ratings, F_o, is the same as the previous year's distribution of employee performance ratings, F_e.
	H_1: $F_o \neq F_e$. The current year's distribution of employee performance ratings, F_o, is different from the previous year's distribution of employee performance ratings, F_e.
2. Identify the test statistic.	χ^2 goodness of fit test, where $$\chi^2 = \frac{\Sigma(\text{Observed Frequency} - \text{Expected Frequency})^2}{\text{Expected Frequency}}$$
3. State the statistical decision rule.	Reject H_0 if the computed χ^2 is equal to or greater than the critical $\chi^2_{(2, .95)}$ of 5.99, $\alpha = .05$.
	The critical value is a function of the test statistic, the degrees of freedom, and the level of significance or α level. Critical value tables are provided in statistics books, and statistical software packages generate critical values for you. For a χ^2 test of goodness of fit, the number of degrees of freedom is equal to the number of categories minus 1, or, in this example, $3 - 1 = 2$. The critical value of χ^2 for level of significance or α of 0.05 and 2 degrees of freedom is 5.99. This means that the probability of a χ^2 value equal to or greater than 5.99 is .05, or 5 percent.

Figure 36.6. Example of a Chi-Square Test for Goodness of Fit.

4. **Calculate the test statistic.**	$\chi^2 = \dfrac{(78-48)^2}{48} + \dfrac{(546-540)^2}{540} + \dfrac{(26-12)^2}{12} = 35.15$
5. **Make a statistical decision.**	The computed χ^2 of 35.15 is greater than the critical $\chi^2_{(2,.95)}$ of 5.99, therefore reject H_0.
6. **Interpret the results.**	The result of the chi-square test, $\chi^2_{(2,n=3)} = 35.15$, $p < .05$, indicates that the current year's distribution of employee performance ratings is significantly different from the previous year's ratings distribution.

Figure 36.6. (*Continued*).

upgrades. An example of a dependent-groups *t*-test is provided in Figure 36.7. It is inappropriate to conduct multiple *t*-tests to compare more than a single variable collected from more than two groups. As the number of pair-wise comparisons increases, the probability of obtaining a spurious result also increases (Kirk, 1968). For multiple comparisons, analysis of variance is appropriate.

Analysis of Variance

Analysis of variance (ANOVA) is appropriate for testing differences among parametric data from more than two groups. For example, we could compare response times from three shifts of emergency workers or call volumes from five different call centers. These examples illustrate the simplest form of ANOVA, which is called a one-way analysis of variance. A one-way analysis of variance has one grouping factor, or independent variable, and there are more than two groups within this factor. Here, the grouping factor is the three shifts or the five call centers, and data from the three shifts or the five call centers are compared on a single dependent measure, the response times or the call volumes. A simple one-way ANOVA is illustrated in Figure 36.8. Here response times, the dependent variable, are compared across three groups, the independent variable. Also shown in Figure 36.8 are basic examples of comparisons using factorial designs. There are multitudes of factorial designs, and the computations are complex. Some classic sources of information about experimental designs include Campbell and Stanley (1963), Keppel (1973), Kirk (1968), and Winer (1971).

Regression

Not only can we compute the degree to which variables are related, we can also use a correlation coefficient to predict the value of one variable, given that we know the value of its related variable. To predict a value, we create a regression equation to plot a regression line. A regression line reflects a best guess as to what value of *Y* would be predicted by a given value of *X*. In a scatter plot, the

Situation	Prior to companywide implementation, a new sales incentive program is piloted on a random sample of thirty sales employees. Sales are recorded for each of the thirty sales employees before the pilot incentive program and then again after the pilot incentive program. Does the company have reason to conclude that average sales are greater following the pilot incentive program compared with sales before the pilot incentive program? Furthermore, if the incentive program does improve sales, is the magnitude of the improvement sufficient to invest in program implementation?
Descriptive statistics	Sample size, $n = 30$ Sales data before (in $1,000) pilot incentive program / Sales data after (in $1,000) pilot incentive program $M_1 = \$14.50$ $M_2 = \$18.57$ $SD_1 = \$2.30$ $SD_2 = \$5.56$ $Min_1 = \$10.00$, $Max_1 = \$19.00$; $Min_2 = \$5.00$, Max_2 $\$31.00$, $Range_1 = \$9.00$ $Range_2 = \$26.00$ Mean Difference, M_D (in $1,000) $= \$4.07$ This is the average of the differences between each individual pair of before and after scores. Standard deviation of difference scores, $SD_D = \$6.25$

1. State the statistical hypotheses.	H_0: $M_D = \mu_D$, where $\mu_D = 0$
	
	   This null hypothesis states that the incentive program has no effect on mean sales. Mean sales before pilot, M_1, of the incentive program is the same as mean sales after pilot, M_2, of the incentive program. This hypothesis is stated in terms of the average of the differences between each individual pair of before and after scores. Under this null hypothesis, we expect before and after sales to be the same, therefore we expect μ_D to be zero.
	
	H_1: $M_D > \mu_D$
	
	   This alternative hypothesis states that sales after pilot of the incentive program are greater than sales before pilot of the incentive program. That is, sales are expected to increase, and M_D is greater than zero. This

Figure 36.7. Example of a Dependent-Groups *t*-Test.

	statement is set up to subtract the larger after-incentive values from the smaller before-incentive values simply as a matter of convenience to avoid working with a negative value for M_D. Furthermore, this is a directional hypothesis.
2. Identify the test statistic.	Dependent-groups t-test for mean of a normally distributed population. $$t = \frac{M_D - \mu_D}{SD_D/\sqrt{n}}$$
3. State the statistical decision rule.	Reject H_0 if the computed t is greater than or equal to critical $t_{(29, .95)}$ of 1.7, $\alpha = 0.05$, one-tailed
4. Calculate the test statistic.	$$t = \frac{M_D - \mu_D}{SD_D/\sqrt{n}}$$ $$t = \frac{4.07 - 0}{6.25/\sqrt{30}} = 3.57$$ Effect Size: $d = \dfrac{M_D}{SD_D}$ $$d = \frac{4.07}{6.25} = 0.65$$ t-test for effect size: $t = d(\sqrt{n})$ $= (0.65)(\sqrt{30}) = 3.57$
5. Make a statistical decision.	The computed $t_{(29)}$ of 3.57 is greater than the critical $t_{(29, .95)}$ of 1.7, $p < .001$, one-tailed. Therefore, H_0 is rejected in favor of H_1. That is, the probability is less than 0.001 that the computed t occurred by chance alone.
6. Interpret the results.	We can conclude that the piloted incentive program positively affected sales. Given that the pilot conditions, including the pilot participants, are indeed representative of the entire company, then we have good reason to believe that companywide implementation of the sales incentive program should produce improvement in sales. Next, we consider the effect size, which tells us about the magnitude of the difference. This consideration helps us to relate the cost in time, money, and other resources needed to implement the independent variable, the incentive program, in relation to the importance of the dependent

Figure 36.7. (*Continued*)

variable, sales. The effect size of 0.65 indicates that the piloted incentive program increased sales by a bit more than one-half (0.65) of one standard deviation, SD_D = $6.25, or about $4.063. The company must consider whether the $4,070 increase in sales exceeds the cost of the incentive program.

On the basis of analyzing one descriptive statistic, the mean, the results of this pilot study indicate that the incentive program may be effective. The dependent mean t-test is statistically significant, and the effect size is moderate and statistically significant. It is prudent, however, to consider whether the effect of the incentive program would be stable over time or whether the incentive may lose its luster as the initial increase in sales attenuates.

We have considered the differences in the means, now we will consider the variability. Although mean sales increased, so did the variability. Notice that sales following the incentive pilot were more variable, SD_2 = $5.56, $Range_2$ = $26.00, than before the pilot, SD_1 = $2.30, $Range_1$ = $9. It is prudent to consider such questions as, is the increase in variability disproportionate to the mean difference? What else might be going on here? What changed other than the intervention of the incentive program that may have induced variability in sales?

Figure 36.7. Example of a Dependent-Groups t-Test (*Continued*).

regression line is the line that minimizes the distances between the line and each of the points of the predicted Y variable. This line is the regression of the Y variable on the X variable and is the line of best fit. The line best fits these data because the line minimizes the distance between each individual point and the line. The formula for linear regression, $Y = bX + a$, is the same as the formula for a straight line, $y = mx + b$; the two equations just assign different letters to the variables. The distance between each individual point and the regression line is the error in prediction. If all of the predictions were perfect, then all of the points would fall perfectly on the line. The coefficient of determination, r^2, is the measure of how well the line best fits the observed data. The coefficient of determination helps us decide whether the regression equation is likely to be useful for prediction and estimation.

Simple ANOVA		
Shift		
A$_1$: Morning	**A$_2$: Afternoon**	**A$_3$ Evening**
A$_1$ response time	A$_2$ response time	A$_3$ response time

Independent Groups Factorial ANOVA

Factor B: Location	**Factor A: Shift**		
	A$_1$: Morning	**A$_2$: Afternoon**	**A$_3$ Evening**
B$_1$: Urban	A$_1$B$_1$ response time	A$_2$B$_1$ response time	A$_3$B$_1$ response time
B$_2$: Rural	A$_1$B$_2$ response time	A$_2$B$_2$ response time	A$_3$B$_2$ response time

Mixed Groups Factorial ANOVA

Factor B: Group This is the independent groups factor because different participants are assigned to each group.	**Factor A: Test** This is the dependent or repeated measures factor because each participant is measured twice.	
	A$_1$: Pretest	**A$_2$: Post-test**
B$_1$: Treatment	A$_1$B$_1$ pretest score	A$_2$B$_1$ post-test score
B$_2$: Control	A$_1$B$_2$ pretest score	A$_2$B$_2$ post-test score

Figure 36.8. Examples of ANOVAs.

MULTIVARIATE TECHNIQUES

Multivariate techniques accommodate the realities of complex and multifaceted phenomena such as behavior when multiple factors interact in complicated ways. In multiple regression, for example, multiple independent variables are used to predict values of a single dependent variable. The design is easily extended to examining relationships among multiple independent and dependent variables. The general linear model underlies univariate, and by extension multivariate, techniques. Although statistical software packages make short work of the complex computations, our job of deciphering the reams of printouts can be daunting. As the number of variables increases, so does the challenge of interpretation. Recommended sources on multivariate techniques include Harris (1975), Kerlinger and Pedhazur (1973), Kim and Mueller (1978a, 1978b), and Tatsuoka (1970, 1971). Brief descriptions of several multivariate techniques follow.

Multiple Regression

We are not limited to a single variable predicting just one other variable. Instead, we may wish to examine relationships among multiple variables. Multiple regression is an extension of linear regression for use with multiple variables. The general linear model accommodates multiple Xs to predict multiple Ys. The equation, $Y = b_1X_1 + b_2X_2 + a$, shows two X variables, each with different beta weights, the bs, forming a regression line crossing the y axis at point designated "a" all together predicting a Y. Kerlinger and Pedhazur (1973) emphasize, "We do not simply throw variables into regression equations; we enter them, wherever possible, at the dictates of theory and reasonable interpretation of empirical research findings" (p. 49).

Canonical Correlation

Canonical correlation is a generalization of multiple regression that addresses multiple dependent variables. That is, any number of Y variables, the dependent or predictor variables, is correlated with any number of X variables, the independent or criterion variables. Canonical analysis seeks an optimal combination of these two sets of variables (Tatsuoka, 1970, 1971) to yield the maximum canonical correlation coefficient (Kerlinger and Pedhazur, 1973).

Multivariate Analysis of Variance

Multivariate analysis of variance (MANOVA) is an extension of factorial univariate analysis of variance (ANOVA) and analysis of covariance (ANCOVA) to accommodate multiple independent as well as multiple dependent variables. The difference between univariate and multivariate techniques is the dependent variable. An ANOVA tests only one dependent variable at a time, whereas a MANOVA tests multiple dependent variables. Perhaps we wish to examine the effects of two independent variables, instructional methods A_1 and A_2, and types of incentive B_1 and B_2, on two dependent variables, certification test score and the job performance assessment. A MANOVA is appropriate here to evaluate whether the means of the two dependent variables, considered simultaneously, are equal (Kerlinger and Pedhazur, 1973).

Discriminant Analysis

Discriminant analysis seeks the optimal combination of variables that best differentiate among several groups (Tatsuoka, 1970, 1971). Individuals, or other entities of interest, are classified or assigned to two or more groups on the basis of any number of variables. For example, discriminant analysis could be used to group product quality measures as acceptable or unacceptable based on assessment scores and attitude scores. Then the resulting discriminant function can be used to predict, before problems arise, whether the quality of a performer's output is likely to be acceptable or unacceptable based on that performer's assessment score and attitude score.

Factor Analysis

Factor analysis uses the intercorrelations among multiple variables to identify a smaller set of common factors or hypothetical constructs assumed to underlie the various measures. For example, factor analysis studies of intelligence tests have identified underlying verbal, numerical, spatial, memory, and reasoning factors (Ary, Jacobs, and Razavieh, 2002). The results of such exploratory analysis become the input for confirmatory factor analysis to test hypotheses not only about the constructs but also whether certain variables contribute to certain factors (Kim and Mueller, 1978a, 1978b).

META-ANALYSIS

Glass (1976) defines meta-analysis as "the analysis of analyses . . . the statistical analysis of a large collection of analysis results from individual studies for the purpose of integrating the findings" (p. 3). Meta-analysis is of great value to both producers and consumers of research. Meta-analysis helps research producers to synthesize a body of knowledge before planning further research. Meta-analysis studies allow research consumers or practitioners to more readily assess a synthesized body of knowledge before deciding on a course of action. Rosenthal and DiMatteo (2001) examine the advantages and criticisms of meta-analysis and provide a basic overview of the steps for conducting meta-analyses.

GENERAL RECOMMENDATIONS

In the end, after all the data have been collected, summarized, graphed, and analyzed, and you are staring numbly at the printouts, it comes down to the only test that really counts: the test of meaningfulness. Only you can tell the rest of us what it means. In summary:

- Begin with a worthwhile and researchable problem. The most well-designed research will not improve a poor idea.
- Design your research to address your research problem. Without sound planning, quantitative analysis is little more than number crunching.
- Choose statistical techniques that are appropriate for your data, the scale of measurement, and distributional and sampling assumptions.

- Examine your data thoroughly. Focus first on descriptive statistics, rather than on the rush to cookbook inferential techniques.

- Consider both the statistical significance and practical significance of your findings.

- Throughout the entire process, remember: statistics do not make decisions, people make decisions.

To better ensure meaningful results from data-analysis efforts, consider the general recommendations for before, during, and after data collection listed in Figure 36.9.

Before data collection	Partner with an expert on quantitative research methods. Even research veterans benefit from the advice of fellow experts.
	Plan, plan, plan. Planning is perhaps the single most important activity.
	Confirm that the purpose of your investigation has value. A worthless study is not worth doing well.
	Precisely define the population to which you wish to apply your results. This definition affects data collection, analysis, and, most important, your conclusions and recommendations.
	Carefully plan the steps you will take and the tools you will use to collect and analyze your data. Remember, sloppy methods produce garbage.
	Specify the rules or heuristics you will use to make decisions about your data.
	When justifying the choice of a statistical procedure, refer to the statistical literature.
	When justifying the use of a statistical software program, refer to the software's documentation.
	Choose a minimally sufficient analysis. Given the sophistication, complexity, and affordable availability of statistical software packages, investigators face a daunting challenge to match the analysis to the research problem.
During data collection	Record the exact steps you take and the tools you use.
	Note all deviations, complications, and unanticipated events.
	Use these records to accurately interpret and report your results.

Figure 36.9. General Recommendations.

After data collection	Check all data. Correct data-entry errors, missing data, data-coding inconsistencies, and database bugs.

Construct and carefully inspect tables and graphs of your data. Get to know your data.

Verify the results of the data analysis, understand how the results were computed, and understand what the results mean.

Do not conduct analyses or report results that you do not understand or that you did not specifically plan to run.

Avoid fishing expeditions. Just because statistical software can compute dozens of statistics does not mean that the computations are appropriate or meaningful. Such indiscriminate analysis may do more harm than good in contaminating the body of knowledge with unreliable and invalid reports.

Interpret your results in light of the strengths and weaknesses of your study. Consider the limitations of your results, including threats to reliability and validity and their impact on the results.

Do not overgeneralize. Unless your sample was randomly selected, or otherwise met criteria for representativeness from a well-defined population, then your results apply only to the specific participants or events that you measured. Interpret a single study's results as a single piece of the puzzle, not as the entire picture.

Relate your results to previous studies. Consider the extent to which your results support or deviate from the current body of knowledge.

Report your study accurately and clearly. Ensure that the study's purpose, methods, and analysis all align. Ensure that the write-up of your methods is sufficiently accurate and detailed so that another investigator could replicate your findings. |

Figure 36.9. (*Continued*).

RESOURCE GUIDE

The wealth of resources on quantitative methods accommodates a wide range of expertise levels, content topics, and media preferences. Content ranges from basic methods to highly focused topics, targeted for audiences ranging from novice to advanced, and in formats ranging from heavy textbooks to light multimedia tutorials. Some recommended sources are provided in Figure 36.10.

Research methods	General sources for research methods for social sciences, education, and applied settings. Ary, Jacobs, and Razavieh, 2002 Fraenkel and Wallen, 2003 Tashakkori and Teddie, 2002 Babbie, 2003 Salkind, 2003
Statistics	General sources for statistics for social sciences, education, and applied settings. Levine, Stephan, Krehbiel, and Berenson, 2005 Hays, 1973 Siegel and Castellan, 1988 Daniel and Terrell, 1986 Salkind, 2004
Multivariate statistics	Classic sources for multivariate statistics for social sciences, education, and applied settings. Harris, 1975 Kerlinger and Pedhazur, 1973 Tatsuoka, 1971
Experimental design	Classic sources for experimental design for social sciences, education, and applied settings. Campbell and Stanley, 1963 Kirk, 1968 Keppel, 1973 Winer, 1971
Statistical software	Statistical software packages abound and range in price from free to thousands of dollars. Very likely you already have one; check out the data-analysis tool pack add-on, which comes standard with Microsoft Excel. This add-on accommodates, for example, regression, analysis of variance, and graphing, and will even do sampling. On the more expensive and feature-packed side is SPSS (statistical package for the social sciences), which since its debut in 1968 has evolved into a family of products spanning planning, data management, analysis, and reporting results. Some authors gear their texts toward particular software, such as Levine, Stephan, Krehbiel, and Berenson (2005), who orient their business statistics text for use with Microsoft Excel, or Salkind (2004), who provides introductory "how to's" for SPSS.
Professional organizations and journals	For current thinking on quantitative techniques, consult professional organizations such as those listed below. Also browse the journals published by these organizations. American Psychological Association (www.apa.org) American Educational Research Association (www.aera.net) American Evaluation Association (www.eval.org)
Reporting results	Guidance on organizing and reporting results. American Psychological Association, 2001 Wilkinson, L., and American Psychological Association Task Force on Statistical Inference, 1999
Internet sites	A search of Internet sites on quantitative data analysis will return pages of hits. However, because of the perishable nature of Web addresses as well as the problem of vetting sources, specific recommendations are not included here. Keep in mind, as with all Internet sources, some are credible while others are not. Just because you see it in print, whether online or on paper, does not guarantee accuracy.

Figure 36.10. Quantitative Analysis Resource Guide.

References

American Psychological Association. (2001). *Publication manual of the American Psychological Association* (5th ed.). Washington, DC: American Psychological Association.

Ary, D., Jacobs, L., and Razavieh, A. (2002). *Introduction to research in education* (6th ed.). Belmont, CA: Wadsworth.

Babbie, E. (2003). *The practice of social research* (10th ed.). Belmont, CA: Wadsworth.

Campbell, D. T., and Stanley, J.C. (1963). *Experimental and quasi-experimental designs for research.* Boston: Houghton Mifflin.

Cohen, J. (1988). *Statistical power analysis for the behavioral sciences* (2nd ed.). Hillsdale, NJ: Lawrence Erlbaum Associates.

Daniel, W. W., and Terrell, J. C. (1986). *Business statistics: Basic concepts and methodology* (4th ed.). Boston: Houghton Mifflin.

Fraenkel, J. R., and Wallen, N. E. (2003). *How to design and evaluate research in education* (5th ed.). New York: McGraw-Hill Higher Education.

Glass, G. (1976). Primary, secondary, and meta-analysis of research. *Educational Researcher, 5,* 3–8.

Graziano, A. M., and Raulin, M. L. (2004). *Research methods: A process of inquiry* (5th ed.). Boston: Pearson Education Group.

Green, B., and Hall, J. (1984). Quantitative methods for literature review. *Annual Review of Psychology, 35,* 37–53.

Harris, R. J. (1975). *A primer of multivariate statistics.* New York: Academic Press.

Hays, W. L. (1963). *Statistics for psychologists.* New York: Holt, Rinehart and Winston.

Hays, W. L. (1973). *Statistics for the social sciences* (2nd ed.). New York: Holt, Rinehart and Winston.

Keppel, G. (1973). *Design and analysis: A researcher's handbook.* Englewood Cliffs, NJ: Prentice-Hall.

Kerlinger, F. N., and Pedhazur, E. J. (1973). *Multiple regression in behavioral research.* New York: Holt, Rinehart and Winston.

Kim, J., and Mueller, C. W. (1978a). *Factor analysis: Statistical methods and practical issues.* Sage University paper series on Quantitative Applications in the Social Sciences (No. 14). Beverly Hills, CA: Sage.

Kim, J., and Mueller, C. W. (1978b). *Introduction to factor analysis: What it is and how to do it.* Sage University paper series on Quantitative Applications in the Social Sciences (No. 13). Beverly Hills, CA: Sage.

Kirk, R. E. (1968). *Experimental design: Procedures for the behavioral sciences.* Belmont, CA: Brooks/Cole.

Kirk, R. E. (1972). *Statistical issues: A reader for the behavioral sciences.* Belmont, CA: Brooks/Cole.

Kirk, R. E. (1996). Practical significance: A concept whose time has come. *Educational and Psychological Measurement, 56,* 746–759.

Lehmann, R. D. (1989). *Market research and analysis* (3rd ed.). Boston: Irwin.

Levine, D. M., Stephan, D., Krehbiel, T. C., and Berenson, M. L. (2005). *Statistics for managers using Microsoft® Excel* (4th ed.). Upper Saddle River, NJ: Prentice-Hall.

Rosenthal, R. (1994). Parametric measures of effect size. In H. Cooper and L. V. Hedges (Eds.), *The handbook of research synthesis* (pp. 231–244). New York: Sage.

Rosenthal, R., and DiMatteo, M. R. (2001). Meta-analysis: Recent developments in quantitative methods for literature reviews. *Annual Review of Psychology, 52,* 59–82.

Salkind, N. J. (2003). *Exploring research* (5th ed.). Upper Saddle River, NJ: Prentice-Hall.

Salkind, N. J. (2004). *Statistics for people who (think they) hate statistics* (2nd ed.). Thousand Oaks, CA: Prentice-Hall.

Siegel, S. (1956). *Nonparametric statistics for the behavioral sciences.* New York: McGraw-Hill.

Siegel, S., and Castellan, N. J. (1988). *Nonparametric statistics for the behavioral sciences.* New York: McGraw-Hill.

Stevens, S. S. (1972). Measurement, statistics, and the schemapiric view. In R. E. Kirk (Ed.), *Statistical issues: A reader for the behavioral sciences* (pp. 66–78). Monterey, CA: Brooks/Cole. (Abridged from Measurement, statistics, and the schemapiric view, *Science, 161,* 849–856, by S. S. Stevens).

Tashakkori, A., and Teddie, C. (2002). *Handbook of mixed methods in social and behavioral research.* Thousand Oaks, CA: Sage.

Tatsuoka, M. M. (1970). *Discriminant analysis: The study of group differences.* Selected topics in advanced statistics: An elementary approach (No. 6). Champaign, IL: Institute for Personality and Ability Testing.

Tatsuoka, M. M. (1971). *Multivariate analysis: Techniques for educational and psychological research.* New York: Wiley.

Townsend, J. T., and Ashby, F. G. (1984). Measurement scales and statistics: The misconception misconceived. *Psychological Bulletin, 96,* 394–401.

Tufte, E. R. (2002). *The visual display of quantitative information* (2nd ed.). Cheshire, CT: Graphics Press.

Vaughan, G. M., and Corballis, M. C. (1969). Beyond tests of significance: Estimating strength of effects in selected ANOVA designs. *Psychological Bulletin, 72,* 204–213. Reprinted in R. E. Kirk (Ed.), 1972, *Statistical issues: A reader for the behavioral sciences* (pp. 66–78). Monterey, California: Brooks/Cole.

Wilkinson, L., and American Psychological Association Task Force on Statistical Inference. (1999). Statistical methods in psychology journals: Guidelines and explanations. *American Psychologist, 54,* 594–604.

Winer, B. J. (1971). *Statistical principles in experimental design* (2nd ed.). New York: McGraw-Hill.

Wolf, F. M. (1986). *Meta-analysis: Quantitative methods for research synthesis.* Sage University Paper Series on Quantitative Applications in the Social Sciences, 07–059. Newbury Park, CA: Sage.

CHAPTER THIRTY-SEVEN

Evidence-Based Practice
and Professionalization of
Human Performance Technology

Ruth Colvin Clark

Scene: Waiting in Line by the Company Espresso Bar

CLIENT: I am glad I ran into you! We have got to have a training program to pump up our sales numbers. You know, something on product knowledge and sales techniques. The pressure is on. We have got to have it right away!

YOU: Great. Let's make an appointment to discuss our options. Let me check. . . .

CLIENT: No need to discuss! We need action, not words. Anyway, I have got it pretty well worked out. We need to start the training class soon, say in three or four weeks. And I can't take my salespeople off the phones for long. Four hours at the most! Say, you know how salespeople just love competition and games! Let's focus on that recent product roll-out using something fun and fast-moving like *Jeopardy*. And we could save travel costs if you would use that new virtual meeting software so they could attend from their desktops. I have got to run to a meeting but give me a call tomorrow and I will fill you in on my other ideas!

In less than a minute at a chance meeting, your client has told you (1) she has an operational gap which can be filled by training, (2) the content you should include in the training, (3) how long the training should last, (4) how long you should take to develop it, and (5) the delivery medium you should use. Since our clients have generally completed years of education, most of them see training as the best solution to performance gaps and consider themselves experts in training. Rather than professional partners, human performance technology (HPT) and training professionals are seen as a pair of hands to implement the clients' ideas. With everyone an expert in instruction and learning, it is challenging to establish ourselves as professionals.

This is a chapter on evidence-based practice: what it is, why we need it, and the barriers we face getting there. Recent certification programs from professional organizations such as the International Society for Performance Improvement (ISPI) and the American Society for Training and Development (ASTD) accompanied by supporting training programs are harbingers of the professionalization of human performance improvement practitioners. *Merriam-Webster's Collegiate Dictionary,* 10th edition, defines a professional as "one who conforms to the technical or ethical standards of a profession." The grounding of our professional decisions in systematic and evidence-based practice is an essential requisite to achievement of professional status and recognition that is accorded to professionals in medical, legal, and other recognized professions.

A SHIFT TOWARD EVIDENCE-BASED PRACTICE?

"At the dawn of the 21st Century, educational research is finally entering the 20th Century. The use of randomized experiments that transformed medicine, agriculture and technology in the 20th Century is now beginning to affect educational policy" (Slavin, 2002, p. 15). So begins a report in the *Educational Researcher* summarizing recent trends toward evidence-based practice in the field of education. In 1998, for the first time in history, the U.S. Department of Education made school funding contingent on use of the funds for programs based on "proven, comprehensive reform models." The No Child Left Behind Act of 2001 (2002) mentions scientifically based research one hundred times. The Act defines scientifically based research as "The application of rigorous, systematic, and objective procedures to obtain reliable and valid knowledge relevant to education activities and programs which includes research that is evaluated using experimental or quasi-experimental designs preferably with random assignment." U.S. government funding appropriations of $150 million per year are available to schools willing to base their programmatic decisions on valid evidence.

Furthermore, the Office of Educational Research and Improvement specifies that 75 percent of all their funded research will use random-assignment experimental designs. This legislation signals a shift from educational practice based solely on experience and trends to practice rooted in evidence of what works. The recent movement toward certification by major human resource professional organizations including ISPI and ASTD is a harbinger of a more formalized definition of the HPT and training profession based on a set of standards that define best practices. The outcome of the professionalization movement could be "the progressive, systematic improvement over time that has characterized successful parts of our economy and society throughout the 20th Century in fields such as medicine, agriculture, transportation, and technology" (Slavin, 2002, p. 16).

There is considerable economic incentive for commercial organizations to embrace evidence-based practice. Compared with the resources of the commercial sector, the $150 million dollar U.S. government educational appropriation is small. You might be surprised to find out that in the United States, investments in organizational training fall into the *$50 to $60 billion* range (Dolezalek, 2004). And this is a conservative figure, since it does not factor in the most expensive element of all organization training programs, the salary time and lost opportunity costs of the training participants. What, you might wonder, is the return on that investment? The answer is, of course, that we rarely know since so few training programs are ever evaluated beyond learner satisfaction ratings. However, since few training and HPT programs incorporate evidence of what works, it would be surprising to find that a large proportion of that investment translates into better organizational bottom-line results.

BARRIERS TO EVIDENCE-BASED PRACTICE

While there is quite a bit of rhetoric right now for evidence-based practice in the public education arena, the reality is a far cry from the goal. In this section I will review the following questions, which represent barriers faced by training and HPT professionals who want to ground their organizational interventions and training programs on valid evidence:

1. Where is the evidence?
2. Does this evidence apply to my HPT and training interventions?
3. How can I access meaningful evidence?
4. How can I influence my clients to make evidence-based decisions?

Barrier 1: Where Is the Evidence?

Last year I worked briefly with a small group of talented and experienced professionals planning a book on best practices in use of on-line collaborative facilities for learning. After two months of sifting through hundreds of articles and a few books, I concluded that as of that time, there was insufficient solid evidence on which to base reliable recommendations. There was a lot of advice in the literature, including many case studies and a number of descriptive articles. But there were very few controlled research studies. Why is there not more research we can use to inform our instructional practices and programs?

Most educational experimental research is conducted as *one-shot* studies by individual graduate students to meet dissertation requirements. Why? For one thing there is relatively little funding for the kind of long-term sustained team research efforts that we see in fields of medicine or the basic sciences. Commercial organizations such as pharmaceutical and engineering companies typically invest 5 to 15 percent of their expenditures on research and development. Twenty percent of that investment is in basic research and 90 percent in design and systematic development. The United States spends $300 billion a year on public education and less than $30 million on education research. In 1998 a single pharmaceutical company reported spending over $200 million dollars a year on animal health care research (Burkhardt and Schoenfeld, 2003). Why is there such a large discrepancy in funding? First, in contrast to animal health products, educational products yield relatively low profits. Second, unlike findings from medical research, educational research has generally not paid off in widely adopted programs that made a demonstrable difference in learning outcomes. As a result, we face a self-perpetuating cycle. Since there is little educational research funding and there are almost no large-scale, team-based educational research programs, there is relatively little payoff, and since there is little payoff, there continues to be little funding.

While we have a plethora of journals filled with articles, some of which are labeled as "research," only a few of these represent controlled experimental studies. Slavin (2004) found that only 5.4 percent of the studies reported in the *American Educational Research Journal* from 2000 through 2003 involved experimental studies. Not that experimental research is the only good source of evidence. However, it is the most valid resource from which to derive guidelines regarding the value of one instructional intervention over another.

So our first barrier is that in 2005 there is relatively little evidence based on randomly controlled experiments on which to base educational policy and practice. But a large and accumulating body of scientific research alone would not necessarily translate into better instructional programs. To get to the next step, practitioners need evidence-based guidelines that apply to their specific training and performance needs. This requires evidence that has been demonstrated to apply to diverse settings or that specifies the conditions under which a specific intervention works best.

Barrier 2: Does This Evidence Apply to My HPT and Training Interventions?

Even if we find a wealth of research with conclusions based on experiments involving random assignment, how confident can we be when applying the guidelines to our daily instructional decisions? In 2003, *Performance Improvement* published

---

❑ What are the features of the tested intervention?
❑ What is the functionality of the tested intervention?
❑ What was the performance metric?
❑ Who were the learners?
❑ What was the learning context? For example, what were the length and the content of experimental lessons
❑ When was learning measured?
❑ Are there a statistical significance and a clinical significance?
❑ What is the theoretical context?
❑ Have the findings been replicated?

Figure 37.1. Evaluating the Applicability of Research.

---

a review of my book *e-Learning and the Science of Instruction,* coauthored with researcher Richard Mayer. In that review, Thalheimer (2003) described some of the limitations of the research that we used as evidence for our guidelines and suggested that we should have been more explicit in pointing these out to readers. He was right. The challenge is that no one study or even a series of studies can form the basis for guidelines that are applicable to all learners and all instructional goals. Figure 37.1 lists some of the questions that you need to consider when evaluating research for its applicability to your instructional decisions.

One of the guidelines we presented in *e-Learning and the Science of Instruction* (Clark and Mayer, 2003) recommended that audio narration be used to explain onscreen visuals. This principle is known as the "modality effect." The modality effect states that learning is better when visuals are explained by words presented as audio narration than when the same words are presented as written text. Table 37.1 summarizes some of the details from research studies that have found significant results in favor of the modality effect. I will use these data to illustrate the questions summarized in the next section.

Will the Real Intervention Please Stand Up? One of our challenges in reviewing research is to determine what instructional or HPT method was actually being tested. Because our field lacks consistent definitions or a taxonomy of terms, words such as *e-learning, simulation,* or *graphic* can reflect drastically different interventions in different studies. For example, there have been hundreds of studies on "advance organizers" but very few results in the form of solid conclusions or prescriptions (Slavin, 2002). The reason is that the advance organizer is what I call a fuzzy construct: one lacking a consistent and clear statement of features. Therefore, researchers created their own unique

Table 37.1. A Summary of Experiments Demonstrating a Modality Effect.

Research Team	Learner Population	Lesson Topic	Lesson Length	Outcome Measures
Mousavi, Low, and Sweller, 1995; Experiment 1	Eighth-graders Australian	Geometry examples	Learner-determined, up to five minutes per example on text and time to listen to audio twice	Scores on similar and different geometry problems
Mousavi, Low, and Sweller, 1995; Experiment 2	Eighth-graders Australian	Geometry examples	151 and 157 seconds for each example	Scores on similar and different geometry problems
Mousavi, Low, and Sweller, 1995; Experiment 3	Eighth-graders Australian	Geometry examples	Varied by treatment	Learning time, testing time, scores on similar and different geometry problems
Mousavi, Low, and Sweller, 1995; Experiment 5	Eighth-graders Australian	Geometry examples	Varied by treatment	Test solution times
Mousavi, Low, and Sweller, 1995; Experiment 6	Fourth-graders Australian	Geometry examples	Fifty-five seconds up to three minutes per example	Learning time and test solution times

Tindall-Ford, Chandler, and Sweller, 1997; Experiment 1	Trade apprentices Australian	How to conduct electrical tests	Five minutes	Recognition and application
Tindall-Ford, Chandler, and Sweller, 1997; Experiment 2	Trade apprentices Australian	How to interpret an electrical table	100 seconds and 170 seconds	Recognition, application, and efficiency
Tindall-Ford, Chandler, and Sweller, 1997; Experiment 3	Trade apprentices Australian	Electrical symbol identification and how to interpret electrical circuit diagram	Approximately three minutes	Recall and application, test solution times, and efficiency
Mayer and Moreno, 1998; Experiment 1	College students United States	How lightning forms	140 seconds	Retention, recognition, and application
Mayer and Moreno, 1998; Experiment 2	College students United States	How car brakes work	Forty-five seconds	Recall, recognition, and application
Moreno, Mayer, Spires, and Lester, 2001; Experiment 1	College students United States	Botany concepts Game format with agent	Twenty-five minutes	Recall and application

(Continued)

Table 37.1. A Summary of Experiments Demonstrating a Modality Effect. (*Continued*)

Research Team	Learner Population	Lesson Topic	Lesson Length	Outcome Measures
Moreno, Mayer, Spires, and Lester, 2001; Experiment 2	Seventh-graders United States	Botany concepts Game format with agent	Self paced, up to forty minutes	Recall and application
Moreno, Mayer, Spires, and Lester, 2001; Experiment 4	College students United States	Botany concepts Game format with agent	Self-paced, twenty-four to twenty-eight minutes	Recall and application
Moreno, Mayer, Spires, and Lester, 2001; Experiment 5	College students United States	Botany concepts game format with agent	Self-paced, twenty-four to twenty-eight minutes	Recall and application
Craig, Gholson, and Driscoll, 2002; Experiment 2	College students United States	How lightning works, explained by agent	180 seconds	Recall, recognition, and application
Leahy, Chandler, and Sweller, 2003; Experiment 1	Fifth-graders Australian	Interpretation of a line graph	No time limit and 185 seconds	Recognition and application
Mayer, Dow, and Mayer, 2003; Experiment 1 ES = .85	College students United States	How an electric motor works	Approximately twenty minutes	Application

implementation of an advance organizer, likely no two of which were the same. Likewise it is left to practitioners' imaginations to apply this fuzzy concept to their own instructional products. No doubt if you asked ten instructional professionals to show you advance organizers they created, you would see ten quite different implementations.

Getting Beneath the Surface. The problem, however, goes a little deeper than agreeing on a consistent definition for instructional treatments. It turns out that the effectiveness of any instructional intervention depends not only on its surface features but also on its functional properties. In 2003 I devoted over six months to gathering and reviewing research on graphics for my book *Graphics for Learning* (Clark and Lyons, 2004). Much of the research on graphics published prior to 1980 yielded little in the way of usable guidelines. In fact, a review of hundreds of research studies on graphics conducted in the 1970s and 1980s involving over forty-eight thousand students concluded that "visuals are effective some of the time under some conditions" (Rieber, 1994, p. 132). Nothing more helpful than that generality had come out of the research because most of the studies defined graphics in terms of their surface features rather than their functions. As we will see in the next paragraph, graphics that work in harmony with human psychological processes will have a positive effect on learning, whereas graphics that disrupt these processes will depress learning. The effects of graphics on learning are more about how the graphics function psychologically than about whether they are line drawings or photographs.

As instructional scientists have taken a closer look at the effects of graphics, they find that some graphics do indeed support learning while others either make no difference or in fact depress learning. Mayer (2001) conducted a number of studies comparing learning of scientific processes such as lightning formation from text alone with lessons that added relevant graphics to the text. He found large and significant positive learning effects for graphics. However, he found that when he added different graphics to those same lessons in order to add interest, learning was actually depressed. For example, he added visuals illustrating people and airplanes struck by lightning. These visuals did add interest to the basic lesson on how lightning works but they also depressed learning compared to lessons that simply included relevant visuals. In another research study on graphics, Gyselinck and Tardieu (1999) compared the effects of different types of visuals on understanding of scientific processes. For example, in Figure 37.2, I show two versions of graphics they used to illustrate the relationship between gas pressure and altitude. The figure on the right is a representational graphic; it simply depicts the objects mentioned in the text. In contrast, the figure on the left is an interpretive graphic; it uses arrows and a series of bags to illustrate state changes in gas pressure at different altitudes. The authors found that both illustrations improved learning, compared with text alone. However, the interpretive visual promoted better understanding of the principles involved.

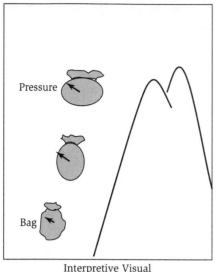 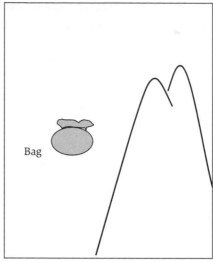

| Interpretive Visual | Representational Visual |

As the bag goes up in altitude, it will inflate because of the pressure.

Figure 37.2. Examples of Interpretive and Representational Graphics.

Source: Adapted from Gyselinck and Tardieu, 1999; used with permission.

From these studies we learn that we cannot make any generalizations about the effects of graphics on learning without considering the functional features of the graphics that lead to different psychological effects. An interesting visual related to the topic of lightning but irrelevant to the goal of the lesson depressed learning. A visual that depicted the elements in the text improved learning somewhat but not as much as did a visual that illustrated the relationships depicted in the text and thus promoted understanding. In conclusion, as we become more sophisticated about the psychological effects of interventions, we will adopt better labels for instructional methods that reflect their functional properties. For example, Table 37.2 is a taxonomy of visuals we adapted from Carney and Levin (2002). The goal of this taxonomy is to help us view graphics in terms of their functionality and not just their surface features.

Different Learners, Different Functions. The effectiveness of any instructional method will be shaped by the prior knowledge of the learner. For example, Mayer and Gallini (1990) compared learning outcomes among high- and low-prior-knowledge learners from lessons containing relevant graphics and text with lessons containing text only. In three experiments they found that the relevant graphics dramatically improved learning of individuals unfamiliar with the instructional content. However, learners with related content background learned as effectively from the text alone as from the text plus graphics. The experienced learners had sufficient mental models in memory to interpret and learn from the

Table 37.2. Communication Functions of Graphics.

Function	Graphic	Examples
Decorative	Used for aesthetic purposes or to add humor	Art on book cover Cartoon character in lesson
Representational	Used to represent the object being depicted	A screen capture of a computer screen A photograph of equipment
Mnemonic	Used to support memory of factual information	An image of a letter in a grocery cart to recall the meaning of carta
Organizational	Used to show qualitative relationships among content	A course map A concept hierarchy chart
Relational	Used to show quantitative relationships among two or more variables	A line graph A pie chart
Transformational	Used to show changes in objects over time or space	An animation of the weather cycle A video showing how to operate equipment
Interpretive	Used to model theory or principles	A simulation of molecular action A schematic diagram

Source: Clark and Lyons, 2004; adapted from Carney and Levin, 2002.

text alone. The graphic representations did not add anything they could not construct for themselves. Similar results were reported by Brewer, Harvey, and Semmler (2004), who compared the use of visuals to improve comprehension of legal instructions to mock juries consisting of law students, considered experts in this study, or general population participants, who were considered to be novices. They found that the novice juries had better comprehension of legal instructions from explanations that incorporated visuals, whereas the experts learned as much from audio explanations lacking visuals.

In summary, to evaluate the applicability of an experimental study to your own instructional environment, you need to go beyond the label the researchers used for their intervention. You will need to read the fine print in order to

(1) define the exact features of the intervention used in the study and (2) go beyond the surface features to consider the functionality of the intervention as well as how it might interact with the learner population used in the study.

Defining the Modality Effect Intervention. In the case of the experiments on the modality effect summarized in Table 37.1, the treatments are pretty consistent among all of the experiments. The test lessons involved explanations of a visual such as a graph or an animation showing a scientific process. One version explained the visual with words presented in text while the comparison version explained the visual with the same words presented in audio narration. The versions using audio narration resulted in significantly better learning than did the text versions, but only for novice learners. Learners with some background and experience with the content learned as well from either text or audio narration of words (Clark, Nguyen, and Sweller, 2006).

Is the Performance Measure an Application or Recall Metric? The effect of any instructional intervention that is evaluated in an experiment must be quantified with some kind of outcome measure. Some educational research studies use recall of lesson content as their measure, whereas others use application assessments. Two recent studies on the value of adding signals to texts and lectures offer illustrative examples. Signals are devices inserted into text or lectures to clarify the structure and importance of the content. Signals include section headings, cues to draw attention to important words or sentences, such as bolding in text or stress and pauses in lectures, and transitional and clarifying words and phrases, such as "The next section describes the four main reasons for. . . ." The purpose of signaling is to help learners select, organize, and integrate the content. Is there any evidence that signals enhanced learning? A recent study by Rickards, Fajen, Sullivan, and Gillespie (1997) compared the effects of signaled lectures on learning of students who did and did not take notes while listening. As you can see in Figure 37.3, signals led to better learning when learners took notes. In contrast, note-taking was detrimental to learning when the lecture was not signaled. It is likely that having to take notes imposes considerable cognitive load and is only helpful when the lecture reduces load by adding signals. Otherwise, note-taking becomes a divided-attention activity. This result gives us a useful guideline: add signaling to lectures and require learners to take notes. However, there is one problem. In this study, learning was measured by recall of the ideas presented in the lecture. In organizational learning, our goal is application of new knowledge and skills to work tasks, not recall of information.

Now we might assume that if learners could recall content, they could also apply it. However, this is not always the case. For example, in another experiment on signaling, Mautone and Mayer (2001) compared learning from signaled and unsignaled versions of a text passage describing airplane lift. They

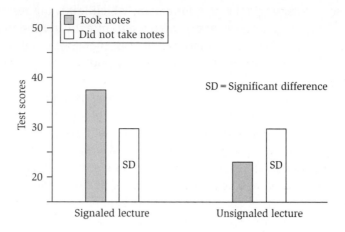

Figure 37.3. Effects of Signals on Learning with and Without Note-Taking.
Source: Clark, Nguyen, and Sweller, 2006.

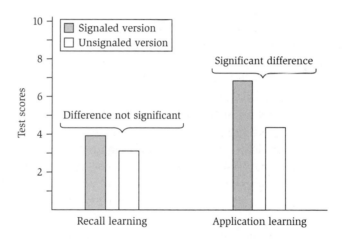

Figure 37.4. Effects of Signaling of Text on Recall and Application Learning.
Source: Adapted from Mautone and Mayer, 2001.

measured learning with recall and with problem-solving tests that required learners to apply the concepts in the passage to questions such as, How could a plane be redesigned to achieve lift more rapidly? As shown in Figure 37.4, signaling had a significantly positive effect on application learning but not on recall. The authors concluded, "In several studies the groups did not differ on retention tests but did differ on transfer tests, so it appears that signaling does more than just help people select and retrieve information. Learners in the signaled groups did not have to use all of their limited cognitive resources in the process of selecting relevant information, which left some resources available for the higher processes of organizing and integrating the information" (p. 387). In other words, by reducing mental load, signals free up working memory to process the content more deeply and thus lead to a richer understanding that pays off in better problem solving.

For most of us working in organizations, our goal is application, not recall. While instructional treatments that lead to better recall may at the same time promote deeper understanding, we cannot make that assumption. Studies that base conclusions only on recall measures will have limited application to practitioners. Most research reports display their results in tables or, if you are lucky, in graphs that clearly label the outcome measure. Therefore you can usually easily identify the performance measure. If the data only presents scores, review the materials or procedure section of the report to determine the nature of the test from which the score was derived.

How Is the Modality Effect Measured? Regarding the performance measures in experiments related to the modality effect, as you can see in Table 37.1, a variety of outcomes have been measured, including recall, recognition, and application test scores, learning times, and instructional efficiency. Since all of these measures showed significant and positive effects for audio narration, we can feel confident recommending guidelines based on the modality effect for application learning.

Will the Findings Generalize to My Learners? All research studies use a pool of subjects that, in most cases, tends to be relatively homogeneous. In experimental studies the subjects are randomly assigned to interventions to rule out any effects of individual differences. But you still need to ask yourself about the original population from which the subjects are drawn. Many educational studies are conducted with college students who must participate in one or more studies as a course requirement. In fact, over 90 percent of the studies we cited in *e-Learning and the Science of Instruction* (Clark and Mayer, 2003) were conducted with college students. To what extent do results derived from college students apply to your learners?

One of the most significant individual differences that affect learning outcomes is prior knowledge and experience. In fact, Kalyuga, Ayers, Chandler, and Sweller (2003) found that instructional techniques that worked well for novices, including the modality principle, not only *did not help* more advanced learners but actually hindered their learning. They call this phenomenon the *expertise reversal effect* and have demonstrated it with diverse instructional treatments. The reason for expertise reversal is that many instructional interventions are helpful because they support a limited working memory capacity. As learners gain expertise, they build schemas in long-term memory that can compensate for limited working memory capacity. Therefore they no longer need the support that benefits novices. In fact, after they have acquired quite a bit of expertise, they are better off using their own schemas to process new information and are disrupted when forced to use methods imposed by instruction. To reduce variation in results due to expertise, most educational research studies select subjects who are new to the skills being trained.

The subject pool can make a difference to motivational outcomes as well. For example, a recent review of problem-based learning (PBL) in medical education by Hmelo-Silver (2004) reported the frequent finding that medical students engaged in PBL classes were significantly more satisfied than were learners in traditional classes. However, the author cautions, "It is important to note that in medical schools, the students are a fairly select group and the PBL curricula are well established. Moreover, PBL is used throughout the entire curriculum" (p. 259). Therefore, similar positive attitudes may not be seen among learners who represent a broader cross-section of the population and who are not used to learning in this format. When you review research studies, you will need to consider how similar the experimental subjects are to your population, especially in terms of prior knowledge and experience.

Subjects in the Modality Research. As you can see in Table 37.1, the range of learners who benefited from the modality effect is quite broad; from fourth-graders to adult learners in college or trade schools in Australia and the United States. Most of the studies used novice learners. The applicability of this effect across such diverse learners supports the modality effect as a universal instructional principle applicable to novice learners of diverse ages and backgrounds.

Will the Intervention Apply to My Instructional Context? In *e-Learning and the Science of Instruction* (Clark and Mayer, 2003), we summarized a number of controlled experiments that Mayer has published on the effects of various instructional methods, such as the modality effect on learning from computer-delivered training. When you read Mayer's studies you will find that the topics included in his experimental lessons focused on science or mechanical processes, such as how lightning forms or how automobile brakes work. Furthermore, most of the experimental lessons were quite brief and lasted one to three minutes.

Multiple Contexts for the Modality Effect. As you can see in Table 37.1, the modality effect has been observed with a variety of skill-building lessons, including solving geometry problems, conducting electrical tests, interpreting data tables, applying botany concepts, and understanding scientific and mechanical processes. The commonality among all of these test lessons is an audio explanation of a complex visual from a fairly structured domain. Because structured domains such as mathematics and science tend to have right or wrong answers, the effects of instructional treatments in such domains are easier to measure than those in less clearly defined domains for which there are multiple correct answers. Therefore, you will see a preponderance of structured subject domains used in experimental studies.

Not only has the modality effect proven robust across different content topics, it also has been shown to apply to lessons of various lengths ranging from a few seconds to twenty-five minutes. Of course, real-world instruction is measured in units of hours and days, not minutes. Therefore, for practical application, we need to know whether the modality principle would apply in much longer instructional sequences than those tested so far, as well as whether it applies to more ill-defined domains.

Do Positive Learning Effects Last? Even a very significant positive learning result needs to last more than a few minutes to be of value to training professionals. We need instructional treatments that have lasting effects; treatments leading to learning that can be demonstrated days and weeks after the training. Unfortunately, very few educational research studies report learning results beyond a short period after the instructional treatment. Gyselinck and Tardieu (1999) compared recall and application learning of science text passages that were or were not illustrated with relevant graphics. As is typical of most experiments, they measured learning immediately after the study period. They also reported beneficial effects of visuals on a delayed measure of learning. The delay, however, was only one day. I did not feel that this was adequate support for their claim that "it appears that the presentation of pictures has not only a superficial and transient effect on the processing of the text, but that it also leads to an elaborated and long-lasting representation" (p. 206). While the results do offer some encouragement about the lasting benefits of visuals, we need data from much longer delay periods.

There are a few experiments that do report delayed learning effects. A recent study reported by Haidet, Morgan, O'Malley, Moran, and Richards (2004) compared learning and attitudes of medical residents after instruction in the form of a didactic lecture or a lecture combined with problem solving in collaborative learning groups. They measured outcomes both immediately after the training session and one month later. There were no significant differences in learning or attitudes toward the content between the two groups either immediately after the study or one month later. Interestingly enough, however, participants in the didactic session perceived significantly higher value and believed they met the objectives more than did participants in the collaborative session. The research team suggests that "[s]ince the culture of medical education has traditionally emphasized the value and legitimacy of didactic lectures over other methods of instruction, we hypothesize that when learners found themselves in a situation where the methods were unusual (i.e., the small-group/large-group format of the active session), these methods were marginalized and the session was seen as less useful" (p. 23).

How Long Does the Modality Effect Last? None of the studies on the modality effect listed in Table 37.1 measured retention of learning. Therefore, we will need additional studies to demonstrate the longevity of the modality effect.

What Do the Numbers Mean? Experimental studies will use some form of statistical analysis to determine whether or not an average score of say 75 percent is better than an average score of 70 percent. First, the study will report statistical significance. Statistical significance tells us that the results most likely did not occur by chance. Typically, studies use a standard of .05 that tells us that there is less than a 5 percent probability that the results occurred by chance alone. However, statistical significance does not necessarily translate into practical significance. A very small difference in learning can be statistically significant, especially when the sample size is large. In the past few years, most studies reported a statistic called "effect size" that gives us a better indication of practical significance. The effect size tells how many standard deviations the test group is from the control group. A standard deviation is an average deviation of each score from the mean in a set of scores. The larger the standard deviation, the greater is the dispersion among the scores in the set. An effect size of .5 means that you could expect any individual score of someone studying the less effective lesson version to increase by half a standard deviation if they took the more effective version.

Mayer (2001) reports an average effect size of 1.17 among four experiments testing the modality effect. This indicates a lesson that explains that visuals with auditory narration will result in a learning improvement that is 1.17 of a standard deviation higher than if the lesson used text. Assume a group studying the version with text descriptions had an average score of 60 percent and a standard deviation of 10; if they were assigned to the audio version, you could expect an improvement of 60 plus 11.7 points for an average of 71.7. As a general guideline, effect sizes less than or equal to .20 are considered small and are of negligible practical importance. Effect sizes around .50 are considered medium and are of moderate practical importance. Finally, effect sizes of .80 or higher are large and are of crucial practical importance (Hojat and Xu, 2004). Beyond statistical significance and clinical significance, you will also have to decide whether the results are effective. In other words, will the improvement in learning warrant the investment in constructing an instructional program that applies the guidelines or principles? This question of course requires a value judgment that will depend on the criticality of the skills being trained and the size of the learning audience, as well as the costs involved in implementing the guideline.

Is There a Theoretical Context for the Results? Why should practitioners care about the theory behind instructional guidelines? Should we not leave the theory to the researchers? We have all heard the expression, there is nothing as practical

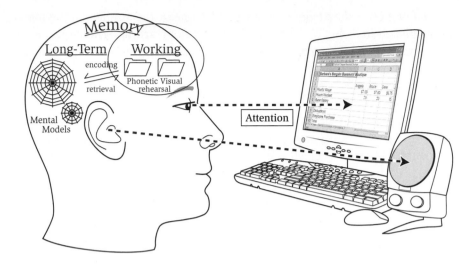

Figure 37.5. Subcomponents of Working Memory.

Source: Clark, Nguyen, and Sweller, 2006.

as a good theory. This is especially true in our field because, as we have discussed throughout this chapter, the effects of instructional treatments depend on so many variables. No matter how many studies you review, you are not likely to find one that exactly duplicates your instructional context. In all cases, the learners, the content, the performance outcomes, the lesson length, and so on will differ from your situation. Even in the best of circumstances, you will have to adapt guidelines, and knowing the theoretical rationale for any given guideline should help.

What Theory Explains the Modality Effect? The modality effect provides a good example of an instructional method with a good theoretical basis. The modality effect is based on cognitive load theory, which states that the acquisition of new knowledge and skills that are complex imposes a heavy load on working memory (Clark, Nguyen, and Sweller, 2006). Anything instructional professionals can do to minimize cognitive load imposed by the instructional materials will lead to more capacity being available for learning. Figure 37.5 illustrates the two subcomponents for working memory: one for auditory information and one for visual information.

When your instruction includes a complex visual that must be explained to be understood, you can maximize working memory by presenting the explanatory words in an auditory format. By doing this you balance the instruction across the visual and auditory resources in working memory. Based on cognitive load theory, when would the modality principle be most applicable? Working memory will be most taxed when the learners are unfamiliar with the content and when the content is complex. Working memory will also be more taxed when instructional content is presented to learners under instructional control of pacing rather than learner control. In fact, recent research has shown that the modality effect *did not apply* to lessons with simple content, to experienced learners, or to situations in which the learners had control over pacing (Clark, Nguyen, and Sweller, 2006). All of these circumstances impose relatively low cognitive load.

Understanding the mechanisms behind instructional guidelines enables us to adapt and adjust them to our situations. The hallmark of a professional is that he or she is someone who not only knows the best approach to resolve a practical problem but also knows the reasons for that approach. For example, workshop participants have asked me whether the modality effect applies to different cultures. It is a great question, and I cannot respond from evidence because all of the studies involve subjects from Western cultures. However, given its mechanism of action, I would expect the modality effect to apply to any cultural group, because as humans we share the challenges of a limited working memory.

Have Findings Been Replicated? Since no single experiment will meet all of the criteria we have discussed, we need replicated studies in order to recommend general guidelines that apply to diverse situations. Ideally, similar positive effects will be replicated among learners of different ages and with lessons containing different instructional content and of various lengths. As an instructional method like the modality effect is tested under more and more diverse conditions, we can get specific about the conditions under which it applies. Based on research to date, we can generalize that the modality effect applies to immediate learning among Western culture novice learners of diverse ages who must master complex skills that involve explanations of visuals in lessons lasting up to thirty minutes. It is hoped that as more evidence accumulates, we will be able to expand this guideline to content that is less structured, to lessons of greater length, and to learners from other cultural backgrounds.

We have discussed a number of issues you must consider when interpreting research reports. But that is only one set of challenges. Suppose there are a number of research studies relevant to your instructional issues. What barriers will you face trying to access and integrate them in a way that will give you meaningful guidance to your instructional issues?

Barrier 3: How Can I Access Meaningful Evidence?

Let us suppose that there is a sizeable number of studies that are not only methodologically valid but also are varied enough that many of the criteria previously listed are met. For example, positive application learning effects from well-specified instructional methods have been documented in diverse populations, with different instructional content, that have lasting effects, and so on.

In other words, we have sufficient evidence to warrant a relatively robust instructional principle. But even when good research evidence is out there, how easy is it for practitioners to obtain it and translate it into meaningful guidelines? From personal experience I can respond, "only with a great deal of time and difficulty," and I am not alone. In the medical field, in which there is an abundance of published studies, physicians reported that information overload was a significant barrier to accurate diagnosis and effective management of heart failure in primary care settings (Fuat, Hungin, and Murphy, 2003). There are three main routes whereby practitioners can access evidence-based instructional guidelines: (1) by finding and reading individual research studies and attending conferences that present research, (2) by reading articles and books that present narrative reviews of research, and (3) by accessing systematic reviews of research. There are trade-offs to each of these, as follows:

Problems with Accessing and Reading Research Studies. Most research reports are found in diverse technical journals or reported at academic research conferences. Since researchers and practitioners represent separate communities of practice, practitioners must make a special effort to find relevant research reports. Fortunately, the Internet is making more recent reports more readily accessible. University libraries have subscription services that offer their users these on-line resources on a no-cost or low-cost basis. For individuals, however, and many organizations, there is a charge of from $10 to $25 to download a research article. As an individual practitioner, I find it more economical to visit my local university library, where I can get older reports from hardbound journals and newer ones from their on-line subscription services.

Once I have the article in hand, the next challenge is to read it. Most research reports are not written for practitioners. In fact, some are only intelligible to a select group of like-minded researchers familiar with the unique jargon of that research domain. For example, Figure 37.6 includes an excerpt from an article from a social psychology journal. The number of technical terms makes it difficult for practitioners unfamiliar with the constructs to decipher the meaning. The bottom line to accessing research one study at a time is that busy practitioners simply do not have the time to find research reports, read through them, assess their relevance to their research issues, and synthesize them into meaningful guidelines. Narrative reviews and systematic reviews of evidence, discussed in the next sections, offer two alternative vehicles that busy professionals can use to find and apply research evidence relevant to their practice.

Problems with Narrative Reviews. The last four books I have written fall into the category of narrative reviews of research. A narrative review is a synthesis of evidence gathered to support specific instructional interventions or methods. For example, in *e-Learning and the Science of Instruction* (Clark and Mayer, 2003)

The article presents the basic tenets of social cognitive theory. It is founded on a causal model of the triadic reciprocal causation in which personal factors in the form of cognitive, affective, and biological events; behavioral patterns; and environmental events all operate as interacting determinants that influence one another bidirectionally. Within this theory human agency is embedded in a self theory encompassing self-organizing, proactive, self-reflective and self-regulative mechanisms. Human agency can be exercised through direct personal agency, through proxy agency relying on the efforts of intermediaries, and by collective agency operating through shared beliefs of efficacy, pooled understandings, group aspirations and incentive systems, and collective action.

Figure 37.6. Journal Article Excerpt.

Source: Bandura, 1999.

we included guidelines with examples and research supporting instructional methods that lead to learning implemented in asynchronous e-learning. Unlike systematic reviews, narrative reviews typically do not apply statistical techniques such as meta-analysis to the accumulated data, and the criteria and processes for collecting and including evidence are more informal and usually not documented.

In writing these reviews, I have done the legwork I described in the previous sections in order to distill and illustrate evidence-based guidelines that are useful for practitioners. In two of my books I have partnered with the researchers who produced much of the evidence behind the guidelines. Based on book sales, practitioners have found these useful. However, narrative reviews have inherent limitations. First, I gathered published evidence that was readily available from journals and books. This imposes a bias in that many research studies, such as dissertations that do not demonstrate any positive effects, are not published in these sources. As a result, my guidelines may be overinflated, since they are based on published studies. Second, in *e-Learning and the Science of Instruction* (Clark and Mayer, 2003), I did not invest much effort in pointing out the limitations of the guidelines presented, as discussed in the preceding section. I believe this is a common shortcoming of narrative reviews. Last, there are the limitations inherent in the delivery and updating of books as a delivery device. First, after completing a manuscript, there is typically a nine-to-twelve-month period before the book is released. Second, as new research becomes available, revised guidelines will need to wait for a second edition of the book to be documented. To maintain a more timely and updatable resource, narrative reviews must be available on the Internet. This brings us to the topic of systematic reviews.

Problems with Systematic Reviews. I believe that many of the problems summarized in the previous sections can be solved with systematic reviews. A systematic review is a synthesis of research that uses an exhaustive search process to identify the accumulated research evidence on a topic or question, critically appraises it for its methodological quality and findings, and determines the consistent and variable messages that are generated by this body of work (Davies, 2004). Compared to narrative reviews, the systematic review follows a much more rigorous and resource-intensive process. The systematic review begins with a precise crafting of the question to be answered in order to focus the goal of the review and to build an appropriate search strategy. Then a comprehensive search process attempts to find and critically appraise all of the available research literature on the question at hand, including unpublished sources. The search procedures are explicitly identified in the review so readers can assess for themselves the comprehensibility of the materials on which the findings are based. Once identified, all sources are carefully evaluated regarding their quality, and published studies that do not meet the stated criteria are discarded. To aid the reader, all criteria used to include or exclude studies are included in the report.

The Cochrane Collaboration was founded in 1993 as an on-line resource of systematic reviews in health care. The Cochrane Collaboration currently includes two thousand Cochrane reviews reflecting the participation of over ten thousand professionals worldwide. The reviews are available on a subscription basis, although several countries have contracted with the Collaboration to make the library freely available to anyone with Internet access. You can see samples of systematic reviews included in the Cochrane Collaboration at www.Cochrane.org.

The Cochrane Collaboration was created because

> People making decisions about health care, including patients, health care professionals, policy makers and managers, need high-quality information and, unfortunately, much of what is available is of poor quality. As a consequence, vast resources are wasted each year on health care that is not effective and may even be harmful, effective forms of care are often under utilized, and people sometimes suffer and die unnecessarily. To overcome these barriers to better health care, and to provide a key piece of the evidence needed for this, results from similar randomized trials need to be brought together. Trials need to be assessed and those that are good enough can be combined to produce both a more statistically reliable result and one that can be more easily applied in other settings. This combination of trials needs to be done in as reliable a way as possible. It needs to be systematic [Clarke, 2004].

The Cochrane Collaboration estimates that currently it needs ten thousand reviews to cover all health care interventions that have been investigated in controlled trials, and that these reviews will need to be updated at the rate of five thousand per year. At the Collaboration's current rate of growth, it anticipates reaching this target within the next ten to fifteen years.

The Cochrane Collaboration has a sister organization called the Campbell Collaboration, which was established in 1999 with the goal of providing systematic reviews in the social sciences, including interventions in education, crime and justice, and social welfare. However, when I visited the site during the summer of 2004, I was unable to access any completed reviews in the education section, although there were several topics listed as in progress. This dearth of reviews, in contrast to the Cochrane Collaboration, may reflect recent origins or the smaller number of controlled research studies available in the social sciences, as well as a difference in funding.

In summary, systematic reviews available on the Internet would offer a useful way for busy practitioners to obtain guidelines based on comprehensive search and synthesis of research. However, whether there will be adequate funding for a sustained effort in the social sciences remains to be seen.

Barrier 4: How Can I Influence My Clients to Make Evidence-Based Decisions?

Once you access guidelines based on systematic reviews and therefore feel confident in recommending instructional treatments that lead to better learning, you will still face the challenge of convincing your clients. This issue brings us back to where I started this chapter and points to the heart of our challenge of being seen and accepted as professionals. Gaining professional status will take a long time, and no doubt we will experience uneven progress as we move along this path. There are no silver bullets, but some helpful guidelines include the following suggestions.

First we must embrace evidence-based practice ourselves. That means questioning the many transient trends that surface in our field on a regular basis. Some of my favorite examples include visual and auditory learning styles, edutainment, and discovery learning. Each of these fads has evidence to disprove it. We can draw encouragement that other professions have evolved beyond a fads and folklore basis for practice. For example, in the health sciences, "for all but the last century, decisions on how to treat patients were almost always based on personal experience, anecdotal case histories, and comparisons of a group of patients who received one treatment with an entirely separate group who did not" (Clarke, 2004).

Second, we need better mechanisms to evolve research findings from the laboratory into practice. Currently we have a relatively large body of instructional scientists who do basic laboratory work and report research findings, and we have a very large group of practitioners who seek the most effective instructional methods. But there are few individuals between these two communities whose work involves taking instructional methods proved effective in the laboratory and first adapting them based on larger-scale real-world trials and then promoting their adoption in the practitioner community. Third, we need to build business relationships with our clients in which we learn to speak with them in terms of their operational goals and challenges and over time build alliances based on trust and mutual respect.

EVIDENCE-BASED PRACTICE AND THE PROFESSIONALIZATION OF HPT

The bulk of this chapter has focused on the challenges we face in integrating evidence in a meaningful way into our professional decisions and relationships. While there are a number of hurdles, consider that one hundred years ago the medical profession was more or less in the same position that we are in today. For some time research had identified the relationship between bacteria and disease, and by 1865 Joseph Lister had demonstrated the effectiveness of antiseptic procedures in surgery. Still it took over thirty years to convince tradition-bound physicians to abandon the practice of dropping a scalpel, picking it up, wiping it off, and continuing with the surgery. "The most important reason for the extraordinary advances in medicine, agriculture, and other fields is the acceptance by practitioners of evidence as the basis for practice" (Slavin, 2002, p. 16).

Since we have a long way to go, ever more do we bear the responsibility to do our part in moving our practice toward professional status by factoring evidence into our decisions. Of course, research evidence can never be the sole basis for our decisions. All practitioners must consider other major factors that will shape their products and programs, such as their organization's culture; the availability and use of technology; and pragmatic issues including time, budget, and politics. However, the time is ripe to ensure that evidence be weighed as heavily as any of these factors when planning a new program or policy related to learning or HPT. To do less diminishes us as a fledging profession and our opportunities to support the organizations and the staffs within them that we serve.

References

Bandura, A. (1999). Social cognitive theory: An agentic perspective. *Asian Journal of Social Psychology, 2,* 21–41.

Brewer, N., Harvey, S., and Semmler, C. (2004). Improving comprehension of jury instructions with audio-visual presentation. *Applied Cognitive Psychology, 18,* 765–776.

Burkhardt, H., and Schoenfeld, A. H. (2003). Improving educational research: Toward a more useful, more influential, and better-funded enterprise. *Educational Researcher, 32*(9), 3–14.

Carney, R. N., and Levin, J. R. (2002). Pictorial illustrations still improve students' learning from text. *Educational Psychology Review, 14*(1), 5–26.

Clark, R. C., and Lyons, C. (2004). *Graphics for learning.* San Francisco: Jossey-Bass/Pfeiffer.

Clark, R. C., and Mayer, R. E. (2003). *e-Learning and the science of instruction.* San Francisco: Jossey–Bass/Pfeiffer.

Clark, R. C., Nguyen, F., and Sweller, J. (2006). *Efficiency in learning: Guidelines for applying cognitive load theory.* San Francisco: Jossey–Bass/Pfeiffer.

Clarke, M. (2004). Systematic reviews and the Cochrane collaboration. Retrieved July 2004 from www.cochrane.org/docs/whycc.htm.

Craig, S. D., Gholson, B., and Driscoll, D. M. (2002). Animated pedagogical agents in multimedia educational environments: Effects of agent properties, picture features, and redundancy. *Journal of Educational Psychology, 94*(2), 428–434.

Davies, P. (2004). Systematic reviews and the Campbell collaboration. In G. Thomas and R. Print (Eds.), *Evidence-based practice in education.* Berkshire, UK: Open University Press.

Dolezalek, H. (2004). Industry report. *Training Magazine, 41*(9), 20–36.

Fuat, A., Hungin, A.P.S., and Murphy, J. S. (2003). Barriers to accurate diagnosis and effective management of heart failure in primary care: Qualitative study. *British Medical Journal, 326,* 196. Accessed March 7, 2004, from http://bmj.bmjjournals.com/cig/content/full/326/7382/196.

Gyselinck, V., and Tardieu, H. (1999). The role of illustrations in text comprehension: What, when, for whom, and why? In H. van Oostendorp and S. R. Goldman (Eds.), *The construction of mental representations during reading.* Mahwah, NJ: Lawrence Erlbaum Associates.

Haidet, P., Morgan, R. O., O'Malley, K., Moran, B. J., and Richards, B. F. (2004). A controlled trial of active versus passive learning strategies in a large group setting. *Advances in Health Sciences Education, 9,* 15–27.

Hmelo-Silver, C. E. (2004). Problem-based learning: What and how do students learn? *Educational Psychology Review, 16*(3), 235–266.

Hojat, M., and Xu, G. (2004). A visitor's guide to effect sizes. *Advances in Health Sciences Education, 9,* 241–249.

Kalyuga, S., Ayers, P., Chandler, P., and Sweller, J. (2003). The expertise reversal effect. *Educational Psychologist, 38*(1), 23–31.

Leahy, W., Chandler, P., and Sweller, J. (2003). When auditory presentations should and should not be a component of multimedia instruction. *Applied Cognitive Psychology, 17,* 401–418.

Mautone, P. D., and Mayer, R. E. (2001). Signaling as a cognitive guide in multimedia learning. *Journal of Educational Psychology, 93*(2), 377–389.

Mayer, R. E. (2001). *Multimedia learning.* New York: Cambridge University Press.

Mayer, R. E., and Gallini, J. K. (1990). When is an illustration worth ten thousand words? *Journal of Educational Psychology, 82*(4), 715–726.

Mayer, R. E. and Moreno, R. (1998). A split attention effect in multimedia learning: Evidence for dual processing systems in working memory. *Journal of Educational Psychology, 90*(2), 312–320.

Mayer, R. E., Dow, G. T., and Mayer, S. (2003). Multimedia learning in an interactive self-explaining environment: What works in the design of agent-based micro worlds? *Journal of Educational Psychology, 95*(4), 806–813.

Moreno, R., Mayer, R. E., Spires, H. A., and Lester, J. C. (2001). The case for social agency in computer-based teaching: Do students learn more deeply when they interact with animated pedagogical agents? *Cognition and Instruction, 19*(2), 177–213.

Mousavi, S. Y., Low, R., and Sweller, J. (1995). Reducing cognitive load by mixing auditory and visual presentation modes. *Journal of Educational Psychology. 87*(2), 319–334.

No Child Left Behind Act of 2001. (January 8, 2002). 107 U.S.C. Public Law 107–110.

Rickards, J. P., Fajen, B. R., Sullivan, J. F., and Gillespie, G. (1997). Signaling, note taking, and field independent-dependence in text comprehension and recall. *Journal of Educational Psychology, 89*(3), 508–517.

Rieber, L. P. (1994). *Computers, graphics, and learning.* Madison, WI: WCB Brown & Benchmark.

Slavin, R. E. (2002). Evidence-based educational policies: Transforming educational practice and research. *Educational Researcher, 31*(7), 15–21.

Slavin, R. E. (2004). Education research can and must address "what works" questions. *Educational Researcher 33*(1), 27–28.

Thalheimer, W. (2003). E-learning and the science of instruction: Proven guidelines for consumers and designers of multimedia learning. *Performance Improvement, 42*(5) 41–43.

Tindall-Ford, S., Chandler, P., and Sweller, J. (1997). When two sensory modes are better than one. *Journal of Experimental Psychology: Applied, 3*(4), 257–287.

PART SIX

PERFORMANCE TECHNOLOGY IN ACTION

DEBRA HANEY

The previous parts of the handbook have presented the foundation, process, interventions, and measurement and assessment of human performance technology (HPT). The emphasis in this part of the book turns to improving the efficiency, effectiveness, and conduct of HPT practitioners. Improving HPT practice was a goal of the first two editions of the handbook; that goal has not changed with this edition. Part Six continues supporting practitioners by presenting chapters that both inform our work and provide, for some of us, new professional goals. The themes of these chapters are both external to the practice environment and internal to the practitioner: leadership, change, planning, self-reflection, ethics, and standards. These internal and external aspects must be incorporated for successful interventions and rewarding careers. The chapters in Part Six do not just discuss these themes in general terms; they all present specific and actionable steps that support performance improvement. They are a balance of theory and application, logic and results, and planning and execution.

Many HPT practitioners have dual responsibilities in training and nontraining interventions. Making the transition from training to performance may seem obvious, but it is not necessarily easy to accomplish. Part Six starts with a chapter by Dana Gaines Robinson and James Robinson that supports this transition with a transformation framework and guidance. The theme of successful practice continues with Chapter Thirty-Nine by Danny Langdon, which discusses successfully partnering with management for efficient and effective practice.

Chapter Forty, by Nicholas Andreadis, presents formal project management for HPT interventions. Partnering with both management and project management is requisite for success. These chapters have different perspectives on successful practice; these different perspectives complement each other.

Chapter Forty-One, the fourth chapter of Part Six, reinforces the importance of managing projects by focusing on the performance consultant's leadership role in client interactions. It is not enough to lead or manage the project steps; one must also manage the client relationship and lead the client, especially in the analysis process, by asking questions. The concept is simple; the application is not. Chapter author Roger Chevalier gives numerous specific ways to lead.

A framework can be likened to an anatomy. Chapter Forty-Two, by Geary Rummler, uses anatomy to guide understanding of the organization, performance, and the performance-improvement project. Knowing the factors that compose an organization's anatomy leads to accurate understanding of critical success factors and their linkage to successful project actions.

Since publication of the last handbook edition, certification for practitioners has become a reality. Chapter Forty-Three, by Judith Hale, describes the International Society for Performance Improvement's certification program's history, components, and benefits to practitioners. It will be fascinating reading for many of us, and is the documentation of a milestone in our field.

Certification involves standards and ethics. Chapters Forty-Four and Forty-Five, by Ingrid Guerra and Jim Hill, respectively, focus on standards and ethics. They give both the formal background and the practical application that HPT practitioners need to know in their professional lives. The realistic examples of ethically ambiguous or challenging situations are thought-provoking because they occur to all of us, sooner or later. These authors make a persuasive argument that HPT practitioners have ethical responsibilities to the client, society, themselves, and the profession.

In the final chapter in Part Six, Chapter Forty-Six, Dennis Duke, Robert Guptill, Mark Hemenway, and Wilbur Doddridge give a step-by-step history of HPT analysis supporting the linkage between acquisition and operational support of a complex system, aircraft, in the U.S. Navy. This is an unusual chapter for the handbook because it is based in a military environment that many readers typically do not think about. It is worth reading not because of that unusualness, but because it demonstrates the soundness of basic HPT methods in a complex situation in which mistakes can be costly.

The chapters that compose Part Six are thematically sequenced. Some readers will start with the first chapter and work their way through to the last chapter. Others will read whichever chapter seems most interesting at the time. Some readers will read only some of the chapters. Different readers will take different approaches. However, all the chapters are pertinent. All the chapters contain useful information that supports our work and our professional development. However the reader approaches the chapters, reading all of them will be beneficial.

As a group, the authors of Part Six have decades of practice and research. They represent the worlds of consulting, professional organizations, and academe. They act as both internal and external consultants. They have a wide range of experience in different arenas: corporations, government, not-for-profit organizations, and institutions of higher learning. They have different orientations, philosophies, and professional interests. Despite these disparate backgrounds and differences, they share important commonalities. They have a talent for astute observations and thoughtful, balanced reflection on those observations. They have a talent for clear communication in writing. The readers of the chapters in Part Six will benefit from the authors' talent and willingness to share their expertise.

CHAPTER THIRTY-EIGHT

Making the Transition from a Learning to a Performance Function

Dana Gaines Robinson, James C. Robinson

ow do I facilitate the transition of this learning department into one that is focused on performance improvement? This question is being asked by Elizabeth, the newly appointed manager of retail learning and development. The same question is being asked by Randal, a line manager, who has just been appointed director of learning and performance in a financial services organization. Actually, this question is often asked by training and development professionals, performance consultants, performance technologists, and others who have been appointed as managers of the learning function. In this chapter we will answer the question of how to successfully make this transition. We will provide a framework of five major steps for transforming a traditional learning department into one that has a performance focus. We will also provide guidelines for navigating through the crosscurrents of transition.

KEY CONCEPTS

Before discussing the five transition steps, it is important to note two concepts: the need hierarchy and the three kinds of work expected of learning and performance functions. Both of these concepts will have implications for how your performance function is structured and must be considered as you plan the transition to a performance focus.

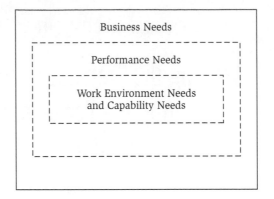

Figure 38.1. The Need Hierarchy.

The Need Hierarchy

A short definition of the role of performance consultants is that they are individuals who partner with managers and leaders to define and align the four types of needs within the organization. Figure 38.1 illustrates these four needs. As you will note, these needs rest like boxes within a box, with business needs at the top of the hierarchy.

Business Needs are the highest-order need, and all other needs emanate from them. If business needs go unmet for a long period of time, the future of the enterprise can be threatened. Business needs have three characteristics; they are

- Operational in focus
- Measured in a quantifiable manner
- Goals or needs for an entity, such as a business unit, department, plant, region, or the entire enterprise

To grow market share by 2 percent, to improve customer satisfaction by five points, and to reduce operational expense by $500,000 are examples of business needs.

While business needs focus on entities, *performance needs* focus on people. Performance needs identify the on-the-job behavior and activities that employees must carry out if the business needs are to be successfully achieved. In essence, performance needs answer the questions, What must people do more, better, or differently if we are to achieve our business goal? and How does that compare to what people are typically doing now? Performance needs focus on one or more specific groups of employees: those people who share a common job or role and who through their day-to-day performance most directly contribute to the achievement of the business needs. Figure 38.2 illustrates some examples of performance needs and how they link to specific business needs or goals.

Business Need	Employee Group and a Related Performance Need
Increase revenue by $1 billion in three years	*Sales representatives* need to tier their customers into A, B, C groupings. They then need to build account penetration plans for customers in the A group, those customers currently generating at least $1 million or more of revenue per year with the organization.
Achieve customer satisfaction rating of 87 percent	*Customer service representatives* (CSRs) need to ask open-ended questions of customers to identify their specific needs. Then the CSRs should summarize what they have learned to ensure mutual understanding.

Figure 38.2. Linkage of Business and Performance Needs.

Work environment needs are the organization's infrastructure within which employees work. This infrastructure includes work processes, information flow, reward and recognition systems, access to coaching, and clarity of expectations. The infrastructure either enables employees to perform as needed or acts as a barrier to the desired performance.

Capability needs are the skills, knowledge, and attributes that are required of employees to perform as needed in their jobs. For example, it would be difficult for a sales representative to perform successfully and accomplish the required revenue goals if the representative lacked knowledge of the products to be sold.

So what is the implication for a learning function wanting to make the transition into a performance-improvement function? A learning function focuses on identifying and addressing capability needs; a performance function focuses on identifying and addressing performance needs. Enlarging the focus of the function to the performance level requires that the function also have a role in identifying and addressing work environment needs, as these needs are integral to successful on-the-job performance. It also requires that people in the function have in-depth knowledge of the organization's business needs, as these establish requirements for performance. The result is a larger mission with additional services than is typically true for traditional learning functions.

Three Categories of Work

There are three kinds of work required of those who work in learning and performance functions: transactional, tactical, and strategic. In a performance function, the percentage of work that is strategic will likely increase. Let us look more closely at what qualifies as each type of work.

Transactional work is done to identify and address the needs of an individual. It is typically completed quickly and provides the individual with some type of information or guidance. Examples of transactional work for a learning function include counseling an employee as to a workshop that will develop the employee's skill in a specific area or coaching a former workshop participant on how to apply a skill.

Tactical work is done to identify and address the needs of work groups. This is often the primary focus of a learning function because a learning solution is often a tactic that supports a business goal. What is interesting about tactical work is the process used to implement it. Tactical work can be implemented in a programmatic manner: "We are rolling out a new leadership training program." Tactical work can also be implemented as part of an overarching strategic initiative: "We are creating greater flexibility in the workforce to support our business goal of operational efficiency. For this to succeed, our managers need to operate in a more empowering and flexible manner, so we are implementing a leadership development program to build their capability in this area."

The third category is *strategic* work. This is work done to give direct advantage to the business or organization. Strategic work

- Focuses on departments, business units, or the entire enterprise
- Is long-term in scope, often looking ahead two or more years
- Is directly linked to one or more business goals of the organization
- Is solution-neutral in the early stages of exploring the need
- Requires multiple solutions or tactics to be implemented; single solutions do not yield results in strategic initiatives

The implication for planning your transition is that strategic work is the type of work that performance functions seek. You want work that is directly linked to business goals. You want the solutions implemented by the performance department to be aligned with other solutions that might arise from other functions, such as marketing, manufacturing, and finance. Therefore your transition must work toward a structure and process that support strategic work.

With these two concepts in mind, let us now explore the five steps used to transform from a learning to a performance function.

STEP 1: AGREE ON A DESIRED END STATE

In his acclaimed book *The 7 Habits of Highly Effective People* (1989, p. 95), Stephen Covey states, "Begin with the end in mind." Before you begin the change process, determine two things: (1) the mission of your department and

(2) how your department will look when the transition is completed. A mission statement describes why your department exists. It indicates the value of your department to the enterprise. If you are a sales organization, your mission might be "to generate profitable revenue for the corporation." As a performance department, your mission statement might be "to enhance the capability and performance of employees and management in support of business goals." Another way of expressing this may be "to help our business leaders improve overall business performance and long-term success by enhancing the performance of the associates and the environment within which they work."

When forming the mission statement, make sure to obtain input from a variety of sources. What do the business leaders expect from your department? If you hope to hear answers other than "to train employees and managers," you will need to make business leaders aware of the options, other than training, that your department can provide. You can provide examples of how performance functions in other organizations have supported leaders in achieving their business goals. In addition to organizational leaders, obtain input from colleagues within your own department and within related departments such as human resources, organizational development, or organizational effectiveness. Your goal is to form a synergy with these other functions, identifying how all of you can work together toward the common goal of enhancing workplace performance.

In addition to obtaining input from people within your organization, it is beneficial to network with professionals in other organizations who have successfully made the transition to a performance function. Ask questions to determine what they see their mission and purposes to be. Discuss the techniques that worked for them and the roadblocks they encountered during the transition. Finally, we suggest you conduct a review of literature to determine how leaders in the human performance improvement field view the role of performance functions within today's organizations.

It is also important to gather information regarding how successful performance-improvement departments operate. This way you can gradually form a picture of what your function should look like when the transition into a performance-improvement function is completed. Figure 38.3 contrasts the characteristics of traditional learning departments as compared to performance-improvement functions. We compiled this information as we worked with several hundred learning functions making the transition from a traditional to a performance focus. This figure describes each of the eight characteristics for both a traditional learning function and a performance-improvement function. Because most departments are not totally traditional or totally performance in their approach, consider the paired characteristics as being opposite ends of a continuum. Place your department on the point in the continuum that best describes the current state of your function using the scale shown at the top of the figure.

TRADITIONAL APPROACH	PERFORMANCE APPROACH
Definitely traditional in approach	Mostly traditional; sometimes performance	Mostly performance; sometimes traditional	Definitely performance in approach

1. Focus is on the solution that is implemented; the solution (learning) is the end.	Focus is on what people need to do; the solution is a means to an end.
2. Approach is event-oriented; contact with client, before or after solution is implemented, may be minimal.	Approach is process-oriented; uses a continuous-improvement approach that involves clients on an ongoing basis.
3. Entry is primarily reactive, frequently in a "firefighting" mode.	Entry is both reactive and proactive. Projects should be sought that are longer-term and directly connected to a business goal.
4. Approach is biased to a solution during initial discussions.	Approach is solution-neutral during initial discussions.
5. Approach relies on single solution (generally the learning department's specialty).	Approach facilitates access to multiple solutions, both within and outside the learning department.
6. Department can work independently of client partnerships. Accountability for success is segmented, with the learning department "owning" the learning solutions and the client "owning" the business results.	Department is always partnered to a client who is active in the project. Accountability is shared, with both performance department and client owning accountability for business and performance results.
7. Learning needs assessments are conducted; identifying work environment barriers to performance is rarely done.	Organization or performance assessment is mandatory; performance gaps and causes for gaps are identified.
8. Evaluation of the solution is typically completed (that is, reaction and learning evaluation).	Evaluation is completed to determine the performance and operational impact resulting from the solution.

Figure 38.3. Characteristics of Traditional and Performance Approaches.

Our experience has been that some of these characteristics are easier to change than others. For example, changing characteristic 1 is often easily accomplished. Perhaps this is because the focus of the department is within the control of the department manager. Also we find that changes in characteristics 2, moving from event-oriented to process-oriented, and 7, moving from a learning needs assessment to an organizational or performance assessment, are also relatively easy to complete. Again, this may be because these characteristics are more directly under the control of the performance-improvement department. The transitions that are more difficult are those for the following characteristics, numbered as in Figure 38.3:

3. Moving from reactive entry to both reactive and proactive entry. The problem often encountered is that many learning functions are in the firefighting mode and therefore consultants within them do not find the time to proactively meet with their clients.

4. Moving from being biased toward a solution to being solution-neutral during initial discussions. Here the barrier is that learning consultants are often more comfortable with, and more knowledgeable about, learning solutions than other possible solutions, particularly those outside their department. Therefore, there is a tendency for learning consultants to migrate toward what they know; in other words, to migrate toward learning solutions.

6. Moving from working independently of client partnerships to always being partnered with the client on projects. The barrier is that many performance consultants are more skillful and comfortable with the technical skills, such as assessment and solution selection, than with the consultative and business skills needed to partner with clients. Therefore, they often move ahead with performance assessment, root cause analysis, and solution selection without first establishing a clear business need and without forming a partnership with their clients. The downside is that typically only learning solutions are implemented when a strong client partnership is absent.

8. Moving from evaluation of the solutions to evaluation of performance and operational impact. Measuring the impact of performance change and operational impact is more complex and difficult than measuring the amount of learning that has occurred. In addition, during the transition of a department, performance consultants are often overloaded with new responsibilities. These factors many times result in the evaluation of performance and operational impact taking place in the later stages of transition.

Go Wrongs

What can go wrong in this first step of the transition? Here are a couple of "go wrongs" we have observed.

- The learning department creates a new mission statement and changes its name. Learning consultants make the transition to the role of performance consultants. They are provided with new position descriptions and attend a performance-consulting-skills workshop. However, the workflow process and organizational structure are not changed. This being the case, performance consultants have been provided knowledge and skill regarding the consultative approach, but have been asked to perform in an unchanged work environment. Eventually, the lack of alignment between the work environment and the new skills results in the performance consultants continuing to follow the traditional approach. The work environment always prevails in situations in which skills and work environment are not aligned.

- The learning department begins the transition to a performance department without creating a transition plan. In this situation the learning consultants are asked to perform as performance consultants. However, without mileposts and transition goals, there is ambiguity. And this ambiguity typically results in a continuation of what has been done in the past. Goals must be established and progress monitored if there is to be a sustained change in on-the-job performance.

STEP 2: ALIGN THE PROCESS WITH THE PERFORMANCE MISSION

In his book *Serious Performance Consulting According to Rummler* (2004), Geary Rummler describes the need for alignment between organization goals, workflow process, and job requirements. He also makes the point that management must do the aligning. These principles are very relevant when making the transition to a performance department. The manager has the responsibility of aligning the workflow process, the structure, and the individuals within the department with the new mission statement. A process that is not aligned will result in the performers creating additional procedures that work around the process and that enable them to achieve the requirements of the job. How many times have you created a workaround for a software program that was not aligned with your job requirements? These workarounds take time away from more important tasks that have an impact on goal achievement.

Therefore, once you have determined the mission of your department, it is important to focus your attention on creating a workflow process that enables the department to achieve this new mission. Within the area of human performance improvement, many workflow processes have been described by various authors and practitioners. We encourage you to become familiar with the major performance-improvement processes that are most frequently described in the literature. Select two or three you believe are applicable to your department. Analyze each to determine how it can help you accomplish your department's mission and how it will support the department's characteristics that you determined as key. Also identify any potential challenges posed by each process.

A high-level process that we believe can support a performance department mission is shown in Figure 38.4. We offer it as one option to consider when designing the process for your department. Let us look at each of the four process phases separately.

Partnership Phase

In this phase you identify opportunities to work with clients on performance-improvement projects. Why is the partnership phase first? An experienced performance consultant provided the answer. When asked what was the most critical element of consulting, he answered, "your partnership with the client; without a partnership you can accomplish nothing." Our experience has been the same. To work effectively on performance-improvement projects, you must create a positive working partnership with your clients. This, of course, raises

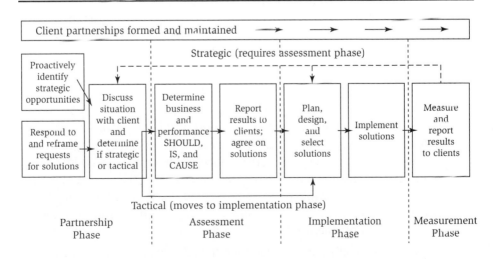

Figure 38.4. Four Phases of a Performance-Improvement Process.

two questions: Who is the client? How do you form partnerships with these individuals?

Let us first answer the question about who is the client. Your client is a person or team who

- Is responsible for achieving the business goals of the organization
- Manages, often through others, the performance of employees within the organization
- Has the most to gain or lose by the business goals being achieved
- Has the authority to make decisions and implement solutions associated with business goals and employee performance
- Can obtain the needed resources to build employee capability and address work environment barriers.

Now let us look at how you form partnerships with clients. In our book *Strategic Business Partner: Aligning People Strategies with Business Goals* (Robinson and Robinson, 2005), we describe three elements that are required in order to build and maintain ongoing partnerships with business leaders and managers. These are access, credibility, and trust: the ACT approach to partnering.

- *Access* consists of two components: (1) determining the specific owners of the business and performance needs and (2) gaining face time with those individuals. Performance consultants need to identify the managers who are the strategic decision makers. These are the managers who drive the business goals and are responsible for obtaining results. These managers are the ones with whom sustained client relationships are formed, when you invest time independent of any project work. It is important that performance consultants periodically meet, either personally or by phone, with each of their sustained clients. They need to stay current with the clients' business requirements, challenges, and strategic initiatives. These meetings are an excellent venue in which to clarify the performance consultant's role and to build credibility.
- *Credibility* refers to the client's confidence that the performance consultant can and will deliver results in support of the business. This requires a deep understanding of the client's business goals and strategies. Clients want to partner with performance consultants who understand both the organization's business model and the external forces having an impact on the organization. To build credibility, performance consultants need knowledge of both human performance improvement processes *and* business systems; knowledge of only one is insufficient.
- *Trust* means the client is confident that the performance consultant will work with integrity and reliability to achieve results in support of the

business. Developing trust requires congruence between what the consultants say and what they do. Trust has been developed with a business leader when that person has confidence in the moral and ethical code of the consultant. Performance consultants can demonstrate that code in multiple ways: by honoring the confidentiality of information and sources and by openly discussing and confronting issues of potential conflict and ethics with their clients. Trust is also developed when clients see that consultant's actions are in the best interest of the organization and demonstrate respect for individuals affected by those actions.

Developing partnerships is key to success in this phase of work. The goal is to leverage these partnerships so that strategic performance-improvement projects are identified. These projects can be identified in a reactive or proactive manner. When working reactively, the performance consultant is responding to a request from someone in the organization. Typically these requests are of a tactical nature, for example, "I would like to discuss bringing some type of negotiation training to employees within procurement." It is vital that the performance consultant reframe this type of request into a discussion about the performance and business results the manager is seeking. Some of the requests that begin reactively will transform into strategic performance-improvement opportunities.

Performance-improvement projects can also be identified proactively. In this option the performance consultant initiates the discussion, using the time to discuss the leader's business goals and needs. This in-depth business discussion often results in a performance-improvement project that would not have been identified but for this discussion. The good news with this option is that almost any need identified *will* be strategic in purpose, as it is emanating directly from a business need.

Clearly one of the key performance accomplishments of the partnering phase is to identify strategic performance-improvement opportunities. It is also vital that performance consultants be able to clearly delineate those projects that should be managed in a tactical manner from those that qualify for a strategic approach.

Assessment Phase

In this phase you obtain the information needed to ensure that appropriate solutions can be taken. This generally involves identifying what *should* be happening for both business goals and the on-the-job performance of specific workgroups. It also includes a gap analysis to identify specific areas where the *should* business goals are not being achieved or where *should* performance is not being demonstrated. When the gaps are identified, you conduct a cause analysis to determine the root causes for the gaps. This cause information enables you and your clients to determine the appropriate solutions for closing the gaps.

Implementation Phase

Here you design or purchase the appropriate solutions and implement them in a manner that closes the gaps, enabling the organization to achieve its business goals. The primary concept, of course, is that a single solution by itself will not bring about sustained change, because almost always there is more than one root cause of a workgroup's performance gap. Therefore, multiple solutions are needed to change workgroup performance and to close the gap between actual business results and business goals. Often in this phase some solutions are managed by the performance department and some are managed by other functions, both within and outside the organization.

Measurement Phase

In this phase you determine the effectiveness of the solutions that have been implemented. Because multiple solutions have been utilized, the measurement phase should focus on the results achieved by the total set of solutions, including the changes in workgroup performance and the business results. Following are some questions for which you may want answers on each performance-improvement project:

1. Did each solution produce the intended results? What were the actual results of each solution? How do these compare to the intended results?

2. Did the on-the-job performance change as expected? If sufficient performance change did not occur, what are the reasons?

3. Were the desired business results achieved? If there is still a gap between desired and actual business results, what are the reasons for the gap?

4. Were your clients satisfied with the results achieved and the manner by which the work was done? If they were not satisfied, what are the causes of this dissatisfaction?

Other Issues to Consider

When designing the workflow process for your department, make sure to consider the relationships with other people functions within your organization. How is the role of your department unique from, and yet supportive of, the roles of human resources, organization development, and organizational effectiveness? If the roles of each department are overlapping or unclear, there will be problems in the future. You are always better off to anticipate this type of conflict before it occurs. So initiate discussions with the leaders of those functions. This way you can carve out a process that does not overlap and will facilitate synergy between the functions.

Now that the workflow process has been determined, it is important to communicate with everyone within your own function so they clearly understand the process and their role in it. In addition, discuss the process with those in other people functions, clarifying the interfaces and handoffs from one department to another.

Go Wrongs

What can go wrong in this step? There are two potential problems we have observed:

- The performance department fails to clarify the process and techniques for forming partnerships with key line managers. Therefore, the performance consultants use trial and error to form those partnerships with limited success. This results in many performance consultants continuing to do traditional, rather than strategic, work with their clients.

- The performance department forms its performance consulting process independent of the other people functions such as human resources. While this enables the department to quickly form the process, it also invites problems further down the road. As the performance consultants form partnerships with line manager clients, conflict can occur with the human resource consultants, who believe that they are primarily responsible for the client partnerships. This not only results in conflict between the performance-improvement and human resources departments, but can create confusion for the client about the role of each department. Our experience has been that line managers prefer to have a single point of contact for the people functions. Clarifying accountability for client partnerships is key to supporting this client preference.

STEP 3: ALIGN STRUCTURE WITH THE PERFORMANCE MISSION

Structure follows process. Now that you have determined the workflow process for your function, it is time to align the structure with that process. There are two primary components to structure: the organization chart and the type of work to be done.

Let us look at the organization chart first. Here you are structuring your department in a manner that supports the process. This means arranging the boxes on the organization chart so that your function can be successful in accomplishing its mission. Figure 38.5 shows two possible configurations.

In option 1, the performance department is aligned so that each performance team supports a specific line of business. Each team typically consists of two or more individuals, headed by a lead consultant. The makeup of the other team members depends on the responsibilities of the team. For example, does each

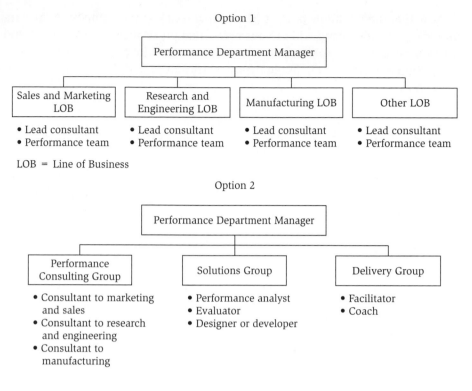

Figure 38.5. Options for Organizational Structure.

team do its own assessment, or is that done by a central group? Does each team facilitate the delivery of learning, or is that done by another group? The advantage of this approach is that each team is dedicated to a specific line of business. The risk is that a team may be influenced by the line of business to deviate from the performance-improvement process, resulting in a more traditional approach to learning. This option also can result in duplication of work. It is vital that communication links be developed across the lines of business so each team can benefit from the work of other teams.

The option 2 shows a department structure in which a performance consulting group supports several lines of business. The performance consultants in this group form the partnerships and identify performance-improvement opportunities. When analysis or delivery is required, the performance consultants use the services of the solutions or delivery group. One of the primary benefits from this structure is the operational efficiency that can result. There is a central group of experts in the area of analysis or delivery that any performance consultant, working with a line of business, can utilize. A problem can result when those in the performance consulting group act as gatekeepers, making it difficult for those who design and deliver the solutions to have direct access to the clients whose project they are supporting.

A second element in forming structure is to consider how the three types of work will be accomplished. You may recall our discussion about transactional, tactical, and strategic work earlier in this chapter. In the transition to a performance-improvement focus, the percentage of strategic work will increase. For the performance department manager, a challenge will be to balance and accomplish these three very different types of work. What will be done to reduce the amount of transactional and tactical work so that there is room on the plates of the performance consultants and others to identify and address strategic business needs? Many leaders of learning functions look to technology and outsourcing as options for managing tactical and transactional work. The bottom line is that you need to structure your department so that there is time for people to work on strategic performance-improvement initiatives. In this way they are working on the important, not just the urgent.

Go Wrongs

A couple of items we have seen go wrong in this step are

- The performance-improvement manager creates an appropriate mission and a process that supports that mission, but does not change the organizational structure. This often results in the performance consultants continuing to support the type of work and business units that they previously supported. There is little time or incentive to change the type of work they are doing, including the time needed to form partnerships with clients, so everything remains the same.

- The performance department manager does not take steps to reduce the amount of transactional work. The result is that the performance consultants lack time to proactively identify strategic projects. Therefore, they continue to react to requests from the business leaders, most of which are for standalone learning solutions.

STEP 4: ALIGN PEOPLE WITH THE PERFORMANCE MISSION

Once you have formed the structure of your department, it is time to identify those individuals who will be placed in each of the jobs within your department. Your goal is to have the right people for the right jobs. While there are often several different jobs within a performance department, including instructional designers and e-learning specialists, we will focus on the job of performance consultant. Of course this job actually has a variety of job titles, including performance technologist, learning and performance consultant, relationship manager, and performance solutions consultant. In this chapter we have chosen to use the title of performance consultant. Whatever the job title, the first step is to determine the competencies required for success. Figure 38.6 lists and describes twelve

---

COMPETENCIES

1. *Analysis skill:* Obtaining, synthesizing, and reporting data, both narrative and quantitative.

2. *Business knowledge:* Knowledge of how businesses function and achieve success; knowledge of these factors for the organization specifically being supported.

3. *Change management skill:* Guiding others to identify and take required actions in support of a performance change initiative.

4. *Facilitation skill:* Managing meetings and group processes to ensure that the objectives of the group are achieved.

5. *Human performance technology understanding:* Knowledge of HPT as a discipline, as well as knowledge of the work of those who are its primary leaders and thinkers.

6. *Influencing skill:* Gaining acceptance of an idea through interpersonal skills and persuasion.

7. *Learning systems and process knowledge:* Knowledge of multiple learning interventions and systems that can be used as solutions when addressing performance and learning needs relative to business goals.

8. *Project management skill:* Planning, organizing, and monitoring work done by others in support of a specific project or assignment.

9. *Questioning skill:* Gathering information through the process of interviews and other probing methods.

10. *Relationship-building skill:* Establishing and maintaining collaborative partnerships with individuals across a broad range of people and groups.

11. *Strategic thinking skill:* Obtaining information and identifying key issues and requirements relevant to achieving an organization's long-range goal or vision.

12. *Systemic thinking skill:* Viewing the organization as a system, recognizing that the success of the whole is dependent on the integration, understanding, and inclusion of all segments; considering the "big picture."

ATTRIBUTES

1. *Behavioral flexibility:* Readiness to modify approach or performance when the situation requires it.

2. *Objectivity:* Maintaining a bias-free approach to situations and people.

3. *Self-confidence:* Managing one's own performance in an effective manner when placed in new or challenging situations.

4. *Tolerance for ambiguity:* Demonstrating comfort in situations in which the goals or process to achieve goals are unclear and difficult to determine.

Figure 38.6. Competencies for Performance Consultants.

competencies that we have found critical to the success of performance consultants. These competencies reflect skills and knowledge that individuals must develop to be successful in their jobs. In addition, the table lists four attributes which are also critical to the success of performance consultants. Attributes describe characteristics or traits that are more difficult to develop on the job. Therefore, it is wise to select people who have these attributes rather than attempt to develop them through skill development.

Why are we providing you with a list of competencies and attributes for performance consultants and not for other jobs in a performance department, such as performance analyst or learning strategist? Because the role of performance consultant is typically a new role for learning functions that are making the transition into performance-improvement functions, many of the results expected of performance consultants have not been focused on in a traditional function. Performance consultants are expected to

- Form and build business-based partnerships with key clients in the organization
- Identify, in both a reactive and proactive manner, strategic performance-improvement projects to support
- Influence and guide clients in making decisions regarding the solutions required to address the performance and business needs
- Manage performance-improvement projects, ensuring that the completed work is yielding the results desired by the client
- Partner with clients throughout projects, ensuring that the client is actively engaged throughout
- Coordinate the work of others who design and deliver solutions throughout the project

The success of your department's transition will be largely influenced by the effectiveness with which your performance consultants fulfill these expectations. While your current department may have experienced individuals, it is important to determine if those individuals have or can develop the competencies and attributes shown in Figure 38.6. Individuals who are in the role or job of performance consultant, but lack some of the competencies and attributes, will most likely disappoint both themselves and you. Now is the time to make the tough decisions regarding staffing of your function.

Most likely those individuals identified as performance consultants will require some development. The competencies most often requiring additional skill include business knowledge, influencing skill, questioning skill, and strategic thinking. Of course, there are many ways to develop people other than through classroom experience. Having designated coaches assigned to new performance consultants is an effective option. Coaches can help individual performance consultants prepare for an activity, such as a proactive business goals discussion with a client. They can also observe the new performance consultant during the proactive meeting, providing feedback after the meeting. This is a great way to develop members of your team.

Go Wrongs

Even when aligning people with the performance mission, things can go wrong. A couple of go wrongs we have observed are noted here.

- Providing skill development without on-the-job coaching and reinforcement. There will always be new and challenging situations to be faced, for example a resistant client or a business situation filled with ambiguity. Performance consultants need continued support to ensure skill application and continued growth in competence.

- Assigning individuals to the role of performance consultant when they lack tolerance for ambiguity. When forming partnerships with business leaders and working on strategic projects, performance consultants encounter numerous situations in which uncertainty reigns. One new performance consultant who was just beginning to work on a strategic project was asked, "How is it going?" Her response was, "Pretty good, but I would feel a lot better if I knew what the answer was to this problem." Unfortunately, individuals who are uncomfortable with ambiguity are likely to focus on solutions too quickly. Performance consultants need to trust the process, acknowledging that it may take some time before appropriate solutions can be identified.

STEP 5: START SMALL; GET SOME EARLY WINS

There is a go wrong in this step that you want to make sure you avoid. The go wrong is that it takes too long to show results from your transformation. Therefore, you want to make sure that your performance consultants identify performance-improvement projects quickly and complete those projects expeditiously. This way you show your clients some early wins. First projects should be relatively small in scope and have a high probability of success. The project must be completed within a few weeks rather than a few months. An example of a fast-moving project took place in a large regional bank in which a performance consultant was asked by a vice president to determine the reasons why a new operations center was not achieving its business goals. The workgroup having the greatest impact on these business results were operators who processed the transactions through the center. Because the work process had been well-defined and the desired performance of the operators had been determined, the performance consultant focused on a cause analysis to determine the reasons for the operators not performing at the level required. Through documentation review, interviews with both the center's managers and supervisors and focus groups with operators, the performance consultant was able to identify the major factors affecting the operators' performance. Within one week, the performance consultant obtained this information and reported the results of the analysis to her client. Appropriate solutions were implemented immediately. Within a few weeks the performance of the operators was improving, and at the end of six months the center was achieving its operational goals. This project is a good example of what types of situations can help you "start small and get some early wins." Look for situations in which

- There is a clear-cut business need with operational metrics.
- The client will provide you with access to the appropriate people and information.
- You can focus on one location and one workgroup.
- The required information can be gathered within a few days.

TRANSITION STRATEGIES

A major challenge during a transition is to identify and initiate strategic projects without neglecting the traditional work that your current clients expect. There are several strategies that can enable some of your staff to be working on strategic projects while others continue to operate in a business-as-usual manner:

Project-based pilots: This transition strategy is often appropriate when a business need within a line of business is apparent. You initiate a meeting with the client and agree on a performance-improvement project. The remainder of the performance department operates in a business-as-usual mode, while the project is implemented within that line of business. Given success, the client for the project is encouraged to assist the performance department in marketing this new approach to others. For this strategy to be successful, agree with your team on the criteria for identifying a first project. Also ensure that there is an obvious business need to which the project is linked.

Client assignment: In this option, some members of the department are redeployed to work as performance consultants to one or more lines of business. These performance consultants build quality relationships with clients and identify opportunities for strategic performance-based work. As the projects are identified, others within the department are asked to support the projects for the assessment, implementation, and measurement phases. This strategy requires that one or more individuals are dedicated to the role of performance consultant. Be certain to provide them with sufficient time to build client relationships.

Project scope enlargement: In this option, the performance consultants use a "yes, and" approach to reframe the solution. When the client asks the performance consultant to implement the solution, the consultant responds, "Yes, we can do that, and it will be important also to discover any work environment factors that might derail the solution." Here the initial scope of the solution is enlarged to include determining work environment factors that would be barriers to project success. The client's request for a solution is reframed into a performance-improvement project. This strategy requires that performance consultants have the expertise to question clients and reframe requests for a solution into discussions of the business and performance results needed.

Some additional factors to consider when making the transition to a performance-improvement department include the following:

Commit strong leadership to the transition. As with any change, the transition to a performance-improvement department will not come without pain. When this pain does occur, you, as department manager, must demonstrate resolve to continue the transition. If your resolve is not evident, the transition will slow down and eventually stop. Do not be blindsided. Expect that there will be resistance to the transition. In fact, the most common resistance comes from those within your own department. Often individuals who are comfortable in their current positions will try to protect the status quo. They may attempt to enlist others to help them with the resistance. So throughout the transition, it is important that you stay in touch with the people within your department, acknowledging and responding to concerns while evidencing commitment to the transition.

Ensure that performance consultants have direct access to clients. Without direct access to the business leaders, it is impossible for the performance consultants to build partnerships. Partnerships are built on credibility and trust, which can be developed only through ongoing contact with clients. If there are barriers to client access, take action to remove them.

Execute, execute, execute. Many managers have the mistaken belief that once a decision is made and people have been informed, the decision will be implemented quickly and successfully. In their book *Execution: The Discipline of Getting Things Done,* Larry Bossidy and Ram Charan (2002) indicate that good execution is the best means for bringing about change and transition within an organization. So look at the transition of your department as an evolution, not a revolution. Realize that it will take months to complete the transition, and the function operates as you envisioned when you formed the mission. Your role is to create mileposts to measure progress toward the transition. In addition, you must monitor the transition, so that if there is a derailing, you can take appropriate action.

SUMMARY

When making the transition from a learning department to a performance department, use human performance technology concepts to develop a transformation plan. The major steps in a plan are

1. Agree on a desired end state
2. Align the process with the performance mission
3. Align structure with the performance mission
4. Align people with the performance mission
5. Start small; get some early wins

Be alert to what can go wrong. Monitor your department's progress during the transition. View the transition as an evolution, not a revolution.

References

Bossidy, L., and Charan, R. (2002). *Execution: The discipline of getting things done.* New York: Crown Business.

Covey, S. R. (1989). *The 7 habits of highly effective people.* New York: Free Press.

Robinson, D. G., and Robinson, J. C. (2005). *Strategic business partner: Aligning people strategies with business goals.* San Francisco: Berrett-Koehler.

Rummler, G. A. (2004). *Serious performance consulting according to Rummler.* Silver Spring, MD: International Society for Performance Improvement.

CHAPTER THIRTY-NINE

Using an HPT Model to Become Management's Partner

Danny Langdon

Human performance technology (HPT), as noted throughout this book, can bring enormous results-based, valued-added benefits to organizations at every level of work performance. These benefits range from those of the individual workers or jobs to those of teams, core processes, performance management of work execution, business problem solving, and the alignment of work levels to cultural issues and to their resolutions. HPT not only concerns itself with how work is executed and how it can be improved but also addresses the entire culture that supports the execution of work. HPT can be used as an analytical, systemic problem-solving methodology. The work of HPT researchers and practitioners such as Gilbert, Rummler, Tosti, Lineberry, Kaufman, Langdon, Brethower, Carleton, and many others has contributed mightily to the overall understanding of performance and the improvement of organizations (Dean and Ripley, 1997).

How is it that these exemplary human performance technologists are trusted by business to be of help in improving performance? Certainly the use of a systematic methodology that has evolved over four decades has been a key factor. Through research and practice, the exchange of ideas and case studies, we simply know more about what performance is today and how to improve it. We have a better idea of how to identify performance gaps, select interventions, develop solutions, implement, and assess for performance effectiveness than we did just a few years ago. Furthermore, the use of techniques such as partnering, best practices, branding, modeling success with others, and using HPT within other programmatic approaches such as total quality, Six Sigma, competency management, and others has helped the HPT field to come closer to becoming management's partner.

Still, it remains common knowledge based on all too common experience that, with very few exceptions, HPT has generally not yet become management's ongoing partner in the same ways that such disciplines as information technology (IT), health and safety, quality assurance, and other support functions have. Can HPT ever be management's partner on an ongoing basis? Can it be the partner that they cannot do without, their *must-have* partner, the *go-to* partner to continuously identify or help solve issues of work performance as they emerge? Can HPT become a partner that is not eliminated or severely reduced in numbers and influence in hard economic times? Is it not the hard times when work performance improvement is even more needed by management? Should HPT be part of the solution, rather than being perceived as part of the problem or something to be ignored? We are well on the way to that partnership goal, but we are certainly not there yet. This chapter proposes a step in the direction of partnership based on experience and use of an HPT model in successfully meeting management's ongoing needs.

With a few exceptions, such as the work of Geary Rummler and Alan Brache (1990), it is my view that the HPT model espoused by the International Society for Performance Improvement (ISPI) and the American Society for Training and Development (ASTD) does not address operationally how to become management's partner. That is not to say that the model advocated by both professional groups when used in organizations has not contributed to making significant strides in meeting various business needs. However, its success has been hit or miss rather than systemwide, and the model is not continuously used in recognizable business applications. I contend that a significant reason for lack of continuous partnering with management has been the absence of a model of performance that mirrors or reflects how business executes work, supports that work, and uses HPT interventions to make improvements or to solve knotty business problems. Furthermore, whatever models exist have not been placed squarely in the control and use of management but rather have been held for internal use by HPT specialists, whether they work internally for an organization or are external consultants. This chapter will suggest one step in the direction of emulating work execution and building on it through the principles and procedures of the generally accepted HPT Model (see Figure 39.1). It will also suggest a mode of work improvement that can reside under the control of management both in its initial analytical use and thereafter as part of the execution and improvement of

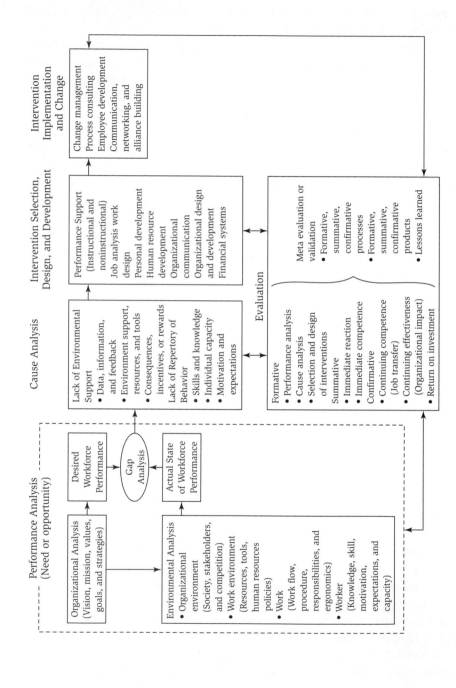

Figure 39.1. The ISPI Human Performance Technology Model.

Source: International Society for Performance Improvement. Used with permission.

work. This version of an HPT model, known as the "Language of Work," has been used successfully in a number of business applications to emulate and improve work performance successfully on an ongoing basis. Management has found it a user-friendly model, and one they can continue to use to understand and make their work performance better, as well as to respond to changes that are always certain to emerge or to be planned. The Language of Work Model is not complete, as of yet, and should be expanded upon through further research and practice so that it can reach the ultimate goal of being totally valued by management as a cannot-do-without tool. Indeed, it has the potential of being a viable "dashboard" approach to reflect, measure, and improve business operations as they happen in real-world time. By presenting the Language of Work HPT model here in the context of the existing and generally accepted HPT Model, I invite your consideration of its merit, as well as challenge you to expand upon your own HPT experience and then communicate that experience to the general community of HPT practitioners.

BUILDING ON THE CURRENT HPT MODEL

Having been in the HPT field for about forty years now, it seems to me that we have to recognize that businesses and organizations could benefit and would want to partner with us more closely if we were but able to do two fundamental things for them regarding their work: (1) provide a work performance model that emulates what work is to be accomplished and how, and (2) provide them access to that work model so that they own and continuously use it to understand and improve their work on their own. We would, of course, provide any ongoing support they need, especially through an integrated HR system, as will be suggested later.

A Model of Work Performance for Work Execution

Traditionally, we have based our understanding and definition of performance solely on statements in the forms of objectives, competencies, outcomes, or what has been labeled generically in the performance technology field as performance gaps. Certainly, these orientations to defining performance and then measuring and developing solutions, that is, interventions, have been useful since it is hoped they provide management and workers with a clear sense of what is to be achieved and, if necessary, improved upon through use of the rest of our technology, namely the right interventions, good implementation, and measurement to ensure that performance has been improved. However, this sort of goals- and results-based-only orientation to work performance has unfortunately thus far limited our understanding of and ability to operationalize work for those who perform it, as well as for those of us trying to help performers improve it. What is absent from our current definition of work performance is the way those results are intended to be achieved, and I am not referring to interventions and solutions.

Performance is a cause and an effect, or, better said for our purposes here, an effect and a cause relationship. Typically, HPT practitioners have defined only the effect, or desired result, but not the cause as part of the performance definition. This will be described in more detail later. Cause is what the organization or person does to execute work or performance in order to produce the results. I argue that a more complete definition of what constitutes performance, both effect and cause, is needed. Thinking in terms of effect and cause will better define performance gaps and improve understanding and work performance; it will mirror or reflect what performance is supposed to be. To do our work as HPT professionals we need to teach management an expanded definition of performance and then show managers how to measure that performance and how to use the knowledge gained to improve their collective work performance with workers. When we do this, we have found that management and workers are more accepting and more willing to partner with us and to use our technology.

Management Owning and Using HPT Continuously

There is no better way to ensure that managers will use our human performance technology than to ensure that they own it, rather than perceiving that we own it and have come to use it on them. Unless management and workers are convinced that the work execution model is something they can use on their own, they are unlikely to be committed to using it on an ongoing basis. Is it possible to work in such a way that management owns the model? Actually, my experience shows that it is quite possible.

My experience shows that providing management with a facilitated process in which we introduce a model of work execution in ten short minutes and then immediately engage managers in defining their work to better understand it, usually in the form of core processes and jobs, works superbly. Managers immediately see the value of the model in defining clearly what their work is and how, with newfound clarity, they can make improvements. It is to some extent a forest-for-the-trees phenomenon: because managers are so close to the work, they need our technology, that is, both a telescope and a microscope, to observe the work and share a common understanding of it.

A key to owning and using a work execution model is being able to define work at the various levels at which it exists within an organization. You will be introduced to four levels of work within an organization. However, defining work at the level of the individual or the job level is most important and relevant to management's acceptance of our technology. I consider the individual job to also include the performance of workers in teams. Until such time as the individual workers, with the manager, understand and use an HPT model together, they will not know, perceive, or use HPT on an ongoing basis to make improvements in their own work. They will, frankly, just continue doing their jobs. They generally do not like change anyway since it is upsetting, so their feeling will be "Why bother?" Even when employees are change-agile and look forward to change, they generally do not know how to go about making such changes themselves, let alone collectively. As with management, in using any approach to performance execution and performance improvement, there is a What's in it for me? focus. What is needed is an easy way for a worker to use a performance model to improve his or her own performance. Combine the individual acceptance of HPT with a manager's use of the same performance model, and then you have a powerful, mutually beneficial performance tool. And because both workers and management own it and use it on their own and collectively, they are more disposed to accept additional support from other departments such as human resources (HR), training, organizational development (OD), and others.

The refinements to the current HPT model that will be suggested here would be owned by managers and workers, using our help as experts in the application and use of the performance model. But the managers and workers would conduct their own analyses, do their own assessment to identify performance gaps, do their own identification and selection of needed solutions and accompanying interventions, and do their own implementation and evaluation to prove what has worked and what remains to be improved. In all this, HPT is *their* model to meet *their* work needs. Our role as HPT specialists is to serve as educators, practitioners, consultants, experts in theory and interventions, and facilitators who help the business use the HPT model we have developed for them: a model that we help to improve in speed and effectiveness year after year through practice and research. From my perspective, this approach to HPT recognizes that they, managers and workers, do the work; they know the work intimately and simply need our help to see it clearly. It is their work; they are best suited to improve it. What they need from us, their performance partners, is a way to define that work clearly in order to achieve full understanding and consensus; to ask the right questions and measure the results, and to analyze the situation completely in order to develop and implement the right solutions. Management becomes its own change agent using an HPT model as the preferred competency of work understanding, implementation, and improvement.

THE LANGUAGE OF WORK AS AN HPT MODEL OF WORK EXECUTION

The Language of Work Model is an HPT model that I devised in the early 1990s. I have written books (Langdon, 1995, 2000) and numerous articles about it, and white papers on various business applications, but most important, I have refined it in many business settings. In the past few years, the approach has been used successfully in a few companies, has become management's and workers' performance model, and is being used within an arsenal of various programmatic approaches that these organizations have also been using, such as Six Sigma, competency initiatives, and so on. I have noted in this context that using the Language of Work Model has been easier and more widely accepted because, I believe, programs such as Six Sigma have made managers and workers more receptive to HPT models such as the Language of Work. This is said to help the reader recognize that my efforts in business have been successful not just because of the Language of Work Model but because of the effective use of a combination of initiatives. The contribution is, I hope, that the model of performance is one that managers and workers can readily accept, use, and continue long after I have moved on to other parts of an organization or other companies.

The Language of Work Model will be described here in the context of the generally accepted HPT methodology as defined by ISPI (Figure 39.1). Rather than a mere recounting of the five basic stages of HPT, a view of performance will be delineated that models or replicates work performance in organizations. This subtle but very powerful difference between merely identifying and stating performance gaps, as is the usual practice of HPT professionals, and moving toward replicating work execution as espoused in the Language of Work Model, is key to becoming management's partner. We shall also see that it is the key to the use of my performance model by management and, as important, is an operational performance model that can be used by human resources and other business support groups to further assist management's use of HPT on an ongoing basis.

It is noteworthy to mention that there are multiple ways to introduce the Language of Work Model to management. On a macro level there is the reorganization of a company or department, while at the micro level there is the approach of individual job modeling and improvement of performance for or by individuals. The emphasis in this chapter will be more on the macro application, since that allows a more extensive partnering with management at different levels in the organization, and it exemplifies the broader use of HPT in several of its possible dimensions. I place the Language of Work Model within the existing ISPI HPT paradigm so as to emphasize its value in partnering with management. I will be glad to provide to those who inquire the several other ways in which the Language of Work Model has been successfully used to analyze and implement business and organizational improvement and job-level applications, to manage performance, and to solve specific business problems.

PLACING THE LANGUAGE OF WORK MODEL WITHIN THE ISPI HPT MODEL

As noted in Figure 39.1, the HPT Model is defined as a five-stage, continuous-looped technology or systems approach. The steps include (1) performance analysis; (2) cause analysis; (3) intervention selection, design, and development; (4) intervention implementation and change; and (5) evaluation.

Performance Analysis

In describing the Language of Work as a model for management partnering, I shall give primary attention to performance analysis. It is the first and most critical stage in getting managers and workers to understand a way to model their work execution and work support. The success of each of the four steps that follow the performance-analysis step is dependent on the reflection, clarity, and accuracy of the model used to do a performance analysis, in this case, the Language of Work Model. Cause analysis; intervention selection, design, and development; intervention implementation and change; and evaluation will be described as affected by the Language of Work Model, but to a lesser extent. This is not to suggest that any step is any less important.

As noted in the ISPI HPT Model, performance analysis is divided into three parts: organizational analysis; environmental analysis; and gap analysis, including desired and actual workforce analysis. For our purposes here, I assume that the organizational analysis has been done. We call it the value proposition in most of our engagements.

I will begin the description of the Language of Work Model as an HPT model for partnering by describing how it is used by managers and workers to define, in order, the elements of "work," "worker," and "work environment" found collectively in the HPT Model under environmental analysis. It is suggested that as the Language of Work Model is described, you periodically review the HPT model in Figure 39.1. Assume that the organizational analysis and the organizational environment, within the environmental analysis, have already been defined by management with or without your help, but with your full understanding.

Defining Work as an Element of Environmental Analysis

The goal of becoming management's partner builds on the direction management has set by defining work as identified in the HPT model under environmental analysis. What is critical for practitioners is to recognize that we need to provide managers with a work and performance model that mirrors or reflects operationally how they currently operate, that is, *As Is,* as well as how they intend to do their work to achieve their organizational analysis, that is *To Be,* in light of their organizational environment (see the HPT Model in Figure 39.1). Sometimes you might proceed directly to the To Be work definition, but more often both As Is and To Be would be defined. In doing this analysis, management and the workforce move from a vague notion of *work* to a clear and concise consensus of *work* that is not just results-driven but *execution*-defined and driven to results.

The operational *execution of work* model being proposed here is fundamentally different from the approach more often used by management and by most practitioners of HPT. In current practice, emphasis is given to a results-only approach to defining performance or work. The emphasis is on defining work as a combination of such statements and descriptions in the form of goals, objectives, outcomes, competencies, so-called performance gaps, or other versions of results-only analysis. The reader will note that these are all definitions of only the desired results, which are important but do not describe *how* the work will be executed to achieve these results. By contrast, the Language of Work Model calls for the definition of *work* in terms of both results, or effect, and work execution, or cause. The Language of Work Model identifies six systemic elements that reflect and represent the totality of work performance. These are illustrated in Figure 39.2. They are *outputs* and *consequences* as the results specification, and *inputs, conditions, process steps,* and *feedback.* All six elements together should be used to reflect or mirror what I call *work execution.*

When the model of work execution, implicit in the Language of Work Model, is applied by management and workers to define, to measure, and to improve work, then they can paint clear work definitions for their business as a whole using the *business-unit model.* For their key core processes they can use the *core-process model.* For individual work, the *job model* is of use, and for work groups and teams, the *work-group model* can be used (see Figures 39.3 and 39.4).

Furthermore, when all four levels of work are defined in an organization using the common Language of Work six-element model, these four levels of work definition can be *aligned* to each other to more clearly achieve the organization's purposes, including vision, mission, goals, and so on. When we as HPT practitioners are able to bring such a model of work execution to management and workers through skilled facilitation, they can then define and improve *their* business by *their* own efforts, and then they understand and use us as partners. We have helped them with what they have not achieved on their own, an operational understanding of what work performance is and how it is and

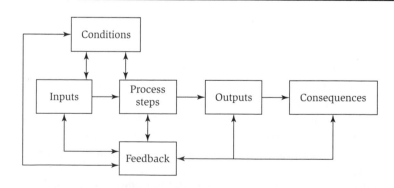

Figure 39.2. The Language of Work Model.

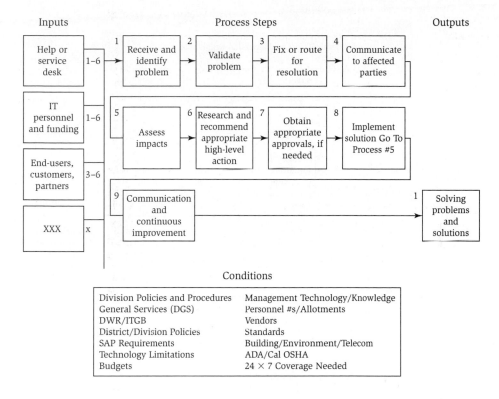

Figure 39.3. IT Core Process (partial).

Note: Consequences, Feedback, and other processes are not illustrated here.

should be performed. To this operational understanding of work execution we can then add many other work-improvement tools, such as how to measure, how to set standards, and how to meet work-support needs as well as interventions that are all part of being the best they can be for the benefit of the entire organization. When we make them look good, then they value us for our contribution to their success. We are partners.

Defining Worker as an Element of Environmental Analysis

In using the Language of Work Model, note that the definition of work takes the form of "business-unit" and "core-process" models. The business-unit model captures *what* the business will be. The core-process models capture *how* the business will produce the *what,* namely products and services. A much abbreviated core process model for illustrative purposes of the six key elements is shown in Figure 39.3.

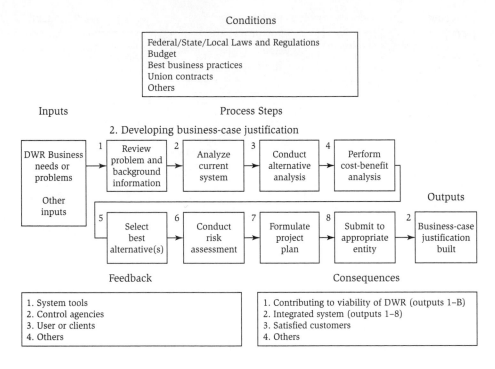

Figure 39.4. Business Analyst Job Model (partial).

The key to partnering with management at the worker level is to have a way for the individual and teams of individuals to know specifically how they are supposed to execute the work as defined in a core-process model. How they do their work is supposed to be, in this sense, aligned to the intent defined by management in the core processes. Since the Language of Work Model can be used to define core processes and jobs using the same six elements of work, it is relatively easy to align or match the two levels of work. Indeed one of the difficulties faced by management and technical personnel has been how to get the worker to see exactly how to execute the well-defined core processes. This has been solved by the use of job models that match perfectly to the core-process models through use of the same six-word performance paradigm.

A *job model,* a partial version of which is illustrated in Figure 39.4, as a definition of worker, is composed of the same six elements of work previously defined as part of the Language of Work Model: inputs, conditions, process steps, outputs, consequences, and feedback. Once these jobs or roles are defined, it is a relatively easy matter to attach or specify the underpinning skills and knowledge for the inputs, conditions, process steps, and feedback that are required to execute the four elements of work that achieve the outputs and consequences. For HPT practitioners, this method removes brainstorming about the needed skills and knowledge identification because we can now tie skills and knowledge directly to the work execution. Equally so, other perceived job- or worker-specification needs, such as competencies, attributes, capacity, entry skills, and so on, can also be identified and attached with the job models. In so doing, the worker knows explicitly what and how to perform, the manager knows what and how the workers are to perform, and meaningful measurements and discussions between both parties can be much more explicit. For example, I have found that the Language of Work Model serves as a far more meaningful performance-review process when based on results, that is, outputs and consequences as well as cause, which is inputs, conditions, process steps, and feedback. Managers and workers can then see what skills, knowledge, motivational attributes, and other work influences need to be worked on, since they are directly tied to the job model. In turn, HR can more easily select the right person for the right job when basing that selection on the job model and related attributes.

The description of job models using the six-element Language of Work Model can be easily applied to define teams of workers. The worker element of environmental analysis in the HPT model is not just about individual workers. It must also concern workers working in teams, or what the Language of Work Model defines as *work groups.* It is not difficult to see that the six-element Language of Work Model can be used to define, communicate, and improve work groups, including teams. In so doing, we can align the work-group performance with the other three levels of work: business unit, core processes, and jobs.

Defining the Work Environment as an Element of Environmental Analysis

All work execution must operate and be managed within a work environment. The more clearly that work environment can be specified, understood, and aligned to work execution, the more overall, systemic improvement can be ensured.

In the Language of Work Model, work environment is labeled "work support." A detailed matrix of organizational work-support needs can be found in Langdon, 2000. As Don Tosti, Claude Lineberry, and Bob Carleton have noted, these work-support needs represent the elements that any healthy organization would want to provide to workers and managers so they can execute the work with as few obstacles as possible (Dean and Ripley, 1997; Carleton and Lineberry, 2004). Healthy organizations are able to achieve maximum organizational effectiveness and efficiency though attention to ensuring a good work environment.

Without reviewing the work-support matrix in detail here, work support essentially maintains that a variety of interventions must be provided by an organization, that is, management, for everyone in the organization to use the inputs, follow the conditions, implement the process steps, and use and attend to the feedback to produce the outputs and achieve the consequences of work. This is just as true at the individual job level as it is at the other three levels of work: business unit, core processes, and work groups. This *cultural due diligence,* as it is often referred to by authors such as Carleton and Lineberry (2004), is the responsibility of management. When managers are aware of, assess, and use a work-support matrix, they understand how to view and improve work support in relation to work execution, a performance-alignment need in all organizations. As HPT practitioners, our task is to bring this knowledge of work-support needs to management in light of the attention we have given to the work and worker models previously described. For example, in the course of a performance-consulting engagement, when the core-process models, that is work and job models and worker definitions, are completed, managers and workers are asked "What needs fixing?" in the work environment relative to each model of work execution. These *performance gaps* in work support become important needs to improve upon, just as the gaps in work execution need to be identified and improved. In other, more formal organizational scans for work support, such as described by Carleton and Lineberry (2004), the performance gaps are identified by surveys and focus groups that detail the range of support that should be improved in organizational improvement efforts in general and specifically in business reorganizations and mergers.

As another consideration of work support, HPT practitioners in general must attend to the human resources support function in order to become partners with management. Human resources, including personnel selection, personnel development, career development, and so on, is a work-support function as defined in the Language of Work Model. Rather than being merely a service to management, or worse yet viewed as a necessary evil, HR needs to find a new and better way to partner with management. Such a partnership is possible when the very model used to define and align the organization's work execution and culture is also used to organize and support the work. The Language of Work Model refers to such a need and solution as an *integrated human resource system* (IHRS).

An IHRS system is one in which the job models serve as a focal point for meeting management's personnel needs. Job models are more functional versions of job descriptions that can be developed much more quickly, be responsive to work changes, are better understood by management and worker together, and can be used more accurately and completely to select employees, assess work execution as well as skill and knowledge performance, identify performance gaps, and fit well into career-development programs. Because job models specify work execution, with related skills, knowledge, attributes, and competencies, they can be used by managers and workers together to do meaningful and useful performance reviews. An effect-and-cause discussion between managers and workers on a periodic basis results in the identification of performance gaps, and when linked to available internal and external intervention resources, individual- and group-development plans are easy to define and execute. This continuous feedback to HR based on job models and evaluation of performance is a vital resource that keeps the employee-development program centered on continuous and realistic needs. Managers do the assessment, that is, their output is input to HR; HR provides the meaningful work-support resources, that is, interventions are HR's outputs, serving as inputs to management. They are partners.

In a similar way, the job models can also serve to help select personnel more accurately in relation to work execution, skills, knowledge, attributes, and other requirements specified in the job models. Again, HPT and management are partners. Career development, performance management, and other HR requirements are enhanced in their effectiveness through the job models. These are other forms of partnership between HPT and management. The various needs of HR are thus integrated under a common Language of Work HPT model, and the model itself can be used to implement and improve many of the HR and management performance needs.

This leads us to a further elaboration on how to partner with management and workers using the Language of Work Model in identifying gaps and finding solutions, the next two phases of the overall HPT model, as depicted in Figure 39.1.

Gap Analysis

Partnering with management and the workforce does not stop with defining their work, nor does improving work performance begin with a *gap analysis,* a practice too common with many HPT practitioners. Without a complete and concise work-performance model on which to base and do gap analysis, gap analysis becomes a brainstorming, guessing exercise that may result in lost and even misguided performance-improvement opportunities.

Partnering with management to do a gap analysis is actually embedded for the greater part in proper performance analysis. There is a systemic relationship between performance and performance gaps between analysis of work, worker, and work environment, as well as organizational environment. Gap analysis is usually, but not entirely, done in two related aspects of work: work execution and work support.

Work Execution Gap Analysis. Gaps in work execution are either identified as the difference between As Is and To Be business-unit, core-process, job, or work-group models, identified through an analysis of the As Is model, or both. For example, when As Is job models are defined, we have generally executed on-line assessments of workers through the self-evaluation of their performance on the use of inputs, process steps, attention to conditions, and use of feedback, as well as related their skills and knowledge in the form of competencies. A version of 360-degree feedback (Lepsinger and Lucia, 1997) or direct observation of performance based on the job models is possible as well. These all result in performance gap identification of work execution. The assessment is a partnership between management, worker, HR, and the HPT practitioner. An ongoing extension of this kind of gap analysis involves using the job models to do performance reviews and cycling the performance gaps to HR on a continuous basis.

Work Support Gap Analysis. As managers and workers are taught to define work using the business-unit and core-process models and the job and work-group models, they can perform an organizational scan of work-support needs. This usually takes the form of asking what needs fixing relative to and in the context of the work models. The results are performance gaps being identified in the work and support environment. For example, in conjunction with job modeling, managers and workers together identify what is needed from management to better execute their work in the work environment.

These various stages of gap analysis, whether in work execution or work support, carried out by and in the hands of management, are more likely to be acted on than when gap analysis is in the hands and control of HPT personnel. Managers and workers merely need the means, work models, and techniques, such as facilitated guidance, scans, performance reviews, and so on, to base and conduct useful gap analysis.

Cause Analysis and Intervention Selection

While *cause analysis* and *intervention selection* are listed separately in the HPT Model in Figure 39.1, they are so intertwined in practice that they will be addressed together in relation to the implementation of the Language of Work Model. Conventional practice around the use of cause analysis suggests that management and workers help identify which of the six causes, or a combination thereof, is responsible for the performance gaps. Then the appropriate intervention solutions are selected. A slight variation of this practice will be described in light of the Language of Work model.

The Language of Work Model uses cause analysis in a hybrid form labeled in recent articles (Langdon and Whiteside, 2004) and in presentations as "change-of-state analysis." Because analyses are aimed at determining appropriate interventions for performance gaps, the key question is, Which kind of analysis works best with or better by management? My aim is not just analysis and selection of interventions, but ownership and partnering with management in doing so.

I maintain that change-of-state analysis is easier and more user-friendly, and results in a more appropriate intervention mix. There are two reasons for this. First, my experiences have shown that management and the workforce often try to forcefeed many causes and therefore end up at times with unneeded and perhaps too many interventions. An example is management's common perception and resulting suggestion that the problem or gap must be skill deficiencies. Second, management finds change-of-state analysis easier to use because it has fewer *categories,* speaks to the desired performance changes as management has defined and understands them, and links more easily to the most desired interventions that will help to change performance within the work environment. A brief description of change-of-state analysis should demonstrate how gap analysis and intervention selection can be more management friendly. The emphasis again is on partnering with management and workers so that they use and own the interventions they identify to develop and implement.

Change-of-state analysis suggests that there are four fundamental ways in which performance changes. A single performance change usually involves a single occurrence, but may also be a combination of these changes. The four possible changes to performance are establishing, improving, maintaining, and extinguishing performance.

From my experience in orienting managers and workers to use change-of-state analysis, I call describing these changes the "nine-minute-teach." It only takes a few minutes to relate to them the meaning behind each of these four types of changes. A definition and a sample job aid, as partly illustrated in Figure 39.5, work well. From there, management and workers can be helped in selecting interventions based on the performance analysis and already completed assessment. When linked to interventions that can be used within the organizational environment to make such changes as partially illustrated in Figure 39.5, the

Improve Performance		Establish Performance	
Current performance exists, but needs to be made better		Current performance does not exist and needs to be put in place	
Sample interventions:	Business planning Career development Coaching Training	Sample interventions:	Employee selection Job aids Mentoring Training
Maintain Performance		Extinguish Performance	
Current performance exists and needs to be retained at its current level		Current performance exists, but needs to be eliminated	
Sample interventions:	Compensation Feedback Work schedules	Sample interventions:	Outplacement 360-degree evaluation Withholding rewards

Figure 39.5. Intervention Taxonomy by Change-of-State Analysis.

methodologies are easy for managers to understand and use to observe resulting values. They conduct the analysis and selection themselves, and therefore have more direct ownership of the overall performance-improvement effort. Management, again, owns the HPT model in this sense.

If we recognize that management really does know its work and does have the answers, but does not know how to formulate or approach the question of work analysis and solution selection in this instance, we go a long way toward partnering with management by putting our HPT model in managers' hands and under their control. As it turns out, it does not take extensive training to impart this so much as it does a functional work performance definition model, a series of quick ways to introduce the model and analytical methodology, and an approach that engages management and workers in analyzing and solving their needs immediately and in a context they know well.

Intervention Implementation and Change

There are too many aspects of *implementation and change* to be addressed here in terms of partnering with management, but one experience in using the Language of Work Model serves as a best practice for the HPT practitioner in carrying out implementation and change. Using the Language of Work Model with managers and workers together to do the performance analysis, identify the gaps, do cause or change-of-state analysis, and intervention selection takes care of many important aspects of change management itself. These include communicating change through core-process and job- and work-level models, buy-in to the change because those involved in the process are saying what should be changed and how, and a methodology to measure what should be measured, when and if the changes occur. Change is particularly difficult to achieve when those affected by the change do not agree, understand, or buy into it. Traditionally, we HPT interventionists have imposed change through our own somewhat distant analyses and methodologies; this has required *selling* our interventions and solutions to management and the workforce. When a change is identified through our client's own analysis and intervention selection, partnering with management is much easier to accomplish.

Evaluation

The HPT Model specifies three key evaluation points along the continuum of formative, summative, and confirmative evaluation (see the HPT Model in Figure 39.1). The emphasis on evaluation in all of these phases is intended to ensure that what has been identified as change has indeed been achieved to the desired level; where it has not, further analysis identifies how to achieve success. In my thinking, the problems in evaluation have long persisted not so much in terms of how to measure, but rather in identifying what should be measured. The genesis of this difficulty, it turns out, is centered at the very beginning point of our human performance technology process; that is, how we define and identify performance or work. The dilemma in evaluation we face is achingly similar to Robert Mager's poignant comment concerning behavioral objectives: "If you're not sure where you're going, you're liable to end up some place else" (Mager, 1997, p. vi). Similarly, if you cannot define the performance paradigm accurately and completely, including work execution that matches the work, worker, or work environment in environmental analysis, then it is really hard to know what to measure in terms of cause and effect.

The Language of Work Model solves this problem of what to measure by offering a paradigm that (1) matches or mirrors work through the six elements of performance as depicted in Figure 39.2, (2) is specified and linked to the other aspects of work execution found in the work-support matrix, (3) aids in setting standards more systematically, and (4) identifies where human relations get in the way of work. For more details on items 3 and 4, see Langdon, 2000. The key point to observe in terms of partnering with managers is that they will know what to measure within a model of performance that they have used to understand, operationalize, improve, and measure work. The outputs and consequences of work tell them what effect they want; these can be measured with any number of metrics. When they find a problem in achieving any output and consequences combination, they can readily measure inputs, conditions, process steps, feedback, and work support and then find the cause or performance gaps, continue to identify solutions, implement, and close the loop.

CONCLUSION

The Language of Work Model can make the overall use of HPT a true partnership with both management and workers together. We are the stewards of our human performance technology, but management should be the holder and user of it. This model makes for a very nice partnership, with the result that we are valued for our contribution to the total organizational effort.

References

Carleton, J. R., and Lineberry, C. (2004). *Achieving post-merger success: A stakeholder's guide to cultural due diligence, assessment, and integration.* San Francisco: Jossey-Bass/Pfeiffer.

Dean, P. J., and Ripley, D. E. (Eds.). (1997). *Performance improvement pathfinders: Models for organizational learning systems.* Washington, DC: International Society for Performance Improvement.

Langdon, D. G. (1995). *The new language of work.* Amherst, MA: HRD Press.

Langdon, D. G. (2000). *Aligning performance: Improving people, systems and organizations.* San Francisco: Jossey-Bass/Pfeiffer.

Langdon, D. G., and Whiteside, K. (2004, August). Bringing sense to competency definition and attainment. *Performance Improvement, 43*(7), 10–21.

Lepsinger, R. L., and Lucia, A. D. (1997). *The art and science of 360° feedback.* San Francisco: Jossey-Bass/Pfeiffer.

Mager, R. F. (1997). *Preparing instructional objectives.* Atlanta: Center for Effective Performance.

Rummler, G. A., and Brache, A. P. (1990). *Improving performance: How to manage the white space on the organization chart* (2nd ed.). San Francisco: Jossey-Bass.

CHAPTER FORTY

Managing Human Performance Technology Projects

Nicholas Andreadis

In today's demanding, highly competitive, and complex environment, project management can no longer be considered a nice-to-have tool for performance analysts. Problems must be solved quickly and completely and opportunities grasped when presented.

This chapter presents time-tested concepts, methods, and tools of project management, with the critical success factors that support successful human performance technology (HPT) projects.

HPT is an area of practice that brings together three distinct but related management disciplines: total quality management, change management, and project management (see Figure 40.1).

Each of these management disciplines is embedded in the HPT model developed and published under the auspices of the International Society for Performance Improvement. Scrupulous attention to the concepts, methods, and tools of all three disciplines is essential to achieving the results desired from HPT projects.

Project management is the application of knowledge, skills, tools, and techniques to project activities in order to meet or exceed stakeholder needs and expectations from a project (Duncan, 1996). It involves the acquisition and use of organizational resources to achieve defined goals and objectives. HPT has four characteristics that make it an excellent model of a project-based, quality-oriented discipline. HPT projects are process-driven, temporary, unique, and naturalistic. The process orientation is evident in that the execution of each element of the HPT Model transforms inputs into outputs. At the macro level, HPT transforms

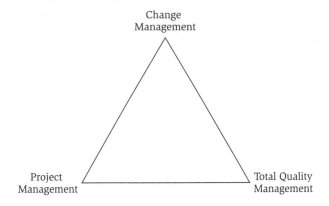

Figure 40.1. The Three Management Disciplines of Human Performance Technology.

problems into solutions and opportunities into realized gains. It comprises five work steps or processes: analysis, design, development, implementation, and evaluation (ADDIE). Ideally, each process is designed to meet the expectations and needs of project clients and stakeholders. Project-management tools are uniquely suited to facilitate the methodical work of HPT. The work of performance technology flows horizontally and vertically through the organization across organizational functions and hierarchy. Because project-management methods are designed to work across different functions and disciplines, project management facilitates collaboration and cooperation among project team members. Each HPT project is temporary in that its start and end points are defined, as are its stakeholders, goals, and deliverables. This feature distinguishes project management from the so-called regular work of the organization. Projects have unique and specific timelines, quality requirements, and organizational contexts. Finally, HPT projects are naturalistic. They are conducted in the "natural setting" of the organization with its embedded culture, characteristics, and members. The problems or opportunities under study evolve from the natural course of the organization's business affairs.

There are sound reasons for using project-management concepts, methods, and tools for HPT projects. Good project management saves organizational resources, increases productivity, and increases the likelihood that projects will be successful. Successful projects are those that deliver business value for their customers, are completed on time and within budget, and meet the technical and quality requirements expected by project sponsors and stakeholders. Given the benefits provided to HPT projects, one would expect that the concepts, methods, and tools of project management would be used on a regular basis. However, when the author queried managers and professionals taking an introductory course in

Reflect on your own experience with HPT projects. On a scale of 1 to 4, score as follows: 1 = never, 2 = occasionally, 3 = usually, 4 = always.

- The project team had a clear idea of what the project was expected to accomplish.
- The needs and expectations of the project's customers were clearly identified.
- A thorough project plan was written.
- Project team members gave and got adequate commitment to the project's success.
- The project was "broken down" into tasks that were the right size for people to manage.
- The team knew early in the project which resources were needed and where they were coming from.
- Some of the risks to the project success and completion were proactively identified.
- The team confidently and consistently knew the status of the project as it unfolded.

Figure 40.2. Project-Management Self-Assessment.

project management, a different reality was revealed. Take a moment and review the self-assessment statements presented in Figure 40.2. Score them based on your own experience with HPT and related projects.

If you answered with a "1" or "2" on three or more of the statements, then it is likely that your experience with projects ranges from frustrating to painfully difficult. The problems suggested by these statements are typical of the kind that performance consultants face when approaching a problem without an organized project plan. But beyond the purely analytical reasons for regularly using project-management methods and tools, experience teaches us that they simply make working on projects much more satisfying.

PROJECT-MANAGEMENT LIFE CYCLE

HPT projects are created because individuals or teams perceive a need or opportunity that needs systematic attention. This realization, when acted on, initiates a series of work processes collectively called a project life cycle. The underlying principles of the project life cycle are based on systems theory, in which inputs are transformed into outputs or deliverables. There are five major processes in the life cycle.

1. Initiating
2. Planning
3. Organizing
4. Executing
5. Closing

These five processes include eighteen subprocesses that further describe the work of the project. These eighteen subprocesses are presented in Figure 40.3.

Initiating

　　Defining the request

　　Analyzing stakeholder requirements

　　Establishing project goals and deliverables

　　Defining constraints and boundaries

　　Creating a scope document

Planning

　　Building a work breakdown structure

　　Creating a network diagram

　　Scheduling the work packages

　　Estimating resource needs

　　Identifying project risks

Organizing

　　Defining roles and responsibilities

　　Selecting project team members

　　Delegating the work

Executing

　　Implementing the plan

　　Controlling for variances

　　Communicating with stakeholders

Closing

　　Terminating the project

　　Conducting an evaluation

Figure 40.3. Project Life Cycle Processes.

Planning and organizing the project are conducted continuously throughout the life cycle, running concurrently with the executing phase. This allows for changing some aspects of the project and permits a degree of necessary flexibility.

Initiating

The importance of the initiating phase cannot be overstated. When the initiating steps are not completed or are done poorly, misunderstandings, missteps, and project delays generally result. The project team should conduct each step of the initiating phase thoughtfully and thoroughly.

Defining the Request. Prior to doing the hard work of HPT, it is essential that the performance consultant completely understand what problem or opportunity is to be addressed. The first step in the initiating phase of the project is to meet with the client to define the project. It is essential that the consultant develop a clear understanding of what problem the client wishes to have solved. All too often, extensive effort and resources are expended without assurance that the problem has been accurately identified or is worth the time and expense to resolve. Effective consultants listen carefully to the client, paying particular attention to learning what the client wants to achieve from the project. This information is critical, as it identifies the strategic value of the project. For example, the client may want you to conduct a training needs assessment. On probing beyond the expressed want, you may discover that what the client really wants is an increase in worker productivity. When presented with a client's want, the performance consultant should redirect the client's request to a desired outcome beyond the want. There are two benefits to this approach. First, this discussion provides an opportunity for the consultant to affirm the organizational need, particularly when resources are scarce and negotiations are necessary. Second, the consultant, as project manager, can now emphasize the strategic value of the work to project team members because the client has stated that value clearly.

Analyzing Stakeholder Requirements. While the typical performance project often has a single client, both the client and the project have multiple stakeholders. As the name implies, stakeholders are all persons, units, departments, or agencies who have a stake or major interest in the outcome of a project. Typical stakeholders are the client, the client's customers, project team members and their bosses, line managers who provide resources and whose work is affected by the project, and external constituencies. Clearly identified stakeholder expectations and information needs are key components of change management. Stakeholders need reassurance throughout the project that their interest and expectations are respected by the project team. This is achieved by attending to their needs throughout the project and regularly communicating the status of progress made toward meeting their expectations. This attention will pay enormous dividends when the project moves into the implementation phase. Clearly identified stakeholder

Table 40.1. Stakeholder Management Worksheet for a Vendor-Invoice-Processing Project.

Stakeholder	Expectations	Information Needs
Accounts payable clerk	New software will decrease vendor invoice processing time by 30 percent	What new knowledge and skills will clerks need to operate the software successfully?
		How much lead time will we have to prepare for the installation and "go live" of new software?
Manager of accounts payable department	New software will reduce overall costs of invoice processing and payment by at least 25 percent	Will training on new software require our department to shut down for any length of time?
		Can I anticipate that the new software will result in loss of jobs in the department?
Vendors	New software will result in faster payment of invoices	Do we need to change our billing forms or processes to be compatible with your system?

expectations and information needs are key components of successful change management. Many project managers will use a stakeholder management worksheet to document the needs of stakeholders and identify how they will manage their interests. The stakeholder worksheet identifies each stakeholder, his or her expectations for the project, and the essential information the stakeholders need from the project team. Table 40.1 provides an example of a stakeholder management worksheet for a project that involves the installation of new software to process vendor invoices in an accounts payable department.

It is useful for members of the project team to be assigned to one or more stakeholders whose interests they will represent during the planning and executing phases. Once the interests and expectations of the client and other stakeholders are clarified, the next step in the initiating phase is to define the project's goals and deliverables.

Establishing Project Goals and Deliverables. Project goals and deliverables are the products or outputs of the HPT project. Project goals are considered

Organizational performance assessment

Competency profiles for successful job performance

Training courses

Work process maps

Improvements in the performance-support system

Creation of job aids to support work performance

Recommendations to align an incentive plan with performance objectives

Figure 40.4. Common HPT Deliverables.

---

effective when they are specific, measurable, and time-bound. Goals and deliverables are defined collaboratively by the client and project team. The goals and deliverables of the project must be stated in a manner that makes it clear that they are linked and aligned with the strategic business goals of the organization. For example, stating that the project's goal is to "contribute to the organization's profitability by analyzing workflow efficiencies and recommending improvements" is better than simply describing the project as a "workflow productivity analysis." Since the project's success will ultimately be based on the impact the project deliverables have on improving business results, each project team member should be able to see the alignment of deliverables with those results. A list of common HPT deliverables is presented in Figure 40.4.

Defining Constraints and Boundaries. Once the project's goals and deliverables are established, the next step is to define the project's boundaries and constraints. All projects are bounded and constrained in some way. The classical description of project constraints is presented as the "Triple Constraints": limits on time, money, and quality. Constraints pose limits on the team's options in executing the project, as time, money, and quality battle for supremacy during the project. Constraints produce discussions about trade-offs. Can time be added if resources are limited? Can quality requirements be modified if meeting the schedule is critical? Often the client is unaware of the implications that constraints impose on a project, so it behooves the project manager to be both patient and assertive in any negotiations. Not all constraints are defined by the Triple Constraint model. Other common constraints include the availability of key experts being limited to a specific week or month during the project, limited access to key data sources for the analysis, and a need for an excessive number of approvals during the planning or executing phases.

Some constraints are stronger than others and end up being not-so-subtle drivers of the project (Dobson, 2003). For example, if the schedule for completing the analysis is absolutely firm and unchangeable, then it becomes the driving constraint, even if that means spending more money to get the project done. If, however, the client balks at spending the additional money to meet the schedule, then it becomes evident that cost is the real driver. The nature and number of constraints has a huge influence on the success of the project, and savvy project managers attempt to identify them early in project planning. This gives the project manager time to negotiate with the client for some relief if constraints are too restrictive.

Boundaries define what is and what is not in the project. There are two main types of project boundaries. The first, a start-finish boundary, defines the point at which a project begins and the point at which it ends. To illustrate, let us say you are asked to analyze the performance of a manufacturing organization's supply chain. If you are told that your analysis is to begin with the packaging of finished goods and to end on the shipping dock, then you know that the processes of purchasing raw materials and delivering goods to the customer are not in the analysis. The second type of boundary is one that includes or excludes various analyses within the larger start-finish boundary. You may, for example, be instructed not to analyze the package-labeling aspect of the packaging process or any of the incentive systems for individuals working on the shipping dock. As with constraints, identifying the project's boundaries is a proactive step in minimizing unwanted work and team member frustration.

Creating a Scope Document. The final step in the initiating phase is the development of the project scope document. The scope document provides the overall project governance, succinctly describing the main goals and operational aspects of the project. Generating a scope document is an essential part of initiating a project and should not be overlooked. A scope document serves as a useful means of communicating project essentials to the organization. The scope document presents in narrative form an overview of the project, describing its key parameters: the project's reason for being, its goals and deliverables, a description of the project's work, and the project's boundaries and constraints. It requires the client and analyst to think through and validate each of the major elements of the project. A scope document can help you and your client manage expectations and understand exactly what to expect before and during the project. The reason for the project is rooted in the customer's needs. People hear and recall verbal agreements in different ways. The essence of the scope document is to say to your client, "This is what I heard you say, this is what I plan to do, this is how long it will take, and this is how much it will cost."

The level of detail in a scope document varies from project to project and from client to client. Once you get into the habit of creating scope documents, they will become easier and quicker to complete. Figure 40.5 presents the key elements that should be included in a scope document.

Business purpose

Goals

Statement of deliverables

A description of technical work

Measures of success

Milestones

Boundaries

Major assumptions and constraints

Figure 40.5. Essential Elements of Scope Documents.

Planning

With the overall governance and direction established in the initiating phase, the performance consultant and team can now begin the planning phase of the project. Most readers with a working familiarity with project management will recognize the methods and tools commonly used in project planning. These tools have considerable usefulness in managing HPT projects, and it would benefit performance consultants to learn them. Whole chapters have been written on each of the following subjects in texts devoted solely to project management. Space constraints of this chapter permit only an introduction to these methods and tools.

Recently, the author was involved in a project with a school district. I use this project to illustrate several of the planning concepts and tools discussed in this section. The project was commissioned by school officials who wanted a new set of performance-management forms designed. Once designed and approved by managerial staff, the new forms were then to be made available on the school's internal computer network.

Building a Work Breakdown Structure. There are times when a project is so complex that it can seem overwhelming and unwieldy. It is useful to divide the project into manageable parts or chunks called "work packages." A work package is the basic process unit of a project and consists of a set of inputs that the process transforms into an output, a deliverable, or an intermediate to the deliverable. The collection of work packages associated with a project can be displayed in a work breakdown structure (WBS) (see Figures 40.6 and 40.7). The WBS presents the work packages in a way that facilitates overall planning, management, and control of the project. It is also useful for defining roles and responsibilities, project costing, milestone management, reporting, and coordination. Like other

Name of project:

Assess Performance Gaps
- Perform environmental analysis
- Define To Be (desired) workforce performance
     Benchmarking
     Literature review
- Define As Is (actual) state of workforce performance
     Process mapping
     Measurement of key work parameters
- Generate gap analysis report

Perform Causal Analysis
- Generate hypotheses
- Gather data and test hypotheses
- Identify probable causes

Select and Design Intervention
- Identify intervention objectives
- Select intervention components
     Define criteria
     Evaluate options
- Design intervention

Implement Intervention
- Select development team
- Prepare the development plan
- Develop and test prototype of the plan
- Revise the development plan
- Produce the final intervention materials

Evaluate Project
- Identify the purpose of evaluation
- Design the evaluation
- Prepare evaluation materials
- Implement the evaluation
- Communicate results to clients and stakeholders

Figure 40.6. Work Breakdown Structure (text form).

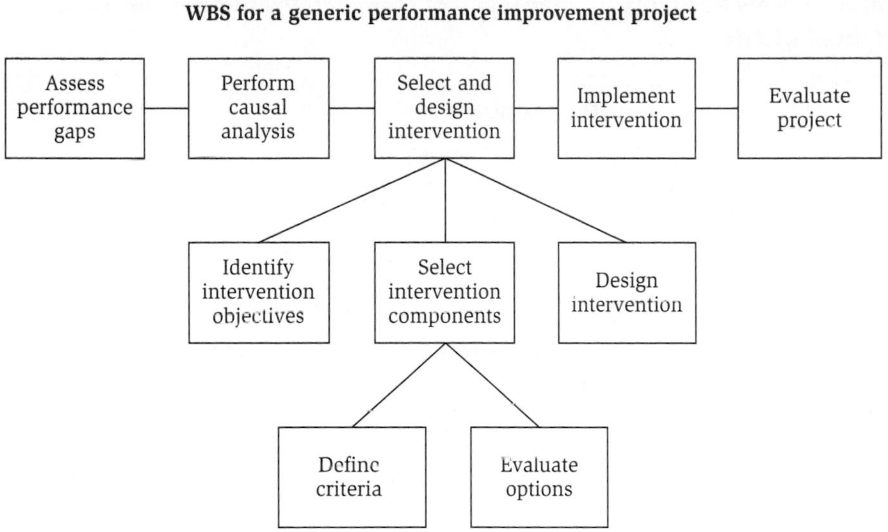

WBS for a generic performance improvement project

Figure 40.7. Partial Work Breakdown Structure (graphic form).

planning documents, it can also serve as a means for communicating about the project work or status.

Creating a Network Diagram. Creating a project WBS requires a general understanding of HPT work processes, project boundaries, and the work environment surrounding each project. A full description of building a WBS is beyond the scope of this chapter, but a few suggestions are offered. I recommend that all team members be involved in building the WBS. The scope document provides useful data for building the WBS. Construction can start with a list of either the major project deliverables or major work steps. I prefer the latter, using verbs and action words to describe the work to be done in each package. This list, often called a task list, is used to create the WBS and provides input into developing the project schedule. See Figure 40.8 for the task list for the school's project. Sticky notes are useful tools for drafting a task list and building the WBS. It is not necessary for the project to be broken down into painful detail. The process begins by dividing the large work steps into smaller, more manageable and measurable work packages. Milosevic (2003) provides useful advice on how to construct a WBS. He suggests that the structure have three to four tiers with a total of fifteen to twenty work packages, with each work package representing 3 to 7 percent of the overall hours estimated for the project. When complete, the WBS should provide all team members with a clear representation of the work to be done during the project.

Project: New Performance Management Form and Procedures for School District

Task	Description
A	Define project objectives
B	Conduct stakeholder analysis
C	Conduct focus group with managers
D	Conduct focus groups with associates
E	Develop specifications for forms and procedures
F	Develop prototype of forms
G	Write program code for forms
H	Install new forms on network
I	Test forms in focus group with managers
J	Test forms in focus groups with associates
K	Revise forms based on focus groups
L	Conduct training with associates
M	Conduct training with managers
N	Pilot new forms and system
O	Evaluate pilot

Figure 40.8. Project Task List.

Work breakdown structures can be presented in either text or graphic formats (see Figures 40.6 and 40.7).

Using the WBS, the project team can

- Assign work package responsibility to team members
- Define inputs and outputs for each work package, leaving no room for dispute about what the completed work package contains
- Schedule the project
- Estimate resource needs for each work package
- Build milestones and a control plan around work package outputs

Scheduling the Work Packages. To many people the phrase *project management* brings to mind the image of a commonly used scheduling device called a Gannt chart. However, before a Gannt chart can be created, the project team must identify the most sensible order in which to conduct the project's work. Although the WBS provides an overview of the work that is to be done in the project, it does not describe the sequence of those work steps. For that we must transform the task list into a network diagram. A network diagram is a graphical description of the work packages in order of execution. The next step is to identify all work package dependencies. The word *dependency* is used to describe the temporal relationship between two or more work packages. When one work package must be completed before another can start, we say that the second work package is dependent on the first. The most common type of dependency is the finish-start dependency. For example, before you can change a flat tire, you must first remove the deflated one. Changing the tire is dependent on removing the flat one. If every work package after the first is dependent on the completion of its preceding work package, then the network diagram is linear. When more than one work package can be done independently of others, the diagram takes on a more web-like appearance. Ideally, projects will have few finish-start dependencies, permitting some tasks to be done concurrently rather than consecutively. Once all the dependencies are identified, the project team can again use sticky notes to sequence the work packages, respecting the finish-start dependencies and exploring options for doing work concurrently. Using this task list, a network diagram is created (see Figures 40.8 and 40.9). Each letter in the diagram corresponds to a work package presented in the project's task list.

The next step in the scheduling process is to estimate the amount of time it will take to complete each work package. One method for arriving at a time estimate for each work package comes from a technique called PERT, or Project

Each letter in the network corresponds to its respective work package on the task list.

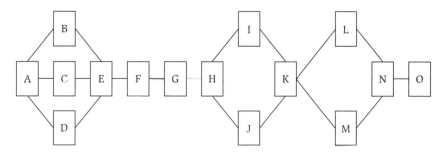

Figure 40.9. Network Diagram for a Performance Management Project.

Evaluation and Review Technique (Wren, 2004). The PERT method uses a method of time estimation based on probability. Team members are asked to provide three time estimates for completing a given work package: optimistic, or fastest; pessimistic, or slowest; and the most likely time estimate. These estimates are then inserted into the following equation to calculate a time estimate that can be used for planning.

$$\text{Time estimate} = (a + 4m + b)/6$$

where:

a = optimistic time estimate

b = pessimistic time estimate

m = most likely time estimate

When all the dependencies and time estimates have been identified, the task list can be expanded to include them, as illustrated in Figure 40.10.

When the network diagram and time estimates are complete, the team can now construct a Gannt chart. In developing the chart, all constraints that are imposed on the project must be respected. For example, a much-needed subject-matter expert may only be available from Tuesdays through Thursdays. All constraints should be collected in one place and be available to the team as they are creating the schedule. A Gannt chart is a commonly used graphical representation of the schedule. Figure 40.11 presents the Gannt chart for our school's performance-management project. Developing a Gannt chart is a useful step in project management, and readers are encouraged to review common project-management texts for detailed instructions on how to construct them. See the end of this chapter for selected resources.

Estimating Resource Needs. All HPT projects consume resources, but rarely are the costs of projects fully accounted for. Even if the analyst is an internal consultant, the project will cost the client money, time, and opportunity. A common method for calculating project costs is to estimate the anticipated resource needs of each work package. This bottom-up approach is useful for creating the project budget and also useful as a communication device to inform management of the anticipated cost of a project.

Resource planning goes beyond cost estimates; it includes scheduling scarce resources to be available when the project needs them. A project may require a subject-matter expert whose time and availability are limited. Failure to account for this constraint in the schedule will delay the project. The project manager is more likely to secure time on the expert's busy calendar by providing a specific time frame. Using the WBS and a scheduling device like the Gannt

Project: New Performance Management Form and Procedures for School District

Task	Description	Estimated Completion Time	Dependency
A	Define project objectives	One day	None
B	Conduct stakeholder analysis	Four days	A
C	Conduct focus group with managers	Two days	A
D	Conduct focus groups with associates	Two days	A
E	Develop specifications for forms and procedures	One day	B, C, D
F	Develop prototype of forms	Two days	E
G	Write program code for forms	Three days	F
H	Install new form on network	Fourteen days	G
I	Test forms in focus group with managers	One day	H
J	Test forms in focus groups with associates	One day	H
K	Revise forms based on focus groups	Three days	I, J
L	Conduct training with associates	Two days	K
M	Conduct training with managers	Two days	K
N	Pilot new forms and system	Two days	L, M
O	Evaluate pilot	Two days	N

Figure 40.10. Expanded Project Task List.

chart, project managers are able to identify specific time frames when scarce resources are needed.

The project team is responsible for identifying the expenses that will be incurred in the project and constructing a budget. The budget should contain sufficient detail regarding costs to allow it to be useful in the control phase of the project. Experienced project managers realize that cost overruns are a realistic possibility in performance projects. To prepare for this possibility, they will often add 10 percent

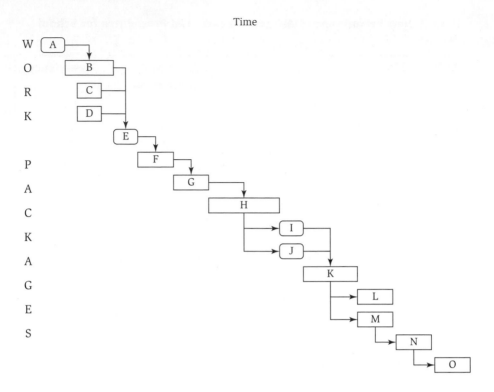

Figure 40.11. Gannt Chart for School Project.

to budget estimates. Project costs are either variable or fixed. Variable costs are those incurred specifically and uniquely for the project and include items such as supplies, consultant fees, and project-related travel. Fixed costs are costs for resources incurred by the organization irrespective of their use in completing the project. Examples of fixed costs include team member salaries, a conference room, and a photocopier. The cost of purchasing a copier for the project is a fixed cost, while the paper consumed is a variable cost.

A useful method for developing a project budget is to estimate all costs for each work package in the WBS. These estimates are then added together to arrive at a rough estimate of total project cost.

Identifying Project Risks. Risk is inherent in every project. It behooves the project team to anticipate the likely risks to project success and identify ways to prevent their occurrence or minimize their impact. Good planning may not eliminate all risks to a project, but it can reduce the likelihood of significant disruption. Risks include unexpected changes in project goals or scope, unresolved conflicts among team members, or the loss of much-needed resources. While risk management begins in the planning phase, it is an ongoing activity for the project team. Risk is best managed by having information systems that provide real-time data on all aspects of project status. By acknowledging the potential for projects to go off track, the project team prepares itself by developing early warning systems that alert the team to variances from plans. Project control mechanisms, described later in the chapter, help the team identify those variances when they arise.

Organizing

In the organizing phase, the project manager defines the major roles and responsibilities needed to implement the project plan, recruiting people to the project and delegating the work to them.

Defining Roles and Responsibilities. One of the project manager's key organizing tasks is to identify the technical and organizational skills needed to complete the project. Based on this analysis, individual roles and responsibilities can be constructed. The project manager must bring two perspectives to this analysis. The first is a careful review of each work package to determine which technical skills are needed to execute the steps required of each package. Second, an analysis of the organizational and team skills is needed to create a high-performing project team.

Selecting Project Team Members. Most project teams require expertise from a variety of organizational functions and units. By their very nature, HPT projects are multidisciplinary, and the principles of classic matrix management apply. All project managers have to cope with the reality that they are borrowing resources from the line organization, and must manage these resources through influence. Nowhere is influence more important than in the project manager's relationship with line managers. Recruiting the right person for the right task is an essential function of the project manager and one done in collaboration with line managers. Because it is difficult to pry good people away from the day-to-day tasks of an organization, project managers need good negotiation skills to secure the human resources necessary for project completion. Not only do line managers provide access to the talent in an organization, they often control access to the data needed to solve problems. Project managers must also be cognizant of the political demands being placed on team members who report upward to their bosses as well as horizontally to other team members.

Delegating the Work. The final organizing step is to delegate responsibility and accountability for the project's work to team members. The WBS is a useful tool for defining the specific work packages and deliverables for which each team member will be accountable. A major challenge for project teams is that their members come and go as phases of the project start and end. The potential for disrupting the high performance of a team is a real risk. The project team must also contend with a range of organizational issues that arise during the execution of the project. Some of these include changing organizational priorities, competition for resources, power and authority problems, and resistance to proposed changes. It often falls to the project manager to be the one constant that keeps the project focused, aligned, and on track. As can be seen from these few paragraphs, project managers must possess outstanding people skills.

Executing and Implementing the Plan

Executing is the carrying out of the steps for the project as defined in the project plan. For a typical HPT project, this means conducting the analysis, design, and development of proposed interventions as depicted in the ADDIE process. The specifics of each of these activities are thoroughly discussed elsewhere in this handbook and will not be repeated here. During the executing phase, the project team is also involved in monitoring the status of the project, communicating progress to stakeholders, and managing variances and risks that emerge during the execution of the project.

Controlling for Variances. It is essential that the project team regularly monitor and evaluate the status of the project throughout the execution phase. Monitoring, generally referred to as "controlling the project," is the ongoing surveillance for variances, or deviations, from the plan as the project progresses through the execution phase. Control is the "plan-do-check-adjust" activity commonly associated with total quality management. Each team member is responsible for controlling the project and accordingly must have accurate and timely information on project costs, schedule, and quality. It is in the controlling phase that the project benefits from careful attention to detail given in the planning phase. Without a good plan, specific goals, and measures, control is weak at best. Though project control is an ongoing activity, teams typically check for variances when each project milestone is achieved. Developing a control plan is particularly useful for projects that are complex and involve high risk, and for which regular progress reports to stakeholders have been promised. The purposes of the control can only be achieved when milestones, cost estimates, schedules, and quality or technical objectives are clearly defined, documented, and rigorously measured. Accordingly, control can only be achieved if team members are accountable for regular assessment of key project variables. When variances are discovered, it is essential that the project team determine whether the size and importance of the variation require the team's immediate attention. The project team must be sufficiently empowered to take actions necessary to return the project to plan. This empowerment comes from the project sponsor and is documented in the project charter. Controls should promote self-management and not micromanagement of project team members. When project-management controls are used effectively, team members feel a sense of ownership for the project and its outcomes.

Communicating with Stakeholders. No organization's members like living in an information vacuum. This is especially true when organizations are experiencing the kind of problems for which performance technology is employed. In the initiating phase of the project, the team creates a stakeholder management plan that identifies the interests and information needs of each stakeholder. During project execution, the plan is implemented. All project team members need to understand their responsibility for keeping stakeholders informed. Each project team meeting agenda should include an item focused on communication to stakeholders. It is this kind of attention to detail that maintains the good will of stakeholders and builds project team credibility.

Closing Out a Project

Experienced project managers know the value of properly closing out a project. By the time of closure the project team members, having completed the work of execution, often are tired and ready to return to the work of their regular assignments. It is tempting to leave several project loose ends. The same discipline that members applied to other phases of the project must now be applied to terminating and evaluating the project.

Terminating the Project. Proper closure of an HPT project involves more than presenting the final deliverables to the client. Deeprose (2001) provides a checklist of closing activities that include

- Ensuring the completion of all project deliverables
- Documenting the project
- Reconciling any budget and financial issues
- Notifying all key stakeholders that the project is complete
- Acknowledging team member contributions

The project team needs to review the stakeholder management plan and assess whether all the customer and stakeholder requirements have been met or fulfilled. Of particular importance is the formal transfer of responsibility for implementing any or all of the recommendations and outputs from the project. A poorly executed handoff of responsibilities can negate the good work that has been done during the project.

Conducting an Evaluation. Closure also provides the opportunity to formally assess your customer's overall satisfaction with the team's work. One of the most important tasks of closure is a project evaluation, wherein the team takes the time to review and reflect on the project. Assessing your team's performance on the project does not necessarily involve requiring formal evaluation methods. A few well-chosen questions can provide considerable information that is valuable for use in future projects. I suggest the following questions as a starting point for your evaluation:

- What went well during the project?
- What could have gone better?
- Were there any surprises? What could we have done to anticipate them?
- How close were we on time and cost estimates?
- What aspects of the project could have been simplified?
- What did we learn in this project?
- What advice can we give to other project teams?

BUILDING CREDIBILITY AS A MANAGER OF HPT PROJECTS

Ultimately, the capability of HPT professionals is determined by whether the project produces positive results for the client. The credibility that is earned by repeatedly performing well is an enormous asset to the professional. This credibility is essential for the project manager to be able to exercise the necessary power, influence, and authority to overcome problems. In most organizations power is located with the line managers. The project manager gets the work done through referred power and persuasion. Clients and team members will form their impressions of the HPT professional based on a series of observations made as the project progresses. If the project manager is deemed credible, the team will follow and perform under his or her direction. The criteria on which a project manager's credibility is based can be organized into five categories:

- A clear sense of purpose, including a focus on results and customer satisfaction
- Knowledge of essential project-management concepts, methods, and tools
- Analytical skills and problem-solving skills
- Interpersonal effectiveness
- Personal characteristics such as resilience, composure, and adaptability

CONCLUSION

This chapter began with an acknowledgment that the competitive environment that most organizations face will only become more intense. Leaders who sponsor performance-improvement initiatives position their organizations to succeed in this environment. Project management can serve as an effective tool for managing performance-improvement projects. The concepts, methods, and tools presented in this chapter will not guarantee perfect projects, but careful attention to the following list of critical success factors will go a long way in improving results.

- Balancing the triple constraints of cost, schedule, and quality
- Maintaining a sense of urgency
- Team building and ongoing team management
- Communicating the project in vivid detail
- Aligning project deliverables to original needs defined in the charter and the scope document
- Keeping sponsors and stakeholders fully informed
- Ability of the project manager to clear obstacles for the team
- Having fun while doing serious work

References

Deeprose, D. (2001). *Smart things to know about managing projects.* Oxford, UK: Capstone.

Dobson, M. S. (2003). *Project management: How to manage people, processes, and time to achieve the results you need.* Avon, MA: Adams Media.

Duncan, W. R. (1996). *A guide to the project management body of knowledge.* Darby, PA: Project Management Institute.

Milosevic, D. Z. (2003). *Project management toolbox: Tools and techniques for the practicing project manager.* Hoboken, NJ: Wiley.

Wren, A. (2004). *The project management A–Z: A compendium of project management techniques and how to use them.* Hampshire, UK: Ashgate.

Additional Resources

Cleland, D. I., and Ireland, L. R. (2002). *Project management: Strategic design and implementation* (4th ed.). New York: McGraw-Hill.

Project Management Institute. (2000). *A guide to the project management body of knowledge* (PMBOK® Guide). Drexel Hill, PA: Available from Project Management Institute at www.pmi.org.

CHAPTER FORTY-ONE

Leadership in Performance Consulting

Roger Chevalier

Although there are many models that guide the performance consultant in the overall performance-improvement process, little has been written about the leadership skills necessary to successfully interact with the client. These leadership skills are particularly important as performance consultants partner with their clients to identify performance gaps and causes. This chapter presents the performance consultant's leadership role, models, and performance aids for leading clients in the performance-analysis process. Special attention will be paid to the way in which performance consultants lead their clients with questions.

SITUATIONAL LEADERSHIP

The Situational Leadership Model provides performance consultants with the underlying framework they need to lead their clients in the performance-improvement process (Hersey, Blanchard, and Johnson, 2001). This widely accepted leadership model has been used by over ten million managers worldwide. The underlying premise of situational leadership is that leaders should adjust their leadership styles by varying the amount of direction and psychological support they give based on the followers' readiness level, that is, the followers' degree of ability and willingness to perform a given task (see Figure 41.1).

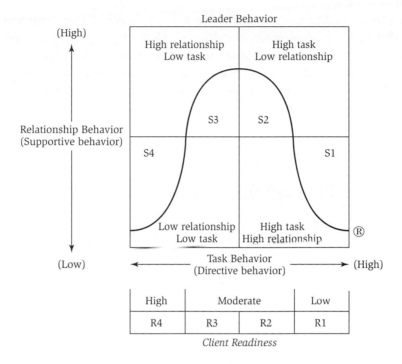

Figure 41.1. Situational Leadership.

The same idea applies to the leadership roles in the performance consulting process. To be effective, consultants must adjust the amount of direction and support they give their clients based on the clients' level of readiness for each step in the performance-improvement process. As such, performance consulting is a unique application of situational leadership.

The lowest readiness level for a group or individual is described as being not willing and not able to do a given task and is labeled R1. The appropriate leadership style, labeled S1, is that of providing high amounts of task behavior or direction, and low amounts of relationship behavior or support. The next readiness level, labeled R2, is described as willing but not able. The appropriate leadership style is that of high amounts of both task and relationship behavior and is labeled S2.

The next readiness level, labeled R3, is described as able but unwilling, in that the individual lacks confidence or commitment. The appropriate leadership style is that of high amounts of relationship behavior and low amounts of task behavior and is labeled S3. The highest readiness level for a group or individual to do a given task is willing and able, and is labeled R4. The appropriate leadership style is that of low amounts of both relationship and task behavior and is labeled S4.

The Situational Leadership Model provides a framework from which to diagnose different situations and prescribes which leadership style will have the highest probability of success in a particular situation. Use of the model will make performance consultants more effective, in that it illustrates the connection between their choice of leadership styles and the readiness of their clients. As such, situational leadership is a powerful tool for performance consultants to use as they work with their clients to identify and determine causes for their performance problems.

THE PERFORMANCE CONSULTING GUIDE

But how do consultants interact one-on-one with clients? The answer became clear in the International Society for Performance Improvement's Principles and Practices programs (International Society for Performance Improvement, 2001), in which participants were asked to describe how they worked with their clients. With a minimum of coaching by the instructor, the Principles and Practices participants described a process of preparation, assessment, diagnosis, prescription, partnering, reinforcement, and follow-up.

Preparation

The first step happens away from the client but greatly influences the interaction process with the client as well as the outcome of the meeting. Preparation includes researching the industry and the organization as well as the specific client within the organization. Internal consultants have access to a great deal of information; external consultants can use the Internet to access industry and organization-specific information. The client will know how well prepared the consultant is by the quality of the questions the consultant poses.

Assessment

The next step centers on building rapport with the client and asking open-ended questions to gain the client's perception of the overall situation. This phase is necessary as the performance consultant builds trust and begins the process of assessing the client's situation and organizational needs. The message from the Principles and Practices participants was that this step is necessary but often overlooked by new consultants who are anxious to get to the problem. This step is critical to building trust with the client as the overall situation is gently probed.

Diagnosis

Once the overall situation has been identified, the performance consultant needs to explore the client's perception of the problem, the implications of the problem, and the value of resolving the problem. This is done with direct questions that guide the discussion as the performance consultant identifies the performance gap and causes with the client. The Principles and Practices participants agreed that these first three steps were necessary to *earn the right* to make a recommendation as to how to improve performance.

Prescription

After identifying the overall situation, problems, implications, and value of improving performance, the performance consultant is ready to make a recommendation as to alternative courses of action. This phase is called "prescription" rather than "presentation" to reinforce the idea from the medical community that "prescription without diagnosis is malpractice." The Principles and Practices participants reinforced this idea, as many had experienced outside vendors who recommended their one prescription, such as a training program, without knowing what the problem was.

Partnering

To work with the client to decide the best course of action, the performance consultant must define what roles each will play. In effect, a partnership is formed in which the client is responsible for correcting the problem, but the performance consultant has a clearly defined role to play in seeking to resolve that problem. The Principles and Practices class was quick to point out that the roles in this partnership are different for each client and problem.

Reinforcement

Before ending the session, the performance consultant should reinforce the client's decision to work together. A member of the class commented that this was tantamount to dealing with buyer's remorse in advance, and it is important that the consultant addresses this before it happens rather than afterward. It is natural for the client to feel apprehensive about taking risks and committing resources to a new course of action.

Follow-Up

Obviously, consultants need to "walk the talk" by making sure that all promises made to the client are fulfilled. Once again, the class was in agreement that all of our good work would be for nothing if the consultant did not meet the expectations created with the client.

The Performance Consulting Guide was developed as part of a family of performance aids developed by the author that apply situational leadership to performance consulting, coaching, sales, and customer service (see Figure 41.2).

Assessment of Client's Readiness

Prepare Low Direction Low Support	**Assess** Low Direction High Support	**Diagnose** High Direction High Support
1. Research organization, industry, and problem.	1. Build rapport, trust, and personal power.	1. Focus discussion with direct questions.
2. Identify measures of success or effectiveness.	2. Probe gently with open-ended questions.	2. Identify present and desired performance outcomes.
3. Set meeting goals; develop an agenda.	3. Actively listen; identify key issues.	3. Select an appropriate style for intervention.

Follow-up Low Direction Low Support	**Reinforce** Low Direction High Support	**Partner** High Direction High Support	**Prescribe** High Direction Low Support
1. Design and develop change strategy.	1. Actively listen; ensure mutual understanding.	1. Discuss available alternative strategies.	1. Summarize what you have learned.
2. Follow through on all commitments.	2. Reinforce decision to move forward.	2. Reach agreement on best course of action.	2. Present needed actions and desired results.
3. Observe, monitor, and track performance.	3. Encourage, motivate, support, and empower.	3. Explain, persuade, guide, and train.	3. Inform, describe, instruct, and direct.
Informed and Committed	**Informed, Committed but Apprehensive**	**Somewhat Informed and Somewhat Committed**	**Neither Informed nor Committed**

Intervention Style Matched to Client's Readiness

Figure 41.2. The Performance Consulting Guide.

Participants of the Principles and Practices programs have validated its structure by describing the process they use when working with clients.

The most important part of the performance consulting process is found in the first three steps, as the performance consultant prepares, assesses, and diagnoses. By gaining an understanding of the client's perception of the problem, the performance consultant is also identifying the client's readiness level to commit to change. A new addition is the ability to skip steps based on how well-informed and committed the client is to the process. Figure 41.2 illustrates how the performance consultant, in effect, is backing through the Situational Leadership Model. The consultant is preparing in style 4, assessing in style 3, and then diagnosing in style 2. If the client is poorly informed and not committed, the performance consultant will need to use style 1 to prescribe alternative strategies and guide the client in the selection of the best alternative. If the client is informed but not committed, the performance consultant should use style 2 to partner with the client to develop a course of action. If the client is informed and committed but apprehensive, the performance consultant should use style 3 to reinforce the client's decision to move ahead. The Performance Consultant Guide provides the overall structure for working one-on-one with clients while allowing flexibility for adjusting to the client's readiness level.

QUESTIONS: THE KEY TO OUR SUCCESS

The key to the performance consulting process is in asking the right questions in the right order. Our goal is to identify the overall situation, specific performance gaps, implications, and value for improving performance. These questions can be incorporated into the overall performance consulting process.

A very useful questioning technique comes from Neil Rackham's book *SPIN Selling* (1988), in which he describes how to use questions in selling to (1) assess the situation, (2) identify the client's perception of the problem, (3) explore the implications of the problem, and (4) gain the client's perception of the need-payoff. These items have been adapted for use in the performance consulting process and are described in the following discussion.

Situation Questions

Situation questions gather background information from the client. Unfortunately, new consultants tend to spend too much time "picking the brain" of their clients by asking too many open-ended questions, usually to make up for their lack of preparation. Examples of situation questions are, How has business been? and Is your business growing or shrinking?

Problem Questions

Problem questions identify the client's perception of current problems and performance shortfalls. These questions are necessary to set up the implication and need-payoff questions that will follow. Examples of problem questions are, What new problems has your rapid growth created for your managers and supervisors? and Do you foresee any shortfalls in your ability to deal with increased demand for your products and services?

Implication Questions

Implication questions explore the effects of the problems on the success of the business. This exercise in "cause and effect" leads the client to a clearer understanding of the problems and their cost in terms of lost productivity, efficiency, profitability, and retention. Examples of implication questions are, How has your rapid growth affected your ability to develop your people? and How would a decrease in employee retention affect the quality of the products you produce?

Need-Payoff Questions

Need-payoff questions gain the client's perception of what would be gained by solving the problem. These questions establish the value of improving performance. At this point, the performance consultant is now able to customize the presentation to meet the specific needs of the client. The consultant has earned the right to give a presentation that has the best chance of being successful. Examples of need-payoff questions are, Why is it important to solve this problem now? and What value do you see in improving the performance of your managers and supervisors?

By helping the client to define the situation, identify current problems, explore the implications of these problems, and determine the value of solving the problems, performance consultants are in a better position to recommend a course of action to improve performance (Chevalier, 2001). These questions can be used in conjunction with the Performance Consulting Guide as depicted in Figure 41.3.

Performance consultants prepare, assess, and diagnose to gain an understanding of the performance gap and causes from the client's point of view and then choose the appropriate style with which to intervene based on how informed and committed the client is. The performance consulting process is an application of leadership in which the consultant becomes a trusted resource for the client. The Performance Consulting Guide and the SPIN questions are job aids that structure the process used by performance consultants to lead their clients.

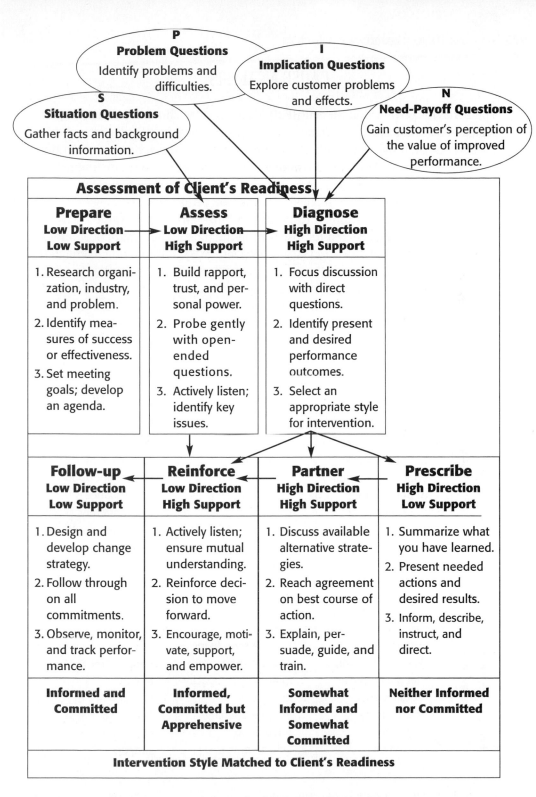

Figure 41.3. SPIN Questions and the Performance Consulting Guide.

CAUSE ANALYSIS

The Behavior Engineering Model (BEM), developed by Thomas Gilbert and presented in his landmark book, *Human Competence: Engineering Worthy Performance* (Gilbert, 1978), provides us with a way to systematically and systemically identify barriers to individual and organizational performance. The BEM distinguishes between what the individual brings to the performance equation and his or her work environment that either promotes or limits job performance (see Figure 41.4).

The BEM has been adapted to provide a more efficient method for troubleshooting performance and for discovering the most important opportunities for improving individual performance (Chevalier, 2003). Like the original model, the updated model, shown in Figure 41.5, serves as a diagnostic tool to be used by the performance consultant in leading clients to identify the underlying causes of their performance shortfalls. Cause analysis provides a framework for discovering the underlying causes but does not direct the performance consultant to the best solutions for correcting the problem.

	Information	**Instrumentation**	**Motivation**
Environmental Supports	*Data* 1. Relevant and frequent feedback about the adequacy of performance 2. Descriptions of what is expected of performance 3. Clear and relevant guides to adequate performance	*Resources* 1. Tools and materials of work designed scientifically to match human factors	*Incentives* 1. Adequate financial incentives made contingent upon performance 2. Nonmonetary incentives made available 3. Career-development opportunities
Person's Repertory of Behavior	*Knowledge* 1. Systematically designed training that matches the requirements of exemplary performance 2. Placement	*Capacity* 1. Flexible scheduling of performance to match peak capacity 2. Prosthesis 3. Physical shaping 4. Adaptation 5. Selection	*Motives* 1. Assessment of people's motives to work 2. Recruitment of people to match the realities of the situation

Figure 41.4. The Behavior Engineering Model.

Source: Gilbert, 1978, p. 88.

	Information	**Resources**	**Incentives**
Environment	1. Roles and performance expectations are clearly defined; employees are given relevant and frequent feedback about the adequacy of performance. 2. Clear and relevant guides are used to describe the work process. 3. The performance management system guides employee performance and development.	1. Materials, tools, and time needed to do the job are present. 2. Processes and procedures are clearly defined and enhance individual performance if followed. 3. Overall physical and psychological work environment contributes to improved performance; work conditions are safe, clean, organized, and conducive to performance.	1. Financial and nonfinancial incentives are present; measurement and reward systems reinforce positive performance. 2. Jobs are enriched to allow for fulfillment of employee needs. 3. Overall work environment is positive, in which employees believe they have an opportunity to succeed; career development opportunities are present.
	Knowledge and Skills	**Capacity**	**Motives**
Individual	1. Employees have the necessary knowledge, experience, and skills to do the desired behaviors. 2. Employees with the necessary knowledge, experience, and skills are properly placed to use and share what they know. 3. Employees are cross-trained to understand each other's roles.	1. Employees have the capacity to learn and do what is needed to perform successfully. 2. Employees are recruited and selected to match the realities of the work situation. 3. Employees are free of emotional limitations that would interfere with their performance.	1. Motives of employees are aligned with the work and the work environment. 2. Employees desire to perform the required jobs. 3. Employees are recruited and selected to match the realities of the work situation.

Figure 41.5. The Updated Behavior Engineering Model.

Using the Updated Behavior Engineering Model

As was the case with the original BEM, the updated model focuses attention on the distinction between environmental and individual factors that affect performance. Environmental factors are the starting point for analysis because they pose the greatest barriers to exemplary performance. When the environmental supports are strong, individuals are better able to do what is expected of them. Environmental causes are analyzed first because, in the words of Geary Rummler and Alan Brache (1995, p. 13), "If you pit a good performer against a bad system, the system will win almost every time."

Environment. The work environment gives three types of performance support: (1) information: communicating clear expectations, providing necessary guides to do work, and giving timely, behaviorally specific feedback; (2) resources: ensuring that the proper materials, tools, time, and processes are present to accomplish the task; and (3) incentives: ensuring that the appropriate financial and nonfinancial incentives are present to encourage performance.

Individual. The individual brings to the job (1) individual motives, aligned with the work environment so employees have a desire to work and excel; (2) capacity, whether the worker is able to learn and do what is necessary to be successful on the job; and (3) knowledge and skills, whether the worker has the necessary knowledge and skills to do a specific task needed to accomplish a specific goal.

The model gives us the structure needed to assess each of the six factors: *information, resources, incentives, motives, capacity,* and *knowledge and skills* that affect individual and group performance. These factors should be reviewed in the order described in Figure 41.6, since the environmental factors are usually less expensive to improve and have a greater impact on individual and group performance. It would also be difficult to assess if the individual had the right motives, capacity, and knowledge and skills to do the job if the environmental factors of information, resources, and incentives are not sufficiently present.

As presented in Figure 41.6, performance can be improved by addressing the information present in the work environment by communicating clear expectations, providing the necessary guides to do the work, and giving timely, behaviorally specific feedback. This can be done at relatively low cost and it benefits performance. Similarly, shortfalls in the resources necessary to do the job can be addressed by ensuring that the proper materials, tools, time, and processes are present. This is also relatively inexpensive and benefits performance. In contrast to these highly leveraged solutions, changes to the individual's motives, capacity, knowledge, and skills will be expensive and may not have the impact made when dealing with the environmental issues.

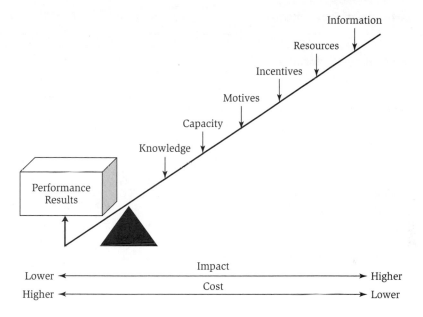

Figure 41.6. Leveraging the Solution.

Source: Adapted from International Society for Performance Improvement, 2001, p. 6.3, Figure 6.2.

Performance Analysis Worksheet

Conducting a thorough cause analysis helps define the reasons why a gap in performance exists. The starting point in using the Performance Analysis Worksheet is identifying the individual's or the organization's present level of performance, where they are, and their desired level of performance, where they want to be. The difference between where they are and where they want to be is the performance gap. Another useful step is to identify a reasonable goal, something that can be accomplished in a short time and that moves the organization in the direction of where it wants to be. This should be defined clearly with measures of quality, quantity, time, and cost delineated for the goal.

Next, assess the impact of the environmental factors, and then move to the individual factors in the order described in Figure 41.7. Environmental factors such as information, resources, and incentives are usually more cost-effective to fix than are individual factors such as motives, capacity, and knowledge. Even if individual factors were successfully changed, performance will most likely not improve if negative environmental factors exist.

The process begins by asking questions to identify how each of these factors is presently affecting the performance gap. Developed by Kurt Lewin (1947), force-field analysis provides a methodology for identifying and weighting the relative strength of factors at the present level of performance (see Figure 41.8).

Present Level of Performance:

_____

_____

Desired Level of Performance:

_____

_____

Reasonable Goal:

_____

_____

Factors	Driving Forces					Restraining Forces			
	+4	+3	+2	+1	0	−1	−2	−3	−4
Information									
Clear expectations	.	.	.	.		.	.	.	.
Relevant feedback	.	.	.	.		.	.	.	.
Relevant guides	.	.	.	.		.	.	.	.
Performance management system	.	.	.	.		.	.	.	.
Resources									
Materials and tools	.	.	.	.		.	.	.	.
Time	.	.	.	.		.	.	.	.
Clear processes or procedures	.	.	.	.		.	.	.	.
Safe and organized environment	.	.	.	.		.	.	.	.
Incentives									
Financial	.	.	.	.		.	.	.	.
Other incentives	.	.	.	.		.	.	.	.
Enriched jobs	.	.	.	.		.	.	.	.
Positive work environment	.	.	.	.		.	.	.	.
Motives									
Motives aligned with work	.	.	.	.		.	.	.	.
Employees' desire to perform	.	.	.	.		.	.	.	.
Realistic expectations	.	.	.	.		.	.	.	.
The right people recruited or selected	.	.	.	.		.	.	.	.
Capacity									
Capacity to learn	.	.	.	.		.	.	.	.
Capacity to do what is needed	.	.	.	.		.	.	.	.
The right people recruited or selected	.	.	.	.		.	.	.	.
Emotional limitations	.	.	.	.		.	.	.	.
Knowledge and Skills									
Necessary knowledge	.	.	.	.		.	.	.	.
Necessary skills	.	.	.	.		.	.	.	.
Proper placement	.	.	.	.		.	.	.	.
Cross-training	.	.	.	.		.	.	.	.

Figure 41.7. Performance Analysis Worksheet.

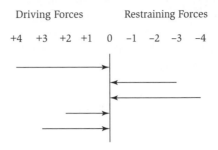

Figure 41.8. Force-Field Analysis.

Driving forces are those factors that are already working to close the gap between the present level of performance and the desired level of performance. These are identified and evaluated as to their relative strength on a +1 to +4 scale. Restraining forces are those factors that are working against closing the gap. These are identified and evaluated as to their relative strength on a –1 to –4 scale.

Figure 41.7 depicts a one-page worksheet that brings together gap analysis, cause analysis, and force-field analysis into a useful performance aid. Whether the consultant is working with an individual or a group, the worksheet gives the needed structure to guide questions to identify the driving and restraining forces.

Leading with Questions

In 1982, Thomas Gilbert published a collection of questions used to assess the state of the six cells in his Behavior Engineering Model. He called these questions "The PROBE Model," a contraction of "*PRO*filing *BE*havior" (Gilbert, 1982). The PROBE model consisted of forty-two questions to be used to assess the accomplishment of any job in any work situation.

Following Gilbert's lead, I developed the PROBE questions depicted in Figure 41.9 to support the Updated Behavior Engineering Model. In addition to the direct questions that follow from the original PROBE questions, an open-ended question has been added to start the discussion with the client. It is important to start the discussion with an open-ended question to keep the client from getting defensive from a series of direct questions.

CASE STUDY: PERFORMANCE ANALYSIS

The following performance-improvement intervention started the way most do, with a request for training. A company provided software products and services for very large financial organizations and government agencies. Management had recently decided to develop products and services for

A. Information

Open-ended, exploratory question: How are performance expectations communicated to employees?

Direct, follow-up questions:

1. Have clear performance expectations been communicated to employees?
2. Do employees understand the various aspects of their roles and the priorities for doing them?
3. Are there clear and relevant performance aids to guide the employees?
4. Are employees given sufficient, timely, behaviorally specific feedback regarding their performance?
5. Does the performance management system assist the supervisor in describing expectations for both activities and results for the employee?

B. Resources

Open-ended, exploratory question: What do your employees need in order to perform successfully?

Direct, follow-up questions:

1. Do employees have the materials needed to do their jobs?
2. Do employees have the equipment to do their jobs?
3. Do employees have the time they need to do their jobs?
4. Are the processes and procedures defined in such a way as to enhance employee performance?
5. Is the work environment safe, clean, organized, and conducive to excellent performance?

C. Incentives

Open-ended, exploratory question: How are employees rewarded for successful performance?

Direct, follow-up questions:

1. Are there sufficient financial incentives present to encourage excellent performance?
2. Are there sufficient nonfinancial incentives present to encourage excellent performance?
3. Do measurement and reporting systems track appropriate activities and results?
4. Are jobs enriched to allow for fulfillment of higher-level needs?
5. Are there opportunities for career development?

Figure 41.9. Updated Behavior Engineering PROBE Questions.

D. Motives

Open-ended, exploratory question: How do your employees respond to the performance incentives you have in place?

Direct, follow-up questions:

1. Are the motives of the employees aligned with the incentives in the environment?
2. Do employees desire to do the job to the best of their abilities?
3. Are employees recruited and selected to match the realities of the work environment?
4. Do employees view the work environment as positive?
5. Are there any rewards that reinforce poor performance or negative consequences for good performance?

E. Capacity

Open-ended, exploratory question: How are employees selected for their jobs?

Direct, follow-up questions:

1. Do the employees have the strength necessary to do the job?
2. Do the employees have the dexterity necessary to do the job?
3. Do employees have the ability to learn what is expected for them to do to be successful on the job?
4. Are employees free from any emotional limitations that impede performance?
5. Are employees recruited, selected, and matched to the realities of the work situation?

F. Knowledge and Skills

Open-ended, exploratory question: How do employees learn what they need to be successful on the job?

Direct, follow-up questions:

1. Do the employees have the knowledge necessary to be successful at their jobs?
2. Do the employees have the skills needed to be successful at their jobs?
3. Do the employees have the experience needed to be successful at their jobs?
4. Do employees have a systematic training program to enhance their knowledge and skills?
5. Do employees understand how their roles affect organizational performance?

Figure 41.9 *(Continued)*.

medium-size financial institutions and had formed a sales team to bring these products to market.

While the sales manager was looking for training to enhance the selling skills of his sales team, he was also interested in a broader solution to build systems that would systematically track and continuously improve the performance of his people. Not only would the solution have to contain selling and sales-management systems to support the training given the sales team, it also would have to bridge the gap between the sales team and the customer service people in another division.

The new sales manager had recently joined the company. While he had some experience with the products and services offered by his new company, he had little sales experience. One month before he had joined his new company and while working at his former company, he had been involved in the purchase of the new products and services. He was very enthusiastic about the services being offered, understood their potential, and wanted to join his new company to be a part of the team that brought the new products and services to a broader market. He had sold his interest in his former business to his old partners and reinvested the money to become a partner in the new company, becoming the sales manager.

During an interview with the sales manager, the following information was revealed:

1. The six salespeople hired had a wide range of sales experience and knowledge of the products and services being offered. Two of them had been involved in the products' development but knew little about sales. Two of them had excellent track records in selling software and technical products but knew little about the new products and services being offered. Another had some experience with the products and services and some sales experience. The last member of the sales team was the brother-in-law of the owner and founder and had some experience in real estate sales.

2. The sales manager had tried cross-training the different salespeople by sending them out together on sales calls, and he would try to match salespeople with different backgrounds. He would also go on sales calls with each salesperson to observe and provide feedback. He was not happy with the results to date and thought he was running out of time. The company had not made a sale since the deal with the sales manager's former company.

3. The sales manager indicated that they had three months in which to obtain one sale per salesperson; this would allow the company to break even and provide each salesperson a living wage. Salespeople had a base salary and worked on commissions. They were taking advances against future commissions.

4. The software product was very expensive, just over $100,000. In addition, the customer would pay about $5,000 a month for related services. While the sales manager's old company had had the software in place for only two months, the increased profits would pay off the initial investment in six months and then start producing a substantial profit.

5. There were no tracking systems in place to manage the leads they obtained from three sources: (1) from their present customers, large financial institutions that referred smaller companies to them; (2) from trade shows, where they would meet potential customers; and (3) from government reports that would identify and qualify potential customers. All salespeople followed up on the leads they were given, but there was no overall tracking system in place.

6. The selling process was not defined. Since the only sale made to date was unique, with the CEO selling the product and service to an old friend, there was no model of the selling process that could be followed.

7. The best leads were generated by the large financial institutions, which would invite their customers in for a sales presentation. What had been discovered was that typically only one of the decision makers needed for the sale would attend. They needed to reach the company's CEO or owner, CFO, and IT manager if the sale was to be approved. Each of these individuals had different information needs in order to make their part of the decision.

8. Interviews with the salespeople indicated that they were aware of the goal of one sale per salesperson in the next three months. They were becoming concerned about making the goal. They were well equipped with laptop computers and demo programs but lacked a structured way to approach the selling process and analyze their progress with prospects. They received feedback from each other and when the sales manager went on a sales call with them. While they liked the sales manager and the job itself, they were becoming discouraged.

9. The salespeople were a very mixed group. While the team together had what it needed to be successful, individually each salesperson was lacking some knowledge and skills necessary to be successful. Guidance was limited at best, and feedback from their prospects was nonexistent. All wanted to do a good job and appeared to be highly motivated but did not know what it would take to make them successful. There was no performance-management system in place to clearly define the activities needed to be successful.

10. Because of the time constraints, the intervention would have to be designed and implemented within two weeks.

The Performance Analysis Worksheet was used to guide the gathering of the needed information and to display the overall picture of what was found. It combines gap analysis, cause analysis, and force-field analysis to develop a graphic depiction of the situation and the forces affecting it. Figure 41.10 is a completed Performance Analysis Worksheet that displays the information from the case study.

After this picture of the performance gap and the factors working for and against closing the gap was developed, the strategy for closing the gap became one of adding to or strengthening driving forces and minimizing or removing restraining forces.

After the consultant met with the sales manager and several of his salespeople, a proposal was developed that included four hours of leadership and coaching training for the sales manager and the other managers associated with the customer service process. This was followed by sixteen hours of consultative sales and customer service training for all sales and customer service personnel.

Since coaching, sales, and customer service are all applications of leadership, the training programs were designed around performance aids derived from Situational Leadership to assist managers in the performance coaching process and employees in their sales and service roles. By capturing the parallel processes of coaching, sales, and service in three similar performance aids, the basis for an integrated system was established.

Two sales management systems were developed from the coaching and sales performance aids and from employee input given during the training programs. The systems focused on the means (how salespeople were working with clients) as well as the ends (how clients moved through the sales funnel to become customers).

A client and customer survey, derived from the sales performance guide, was developed to gather information from clients and customers regarding the selling process and the value of the products and services being offered. As soon as a lead was declared dead, a one-page survey was sent to the potential client who had failed to make a purchase. A more comprehensive two-page survey was sent to customers after the software was installed and the first month of service was provided.

When the surveys were returned, a copy was immediately given to the salesperson who handled that client. The sales manager's administrative assistant would analyze the feedback received for each salesperson and prepare a monthly summary for the sales manager, who would then provide feedback on selling tendencies to each salesperson.

A parallel survey was also developed to gather information every three months from the salespeople on areas in which they needed to improve and on the leadership they were receiving from the sales manager. The net effect was an interrelated survey system for systematic assessment and continuous

Present Level of Performance: *A sales group of mixed readiness levels, with an inexperienced sales manager, in danger of floundering*

Desired Level of Performance: *A trained, confident, productive and continuously improving sales team*

Reasonable Goal: *One sale per sales person per month in three months*

Factors	Driving Forces					Restraining Forces			
	+4	+3	+2	+1	0	−1	−2	−3	−4

Information
- Clear expectations
- Relevant feedback
- Relevant guides
- Performance management system

Resources
- Materials and tools
- Time
- Clear processes or procedures
- Safe and organized environment

Incentives
- Financial
- Other incentives
- Enriched jobs
- Positive work environment

Motives
- Motives aligned with work
- Employees' desire to perform
- Realistic expectations
- The right people recruited or selected

Capacity
- Capacity to learn
- Capacity to do what is needed
- The right people recruited or selected
- Emotional limitations

Knowledge and skills
- Necessary knowledge
- Necessary skills
- Proper placement
- Cross-training

Figure 41.10. Completed Performance Analysis Worksheet.

improvement of the sales and coaching processes. Customer service surveys were later developed to bring the customer service division under the same system.

The feedback from potential clients, customers, and salespeople that was obtained from the various surveys also aided in identifying specific knowledge and skill deficiencies in the sales team as a group. These were remedied with short training sessions held during the weekly sales meetings and were presented by either the sales manager, one of the salespeople, or the outside consultant.

Another element of the system was the creation of weekly sales meetings to reinforce the idea that the salespeople were members of a team rather than just individuals working on their own. Salespeople who were on the road phoned in to participate in the one-hour meeting whenever possible. The agenda allowed salespeople to describe their progress and get credit for their victories by ringing a bell for each victory.

The combination of these interventions provided the needed training and built a basic sales system that helped the fledgling sales team surpass all sales goals during the first two quarters following the training while developing a strong foundation for their future success. Bringing the customer service team under the same systematic assessment and continuous improvement survey system the following quarter further integrated the two divisions. The group made its sales goal of one sale per salesperson in the third month by making five sales and terminating one salesperson. They went on to great success and were eventually bought out by a major software producer.

CONCLUSION

Leadership plays an important role throughout the performance-improvement process. It is most important in guiding clients and during the performance-analysis phase. Situational leadership can serve as the underlying model for the performance consulting process, in which the consultant prepares, assesses, diagnoses, presents, partners, reinforces, and follows up in leading the client as described in the Performance Consulting Guide.

Gilbert's Behavior Engineering Model has been a valuable tool for systematically identifying barriers to individual and organizational performance. With some updating and the addition of a performance aid to guide its use, a more clearly defined process for identifying the causes that contribute to a performance gap is defined. The Performance Analysis Worksheet brings together the concepts of gap analysis, cause analysis, and force-field analysis into a job aid that can serve as a useful tool to guide the assessment process for performance-improvement professionals as they lead their clients.

Used together, the Performance Consulting Guide, SPIN Questions, the Updated Behavior Engineering Model and PROBE Questions, and the Performance Analysis Worksheet can guide the performance consultant in leading clients as they work together to identify performance gaps and their causes.

References

Chevalier, R. D. (2001). Performance consulting: Job aids for interacting with clients. *Performance Improvement, 40*(1), 28–31.

Chevalier, R. D. (2003). Updating the behavior engineering model. *Performance Improvement, 42*(5), 8–14.

Gilbert, T. F. (1978). *Human competence: Engineering worthy performance.* New York: McGraw-Hill.

Gilbert, T. F. (1982, September). A question of performance, part I: The PROBE model. *Training & Development Journal, 36*(9), 21–30.

Hersey, P., Blanchard, K. H., and Johnson, D. E. (2001). *Management of organizational behavior* (8th ed.). Upper Saddle River, NJ: Prentice-Hall.

International Society for Performance Improvement. (2001). *Online institute: Principles and practices of human performance technology participant manual.* Silver Spring, MD: International Society for Performance Improvement.

Lewin, K. (1947). Frontiers in group dynamics: Concept, method, and reality in social science; social equilibria and social change. *Human Relations, 1,* 5–41.

Rackham, N. (1988). *SPIN selling.* New York: McGraw-Hill.

Rummler, G. A., and Brache, A. B. (1995). *Improving performance: How to manage the white space on the organization chart* (2nd ed.). San Francisco: Jossey-Bass.

CHAPTER FORTY-TWO

The Anatomy of Performance

A Framework for Consultants

Geary A. Rummler

Sara was ecstatic as she left the meeting and headed for her office. This was the third successful performance analysis and improvement project she had completed in the past eighteen months at JAX, Inc. Plus her boss, the vice president of the JAX Corporate Performance Support Group, had just asked her to make a presentation to a group of new performance consultant candidates on what it takes to be a successful performance consultant. It could not get much better than this!

BACKGROUND

Three years ago, Sara had joined the JAX Corporate Performance Support Group (PSG), which had recently evolved from a traditional training organization to a performance-improvement department. The organization continued to deliver training when appropriate, but it also provided or managed the implementation of other performance-improvement interventions. The resources in the JAX Corporate PSG were organized into teams that were assigned to support particular JAX subsidiaries or corporate functions. Although Sara occasionally did some training design, her responsibilities on the team were more about analyzing requests for assistance and determining the most appropriate action to close performance gaps identified during needs assessments.

Because of her successful work, and as part of her professional development plan, Sara was promoted eight months ago to a different PSG team, supporting a much larger subsidiary, AJAX, Inc. Her most recent project, her first at AJAX, had required learning a new client organization and understanding the performance issue.

FOUR CRITICAL SUCCESS FACTORS FOR PERFORMANCE CONSULTING

Back in her office, Sara began to think about her upcoming presentation for the new performance consultant candidates. She reflected on what had contributed to her success as a performance consultant over the past three years. By success she meant the positive reaction of the client to her findings, the client's commitment to implementing her recommendations, the relatively short time it took to look at the problem and develop appropriate recommendations, and, finally, the impact on measurable organization results. After some thought, Sara isolated four critical success factors (CSFs) that lead to successful performance consulting:

CSF 1: Focus on Results

Since becoming a performance consultant, Sara had made results a priority. Regardless of the issue confronting the team, she insisted on understanding the gap in results that she and the team were to close. This meant clarifying the current, or *is,* results and the desired, or *should,* results of the client organization. Because she was a *performance* consultant, she saw her job and that of the PSG as closing gaps in job, process, and organization results.

CSF 2: Understand Reality

The typical situation faced by Sara and her team can be represented by the diagram in Figure 42.1. It usually works like this: the majority of consulting work begins with a request for help from an executive or manager of some operation who sees or hears something (A) that causes that person to believe a problem exists. Moreover, in many instances the requester also reaches a conclusion as to what an appropriate solution should be, such as team building, training, and personal coaching. The requester, or worse yet, an intermediary, with his or her own interpretation of the problem and solution, then contacts a resource (B) and requests that particular solution, seldom mentioning any gap in job performance or organization results (C) that might have occurred because of (A).

Now the scenario gets interesting. What will the resource (B) do? The most common option is to follow path (D) and just say yes to the request and faithfully deliver the requested solution. Alternatively, the resource could follow path (E) and

- Examine the situation (A) for himself or herself
- Determine if the apparent problem can be linked to a gap in results (C)

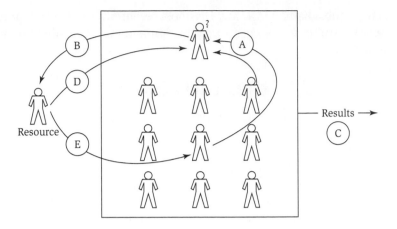

Figure 42.1. The Typical Performance Consulting Situation.

- Employ a sound analysis methodology and arrive at his or her independent conclusions regarding the problem and solution

- Work with the requestor to define a project that will solve the
  problem as perceived by the requester *and* deliver measurable
  results (C)

Sara and the vice president of the PSG believe that the preferred path is
(E). Sara and her team follow path (E) whenever feasible because they
believe the result is better for the customers and the financial stakeholders
of JAX.

However, Sara and her colleagues in the PSG have learned that there are
times to follow path (E) and there are times not to. In some cases, it is best
either to pursue path (D) or to convince the requester that no action is really
necessary. The organizational reality is that performance consulting represented
by path (E) is a role Sara plays only from time to time. That is to say, not every
request for help that comes her way merits application of her performance
analysis and performance consulting skill set.

She applies the rigor of performance analysis underlying performance consulting only if

- The situation involves a significant gap in results.

- The solution to closing the gap will most likely require more than just a
  training solution.

- The requester has some tolerance for conducting some brief initial
  analysis.

Many times, Sara can put on her performance consulting hat, but not always. Being sensitive to this reality and knowing when to follow path (E) and when not to have been critical to the success of Sara and her team.

CSF 3: Apply the Anatomy of Performance Model

Sara believed that the mental model she called the *anatomy of performance* (AOP) was the foundation of all her success. It was the basis for what she did as a performance analyst and performance consultant. What is the AOP? The AOP is to a performance consultant what human anatomy is to a physician. Knowledge of human anatomy provides the physician with a framework for understanding how components of the human body interact. Every physician knows the factors that determine good health, the consequences of a failure in any of those factors, and what must be done to correct a failed factor and return the patient to good health. Physicians also know that symptoms in one area may result from problems in another. This understanding requires them to take a systems view of the problem. Even though patients come in different sizes and colors, physicians know that inside they all have the same parts, located in basically the same physical area, and that they are supposed to perform the same function within the system (Rummler, 2004).

The AOP provides a similar framework for the performance consultant. It identifies the basic factors or variables that intersect in an organization and affect individual performance and organizational results. Sara knew that all organizations, including AJAX and its subsidiaries, contain the components of the AOP. She used the AOP framework to gain a quick understanding of which variables were causing a gap in results and what was required to close the gap. The utility of this framework starts with the situation Sara described in Figure 42.1, a request from within an organizational unit. The AOP is all about quickly understanding what is going on in that organizational unit box from which the request emanated. Sara, or any other good performance consultant, wants to understand the dynamics of that organizational box because gaps in human behavior, performance, and job results *never* take place in a vacuum. They always occur in the organizational context of other performers, functions, processes, procedures, systems, policies, and management practices, and the cause of most gaps in job and organization results is a function of those many interacting factors. It is essential, therefore, that performance consultants find out what those interacting factors are as quickly as possible, usually when they first try to identify a rational explanation for gaps in results. To novice performance consultants, this task may sound like a major challenge, because they can expect to look at a great variety of problems in many kinds of organizational units over the course of their careers. Fortunately, the AOP model makes it possible to see that all organizations are essentially the same, at least in regard to the factors that affect individual performance and influence organization results.

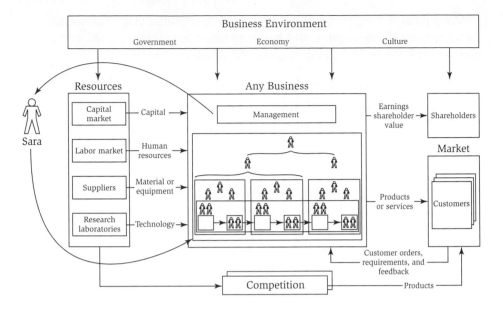

Figure 42.2. The Anatomy of Performance (AOP).

For her latest project, Sara was fielding a request from an executive in a business she had never seen before. Yet, in a matter of two weeks, Sara was in control of the situation. She had an understanding of the performance context of the initial request and even proposed enlarging the scope of the initial project. How had she done that?

When Sara looks at or thinks about AJAX or any organization, what she envisions is the AOP, shown in Figure 42.2. The anatomy of performance boils down to these two points:

- An organization is a complex system of individuals, jobs, processes, functions, and management.

- Organizational performance or results are a function of how well these interdependent components are aligned and working toward clearly specified results.

In the eyes of the serious performance consultant, every performance issue, whether it is an individual, a job, or a process, must always be seen in the overarching *organizational* context: the anatomy of performance. Referring to the diagram in Figure 42.2, Sara understood the following about the AJAX organization before she had ever asked a question about the company:

- AJAX is a processing system. AJAX's primary function is to convert customer needs or orders into valued outputs. AJAX uses the resources you see on the left side of Figure 42.2 to create those valued outputs. The more effective the processing system is in delivering value to the customers, the more value, also known as return on investment, the organization can provide its shareholders (Rummler, 1998).

- AJAX is an adaptive system, represented by the box labeled "Any Business" in Figure 42.2. AJAX in turn exists in a super-system comprising all the elements outside the Any Business box. AJAX must continually adapt to changes in those elements as it tries to deliver value to its customers and shareholders. These changes might include a shortage of materials, changing customer expectations, a new competitive product, or a decline in the general economy. The bottom line is that AJAX must adapt or die.

- Jobs or roles and functions in AJAX exist to support processes. Functions and jobs represent nonvalue-added cost until they are linked to processes that deliver value to customers. Customer requirements should drive process requirements. Subsequently, process requirements should drive function and job requirements.

- All performers in AJAX exist in a human performance system. Figure 42.3 represents the reality of any of the performers shown in Figure 42.2. They all exist in their own unique human performance systems. All the conditions shown in Figure 42.3 must be met if an organization is going to get the desired behavior or performance from a particular individual (Rummler, 1988).

- AJAX's effectiveness requires alignment of the organization, process, and function or job levels. The goals of AJAX must be aligned with the expectations of customers and investors. The goals of the major processes must be aligned with the organization goals. Finally, the goals of functions and jobs must be aligned to the processes that they perform. This alignment forms a value-creating system within AJAX. Figure 42.4 presents a summary of the major variables affecting results at each level. The *should* requirements of each variable are also identified. Failure to achieve desired results at any of the three levels can be traced to a failure of one or more of the variables at that level to meet the necessary requirements.

- The role of AJAX management is to keep all the system components shown in Figure 42.2 aligned. Management must see that AJAX's goals and strategy align with the reality of its super-system, the internal process goals align with AJAX's corporate goals, and function and job goals align with process goals. Finally, they must see that the components of an individual's human performance system are aligned to support the desired behavior or performance of that individual.

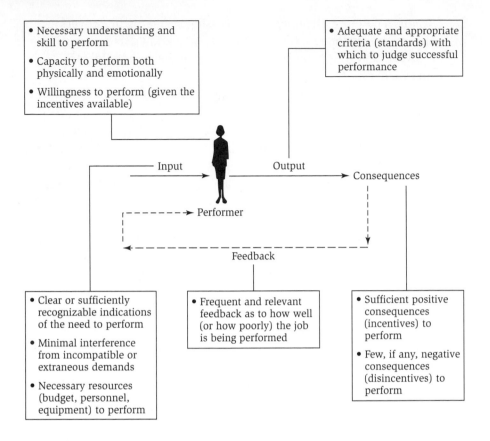

Figure 42.3. The Human Performance System (HPS).

Sara has come to think of organizations as giant value machines, whose primary goal is to deliver value to customers and investors. The job of Sara as a performance consultant is to continually improve the effectiveness and efficiency of that machine. Essentially, the AOP is a template that guides Sara in looking for causes of breakdowns or inefficiencies in the value machine.

CSF 4: Establish a Chain of Results

This point is really a corollary of CSF 3. The AOP framework stresses the connections among customer, organization, process, and job requirements that are necessary to produce customer-valued outputs. This connection makes it possible and useful to establish a results chain linking job, process, and organization issues, as displayed in Figure 42.5.

C. Organization Results

Requirements

1. Super-system monitored and action taken
2. Organization direction aligned with super-system
   a. Mission or vision
   b. Strategy
   c. Business model
   d. Goals
3. Processes aligned and optimized to achieve desired organization results
   a. Goals aligned
   b. Processes capable
4. Process results, as described in "B"

B. Process Results

Requirements

1. Process outputs and requirements are
   a. Linked to organization and customer requirements
   b. Clear
   c. Communicated
2. Process is designed to meet output requirements
3. Inputs or triggers meet input standards
4. Necessary resources are available
5. Job results, as described in "A"

A. Job Results

Requirements

1. Job outputs and requirements are
   a. Linked to process, organization, and customer requirements
   b. Clear
   c. Communicated
2. Job is designed to meet job output requirements
3. Inputs or triggers meet input standards
4. Necessary resources are available
5. Performer has capacity
6. Performer has necessary knowledge and skill
7. Appropriate balance of consequences
8. Appropriate feedback on performance

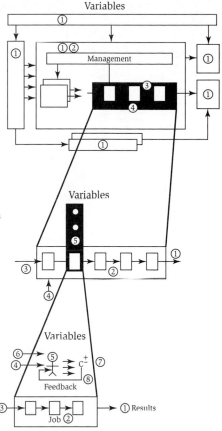

Figure 42.4. Major Variables Affecting Organization, Process, and Job Results.

The results chain is a set of linked issues and associated results gaps at the job, process, and organization levels. A complete results chain includes

- A critical job issue (CJI): a gap between desired and actual results regarding a key job output or outcome

- A critical process issue (CPI): a gap between desired and actual results regarding a key process output or outcome

- A critical business issue (CBI): a gap between desired and actual results regarding a key organization output or outcome

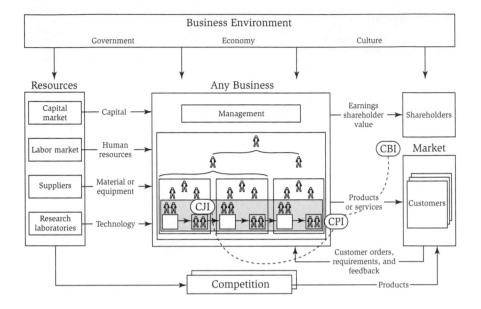

Figure 42.5. The Results Chain.

Consider this example of a results chain: business office representatives in a telecom company fail to capture critical information from a new customer about when the customer will be home to provide access for a service person to provide the necessary hook-up, a critical job issue. Because all jobs are part of a process or processes, it is necessary to ask if this CJI affects a critical process issue. In this case the answer is yes since the business office representative's job affects the installation process, which has a CPI having to do with the time to install new service. If the property access time is incorrect, the installer will have to return to the property a second time, leading to additional installation expense and a delay in installation of the service and revenue. Finally, does this CPI have an effect on the business at large; that is, does it constitute a critical business issue? Yes, because failing to show up at the customer's domicile for service installation at the time promised leads to that customer and probably several of his friends and acquaintances defecting to the competition.

If the performance consultant can establish a results chain connecting a CJI to a CPI to a CBI, then he or she can move the scope of the potential project up the results chain. Closing a gap in job performance leads to closing a gap in process performance, which may then close a gap in organizational performance.

Why would a performance consultant want to do this? First, a project has a greater potential impact on organization results as one moves up the results chain. Second, it is easier to garner management support for implementing a project if it can be shown that there may be organization-level results in the offing: "I know we are cutting costs in the organization, but we simply cannot halt Sara's project. It is going to improve market share." Third, if the apparent CJI cannot be linked to a CPI, then there may not be much value in pursuing the project, and the performance consultant should back away if at all possible.

Sara concluded that the four CSFs were the points she wanted to stress to the performance consultant candidates. She also decided she would use her most recent project, the one for the AJAX subsidiary, to illustrate these four critical success factors. To that end, Sara began making some notes on how that project had evolved.

PROJECT REDUX: THE REQUEST FOR HELP

The project started with this phone message from the vice president of sales at AJAX:

> It has been brought to my attention that some of our sales reps continue to submit incomplete sales orders to production. Is it possible for you to develop a one-day refresher training session for the sales reps addressing this issue, maybe something we can deliver during our quarterly sales meetings? The next one is in six weeks. Please let me know what you think.

During a follow-up phone conversation with an assistant to the vice president of sales, Sara received approval to spend two weeks gathering more information about this issue before committing to a particular plan of action. She immediately set out to take stock of what she knew about the request and about AJAX to see if it was realistic for her to apply the rigor of performance consulting (CSF 2: Understand Reality). Basically, Sara found herself in the situation depicted in Figure 42.1. She had received a request for help from an executive within an organizational unit box. She had already been granted time to start down path E. Now she had to learn quickly what went on inside the box that might have an effect on the request. Thanks to Sara's understanding of the AOP framework, she already had a head start on this task.

Using AJAX's organizational chart (Figure 42.6) and her basic knowledge of AJAX, Sara generated a first approximation of an AOP diagram for AJAX (Figure 42.7) on a whiteboard (CSF 3: Apply the Anatomy of Performance Model). This diagram summarized what she knew and what she had yet to learn about AJAX and the request for help. Sara was pleased with what she had diagrammed, given that she had yet to set foot on AJAX property or interview any AJAX staff.

Stepping back from the whiteboard, Sara reflected on what she already knew about this request and AJAX and what she needed to learn to complete her analysis. Looking at the rough AOP she had developed, Sara knew that the sales rep job was at the bottom of the sales hierarchy in the sales department.

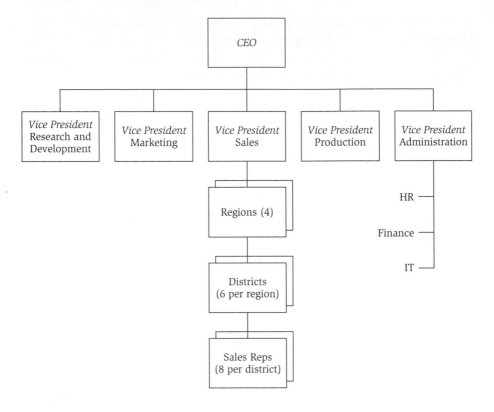

Figure 42.6. AJAX's Organizational Chart.

It appeared that the sales order was a key output of the sales rep job. The failure of the sales reps to consistently submit complete sales order forms appeared to be a CJI, representing a definable gap between the desired result of 100 percent complete orders and the current, or *is,* results that fell short of the 100 percent *should* results—the gap in results. She had yet to discover the exact percentage of sales orders that were currently being completed properly.

What Sara needed to learn next was

1. What exactly was the gap in results, the difference between *is* and *should* performance, and was it significant (CSF 1: Focus on Results)?

2. Was there a pattern as to when and where this gap occurred?

3. What were the causes of the gap in job-level results?

4. What processes were affected by the sales rep job in general? How did the sales rep job affect the customer in particular? Although the initial focus was on the sales rep job, it was necessary to understand the process context of the sales rep job because jobs are always part of a process and exist to perform or support that process.

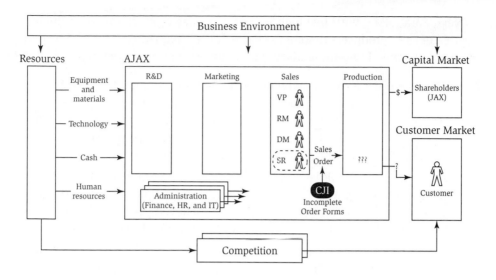

Figure 42.7. AJAX Anatomy of Performance Approximation I.

Given what she knew and needed to know, Sara then planned a two-pronged approach for the next two weeks of data gathering: she needed to learn more about the sales rep job and the CJI, and she needed to learn how the sales rep job connected to the customers.

PROJECT REDUX: JOB-LEVEL ANALYSIS

Sara was aided in her analysis of the sales rep job by the job-level variables and requirements shown in section A of Figure 42.4. Sara used this diagram as a job results template and set about to compare the *should* requirements shown for each variable against the *is* reality of the sales rep job.

Guided by the job results template, Sara talked with representatives of the AJAX production department who quickly verified that incomplete order forms had been an increasing problem for the past eighteen months and that incomplete forms had been running around 8 percent to 10 percent for months. The problem of incomplete forms occurred in all the sales districts, across all products produced by AJAX. There definitely was a gap between desired and current results. This gap, however, did not affect sales in a negative way, as all the orders were eventually processed. When incomplete order forms were submitted, clerks in the production organization had to call the customer to get the missing details, such as desired shipping date, receiving address, or product and market codes, to enter the order into their system. This step added time and cost to the production process and, on occasion, irritated the customer.

Next, Sara talked with five high-performing sales reps who were in the top quartile of sales producers despite the fact that they frequently submitted incomplete order forms. From these discussions, she learned the following:

- The sales order form was submitted to sales administration and then sent to production. A sale was deemed complete for commission purposes as soon as it was received by sales administration whether the sales order form was completed correctly or not. In other words, sales reps were rewarded for the undesired behavior of submitting an incomplete order form.

- Although the sales order forms were not hard to complete, sales reps found completing all sections of the form to be a time-consuming aggravation while they were on the road. They believed they could produce healthier sales numbers if they did not have so much paperwork.

- The sales reps also thought it a major inconvenience to cart around the order code manual. They could not keep up with the frequent code changes, and the information was often out of date.

- Infrequently, the vice president of sales would send a memo to the four regional sales managers urging them to make sure that their sales reps understood the importance of completing the order forms. The situation would usually improve for a couple of weeks following one of these memos, but the number of incomplete forms would quickly rebound.

Sara also learned that she could not apply the job results template just to the sales rep job. She had to apply it to all the jobs in the sales hierarchy because it was essential that the human performance systems, particularly in terms of expectations, measures, consequences, and feedback, be aligned from top to bottom for all the people in the hierarchy.

When she discussed the problem of incomplete sales orders with a sample of district and regional sales managers, she learned that they cared only about the number of sales orders entered, not their completeness. Sheer numbers had become the unspoken priority ever since the new vice president of sales had taken over two years ago. There were no negative consequences for incomplete order forms, only positive consequences in the form of the commissions received regardless of the completeness of the order forms.

Sara summarized her conclusions regarding the CJI and the gap in results as shown in Table 42.1.

From these data, Sara concluded that the gap in results was not something that was going to be corrected through training. An effective solution would have to address other components in the human performance system as well, including

- Clarifying what is expected of and by the sales reps and their managers
- Modifying the sales order form

Table 42.1. Sales Rep Job Findings Regarding Incomplete Sales Order Forms.

Requirements for Job Results	AJAX Sales Rep Findings
1. Job outputs and requirements are clear and effectively communicated.	Mixed signals: The occasional memo stating need for complete order forms is at odds with pressure from managers to just get the orders in.
2. Job is designed to meet job output requirements.	Yes: not an issue.
3. Input and triggers meet input standards.	Yes: not an issue.
4. Necessary resources are available.	No: The order code manual is an issue and it is awkward to use.
5. Performer has capacity.	Yes: not an issue.
6. Performer has necessary knowledge and skill.	Yes: There is no evidence that sales reps do not know how to complete sales order forms.
7. Consequences are balanced appropriately.	No: Manager priorities and current sales commission policies support submission of incomplete sales order forms.
8. Appropriate feedback is provided for performance.	No: No specific feedback is given to sales reps on the number of times incomplete order forms are submitted and the subsequent impact on AJAX and the customer.

- Finding an alternative to the code manual
- Modifying consequences so that sales reps are not automatically paid for their failure to meet standards
- Providing specific feedback to sales reps and their bosses regarding their performance against standards

Based on this analysis, Sara was confident she knew how to close the results gap attributable to the CJI. Closing the results gap regarding incomplete sales order forms, however, was not going to be a slam-dunk training program as the vice president of sales had anticipated and requested. The vice president of sales was feeling no pain around this CJI because, after all, it did not affect the number of sales booked. Sara was betting that to get support for the kind of changes required to close this gap in results she would have to move up the results chain to link to some significant results at either the process or the organization level.

She therefore decided to investigate the process context of the CJI to see if there was a potential CPI.

PROJECT REDUX: PROCESS-LEVEL ANALYSIS AND BEYOND

Now Sara had to expand her understanding of the AJAX AOP as it related to this project. Based on her interviews with the sales reps and some people in production, Sara knew that sales reps were participants in the customer order process. The completed sales order form, a principal output of the sales rep job, was also the critical input to the customer order process that ultimately delivered the product to the customer. Next question: Did a CPI exist regarding the customer order process?

Sara learned from the marketing and sales managers that customers were expressing increasing dissatisfaction about the length of time required to receive their orders. AJAX filled orders in an average of twenty days, compared with five days by some of its competitors. This problem certainly constituted a legitimate CPI and represented a significant gap in results regarding the customer order process. There certainly seemed to be an opportunity to affect this gap in process results. In fact, Sara believed she most likely could fix the CJI in the context of the CPI because the CPI of the customer satisfaction was influenced by the CJI of incomplete sales order forms. Moving up the results chain to the CPI of customer satisfaction and time to receive orders garnered significant leverage for implementing job-level changes in the customer order process.

With her new-found knowledge, Sara updated her AOP diagram as shown in Figure 42.8 (CSF 3: Apply the Anatomy of Performance Model). But before looking closer at what could be done regarding the CPI, Sara wondered if she could link the CPI to a CBI (CSF 1: Focus on Results). The vice president of marketing showed her a recent memo announcing an initiative to regain market share, which had slipped from 60 percent to 52 percent in sixteen months. Although AJAX's sales to new customers had continued to grow, sales to existing customers had declined for seven consecutive quarters. Consequently, net sales for AJAX had been flat for almost two years while the sales of competitors had continued to grow. The result was a loss of market share for AJAX.

Sara had established a tight results chain. Incomplete sales order forms, a CJI, contributed directly to delays in filling customer orders and the resulting customer dissatisfaction with AJAX, a CPI. This CPI, in turn, played a role in the decreased number of sales to existing customers and the corresponding drop in market share, a CBI. Sara updated her AJAX AOP as shown in Figure 42.9 (CSF 3: Apply the Anatomy of Performance Model).

Sara now understood how the initial request and CJI linked to a CPI and a CBI. Next, she had a decision to make regarding the scope of the project she

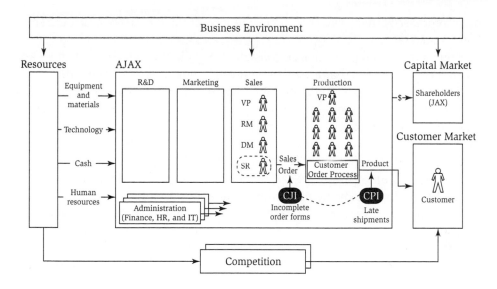

Figure 42.8. AJAX Anatomy of Performance Approximation II.

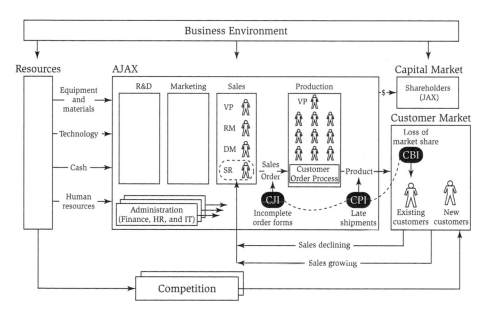

Figure 42.9. AJAX Anatomy of Performance Approximation III.

wanted to undertake. Did she want to quietly address the CJI as initially requested, even though there would be only a limited impact on results? Or did she want to push to look at the CPI, understanding that the CJI of incomplete sales order forms would be addressed in the course of improving the customer order process? Perhaps she should push to look at the CBI. How much did she want to tackle?

Being a top-notch performance consultant, Sara knew that even when looking at a CJI, she needed at least a basic understanding of the process that that job is part of. Sara talked to the vice president of sales and received her support to explore the impact the sales reps were having on the customer order process. She then gained the support of the finance director and vice president of production to take a look at the customer order process, the CPI. She elected not to pursue the CBI at that time because she hypothesized that closing the results gap in the customer order process would have a large impact on the CBI. Expanding the scope of the project to include all possible root causes of the decrease in market share would be too large an initial undertaking for the organization and for her.

Sara formed a small team of representatives from the sales, finance, and production departments. After two days of working together, they developed the flow chart shown in Figure 42.10 (CSF 3: Apply the Anatomy of Performance Model).

This cross-functional process map was a useful tool for examining the customer order process because it made it possible to see when, where, and how the various jobs in sales, finance, and production affected the process and the customers. From this detailed look at the customer order process, Sara learned the following about the time required to fulfill a customer's order:

- In addition to submitting incomplete order forms, many sales reps waited until the end of the week to submit their orders, leading to delays of up to five days.

- Both new and existing customer orders underwent a credit check by the finance department. Because this task was disruptive to other tasks, clerks in finance batched the orders and did the credit checks at the end of the week, a practice that sometimes delayed orders by five days.

- The available inventory was not checked for an order until it reached production, now several weeks after the customer placed the order. This might necessitate a call back to the customer about the additional delay.

- Because of an attempt to control the cost of inventory, some products were produced only when ordered instead of filling orders from inventory. In some cases, the resulting delay was five to eight days.

- A long-standing policy of shipping orders by surface transportation only added another four or five days to receipt of the order by customers.

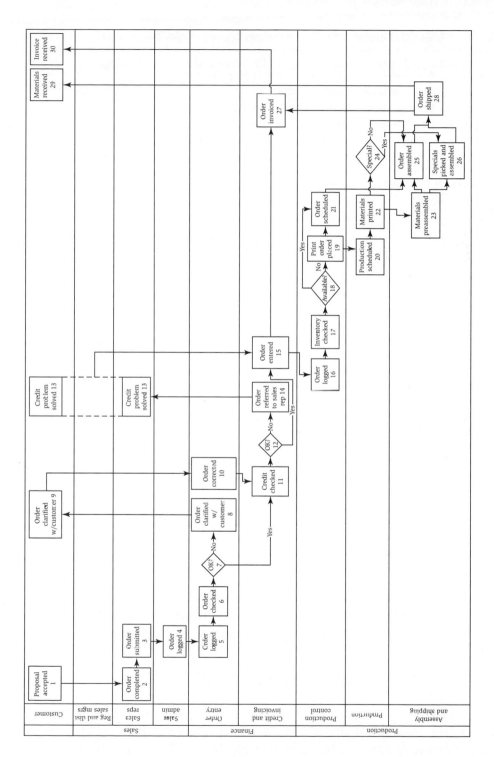

Figure 42.10. The AJAX Customer Order Process: The *Is* Map.

Table 42.2. Customer Order Process Findings Regarding Order Delivery Time.

Requirements for Process Results	Customer Order Process Findings
1. Process outputs and requirements are linked to the organization's and the customer's requirements; they are clear and effectively communicated.	No: Outputs and requirements are not linked to customer expectations. Customer expects orders in five days but AJAX has been content with a twenty-day delivery time.
2. Process is designed to meet output requirements.	No: Process is not designed to deliver orders in five days.
3. Inputs and triggers meet input standards.	No: The input from the sales rep job does not meet the standards of being complete and timely.
4. Necessary resources are available.	No: Implementation of a process to deliver orders in five days will require additional resources of various types.
5. Job results meet requirements as outlined in section A of Figure 42.4.	No: Job results do not meet requirements for the sales rep job or for several jobs in the finance function.

As she had done with the job-level analysis, Sara used section B of Figure 42.4 as a process-results template to analyze the AJAX customer order process. She summarized her findings as shown in Table 42.2.

Based on these process-level findings, Sara's team recommended the following:

- Require the sales reps to submit complete order forms daily.
- Install an order-entry system that automatically checks credit through an on-line credit service, checks product inventory levels, and simultaneously enters orders in the sales administration, finance, and production departments.
- Alter the sales commission system so that orders are approved for commission purposes only when the order actually ships to the customer.
- Offer the alternative of air shipment to customers at a discounted rate.

PROJECT REDUX: RESULTS

Once AJAX managers understood the factors contributing to the CPI, they quickly approved and implemented the job-level and process-level changes recommended by Sara and her team. During the meeting Sara attended this morning, the AJAX chief executive office congratulated Sara and her team, because in only six months the average time to receive orders had dropped from twenty to five days and customer satisfaction results had begun to turn around.

THE CONTINUING USEFULNESS OF THE AOP FRAMEWORK

The AOP framework had not stopped with Sara's sales representative or customer order process project recommendations seven months ago. At that point, she had gained a good understanding of how parts of AJAX worked. Since then, she studiously used every meeting, memo, and press release to expand her understanding of the AJAX AOP, including its external super-system. The AOP was an effective guide as to what must be learned and a great framework for sorting and storing what she was learning. This increased knowledge of AJAX had already begun to benefit her in several ways:

- First, it added to her credibility with AJAX managers at all levels. They are granting her even greater latitude and access as she investigates gaps in performance and results.

- Second, it increased the speed and accuracy of her responses to requests for assistance. Response time is critical because the biggest objection to performance consulting and performance analysis is a legitimate fear of analysis paralysis. As her understanding of the AJAX AOP grew, she was able to link a request to a significant gap in results worth closing, thus building the business case for responding to the request. She could also question the appropriateness of requested solutions, identify alternative explanations for gaps in results, or transform or redirect original, questionable requests into a project that would make a difference.

- Third, it increased her chances to proactively identify opportunities to improve performance, rather than continually reacting to requests for help.

A good example of this last point was what she had begun to do to address the market share CBI opportunity identified during the project. Sara learned that market share was affected most directly by three primary processes: (1) the new product-development process: Are we introducing products the customer wants?; (2) the marketing and sales process: Are we effectively selling products?; and (3) the customer order process: Are we able to deliver products to the quality and timeliness requirements of our customers? She had already addressed the latter process with the sales representative or customer order process project, which would have a significant impact on the CBI of market share. This project could not completely close the gap in results, however.

Sara was now seeking opportunities to improve the other two critical processes having an impact on market share. Among other things, she was now looking for other CJIs that could be linked via a results chain to a CPI that affects the CBI market share. Sara was confident she would eventually have an even greater impact on the CBI. Her confidence was due in part to section C, organization results, in Figure 42.4 that would guide her analysis of the market share results gap in the same way that the job and process templates had guided her on this most recent success.

SUMMARY

Sara glanced at the clock and realized she had better stop reliving her most recent success and get started on an outline for her presentation to the performance consulting candidates.

What did she want to cover in addition to the four critical success factors and the sales representative or customer order project?

First, Sara wanted to build on the analogy between human anatomy and organizational anatomy because knowledge of the underlying anatomy, whether for a human being or for an organization, is critical for arriving at an accurate diagnosis. The physician knows what a healthy human anatomy looks like. As physicians examine X-ray results, for example, they are comparing the *is* X-ray of a patient against the *should* model they have in their head or in medical references. The same is true for performance consultants. They know the requirements of an effective and healthy AOP for an organization. Their diagnostic phase or analysis is comparing the *should* AOP requirements summarized in Figure 42.4 against the *is* reality they see in an organization, just as Sara did in the sales representative or customer order project.

Second, she wanted to stress the value of using the AOP framework as a template for performance consulting in any organization. All organizations contain the components of the AOP; the performance consultant just needs to find the specifics for each project. The AOP guides performance consultants as they seek to understand each client organization, identify gaps between *is* and *should* results, and recommend ways to close those gaps in results.

Third, Sara wanted to emphasize the value of using the AOP framework as a guide during the project. Throughout the sales representative or customer order process project, the AOP picture of AJAX served as a road map showing Sara where she was in her project and what she still needed to learn. The framework was also a visual guide for evaluating when and where to expand the scope of the project and when to consider moving up the results chain.

Finally, she wanted to describe how the AOP framework provided a common mental model and vocabulary for all the members of the AJAX PSG. All the members of a project team shared the same view of the business and of the variables that affected individual performance and organization results. This common ground enhanced communication and understanding among team members and contributed significantly to the efficiency and effectiveness of the project teams.

Well, Sara thought, that about covered it. Tomorrow she would review her notes and finalize her presentation to the performance consultant candidates. Sara turned off the lights and was starting out her office door when she thought of one more thing—a point to make to the new performance consultants. She flipped on the lights, went to the whiteboard, and wrote, "Here's the bottom line: you *must* know your client's business."

The AOP framework provides the perfect road map for doing just that, she thought, as she turned off the lights and headed for her car.

References

Rummler, G. (1988, September). A systems view of performance. *Training*, 46.

Rummler, G. (2004). *Serious performance consulting according to Rummler.* Silver Spring, MD: International Society for Performance Improvement.

CHAPTER FORTY-THREE

Certification

An Alignment Intervention

Judith A. Hale

This chapter is about how professional associations and business enterprises can use certifications to ensure that their training programs build the right type of capability. Well-designed certifications link developmental activities with the knowledge and skills required for performance. Certifications can also ensure that performance standards are true measures of proficiency. The process of creating a certification program can result in by-products such as competencies, codes of conduct, training, and other development activities that are focused on what people require in order to be effective in the workplace. The process can also force vested parties to define what evidence of competence is, agree on the required body of knowledge, develop and agree on a set of standards, promote the adoption of common procedures and performance measures, and modify their education and training programs to include the required body of knowledge. The results are developmental activities that will be better aligned with what the organization requires to fulfill its mandate. See Figure 43.1.

For example, the International Society for Performance Improvement (ISPI) developed the Certified Performance Technologist (CPT) designation in 2001. The process produced a set of standards and a code of conduct. The creation of this credential resulted in the American Society for Training and Development (ASTD), the other association that represents the field of learning and development, endorsing the standards and code of conduct in 2003. These endorsements have encouraged universities to align their academic programs with the standards and spawned private vendor-training programs based on the standards.

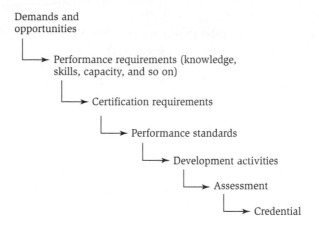

Figure 43.1. Alignment.
Source: Adapted from Hale, 2004b.

Corporations also use certifications to align their hiring criteria, development activities, and performance standards with what is needed to meet business demands. For example, some companies encounter situations in which it becomes necessary to quickly deploy workers from around the world to a single site due to an emergency, such as to restore gas pipelines after an earthquake or to help a customer resume production after a fire damaged its equipment. In these emergency situations, the task is too large for local workers alone to handle.

RAPID DEPLOYMENT

One company, when faced with an emergency at a client site, sent out an emergency call to its most experienced technicians, only to discover that the technicians did not do the job in the same way or perform at the same level of proficiency. The technicians disagreed on the procedures for doing the job. Typically these technicians had received ratings of "meets or exceeds expectations" on their performance reviews and were considered high performers by their supervisors. However, when asked to work at a different site, they were ineffective. A decision was made to develop a certification program that all technicians had to complete. The process of deciding what constituted proficiency led to a decision to define the competencies for the job. The process of defining the competencies uncovered four different sets of procedures being used that varied by location and length of time of employment. Depending on when a technician was hired, the training covered the most recently purchased equipment, not the range of machines used in the field. The training also stressed the procedures used by the subject-matter expert in residence at the time. Management decided to evaluate all of the procedures and agree on the one most suitable to emergency situations. Next, a decision was made to develop a universal set of performance standards against which all technicians would be judged. To be certified, technicians had to complete a two-day course on the procedures, pass a test given at the end of the training on the procedures, and demonstrate to their supervisor when back on the job that they could apply the procedures appropriately. As a result of developing a certification, the company had a standard set of operating procedures, training, and skill assessments based on those procedures. The next time an emergency situation occurred, it could rapidly deploy technicians who capably followed the same set of procedures.

SUCCESSION PLANNING

Another company discovered that about 60 percent of the people in key positions would be eligible to retire within thirty months. This discovery became the impetus to use certification as a way to qualify and prepare job candidates. The process of creating the certification resulted in the company doing a job task analysis, setting performance standards, and developing on-the-job performance support tools to assist in trouble shooting and emergency response. The company also developed a skill-based training program and created a series of assessments to confirm that candidates were acquiring the required knowledge and skills as they progressed through the training program.

EXTERNAL AND INTERNAL PROGRAMS

There are two types of certifications: (1) external programs developed by credentialing boards, professional societies, and vendors to recognize practitioners and product users; and (2) internal programs developed by employers to recognize their employees, contractors, suppliers, partners, and customers. Examples of external certifications are programs offered by credentialing boards, such as the American Board of Oral and Maxillofacial Surgery, which certifies oral surgeons; professional societies such as the Society for Human Resource Management, which certifies human resource generalists; and Microsoft, which certifies system engineers. Examples of internal certifications are those companies that certify their sales personnel in product knowledge and the selling process, customer service personnel in customer-handling techniques, technicians in product repair and maintenance, distributors in product installation, and customers in product operations.

External certification programs are more likely to be created to protect society. Internal programs, by comparison, are usually created in response to a business need. External and internal programs share some attributes and differ in others. Both require people who want to be certified to satisfy a set of requirements. However, they differ in the breadth and scope of those requirements. For example, both may require applicants to complete an educational program and pass a test. The educational content for an external program would include the general principles and rules related to the practice at large. The educational content for an internal certification, however, would focus on proprietary information unique to the organization's products or way of doing business.

THE PROCESS

The process for developing a certification includes twelve phases, as shown in Figure 43.2. The phases are both linear and iterative. Logically, each phase follows or precedes another; however, each produces information that can be used to advance or modify another phase.

Phase 1: The Need

As shown in Figure 43.2, the process begins with defining the organization's need. There are a number of reasons why organizations develop certification programs. The reasons include exercising due diligence on behalf of the public, satisfying a regulatory requirement, striving for a competitive advantage,

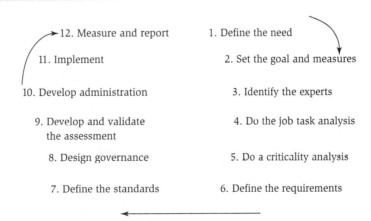

Figure 43.2. The Twelve-Phase Credentialing Process.

Source: Adapted from Hale, 2004a.

wanting to reduce developmental costs, and ensuring that people can do a job to a standard. ISPI, for example, described the need this way: "Consumers and customers are entitled to ways that better enable them to discriminate effective from ineffective performance improvement products, services, and practices" (International Society for Performance Improvement, 2001a). Practitioners are entitled to a set of standards that better enable them to judge their own work and manage their professional development.

A manufacturer of industrial equipment that I worked with that chose to certify its field technicians described the need to me this way: customers had complained that they got different levels of service from the company's technicians depending on which dealership they used. Customers deserve technicians with the same level of proficiency in every dealership worldwide.

When an organization decides to certify, other questions surface, such as, What constitutes good enough? and What is the best way to develop and assess capability? The act of answering these and similar questions usually produces a design document that describes the societal or business reason for the certification, measures of success, intended audience, requirements, assessment method, and implementation plan.

Phase 2: The Goal and Measures

Certifications alone usually do not completely satisfy a larger need; however, they can contribute to solving a problem. The goal is a statement of what the certification is intended to accomplish in reference to addressing the need. For example, the goal of external certification programs concerned with public safety might be to ensure that people sufficiently know a body of knowledge, such as safe food-handling procedures. The goal of internal programs may be to ensure that people can do a task to standard, at least in a controlled environment, such as assemble a piece of equipment. ISPI's goals for its certification are to

- Encourage practitioners to pursue further professional education and development

- Improve practitioners' career opportunities through professional contacts

- Result in greater recognition by colleagues and employers because certified practitioners have demonstrated their expertise in performance improvement [International Society for Performance Improvement, 2001a]

The measures are the criteria for judging the effectiveness of the program, how well the certification delivered on the goal and contributed to satisfying the need. The measures are not concerned with judging the knowledge or proficiency of candidates; those are defined in phases 6 and 7, in which the requirements are defined and the standards set. For example, ISPI's program measures of the success and effectiveness of the CPT credential are based on

- The number of practitioners actively pursuing the credential
- The number of employers endorsing the credential by embracing its principles and systematic process, by using it in their hiring and development decisions, or by becoming Advocate members of the Society
- The number of providers offering training based on the standards
- The perceptions of those with the credential that it aided their career advancement
- The ability of the program to be self-funding
- The degree the program generates other income such as conference registration, membership, and the purchase of other services [International Society for Performance Improvement, 2001b, p. 1]

The manufacturer of industrial equipment, for example, may have the following goals for its certification program:

- Assess the proficiency of every technician worldwide (thirty-five thousand) to determine what developmental gaps exist by product line, such as trucks, tractors, or hydraulic and electronic systems
- Develop a competency-based development program that addresses the developmental gaps and is accessible to technicians worldwide
- Recognize technicians who demonstrate proficiency on the job

The measures the manufacturer uses to judge the success of the program include

- The percentage of reduction in dealers' warranty work
- The increase in the sale of parts
- The number of dealers supporting the program
- The number of technicians certified by product line and system
- Customer perceptions about the quality of the technicians

Phase 3: Experts

Most certifications depend on the opinions of experts: people with the knowledge and experience to dictate what constitutes proficiency. External certifications rely on the opinions of academics and members in good standing to determine what it is people should know and be able to do to obtain certification. Associations and credentialing boards may include the opinions of other vested parties, such as representatives from health agencies, insurers, police and fire departments, suppliers, and consumer groups. Certifications that are based on multiple voices are more likely to be seen as valid and accepted by practitioners and the public. ISPI solicited the opinions of employers, experienced practitioners, and academics. The manufacturer of industrial equipment solicited the opinions of dealers, customers, instructors, and technicians.

Phases 4 and 5: Job Task and Criticality Analyses

A job task analysis is a formal study to identify what people do; what they have to know to do it; what they use to do it, including equipment, materials, systems, and information; and under what conditions they do it. A job task analysis may be done by soliciting the opinions of the experts or by observing competent people performing the job. A criticality analysis is done by having the experts rank the required knowledge and steps that make up a task in order of difficulty, importance, and frequency. The results of the job task and criticality analyses are used to define the requirements and standards of the certification and to design the assessment tools.

ISPI started with an extensive review and synthesis of the literature and research projects submitted by members. It then polled the opinions of its experts to identify what performance technologists do, what they need to know, and what constitutes proficiency. The criticality analysis was done through debate and eventual consensus by the experts. The industrial equipment manufacturer in the example would have interviewed and observed competent technicians. It would have polled the opinions of other technicians, dealers, and instructors to rank the tasks in order of importance.

Phases 6 and 7: Requirements and Standards

Phases 6 and 7 define the requirements and standards for certification. The two phases are closely related, yet distinct. Requirements are the conditions a person has to meet either to be eligible to apply or to be certified. They include things such as pass a test, have experience, and complete an educational program. Standards describe how much or to what level people must demonstrate their knowledge and skills to satisfy the requirements. They include how well people have to do on the test, the passing score, what the experience must consist of, and what criteria educational activities they must satisfy to be accepted.

The term *to certify* means to attest that someone or something satisfied a set of requirements. Most certifications are given to people; however, work products are also certified. Whether the goal is to certify people or products, the designation means that someone or something fulfilled or satisfied the requirements.

Requirements of Certification. A certification may require applicants to satisfy all or any combination of requirements. The term *certification* usually conjures up an image of a test, because passing a test has been a traditional requirement to being certified. However, organizations impose other requirements in addition to or as a substitute for testing. The more common requirements are

- Successfully complete an approved or accredited education or training program
- Successfully demonstrate knowledge and skills through either a test or performance on the job
- Have a minimum amount of experience, usually in a specified area
- Commit to a code of ethics
- Commit to being recertified or complete a minimum amount of continuing education annually

Less common requirements are

- Obtain a certificate or certification in an enabling or related area
- Work under the supervision of a qualified person for a specified period of time
- Gain the endorsement, sponsorship, or attestation of competence by a recognized entity
- Continue to practice or stay involved in the field

Whatever the reason for the certification, the requirements can be looked at either as gates that must be cleared or as recognition for proven capability. Historically, certifications were designed to be gates, allowing only those who successfully passed to claim a title or perform a task. Those gates usually include education or training and then passing a test. The fidelity and validity of the gates become more important when achieving the designation means a person is qualified to perform a task or fulfill a business need. Other certifications are more like recognitions as people are allowed to practice or work in a field without being certified. See Figures 43.3 and 43.4.

Another way to view certification is the degree to which there is an emphasis on knowledge compared to the application of the knowledge in the workplace or society. Certifications that place greater weight on knowledge tend to

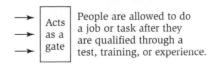

Figure 43.3. When Certification Qualifies.

Source: Adapted from Hale, 2004a.

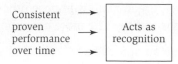

Figure 43.4. When Certification Means Competence.

Source: Adapted from Hale, 2004a.

require completion of an accredited academic or education program and the successful completion of a knowledge-based test. More performance-oriented programs place greater emphasis on experience and proven capability in the workplace or settings that emulate it, such as a laboratory.

ISPI values proven performance, so its requirements consist of at least three years of experience in activities related to improving human performance, commitment to a code of conduct, recertification, and the submission of at least three but no more than seven projects that demonstrate candidates' adherence to the principles and the application of the systematic process (International Society for Performance Improvement, 2002). The manufacturer of industrial equipment values knowledge and performance; therefore, its requirements for them would include knowledge tests, skill tests, and performance tests.

Standards. Standards are statements that describe how much knowledge or what level of proficiency a person must demonstrate. One approach is to use the model described by Robert Mager in his book *Preparing Instructional Objectives* (Mager, 1962), which suggests a three-part objective:

- A condition statement that describes under which circumstances people are expected to perform or demonstrate their knowledge, whether that be in the classroom, on-line, or at the job site, for example, and what they will have available to them when demonstrating their knowledge or skills, including reference materials, calculators, and job tools.

- One or more performance statements that describe what the person is expected to know or do.

- One or more criteria statements that describe the evidence or results that will be used or accepted to judge the adequacy of people's knowledge or sufficiency of performance. The criteria can include the percentage of questions that have to be answered correctly, the maximum amount of time in which a task must be completed, or how accurately a task must be done.

Another method is to describe in narrative form the behaviors, results, or knowledge people are expected to demonstrate. This is the approach ISPI took in the development of its standards. The manufacturer of industrial equipment modeled its standards after the model recommended by Mager. Whatever approach is used, the standards should be written to a level of detail that supports measuring knowledge and ability. Well-formed standards also support the creation of education or training activities.

Phase 8: Governance

Governance is the creation of a body authorized to make decisions about the design and operation of the certification. In the beginning, decisions about what the certification should entail and how best to communicate it to the people who will be affected are made by the design team with input from experts and other vested parties. In time, the decision making body evolves to a more formal policy-making group. Policies and procedures should be created about how to handle disputes or appeals and whether or not to exempt very experienced practitioners or employees before the need arises. When governance policies are not in place and issues arise, organizations risk making decisions that could set precedence for future actions. The organization could later find itself in conflict over how to handle disputes, appeals, and changes to the requirements or standards. Governance is one of the most frequently overlooked phases when creating a certification, yet planning for it can be very helpful. The range of issues the governance group might address includes questions such as

- What information should be retained and shared about candidates?

- Who will have access to individual test scores?

- Should candidates be given credit if they complete equivalent programs offered by other groups?

- How recent must the experience or the training be?

- Can people earn or retain the certification if they cannot work for an extended period of time due to health, military service, or other obligations?

- How long will data about candidates and certificants be retained?

- Will achieving the certification affect salary? Will successful candidates get a bonus?

- How many times can a person fail the assessment? May people who fail the test be allowed to retake the assessment or training? Will some type of remediation be made available to them? What kind of feedback will they be given?

The National Organization for Competency Assurance has standards and guidelines for how to structure the governing group, what its role should be, and how to address many issues (Browning, Bugbee, and Mullins, 1996). At a minimum, the governing body's members should represent the same groups who were represented by the experts. Development of the test and administrative system are usually done in parallel with the creation of the governance group; however, it is best to formalize the governance process before the certification is launched.

ISPI set up a certification governance committee, in which members represent employers, practitioners, and academics. ISPI created a policy and procedures manual that describes the procedures for responding to disputes or appeals and accusations of ethical violations. The certification governance committee approves policies, reviews requests, and makes recommendations to the board of directors on how to best respond. The industrial equipment manufacturer chose to leverage an already standing group known as the Global Council, whose members represent geographic regions and are elected by the dealerships. Also on this council are corporate representatives from marketing and service training.

Phase 9: Assessment

This phase focuses on developing tools and processes for assessing people's capability, whether it be knowledge, skills, performance, or some combination, and then validating that the methods discriminate in the ways intended. Some organizations start their certification process with building a test, usually a set of multiple choice questions. However, there are other ways to assess people's knowledge, skills, and performance besides traditional tests. For example, capability can be determined by observing people at task on the job or with a simulation, or by comparing people's work products to a standard by using performance checklists. Interviews and surveys can also be used to poll customers or coworkers about their experience with and level of confidence in people's work. Reviewing control charts and production records are other ways to judge people's capability. It is easier to decide how best to assess capability when there is agreement on the goal, requirements, and standards. The job task and criticality analyses results can provide valuable input on what people must know and do and how much emphasis to put on each topic or skill area.

The more the certification relies on a single requirement to discriminate people who meet the standards from those who do not, the more important is the validity and fidelity of that method, as shown in Figure 43.5. Fidelity is the degree to which the training or assessment emulates the work environment, and validity is the degree to which the successful completion of the requirement correlates with job performance. Increasing the number of requirements, such as completing an assessment and an educational program or having experience, lessens the burden on the assessment tool to accurately discriminate people who are capable from those who are not.

ISPI's assessment is in two parts. Applicants are required to submit a description of their work. The first part of the assessment is an attestation by clients as to the accuracy of the work description. The second part is a review of the description by two qualified jurors who judge the degree to which applicants

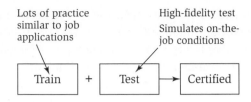

Figure 43.5. Effectiveness Depends on Fidelity.

Source: Adapted from Hale, 2004a.

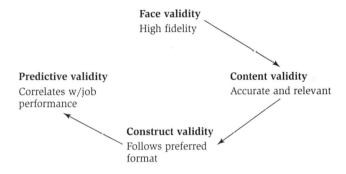

Figure 43.6. Validity.

Source: Adapted from Hale, 2004a.

---

satisfied the standards when executing their work (International Society for Performance Improvement, 2002). The manufacturer of industrial equipment in the example requires technicians to successfully complete a series of knowledge tests that are administered at the end of the training, a series of skill tests that are done in a laboratory setting and evaluated by a qualified reviewer, and a series of proficiency tests that are demonstrated through work orders completed on the job and reviewed by a qualified reviewer.

There are multiple measures of validity. Four of these validity measures—face, content, construct, and predictive—are shown in Figure 43.6. The ultimate measure of validity is the degree to which the certification's requirements, standards, and assessment methods collectively correlate with job performance and accomplishment of the certification's goals. There are two tests to determine an assessment's validity: the usability test and the discrimination test. Both tests are formative evaluations in that they are done prior to implementing an assessment.

Usability or User Acceptance Test. This test is done to confirm that the assessment instructions and questions or simulations are clear. The results are used to improve the clarity of the instructions, test questions, and simulations. If the assessment is administered electronically, the test is used to confirm the software and hardware work as intended.

Discrimination Test. This test is sometimes called a small statistical sample pilot. This pilot is done to determine if the assessment discriminates competent performers from less competent performers. For this type of pilot, an equal number of people who are known to be competent and those who are not are asked to take the assessment. The assessment is administered to both groups at the same time under conditions most similar to the actual assessment. The results include how long it takes everyone to complete the test and whether or not the accomplished performers' responses are significantly different from the noncompetent performers. The results help determine if the assessment discriminates on the basis of capability.

Phase 10: Administration

The issues this phase addresses are (1) what information is required, in what form, and how frequently; (2) if the system is to interface with other databases, such as a learning management, learning content management, or test administration system; and (3) which reports are required and how often they can or should be made available. The administrative process addresses issues such as how to efficiently collect, retain, and compile data about people and the requirements. For example, some organizations want a system that permits on-line registration for training and assessment. Some want the system to score the assessments and analyze the results. Others want the system to track training content, automatically print and issue certificates of course completion, bill candidates, and update personnel records. Few systems are able to accomplish all that is expected.

ISPI uses its Web page to allow candidates to download the standards, code of ethics, and application forms (see www.ispi.org). Candidates can submit their applications electronically, although attestations must be submitted by mail. The applications are initially reviewed by staff for completion, and the descriptions without the attestations are forwarded electronically to qualified reviewers. Reviewers complete an electronic checklist and submit their assessment electronically to the national office. The manufacturer of industrial equipment tracks candidates and training with a learning management system (LMS). The company also has a test administration system that interfaces with the LMS. The performance assessment of technicians is done by certified instructors.

Phase 11: Implementation

This phase focuses on how best to implement a certification. It includes how to communicate the benefits and requirements to the target audience. Questions come up as to whether or not to use a staged approach, perhaps by geography, work unit, or level of experience. A significant part of implementation is marketing the certification. Even organizations that want to certify their own employees must get the support of management. The implementation phase should include a communication plan that contains information for managers and candidates about how to apply, what the credential means, what the requirements are, and how it will benefit the candidate and the organization.

ISPI announced its certification at its international conference. Candidates can find answers to the most frequently asked questions on ISPI's Web page (www.ispi.org). ISPI also established a special interest group in which candidates and certificants can exchange information and respond to questions about how the processes benefited them. The manufacturer of industrial equipment launched its certification by first certifying its company instructors, then its dealers' instructors, and finally the community college instructors who teach the manufacturer's courses. Once the instructors are qualified by successfully completing the knowledge and skill assessments, they are then trained to administer the same assessments plus the performance assessments to technicians.

Phase 12: Measuring and Reporting

The final phase is the ongoing measurement of the success of the program and reporting the results. Information should be sent to the governance committee and the program administrator to identify opportunities for improvement. Any lack of alignment between the certification's requirements and the organization's needs will be most evident in this phase. ISPI monitors candidate participation and comments on an ongoing basis. The results of the semiannual enrollment period are shared with the governance committee. Staff uses the results to identify ways to recognize and support candidates at conferences, on the Website, and in ISPI's publications. The manufacturer of industrial equipment monitors participation and correlates it against the primary business measures. The results are reported quarterly to senior management and the Global Council.

SUMMARY

The more common mistakes organizations make when they develop a certification program are that they

1. Fail to fully define the need
2. Fail to set goals and measures for the program, making it difficult to prove the worth of the program
3. Fail to fully analyze the job or task
4. Fail to do a criticality analysis, therefore increasing the risk of either under-representing key tasks or knowledge elements in the assessment or assessing factors that are not relevant to performance
5. Rely on the views of too few groups, which produces biased information and criteria

6. Overly rely on too few requirements or assessment methods, which overly burdens those methods to appropriately identify knowledgeable or competent people

7. Generate task lists instead of developing the standards sufficiently to support the development of education programs or assessment tools

8. Fail to validate the assessment methods

9. Fail to link the requirements, standards, and assessment results to the satisfaction of the need

10. Underestimate the costs associated with assessment and the administration process

However, there can be a number of benefits to a well-designed certification program. For example, the criteria for being certified can be used

1. In the hiring and selection process

2. To assess people's readiness and developmental needs

3. To identify and develop programs and materials to help people achieve proficiency

4. To judge the proficiency of incumbents and candidates

5. To demonstrate the degree to which the program supports the organization's need or social mandate

Not all certifications produce the desired results or side benefits; however, the ones that do share some common attributes. For example,

1. They are based on a well-defined business need or social mandate.

2. The requirements and standards are based on the input from multiple stakeholders.

3. The requirements, standards, and assessment results are sufficiently rigorous to positively correlate with satisfying the need or mandate.

4. The assessment process is valid and supports measuring the requirements and standards.

5. The administrative process is efficient and produces data that enables sponsors to judge the adequacy of the requirements, such as training programs, and make decisions about how to improve the program.

6. The governance process monitors the usefulness of the program and provides an avenue to allow for exceptions or exemptions from the requirements and standards.

7. There is a public relations and marketing plan to encourage recognition of certificants and increase participation.

References

Browning, A., Bugbee A., and Mullins, M. (Eds.). (1996). *Certification: A NOCA handbook.* Washington, DC: National Organization for Competency Assurance.

Hale, J. (2004a, June). *How to design an effective certification.* Presentation made at the annual Training Director's Forum by VNU Learning, Atlanta.

Hale, J. (2004b, October). *New marketers of standards, accreditation, and certification.* Presentation made at the annual meeting of the Association for Education and Communication Technology (AECT), Chicago.

International Society for Performance Improvement. (2001a). *Certified performance technologist.* Retrieved June 1, 2005, from www.ispi.org.

International Society for Performance Improvement. (2001b). *ISPI certification business case* (Working paper). Silver Spring, MD: International Society for Performance Improvement.

International Society for Performance Improvement. (2002). *Certified performance technologist* (Program brochure). Silver Spring, MD: International Society for Performance Improvement.

Mager, R. (1962). *Preparing instructional objectives.* Atlanta: Center for Effective Performance.

Additional Resources

Following are some resources to learn more about how to develop an effective certification program. Other resources are noted in the preceding references section.

Hale, J. (2000). *Performance-based certification: How to design a valid, defensible, cost-effective program.* San Francisco: Jossey-Bass/Pfeiffer.

   The book comes with approximately two dozen tools on a CD.

Knapp, L. G., and Knapp, J. E. (2002). *The business of certification: A comprehensive guide to developing a successful program.* Washington, DC: American Society for Association Executives.

   The book comes with checklists and guidelines.

Here are some resources on how to link human resource development products and services such as certification to the organization's needs.

Becker, B., Huselid, M., and Ulrich, D. (2001). *The HR scorecard: Linking people, strategy, and performance.* Boston: Harvard Business School Press.

Fitz-enz, J. (2000). *The ROI of human capital: Measuring the economic value of employee performance.* New York: AMACOM.

CHAPTER FORTY-FOUR

Standards and Ethics in Human Performance Technology

Ingrid J. Guerra

What is the right thing to do in the following situations?

Should I tell the truth even though it may mean losing a potential client? For example, what if what the client is requesting is not likely to solve the performance problem; we have no proof or indication it will do so; comparable attempts in comparable situations have not worked before; and so on? Should I report my coworker for cheating the company? Must I give credit to the originator of every idea or concept that I use in my work? Is it appropriate to reveal the identity of the subjects who provided me with data for my analysis findings, if the client asks me to do so? Is it fair to fire an employee for not accomplishing the results we expected, when we did not give the employee the tools required to do the job? Is it my responsibility to do something about my organization's current production process, which is dumping waste by-products into a nearby stream? Should I report my boss for misusing her power? Is it appropriate to accept a gift from a vendor? Is it inappropriate to make flirtatious comments to my coworker? Should we look further into the potential health risks of a new product line, when three out of five studies indicate nonthreatening side effects from using the products? Should profit be our only guiding criteria? Are opportunism and self-interested competition right or wrong? These and many other types of questions and accompanying decisions and actions are what ethics, ethical codes, and standards are intended to guide us through as practicing professionals.

If you ask, most if not all professionals will probably say they are competent and ethical, and they conduct business in ethical ways. Interestingly enough, "a vast new industry worth hundreds of millions of dollars is springing up to help companies be ethical—whether they need it or not" (Warner, 2004, p. 47). Warner identifies management consultants as one of the leaders in this industry. Leaders in the human performance technology (HPT) field and others have challenged professionals to rethink many traditional practices within the field and to consider the ethical responsibilities associated with its application (Westgaard, 1988; Kaufman, 1992; Dean, 1993; Kaufman and Clark, 1999; Farrington and Clark, 2000). A typical example of this is providing preferred or requested solutions without data to support their utility in a given situation and without regard to consequences of doing so. The field of performance improvement should continuously evaluate itself in order to help practitioners add a demonstrable value to the field and society as a whole (Dean, 1997; Kaufman, 2000; Westgaard, 1988; Guerra, 2003). Clear expectations, such as those illustrated through standards and codes of ethics, can help HPT professionals do just that. Stolovitch, Keeps, and Rodrigue affirm, "performance standards can serve as a means to officially recognize the achievements a professional has made in his or her area of practice" (1999, p. 683).

Ethics and performance standards are integral to the competence of HPT professionals and the value they add. Just as the basic analysis, design, development, implementation, and evaluation (ADDIE) model and its numerous variations shape the way we view, solve, and avoid performance problems, ethics and performance standards also do so, whether we acknowledge it or not.

We are better prepared to make professionally sound and ethical decisions when we are aware of the factors that have an impact on such decisions. Ignorance of such factors is not a valid justification for poor decisions. Increasing our awareness of ethical and professional standards will increase our likelihood of adding value to our clients, our organizations, our communities, and not least of all ourselves and our families. The goal of this chapter is to raise your awareness about some key factors that affect the value you potentially add or subtract through your work as an HPT professional.

ETHICS AND MORALITY

Ethics, or moral philosophy, is concerned with the analysis of morality, moral problems, and moral judgment. In philosophy, the terms *ethics* and *morality* are often used synonymously (Pojman, 1996). Ethics is concerned with values, that is, with what ought to be rather than with what is. It seeks to analyze what is considered right and wrong in a moral context, and consequently to establish principles of right behavior to guide the actions of individuals and groups. Ethics distinguishes itself from law or etiquette in that it examines issues beyond the adherence to social convention; it explores rational existence. It also differs from religion in the sense that it seeks logic, rather than supremacy, to justify its principles. The following definitions, offered by Dean (1993, p. 3), are helpful in clarifying a common language for this discussion:

- *Ethics:* The rules or standards that govern the conduct of the members of a group
- *Morals:* Personal judgments, standards, and rules of conduct based on fundamental duties of promoting human welfare, acknowledging human equality or justice, and honoring individual freedom or respect of persons
- *Values:* The core beliefs or desires that guide or motivate the individual's attitudes and actions, such as honesty, integrity, and fairness
- *Business ethics:* Moral principles or standards that guide behavior in the world of business

Is There One Correct Ethical Theory?

Ethics are usually divided into three general areas: *Metaethics, Normative Ethics,* and *Descriptive Ethics.* Metaethics explores the origins and meaning of our ethical principles, and tackles issues such as universal truths, the role of God, and the role of reason. Normative ethics focuses on the more practical task of establishing moral standards and acceptable behaviors, which includes the articulation of our duties and the consequences of our actions. Finally, descriptive ethics describes how people actually behave, and thus lends itself to scientific inquiry better than do other approaches. It integrates aspects of psychology, anthropology, and sociology. In keeping with the purpose of this chapter, facilitating ethical and professional actions through awareness of what ought to be, the central focus of this discussion is dedicated to normative ethics. It concludes with a brief review of decision-making models that integrate both normative and descriptive perspectives.

Consequentialist Theories: Based on Consequences

An approach we commonly take to making decisions is the weighing of the consequences of our actions. According to consequentialist, formally known as teleological, theories first proposed by Jeremy Bentham (1979 [1789]), John Stuart Mill (1998 [1861]), and Henry Sidgwick (1907 [1874]), the morality of an action is solely determined by its consequences, and thus appropriate moral action should be based on an analysis of the consequences of that action. More specifically, if the positive consequences of an action outweigh the negative consequences, then that action is indeed morally proper. If the converse is true, then the action is morally improper.

We cannot always predict with assurance all potential consequences of a given action. Consequentialists did not intend for us to use the costs and benefits approach as a decisional procedure, but rather encouraged us to recognize consequences as the criterion for what is deemed morally right or wrong (Bales, 1971).

Weighing positive and negative consequences seems straightforward enough. However, if we analyze this issue closer, the natural question becomes *consequences for whom*? An important consideration is that what is positive for one may be the stark opposite for someone else. So whose benefit should we be looking out for? Three different schools of consequentialism—ethical egoism, ethical altruism, and utilitarianism—provide three different answers.

Ethical Egoism, Ethical Altruism, and Utilitarianism. Ethical egoism essentially holds that our actions should be taken from the perspective of our own self-interests, and at the core, all moral duties have an underlying principle of self-interest. Pojman (1996) presents Ayn Rand's 1959 *Atlas Shrugged* as the work that set forth a new form of ethical egoism, called objectivism. Objectivism proposes that the proper life for rational beings is the pursuit of their own happiness. Under objectivism, altruism is incompatible with rational morality, and in fact, it is demeaning to others since it makes them the objects of charity.

One important counterargument to this view is that the happiness of others is not necessarily incompatible with our own happiness. Moreover, the happiness of others might be precisely what makes us happy. Along the lines of this counterargument, ethical altruism holds that an action is morally right if the consequences are more favorable to others than to oneself. A premise to this view is that life is sacred, and because of this sacredness, we must offer our own in the service or sacrifice for others.

A problem common to both ethical egoism and altruism is that they are simply too extreme. In the work that would become the foundation of English utilitarianism, *An Introduction to the Principles of Morals and Legislation,* Bentham (1979 [1789]) resolved this issue by suggesting that the morally correct action is that which results in the greatest good for the greatest number.

HPT professionals would be well served by recognizing which of these views they adhere to, both generally and in specific situations, since it may directly influence both the means and results of their work. While it is appropriate to consider consequences during all stages of HPT work, some obvious stages worth mentioning are contracting, planning, assessment, and solution selection stages. Here we make attempts at clarifying deliverables and expectations for ourselves, our clients, employees, subcontractors, and other stakeholders. In so doing, we are realizing that there is a range of consequences for various parties. The clearer we are on *who* is affected and *how,* the more proactive and effective we can be at avoiding and solving problems down the road. Some specific tools that we use in these stages are return-on-investment estimates, cost-benefit analyses, forecasting methods, cost-consequences analysis, methods-means analysis, and trend analysis.

Intentionality. Whereas consequentialism focuses on consequences as the criterion for determining which actions are moral, intentionality, formally known as deontology, is characterized by adherence to independent and objective moral duties. According to intentionality, when we follow our moral duties, we are behaving ethically. In addition to following our moral duties, it is also important to have the right motivation for doing so, regardless of the consequences. In one of the more important works in the development of intentionality, Kant (1964 [1785]) argued that only *good will* was unconditionally good. Moreover, our will to do *good* is the only thing within our control, since there are many variables that influence results that are not under our control. Take for example an employee who, though with trepidation, reports out of her sense of duty that her boss is stealing from the company. An investigation turns up no credible evidence of this, and, as a result, the boss gets away with it and continues to astutely steal from the company. The fact that the employee's actions did not stop the stealing does not make her any less ethical. Her actions were driven by a moral duty to tell the truth.

Though this good-will element may seem to overlap with altruism, Kant would argue that a truly moral person is one who acts out of moral duty, despite his or her inclinations not to do so, while it does not take much effort or conviction for an altruist to do so (Russo, n.d.).

What does this mean to HPT? While the consequentialist perspective would be more evident in clarifying the potential consequences and deliverables of a contract, the intentionalist perspective would be most evident in meeting all expectations and terms of the contract and proposed scope of work adhering to the law and other rules, including keeping one's word.

Virtue Ethics. While consequentionalist and intentionalist ethics theories are both based on actions, virtue ethics emphasizes moral character. Virtue ethics is concerned with helping people develop good character traits such as honesty and responsibility, as well as change negative traits or vices such as greed and dishonesty, all of which will enable them to make moral decisions.

Virtue ethics dates back to Greek times with Aristotle as perhaps its first formal proponent, as presented in his landmark work *Nicomachean Ethics,* written in 350 B.C. (Ross, n.d.). Aristotle's basic premise was that if people learned or acquired good moral traits, they would be better judges of what is moral and what is not. For how could one be a good judge in the context of a topic one did not know?

An important counterargument here is that having a moral character or possessing moral qualities, while perhaps a helpful foundation, does not necessarily guarantee moral action. Some morally ambiguous situations may indeed require critical thinking and reasoning before a morally acceptable action is chosen. For instance, for an HPT professional with a good moral character, not making false promises about the expected value of her services and products would probably require little to no critical thinking. Now suppose that a potential client contacts a consultant requesting a service or product that is not appropriate for the suspected problem. The consultant is honest with the potential client and explains her concerns. The eager client-to-be agrees with the explanation given, but tells the consultant that the request still stands. Taking a moral action in this case will take more than moral character; it requires critical thinking about all relevant elements affecting the consultant and the potential client.

The development of our moral character begins when we are children and continues throughout our lives. One indicator of the importance of developing moral character in business and beyond is illustrated by the increase in ethics courses being required across college programs outside of philosophy. While most of us may not have been given a choice of the moral qualities we learned as children, we certainly have choices as adults. There are many relevant information and learning resources. Given the wealth of electronic mediums today, we have even more convenient avenues through which to pursue the development of our own moral character, if we choose to do so.

IS ETHICAL BEHAVIOR ABSOLUTE OR RELATIVE?

One fundamental question in ethics is whether morality is relative or absolute and universally imposed on all human beings. Ethical relativism makes the case that there are no universally valid moral principles, but rather that these are dependant on cultural and individual choices. The American anthropologist Ruth Benedict (1934) was a supporter of the relativist view and described a social system as a community with common beliefs and practices that chooses which repertoire of dispositions and habits to emphasize. Likewise, Jarvis (n.d.) sites Mackie's 1975 argument that ethics, or morals, is a subjective, dynamic matter, which is subject to individual and collective interpretations. Rationality, for ethical relativists, is based on social interactions, which integrate the historical and economic contexts and includes a concern for liberty and justice for others, both in terms of self-interest and self-referencing altruism.

In response to ethical relativism, Pojman (1996) cites James Rachels's argument that the cultural difference argument is invalid. The fact that moral differences exist among different cultures does not negate that there are absolute truths about morality. For example, two HPT professionals could differ on their interpretation of the same analysis data, leading each to different conclusions about the performance problem. It is worth noting that this is also not uncommon in the medical profession. However, their differences do not disprove that there is one independent truth, whether one or neither of these conclusions correspond to that truth.

Sidgwick (1907 [1874]), a proponent of ethical objectivism, argued that ethics dealt with what should or ought to be, and that ultimate goodness was the same across all human purposes and cultures. This ultimate goodness, or ideal vision (Kaufman, 2000), is universal. It is the ultimate end or target that all humankind, at its core, wants and depends on. An example is a world without murder, abuse, unnecessary violence, and so on. Sidgwick contended that a fixed target is needed to determine which means or behaviors are appropriate. In his view, moral actions involve meeting basic and high-order duties that bind every single human being, independent of culture, profession, religion, class, or any other variable.

The moral absolute perspective struggles against the dangers of the abuse of power and force (Jarvis, n.d.). Relativists would argue, so what if my moral truth is different than yours? Is it appropriate for me to superimpose my view of morality on another? What if a culture viewed hiring children to work in sweatshops as consistent with their moral truth? What if a particular culture thought releasing products in the market without proper safety testing was morally appropriate? Absolutists would argue that regardless of the differences in beliefs or practices between groups, there is an overarching goal of humanity, or an ultimate truth, that guides our judgment of right or wrong and, in turn, should guide our behavior. For example, in some cultures stoning women to death for leaving the house without being escorted by a male relative may be legal and in accordance with tradition. However, is it right? Without a common goal of goodness, there is no standard by which to judge if this practice is moral or immoral. The fact that a practice is both traditional and legal does not make it moral or ethical.

The views of the absolutist are also relevant to the business culture. If a variety of moral beliefs exist for an organization, consultants, vendors, creditors, employers, employees, and clients, it will be challenging to agree on what is morally appropriate and what is not, independent of the law.

Shaub, Finn, and Munter (1993) found that accountants' ethical orientation as either relativist or absolutist influences their ability to recognize the ethical nature of a situation in a professional context. Carliner (2003, p. 97) cited a number of relevant and interesting studies that illustrated how differences in our moral philosophies affect behavior:

> Related studies explore the differences in moral philosophies guiding ethical decisions between marketers and the general public. Research reported by Singhapakdi, Vitell, Rao, and Kurtz (1999) suggests that marketers take a more relativistic view of the world than others. They define relativism as the extent to

which an individual rejects universal moral rules. Relativists feel that moral actions depend on the nature of the situation and the individuals involved, and weigh circumstances more than the ethical principal that was violated. In contrast, idealism is the degree to which individuals assume that the "right" action results in desirable consequences. The researchers also found that relativistic marketers tended to exhibit lower honesty and integrity than idealistic ones.

Answering the question about the relative or absolute nature of ethics is beyond the scope of this chapter. The critical point of this discussion is that our perception of ethics as either relative or absolute may indeed affect the decisions we make. Clarifying our perspective and assumptions would help us understand what we consider ethical, regardless of whether or not we think others should agree, and help us make morally justifiable decisions.

ETHICAL DECISION MAKING IN AMBIGUOUS SITUATIONS

One important factor in making ethical decisions is whether you will recognize an ethically ambiguous situation. Butterfield, Treviño, and Weaver (2000) define moral awareness as "a person's recognition that his/her potential decision or action could affect the interests, welfare, or expectations of the self or others in a fashion that may conflict with one or more ethical standards" (p. 982). Rest (1986) includes moral awareness as the first step in his four-stage process for ethical decision making:

1. Recognizing a moral issue, that is, *moral awareness*
2. Making moral judgments
3. Establishing moral intent
4. Engaging in moral behavior, that is, taking action

Ferrell and Gresham (1985) found that this moral awareness or intent is regulated by significant others, individual characteristics, and opportunity. Furthermore, Treviño (1986) found that both individual and situational characteristics affected moral intent (cited in Loe, Ferrell, and Mansfield, 2000). From a review of empirical studies on ethical decision making, Loe, Ferrell, and Mansfield found that "people in organizations are influenced by the corporate culture and role relationships" (p. 200). The Ford Pinto fiasco during the 1970s is a good illustration of this conclusion. Dennis Goia, the recall coordinator for Ford during the early 1970s, along with his team, voted against the recall of the Ford Pinto while knowing that low-impact collisions could set them on fire, which had already caused deaths and injuries (cited in Butterfield, Treviño, and Weaver, 2000). In the reflections he published years after leaving the company, he indicated that his decision-making process relied on scripts, which did not include one for the Pinto situation, and thus the realities of the situation were not revealed for what they were. He further indicated that the decision not to recall the Pinto was not based on the wrong ethical premise, but rather that no ethical dimension was even considered (cited in Butterfield, Treviño, and Weaver, 2000). Goia's decisions were influenced by both the organizational context and his lack of moral awareness at the time.

This brief discussion on ethics is intended to promote the moral awareness of HPT professionals. While this discussion may not be sufficient to do so, it can be an important preliminary step in recognizing our own responsibility for moral awareness.

SOCIAL, CORPORATE, AND PROFESSIONAL CONSCIOUSNESS

In a review of several empirical studies, Loe, Ferrell, and Mansfield (2000) reported that the majority of the studies dealing with codes of ethics revealed that these codes influence ethical decision making and assist in raising the general level of awareness of ethical issues. However, the utility of professional codes of ethics should not be focused only on the guidance they lend for general practice, but also on the not-so-common dilemmas professionals can face throughout the course of their careers.

Codes of ethics can be developed from the standpoint of a profession, an organization, an individual, or society as a whole. While it is possible for a comprehensive code to align some of these perspectives, the reality is that what is considered ethical from one perspective may be in conflict with another perspective. For instance, an HPT professional, after a sound assessment and analysis, determines that the best solution for a performance problem is to automate a process that is currently being performed by workers. One might or should ask, "best" according to what criteria? The organization itself might consider this best because this approach will translate into large savings in time and money for the company. The local community may not consider this the best solution because it would mean eliminating the jobs of thousands of workers. There may be other solutions that would not render as much savings to the company but still satisfy the requirements of multiple parties, including the workers. But who are the stakeholders? To whom is the HPT professional ultimately responsible?

Our previous discussion addressed the importance of weighing the consequences for multiple stakeholders. The preceding questions suggest that codes of ethics must take into account the complexities and potential conflicts performance technologists will likely deal with concerning ultimate responsibilities at some point in their career.

With a growing focus on results, the performance-improvement field is beginning to examine the various stakeholders and varying degrees of results it is responsible for improving. Though some companies may be conducting business in an irresponsible manner, others are realizing that doing societal good is not just an option, but a requirement for success, and are now embracing social responsibility (Popcorn, 1991; Hatcher, 2000). Today, we see worldwide organizations increasingly including societal value added as a major component of their mission (Watkins, Leigh, and Kaufman, 2000).

When working with organizations, performance-improvement consultants traditionally have either overlooked the benefits to internal and external clients as well as society or assumed that they were being taken into account (Kaufman and Clark, 1999; Farrington and Clark, 2000). Today, however, performance-improvement professionals are assuming leadership roles in helping organizations realize the ethical and financial power of corporate social responsibility (Hatcher, 2000).

Consistent with the social responsibility of professionals and clients, there has been a growing effort to establish an ethical foundation for performance-improvement professionals. In 1988, Westgaard developed a credo for performance-improvement professionals in which social mandates were outlined. These social mandates were obtained from a consensus of performance-improvement professionals using the Delphi technique. Some of these included: use performance improvement only in support of humane, socially responsible, and life-fulfilling ends for both the individual and the organization; maintain the widest view of the usefulness for, and impact of, their interventions; support organizational goals that are aware of impacts to society as a whole; take moral and ethical positions on societal issues and make professional decisions according to those positions; help clients make informed decisions by providing supportable intervention options with objective data, consequences, and recommendations; use the highest professional standards of ethics, honesty, and integrity in all facets of their work; and withdraw from clients who cannot act ethically.

Peter Dean has also written extensively on ethical responsibility, specifically within the performance-improvement field. In 1993, he reviewed the basic ethical theory and relevant empirical research with the goal that this would serve as part of the preliminary requirement for developing a code of ethics. Dean (1993, p. 3) proposed,

> By examining these [HPT strategies] in the context of ethics, they [performance-improvement professionals] may broaden their "vantage points" (Dean 1992) on these systems and strategies so they can see more precisely how ethical issues influence performance and how what they do can influence the ethical climate of an organization.

Furthermore, Dean provides evidence of the importance of ethical awareness and practice for professionals by citing a study conducted by Hammond (1992), in which it was found that 63 percent of business executives and recruiters indicated that a sense of social, professional, and ethical responsibility was one of the most sought-after qualities in new recruits.

In 1999, the Academy of Human Resource Development (AHRD) produced the first edition of *Standards on Ethics and Integrity* for anyone with membership in the International Society for Performance Improvement (ISPI), the American Society for Training and Development (ASTD), the Organizational Development Network, and similar professional societies (Academy of Human Resource Development, 1999). Dean (1999, p. 3) explains the rationale:

> The purposes of these standards are to provide guidance for professionals engaged in practice, research, consulting, and instructional/facilitation/teaching. The standards identify a common set of values upon which we can build our research and/or practice. The primary goal is for the welfare and protection of the individuals, groups, and organizations with whom we work.

These general principles of identified ethics are displayed in Table 44.1.

Building on these standards and other relevant literature in management ethics and conduct, Watkins, Leigh, and Kaufman (2000) proposed a code of professional conduct for performance-improvement professionals. They state that in today's management environment there is a growing requirement to deliver measurable value to external clients and society. Moreover, the new era of management and performance improvement is focused on defining, justifying, and delivering useful results for all internal and external stakeholders. To this end, the following items represent the introduction to the preliminary code of professional conduct suggested by these authors:

1. The objectives of a performance-improvement professional are (a) to provide organizations and individuals with the skills, knowledge, abilities, and attitudes necessary to create opportunities for achieving desired and required individual, organizational, and societal results; (b) to assist in the generation of new and valid knowledge that will lead to the attainment of results that meet the performance criteria demanded by individuals, organizations, and society; (c) to acquire the knowledge through systematic and valid research methods without jeopardizing the success of clients, the clients' clients, or society; and (d) to produce the results required by the client.

2. The performance-improvement professional will not enter into any engagement (a) that violates one or more of the stated codes of conduct or the profession's standards on ethics and integrity; (b) in which the pending results cannot be linked to or are not aligned with the organizational mission and positive contributions to society; (c) that will not lead to the achievement of measurable contributions to the

Table 44.1. General Principles Based on the AHRD *Standards on Ethics and Integrity.*

A: Competence	HRD/HPT professionals must recognize the boundaries of their particular competencies and the limitations of their expertise, as well as realize that these will differ from situation to situation.
B: Integrity	HRD/HPT professionals must be honest, fair, and respectful, seeking to promote integrity in their research, teaching, and practice and never making statements that are false, misleading, or deceptive. In addition, they must strive to be aware of their own belief systems, values, needs, limitations, and the effect of these on their work, as well as avoid potentially conflicting relationships.
C: Professional responsibility	HRD/HPT professionals must uphold professional standards of conduct, clarify their professional roles and obligations, accept appropriate responsibility for their behavior, and adapt their methods to the needs of different populations. In addition, they should concern themselves with the ethical compliance of their colleague's research and professional conduct and likewise should consult with colleagues in order to prevent unethical practice themselves.
D: Respect for people's rights and dignity	HRD/HPT professionals should respect the right of individuals to privacy, confidentiality, self-determination, and autonomy, mindful that legal and other obligations may lead to inconsistency and conflict with the exercise of such rights. In addition, they are aware of cultural, individual, and role differences, including those due to age, gender, race, ethnicity, national origin, religion, sexual orientation, disability, language, and socioeconomic status and do not knowingly participate in discriminatory practices.
E: Concern for others' welfare	HRD/HPT professionals seek to contribute to the welfare of those individuals with whom they interact professionally by weighing the welfare and rights of their clients. If conflicts arise, they should attempt to resolve them and perform their roles in a responsible manner that avoids or minimizes harm.
F: Social responsibility	HRD/HPT professionals must be aware of their professional responsibilities to the community, the society in which they work and live, and the planet. They work to minimize adverse affects on individuals, groups, organizations, societies, and the environment and understand that a healthy economy, healthy organizations, and a healthy ecosystem are intricately interconnected. Further, they are concerned with and work to eliminate the causes of human suffering, and when undertaking research, they work to advance human welfare, human development, and a sustainable future.

Source: Academy of Human Resource Development, 1999.

attainment of the ideal vision, that is, creating a measurably better world for future generations.

3. An engagement with a client requires certain responsibilities for the consultant or employee, as well as for the client organization. The performance-improvement professional will state these responsibilities as well as biases explicitly to provide all stakeholders with the necessary information and expectations prior to making a decision regarding the acceptance of position or engagements.

4. Missing data are data. Thus, when efforts uncover performance issues for which the client currently has no measures, the performance-improvement professional will include these "missing cells" in a report and suggest means by which the client can develop measures of successful accomplishment of required performance [Watkins, Leigh, and Kaufman, 2000, p. 19].

These authors also propose specific obligations and general professional practice suggestions for the professional as well as responsibilities for the client: for example, use the code of conduct as a contract discussion check sheet; use an ideal vision as the starting place for all decision making; standardize our language; and ask tough questions.

The International Society for Performance Improvement *Code of Ethics* (2002a) integrates many of the concepts just described. It is summarized in the following lists, organized into two categories: objectives and principles.

ISPI Objectives of HPT Professionals

1. Provide organizations, individuals, or both with the skills, knowledge, abilities, and attitudes necessary to create opportunities for achieving desired or required individual, organizational, and societal results.

2. Assist in the generation of new and valid knowledge that will lead to the attainment of results meeting the performance criteria demanded by individuals, organizations, and society.

3. Acquire the knowledge through systematic research methods without jeopardizing the success of my client, my client's clients, or society.

4. Produce the results required by the client.

Founding Principles for ISPI Code of Ethics

1. *Add value principle:* Strive to conduct yourself, and manage your projects and their results, in ways that add value for your clients, their customers, and the global environment.

2. *Validated practice principle:* Make use of and promote validated practices in performance technology strategies and standards.

3. *Collaboration principle:* Work collaboratively with clients and users, functioning as a trustworthy strategic partner.

4. *Continuous improvement principle:* Continually improve your proficiency in the field of performance technology.

5. *Integrity principle:* Be honest and truthful in your representations to clients, colleagues, and others with whom you may come in contact while practicing performance technology.

6. *Uphold confidentiality principle:* Maintain client confidentiality, not allowing for any conflict of interest that would benefit you or others.

The International Board of Standards for Training, Performance, and Instruction (IBSTPI) (2003a) has also released professional codes of ethical standards, which have been specifically designed for instructional designers and training managers.

IBSTPI Code of Ethical Standards for Instructional Designers

I. Guiding Standards: Responsibilities to Others
   A. Provide efficient, effective, workable, and cost-effective solutions to client problems.
   B. Systematically improve human performance to accomplish valid and appropriate individual and organizational goals.
   C. Facilitate individual accomplishment.
   D. Help clients make informed decisions.
   E. Inform others of potential ethical violations and conflicts of interest.
   F. Educate clients in matters of instructional design and performance improvement.

II. Guiding Standards: Social Mandates
   A. Support humane, socially responsible goals and activities for individuals and organizations.
   B. Make professional decisions based on moral and ethical positions on societal issues.
   C. Consider the impact of planned interventions on individuals, organizations, and the society as a whole.

III. Guiding Standards: Respecting the Rights of Others
   A. Protect the privacy, candor, and confidentiality of client and colleague information and communication.
   B. Adhere to intellectual property regulations.
   C. Do not use client or colleague information for personal gain.
   D. Do not represent the ideas or work of others as one's own.
   E. Do not make false claims about others.
   F. Do not discriminate in actions related to hiring, retention, and advancement.

IV. Guiding Standards: Professional Practice
   A. Be honest and fair in all facets of one's work.
   B. Share skills and knowledge with other professionals.
   C. Recognize the contributions of others.
   D. Support and aid colleagues.
   E. Commit time and effort to the development of the profession.
   F. Withdraw from clients who do not act ethically or when there is a conflict of interest.

IBSTPI Code of Ethical Standards for Training Managers

   I. Guiding Standards: Responsibilities to the Organization
   A. Provide efficient, effective, workable, and cost-effective solutions that advance organizational performance goals.
   B. Initiate and collaborate in organizational decision making.
   C. Educate the organization in matters of instructional design and performance improvement.
   D. Inform the organization of potential conflicts of interest and ethical, legal, and due process violations.
   E. Protect the privacy, candor, and confidentiality of information and communication of the organization and its members.
   F. Do not misuse organizational information for personal gain.
   II. Guiding Standards: Responsibilities to Others
   A. Be honest and fair in interactions with others.
   B. Treat others with dignity and respect.
   C. Facilitate individual accomplishment.
   D. Do not engage in exploitative relationships.
   E. Do not discriminate unfairly in actions related to hiring, retention, salary adjustments, and promotion.
   F. Do not represent the ideas or work of others as one's own.
   G. Do not make false or deceptive claims about self, others, or the work of the training function.
   III. Guiding Standards: Responsibilities to the Profession
   A. Seek and acknowledge the contributions of others.
   B. Aid and be supportive of colleagues.
   C. Commit time and effort to the development of the profession.
   D. Promote the enforcement of ethical standards.
   IV. Guiding Standards: Responsibility to Society
   A. Support humane, socially responsible goals and projects for the organization.
   B. Ensure that training products and procedures reflect moral and ethical positions on societal issues.
   C. Consider the consequences of proposed solutions upon individuals, organizations, and the society as a whole.

STANDARDS

Both standards and codes of ethics are intended to guide professional practice in a given field. Clients, employers, consultants, and employees look to standards to help them distinguish professionals who can demonstrate their competence and the value they add. Without accepted standards and related criteria, it is difficult for HPT professionals to prove they are accomplishing worthy results. The International Board of Standards for Training, Performance, and Instruction (2003b, paragraph 1), cites several benefits from the development of standards:

> The development of standards for professional practice (as indicated by competency and performance standards), and perhaps formal certification, promotes several immediate, and highly desirable, outcomes. It establishes a basis for selecting new members into the profession. It establishes a sound basis for faculty members to train new professionals. It provides a basis for employers to hire professionals with the specific knowledge and skill required to satisfy organizational demands. It provides a clear criterion for supervisors to judge the work performance of, and to assist in upgrading the knowledge and skill of established practitioners.

Broadening the Vantage Point

The HPT field, like many others, is in continuous development, expanding the boundaries of performance-improvement professionals by shifting from a focus on training to a focus on performance results. It has emerged from the fields of behavioral and cognitive psychology, systems theory, communication and information theory, instructional technology, training design, organizational development, ergonomics, and human resource management (Rosenberg, Coscarelli, and Hutchinson, 1999; Stolovitch and Keeps, 1999). Of these, many believe that its major influences have been instructional systems design and programmed instruction (Sanders and Ruggles, 2000), which themselves evolved from the fields of communication, management science, and behavioral sciences (Morgan, 1978). Each time it has evolved, it has done so by consistently expanding its scope and incorporating a bigger part of the performance context. This evolution even has led professionals to begin to consider the societal context influenced by individual, small group, and organizational performance (Dean, 1997, 1999; Hatcher, 2000; Kaufman, 2000).

Professional Accountability and Credibility Through Standards

While consideration of the societal context is a positive sign, signaling the continuous demand for and value of our services, it also brings with it the risk of inconsistent behavior and poor performance. Professional standards can be a useful resource in promoting consistency in the quality of the contributions HPT professionals make to their clients. At the same time, standards can provide the criteria used to hold HPT professionals accountable to their clients and colleagues (Dean, 1999). HPT being a field that encourages observable and measurable results, its professionals have an especially good understanding of the importance and utility of standards that are objective-based, that is, standards that lend themselves to being used as clear guides of what to accomplish and how well it has been accomplished.

Standards can also provide a common language (Dean, 1999) with which clients, consultants, academics, students, and other stakeholders can clearly communicate: "What is it that you do again?" Many HPT professionals have likely heard that question numerous times, even after having previously explained it to the same individual. Standards can provide clear and practical explanations for the processes that we use and the results we deliver, something particularly useful in communicating with and marketing to potential clients the value we can add to their organizations.

ESTABLISHED STANDARDS

IBSTPI Standards for Instructional Designers

In 2000, IBSTPI released the third edition of *Instructional Design Competencies: The Standards* (Richey, Fields, and Foxon, 2001). It was published to provide instructional designers with a foundation for the establishment of professional standards. IBSTPI defines a competency as "a knowledge, skill, or attitude that enables one to effectively perform the activities of a given occupation or function to the standards expected in employment" (Richey, Fields, and Foxon, 2001, p. 31). As part of the revision and updating process of the previous versions, the IBSTPI competency model went through three major phases: identification of foundational research, competency drafting, and competency validation and rewriting. Following is a summary of the resulting instructional designer competencies (Richey, Field, and Foxon, 2001, pp. 46–55):

Professional Foundations

1. Communicate effectively in visual, oral, and written form. (Essential)

2. Apply current research and theory to the practice of instructional design. (Advanced)

3. Update and improve one's knowledge, skills, and attitudes pertaining to instructional design and related fields. (Essential)

4. Apply fundamental research skills to instructional-design projects. (Advanced)

5. Identify and resolve ethical and legal implications of design in the work place. (Advanced)

Planning and Analysis

6. Conduct a needs assessment. (Essential)

7. Design a curriculum or program. (Essential)

8. Select and use a variety of techniques for determining instructional content. (Essential)

9. Identify and describe target population characteristics. (Essential)

10. Analyze the characteristics of the environment. (Essential)

11. Analyze the characteristics of existing and emerging technologies and their use in an instructional environment. (Essential)

12. Reflect upon the elements of a situation before finalizing design solutions and strategies. (Essential)

Design and Development

13. Select, modify, or create a design and development model appropriate for a given project. (Advanced)

14. Select and use a variety of techniques to define and sequence the instructional content and strategies. (Essential)

15. Select or modify existing instructional materials. (Essential)

16. Develop instructional materials. (Essential)

17. Design instruction that reflects an understanding of the diversity of learners and groups of learners. (Essential)

18. Evaluate and assess instruction and its impact. (Essential)

Implementation and Management

19. Plan and manage instructional design projects. (Advanced)

20. Promote collaboration, partnerships, and relationships among the participants in a design project. (Advanced)

21. Apply business skills to managing instructional design. (Advanced)

22. Design instructional-management systems. (Advanced)

23. Provide for the effective implementation of instructional products and programs. (Essential)

Although Sanders and Ruggles (2000) conclude that most accounts indicate HPT is an outgrowth of instructional systems design and programmed instruction, these instructional-design competencies do not cover the entire spectrum of competencies required for performance-improvement professionals (Kaufman and Clark, 1999; Guerra, 2003). The ISPI standards, discussed in the next section, are geared toward general HPT professionals.

ISPI Standards for HPT Professionals

In 1999, under the leadership of Dale Brethower, then ISPI's president, the ISPI board of directors approved a study of the feasibility of developing a professional certification for HPT professionals. Following positive feedback about this idea, Judith Hale, then ISPI president elect, convened the "Kitchen Cabinet," a representative group of thirty HPT professionals from industry, academia, and business. This group began the development of HPT standards for the certification effort. The result was the articulation of ten standards, which were further validated by a group of graduate students under the guidance of James Pershing, a professor at Indiana University (International Society for Performance Improvement, n.d.). The ten HPT standards are as follows:

1. Focus on results and help clients focus on results.
2. Look at situations systemically, taking into consideration the larger context, including competing pressures, resource constraints, and anticipated change.
3. Add value in how you do the work and through the work itself.
4. Utilize partnerships or collaborate with clients and other experts as required.
5. Be systematic in all aspects of the process, including the assessment of the need or opportunity.
6. Be systematic in all aspects of the process, including the analysis of the work and workplace to identify the cause or factors that limit performance.
7. Be systematic in all aspects of the process, including the design of the solution or specification of the requirements of the solution.
8. Be systematic in all aspects of the process, including the development of all or some of the solution and its elements.
9. Be systematic in all aspects of the process, including the implementation of the solution.
10. Be systematic in all aspects of the process, including the evaluation of the process and the results [International Society for Performance Improvement, 2002b].

Measurement of Standards and Certification

Hale (2003) proposes that certification changes the nature of the conversations between HPT professionals and their clients, which consequently changes the expectations, the relationships, and the reputation of the HPT field as a whole.

Professional certification is usually based on the voluntary action of an occupational or professional group to institute a system by which it can grant recognition to those practitioners who have met some stated level of competence, experience, and training. Such individuals are granted a certificate attesting to the fact that they have met some set of agreed upon standards of the credentialing organization and are entitled to make the public aware of their credentialed status.

While established standards provide the objectives or expectations, certification provides the vehicle through which a professional society or field can evaluate whether or not its professionals have attained such objectives or expectations. According to the International Board of Standards for Training, Performance, and Instruction (2003b), a professional certification process, based on predetermined standards or criteria, is the most typical means for evaluating the competence of a professional.

Certified Performance Technologist

In April of 2002, the Certified Performance Technologist (CPT) certification was developed and implemented by ISPI, under Judith Hale's leadership. This was in response to requests from public and private organizations for criteria to better distinguish proficient practitioners of human performance technology. Currently, this performance-based, as opposed to education- or training-based, certification requires three years of experience in performance-improvement work, demonstration of proficiency in the ten HPT standards, commitment to the Code of Ethics, and recertification every three years (International Society for Performance Improvement, n.d.).

SUMMARY

Ethics and performance standards are integral to both the competence of HPT professionals and the value they add. Both, inevitably, shape our views, decisions, and actions. To make professionally sound and ethical decisions and contributions, we must be aware of the factors that influence our work. Increasing our awareness of ethical and professional standards, and adhering to them, will increase the likelihood of adding value to our clients, our organizations, our field, ourselves, and the communities we affect through our work. As the HPT field continues to grow, so do the resources and support available through vehicles such as codes of ethics and professional standards. Such phenomena increase the quality and credibility of our profession, if we choose to make good use of them.

References

Academy of Human Resource Development. (1999, May). *Standards on ethics and integrity* (1st ed.). Retrieved November 7, 2005, from http://64.233.167.104/search?q=cache:ZU3v5wjeragJ:www.ahrd.org/publications/ethics/ethics_standards.PDF+Standards+on+ethics+and+integrity&hl=en.

Bales, R. E. (1971). Act-utilitarianism: Account of right-making characteristics or decision-making procedures? *American Philosophical Quarterly, 8,* 57–65.

Benedict, R. (1934). *Patterns of culture.* Boston: Houghton Mifflin.

Bentham, J. (1979). *An introduction to the principles of morals and legislation.* Garden City, NY: Doubleday. Originally published publicly in 1789.

Butterfield, D., Treviño, L., and Weaver, G. (2000). Moral awareness in business organizations: Influences of issue-related and social context factors. *Human Relations, 53*(7), 981–1018.

Carliner, S. (2003). Ethics and the marketing of technology for training and performance improvement: A commentary. *Performance Improvement Quarterly, 16*(4), 94–106.

Dean, P. (1992). Allow me to introduce . . . Tom Gilbert. *Performance Improvement Quarterly, 5*(3), 83–95.

Dean, P. (1993). A selected review of the underpinnings of ethics for human performance technology professionals—Part one: Key ethical theories and research. *Performance Improvement Quarterly, 6*(4), 6–32.

Dean, P. (1997). Social science and the practice of performance improvement. *Performance Improvement, 10*(3), 3–6.

Dean, P. (1999). Editorial: Standards on ethics and integrity for professors and professionals in the field of learning and performance improvement and for the practice of HRD/HPT. *Performance Improvement Quarterly, 12*(3), 3–4.

Farrington, J., and Clark, R. E. (2000). Snake oil, science, and performance products. *Performance Improvement, 39*(10), 5–10.

Ferrell, O. C., and Gresham, L. G. (1985). A contingency framework for understanding ethical decision making in marketing. *Journal of Marketing, 49,* 87–96.

Guerra, I. (2003). Key competencies required of performance improvement professionals. *Performance Improvement Quarterly, 16*(1), 55–72.

Hale, J. (2003). Certification: How it can add value. *Performance Improvement, 42*(2), 30–31.

Hammond, J. (1992). Internal communication, Smeal College of Business, Pennsylvania State University, cited in P. Dean (1993). A selected review of the underpinnings of ethics for human performance technology professionals— Part one: Key ethical theories and research. *Performance Improvement Quarterly, 6*(4), 6–32.

Hatcher, T. (2000). Building socially responsible companies through performance improvement outcomes. *Performance Improvement, 3*(7), 18–22.

International Board of Standards for Training, Performance, and Instruction. (2003a). *Codes of ethical standards.* Retrieved December 8, 2004, from www.ibstpi.org.

International Board of Standards for Training, Performance, and Instruction. (2003b). *Certification.* Retrieved December 8, 2004, from www.ibstpi.org.

International Society for Performance Improvement. (2002a). *Code of ethics.* Retrieved December 5, 2004, from www.certifiedpt.org/forms/Code%20of%20Ethics.pdf.

International Society for Performance Improvement. (2002b). *Performance improvement standards.* Retrieved December 5, 2004, from www.certifiedpt.org/standards.pdf.

International Society for Performance Improvement. (n.d.). *Certification.* Retrieved December 5, 2004, from www.certifiedpt.org/index.cfm?section = WhatisCPT.

Jarvis, C. (n.d.). *The absolute-relative puzzle.* Retrieved December 1, 2004, from www.brunel.ac.uk/~bustcfj/bola/ethics/relative.html.

Kant, I. (1964). *Groundwork of the metaphysics of morals.* (H. J. Paton, trans.). New York: Harper and Row. Originally published in 1785.

Kaufman, R. (1992). *Strategic planning plus: An organizational guide* (Revised). Newbury Park, CA: Sage.

Kaufman, R. (2000). *Mega planning.* Thousand Oaks, CA: Sage.

Kaufman, R., and Clark, R. (1999). Re-establishing performance improvement as a legitimate area of inquiry, activity, and contribution: Rules of the road. *Performance Improvement, 38*(9), 13–18.

Loe, T., Ferrell, L., and Mansfield, P. (2000). A review of empirical studies assessing ethical decision-making in business. *Journal of Business Ethics, 25,* 85–204.

Mill, J. S. (1998). *Utilitarianism.* (Roger Crisp, ed.). New York: Oxford University Press. Originally published in 1861.

Morgan, R. (1978). Educational technology: Adolescence to adulthood. *Educational Communication and Technology, 26,* 142–152.

Pojman, L. (1996). *Philosophy: The quest for truth* (3rd ed.). Belmont, CA: Wadsworth.

Popcorn, F. (1991). *The Popcorn report.* New York: Doubleday.

Rest, J. (1986). *Moral development: Advances in research and theory.* New York: Praeger.

Richey, R., Fields, D., and Foxon, M. (2001). *Instructional design competencies: The standards.* (3rd ed.). Iowa City: International Board of Standards for Training, Performance, and Instruction.

Rosenberg, M., Coscarelli, W., and Hutchinson, C. (1999). The origins and evolution of the field. In H. D. Stolovitch and E. J. Keeps (Eds.), *Handbook for Human Performance Technology: Improving individual and organizational performance worldwide* (2nd ed.). San Francisco: Jossey-Bass.

Ross, W. (n.d.). *Nicomachean ethics.* Retrieved December 1, 2004, from people.bu.edu/wwildman/WeirdWildWeb/courses/wphil/readings/wphil_rdg09_nichomacheanethics_entire.htm.

Russo, M. (n.d.). *Deontology and its discontents: A brief overview of Kant's ethics.* Retrieved November 12, 2004, from www.molloy.edu/academic/philosophy/sophia/kant/deontology.htm.

Sanders, E., and Ruggles, J. (2000, June). HPI soup: Too many cooks haven't spoiled the broth. *Training and Development,* pp. 27–36.

Shaub, M., Finn, D., and Munter, P. (1993). The effects of auditor's ethical orientation on commitment and ethical sensitivity. *Behavioral Research in Accounting, 5,* 145–169.

Sidgwick, H. (1907). *The methods of ethics* (7th ed). London, UK: Macmillan. First edition published in 1874.

Singhapakdi, A., Vitell, S., Rao, C., and Kurtz, D. (1999). Ethics gap: Comparing marketers with consumers on important determinants of ethical decision-making. *Journal of Business Ethics, 21*(4), 317–328.

Stolovitch, H., and Keeps, E. (1999). What is human performance technology? In H. D. Stolovitch and E. J. Keeps (Eds.), *Handbook for Human Performance Technology: Improving individual and organizational performance worldwide* (2nd ed.). San Francisco: Jossey-Bass.

Stolovitch, H., Keeps, E., and Rodrigue, D. (1999). Skill sets for the human performance technologists. In H. D. Stolovitch and E. J. Keeps (Eds.), *Handbook for human performance technology: Improving individual and organizational performance worldwide* (2nd ed.). San Francisco: Jossey-Bass.

Treviño, L. K. (1986). Ethical decision making in organizations: A person-situation interactionist model. *Academy of Management Review, 11,* 601–617.

Warner, J. (2004). Ethics for sale. *Chief Executive Magazine, 203,* 6–50.

Watkins, R., Leigh, D., and Kaufman, R. (2000). A scientific dialogue: A performance accomplishment code of professional conduct. *Performance Improvement, 38*(4), 17–22.

Westgaard, O. (1988). *A credo for performance technologists.* Western Springs, IL: International Board of Standards for Training, Performance and Instruction.

CHAPTER FORTY-FIVE

Professional Ethics

A Matter of Duty

Jim Hill

Six principles serve as the foundation on which certified performance technologists base their practices.

- Add value
- Make use of and promote validated practices
- Work collaboratively
- Continuously improve proficiency
- Exhibit integrity
- Uphold confidentiality

They are the bedrock of the code of ethics espoused by the International Society for Performance Improvement (2002b) and are intended to promote ethical practice in the profession of human performance technology (HPT). As noted in the International Society for Performance Improvement (ISPI) certification materials (2002a), to be certified or recertified, performance technologists must sign a statement that they agree to conduct themselves in ways that are in keeping with these principles. No signature equals no certification and no professional designation.

The purpose of this chapter is to provide an outline and an overview of ethical considerations in general, and then tie those considerations to the work of human performance technologists.

WRITING ABOUT ETHICS

The ethical dialogue within the HPT profession is not a new one. Led by forward-thinking members of ISPI such as George Geis, Carol Haig, Peter Dean, and Stephanie Jackson, members of the Society have been discussing and debating the topic for years. With the development of the Certified Performance Technologist (CPT) program came the formalization of an ethical code for use and adherence by ISPI members so inclined to gain certification.

Still, writing about ethics on behalf of an international body is not easy. It is always a challenge, and it continues to be a topic of interest and importance not only for the HPT profession but for all professions. Ethics requires trust, and trust is built on a foundation of moral and cultural norms. A significant issue facing ethicists and writers on the subject is that there is no common global culture. As Francis Fukuyama (1995) points out, one commonly used anthropology book provides 11 definitions of culture (Geertz, 1973). Another identifies 160 more (Jamieson, 1980). Because of the diversity across cultures, any attempt to write an all-encompassing ethical overview is bound to fall short.

Given this explanatory caveat, we begin this particular ethical journey by knowing that some readers will take exception to the approach, terms, definitions, and references used in the creation of this chapter. Some may find their ethical concerns unmet. But I have done my best and, I hope, most readers will gain insight into an increasingly necessary part of the business environment for the human performance technologist. More than likely, the ethical foundations put forth on these pages will be described in Western terms. There are a few good reasons for this. The writer is from the West, ISPI's roots are firmly planted in the West, and the majority of large-scale international business practices are based on Western norms.

PROFESSIONAL REQUIREMENTS VERSUS PERSONAL NEEDS

There is a need for ethics in the conduct of business. We know it instinctively, but there is a growing body of research that points to measurable economic impacts. Webley and More (2003) have noted that firms not explicitly committed to ethical dealings have profit and turnover ratios 15 percent lower than others. Previously, Varca and Valutis (1993) showed that the performance and productivity of an organization's highly skilled workers drops as much as 25 percent when others in the organization engage in unethical behavior. There are also findings which suggest that unethical behavior within an organization may lead to the departure of highly skilled employees, since they are the ones most able to switch jobs easily (Cialdini, Petrova, and Goldstein, 2004). This turnover is expensive: Fitz-enz (1997) notes that the average company loses approximately

$1 million for every ten managerial and professional employees who leave the organization. In sum, a lack of ethics is economically costly.

Defining the Objectives of a Profession

When one enters a profession, he or she faces a wide variety of situations, some of which pull personal and professional needs in opposite directions. As members of a work society determine the proper balance as individuals through their combined decisions, they are also shaping the identity of their profession. But what exactly does the term *professional* mean? What does it require? Again, the ISPI Website provides guidance for human performance practitioners by suggesting a framework for these considerations and outlining the objectives of a profession. These include the following:

- Provide organizations and individuals with the skills, knowledge, abilities, and attitudes necessary to create opportunities for achieving desired or required individual, organizational, and societal results.

- Assist in the generation of new and valid knowledge that will lead to the attainment of results meeting the performance criteria demanded by individuals, organizations, and society.

- Acquire the knowledge through systematic research methods without jeopardizing the success of a client, a client's clients, or society.

- Produce results required by the client.

Our Group: Building a Community

We know from both science and practical experience that humans are instinctively selfish, yet they also carry an obligation to others. Maintaining a balance between the two instincts is a continuous internal challenge. When every other person we come into contact with is conducting the same balancing act, the world gets a little messy. So, when we discover like-minded others, or we can establish a principle that is generally accepted within our group, it makes daily functioning more efficient, more dependable, more cooperative, and less stressful. It holds us together as a society (Abegglen and Stalk, 1985). Bardwick (1998) reinforces this notion by reminding us that community requires morality, and without community, we are alone (p. 248). This leads us to one of our first questions when making ethical determinations: Who is in our group?

"Trust is the expectation that arises within a community of regular, honest, and cooperative behavior based on commonly shared norms, on the part of members of the community" (Fukuyama, 1995, p. 26). Groups must adapt to common norms as a whole before trust can become generalized among their members (Fukuyama, 1995). The challenge for ISPI is that *our group* is becoming larger and more physically disconnected in a global Internet society. This begets a second consideration for ethical decisions: What is your obligation to me and what is mine to you? Said another way, What is our duty?

Because we define our groups and our obligations differently, we find, unsurprisingly, that there are different definitions of *ethics.* The easy part is selecting a few general terms, values, or characteristics such as those cited by Ivaturi (2001): loyalty, honesty, fairness, respect, tolerance, and moral courage. The challenge these terms present is that they are universally noncontractual, as is duty.

THE CHALLENGE OF COMMON TERMS

There is no doubt that we live in a pluralistic world (Dippman, 2003). Within that world there are independent sources of value and multiple groups with competing interests (Blais, 1997). In the realm of nation-state politics, the challenges associated with common rules and definitions are crystallized. As reported by the U.S. Department of State (2004), two million people have been killed and four million more displaced in the internal conflict in Sudan. There is also ample eyewitness evidence of rape, killing of male babies, use of racial epithets, and burning of villages. However, leaders from varying cultures disagree about what to call the situation. Among representatives of the United Nations there is no agreement that there is *genocide* or that the situation even represents a *humanitarian crisis* (Wax, 2004a). As Wax (2004b, p. A17) also reports, "Use of the word genocide is 'a political question now,' a high-ranking State Department source said. 'Not a legal one.'" If globally *we* cannot agree on what is or is not a humanitarian crisis, we are unlikely to tackle what is or is not honesty, fairness, and respect. This again corresponds to the comment of Ivaturi (2001), who notes that our daily challenges rarely involve violations of contractual obligations but rather those that are noncontractual: how we act and what we do when there are no clauses to reference.

TAKING LESSONS FROM MEDICINE

In the realm of performance consulting, there are scores of easy targets for those looking for ethical violations. A starter set might include the following:

- Simply agreeing with clients' assessment of what is needed or what they want to hear versus recommending interventions that are truly necessary
- Accepting a job without having the expertise the client is requesting
- Recommending a colleague who does not have the necessary expertise
- Skewing data to make an intervention look more attractive

- Promising results you cannot deliver
- Deliberately delaying delivery of a task
- Attempting to be a "jack-of-all-trades"
- Not educating the client

Any of these would be unthinkable if they were the actions of a physician:

- You want LSD for that headache Mrs. Johnson? No problem!
- You want me to perform minor brain surgery, even though I'm your podiatrist? OK! I'll give it a try!
- Let's just change Mr. Rodman's charts so that we can prescribe him some Percodan.
- I promise that if you take these pills, you will be smarter by next month!

Or consider an actual newspaper ad for cosmetic surgery. A gorgeous blonde woman graces the page. Lithe, tanned, and clear-eyed, she is confident in her superior beauty. The ad makes one think, "This doctor really knew what he was doing!" Below the woman's photograph is the rest of the story: "Not an actual patient." As potential patients, now what do we do?

The unfortunate reality is that in the field of performance improvement, and in similar consulting engagements, situations similar to these are common. On a daily basis, many of our performance consulting brethren think nothing of attempting the organizational equivalents. Regardless of capability, many practitioners, as distinguished from professionals, via their all-encompassing approach, provide "solutions" in the areas of training, process improvement, organizational design, leadership development, and compensation planning without hesitation. Still, many customers accept this as the norm. Why? Even automotive mechanics specialize.

THE DEVELOPMENT OF OUR ETHICAL CENTER

According to Vice Admiral James Stockdale (Brennan, 1992), integrity consists of knowing the limits of what you are responsible for. This requires personal honesty. Those who fail the moral test often require the approval of others to build their self-respect. People who change at a moment's notice, those who exchange principles for approval, and those with weak character may never be truly tested in the moral and ethical arena.

The Need for a Moral Center

Business life is generally easy and presents no serious challenge. However, when difficult circumstances arise, they often bring out the best, and worst, in people.

As LaFave (2003) notes, a failure of integrity might be entirely harmless in less stressful situations. But sometimes people are unlucky. They find themselves in times of challenge, facing more than they can ethically handle. We cannot blame people whose lives fall into such events. What we can do is hope that our employees, our partners, and our consultants each have a moral center. In many cases, this sense of duty is based on culture, and culture frequently is based on religion.

Colero (2000) suggests that, closely aligned to the notion of a moral center, a universal set of principles is compatible with our ability to follow our intuition and a reliance on our inner voice. But Stockdale (Brennan, 1992) would urge caution, noting that while rarely arguable and generally given an approving head nod by a wide set of people in common situations, our personal set of standards may fall short on the day it is required.

Trust Leads to Prosperity

Many ethicists lean heavily on the human desire for unconditional love and compassion, two constructs found in nearly all religions. Another common ethical and religious construct is empathy, which might best be defined in the form of a question: If you knew everything that I knew, what would you do? Yet, every year across the globe, we learn of corporate scandal and fraud in caregiving organizations, and governmental contract violations or impropriety. If the principles are so easy, why do we have so much difficulty adhering to them? The answer to this question is complex, but it may be found in the nuances of our cultural beliefs, our determinations of who is in our group, and our definitions of trust. The ramifications of our answers to this complex question form much more than the foundations of our beliefs. As Fukuyama (1995) points out, they are the cornerstone for our economic prosperity. Low-trust society? Low prosperity. High-trust society? Great prosperity. Across the globe, the equation is truly that simple.

DIFFERING CULTURES: CORE BELIEFS

While more has been written on ethical and religious linkages than can fill an entire library, it is helpful to take a glimpse into some of the major cultures to see where differences and similarities lie. Our world is more complex and our interactions with others will not get easier. Cultural superiority and its supporting religious beliefs form the underpinnings of many, if not most, of the world's battles. The ethical challenges we will continue to face will lead us to poor decisions, and ultimately organizational conflict and division, if we are not aware of cultural norms and their foundations. Consider the following very brief snapshots.

East Asia

The members of many East Asian cultures are followers of Buddhism, which is viewed mainly as a peaceful religion. Buddhists are asked to adhere to the "Five Precepts," training rules meant to cultivate a peaceful mind. Ethical and moral principles are governed by examining whether certain actions are likely to be harmful to one's self or others. Buddhists say that a skillful mind avoids actions that are likely to cause suffering or remorse, and they believe that

- All beings have a right to their lives, and that right should be respected.
- One should avoid taking anything unless one can be certain that it is intended for them.
- One should avoid overindulgence in any sensual pleasure.
- One should avoid lying, deceiving, slandering, and communicating in ways that are not beneficial to the welfare of others.

Most people, Buddhist or not, would agree with these guidelines. However, even in Buddhist countries, practice diverges from principle. For example, in Thailand, there is widespread environmental vandalism, and in Japan, the killing of whales and dolphins is still prevalent regardless of international norms (Buddha Dharma Education Association, 2004).

China

While China is another predominantly Buddhist country, it is also influenced by strong Confucian beliefs (Emery, 1999). The result is a need for loyalty that often overrides more rigid Buddhist practices. The Chinese stress five primary relationships:

- Ruler and subject
- Parent and child
- Elder and younger
- Husband and wife
- Friend and friend

The concept of *our group* is especially strong in Asian cultures, and businesspeople will tend to display group orientations. Asians are also more likely than Westerners to accept the norms and rules of the organizations to which they belong. Business decisions are often made based on a hierarchy of loyalty.

In China, visitors will experience overriding reverence and respect for family. Westerners will find that in Chinese businesses, family members tend to make up a large part of the organizational relationships. This further compounds the loyalty issues when matters of dealmaking are at hand. Because of the need to maintain strong ties to relationships higher in the hierarchy, Chinese may distance themselves from difficult decisions. Strangers, new customers, and new business partners are likely to fall in the lower rung of the loyalty ladder. While Westerners are likely to seek out those who are more capable or possess the better skills, Chinese are likely to place greater importance on friends or family connections. That is where one's first duties lie.

Korea

Shifting our view to Korea, another Buddhist country, we find similarities. As in many other Asian countries, business is personal and everything takes a backseat to those relations. One's sense of duty is tied to family relations, school affiliations, and hometown similarities, which often take precedence over job seniority and rank (De Mente, 2001). Trust is an enormous component of the business relationship. To increase trust it is important to have the right relationships, and that requires the right introductions on the right level.

Any outsider looking for a quick win in Asia is bound to be disappointed. In starting my own company, I had a desire to gain a foothold in Korea, knowing that their economy was booming and believing that our products would align with their desires to create organizational harmony. Still, I had no clear method of entering into fruitful relationships. A *business matchmaker* helped me by providing our company's information to her contacts. This took about a year. Then I was instructed to send Christmas greetings to senior executives that I had never met. It seemed strange to me but I did as I was instructed. That is the essence of Asian business. Being independently successful or boldly calling on company presidents or C-level executives would have produced few tangible results.

As a result of their fierce loyalties, Asians can also be relentless in their negotiations with outsiders. In particular, when dealing with Westerners, they have a strong feeling that their tactics are fair, since they believe that foreigners have so much. So there is little sense of taking an unfair advantage.

Japan

The core religious thread running through Japanese society is the Shinto religion. Where many other cultures are concerned with what awaits them in the afterlife, Shintoists have few such concerns. They are more focused on fitting into this life, and the Shinto religion is a collection of rituals and methods meant to mediate the relations of living humans. Shintoists have no absolute commandments (De Mente, 1999). Their goal is to live a harmonious life. Shinto also does not focus on sin but, rather, on impurity. When one is impure, it is his or her duty to undertake a cleansing ritual. The cleansing is not for others, but for one's self, one's peace of mind. In fact, evil is called *kegare,* literally meaning dirtiness. The opposite is *kiyome,* which means purity (De Mente, 1999).

In Japan, rituals are important. They often focus on the need to cleanse, to show appreciation, or to show humility. I am married to a Japanese citizen, and before every meal, we say, "*i-tadaki-masu*," or, "I will humbly receive." In doing so, we show proper gratitude to those who prepared the meal, and also to those living things that lost their lives to make the meal. As De Mente (1999) notes, failure to show proper respect is a sign of pride and lack of concern for others. Such an attitude is looked down on, because it is believed to create problems for all. Those who fail to take into account the feelings of other people only attract ruin.

South Asia

In India and some other parts of South Asia, Hindu ethics predominate. In India, for example, there is a strong belief in reincarnation, and this leads to the need for reciprocity in one's current life, as a person may end up in another's shoes in a future life. These beliefs, however, may also help to excuse not assisting someone in distress, due to the beliefs that one deserves the life one gets and that the future is already set, so human deliberation and actions will sort themselves out in the way they have to be (*Hinduism*, 2004). Followers of Hinduism believe that the future is already set and, therefore, that human deliberation and actions are pointless because things have to be the way they have to be.

West-Southwest Asia

In Western Asia, Islam dominates. Regardless of a thousand years of conflict, there are a number of Islamic tenets that seem to suggest at least surface-level alignment with Judeo-Christian beliefs. For example, within the practice of Judaism it is forbidden to hurt with words, to mislead people, or to cheat in business transactions (Karlinsky, 2000). A seller must inform a purchaser if his products are defective. Sellers cannot misrepresent one thing as another, or give the impression that they are doing something for another, when they really are not.

The Hanafis' interpretation of Islamic law (Al-Majalla, n.d.) is similar and also reinforces the need for equity and fairness. It says that if "the vendor sells property as possessing a certain desirable quality and such property proves to be devoid of such quality, the purchaser has the option of either canceling the sale, or of accepting the thing sold for the whole of the fixed price." This is called an option for misdescription. It is just one example among hundreds of similarities.

Muslims also believe in the afterlife, and their actions in this life are meant to support a pleasurable experience in the next. To practitioners of Islam, the decay and eventual disappearance of honesty is a sign of the imminence of the Day of Judgment (Beekun, 1997).

Muslims look to their Holy Prophet for the ultimate example, and seek to emulate his example in their lives. They believe in respect for the person first, then respect for the message. People can be respected for many qualities but most importantly for their integrity and honesty, which when combined serve as the cornerstone of ethical behavior.

There are six major principles in Islamic ethical thought, and within the Islamic business community it can be expected that ethical decisions will be made based on the following guidelines:

1. On the basis of self-interest.

2. On the basis of the outcome. For example, an action is ethical if it results in the greatest benefit for the largest number of people.

3. On the basis of universalism.

4. On the basis of individual entitlement, ensuring freedom of choice.

5. To ensure equitable distribution of wealth and benefits.

6. On the basis of Eternal Law, rather than what they perceive as the transient law of secular religions.

The order of these guidelines may be the most important differentiator between Islam and other cultures. Where self-interest is high on the preceding list, other cultures seem to focus more on others before self. For those interested in nuances, further investigation would be appropriate.

The West

According to Cunningham (1998), best practices within Western businesses include

- Compliance with standards

- Clearly defined and effectively communicated operational values

- Clearly defined and communicated aspirational values

- Effective ethical leadership, in which leaders are effective role models

- Effective systems in place to facilitate ethical conduct; for example, a code of ethics, a communications strategy, monitoring of stakeholder perceptions and behavior, reporting mechanisms, and governance

- A commonly understood system of ethical reasoning and decision making

- A culture in which making ethical decisions is the priority

Most Westerners follow some type of Judeo-Christian religion. Of all Judeo-Christian principles, probably the most common and most functional is the "Golden Rule": Do unto others as you would have others do unto you. Christians believe that people function best when people can count on others and when they are willing to collaborate with their colleagues and customers on mutual goals (Cunningham, 1998). As businesspeople, followers of Judeo-Christian faiths believe it essential to treat clients as equals, with consideration and respect. Within Western organizations, the Golden Rule is a helpful guide to prevent infighting, authoritarianism, and excessive status seeking. The Golden Rule is meant to pull people together so they can accomplish worthy tasks. Every workplace that has long-term success rests on community values: mutual support, caring for each other and our customers, and being responsible to learn and change so as to produce unquestionable positive value (Pinchot, 2004).

COEXISTENCE OF PRINCIPLES

Principles only provide guidance. There is no easy ethical formula. Principles, whether developed by a group of business ethicists or religious leaders, serve, at best, as decision guides. Wars are fought over principles, and the principles of personal ethics are the first checkpoint in any situation, often overriding those at the professional and global levels. When, for example, we judge whether or not a corporation has been socially responsible, we still need to consider principles of personal ethics as prerequisites. Contributions to charities and other attempts to do good may appear to be in the interests of society, but they lose their significance if the corporation has not also taken responsibility to minimize the damage done by its core business operations.

Consistency of Practice

For an excessive example of diminishing ethical impact, consider the organizational entity known as La Cosa Nostra. The name is one of honor, this thing of ours, and bears a strong similarity to a term used earlier in the chapter, *our group*. La Cosa Nostra operates under a rigid code of internal ethics in which trustworthiness is highly valued and there is a strong sense of justice. Members are known to give gifts and support to local charities and those in need. Many smaller organizations with related business interests are known to operate under a similar code. But the core businesses of these entities are illegal and harmful. In the conduct of their revenue-generation activities, organizational members would likely have no issues with robbing you, but they would never rob another family member (Navran, 2003). As a result, regardless of the organization's contributions, donations, and strong internal ethics, any outside observer would agree that its members' situational application of ethics weakens their basic principles.

What happens when these concepts are moved from criminal organizations to larger ethnic, racial, and nation-state applications? It is easy to make a claim that the Mafia is wrong in its approach, but when the same comment is made about a specific nationality, it starts to sound like prejudice.

Frameworks for Personal and Professional Ethics

Every list of ethical considerations provides a similar general framework. For example, Colero's basic principles of personal and professional ethics (2000) include the following:

Personal Ethics

- Concern for the well-being of others
- Trustworthiness and honesty
- Willing compliance with the law, excepting civil disobedience
- Being fair
- Refusing to take unfair advantage
- Doing good
- Preventing harm

Professional Ethics

- Objectivity
- Full disclosure
- Confidentiality
- Due diligence
- Avoiding conflict of interest
- Fidelity to professional responsibilities

The Colero list is an attempt to address the needs of all cultures, philosophies, faiths, and professions. As well-meaning as it is, his list only adds further to the confusion. If ethics could be ensured by means of a list, we would only need a single set of guidelines. But in addition to the one just shown, the ethics institute at the Illinois Institute of Technology has collected 850 other codes of ethics.

A Societal Framework

In any event, Colero suggests that the personal ethics reflect general expectations of any person in any society, acting in any capacity without needing to articulate the expectation or formalize it in any way. Even when not written into a code, principles of professional ethics are usually expected of people in business, employees, volunteers, and elected representatives. Many, including Colero (2000), suggest a third category of ethics worthy of consideration: global, or what some might classify as societal, ethics. But these are also the most controversial. Because, by definition, they include perceptions and beliefs from all corners of the world, they can create great chasms of misunderstanding and intolerance. Requiring societal considerations in our business conduct is a worthy request, but since we are dealing with humans and their multiple societies, it may be too much to ask. There is too much complexity, and the cost and time requirements are often too great for us to implement a truly global model.

Yet performance-improvement professionals can adhere to a set of general principles that can be practiced in many different ways. People from different cultures might agree in principle that deceit is unethical and trustworthiness is ethical, but misunderstandings can arise when the underlying principle is embodied in diverse ways that reflect different cultural values and virtues. Keeping us aligned are our professional principles, recurring patterns of ethically responsible behavior that our conscience can use as landmarks.

DUTY

I slept and dreamed that life was Beauty.
I woke and found that life was Duty.
—Hooper, 1840, p. 123

The common vein that runs through the preceding cultural overviews, and that is outlined in the ethical models, is one of duty. Mostly, the order of one's dutiful responsibilities as outlined by cultural norms is others first, then self. Problems in business ethics arise when the order is reversed. With an agreement to focus first on the needs of others, the subsequent consideration is to determine who among the others is most important.

As performance-improvement professionals, we can, however, create a model that supports our profession. We have a duty. If, in this professional model, we ask people to consider the implications of that duty and their responsibilities and authority to ensure that their duty is carried out, we might have an easier time of gaining a common ethical foothold—and get closer to the common societal results.

Local Focus; Global Impact

Although many practitioners may begin their professional journey with a local focus, their larger perceptions regarding the impact of their actions can be influenced. Through the rules of ISPI and similar organization and the use of various awareness methods, performance-improvement professionals will increasingly ask themselves, "Do I want to be responsible for the outcome of a poor decision?" Because the answer is often, "No," behaviors will change and our clients, and our society, will be better off. The individual performance consultant operating on a local level has power to influence the good of society. That power may not be on a large scale, but it is power nonetheless, and, as statesmen know, with power comes responsibility.

Accepting Our Global Duty

As professionals, we bear an ethical burden of global proportions. Our duty is global. We must be able to withstand cross-cultural demands and deliver consistent and reliable services to our customers regardless of geographic location. Our body of experts cannot be successful if its members contribute to human suffering, environmental damage, or business loss. In support of a global practice, there must be, and there is, a universal set of standards. A modern and complete model of success requires our individual and unified consideration of the effect of our actions, recommendations, and products on humanity and our society. Each individual must decide whether or not to accept it. This is true in any business environment and in any cultural circumstance. Ethical relativity is a dangerous destination that relieves people of responsibility other than what they choose in their own interests.

INCREASING OUR ABILITY TO TRUST AND BE TRUSTED

Trust is an essential element of long-term success at the individual, organizational, and societal levels. Attention to each element in that triad will help us create an ethical work environment and allow us to reap recognizable benefits.

Start with the Personal

In presenting a definition of trust, Navran (2003) cites a vague memory from a science fiction paperback that suggested trust as an expectation, the residue of promises fulfilled. Trust in this sense is a consequence, a result of certain specific actions. Under this definition, trust is tied to the predictability of one's actions or behavior. So trust is both an outcome and an expectation.

When we are new to a relationship, trust is something hoped for. Once the relationship has been established and we are seeking to add depth to it, trust becomes an expectation or a predictor. People are willing to continue their relations with us based on previously delivered trust. This makes things very neat, but it can also make things dangerous. For example, it is common for swindlers to begin their relationships with some small token of trust in order to move in for the big kill later.

A Story: High Tech, Low Trust

A few years ago, the executive vice president (EVP) of human resources for a large computer manufacturer met with a consultant to the organization. The consultant had spent a few months working in different departments, discovering in the process that the one unifying characteristic among mid- to senior-level leaders was a near universal lack of trust. It was absolutely *every man for himself*. The organization was disintegrating, customers were fleeing, and the stock price was plummeting. The consultant asked the EVP how he would classify the trust environment within the company. The EVP was not about to be cornered, so he turned the question back to the consultant. The disappointing response was, "low trust." At that point, the EVP opened up and granted a two-word response, "I agree." He needed help, and he knew it.

Cultures take a long time to change. In this organization's case, the EVP was unable to facilitate a shift from low to high trust. Even now, four years after our chat, mid-level managers characterize the organization as one with extensive communication disconnections, mixed agendas, and widespread passive resistance. Moreover, they say, there are no consequences for a lack of positive action. It should come as no surprise to learn that this Fortune 500 company trails its industry counterparts in every measurable financial category.

Trust as Understanding

Knowing what you are working with is helpful. Snake charmers are unsurprised when they are bitten. Similarly, some ethicists suggest that trust does not have to imply agreement or admiration. It can also mean understanding. "I know what I am likely to get when I work with this person." When a person's actions are consistent over time and consistent with the principles he or she espouses, that person can be said to have integrity. The person predictably acts according to his or her principles and, therefore, can be trusted. This might be a stretch for some, and it certainly does not align with the previous assertion of duty to others as the core of ethical values. Still, it is a data point that some may want to consider.

If you decide to adopt this as a reasonable consideration, what will your action be once you know someone does not share your values or your definition of trust? What does it mean for an individual or an organization to be trustworthy? If we know that others have a duty and an obligation to our legitimate needs, we will trust them.

Trusting an Organization

Organizational trustworthiness is based on internal phenomena that lead others to make a perception. This perception is formed as a function of three things:

- *Intentional communication:* what an organization chooses to say
- *Unintentional communication:* what an organization communicates that differs from what was intended
- *Third-party communication:* what others say about an organization

An organization can control only one of those, intentional communication. The most trusted intentional communications are those that are believed to be diametrically opposed to *spin*. Guidelines on avoiding the perception of spin include

- Being the first to report one's own mistakes
- Accepting responsibility
- Showing that the event was an exception
- Focusing on fixing the problem, not the blame
- Inviting public scrutiny of the issue and your proposed responses

Perceptions become reality when organizations demonstrate a commitment to their values even when the cost of doing so is high. The reality is reinforced when the organization's agenda is deemed acceptable by others—that its purpose for being is legitimate and in line with society's needs and expectations.

BUILDING AN ETHICAL ENVIRONMENT

This chapter highlights some of the challenges we face, but it is only when difficulties arise that we can truly find out who we are in an ethical context. We do so knowing that we must earn a fair wage for what we do and that in a competitive world the word of the client is gold. Performance technologists are employed to improve organizational health on behalf of shareholders, clients, and employees. If the client is engaging in unhealthy activities, the performance technologist cannot ethically provide support. The ethical consulting requirement is that the consulting mission shift to one of redirection and education.

Borrowing from the military, R. E. Bryant (personal communication, January 31, 2005) suggests that a true profession is one in which a sense of duty is honed, reinforced, and rewarded. In developing an ethical performance-improvement team, we should look to our own performance technologies.

Hire Ethical People

The first requirement when developing an ethical team is to hire ethical people committed to supporting our professional code. Training unethical people is a waste of time, effort, and money. Those we select must meet the standards we aspire to, must help a client maintain the appropriate standards, and must quickly identify ethical situations that may arise from time to time before they become mired in less than desirable situations. Those who develop the sense of duty in others must be specially selected. They should be recognized for their combination of business success and ethical fortitude, and for their willingness to look out for the team interests before their own. In considering future politics, Heinlein (1959) painted a similar need for a strong ethical community and suggested that only those individuals who serve the common good of the whole are entitled to vote for the whole, and *only* after they step down from serving for the whole group.

Set Clear Expectations

Our hiring criteria give the first hint of who we are, what we stand for, and what we expect. As our organizations form, leaders must set clear expectations and send messages that support clear, observable, and measurable ethical standards. In conjunction with their expectations they must establish procedures for dealing with unusual ethical situations, so that people, both employees and clients, have a good idea of what to expect. Management would also be wise to have consistent procedures for rewarding those who exemplify the ethical standards subscribed to by the organization, and addressing those who do not. The organization and its leadership clearly have the primary responsibility for ensuring that an ethical environment is created, maintained, and recognized.

Provide the Necessary Support

A successful team, regardless of environment, will be one whose capabilities are fully integrated, one in which all are united toward a common goal, and one that operates with clearly and fully understood methods, tools, and capabilities to produce the outcome that is desired. The leader of that team will set the objective and desired outcome, and the rest of the organization will complete the task with limited interactions until the desired result is achieved. The leader's approach will be supported by just a few fundamental factors (R. E. Bryant, personal communication, January 31, 2005):

- Well-defined doctrine
- An efficient organizational structure
- Effective training
- Available and useful materials and facilities
- Focused leadership
- Capable people

In any environment, a foundation of good and honest people backed with the support of the functional factors just listed will contribute to a strong ethical environment and ensure that the organization can accurately respond with the best course of action to produce the results desired by customers.

Personal Decisions: Huge Impact

As performance technologists, we will work with a wide range of cultures, organizations, and people. All of these constituents will have a desire to improve their current circumstances. Our job is to help them get there if those circumstances are legal and ethical. In doing so, we will improve our personal circumstances, in terms of reputation, mental well-being, and financial security.

Wanted: Moral Exemplars

Case Western Reserve's Online Ethics Center for Engineering and Science presents the case for *moral exemplars,* people in difficult circumstances who have demonstrated wisdom that enabled them to fulfill their responsibilities as scientists and engineers. Through their actions, they provide guidance for others who want to do the right thing in circumstances that are similarly difficult. In our profession, we must focus on needs, even if they diverge from client wants. Our goal is to help clients help their organizations. Sometimes our analyses and reports are unpopular, but they must be provided. This may put us in danger of losing a relationship, but it is a requirement.

THE GOAL? BUILDING A WORTHY LIFE

Bardwick (1998) reminds us that people need the structure of powerful and unambiguous values. "They need clarity in order to achieve worthwhile lives. A preoccupation with rights without responsibility leaves people without bonds or belonging. For people to know they've made a contribution, they need criteria for what is worthy" (p. 248). At the end of the day, if we can provide a path to improved performance, not hurt others, and ensure that our family names remain in good standing, we will have done good and done well.

References

Abegglen, J. C., and Stalk, G. Jr. (1985). *Kaisha: The Japanese corporation.* New York: Basic Books.

Al-Majalla. (n.d.). Option for misdescription. *The Ottoman courts manual [Hanafi],* Section II, 310.

Bardwick, J. M. (1998). *In praise of good business.* New York: Wiley.

Beekun, R. I. (1997). *Islamic business ethics.* Herndon, VA: The International Institute of Islamic Thought.

Blais, A. L. (1997). *On the plurality of actual worlds.* Boston: University of Massachusetts Press.

Brennan, J. G. (1992). *Foundations of moral obligation: The Stockdale course.* Newport, RI: Naval War College.

Buddha Dharma Education Association. (2004). *Buddhist studies: Buddhist ethics.* Sydney, Australia. Retrieved December 1, 2004, from www.buddhanet.net/e-learning/budethics.htm.

Cialdini, R., Petrova, P., and Goldstein, N. (2004). The hidden costs of organizational dishonesty. *MIT Sloan Management Review, 45*(3), 67–73.

Colero, L. (2000, February 21). *A framework for universal principles of ethics.* Crossroads Programs, Inc., University of British Columbia Centre for Applied Ethics. Retrieved on December 1, 2004, from www.ethics.ubc.ca/papers/invited/colero.html.

Cunningham, W. P. (1998). The Golden Rule as universal ethical norm. *Journal of Business Ethics, 17,* 105–109.

De Mente, B. L. (1999, June). Asian business codewords: The personal of business. Excerpted from *Japanese etiquette and ethics in business.* Lincolnwood, IL: NTC Business Books. Retrieved June 13, 2005, from Asia Pacific Management Forum Website: www.apmforum.com/columns/boye49.htm.

De Mente, B. L. (2001, October). Asian business codewords: Negotiating Korean style. Excerpted from *Korean etiquette and ethics in business.* Lincolnwood, IL: NTC Business Books. Retrieved June 13, 2005, from Asia Pacific Management Forum Website: www.apmforum.com/columns/boye46.htm.

Dippman, J. (2003). *Philosophy 202: Introduction to ethics.* Central Washington University. Retrieved June 13, 2005, from www.cwu.edu/~dippmanj/ethicssylfl03.htm.

Emery, G. A. (1999, October). Chinese business and Confucianism. *Moral Musings, 3*(1). Retrieved June 20, 2005, from http://epe.lac-bac.gc.ca/100/202/300/moral_musings/v3n1/Emery.html.

Fitz-enz, J. (1997). It's costly to lose good employees. *Workforce, 76*(8), 50–51.

Fukuyama, F. (1995). *Trust: The social virtues and the creation of prosperity.* New York: First Free Press.

Geertz, C. (1973). *The interpretation of cultures.* New York: Basic Books.

Heinlein, R. A. (1959). *Starship troopers.* New York: G. P. Putnam's Sons.

Hinduism. (2004). Retrieved December 1, 2004, from www.fact-index.com/h/hi/hinduism.html.

Hooper, H. S. (1840). The dial. *Dial Magazine.*

International Society for Performance Improvement. (2002a). *Certified performance technologist.* Retrieved June 13, 2005, from www.certifiedpt.org/standards.pdf.

International Society for Performance Improvement. (2002b). *Code of ethics.* Retrieved June 13, 2005, from www.certifiedpt.org/forms/Code%20of%20Ethics.pdf.

Ivaturi, R. M. (2001). *Business ethics for the ERP industry.* Retrieved December 1, 2004, from www.cibres.com/articles/20010726.

Jamieson, I. (1980). *Capitalism and culture: A comparative analysis of British and American manufacturing organizations.* London, UK: Gower.

Karlinsky, R. S. (2000). Business, spirituality, and management-labor relations: Source#3—Shulchan Arukh Choshen Mishpat 228:6, as presented in *Darche Noam.* Retrieved December 5, 2004, from www.darchenoam.org/ethics/labor/manlab_rsk.htm.

LaFave, S. (2003). *What is philosophy?* Department of Philosophy, West Valley Community College, Saratoga, California. Retrieved January 13, 2005, from instruct.westvalley.edu/lafave/whatis.htm.

Navran, F. (2003, April). How does an organization gain a reputation for being trustworthy? *Ethics Today.* The Ethics Resource Center, Washington, DC. Retrieved December 5, 2003, from www.ethics.org/ask_e5.html.

Pinchot, E. (2004). *Can we afford ethics?* Retrieved January 13, 2005, from www.pinchot.com/MainPages/BooksArticles/OtherArticles/CanWeAffordEthics.html.

U.S. Department of State. (2004, September). *Documenting atrocities in Darfur.* State Publication 11182. Released by the Bureau of Democracy, Human Rights, and Labor and the Bureau of Intelligence and Research. Washington, DC: Author.

Varca, P. E., and Valutis M. J. (1993). The relationship of ability and satisfaction to job performance. *Applied Psychology: An International Review, 42*(3), 265–275.

Wax, E. (2004a, June 27). In Sudan, death and denial: Officials accused of concealing crisis as thousands starve. *Washington Post,* p. A1.

Wax, E. (2004b, September 8). U.S. report finds Sudan promoted killings: Use of term "genocide" debated ahead of Powell testimony on Darfur atrocities. *Washington Post,* p. A17.

Webley, S., and More, E. (2003). *Does business ethics pay? Ethics and financial performance.* London: Institute of Business Ethics.

CHAPTER FORTY-SIX

Improving Human Performance by Employing a Top-Down Function Analysis Methodology in Navy Aircraft Design

Dennis Duke, Robert Guptill, Mark Hemenway, Wilbur Doddridge

Significant changes are occurring within the U.S. Navy in the area of human performance. Similar changes are also occurring within the other military services, but not to the extent they are in the Navy, in which an organizational "revolution" has taken place. This revolution has resulted in a reorganization of several commands and the creation of the Human Performance Center, the mission of which is to reexamine the Navy's workforce and organizational structure with the intent of improving human performance by determining a more effective and efficient way of growing and using the knowledge and skill mix of today's sailors in the fleet.

Another significant impact on human performance has been made by the Department of Defense's recent changes in the system acquisition process. This is evident in the revision of Department of Defense Directive 5000.1 (2003a) and Department of Defense Instruction 5000.2 (2003b), which are the primary regulations that govern major military system acquisitions. Both of these regulations now mandate that human systems integration will be incorporated early and throughout the system acquisition process.

This chapter will provide a brief example of how the U.S. Navy is applying the principles of human performance technology early in the acquisition of new

---

aircraft. More specifically, this chapter will concentrate on the Top-Down Function Analysis (TDFA) process, which analyzes, documents, and optimizes the performance requirements of the sailors who have the ultimate responsibility for operating and maintaining the aircraft system. The process also leads to optimal training solutions that enable the sailor to achieve maximum proficiency on the job.

Traditionally in the U.S. military, the procurement process has focused primarily on developing the hardware systems and embedded software needed to meet operational requirements. More often than not the human perspective in system design was relegated to integrated logistics support efforts that included developing, training, and writing operator and maintenance manuals. In addition, logistics support was usually an independent effort that was performed out of the mainstream design and development process. Logistics support decisions were often made without the benefit of inputs by the design engineering team. As a result, training and human systems integration investments were thought of as add-on costs without comparable return on investment. When system acquisition budget cuts were made, human-centered design and training activities were often the first investments cut from the program.

Fortunately, the tide is turning. The Navy has instituted Sea Power 21, which is a Navy vision for delivering enhanced military capabilities through new concepts, technologies, organizational initiatives, and improved acquisition processes. In support of Sea Power 21, the chief of naval operations, Admiral Vern Clark (2002), has instituted a human-centered approach for new system developments and quality of service initiatives. In support of this concentration on the human, Vice Admiral David Balisle (Nagle, 2002) said,

> The Fleet is also Sailors: energetic, talented and exceptionally dedicated Americans who have volunteered to perform incredibly complex duties in a harsh and often hostile environment. Without highly motivated and well-trained Sailors, our ships, airplanes, and submarines are lifeless and inanimate platforms. When viewed from this perspective, Sailors clearly are the "Navy's most valuable shipboard system," and our duty is to ensure that every ship we build and system we deliver is designed, acquired, and supported with their performance, training, safety, and survivability in mind.

HUMAN PERFORMANCE IMPROVEMENT

Human performance improvement is a results-driven process that aims to improve organizational performance by helping people perform their jobs better. Human performance improvement takes a systems view of the process and focuses improvement efforts on the organization as a system. While its goal is the improvement of organizational performance, it must be applied at both the

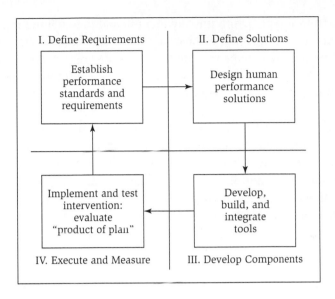

Figure 46.1. Human Performance System Model.

individual and organizational levels to identify and resolve barriers to optimal performance. Finally, it must use a variety of disciplines and techniques to identify, measure, and resolve human performance issues.

The human performance system model used by the Navy's Human Performance Center, shown in Figure 46.1, is the foundation for human performance improvement. The model comprises four quadrants. In quadrant I, human performance professionals define human performance requirements in terms of competencies and standards. Requirements are derived from missions that need to be performed. Competencies are the knowledge, skills, and abilities that sailors need in order to perform their specific jobs in support of the mission. In quadrant II, human performance professionals and subject-matter experts determine how to meet human performance requirements. Here, individual and organizational performance issues are diagnosed and solutions are developed. Solutions do not consist only of individual-, organizational-, or system-oriented training. They may involve numerous other entities that may affect human performance such as facilities, logistics solutions, or systems engineering modifications. Planning and execution of the solutions identified in quadrant II begin in quadrant III. In this third quadrant the recommended solutions, for example, facility renovations, engineering modifications, or training devices, are made or developed, and implementation begins. The implementation is completed in quadrant IV, and the results are measured and evaluated. The process then begins another iteration based on the results of the evaluation.

The quadrant I approach to initially identify and define human performance requirements is accomplished via a structured process that centers on identifying specific mission requirements from the top of the organization. This approach is similar to the International Society for Performance Improvement's (ISPI's) human performance improvement model, which first suggests identifying organizational goals and documenting what must be accomplished to achieve them (Deterline and Rosenberg, 1992). The U.S. Navy has determined that the most effective means to make accurate, cost-effective determinations of manpower, personnel, and training needs is to closely examine the performance requirements resulting from carefully executed mission analyses and systematic functional allocations. They use a structured process, called the Top-Down Function Analysis methodology, that decomposes the mission requirements and system functions down to the level of human tasks and ultimately to the individual human-system interfaces and crew designs needed to meet the mission requirements. This process produces an audit trail that connects individual tasks to system functions and ultimately to top-level organizational missions.

THE NAVY'S TOP-DOWN FUNCTION ANALYSIS METHODOLOGY

The Navy is approaching performance improvement in a manner similar to Kaufman (2003). Training, as a means to an end, is being replaced by performance improvement, which focuses on achieving optimal performance results and payoffs. The TDFA methodology is representative of how the Navy is focusing on identifying and defining what has to be accomplished to successfully complete its missions. The methodology is a systems engineering approach used in naval aviation to determine and manage the integration of human performance requirements within the systems design process. When incorporated in the systems acquisition process, it provides a documented hierarchy that quantitatively describes the human skills, knowledge, and materiel systems required to successfully achieve its missions. As shown in Figure 46.2, the TDFA methodology comprises nine analysis phases. Those nine phases are

1. Mission analysis

2. Human performance goals analysis

3. Function analysis

4. Function allocation

5. Task design and analysis

6. Interface concepts and designs

7. Crew or team concepts and designs

8. Performance, workload, and training estimation

9. User and requirements review

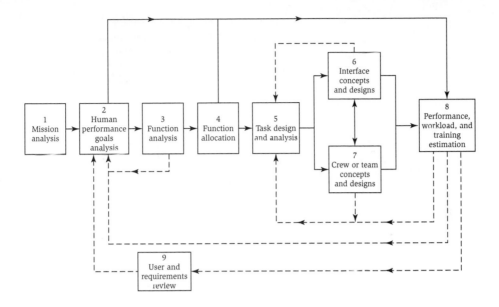

Figure 46.2. The Top-Down Function Analysis Methodology.

The TDFA methodology provides a formal design process that is consistent and integrated with the systems engineering process. Figure 46.3 shows the overall relationship between systems and human engineering. The major phases of the systems engineering process are highlighted in this figure. TDFA phases are shown in relation to the systems engineering process. Although it is well beyond the scope of this process summary, formal points of intersection between the two processes have been identified and described by Wallace, Winters, Dugger, and Lackie (2001) and Winters, Dugger, and Parker (2000). In the following TDFA methodology description, examples are provided using aircraft acquisition applications.

Mission Analysis Phase

Mission analysis is the first phase of the TDFA methodology. The objective of the mission analysis phase is to document the top-level missions that the system is required to support and then to identify the capabilities required to effectively support those missions. This is similar to organizational headquarters developing their corporate mission statement, identifying subordinate roles within the organization, and identifying the capabilities required of each of the supporting operating divisions.

Military personnel know that in any military exercise or mission each echelon is assigned a specific responsibility. Great efforts are taken to ensure that soldiers, sailors, airmen, or marines assigned to that echelon understand exactly

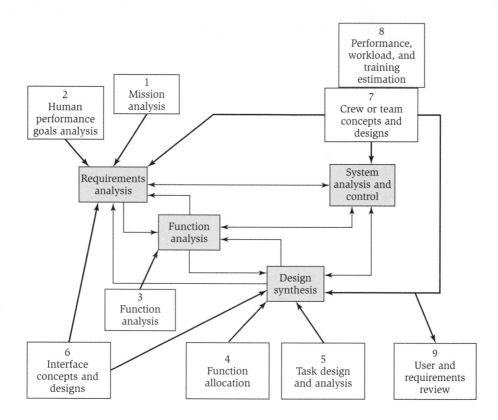

Figure 46.3. TDFA Methodology and Systems Engineering Model Relationships.

what they are supposed to do in order to carry out the echelon's combat responsibility. To ensure readiness and optimal performance under different conditions, military personnel are continually trained as they would fight. This is done via training maneuvers, live-fire exercises, electronic simulations involving realistic scenarios, and so on, which depict various situations that they would face. Action reports are prepared after each training exercise to systematically discuss lessons learned and incorporate them into what will be done the next time. "The heart of this [alignment and training process] is the Mission Essential Task List (METL). Derived directly from the unit's war plans, those tasks are fundamental to the real-world combat mission it has been given. Those operational plans constitute the core of what the unit is expected to do if push comes to shove . . ." (Allard, 2004, p. 181). For a description of how the military's Mission Essential Task List (METL) can be applied to the roles of CEOs in private organizations, see Chapter Nine, "Testing Your METL or What to Do When the Mission Really Is Essential," in Allard (2004).

The missions defined in this initial TDFA phase play a critical role in initiating and anchoring the system's performance requirements hierarchy. As shown in

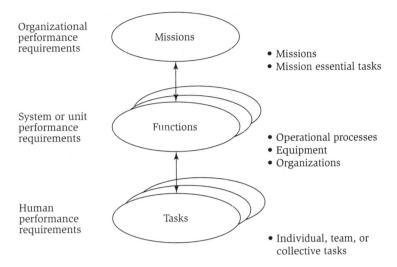

Figure 46.4. Mission-Based Performance Hierarchy.

Figure 46.4, the missions provide the highest level of performance requirement for the system. All subsequent TDFA phases flow down from these mission tasks and provide a powerful means for linking all system and human performance requirements with engineering design decisions.

During the mission-analysis phase, the boundaries of the system as well as the system's interactions with its environment and with other external systems are identified. The mission analysis determines the general capabilities the system should provide and identifies the typical scenarios in which the system will operate. These scenarios are determined by carefully analyzing the system's mission using operations templates, requirements documents, the Universal Joint and Navy Task Lists, and input from subject-matter experts. Specific Navy mission essential tasks that apply to the system under analysis are then analyzed to determine performance measures.

The basis for identifying most mission tasks is the Universal Navy Task List, which is a hierarchical organization of mission-oriented tasks at the strategic national, strategic theater, operational, and tactical levels of war. Mission tasks at higher levels are part of the Universal Joint Task List and are not service specific. These military mission tasks serve as a common language and reference system for joint force commanders, combat developers, systems acquisition specialists, and trainers. They can also be useful to military analysts and planners for understanding and integrating joint operations.

These operations are documented in operations templates, which are developed to aid the identification of mission tasks. Operations templates are flow charts that describe mission execution. They provide a graphical depiction of the order and relationship of mission tasks as they are performed as part of a military operation. The operations templates are similar to high-level flow charts that illustrate the various entities involved in a typical manufacturing supply-chain analysis.

Human Performance Goals Analysis Phase

The second phase of the TDFA methodology is the human systems performance goals analysis phase. In this phase, system requirements documentation and mission analysis results are reviewed to identify human performance goals and strategies in the human systems integration domains. The objective of this analysis phase is to document known human system performance requirements. In a new system acquisition such as an aircraft, general information about human performance has to be documented prior to the design and development of many technical systems that will be placed on board the aircraft. High-level presumptions must be made based on predecessor systems. The human performance data are constantly revisited as the system matures and additional information becomes available. Milestones for when these analytical iterations occur are based on key dates in the acquisition cycle, especially aircraft design reviews. As the system design evolves, the human performance assessments become the baseline for trade studies and analysis of alternatives.

Typically, the results of this phase might include manning goals and proposed manning sources, operational and logistics deployment time goals, physical constraints, logistics maintenance time goals, desired skills and knowledge, education levels, and so on. Examples of human performance goals might include "Manning requirements for the XYZ system will not exceed current manning levels." A human performance requirement might be "Reduce squadron manning levels by 50 percent." An example of a physical constraint might be "Will accommodate a 98th percentile female sailor." A human performance strategy might be "Reduce maintenance manning requirements by 50 percent through the design of an enhanced test built in to the onboard equipment."

Function Analysis Phase

The third TDFA methodology phase is the function analysis phase. Here the mission performance requirements are refined and system functions are identified. This involves defining what the aircraft has to do in order to satisfy mission requirements. For example, if a mission requirement is surveillance, then the aircraft has to perform a surveillance function via a radar system. During this phase, all the functions are identified that will be needed to meet mission requirements.

Functions describe what the system must do to accomplish mission requirements. Function analysis includes the identification of the functions the system will perform, enumeration of performance measures for each function, and description of the logical relationship between them. The logical relationships between functions may be described graphically in a functional block diagram that shows the sequence and temporal relationships of the functions. Fault trees, information flows, data architectures, and so on may also describe function relationships. Graphical methods are selected based on the types of functions and the objectives of the study.

The product of function analysis is a functional architecture. The functional architecture may be derived analytically. However, there are standardized authoritative models available to support analysis. The use of these models provides several benefits. First, the analysis process can be streamlined by providing a template of validated functions, definitions, and functional relationships. The analyst is rescued from the need to "reinvent the wheel" for each application. Second, the use of authoritative models ensures consistency with other applications and with the broader community. For example, the use of the National Air and Space Model (NASM) for assessment of aircraft ensures the use of common terms and a standardized analysis approach across the aviation community. It also supports consistency in a joint environment.

The model was developed by the Defense Modeling Simulation Office to support the development of constructive simulation models within the military aviation domain. Since the model is a hierarchical model, it provides a functional view of system operations at several levels of detail including mission, flight phase, function, and function step.

Mission analysis, function analysis, and task analysis processes use similar labels for missions, functions, and tasks. It is important to note the distinctions among the different usages. NASM missions are equivalent to the mission tasks used in the mission analysis process. The mapping of mission analysis tasks to missions is the entry point to function analysis. Flight phases decompose or break down a mission into discrete time periods. Functions and function steps decompose flight phases into lower levels of activity detail, as shown in Figure 46.5.

The function analysis may be revisited several times during the acquisition process. The initial iteration of function analysis may consist of the creation of a complete functional architecture for the system. This is appropriate when a preliminary design is not available. In this case, the functional architecture is analytically derived. As the system develops and design decisions are made, design changes are assessed and the functional architecture is modified to reflect changes in system missions, performance requirements, or design approach.

Function analysis is an essential component of the systems engineering process and an essential link between mission and system design. As such, it is a critical analysis phase in almost every systems engineering domain. Ideally, the functional architecture is developed and maintained by an integrated project team representing all the critical domains and led by the systems engineering discipline. However, in the current environment of compressed acquisition

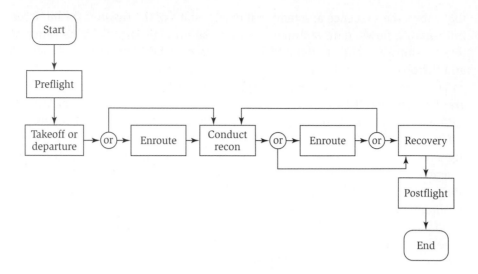

Figure 46.5. Sample Function Decomposition.

schedules and austere funding, this ideal condition is rarely achieved. This circumstance does not reduce the importance of function analysis and the following function allocation process to the human systems integration process. These processes are essential to establishing human systems integration requirements and for influencing system design. Therefore, although the primary responsibility for function analysis may rest with the systems engineering domain, in the absence of a usable product, it is essential for the human engineering domain to undertake its own analysis.

Function Allocation Phase

Function allocation is the next TDFA phase. Function allocation is the process of assigning the performance of system functions to human operators and maintainers or to the hardware and software components of a system. Several criteria are used to make function allocation decisions. Mandatory allocations are directive in nature and are based on design criteria, design standards, or policy. For example, service policy may require a human in the loop to fire a weapon, or safety considerations may preclude human performance of dangerous tasks. Military policy often requires task performance by a commissioned or noncommissioned officer. Once mandatory allocations are made, a number of criteria can be applied to perform the remaining allocations. Examples of the criteria that may be applied include the following:

- *Ability to perform the task.* Machines perform repetitive calculating tasks better than humans. Humans perform tasks requiring complex reasoning better than machines. The physical requirements for task performance may exceed human capabilities.

- *Cost.* Humans represent over 70 percent of system life cycle cost.
- *Cognitive workload.* The cognitive demands of automated information delivery systems can easily overwhelm a human's ability to process that information without automated support.
- *Physical workload.* Physical workload may exceed the possible crew size.
- *Frequency of performance.* Highly repetitive tasks requiring sustained accuracy are candidates for machine or software allocation.
- *Training requirements.* Training is a significant expense in terms of dollars and time. To the extent that allocating tasks to machine performance can reduce training requirements, associated costs are also reduced. In some cases training to perform difficult tasks may be infeasible.
- *Manning criteria.* Efficient function allocation is an extremely effective means of achieving manpower reductions.

In developing allocation options systems, engineers consider the project constraints, the requirements, and the capabilities and limitations of both technology and the users, operating as individuals or as a team. The constraints and requirements to be considered are developed early in the overall process when the systems engineer is assessing all the constraints on the system and its operational requirements. The systems engineer determines the capabilities and limitations of the potential technologies, as well as the possible use of commercial off-the-shelf products, while information about operator capabilities and limitations comes from the human engineer.

Often the prime contractor will present a preliminary design at the outset of the acquisition process. In this case, function allocation documents the allocation decisions represented by the design. Table 46.1 shows a sample functional allocation.

Task Design and Analysis Phase

The fifth phase of the TDFA methodology involves identifying human tasks. From the human performance perspective, tasks describe the basic unit of work performed by humans in the system. Human tasks include tasks that humans do alone and tasks that involve coordinated action with other system components. The order and interactions of the tasks can be defined and modeled to verify that they meet the technical system function requirements.

The objective of the TDFA process is to define the human systems integration requirements. Therefore, analytical focus during the function and task

Table 46.1. Sample Function Allocation.

| Mission | Flight Phase | National Air and Space Model | | Functional Allocation |
		Function	Function Step	
Antisubmarine warfare (ASW) mission	Conduct anti-submarine phase	Communicate with WD/ATC controllers/C2	Receive message/information	Supervisory
			Transmit message/information	Interactive
		Subsurface prosecution	Coordinate with ship and/or other ASW asset	Interactive
			Track submarine	Manual
			Maneuver for torpedo drop	Interactive
			Drop torpedo	Interactive
		Subsurface surveillance	Coordinate with ship and/or other ASW asset	Interactive
			Plan/update tactics	Interactive
			Employ/deploy submarine	Interactive
			Detect submarine	Interactive
			Localize submarine	Manual
			Track submarine	Manual
	Recover phase	Change flight path	Change heading	Interactive
			Change altitude	Interactive
			Change speed	Interactive
		Communicate with WD/ATC controllers/C2	Receive message/information	Supervisory
			Transmit message/information	Interactive

analysis phases is on identifying those tasks requiring some level of human performance. Functions allocated to system hardware or software are documented and archived for future reference.

Task analysis begins with the extraction of functions allocated to humans during the function allocation process. These functions are then broken down into smaller units of work to create tasks. This is called a top-down analysis approach.

Legacy or predecessor systems are a primary source for initial task data. Legacy system tasks may be adopted as is, or they may be modified to reflect changes in functions of the new system. The use of legacy system tasks is known as bottom-up task analysis. In either case, the integrity of the linkages in the mission, function, and task structure guides the analysis.

Interface Concepts and Designs Phase

The next phase involves determining interfaces. Human system interfaces are the physical or virtual junctions at which data or information is exchanged or where the human manipulates the system. Designs and concepts for the interfaces between humans and the system software or hardware determine cues and responses and dictate human performance levels. They are an essential component of system crew or team design because they provide a specific location and interaction for each task and crew member, both individually and collectively. These interfaces can be considered at three different levels:

- Individual interfaces that represent a particular interaction based on the task analysis as well as performance and design requirements. Piloting an aircraft requires the pilot to exercise positive control over the aircraft during some maneuvers. In other words, the pilot interfaces with the flight controls to maneuver the aircraft as required.

- Combinations of interfaces for a design at the individual-operator level based on the combination of tasks into roles. Tasks are grouped and aggregated to form jobs or roles. Interfaces at this level are often described as workstations and support a variety of complex interactions between the human and the system.

- Interface designs and concepts for multiple operators based on the combination of individuals into crews or teams. At the next higher level of complexity, workstations are aggregated to support the coordinated action of several members of a team. For example, the signal analyst positions on an electronic surveillance aircraft are located in the same area to support collaboration and load sharing among the analysts.

Interface design decisions are based on the functional architecture and allocation, task model, design guidance, and human engineering design criteria.

Clearly, this analysis step is closely related to crew or team design and the two processes are highly recursive. For example, a concept for a four-man crew design is assumed during interface design. However, as the interface concept emerges, the realities of that design, including workload, physical layout, working conditions, and so on may influence the initial crew design concept. In our example, an assessment of cognitive workload combined with hardware constraints may indicate that a five-man or a three-man crew design is necessary.

Crew and Team Concepts and Designs Phase

The seventh phase of the TDFA methodology involves the design of crews and teams. In this phase, individual workload represented by tasks is aggregated and integrated to define team and crew workload. A crew is defined as a group of individuals working together onboard the aircraft to perform tasks necessary to satisfy technical system functions. A team involves individuals located outside the aircraft, such as those receiving information at a ground station, who are integral to the effective performance of technical functions in support of mission requirements. Functional architecture, interface design, knowledge, skills and abilities, and workload optimization are all primary criteria for crew or team design. During this step, individual tasks are grouped together to form crew and team structures. A variety of criteria are used in this process. Policy guidelines, design standards, and human factors design criteria are examples of sources for crew and team design criteria.

Work in complex systems is rarely performed in isolation. Each crew member is part of a team that combines the capacity, knowledge, and skill of individual members to perform technical system functions. Crew and team workload is more than the sum of individual tasks. It requires communication, coordination, and resource sharing. As such it influences the performance requirements of individual tasks and often represents workload not accounted for in analysis of individual tasks. For example, some signal analysts in an aircraft operate independently to perform technical analysis at assigned workstations. However, prioritization of analysis opportunities and the decision process for distribution of analysis results requires interaction and communication with other operators and evaluators. The coordinated assessment and prioritization of signals is crew and team workload, which individual analysts share with the team.

Crew and team design is influenced by a variety of factors. The physical layout of equipment, workspace, and workstations often determines crew and team design. A four-workstation layout will not accommodate a five-person crew, nor will it be used efficiently with a three-person crew. Crew and team design is often influenced by policy. Supervisory positions are often based on span of control or the criticality of activities performed in the work center. For example, some decisions require approval or execution by a commissioned officer.

Crew and team design is achieved by shifting tasks between positions to level workload, to group similar performance requirements, and to leverage skill and knowledge requirements for the operators. For example, technical specialists in an aircraft may perform similar analysis tasks. However, one group of technical specialists in that same aircraft may have additional, specialized responsibilities to integrate and distribute the technical information provided by the other technical specialists. From a human systems integration perspective, the aircraft will be designed to enable the two groups to be seated separately to facilitate task and function performance.

Performance, Workload, and Training Estimation Phase

The primary objective of the TDFA methodology is to determine the human performance and human resource requirements of a system design. This analysis objective is achieved during this phase by determining the manning, personnel qualifications, and training requirements using information determined in preceding TDFA phases. These results are inputs to the systems engineering and other human systems engineering processes. As such, they measure human performance impacts of a given design or design concept or as human performance requirements.

The process begins with the estimation of both physical and cognitive workload based on the functional architecture, task models, measures of performance, and use scenarios. Individual human performance requirements are derived from cognitive and physical workload data. Crew, team, and human-system interface designs and concepts are applied to individual performance requirements in order to estimate crew workload. Individual and crew workload provide the basis for determining manpower requirements and for determining the characteristics of humans selected to operate or maintain the system. Physical and cognitive workload analysis techniques are well documented in the human performance literature.

The quantity and nature of the workload also determine training requirements and lead to the development of a training strategy in conjunction with the consideration of manpower and personnel requirements. Training requirements estimation includes the preliminary determination of student throughput; courses of instruction; course resource requirements, for example training man-days, instructor contact hours, and instructor requirements; training devices; and unit training products.

User and Requirements Review Phase

The last phase of the TDFA methodology involves user feedback. The objective of the systems engineering processes is to develop a system design that satisfies user needs. The methodology supports this objective in the area of human performance by linking human performance aspects of system performance with the system design and system design process. The methodology is designed to identify human performance requirements and to assess the ability of the system design to meet those requirements. A number of design decisions about both the human and hardware aspects of system design are called for during the analysis process. As the system evolves, it is essential that TDFA results be assessed for their ability to satisfy or contribute to system performance requirements.

During this step, high drivers are identified. High drivers are high-cost or high-risk tasks or functions. High-driver criteria vary by system and circumstance, but often include such factors as high acquisition or maintenance cost, extraordinary personnel qualifications or prerequisites, high training demand, safety, or human performance issues of many types. High drivers may require mitigation in the system design to meet system performance requirements or baselines. For example, safety issues always require mitigation to reduce risk. From a positive point of view, they may present opportunities for high payoff design changes in which a small design change may produce a disproportionate reduction in manpower costs.

During the earliest phases of system development, the identification of high drivers is an important contribution of the TDFA process to overall system design. High drivers become critical issues to be addressed as the design evolves. As a minimum, they require management attention and follow-up to preclude negative impacts on the system design process and system performance.

Several other activities may occur during user and requirements review. These include testing to validate analysis results, constructive modeling to confirm predicted performance levels, audits against performance requirements and specifications, sensitivity analyses to identify human performance and design alternatives, and trade-off analyses to assess those alternatives.

SUMMARY

For organizational performance problems to be effectively solved, the resources and tactics for that problem must be identified and aligned with the organization's mission. The TDFA methodology is a clear illustration of how performance needs are being applied at three levels: (1) societal, the military; (2) organizational, that is, aircraft platform and associated squadrons and battalions; and (3) individual and team, that is the aircrew. The identification and satisfaction of the aircraft's role, with associated conditions and standards, in satisfying specific mission tasks is representative of the societal need advocated by Kaufman (1999). In the case of the military society, effective performance in the accomplishment of assigned mission tasks contributes to the betterment of overall modern warfighting techniques. The successful accomplishment of various functions performed on an aircraft or in the squadrons and units in support of the specific mission requirements are illustrative of the satisfaction of an organizational need. Last, the effective and efficient performance of sailors and soldiers who are associated with the operation and maintenance of an aircraft platform is illustrative of an individual need.

The TDFA methodology provides a template that allows the U.S. Navy to objectively document the organizational and individual elements and their associated resources, as well as their relationships needed for optimal performance in specific mission scenarios. In addition, since the data contained in the methodology are quantitative, the program manager can use the information to establish priorities when having to deal with budget cuts. This methodology is applicable not only to the military, but to civilian organizations as well.

References

Allard, K. (2004). *Business as war: Battling for competitive advantage.* Hoboken, NJ: Wiley.

Clark, V. (2002, October). Seapower 21: Projecting decisive joint capabilities. *Naval Institute Proceedings Magazine, 128*(10), 32–41.

Deterline, W. A., and Rosenberg, M. J. (1992). *Workplace productivity: Performance technology success stories.* Washington, DC: International Society for Performance Improvement.

Kaufman, R. (1999). *Mega planning: Practical tools for organizational success.* Thousand Oaks, CA: Sage.

Kaufman, R. (2003). Debunking conventional wisdom: Selecting methods and processes that add value. *Performance Improvement, 42*(6), 5–8.

Nagle, D. (2002, October 8). New NAVSEA directorate to focus on sailor performance in new systems. *Navy Office of Information.* Story Number NNS021007–03.

U.S. Department of Defense. (2003a, May 12). The defense acquisition system. Department of Defense Directive (DODD) 5000.1.

U.S. Department of Defense. (2003b, May 12). Operation of the defense acquisition system. Department of Defense Instruction (DODI) 5000.2.

Wallace, D., Winters, J., Dugger, M., and Lackie, J. (2001). Human-systems engineering: Understanding the process of engineering the human into the system. ONR/SC-21. *Manning Affordability Initiative.*

Winters, J., Dugger, M., and Parker, C. (2000, March). Human engineering task analysis operational sequence diagrams (OSDs). ONR/SC-21. *Manning Affordability Initiative.*

PART SEVEN

LOOKING FORWARD IN HUMAN PERFORMANCE TECHNOLOGY

DARLENE M. VAN TIEM

Human performance technology (HPT) is a rapidly emerging field combining many disciplines, such as instructional systems design, organizational development and change, communications, psychology, economics, systems theory, and many other fields. This blending leads to flexibility and a willingness to consider almost any approach that will support human performance improvement. HPT has a mind-set that is systemic and systematic, enabling professionals to be creative and to extend previous experience into new realms. Certified performance technologists can attest to positive energy and success when using the standards of performance technology.

It is clear that HPT will be moving forward with the same dynamic that has been evident in the recent past. Since the second edition of the Stolovitch and Keeps handbook in 1999, the human performance technology model has been revised, standards of performance technology have been developed, the certification of performance technologists program has been instituted, and over one thousand performance technologists have been certified.

In the second edition of the *Handbook for Human Performance Technology,* it was stated that the final part of the handbook engages in some crystal ball gazing. Yet most of the ideas discussed in the HPT-future section of that edition are now considered part of the mainstream of HPT thinking. For HPT, crystal ball gazing often becomes reality. We cannot underestimate the speed with which experimentation and futuristic thinking collide with tomorrow. What seems like the future today will probably be the present before the fourth edition of the handbook is published.

Part Seven of this edition, "Looking Forward in Human Performance Technology," begins with Chapter Forty-Seven, in which Doug Leigh introduces SWOT (strength, weakness, opportunity, and threat) analysis and promotes comparison of SWOTs both visually and numerically to enhance data-driven decision making focused on desired outcomes and organizational results.

The next three chapters, Forty-Eight, Forty-Nine, and Fifty, assert the importance of contemplation in the practice of HPT. Scott Schaffer and Therese Schmidt's "sustainable development" urges that HPT efforts meet current needs without compromising the opportunities of future generations to meet their future needs by creating win-win solutions having a positive impact economically, environmentally, and socially. Sharon Korth and Brenda Levya-Gardner advocate "rapid reflection" as a way to systematically think through issues without creating delay or increasing costs. Darlene Van Tiem and Julie Lewis endorse "appreciative inquiry" as a way to foster the positives within organizations to advance further performance improvement while minimizing resistance to change.

Chapters Fifty-One, Fifty-Two, and Fifty-Three consider the necessity of systematic HPT practice. Barbara Bichelmeyer and Brian Horvitz advocate "comprehensive performance evaluation," beginning with logic models that represent the variables: inherent capabilities, knowledge and skills supports, incentives, organizational systems, tools and resources, and environmental elements. John Amarant and Donald Tosti discuss aligning the human performance system by presenting the evolution of HPT, enabling readers to glimpse into HPT's foundation, while asserting that HPT uses a cacophony of terms and concepts, overemphasizes the individual over the organization, and does not sufficiently integrate solutions within the organization. Don Winiecki discusses the relationships between systems, measures, and workers, cautioning that producing and obscuring the system can make systemic performance improvement difficult.

As HPT advances practice, Darlene Van Tiem, Swati Karve, and Jennifer Rosenzweig in Chapter Fifty-Four point out the growing awareness that situations often appear complex and chaotic. By understanding the application of chaos and complexity theories, HPT professionals will see patterns in complex situations and realize that most situations are chaotic as they move toward orderliness.

In Chapter Fifty-Five, the final chapter, Klaus Wittkuhn challenges the HPT profession to understand the *quantulumcunque* of our assumptions, to consider eliminating our term *technology* for more descriptive words, and to gradually integrate the HPT field into a mature approach.

Clearly, the HPT future will rely more on data-driven decision making as well as on contemplation and reflection to ensure that HPT practice optimizes the future using positive approaches. HPT professionals will approach their practice more systematically and systemically by creating better models for each project, streamlining terminology and concepts, and maximizing the HPT evolution. Finally, as our field advances, HPT will challenge assumptions and begin to see patterns in situations that now seem complex and chaotic, leading to a more mature comprehensive practice.

CHAPTER FORTY-SEVEN

SWOT Analysis

Doug Leigh

The intention of SWOT, or strength, weakness, opportunity, and threat, analysis, is to identify those internal strengths and external opportunities that an organization can leverage to accomplish its objectives, while also seeking to mitigate internal weaknesses and external threats (Lewis and Littler, 1997). This chapter provides a definition of SWOT analysis, discusses the origins of the method and its relevance to human performance technology (HPT), illustrates two conventional approaches to utilizing SWOTs, offers applications of SWOT analysis, and concludes with recommendations for the enhancement of the method.

SWOT ANALYSIS DEFINED

As commonly defined, SWOT analysis is an approach to considering the inhibitors and enhancers to performance that an organization encounters in both its internal and external environments. Strengths are enhancers to desired performance while weaknesses are inhibitors to desired performance, with both being within the control of an organization. Opportunities are enhancers and threats are inhibitors to desired performance, though these are considered outside of an organization's control. Examples of these factors are presented in Figure 47.1.

Internal Factors	
Strengths	**Weaknesses**
Market dominance	Market share weakness
Core skills	Few core strengths and low key skills
Economies of scale	Old equipment, higher costs than the competition
Low-cost position	
Leadership and management	Weak finances and poor cash flow skills
Manufacturing ability	Management skills and leadership lacking
Age of equipment	
Innovative processes and products	Poor record of innovation
Architecture network	Weak organization with poor architecture
Reputation	
Differentiated products	Low quality and poor reputation
Product or service quality	Products not differentiated
	Dependent on few products

External Factors	
Opportunities	**Threats**
New markets and segments	New market entrants
New products	Increased competition
Diversification opportunities	Increased pressure from customers and suppliers
Market growth	
Competitor weakness	Substitutes
Demographic and social change	Low market growth
Change in political, economic environment	Economic cycle downturn
	Technological threat
New takeover or partnership opportunities	Change in political or economic environment
Economic upturn	Demographic change
International growth	New international barriers to trade

Figure 47.1. Examples of SWOTs.

Source: Datamonitor (n.d.). Reprinted with permission.

ORIGINS OF THE SWOT ANALYSIS

Much of the original groundwork for what is today referred to as SWOT analysis was established over fifty years ago. In 1951, Kurt Lewin's landmark posthumous text, *Field Theory in Social Science,* contended that the results to which an organization aspires are influenced by various driving forces or enhancers and by limiting forces or inhibitors. Around the same time, two Harvard professors of business policy, George Albert Smith Jr. and C. Roland Christensen, were interested in a related issue: that of identifying the extent to which a firm's strategy matched its competitive environment. Using case studies, Smith and Christensen instructed students to address whether a company's policies adequately took into account the requirements of a competitive situation. To do so, the students were asked to investigate the growth trends of the relevant industry, and to develop an argument for the competencies required by a company to compete with others in that industry (Ghemawat, 2002).

Within a decade, discussions in Harvard's business policy course emphasized the analysis of a company's distinctive competence and strengths as well as noncompetence and weaknesses along with the opportunities and threats or risks the company encountered in the marketplace. In the early 1960s, another Harvard business policy professor, Kenneth Andrews, explored the ways in which Smith and Christensen's approach, which had by then become known by the acronym SWOT, could be used to explore the ways in which competitive thinking influences business strategy. Soon thereafter, in 1963, Harvard held a well-attended business policy conference that aided in the diffusion of SWOT within the academic community as well as among practicing business managers (Ghemawat, 2002).

Two years later, Igor Ansoff, who coined the term *strategic management,* introduced the "Product-Market Matrix" (1965). This framework was intended to provide a means by which business decisions could be made on the basis of the product or service a firm delivers as well as the market into which it delivers that product or service. In both cases, the product and market were defined as current or new. New products within current markets were assumed to call for product development, while market development was justified for current products within new markets. Alternatively, diversification was seen as suited to new products within new markets, while market penetration was deemed appropriate for current products within current markets. Along with SWOT analysis, the Product-Market Matrix became one of the first conceptual frameworks to forward the modern practice of business strategy (Lowy and Hood, 2004).

What these two strategic frameworks share in common is the simultaneous dialectic comparison of two levels of two factors involved in an organization's operating environment. Dialectics concerns the "contradiction between two conflicting forces viewed as the determining factor in their continuing interaction"

(Dictionary.com, 2000). Lowy and Hood (2004) describe such approaches as 2×2 matrices and argue that they offer an organizing framework for deconstructing and reconstructing problems, a means for the visualization of complex situations, and safe grounds within which to conduct "if-then" experiments.

SWOT ANALYSIS AND HPT

The International Society for Performance Improvement's HPT Model contains five primary components: (1) performance analysis, (2) cause analysis, (3) intervention selection, design, and development, (4) intervention implementation and change, and (5) evaluation (Van Tiem, Moseley, and Dessinger, 2004). SWOT analysis is most useful in the front end of the model for determining environmental influences within performance analyses and for gauging the level of knowledge, skills, attitudes, abilities, and environmental support within cause analyses.

As is illustrated in Figure 47.2, new products or interventions are put in place to *extinguish* old practices or *establish* new ones when current "As Is" results are undesirable. In situations within which current results are desirable, actions are taken to *maintain* or *improve* upon the performance (Langdon, 2003). While eliminating value-subtracted performance, labeled "V−," is the aim of extinguishing performance, creating, keeping, and bettering value-added performance, labeled "V+," is the intention of establishing, maintaining, and improving performance.

Performance Analysis

Performance analysis serves to identify a gap between desired and actual performance by way of "organizational analysis" and "environmental analysis."

| | | Accomplishments (results) | | Goal of Interventions |
		As Is (current)	To Be (desired)	
Actions	**Extinguish**	✓	✗	Eliminate V−
	Establish	✗	✓	Create V+
	Maintain	✓	✓ (same)	Keep V+
	Improve	✓	✓ (better)	Better V+

Figure 47.2. Alternatives for the Accomplishment of Performance.

Key: Value subtracted (V−); value added (V+); desired result (✓); undesired result (✗).

Source: Adapted from Langdon, 2003.

Organizational analyses are typically employed to specify desired To Be performance. Conducted at different organizational levels, these analyses yield a vision, a mission, values, goals, and strategies. Environmental analyses can assist in the identification of internal factors affecting As Is performance that focuses on work, the worker, or the work setting as well as external influences on performance, including those factors existing within society as well as among stakeholders and the competition.

SWOT analysis is intended neither to extol organizational strengths and opportunities nor to denounce weaknesses and threats. Rather, it simply serves to identify the degree to which various interventions, activities, and practices influence the accomplishment of current As Is results. Without data regarding these results, the specification of To Be performance provides an objective but without a clear sense of the discrepancy between current and desired results. Without a specification of To Be performance, current results data provide only evaluative information with no utility for making decisions regarding which objectives to pursue or abandon.

SWOT analysis can be a useful tool for differentiating As Is performance on the basis of its presence or absence in the current organizational context. Combined with a specification of To Be performance, better informed decisions can be made regarding which performance to extinguish, establish, maintain, or improve.

Cause Analysis

Cause analysis provides a means for distinguishing performance gaps resulting from a lack of environmental support from those that involve inadequate knowledge, skills, attitudes, and abilities. Using the results of a cause analysis, better-informed decisions can be made regarding the selection, design, and development of means to eliminate the root causes of performance gaps (Rosenberg, 1996).

Information regarding the reasons for the results currently being achieved by an organization can inform what practices should be continued or expanded in the future, as well as those that should be discontinued or complemented by other methods and tools. Within a cause analysis, SWOT analysis provides an indication of the factors to be considered in determining such operational requirements and tactics.

CONVENTIONAL APPROACHES TO SWOT ANALYSIS

SWOT analysis typically consists of using four sequential steps within focus group settings: identifying stakeholders, generating SWOTs, categorizing SWOTs within a 2×2 matrix, and deliberating how best to address those SWOTs. An alternative approach to data collection involves the use of market-analysis research conducted outside of focus group settings. Both approaches can be effective means of

Internal Factors	
Strengths	**Weaknesses**
Financial resources	Reliance on U.S. market
Global presence	Rapid build-out hangover
A disciplined innovator	Reliance on beverage innovation
Consistent strength of core product	Performance of international operations unit
External Factors	
Opportunities	**Threats**
International operations	Supply risk
Growth market	Slowing U.S. retail sales
Starbucks Visa card	Competition
Clustering of company units	Volatility of market
	Rising dairy costs

Figure 47.3. SWOT Analysis: Starbucks Corporation.

Source: Datamonitor, 2004. Reprinted with permission.

identifying internal and external inhibitors and enhancers to performance. However, given that such research is more typically within the purview of marketing and research and development departments rather than of HPT, the group-facilitation model is the primary focus of this chapter. SWOT analysis grounded in market research can, however, prove useful to HPT practitioners when cross-checking focus group data from performers and other stakeholders against existing performance data available within the organization. An example of such a market research approach to SWOT analysis is presented in Figure 47.3.

USING MARKET RESEARCH DATA FOR SWOT ANALYSIS

Datamonitor, a business information firm, creates company profiles that summarize the strengths, weaknesses, opportunities, and threats affecting various organizations. Sources used include internal Datamonitor data reports, investment analyst research, regulatory filings and press releases, trade journals, and interviews with key company personnel. Its comprehensive reports offer a company overview, key facts, a business description and history, a listing of key employees, an analysis of the company's major products and services, an identification and discussion of key SWOTs and top competitors, a statement on the company's future outlook from one of its executives, and a listing of the company's locations and subsidiaries. The SWOT analysis in Figure 47.3 is excerpted from Datamonitor's profile of Starbucks Corporation, a leading specialty coffee retailer with more than 7,500 retail store locations around the world (Datamonitor, 2004). Datamonitor's full reports provide a detailed discussion of each of the SWOTs in their company profiles. For more information on their products and services, visit www.datamonitor.com.

USING FOCUS GROUP DATA FOR SWOT ANALYSIS

Focus group data can augment market research and performance data meaningfully within HPT settings by providing perspectives from performers and other stakeholders regarding the results achieved by an organization. The four steps typical of such SWOT analyses are provided in this section, followed by a discussion of the ways in which this approach can be enhanced.

Step 1: Identifying Stakeholders

The context within which organizational decisions will be made is the primary consideration during the identification and invitation of stakeholders to participate in a SWOT analysis. It is advisable to invite participation from multiple constituencies when data from a SWOT analysis will influence the decisions made regarding various groups. Relevant stakeholders often include individuals from outside the organization such as customers, vendors, community members, and partners. Internal stakeholders may include associates, managers, union representatives, owners, and directors. What types of participation will be solicited, how information will be solicited during the analysis, and the degree to which the process will influence decision making will be described in steps 2, 3, and 4 of this section of the chapter.

Whether to conduct a SWOT analysis session with a homogenous group of stakeholders or with a cross-section of representatives from all stakeholder groups largely depends on two issues: the importance of consensus opinion versus having a variety of perspectives, and the degree to which honest and meaningful contributions can be expected. If it is reasonable to expect that participants from mixed stakeholder groups, such as bargaining unit members grouped with managers, might fear voicing dissenting or unpopular perspectives on an organization's performance, it is advisable to conduct multiple SWOT analyses, each consisting of homogeneous groups of stakeholders. While this approach allows for comparisons to be made between stakeholder groups, it is also less likely to represent a multiplicity of perspectives than when diverse groups are mixed and able to interact (Weisbord, 1993). Regardless of whether homogenous or heterogeneous stakeholder groups are used to generate SWOT data, SWOT analyses should typically be conducted in focus group settings consisting of eight to forty stakeholders. Groups of this size allow for a variety of opinions to be expressed while at the same time increasing the manageability of group facilitation and data analysis.

Capon and Disbury (2003) recommend the participation of both internal and external stakeholders during SWOT analyses. To identify prospective participants, they suggest selecting stakeholders on the basis of their relative decision-making power or influence and level of interest or stake in the organization's success (Johnson and Scholes, 1999). *Key players* are those with both high power and interest, and clearly should be invited as participants. Conversely, only minimal effort should be directed toward seeking the participation of those stakeholders who possess neither power over decision making nor interest in the organization's stake. However, a good working relationship should be developed with those stakeholders possessing high power but low interest, as they may be able to influence the participation of key stakeholders. Last, those stakeholders with low power but high interest are likely to be eager to participate in a SWOT analysis and at minimum should be kept informed of the process. While this last group of stakeholders may individually possess little power, it is possible that they may gain power through collective action and reposition themselves as key stakeholders.

Step 2: Generating SWOTs

Prior to being tasked with the generation of SWOTs, participants should have a clear understanding of the meaning of each of the four SWOT factors. Capon and Disbury (2003) offer the following definitions:

- *Strength:* an internal competence, valuable resource, or attribute that an organization can use to exploit opportunities in the external environment
- *Weakness:* an internal lack of a competence, resource, or attribute that an organization requires to perform in the external environment
- *Opportunity:* an external possibility that an organization can pursue or exploit to gain benefit
- *Threat:* an external factor that has the potential to reduce an organization's performance

After the definitions of SWOTs are clarified, a variety of approaches can be used to facilitate the generation of SWOT factors. SWOT analyses are typically conducted within a conference room or work area large enough to accommodate the number of participants involved. Participants may be asked to independently list SWOT factors, and then report their findings back to the larger group of participants. More collaborative approaches include

1. Facilitating the analysis among the entire focus group in which participants call out factors to a recorder
2. Forming four break-out groups, each responsible for the generation of one of the four SWOT factors, followed by reporting back to the entire group
3. As in number 2, but rotating the identification of each SWOT factor according to a preset schedule
4. Forming break-out groups based on similar or divergent power and interest, each tasked with generating all four SWOT factors, followed by reporting back to the entire group
5. As in number 4, but rotating participants between break-out groups according to a preset schedule

As an example of SWOT generation, consider a construction company that is interested in reducing the amount of scrap generated by cutting electrical conduit. Figure 47.4 provides a list of potential SWOTs that might be generated by

---

Strengths
S_1) Referrals frequent
S_2) Overhead costs relatively low
S_3) Storage space for inventory sizable

Weaknesses
W_1) Scrap production high
W_2) Purchases not coordinated across jobs
W_3) No standards for returning surplus inventory

Opportunities
O_1) Discounted pricing from vendors
O_2) Waterfront revitalization project
O_3) Tax incentives for waste management initiatives

Threats
T_1) New competitors entering the market
T_2) Disincentives for nondomestic goods
T_3) Improper waste disposal fines

Figure 47.4. Sample SWOT Factors.

managers, sales personnel, foremen, and construction workers in a focus group facilitated by an HPT consultant. An elaborated version of this example is provided in the article "How to Conduct Better SWOT Analyses" (Leigh, 2005).

Once SWOTs have been adequately generated, fact checks using market research data such as those discussed earlier may be employed prior to moving on to the next step of the analysis. Depending on the level of detail and validation required, this activity may require only a few hours to a month or longer.

Step 3: Categorizing SWOTs

Most SWOT analysis models ask two binary questions concerning the factors influencing an organization: Is this factor a benefit or cost? and Is this factor occurring within or outside this organization? (Leigh, 2000). Figure 47.5 displays a common format for categorizing factors according to a nominal scale with factors simply labeled a strength, a weakness, an opportunity, or a threat without regard for the relative impact of each. A greater degree of measurability can be accomplished by ranking SWOTs according to the perceived influence of each factor on the organization's performance.

While more information can be obtained by ranking SWOTs, equal-scale cross-factor comparisons *between* strengths, weaknesses, opportunities, and threats rather than *within* each factor are often difficult. In addition, stakeholders are likely to rank SWOTs differently due to their own definition of importance. Both of these limitations to conventional SWOT analysis are addressed in the "SWOT Analysis Critiques and Advancements" section later in this chapter.

	Strengths	Weaknesses
Internal	a. b. c.	a. b. c.
External	Opportunities a. b. c.	Threats a. b. c.
	Benefit	*Cost*

Figure 47.5. A Conventional SWOT Matrix.

Step 4: Deliberation

After categorizing SWOT statements within a SWOT matrix, discussions regarding the appropriate actions to take with regard to items in each quadrant typically follow. This deliberation may address a variety of decisions to be made regarding the leveraging of performance enhancers and mitigation of performance inhibitors (Capon and Disbury, 2003). An initial discussion typically addresses the prioritization of SWOT factors and the implications this will have on management practice. This often leads to discussions regarding the importance of various SWOTs and the urgency with which each should be addressed (Covey, 2004). Often, further deliberation pursues the potential vulnerabilities of ignoring threats and weaknesses, the means by which threats can be turned into opportunities, and alternative approaches for leveraging weaknesses into strengths. Such conversation commonly includes a consideration of how ambiguities regarding changing external environments can be best addressed. Methods such as Ansoff's Product-Market Matrix (1965), described earlier, and scenario planning, as described by Schwartz (1996), may be used to generate scenarios under which existing markets may change and new markets may emerge. These deliberations may occur within the SWOT analysis session, at a follow-up focus group, or by independent work groups tasked with conducting formal inquiry into these matters.

APPLICATIONS OF SWOT ANALYSIS

SWOT analysis allows an organization to analyze the causes of As-Is results and thus can inform the consideration of alternative solutions to suboptimal performance. To this end, the technique is relevant to two aspects of performance analysis—strategic planning and needs assessment—as well as to the evaluation of change initiatives.

Strategic Planning and Needs Assessment

Strategic planning is the process of identifying the direction in which an organization should head, why it should do so, and how it should determine progress along the way. The process serves to aid in the alignment of what an organization uses, does, produces, and delivers while at the same time defining the value to be established, maintained, or improved, or costs to be eliminated for external clients (Kaufman and Watkins, 1999). Needs assessment typically serves as the first step within strategic planning efforts as it prepares for the process of selecting appropriate solutions to the challenges and opportunities at hand while building shared commitment to an organization's future direction.

As a form of performance analysis, needs assessment provides a formal process for identifying gaps or needs between As Is or What Is, and To Be or What Should Be results, prioritizing those needs on the basis of the cost of

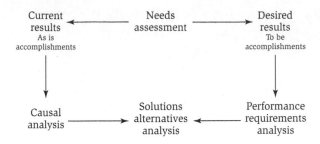

Figure 47.6. The Performance Accomplishment Model.

Source: Kaufman, Watkins, and Leigh, 2001.

ignoring gaps in results and the benefits of closing them, and identifying the performance to be extinguished, maintained, established, or improved (Kaufman, Oakley-Browne, Watkins, and Leigh, 2003). Within this basic problem-identification, analysis, and resolution framework, as illustrated in Figure 47.6, needs assessment serves to identify discrepancies between current and desired results. After the completion of this task, it is often necessary to explore the reasons for and solutions to identified gaps in results.

Needs assessments identify gaps between current and desired results that occur both within and outside an organization. Because SWOT analysis is most useful for identifying the factors that contribute to or detract from organizational effectiveness, the accurate identification of current As Is accomplishments becomes critical for the identification and selection of appropriate solutions to needs.

The identification of current As Is or What Is results typically involves a substantial amount of new data collection, especially when no prior needs-assessment or evaluation data have been collected. However, since many organizations regularly collect results data, available documentation such as annual reports, documentation from previous projects and program evaluations, audits, and internal correspondence, among other sources, should first be reviewed. If What Is data are not available from extant sources, plans should be developed for collecting new or supplemental data. Methods for the collection of such data may include direct observation, individual interviews, group interviews or focus groups, document searches, questionnaires or surveys, criterion tests, assessment centers, critical incidents, artifacts or work products, examination of public data, and review of existing research and statistical databases.

Evaluation of Change Initiatives

While the identification of SWOTs typically occurs during program planning, it can also be used for program evaluation. The utility of SWOT analysis in evaluative contexts is similar to that in performance analyses. However, whereas performance analyses serve to identify the discrepancy between As Is (What Is), and To Be (What Should Be) results, evaluation provides information regarding the gap between objectives that were intended to be accomplished (What Was Intended), and those results that were actually accomplished (What Is). SWOT analysis can be useful within evaluation settings that are formative or during program implementation, as well as those evaluation settings that summatively provide an overall judgment of a program's worth.

In formative evaluation settings, SWOT analysis can be used to monitor changes over time in the internal and external environments of a program. For this purpose, SWOT analyses are typically conducted along with program reviews, often on a quarterly basis. Program reviews help identify progress against stated benchmarks or objectives, and SWOT analyses can assist in tracking the stability of SWOT factors over time. For example, an organization may discover that an effective program has succeeded in capitalizing on external enhancers to performance (opportunities); or in mitigating internal performance inhibitors (weaknesses). Conversely, it may be discovered that a program has become more susceptible to external inhibitors to performance (threats), or that it has lost ground with regard to previously existing competitive advantages (strengths). Last, SWOT analyses used within formative evaluation contexts can also be useful for tracking new SWOTs as they emerge, and for documenting previously existing SWOTs as they become less influential on a program.

Scriven (2000) explains that summative evaluation does not involve the determination of how to improve a program, but rather provides determination of a program's merit or intrinsic quality; its worth or value given its costs; or its significance or importance. Because the purpose of formative evaluation is to gauge a program's ability to do what it was designed to do in terms of the accomplishment of programmatic objectives as well as unintended consequences, SWOT analysis can provide information regarding the areas in which a program may or may not have had an impact on the external environment.

SWOT ANALYSIS CRITIQUES AND ADVANCEMENTS

While needs assessment provides data useful for comparing the costs of ignoring gaps in results against the benefits of closing them, it does not help determine the costs and benefits of alternative performance solutions. Unfortunately, as traditionally conducted, SWOT analysis lacks this ability as well.

As environmental scans, conventional SWOT analyses are not new to many organizations' strategic planning efforts. Nevertheless, SWOT analysis has been criticized by some for its inability to prioritize SWOTs in relation to one another, yielding little in the way of data that can be used to inform decision making (Marshall, 1997). Put differently, most SWOT analyses do not allow practitioners a means for determining the degree to which a given SWOT factor serves as an enhancer or inhibitor to the performance desired of an organization.

In conventional SWOT analyses, stakeholders are rarely asked to do more than identify, or at best rank the strengths, weaknesses, opportunities, and threats affecting organizational operations. Conventional approaches to SWOT analysis do not assist decision makers in gauging the relative costs and benefits of any single SWOT factor in relation to all other factors generated. This is because traditional SWOT analyses are limited to simply naming strengths, weaknesses, opportunities, or threats without regard for the impact of each on actual performance, and their potential impact on desired performance. Furthermore, most SWOT analyses provide minimal information regarding the degree to which an organization or work team possesses influence over the factors that have been identified.

Fortunately, the utility of SWOT analysis can be enhanced. Doing so requires that SWOTs be examined in relation to one another according to (1) approximations of the degree to which an organization can exert control over each factor, and (2) estimates of the costs and benefits of those factors. Specifically, better informed decisions regarding what performance to extinguish, establish, maintain, or improve are available when SWOT analysis involves systematically asking and answering two essential questions (Leigh, 2000):

- How much control does the organization have over each SWOT factor?

- How much does each SWOT factor cost or benefit the organization?

Answers to these questions add quantitative measures to what traditionally has been a purely qualitative undertaking. Termed "IE^2" (internal-external, inhibitor-enhancer), this expanded approach so foundationally changes the nature of SWOT analysis that the practice is reconceptualized as

> an analytic process in which a group of stakeholders (a) identify enhancers and inhibitors to desired performance, (b) rate those factors based on their perceived control and cost-benefit, and (c) decide what future actions to take with regard to those factors [Leigh, 2005, p. 240].

This approach allows the consideration of SWOTs in terms of the four quadrants represented in Figure 47.7.

ORGANIZATIONAL CONTROL OVER SWOTS

An IE^2 analysis proceeds much as described earlier in the section "Using Focus Group Data for SWOT Analysis." However, following the identification and categorization of SWOTs, the degree to which each factor is within or outside the control of the organization is estimated. This is accomplished by asking

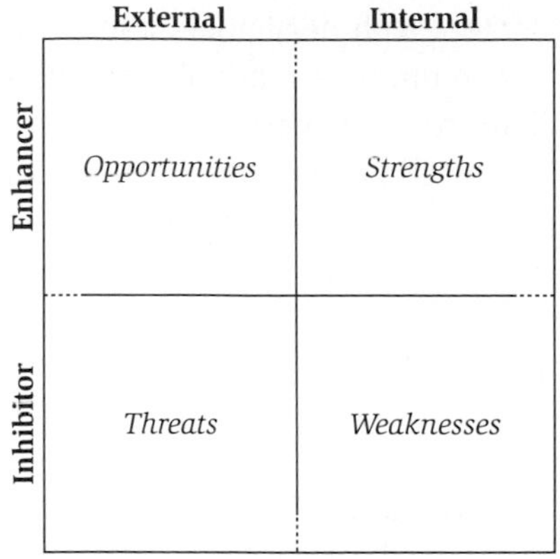

	External	Internal
Enhancer	*Opportunities*	*Strengths*
Inhibitor	*Threats*	*Weaknesses*

Figure 47.7. SWOTs as Internal and External Inhibitors and Enhancers of Performance.

participants to rate the degree to which each factor is within the control of their organization for strengths and weaknesses, or outside for opportunities and threats. A scale ranging from −5 (complete external control) to +5 (complete internal control), with 0 indicating a balance of internal and external control, is used to quantify these estimates.

Because this determination is obviously subject to participants' individual interpretations, consensus regarding organizational control over SWOTs is rare. Thus, as noted earlier, it is important to obtain the participation of stakeholders with sufficient organizational power and interest to diminish the potential for hostility among stakeholders. A skilled IE^2 facilitator leverages disagreement to creatively identify additional factors that may qualify the estimates of the controllability of SWOTs. To do so, SWOT analysis facilitators should remind participants that internalizing the control of SWOTs might not be either necessary or advantageous. Simply because opportunities and threats are susceptible to external control does not make them uncontrollable or out of control. Indeed, as Scriven (1991) points out, seeking to internalize all SWOTs may actually be indicative of unrealistic or unfounded ambitions.

COSTS AND BENEFITS OF SWOTS TO AN ORGANIZATION

After facilitating the estimation of internal and external control, the IE^2 facilitator should ask participants to rate the degree to which each SWOT factor acts as an enhancer of strengths and opportunities, or as an inhibitor of weaknesses and threats. Again, this is done according to an eleven-point scale, this time with highly costly inhibitors receiving a rating of −5, highly valuable enhancers receiving a rating of +5, and those factors with negligible financial impact receiving a rating of 0. As cost-benefit data can often be more objectively quantified than those of organizational control, data from this part of the analysis may be generated outside of the focus group setting through a financial analysis of those SWOT factors that have been identified. The degree to which stakeholders' impressions, as opposed to market analysis data, are used to guide decision making typically determines whether additional data should be collected. In many circumstances, it is not uncommon for both stakeholder input and financial data to inform this process.

PLOTTING IE^2 DATA

The generation of control and cost-benefit data produces four sets of bivariate data that allow SWOTs to be compared to one another both numerically and visually. As an example, consider that an IE^2 analysis of the factors in Figure 47.4 resulted in the data set illustrated in Figure 47.8.

	External(−)/ Internal (+)	Inhibitor (−)/ Enhancer (+)
Strength		
S_1	+3	+2
S_2	+2	+3
S_3	+3	+1
Weakness		
W_1	+1	−4
W_2	+5	−2
W_3	+5	−5
Opportunity		
O_1	−3	+3
O_2	−4	+1
O_3	−5	+5
Threat		
T_1	−4	−3
T_2	−5	−1
T_3	0	−1

Figure 47.8. Sample IE^2 Data.

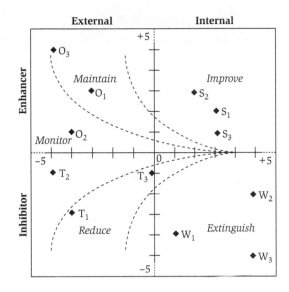

Figure 47.9. Sample IE^2 Grid.

Note: See Figures 47.4 and 47.8 for key.

These data can then be plotted within an IE^2 grid, as represented in Figure 47.9. Overlaying this IE^2 grid are thresholds that can be used to inform decision making, as discussed in the following section.

USING IE^2 DATA TO INFORM DECISION MAKING

The unique contribution of IE^2 analysis is its applicability in informing the means by which desired, To Be performance, as illustrated in Figure 47.2, can be accomplished. This approach allows for individual SWOTs to be examined in relation to one another based on data regarding the cost-benefit of each factor, along with estimations regarding the degree to which each factor is or is not within an organization's control. Decision guides, such as those represented by the dotted lines in Figure 47.9, may be superimposed over the IE^2 grid to facilitate decision making. While the thresholds of these guides are best established prior to the identification of SWOTs so as to preclude the manipulation of data that might come across as "bad news," it is also possible to adjust them on the basis of stakeholder input. These decision thresholds, from left to right within the IE^2 grid, are described in the following sections.

Monitor

Because their current cost-benefit is relatively low, those factors close to the horizontal axis of the grid are likely candidates for *monitoring*. Their stability over time should be tracked. However, it may also be prudent to act on opportunities and threats should the organization be able to gain influence over their impact on performance.

Reduce Threats and Maintain Opportunities

Inhibitors more costly to performance, and those that are under greater internal control, are typically of high priority. For this reason, their *reduction* is warranted if the cost of doing so is less than the cost of simply monitoring them. Similarly, as opportunities surface to enhance performance, those which are more beneficial to the organization or are under greater organizational control should be *maintained*.

Extinguish Weaknesses and Improve Strengths

Costly internal weaknesses that serve as inhibitors to desired performance are likely candidates for *extinguishing*. Conversely, internal strengths that add the greatest value and are relatively controllable are often those factors that should be *improved* upon.

CONCLUSION

Data-based decision making is at the heart of HPT's systemic approach to helping individuals and organizations accomplish results. Essential to this effort is the systematic identification of gaps in results and the analysis of those factors that limit or enhance performance (International Society for Performance Improvement, 2002). SWOT analysis provides a means for identifying the inhibitors and enhancers to desired results by providing information regarding the factors that contribute to current results. When coupled with an estimation of the relative cost-benefit ratio and controllability of SWOTs, the method provides a powerful tool for HPT practitioners as they work with internal and external stakeholders to select, develop, and implement interventions that achieve results and add value.

References

Ansoff, I. (1965). *Corporate strategy.* New York: McGraw-Hill.

Capon, C., and Disbury, A. (2003). *Understanding organisational context: Inside and outside organisations.* London: Financial Times/Prentice-Hall.

Covey, S. R. (2004). *The 8th habit: From effectiveness to greatness.* New York: Free Press.

Datamonitor. (2004, October). *Starbucks Corporation: Company Profile* (Datamonitor Publication Code No. 1586). New York: Author.

Datamonitor. (n.d.). Untitled internal document. New York: Author.

Dictionary.com. (2000). *Dialectics.* Retrieved September 24, 2004, from dictionary.reference.com/search?q=dialectics.

Ghemawat, P. (2002). *How business strategy tamed the "invisible hand."* Harvard Business School. Retrieved September 24, 2004, from http://hbswk.hbs.edu/item.jhtml?id=3019&t=bizhistory.

International Society for Performance Improvement. (2002). *ISPI's performance technology standards.* Retrieved November 05, 2004, from http://ispi.org/hpt_institute/Standards.pdf.

Johnson, G., and Scholes, K. (1999). *Exploring corporate strategy* (5th ed.). London: Prentice–Hall.

Kaufman, R., and Watkins, R. (1999). Strategic planning. In D. G. Langdon, K. S. Whiteside, and M. M. McKenna (Eds.), *Intervention resource guide: 50 performance improvement tools.* San Francisco: Jossey-Bass.

Kaufman, R., Watkins, R., and Leigh, D. (2001). *Useful educational results: Defining, prioritizing, and accomplishing.* Ringwood, NJ: Proactive Publishing.

Kaufman, R., Oakley-Browne, H., Watkins, R., and Leigh, D. (2003). *Strategic planning for success: Aligning people, performance, and payoffs.* San Francisco: Jossey-Bass/Pfeiffer.

Langdon, D. (2003). Should we conduct cause analysis or change-of-state analysis? *Performance Improvement Journal, 42*(9), 8–13.

Leigh, D. (2000). Causal-utility decision analysis (CUDA): Quantifying SWOTs. In E. Biech (Ed.), *The 2000 annual, volume 2: Consulting* (pp. 251–265). San Francisco: Jossey-Bass/Pfeiffer.

Leigh, D. (2005). How to conduct better SWOT analyses. In M. Silberman (Ed.), *The 2005 ASTD team and organization development sourcebook.* Princeton, NJ: Active Training and the American Society for Training and Development.

Lewin, K. (1951). *Field theory in social science.* New York: Harper & Row.

Lewis, B. R., and Littler, D. (Eds.). (1997). *The Blackwell encyclopedic dictionary of marketing.* Malden, MA: Blackwell.

Lowy, A., and Hood, P. (2004). *The power of the 2×2 matrix: Using 2×2 thinking to solve business problems and make better decisions.* San Francisco: Jossey-Bass.

Marshall, S. (1997). *Strategy formulation—SWOT analysis—An indictment: Strengths, weaknesses, opportunities and threats.* Retrieved September 24, 2004, from www.mindspring.com/~stevenmarshall/Strategy.htm.

Rosenberg, M. J. (1996). Human performance technology. In R. L. Craig (Ed.), *The ASTD training and development handbook* (4th ed.). New York: McGraw-Hill.

Schwartz, P. (1996). *Art of the long view: Planning for the future in an uncertain world.* New York: Currency.

Scriven, M. (1991). *Evaluation thesaurus* (4th ed.). Newbury Park, CA: Sage.

Scriven, M. (2000). *Evaluation context index.* Retrieved September 24, 2004, from http://eval.cgu.edu/lectures/lecturen.htm.

Van Tiem, D. M., Moseley, J. L., and Dessinger, J. C. (2004). *Fundamentals of performance technology* (2nd ed.). Washington, DC: International Society for Performance Improvement.

Weisbord, M. R. (1993). *Discovering common ground: How future search conferences bring people together to achieve breakthrough innovation, empowerment, shared vision and collaborative action.* San Francisco: Berrett-Koehler.

CHAPTER FORTY-EIGHT

Sustainable Development and Human Performance Technology

Scott P. Schaffer, Therese M. Schmidt

Motivated by recognition of the harmful effects of rapid economic growth in the last century, an increasing number of organizations are now taking responsibility for the societal impact of their products and processes. With this recognition and responsibility, concepts such as sustainability and sustainable development have begun to appear in corporate vision and mission statements. Performance-improvement professionals can play a key role in supporting an organization's shift from goals that reflect a sole concern for profits to those that incorporate concerns for the present and future economic, social, and ecological health of society. The purpose of this chapter is to build conceptual relationships between sustainability, as it is currently defined, and the theory and practice of human performance technology (HPT).

Performance technologists have access to and expertise in a powerful technology. The Code of Ethics of the International Society for Performance Improvement (ISPI) dictates that this technology must be used to add value to clients, their customers, and the global environment (International Society for Performance Improvement, 2002a). The implications of this principle were explored in a *Performance Improvement* article titled "Saving the World with HPT: Expanding Beyond the Workplace and Beyond the 'Business Case,'" and subsequently in a Silicon Valley ISPI chapter meeting at which there were discussions about the possibilities, pros, and cons of using HPT to address issues such as world peace, world hunger, water availability and quality, living in balance with nature, and so on (Andrews, Farrington, Packer, and Kaufman, 2004). Some of the challenges and obstacles discussed centered on the difficulty in taking HPT outside of the workplace and widening the scope of HPT.

A major premise of this chapter is that it is possible to add value to the global environment from within the workplace. HPT practitioners can address important global issues within organizations by using their expertise of the HPT process and by working with sustainability experts to help move organizations toward sustainable development.

SUSTAINABILITY DEFINED

Many definitions for sustainability exist, but perhaps the best known is the related definition of sustainable development that came out of *Our Common Future,* the 1987 report of the World Commission on Environment and Development. The commission defined sustainable development as development that "meets the needs of the present without compromising the ability of future generations to meet their own needs" (p. 8). In another definition, Newton (2003) describes sustainability in the following way: "[W]e will understand a community, economic system, or other human activity to have reached sustainability when it can be maintained profitably and indefinitely, without degrading the systems on which it depends" (p. 5). Finally, Smith (2004) says that sustainability is "finding win/win/win solutions for both the short- and long-term effects of design on social responsibility, environmental performance and business results—the triple bottom line" (p. 23). Definitions of sustainability and sustainable development share a common theme of concern for the economic, environmental, and social impacts of an organization and for whether or not an organization can lead to healthy and prosperous lives for current and future generations.

Economic Dimension

In thinking about the sustainability of an organization, it is typical to consider an organization's longevity, and especially its financial well-being. This is understandable, as the focus for much of the twentieth century has been on developing and nurturing an infrastructure and system of economic growth. The economic dimension of sustainability is also concerned with financial issues related to the internal health of an organization, including the traditional bottom line, value provided to shareholders, and profitability of the organization over the long term. Externally, organizations may be concerned about the sustainability of world markets and global economic growth. Thus, both internal and external economic sustainability are crucial to success. Furthermore, many organizational leaders are beginning to see the direct linkages between the economic sustainability of their organization and society, and the sustainability of the global environment and social systems.

Environmental Dimension

Interest in the environmental dimension of sustainability has grown in recent years, partially due to increases in environmental legislation. Many organizations, for example, have developed environmental management systems to measure and control their impact on the environment. Organizations concerned with environmental sustainability focus on minimizing their use of nonrenewable resources and minimizing the pollution and waste they add to the environment. This is what is known as eco-efficiency, a term promoted by the Business Council for Sustainable Development in 1992 (McDonough and Braungart, 1998). The eco-efficiency movement, with its "reduce, reuse, recycle" mantra, has gained great popularity within the business world and communities. Not only have eco-efficiency practices helped organizations go beyond compliance, they have also benefited them financially. Increased operating efficiency may be obtained by focusing on practices that increase the productivity of natural resources and enhance material recyclability. For example, 3M reported that between 1986 and 1997 it saved more than $750 million through pollution-prevention projects (McDonough and Braungart, 2002).

William McDonough and Michael Braungart (2002) argue that eco-effectiveness rather than eco-efficiency is a more compelling future direction. Eco-efficiency lacks sustainability because it only slows down destruction and depletion, while eco-effectiveness is aimed at changing the results we expect. According to McDonough and Braungart, recycling is really just down-cycling, resulting in a product of less quality that will still eventually end up in the landfill. Alternatively, they suggest a focus on up-cycling products and materials for use in products that may continually be reused. Eco-effectiveness involves creating the following:

- Buildings that, like trees, produce more energy than they consume and purify their own waste water
- Factories that produce effluent that is cleaner than drinking water
- Products that, when their useful life is over, do not become useless waste but can be tossed onto the ground to decompose and become food for plants and animals and nutrients for soil, or, alternatively, that can return to industrial cycles to supply high-quality raw materials for new products
- Billions, even trillions, of dollars' worth of material accrued for human and natural purposes each year
- Transportation that improves the quality of life while delivering goods and services
- A world of abundance, not one of limits, pollution, and waste
  [pp. 90–91]

Social Dimension

As the demands placed on organizations to contribute to the well-being of their employees and to the greater society have increased, so has the adoption of corporate social responsibility, employee wellness, and work-life programs. Hiring, nurturing, and retaining valued employees and maintaining public respect and confidence is crucial to the sustainability of an organization and to the sustainability of society. Organizations that focus on the social dimension of sustainability realize that they must invest in the development and career goals of their employees, provide a safe and healthy workplace, respect human rights, and take actions toward a just society.

Incorporating the ideas of sustainability by designing new products and processes that lead to improved economic, social, and environmental well-being of the greater community has become a driving force in several organizations. Whereas the focus of the last century was on economic growth, the focus of this century will be on "sustainability—that is, how to redesign the industrial system— the triumph of the twentieth century—to support a just and equitable social order and to sustain rather than damage the biosphere" (Dunphy, 2003, p. 2). Dunphy backs up this claim by citing the authors of a worldwide survey commissioned by the Millennium Project that concluded, "Never before has the world opinion been so united on a single goal as it is on achieving sustainable development" (Dunphy, 2003, p. 2).

WHY ORGANIZATIONS ARE CONCERNED WITH SUSTAINABILITY

At the most fundamental level, corporations are concerned about environmental and social impact because of the necessity for compliance with government regulations. In a business that is determined to cut costs, noncompliance with environmental and health and safety regulations of the government does not pay. For example, penalties assessed by governmental agencies such as the Environmental Protection Agency are large, avoidable costs.

In addition, organizations feel that it is important to consider sustainable business practices in order to manage risk. As J. Elkington stated in *The Chrysalis Economy,* "While many managers may argue that 'it could never happen to us,' the issues of liability and risk stand out as a powerful leverage point for organizations to change course on sustainability issues before they become the subject of the next crisis of confidence" (as quoted in Dunphy, Griffiths, and Benn, 2003, p. 106). Recognizing the potential for large claims against the companies that they insure, insurance companies are now requiring that all public companies report on the policies they use to identify and mitigate risks related to their social and environmental impact (Dunphy, Griffiths, and Benn, 2003, p. 107). Like insurance companies, lending agencies are also very interested in a company's environmental policy and performance: according to Curcio and Wolf (1996), "few commercial loans are made without first performing environmental audits" (p. 22).

Alternatively, some organizations consider sustainable design and development practices proactively as a strategy to gain a competitive edge and possibly increase profits. Larson, Teisberg, and Johnson (2000, p. 1) state:

> Firms that succeed with sustainable business are not being altruistic, and they are not choosing between profitability and environmental responsibility. They achieve dramatic gains in efficiency, product differentiation, and strategic advantage from the innovations they make after adopting this new perspective.

Rising world incomes and an increased interest in corporate responsibility will likely accelerate the potential for increasing the public's loyalty to businesses that incorporate the practices of sustainable development.

As the world population continues to increase, natural resources become depleted, and waste continues to amass, it is likely that all organizations will eventually incorporate some form of sustainable design and development into their operational practices. Organizations that already have such practices in place will, therefore, have a great competitive edge.

SUSTAINABLE DESIGN IN ACTION: FORD MOTOR COMPANY

In late 2002, Ford Motor Company adopted the Ford Business Principles to guide its actions as a company for the next one hundred years. The principles focus on the following areas: accountability, community, environment, safety, products and customers, financial health, and quality of relationships. The goal of these principles is to help put Ford's values concerning sustainability issues into action. William Clay Ford, Jr., chairman of Ford Motor Company, argues that these sustainability issues are at the heart of the company's business (Ford, 2003).

One of the best examples of the application of the Ford business principles, and of the integration of sustainable design, is Ford's $2 billion investment in the renovation of its River Rouge factory complex in Dearborn, Michigan. This assembly plant, built from 1917 to 1925 for the Model A, and the home of the Ford Mustang since its 1964 debut, had once covered hundreds of acres and employed more than one hundred thousand workers. However, by the end of the century, the number of employees had dwindled to about seven thousand, and much of the land had become unusable due to the abuse of the manufacturing processes (McDonough and Braungart, 2002).

However, instead of closing the aging plant and spending money to purchase new land, William Clay Ford, Jr., decided to redesign it and make it a model of sustainable design and development. The plant was redesigned to incorporate lean and flexible manufacturing that made it capable of producing nine different vehicle models based on three platforms (Ford Motor Company, 2003). This enables the company to be more efficient and increases its capability to respond quickly to consumer demands, thereby increasing the sustainability of the plant.

In addition, the Rouge is a model of sustainable design in the way that it incorporates McDonough and Braungart's (2002) principles of eco-effectiveness. One of many examples is the design of its new storm-water management system (Ford Motor Company, 2005). On the Ford Rouge Dearborn Truck Plant, Ford has incorporated a ten-acre living roof lined with sedum plants that can hold several inches of rainwater. It has also included porous pavement and a system of shallow green ditches lined with plants through which the storm water flows. These swales naturally cleanse the water before it is released into the river. By designing these features into the regeneration of the plant, Ford has created habitat for wildlife and used a natural and sustainable process for storm-water management.

Finally, the Ford Rouge Center site management committed to conducting a community impact assessment to identify and involve key stakeholders in the plant's operations and community involvement. Discussions during this assessment opened a dialogue in which community concerns can be voiced, and opportunities for the plant to make positive contributions to the greater community are being discovered (Ford Motor Company, 2003).

SUSTAINABILITY AND HUMAN PERFORMANCE TECHNOLOGY

How are these ideas related to human performance technology (HPT)? Human performance technology practitioners can apply the existing interest in societal value in our field and their expertise in the systematic HPT process to facilitate an organization's shift to sustainable development.

Groundwork in Our Field

A concern for societal value is not new in our field. Hamblin (1974) developed a five-level evaluation framework for training and development that emphasized the importance of *ultimate value*, or human good relative to organizational effectiveness. Roger Kaufman built much of his career around making individuals and organizations more aware of societal value, especially as it relates to strategic planning and needs assessment (Kaufman, Oakley-Brown, Watkins, and Leigh, 2003). Performance-improvement theorists have recognized the necessity of addressing the societal value added of performance-improvement interventions most directly within the realm of evaluation. Kaufman and Keller (1994) suggest adding an additional level to the Kirkpatrick evaluation framework to address the societal impact of a performance-improvement intervention. In discussing Kaufman and Keller's Kirkpatrick Plus framework, Watkins, Leigh, Foshay, and Kaufman (1998) go a step further by suggesting that evaluation should start at the societal level and related evaluation criteria should be part of the initial design of an intervention. In other words, a performance-improvement professional should begin by identifying the impact of the intervention outside the organization, and only after that investigate the impact on the organization and individual performers. This approach places societal impact at the forefront of the design of the intervention and addresses the challenge of aligning interventions with the goals of the growing number of organizations that are concerned with having a positive impact on society.

While Kaufman and Keller address the new societal focus of many of today's organizations, their ideas must be reinforced with practical applications. Kaufman speaks of applying these ideas by using an "ideal vision" to guide organizational initiatives. An example of an ideal vision follows:

> All people will live in a healthy, positive, safe, and satisfying environment where all things both survive and thrive. There will be no losses of life or elimination or reduction of levels of well-being, survival, self-sufficiency, quality of life, livelihood, or loss of property from any source. Poverty will not exist, and every person will earn at least as much as it costs to live (unless they are progressing toward being self-sufficient and self-reliant). No adult will be under the care, custody, or control of another person, agency, or substance. All adult citizens will be self-sufficient and self-reliant as minimally indicated by their consumption being equal to or less than their production [*Roger Kaufman and Associates*, 2004].

This ideal vision is noble, but it is likely to have greater impact if it is phrased in language that is more familiar to corporations and communities throughout the world. The concept of sustainability offers that language and provides practical direction for taking steps toward making the ideal vision a reality.

Role of Human Performance Technology Processes and Practices

The HPT process is uniquely positioned to support a strategic shift from an organization's current state to one that incorporates sustainable development. Furthermore, the processes that an organization must implement to move toward sustainability align well with the theory and practices of HPT. A fundamental principle of HPT is the practice of taking a systems view by looking at the interconnectedness of the components of a system to examine how the effectiveness of each component depends on the success of the whole and vice versa (International Society for Performance Improvement, 2002b). The concept of sustainability is also derived from taking a systems view, as it involves accounting for the economic, environmental, and social systems in and around the organization.

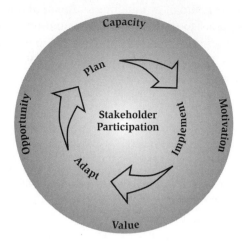

Figure 48.1. HPT Change Framework.

Source: Adapted from Schaffer and Keller, 2003.

Sustainability involves solving problems by addressing the problem not from one of these dimensions, but instead, from all three. Interconnections are explored, barriers and leverage points are identified, and ideally solutions that address all three system elements are selected.

Operating from the systems view is inherent in the concept of sustainability. HPT professionals can facilitate an organization's shift to sustainable development by leading them through the change process. The HPT Change Framework (Schaffer and Keller, 2003) was developed specifically to assess and lead large, complex process innovations such as sustainable development (Figure 48.1). Process innovations require the involvement of many organizational levels to be successful, and differ from product innovations in that the success of the innovation is difficult to measure (Damanpour and Gopalakrishnan, 2001). As shown in Figure 48.1, the HPT Change Framework incorporates the major domains of influence on human performance: opportunity, capacity, and motivation (Keller, 1999), as well as results or value orientation. Stakeholder participation represents the collaborative nature of successful change process that drives the ongoing reflection, assessment, and evaluation necessary for complex innovations to gain traction. The framework also stresses the importance of both ongoing collaboration among stakeholders and the importance of creating the conditions necessary for successful implementation. Organizational change research has shown that a process of mutual adaptation occurs when an innovation is introduced to an organization. The organization and its people and processes change to accommodate it, and the innovation itself is adapted to more closely resemble the immediate context in which it is introduced (Orlikowski, 1992; Leonard-Barton, 1995).

PLANNING TOOLS

To define the opportunities related to sustainable development, performance technologists work with organizational stakeholders to complete an organizational and environmental analysis. The analysis team can work with sustainability experts to define the desired state and to determine subsequent gaps in current strategies, operations, and tactics relative to sustainable development. A good starting point for beginning such an analysis may be the Global Reporting Initiative, an independent institution that provides guidelines for organizations to follow when reporting on the economic, social, and environmental dimensions of their activities (Global Reporting Initiative, 2002).

Another tool that may be useful during this opportunity assessment stage is the Sustainability Readiness Assessment, or SRA, developed by Schaffer and Schmidt (2004). The SRA is both an assessment tool and a facilitator guide in that it may be completed by a large number of stakeholders in an organization to create a sustainability readiness score, or it can be used to facilitate exploratory dialogue within focus groups or other similar settings. An excerpt of SRA items to accomplish the latter is shown in Figure 48.2.

When assessing opportunities within organizations where stakeholders are already quite knowledgeable of the organization's sustainable development practices, the SRA items displayed in Figure 48.3 may be most appropriate.

IMPLEMENTATION

Change theorists and practitioners (Rogers, 1995; Conner, 1992) strongly assert that learning precedes change. Performance technologists can facilitate the implementation of sustainable development interventions by identifying and developing stakeholder capacity and motivation levels that are major predictors of eventual innovation adoption. Once capacity and motivation levels are sufficient to address sustainable development opportunities, performance technologists can use their expertise in cause analysis to help stakeholders identify internal and external barriers and deficiencies that are preventing the organization from meeting its sustainable development goals. They can then work with stakeholders to select, design, and develop interventions to address these barriers and deficiencies.

Change Leadership, Alignment, Opportunity

1. To what degree will leadership and stakeholders support efforts to implement sustainable development practices?
2. What are the key business issues for the next several years, and what role do sustainability issues play in strategy development?
3. Does the organization have specific sustainability-related requirements from customers, regulatory agencies, and so on?
4. Are there forces within or outside of the organization that will have an impact on this strategy?
5. Where are the best opportunity areas for adopting sustainable development practices?
6. What are barriers to successful implementation of an action plan to address opportunities?

Capacity, Motivation, Value

1. What is the current level of understanding or awareness of

   - Sustainability
   - Sustainable development
   - Sustainable design
   - ROI of sustainable development

2. What is the current level of knowledge or organizational expertise relative to sustainable development?

3. Do current best practices related to sustainability exist in the organization?

4. Is there a willingness to experiment with sustainable development projects?

5. What would it cost to modify current processes?

6. What impact would modified processes have on other processes?

Figure 48.2. Sample of SRA Items to Facilitate Exploratory Dialogue.

Because the sustainable development process requires adoption and mutual adaptation by many different levels of the organization, the implementation phase may be where the expertise of skilled performance technologists is most needed. Change leadership and management processes will be crucial for the organization to reach its sustainable development goals. Ongoing collaborative review and evaluation at all stages of development and implementation will be necessary to ensure that the process is following the most effective path and that real value is being added.

Identify the *current state* and *desired state* of social and environmental performance. Using the scale below, circle the rating for each of the indicators to indicate the *current state* of the organization and place a box around the organization's *desired state* for each of the indicators. If there are any additional indicators that you feel are important for the organization, include those in the blank rows provided.

> 1 = No concern
>
> 2 = Lip service, but no action
>
> 3 = Action taken is minimum required by law or regulatory agencies
>
> 4 = Action taken is more than required by law or regulatory agencies
>
> 5 = Model for industry

Social Indicators					
Employee training	1	2	3	4	5
Career advancement support for employees	1	2	3	4	5
Health and safety programs	1	2	3	4	5
Employee benefits	1	2	3	4	5
Working conditions	1	2	3	4	5
Human rights	1	2	3	4	5
Impact on community	1	2	3	4	5
Community support	1	2	3	4	5
Equal opportunity policies	1	2	3	4	5
Corporate ethics	1	2	3	4	5
Customer health and safety	1	2	3	4	5
	1	2	3	4	5
	1	2	3	4	5

Environmental Indicators					
Minimization of material use	1	2	3	4	5
Energy efficiency	1	2	3	4	5
Use of renewable energy sources	1	2	3	4	5
Recycling and reuse of water	1	2	3	4	5
Impact on water sources and habitats or ecosystems	1	2	3	4	5
Minimization of greenhouse gas emissions	1	2	3	4	5
Minimization of use and emissions of ozone-depleting chemicals	1	2	3	4	5
Minimization of waste	1	2	3	4	5
	1	2	3	4	5
	1	2	3	4	5

Figure 48.3. Sample of SRA Items to Assess Social and Environmental Gaps.

CONCLUSION

Sustainability will continue to become a strategic imperative for an increasing number of organizations that HPT professionals serve. HPT provides a powerful process for systematically transforming an organization from one that has its main focus on profits to one that is focused on sustainable development. HPT professionals have a systemic change perspective, process expertise, and a responsibility to use this expertise to support and lead this societal transformation.

References

Andrews, J., Farrington, J., Packer, T., and Kaufman, R. (2004). Saving the world with HPT: Expanding beyond the workplace and beyond the "business case." *Performance Improvement, 43*(2), 44–47.

Conner, D. (1992). *Managing at the speed of change.* New York: Villard Books.

Curcio, R. J., and Wolf, F. M. (1996). Corporate environmental strategy: Impact upon firm value. *Journal of Financial and Strategic Decisions, 9*(2), 21–31.

Damanpour, F., and Gopalakrishnan, S. (2001). The dynamics of the adoption of product and process innovations in organizations. *Journal of Management Studies, 38*(1), 45–65.

Dunphy, D. (2003). The sustainability of organizations. In S. Chowdhury (Ed.), *Organization 21C* (pp. 259–271). Indianapolis: Financial Times Prentice-Hall.

Dunphy, D., Griffiths, A., and Benn, S. (2003). *Organizational change for corporate sustainability: Understanding organizational change.* New York: Routledge.

Ford, W. C., Jr. (2003). *Letter from Bill Ford.* Retrieved July 24, 2004, from http://www.ford.com/en/company/about/corporateCitizenship/report/overviewLetter.htm.

Ford Motor Company. (2003). *Regeneration of the Rouge.* Retrieved July 24, 2004, from http://www.ford.com/en/goodWorks/environment/cleanerManufacturing/rougeRenovation.htm.

Ford Motor Company. (2005). *Rouge renovation.* Retrieved January 28, 2005, from www.ford.com.

Global Reporting Initiative. (2002). Performance indicators. In *Sustainability reporting guidelines* (Part C). Retrieved July 25, 2004, from www.globalreporting.org/guidelines/2002.asp.

Hamblin, A. C. (1974). *Evaluation and control of training.* London: McGraw-Hill.

International Society for Performance Improvement. (2002a). *Code of ethics.* Retrieved July 24, 2004, from www.certifiedpt.org/index.cfm?section = standards.

International Society for Performance Improvement. (2002b). *Performance technology standards.* Retrieved July 24, 2004, from www.certifiedpt.org/hpt_institute/standards.pdf.

Kaufman, R., and Keller, J. (1994, Winter). Levels of evaluation: Beyond Kirkpatrick. *Human Resources Quarterly, 5*(4), 371–380.

Kaufman, R., Oakley-Brown, H., Watkins, R., and Leigh, D. (2003). *Strategic planning for success: Aligning people, performance and payoffs.* San Francisco: Jossey-Bass.

Keller, J. M. (1999). Motivational systems. In H. D. Stolovitch and E. J. Keeps (Eds.), *Handbook of human performance technology: Improving individual and organizational performance worldwide* (pp. 373–394). San Francisco: Jossey-Bass.

Larson, A. L., Teisberg, E. O., and Johnson, R. R. (2000). Sustainable business: Opportunity and value creation. *Interfaces, 30*(3), 1–12.

Leonard-Barton, D. (1995). *Wellsprings of knowledge: Building and sustaining the sources of innovation.* Boston: Harvard Business School Press.

McDonough, W., and Braungart, M. (1998). The next industrial revolution. *The Atlantic Monthly, 282*(4), 82–92.

McDonough, W., and Braungart, M. (2002). *Cradle to cradle: Rethinking the way we make things.* New York: North Point Press.

Newton, L. H. (2003). *Ethics and sustainability: Sustainable development and the moral life.* Upper Saddle River, NJ: Prentice-Hall.

Orlikowski, W. J. (1992). The duality of technology: Rethinking the concept of technology in organizations. *Organization Science, 3*(3), 398–427.

Roger Kaufman and Associates. (2004). Retrieved May 2, 2004, from www.megaplanning.com.

Rogers, E. M. (1995). *Diffusion of innovations.* New York: The Free Press.

Schaffer, S. P., and Keller, J. (2003). Evaluating organizational results. *Performance Improvement Quarterly, 16*(1), 7–26.

Schaffer, S. P., and Schmidt, T. M. (2004). *Sustainability readiness assessment (SRA).* Unpublished manuscript.

Smith, J. (2004). The triple top line. *Quality Progress, 37*(2), 23–31.

Watkins, R., Leigh, D., Foshay, R., and Kaufman, R. (1998). Kirkpatrick plus: Evaluation and continuous improvement with a community focus. *Educational Technology Research and Development, 46*(4), 90–96.

World Commission on Environment and Development, The (1987). *Our common future.* Oxford: Oxford University Press.

CHAPTER FORTY-NINE

Rapid Reflection Throughout the Performance-Improvement Process

Sharon J. Korth, Brenda S. Levya-Gardner

Today the world of business is characterized by rapid growth, technological changes, and increasing global competition. Organizations require quicker and more effective responses to their problems; the effect this has on the role of human performance improvement professionals is substantial. As they manage performance-improvement projects, the demand to increase their own efficiency and speed up their own processes is increasing. While it is important that the performance-improvement professional follow the steps in the human performance technology (HPT) model to help the client meet business objectives, it is also important that the consultant is sensitive to the extreme time pressures on business leaders to deliver results. There have been a number of books written in the past five years addressing the need for speed in the performance-improvement process (Barksdale and Lund, 2001a, 2001b, 2002; Rossett, 1999; Piskurich, 2000). Holton (2003) has suggested that the stature of HPT as a field and our ability to address the strategic needs of organizations is dependent on our ability to move as quickly as organizations need us to move.

Reflection can be described simply as a way of exploring experience to learn new things from it and to use the learning in future planning and action. As a concept and deliberate practice, reflection has been determined to be very important to the long-term success of both profit and nonprofit organizations (Davenport, DeLong, and Beers, 1998; Dotlich and Noel, 1998). Reflection helps human performance improvement professionals become better critical thinkers and contribute to enhanced organizational learning and performance. In 1997, in fact, *Fortune* magazine's article "The Power of Reflection" stated that "successful organizations fail in many different ways, but they share one underlying cause: a failure to reflect" (Hammer and Stanton, 1997, p. 292). Conversely, Edgar Schein (2002) discusses the responses of various organizations to spending time on learning. "When I say to companies that learning requires 'slack' time, I get outraged responses that there is no slack time anymore, but even if there were, the stakeholders would never approve of time being used unproductively. So how do we 'find' time in a world that claims there is no time to be found?" (p. 79).

Herein lays the paradox between reflection and cycle time. Reflection has been shown to increase one's learning from experience. When reflection occurs *during* action, it can help improve on-the-spot, in-process decisions. When reflection occurs *after* action, it can provide valuable perspectives that guide iterative steps and inform future actions. While the benefits of reflective practice are widely acknowledged (Ayas and Zeniuk, 2001; Davenport, DeLong, and Beers, 1998; Dotlich and Noel, 1998), the problem with reflection is that it takes time, a valuable commodity.

How can performance-improvement professionals meet the needs of their clients for quick results, follow the HPT process, and build in time for valuable reflection? The Rapid Reflection Model and process proposed in this chapter will describe ways to harness the advantages while compressing the time required for reflection.

Rapid reflection involves mini-cycles of deliberation that occur *in the moment* or *between* phases of a project. These reflective activities are opportunities to step back from the action, to learn from the experience, and to apply what is learned. Streamlining occurs with up-front planning, consolidation of steps, and efficient use of appropriate tools and techniques. In HPT projects, reflection takes place *within* each phase of the process, performance analysis, cause analysis, intervention selection and design, intervention implementation and change, and evaluation, as well as *between* each phase (Van Tiem, Moseley, and Dessinger, 2004). The rapid reflection process can be employed with any HPT project, big or small, regardless of the business issue, type of intervention, or whether the human performance improvement professional is internal or external to the organization.

Long ago Socrates claimed, "The unexamined life is not worth living." Applying this concept to reflection during the HPT process, perhaps it can be said, "The unexamined HPT process is not worth undertaking." The follow-up might be, "And if the examination takes too much time, the opportunity will be lost."

Typically, reflection is thought of as a deliberate, time-consuming activity that takes people away from the work at hand. The value of the Rapid Reflection Model is that it takes advantage of the benefits of reflection but integrates reflection into the overall HPT process, therefore making efficient use of the important commodity, time. Rapid reflection provides a venue for ongoing, real-time dialogue between the HPT professional and the client, which aids in judicious decision making. Therefore, it helps ensure that the project stays on course and that the right things are done by the right people at the right time, using the least amount of time.

FOUNDATIONS OF REFLECTION

Many authors and practitioners have discussed reflection as part of a process for individual learning, group learning, and organizational learning. Dewey, in his treatises on education, felt that reflection was the "heart of intellectual organization and of the disciplined mind" (1938, p. 110). Schön opened debates in the 1980s about how reflection related to professional practice. He initiated the term *reflection-in-action,* which characterizes real-time thinking on your feet as a tool to develop reflective practitioners (1983, 1987). Seibert and Daudelin (1999) take this one step further and note that reflection-in-action will occur in situations of uncertainty, instability, uniqueness, or value conflict. Schön's "reflection-on-action" mirrors retrospective thinking about a professional or personal situation.

Kolb (1984) builds reflection into his much-discussed and debated experiential learning cycle as part of the second stage of the cycle: concrete experience, reflective observation, abstract conceptualization, and active experimentation. "Immediate concrete experience is the basis for observation and reflection. These observations are assimilated into a theory from which new implications for action can be deduced. These implications or hypotheses then serve as guides in acting to create new experiences" (p. 21). He theorizes that individuals may have learning preferences related to various stages of the cycle but that the cycle can be applied to a variety of situations in which the active part of the learning may be simultaneous with the reflective part. Primarily developed as a tool for educators in helping their students learn from experience, the experiential learning cycle has been applied to a variety of professional, organizational, and managerial situations.

In addition to the emphasis reflection has on individual learning, many authors have also related reflection to group and organizational learning. Argyris and Schön's writings on using experience for single-loop, or adaptive, and double-loop, or generative, learning do not explicitly use the term *reflection,* but their discussions on how to increase double-loop learning in organizations by using deep and intense challenges to assumptions imply that reflection is a necessary requirement for this process to occur (1978). Senge's "learning organization" has professionals continually learning from experiences faced by their organizations, using reflection as one developmental tool to help this process (1990). Marsick and Watkins' "continuous work/learning" model includes reflective practice, both in-action and on-action, but states that observation and reflection are interwoven throughout their model (1992, 1997). Even the Society of Jesus, whose members are called Jesuits, using St. Ignatius Loyola, their founder in the sixteenth century, as a role model, proclaims that their recruits should be *simul in actione contemplativus,* translated to contemplative even in action, to address the busy lifestyle and pressures they face daily (Lowney, 2003).

Boud describes three ways to view reflection: in *anticipation* of events, in the *midst* of action, and *after* events (2001). Loughran describes anticipatory reflection as a "means of accessing or framing a problem situation before it occurs" (1996, p. 20). Langer (2003), discussing his work with inner-city adults, proposes that the work of both Dewey (1991) and Hullfish and Smith (1961) on reflection implies the *future* orientation, what he calls "reflection-to-action." Moore and Pennington's work with physicians describes reflection-in-action as a form of temporary learning and experimentation that can lead to reflection-on-action and more permanent changes in behavior or knowledge (2003).

Seibert and Daudelin's research on active reflection, which occurs *during* a developmental experience, and proactive reflection, which is learning *from* a developmental experience, indicates that the traditional view of debriefing after an event cannot be used as the only manner in which to learn and plan for the future. Their model of managerial reflection relies on organizations creating environments where proactive reflection can occur, as well as the ability for the managers to reflect individually, with peers, and with tutors or coaches (1999). Coaches could be members of other organizational units, trusted peers, superiors, or consultants hired specifically to help with the overall process.

This raises the question, Should reflection be an individual or collaborative process? Seibert and Daudelin (1999) report that managers' learning is maximized when they engage in individual reflection and also interact with other people, and Osterman and Kottkamp (1993) assert that individuals have limitations in analyzing their own behavior, so that "analysis occurring in a collaborative and cooperative environment is likely to lead to greater learning" (p. 25). Research on successful learning organizations implies that the organization cannot be successful until the individual, team, or group initiates the reflection, either in-action or on-action, and then shares, discusses, or analyzes the learning with others and infuses the learning throughout the organization. Regardless of the method or timing, it is clear that individual learning can be better sustained and further developed when others are involved in either a mentoring or consulting fashion.

THE RAPID REFLECTION MODEL

"And the Grinch, with his grinch-feet ice-cold in the snow, stood puzzling and puzzling: 'How could it be so?' . . . And he puzzled three hours, till his puzzler was sore. *Then* the Grinch thought of something he hadn't before" (Dr. Seuss, 1957, p. 46).

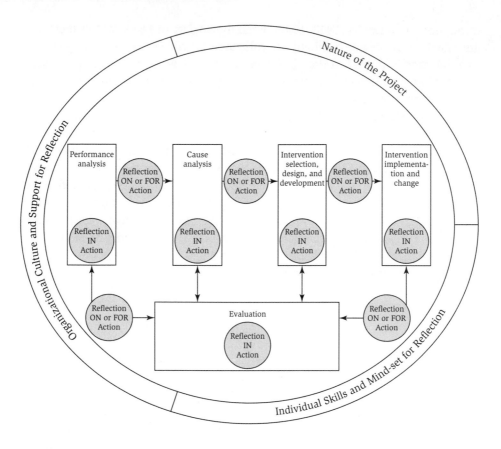

Figure 49.1. Rapid Reflection Model for HPT Projects.

Unlike the Grinch, performance-improvement professionals do not have the luxury of puzzling for three hours until their "puzzlers" are sore. Reflection is a critical component of learning from experience; however, reflection must take place within the time constraints of the fast-paced work environment. The Rapid Reflection Model provides a systemic framework to help performance-improvement professionals, clients, and stakeholders incorporate reflection efficiently throughout the entire HPT process.

In the Rapid Reflection Model for HPT Projects, shown in Figure 49.1, reflection occurs *within and between* each phase of the HPT process, resulting in mini-cycles of reflection. The goals are to learn from ongoing experience by making adjustments in real time, by gathering quick feedback on the value and success of each phase, and by looking forward before proceeding to the next phase. *Within* each phase of the HPT process the performance-improvement professional ensures that the conditions exist so that reflection occurs in a natural setting and becomes a spontaneous, ongoing, real-time, informal activity. In Figure 49.1, this is depicted by the circles, Reflection-IN-Action, embedded in each of the phases. *After* each phase of the HPT process the performance-improvement professional engages in more formal, structured, contemplative reflection on that phase and strategic planning for the next phase. In Figure 49.1, this is illustrated by the circles, Reflection-ON-Action and Reflection-FOR-Action, positioned between each pair of phases. The model also highlights important factors that affect the overall reflective process, shown in the outer rings of Figure 49.1: organizational culture and support for reflection, the nature of the project, and individual skills and mind-set for reflection.

Reflection that occurs within or during each phase of the HPT process is what Schön (1983, 1987) calls reflection-in-action. Other terms to describe it are thinking on your feet, decisions in the heat of the moment, keeping your wits about you, thinking on the fly, just-in-time decision making, contemporaneous reflection, active reflection, on-the-spot experimenting, real-time reflection, informal learning, or reflective thinking. Reflection-in-action occurs informally when there is a surprise, a challenge, a problem, or a value conflict; it involves exploration of underlying issues and assumptions in what Argyris and Schön (1978) call double-loop learning or critical reflection. It occurs when something other than routine action is needed to advance the project. As such, it is "an internal dialogue involving moments of inquiry and interpretation intended to produce increased insights into experience" (Seibert and Daudelin, 1999, p. xvii).

Reflection-in-action can occur *in the moment* or it can occur during brief getaways or respites from the interactions in the HPT process. For example, if a problem surfaces during a meeting with stakeholders in the cause analysis phase, the performance-improvement professional can reflect on the spot and bring new insights to the discussion. If there is a break in the meeting, performance-improvement professionals can use the breaktime as an additional opportunity to reflect on the issue. Finally, if the problem is not resolved by the end of the meeting, the performance-improvement professional can use the travel time immediately after the meeting to reflect back on the situation and consider alternative approaches.

While performance-improvement professionals can engage in reflection as an individual activity, they can also leverage the benefits of reflection-in-action by sharing their thoughts, questions, and alternatives with the client and other stakeholders and by encouraging them to reflect and do the same. There may be opportunities as well, during brief getaway moments, to solicit input from an outsider or coach who might be able to provide a fresh perspective. These coaches, who could be internal staff, managers, or external consultants hired for this process, may also work ahead of time with performance-improvement professionals, clients, and stakeholders to help them develop their reflective skills, or even facilitate individual or collaborative reflection. Therefore, reflection-in-action can be an individual, a collaborative, or a coached activity (see Table 49.1).

Table 49.1. Reflection-in-Action Within the Phases of the HPT Process.

Mode	Description
Individual Reflection	Individual reflects in the moment.
	Individual reflects during brief "getaways" or respites.
Collaborative Reflection	Reflector shares thoughts with others in the moment or after respites.
	Reflector gets an outside perspective about the situation during a respite.
Coached Reflection	Coach works ahead of time with human performance professionals, clients, or stakeholders to develop reflective skills.
	Coach provides a fresh perspective on the situation in the moment or during respites.
	Coach facilitates individual or collaborative reflection.

Engaging in reflection-in-action and folding the insights into the HPT process in real time are efficient ways to maximize the benefits of reflection. In addition, the performance-improvement professional, client, and stakeholders should apply these new perspectives to other projects throughout the organization to leverage and maximize the overall learning.

Between Phases, of the HPT Process: Reflection-on-Action and Reflection-for-Action

Two types of reflection take place between phases of the HPT process. One type is what Schön (1983, 1987) calls reflection-on-action. This retrospective reflection occurs after the fact and is a planned, formal, critical analysis of past events undertaken to learn from them for future action. While reflection-on-action looks back, another type of reflection that transpires between phases is reflection that looks forward, or reflection-for-action. This is also called anticipatory reflection, reflection-before-action, preparatory reflection, reflection-to-action, and reflective planning. These two types of reflection commonly occur as separate processes; however, in the Rapid Reflection Model they are consolidated to save precious time.

This combined approach is similar to the After Action Review (AAR) process used by the Army and other organizations (Darling and Parry, 2001):

> In the AAR practice that the U.S. Army has evolved during the past 19 years, several AAR meetings typically take place *through the life* of the project, rather than *after* the project is done and people are about to disperse. These sessions are generally planned into the project up front and focus on behaviors the participants can implement. A true AAR pays attention to future actions, not just reflection on what has happened to date. . . . The result is reflection-planning, a brief period of action, reflection-planning again, more action, and so on. Reflection and planning are thus closely tied together, interspersed between actions, which shortens and steepens the improvement curve [pp. 64–65].

As with reflection-in-action, the combined reflection-on-action or reflection-for-action process can be individual, collaborative, or coached, as described in Table 49.2. Performance-improvement professionals, clients, and stakeholders can spend time independently assessing past events and planning for future tasks in the upcoming phase in the HPT process. Also, reflection-on-action or reflection-for-action can be a public event, in which subgroups of stakeholders engage in open dialogue about their thoughts and feelings related to past and future project-related actions. In individual reflection, stakeholders can explore their ideas in

Table 49.2. Reflection-on-Action or Reflection-for-Action Between the Phases of the HPT Process.

Mode	Description
Individual Reflection	Reflection takes place in the head of the reflector.
	Reflection is done in written form.
Collaborative Reflection	(Oral) Performance improvement professionals, clients, and stakeholders hold meetings or discussions.
	(Written) Performance-improvement professionals, clients, and stakeholders share written communication.
Coached Reflection	Coach helps human performance professionals, clients, and stakeholders develop reflective skills.
	Coach provides a fresh perspective on the situation.
	Coach facilitates individual or collaborative reflection.

their heads or in writing, whereas in collective reflection, communication can take place orally or in writing, and can be face-to-face or virtual.

A coach, either internal or external, may be a valuable aid to the reflective process. Coaches can provide fresh perspectives on the situation, facilitate individual or collaborative reflection sessions, and help performance-improvement professionals, clients, and stakeholders develop reflective skills. The advantage of having a coach is that people directly involved in the HPT project may be so close to the situation that they need assistance in stepping back, challenging assumptions, probing difficult issues, dealing with interpersonal challenges, and envisioning alternative scenarios.

Perhaps the Grinch, who stood puzzling for three hours, could have benefited from a reflection coach!

Leveraging the learning from these individual, collective, or coached reflective activities within the current HPT project is critical. Insights may inform future steps or lead back to prior steps, thus reinforcing the iterative nature of the HPT process. Furthermore, all stakeholders must share their new knowledge throughout the organization in places where it can be useful, in different projects, and in other client or stakeholder relationships.

Factors Affecting Reflection

Surrounding the overall process for reflection, whether in-action, on-action, and for-action, are three factors that affect reflection and its benefits: individual skills and mind-set for reflection, the nature of the project, and organizational culture and support for reflection.

Individual Skills and Mind-Set for Reflection. Certain individual skills and mind-sets enhance the ability to reflect and learn from experiences. The American Society for Training and Development's 2004 workplace learning and performance competency model includes two personal competencies related to reflection: demonstrating adaptability and modeling personal development (Bernthal, Colteryahn, Davis, Naughton, Rothwell, and Wellins, 2004, p. xxi). Both of these competencies require open-mindedness, flexibility, and tolerance of ambiguity, which are important foundations for effective reflection, as mentioned in general literature on reflection (Loughran, 1996; Robinson and Wick, 1992; Seibert and Daudelin, 1999). Perhaps commitment is even more important. According to Anderson, Knowles, and Gilbourne (2004), "Becoming a reflective practitioner is more than a collection of techniques. Reflective practice involves an all-encompassing attitude to practice that requires the practitioner to commit to professional and personal development" (p. 193).

Raelin (2001, 2002) builds on this attitudinal component, which he calls *being*, and acknowledges communication skills, listening in particular, as basic requirements for reflective practice. He advocates public reflection and the interplay of individual and collective reflective activities.

The implication, therefore, is that reflective practitioners must be flexible and open-minded, and have foundational and advanced communication skills. The integrated use of these skills and mind-set will enhance individual growth and organizational results.

Nature of the Project. All HPT projects are not created equal. Certain preconditions surrounding the project affect the efficiency and effectiveness of the reflective process, including the time frame of the project; prior experience with a similar situation; the complexity of the performance issue; and former working relationships between performance-improvement professional, client, and stakeholders. Reflective practitioners need to be cognizant of these issues and discuss their implications with the client in the up-front planning process.

Organizational Culture and Support for Reflection. Finally, organizational culture and support are critical components for successful reflection. Research with managers in challenging developmental experiences showed that reflection is more likely to appear in an environment that is rich in autonomy, feedback, meaningful interactions with other people, pressure, and opportunity for momentary solitude (Seibert, 1999; Seibert and Daudelin, 1999). Other important conditions are a nurturing environment, characterized by openness and trust (Osterman and Kottkamp, 1993).

Model Summary

In sum, the overall Rapid Reflection Model proposes an integrated approach for reflection, including reflecting in-action, on-action, and for-action; involving the performance-improvement professional, client, and stakeholders; leveraging the resulting learning within the current project and across the organization; addressing the skills and mind-set of the reflectors; considering the nature of the project; and orchestrating organizational conditions and support. While reflective activities are normally thought of as time consuming, much like those of the Grinch, the Rapid Reflection Model emphasizes the time-efficient process of reflection-in-action and consolidates reflection-on-action and reflection-for-action into one step. Additional techniques for enhancing and streamlining the reflective process will be described in the next section on the implementation process.

IMPLEMENTING THE RAPID REFLECTION PROCESS

Guidelines for implementing rapid reflection related to the role of the performance-improvement professional will be described along with issues concerning the ever-important work environment conditions. Helpful tools, techniques, and templates to enhance reflection-in-action, -on-action, and -for-action will also be provided.

Leveraging the Role of the Human Performance Professional

Performance-improvement practitioners serve in a collaborative, consulting role with clients and stakeholders. To leverage that role, Bellman (1998) advocates an open-partner relationship that involves sharing underlying assumptions, risks, values, and expectations. Bellman also provides specific advice to put this into action, such as building in regular meetings with the client to talk about how the work is going and how the partnership contributes to or detracts from that; checking informally with the client to see how things are working today; and telling the client how things are working. These suggestions are reinforced by the Robinsons (Robinson and Robinson, 1995), who suggest regular updates with clients throughout the assessment process and an agreement to contact the client team if unusual situations or problems arise. Schön (1983) takes this one step further and recommends the creation of a reflective contract between the client and consultant. This reflection contract includes addressing issues such as bringing misunderstandings to the surface to reconcile them and anticipating issues, barriers, and resistance (Van Tiem, Moseley, and Dessinger, 2004).

To summarize, performance-improvement professionals can leverage their role by discussing the function of reflection in the overall process during the contracting phase, building reflection steps into the overall project plan, and creating a reflection contract with the client that includes an agreement to share questions and concerns when they occur throughout the project. Furthermore, they can serve as reflection *role models* and *educators* by engaging in private and public reflective practice and by sharing the process and benefits of reflection with others across the organization.

Enhancing Work Environment Conditions to Support Reflection

Reflection does not occur in a vacuum. What work environment conditions support rapid reflection? What is the role of the human performance improvement professional in creating those conditions?

First, the organizational culture must embrace learning from experience and grant employees the autonomy to challenge assumptions and beliefs without fear of reprisal. Second, the organization must provide the time and resources required for people to engage in private reflection, which includes both brief moments of solitude and longer periods of private contemplation, as well as collaborative and coached reflection, which involves dialogue, feedback, and positive pressure to perform. According to Edgar Schein (2002), "Most of us do not smoke anymore, but maybe the 'smoke break' should be brought back as an institution to provide 5 to 10 minutes of reflection time out on the balcony. Instead of bringing our coffee back to the desk, what about taking a coffee break to walk around the block or to sit alone staring at the landscape and reflecting?" (p. 79).

Perhaps even more important, however, is a culture that expects all members to share lessons learned across the organization to other individuals and project teams. This sharing of new insights and best practices characterizes the learning organization characterized by Senge (1990), "where people continually expand their capacity to create the results they truly desire, where new and expansive patterns of thinking are nurtured, where collective aspiration is set free, and where people are continually learning how to learn together" (p. 3).

If these conditions do not exist, the performance-improvement professional has an additional responsibility to inform key stakeholders of their importance in the project and the overall capability of the organization. Moreover, the performance-improvement professional becomes a change agent in creating a learning organization by fostering the development of these important workplace conditions. The tools and methods described in the following section can be used to help create the culture of learning from experience through reflection.

Tools, Techniques, and Templates

Where to begin? What resources and guidelines are available to help performance-improvement professionals engage in rapid reflection throughout the HPT process?

Template of Guiding Questions. "Regardless of the method chosen, posing and answering questions appears to be an important part of any formal reflection process" (Seibert and Daudelin, 1999, p. 25). As such, a template of reflective questions as depicted in Table 49.3 can be a valuable tool for human performance professionals, clients, and stakeholders.

These questions can serve as guides for the reflective processes that occur throughout the HPT project. Furthermore, a worksheet or job aid can be created from the template to have as a handy resource. As reflection becomes more natural and routine, it will become more common and beneficial.

Questions are the core of the reflective process; however, these questions can be explored in different ways. The Framework for Rapid Reflection Questions, shown in Figure 49.2, illustrates three important dimensions: focus, timing, and mode. The *focus* of the reflection can be on various elements important to the success of the overall project, thus the categories of questions in the Template of Guiding Questions in Table 49.3 of progress, process, partnerships, personal and professional development, and application; the *timing* of the reflection can be *within* phases of the HPT process (reflection-in-action), or *between* phases of the HPT process (reflection-on-action and reflection-for-action), as shown in Figure 49.1. The *mode* of reflection can be individual, collaborative, or coached, as described in Tables 49.1 and 49.2. So, for example, in a particular situation the HPT professional might employ questions with a *focus* on partnerships, with the *timing* being between phases of the HPT process and the *mode* being a collaborative reflection with the client.

Table 49.3. Template of Guiding Questions for Rapid Reflection-in-Action, Reflection-on-Action, and Reflection-for-Action in the HPT Process.

Focus	Reflection Questions
Progress (toward project goals)	**In:** How and why are the current actions contributing to the overall goal? **On:** How and why did this HPT phase help or hinder progress toward the overall goal? **For:** What are potential obstacles to achieving the overall goal in the upcoming HPT phases and how can we overcome them?
Process (HPT process, reflection process)	**In:** How well are we following the steps in the HPT process? **On:** How did we use reflection to aid in the overall process? **For:** What can we do to enhance the implementation of the HPT and reflection processes?
Partnerships (performance-improvement professional, client, stakeholders)	**In:** How well are we working together in our interactions? **On:** How effectively did we address the interpersonal issues in the last phase of the process? **For:** What interpersonal challenges do we foresee in the upcoming phases and how can we avoid or minimize them?
Personal and professional development	**In:** What skills am I using effectively and what skills need improvement? **On:** How did I enhance my skills during the last HPT phase? **For:** What assumptions are limiting my personal and professional growth?
Application (within the current project, throughout the organization)	**In:** What am I learning and how can it be applied to this project? **On:** What did we learn from this phase that can be utilized throughout the rest of the project? **For:** How can we leverage what we have learned in this project across other projects and throughout the organization?

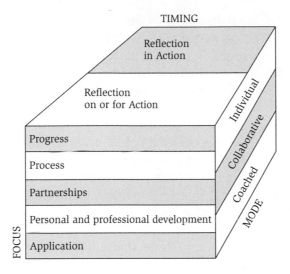

Figure 49.2. The Framework for Rapid Reflection Questions.

Reflective Questions in-Action. Responses to reflection questions in-action will be less formal than responses to reflection questions on-action or for-action. For example, when reflecting in-action and in-the-moment, these questions will likely be explored in one's head. When reflecting in-action during brief respites, it may help to jot down responses or ideas so that they are not lost or forgotten. If the template of guiding questions is available, brief notes could be recorded on the form. If it is not available, other "idea cisterns," a term used by Seibert and Daudelin (1999), can be used, such as jotting ideas down on a scrap of paper, calendar, napkin, or electronic notepad when they first occur; dictating them; or e-mailing them to someone. The point is to record the interpretation before it is lost in the urgency of the moment. In addition to individual reflection, the performance-improvement professional can foster dialogue with the client and stakeholders or consult with a coach about responses to these questions, particularly the logic behind the thought process.

Reflective Questions on-Action and for-Action. When individuals reflect on-action and for-action between the phases in the HPT process, they can either explore the questions in their heads or write their responses. Writing may take the form of a journal, which is a very common tool for capturing reflective thoughts and allowing for deeper processing (English and Gillen, 2001; Gardner and Korth, 1996; Honold, 2000; Moon, 2004). As Boud (2001) states, "the journal is both the place where the events and experiences are recorded and the forum by which they are processed and re-formed" (pp. 10–11).

Collaborative reflection-on-action and reflection-for-action can take both oral and written forms. Oral communication between the performance-improvement professional, client, and stakeholders, in which they share responses to the reflective questions, can be via phone calls, live meetings, or virtual meetings with audio. Written communication can take the form of e-mail, document sharing, text messages, electronic discussion boards, or virtual meetings using text.

Coached reflection-on-action and reflection-for-action involves a facilitator or trusted peer using the questions on the template as a guide to help the performance-improvement professional, client, and stakeholders reflect individually or collectively, as appropriate. The coach can ask probing questions, help people clarify their meanings and intentions, serve as a sounding board for new ideas, provide a fresh perspective, aid in the communication process, and provide overall support for reflection and learning at the individual, group, and organizational levels.

Tips and Techniques for Rapid Reflection. In addition to the suggestions regarding use of the template and the reflection questions, the following tips and techniques can also enhance rapid reflection.

Build Reflection into the Initial Contract and Project Plan with the Client. Discussing reflection up front will foster the reflective mind-set and ensure that expectations are clear. Meetings and milestones should include reflective activities and checkpoints. Peter Block (2000) provides useful guidelines for contracting with clients and for managing the ongoing feedback process. For example, he encourages consultants to be authentic, to clarify their roles and relationships with clients, and to build trust by dealing with difficult issues.

Use Brief Moments Alone as Prime Opportunities for Reflection. One way to demonstrate the mind-set for reflection is to look for *reflective moments* such as while "waiting for a meeting to start (or even during an unproductive meeting), while on hold on the telephone, while waiting in line, and even while walking from a parking space to the office" (Seibert and Daudelin, 1999, p. 207). Furthermore, it helps to realize that reflection can also occur spontaneously and subconsciously, during seemingly mindless activities such as jogging, mowing the lawn, commuting the same route each day, or even while sleeping. Ideas spawned during these moments can often bring a fresh perspective to challenging problems (Daudelin, 1996).

Use Technology When Appropriate. Face-to-face interactions are very important, especially in the beginning stages of the HPT project, when trust is being established and contracts are being created. However, various forms of technology, such as e-mail, groupware, or discussion boards, can help streamline parts of the reflective process. Project-management software can be used to monitor the overall HPT process, with reflection activities and milestones built in.

Consolidate Reflection-on-Action and Reflection-for-Action into One Meeting. Whereas retrospective and anticipatory reflections normally occur as two separate events, combining them into one meeting can save precious time.

Performance-improvement professionals, clients, and stakeholders can use the questions in the template to record and share their individual thoughts in advance of the meeting, which will allow meeting time to be spent on valuable face-to-face dialogue.

Develop Reflective Skills So They Become Natural and Routine. Besides open-mindedness, flexibility, and tolerance of ambiguity, basic communication skills such as listening, speaking, disclosing, testing, and probing are needed for effective and efficient reflection. These skills can be developed through a variety of educational options so that they are not obstacles to the successful execution of the HPT project.

Use Reflection Options Based on the Individuals' Strengths or Preferences. Even when developmental opportunities are employed, individuals have different strengths and preferences. Kolb's (1984) model has been used to identify preferred learning styles and as a foundation for categorizing reflective activities in the areas of reading, writing, doing, and telling (Eyler, Giles, and Schmiede, 1996). For example, some people are more comfortable writing versus speaking, or engaging in individual versus collaborative activities. Allowing individuals to work from their strengths is another way to maximize the reflective part of the HPT process.

Apply Established and Creative Tools to the Reflection Process. Numerous tools have been created to help surface tacit beliefs and assumptions. Argyris' "Ladder of Inference" helps people understand how they may be jumping to incorrect conclusions based on their interpretations of others' actions. Argyris and Schön's "Left Hand/Right Hand Column Exercise" has people reflect back on a situation, writing what they did in one column and what they were really thinking in another column, which often exposes inconsistencies that affect interpersonal relationships (1978). More information about the use of these tools can be found in the *Fifth Discipline Fieldbook* (Senge, Kleiner, Roberts, Ross, and Smith, 1994). These and other problem exploration tools, such as force-field analysis, which presents the positives and negatives of a situation so they are easily compared, and Pareto charting, which helps focus efforts on the problems that offer the greatest potential for improvement (Brassard and Ritter, 1994) may be beneficial to the reflective process, especially if those involved in the HPT process are familiar with these tools from other applications. See *The Memory Jogger II* (Brassard and Ritter, 1994) for explanations on the use of these tools. New and creative tools can be valuable as well. Activities such as story making, storytelling, using metaphors and images, standing back from oneself, employing a critical friend, group journals, self-awareness tools, graphic depiction, mind-mapping, storyboarding, brainstorming, guided imagery, and scenario planning can be employed to aid in the reflective process (Daudelin and Hall, 1997; Eyler, Giles, and Schmiede, 1996; Honold, 2000; Moon, 2004; Martin and Tate, 1997; Brassard and Ritter, 1998). Use of these tools may provide insights or perspectives on the HPT project that would not surface during conventional reflective activities. See the "Resources" section at the end of this chapter for more information about these and other tools.

CHALLENGES AND SUCCESS STRATEGIES FOR RAPID REFLECTION

Much research has been done to determine some of the best ways to ensure that quality reflection processes will occur and that the learning acquired will be fed back into the organization.

Keegan and Turner's 2001 study of European organizational learning practices concluded that databases of lessons learned, after-action and project-end reviews, learning resource centers, and process documentation were some of the ways that project-based firms succeeded in learning from and through projects. Ayas and Zeniuk's 2001 study of project-based learning showcases projects that were successful and discusses the issues involved in building long-term, large-scale learning throughout the organization. They reported that Fokker Aircraft's Jetline Avionics project team outperformed other teams in time, cost, and quality when there was an investment in reflective practices; and long-term success was supported by changes in human resource and career development policies, changes in reward systems, and evaluation of teams. In addition, their study indicated that the Ford Motor Company formed a leadership group to practice using organizational learning tools within a specific behind-schedule project. Use of reflective practices such as journals not only helped the project to exceed its objectives, the practices were continued over the years with other Ford projects. The U.S. Army's After Action Reviews (Darling and Parry, 2001) highlight success strategies in using reflection to improve performance; project and team audits as well as databases of lessons learned have proven to be beneficial in learning from experience. These studies all provide examples of organizational culture and support that can be applied to HPT projects as well.

The use of collaborative or coached reflective techniques is highlighted in many studies as being a key element in successful projects. Anderson, Knowles, and Gilbourne (2004) conducted a study of sport psychologists and determined that a list of reflective questions that were individually addressed and addressed in learning groups with supervisors or mentors led to deeper learning and action. Raelin noted that "public reflection," in the presence of peers, kept managers from excusing or justifying their behavior and led to in-depth behavioral changes (2001). Langer's work with inner-city adults concluded that multiple methods, including mentoring, group meetings, and individual reflection techniques, were instrumental in increasing reflection-for-action (2003). Lyon and Brew's work with medical students who were learning operating techniques used a template to help students monitor their own learning but followed up with reflective facilitators; the medical students who used these reflective practices reported the most learning (2003).

There are, of course, challenges or barriers to the effective use of reflective practices in organizations. Platzer, Blake, and Ashford (2000) studied student nurses whose learning was structured around a reflective practice module and group reflective facilitation. The results indicated that although the practices could be very beneficial to the nurses' learning, barriers to their learning needed to be overcome in order for this to happen. These barriers included previous educational experiences and the organizational culture. In particular, many of the students felt vulnerable to criticism and public scrutiny and were unwilling to engage in group reflection until the group was able to fully mature. This same feeling of vulnerability was reported in a study of Japanese nurses, which indicated that initiators of structured reflective practices need to take into account the cultural background of the reflectors (Stockhausen and Kawashima, 2002). Consistent with any HPT project, measuring the results of reflective practices and managing a multilayered, complex project are continual challenges for performance-improvement professionals.

What may be the most significant conclusion of all the studies is the need to increase the use of *in*-action reflection in all phases of a project. Deferring project reviews until the end of a project results in lost opportunities for learning as well as reduced potential for long-term success. Reflecting between phases of a project increases the likelihood that issues will be addressed or that lessons learned will be applied in a more efficient and effective manner. A critical success strategy is to heed the *rapid* components of the proposed process to avoid the reflection version of analysis-paralysis, or reflection rigor mortis. The Rapid Reflection Model builds reflection into the process, it integrates thought and action, it makes doing and thinking complementary, and it enhances real-time decision making. Some of the challenge may come from mental models about the word itself. It would appear that the term *reflection* produces stereotypes of professionals lounging about, not actively *working*; perhaps the Grinch needs not to *reflect* but to *process* or *examine* information in order to be seen as more industrious and professional.

RAPID REFLECTION EXAMPLE

The following is a hypothetical example of the Rapid Reflection Model in action, created to illustrate key points. Lee, the head of the customer service division, approaches Chris, an internal performance-improvement professional, to collaborate on ways to address recent business challenges related to customer satisfaction, retention, and sales of additional services. During the contracting process, which uses Block's model, Lee and Chris discuss the phases of the HPT process as well as the reflective process that will occur throughout the project. They agree to raise issues as they occur during the phases, to create reflective checkpoints between each phase, and, based upon their communication preferences, to use groupware to share information. They also discuss factors that will affect the overall success of the project, such as organizational culture and support for reflection, the nature of the project, and individual skills and mind-set for reflection, and then how they plan to address them up front.

In the debriefing meeting after the performance analysis phase, Lee, Chris, and a few key stakeholders invite a facilitator to help them use the creative tools of storyboarding and scenario planning to discuss their reflection-on-action and reflection-for-action. The coach structures the activities using the guiding questions in the template related to the five areas: progress, process, partnerships, personal and professional development, and application. As a result, the group makes several application decisions: to use different communication tools because the current ones have not been effective; to use the storyboarding technique as a reflection tool within their respective units on other projects; and to bring a new stakeholder into the project to head off potential obstacles that have been identified.

During a meeting within the cause analysis phase, one of the stakeholders shares new information about business goals, which triggers reflection-in-action for Chris. Chris uses a break in the meeting for further thought and then initiates a discussion between Lee and the stakeholders about the implications of this change on the overall project and the performance analysis phase just completed. Consequently, they decide to revisit one part of that prior phase.

Throughout the project, Chris serves as a model for reflective practice, capturing thoughts in an electronic notepad and sharing them with others when appropriate. At one point in the intervention, implementation, and change phase, Chris receives a curt note from Lee. Concerned about the implications for the project, Chris uses the Ladder of Inference tool to help surface underlying assumptions and beliefs that might be affecting their relationship. This reflection leads to a brief meeting between the two in which the misunderstanding is resolved. Chris, Lee, and the stakeholders continue to practice reflection-in-action, -on-action, and -for-action, folding new learnings into the project and applying them to other projects across the organization. At the end of the project, they conclude that the reflective activities helped their overall communication so that they avoided major derailments or setbacks during the HPT project.

This example of the Rapid Reflection Model highlights key points, such as the importance of up-front planning and attention to the client-consultant relationship. In addition, it demonstrates how reflective practice reinforces the iterative nature of the HPT process and contributes to organizational learning.

OPPORTUNITIES TO INCREASE THE USE
OF THE RAPID REFLECTION MODEL

While the Rapid Reflection Model has been described within the context of individual HPT projects, it is important to keep the broader organizational context in mind. Human performance professionals, clients, and stakeholders should constantly be looking for opportunities to transfer their learning from reflections to other situations throughout the organization. Furthermore, the foundation of the model is universal, so it can be applied to any type of project, not just HPT projects.

The Universal Rapid Reflection Model, shown in Figure 49.3, is built around a generic project framework divided into phases. In any type of project or activity, reflection can occur during, after, and before events. The center circle in the figure

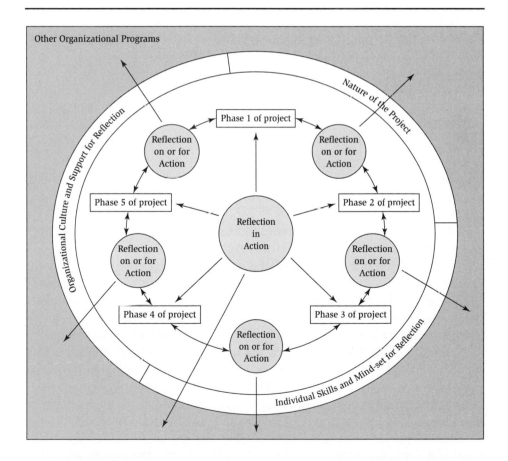

Figure 49.3. The Universal Rapid Reflection Model.

illustrates Reflection-in-Action, which can transpire within any of the phases. The circles positioned between the phases of the project represent Reflection-on-Action or Reflection-for-Action, which take place after each phase and before the next. The Universal Rapid Reflection Model also includes the factors that affect any type of project, shown in the ring surrounding the generic process: organizational culture and support for reflection; the nature of the project; and individual skills and mind-set for reflection. In any project, speeding up the reflection process involves building it into the plan up front, combining steps, using tools and techniques so that they become routine, and streamlining communication among stakeholders. This communication extends beyond individual projects, however, and involves sharing the learning that comes from reflection in one project to other parts of the organization, shown by the arrows pointing outward to other organizational programs. Organizational learning and productivity will be enhanced by distributing information about lessons learned and best practices.

The benefits of reflection have been demonstrated across many organizations. The Rapid Reflection Model leverages those advantages while addressing the critical time challenges in today's fast-paced world. By incorporating rapid reflection into everyday practice, performance-improvement professionals will be able to more effectively manage their projects and help the organization meet its strategic goals and priorities.

RESOURCES

To gain more *how to* tips and techniques, you might want to pay particular attention to the following specific resources.

The Fifth Discipline Fieldbook by Senge, Kleiner, Roberts, Ross, and Smith (1994) has a host of practical exercises to help performance-improvement professionals in their journey discover ways to help them reflect-in-action, -on-action, and -for-action. The authors' descriptions of "Mental Models" and how understanding and reflecting upon assumptions and beliefs can lead to deeper learning and change build upon Argyris, Schön, and Senge's work on organizational learning models. There are practical exercises and examples on reflection and collaborative dialogue in all chapters; particularly relevant are the ones in "Mental Models," "Team Learning," and "Personal Mastery." Another excellent resource with a number of exercises on individual and collaborative learning tools is Honold's *Developing Employees Who Love to Learn* (2000); information on different reflective techniques depending on one's preferred learning style is interesting and relevant to the Rapid Reflection Model.

One tip to using the Rapid Reflection Model effectively is to collaborate with the client and key stakeholders to build critical reflective moments into your HPT projects; the use of a consulting model such as the very practical one proposed by

Block in *Flawless Consulting* (2000) can help you establish the consulting contract in an efficient and effective manner. Be sure to build in those checkpoints for reflection as Lee and Chris did in the hypothetical rapid reflection example.

Journaling is one of the most common tools reflective practitioners use to capture their personal and organizational learning. Much of the research on the most effective journaling techniques has been done by educators to help their in-service students learn from their practicums and internships, but the tool has also been effective in managerial learning as well. O'Brien's *Profit from Experience* (1995) describes a twenty-one-day change process that uses journaling to enhance personal reflection. The chapter "Tell Yourself a Story" has a good, short exercise on focused reflection. Another resource for a variety of journaling examples and *how to* tips is the *Promoting Journal Writing in Adult Education* monograph (English and Gillen, 2001); specific information on journaling for reflection and issues regarding women and journal writing are particularly helpful.

Discussed earlier in this chapter is the U.S. Army's experience with After Action Reviews and their use during a project, after a project is completed, and long after a project is completed. It is well worth reading Darling and Parry's 2001 discussion of the AARs and the original document published by the Army, *A Guide to the Services and the Gateway of the Center for Army Lessons Learned* (U.S. Army TRADOC, 1997). Its systematic approach to team and organizational learning will provide a real-life example that may help you conceptualize your HPT project in a broader and more long-term manner.

Last, but most important, the key resource you have is *you,* your motivation to learn from experience and your desire to increase your own and your organization's capabilities. Rapid reflection is one tool that builds upon this motivation; take the initiative to build it into your HPT projects, learn from the experience, and keep the process in motion. By viewing the Rapid Reflection Model as a process from which to learn, there is only one outcome: success!

References

Anderson, A. G., Knowles, Z., and Gilbourne, D. (2004). Reflective practice for sport psychologists: Concepts, models, practical implications, and thoughts on dissemination. *The Sport Psychologist, 18,* 188–203.

Argyris, C., and Schön, D. A. (1978). *Organizational learning: A theory of action perspective.* Reading, MA: Addison-Wesley.

Ayas, K., and Zeniuk, N. (2001). Project-based learning: Building communities of reflective practitioners. *Management Learning, 32*(1), 61–76.

Barksdale, S., and Lund, T. (2001a). *Rapid evaluation.* Alexandria, VA: American Society for Training and Development.

Barksdale, S., and Lund, T. (2001b). *Rapid needs analysis.* Alexandria, VA: American Society for Training and Development.

Barksdale, S., and Lund, T. (2002). *Rapid strategic planning.* Alexandria, VA: American Society for Training and Development.

Bellman, G. (1998). Partnership phase: Forming partnerships. In D. G. Robinson and J. C. Robinson (Eds.), *Moving from training to performance* (pp. 39–61). San Francisco: Berrett-Koehler.

Bernthal, P. R., Colteryahn, K., Davis, P., Naughton, J., Rothwell, W. J., and Wellins, R. (2004). *ASTD 2004 competency study: Mapping the future: New workplace learning and performance competencies.* Alexandria, VA: American Society for Training and Development.

Block, P. (2000). *Flawless consulting: A guide to getting your expertise used* (2nd ed.). San Francisco: Jossey-Bass.

Boud, D. (2001, Summer). Using journal writing to enhance reflective practice. In L. M. English and M. A. Gillen (Eds.), *Promoting journal writing in adult education* (pp. 9–18). New Directions for Adult and Continuing Education, No. 90. San Francisco: Jossey-Bass.

Brassard, M., and Ritter, D. (1994). *The memory jogger II: A pocket guide of management and planning tools for continuous improvement and effective planning.* Salem, NH: GOAL/QPC.

Brassard, M., and Ritter, D. (1998). *The creativity tools memory jogger: A pocket guide for creative thinking.* Salem, NH: GOAL/QPC.

Darling, M. J., and Parry, C. S. (2001). After-action reviews: Linking reflection and planning in a learning practice. *Reflections, 3*(2), 64–72.

Daudelin, M. W. (1996). Learning from experience through reflection. *Organizational Dynamics, 24*(3), 36–49.

Daudelin, M. W., and Hall, D. T. (1997). Using reflection to leverage learning. *Training and Development, 51*(12), 13–15.

Davenport, T. H., DeLong, D. W., and Beers, M. C. (1998). Successful knowledge management projects, *Sloan Management Review, 39*(2), 43–57.

Dewey, J. (1938). *Experience and education.* New York: Macmillan.

Dewey, J. (1991). *How we think.* New York: D. C. Heath.

Dotlich, D. L., and Noel, J. L. (1998). *Action learning: How the world's top companies are re-creating their leaders and themselves.* San Francisco: Jossey-Bass.

Dr. Seuss. (1957). *How the Grinch stole Christmas.* New York: Random House.

English, L. M., and Gillen, M. A. (Eds.). (2001, Summer). *Promoting journal writing in adult education.* New Directions for Adult and Continuing Education, No. 90. San Francisco: Jossey-Bass.

Eyler, J., Giles, D. E., and Schmiede, A. (1996). *A practitioner's guide to reflection in service learning: Student voices and reflections.* Nashville, TN: Vanderbilt University.

Gardner, B. S., and Korth, S. J. (1996). Using reflection in cooperative learning groups to integrate theory and practice. *Journal of Excellence in College Teaching, 7*(1), 17–30.

Hammer, M., and Stanton, S. A. (1997). The power of reflection. *Fortune, 136*(10), 291–294.

Holton, E. F. (2003). Cycle time: A missing dimension in HRD research and theory. *Human Resource Development Review, 2*(4), 335–336.

Honold, L. (2000). *Developing employees who love to learn: Tools, strategies, and programs for promoting learning at work.* Palo Alto, CA: Davies-Black.

Hullfish, H. G., and Smith, P. G. (1961). *Reflective thinking: The method of education.* New York: Dodd, Mead.

Keegan, A., and Turner, J. R. (2001). Quantity versus quality in project-based learning practices. *Management Learning, 32*(1), 77–98.

Kolb, D. A. (1984). *Experiential learning: Experience as the source of learning and development.* Englewood Cliffs, NJ: Prentice-Hall.

Langer, A. M. (2003). Forms of workplace literacy using reflection-with-action methods: A scheme for inner-city adults. *Reflective Practice, 4*(3), 317–336.

Loughran, J. J. (1996). *Developing reflective practice: Learning about teaching and learning through modeling.* London: Falmer Press.

Lowney, C. (2003). *Heroic leadership: Best practices from an unlikely 450-year-old company that changed the world.* Chicago: Loyola Press.

Lyon, P., and Brew, A. (2003). Reflection on learning in the operating theatre. *Reflective Practice, 4*(1), 53–66.

Marsick, V. J., and Watkins, K. E. (1992). Continuous learning in the workplace. *The Reflective Practitioner, 3*(4), 9–12.

Marsick, V. J., and Watkins, K. E. (1997). Lessons from informal and incidental learning. In J. Burgoyne and M. Reynolds (Eds.), *Management learning: Integrating perspectives in theory and practice* (pp. 295–311). Thousand Oaks, CA: Sage.

Martin, P., and Tate, K. (1997). *The project management memory jogger: A pocket guide for project teams.* Salem, NH: GOAL/QPC.

Moon, J. A. (2004). *A handbook of reflective and experiential learning: Theory and practice.* London: RoutledgeFalmer.

Moore, D., and Pennington, F. (2003). Practice-based learning and improvement. *Journal of Continuing Education in the Health Professions, 23*(2), S73–S80.

O'Brien, M. J. (1995). *Profit from experience: How to make the most of your learning and your life.* Austin, TX: Bard & Stephen.

Osterman, L., and Kottkamp, R. (1993). *Reflective practice for educators.* Newbury, CA: Corwin Press.

Piskurich, G. M. (2000). *Rapid instructional design: Learning ID fast and right.* San Francisco: Jossey-Bass.

Platzer, H., Blake, D., and Ashford, D. (2000). Barriers to learning from reflection: A study of the use of groupwork with post-registration nurses. *Journal of Advanced Nursing, 31*(5), 1001–1008.

Raelin, J. (2001). Public reflection as the basis of learning. *Management Learning, 32*(1), 11–30.

Raelin, J. (2002). "I don't have time to think!" versus the act of reflective practice. *Reflections, 4*(1), 66–79.

Robinson, D. G., and Robinson, J. C. (1995). *Performance consulting: Moving beyond training.* San Francisco: Berrett-Koehler.

Robinson, G. S., and Wick, C. W. (1992). Executive development that makes a difference. *Human Resource Planning, 15*(1), 63–76.

Rossett, A. (1999). *First things fast: A handbook for performance analysis.* San Francisco: Jossey-Bass/Pfeiffer.

Schein, E. H. (2002). Commentary to J. A. Raelin, "I don't have time to think! versus the art of reflective practice." *Reflections, 4*(1), 79.

Schön, D. A. (1983). *The reflective practitioner: How professionals think in action.* New York: Basic Books.

Schön, D. A. (1987). *Educating the reflective practitioner: Toward a new design for teaching and learning in the professions.* San Francisco: Jossey Bass.

Seibert, K. W. (1999, Winter) Reflection-in-action: Tools for cultivating on-the-job learning conditions. *Organizational Dynamics,* 54–65.

Seibert, K. W., and Daudelin, M. W. (1999). *The role of reflection in managerial learning: Theory, research, and practice.* Westport, CT: Quorum.

Senge, P. M. (1990). *The fifth discipline: The art and practice of the learning organization.* New York: Doubleday/Currency.

Senge, P. M., Kleiner, A., Roberts, C., Ross, R. B., and Smith, B. J. (1994). *The fifth discipline fieldbook: Strategies and tools for building a learning organization.* New York: Doubleday/Dell.

Stockhausen, L., and Kawashima, A. (2002). The introduction of reflective practice to Japanese nurses. *Reflective Practice, 3*(1), 117–130.

U.S. Army TRADOC. (1997). *A guide to the services and the gateway of the Center for Army Lessons Learned. CALL guidebook No. 97–13.* Ft. Leavenworth, KS: Author.

Van Tiem, D. M., Moseley, J. L., and Dessinger, J. C. (2004). *Fundamentals of performance technology: A guide to improving people, process, and performance* (2nd ed.). Washington, DC: International Society for Performance Improvement.

CHAPTER FIFTY

Appreciative Inquiry

Unraveling the Mystery of Accentuating the Positive

Darlene M. Van Tiem, Julie Lewis

It is not difficult to construct a series of inferences, each dependent upon its predecessor and each simple in itself. If, after doing so, one simply knocks out all the central inferences and presents one's audience with the starting-point and the conclusion, one may produce a startling, though perhaps a meretricious, effect.
—Sherlock Holmes in "The Adventure of the Dancing Men"
—(Sir Arthur Conan Doyle, 1905)

Appreciative inquiry (AI), not unlike Holmes's methods of deduction, offers a different perspective of viewing and promoting organizational buy-in for purposed and needed organizational change. The instinct over many years when viewing organizations with poor performance has been to focus on desired performance and actual performance, and to *fill* the gaps that exist. By *knocking out* this negative-based instinct, the AI approach begins by viewing the best aspects of the past and present to drive the organization to its future ideal. By focusing on the positive aspects that are inherent within the organization, the conclusion is the creation of a dynamic environment that provides an atmosphere in which input from all levels is valued and affirmed.

As the fictitious detective Sherlock Holmes proclaimed, "The game is afoot." Appreciative inquiry provides performance-improvement specialists with a positive-based tool to bring out the best within organizations. The *game* of AI seeks to involve top-to-bottom and bottom-to-top input and buy-in to promote positive performance outcomes. Through this involvement the outcomes created produce personal drive to make the good within the organization better (Cooperrider and Whitney, 1999). Appreciative inquiry may be viewed as a cultural transformation within an organization that provides a robust tool of which individuals, departments, and ultimately the organization can proudly take ownership.

The purpose of this chapter is to present a new mind-set in viewing performance improvement as a win-win situation for all participants involved. In this chapter, appreciative inquiry is defined, a brief discussion of appreciative inquiry's founders is presented, and the framework of the AI approach is outlined. This chapter compares and contrasts the AI approach with human performance technology (HPT) and traditional performance solutions, and also presents the challenges that have emerged with the use of the AI approach. The intent of this chapter is to present an overview of appreciative inquiry as an alternative tool to use in conjunction with, or as a new approach to, human performance improvement.

APPRECIATIVE INQUIRY DEFINED

Appreciative inquiry has been viewed as a theory of action research that originated in psychology and organizational development practices. The fundamental principles of AI can be traced hundreds of years before Freud and the industrial age. Through the centuries, tenets of various religions have sought to recognize the positive and good within people and situations. AI promotes recognition of positive aspects that provide self-knowledge to encourage individual and organizational well-being and growth.

"Over 2000 years ago Socrates declared that the attainment of self-knowledge is humanity's greatest challenge; Aristotle added that this challenge was about managing our emotional life with intelligence" (Wieand, 2003). Appreciative inquiry considers people as beings that in totality share a wealth of information to be bestowed, disseminated, and learned.

Webster's Collegiate Dictionary, Ninth Edition defines the word *appreciate,* base of the word *appreciative,* and the word *inquiry* as follows:

> **appreciate**—1 a: to grasp the nature, worth, quality or significance of b: to value or admire highly c: to judge with heightened awareness or understanding having or shown appreciation: be fully aware of d: to recognize with gratitude 2: to increase the value

> **inquiry**—1: request for information 2: a systematic investigation often of a matter of interest

The word *appreciative* is based on awareness and increasing value, while *inquiry* describes a means of research and exploration. The AI approach empowers those within the organization with a means of discovery to seek the best within the organization. This discovery encourages the organization to envision itself in the present and the future. Through this vision, the best possible outcomes and practices within the organization are sought and built upon, so that a new and better destiny can unfold.

An analogy that brings insight into AI is the concept that when we are infants, our parents encourage us to talk, walk, and a myriad of other milestones that bring us to be productive adults. The first smiles, coos, and gurgles bring us attention that is positive and invites us to continue to form the initial verbal sequences that begin our vocalization. We are continually encouraged to expand our vocabulary, as parents and other members of our world guide us in our socialization. This eventually leads to two-syllable sequences, short sentences, and fluency with our language until we have learned to communicate within our world.

Though this analogy is simplistic in its description, it provides a framework for the AI approach. The ideal is for us to communicate within our world. Through positive reinforcement, we attain this goal. Positive encouragement of initial milestones from infancy to toddler to adolescence to adulthood builds our self-confidence and provides us with the affirmation to succeed in our endeavors.

Appreciative inquiry does not demean or trivialize aspirations, hopes, experiences, or ideas. Appreciative inquiry seeks to focus on accomplishments and to reinforce these accomplishments by embracing positive aspects, not unlike our parents' encouragement at our first coos as infants.

THE FOUNDERS

The recognized cofounders of appreciative inquiry are David Cooperrider and Suresh Srivastva from Case Reserve Western University in Cleveland, Ohio. As a doctoral student in the early 1980s at Case Western Reserve, Cooperrider sought to "bring to light the inadequacies of the human side to organizations" under his adviser Srivastva (Watkins and Mohr, 2001, p. 15). Through his investigation of this subject at the Cleveland Clinic in Ohio, Cooperrider discovered an organization that focused on its positive aspects and functioned as an active, caring, collaborative team (Watkins and Mohr, 2001). "Influenced by the writings of Schweitzer on the 'reverence of life,'" and the innovative framework within the Cleveland Clinic from the highest levels of the organization down, Cooperrider was inspired (Watkins and Mohr, 2001, pp. 15–16). Srivastva agreed that Cooperrider should further research the Cleveland Clinic and the positive dynamics observed within this organization (Watkins and Mohr, 2001).

With permission from the clinic's chairman, Dr. William Kisner, Cooperrider made his focus a study that sought to uncover what was going right within this organization (Watkins and Mohr, 2001). The term *appreciative inquiry* was born "in an analytic footnote . . . in the feedback report by Cooperrider and Srivastva for the Board of Governors of the Cleveland Clinic" (Watkins and Mohr, 2001, p. 15). This study provided Cooperrider with the research for his seminal dissertation and the foundations of the AI approach (Watkins and Mohr, 2001).

Today Cooperrider is chairman of the SIGMA Program for Global Change and associate professor of organizational behavior at Case Western Reserve University's Weatherhead School of Management. He is also cofounder of the Taos Institute and has served as a consultant and facilitator to numerous organizations including GTE, the United Religions Initiative at the invitation of the Dalai Lama, and Hunter Douglas, to name but a few (Watkins and Mohr, 2001). As a consultant Cooperrider has applied the AI approach to provide "a shift in the field from its deficit-based theory of change to a positive, life-centric force" (Watkins and Mohr, 2001, p. 15).

Srivastva has been a professor of organizational behavior at Case Western Reserve University's Weatherhead School of Management since 1970. He served as department chair from 1970 through 1984 at Case Western. He is also cofounder of the Taos Institute and has been involved in developmental research and consulting with firms including the Texas Heart Institute, Vick Chemical Co., Xerox Corporation, Polaroid, and GE. Srivastva and Cooperrider have continued to publish findings on AI and have worked together to develop AI within organizations (Watkins and Mohr, 2001).

THE APPRECIATIVE INQUIRY APPROACH: THE 4-D CYCLE

Whitney and Bloom acknowledge that no two applications of the AI process will be the same because it "is an approach rather than a single methodology" (2003, p. 23). From an approach-based standpoint, AI *generally* follows the flow of the 4-D Cycle (Figure 50.1). With each AI application, the reasons for using AI and

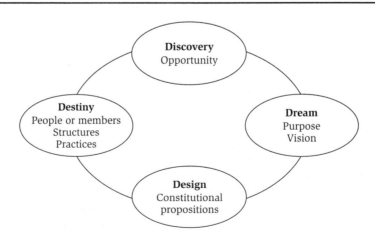

Figure 50.1. Appreciative Inquiry 4-D Process Cycle.

Source: Cooperrider and Whitney, 1999.

Table 50.1. AI and HPT Methods.

Appreciative Inquiry Approach	HPT Methodologies
Change agenda	Performance analysis
Form of engagement	Cause analysis
Inquiry strategy	Intervention selection and development
	Intervention implementation and change
	Evaluation

the way the key steps in the process are carried out may differ (Whitney and Bloom, 2003). From the HPT methodology standpoint, steps are followed in a precise manner and follow set procedures. Table 50.1 outlines the AI approach that normally begins with setting a change agenda, such as purpose and results; establishing an appropriate form of engagement by describing the organizational culture, timeframe, and resources; and defining the inquiry strategy, such as decisions related to the 4-D Cycle in comparison with the HPT methodology.

When using the AI approach, a "4-D" cycle of discovery, dream, design, and destiny (see Figure 50.1) is adapted to fit organizational needs. While undertaking a project with Romania's health care system in 1990, Cooperrider and Fry created the discovery, dream, and destiny model to outline the AI approach. During work with Save the Children later that same year, the initial 3-D Cycle became the 4-D Cycle with the addition of design (Watkins and Mohr, 2001).

The 4-D Cycle first seeks to *discover* positive aspects within the organization. *Dreams* of optimal performance within the organization are expressed. *Designs* to bring these dreams to fruition are created, based on the discoveries of the vocalized dreams. Through continued visualization of these dreams, the dreams are shaped and sustained, providing the *destiny* of the organization's potential. Though stress, tension, the pursuit for power and territory, and other negative-based aspects may be occurring within an organization, AI purposefully frames questions to discover what is working best.

Discovery

The discovery phase begins with dialogue and shaping or reshaping a question or questions within a positive, unconditional framework, which allows individuals, departments, and the organization to envision positive cores. By framing positive questions on effective processes inherent within the organization, the organization itself can emphasize factors that have proven successful and that do not promote fear and resistance.

Within the AI approach, reshaping negative-based discussions to positive-based questions or topics is called *affirmative topic choice* (Whitney and Bloom, 2003).

Ray Metz, the chief of staff at the University of Michigan-Dearborn, provided the following example of this type of question reshaping.

Metz passed through a computer lab and saw a stack of documents on a desk. He questioned "Why are these here?" He was just trying to say "Good morning," but throughout the day, he heard through various sources that there was concern about his question. People were asking if the documents should be where they had been placed and what he had meant by that question. The next day he returned to the computer lab and asked, "Do you have everything at your desk to get the service you want out to the public?" (Metz, personal interview, August 9, 2004).

By simply restating his question in a positive manner, Metz relieved those involved in this event of their fears that they had done something amiss. Through restructuring of a comment or question that seeks to inquire about the true needs of individuals, these individuals in turn feel valued within the organization. From this standpoint, individuals, groups, and the organization can fully appreciate their value by the questions framed and the input that they provide, without fear of repercussion.

Dream

The dream phase promotes the affirmative topic choice. By focusing on the already effective processes inherent within the organization, the organization can build on what has already proven to be successful. "People have more confidence and comfort to journey to the future (the unknown) when they carry forward parts of the past (the known)" (Hammond, 1998, p. 21). Individuals, groups, and the organization can fully appreciate what has worked in the past and apply these successes to the present and the future.

Design

The design phase allows participants to gather to build new systems within the organization. The strengths uncovered during the discovery and dream phases are acted on to build these new systems and processes. Acceptance is inherent because individuals and departments shape their own processes and systems for optimum organizational performance. The design phase allows individuals and departments within the organization to create their own destiny in order to build on the best within the organizational system.

Destiny

The destiny stage cycles the discovery, the dream, and the design phases to sustain the empowerment that AI provides. The 4-D Cycle continues to work back on itself during this phase by emphasizing the successful practices within the organization. A positive vision that acknowledges further research when an answer is not readily available is not viewed as a weakness. This vision seeks to frame positive outcomes, creating optimum performance. Destiny provides an ongoing vision for the future.

In *The Thin Book of Appreciative Inquiry*, Hammond (1998, pp. 20–21) suggests operating from eight assumptions in approaching AI and the 4-D Cycle:

- In every society, organization, or group something works.
- What we focus on becomes our reality.
- Reality is created in the moment, and there are multiple realities.
- The act of asking questions of an organization or group influences the group in some way.
- People have more confidence and comfort to journey to the future, that is, the unknown, when they carry forward parts of the past, that is, the known.
- If we carry parts of the past forward, they should be what is best about the past.
- It is important to value differences.
- The language we use creates our reality.

Hammond's assumptions highlight the core values in seeking the affirmative topic choice and the 4-D Cycle as a whole. By affording people the assurance that what they value is important and acting on the contributions of those involved within the organization, a powerful transformation occurs. Not unlike in the Hawthorne[1] studies of the early twentieth century, workers who felt valued at the Western Electric plant under study continuously increased production regardless of physical, environmental, or psychological conditions set upon them. Cooperrider, Sorensen, Yaeger, and Whitney view the AI approach as "heliotropic . . . just as plants of many varieties exhibit a tendency to grow in the direction of sunlight, symbolized by the Greek god Helios, there is [a corresponding] process going on in all human systems" (2001, p. 32).

Whitney and Bloom agree that different situations call for variations in the way in which AI is approached (2003). The change agenda seeks to discover the purpose for change. Change may come in the form of organizational change, alliance building, participatory planning, global transformation, meeting management, or personal and relational transformation, to name a few applications for AI (Whitney and Bloom, 2003). Form of engagement seeks to discover the best "time-line, resources and other circumstances" that are most appropriate for the change agenda to be undertaken (Whitney and Bloom, 2003, p. 30). The inquiry strategy develops and applies the 4-D Cycle approach based on the change agenda determined, and the form of engagement desired. Appreciative inquiry seeks to include input from many, if not all, facets of the organization. Positive aspects within the organization are focused on and affirmed, creating momentum to continue this process that offers self-fulfillment, acceptance, and growth for and within the organization.

THE DIFFERENCES BETWEEN THE HPT MODEL AND THE APPRECIATIVE INQUIRY APPROACH

Human performance technology seeks to allow a performance-improvement practitioner to "diagnose human behavior and its impact on the organization and vice versa" (Van Tiem, Moseley, and Dessinger, 2000, p. 2). Appreciative inquiry may be viewed as counterintuitive, because it is instinctive to seek and identify negatives in the framework of the HPT model rather than focusing on positive aspects within organizations (Lewis and Van Tiem, 2004). Within the HPT model, the methodology of organizational and environmental analysis (see Table 50.2) seeks to find gaps between desired performance and actual performance (Van Tiem, Moseley, and Dessinger, 2000). Causes for the gaps in performance are verified, the design of the intervention is determined, and implementations of the intervention are undertaken (Van Tiem, Moseley, and Dessinger, 2000). Contracted human performance specialists or persons outside the department under investigation for

Table 50.2. Organizational and Environmental Analyses.

Organizational Analysis	Environmental Analysis
Vision	Organizational environment • Stakeholders and competition
Mission	Work environment • Resources • Tools • Human resources policies
Goals	Work • Work flow • Procedure • Responsibilities • Ergonomics
Strategies	Worker • Knowledge • Skill • Motivation • Expectations • Capacity

Source: Adapted from Van Tiem, Moseley, and Dessinger, 2000, p. 3.

poor performance undertake this process. From the standpoint of the HPT model, to seek the cause of poor performance is to seek negative-based gaps to be remedied through intervention, usually by an outside source.

Appreciative inquiry seeks to use those closest to the source of performance to determine what works best and to focus on the positive aspects of the past and present. Within this framework employees are asked to *discover* and *dream* about what is happening when the organization is at its optimum. By allowing employees to focus on the need to continually strengthen the organization, acceptance of change is more readily agreed to, due to the fact the redesign is coming from the employees themselves.

AI Approach: Affirmative Topic Choice

AI begins by seeking aspects within an organization that are working well. Interviews with an AI facilitator take place individually or in groups with as many participants from varying departments as possible. As individuals are interviewed, they experience validation and support. By telling their stories and being witnessed by other people in an open, accepting environment, they are transformed by the affirmation within this forum. Dialogue of concerns and topics are validated and then actualized into positive-based questions to discover the best within the company. This type of discovery brings about meaningful connections as the validation of experiences of those being interviewed is expressed.

Through this *discovery* affirmative topic choice is determined by selecting the best single topic "that carries the spirit, essence, and intent of the original organizational topics and stories" (Whitney and Bloom, 2003, p. 144). As outlined by Hammond, "The act of asking questions of an organization or a group influences the group in some way" and "What we focus on becomes our reality" (1998, p. 20). Affirmative topic choice lays the foundation for the organization's direction and goals. Through this foundation the *dreams* of the organization are envisioned and the best of what is is then brought to life.

The HPT Model: Performance Analysis and Cause Analysis

Performance analysis seeks to determine factors including but not limited to problems, causes, and gaps between what is and what should be. These problems, causes, and gaps can stem from environmental, physical, and psychological factors as well as disharmony within a department or work group. Management at varying levels throughout the organization discerns what is working and what is not. Through these observations, the human resource department or a consultant is brought in to discover what is going wrong. Table 50.3 compares factors relative to problem solving and their appreciative inquiry counterpart.

Following the HPT model, a consultant begins a cause analysis by conducting interviews with low and high performers—speaking with management concerning performance outcomes and consulting with those who have sought to improve performance to provide input for the creation of interventions. By

Table 50.3. Comparison of Problem Solving and Appreciative Inquiry.

Problem Solving and HPT	Appreciative Inquiry
"Felt need": identifying the problem	Appreciating: valuing the best of "what is"
Cause analysis: environmental or human	Envisioning: "what might be"
Analysis of possible interventions or solutions	Engaging in dialogue: "what should be"
Implementation: action planning	Innovating: "what will be"

Source: Adapted from Barrett and Cooperrider, 1990. Republished in Cooperrider, Sorensen, Yaeger, and Whitney, 2001.

viewing the *negative-based gaps,* the performance-improvement specialist seeks to bridge actual performance and desired performance.

AI Versus the HPT Model

AI and the HPT model both seek to improve performance. "Appreciative Inquiry, in itself, is not an intervention . . . it is an innovative process for organizational assessment and intervention design" (Cooperrider, Sorensen, Yaeger, and Whitney, 2001, p. 380). AI affords the opportunity for all within the organization to participate in job enrichment for themselves and promotion of their own self-image and worth (Cooperrider, Sorensen, Yaeger, and Whitney, 2001).

The HPT model unquestionably has provided performance improvement in numerous organizations over many years. The questions to be asked are, How can performance continually be enhanced? and How best to achieve results without blame or ramifications? The answer to these questions is the positive approach: appreciative inquiry.

AI provides a shift from the negative-based aspects of the HPT model. Appreciative inquiry does not seek best solutions but asks the question, What are the possibilities when performance is at its best? (Whitney and Bloom, 2003). AI seeks these answers not from a few, but from all within the organization. AI focuses on ongoing positive change rather than on *fixing* specific poor-performance issues (Whitney and Bloom, 2003).

TRADITIONAL PERFORMANCE SOLUTIONS

Traditional performance solutions may be viewed as a control system to increase productivity (Chenhall and Smith, 2003). Traditional performance solutions include motivation, incentive, and feedback, which primarily focus on negative-based performance and seek to improve performance by providing intrinsic or extrinsic interventions. At the onset of these traditional performance solutions performance does increase, but in the long term these initiatives fail or require redesign. In a fifteen-year study by Chenhall and Smith, a manufacturing plant offering a gainsharing plan to its employees to decrease resistance to proposed change and to increase production found that after ten years, gainsharing was not enough to sustain increased performance (2003). The last five-year period in this study sought to build trust and teamwork between management and employees with less emphasis on monetary rewards (Chenhall and Smith, 2003). It was discovered that "Trusting relationships provide[d] a basis for employees and management to work in concert toward achieving organizational objectives and to contribute to developing and implementing innovative strategies" (Chenhall and Smith, 2003, p. 120).

AI Versus Motivational Systems

Motivation theory seeks to stimulate individuals psychologically and emotionally to influence optimum performance and to promote belonging within the organization. Motivation can come in the form of pay for performance (individual); pay for knowledge (individual); profit-sharing plans (group); and gainsharing plans (group) (Van Tiem, Moseley, and Dessinger, 2001). The drawback to this concept is that motivations can change over time due to personal, departmental, and organizational shifts.

Within AI, individuals are asked to view positive perspectives in their work environment and *discover, dream, design,* and create their own future and *destiny.* By providing individuals a voice that is heard and acted on, AI perpetuates the emotional and psychological needs of individuals. Appreciative inquiry offers individuals affirmation and self-worth within the organization.

AI Versus Incentive Systems

Incentives are directly linked to a job or task (Van Tiem, Moseley, and Dessinger, 2001). Sales commissions, bonuses, and profit-sharing plans have been used as incentives in many organizations to improve performance and reduce turnover (Van Tiem, Moseley, and Dessinger, 2001). A fundamental challenge of incentives, not unlike the motivations listed previously, is the inability or apathy of individuals to perceive the extrinsic and intrinsic value of the incentives provided.

As stated by Hammond, "What we focus on becomes our reality" (Hammond, 1998, p. 20). Appreciative inquiry offers individuals the incentive to create the environment in which they work. This opportunity provides buy-in to perform at ideal levels and creates opportunities to make the individuals' role within the organization their own, due to the strength of possibilities to excel without fear of repercussion. The Chenhall and Smith study outlined earlier also found that "although financial rewards were important, employees understood that their cooperative efforts produced these rewards" (2003, p. 132). The validation that AI provides challenges individuals to continue on the AI path.

AI Versus Feedback Systems

AI is a continuous feedback system unto itself, focusing on positive aspects within the organization. Traditionally, feedback has taken the form of constructive criticism linked to semi-yearly or yearly employee evaluations, if feedback is provided at all. These evaluations, when provided, are usually related to pay raises. Appreciative inquiry provides a forum for a continuous feedback loop that provides innumerable possibilities and provides hope for the future for those involved. As stated by Cooperrider, Sorensen, Yaeger, and Whitney, "hope can thrive under all conditions . . . hope draws on people's resources . . . in search of even more vital possibilities" (2001, p. 451).

The Selection of AI Versus Traditional Solutions

Interventions such as motivational systems seek to stimulate desired performance. Incentive systems offer rewards for desired performance, while feedback systems predominately provide constructive criticism. These traditional performance solutions do have a place in the AI approach, but they should not be viewed as a means to meet or exceed a desired performance outcome unless they are proposed within a positive framework.

Motivation and incentives are inherent in AI. By providing those within the organization a means to communicate their wants and needs, and meeting these wants and needs, motivation and incentive are both reinforced because the employees perceive their value to and within the organization. From an AI perspective, feedback can be viewed as a positive reinforcement rather than a negative-based correction of performance. Bandura and Locke state, "Feedback framed as gains toward goal attainment sustained high perceived self-efficacy, raised self-set goals, and supported self-satisfaction and group productivity in the management of a simulated organization" (2003, p. 91). AI provides a means to meet the intrinsic and extrinsic needs of those within the organization by providing self-fulfillment that results in positive performance outcomes through inherent motivation, incentive, and feedback within the AI approach. Bandura and Locke have found that "it is not discrepancies that people seek to eliminate but goals and valued outcomes they seek to attain" (2003, p. 91). AI creates the environment in which employees want to succeed.

LEADING AI

Leading AI necessitates positive approaches. As David Cooperrider noted, "It could be argued that all leadership is appreciative leadership. . . . It is the capacity to see the best in the world around us, in our colleagues, and in the groups we are trying to lead. . . . It's the capacity to see with an appreciative eye the true and the good, the better and the possible." (Creelman, 2001). The goal of appreciative leadership is to capture everyone's imagination (Quinn, 2004). Appreciative leadership taps into "the core of the culture, listening to the collective voice of the organization in order to access the essence of the existing system" (Quinn, 2004, p. 126).

Initially, the organization's reaction is often that the leader appears to lose credibility, and few people take the questioning seriously because the leader is viewed as ignoring reality and looking for improbable opportunities. Eventually, some people realize that the new mind-set is practical and applicable. Gradually there is consensus that the positive approach will work. Clearly, appreciative leaders need to anticipate skepticism and enable quick wins so that those involved in positive change understand the value of this positive approach.

AI AT WORK

Ray Metz, chief of staff at the University of Michigan-Dearborn, has been applying AI concepts personally to promote organizational change. His AI mantra is "This is an evolution not a revolution," and he relies heavily on framing questions in a positive manner. Metz states, "The power of questions does shape things. Asking a question changes things and by shaping the question it helps individuals answer their own questions" (Ray Metz, personal interview, August 9, 2004).

Before his appointment at the University of Michigan, Metz was employed at Bucknell University. His function at the university was to bring together the library and computing and telecommunication departments into one organization. The interview with Metz, excerpted here, provides insight into real-world AI applications.

> There had been a director for the library and the computing and telecommunication groups before I was hired. Between these departments, there were one hundred employees. Initially the two organizations assumed that they were unlike and saw problems when they viewed each other's department. I brought in a consultant from the library group and the computing group because they had strong organizational awareness, and we met individually, for the most part, over a two- to three-year period.
>
> One day, one of these individuals asked if I was "familiar with appreciative inquiry, because what I was doing was similar to this approach." I had never heard of appreciative inquiry, but I went out and bought *The Thin Book of Appreciative Inquiry* by Hammond. A leadership group with three organizational directors and me had been formed, and we all became familiar with appreciative inquiry and started incorporating AI aspects into what we were doing.
>
> Asking questions, shaping questions, and focusing on positives are the first things that come to mind. We did not ignore the negatives, but we balanced the positive and the negative. When we did have a problem, I would try to approach

it in a positive way. It was very rewarding over the years working with the positive and having a positive impact. When I left Bucknell University, of the one hundred employees who had gone through the organizational change process, with aspects of appreciative inquiry, seventy-four individuals remained employed [Ray Metz, personal interview, August 9, 2004].

LARGE-SCALE CHANGE

Although many AI projects use conventional consulting models such as Block's contracting, data collection and diagnosis, feedback and the decision to act, results, and accountability with departments of small and middle-size organizations, large-scale change methods known as appreciative inquiry summits have been effective and shortened the inquiry process considerably (Block, 1981). Large groups of people convene in one location, such as a large hotel, and work in large-group sessions in which all participants gather and small-group dialogue sessions take place. Ideas are often recorded on flip-chart pages that are word-processed on computers. Reports are quickly prepared, enabling the entire group to make decisions and move ahead.

In preparation for the summit, interviews, data synthesis, and sense-making meetings are conducted. An interview guide is prepared to foster consistency and to structure the interaction. In many cases, hundreds of interviews of employees and customers are conducted. Data synthesis and sense-making can be completed in a few sessions. A document is prepared and distributed to all involved in the large-scale summit. In addition, a participant's workbook is provided, covering such topics as (1) the summit purpose, objectives, and agenda; (2) appreciative inquiry; (3) the AI 4-D Cycle; (4) an appreciative interview summary; (5) mapping the positive core; (6) creating a shared dream; (7) writing provocative propositions; and 8) forming innovative teams: from inquiry to action (Ludema, Whitney, Mohr, and Griffin, 2003).

Large-scale change has been successful in many corporations and organizations. Kathie Dannemiller developed processes and concepts based on the one-head and one-heart holistic principle, open forum configuration, and *max-mix*, or the maximum mix of people to represent the microcosm of the entire organization. Dannemiller Tyson Associates conducted numerous large-scale events for Ford Motor Company that proved successful (Dannemiller Tyson Associates, 2000a, 2000b). Margaret Wheatley, in the preface for *Whole-Scale Change: Unleashing the Magic in Organizations,* stated, "When the entire organization or community is engaged in the work of planning its own future, or dealing with a difficult and meaningful issue, wondrous possibilities emerge" (Dannemiller Tyson Associates, 2000a, p. xx). Using the term *magic* is appropriate.

Harrison Owen, founder of Open Space Technology, explains that "diverse people facing complex issues, for whom conflict is a present reality or a real possibility, nevertheless manage to achieve quite uncommon results quickly and with a sense of pride" (Owen, 1997a, p. 20). Open Space Technology and large-scale change summits are able to unite enormously diverse groups, including differences in education, ethnicity, economics, politics, culture, and social position (Owen, 1997b). Clearly, there are distinct advantages to using an open, large-scale summit approach.

CHALLENGES OF AI

Not unlike other human performance improvement approaches, challenges exist in implementing AI. The challenges most cited include control of power within the organization, resistance, the necessity to learn from both the negative and the positive, the evaluation of results and hard data, and the need for trained facilitators in implementing the AI approach. The control of power and resistance has been an inherent issue in organizations for many years (Reed, Pearson, Douglas, Swinburne, and Wilding, 2002). Resistance usually surfaces with any change effort. As stated earlier, AI can seem counterintuitive as a means to increase performance. Some organizations rely on both the negative and the positive to learn from their experience. Whitney and Bloom acknowledge that no two applications of the AI approach will be the same, which provides challenges in evaluating and hard-data gathering (2003). A further challenge is the need for a facilitator who is familiar with reshaping a negative-based question into affirmative topic choice.

Hierarchies are developed within organizations, and within these hierarchies set rules of control are established. "Hierarchies all too often exclude those most significantly impacted" (Whitney and Bloom, 2003, p. 4). In the article *Going Home from the Hospital: An Appreciative Inquiry Story* by Reed, Pearson, Douglas, Swinburne, and Wilding (2002), the challenge of *power* in a patient discharge study found that senior management caused group members to feel powerless to promote needed change. "Lack of support from senior management was interpreted as a lack of the value placed on the appreciative inquiry approach that had been implemented" (p. 45). From an AI standpoint, the culture should not be hierarchical, but instead one of discovery and cooperation (Whitney and Bloom, 2003).

Resistance results from any type of change. Resistance can occur at any level of the organization and prove detrimental to the change effort. The appreciative inquiry approach differs from traditional approaches because it provides involvement and input from all within the organization. "If we carry parts of the past forward, they should be what is best about the past" (Hammond, 1998, pp. 20–21). By carrying parts of the past forward, individuals find comfort within the change effort. Due to the factors listed earlier, AI removes and reduces underlying causes of resistance to change as individuals move through the 4-D Cycle (Cooperrider, Sorensen, Yaeger, and Whitney, 2001).

Some organizations feel that it is necessary to learn from both the negative and the positive, and that both must be examined to provide the best outcomes for the organization (Murphy, 2002). In the article *No More Catch Phrases Please*, Chief Cryptologic Technician Interpretive J. M. Murphy, United States Navy, challenges the AI focus on viewing and learning from only the positive aspects of an organization. "We do our sailors a disservice if we overlook their deficiencies . . . missteps we make during our careers are very much part of our learning process" (Murphy, 2002, p. 32). Appreciative inquiry does not attempt to dismiss the negative, but to "validate them as lived experience, and . . . to reframe them" (Whitney and Bloom, 2003, p. 16).

As with any process, challenges have occurred during the implementation of AI, and it has been stated that further study of these challenges has not been fully interpreted or described (Michael Quinn Patton, cited in Preskill and Coghlan, 2003). Questions include hard data of the effects AI has on an organization's bottom line, evaluation of AI's use, and the need for skilled facilitators. Rogers and Fraser argue that "Overenthusiastic promotion of any new approach to evaluation risks oversimplifying the process involved and the demands it makes on those to seek to use it" (2003, p. 75). Each organization has unique features and challenges that require skilled implementation and evaluation to drive AI effectively (Michael Quinn Patton, cited in Preskill and Coghlan, 2003).

Despite the recognized challenges, as just outlined, AI is gaining attention in training and performance literature. In the publication *Using Appreciative Inquiry in Evaluation* (Preskill and Coghlan, 2003), case studies are presented and evaluated that address these challenges, as well as evidence that AI can and does work. As with any new tool, appreciative inquiry provides a new scope of viewing and promoting performance improvement.

CONCLUSION

Some consider AI as a *Pollyanna* approach that seeks to fix the ills of the world, or at least within the organization. AI does not guarantee a quick fix, but provides an alternative or an added tool to past performance approaches. This chapter has sought to unravel the *mystery* of appreciating the positive. The root cause of peak performance is investigated, and the implications found through this investigation are built on to make the best within the organization better. When individuals and groups are afforded the opportunity at the start of a change effort to provide their opinions, which are acted on, these individuals and groups relish that their input was given credence. The outcome AI provides is an environment that is dynamic and seeks the positive in a world that all too often focuses on the negative.

Note

1. The Hawthorne Studies were conducted in the late 1920s and early 1930s by Harvard Business School professor Elton Mayo, at the Western Electric Hawthorne Works in Chicago, Illinois. These studies sought to determine the effects on productivity as variables such as hours worked, break periods, lighting, and temperature were increased and decreased. The individuals under study increased productivity regardless of the variables that were put into place. It was determined that this productivity increase was due in large part to the feeling of belonging and teamwork that individuals felt in being a part of these studies (Shivers, 1998).

References

Bandura, A., and Locke, A. E. (2003). Negative self-efficacy and goal effects revisited. *Journal of Applied Psychology, 88*(1), 87–112.

Barrett, F. J., and Cooperrider, D. L. (1990). Generative metaphor intervention: A new approach to intergroup conflict. *Journal of Applied Behavioral Science, 26*(2), 219–240.

Block, P. (1981). *Flawless consulting: A guide to getting your expertise used.* Austin, TX: Learning Concepts.

Chenhall, R. H., and Smith, K., L. (2003). Performance measurement and reward systems, trust and strategic change. *Journal of Management and Accounting Research, 15,* 117–143.

Cooperrider, D. L., and Whitney, D. (1999). Appreciative inquiry. San Francisco: Berrett-Koehler.

Cooperrider, D. L., Sorensen, P. F., Yaeger, T. F., and Whitney, D. (Eds.). (2001). *Appreciative inquiry: An emerging direction for organization development.* Champaign, IL: Stipes.

Creelman, D. (2001, July 9) Interview: David Cooperrider and appreciative inquiry. HR.com. Retrieved October 10, 2004, from www.hr.com.

Dannemiller Tyson Associates. (2000a). *Whole-scale change: Unleashing the magic in organizations.* San Francisco: Berrett-Koehler.

Dannemiller Tyson Associates. (2000b). *Whole-scale change toolkit.* San Francisco: Berrett-Koehler.

Hammond, S. A. (1998). *The thin book of appreciative inquiry* (2nd ed.). Bend, OR: Thin Book Publishing.

Lewis, J., and Van Tiem, D. (2004). Appreciative inquiry: A view of a glass half full. *Performance Improvement, 43*(8), 19–24.

Ludema, J. D., Whitney, D., Mohr, B. J., and Griffin, T. J. (2003). *The appreciative inquiry summit: A practitioner's guide for leading large-group change.* San Francisco: Berrett-Koehler.

Murphy, J. M. (2002, June). No more catch phrases please. *Proceedings,* 30–31.

Owen, H. (1997a). *Expanding our now: The story of open space technology.* San Francisco: Berrett-Koehler.

Owen, H. (1997b). *Open space technology: A user's guide* (2nd ed.). San Francisco: Berrett-Koehler.

Preskill, H., and Coghlan, A. T. (Eds.). (2003, Winter). Using appreciative inquiry in evaluation. *New Directions for Evaluation: A Publication of the American Evaluation Association.* No. 100. San Francisco: Jossey-Bass.

Quinn, R. E. (2004). *Building the bridge as you walk on it: A guide for leading change.* San Francisco: Jossey-Bass.

Reed, J., Pearson, P., Douglas, B., Swinburne, S., and Wilding, H. (2002, January). Going home from the hospital: An appreciative inquiry story. *Health and Science Care in the Community, 10*(1), 36–45.

Rogers, P. J., and Fraser, D. (2003). Appreciating appreciative inquiry. In H. Preskill and A. T. Coghlan (Eds.), *New directions for evaluation: A publication of the American Evaluation Association.* No. 100. San Francisco: Jossey-Bass.

Shivers, H. C. (1998, March). Halos, horns and Hawthorne: Potential flaws in the evaluation process. *Professional Safety, 43*(3), 38–41.

Van Tiem, D., Moseley, J. L., and Dessinger, J. C. (2000). *Fundamentals of performance improvement: A guide to improving people, process, and performance.* Washington, DC: International Society for Performance Improvement.

Van Tiem, D., Moseley, J. L., and Dessinger, J. C. (2001). *Performance improvement interventions: Enhancing people, processes and organizations through performance technology.* Washington, DC: International Society for Performance Improvement.

Watkins, J., and Mohr, B. (2001). *Appreciative inquiry: Change at the speed of imagination.* San Francisco: Jossey-Bass.

Whitney, D., and Bloom, T. A. (2003). *The power of appreciative inquiry: A practical guide to positive change.* San Francisco: Berrett-Koehler.

Wieand, P. (2003, July–August). Drucker's challenge: Communication and the emotional glass ceiling. *Ivey Business Journal, 67*(6), n.p.

CHAPTER FIFTY-ONE

Comprehensive Performance Evaluation

Using Logic Models to Develop a Theory-Based Approach for Evaluation of Human Performance Technology Interventions

Barbara A. Bichelmeyer, Brian S. Horvitz

The quintessential goal of every human performance technologist, as well as every educator, professional development specialist, corporate trainer, human resources professional, middle-level manager, corporate executive, psychologist, coach, and self-help guru, is to create better human performance.

This statement is not an exaggeration: the fundamental purpose of each of these professions is to help others do things better than they have previously been able to. Managers, by definition, are those who have the responsibility for ensuring that employees are able to successfully perform their work. Teachers and trainers want their students to be more capable when they leave the classroom than they were when they came into it. The very reason that coaches coach is to help the athlete or the musician or the actor perform better within their arenas of expertise.

Billions, probably trillions, of dollars are spent annually for education, coaching, training, management, and performance support. These vast sums of money are spent with the overarching goal of helping individuals achieve better human performance in all manner of contexts: in their professional work, on tests at school, in recreational activities that interest them, and at home in personal relationships.

The authors would like to thank Arlen Gullickson, director of The Evaluation Center at Western Michigan University, and Goldie MacDonald, associate director of the National Center for Chronic Disease Prevention and Health Promotion, for their contributions to our understanding of the literature of program evaluation.

We who have the title of "human performance technologist" bring to our work the assumption that human performance is "lawful." By using the term *lawful,* we mean to convey the idea that human performance is somewhat predictable; that performance can to some degree be managed or engineered through the application of human performance theory to the practical problems of human performance in day-to-day activities. Yet despite the fact that human performance improvement is a multibillion dollar enterprise, and despite the fact that human performance technologists have documented numerous theories that predict human performance, the literature on human performance improvement does not provide a comprehensive evaluation methodology that is grounded in this overarching theory about the lawfulness of human performance that is the basic assumption of our field. The fact that the field of human performance technology is primarily concerned with improving human performance and yet does not have a coherent and consistent evaluation methodology that reflects our basic assumptions is a critical gap that must be addressed.

Cicerone, Sassaman, and Swinney (2005) tell us that "the success of efforts to enhance performance is determined by the theory that guides the analysis of the performance" (p. 10). The field of human performance technology is in need of an evaluation framework that will allow theorists and practitioners to consistently and coherently collect data on the underlying variables that contribute to successful human performance within its many contexts. This chapter seeks to address this need.

The premise of this chapter is that comprehensive performance evaluation (CPE), which is systemic and systematic, may serve well as an activity that brings theorists and practitioners together in a shared commitment (1) to describe human performance improvement interventions, (2) to describe the theories that support these interventions, (3) to evaluate the success of these interventions, and (4) to critically tie theory, practice, and research together in a way that will advance knowledge of the field.

In the remainder of this chapter, we will provide a brief overview of the historical development and variety of theories in the field regarding the lawfulness of human performance, introduce the evaluation models that are currently most commonly referenced in the human performance technology (HPT) literature, and note the gap between the theories of lawfulness and the structure of our evaluation models. We will then draw from the literature of program evaluation documented by the American Evaluation Association to introduce logic modeling as a theory-based approach that may be used to design and evaluate human performance improvement initiatives in a manner that is consistent with our field's assumptions about the lawfulness of human performance. Finally, we will provide an example of how CPE has been used as a framework for the understanding of actual human performance improvement interventions. We will draw conclusions based on the examples about the strengths and limitations of the model and discuss opportunities for its further development.

THE LAWFULNESS OF HUMAN PERFORMANCE

In 1951, Kurt Lewin wrote, "there is nothing so practical as a good theory" (p. 169). One of the theories for which Lewin is most famous is his "field theory," which was one of the first expressions of the lawfulness of human performance, and a precursor to later "performance equations" in the literature of human performance technology. Lewin's field theory proposed that human behavior (B) is a function of both a person's activity (p) and the environment (e) within which a person acts: [B(p,e)].

In 1978, Tom Gilbert wrote one of the seminal works of HPT literature, *Human Competence: Engineering Worthy Performance*. In that work, Gilbert extended Lewin's performance equation to include an additional variable, arguing that the "worth" of human activity (W) is a function of human accomplishments (A) that are derived from behavior (b), environment (e), and management (m): [W = A(b + e + m)].

Joe Harless (1970), another pioneer in the field of HPT, proposed his own version of the performance equation, arguing that human performance (P) is a function of a person's inherent capabilities (ic), skills and knowledge {s,k}, motivation and incentives {m,i}, and environmental supports (e): [P = ic + {s,k} + {m,i} + e].

Numerous other variations on the performance equation have followed these foundational theories. Two of the most prominently cited are from Mager and Pipe (1997) and Rossett (1992). Mager and Pipe proposed that human performance (P) is the result of a combination of resources (r), consequences (c), skill and knowledge {s,k}, and the nature of a task (t): [P = r + c + {s,k} + t]. In a streamlined version of Harless's model, Rossett proposed that (P) is simply a function of environment (e), skills and knowledge {s,k}, and motivation and incentives {m,i}: [P = e + {s,k} + {m,i}].

The most current and comprehensive performance equation comes from Wile (1996), who synthesized five of the previous theoretical expressions of the performance equation and concluded that performance (P) is a function of variables internal (I) to a performer such as skills/knowledge {s,k} and inherent ability (ia), as well as variables external to the performer including environmental factors (E) such as organization systems (os) and incentives (i), as well as tangible resources (R) such as cognitive supports (cs), tools (t), and the physical environment (pe) within which performance occurs: [P = I({s,k} + ia) + E(os + i) + R(cs + t + pe)].

So what are the practitioners whose goal is to improve human performance to make of this plethora of performance equations? How are they supposed to make an informed decision about which equation is most appropriate to apply to their particular context? How might their experiences in using a particular equation be captured, and how can the knowledge gained from their experiences in any rigorous way add to the knowledge base of the field?

The strategy proposed in this chapter is to bring theory and practice together in a way that adds to the knowledge base of the field by introducing a comprehensive performance evaluation model that is based on a human performance equation. Using this model, practitioners can describe and evaluate their performance interventions based on the variables in their performance equation, while theorists and researchers can study evaluation reports from those interventions to determine how the variables of the performance equation reflect and work in the real world. Using this approach, practitioners, theorists, and researchers may be able to work together to answer questions such as, Which variables are most commonly used by practitioners? Which variables are least likely to be addressed in various contexts? Which variables provide the greatest return on investment? Which combinations of variables are most powerful for affecting human performance? and, most important, Which of the many variations of the performance equation is the most efficient and effective to facilitate human performance?

Using the CPE model may give us a means by which we are able to view each human performance technology intervention and each evaluation report as an opportunity to study the application of one of the foundational theories of the field, with the result that we can more systematically advance our knowledge base with each project we complete.

CURRENT EVALUATION MODELS IN HPT LITERATURE

The most commonly cited approaches to evaluation in the HPT literature are those based on the examination of interventions at a series of levels, progressing from a focus on individual performers and beyond to the larger organization.

The most prominent and influential of the "levels" approaches to evaluation is Donald Kirkpatrick's (1998) model, commonly known as "The Four Levels of Evaluation."

Kirkpatrick's approach to evaluation has as its main focus the evaluation of training programs, and the subsequent impact of training on the performance of the individual and the larger organization. Kirkpatrick's model directs the evaluator to focus on four levels described as (1) reaction, (2) learning, (3) behavior, and (4) results. At the reaction level the evaluator measures the satisfaction of the trainees with the training intervention. At the learning level the evaluator measures the extent to which trainees experienced a change in knowledge, skill, and attitude as a result of a training intervention. At the behavior level the evaluator measures the extent to which the change in behavior of trainees can be attributed to their participation in the training intervention. This is also commonly referred to as "transfer" of learning to the job. At the results level the evaluator measures the extent to which the learning among trainees that is attributed to the training intervention results in value added to the organization. This may include increased production, improved quality, decreased costs, reduction of accidents, increased sales, and higher profits.

According to Kirkpatrick (1998), the four levels represent a sequence in which each level has an impact on the next one, and each subsequent level is more important than the previous one. Kirkpatrick also suggests that each subsequent level is more difficult and time-consuming to measure, but the higher levels also provide increasingly valuable information about the training program and the organization.

Kirkpatrick is not the only prominent name in the HPT literature to advocate a level-based approach to evaluation. Kauffman and Keller (1994) support a similar approach, which retains Kirkpatrick's four levels and adds a fifth level called "societal outcomes" that aims to look beyond the organization to determine how much a program has affected the surrounding environment and society.

Jack Phillips (1997) adds his own fifth level, called "return on investment." At this level, the evaluator examines whether or not the business impact achieved was worth the costs of the program. Robinson and Robinson's (1989) approach to evaluation also retains four levels, though the authors distinguish between two systems within an evaluation. The first two levels, reaction and learning, are part of the evaluation system that takes place concurrently with or immediately after a training intervention, while the next two levels, behavior and results, constitute the tracking system that takes place during a period of time after the training. A more recent iteration of Kirkpatrick's model comes from Van Tiem, Moseley, and Dessinger (2000), who distinguish between formative, summative, confirmative, and meta evaluations, though their approach to summative evaluation essentially reflects Kirkpatrick's four levels with no changes.

Strengths of Level-Based Evaluation

It is no accident that these level-based approaches to evaluation are the most well-recognized and widely used among HPT practitioners, for they share some significant strengths.

When used appropriately, the level-based approaches can clearly guide the evaluator toward the collection and analysis of data that will inform judgments regarding the overall effectiveness and worth of a performance intervention. At each of the levels built into these approaches, it is possible to make some determination regarding the effectiveness of an intervention, whether one is most concerned with satisfaction, learning, transfer, or organizational impact. When such summative judgments are the goal of the evaluator, these approaches may be suitably effective.

These level-based approaches are not difficult to understand or to explain to those without a background in HPT, such as clients, managers, and other stakeholders. An HPT professional can easily summarize the four levels and explain to someone unfamiliar with the approach about the progression from one level to the next. Thus, these approaches have a significant and powerful attribute in that they are easy to communicate to stakeholders of the human performance intervention and therefore facilitate agreement between the evaluator and other stakeholders and may help to engender stakeholder support for the evaluation.

While these level-based approaches guide the evaluator through a logical series of stages in data collection and analysis, they do not restrict the evaluator to any specific set of methods for performing these tasks. This provides evaluators with the flexibility and opportunity to select whatever type and mixture of data collection and analysis methods they prefer, using those that seem most appropriate for their particular situations, and with which they are most comfortable.

Limitations of Level-Based Evaluation

While the level-based approaches to evaluation have significant and attractive characteristics, these approaches also have limitations that can adversely affect the quality of the evaluation and, even more important, the human performance intervention.

As stated, these approaches are well-suited for helping evaluators make summative judgments of the overall effectiveness and worth of a performance intervention. What they are not well-suited for is helping evaluators gain insights regarding what aspects of programs are or are not working well, and, similarly, they do not help to inform decisions about how best to improve an intervention. These level-based approaches to evaluation focus the evaluator on the intervention as a whole, not on its parts.

Related to the previous point, the level-based approaches focus primarily on intervention outcomes. This can have the effect of reducing an intervention in the evaluator's mind to only a set of outcomes and not to a complex set of programmatic elements that work and interact together to cause those outcomes. In so doing, an intervention can be oversimplified to the point at which the findings of an evaluation reflect more of an abstraction of the intervention that, while possibly interesting, risks providing little information that provides actual useful insights about the intervention.

Another potential weakness of these level-based approaches is that they guide the evaluator to examine an intervention as it actually happened by answering questions such as, Were performers satisfied with the program? What did employees learn from the training? What are performers doing on the job? and so on. While answers to these types of questions and findings from these types of evaluations can provide some insights about the intervention as it happened, the evaluator gains no insight into whether the intervention was actually implemented as intended and, if not, what effect this may have had on the success of the intervention. How often does any intervention or program get implemented without a hitch, exactly as it was planned? Such deviations from a plan ought to be accounted for in an evaluation so that a determination can be made as to whether problems occurred in the design or in the implementation or, most likely, in some combination of the two.

One more area for improvement on these level-based approaches to evaluation concerns a significant assumption that they make about the analysis that went into an intervention's design. A human performance intervention may have been designed to perfectly match the objectives of the intervention as agreed upon by stakeholders, and the agreed upon design may have been developed and implemented perfectly as well. But what if all of the work of designing, developing, and implementing the intervention was based on a flawed decision regarding which performance problems existed in the particular situation and which changes needed to occur? An evaluation ought to address such a possibility, especially when the person or people who designed an intervention were different from those who made the decision to enact it, and the people who implemented the intervention were different from the people who designed and developed it.

Finally, the greatest limitation of level-based evaluation models, as pointed out in previous sections of this chapter, is that they provide no clear, obvious, or direct links to the overarching theory of the lawfulness of human performance, which is the basic assumption of our field. This means that these evaluation models do not draw upon the unique assumptions that make HPT a distinct field. Since the results of these evaluations are not theory-based, the findings from these types of evaluations do little to advance the knowledge base of the field.

CURRENT MODELS FROM PROGRAM EVALUATION

For guidance regarding how to address the limitations of these prominent approaches to evaluation used by HPT practitioners, the authors turned to the field of program evaluation. Program evaluation, as a contemporary field, has been active since at least the 1960s (Worthen, Sanders, and Fitzpatrick, 1997). The field comprises scholars and practitioners primarily interested in developing improved methods for evaluating social programs. Historically, program evaluations have been used to determine the worth or merit of evaluation objects such as military initiatives, health promotion programs, social programs, instructional programs, and government interventions.

Theory-Based Evaluation

As in HPT, the most prevalent approaches to program evaluation have involved collecting and analyzing data that speak to how well a program's objectives were met. In response to the limitations of such approaches and the perceived need to move beyond evaluations that are simply judgments of the overall worth and effectiveness of a program, and to develop evaluations that aid in program improvement, scholars and practitioners have proposed and advocated a theory-based approach to evaluation. Theory-based evaluation has been discussed in the program evaluation literature for at least thirty years (Weiss, 1972; Fitz-Gibbon and Morris, 1996; Wholey, 1979; Chen and Rossi, 1980; Chen, 1990). Weiss (1997) summarizes this approach as follows:

> The root idea behind TBE (theory-based evaluation) is that the beliefs and assumptions underlying an intervention can be expressed in terms of a phased sequence of causes and effects (i.e. a program theory). . . . The evaluation is expected to collect data to see how well each step of the sequence is in fact borne out. This approach to evaluation offers a way in which evaluation can tell not only how much change has occurred but also, if the sequence of steps appears as expected, how the change occurred. If the posited sequence breaks down along the way, the evaluation can tell at what point the breakdown occurred [pp. 501–502].

Put another way, in theory-based evaluation, the evaluator develops a model, which will be explained in more detail further on, of how a program is supposed to work. The model identifies and explains the program activities, what changes these activities are supposed to effect in the program's participants, and how these changes lead to the program's intended outcomes. This program model can then guide the evaluator to strategically collect and analyze targeted data that can shed light on the various mechanisms and components that comprise a program. In doing this, the evaluator can gain insights on what aspects of a program are or are not working, which can then inform decisions not only about how well a program is working overall, but also on how best to improve it.

Logic Modeling for Program Evaluation

As discussed previously, a theory-based approach to evaluation requires the development of a program model, or, for HPT practitioners, an intervention model. What exactly does this involve? Several advocates of this evaluation approach suggest the use of logic models (Weiss, 1997; Rogers, 2000; Chen, 1990; Yampolskaya, Nesman, Hernandez, and Koch, 2004).

Figure 51.1. A Generic Logic Model for Program Evaluation.

A program logic model links short-term and long-term outcomes with the program's activities and processes as well as the theoretical assumptions that ground the program (Kellogg Foundation, 2001). If designed well, with the input of key personnel related to a program or intervention, a logic model can help the evaluator determine which data need to be collected to guide program improvement.

A basic, generic logic model depicts the inputs, activities, outputs, outcomes, and impact of a program (see Figure 51.1; Kellogg Foundation, 2001).

The "inputs" to a program are the resources that are needed to operate a program; such resources may be human, financial, organizational, or material. The key feature of any input is that it is the raw material from which an intervention is built. The "activities" of a program are the events of the intervention; they are what the program does with the inputs. They are the processes, tools, technology, and actions that make up the implementation of the program. "Outputs" are the direct and immediate results of the program activities, while "outcomes" are the short-term, intermediate, or long-term results of the program that are evident in specific changes created by the program, such as a change in the skills, knowledge, behavior, or performance of program participants. "Impact" is the ultimate change in an organization or system as a result of the program or intervention.

Programs such as HPT interventions rarely are simple enough to have a linear logic model as shown in Figure 51.1. More typically, there would be a few or several or most of these logic model components. Figure 51.2 is an example of a fairly typical logic model for an HPT intervention; the source of the logic model is the W. K. Kellogg Foundation's "Logic Model Development Guide."

Looking at the example in Figure 51.2, it becomes clear that logic models can be read in different ways. When read from left to right, a logic model describes how a program or intervention should work: particular inputs will feed into particular activities, which will lead to particular outputs, which will result in particular outcomes, which will deliver the desired impact. When read from right to left, a logic model describes the theory behind a program or intervention: creating a certain kind of impact will require accomplishing specific outcomes, which will result from particular outputs, which are the effect of key activities, which require unique inputs. While the shift in emphasis when reading a logic model right-to-left rather than left-to-right may seem insignificant, it in fact illustrates something critically important and valuable about logic models. There are two ways that logic models can help to improve a program or

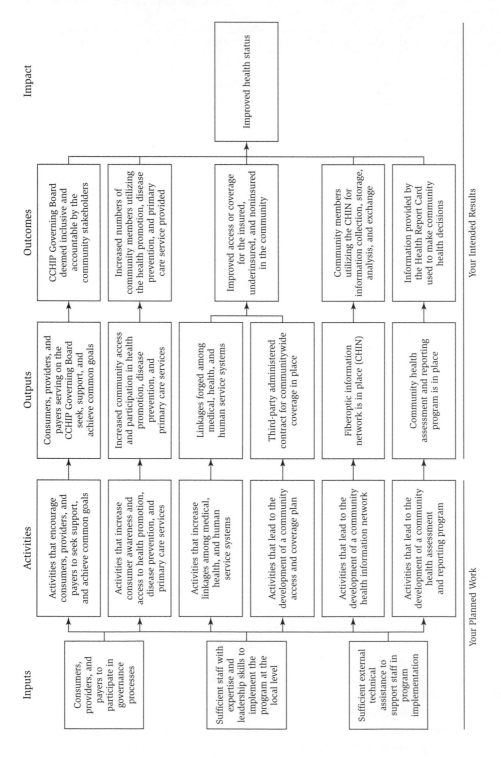

Figure 51.2. Logic Model from the Calhoun County Health Improvement Program.

Source: W. K. Kellogg Foundation, 2001, p. 12.

intervention. First, an evaluator will have to work closely with key program personnel to develop a model that accurately and adequately reflects the program. This collaborative process of model development can help program personnel identify gaps or shortcomings in program logic regardless of how it was implemented. That is, the development of the model helps program personnel examine and reconsider their *program-as-intended* and answer the questions, Should this work? and If not, why? The second way that a logic model can be used is to help the evaluator identify what should be happening at key intervals during implementation and as a result of a program. This will tell the evaluator where and when data ought to be collected to confirm whether or not the *program-as-implemented* reflects the *program-as-intended.*

COMPARING LEVEL-BASED AND THEORY-BASED EVALUATION MODELS

A comparison of HPT's most popular level-based evaluation models with the theory-based, or logic modeling approach detailed in the literature on program evaluation highlights four distinct differences between these two types of evaluation, and suggests that theory-based evaluation offers a means to overcome the key limitations that are inherent in current HPT evaluation models.

First, while HPT evaluation models use the terminology of "levels" to create a "place based" focus on the impact of an intervention, that is, from individual learner to department performer to organization to society, theory-based evaluation models use the terminology of "phases" to emphasize a time-based focus on the impact of an intervention, from immediate results to short-term, intermediate, long-term, and finally ultimate impacts. However, a logic model that represents the impact of an intervention over time also can easily represent the impact on place, while level-based evaluation models do not easily represent time. The combined focus on organizational levels and intervention phases that is possible with logic modeling allows for deep and complex representations of the various impacts of any particular intervention.

Second, the beginning "level" in the most popular HPT evaluation models is an output measure, such as satisfaction or learning, while theory-based evaluation models represent the inputs and activities of an intervention as well as its outputs, outcomes, and impact. The representation of inputs and activities in theory-based evaluation models allows the evaluator to collect data that help to determine what actually happened during the intervention, rather than simply documenting the final results of the intervention. Knowing what actually happened during a program means that the evaluation can help to drive the continuous improvement of the program, rather than simply serve as a judgment of the program's worth.

Third, the most popular HPT evaluation models assume that programs and interventions are atheoretical, while theory-based evaluation provides a means for documentation of program theory that underlies both the implementation and the evaluation of an intervention. Theory-based evaluation approaches may actually fit better with HPT interventions than current HPT evaluation models do because HPT provides detailed guidance about factors that influence performance, yet ignores these same basic assumptions during the planning, data collection, data analysis, and reporting of evaluations. Because systemic views and systematic study of interventions lead to greater understanding, the extension of HPT theory from analysis and design to evaluation may provide a more complete model for human performance improvement.

Fourth, HPT evaluation models specify the collection and analysis of data that only reflect how a program was implemented, while theory-based evaluation models provide a framework that allows an evaluator to capture data that not only reflects the program-as-implemented but, additionally, reflects the program-as-intended. Knowing the difference between the intended intervention and the actual intervention provides the evaluator with an understanding of the gap between what was planned and what actually happened. Understanding this gap provides all of the stakeholders of an intervention with the opportunity to use that knowledge not only to judge the merit of the program, but also to improve the program in future iterations.

AN APPROACH TO COMPREHENSIVE PERFORMANCE EVALUATION

The field of human performance technology is built upon a theoretical assumption that there is a certain degree of lawfulness to human performance, such that human performance can be engineered at least in part if we work systemically and systematically to apply a performance equation in the particular context within which we work. HPT practitioners generally apply some version of this theory when designing interventions; however, we rarely study the application of our theory in the evaluations of our interventions. Theory-based evaluation is an approach that emphasizes the use of theory when evaluating programs, but does not dictate any particular theory that should be applied to programs or interventions. By bringing a basic theory about human performance together with a theory-based evaluation approach, we may be able to create a more coherent approach to the design, implementation, and evaluation of HPT interventions. Building this type of approach requires that we create a framework that fits with the particular theory espoused by HPT practitioners and that we outline a process for how to conduct a theory-based evaluation in HPT. This framework and process, which we call "comprehensive performance evaluation," are outlined in the next section of this chapter.

Theoretical Framework for Comprehensive Performance Evaluation

In a previous section of this chapter, we outlined in part the historical evolution of the performance equation, and identified a few of the most widely referenced versions of the equation. In this section, we present a version of the performance equation that we have created based on those previous models that may be used as a framework for theory-based evaluations of interventions that are focused on human performance improvement.

Drawing from Wile's (1996) model, which is a synthesis of other popular iterations of the performance equation, we have created a visual representation of the theory behind the performance equation that attempts to simplify Wile's organizational scheme by eliminating the super-ordinate categories that create a distinction between performance variables that are internal and external to the performer and by eliminating any repetition of variables, so as to create a framework that is as comprehensive as possible while also being easy to comprehend. This framework is presented in Figure 51.3.

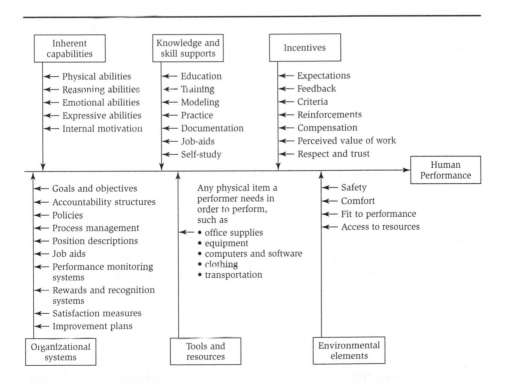

Figure 51.3. Theoretical Variables for Comprehensive Performance Evaluation.

Comprehensive performance evaluation identifies six primary performance variables that should be considered when evaluating a human performance intervention: the inherent capabilities of the performer related to the desired performance; the skill and knowledge supports provided to the performer during the intervention; the incentives, both internal and external, to the performer for completing performance; the organizational systems that have an impact on performance; the tools and resources used for performance; and the more ethereal environmental elements that affect performance.

The six key variables are overarching categories that represent particular types of actual variables that can affect human performance, and there are a large number of possibilities for the exact variables that affect a single human performance intervention in a specific context. It is the responsibility of the program designers, implementers, evaluators, and other key stakeholders of a particular intervention to determine the specific variables that should be studied during the evaluation of the intervention. Determining the specific performance variables that were addressed during the development of a program is the beginning of the process by which the underlying theory of the program is articulated.

Logic Model for Comprehensive Performance Evaluation

To ensure that evaluations of HPT interventions are based on the foundational theory of the lawfulness of human performance, we need to combine the elements of a simple logic model with the key variables of the performance equation. Figure 51.4 is a depiction of a generic logic model for CPE that provides the evaluator with a framework for conducting an evaluation by considering each of the variables that make up the performance equation.

Note that the logic model for CPE is able to incorporate the "levels" that are included in popular HPT evaluation theories in the output and outcome phases of the logic model. Like Kirkpatrick's level 2, the output phase measures whether employees have the skills and knowledge for desired performance, and it additionally recognizes the importance of the other variables of the performance equation by measuring whether capabilities, incentives, systems, resources, and the environment are aligned with desired performance. Like Kirkpatrick's level 3, the outcomes phase measures whether learning has transferred back to the job or to the performance environment, but it also acknowledges the impact that capabilities, incentives, systems, resources, and the environment have on increasing desired performance and decreasing unwanted performance. In addition, the outcomes phase can be expanded to distinguish between short-term, intermediate, and long-term outcomes when an intervention takes place over an extended period of time or if changes to performance occur in developmental phases. Like Kirkpatrick's level 4, the impact phase measures the goals of the intervention, but it goes beyond Kirkpatrick's model by explicitly acknowledging that the ultimate success of the intervention is a result of the combined impact of all of the

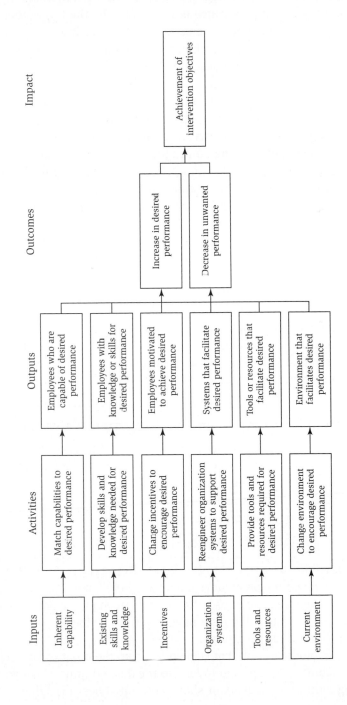

Figure 51.4. Logic Model for Comprehensive Performance Evaluation.

variables of the performance equation, rather than emphasizing the impact of the single variable of skill or knowledge development on performance.

In addition to depicting the outcomes measured by the levels approaches to evaluation, the CPE logic model is able to represent the inputs and activities of an intervention. As mentioned earlier, by depicting the inputs and activities, and their relationship to the outputs, outcomes, and impact of an intervention, the logic model can be used in two important ways. First, the CPE logic model can be used to represent the program-as-intended, depicting what the intervention planners hoped would happen when they developed the program. Second, the CPE logic model can be used to represent the program-as-implemented, depicting what actually happened during the intervention. Using logic models for both the program-as-intended and program-as-implemented, an evaluator can make a comparison that yields important information about how the program implementation deviated from the planned program, and can identify whether the program theory was poorly conceived or whether the implementation was poorly conducted. As a result, the evaluation may help to facilitate continuous improvement of the program, rather than simply serve as a judgment of the program's worth.

In any particular instance of evaluation, the CPE logic model may include any combination of specific variables from the performance equation; the value of the logic model is that it provides the evaluator with a tool that encourages the consideration of the various types of variables and the role of each in creating a successful intervention, so that the logic model serves as a visual depiction of the program in terms of both its theoretical framework and its actual implementation.

Method for Comprehensive Performance Evaluation

Comprehensive performance evaluation is based on the development of a logic model that depicts the variables of the performance equation and the relationships between those variables in support of the activities and outcomes of the program. CPE also outlines a method involving five steps that provide guidance to evaluators for how to develop the logic model and apply it to the evaluation of a performance intervention.

Step 1: Develop a Logic Model That Represents the Program-as-Intended. Document the program-as-intended by documenting the inputs, activities, outputs, outcomes, and impact that were planned by the program designers. Specifically, you need to ask questions to determine what the program designers' intentions were for each phase of the program: (1) What is the ultimate impact, the bottom-line result that is intended from the program or intervention? (2) What outcomes are expected to lead to the desired impact? Do you need to specify long-term, intermediate, or short-term outcomes? (3) What outputs are expected to lead to the desired outcomes? Put another way, what behavioral and performance changes are intended as a result of the program? (4) What are the planned program activities? What are the components that planners expect to make up the intervention or program? (5) What inputs are needed in order to implement the planned program?

When documenting the inputs, activities, and outputs for the program-as-intended logic model, the evaluator should consider each of the six variables of the performance equation to determine whether program planners have planned activities to address each variable. Key stakeholders of the program should be interviewed to get various perspectives regarding whether all appropriate performance variables are addressed for each element and phase of the program.

Once all the elements have been identified, map them into a logic model that depicts the program-as-intended, or the theory behind the program. Note that the questions in the preceding paragraph have been listed in reverse chronological order, the opposite order from how they would occur in real time. Ideally, creating a logic model by "reverse engineering" can help an evaluator keep a tight focus on the relationships between all the elements in each phase of the logic model. If it is not possible to reverse engineer the logic model, then it is helpful to read the logic model in reverse order once it is completed, to check that the relationships between elements and phases clearly represent the theory behind the intended program.

Step 2: Measure Key Indicators of the Program. Once the program-as-intended logic model is agreed upon by the various stakeholders as an accurate representation of the theory behind the program, measurable indicators must be derived for each component of the logic model, including the activities as well as the outputs and outcomes. Then, data must be collected to determine whether each component has been successfully completed during program implementation.

When the data show that a component has not been successfully implemented, this should be noted as a discrepancy on the program-as-intended logic model, in order to clearly identify the disconnection between the intended program and the actual implementation.

Step 3: Develop a Logic Model That Represents the Program-as-Implemented. Having collected and analyzed data that measure the success or failure of the various elements and phases of the intended program, the evaluator is then able to develop a new logic model that represents the program-as-implemented.

The logic model for the program-as-implemented provides a realistic depiction of what actually happened during the program or intervention. This may look very similar to or very different from the program-as-intended logic model, depending on whether the program goals were clearly defined and on the quality of program management. It is appropriate in this step, just as it was in step 1, to verify the program-as-implemented logic model with key stakeholders to ensure that the logic model reflects their experience of what happened during the program.

Step 4: Compare the Program-as-Intended and Program-as-Implemented Logic Models. Once the evaluator has the two logic models for the program-as-intended and program-as-implemented, it is possible to compare the two to clearly identify the discrepancies between the intended program and the implemented program.

Findings from this comparison may lead the evaluator to one of four likely conclusions:

1. The program was implemented as intended and was successful: good planning, good implementation, positive result.
2. The program was implemented as intended and was *not* successful: poor planning, good implementation, negative result.
3. The program was *not* implemented as intended and was *not* successful: good planning, poor implementation, negative result.
4. The program plan was *not* clear and the program was poorly implemented and the program was *not* successful: poor planning, poor implementation, negative result.

If the comparison of logic models shows that the results of the program are less than successful, then a final step should be completed in order to improve the program, by revising either the program theory, the program implementation, or both.

Step 5: Improve the Program Model. Based on lessons learned from the previous steps, the final step of the evaluation method is to develop a new program or logic model that reflects the changes in program logic based on key indicator data collected in step 3 and the comparison of logic models in step 4. The evaluator obviously will need to work with key stakeholders to redesign the program based on the new program or logic model, as well as to monitor the revised program to ensure its continuous improvement.

EXAMPLES OF COMPREHENSIVE PERFORMANCE EVALUATION

Included among the organizations that have been at the forefront of the movement toward logic modeling and theory-based program evaluation are many public health organizations, the government, and social services. The sample logic models provided in this section are based upon publicly accessible information from the National Tobacco Control Program, an initiative supported by the National Centers for Disease Control and Prevention, National Center for Chronic Disease Prevention and Health Promotion, Office on Smoking and Health (OSH) and involving programs in all fifty states in the United States. Though information regarding NTCP program theory and program activities is publicly accessible (go to www.cdc.gov/tobacco to find resource materials), the logic models in this chapter have been generated by the authors to provide examples that should be easy to understand for all readers, using nonproprietary information that is accessible to all readers and that could be customized to fit the CPE logic model framework. Cautionary note: these logic models are *not* endorsed by the National Centers for Disease Control, and are *not* used to officially represent the theory behind the National Tobacco Control Program.

CPE Logic Model for NTCP

The logic model represented in Figure 51.5 provides one possible representation of the program theory behind the National Tobacco Control Program. As stated on the Website, OSH is responsible for leading and coordinating strategic efforts aimed at preventing tobacco use among youth, promoting smoking cessation among youth and adults, protecting nonsmokers from environmental tobacco smoke, and eliminating tobacco-related health disparities.

Program-as-Intended Compared with Program-as-Implemented

A hypothetical example that is more simplistic than the NTCP example demonstrates how the use of logic models in CPE can help an evaluator go beyond solely assessing the overall merit and worth of a program to actually analyzing what aspects of a program need improving. Figure 51.6 is the program-as-intended logic model for an intervention used to improve the performance of a company that sells goods to customers by phone.

This company determined that it was losing sales because customers were displeased with the service they were getting from their phone sales department. The company decided it needed to better train its phone sales workers and give them better tools to improve their performance. Management determined that these actions would improve the workers' call speed and help them to deliver better information, which they assumed would increase the number of calls the salespeople could take, thus reducing the amount of time customers are on hold. Furthermore, this would improve their ability to answer customers' questions, making for more satisfied customers that would create return business.

A few months after having implemented their performance-improvement interventions, the company used CPE to evaluate their success. The evaluator developed the program-as-implemented logic model in Figure 51.7.

While there was a significantly increased rate of customer satisfaction with the quality of information communicated by the phone sales workers, there was

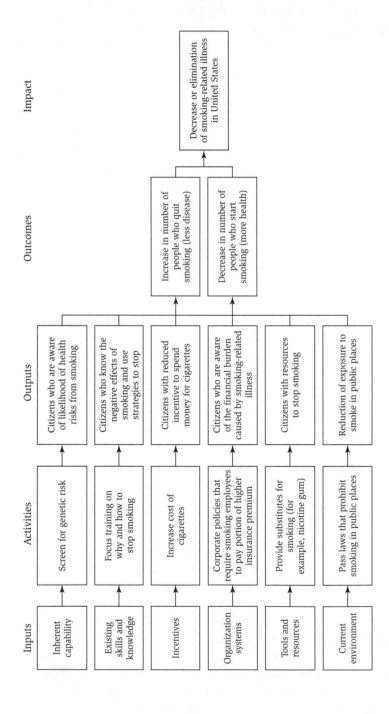

Figure 51.5. Sample CPE Logic Model for National Tobacco Control Program.

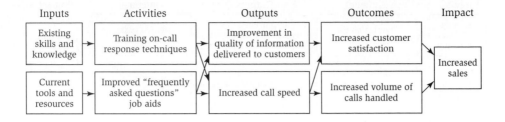

Figure 51.6. Sample Program-as-Intended Logic Model.

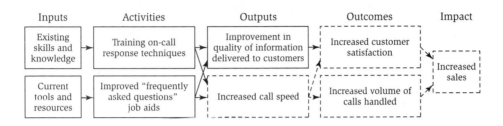

Figure 51.7. Sample Program-as-Implemented Logic Model.

almost no change in average call times. This contributed to the company not reaching their goals for improved overall customer satisfaction and, ultimately, overall sales.

Guided by the generic logic model for CPE (see Figure 51.4), the evaluator collected data not only on the program-as-intended, but also on each of the other inputs that contribute to human performance. In doing so, she determined that there was a problem with motivation and incentives among the phone sales workers. While they understood how to increase the speed of their work, they were not paid any more for increased phone call volume. Therefore, they had little motivation to work harder. Given this finding, the evaluator reported back to management that they needed to seriously reconsider the way they used compensation to create performance incentives for their workers if they wanted to increase call speed. The evaluator was able to communicate this through the use of a new logic model, as shown in Figure 51.8.

A typical, nontheory-based evaluation would likely only have been able to report that the intervention was not a success. It would have been up to the company to speculate as to where it broke down and what else they could do achieve their goals. Using CPE, the evaluator was able to diagnose the aspects of the program that were not functioning as intended and, in this case, was even able to make a specific recommendation for how to fix it.

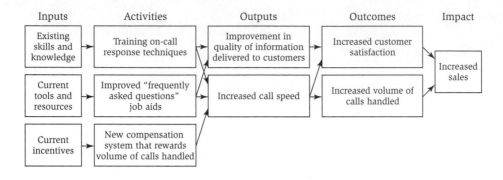

Figure 51.8. Sample Program Redesign Logic Model.

CONCLUSIONS

The assumption on which this chapter is based is that the field of human performance technology needs an approach for the evaluation of our interventions that will bring theorists and practitioners together in a shared commitment to systemically and systematically describe human performance improvement interventions; describe the theories that support these interventions; evaluate the success of these interventions; and, most important, tie theory, practice, and research together in a way that can advance knowledge of the field.

In this chapter, we built a case for why the linkage between theory and practice is important, noted the gap between the theories of lawfulness and the structure of our current evaluation models, and introduced an approach to evaluation that is based on a foundational theory of the field. We recognize that the approach we have outlined in this chapter has its own unique strengths and limitations, which we will explain in the following section. Because of this model's strengths, and despite its limitations, we believe that comprehensive performance evaluation can serve an important role in the field of human performance technology; therefore, we end this chapter with a discussion of ideas for further development of the approach and a call to our colleagues in the field to join us in this endeavor.

Strengths of Comprehensive Performance Evaluation

Comprehensive performance evaluation appears to have several strengths as compared with the "levels" approaches for evaluation of HPT interventions. First, and most important, this approach allows practitioners to apply a foundational theory of HPT, that is, the performance equation, to the evaluation of an intervention, so as to link theory, practice, and evaluation in a way that can help us to systematically develop the knowledge base of the field. A second and related strength is that this is a holistic approach that encourages the integrity of an intervention by attempting to link the design, implementation, and evaluation phases of an intervention through the process of logic modeling. Third, comprehensive performance evaluation provides information not just about the outcomes of an intervention, but also about the inputs and activities of the intervention. Fourth, CPE is a systemic and systematic approach to the process of evaluation. Fifth, this approach can help program stakeholders better understand their own thinking and assumptions about the intervention. Sixth, and finally, because this is a holistic, systematic, theory-based approach, it goes beyond evaluation as program assessment and can lead to systematic program improvement.

Limitations of Comprehensive Performance Evaluation

As noted, there are many good reasons why an HPT practitioner might be interested in conducting a comprehensive performance evaluation. We also recognize that there are limitations to this approach, and it is important, when considering whether to use the CPE framework, to consider its limitations as well as its strengths. First, it can be long and hard work to develop a sound logic model, particularly when attempting to do so as a collaborative effort with a relatively large group. One reason for this difficulty is that the various stakeholders may not agree about a program's guiding assumptions or theories, and, in that case, it may be impossible to create a logic model that will be supported by any kind of group consensus. Second, it is possible that the evaluator may uncover multiple theories, which would require some strategy for deciding which of the derived theories will be the one that is formalized for the evaluation. Third, the evaluation process may require more time and the collection of a larger amount of data than required from other evaluation models, given that the evaluator is documenting program activities as well as program outcomes. Fourth, and finally, stakeholders may be wary or nervous about discussing "theory or logic" when they simply want to complete an evaluation to demonstrate program results. When faced with any of these situations, it may well be advisable for the evaluator to abandon this approach and to use an evaluation model that better fits the needs of the client.

Ideas for Further Development
of Comprehensive Program Evaluation

To those readers who see potential value in comprehensive program evaluation as the model and method has been outlined in this chapter, we invite you to join us in testing the model and method and encourage you to document the results of your evaluations for publication in peer-reviewed journals related to human performance technology, organization development, and program evaluation. Specifically, we believe that the most appropriate strategy for further development of CPE is to begin by testing the approach with small programs, ones that are limited in time and scope, and work toward using it with larger programs over successive evaluations.

Once there is a more robust set of evaluation reports based on the use of the CPE approach, we hope that it will be possible to develop more detailed and prescriptive guidelines for how to develop performance-based logic models, to streamline the evaluation method, and to determine which types of environments fit most appropriately with the use of comprehensive performance evaluation.

References

Chen, H. T. (1990). *Theory-driven evaluations.* Newbury Park, CA: Sage.

Chen, H. T., and Rossi, P. H. (1980). The multi-goal, theory-driven approach to evaluation: A model linking basic and applied social science. *Social Forces, 59*(1), 106–22.

Cicerone, B., Sassaman, R., and Swinney, J. (2005). The path to improved performance starts with theory: A lesson learned from Tom Gilbert. *Performance Improvement, 44*(2), 9–14.

Fitz-Gibbon, C. T., and Morris, L. L. (1996). Theory-based evaluation: What do we mean by theory-based evaluation? *Evaluation Practice, 17*(2), 177–184.

Gilbert, T. F. (1978). *Human competence: Engineering worthy performance.* New York: McGraw-Hill.

Harless, J. H. (1970). *An ounce of analysis (is worth a pound of objectives).* Newnan, GA: Harless Performance Guild.

Kauffman, P., and Keller, J. M. (1994). Levels of evaluation: Beyond Kirkpatrick. *HRD Quarterly, 5*(4), 371–380.

W. K. Kellogg Foundation. (2001). *Logic model development guide: Logic models to bring together planning, evaluation, & action.* Retrieved May 14, 2005, from page 12 at http://www.wkkf.org/Pubs/Tools/Evaluation/Pub3669.pdf.

Kirkpatrick, D. L. (1998). *Evaluating training programs: The four levels.* San Francisco: Berrett-Koehler.

Lewin, K. (1951). *Field theory in social science: Selected theoretical papers.* New York: Harper.

Mager, R. F., and Pipe, P. (1997). *Analyzing performance problems.* Atlanta: Center for Effective Performance.

Phillips, J. J. (1997). *Training evaluation and measurement methods: Proven models and methods for evaluating any HRD program* (3rd ed.). Woburn, MA: Butterworth-Heinemann.

Robinson, D. G., and Robinson, J. C. (1989). Training for impact: How to link training to business needs and measure the results. San Francisco: Jossey-Bass.

Rogers, P. J. (2000). Causal models. *Program Theory Evaluation, 87,* 47–55.

Rossett, A. (1992). Analysis of human performance problems. In H. D. Stolovitch and E. J. Keeps (Eds.), *Handbook of human performance technology: A comprehensive guide for analyzing and solving performance problems in organizations.* San Francisco: Jossey-Bass.

Van Tiem, D., Moseley, J. L., and Dessinger, J. C. (2000). *Fundamentals of performance improvement: A guide to improving people, process, and performance.* Washington, DC: International Society for Performance Improvement.

Weiss, C. H. (1972). *Evaluation research: Methods of assessing program effectiveness.* Englewood Cliffs, NJ: Prentice-Hall.

Weiss, C. H. (1997). How can theory-based evaluation make greater headway? *Evaluation Review, 21*(4), 501–524.

Wholey, J. S. (1979). *Evaluation: Promise and performance.* Washington, DC: Urban Institute.

Wile, D. (1996, February). Why doers do. *Performance and Instruction, 35*(2), 30–35.

Worthen, B. R., Sanders, J. R., and Fitzpatrick, J. L. (1997). *Program evaluation: Alternative approaches and practical guidelines* (2nd ed.). New York: Addison Wesley Longman.

Yampolskaya, S., Nesman, T. M., Hernandez, M., and Koch, D. (2004). Using concept mapping to develop a logic model and articulate a program theory: A case example. *American Journal of Evaluation, 25*(2), 191–207.

CHAPTER FIFTY-TWO

Aligning the Human Performance System

John Amarant, Donald T. Tosti

Over the past forty years, a rich array of human performance concepts, methodologies, and models have been published with the broad purpose of improving various aspects of the performance of people working individually, in groups, or in organizations. The recent history of this literature seems to be that a model or concept demonstrates effectiveness, is used for a while, then ceases to be used. Its value then goes unrecognized until it is rediscovered or reinvented.

An example of this cycle of loss and recovery is one of the first application models to come out of the field of human performance, the RULEG model developed in the late 1950s (Evans, Homme, and Glaser, 1962). The model proposed that to construct an effective programmed instruction frame, one should start with a rule (RUL), provide an example (EG), and then provide an incomplete example for the student to work on. The model is still useful in the design of instructional materials; however, its value goes unrecognized today because the field has become crowded with a rash of solutions. This rush to provide remedies poses some challenges for the field of performance improvement. They include the following:

- Many models describe the same or similar phenomena but with different language. The result is a cacophony of terms and concepts that confuses not only professionals but clients as well, undermining the credibility of serious practitioners seeking to ease their clients' plight.

- Overemphasis on the individual performer results in neglect of other variables in the organization that, if properly leveraged, could yield substantial gains with modest investment. Moreover, the preoccupation with the performer has created a kind of management formula in which "fixing" employees is a key ingredient. The result is employees who are battling defensively with managers who fail to recognize the broader scope of the problem or fail to admit that the fix may be with the manager or the organization.

- Initiatives and solutions are not integrated with other initiatives or with the organization as a whole. The result can be a series of unanticipated consequences that can have disastrous results.

Over the past few years, the idea has emerged that these limitations might be addressed by a performance model that provides a framework for moving between models or approaches. It would facilitate the integration of interventions with the *status quo* or with other initiatives the organization is undertaking. We are proposing a framework that improves understanding of the limitations of various models and that aids in the transition from one model to another to address the different variables within the organization.

At a minimum, such an integrated framework for human performance technology (HPT) should incorporate the following principles:

- Focus on results and contributions to value

- Take a systemic view

- Be scalable so that it can be applied consistently at each level of system complexity from the individual performer level to the organizational level

- Be inclusive, so that all variables that affect performance are incorporated in the system

- Support or encourage the collaboration between professional communities specializing in human performance

As a way forward, we will describe such a framework and demonstrate how it might be applied in light of these principles and used with some of the more common models and concepts for performance improvement.

EVOLUTION OF UNDERSTANDING

The origins of the proposed systems framework for performance improvement lie in the early days of HPT. The late 1950s and 1960s were times of activism and social reform in the United States. The field, initially called behavior technology, was a product of that spirit. In the early 1960s a number of behavioral scientists and their graduate students made the decision to take what they had learned in their *learning laboratories* and apply those lessons to real-world issues of learning and performance. But the real world is much less controllable than the laboratory, and they quickly learned some powerful lessons when dealing with the many variables that can have an impact on individual and group performance.

Early Models

Many of the early models were very useful, but an important advance was provided by Dale Brethower in the mid-1960s (Brethower, 1972). His inspiration was to expand on the fundamental behavior model, a powerful tool for analyzing and influencing behavior. Although valuable, the behavior model was limited by its focus on behavior and the individual performer. The behavior model focuses on the smallest chunk of behavior that is meaningful to a performer, called the *operant*. An operant describes behavior in terms of the relationship between the *stimulus,* or signal for behavior, the *response* to that signal, and the *reinforcing consequences.* The relationship is usually represented this way:

$$S \longrightarrow R \longrightarrow RC$$

In simple terms, the operant states that when someone senses an event or object in the environment (S) and makes an appropriate response (R) to that event, reinforcing consequences (RC) will tend to strengthen the behavior. Brethower recognized that this basic three-term behavioral or contingency model could be viewed as part of an overall system. By setting the contingency model within a broader systems model, he presented analysts with a way to consider a larger number of performance variables. He recast the basic model of stimulus, response, and consequence in the form found in Figure 52.1.

By including the receiving system in the overall model, Brethower provided an opportunity for a second source of feedback to be conveyed from the receiving system back to the performance system, increasing its ability to adapt.

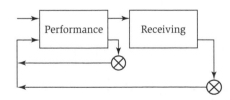

Figure 52.1. The Adaptive Performance System.

However, at the time of its publication the significance of this proposal was not grasped by many in the field, and the opportunity to expand the scope of factors beyond instruction and motivation was overlooked.

Joining the Touchstones

Nearly four decades ago, there were two recognized principles that could serve as touchstones for the development of a comprehensive model of performance technology that could be used to analyze and influence the performance of any human system from individuals to organizations. Those principles are

- Recognition that any behavior or action is but one component of a dynamic system that can adapt in response to input from a receiving system or the environment
- Recognition that effectively influencing performance requires attention to a far more comprehensive range of variables than instruction or motivation, and those variables need to be cast in a categorization scheme to aid in their recognition and application

One of the pioneers in joining these principles is Lloyd Homme. In his seminal article on behavioral engineering (Homme and Homme, 1966), he described the key components of the performance system in terms of its stimulus factors, that is, conditions and direction, and its consequences, that is, reinforcement and feedback. A few years later, Gilbert presented his model of performance, which, though it did not build on systems logic, prompted people to consider a broader range of performance influences. Gilbert offered a taxonomy using the performer and divided the performance variables into two main groupings. That is, he identified three performance influences inside the performer, skills or knowledge, capacity, and motives, and three outside the performer, data, instruments or tools, and incentives (Gilbert, 1996, p. 85).

During this time, most new HPT models, like Homme's behavioral engineering model, continued to focus primarily on the individual performer, but began to strengthen our understanding of where the technology could go and how it could be used. For example, Mager and Pipe (1970) developed an analytical problem-solving model that, although not strictly a systems model, structures the analysis process and helps set priorities as to where to look for opportunities to improve performance.

Practical Analytical Tools

Several early analytic models such as Gilbert's and Mager's relied on taxonomies that they created, but equally early in the development of the field the systems models such as that devised by Brethower were in fairly widespread use as well. For example, systems models were being used in behavioral engineered classrooms as early as 1963 (Homme, Csanyi, Gonzales, and Rechs, 1969; Tosti, 1968). Although taxonomic models such as Gilbert's still have a following, most professionals in the field have moved to systems models in their quest to conduct better analyses. In fact, "taking a systemic view" has been adopted as a major principle of HPT. There are two major advantages of systems models:

- They not only identify variables, just as taxonomies do, but also provide insight into the interdependent relationships between the variables.

- Systems models are scalable. That is, a systems framework can be applied to varying degrees of complexity across levels of systems with any number of people working toward a common result: starting with individuals, moving up in complexity to operations, and ultimately to the administration of the whole organization. In addition, systems models can be applied as well to the organization's interactions with its marketplace and community.

As an alternative to the taxonomic analytical models, Geary Rummler (Rummler and Brache, 1995) applied systems principles to broaden the scope of analysis to include variables outside the performer, focusing on work processes. It took the field a while to grasp the significance of Rummler's work. Among other things, his work demonstrated that much more of the variance in performance is attributable to inadequate processes than to deficiencies in individual performance.

Three Levels of Analysis

It soon became apparent that the systems framework was applicable to analyzing group or team performance. By the late 1970s, the methodology was well established for looking at the entire organization and hunting down key performance variables by analyzing the three major organizational subsystems:

- Organizational-Administrative

- Operations-Process

- People-Job

Note that each level has been identified with two labels: for example, people and job. The purposes of these two labels is to identify the level of system complexity and to ensure clarity that as living systems, people are central at each level of complexity. The three categories or levels of subsystems do *not* connote an organizational hierarchy or structure. Nor is the focus limited to the mechanical performance of the work. There are times, however, when a better understanding of the level comes from using one term or the other.

Rummler proposed a similar three-level approach to organizational analysis, preferring to emphasize the importance of processes and the tasks that support them. In this way, he proposed that effective process improvement requires management not just of the process but of the other levels as well: in other words, "the entire hierarchy must be managed" (Rummler and Brache, 1995, p. 171). This perspective approaches the organization as a processing system. Jobs or roles and functions exist to support the processes of the organization. "All of this is critical if the organization is to successfully deliver results" (Rummler, 2004, p. 17).

The strength of this perspective is twofold. First, it invites analysis of the value chain composed of those who contribute to the result. Second, it allows analysis of issues from the perspective of different levels of the organization. Whether an analyst is working with an individual position, a business unit, a process that links two or more functions, or the entire organization in its environment or marketplace, the principles that apply at all of these levels are consistent. The differences are largely a matter of scale. This is true whether the issue is managing the tasks for one job or managing thousands of people in an organization.

Organizational Alignment

Today, a systems approach to analyzing organizational performance is widely used with good results, and is becoming increasingly accepted both by performance professionals and by the leadership and management of organizations. As noted earlier, "Take a systems view" is an International Society for Performance Improvement (ISPI) standard of its interpretation of performance technology.

Complementing the process view of human performance is the concept of cultural alignment (Tosti and Jackson, 1994). In the mid-1980s there were a number of initiatives to align the culture of organizations to support the implementation of strategy. Such initiatives sought to align the culture of the organizations across the various levels of the process hierarchy in a way that would incorporate both the sociological model of work and the industrial engineering model of work (Carleton and Lineberry, 2004, p. 36). This model proved immensely successful with a number of initiatives and offers an alternative view of the organization to the process hierarchy.

The decade of the 1990s was filled with rapid change attributable to globalization and the introduction of new technologies. Managing change emerged as an important discipline in the human performance field. As with the process analysis and culture analysis, practitioners have come to recognize that an effective change plan looks at the change initiative in light of the organization as a whole. This allows the analyst and planner to assess the organization as a dynamic system and consider how proposed changes are likely to affect the system at all three levels: organizational, process, and people. The relationship between these levels is typically represented this way:

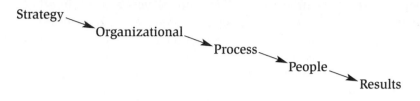

FULLY INTEGRATED FRAMEWORK

It has long been a standard of ISPI to measure results in order to demonstrate the effectiveness of methods or interventions. In that tradition, the integrated framework should be an evolutionary step in the four-decade development of HPT. As the preceding review demonstrates, there already exists an adequate body of work that offers sound and tested components for a fully integrated framework by applying two fundamental themes, both of which have already been embraced as standards of ISPI. The first is the systems approach to organizations. The second is a focus on results as the means to align the organization's culture to enable achievement of its strategy.

Systems Analysis

Within any organization, there are multiple systems:

- There are people working individually as performers, doing the work.
- There are operational processes that involve and link people working in concert.
- There is the overall organizational and administrative system that must be led and governed, responding to the marketplace and external conditions.

From an HPT viewpoint, the basic systems model underlying each of these levels is the same as that used to generally describe the seven interrelated performance components for a process system:

- Conditions
- Inputs
- Processes
- Outputs
- Operational or corrective feedback: coming from the measures of the operational outputs

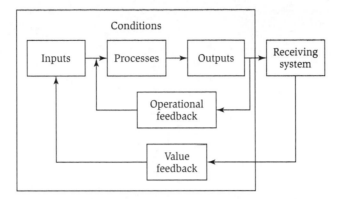

Figure 52.2. The Basic System.

- Value feedback: based on the measure of the receiving system's satisfaction with the outputs
- Receiving system or receiver

The graphic representation in Figure 52.2 shows the interrelationship of these system components.

The definitions of these components appear in Figure 52.3. Typically, these seven components can be readily measured when analyzing a process. In fact, they are commonly used in process engineering. These processes are often interlocked with other processes in a maze of organizational systems that form a value chain linking organizational input to products or services delivered to customers.

Scalability. The term *scale* connotes maps drawn to a variety of scales or models built to replicate the detail of the original but in a smaller, more manageable size. Although the size may vary, what is important is the preservation of the relationship among the variables. The relative positions of components are preserved. Scale is important because it allows the viewer to analyze a range of objects, such as the terrain or even the sky, by employing a common methodology. This concept gives us confidence as experts. Based on our experience, we enter new situations and can grasp what they have in common with previous situations (Brethower, 2002).

The notion of *scalability* has utility in human performance when there are common patterns of relationships among the variables influencing the performance of people working alone or together. James Grier Miller, in his general theory of living systems (Miller, 1978), makes the case that beginning with a few common coordinates it is possible to scale up from a single cell to more complex systems such as an organism, to a group, to a society, and even to a nation. This concept of scale is inherent in a systems approach to human

Component	Description
Conditions	The surroundings or environment within which performance occurs, including tools, equipment, information and guidance, and support, as well as physical conditions and the business and social environment
Input	What initiates an action or process or is used by it, including such things as customer requests, stakeholder demands, information, and raw materials
Process	The actions that convert an input into an output or accomplishment
Output	The accomplishment: what is produced or created by a process, including products and services as well as changes in the environment or situation
Operational feedback	Information about the quantity or quality of outputs that is "fed back" to an individual, work unit, or organization and that can be used to make adjustments or corrections that will improve results
Value feedback	Information about the relative value or benefits of outputs to stakeholders that is "fed back" to an organization for the primary purpose of allowing the organization to adapt to create greater stakeholder value and maintain the organization's long-term viability
Receiving system or receiver	The system stakeholder that receives or is directly affected by the output

Figure 52.3. Definitions for the Basic Systems Model.

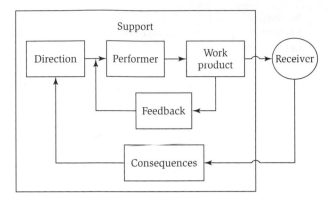

Figure 52.4. The Individual Performer System.

performance. The same performance logic applies both to the individual performer and to the performance of the organization as a system. The difference is one of scale, involving such factors as the number of variables, numbers of performers, volume of inputs, or size of the receiver system.

Individual Performer System. Most applications of HPT have focused on the individual performer; the most common of these is instruction. The basic rationale for using instruction as an intervention is a belief that the individual performer has some deficiency in skill, knowledge, or practice and therefore needs to learn something to improve the deficient repertoire. But individual performance problems often occur not because an individual lacks something but because of some other system deficiency, such as lack of clear direction or feedback. When the individual performer is cast within the context of the basic systems framework (see Figures 52.4 and 52.5), this interdependency of alternate variables is immediately apparent.

These are the same seven components as portrayed in the basic systems model but labeled differently to reflect the nature of the performance level and the language of performers.

These seven general systems elements are commonly condensed into five and relabeled to reflect those variables perceived by the performer: support, direction, performers, consequences, and feedback. This is because the performers often do not see the receiving system, nor do they distinguish between operational and value feedback. Typically, performers in a large organization do not see how their output is put to use. Their awareness is limited to the feedback and consequences arising from their work results and how those results are measured or are used by their immediate receiving system. Whether there are five or seven variables, the power of the systems framework is not diminished.

Comparable Basic Process Component	Individual Performer Component	Individual Performer Component Descriptions
Conditions	Support	The physical and social environment that enables the performer to take action to achieve desired results; it consists of the workspace, working conditions, tools, and support personnel.
Inputs	Direction	Clear communication of what the performer is expected to accomplish; it may also include information on the means by which it is to be accomplished and the priorities for action.
Processes	Performer	The people who, through their conduct and their execution of task, produce the desired results; this includes the performer's own history, capabilities and skills, interests, and so on.
Outputs	Work product	That which is produced by the individual in the execution of the process.
Receiving system	Receiver	The person or persons who receive the work product or output.
Operational feedback	Feedback	Information, provided to the performer, about the outcome or results to change actions if need be, or to maintain performance if it is effective.
Value feedback	Consequences	Events occurring as a result of performer's efforts that either increase or decrease the likelihood of future action by the performer.

Figure 52.5. Definitions for the Individual Performer System.

It is important to note that the people who work in the organization are at the heart of the system and system variables we are describing. Without people, there is no human performance system.

To illustrate the potency of the individual performer model, consider the questions listed in Figure 52.6. Consultants often use such questions to probe for factors that may be supporting or hindering effective individual performance, including factors that may be creating positive or negative consequences for simply being in the workplace.

Thinking systemically, viewing performance as the result of a system is a fundamental principle for performance improvement. Performance is a function of all the system variables. Limiting attention to performers ignores major sources of performance variance that occur at other levels of the organization.

Performance System Factor	Question
SUPPORT	***Do people get support that contributes to effective performance?***
Physical and social environment	Do people have the *tools* they need to do the job well? Are they in good condition, easy to use? Are *resources* readily available and accessible when performers need them, including good information, resource personnel, and raw materials? When performers are faced with conflicting demands, heavy workloads, or interfering tasks, do they have guidelines for setting *priorities*?
DIRECTION	***Do people get effective direction?***
Expectations and information	Are appropriate *expectations* set with performers? Do standards exist? Are the objectives reasonable? Are they clear? Are they presented in a way that is positive and respectful? Is *information* about how to perform clear? Is it accurate and logical? Is it given when people need it? Are people provided with information about *priorities* for their work?
PERFORMERS	***Are people able to perform well?***
Repertoire and capacity	Do they have the right *repertoire*: the skills, knowledge, and experience they need? Do they have the *capacity* to perform the job well: the physical strength, manual dexterity, and intellectual ability? Does the work fit with the performer's psychological, emotional, and working style characteristics?
CONSEQUENCES	***Are there appropriate consequences for good performance?***
Contingencies and timing	Do people view the *balance* of *consequences* for good performance as positive? Are *contingencies* clear? Are consequences clearly linked to good performance, from the performer's viewpoint? Are consequences *timed* to come as soon as feasible following good performance?
FEEDBACK	***Do people get helpful feedback about their performance?***
Fit, focus, and timing	Does feedback *fit* the performer's needs? Is there the appropriate amount of detail, given in a way people can understand? Is feedback clearly *focused* on improving performance—on how to improve, rather than what went wrong, or on improving the work, rather than criticizing the person? Is feedback given at a *time* when people can use it to improve?

Figure 52.6. Sample Probes for an Individual Performer System.

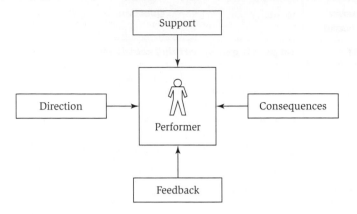

Figure 52.7. The Performer System at the People-Job Level from the Performer's Perspective.

Performers and their actions should not be the center of scrutiny, but *one* of the variables to be analyzed.

Organizational Performance. As mentioned earlier, an advantage of using the HPT systems approach when analyzing performance is that the analysis can readily be scaled up to the more complex organizational level or scaled down to the job level. This scalability offers consistency of troubleshooting at each level of system complexity, and it invites analysis between levels as well. This approach accommodates the need to develop complex solutions when problems at one level are magnifying the consequences of problems at another level. For example, HPT applied at the organizational level can be used to streamline governance procedures, maximize leaders' effectiveness, enhance customer value, create agile cultures, or align organizations to produce far better results for all stakeholders. For every aspect of the organization that involves people, there is an HPT application.

To illustrate this point, consider the schematic in Figure 52.7, which depicts the relationship among the three levels of organization.

People Level. At this level, the performer is central to the system, but constitutes only one set of variables. From the performer's perspective, there are four sets of system variables. Figure 52.7 illustrates this view, with the performer in the center being influenced by the other variables.

In terms of system complexity, the performance system influencing an individual performer is the least complex. The relationship of system elements applies to the entire range of jobs performed at all levels of the organization's hierarchy. Although there are receivers who determine the value of the performer's task results, the central issue from the performer's perspective is the value received for performing the task. This return of value for people working in organizations, at any position within the organization, can be depicted from a systems view in Figure 52.8.

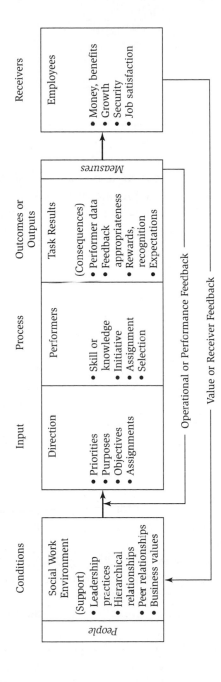

Figure 52.8. The Performance System at the People-Job Level from a Whole Systems Perspective.

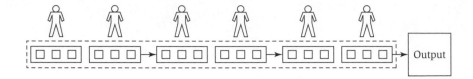

Figure 52.9. The Performance System at the Operations-Process Level from the Performer's Perspective.

Operations Level. The processes that guide people's work are intended to convert inputs into goods or services that provide customers with value. Within each process are sequences of tasks that are supported by management. Under optimal conditions, the contributions of workers form a value chain that produces the goods and services that create value for customers. Such processes are illustrated from a worker's or supervisor's perspective in Figure 52.9. This is the level at which the operations of the organization come together to deliver products or services for its customers. The processes are influenced by variables that have an impact on the outputs and ultimately on the results. This relationship becomes more apparent when viewed from a systems perspective, as illustrated in Figure 52.10.

Organizational Level. Finally, the organization is not an abstraction. It is a dynamic entity that must be managed and governed by people. This requires executives, functional managers, and administrative systems to lead the organization as a whole. From their vantage point, and perhaps from the perspective of all performers within the organization, this portion of the organization is typically mapped in the manner shown in Figure 52.11.

However, governance and leadership of the organization at this level follow the same principles that apply at the other levels. Figure 52.12 shows the system elements at play at this level. They have the same relationship to one another as at other levels; however, they are adapted to reflect the scale or magnitude of the tasks to be performed.

Of course, some administrative systems consist of a number of processes and can be analyzed as such. The result or value created by these systems, however, focuses on supporting the integrity or discipline of the organization's value chain processes. That is, they enable the organization as a whole to produce the intended results. In analyzing this level of the performance system it is important not to mistake the organization's hierarchy or structure for system components.

In Figure 52.13, we have adapted a schematic first proposed by Rummler to show how these three levels can be combined to illustrate the interaction among them as subsystems of the whole organization.

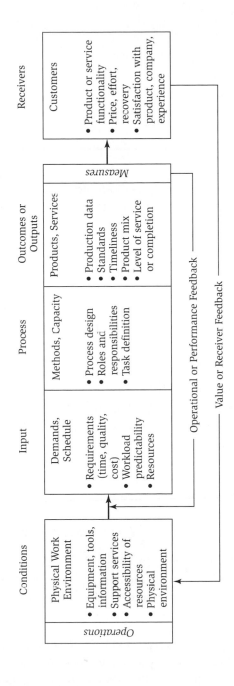

Figure 52.10. The Performance System at the Operations-Process Level from a Whole Systems Perspective.

Figure 52.11. The Performance System at the Organizational-Administrative Level from the Performer's Perspective.

To conduct a comprehensive analysis of an organization, we need to probe each component of the entire human performance system as shown in the previous schematic. Such an examination requires an organizational performance systems framework. This approach allows the analysis of the organization to occur in an integrated fashion across all three levels. Figure 52.14 illustrates the power of the human performance systems logic brought to bear at the three levels of the organization.

Just as there are questions to probe each component of the system at the individual performer level or at the process level, so there are a series of questions that can be used to probe the human performance system at the organizational level. These questions have been grouped in Figure 52.15 by system component.

Organizational Alignment

The systems framework offers a perspective of performance that concentrates on the relationship among system elements at a given level. System scalability supports a common approach to analysis of varying levels of complexity, but the analysis is limited to the horizontal system flow at one level. Obviously, there is a need for the various system levels to work together. The Organizational Alignment Model provides a framework for analyzing the linkage across levels.

In many ways a business organization is an ideal environment for analyzing behavior and developing a technology of performance. It is relatively self-contained:

- It has outcomes that are relatively easily measured.
- It is complex enough to support the application and development of a sophisticated performance technology.
- It is self-sustaining.

As performance technologists began to apply the lessons learned with the operant model that had worked so well for individual performance, they quickly discovered that it was insufficient to account for all the variance in organizational performance. The systems approach provides the means for effectively handling such complexity, but it does not address alignment across the levels. Alignment is

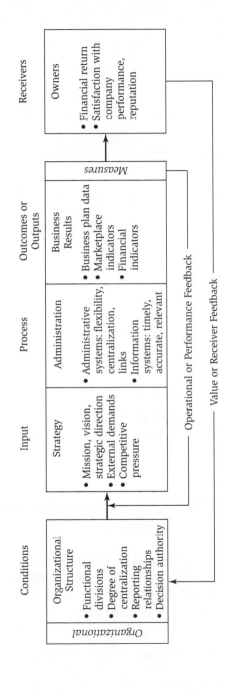

Figure 52.12. The Performance System at the Organizational-Administrative Level from a Whole Systems Perspective.

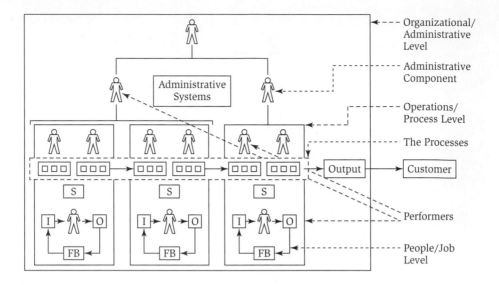

Figure 52.13. The Subsystems of the Organization from the Performer's Perspective.

critical to optimum performance of any complex system: an organization, the human body, or an automobile. If system components are not aligned, they cannot work together to produce optimum results. A primary management function, then, is to ensure alignment across levels.

The Strategy Factor: Aligning Processes. Managers often see their job as making sure that the three levels of organizational complexity are vertically aligned in the execution of a process. They do so by aligning goals and objectives with the organization's mission statement, aligning processes with those goals in order to produce the required services and products, and finally by aligning the tasks that people perform with the processes to produce results. This form of alignment is a common topic of discussion and is often referred to as process alignment, as illustrated in Figure 52.16.

When practitioners are looking at how to strengthen performance, or solve performance problems, it is critical to consider all three levels. A large part of our analysis and intervention, however, occurs at the operations level. By analogy, this is similar to physicians who focus much of their effort on the body's functions and systems, rather than on the cellular level of the body or on the person as a whole.

The Culture Factor: Aligning Practices. A closer look at performance at the operations level makes clear that results depend not just on *what* performers do, the processes people follow, but also on *how* they behave while doing things, the practices people demonstrate. Even with well-designed processes, the behavioral practices of groups and individuals can make the difference

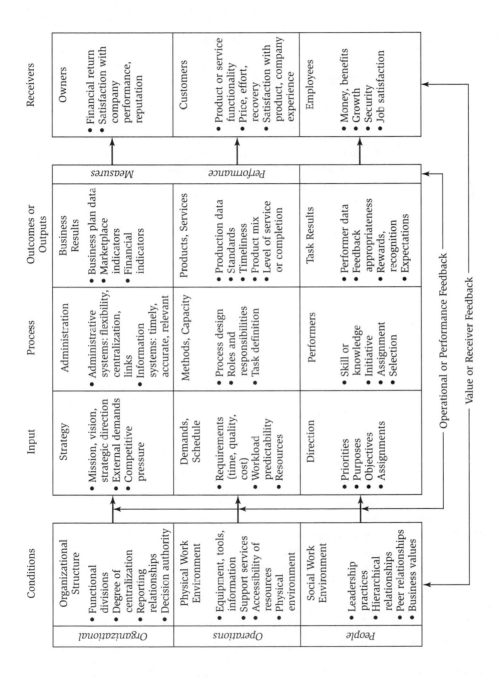

Figure 52.14. The Whole Organizational Performance Systems Framework.

Conditions

Performance System Factor	Questions
STRUCTURE	**Is the organization structured in a way that contributes to effective and efficient performance of the work?**
Functional divisions	Are organizational functions set up to produce clear outcomes that are useful to other units or the organization as a whole? Do people typically know what other functional groups do and how it is related to their own work or that of the organization?
Degree of centralization	Are support functions sufficiently decentralized so that geographically or functionally separate groups can easily obtain support that matches their situation and needs? Are support functions sufficiently centralized so that they can provide support cost-effectively?
Reporting relationships	Do people who do similar or closely related work typically report to the same manager or management group? Do managers in the organization have a reasonable span of control?
Decision authority	Is decision-making authority placed at the lowest feasible level? Do groups have the authority to make most of the decisions that directly affect their work?
PHYSICAL WORK ENVIRONMENT	**Is the work environment set up to make it as easy as possible to work efficiently and effectively?**
Equipment, tools, information	Are necessary equipment, tools, and information available? Are they designed to be easily used and to effectively support the work? Are they cost-effective?
Support services	Are necessary support services available? Are they designed to be easily used and to effectively support the work? Are they cost-effective?

Figure 52.15. Sample Probes for the Organizational Performance Systems Framework.

Performance System Factor	Questions
Accessibility of resources	Are equipment, tools, and information readily accessible when and where they are needed? Are support services easily accessed when needed? Are supplies and raw materials readily accessible when needed?
Physical environment	Are space, light, and temperature adequate to work effectively? Is the environment free of physical obstacles that get in the way of doing the work?
SOCIAL WORK ENVIRONMENT	**Do people throughout the organization typically behave in a way that supports effective performance?**
Leadership practices	Do organizational leaders typically: • Provide people with clear direction about goals? • Create a compelling vision about purposes and what the future could be like? • Provide advice and coaching when needed? • Demonstrate through their own behavior what they expect of others? • Offer recognition or rewards for improved or excellent performance? • Encourage initiative?
Hierarchical relationships	Do people accept and even encourage information, opinions, and ideas from people who are below them in the organizational hierarchy? Do people readily provide relevant information, ideas, and opinions to people who are both above and below them in the organizational hierarchy?
Peer relationships	Do organizational peers or colleagues typically: • Share relevant information with each other as well as encourage and accept suggestions and feedback from each other? • Treat each other with respect? • Share the risk and responsibility for mutual efforts?

Figure 52.15 (*Continued*).

Performance System Factor	Questions
Business values	Has the organization defined and communicated its business values to people within the organization, to suppliers, and to customers as well? Do people in the organization typically behave in a way that reflects those values? Are the values compatible with the organization's strategy and goals? Are the values compatible with the needs and expectations of the organization's customers?

Input

Performance System Factor	Questions
STRATEGY	**Is the organization's strategy clear and appropriately responsive to the demands of the business and competitive environment?**
Mission, vision, strategic direction	Does the organization have: • A clear mission: what the organization is in business to do? • A vision of the desired future and why it matters? • A strategic direction: how the organization intends to succeed? Do people throughout the organization understand the mission, vision, and strategy? Do people "buy into" the mission, vision, and strategy?
External demands	Does the organization have a clear picture of the external demands that are now being placed on it? Do the organization's leaders regularly scan the external environment to assess and adapt to potential changes in demands? Are the organization's mission, vision, and strategy responsive to external demands?
Competitive pressure	Does the organization have a clear picture of its competition? Who are they and how are they positioned in the marketplace? Does the organization keep abreast of what the competition is doing? Are the organization's mission, vision, and strategy responsive to the competition?

Figure 52.15. Sample Probes for the Organizational Performance Systems Framework (*Continued*).

Performance System Factor	Questions
DEMANDS, SCHEDULE	**Are the demands placed on the work clearly defined and managed so that work can proceed efficiently and effectively?**
Requirements (time, quality, cost)	Are the requirements for successful completion of the work clearly understood? Do requirements match the organization's strategy and customer needs?
Workload predictability	Is the workload sufficiently predictable so that people can respond to it successfully or are plans in place for dealing with unpredictable changes in the workload? Is the workload effectively monitored and managed to minimize surprises? Are those who will be directly affected by workload changes informed of them as soon as possible?
Resources	Are sufficient resources available to effectively respond to the workload and meet requirements? Are resources managed so that the right resources are available when needed?
DIRECTION	**Do leaders and managers provide clear direction that supports the organization's mission, vision, strategy, and desired business results?**
Priorities	Do priorities match the mission, vision, and strategy? Are priorities clearly communicated and followed?
Purposes	Are purposes communicated? Do people understand how their work contributes to larger organizational goals and purposes?
Objectives	Are unit objectives derived from the organization's strategy? Are objectives compatible across business units? Are objectives clearly communicated to those who are expected to accomplish them? Do the objectives as a whole represent full accomplishment of the organization's strategic goals?

Figure 52.15 (*Continued*).

Performance System Factor	Questions
Assignments	Are work assignments, both ongoing work and special projects, derived from organizational strategy and objectives? Are work assignments compatible across individuals and groups? Are work assignments clearly communicated; do people know what they are expected to do? Do work assignments as a whole represent full accomplishment of objectives?

Process

Performance System Factor	Questions
ADMINISTRATION	**Do administrative systems and policies support performing the work of the organization effectively and efficiently?**
Administrative systems: flexibility, links, centralization	Are administrative systems flexible enough that people can effectively respond to the variety of work situations they encounter? Are systems linked so that controls and guidelines in one area of the organization are compatible with those in other areas? Are systems centralized enough that compatibility and efficiency are maintained? Are systems decentralized enough to allow for local solutions?
Information systems: timely, accurate, relevant	Do information systems provide people with the information they need when they need it? Is the information accurate and reliable? Do information systems provide people with information that is directly relevant to the decisions they need to make? Is irrelevant information omitted? Is information provided in a form that is easy to use and understand?

Figure 52.15. Sample Probes for the Organizational Performance Systems Framework (*Continued*).

Performance System Factor	Questions
METHODS, CAPACITY	**Do work methods support effective performance? Does the system have the capacity to perform as desired?**
Process design	Are process goals clear? Are all relevant functions in place? Are they free of redundancies and unnecessary work? Is there clear and appropriate flow of inputs and outputs throughout the process? Are process steps documented?
Roles and responsibilities	Are roles and responsibilities clear? Are responsibilities compatible? Free of conflicts? Are process interfaces managed?
Task definition	Are tasks defined and documented as needed? Is documentation clear, useful, and up to date?
PERFORMERS	**Do people have the capability to perform their work efficiently and effectively?**
Skill or knowledge	Do people know what they are expected to accomplish and why? Do people know how to perform successfully? Do people have the skills to perform successfully?
Initiative	Are people encouraged to take initiative to improve their performance or to adapt it to changing situations and demands whenever feasible? Do people clearly know when it is appropriate to take initiative and when it is not?
Assignment	Are people given clear work assignments? Do work assignments match the capabilities and skill levels of performers?
Selection	Do selection or hiring criteria match job requirements? Are people selected for positions based on both their capability to perform and their interest in the kind of work being performed?

Figure 52.15 (*Continued*).

Outputs

Performance System Factor	*Questions*
BUSINESS RESULTS	**Are expected business results defined and linked to organizational strategy? Are they measured and monitored?**
Business plan data	Do business plans reflect strategic input? Are they compatible across functions? Are plans monitored and managed? Is reliable information about performance against the plan available to those who need or can use it?
Marketplace indicators	Are measures in place to track key aspects of the organization's performance in the marketplace? Is information about marketplace performance made available to those who need it or can use it?
Financial indicators	Are measures in place to track key aspects of the organization's financial performance? Is information about financial performance made available to those who need it or can use it?
PRODUCTS, SERVICES	**Are expectations for product and service performance defined and linked to organizational strategy? Are they measured and monitored?**
Product data	Is information about product or service quality gathered? Is information accurate, reliable, and timely? Is information made available to those who need it or can use it?
Standards	Are product or service standards defined and is performance against those standards measured? Is the information made available to those who need it or can use it?
Timeliness	Are requirements for timely delivery defined and is performance against those requirements measured? Is the information made available to those who need it or can use it?

Figure 52.15. Sample Probes for the Organizational Performance Systems Framework (*Continued*).

Performance System Factor	Questions
Product mix	Are product mix guidelines or expectations established and information about the actual mix gathered? Is the information made available to those who need it or can use it?
PERFORMER'S RESULTS	**Are there appropriate consequences for effective performance: information, rewards, and recognition?**
Performer data	Is information gathered about individual performance in relation to standards? Are those standards linked to company strategy and goals? Are data made available to people who need it or can use it?
Feedback appropriateness	Are feedback sources reliable? Is feedback timely, constructive, and useful?
Rewards, recognition	Are rewards and recognition provided for performance? Are rewards and recognition clearly linked to performance that meets or exceeds standards? Are rewards and recognition valued by performers and seen as commensurate with the quality of performance?
Expectations	Is information about business behavior in relation to expectations gathered? Is information made available to people who need it or can use it?

Receivers

Performance System Factor	Questions
OWNERS	**To what extent is the organization creating value for owners? To what extent is it using owner feedback to continue to create or increase value?**
Financial return	Do owners receive what they see as an adequate return on their investment? Are expectations about financial return monitored and used to look for ways to adapt as appropriate?

Figure 52.15 (*Continued*).

Performance System Factor	Questions
Satisfaction with company performance, reputation	How satisfied are owners with the company's performance and reputation? Are expectations about company performance and reputation monitored and used to look for ways to adapt as appropriate?
CUSTOMERS	**To what extent is the organization creating value for customers? To what extent is it using customer feedback to continue to create or increase value?**
Product or service functionality	To what extent do products or services function as customers want or need them? Are expectations about product or service function monitored and used to look for ways to adapt as appropriate?
Price, effort, recovery	To what extent do customers consider the price and effort associated with products and services reasonable in relation to the value they receive? To what extent are customers pleased with the company's recovery efforts when they have problems or complaints? Are expectations about price, effort, and recovery monitored and used to look for ways to adapt as appropriate?
Satisfaction with product, company experience	How satisfied are customers with: • Their overall experience with products and services? • Their experience with the company and its people? Are expectations about product or service and company experience monitored and used to look for ways to adapt as appropriate?
EMPLOYEES	**To what extent is the organization creating value for employees? To what extent is it using employee feedback to continue to create or increase value?**
Money, benefits	Do employees receive what they see as adequate money and benefits for their performance? Are expectations about money and benefits monitored and used to look for ways to adapt as appropriate?
Growth	Do employees see adequate opportunity for growth in their jobs? Are expectations about growth monitored and used to look for ways to adapt as appropriate?

Figure 52.15. Sample Probes for the Organizational Performance Systems Framework (*Continued*).

Performance System Factor	Questions
Security	Are employees satisfied with job security? Are expectations about job security monitored and used to look for ways to adapt as appropriate?
Job satisfaction	How satisfied are employees with their work, including the work itself, the environment, and the value they create? Are expectations about job satisfaction monitored and used to look for ways to adapt as appropriate?

Figure 52.15 (*Continued*).

Level	Alignment
	Mission
Organizational	Goals
Operations	Processes
Job	Tasks
	Result

Figure 52.16. Organization Processes Alignment.

between merely adequate results and outstanding results. In the worst case, poor practices can destroy good processes.

Thus, what people do is sometimes less important than *how* they do it, especially over the long term. Products, services, and technology, even unique, first-class ones, often give organizations a short-lived edge over their competition. Sustained success depends on how an organization's people deliver those products and services.

When reengineering was first introduced as a performance intervention, many organizations spent a lot of time and money only to achieve little in the way of improved results. Follow-up studies found that in almost every case, the reason was a failure to recognize that the change in process required a realignment of practices for the new process to be effective. Despite this, it is only in relatively recent years that managers and performance consultants have given serious attention to practices. There appear to be at least two reasons for this, according to Tosti and Jackson (1994):

Practices are often companywide. In performing their jobs, most people in the organization exhibit behavior patterns that reflect common company practices. There are prevailing norms, expectations, and rewards that support these practices. People whose behavior does not fit those norms and expectations may find themselves quite uncomfortable. This makes it difficult for people to change their practices unless the behavior of others around them changes at the same time or the environment changes in a way that clearly supports new behavior. Under ideal change circumstances, both will change to reinforce the new behavioral practices.

The relationships to results may not be obvious. People usually know how their task or process behavior affects the results of their work. A good deal of effort often goes into designing processes and tasks. Practices typically develop over time, without the same kind of planning that went into process development, and may become virtually unnoticed habits. People may not see how the practices that define their approach to the work or their treatment of their coworkers affect results.

As an example, consider organizations in which a high degree of internal competitiveness affects the way people work with other departments, as well as their view of external competitors. The resulting working relationships are far less effective than if guided by practices that foster cooperation or partnering. But that connection is not always visible to people in the organization who are simply behaving the same way everyone else does.

Thus, if a person is asked to change task-related behaviors, for example, to organize information in a business case differently, or to assemble equipment in a new sequence of steps, the change will not usually fly in the face of prevailing norms. If someone is asked to work differently with others, however, for example, to consult widely in preparing a business case or share equipment assembly tasks, this may violate expectations about how things have always been done. Practices can be viewed in the context of an alignment framework similar to that for processes. We call this the practices alignment and typically show it as depicted in Figure 52.17.

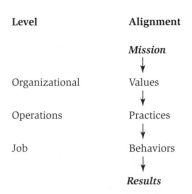

Figure 52.17. Organization Practices Alignment.

Alignment

Mission or Vision

Goals   Values

Processes   Practices

Tasks   Behaviors

Results

Figure 52.18. Organization Alignment.

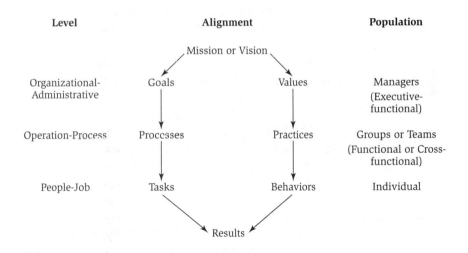

Level	Alignment	Population
	Mission or Vision	
Organizational-Administrative	Goals Values	Managers (Executive-functional)
Operation-Process	Processes Practices	Groups or Teams (Functional or Cross-functional)
People-Job	Tasks Behaviors	Individual
	Results	

Figure 52.19. The Extended Organizational Alignment Framework.

Putting those two alignment frameworks together (see Figure 52.18) allows us to create a balanced model for organizational alignment.

To further illustrate the linkages between this model and the organization, consider the graphic found in Figure 52.19, which seeks to better amplify relationships between levels of system complexity and the levels of populations within the organization.

CONCLUSION

Understanding that every organization at its most basic level is a human performance system is critical for the success of virtually any attempt to improve or maintain performance. It is as important for every manager and every consultant to management to grasp this reality as it is for a medical doctor to recognize that the human body is at its basic level a biological system. Too many so-called *solutions* have either failed or are short-lived precisely because they failed to adequately address the *people* issues with this understanding.

The HPT systems framework supports an assessment of the interrelationship of the functional flow of the organization and the vertical alignment of the organization, integrating the whole in terms of the contributions of the subsystems to the results. Using both the organizational alignment and systems frameworks accommodates all HPT variables within an organization and clarifies the interdependency between such variables. This integrated framework enables consultants to test new concepts or models against an existing understanding of organization systems and the need for alignment for results. These two themes have the potential to serve as a foundation for all forms of organizational consulting. With such a foundation, the future is unlimited.

References

Brethower, D. (1972). *Behavior analysis in business and industry: A total performance system.* Kalamazoo, MI: Behaviordelia Press.

Brethower, D. (2002). *Notes on value-added, scalability, and alignment.* Phoenix, AZ: Circulated Paper.

Carleton, J. R., and Lineberry, C. S. (2004). *Achieving post-merger success.* San Francisco: Jossey-Bass/Pfeiffer.

Gilbert, T. F. (1996). *Human competence: Engineering worthy performance* (Tribute Ed.). Washington, DC: International Society for Performance Improvement and HRD Press.

Evans, J. L., Homme, L. E., and Glaser, R. (1962). The RULEG system for the construction of programmed verbal learning sequences. *Journal of Educational Research, 55,* 513–518.

Homme, L., and Homme, A. (1966). What behavioral engineering is. *Psychological Record, 16.*

Homme, L. E., Csanyi, A. P., Gonzales, M. A., and Rechs, J. R. (1969). *How to use contingency contracting in the classroom.* Champaign, IL: Research Press.

Mager, R. F., and Pipe, P. (1970). *Analyzing performance problems.* Belmont, CA: Fearon.

Miller, J. G. (1978). *Living systems.* New York: McGraw-Hill.

Rummler, G. A. (2004). *Serious performance consulting: According to Rummler.* Silver Spring, MD: International Society for Performance Improvement and American Society for Training and Development.

Rummler, G. A., and Brache, A. P. (1995). *Improving performance: How to manage the white space on the organization chart* (2nd ed.). San Francisco: Jossey-Bass.

Tosti, D. T. (1968). PRIME: A General model for Instructional Systems. *NSPI Journal, VII*(2), 11–15.

Tosti, D. T., and Jackson, S. F. (1994, April). Organizational alignment: How it works and why it matters. *Training Magazine,* 58–64.

Additional Resources

Ackoff, R. L. (1999). *Ackoff's best: His classic writings on management.* New York: Wiley.

Ackoff, R. L. (1999). *Recreating the corporation: A design of organizations for the 21st century.* New York: Oxford University Press.

Carleton, J. R., and Rummler, G. A. (2004, April). *Serious total organizational system integration in mergers and acquisitions.* ISPI Annual Conference, Tampa, Florida.

Langdon, D. (2000). *Aligning performance: Improving people, systems, and organizations.* San Francisco: Jossey-Bass/Pfeiffer.

Tosti, D., and Ball, J. (1969, Spring). A behavioral approach to instructional design and media selection. *Journal of Audio-Visual Communication Review, 17,* 5–25.

CHAPTER FIFTY-THREE

Systems, Measures, and Workers

*Producing and Obscuring the System
and Making Systemic Performance
Improvement Difficult*

Donald J. Winiecki

Early in the preparation of this chapter, James A. Pershing, the editor of this volume, suggested that systems thinking in instructional and performance technology is more metaphorical than systems thinking in the physical or biological sciences and does not have the same status. In other words, for us, systems are more abstract depictions when applied to social phenomena rather than physical processes and serve as a convenient tool to think with as we attempt to learn and know things, create new knowledge, develop and control social phenomena, and analyze and try to reorient social phenomena when they do not work as we intended or when we change our minds about how we want organizations to function. Indeed, all theories are properly thought of as tools to think with. This chapter accepts that view of systems as accurate. As we continue to learn about our systems, our theories of how they function should change. Of course, this does not necessarily mean they become more true or closer to perfection, only that our theories are changed to fit what we are experiencing in the real world. In other words, systems thinking appears to do things to us, and we do things to systems thinking that changes how we know it and can use it in our work.

In a small company, the organization is fairly compact and it is relatively easy for one person to know and understand everything at once. However, as organizations grow in size and perhaps even occupy space in more than one town, city, or country, they begin to be difficult if not impossible to fully know and understand. There are just so many subsystems internal to the organization to keep track of that no one individual can know it all. General systems theory and management theory provide us with tools to think with and with which to break down such large systems into components so they can be intentionally designed, managed, and regulated by separate individuals who are all aware of the goals of the overall organization (Hoskin, 1998; Hoskin and Macve, 1994). Also, see Brethower (1999) for a treatment of general systems theory related to the field of human performance technology (HPT).

Principally, general systems theory has several fundamental principals. Systems (1) require constant consumption of resources to maintain or grow, (2) follow particular rules for adapting to or constraining factors surrounding them, (3) can be guided to satisfy certain desired ends by manipulating access to resources or surroundings, and (4) have subcomponents that can be measured, regulated, and compromised in ways that may constrain parts but that allow the whole system to survive.

When a large system is broken down into subsystems, individual managers assigned to oversee subsystems translate their knowledge of how the overall organization is supposed to operate into day-to-day thinking and actions. That is, while systems-oriented thinking allows us to envision them in unique and beneficial ways, when systems get large, we adopt tactics and strategies that allow us to reduce their complexity so we can work with them in terms of discrete inputs and outputs. When many such subsystems are connected, we might aim to have their relatively smaller inputs and outputs accrue to what has been called outcomes at a larger, perhaps societal level (Kaufman, 1992).

As a side effect of these rationalizing tactics and strategies to reduce complexity, and depending on one's position in a system, the system is experienced and known differently. To the high-level manager, the system typically appears in the form of reports or spreadsheets detailing how the organization is functioning against particular measures. To the middle manager, the system appears as a hectic environment in which business happens, and which has to be maintained according to particular rules of the organization in order to keep the organization functioning. Not only that, but the middle manager also has to translate the hectic environment of business and performance into reports and spreadsheets for delivery to high-level management so they can know what is happening. To the worker, the system appears as a set of more or less rationalized and more or less well-defined activities, data, tools, feedback, and incentives with which to perform those activities. The worker is also usually aware of at least part of the reporting described earlier. These are not new ideas. They have been part of the landscape and logic of business for at least several hundred years (Durkheim, 1997; Smith, 1991 [1776]; Weber, 2001).

This reporting becomes known through feedback on performance delivered either individually or to a group of workers. This feedback usually takes the form of comparisons between what the company wants and what it is doing, that is, the presentation of gaps. These comparisons are usually in the form of charts, tables, graphs, and other media that allow the difference between desired and actual to be communicated efficiently. While all of the stakeholders, high-level managers, middle managers, and workers, are focused on very different things, they all come to have knowledge of the system in a similar way, through reports and statistics. All of these groups of individuals also carry with them knowledge, skills, and values that are not specific to the workplace but are deployed in the context of things that happen in the workplace.

In all scientific and technical fields, statistics are a common language. They permit huge quantities of data to be rendered into very compact forms that provide a totalizing sort of gaze over the field from which the data were collected. They also permit each individual in the system or, more correctly, the data representing that individual, to be pinpointed in the array of data. With this, a measure of difference between desired and actual is thus possible for both the entire organization and each individual in it. This has been called a totalizing and individualizing effect (Foucault, 1995; Hopper and Macintosh, 1998). These data are essential in many forms of front-end analysis and evaluation in organizations. Figure 53.1 shows how this totalizing and individualizing gaze can be simply accomplished (Durr, 1996). The figure displays the total team of call center agents and their individual scores on both quality ratings and quantity along normalized scales. The organization dubs this productivity. The horizontal and vertical bands represent the minimum standards expected on quality and

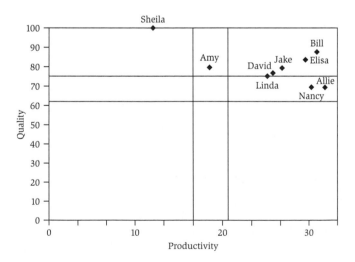

Figure 53.1. Totalizing and Individualizing with Statistics.

Source: Durr, 1996, p. 92.

quantity measures for the call center agents in this team. Durr (1996) recommends the use of this sort of display to highlight to both management and the agents themselves who is doing what level of work as compared with both the organizational expectations and others on the team.

The statistics and their display on this chart are considered to be a sufficient representation of work to allow management to identify who is not performing to expectations and thus where to direct energies for producing change. Similarly, across subsystems in a single organization, statistics provide management and workers with the ability to see how things are going in many places, without having to have intimate knowledge of the day-to-day activities being conducted in those places. Management and workers at any level of an organization can see statistics as a representation of how others are doing or how one is doing in terms common to the organization or work group.

MANUFACTURING KNOWLEDGE

The data from which statistics are produced come from observations of some kind. The value asserted by these observations is measured as a distance from a baseline. Observations can be objective, meaning that the observation does not rely on human judgment but rather is just there, or waiting to be noticed by an observer. Objective observations in a call center include the number of calls that are handled in a call center per day and by each agent per day, or the duration of each call handled by a call center agent. Observations can also be subjective, meaning that they depend on human judgment. Subjective observations include things such as the quality of a call center agent's conduct when talking with customers. The value of the number of calls handled per day by a call center agent is established by measuring the difference between the number of calls actually handled and the organization's desired target number of calls to be handled per day.

To place some reliability on both objective and subjective observations, it is common for rules to be established for producing the observation. When counting the number of calls handled by each agent, we establish what defines a call. We may say that we do not count those calls that were misrouted to the agent, or we establish a count per hour as the basic framework of the observation. We can even program these rules into the phone system of a call center so that such observations are made and recorded continuously and automatically. When scoring the quality of a call center agent's conduct with customers, we may establish a set of rules and codify those rules on a form to be used when doing quality evaluations. We may train those individuals responsible for doing quality evaluations so that they are all aware of particular details that we want to be considered and particular scales with which to score those details. Each of these interventions acts to improve the probability that all quality evaluations done by anyone will follow the same basic framework, thus permitting all evaluations to be totalized into an average level of performance, and permitting each individual agent's quality score to be compared to the average or other points in the total range of scores.

The product of this activity, whether objective or subjective, is knowledge. By aggregating measurements of the same or definably similar activities over time, we produce a particular kind of knowledge of those activities and the individuals who perform them. As shown in Figure 53.1, Bill has the highest combined quality and productivity rating of any agent on this team while Sheila has the highest quality but lowest productivity rating on the team. The remaining agents meet or exceed the expectations for combined quality and productivity scores. These findings are produced through various objective and subjective observations and the statistical processing of the data collected through those observations. By hybridizing (Latour and Woolgar, 1990) the different observations and statistical representations of quality and productivity, we can produce a general indication of value. For example, in terms of the quality and productivity hybrid shown in Figure 53.1, Bill can be said to be a more valuable agent than Sheila. In call centers participating in my research, this is usually considered the right way to view the data. As will be shown further on, however, there are times when management, supervisors, and agents would like us to see and interpret the data otherwise. That is, depending on context or other knowledge, management, supervisors, and agents can deploy the same data to justify and prove different things. In other words, our ways of producing knowledge, and thus ways of knowing, permit us to selectively combine or exclude things depending on factors that are local to the user and which may not have been considered when the data were collected.

MANUFACTURING OFFICIAL IGNORANCE

Besides establishing some reliability of our observations, an essential characteristic of data to be used in any statistical process, the rules we set have another effect. These rules also indicate what we are not supposed to pay attention to when doing observations; they are supposed to impose boundaries or filters on our observations and thus protect the statistical product of those observations from presumably corrupting factors (Latour and Woolgar, 1990). For example, by designing a training course on how to carry out an evaluation, or by designing evaluation instruments in a particular way, we implicitly expect individuals doing quality evaluations not to consider any factors we have not included on the scoring forms they use or that are not included in their training on how to do quality evaluations.

Similar to the simplifying tactics and strategies we use to subdivide large systems into subsystems, sub-subsystems, and so forth, methods of collecting data and combining those data into statistics translate the complexity of everyday activity in an organization into a simplified form. In both cases this is accomplished by (1) telling each worker what to pay attention to and do, and (2) implying what the organization wants to ignore, thus, implicitly, what the organization does not want to pay attention to. Systems thinking and doing and all of the processes encompassed can be considered as ways of conceptualizing large-scale organizations and then simplifying them into forms that can be more easily handled. They are tools to think with and ways of producing knowledge or identifying gaps in knowledge for our organizations. As suggested earlier, knowledge and ignorance can be selectively deployed by individuals at many levels in organizations to justify what seems relevant at the time, while at the same time obscuring from view or mitigating contextual knowledge that was used along the way.

It will come as a surprise to nobody that despite these rules, even the most diligent worker will occasionally, maybe even frequently, deploy his or her local knowledge of the workplace and personal knowledge, skill, and values in ways that corrupt the official production of knowledge. However, this is frequently done in ways that are obscured and that permit the system to keep functioning in the face of incorrigible situations. While official ignorance may not be bliss, in many cases, it is a very practical thing for workers who find themselves in incorrigible situations to use.

Getting Performance, Obscuring Gaps, and Impeding Improvement

Intuitively, simplification of any complex concept or organization will result in the loss of some data. Whenever we begin with a vision of a system or assemblage of subsystems and then reduce our focus to particular inputs, outputs, and so forth in the form of measures, we lose detail. As previously indicated, this is a pragmatic decision. We simply cannot pay attention to everything at once. And, even with the best of intentions, careful planning, and application of technical knowledge, some things are bound to be missed. In human performance technology, our hope is that we will gradually but methodically catch those missed items and incorporate them into our system. In doing so, we will realize continuous improvement.

Examples are provided further on to show that most actors will develop practices to ensure they are observed and measured to be in compliance with performance expectations made of them. The workers will act such that their managers can produce statistical or other forms of reports that show their activity and output of their work is within the expected or desired range. Upon seeing these reports, higher-level management will see that the organization is operating as expected. It is only when the statistical reductions of performance data are not within the expected range that higher-level management will take notice and put pressure on managers to remedy the situation. It is not a new contention, however, that workers and managers can and do take steps to effect change in performance informally and locally with the explicit goal to avoid drawing the ire of higher-level personnel (Argyris, 1952; Winiecki, 2002, 2003). In effect, workers have an interest in addressing their own problems, even if those problems are systemic and not of their own making. In so doing, the simplified statistical representations of work appear to represent normal activity, while the actual activity is much more intensive and interactive. That is, what actually happens is made officially invisible to those who read the reports and concentrate only on the statistics.

It is also the case that workers have knowledge of local processes relevant to the solution of local problems that can and will be invoked not with the goal of avoiding the attentions of management, but rather to ensure that other local and perhaps informal values and systems are maintained or to protect worker authority not formally regulated by the organization (Button and Harper, 1993). In such cases, the formal aims of the organization continue to be met in ways that obscure the actual conduct of workers, including management at all levels. In a trenchant study of institutions in modern America, sociologist Erving Goffman called such cases "continuous secondary adjustments" to indicate that the interest of the organization was maintained, while the members adjusted their practice to effect secondary or informal goals (1961, pp. 54ff, 199ff), while no practical harm comes to the organization or its members.

These practices, while reinforcing the appearance that everything is happening as expected or desired, also have an effect of obscuring what might be systemic problems that the workers should not have to take responsibility for. In a marvelous example of secondary adjustments, Button and Harper (1993) document how workers actually maintained a shadow organization that allowed them to support a highly respected but somewhat incompetent boss through a set of radical changes he instituted in the organization.

This is not to say that no performance improvements are called for, however. When workers act locally to maintain the present system, they may cover up problems and in so doing make it possible for observations and statistical records to indicate the system is operating as expected. That is, they may actually obscure systemic problems through their day-to-day heroic efforts to keep the system functioning; workers act in ways that may actually conspire against them by taking responsibility for and compensating for problems located at the organizational level.

The next sections of the chapter will introduce and then draw upon data from a multiyear ethnographic study in call centers to illustrate the issues just identified.

SETTING THE STAGE: HOW CALL CENTERS MANUFACTURE KNOWLEDGE AND PERMIT GAPS IN KNOWLEDGE

Call centers are a growing field of employment in all Westernized countries. They are but one component of a huge, cross-national shift from production work to service work called post-industrialization by Daniel Bell in the 1970s (Bell, 1973). Generally acknowledged to have begun in the early 1970s with a movement toward telephone-based service in High Street banks in London (Call Center News Service, 2000), recent reports set the number of U.S. call center workstations at 2.86 million in 50,600 call centers and international workstations at 109,000, with a trend toward decreasing U.S. workstations and increasing those located outside of the United States (Datamonitor, 2004).

The development of telephone-based service work to replace or augment walk-up service work is attributed primarily to economic pressures to reduce the cost of direct interaction with customers, otherwise known as customer-facing work. However, to realize the potential cost savings of consolidating the customer-facing work of individual branch offices into a single or a few call center locations, other changes in the way customer-facing service work was conducted had to be developed and implemented. As in all cases of business process reengineering, this included the rationalization of what services the company would offer to customers and the routinization of procedures that would have to be followed in order to accomplish those services. At the same time, new tools and technologies were developed that regulated workers in their performance of routine procedures and at the same time automatically observed them in this work and recorded call-by-call observations into databases that allowed for a totalizing and individualizing gaze over the workers.

This imbrication of routinization and observation was made economically possible with the development of a computer interface between the customer and the call center agent. This interface is called the automated call distributor, or ACD (Bodin and Dawson, 1999; Taylor and Bain, 1999). The ACD fulfills several functions. First, the ACD routes calls to the next available agent so that callers' hold times are kept to a minimum and more calls can be handled per agent per day. This also transforms an irregular pattern of incoming calls into a series that can be distributed to agents in an orderly way. This produces a queue similar to what one would find in an assembly line process. Once calls are organized into a queue and agents can be expected to answer approximately the same number of calls per shift, the work of agents becomes statistically comparable. Note that the call centers participating in this study are inbound call centers, meaning they accept only inbound calls from customers. Call centers that conduct telemarketing work are considered to be outbound call centers. For inbound call centers, the

ACD is as just described. For outbound call centers, ACD stands for automated call dialer. Its purpose is to estimate when the next agent will end his or her current telemarketing call, and prospectively dial another phone in order to connect the customer with an agent just as the agent finishes his or her current call.

In addition, the ACD is programmed to automatically detect and record particular artifacts of each call center agent's work, either directly or by statistical operations that combine individual observations. In the call centers participating in this project, as many as twenty different statistics are computed for each agent and the call center as a whole on a continuous basis by the ACD. Examples include how long each call takes, how long an agent pauses between calls, how many minutes are spent on other work products such as the preparation of database records documenting the call, and so on, as well as if the agent arrives to work late or leaves early, the times breaks are taken, the duration of breaks, and so forth. In fact, many more than twenty different types of observations and generation of statistics can be performed by the typical ACD. However, the management at individual call centers has the discretion to decide which of these statistics will be used in their management of the operation. Each of the observations and resulting statistics produced by the ACD is derived from only three pieces of data, (1) the clock time, (2) the time a call was picked up, and (3) the time a call was ended.

The use of the ACD provides the call center management with a continuous stream of objective data on the operation of the entire call center and each individual agent. Figure 53.2 shows an ACD report from one of the call centers participating in this study. Shaded or circled cells provide nominal evaluation of statistics that comply with or deviate from organizational limits. The notes at the lower left indicate desired goals, the meaning of each marking, and feedback to selected workers in terms of statistical representations of their work.

In addition, in each of the call centers participating in this study, covert observation of each agent is to be accomplished on a regular basis in order to evaluate the quality of each agent's work. These quality observations are to be accomplished in accordance with a company-provided form that frames what the evaluator is to look for and rules for evaluating and coding the agent's performance on these items. Figure 53.3 displays an example of the form used in one of the call centers participating in this study. Covert observations are accomplished through a phone-tapping apparatus commonly known as a "barge." The barge allows the evaluator to listen to the on-phone activity of the agent and customer in real time or to record it. The barge is not able to capture things said or done when the agent has muted his or her phone, or placed the customer on hold.

At "A" in Figure 53.3, a set of seven items that must be included in each call is listed. The evaluator puts a check mark in the space under each item if the

Agent Name	ACD Calls	Average Talk Time	In-Bound Exterior Calls	Out-Bound Calls	Out-Bound within Center	Total Out-Bound Time	Out-Bound Percentage	Total AUX Time	Total Train Time	Total ACW Time	Available Time	Staffed Time, Percentage Available	Percentage Available	Calls Per Hour	NCPH
Totals	**929**	**2:16**	**9**	**108**	**27**	**3:06**	**10.4**	**4:06**	**:00**	**3:35**	**6:18**	**52:33**	**93.17**	**17.7**	**20.1**
	151	1:40	2	19	3	:33	11.2	:36	:00	:36	1:03	7:03	91.50	21.4	25.2
	144	2:17	1	13	5	:11	8.3	:21	:00	:37	1:00	7:46	91.96	18.5	21.3
	58	2:25	0	17	3	:21	22.7	:25	:00	:15	:25	3:47	93.36	15.3	17.2
	64	2:08	3	8	0	:08	11.1	:09	:00	:22	:14	3:23	68.74	18.8	20.3
	115	3:06	1	3	2	:06	2.5	:14	:00	:19	:47	7:36	95.73	15.1	14.9
	148	2:05	2	17	7	:35	10.4	:49	:00	:27	:54	7:33	93.90	19.3	21.9
	100	2:30	0	14	6	:22	12.3	:34	:00	:42	:52	7:40	90.78	13.0	14.7
	151	2:07	0	17	1	:47	19.1	:52	:00	:14	:50	7:40	95.54	19.7	22.6

Team Goals
Talk Time ≤ 2:00
Out-Bound ≤ 15%
Available ≥ 95%
NCPH ≥ 25 calls per hour

Wow! Great job!
Almost! Keep working!
Please work on this

Figure 53.2. Totalizing and Individualizing Gaze of the ACD.

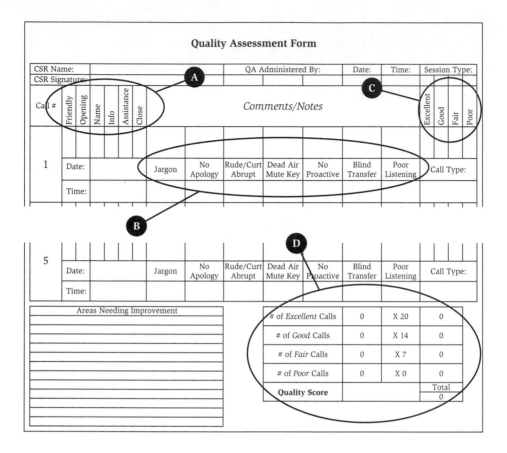

Figure 53.3. Quality Rating Form.

agent includes it in the call being rated. At "B" in Figure 53.3, what some colloquially call "the seven deadly sins" are listed. If an agent commits one of these items during a call, the evaluator marks it in the space above that item. The evaluator refers to a companion set of rules, not shown here, that indicate how accomplishment of the items at "A" and commission of the items at "B" accrue to produce an overall rating of excellent, good, fair, or poor for that call: "C" in Figure 53.3. After five calls are rated, the evaluator converts these nominal ratings to a numeric score at "C." Because the evaluator interprets the agent's performance in terms of the rules provided, these ratings are considered subjective. However, following ongoing training and calibration activities for the evaluators, and given that the ratings are regulated by the form shown in Figure 53.3, including a companion set of rules, ratings are considered to be generally reliable across evaluators and agents.

As is done with the ACD data and statistics, the numeric quality scores of agents are archived to produce a continuous database of agent performance over time. However, unlike the continuously collected ACD data and statistics just described, in the call centers participating in this study, quality ratings are performed on between five and ten calls per agent per month. Agents in these same call centers answer between two hundred and thirty-six hundred calls per month, and the duration of these calls can be as little as forty-five seconds or as long as several hours, depending on the call center and the issue being addressed. Officially, quality ratings are to be used to inform feedback, coaching, and ongoing training of agents in addition to providing data to be included in each agent's semiannual or annual evaluation.

In some of the call centers participating in this project, monthly paper-pencil tests, biweekly interactive quizzes over the contents of a database used in day-to-day answering of customer questions, also account for portions of the call center agent's performance rating. In addition, supervisors or management personnel are expected to subjectively rate each agent based on his or her willingness to comply and actual compliance with local policies and ad hoc shifts, such as schedule changes, meeting attendance, communication skills, professionalism, and responsibility, as defined by the organization. Despite the regulatory function of the quality rating form, the evaluator has access to substantial information in the course of the call that can be considered in addition to the line items included. Access to this additional information provides the evaluator with a substantial resource and unregulated authority to handle issues locally without reporting them on the form. In many cases, this is known by the organization but permitted in the interest of exploiting the knowledge of agents, reducing management labor, or exposing the call center to the attention of higher-level management.

Finally, in two of the four call centers included in this project, internal personnel or contractors conduct what is called a mystery caller audit of the call centers. In the mystery caller audit, a representative of the organization or a subcontractor acting on higher-management direction completes a set number of calls into the call center each month and asks scripted questions of agents. The agents are rated on their politeness, friendliness, correctness, and completeness of their responses in terms of company policy and current promotions or programs. Data from these audits are compiled and reported back to the call center. In organizations with more than one call center, these data are used to rate and rank call centers.

With respect to the mystery caller audits, agents in these call centers indicate that there are particular cues present in these audit calls that "give them away" to the agent. These include a familiar person's voice or questions that sound as if they are scripted, use of technical jargon a typical customer would not be expected to know, or questions asked in a way that the experienced agent or evaluator says just does not sound right. If an agent suspects he or she is taking an audit call, it is common practice to alter the manner of providing information so that one is more likely to be scored highly and broadcast an alert to other agents, local supervisors, and management to be on the lookout for these audit calls. Novice agents, who may not be savvy to the subtle cues that mark an audit call, are provided with informal training by experienced agents so they can identify such calls. In addition, if management learns that audit calls will be conducted on a particular day, it is not unusual for this knowledge to be broadcast to agents. The effect of this should be apparent; agents and management conspire to alter their day-to-day practice in order to manufacture conditions for good evaluation scores.

Workers, including management, are very aware of how they are evaluated at each level of the organization and actively mobilize this knowledge in ways that serve to both obscure variance and selectively manufacture evidence that everything is going as expected. In some cases, this provides a screen that protects the workers and management from undesired inspection, and in other cases, this obscures problems that point to systemic problems in the organization that should not be the responsibility of agents or individual managers. Workers protect themselves and in so doing sometimes take responsibility for problems that can be said to belong to higher-level management. This is commonly done following experiences that demonstrate how higher-level management is unwilling to address the problems or to blame it on lack of discipline or knowledge on the part of other persons.

As alluded to earlier, the tactics workers and management use to accomplish these things are definably outside of the official knowledge created by the organization in the form of official observations and production of statistical records of work. In other words, through its official methods for producing knowledge, an organization actually blinds itself to some of the informal methods that are at play in producing the actual operation of the organization.

TALES FROM THE FIELD: OBSCURING VARIANCE FROM MANAGEMENT AND HELPING OR HURTING ONESELF IN THE PROCESS

In this section, several detailed examples from an ethnographic study of call centers will be given to illustrate the points made previously. All of the examples provided here show how employees and management deploy both official and unofficial knowledge to accomplish day-to-day responsibilities. These examples also show how such actions by workers can actually produce the appearance that the organization's systems are functioning well, even if they are not. In so doing, workers become intimately aware of systemic problems while at the same time creating a situation in which the organization is officially blinded to them, thus making systemic performance improvement difficult.

Ethnographic methods include detailed and long-term observation and the production of extensive field notes of what is observed, interviews, and collection of official documentation produced by an organization. In combination, the analysis of these three forms of data provides the ethnographic researcher with the opportunity to see into and even see through an organization on its own terms (Emerson, Fretz, and Shaw, 1995; LeCompte and Schensul, 1999; Lincoln and Guba, 1985; Patton, 1990; Schwartzman, 1993; Strauss and Corbin, 1998). The ethnographic research from which these cases arose involved over two thousand hours of participant observation in four different call centers, 138 interviews, and the collection of over two thousand pieces of official documentation produced by the organizations.

Quantity Is More Important Than Quality

DeliveryWorldwide is an international freight carrier. (*DeliveryWorldwide* is a pseudonym. All other personal and corporate names in this chapter are also pseudonyms. This is to protect the specific identity of individuals and organizations.) There are eight domestic call centers in the network. There are approximately one hundred agents employed in the call center for *DeliveryWorldwide* where a portion of my ethnographic research was conducted. About eighty of these are full time, forty hours per week, and about twenty of them are part time, ten to twenty-plus hours per week. In this call center, team leaders are expected to accomplish quality evaluations of each agent, two times each month. Each evaluation covers five separate calls out of approximately thirty-six hundred calls handled by each agent per month. During the span of fieldwork at this call center, team leaders were assigned to work more hours per day in regular agent work while cutting back on time taken for other responsibilities, such as the accomplishment of quality evaluations. This was due to the closing of several call centers in the company's domestic system and the rerouting of calls to those left standing, resulting in a dramatic increase in the number of calls handled by each remaining call center. While quality evaluations were cut back, the objective observations and statistics accumulated by the ACD, as previously described, went on uninterrupted.

From the sheer difference between the volume of quantitative data collected by the ACD and qualitative data collected in quality evaluations, one can say that the organization has a much stronger interest in quantitative than in qualitative measures of work. Representatives of the organization told me that this was not an intentional outcome, but rather one that is based in the economics of the work. Quantitative data are simply less expensive to collect and process than are qualitative data. It was the view of these individuals that the accomplishment of any quality evaluations at all indicated a commitment to quality assurance. Indeed, these quality evaluations remained a component of the agents' six-month personnel evaluations even through this time of dramatically increased call volume. Since all of the quality evaluations performed during each six-month period were averaged to produce an average quality score for that period, fewer quality evaluations only meant that those accomplished would count for relatively greater weight when the six-month personnel evaluations were performed.

Team leaders were very aware of the increase in stress felt by agents due to increased call volume. Indeed, they felt it themselves. During this period, Rhonda, a team leader, conducted several quality evaluations of Bruce, an experienced agent, and allowed me to observe her performance of quality evaluations. During the course of listening to recordings made earlier in the day, Rhonda pointed out several instances when she interpreted the prosody of Bruce's talk to indicate he was rushed, and that this was why he overlapped the customer's speech with replies or provisions of additional information, an act that could be interpreted as rude interruptions and thus a violation of one of the criteria for quality work. During one call, Bruce was heard to say to the caller, in what sounded a harried tone of voice, "Ma'am, I'm sorry but I've got a lot of other callers waiting in queue and I just don't have any other information to give you." Rhonda indicated that this was clearly a violation of several criteria for quality work. She paused, however, when producing her rating of the calls:

> Sure he was rushed, and I'd say he was even rude to that one caller. At the same time, who isn't rushed right now? On top of that, it's not just us but the whole system is messed up—we can't get current transit information on freight right now because the network isn't working reliably, and when it is, our computers are so old they can't display the information fast enough—sometimes the computers even crash! It's just not fair to give Bruce a low rating because of things that aren't anybody's fault. I'll write this up without those details and talk to him later.

When Rhonda did talk to Bruce a few minutes later, he acknowledged the incident but remained frustrated by what was palpably excessive pressure from both the organization and callers. In cubicles surrounding Bruce's, other agents overheard this conversation even though they too were on calls. One agent muted his headset so the customer on the line could not hear, and echoed remarks Rhonda had made to me earlier:

> How can the organization expect us not to work so fast that we sound like we're interrupting callers? There's always a display on my computer of how many callers are waiting in queue, and every day we're told that our service level is way below standards. What do you want us to do? Try to maintain service level or quality?

Note: service level is perhaps the central statistic in call centers. It is the percentage of all calls answered within a target time. At *DeliveryWorldwide,* the service level was set at 80 percent of all calls answered in fifteen seconds or less, or eighty in fifteen. At the time of this incident, service level was well below this target.

Later, Rhonda told me that she knows the company wants them to maintain both service level and quality, but she also admitted that the current situation is such that they are not readily able to do that. She sighed and admitted that it was hard for everyone, "but the boss keeps telling us that the company isn't going to hire more people or ease the service level right now." And the boss tells her that her coaching of agents while producing quality evaluations that do not reflect violations such as that noted earlier is the best she can do.

Rhonda reflects an intractable situation. The fact the company has just closed several call centers indicates to her and her boss that finances are tight in the organization and additional resources are not going to be forthcoming, even if asked for. It has also initiated a very understandable fear among agents and management that this very call center might even be closed if statistical representations of its work products reflect what the organization thinks is poor performance. In response, Rhonda's actions admit her understanding that quantitative measures are more important at present, all but stating to the agent in the example that he should focus on service level and not on quality. Her concern about how an agent's six-month evaluation may be affected by present circumstances is addressed by obscuring data that she considers not to be the agent's fault, but rather is attributable to the anonymous economic and market forces in which the company and its workers are situated. Through her practices and her silence, the workers and the organization are made to look as good as possible.

Inquiries made by myself to local and higher-level management indicated that call centers had already been allocated their budgets for the year and were expected to handle the work sent to them within that budget. That is, no new agents could be hired to handle the crush of calls. Subsequently, the organization modified its service level to 60 percent of all calls answered in thirty seconds. While this made it possible for the agents to meet service level with less difficulty, it did not affect the pressures felt by agents when they knew there were more customers waiting to be served. In this case, the organization, faced with what were characterized as intractable economic pressures, simply changed the definition of acceptable service level.

"Maybe This Isn't the Right Place For You . . ."

MHealth is a small insurance company specializing in EAP services. EAP is an acronym for "employee assistance plan," a relatively new innovation in managed care that aims at the emotional well-being of employees. By definition, the

EAP aims to provide counseling and other services to employees who are identified as having mental, emotional, or stress-related issues in their lives that somehow impede their productivity at work. The goal of the EAP is to provide these people with interventions that allow them to manage these issues and return to or attain productivity at work. In most cases, *MHealth* subcontracts with major insurance carriers to offer its services under the umbrella of that larger organization.

As part of its single-office location, *MHealth* maintains a small call center with five seats. One of these agents is designated to be a team leader with responsibilities for scheduling, coaching, and quality evaluation of the other agents. The team leader and other agents take calls from prospective clients who are subscribed to *MHealth*'s services through their insurance plan at work. The work involves intensive data entry as the agent conducts a scripted interview to collect information from the caller, consults several databases, processes additional data to produce a record of the interaction, and provides the caller with either a referral to see professional counseling or some other service.

During my fieldwork at *MHealth* the call center experienced the following employee turnover: over a span of nine months, three agents resigned and, twice, new personnel were hired to fill those three places. The first group of agents hired in this period was selected based on their education in clinical psychology or experience in customer-facing work. The second group of agents was hired for their prior experience in call centers or insurance claims processing. For all agents hired in each group, frequent feedback was offered to their team leader and higher-level management both in regular meetings and informally that the computer tools they had to use were inadequate. The computer tools were prone to frequent failure in the course of a call or after call processing, and this required the agents either to redo the data processing from memory, which resulted in the loss of details about each case, or to take notes during a call on paper instead of on the computer. In either case the attempt to do the data entry and data processing after the customer hung up and before the next call rang in adversely affected service level.

It was at this point, when the technical problem affected the service level of the call center, that it became of urgent interest to management. Service level had to be maintained in order not to default on one major contract held by the company. The solution instituted by the call center was to avoid the interruption of technology failures by saving up all the paper notes until a time when call volume dropped and then rushing to complete the data entry before another call rang in. Other agents surreptitiously completed the work on a scheduled break or at the end of their shift. When agents were caught working through breaks or after hours, management was duly alarmed and strongly urged "This is not that kind of company!" In response to an e-mail memo to this effect, one agent told me, deflated, "Yeah. What do they expect us to do? We cannot get the work done during a call because if the computer crashes we have to reboot and that just makes matters worse, and even if we try to do it during slack times, and the computer crashes, we are already in trouble if another call comes in. We need this job and the clients are depending on us to do the work so they can get the help they are calling for. I'll just make do the best I can."

Management resisted replacing the software tools because of the cost of new software, because other departments' processes in the organization relied on databases that were produced by these tools, and because the managers of those departments expressed concern that they would not be able to complete their backlog of work if they were expected to change their processes. Instead, and predictably, training of the call center agents in the use of their tools was recommended. In all fairness, the agents did learn new methods of using the tools that speeded some work, but the training did not repair the technical problems noted. Subsequently, several versions of paper forms were developed by agents that they thought eased the burden by effectively altering the script for the most common type of calls and speeded the taking of notes by hand.

The agents' practice of taking handwritten notes and trying to complete data entry in between calls, during breaks, or after shift remained in place. Agents traded stories of increasing levels of stress, nightmares, and physical ailments. Dark humor concerning their own impending need for counseling was common in the call center and the break room.

Three of the most vocal critics of the technical problems and subsequent recourse to handwritten notes and overtime were told by a supervisor, perhaps out of exasperation due to management's resistance to her own appeals for the call center, "We've all got to be team players. Maybe this isn't the right place for you." Indeed, it appeared not to be, because these individuals resigned soon after. Those agents who remained longer and those subsequently hired learned, either vicariously by watching the organization's response to agent feedback or from incumbents, that such feedback was neither likely to produce desired responses nor healthy for one's job prospects. Technology problems and extra burdens on agents became the norm.

This is obviously a situation in which an admittedly expensive technical change would have improved performance of the call center, and would have mandated systemic change through other departments in the organization. However, the solution eventually arrived at by the organization and its employees was to replace workers until protests subsided or became less apparent. This was neither economical nor reflected the organization's responsibility to its employees. The only official knowledge of this problem was its effect on service levels. Instead of repairing the technology problem, other, less expensive but ineffective attempts were made. Workers either quit or accepted the added burden and in so doing allowed an incorrigible problem to persist.

Whose Value Is It?

During my ethnographic fieldwork at *DeliveryWorldwide,* I was sitting with a particularly chatty agent on a day when the incoming call volume was particularly low. Between calls and my questions of her, this agent remarked, "You look kinda stressed. You should go see Bonnie; she's got some pills to help her cope with the stress of this place."

Through the conversation and subsequent talk with Bonnie, I found that these pills were prescribed by a physician in response to clinically identifiable symptoms of stress. I also found that she was not alone. Others in the call center, about 10 percent, were also taking prescription medication for stress-related symptoms. Through the fieldwork it became evident that many other agents experienced substantive stresses but had found other means to address the issues. These included lunchtime basketball in the parking lot and widespread use of other legal drugs. Other agents indicated that they were less able to fulfill family responsibilities for some period after work and required some time to, as one agent told me, "start to care again," thus indicating that spouses and children were frustrated or had subsequently learned to cope with these stresses. Investigating this issue, I encountered another agent who indicated that her family had grown to understand the situation. She went on to report that her husband also worked in a call center, and as a couple, they could understand each other's needs and provide support. Her preteen children, accustomed to the normal stressed affect of both parents, had quickly grown independent enough to fend for themselves while their parents wound down at the end of the day.

At the time of this incident, according to the organization's metrics, the workers and organization at large were doing well. However, good agents were apparently suffering at the hands of the system to the extent that they sought medical assistance and were prescribed mood-altering drugs. This suffering was rendered officially invisible by the metrics and measures themselves, and was underground even for those wary of it. One might even argue that the medical establishment, a system connected to this call center through insurance plans, is in part facilitating this official invisibility by its application of chemical additives that hide physical symptoms of stress sourced in the workplace.

This case shows that there are ways to see and measure an organization in addition to the current and conventional statistical representation of work products and balances on a spreadsheet. However, even for those who are aware of it, these other ways of knowing may be treated as incidental and apparently hardly worth a second thought. While this can be considered a substantive problem for individuals, it is all but invisible to the organization while borne by the employees themselves.

Outstanding Customer Service That Violates Company Policy: Playing Both Sides of the Fence

Call volume at *DeliveryWorldwide* is the highest of all of the call centers included in this research. It is not unusual for agents to handle as many as two hundred calls per day, averaging less than two minutes per call over the course of an eight-hour shift when they are assigned to handle the most highly scripted calls. Even if agents are assigned to handle the most complex and script-resistant calls, they are expected to complete all work on that call in less than seven minutes. In fact, the de facto definition of good work is in part measured by the speed with which agents complete each call, the so-called average talk time, and the normalized calls per hour worked by each agent. The fact that team leaders orient to these items in daily feedback, as noted in Figure 53.2, indicates that these two statistics are of special interest on a day-to-day basis.

In addition to the feedback on quantitative measures provided to agents, periodic evaluations of quality are also conducted. The product of these quality ratings is what may be called an objectified subjectivity, or a subjective rating that is so deeply entrenched in the epistemology of an organization that it is treated as an objective reality. The quality data and quantity data are combined to produce overall rankings of agents' quality within teams and across the entire call center. The overall call center ranking is posted publicly in the form of a table, and the team ranking is posted in the form of a two-dimensional graph on which each agent is plotted in terms of his or her productivity or quantity score and quality score (Figure 53.1).

The display in Figure 53.1 shows how one agent, Sheila, has a very good average quality rating of 100, but a low average productivity rating of twelve calls per hour. This is attributed to Sheila's demonstrated and self-acknowledged disregard for call length and interest in answering all of the customer's questions, including checking all aspects of the customer's account, even in the event that no questions are asked about such things. This latter practice is in direct contradiction to a policy of the company indicating that agents should "not open that can of worms," which means that agents should only perform data entry and data processing to fulfill the customers' direct requests and not go looking for other issues that might complicate and prolong the call. As a consequence, her calls regularly exceed fifteen minutes. This is over twice as long as desired for agents who work script-resistant difficult calls and regularly results in very low productivity ratings.

Regardless, this agent is considered to be one of the best overall agents in the call center by management and other agents and was even named so by the company's vice president for customer service when he visited the call center. In part, this designation arises from the many informal benefits she provides to the call center and fellow agents. In particular, other agents in the call center indicate that when they are assigned a cubicle next to Sheila, they learn a lot about the company's products and how to work with customers. Team leaders indicate that they are consistently amazed at the orientation to detail she exhibits in her calls, also remarking that they often have to make two or even three cassette recordings of her calls before they have recorded five complete calls with which to accomplish a quality rating.

One team leader said, "her calls are sooooo long! But every minute of what she does is exactly what you have to do to do good customer service!" When questioned, team leaders admit that she does open a lot of cans of worms in the process, but they are quick to point out that she is very able to handle whatever she discovers. This, as one team leader indicated, "saves me a lot of work because if she couldn't handle it, she might escalate it to me and I'm not sure I could handle it!"

The call center manager admits that he would like all of the agents to have this attention to detail, but quickly adds that the company would not—because in that case the call center would have to employ three times as many agents to handle the same amount of calls. This, obviously enough, would not be economical for the company.

Similarly, all of the team leaders indicate that they always include a note asking Sheila to "work on bringing your call time down!" when submitting a quality rating of her work. Sheila says, "I just ignore those. . . . I've decided that I'm not gonna rush things just to satisfy the clock. They can fire me if they want, but I'm not gonna do that." When asked, team leaders indicate that they include that note "because we have to; it's so obviously something that goes against the company's policies [that] if we didn't say that to her *we* might get in trouble," but also that they know Sheila will not comply.

It seems, then, that Sheila is considered to be the best agent in the call center. However, all of those who have responsibility for measuring the work of agents indicate that her work is deviant. What is universally acclaimed *good work* in terms of quality is *not* measurably good work in terms of productivity.

The discrepancy is understood when the call center manager and vice president for customer service indicated independently that it really does not matter what one agent's call time is, so long as the average call time of the overall call center is low. That is, there are actually two different ways for the company to signify good work. One is the abstracted and ethereal average of all call times and one is the arguably more real conduct of work as it is done by Sheila and experienced by her customers and overheard by other agents.

Both, however, are turned into targets by the company. In the case of quantitative average calls per hour, the statutory target of twenty-five calls per hour, as shown on Figure 53.1, is drilled in daily feedback as the goal for each agent's work. However, while this productivity goal stands, the organization simultaneously holds up the high degree of quality demonstrated by Sheila as what they can and should aspire to! Obviously, both could not be achieved at the same time.

In this example, the two main measures for determining the value of call center workers are played against each other. The organization valorizes quality and points to an agent who snubs a solitary emphasis on the goal of quantity, what the organization dubs as productivity. That is, the system is designed to discipline a particular aspect of workers' conduct, but ironically is prepared to tolerate, even amplify, noncompliance when it can be held up as an example of something that its policies normally inhibit to the point of prohibition.

Agents know that the company's expectations are based on the charted and tabled performance statistics and feedback they receive from supervisors. However, this example demonstrates how an organization can specify its intentions in objective ways yet dismiss those intentions when it is convenient. The statistics used by members of the organization to know how it is functioning and used by the organization to provide feedback to agents are not always what the organization wants. The problem here is that the organization valorizes particular performance yet initiates policies that inhibit this performance in general practice. This is like acknowledging a world record by a sprinter who is known to use performance-enhancing drugs, while expecting everyone else to refrain from that practice.

CONCLUSION

The Doings of Doings: Obscuring Problems from the Organization's View

The net effect of the tactics described in the previous section is the production of appearances: statistical measures that both (1) represent the official activity of individuals and the entire call center's operation and (2) maintain and obscure a different reality than portrayed by the official record. As suggested earlier, several conclusions can be drawn from this. First, official knowledge of a system, that is, what the organization thinks is real, is at best only partially accurate and is in fact largely produced through the actions of individuals who implement both normal organizational procedures and local knowledge in everyday practice to maintain appearances and day-to-day operations. The workers implement what Goffman called "continuous secondary adjustments" (Goffman, 1961, pp. 54ff, 199ff) to create evidence of normal work products using unofficial and unregulated knowledge and procedures. In effect, the system as the organization thinks it exists does not exist. Instead, the system exists largely as a hybrid of official and unofficial practices, knowledge, and circumstances. Second, the workers demonstrate their orientation to the expectations of the company as they deploy local knowledge so as to protect the appearance that everything is going normally. There are two effects of this practice. First, to conserve their independent authority to exercise local knowledge and expertise so that it will not be taken away or become officially regulated by the organization, and second, a social desire to maintain the organization of which they are a part, in a form that allows them to be experts and deploy their expert knowledge.

Avoiding Jumping to Solutions

At this point one may come to the conclusion that additional or closer observations are called for in order to reduce or eliminate the side effects of producing official ignorance and allowing workers to take responsibility unjustifiably. There are several reasons to hesitate before jumping in this direction. In the first place, attempting to collect more data will produce a cost to the company. In an increasingly competitive marketplace, cost is an enemy to business unless it can be offset with greater market share and profit: things that are increasingly difficult to attain in the present economic and consumption landscape. In the second place, regardless of how many points of observation are adopted, both management and labor will always identify spaces left free in the regime of observation and generation of knowledge about the performance of teams and individuals such that more unknowns will arise even as more knowledge is generated. Finally, workers are very aware of their responsibilities in the workplace and will, despite the existence of spaces left free, actually use this unregulated space as a region for exercising their expert knowledge of the day-to-day functioning of the organization in ways that act to keep the system functioning as the organization expects. Their actions show a practical desire to be good employees and at the same time to exercise their local knowledge in solving day-to-day problems that arise. They are members who continuously act to produce and ensure the adequate functioning of the organization. These workers demonstrate a socially distributed desire to not just be employees, rule followers, or subjects to organizational rules that are not always sensible in local day-to-day practice.

Don't We Already Know How to Handle This?

Of course we know how to handle such situations, but only partially. We have known since before the beginning of the field that we should analyze a situation and identify the most likely causes and then implement solutions that are most economically able to have an impact on them (Taylor, 1947). Analysis of performance and performance gaps has since become one of the most important components of practice in our field (Gilbert, 1996; Mager and Pipe, 1997 [1970]).

However, while we know how to analyze and identify problems, the cases described in this chapter are particularly difficult for the typical HPT practitioner. This is because the HPT practitioner is frequently either an independent contractor hired to fulfill a task already defined by personnel internal to the company or an internal employee or consultant attached to a particular business unit, for example, human resources or the training department, whose job scope and authority are already defined formally or informally. In either case, the HPT practitioner may be institutionally limited in what he or she can do without countering higher-level personnel and perhaps endangering their own job or accepting responsibilities that may detract from other aspects of that individual's life. What does one do when the organization has already chosen its measurement systems, has already formed an idea of what is or is not problematic, and thinks in terms of existing organizational structures and their products?

These are difficult problems without easy solutions for HPT practitioners and the field of performance improvement. In their current configuration, the practical, everyday application of knowledge, skills, and values common to organizations as well as the techniques and other ways organizations come to generate knowledge and develop savvy employees are caught up in a network of intentional and unintentional practices that conspire against systemic performance improvement. While I have alluded to mechanisms for addressing the specific problems noted in this chapter and similarly noted some drawbacks, they are not universal.

Perhaps, as was done in the early days of the medical field, and prior to its emergence as a discipline, it may be the case that HPT practitioners themselves must contribute to our knowledge and present highly detailed case studies of performance-improvement efforts, noting the idiosyncratic details of individual cases and successful and unsuccessful interventions and hypothesizing why things happened as they did. From the rich source of empirical evidence so produced, practitioners and those more experienced in academic forms of research may collaborate to develop theory-based guidance for addressing this and other issues that currently vex our practice. This is a task for the future of the field. Without a toolbox of techniques for breaking down organizational and performance issues that impede systemic solution, we may be left with spot fixes that never accrue to the full vision we all see for HPT.

EPILOGUE

HPT-savvy personnel at both *DeliveryWorldwide* and *MHealth* tried to implement changes in their respective organizations following the systemic nature of HPT principles. Continuously blocked by management, they have since left their positions for another call center that promises more open opportunity to practice performance improvement and work in the public sector.

The cases described in this chapter show how well-meaning activities conducted in the unregulated spaces of organizations actually contribute to problems in organizations. One cannot help but wonder what would happen if we tried to work within the rules of an organization to make change. One more case might be illuminating in this regard.

How Do I Value Thee?

MedAdvise is a telephone triage nurse call center, colloquially known as "dial a nurse." It is affiliated with a hospital in the region and located in the basement of one of the hospital's buildings. *MedAdvise* employs seventeen registered nurses and five personnel to perform nonclinical functions. As in health care companies nationwide since at least the 1970s, this hospital is under pressure to continuously, as one nurse describes, "do more with less." In the recent past, the call center has lost several full-time equivalents and now subcontracts with a similar service in another state to cover midnight to 7 A.M. calls. In an effort to improve its position, *MedAdvise* has merged with the marketing function of the hospital and begun taking general calls to enroll citizens into community service health classes, act as an "after hours" answering service for participating physicians affiliated with the hospital, and perform other nonclinical tasks. Having used the same computer database system for collecting and archiving medical information from callers for years, *MedAdvise* is not able to share data with other departments in the hospital. This has amplified the perception that *MedAdvise* is less and less a functional part of the hospital itself, and the call center manager is fearful that the hospital may outsource all of the functions it provides to the hospital and community.

Recognizing that the primary drivers of such a decision are based in accounting practices and resulting statistics used by the hospital's administrators, the manager of *MedAdvise* has begun reporting statistics that project how the call center actually contributes positively to the bottom line of the hospital. These statistics are based on literature she has found in her research in similar call centers. She was confident that "if I talked their language, that is, accounting, statistics, and bottom-line results, they'd understand and see how valuable we are, and provide us with the resources to grow and more fully interact with the rest of the hospital."

She found the contrary. Faced with statistical procedures and projections that were unfamiliar to him, the controller at the hospital simply dismissed her data, sending her away and leaving the call center to languish for another fiscal year. The accountant advised her to "manage your department, not mine" and that "you may have to lay off nurses and juggle the schedule to get more service from the remaining staff, for less money."

Even when making a case for the value added by the call center that "spoke the language" of the hospital's controller, the addition of bottom-line-enhancing performance-improving technology was deflected, and the call center manager was left with unpleasant options that would only further damage the ability of *MedAdvise* to make a difference to the community and the organization.

This case shows that even when one chooses to reflect the value of one's organization in terms of the organization's conventional and official knowledge, in this case, a fiscal accounting gaze, a willing ear is not necessarily found. Thus, accounting for value-adding performance or making a case for performance-improving interventions continues to be a difficult problem for the individuals who try to make changes that challenge the already decided upon ways that individuals in organizations know the organization. They are viewed as ignorant of the organization and unable to act to improve performances.

References

Argyris, C. (1952). *The impact of budgets on people.* Cornell, NY: Cornell University Graduate School of Business and Public Administration.

Bell, D. (1973). *The coming of post-industrial society: A venture in social forecasting.* New York: Basic Books.

Bodin, M., and Dawson, K. (1999). *The call center dictionary: The complete guide to call centers and help desk technology and operations* (2nd ed.). New York: Telecom Books.

Brethower, D. (1999). General systems theory and behavioral psychology. In H. D. Stolovitch and E. J. Keeps (Eds.), *Handbook of human performance technology: Improving individual and organizational performance worldwide* (pp. 67–81). San Francisco: Jossey-Bass/Pfeiffer.

Button, G., and Harper, R.H.R. (1993). Taking the organization into accounts. In G. Button, (Ed.), *Technology in working order: Studies of work, interaction, and technology* (pp. 98–107). London: Routledge.

Call Center News Service. (2000). *What are the origins of the call center industry?* Retrieved September 5, 2001, from www.callcenternews.com/resources/faqs/faq_5.shtml.

Datamonitor. (2004). *Opportunities in North American call center markets to 2005* (No. DMTC0745). New York: Datamonitor.

Durkheim, E. (1997). *The division of labor in society* (W. D. Halls, trans.). New York: Simon and Schuster.

Durr, W. (1996). *Building a world-class inbound call center.* Boston: TeleProfessional/Avanstar.

Emerson, R. M., Fretz, R. I., and Shaw, L. L. (1995). *Writing ethnographic fieldnotes.* Chicago: University of Chicago Press.

Foucault, M. (1995). *Discipline and punish: The birth of the prison.* New York: Vintage Books.

Gilbert, T. (1996). *Human competence: Engineering worthy performance* (Tribute Ed.). Washington, DC: International Society for Performance Improvement.

Goffman, E. (1961). *Asylums: Essays on the social situation of mental patients and other inmates.* Garden City, NY: Anchor Books.

Hopper, T., and Macintosh, N. (1998). Management accounting numbers: Freedom or prison—Geneen versus Foucault. In A. McKinlay and K. Starkey (Eds.), *Foucault, management and organization theory: From panopticon to technologies of self* (pp. 125–150). Thousand Oaks, CA: Sage.

Hoskin, K. (1998). Examining accounts and accounting for management: Inventing understandings of "the economic." In A. McKinlay and K. Starkey (Eds.), *Foucault, management and organization theory: From panopticon to technologies of self* (pp. 93–110). Thousand Oaks, CA: Sage.

Hoskin, K., and Macve, R. (1994). Writing, examining, disciplining: The genesis of accounting's modern power. In A. Hopwood and P. Miller (Eds.), *Accounting as social and institutional practice* (pp. 67–97). Cambridge, UK: Cambridge University Press.

Kaufman, R. (1992). *Strategic planning plus: An organizational guide.* Newbury Park, CA: Sage.

Latour, B., and Woolgar, S. (1990). *Laboratory life: The construction of scientific facts.* Princeton, NJ: Princeton University Press.

LeCompte, M., and Schensul, J. (Eds.). (1999). *The ethnographer's toolkit.* Walnut Creek, CA: AltaMira.

Lincoln, Y., and Guba, E. (1985). *Naturalistic inquiry.* Thousand Oaks, CA: Sage.

Mager, R., and Pipe, P. (1997). *Analyzing performance problems or "you really oughta wanna"* (3rd ed.). Atlanta: Center for Effective Performance. Originally published in 1970.

Patton, M. Q. (1990). *Qualitative evaluation and research methods* (2nd ed.). Thousand Oaks, CA: Sage.

Schwartzman, H. (1993). *Ethnography in organizations* (Vol. 27). Thousand Oaks, CA: Sage.

Smith, A. (1991). *The wealth of nations.* Amherst, NY: Prometheus Books. Originally published in 1776.

Strauss, A., and Corbin, J. (1998). *Basics of qualitative research: Techniques and procedures for developing grounded theory* (2nd ed.). Thousand Oaks, CA: Sage.

Taylor, F. (1947). *Scientific management.* Westport, CT: Greenwood Press.

Taylor, P., and Bain, P. (1999). An assembly line in the head: Work and employee relations in the call centre. *Industrial Relations Journal, 30*(2), 101–117.

Weber, M. (2001). *The Protestant ethic and the spirit of capitalism* (T. Parsons, trans.). New York: Routledge.

Winiecki, D. (2002, April 23). *Assessing the measure: What are we doing when we're measuring performance?* Paper presented at the annual meeting of the International Society for Performance Improvement, Dallas, Texas.

Winiecki, D. (2003, April 12). *System thinking and system doing: Shadowboxing with ourselves?* Paper presented at the annual meeting of the International Society for Performance Improvement, Boston.

CHAPTER FIFTY-FOUR

Hidden Order
of Human Performance Technology
Chaos and Complexity

Darlene M. Van Tiem, Swati Karve, Jennifer Rosenzweig

To say that we work in a world that is complex is to state the obvious. A new merger or acquisition hits the news almost weekly, and while the intent is to build a financially strong institution, it does so by throwing the two companies' existing systems, processes, and cultures into complete disarray. New technology may intend to make our lives easier, but when cell phones and wireless computers allow for twenty-four–hour-a-day and seven–day-a-week access, the pace of change goes into overdrive. Even how we manage has grown more complex. "Traditionally, managers learn that the 'right' way of supervising employees involves careful planning, coordination, and control. In reality, however, management behavior is unplanned, random, and contingent. In today's fast-changing and competitive work environment, plans often derail and managers have less time to coordinate and control actions of their employees" (Titcomb, 1998, p. 1). As practitioners of human performance technology (HPT), our role is to create order and functionality out of this chaos and complexity. What better way to enhance our profession than to learn from the growing body of knowledge of the fields of chaos theory and complexity studies? *Chaos* is "an ancient word originally denoting a complete lack of form or systematic arrangement, but now often used to imply the absence of some kind of order that ought to be present" (Lorenz, 1993, p. 3).

Despite what we see on the surface, there is in fact a hidden order amongst the chaos of business that provides a path for improvement at all levels. The field of HPT, in combination with new thinking from chaos theory and complexity studies, can provide a means to tap into this potential. By way of example, chaos theory and complexity studies help leaders better understand their organizational environment and provide insight into the skills, behaviors, and attitudes that can be used in practical leadership development (Fairholm, 2004).

In the field of chaos and complexity, HPT is viewed as an aspect of social science that has been studied by chaos and complexity researchers for about fifteen years. HPT has great potential for study because it is inclusive, systematic, systemic, and model-oriented. This chapter will use a case study based on performance technology standards applied to an Indian software development company as a major example so that readers can understand the relationship of HPT to chaos and complexity.

INTRODUCTION

HPT integrates and synthesizes various schools of thought, such as human performance improvement, human resource development, workplace learning and performance, and organizational design, as well as other business and social science disciplines. The field of HPT lies within the scope of the broad study of chaos and complexity due to the number of variables that are involved and the various levels at which performance-improvement interventions can take place. Understanding research and scientific thought related to chaos and complexity can strengthen HPT.

Human behavior is so complex that no one theory or field of study can explain everything (Sanders and Ruggles, 2000). One of the aims of chaos theory applied to the social sciences is the betterment of human beings. Many researchers have moved from mechanistic thought to more complex explanations of behavior.

Increased technology choices, faster connectivity, and globalization plus economic, political, and social changes around the world have redefined businesses. Globalization has brought about various cultural changes as well as complexities in terms of international business processes, labor policy, trade agreements, and so on. Industries designed around bureaucracy and hierarchies are being replaced by more open and flatter systems. To survive the pressures of globalization and competition, organizations must constantly evolve and adapt.

HPT is also a field of complexity because there are no limitations on the interventions or solutions that can be used to solve performance problems. (Van Tiem, 2004; Van Tiem, Moseley, and Dessinger, 2001, 2004). As an eclectic field, HPT draws from communications, quality, instructional design and education, psychology, sociology, economics, human factors and engineering, and many other fields. There are truly infinite possibilities.

In the past, researchers would consider limited variables when trying to understand human situations. Frederick Taylor used task analysis and time and

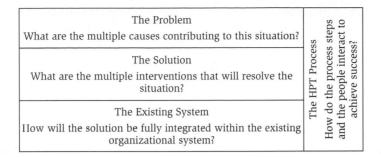

Figure 54.1. Layers of Complexity: HPT and Complex Systems.

motion studies to improve products and services by simplifying jobs so that each worker could focus on clearly defined tasks. Simplification, a form of reductionism, led to efficiencies such as Henry Ford's automobile assembly line. But by focusing on individual tasks, workers became depersonalized and lost their concern for the quality of the entire product. Reductionism leads to thinking about limited variables and separates the situation from the entirety.

HPT thinking is systemic and requires a holistic approach (International Society for Performance Improvement, 2002). "A system implies an interconnected complex of functionally related components. The effectiveness of each unit depends on how it fits into the whole, and the effectiveness of the whole depends on the way each unit functions. A systems approach considers the larger environment that affects processes and other work. The environment includes inputs, but, more importantly, it includes pressures, expectations, constraints, and consequences" (Performance Standard #2: Take a Systems View).

Complex interactions and interconnectivity related to performance mean understanding (1) the work, worker, and workplace; (2) the environment and culture; (3) alignment of goals and objectives, performance measures, rewards and incentives, job work or process designs, systems, tools and equipment, and expectations and capacity; and (4) barriers and leverage points. HPT documents and describes the interrelationships, gains consensus, and looks to improve the full range of issues that hinder performance (see Figure 54.1).

THE PROBLEM

As HPT consultants consider the system as a whole they uncover multiple problems and root causes. Even if not readily apparent, these problems are interconnected. The HPT consultant must therefore consider problems both individually and collectively to better understand the opportunities for improvement.

THE SOLUTION

Just as the problem is due to multiple causes, the solution must in turn offer multiple interventions. For instance, it may not be enough to train personnel; they must also be motivated to apply new skills. Extending this complexity further, other parts of the organization may also need to be aware of the coming changes; communications must, therefore, be designed into the complete solution. Similar to how the problem is approached, the solution must not be viewed as a series of independent interventions but instead as a more complex and interconnected solution.

THE EXISTING SYSTEM

The solution does not exist in a vacuum. It must somehow fit inside many other components of the system, touching areas that are already functioning well. HPT consultants must be aware of the ripple effect their solution will have as it resonates through the system and factor potential concerns into the final implementation plan.

THE HPT PROCESS

As the steps of the HPT process unfold, many ongoing adjustments are required to ensure success. Team members will change, new facts will be uncovered, and priorities will shift, all requiring constant flexibility. The entire HPT experience essentially is its own complex system.

HISTORICAL OVERVIEW OF CHAOS AND COMPLEXITY STUDY

Chaos generally refers to confusion, disorder, and lack of organization. It is a state of disorder and restlessness, which is actually evolutionary. Throughout history many unexpected or substantial changes have occurred that have dramatically altered the way organizations adapt and organize (Farazmand, 2003). Although chaos theory and complexity science are helpful in understanding immediate, unexpected, and rapid changes, it is important to realize that history will probably view change as normal progression.

Chaos as a concept has been described and used in mythologies and religious writings of diverse cultures. It has been a topic of reflection for thinkers and philosophers and a topic of examination and explanation for scientists and mathematicians. In the fifth and fourth century B.C., philosophers such as Plato and Aristotle discussed dialectical discourse theory, including "the interrelationships between parts, the idea that organization is conditioned by the larger environment—social, political and economic—within which a system operates, and that systems contain dialectically conflicting parts that inherently contradict each other, and that systems tend to protect their equilibrium at any cost and crush forces of system challenge" (Julius Weinberg, cited in Farazmand, 2003, p. 343).

Throughout history, chaos has been associated with a negative connotation of disorderliness and mess. As human beings tried to explain the existence of the universe within the limitations of science and mathematical tools and techniques, they explained the existence of chaos in simplistic, reductionism terms. Reductionism is an attempt or tendency to explain a complex set of facts, entities, phenomena, or structures by another, simpler set: "For the last 400 years, science was advanced by reductionism. . . . The idea is that you could understand the world, all of nature, by examining smaller and smaller pieces of it. When assembled, the small pieces would explain the whole" (J. Holland, as cited in *American Heritage Dictionary of the English Language,* 2000).

As human thinking grew through the Renaissance and through new discoveries and inventions in science, it reached new levels. Einstein, Darwin, Freud, and Jung expounded theories in their respective fields that went beyond the obvious. Their explanations for observable phenomena included factors that were beyond what human senses could perceive. There was a revolution in thinking. Chaos, which until then had had a negative connotation, became accepted as a part of life and part of reality. New scientific thought and associated mathematical concepts, developed to accept methodologies such as fuzzy logic, which is algebraic decision making using imprecise data and a range of variables such as artificial intelligence, examined complex phenomena and explained relationships.

One of the factors accelerating these changes has been technology. Beginning at the end of the twentieth century, with the coming of computers and satellite technology, there has been a revolution in telecommunications, including the use of the Internet. In fact, changes are spiraling across all human spheres. "The advent of the new science of complexity has been largely attributed to Prigogine, a 1977 Nobel Laureate in chemistry, whose landmark book *Order Out of Chaos* explored the nature of change through 'dissipative structures' or open systems'" (Jaafari, 2003, p. 49). Titcomb (1998, p. 1) explains the origin of collaborative studies of chaos theory and complexity studies as follows:

> More than 20 years ago, chaos and complexity theory began to take shape in the scientific world. A critical leap occurred in 1977 at the University of California, Santa Cruz, when a group of doctoral students began exploring the ways in which order emerges from chaos. Borrowing theories that physicists and mathematicians had been exploring for decades, they discovered that the universe is a vibrant and chaotic system, not a static machine subject to our control. As their research progressed, the students determined that, while the universe and other systems are extremely complex, they contain patterns that can lead to a greater understanding of their structure and an ability to predict patterns that they will follow.

"In recent years, a new view of learning and learning-based systems has emerged. Researchers have found that the study (and design) of complex, open-ended learning environments requires a framework in which intelligence is shared among multiple agents interacting with each other and their environment" (Titcomb, 1998, p. 5). At the Santa Fe Institute, new ideas emerged leading to more studies at other new scientific centers, spreading chaos and complexity investigations worldwide.

In 1999, James Hite, Jr., published *Learning in Chaos: Improving Human Performance in Today's Fast-Changing, Volatile Organizations,* linking organizational change to classical and technical chaos. Hite related nonlinear organizational systems to leadership, management, networks, self-organization, and creativity, and stressed the importance of incidental learning, measurement of learning, and structures such as corporate universities.

CHARACTERISTICS OF CHAOTIC SYSTEMS

Complex society is evolutionary, exhibiting chaos, open systems, self-organization, and interdependence. According to Jaafari, *open systems* are subject to instability and are changing constantly within networks of interconnections and interrelationships. *Self-organizations* follow autocatalytic processes, leading to autonomous, organic self-steering organizational units based on insights and competence of the actors as well as synergy, flexibility, and teamwork. *Interdependence* makes it difficult, if not impossible, to make predictions based on previous experience. With rising complexity of society due to rapid technological, social, economic, and global change, complexity no longer can be explained by mechanistic, progressive, and linear cause-and-effect discussions based on isolated phenomena (Jaafari, 2003). Hite asserts that complexity today is influenced more by technical chaos resulting from technology than by classical chaos (1999).

Nonlinear Dynamic Systems

Analysis of chaotic systems has shown that under the surface of the chaotic systems lies an order in which the change occurs. There is no need for a direct linear relationship between A and B. By understanding nonlinear dynamic systems (NDS), the underlying nature of the system can be understood. Another important characteristic of variables in the NDS system is that as variables move, they change into a different state and do not return to the same state. Holland describes the relationship between the hare and the lynx, derived from the Hudson Bay Company yearly reports. Generally, as the hare population increases there is more food for lynx; this results in an increased population of lynx and a decreased population of hares. However, this is not a linear relationship because there are too many intervening variables, such as disease, other predators, and prey beyond hares and lynx. Based on the same reasoning, measuring and declaring the impact of training on workplace results is impeded by changes in employee assignments, cultural change, new policies, and competitive or economic situations (Holland, 1995).

Phase Space

Phase space, sometimes referred to as the state space, places variables in an active changing system. Phase space endeavors to place an event on a continuum in time and space. It is not a static model of a system, but looks at a changing system over time. A number of variables may be considered as the number of points in space, and the relationships among these variables change. This leads to valuing timelines and understanding the evolution of change rather than accepting the impression that change is revolutionary. Thinking about organizational, process, or individual change as continuously evolving in ways similar to previous organizational, process, or individual change reduces resistance and feelings of alarm among workers. The energy required, the frequency of transforming change, and the number of significant differences within the change evolution affects the rate of change (Olson and Eoyang, 2001). For example, Internet usage has been evolutionary. What began as a communication system for the U.S. military and universities then became a business communication tool, and eventually a universal source of music, movies, news, general information, and personal communication.

Bifurcation

As changes happen throughout the system, the system bifurcates into two, then four, then multiple numbers of paths. When a system reaches maximum instability, self-organizations are given opportunities for creative reordering (Wheatley, 1994). As the system bifurcates, there are periods of temporary order within the system, but the system remains essentially chaotic and changing. Bifurcation may be slow or fast, depending on the system and the situation, but bifurcation accelerates once it has started, and changes are rapid as the system becomes very complex. Bifurcation helps HPT consultants explain why change may seem slow at first and appear more accelerated as time progresses. For example, HPT efforts often begin with an initiative for one work group or one department. Gradually an upstream or downstream department is affected and decides to also embrace the initiative. Then their upstream or downstream customers begin to adopt the initiative. Later the next level's upstream and downstream customers are involved. Since each work group has many upstream and downstream customers, the initiative eventually increases in speed and the effort grows in geometric proportions.

Attractors

Attractors are variables around which systems come together. Lorenz (1993) suggested a new kind of attractor called a *strange attractor*. With a strange attractor, the behavior of the system cannot be predicted with complete accuracy. It has freedom in all directions, though it is a part of the system itself. The strange attractor can create extreme changes with the system variables or remain in the respective phase space for some time before it jumps to another attractor. Lorenz, a specialist in the chaos of weather, proposed the "butterfly phenomenon." Lorenz made an extremely minor variation in a variable he entered into his weather-related software one day. When he later checked the calculations and actions of the software he found the minimal changes in parameters created an immense weather change. In other words, he realized that the actual minor variation was about the magnitude of the flutter of a butterfly wing, yet the weather change was extensive and far away from the origin of the minor variation. Hence, this minor variation creating an extreme result was described as a butterfly wing fluttering in one part of the world creating extreme weather changes in another part of the world. For HPT, Lorenz's ideas can also confirm the concept of the straw that broke the camel's back. A very minor change can disrupt the organization far beyond the anticipated impact of the situation; very minimal changes can have huge consequences.

Fractals

Fractals refer to similarities at various levels. From a micro perspective to a macro perspective, there are layers within a system. Each layer exhibits some degree of similarity with characteristics of the entire system. Studying fractals provides insight into the geometry of nature (Gleick, 1987). Computers can generate colorful repetitious fractal designs based on algorithmic equations (see Figure 54.2). In nature the repetitions of ferns or snowflakes illustrate chaotic repetitious systems at various levels. Ferns repeat their shape at the individual leaflet level, the fern leaf level, and the fern stem level. Snowflakes repeat their shapes with minor variations. Repetitions enable us to look for patterns within organizations, such as culture, by anticipating change based on repetitions in

Figure 54.2. Computer-Generated Fractal.

---

human issues resulting in almost identical situations throughout cultures, such as how human infants learn to talk and walk. Often situations are believed to be unique when they are probably quite common. Fractals help us focus on commonalities as well as differences. Kauffman emphasizes the repetitious phenomena whereby every living organism begins as a zygote, that is a single-cell organism, and then the species follow their own consistent developmental processes. This consistency is hidden from view by normal sight but visible through microscopes. All humans go through the same stages and so do plants and other animals (1995).

Complex Adaptive Systems

Although all systems are complex and adaptive, complex adaptive systems (CAS) are learning systems that adapt to their environment. They are self-organizing and free to evolve and develop. If organizations do not change, adapt, and learn as they grow and evolve they may collapse. For example, to make a community more responsible for environmental protection, what actions can individuals take? What actions can a group take? And what actions can a local government take?

Organizations are made up of individuals who themselves are complex systems, each with his or her own set of experiences, capabilities, knowledge, and skills. Individuals interact within the organization through established procedures, structures, and communication systems. Every change at any point will lead to changes in the system. The interactions among leaders, managers, and other employees affect the working of the organization. Interpersonal and organizational communications are two important processes that affect the organization and can define the whole organizational culture. CAS organizations are *at the edge of chaos*.

Networks

Network theory has also evolved in recent years, with *network* defined as the architecture or skeleton of complexity (Barabasi, 2003). Network theory gives a means to better understand complex systems and enhance the practice of HPT.

Structure. Networks are mesh-like interfaces in which the individual components of the network are linked in a distributed way. This means the power of the network is spread across the entire network. Figure 54.3 is a visual of a distributed network.

One of the better-known examples of a distributed network is the Internet. Paul Baran, researcher and Internet pioneer, theorized that if the Internet was set up as a net rather than centralized with its power concentrated in one place it would be less vulnerable to failure and more supportive of growth.

Nodes and Clusters. Each individual dot or component in the network is referred to as a *node*. Nodes that are connected to one another form a group known as a *cluster* (see Figure 54.3).

Hubs. Clusters that have many connections are powerful and are called *hubs*. Once formed, hubs tend to become more powerful over time. *Google* and *Yahoo* are examples of powerful hubs on the Internet. Another example of a hub system in action is the airline industry. Certain airports serve as key routes and

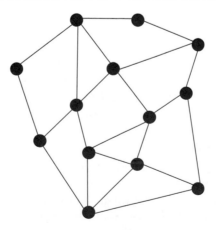

Figure 54.3. Distributed Network Cluster with Nodes.

have a high number of flights traveling through them on a regular basis, allowing for greater efficiencies such as fewer and bigger airports. However, airport hubs also create risk in the system because of the negative impact associated with the loss of a hub.

Network Theory

Network theory offers learning opportunities for HPT consultants. For example, components or nodes within an organization can be people working within the organization at all levels as well as computers, leadership, processes, communication systems, and other resources. In a complex system that is adaptive, self-organized, and free, networks are interconnected, and the people and work flow through the system. Flow refers to communications and linkage in the organization, which may be between humans, between machines, or between humans and machines. As an HPT consultant considers the root cause of a problem or designs an intervention, a more powerful solution can emerge from a dynamic network perspective rather than a reductionist perspective. Solutions should consist of multiple interventions connected to one another and connected to the hubs of the existing system. Networked solutions therefore become stronger and better able to tolerate constant change.

Complex systems are not created equally, with some clusters having more power and influence than others. For instance, a powerful organizational hub is often the compensation system, since employees pay very close attention to their salaries and bonuses. Therefore, an HPT solution that takes into account and leverages the various high-power hubs through the intervention design will realize increased effectiveness. Free interactions between nodes give rise to creativity within the organization. Hite states that creativity will not occur in established rigid organizations "without intervention by organization design (OD) specialists or leaders who know how to exploit the capabilities of the nonlinear dynamical systems" (1999, p. 135). The networks within complex adaptive systems give rise to creativity, making the organization proactive and generative.

A practical application of how network theory relates to the work of the HPT practitioner is displayed in Figure 54.4. In this situation, the administration for a police academy (WCCPA) was out of touch with the activities and needs of the various departments which stayed connected to one another through their formal and informal networks.

To provide some insight on the current situation the HPT practitioner mapped the communications paths, which showed the flow of information and demonstrated that the administration was indeed out of the loop. The focus then turned not to how to control or simplify this flow, but rather how to acknowledge and support it. The team determined that the role of the administrators was to tap into the pipeline, hear the dialogue, and offer ways to move messages through more efficiently and clearly. This was illustrated by drawing a circle all

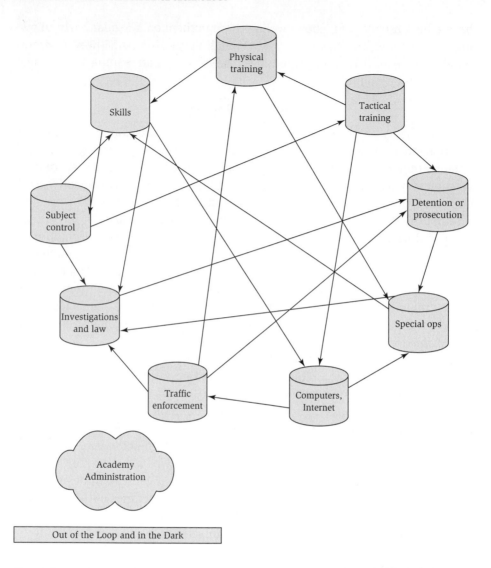

Figure 54.4. WCCPA Current Lines of Communicating Recruit Performance.

the way around the model (see Figure 54.5). The team's actions moving forward therefore focused on building stronger internal relationships, initiating more dialogues, and reviewing information moving through the system.

Finally, networks in action at the social level relate to the phrase "six degrees of separation," which was made famous in the 1960s when Harvard professor Stanley Milgram determined that it took an average of just six progressive links or relationships between one individual and another to connect any two randomly selected individuals. Thus, our world is much smaller than imagined,

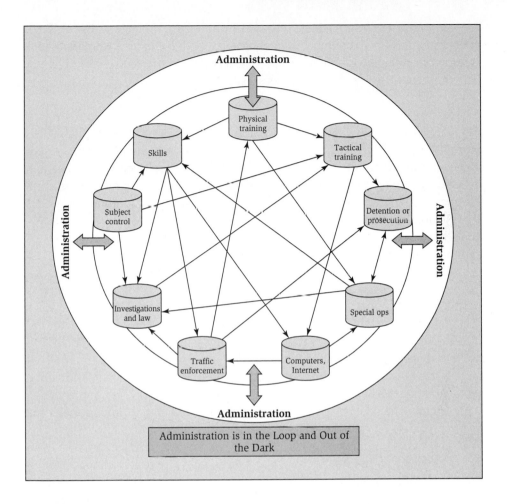

Figure 54.5. WCCPA Future Lines of Communicating Recruit Performance.

and this concept reinforces the importance and value of establishing professional networks. HPT consultants will increasingly partner with experts at all levels. Being a part of a network and tapping into this network will make the possibilities for change almost limitless.

COMPANY ABC CASE STUDY

This case study illustrates the impact of global challenges and actual efforts to resolve associated problems. The approach used is based on the performance technology standards that are part of the certified performance technologist (CPT) designation (International Society for Performance Improvement, 2002). Each intervention involved a number of variables that had to change before that intervention could be fully implemented. The interventions themselves could potentially influence the organization processes and culture.

Context

Company ABC, a software solutions company based in India, was established more than twenty-five years ago and today is a leading global company with offices in more than fifty countries. It employs more than twenty-five thousand people, including local hires in the various countries. The organization is a traditional bureaucracy with a very rigid top-down structure. Human resources (HR) is not very efficient or responsive to organizational needs. Organizational goals are not realistic in terms of today's economy, and frequently managers cannot understand the rationale for the goals.

Organizations are influenced by the broad culture in which they are situated. Culture includes the social structure, definitions of relationships, behavior norms, politics, and the economy. For decades after independence, India was a socialist economy with enormous government controls. The private sector did not readily thrive. Most privately owned large-scale industries belonged to industrial families. Cultural factors, including the family-owned nature of even large businesses, government rules, and the nature of the economy all defined the characteristics of these large industries. Most companies were bureaucratic, with top management serving as patriarchs or benevolent patriarchs, including Company ABC.

Hierarchical management and leadership ensured that companies ran smoothly and that the rules set by the government were followed. However, in the decade of the 1990s, the Indian economy opened, and the private sector got a chance to compete with government industries as well as foreign companies that were set up in India to tap its vast markets. The sudden boom in the Indian software industry resulted in the Indian economy changing at a pace not seen for the past forty years. All the companies, including Company ABC, had to face challenges that came with rapid change.

Current Opportunities and Threats for Company ABC

The opening of the economy and the boom in the software industry provides limitless opportunities. The twenty-five thousand employees, who are highly talented and educated, lend a competitive edge to the company. Company ABC also enjoys immense public confidence and trust and is highly regarded as a company with strict business ethics. Threats come from within Company ABC's own structure and from the complex demands that the economy puts on organizations, compelling them to change and evolve rapidly. Company ABC is at the edge of chaos, and it can collapse if it does not respond fast enough to the changing demands. Threats include the following:

- Due to the outsourcing phenomenon throughout the world, the demands for company services are growing. At the same time the nature of jobs required by clients has become increasingly complex.

- Resourcing is a big problem. To meet the growing demand and the new nature of the work, the company has to hire highly qualified people. Optimum recruitment, with a correct balance between people on projects and people in support roles, becomes very challenging. Retaining resources also is an issue. To place the right resources on the right projects at the right time becomes a challenge.

- Competition from newer and smaller companies is fierce. These companies are also more agile than Company ABC and can respond easily to the demands of changing markets and economies. Company ABC is very process-oriented, and sometimes these processes can lead to red tape that can be detrimental for any company in an environment of constant change.

- Company ABC needs a visionary leader who can transform the company or at least provide some amount of freedom for the managers to work effectively and take on increasing leadership roles.

These issues represent challenges at the organizational level. However, adding to the complexity are problems at the project level. The following human performance improvement (HPI) implementation case illustrates the complex nature of the problem and solutions. The HPI project discussed here was taken up at the request of a project manager of one project located in the U.S. This is just one of the hundreds of projects that the company is engaged in around the world.

Statement of the HPI Problem

A project manager from Company ABC on Project M received a request from a client for the programmers to "improve their client business process knowledge," that is, the knowledge of the business processes of the client, a large-scale manufacturer of auto parts. This request was based on two factors:

- About 20 percent of the errors in coding by the programmers were attributed to the lack of client business process knowledge.

- The lack of business process knowledge also added to the project costs in terms of time, effort, and rework.

This situation was directly related to the company mission and vision, which states that Company ABC desires to be a leader in the software solutions industry by supplying quality software and that it desires to be the preferred vendor of its customers.

Root Cause Analysis

Additional data collection was conducted, and a root cause analysis was completed. Table 54.1 shows the root causes in terms of Gilbert's Human Engineering Model. Rummler's model of organizational structure, process, and

Table 54.1. Company ABC Root Cause Factors.

Environment (Organizational Structure and Processes)		
Information	*Resources*	*Incentives*
Team members may not know the sources of knowledge. Where is the knowledge?	Team members are not aware of resources in the company.	There are no incentives for seeking or getting knowledge.
Sources of knowledge are not fully defined in the company.	Learning systems, training, and development do not consider domain knowledge.	There are no incentives for sharing knowledge.
Information is not easily accessible.	Knowledge base on the company intranet or a similar system may not be sufficient. It may not be an efficient system.	
Initially formal communication channels were not defined, so team members may not have known who was responsible for what, at what stage, and asked questions to the "wrong" individuals.	There is no database of people working in a particular domain. People or experts were a source of knowledge. Existing resources may not be used optimally.	

Individual		
Information	*Resources*	*Incentives*
The individual has a lack of knowledge of business processes.	The individual has a lack of experience in the domain.	The individual may not be motivated to seek knowledge.
The individual has a lack of knowledge in the domain.	Resources may not match in terms of interest and background.	The individual may not be interested.
The individual may not know the sources of knowledge.		The individual may not know the value of tacit knowledge.
		The individual has no incentives to seek knowledge.

individual levels has been integrated into the same table. Communications, incentives, and resources are defined at the organizational level, and not at the project level.

Root cause analysis revealed that the reasons for the programmers' lack of client business process knowledge were not limited to Project M alone. Causes were related to various processes, mainly communications processes and knowledge management processes. Causes were also related to incentive systems and organizational structure. Again, all these factors were interrelated.

Broad culture factors, not directly shown in Table 54.1, also shaped the organization structure and processes in many ways. For instance, organizational culture factors such as hierarchy affected the decision-making process, as decisions were not always made at the point closest to the customer. These overarching issues were considered as solutions were explored.

Performance-Improvement Goal

As a result of the insight from the root cause analysis, the following goals were established:

- Client business process knowledge needed to be defined relating to production, finance, HR, and all other systems within the company. Each company has its own business processes, norms, and specific terms, which are related to *each other* in the way the company defines and organizes them.

- Once the business process knowledge was defined, a knowledge management system was required to transfer knowledge from the clients and the domain experts within the company to the programmers.

- A knowledge measurement system was needed to determine whether the programmers had acquired the necessary business process knowledge.

- There was also the expectation that a universal knowledge management system was needed that could be put in place for all projects.

- A communication system was needed to ensure that business process knowledge was communicated throughout each team.

- Finally, consideration needed to be given to the impact of the organizational structure and culture and how it might affect the chosen solution.

All of the factors related to a knowledge management (KM) system within Company ABC, and the KM system itself depends on the communications process, project management process, company culture, and other factors. It was also acknowledged that there were a number of ways these goals could be tackled, which is discussed in the following section.

Proposed Interventions and Considerations

Interventions at the individual worker level were aimed at bridging the gap between the current state and the desired state, such as training, coaching, mentoring, and incentives to encourage programmers to be more proactive. Interventions at the organizational level involved changing the organizational structure and processes to make them more efficient so that the individuals could be more effective in their jobs. As described in the following sections, an array of interventions were considered, all of which reflected the complexity and nature of the problem itself.

Training. Current team members of Project M could be trained in the client business processes. This would help in the short term for the current team. But a one-time training program is not a solution for a situation in which the team structure is constantly changing. So more robust interventions that ensured continuous transfer of knowledge were needed to improve the client business process knowledge of the team members.

Coaching. Industry and domain experts within the company could coach team members on the client business processes. For this, coaches needed to be identified and incentives given to the coaches. It was proposed that the project manager and team leaders on Project M could become coaches for the team members and help them understand the business processes of the client.

Incentives and Rewards. Prior to HPT analysis, there were no incentives for programmers taking initiative in the area of KM. Existing incentives were based on performance, which was more directly related to meeting deadlines, and so forth. So defining incentives for taking initiatives in the area of KM on Project M was proposed. Incentives for documenting experiences, critical aspects of the projects, and bits of business experience, and for training or taking initiative needed to be defined. Similarly, incentives were considered for trainers, coaches, and managers who took initiative to prepare documents, lead group discussion sessions, and perform other duties that improved the KM process.

Staffing. Staffing was proposed as a long-term strategic intervention. Programmers needed to be matched with their background and interest in a particular project. This kind of intervention requires more elaborate managing of human resources, including establishing real-time databases of existing resources, matching for skills, making manpower projections for future projects, and planning for optimum resources.

Knowledge Management. KM was perhaps one of the most important interventions that could be implemented. However, there was already a KM system in place, and it wasn't as effective as desired. The existing KM system involved putting documents for a project on the internal Website, which was difficult to access and seldom used. As a result, preparing documents was time-consuming and was a low priority among programmers who scrambled to meet project deadlines. It was proposed that the existing KM system be integrated into the project management system, and that the documentation be made simpler for this purpose. Thought was also given to making access to the internal KM system easier for all the team members and across projects.

Job Aids. Programmers normally come into a team that is already formed and working. Programmers may not even have time to go through project documents created by a person who left. In such a situation, a job aid covering the most important and most relevant questions would be very useful, enabling programmers to get the most important knowledge. This would guarantee that the critical knowledge is passed to the incoming person and not left to the memory, motivation, and initiative of the project manager. Similar job aids would be made for managers or module leaders so that information would be passed without forgetting. Job aids would serve as a formal induction of the team members. So preparing job aids for new team members as well as team leaders was proposed.

Documentation. As a part of the project management and quality process, documents are regularly submitted by the team members as a part of their project activities. These documents generally deal with only the technical aspects of the project. It was proposed that documents include knowledge of client's business processes, the critical incidents, experiences on projects, and so on. It was proposed that these documents be integrated into the project management process, to thus form a link between the project management and the KM processes.

Restructuring. Three micro teams exist on Project M: a requirements team that defines the client requirements, a development team that does coding, and a validation team that checks the codes. One of the elements of restructuring would be team design. If the project develops cross-functional teams, then inter-team communications would be streamlined.

Job Rotation. Currently two macro teams exist for Project M: onsite in the U.S. and offshore in India. Naturally, those who interact with the clients have better business process knowledge than the offshore teams who do not. It was proposed that job rotation would be a viable intervention. Business process knowledge as well as communication would improve among team members. Also, creating relationships with the client would create a strong incentive for the offshore team members to perform well.

Leadership. If project managers, project leaders, and others at senior levels make the culture of knowledge management happen, then programmers would accept KM as the norm and take initiative to prepare documents and share knowledge.

Summary of Case Study

Looking at the nature of the problem, a very simplistic solution may first come to mind, such as training individuals in the client's business process knowledge. But as the analysis of potential projects indicated, a deeper view may provide a more effective solution. As HPT looks at solutions at various levels, it inherently looks at complex systems. Root cause analysis helped us to look at factors at different levels, individual and organizational and in terms of process and structure. There were other causes that went beyond the obvious, such as the history of the organization itself, leadership, philosophy of the organization, and the bigger picture of the social and cultural ethos that affect the behavior of seeking knowledge and being proactive. Interventions become learning tools for the people as well as the organization and become a part of the adaptive nature of the organization. Adaptive systems are learning systems because they move to adapt to changing environments.

Some changes initially took place in the organization, but since Company ABC is a large organization, the response was very slow. As a result, the HPT interventions were taken up by the Project M manager as his own initiatives. He became the HPT champion and was determined to make an impact within the scope of his work. Interestingly, one of the first successful interventions was actually the study itself. By participating in the research, team members got to know that this was an issue and became interested, providing ideas and feedback. The study also provided detailed insight on the specific client issues and prompted discussion among project team members concerning the importance of sharing the client process knowledge. The project manager chose to implement the following interventions.

Training and Coaching. The current team was trained and coached by the module leaders and team leaders on the client business processes along with help from domain experts within Company ABC.

Documentation. Team members responded by making a point to document any relevant business process knowledge. For Project M, they made a folder that everyone could share to, which these documents could be uploaded. This made the system very simple and easy to use.

Job Rotation. The team established a rotation schedule so that all members had a chance to work onsite. The team defined a schedule of who would be onsite and offshore for the next year and made plans to allow for maximum opportunities for all team members to be onsite.

Motivation. Motivation became a function of process and not formal rewards. The involvement of the project manager and team members and the acknowledgment of the importance of this performance-improvement initiative added motivation. In addition, the team members were excited for the opportunity to be onsite and took full advantage of the knowledge and learning made available through this experience. Incentives were designed for taking initiatives in sharing knowledge and preparing documents. The project manager stated that he would take up the long-term initiatives such as staffing, integrated KM systems, and project management systems with seniors in the organization.

Results

The project manager reported that errors decreased from 20 percent to about 10 percent, partly because everyone came to know about the importance of the client business processes and tried to learn about them. However, a lot more can be achieved if Company ABC makes policy changes at a higher level.

Being a very large organization, it is slow to respond to demands for changes that emerge from within. Processes are still not efficient for handling the demands for these changes. Its culture still remains a more or less closed and bureaucratic system. HPT initiatives depend on the leadership to drive changes throughout to become a real learning organization. If an organization fails to reward behaviors that create changes, then managers will lose interest in taking any further steps.

RECOMMENDATIONS FOR INCORPORATING CHAOS AND COMPLEXITY INTO THE FUTURE OF HPT

Hite (1999) suggests that the current theories of learning as well as the methodology for performance consulting would change if we were to consider chaos and complexity as realities of organizations. Incorporating chaos and complexity thinking will help to identify other supporting factors that particular interventions need before they can be successfully implemented.

Embrace Complexity During the Analysis Phase of Projects and Beyond

As humans, we often wish for the simple and easy solution. But as human performance technologists, we need to recognize, acknowledge, and appreciate the complexity that exists in our world today. This will lead us to greater understanding of the root cause and direct a more robust solution.

Identify and Make Use of Powerful Nodes

Certain areas of the organizational system or network will be more powerful than others. For example, certain leaders may have a stronger influence than others or existing programs or reward systems may be viewed as critical to the organization's ongoing success. Identify these elements and then factor them into the solution, taking full advantage of them when you are able to do so.

Do Not Be Afraid to Make Concurrent Changes

Because the system is nonlinear, the various solutions should be implemented concurrently rather than one at a time. If the organization is in distress due to the multiple changes, consider increased attention to change management techniques as a way to ease the pain rather than a change to the interventions themselves.

Build in Feedback Loops

Design an evaluation process that allows for ongoing feedback once solutions are put into place. Feedback should be collected at multiple points in the solution, as well as the collection of data that address the accomplishment of end goals.

Plan for Immediate Adjustments During Implementation

Once you have launched your solution, recognize that you have created a disruption in the organizational system, which in turn will require more adjustments on your part. Instead of labeling this need for adjustment as signals of a flawed solution, recognize that they are the result of a complex system in a chaos state and take positive optimistic action.

CONCLUSION

As a field of practice, HPT is clearly a complex science that draws on the learning of many disciplines and many kinds of experts. Chaos theory and the thinking behind complex systems are therefore opportunities to continually evolve the work of HPT practitioners. Given the increasing complexity of the world today, these areas offer untapped potential that can increase the power of service of the discipline in many industries and cultures.

Human performance technology is well positioned to take advantage of the marriage of the many sciences in our world today, as suggested by chaos and complexity. This chapter only scratches the surface of what is sure to be an exciting evolution in our field in the coming years.

References

American Heritage Dictionary of the English Language (4th ed.). (2000). Boston, MA: Houghton Mifflin. Retrieved June 6, 2005, from Dictionary.com.

Barabasi, A. L. (2003). *Linked: How everything is connected to everything else and what it means for business, science, and everyday life.* New York: Plume.

Fairholm, M. R. (2004). A new sciences outline for leadership development, *Leadership and Organizational Development Journal, 25,* 3–4.

Farazmand, A. (2003). Chaos and transformational theories: A theoretical analysis with implications for organization theory and public management. *Public Organization Review: A Global Journal, 3*(4), 339–372.

Gleick, J. (1987). *Chaos. Making a new science.* New York: Penguin.

Hite, J. (1999). *Learning in chaos: Improving human performance in today's fast-changing volatile organizations.* Houston, TX: Gulf Publications.

Holland, J. (1995). *Hidden order: How adaptation builds complexity.* New York: Helix Books.

International Society for Performance Improvement. (2002). *Certified Performance Technologist Performance Technology Standards.* Silver Spring, MD: International Society for Performance Improvement. Retrieved January 7, 2005, from www.ispi.org.

Jaafari, A. (2003, December). Project management in the age of complexity and change. *Project Management Journal, 34*(4), 47–57.

Kaffman, S. (1995). *At home in the universe: The search for the laws of self-organization and complexity.* Oxford, UK: Oxford University Press.

Lorenz, E. N. (1993). *The essence of chaos.* Seattle, WA: University of Washington Press.

Olson, E. E., and Eoyang, G. H. (2001). *Facilitating organization change: Lessons from complexity science.* San Francisco: Jossey-Bass/Pfeiffer.

Sanders, E. S., and Ruggles, J. L. (2000, June). HPI soup: Too many cooks haven't spoiled the broth. *Training and Development, 54*(6), 26–36.

Titcomb, T. J. (1998, July). Chaos and complexity theory. *Info-Line,* no. 9807.

Van Tiem, D. M. (2004). Interventions (solutions) usage and expertise in performance technology practice: An empirical investigation, *Performance Improvement Quarterly, 17*(3), 23–44.

Van Tiem, D. M., Moseley, J. L., and Dessinger, J. C. (2001). *Performance improvement interventions: Enhancing people, processes, and organizations through performance technology,* (2nd ed.). Silver Spring, MD: International Society for Performance Improvement.

Van Tiem, D. M., Moseley, J. L., and Dessinger, J. C. (2004). *Fundamentals of performance technology: A guide to improving people, process, and performance.* Silver Spring, MD: International Society for Performance Improvement.

Wheatley, J. J. (1994). *Leadership and the new science: Learning about organizations from an orderly universe.* San Francisco: Berrett-Koehler.

CHAPTER FIFTY-FIVE

Quantulumcunque Concerning the Future Development of Performance Technology

Klaus D. Wittkuhn

This chapter is a personal statement. You may come to quite different conclusions from the ones I develop here. My hope is that the chapter will trigger a discussion. The clearer that positions are described at the beginning of such a discussion, the easier it is to develop and sharpen arguments. Take it as work in progress, as the result of more than two decades of struggling with systems theory, management challenges, consulting experiences, and desperate attempts to bring these issues together. I have learned a lot during this struggle, but I went through many disappointments as well. This chapter is about sharing my experiences by drawing some conclusions for the future development of the field of performance technology (PT).

This chapter is written from a practitioner's point of view. I am a manager and a consultant, which I consider to be the same side of the coin because both are interested in actions and results in real-world settings. To take action in a responsible way is not easy. If managers take action, they want to improve the company or the organizational unit they are responsible for. This is what responsibility in a business context is all about. But then, how do I know that my action is going to produce the results I am aiming for? Or even more important, how do I know that my action is not going to hurt the company?

Before taking action, some thinking should take place. Great insight, you might say. However, it leads to the heart of the issue I want to discuss in this chapter. How do we gain knowledge about organizations and the outcomes of our actions in those organizations? This is much less trivial than it might appear at first glance.

If you ask someone to describe the company for which they work, you will get all kinds of information ranging from subtle drawings of organizational charts to long and laborious stories about the wrong strategy of top management. Organizations are complex and neither describable nor understandable in simple ways. To understand an organization we need models that help us to reduce this complexity and thus prepare the ground for comprehending and decision making. This leads us back to the question of responsibility: wrong model, wrong decision. Somehow, I have to find out how appropriate the model is that I am using as I prepare for action.

Your understanding of an organization is as good as the models you use. Models are different, they make you see different things: sometimes providing an eye-opening experience, sometimes hiding something essential. Models are neither right nor wrong; they are more or less appropriate for a certain purpose. They are like maps leading you through unknown or even known territory. If your map is not appropriate you will get lost and need to be rescued. However, a map is not the landscape. Moreover, a menu is not a meal as you can easily verify: try to eat it.

As a manager or a consultant you need to have a deep understanding of the models you use in order to make a decision about which model to choose in which situation. Especially, you have to be aware of what models do not show you. Overlooking important aspects of the situation might lead to wrong decisions.

Interestingly, the very same thing holds true for problem definition: the way you describe a problem opens doors for certain solutions and excludes others. With any given problem definition you should be aware that the creative solution is probably hidden in the excluded parts of the problem definition. This should be no surprise, since underlying any problem definition there is a model, explicit or not.

Strangely enough, this leads to the fact that as a practitioner interested in action and results, I have to be interested in models and their underlying theory. So why am I emphasizing the practitioner's point of view? It is because I am interested in the value added of new developments in theory for the everyday business of managing and consulting. When I discuss developments in theory, it is because these developments affect and change the models we use in our decision making.

In the following sections I will outline some possible developments of PT during the coming decade. Moreover, I will outline some developments I personally would like PT to take, because I think they would be fruitful for the whole profession.

PERFORMANCE TECHNOLOGY WILL START QUESTIONING THE PREMISES BEHIND THE CURRENT PT MODELS

Why is this important? An observer does not see what he does not see. There is always a blind spot in observing, and this blind spot includes the observation itself. An eye does not see itself. A model does not show what it does not cover. A mechanism in the scientific community and in any professional community to overcome this problem is to have other people designing other models and then compare the pros and cons of their use in specific contexts. However, too often in a given field of study, many models that are developed and applied tend to be based on the same premises, thus not showing much difference and probably all sharing the same blind spots. This is what one calls a paradigm. Models belonging to the same paradigm are alike in a certain sense.

My impression is that all PT models are based on very similar premises. The most important premise I see is this: there is a reality somewhere, and for performance technologists it is an organization with problems. Those problems can be diagnosed from the outside, for example by a consultant, and then a remedy can be prescribed. This can be seen most clearly in Rummler's anatomy of performance (Rummler, 2004) and the medical analogies he uses. I am not aware of any PT model that is not based on this or a similar premise.

This is not to state that this premise is wrong. On the contrary, I believe it is helpful in many situations. Nevertheless, there are other models that look at organizations based on completely different premises and thus make other things visible. As a practitioner, I am interested in having different models and using the most appropriate one in any given situation. I am interested in the premises of those models being revealed and discussed. Otherwise, I am always working within boundaries and limitations that I do not realize or fully understand.

In my judgment, PT has to develop something similar to what Argyris and Schön (1996) call double-loop learning, not only to discuss and change the current models based on experience, that is, feedback from reality, but also to question the premises of those models.

The single-loop learning of the PT community has led to an unfolding of the insights of the earliest thinkers in the field, who began their work some forty years go. Dean and Ripley (1997) call them "pathfinders." Often the work centers on basic concepts that Brethower (1982), Rummler and Brache (1995), and Rummler (2004) developed during the 1960s, which had been used in workshops for years before they finally were published.

- Brethower's concept of a total performance system
- Rummler's concept of a human performance system

- Brethower's and Rummler's concept of the three levels of performance
- Rummler's concept of the anatomy of performance

These insights serve as premises or building blocks for most models. Later models elaborate on things already embodied in the work of these authors, although sometimes not explicitly. For many readers this might sound a little too "cut and dried," but remember I am talking about very basic premises and not about details elaborated from them.

In my judgment, there is one exception to my generalization: Roger Kaufman and the concept he calls "Mega." Kaufman argues that organizations have to take into account that they are part of a bigger whole, a society, and they need to make sure that they add value to this bigger whole, or at least that they do not damage it. Kaufman (1998) considers Mega to represent a paradigm shift. In my judgment, Mega is not PT specific. It applies to many other ways of thinking about organizations and their performance. In addition, I think that the development of Mega has in part addressed Argyris's double-loop learning. It changed the premise that the limits of a manager's responsibility are more or less the boundaries of his company. Furthermore, the development and application of Mega have thrown overboard the idea that Mega serves only as an ethical imperative but does not have any business impact.

Going beyond current premises in PT model development will open up new doors and lead to new insights, followed by new methods, followed by new approaches. It is in double-loop learning where new opportunities are hidden: discuss and change the current models based on experience feedback from real-world experiences and question the premises of the models.

HAVING CHALLENGED ITS OWN PREMISES, PT WILL EMBRACE OTHER WAYS OF CONCEPTUALIZING REALITY AND INTEGRATE THEM INTO ITS BODY OF KNOWLEDGE

PT claims to be systemic; some of the models are. The PT understanding of a system can be characterized as follows: a system is a whole consisting of parts, which are interconnected in a way that constitutes this whole. And the whole has emerging properties that cannot be reduced to the characteristics of its parts. Many corollaries follow from this definition. For me, *emerging properties* seems to be the core of PT's system understanding. It is a term borrowed from science and used especially in the context of systems theory. For us in PT, it includes things such as learning, adapting, regressing, and, what is most important to us, performance. These factors are integral to the whole system in both constraints, due to the restrictions they impose on any single part, as well as to expansion, due to the interaction of the system's parts. This is predicated on the idea that the system, for example, an organization, is out there and can be analyzed, diagnosed, and changed.

A quite different concept of systems thinking in the context of organizational development is the soft systems methodology (SSM) developed by Checkland (1999) and others. Working on a problem always is the attempt by people to take purposeful action that is meaningful to them. Checkland and his colleagues experienced that "meaning" and "purpose" are quite different for many people, and that there was nothing like an "obvious" problem out there that required a solution. They developed the idea of looking at a problem as a situation that some people, for various reasons, regard as problematical. That means there are always many different models at play, and all of them might be based on sound reasoning. "Obvious," in the sense that it can be analyzed, diagnosed, and changed, seems to be quite different from different perspectives. Instead of trying to discover one truth lying out there, these organizational development specialists changed a basic assumption. Rather than thinking of the world as being systemic, they focused on the process of inquiry. The world might be chaotic, but the process of inquiring about this world can be organized in a systemic way and can be organized as a learning system.

This leads away from the idea of improving a system toward implementing change. And it leads away from implementing change into a given system. A system in SSM only exists as a device to stimulate and structure a debate about the situation that is perceived as problematical. This thinking is also a model, but not a model about something out there to tinker with, that is, some real and tangible thing, but a model relevant to the different ways people conceptualize their views of reality . . . to debate.

Can this approach be helpful in everyday life? Yes, it can. Nobody knows how many change projects and mergers failed because, somewhere and somehow, as projects progressed people were lost as they developed what is called resistance from the point of view of the one who wants change to take place. This finally makes the whole thing fail, as Conner (1992) showed impressively.

SSM is an approach that tries to take into account that there is no "obvious problem" or "obvious solution" for most people and that somehow their perspectives have to be taken into account to successfully change the situation. Given this different modeling of the consulting approach, advocates of applying SSM have developed methods to work with many different subjective models in a change process, as pointed out by Checkland (1999).

I believe that it is not accidental that in the PT literature, implementation is often something that is only mentioned, without genuine approaches having been developed to carrying it out. The basic premises of systems actually in use lead to concepts such as resistance to change and a whole body of knowledge covering implementation from the change and resistance perspectives. Therefore, there is no need for traditional implementation approaches in genuine PT. However, it might be worthwhile to consider that there is no such thing as resistance to implementation and change if you conceptualize differently and take different actions during a performance-improvement project.

Now, this does not at all mean to stop thinking about resistance. In different situations different approaches will be helpful. It is not that one has to abandon a model when theory development leads to different approaches. As a practitioner you do not even have to abandon a model that theory development tells you is outdated. Rather, theory development offers more alternatives for what we do in everyday life. The essential issue is to alter or develop new criteria for when to use the different models and approaches. In essence, to know when they work and why they work when they do work.

I believe it is a good strategy when taking action to go with the simplest model that serves the purpose. Management and consulting are not sciences. They are making changes in the most effective and efficient way. Science helps us to find out how this might work through the development of theories and models. When it finally comes to taking action one should not be judged by scientific criteria, but rather by economical criteria such as effectiveness and efficiency.

What does this mean in management and consulting? If you want to build a tennis court you do not have to take into account that the earth is a ball, you can conceptualize it as flat, as your medieval ancestors would have done, and you quickly will come up with the desired results. Planning a flight from Europe to the United States might ask for a different model of the earth. To take a side step, when something falls on your head, a Newtonian worldview will do. When the object hits your head, Einstein's theory of relativity will most probably only make things more complicated and add nothing to your rescue and treatment. Managing and consulting is not in every case the application of the latest scientific insights; it is getting desired results effectively and efficiently. Focusing on the idea of subjectivity playing part in every human action leads directly in my judgment to a third development.

PT WILL GIVE UP THE CLAIM TO BEING A TECHNOLOGY AND ACCORDINGLY LABEL ITSELF DIFFERENTLY

To illustrate this we have to take a closer look at what is meant by the terms *methodology, method,* and *technique.*

Methodology is the principles of methods, the assumptions behind methods. Those principles are used to gain insight and justify what is actually done in a particular situation that is considered as problematical. Methodology leads to using justified methods to approach problems. If a method, when skillfully applied, guarantees over time that it leads to specific results, it becomes a technique (Checkland, 1999). A comprehensive set of such techniques is a technology.

It is more than unlikely that any method used when working with human beings can become a technique. To demonstrate this requires the distinction between trivial and nontrivial machines (Von Foerster, 1984).

A trivial machine consistently transforms input A into output B. Trivial machines can be engineered. And engineering is all about using techniques. In addition to trivial machines, there is a second category called nontrivial machines. The difference between a trivial and a nontrivial machine is that when a nontrivial machine receives input A at time T1, that input is not only transformed into output B but also changes the way the machine works. The same input A at time T2 is not transformed into output B but into a different output. It might be C, but we cannot know in advance. Every time an input is transformed like this, the working mechanism of the machine is transformed as well. This is the formal description of learning. Living beings learn.

The consequences are easily illustrated. Imagine that some unscrupulous person kicks a dog. The first time the dog runs away. The second time it might run as well or it might try to bite its aggressor. Or it might run away the moment the aggressor enters the room. We cannot know because the reactions of nontrivial machines cannot be reliably predicted.

We all realize that humans do not behave in completely arbitrary ways. People treat each other politely, they know what to answer when they are asked their name, and they know how to solve arithmetic problems. Obviously, it is possible to trivialize people. We have designed whole organizations such as schools and universities that too often trivialize people. But there is always a degree of uncertainty that remains.

To state it differently: nontrivial machines can be influenced. Sometimes they do what we want them to do, but they cannot be controlled. There is always uncertainty. Thus, human performance cannot be engineered but only influenced. To influence somebody one can use a method, but as there will never be a guaranteed result, one cannot claim the use of a technique. "Human performance technology" sounds good, but seems to be a bit overpromising.

PT WILL BECOME MORE SERIOUS CONCERNING THE CLAIM OF BEING SYSTEMIC, AND THIS WILL LEAD TO A MORE COMPREHENSIVE SET OF METHODS TO ANALYZE SYSTEMS

In systems you rarely find causes. Declaring "cause analysis" to be a major step in the performance-improvement process does not at all mirror systemic thinking. It mirrors linear cause-and-effect thinking. Since systems usually show dense

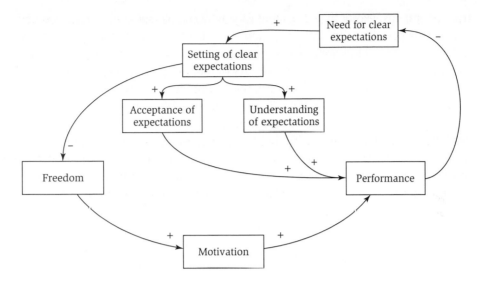

Figure 55.1. A Human Performance System (Detail).

interaction between their elements, there will be circular causality that does not allow linear cause identification. As an example, Figure 55.1 shows the details of a possible conceptualization of a human performance system; the whole system is much more elaborate.

In the figure the plus and minus signs denote positive and negative correlation. Positive correlation means that if one element moves in one direction, the other element moves in the same direction. Negative correlation means that a movement in one direction triggers the opposite movement in the correlated element.

We see that the more insufficient the performance, the higher the need to set clear expectations. The greater the need for clear expectations, the higher the probability that clear expectations will be set. The clearer the expectations are, the greater the chances for their likely acceptance and understanding. And the greater the acceptance and understanding of expectations, the better performance will be. There is an equalizing factor here as well. The clearer the expectations are, the less freedom there is in the system. And if freedom diminishes, motivation diminishes as well. Diminished motivation means diminished performance.

If there is a performance problem, what is the cause? Elements are so interrelated that what seems to be a cause may suddenly turn out to be an effect as well. The meaning of cause as we find it in linear thinking vanishes, with one exception: in linear thinking we would conceptualize performance as the dependent variable and the elements influencing performance as independent variables. Improvements in the independent variables, the causes of performance, would trigger improvement of the dependent variable performance, the effect. This is not true for systems, except that "a given design may contain some slack between variables. This permits us to deal with each variable separately as though it were an independent variable." We find causes again. This is true until the slack between them is taken up. "Then the perceived set of independent variables changes to a formidable set of interdependent variables. Improvement in one variable would come only at the expense of others" (Gharajedaghi, 1999, p. 14).

Cause analysis is popular because most managers and consultants work with systems that contain slack. Still, theory construction has to take cause analysis as a special case when understanding phenomena in systems. On the method level we need tools to understand systems without using cause analysis at all. To date, the focus has been on cause analysis, and there is a void of alternative methods.

PT WILL OPEN TOWARD SECOND-ORDER CYBERNETICS

Checkland (1999) shows that a huge part of theory development in biology, neurophysiology, economics, psychology, sociology, and other sciences during the last twenty years has taken on a constructivist approach. The results conclude in a multidisciplinary approach to systems theory.

The basic premise of the constructivist approach is that every observation and every description, always based on some type of observation, is a construction of the observer himself or herself and does not mirror reality. A brain processes electrical and chemical impulses, not cars or people. And it processes them in a way that is determined by its structure and not by something from outside. The light that hits the cells in the eye of the observer does not transport a picture into the brain. Instead it activates some cells and they start working according to their internal structure. Organs work in an operationally closed structure operating in a self-referential way. It is the contribution of Maturana and Varela (1980) that shows how this leads to adaptation to an environment and finally to successful management and consulting.

Formal arguments for this position have been developed by Spencer-Brown (1973). He developed a calculus of reference that showed that every observation needs a distinction made by the observer. The basic operation needed to make an observation is drawing a distinction to isolate the object of the observation from other objects, and drawing a distinction is done by the observer. The conclusion is obvious: there is no knowledge about objects that is not observer dependent. Objective knowledge disappears. The distinctions being made by the observer are an essential part of the result of the observation and in fact they are part of the observation itself.

Varela (1975) elaborated it to a calculus of self-reference showing the operationally closed structure of systems. And a huge part of Von Foerster's work

(1984) elaborates the concept of self-reference and its meaning in logic, biology, and the social sciences.

This leads us back to the first point: questioning the premises of models. But there is an essential difference. Whereas questioning the premises of models has always been done in the scientific community to get better and better models with the goal of coming closer and closer to reality, here there is no coming closer to reality. Observers behave as operationally closed systems, and observation cannot be separated from the observer.

What are the practical consequences of such an approach? Diagnosing a system is a first-order observation, acting as if it would describe reality. But if you cannot separate the observation from the observer because of the self-referential nature of the observation, it makes sense to watch the observer to find out about the distinctions he or she built into the observation, thus gaining a better understanding of the results of the observation. This is a second-order observation, which is not better in the sense of being closer to reality than is a first-order observation. The essential difference is that now the observer is being watched and not the system: in other words the object of the observation becomes the observer.

For a management or performance-improvement consultant this would mean that instead of diagnosing a system and drawing some conclusions about improvement necessities hoping that management will accept and implement them, it might in many cases be better to discuss the mental models management uses, that is, the distinctions they make. This approach is very close to Checkland's approach (1999).

Once managers understand their distinctions and perhaps even change them, they will make other observations and may not need a consultant because they will come up themselves with a description of the situation that gives them a clear picture of what to do. This is a much more efficient way of consulting; at least it saves consulting time. For a consultant who is interested in successful implementation, the change of management's mental models is probably a condition *sine qua non*. Why has management not already done what you suggest as a consultant if not for their mental models being different from yours? If their mental models are different, they are probably not appropriate to implement what you suggest. And another important reason: there is no guarantee that the distinctions a consultant makes in his or her observation are more appropriate than the ones management makes. This leads to consulting as a debate of mental models and of the differences these models make in managing an organization.

There are many situations in which this approach does not work: management might be in need of more human resources, and this way of consulting might not fit into its mental models. The reasons for nonacceptance might be manifold. Still a constructivist approach comes with additional methods that are worthwhile to consider as making a part of the PT consultant's method repertoire.

SYSTEMS THEORY IN THE FUTURE WILL DEVELOP A NEW FOCUS TO ANSWER THE QUESTION "WHAT ARE THE ESSENTIAL QUALITIES OF A SYSTEM?"

So far theory has focused very much on the emerging properties of a system and on the system being more than the sum of its parts. But a system is also less than the sum of its parts. The emerging properties impose restrictions on the parts of the system and limit their degrees of freedom. The parts of a system can neither behave nor develop into any possible direction; otherwise a system loses its emerging properties and the essential qualities of the system disappear. As an example: you cannot reduce living to the sum of the characteristics of the single organs. A system is more than the sum of its parts. But a system loses the quality of being alive when one of its organs does not function properly to support the system, although the functioning might be sufficient for the organ alone. The system is less than the sum of its parts.

Further research needs to focus more on those limiting phenomena in systems to gain a clearer understanding of how the whole and the parts are connected and to better understand interventions and their results. And here it becomes practical again. A manager's and a consultant's work should be based on such insights. Therefore PT should incorporate such insights.

PT NEEDS TO DEVELOP A MORE COMPREHENSIVE FRAMEWORK HOLDING TOGETHER DIFFERENT MODELS AND APPROACHES CONCERNING PERFORMANCE IMPROVEMENT

This is nothing but a summary of all of the aspects I have outlined. The choice I have made is an eclectic one. The choice was driven by my personal experience. But there is one idea emerging from it: for practitioners, a framework would be helpful that allows integration of linear cause-and-effect thinking as well as systems thinking and integration of first-order observation as well as second-order observation and self-reference.

Thus, such a framework could contain a comprehensive set of methods, and a consultant or manager would choose the most appropriate to serve a particular purpose. But there is one essential requirement for such a framework. That is, to avoid its becoming an "anything goes" collection of methods, which would not be helpful to guide successful practical work. The framework has to provide a set of criteria that helps people make decisions about how to select models and methods. This is not a trivial task, and it would probably involve a research program for the next two decades. But it is worth doing because it will widen our horizons and our practical impact enormously. As Gregory Bateson (1972) would have stated: the result would be a framework making a difference which makes a difference.

References

Argyris, C., and Schön, D. A. (1996). *Organizational learning II: Theory, method, and practice.* Reading, MA: Addison-Wesley.

Bateson, G. (1972). *Steps to an ecology of mind.* New York: Ballantine.

Brethower, D. M. (1982). The total performance system. In R. M. O'Brien, A. M. Dickinson, and M. P. Rosow (Eds.), *Industrial behavior modification: A management handbook.* New York: Pergamon Press.

Checkland, P. (1999). *Soft systems methodology: A 30-year retrospective.* New York: Wiley.

Conner, D. R. (1992). *Managing at the speed of change: How resilient managers succeed and prosper where others fail.* New York: Villard.

Dean, P. J., and Ripley, D. E. (1997) *Performance improvement pathfinders: Models for organizational learning.* Washington, DC: The International Society for Performance Improvement.

Gharajedaghi, J. (1999). *Systems thinking, managing chaos and complexity: A platform for designing business architecture.* Burlington, MA: Butterworth Heinemann.

Kaufman, R. (1998). *Strategic thinking: A guide to identifying and solving problems* (2nd ed.). Washington, DC: International Society for Performance Improvement and American Society for Training and Development.

Maturana, H., and Varela, F. (1980). *Autopoiesis and cognition: The realization of the living.* Dordrecht: D. Reidl.

Rummler, G. A. (2004). *Serious performance consulting according to Rummler.* Silver Spring, MD: International Society for Performance Improvement.

Rummler, G. A., and Brache, A. P. (1995). *Improving performance: How to manage the white space on the organization chart* (2nd ed.). San Francisco: Jossey-Bass.

Spencer-Brown, G. (1973). *Laws of form.* New York: Bantam.

Varela, F. J. (1975). A calculus for self-reference. *International Journal for General Systems, 2,* 5–24.

Von Foerster, H. (1984). Principles of self-organization in a socio-managerial context. In H. Ulbrich and G.J.B. Probst (Eds.), *Self-organization and the management of social systems* (pp. 2–24). New York: Springer.

ABOUT THE EDITOR

James A. Pershing, Certified Performance Technologist, is professor of education in instructional systems technology and educational inquiry methodology at Indiana University. He teaches and advises graduate students in the areas of performance technology and education research. He is also the chief executive officer of Education and Management Research Associates of Bloomington, Indiana. Its clients include leading companies and government agencies in North America, South America, and Asia.

Pershing received his B.S. degree (1968) from Indiana State University with a double major in political science and mathematics. His M.S.T degree (1972) is from the University of Missouri with a major in economics and a minor in mathematics. He earned his Ph.D. degree (1975) from the University of Missouri with a major in education and minor in economics. He joined the faculty of Indiana University in 1977. Prior to that, he was on the faculty at the University of Missouri and was a visiting faculty member at the University of Nevada, Las Vegas.

Over the past thirty years, Pershing has made several contributions to the research, development, and writings that have helped to define and develop the fields of human performance technology, instructional technology, and workforce development. Since 1973, Pershing has published over one hundred books, monographs, articles, or research reports. As executive director of the Office of Education and Training Resources at Indiana University, he was either the principal investigator or project director for over sixty research, development, or service projects that secured over $6 million dollars in external funding from state, national, and international government agencies as well as major corporations. He has made over seventy-five professional presentations at national and international conferences, for organizations including the International Society for Performance Improvement (ISPI), the International Federation of Training and Development Organizations, the American Society for Training and Development, the Association for Educational Communications and Technology (AECT), the International Society for the Systems Sciences, the National Association for Vocational Special Needs Personnel, the American Educational Research Association, and the American Vocational Association.

Some of Professor Pershing's most significant academic and professional contributions have come through his tutelage and mentoring of over three hundred master's or doctoral students. Many of these individuals have assumed leadership positions throughout the world in instructional or performance technology in business and industry, government, the military, and academia. Through the synergism that evolves from dissertation advisement and the coauthoring of articles and reports of findings from research and development projects, several of Pershing's students have become his valued colleagues.

Pershing is former editor of the *Performance Improvement Journal* and *Tech Trends*. He is now a consulting reviewer for *Tech Trends* and is editor of the *Asia-Pacific Cybereducation Journal*. He is a past director of the International Society for Performance Improvement and served as the association manager of the Association for Educational Communications and Technology. He is also a past board member of the Vocational Technical Education Consortium of States as well as a past advisory board member to the National Center for Research in Vocational Education. Pershing has received numerous academic and professional awards and honors, among them awards for outstanding service to ISPI, AECT, the Indiana Department of Elementary and Secondary Education, and the United States Naval Academy. He is a member of the honor societies of Phi Delta Kappa (education) and Omicron Delta Epsilon (economics).

ABOUT THE CONTRIBUTORS

Roger M. Addison, CPT, is an internationally respected practitioner of human performance technology and performance consulting. He is the senior director of human performance technology for the International Society for Performance Improvement (ISPI). Roger was vice president and manager at Wells Fargo Bank. His responsibilities included executive coaching and education, change management, and partnering with line managers to improve performance. He earned his doctorate in educational psychology from Baylor University. Roger is a past president of ISPI, and in 1998 he received ISPI's highest award, member for life. As an international delegate to the International Federation of Training and Development Organizations and ISPI conferences, Roger has worked and presented in North America, South America, Asia, Europe, Africa, and the Middle East.

John Amarant, CPT, is a consultant working in San Francisco in the field of change management. For the first twenty-seven years of his career, John was

---

Certified Performance Technologist (CPT) is a credential that is awarded by the International Society for Performance Improvement (ISPI) to individuals who satisfy a set of requirements that include demonstrated proficiency in ISPI's ten Standards of Performance Technology in ways that are in keeping with ISPI's Code of Ethics.

Certification is performance-based, and individuals who receive the Certified Performance Technologist designation must be re-certified every three years to maintain the credential.

self-employed. He began his career as a change agent as a lawyer. He converted to performance consulting in 1989 and considers the International Society for Performance Improvement his professional home. He has worked with numerous change initiatives to align organizations to better fulfill their strategies. This has included internal branding and brand launches, business process streamlining, introduction of new technologies, service culture changes, and mergers and acquisitions. John's work has taken him throughout the United States, Europe, and the Middle East, where he has worked with a range of industries such as transportation, information technology, publishing, financial services, and telecommunications.

Nicholas Andreadis is dean of extended university programs at Western Michigan University. He is an experienced physician, educator, and consultant whose activities are focused on creating and leading innovative and practical solutions to complex organizational development and performance issues. Scholarly activities are pursued in the area of human performance technology and organizational development. Andreadis received a B.A. degree from Kent State University and an M.D. degree from Creighton University. He is a member of the Academy for Human Resources Development, and the International Society for Performance Improvement, and a fellow of both the American College of Physicians and the American College of Cardiology.

Robert L. Appelman is a clinical associate professor with the instructional systems technology department at Indiana University. Trained initially as a graphic designer, he moved into motion picture and television production and produced award-winning titles in both of these media. He earned his Ph.D. at Indiana University with a focus on message and learning environment design. He now coordinates all technology education courses for preservice teachers for the School of Education, Indiana University, and teaches courses that focus on the integration of technology into teaching and the coordination of production management strategies necessary to create immersive learning environments for K–12 settings, including videogames and simulations.

Sasha Barab is an associate professor in learning sciences, instructional systems technology, and cognitive science at Indiana University. His work involves the design of rich learning environments, frequently with the aid of technology, that are designed to assist children in developing their sense of purpose as individuals, as members of their communities, and as knowledgeable citizens of the world. His research has resulted in dozens of articles, chapters in edited books, and the edited volume *Designing for Virtual Communities in the Service of Learning* (2004).

Barbara A. Bichelmeyer is associate professor of instructional systems technology (IST) in the School of Education at Indiana University. She teaches graduate courses in instructional design, evaluation, and research methods for IST. She consults with numerous corporate, military, and government organizations on instructional design and the evaluation of instruction. Bichelmeyer received her M.S. degree in history and philosophy of education and her Ph.D. degree in curriculum and instruction from the University of Kansas. Her research explores the uses of instructional design and technology to foster intentionality toward learning among students. She has written articles that have been published in journals such as *Educational Technology Research and Development, Performance Improvement Quarterly, College Teaching,* and *Distance Education.*

Christy M. Borders is a doctoral student in the instructional systems technology program at Indiana University. She is an associate instructor, teaching an undergraduate technology skills course to preservice teachers. She also works as project assistant for the Cisco Network Academy Evaluation project and, among other tasks, is the editor of the e-newsletter *E-News.* In August, 2004, Christy was selected to spend one month in Windhoek, Namibia, working with the University of Namibia to increase students' interaction with existing distance education courses. From this experience, she became involved in finding ways to provide quality distance education materials in environments that have little or no access to technology.

Dale M. Brethower is professor emeritus, Western Michigan University, with degrees from the University of Kansas, Harvard, and the University of Michigan. He is widely published, reviews for several professional journals, and presents regularly at professional conferences. One of the pioneers of human performance technology, Brethower has been a consultant for more than thirty-five years. The Organizational Behavior Management Network recognized his contributions with an outstanding contribution award. Dale is a past president of the International Society for Performance Improvement (ISPI). He received ISPI's highest award, member for life, in 2004.

Robert O. Brinkerhoff is an internationally recognized expert in evaluation and training effectiveness and has provided consultation to dozens of major companies and organizations in the United States, South Africa, Russia, Europe, Australia, New Zealand, Singapore, and Saudi Arabia. He is an author of numerous books on evaluation and training, and has been a keynote speaker and presenter at hundreds of conferences and institutes worldwide. He earned a doctorate at the University of Virginia in program evaluation and is currently professor of counseling psychology at Western Michigan University, where he coordinates graduate programs in human resource development. He serves as principal consultant and CEO for The Learning Alliance in Kalamazoo, Michigan, a firm that provides consultation in training effectiveness and measurement.

Megan M. Cassidy has an undergraduate degree from James Madison University in Harrisonburg, Virginia, with a major in communicative sciences disorders. Since completing her bachelor's degree in 2001, she has been employed at Career Development Corporation in Alexandria, Virginia. In May of 2005, Megan earned an M.S. degree in psychological services with a specialization in school counseling from Marymount University. She is currently working toward certification as a licensed professional counselor in the state of Virginia and is a partner in Organizational Improvement Systems.

Michael F. Cassidy is a professor in the School of Business at Marymount University in Arlington, Virginia, where he teaches courses in statistics, research, and group decision making. He has been coeditor of *Performance Improvement Quarterly* since 2002. He regularly conducts cross-disciplinary research on a broad range of topics. Cassidy has published extensively on topics including social capital, semiotics, ethics, measurement, evaluation, diversity, and domestic violence. He is a principal at Innovative Decisions, Inc. and a partner in Organizational Improvement Systems, and he consults regularly within the public and private sectors. Prior to returning to academia in 1995, he worked in business and industry, including twelve years as a technical manager at AT&T Bell Laboratories.

Roger Chevalier, CPT, is the director of certification for the International Society for Performance Improvement. As an independent performance consultant, he specialized in integrating training into more comprehensive performance-improvement solutions. With over twenty-five years experience in performance improvement, Roger is a former vice president of Century 21 Real Estate Corporation's performance division and a former training director for the U.S. Coast Guard's west coast training center. Roger has a Ph.D. degree in applied behavioral science as well as two M.S. degrees, in personnel management and organizational behavior. His formal education includes bachelor's and master's degrees in English Literature.

Richard E. Clark, CPT, is professor of educational psychology and technology in the Rossier School of Education at the University of Southern California, where he is head of the Center for Cognitive Technology and a doctoral program in human performance at work. His recent book *Turning Research into Results: A Guide to Selecting the Right Performance Solutions* (2002) received the 2003 International Society for Performance Improvement (ISPI) award of excellence.

In 2003, he received the SITE Foundation Excellence in Research Award and the Thomas F. Gilbert Distinguished Professional Achievement Award, a presidential citation for intellectual leadership from ISPI. In 2004 he received the Socrates award for excellence in teaching from the graduate students at USC.

Ruth Colvin Clark has focused her professional efforts on bridging the gap between academic research in instructional methods and practitioner application of that research. To that end, she has developed a number of seminars and has written five books (including *e-Learning and the Science of Instruction* [2003], coauthored with Richard Mayer) that translate and illustrate important research programs for organizational training specialists. Ruth studied science as an undergraduate and completed her doctorate in instructional psychology and educational technology in 1988 at the University of Southern California. Ruth is a past president of the International Society of Performance Improvement and a member of the American Educational Research Association.

William R. Daniels is cofounder of American Consulting & Training, Inc. He has been designing management and organizational development programs for thirty years. He has served as keynote speaker at numerous management conferences as well as supervisory, middle, and senior management seminars for several Fortune 100 companies. Bill is the 2005 recipient of the International Society for Performance Improvement's Thomas F. Gilbert Distinguished Professional Achievement Award. He has also served as a member of the board of directors for the International Board of Standards for Training, Performance, and Instruction. Bill has written several books on effective management practices. He holds a B.A. degree in philosophy and English literature, and an M.B.A. degree in finance.

Rodrigo del Valle is an experienced educator and instructional designer from Chile. He worked at the Chilean Ministry of Education nationwide educational technology program and was national coordinator for the world links for development program in Chile. His research and development interests are on-line learning environments for adults and the use of information and communication technologies to enhance quality and access to education. He is especially interested in the use of on-line learning to support teacher professional development, pedagogical agents to support on-line learning, and cognitive and social presence in on-line environments. Currently he works at the Indiana University Center for Research on Learning and Technology.

Brian Desautels, CPT, is president of JB_2D Performance, Inc., a firm specializing in the application of performance technology to human resource management. He is a former senior human resources manager at Microsoft Corporation. He has an M.S. degree in human resource management. His consulting experience includes work for many Fortune 50 organizations. Desautels is a past director and treasurer for the International Society for Performance Improvement (ISPI) and is editor of the *PerformanceXpress* column *CPT@Work*. He has contributed to books on human performance technology and intervention selection and design. He is an instructor with the University of Phoenix and has presented at conferences on the subject of employee performance. He is coauthor of ISPI's workshop *HPT for HR Professionals*.

Joan C. Dessinger, CPT, is senior consultant with The Lake Group, a performance-improvement consulting company. She also teaches graduate courses in instructional technology at Wayne State University and has presented at numerous international conferences. Dessinger is coauthor of the following books: *Training OWLS (Older Worker-Learners): Transitions, Transformations and Opportunities* (2006); *Confirmative Evaluation: Practical Strategies for Valuing Continuous Improvement* (2004); *Fundamentals of Human Performance Technology: A Guide for Improving People, Process*, and *Performance* (2000, 2004); and *Performance Improvement Interventions: Enhancing People and Process Through Performance Technology* (2001). She has also published articles in *Performance Improvement* and coauthored a chapter on full-scope evaluation for ISPI's Pathfinder series (1998); a chapter on evaluating satellite distance learning in *Distance Training* (1998); and a chapter on Ford Motor Company's satellite distance learning program in *Sustaining Distance Training* (2001).

Wilbur Doddridge is a senior instructional systems specialist, recently retired from the Naval Air Systems Command, Orlando, Florida. Mr. Doddridge has over twenty years of experience in training systems acquisition with the United States Department of Defense.

Dennis Duke, CPT, is a senior instructional systems specialist at the Naval Air Systems Command (NAVAIR), Orlando, Florida. He leads interdisciplinary engineering teams in undertaking analyses of systems and organizations from a training perspective. In 2004 he was appointed as a NAVAIR research and engineering fellow, recognizing his significant contributions to naval aviation. Currently he is heading a training analysis for two new U.S. Navy aircraft acquisitions. He has over twenty-five years of experience in the analysis, design, development, implementation, and evaluation of training systems. Duke is also an adjunct professor at the Wayne Huizenga Graduate School of Business and Entrepreneurship at Nova Southeastern University and the Graduate School of Business at Florida Institute of Technology.

John Endicott is a senior instructional designer at DLS Group, Inc. He specializes in writing printed and on-line documentation and e-learning in areas such as securities regulation, telecommunications, pharmaceuticals, and sales training. He has an M.S. degree in technical and scientific communication from Miami University, Oxford, Ohio. Endicott has several years of experience teaching college mathematics and English, and he has participated in conference presentations for several national and international organizations including the International Society for Performance Improvement, the Society for Technical Communication, and the Association for Computing Machinery. He has coauthored several articles and book chapters on project alignment and electronic performance support systems.

Timm J. Esque, CPT, is an independent performance consultant specializing in helping teams and organizations immediately improve performance while creating an environment for sustaining long-term success. His work with product development teams has been featured in *Product Development Best Practices Report* and *Training* magazine. Esque regularly publishes and presents on management and performance topics, usually including data-based results. He has written two books and edited a third. He holds a B.S. degree in psychology and a master's degree in educational technology, both from Arizona State University.

Fang Fang is currently doing research in on-line education in the instructional systems technology program at Indiana University. After getting her M.S. degree in telecommunications with a focus on on-line business management, she switched her interests to how to enhance learning in a Web-based environment with technological initiatives. Her research interests include building on-line learning communities within special organizations, creating various learning environments, promoting new pedagogical designs, and analysis and assessment of on-line learning programs. Major projects she has participated in are: Quest Atlantis 3D simulation gaming environment for elementary schooling, evaluation of self-learning project of e-portfolio, evaluation of IST distance programs, and design and development of a Web-based video streaming system.

Camille Ferond, CPT, is a Vector Europe Director—France and Italy. She is a cofounder and vice president of ASTD's Global Network Italy and is president of the International Society for Performance Improvement Europe. She earned an M.S. degree in applied behavior analysis, administration, and counseling from California State University and pursued a Ph.D. degree in organizational behavior management at Massachusetts State University. She has taught graduate e-courses in research methods, human resource management, and executive leadership. Ferond has led strategic culture change interventions to improve quality, productivity, and safety in education, health care, manufacturing, transportation services, and telecommunication internationally for twenty years. She is an editor for the *European Journal of Behavior Analysis.*

Wellesley R. Foshay, CPT, is senior vice president for curriculum and evaluation, Whitney University. For fifteen years, he was vice president for instructional design and research for PLATO Learning, Inc. His background includes twenty-five years in the private sector and a faculty position at the University of Illinois, Champaign. His doctorate is in instructional design from Indiana University. He has contributed over seventy major articles to research journals and book chapters on a wide variety of topics. He is coauthor of the award-winning textbook, *Writing Training That Works: How to Teach Anyone to Do Anything* (2003). He has served on the board of directors of the International Society for Performance Improvement (ISPI). Foshay was cited by ISPI with honorary life membership and a distinguished service award.

Erika R. Gilmore, CPT, is a performance improvement professional currently working in the pharmaceutical industry, with past experience working in automotive manufacturing and occupational safety and health organizations. In addition to performance-improvement positions, she has worked in operations and quality management roles. Her academic background includes an undergraduate degree from Indiana University and current status as a doctoral candidate at Indiana. Gilmore is nearing completion of a Ph.D. degree in instructional systems technology and organizational behavior and has taught graduate courses in instructional technology, performance analysis, and evaluation. She is a contributor to *Performance Improvement* and has been a presenter at several conferences.

M. Jeanne Girard is the director of the department of engineering professional development (EPD) in the College of Engineering and Computer Science (CECS) at the University of Michigan-Dearborn. She holds a graduate degree in public administration; a graduate certificate in training, design, and leadership; and an undergraduate degree in psychology. She works with college faculty and corporate clients to create programs and courses for the college's continuing education community. In partnership with several representatives from the Ford Motor Company, other CECS colleagues, and several Society for Organizational Learning (SOL) members, she was instrumental in helping to establish EPD's organizational learning program in 1996. Program offerings include a graduate-level course and various workshops and seminars customized for both individuals and teams.

Ingrid J. Guerra is assistant professor at Wayne State University, research associate professor at the Sonora Institute of Technology in Mexico, and a senior associate of Roger Kaufman and Associates. She publishes, teaches, consults, and conducts research in the areas of evaluation, strategic planning, needs assessment and analysis, and learning. She is coauthor of *Practical Evaluation for Educators: Finding What Works and What Doesn't* (2005) and has published chapters in the *Training and Performance Sourcebooks,* as well as the *Organizational Development Sourcebooks.* In addition, she has published articles in *Performance Improvement, Performance Improvement Quarterly, Human Resource Development Quarterly, Educational Technology, Quarterly Review of Distance Education, International Public Management Review,* and the *International Journal for Educational Reform.*

Robert Guptill has over twenty years of experience in the management and performance of training front-end analyses. He is currently the training analysis solutions program manager at Dynamics Research Corporation, where he manages a multidisciplinary group of training analysts, human performance specialists, curriculum developers, and information system professionals.

Carol Haig, CPT, has more than twenty-five years of multi-industry experience partnering with organizations to improve employees' performance. She is known for her skills in project management, analysis, problem and opportunity diagnosis, instructional design, and facilitation. She currently leads Carol Haig and Associates, a consulting firm she founded in 1998. Carol is a past director of the International Society for Performance Improvement (ISPI) and the recipient of ISPI's awards for outstanding organization, outstanding instructional product, and distinguished service. She holds an M.S. degree in secondary English education from the State University College of New York at Buffalo and a B.S. degree in the same discipline from the State University College of New York at Plattsburg.

Judith A. Hale, CPT, is the author of *The Performance Consultant's Fieldbook* (1998), *Performance-Based Certification* (2000), *Performance-Based Evaluation* (2002), *Performance-Based Management: What Every Manager Should Do to Get Results* (2003), and *Outsourcing Training and Development* (2006). She has been a consultant to management in the public and private sectors for over twenty-five years. She specializes in needs assessments, certification programs, evaluation protocols, and the implementation of major interventions. She is a past president of the International Society for Performance Improvement. Judith has a B.A. degree from The Ohio State University, an M.A. degree from Miami University, and a Ph.D. degree from Purdue University.

Debra Haney, CPT, is president of Performance Knowledge, Inc. She consults in performance improvement, knowledge management, and training to Fortune 500 companies. She has presented at the International Society for Performance Improvement, ASTD, and other conferences. She has published in the *Handbook of Human Performance Technology,* 2nd edition (1999), *Performance Improvement,* and other publications. Haney received her Ph.D. degree (2003) and M.S. degree in education (1993) from Indiana University. Her research areas are knowledge management, organizational communications, and group decision making.

Mark Hemenway is the human systems integration (HSI) team leader at Dynamics Research Corporation. He recently performed job task analyses for E-6B and EP-3 aircraft and was the analysis lead for the U.S. Navy aviation simulation master plan (NASMP). He has been conducting HSI analysis for over fifteen years and helped develop the U.S. Army hardware versus manpower methodology.

Jim Hill, CPT, is the CEO of Proofpoint Systems, a global provider of performance analysis software and advisory services. Upon retiring from the U.S. Marine Corps, he joined Sun Microsystems, where he established numerous regional and global sales productivity organizations. In 2001, *Training* magazine recognized him as a leading visionary in the field of organizational performance. He assumed his current role in 2003. Hill is also a past president of the International Society for Performance Improvement and is active on many boards.

Brian S. Horvitz is a Ph.D. candidate in instructional systems technology at Indiana University. He received a B.A. degree (1993) in political science and English literature from Rutgers University, an M.S. degree (1997) in education from the University of Pennsylvania, and an M.S. degree (2002) in instructional systems technology from Indiana University. He works as a senior instructional designer for Option Six, Inc., developing blended instructional solutions for Fortune 500 and other companies. He is an associate instructor in the School of Education at Indiana University. He has worked on NSF-funded projects for The Evaluation Center at Western Michigan University.

Swati Karve has conducted research in organizational behavior focused on individual and organizational factors affecting job satisfaction and job stress among scientists working in the National Institutes and Laboratories in India. Swati was a visiting faculty member at Symbiosis Institute of Management and Human Resource Development, Pune, India and Symbiosis Institute of Business Management, Pune, India, where she taught psychology, industrial sociology, and organizational behavior. Karve has been involved in organizational research and conducted training programs and workshops for various organizations. Her professional interests include use of information technology in human resource management and the practice of Indian thought and culture in management.

Roger Kaufman, CPT, is professor emeritus, Florida State University, director of Roger Kaufman & Associates, and distinguished research professor at the Sonora Institute of Technology. He is a past president, member for life, and Thomas F. Gilbert Distinguished Professional Achievement Award winner of the International Society for Performance Improvement and is the recipient of ASTD's distinguished contribution to workplace learning and performance award. Kaufman has published thirty-six books and over 235 articles on strategic planning, performance improvement, quality management and continuous improvement, needs assessment, management, and evaluation.

Lynn Kearny, CPT, has been a performance-improvement consultant for over twenty years. She specializes in solving human performance problems through work systems improvement and training. She has developed training programs, job aids, and feedback systems for private and public institutions. Her materials and graphics have been used in the United States, Europe, Southeast Asia, and West Africa. Kearny received ISPI's award for outstanding instructional product and the 2004 distinguished service award. She is author of *The Facilitator's Toolkit: Tools and Techniques for Generating Ideas and Making Decisions in Groups* (1995), *Graphics for Presenters: Getting Your Ideas Across* (1995), and *Creating Workplaces Where People Can Think* with Phyl Smith (1994).

Joachim Knuf is an associate professor of lean enterprise development at the center for manufacturing as well as a faculty member in organizational communication, department of communication, University of Kentucky. He is cocreator of two foundational training packages that support companies in their lean transformation.

Sharon J. Korth is associate professor of human resource development at Xavier University in Cincinnati, Ohio. Sharon received her Ed.D. degree from the University of Cincinnati, and master of education and B.S. degrees from Miami University, Ohio. Sharon was formerly a manager of training and senior instructional designer with a large manufacturing and engineering organization. Her research and teaching interests include instructional design and needs assessment, creativity in instructional design, and evaluation processes in organizations. She has published in *Performance Improvement Quarterly, Innovative Higher Education, Journal on Education for Business, Psychological Reports, Performance Improvement,* and the *Journal on Excellence in College Teaching.*

Danny Langdon is a key model maker in the field of performance improvement and work innovation. He has been innovative in designing and developing a number of systems for improving work, most notably the Language of Work Model. He has authored seven books, several book chapters, and many journal articles. He has trained hundreds of practitioners in instructional and performance technology in the United States and internationally. He has been a member of the International Society for Performance Improvement for thirty-eight years and is an honorary life member and past president. He and his partner in life and business, Kathleen Whiteside, run Performance International, a consulting firm dedicated to understanding, aligning, and improving work in business.

Joseph Lapides has been affiliated with the University of Michigan-Dearborn (UMD) for twenty years. He developed the graduate-level course on organizational learning and has been teaching it since 1996. He teaches courses on building high-performing learning organizations for the College of Engineering. He is the former coordinator of the M.A. program in adult instruction and performance technology. Lapides was awarded the UMD 1992 distinguished teaching award and in 1999 the outstanding service award. In 1999 he was selected as the alumni society faculty member of the year. He has a B.A. degree from the City College of New York, an M.Ed. degree from Rutgers University, and a Ph.D. degree from the University of Michigan.

Mark J. Lauer, CPT, is a lead consultant with Performance Knowledge, Inc. He is completing a doctorate in instructional systems technology at Indiana University. His research interest centers on competencies associated with human performance technology and how they may be used to increase organizational performance. Lauer is coauthor of *Lean 101: Lean Manufacturing Foundations for Work Teams* and *Lean 101,* a primary training program for operational level personnel used by major companies in Europe, North America, South America, Mexico, and Russia. He is also coauthor of *FirstLine: A Team Leader's Guide to Lean Thinking,* a training program for supervisors in the lean environment. Mark is a regular contributor to *Performance Improvement* and is also a department editor for *TechTrends.*

Sung Heum Lee is a research fellow for the Educational Research Institute at Kookmin University and a senior consultant with High Consulting Group in Korea. Prior to this, he was director of the cybertraining team with the Central Officials Training Institute, Civil Service Commission in Korea and a research associate with Education and Training Resources at Indiana University. He received his LL.B. degree (1983) in law from Kookmin University, his M.Ed.

degree (1989) in education from Seoul National University, and his Ph.D. degree (1998) in instructional systems technology from Indiana University. His research focuses are in instructional systems design, performance analysis, program evaluation, multimedia-mediated instruction and training, and theories and practices of instructional and performance technology.

Doug Leigh is associate professor of education and director of the Master of Science in Workplace Learning and Performance program at Pepperdine University's Graduate School of Education and Psychology. He earned his Ph.D. degree in instructional systems from Florida State University, where he served as a technical director for projects with various local, state, and federal agencies. His ongoing research, publication, and speaking interests include needs assessment, evaluation, and change creation. Leigh is coauthor of *Strategic Planning for Success: Aligning People, Performance and Payoffs* (2003) and *Useful Educational Results: Defining, Prioritizing, and Accomplishing* (2001). He is an associate director of Roger Kaufman and Associates, two-time chair of the American Evaluation Association's needs assessment topic interest group, and past editor-in-chief of the International Society for Performance Improvement's journal *Performance Improvement*.

Brenda S. Levya-Gardner is associate professor and director of the executive human resource development graduate program at Xavier University in Cincinnati, Ohio. She received her Ph.D. degree in higher and adult education from the University of Missouri, a master's degree in public administration from the University of Southern California-Washington, DC, Public Affairs Center, and a B.A. degree in liberal studies from Providence College. Her research and teaching interests center on group and team behavior, applying organizational behavior concepts to the classroom, and innovative teaching methods. She has published in journals such as *Innovative Higher Education, Journal on Excellence in College Teaching, Workforce Education Forum,* and *Journal on Education for Business.*

Julie Lewis is an adjunct professor at Baker College and was formerly an instructor at Dorsey Schools, a vocational institution for adult learners. Her duties include instructing adult students on software systems used in the business, legal, and medical fields. She served as lead instructor at Dorsey Schools and assisted in the design, development, and implementation of the placement department. Lewis received a B.A. degree from the University of Michigan-Dearborn (1999) and a master's degree in performance improvement and instructional design from the University of Michigan-Dearborn (2004).

Larissa V. Malopinsky is president of KM Concepts, LLC, a consulting firm that provides services ranging from organizational analysis and organizational strategy development to design and development of instructional products. She received a Ph.D. degree in educational administration from St. Petersburg State University, Russia (1998), and has fifteen years of teaching and educational management experience. Currently she is a doctoral candidate in instructional systems technology at Indiana University. Her research focuses on strategic change, organizational culture, and collaborative learning environments.

Anthony W. Marker is an assistant professor of instructional and performance technology at Boise State University. He received his doctoral degree from Indiana University in 2000. Formerly, Marker served as a principal consultant, project manager, and instructional designer for several firms in the Boston area and has experience in the pharmaceutical, financial, telecommunications, and government sectors. He has published in *Performance Improvement Quarterly* and *Performance and Instruction.* His research and teaching interests include performance technology, change management, instructional and interface design, and affective learning.

Karen L. Medsker is professor emerita at Marymount University's School of Business Administration, where she taught courses on instructional design, performance improvement, and management. She consults with business, government, and nonprofit organizations through Human Performance Systems, Inc., a small company she founded. She is coeditor of *Performance Improvement Quarterly,* coeditor with Kristina Holdsworth of *Models and Strategies for Training Design* (2001), and coauthor with Robert M. Gagné of *The Conditions of Learning: Training Applications* (1996). Formerly, she was an instructional designer at AT&T Bell Laboratories and director of instructional development at Indiana University-Purdue University at Indianapolis. She earned her Ph.D. degree in instructional systems at Florida State University.

Michael Molenda is associate professor emeritus in instructional systems technology, Indiana University. His Ph.D. degree is from Syracuse University in instructional technology. He taught graduate courses in instructional technology foundations, instructional development, media applications, simulation and gaming, and distance education. He has held leadership positions in the Association for Educational Communications and Technology (AECT) and the North American Simulation and Gaming Association. Molenda was coauthor through six editions of the widely adopted textbook, *Instructional Media and Technologies for Learning,* with Robert Heinich, James D. Russell, and Sharon Smaldino. In recent years, he has coauthored an annual review of issues and trends in instructional technology; prepared encyclopedia articles for the topics of instructional technology, instructional design, and the ADDIE Model; and written a brief history of AECT.

James L. Moseley, CPT, is an associate professor in family medicine, Wayne State University (WSU) School of Medicine; associate graduate faculty, instructional technology program, WSU; and a performance consultant with the Lake Group Inc. He has presented at the International Society for Performance Improvement and ASTD conferences, published in *Performance Improvement* and *Performance Improvement Quarterly,* coauthored a chapter for ISPI's Pathfinder series (1998), and coauthored four books: *Fundamentals of Human Performance Technology: A Guide for Improving People, Process, and Performance* (2000, 2004), *Performance Improvement Interventions: Enhancing People and Process Through Performance Technology* (2001), *Confirmative Evaluation: Practical Strategies for Valuing Continuous Improvement* (2004), and *Training OWLS (Older Worker-Learners): Transitions, Transformations and Opportunities* (2006).

Monique Mueller, CPT, graduated from the School for Translation and Interpretation in Zurich, Switzerland. She worked in Spain and Switzerland in agricultural exporting; as a social worker for refugees at a nongovernmental organization; and as a translator and interpreter for courts, hospitals, and public sector institutions. After moving to San Francisco, Monique earned an M.B.A. degree. Since her return to Switzerland in 1993, Monique has spent her professional life as a business manager and specialist focusing on human resources development. She directed a company for the training and development of professional women. Monique then worked with UBS Private Banking in Switzerland as head of training and development within the post-merger integration team. In 2001 Monique founded La Volta Consulting, where she focuses on performance improvement, human resources development, and international cooperation. Monique is a founding member of ISPI Europe and was its president in 2002 and 2003. She chaired the first two ISPI conferences in Europe and coedited a special issue of *Performance Improvement.*

Margo Murray, CPT, has earned the International Society for Performance Improvement's (ISPI's) three highest honors: outstanding member, member for life, and president, and serves as mentor to many of its leaders. A preeminent researcher, designer, and evaluator of facilitated mentoring, she has collaborated with clients on strategic planning and mentoring processes in over one hundred organizations in twenty-six countries. Her best-selling book, *Beyond the Myths and Magic of Mentoring: How to Facilitate an Effective Mentoring Process* (2001), is considered the seminal work on facilitated mentoring. Murray has been an invited speaker at many international, regional, and national events, including the United Nations Secretariat, and is faculty for the ISPI Institutes.

José Manuel Ochoa-Alcántar is an associate professor in the department of education at the Instituto Tecnológico de Sonora in México. He teaches graduate and undergraduate courses and has coordinated a master's program in education. He has taught junior high through graduate school and has worked as a graphic designer, pedagogy adviser, and trainer in corporate settings. He received his B.A. degree (1996) in education from the Instituto Tecnológico de Sonora (México) and his M.A. degree (2000) in educational technology from the University of San Francisco. He is in the Ph.D. program in instructional systems technology at Indiana University. He has authored several articles and presented papers, seminars, and workshops at professional conferences and meetings in México and the United States.

Gihan Osman is a lecturer at the Arab Academy for Science and Technology. She has ten years' experience in designing instructional materials in the private and public sectors. For the past few years, she has been working as a researcher, designer, facilitator, and evaluator on international projects to promote systemic educational change and faculty professional development. Her main research interests are Web-based education and training, information exchange in teams, and organizational change in higher education institutions. Currently she is a doctoral student in the instructional systems technology department at Indiana University. She received a B.A. degree (1993) in English language literature from Alexandria University, an M.A. degree (1999) in teaching English as a foreign language from the American University in Cairo, and an M.S. degree (2005) in instructional systems technology from Indiana University.

Jana L. Pershing is an associate professor of sociology at San Diego State University. She is also a senior methodology consultant for Education and Management Research Associates of Bloomington, Indiana. Her areas of research and teaching expertise include research methods, military sociology, and crime and social control. She has recently published articles in the following journals: *Performance Improvement* (2002, 2003), *Human Resource Development Quarterly* (2001, coauthored with J. A. Pershing), *Men and Masculinities* (2006), *Sociological Perspectives* (2003), *Gender Issues* (2003), *Deviant Behavior* (2002), and *Armed Forces and Society* (2001). Pershing received her Ph.D. and M.A. degrees (1997, 1992) in sociology from the University of Washington and her B.A. degree (1990) in sociology from Indiana University.

Dana Gaines Robinson is the president of Partners in Change, Inc., a consulting firm formed in 1981. She is a frequent speaker at national and international conferences. She has been awarded ASTD's distinguished contribution to workplace learning and performance as well as the thought leadership award from ISA. Prior to teaming up in Partners in Change, Robinson was involved in human resources for several years. She led learning organizations in both a financial and a pharmaceutical corporation. She has coauthored and coedited several books, including *Training for Impact* (1989), *Moving from Training to Performance* (1998), the award-winning book *Performance Consulting* (1995), *Zap the Gap!* (2002), and *Strategic Business Partner: Aligning People Strategies with Business Goals* (2005). Books she has coauthored have been translated into more than twenty languages.

James C. Robinson is the chairman of Partners in Change, Inc., a consulting firm formed in 1981. The firm provides services to organizations around the world. He is a frequent speaker at national and international conferences. He has been awarded ASTD's distinguished contribution to workplace learning and performance as well as the thought leadership award from ISA. Prior to teaming up in Partners in Change, he was a vice president at Development Dimensions International, where he was the primary architect for its most successful training program, interaction management. He has coauthored and coedited several books, including *Training for Impact* (1989), *Moving from Training to Performance* (1998), and the award-winning book *Performance Consulting* (1995), and *Strategic Business Partner: Aligning People Strategies with Business Goals* (2005).

Charles M. Roe is a principal in Waves of Change Partnership and a charter consulting member of the Society of Organizational Learning. He was formerly the vice president of Quality Systems at Philips Display Components Company. Roe is a judge for the Michigan Quality Award, an examiner for the Malcolm Baldrige National Quality Award, and a senior examiner for the Michigan Quality Award. He is an instructor in engineering professional development at the College of Engineering and Computer Science at the University of Michigan-Dearborn. He holds a B.S. degree in electrical engineering and an M.S. degree in engineering administration from the University of Tennessee in Knoxville. Roe is a certified Six Sigma black belt through the American Society for Quality.

Jennifer Rosenzweig, CPT, is director of learning and performance solutions for Carlson Marketing Group. She leads a team of consultants who are responsible for training and performance technology solutions for a variety of Fortune 100 clients. Her background includes experience in instructional design, organizational development, organizational communications, and human resources management. Her academic credentials include a B.A. degree in education and English from the University of Michigan and an M.S. degree in education from the University of Michigan-Dearborn. She is currently pursuing an M.S. degree in positive organizational development and change from Case Western Reserve University. She has served as adjunct faculty in the University of Michigan-Dearborn program in performance improvement and instructional design.

Allison Rossett, CPT, is long-time professor of educational technology at San Diego State University and an International Society for Performance Improvement (ISPI) member for life. She is in the *Training* magazine HRD hall of fame. Rossett was ISPI vice president for research and development in the early 1990s. Recipient of ASTD's 2002 award for workplace learning and performance, she is also the editor of *The ASTD E-Learning Handbook: Best Practices, Strategies, and Case Studies for an Emerging Field* (2002). Her books, *Beyond the Podium: Delivering Training and Performance to a Digital World* (2001) and *First Things Fast: A Handbook for Performance Analysis* (1998), were honored with ISPI awards.

Daniel T. Rowe has worked as a training manager and instructional designer at a number of different organizations. He received a master's degree in instructional psychology and technology with an emphasis in design and development from Brigham Young University. One of his main research and development interests is the use of visuals, graphics, illustrations, and animations to improve learning and human performance. He is currently pursuing a Ph.D. degree at Indiana University, where he participates in a research group that studies how people react to, interpret, and learn from instructional visuals.

Geary A. Rummler, CPT, is the founder and chairman of the Performance Design Lab, a Tucson, Arizona–based research and consulting firm specializing in the design of performance systems for organizations in the United States and abroad. He received his M.B.A. and Ph.D. degrees from the University of Michigan. His most recent book is *Serious Performance Consulting According to Rummler* (2004). He is also coauthor of *Improving Performance: Managing the White Space on the Organization Chart* (1990, 1995, with A. P. Brache). Rummler has served as N/ISPI president (1968–1969) and received the ISPI lifetime member award, distinguished professional achievement award, and presidential citation for intellectual leadership. He was inducted into the HRD Hall of Fame in 1986.

James D. Russell is professor emeritus of educational technology at Purdue University. His doctorate is from Indiana University in instructional technology. He taught and conducted instructional research and development at Purdue University for over thirty years before his retirement. He continues to teach instructional design and development courses part time and conducts teaching improvement workshops for Purdue's Center for Instructional Excellence. He offers graduate courses in the instructional systems program at Florida State University. Russell has published over a hundred articles and book reviews. He is a coauthor of two major textbooks: through eight editions of *Instructional Technology and Media for Learning* (2005) and through three editions of *Instructional Technology for Teaching and Learning* (2000).

Scott P. Schaffer is assistant professor of educational technology at Purdue University, where he teaches courses in learning systems design, evaluation, and human performance technology. He holds a doctorate in instructional systems from Florida State University, with an emphasis in performance systems. His research interests include component-based performance systems design, strategic assessment and evaluation, organizational change for sustainability, and cross-disciplinary learning within virtual teams. He has published over fifty articles, books, and book chapters, and recently coauthored the book *Interactive Convergence in Multimedia* (2005). He continues to consult and has worked on more than seventy-five performance improvement projects in manufacturing, education, financial services, transportation, and high technology.

Therese M. Schmidt is a doctoral student in the educational technology program at Purdue University and is an instructional designer for D. E. Foxx and Associates at Eli Lilly and Company. Her research interests include organizational change for sustainable development, performance analysis and strategic evaluation, and cross-disciplinary learning within virtual teams. She received her B.S. degree (1999) in mathematics education from Miami University and her M.S. degree (2004) in educational technology from Purdue University.

Kenneth H. Silber, CPT, has been contributing to the instructional design field since its inception almost forty years ago. Ken is an associate professor of educational technology, research, and assessment at Northern Illinois University, where he teaches human performance technology and instructional design. He is also president of Silber Performance Consulting, a firm specializing in analysis, design, and evaluation of instructional and other performance-improvement interventions. He is a coauthor of IBSTPI's *Instructional Design Competencies: The Standards* (1994) and *Training That Works: How to Train Anybody to Do Anything* (2003). He holds Ph.D. and M.A. degrees in instructional technology with a minor in educational psychology from the University of Southern California.

Deborah L. Stone, CPT, is president of DLS Group, Inc., where she specializes in multimedia, performance support, computer-based training, and instructional systems design. She has extensive experience in the software, financial, and tele-com industries. Stone has received twenty-one professional awards for her work in instructional systems design, technology-based training, and performance support systems. She has developed over three hundred hours of technology-based training and information systems. A frequently published author and international presenter, she was the International Society for Performance Improvement's 1991–1993 vice president, technology applications. Deborah graduated from Ohio State University with a B.S. degree in English, education, and media. She received a full scholarship to complete her graduate work in instructional technology at San Francisco State University.

Ray Svenson, CPT, is president of Ray Svenson Consulting, Inc. He has spent twenty-seven years developing and applying human performance technology strategies, processes, and tools in large corporations. Svenson is coauthor of *The Training and Development Strategic Plan Workbook* (1992), which won the ISPI award for best instructional publication in 1994. Ray has published numerous articles in *Performance Improvement* and other journals and is a coauthor of *The Quality Roadmap* (1993). Ray's degrees are in electrical engineering. He spent sixteen years as a telecommunications systems engineer and engineering man-ager with Bell Labs and AT&T before going into consulting in 1978.

Mary Norris Thomas, CPT, CEO of The Fleming Group, LLC, specializes in performance management systems, armed services command programs, and commissioned studies and analyses. She holds graduate-level adjunct appoint-ments in research methods, applied statistics, and independent research. Her research publications range from experimental analysis of behavior to weapons simulations, and her honors memberships include Phi Beta Kappa and Sigma Xi Scientific Research Society. She received a B.S. degree in psychology from Texas Christian University and M.S. and Ph.D. degrees in biopsychology, with a co-concentration in multivariate statistics, from the University of Georgia. Thomas serves as founding director of the International Society for Performance Improvement's Science and Research Professional Community.

Donald T. Tosti, CPT, has made contributions to the field that have been recog-nized by the International Society for Performance Improvement in several ways. Most notably, he is a member for life and is the recipient of the Thomas F. Gilbert Distinguished Professional Achievement Award. He is the managing partner of Vanguard Consulting, which specializes in the alignment of organi-zational processes and people with the stated strategy of the organization. Don is an expert in organizational systems. His pioneering work on contingency management began in the 1960s. As the principle investigator for the multimedia leadership and management course conducted at the U.S. Naval Academy, he adapted the methods of performance analysis to the study of leadership and management behavior.

Darlene M. Van Tiem, CPT, is associate professor and coordinator of the performance improvement and instructional design graduate program at the University of Michigan-Dearborn. She served as human resource director at Ameritech Yellow Pages and was curriculum manager of General Motors Technical Training, including GM suppliers. She has demonstrated expertise in human performance technology as lead author of two best-selling and International Society for Performance Improvement award-winning books: *Fundamentals of Performance Technology* (2000) and *Performance Improvement Interventions* (2001). She has been recognized as the ASTD national technical trainer of the year (1992) and received the national ASTD excellence in leadership award (1993).

Steven W. Villachica, CPT, is chief learning officer for DLS Group, where he works to improve the performance of people, groups, and organizations in industry and government by leveraging cutting-edge technologies based on proven research, theory, and best practices. In addition to the design and development architectures for Performance Support Systems (PSS), his research interests include representing, supporting, and leveraging human cognition in job-based problem solving and maximizing on-line survey response rates. Villachica has written numerous publications on PSS, rapid application development, e-learning, and alignment. He is a frequent conference presenter and two-time winner of the International Society for Performance Improvement's outstanding systematic approach award. He has a doctorate in educational technology from the University of Northern Colorado.

Guy W. Wallace, CPT, has been in the training and development field since 1979 and has been a performance improvement consultant to government and industry since 1982. He has analyzed, designed, and developed training and development for several types of business functions and processes. He is the author of three books, several chapters, and more than fifty published articles. He has presented more than fifty times at international conferences and local chapters of the International Society for Performance Improvement (ISPI), ASTD, Lakewood Conferences, the Association for Behavior Analysis, and the Conference on Nuclear Training and Education. Wallace served on the ISPI's executive committee as the treasurer for the 1999–2001 boards and as ISPI's president-elect and then president for 2002–2004.

Scott J. Warren has worked as an instructional technology designer, instructor trainer, teacher, and researcher for more than a decade. He has designed and facilitated both on-line and face-to-face instruction in school districts across southeast Texas. Scott's current research focuses on the use of multiple observation techniques to study the effectiveness of 3D on-line instructional environments used to support the development of communities of practice. He is currently employed by the Indiana University Center for Research on Learning and Technology.

Ryan Watkins is associate professor of instructional technology and distance education at the George Washington University in Washington, DC. Ryan has designed and taught courses, both on-line and in the classroom, in instructional design, distance education, needs assessment, and system analysis and design, as well as technology management. He was an assistant professor at Nova Southeastern University and a research faculty member at Florida State University's Learning Systems Institute. He is author of the best-selling books *75 e-Learning Activities* (2005) and *The e-Learning Companion* (2004) and has published more than sixty articles on the topics of distance education, performance improvement, evaluation, needs assessment, and strategic planning. He has served as vice president of the inter-American distance education consortium (CREAD).

John H. Wilson has several years of experience in the field of instructional design. He currently works as a learning strategist for Convergys, designing training simulations for businesses. He is also an adjunct faculty member in the instructional systems technology (IST) department at Indiana University. He has an M.S. degree in instructional psychology and technology and a B.S. degree in education from Brigham Young University. Wilson is completing his doctoral degree in IST at Indiana University. His research interests include coaching and feedback models for on-line role play and strategy simulations.

Donald J. Winiecki is an associate professor in the instructional and performance technology department of the Boise State University College of Engineering. He holds a doctor of education (Ed.D.) degree from Texas Tech University (instructional technology, 1996) and has recently submitted a dissertation in fulfillment of a doctor of philosophy (Ph.D.) degree from Central Queensland University (sociology). He teaches such courses as Ethnographic Research in Organizations; Sociology of Organizations; Sociology of Science, Technology, and Engineering; and Delivery Technology for Instruction. His research interests span the fields of sociology, communication, distance education, instructional technology, and human performance technology. His current research addresses the sociology of labor and technologies. He has published his research in international venues including *Performance Improvement, New Technology Work and Employment,* and *The Handbook of Distance Education.*

He is a past chairperson of the ISPI Research Committee and was instrumental in the development of the ISPI Online Institute.

Klaus D. Wittkuhn, CPT, has published articles on different topics related to performance improvement and has copublished the book *Improving Performance: Leistungspotenziale in Unternehmen entfalten.* He received his master's degrees in the study of political economics and educational science from the Ludwig-Maximilian University, Munich, and the University of Bundeswehr, Munich, Germany. He is an adjunct faculty member of the University of Applied Sciences in Deggendorf, Germany; the University of Applied Sciences in Ludwigshafen, Germany; and the University of Applied Sciences in Winterthur, Switzerland. He is founder and managing partner of Performance Group Ltd., a group of three consulting and two training companies in Germany and South Africa specializing in the design of performance systems and of performance-based training.

About ISPI

The International Society for Performance Improvement (ISPI) *is dedicated to improving individual, organizational, and societal performance.* Founded in 1962, ISPI is the leading international association dedicated to improving productivity and performance in the workplace. ISPI represents more than 10,000 international and chapter members throughout the United States, Canada, and 40 other countries.

ISPI's mission is to develop and recognize the proficiency of our members and advocate the use of Human Performance Technology. This systematic approach to improving productivity and competence uses a set of methods and procedures and a strategy for solving problems for realizing opportunities related to the performance of people. It is a systematic combination of performance analysis, cause analysis, intervention design and development, implementation, and evaluation that can be applied to individuals, small groups, and large organizations.

Website: www.ispi.org
Mail: International Society for Performance Improvement
1400 Spring Street, Suite 260
Silver Spring, Maryland 20910 USA
Phone: 1.301.587.8570
Fax: 1.301.587.8573
E-mail: info@ispi.org

NAME INDEX

SUBJECT INDEX

Addendum to the Copyright Page